OFFICIAL PUBLICATION
OF THE NATIONAL HOCKEY LEAGUE®

TOTAL STANLEY CUP®

DAN DIAMOND
EDITOR

RALPH DINGER JAMES DUPLACEY ERIC ZWEIG
MANAGING EDITORS

ERNIE FITZSIMMONS
CONSULTING STATISTICIAN

PAUL BONTJE
ASSISTANT EDITOR

JOHN PASTERNAK
DATA MANAGEMENT

TOTAL SPORTS

Published in Canada by:
Total Sports Canada
194 Dovercourt Road
Toronto, Ontario M6J 3C8
Canada
e-mail: dda.nhl@sympatico.ca

Published in the United States by:
Total Sports Publishing Inc.
100 Enterprise Drive
Kingston, NY 12401

Trade sales and distribution in Canada by:
Publishers Group West
250 Carlton Street
Toronto, Ontario M5A 2L1
Canada

Trade sales and distribution in the United States by:
Publishers Group West
1700 Fourth Street
Berkeley, CA 94710

Total Sports Canada books may be purchased for educational, business or sales promotional use.
For information please write to:
Total Sports Canada
194 Dovercourt Road
Toronto, Ontario M6J 3C8
Canada
e-mail: dda.nhl@sympatico.ca

ISBN 1-892129-07-8

Printed in the United States of America

10 9 8 7 6 5 4 3 2

TOTAL STANLEY CUP

CONTENTS

The Stanley Cup, shortly after the addition of its five-band barrel in 1958. The inscribed names of each year's winner filled the five bands in 1991. The top band was removed and a new one added at the base. It, too, will be filled after the names of the 2004 Cup winner have been added.

Introduction

If the last 100 years of hockey history have proved anything, perhaps it is that the more things change, the more they stay the same. For example... In 1901, the series to decide hockey's champion opened on a cold January night in Montreal. In 1999, the series began on June 8 in the extreme heat and humidity of Texas. But in both cases, the championship was decided with a 2–1 victory. Of course, Dan Bain of the Winnipeg Victorias needed only four minutes of overtime to give his team the title in 1901. Brett Hull required almost three full overtime periods to make the Dallas Stars champions in 1999.

Much, of course, has changed from the time of the late Victorian era to the dawn of the new millennium, but at least one thing hasn't: In 1901, Dan Bain and the Winnipeg Victorias were going all out to win a championship trophy donated in 1893 by the Governor-General of Canada. Almost a full century later, Brett Hull and the Dallas Stars were doing exactly the same thing.

Welcome to *Total Stanley Cup*, a book that, like *Total Hockey: The Official Encyclopedia of the National Hockey League,* celebrates the history of the sport, pays close attention to the workings of the modern game and, above all, respects the game and the accomplishments of the people who play it.

In *Total Stanley Cup*, you will find the same high standard of in-depth information that made *Total Hockey* the game's best-selling and most comprehensive reference. In fact, *Total Stanley Cup* will be double shifted in the year 2000, being made available to fans wherever books are sold while also serving as the NHL's annual fact guide for journalists and the broadcast media on the playoff beat.

The book is divided into four sections:

- Section I deals with the origins of the trophy and provides background on Lord Stanley, Canada's Governor-General who donated it in 1893 but never saw a Stanley Cup game *(page 4)*. The many changes to the trophy itself and the intricacies and idiosyncrasies of the engraving upon it are described as is Cup competition in the early challenge era *(page 11)*. A chronology of the NHL's evolving playoff format with special emphasis on the setup of the 2000 playoffs is found here *(page 9)*.
- Section II provides comprehensive highlights and playoff records. Each NHL club's all-time playoff record, top playoff scorers and series-by-series results are listed *(page 13)* as are all-time playoff scoring leaders *(page 23)*, year-by-year playoff scoring leaders *(page 24)* and Stanley Cup-winning goal scorers *(page 66)*. Highlights of each season's playoff competition from 1999 to 1893 along with the score of every playoff game and the roster of each Cup-winning team are found here *(page 25)* as are complete team and individual playoff record books *(page 57)*. Also included are lists of every three-goal-game *(page 67)*, overtime game *(page 69)* and penalty shot *(page 72)* in Stanley Cup play.
- Section III offers similar coverage of the Stanley Cup Finals. A team-by-team Final Series history *(page 82)* and a Final Series record book *(page 85)* is supplemented by year-by-year scoring in the Finals *(page 92)*, an alphabetical listing of every player who was a member of a Cup winner from 1893 to 1999 *(page 106)* and Final Series scoring, goaltending and coaching statistics for all NHLers *(page 111)*. There is also a statistical summary of every Final Series game played over the past decade complete with team rosters, scoring and penalty statistics, shots on goal and on-ice officials *(page 119)*.
- Section IV is comprised of two complete statistical registers, providing year-by-year Stanley Cup playoff statistics for every player and every goaltender to appear in the NHL. More than 5,100 players are listed. A comprehensive playoff register has never been assembled or published before. The NHL Playoff Player Register is found on page 131. The Goaltender Register begins on page 221.

Several other features in *Total Stanley Cup* are worth noting: The book begins with an essay by Milt Dunnell, a recipient of the Hockey Hall of Fame's Elmer Ferguson Memorial Award for writing, who has covered playoff hockey since the 1920s. Dunnell's "The Stanley Cup Mystique" *(page 1)* deals with the allure of the silver trophy and the passions ignited by competition for it.

"This Date in Stanley Cup History" *(page 73)* chronicles outstanding and surprising events in the playoffs. April and May have been busy!

"The Post-War Dynasties" *(page 117)* looks at the accomplishments of eight teams of distinction. Three versions of the Montreal Canadiens (1956-60, 1965-69 and 1976-79), two generations of the Toronto Maple Leafs (1947-51 and 1962-64), the Detroit Red Wings (1950-55), the New York Islanders (1980-83) and the Edmonton Oilers (1984-90) make the dynasty list.

"Stranger Than Fiction" *(page 129)* by *Total Hockey* editor James Duplacey details many of the oddest moments in the history of the Stanley Cup trophy. It's been misplaced, drop-kicked and kidnapped in its 107-year existence. This feature also lists misspellings and mystery names on the trophy.

Your comments, suggestion and corrections are extremely valuable to the *Total Hockey* editorial team. Please contact us by e-mail at dda.nhl@sympatico.ca.

Dan Diamond
March 2000

The Stanley Cup, circa 1932, displays the numerous additional silver bands added by various winning teams since the trophy's inception in 1893. Lord Stanley's original gift—The Dominion Hockey Challenge Cup—was just the bowl at the top of the trophy.

CHAPTER 1

The Stanley Cup Mystique

The Allure of the Shimmering Silver Trophy

Milt Dunnell

WHEN LYNN AND MUZZ PATRICK discovered the Stanley Cup in a cardboard box down in the basement of their home in Victoria, British Columbia, they did what any grade-school-age students would be likely to do—especially if their father happened to be Lester Patrick, already a legend in hockey.

They got themselves a nail and attempted to add their names to those of the already anointed. Not being blessed with the powers of Nostradamus, they couldn't even guess their names would be engraved there eventually as members of the New York Rangers.

More than 70 years later, three Russian-born players, their names freshly cut into the Cup, were holding it aloft to the thunderous cheers of 62,000 fans attending a soccer match in Moscow. Among those paying homage to the Stanley Cup was Boris Yeltsin, then head honcho of all the Russians.

The caper of Lester Patrick's kids didn't even make the local prints, of course, but the pilgrimage to Moscow of Igor Larionov, Vyacheslav Kozlov and Viacheslav Fetisov was big news, even in areas that still hadn't entered the debate on the neutral zone trap.

Thoughtful citizens were prompted to comment on the mystique of this trophy which the three Red Wings had lugged back to Moscow. Wasn't that the same bowl that a group of Ottawa celebrants once drop-kicked into the Rideau Canal, after they had closed one bar too many? Nobody seemed to accuse them of being iconoclastic. In fact, people laughed about it when the tale was rehashed at smokers and banquets.

Yes, it is the same old basin, the one that Lord Stanley of Preston left for hockey-crazed colonials when he completed his gig as the sixth Governor-General of Canada. But absolutely nobody, drunk or sober, is kicking the Stanley Cup around any more. Those days definitely are over. And you can take this to the bank: the Stanley Cup probably is the most popular sports trophy in the world at the moment.

Certainly, it is the most recognizable. And it got that way strictly on merit—no costly promotional campaign of flashing lights and crashing cymbals. It comes closer to being a People's Cup than any other trophy in sport. They line up for hours to get a look at it, peering at the names of hockey idols past and present. The secret of its popularity is its availability. It goes where there are people. It's friendly.

During what qualifies as the most successful barnstorming tour in the history of professional sport, the Stanley Cup traveled more than 40,000 miles in 50 days, commencing with the 1998 NHL All-Star Game in Vancouver. In stops at 29 cities, it helped charities to raise more than $2 million. And it didn't find a town that wouldn't just love to have it back.

You might even guess the trustees now responsible for its custody studied the treatment of some other sports cups and decided that mistakes had been made. They might even have known the saga of the America's Cup, the Stanley Cup of yachting. It long enjoyed the title of being the most prestigious prize in sport. But how many would recognize it?

Yes, there are some startling parallels between the America's Cup, and the Stanley. Both have backgrounds in Britain. An English yacht club commissioned the design of the America's Cup as the prize for an 1851 race around the Isle of Wight. After an American yacht won it, the trophy, a bottomless silver ewer that cost $500, narrowly escaped being thrown out as trash from the home of a wealthy sailor.

When the overbearing and unpopular New York Yacht Club came into sole possession of the cup in 1857, the pompous directors knew exactly what to do with it. They secured it to a table in their palatial quarters with a 40-inch bolt. That's where it stayed for 132 years, while the yacht club, frequently revising the rules to their own needs, ran up what was accepted as the longest winning streak in sports history.

And good for the New York Yacht Club. But how many of the unsalty millions in the streets got to see the sport's most publicized award? And good for the trustees of the Stanley Cup, who realize they have something special and want the whole world to help them enjoy it.

Another historic trophy that spent too much time in seclusion, especially during its early years, is the Davis Cup. Dedicated to the purpose of stimulating friendly international interest in tennis, the big silver dish failed in its purpose mainly because of early domination by the Australians. By 1910, both the U.S. and Britain were pleading for a greater display of the cup, in order to revive flagging interest. Where, exactly was the Cup? It was on a sideboard at the home of Norman Brookes, one of the great Aussie players.

Yes, the National Hockey League has been criticized for taking over an award that the donor, Lord Stanley, directed should be for the championship of amateur hockey. At the time, there was no professional hockey and his lordship had no reason to expect there ever would be. His intention was to promote the popularity of hockey, which he and his family had learned to enjoy. It would be difficult to argue that the NHL has not done that. It has used the Stanley Cup to create enthusiasm for the sport in areas that previously were considered barren territory.

And there's more to come. Igor Larionov might have been more of a prophet than he intended to be when he spoke during that night at the stadium in Moscow. He said: "We (the Red Wings) have millions of fans who rooted for us all the way. It would be unfair not to bring this Cup and show it to them."

Those millions of fans—and millions more like them in Sweden and Finland and the former Czechoslovakia—are not going to be content to watch the tube indefinitely, especially after what happened at Nagano. They will want a piece of the action. Who's to say that European teams won't be competing for the Stanley Cup in the future?

Can't happen, you say? Less then 25 years ago, a deuce would get you 10 that a European player never would win one of the major awards in the National Hockey League. You would have been laughed out of the pub for suggesting a sce-

nario such as the Jaromir Jagr story. Four score years before that, the thought of an American team winning the Stanley would have been seen to be equally far-fetched. However, probably buried in the archives, there may be one of the most important decisions ever made concerning the trophy. The Pacific Coast Hockey Association had granted franchises to Portland and Seattle. Was either one of these U.S.-based clubs eligible to play for Lord Stanley's award?

Quietly, it appears now, William Foran, a trustee of the Cup, announced the decision. The Stanley Cup, he said, was emblematic of world championship in hockey and no longer was a challenge trophy, open to bids from organizations or individuals with stars in their eyes. If Foran had decided otherwise, the Stanley Cup might have disappeared down the same faint trail left by the Allan Cup, once the coveted chalice of senior hockey in Canada. For many years, it has suffered anonymity. Seattle, of course, did win the Stanley Cup in 1917, becoming the first team based in the U.S. to do so.

Those first winners deserve to be remembered. Unlike later winners, their names were never inscribed on the Stanley Cup. So here they are, the 1917 Cup champion Seattle Metropolitans: Harry Holmes, Roy Rickey, Ed Carpenter, Jack Walker, Bernie Morris, Cully Wilson, Frank Foyston, Jim Riley and Bobby Rowe. That guy, Morris, scored six goals in one game! In today's NHL, who wouldn't like to be his agent?

Unfortunately, it is true that some of the most colorful chapters in any sport took place during the era in which dreamers could challenge and play for the Stanley Cup. That can't happen now. But reason had to set in somewhere.

There is nothing in the background of any other North American sport that compares to the 1905 bid for Stanley's hardware. It was pure Hollywood stuff outlandish, ridiculous, senseless, laughable—but still admirable.

The gold diggers of the Yukon had a dream. It turned out to be a nightmare but give them credit for trying to prove something they believed—or maybe just suspected. They had a hockey team that could beat the great Ottawa Silver Seven.

Taking off from Dawson City, allegedly by dog team on December 18, 1904, they covered an estimated 4,000 miles by boat, train, even by foot, before they arrived at Ottawa on January 12, 1905. Part of the expenses came out of their own pockets. There was no per diem to take care of shoeshines.

The Silver Seven proved to be impatient hosts. Their attitude was: You're here. Let's get this over with. The gold digger crew scored four goals in the two-game series. Ottawa scored 32. Ottawa star Frank McGee couldn't seem to get warmed up in the opening game and the Yukoners boasted they had his number. McGee scored 14 goals in the second game. Another dream shattered.

There were even nasty rumors that the Silver Seven doctored the ice to ensure that little Rat Portage (Kenora) did not upset the giants to make another absurd shot at the Cup come true. Rat Portage had pulled out all the stops for its bid, hiring some of the best players of the day and equipping them with the new tube skates that were fitted with thin blades.

In the opening game, the Ottawa Silver Seven got an alarming surprise. Those new blades really did work as speedy Rat Portage trounced their hosts by a score of 9–3.

In the second game, however, the thin blades seemed to become a handicap. They sank into the soft ice. One explanation of the ice was that the rink had been flooded shortly before the face-off. There also was some mention of salt. Things like that did happen. And play became so rough that Mike Grant, the referee, donned a hard hat. So much for the question of who wore the first helmet in hockey.

Ottawa won the second and third games. The Portagers went home, poorer but smarter. They had expected to profit handsomely from the proceeds but that didn't work out either. Total receipts were $7,791 before expenses were deducted. That was an Ottawa count, of course.

So spare the sighs of regret for the old days. The truth is that competition for the Stanley Cup, before the NHL took over and got it organized, was pretty much a turkey shoot.

Dawson City may be out of Stanley Cup orbit today but Detroit is in. Los Angeles and Miami are in. Moscow may not be too far away. Take your pick when it comes to return on the entertainment dollar.

And that is not to say the NHL system has been flawless. There seldom has been a dumber ruling in a major sport than Frank Calder, the first president of the NHL, made in 1925 when he fined and suspended the entire Hamilton club for demanding $200 per head for taking part in the playoffs.

But the magic of the Cup was powerful even then. The Hamilton franchise was sold at once to New York interests. Maybe the purchase money did come from rum-running, as was alleged, but the New York Americans, as they became known, demonstrated that hockey belonged in New York. Madison Square Garden jumped into the action and the NHL got one of its strongest franchises, the New York Rangers.

Chicago and Detroit followed within a matter of months in a flurry of expansion. But even the booming NHL had trouble weathering the Depression and World War II.

Jobs were scarce and times were hard in the early 1930s but people still responded to events such as Mud Bruneteau's goal of March 25, 1936, in Montreal—at 2:25 in the morning! It gave the Detroit Red Wings a 1–0 win after 176 minutes and 30 seconds (60 minutes regulation time plus 116:30 of overtime) in the longest game of Stanley Cup history. That broke the record of 104:46 of overtime set at Toronto on April 3, 1933, when Ken Doraty of the Maple Leafs scored the goal that beat Boston 1–0. These were events that helped people forget their troubles, at least briefly.

A student of the occult sciences may even be tempted to conclude that the good old Stanley Cup enjoys powers to make chicken salad out of chicken feathers. A reference point would be the 1942 playoff season.

By this time, the league was about to dwindle to six teams. Money was plentiful but butter and automobile tires were rationed. Hockey players were in a different kind of uniform and the question was whether hockey would be able to hang on until peace was restored. There was no doubt about the public's attitude. You had to know somebody in order to get a ticket.

But the game needed a shot in the arm. Enter Hap Day as freshman coach of the Toronto Maple Leafs. Hap really was far from happy. His team was down three games to zip in a best-of-seven set with the Detroit Red Wings, managed and coached by one of the shrewdest men in hockey, Jack Adams.

It's hockey history now but it was front page news then how Day shook up his lineup and avoided elimination by winning the fourth game of the series, right in Detroit. The ceremonial champagne had to accompany the Red Wings back to Toronto.

But the Leafs won again. This time, it was a 9–3 blowout and the Red Wings realized they were in trouble. And they never did get into that champagne. Day, a teetotaler, fell off the wagon after the Leafs won the series four games to three. He dipped a finger into the bubbly and licked it.

The series became increasingly tense, of course, and a lively sidebar was provided when Adams got onto the ice during the fourth game at Detroit. League president Calder, who was on hand, somehow got the idea that Jolly Jack was about to tackle the referee, Mel Harwood. Adams said that conversation was all he had in mind. Adams was suspended.

Day later went on to win the Cup in three successive seasons—the first time it had been done since the NHL took over Cup custody in 1926. It all added up to a publicity boom and applications for franchises from cities such as Cleveland, Los Angeles and San Francisco. All were rejected while the six-team league sailed serenely into an era of prosperity.

Even more momentous events were on the horizon to maintain the wave of popularity that the Leaf-Red Wings series had touched off. Can any coach in today's game picture himself looking along his bench and seeing Jacques Plante, Doug Harvey, Tom Johnson, Jean Beliveau, Boom Boom Geoffrion, Dickie Moore, Rocket Richard, Bert Olmstead, Henri Richard and Butch Bouchard—all them Hall of Famers?

A better question might be whether any general manager today could picture meeting such a payroll at current prices. Toe Blake had them all when he took his place behind the Montreal Canadiens bench for the first time in 1956. Rocket Richard, alone, was pro sport's best box-office property.

Toe was able to get his players to produce. Beliveau scored five goals in Toe's first playoff series. It was against the New York Rangers. In the finals, against Detroit, he potted seven more. Olmstead contributed ten assists in the two sets.

As just about every hockey fan knows, Blake won the prized jug in his first five tries behind the bench. It never had been done before and it almost certainly never will be again. Free agency, player agents and huge salaries have combined to make Toe's kind of team merely dream material.

Toe had to beat five other teams on his way to the Cup. Future coaches may have to defeat as many as 40 or even 50. The Europeans will be coming and the Asians are looking. One thing that can be said with assurance is that no city will monopolize the Cup as Montreal did through the glory years of Blake and Scotty Bowman.

That was a 15-Cup jog—of which eight were won by Toe's teams and five, including four in a row, by Scotty's. Never had two better rosters ever been billeted in the same town over a comparatively short period of time than those two dynasty teams. And, if it were possible to match them up in a series today, where would you put your pesos?

Would you go with the Pocket Rocket, the real Rocket, the Boomer (Geoffrion) and Le Gros Bill (Beliveau) or would it be with Bowman's crop of Hall of Famers?

Blake may have had a bit of an edge on offense, but Bowman wasn't exactly desperate in that area either. With sharpshooters such as Guy Lafleur, Steve Shutt, Jacques Lemaire and Yvan Cournoyer, in full flight, no goalie ever liked to see the Bowman bunch coming.

Defensively, it had to be said that Bowman was not suffering either. In front of goalie Ken Dryden, he sent out Serge Savard, Larry Robinson, Guy Lapointe and Brian Engblom who were among the game's greatest rearguards. Only one member of that group (Engblom) has escaped Hall of Fame attention. Robinson shares a record with Gordie Howe for most years in the Stanley Cup playoffs—20.

When it comes to collecting the greatest feats of Cup achievement, the Bowman and the Blake teams will get serious consideration. Any coach will say that winning an important trophy is tough enough. Defending it, they'll say, is even tougher. No other team ever did a better chore of defending than the Blake and Bowman clubs.

Al Arbour's powerful Islanders of the early 1980s will get some votes and they will be well-earned. The Isles were not deep in marquee players but they are showing up in the Hall of Fame. Denis Potvin, Bryan Trottier, Mike Bossy and goalie Bill Smith already have made it.

In Mike Bossy, they had one of the most consistent goal-getters in Stanley Cup history. In three successive seasons, he scored 17 playoff goals, a feat not even Wayne Gretzky duplicated. Twice during the Isles' triumphs, Mike's teammate Bryan Trottier was the leading scorer in the playoffs.

Partly because their achievements are so recent, but mainly because they have to be regarded as one of the finest teams ever assembled, the Edmonton Oilers of the Gretzky era scored heavily in the end-of-century polls for Canada's greatest team.

It's inevitable that the Oilers are compared to the Canadiens of Blake and Bowman stewardship. Were they even better than those powerhouses? And where would they rate alongside those Detroit clubs of the early and mid-1950s?

Maybe it's all but forgotten now but the Red Wings of 1952 were hell on wheels when guys such as Gordie Howe, Ted Lindsay and Sid Abel were in full bloom. They swept the Canadiens and the Maple Leafs in eight straight games with goalie Terry Sawchuk logging four shutouts in Detroit. You know that record is for all time because there now are at least 16 teams in the playoffs.

The Edmonton Oilers, of course, don't have those four- and five-year winning strings to match the Bowman and Blake credentials. But five Stanley Cup possessions in seven years will get anyone's attention, especially since there are so many more teams to beat since expansion.

Even a casual glance at the Oilers' roster will impress any pollster. Wayne Gretzky, acclaimed as Canada's athlete of the century, leads off. Then consider these names: Mark Messier, Jari Kurri, Glenn Anderson, Randy Gregg, Kevin Lowe, Paul Coffey, Grant Fuhr, Esa Tikkanen, Dave Hunter, Mike Krushelnyski. The beat goes on. If they are not the best team to come along, they at least create some arguments in the bistros, where such decisions are challenged.

And they have left their skatetracks in the playoff computers. Since Gretzky holds most of the offensive records in the regular season, it's only right that many of the Stanley Cup laurels are his, too. His 122 playoff goals should stand for a long time unless Mark Messier enjoys a huge late career with teams that come up big in the playoffs. Gretzky's 260 assists look safe enough, too. His career points—382—can go to the bank. His closest pursuer, Messier, is almost 100 points behind him.

Polls may be nothing but window dressing, the critics are going to argue. They've got it all wrong when they say it about Stanley Cup polls. This is the People's Cup. And what the people say does matter.

For more than 100 years the Stanley Cup trophy has been the game's talisman, a focal point shared by players and fans. The shimmering silver bowl, collar and barrels have been displayed everywhere from Miami to Moscow where they have been admired and photographed by hundreds of thousands. The Cup's escapades—usually in the possession of a member of a winning team—are an action-adventure story all on their own. It's been the star of the show at small-town rinks and on late-night talk shows, all the while conveying the pride and joy of having reached hockey's pinnacle.

CHAPTER 2

Lord Stanley and His Cup Revealed

The Bearded Gent and the Trophy That Bears His Name

Eric Zweig

A Brief Biography

FREDERICK ARTHUR, LORD STANLEY OF PRESTON, 16th Earl of Derby, was born in London on January 15, 1841. The son of a three-time Prime Minister of England, he himself was a British Member of Parliament from 1865 to 1886. He then sat in the House of Lords, and later served a short stint as the Secretary of State for the British colonies. Publicly shy and politically careful, Lord Stanley was an advocate of closer ties between Britain and its colonies. He was appointed Governor-General of Canada in 1888.

Like most British aristocrats of the day, Lord Stanley was an avid sportsman. He and his family enjoyed the new sports they discovered during his posting to Ottawa. Snowshoeing and toboggan parties became a wintertime feature of life at Rideau Hall, the Governor-General's official residence. Skating and the new sport of ice hockey were also popular. Stanley's daughter Isobel was among the first female hockey players in Canada, while two of his sons, Arthur and Algernon, formed a men's hockey club known as the Rideau Rebels. In 1890, Arthur Stanley helped establish the Ontario Hockey Association. Lord Stanley himself was a patron of the Ottawa Athletic Association, and it was at a dinner for this group on March 18, 1892, that the Governor-General asked Lord Kilcoursie, one of his aides and a member of the Rebels hockey team, to read a letter on his behalf:

> *Gentlemen:*
>
> *I have for some time been thinking that it would be a good thing if there were a challenge cup, which would be held from year to year by the leading hockey club in the Dominion (of Canada). There does not appear to be any outward sign of the championship at present, and considering the general interest which hockey matches now elicit, and the importance of having the game played fairly and under rules generally recognized, I am willing to give a cup which shall be held from year to year by the winning club.*

Lord Stanley's offer was accepted, and a decorative bowl was purchased from a London silversmith for 10 guineas (the equivalent of $48.67). Originally called the Dominion Hockey Challenge Cup, the championship trophy would soon be known by the name of its benefactor. The Stanley Cup was first won by the Montreal Amateur Athletic Association hockey club, champions of the Amateur Hockey Association of Canada (the top hockey league in the country) in 1893. Ironically, Lord Stanley never witnessed a championship game nor attended the presentation of his trophy, having returned home in the midst of the 1893 hockey season. He passed away at Holwood, England, on June 14, 1908.

Terms of the Deal

THE STANLEY CUP REGULATIONS OF 1903 outline the rules that Lord Stanley imposed in a document known as the "Deed of Gift" which states that: the then Governor-General, the Earl of Derby, before his departure from Canada in 1893 donated a challenge cup to be held from year to year by the championship Hockey Club of the Dominion. He appointed Sheriff Sweetland and Mr. P.D. Ross, of Ottawa, to act as trustees of the Cup, and requested them to suggest conditions to govern the competition. Meanwhile, his excellency directed that in 1893 the cup should be presented to the M.A.A.A. Hockey team of Montreal, champions of the A.H.A. of Canada, to be held by them until the close of the ensuing year. His excellency laid down the following preliminary conditions:

1. *The winners to give bond for the return of the cup in good order when required by the trustees for the purpose of being handed to any other team who may in turn win.*
2. *Each winning team to have at their own charge engraved on a silver ring fitted on the cup for the purpose the name of the team and the year won. (In the first instance the Montreal Amateur Athletic Association will find the cup already engraved for them.)*
3. *The cup shall remain a challenge cup, and will not become property of any team, even if won more than once.*
4. *In case of any doubt as to the name of any club to claim the position of champions, the cup shall be held or awarded by the trustees as they may think right, their decision being absolute.*
5. *Should either trustee resign or otherwise drop out, the remaining trustee shall nominate a substitute.*

Lord Stanley, in view of the fact of several hockey associations existing in Canada, also asked the trustees to arrange means of making the cup open to all, and thus representative of the hockey championship as completely as possible, rather than of any one association.

The Trustees' Regulations, from 1893:

1. *So far as the Amateur Hockey Association of Canada is concerned, the cup goes with the championship each year, without the necessity of any special or extra contest. Similarly in any other association.*
2. *Challenges from outside the Amateur Hockey Association of Canada are recognized by the trustees only from champion clubs of senior provincial associations, and in the order received.*
3. *When a challenge is accepted, the trustees desire the two competing clubs to arrange by mutual agreement all terms of the contest themselves such as a choice of date, of rink, division of the gate money, selection of officials, etc., etc. The trustees do not wish to interfere in any way, shape or form if it can be avoided.*
4. *Where competing clubs fail to agree, the trustees have observed, and will continue to observe as far as practicable, the following principles.*

a. Cup to be awarded by the result of one match, or best two out of three, as seems fairest as regards other fixtures. The trustees would be willing, however, if desired, to allow the contest to be decided by a majority of the goals scored in two matches only (instead of best two matches in three).
b. Contests to take place on ice in the home city, the date or dates and choice of rink to be made or approved by the trustees.
c. The net gate money given by the rink to be equally divided between the competing teams.
d. If the clubs fail to agree on a referee, the trustees to appoint one from outside the competing cities, the two clubs to share the expenses equally.
e. If the clubs fail to agree on other officials, the trustees to authorize the referee to appoint them, the expense, if any, to be shared equally by the competing clubs.
f. No second challenge recognized in one season from the same hockey association.

How It Got That Way: Physical Changes to the Stanley Cup

THE ORIGINAL STANLEY CUP BOWL purchased in London in 1892 stood 7½ inches (19 cm) tall and measured 11½ inches (29 cm) across the top. It was mounted on a ebony base that made the trophy about one foot tall (29 cm). In accordance with Lord Stanley's terms, the base was fitted with a silver ring that would be used to engrave the names of the winning teams. The first alteration to the physical appearance of the Stanley Cup was made in 1909, when a new bottom section was added. Again, this base was fitted with a ring for engraving. The Cup now stood about 16 inches (40 cm) tall.

No further changes were made to the Stanley Cup until 1924, when the Montreal Canadiens added a silver band between the two engraved rings. When the Victoria Cougars won the Cup the following year, they added an angled band that covered the area between the bottom of the original bowl and the first ring. The Stanley Cup now appeared completely silver from top to bottom. In future years, the silver area beneath the bowl would be known as the collar.

Following the lead of Montreal and Victoria, Stanley Cup-winning teams recorded their victories and the names of their players by adding new silver bands of varying shapes to the trophy, which saw it increase in size by differing amounts almost every year through 1929. From 1930 through 1939, identical-looking thin bands of engraved silver were added every year to commemorate the champions. During the 1940s, the Stanley Cup was standardized as a long "cigar-shaped" trophy which stood almost three feet (90 cm) high. It remained that way until 1948, when it was rebuilt into a two-piece trophy with a wide barrel-shaped base beneath the removable bowl and collar. The barrel-shaped base was sheathed with the rings that had made up the "cigar" of the 1930s and 1940s.

Additional engraving was added to the barrel annually until 1958, when the modern one-piece Stanley Cup was introduced. The silver from the old barrel was then retired to the Hockey Hall of Fame and replaced with five new wide bands, each of which could accommodate the names of 13 winners. The names of Cup winners beginning in 1928 were engraved on the new barrel before the revamped trophy was first presented.

Though the collar was replaced by a duplicate in 1963, and the original bowl was retired in 1969, the Stanley Cup still appears in the same form as it has since 1958. It stands 35¼ inches (88 cm) tall and 18 inches (45 cm) across the base. It weighs 32 pounds (14.5 kg). For the opening of the new Hockey Hall of Fame in Toronto in 1993, a replica of the trophy (and all the other NHL trophies) was built so that the Hall would always have version of the Stanley Cup to display when the much-modified "original" trophy was on the road. (The trophy hoisted by the winning captain on the ice after the Cup-clinching game is always the "original.")

While the basic look of the Stanley Cup has not changed for 42 years, one further alteration was made after the 1990–91 season. The Pittsburgh Penguins filled the last available spot on the wide barrel bands that year. (When the trophy was remodeled in 1958 it was designed so that the last space would be filled by the winner during Cup's centennial year of 1991–92. This plan went awry when the names of the 1964–65 Montreal Canadiens were engraved over a space than was larger than normal, advancing the date when the Cup would be filled by one season.)

Rather than make the trophy bigger, and thereby change a shape that had become so familiar to hockey fans throughout the world, the decision was made to remove the top band (which contained the Cup winners from 1928 to 1940) and retire it to the Hockey Hall of Fame. The four remaining bands were then moved up the barrel, and a new fifth band was added at the bottom. With room for 13 teams, the Stanley Cup shouldn't require any alteration until 2005.

What's in a Name: How the Practice of Engraving the Stanley Cup Evolved

THE STANLEY CUP IS THE OLDEST PROFESSIONAL sports trophy in North America. It is also the only trophy in the world that records the name of every single player on every single team that has ever won it.

Well, not exactly.

Though many of the early winners of hockey's most coveted trophy are known to have engaged in some freelance silversmithing with a knife or a nail, the formal engraving of player names on the Stanley Cup first occurred in 1907 and did not become an annual rite until 1924. In between, there are several seasons in which the winning teams are not on the trophy.

Let's start at the very beginning.

In 1892, Lord Stanley, Governor-General of Canada, announced his decision to donate a hockey trophy. One of his initial conditions stipulated that, "each winning team to have at their own charge engraved on a silver ring fitted on the Cup for the purpose, the name of the team and the year won."

In accordance with Lord Stanley's wishes, team names in the earliest years of the Cup's history were engraved on this silver ring, but by 1902, the ring was completely filled. When the Montreal AAA successfully defended their third Stanley Cup title against the Winnipeg Victorias in 1903, they carved their team name right into Lord Stanley's bowl. The Ottawa Silver Seven continued this new practice when they took possession of the Cup later that season, only with a twist. When the Silver Seven successfully turned back a challenge, they engraved not only the year and their name on the bowl but also the name of the team that they had beaten. For this reason, the name Rat Portage appears on the Stanley Cup in 1903. (Rat Portage would win the Stanley Cup under its new name of Kenora in 1907.) By the time the Silver Seven were dethroned in 1906, Ottawa had defeated ten teams and there was no room left on the Cup for hockey's new champions; the Montreal Wanderers.

The Wanderers were certainly not about to let their championship go unrecorded (at least not yet!). The Montreal team chose to engrave its name right into the decorative fluting atop the Stanley Cup bowl. They covered half the bowl's circumference with their first win, then filled the other half when they turned back a challenge from New Glasgow, Nova Scotia. When the Kenora Thistles defeated the Wanderers in January 1907, they had to record their triumph inside the Stanley Cup bowl. This must have inspired the Montreal squad, for when they won the trophy back from Kenora in March, they inscribed the bottom of the bowl's interior with their team name and with the names of all of their players.

The 1908 season was the Wanderers' best yet, as they defeated four different Stanley Cup challengers. And how did these great champions, innovators of engraving that they were, commemorate these triumphs? They didn't! Only months after becoming the first team to engrave the names of its players on the Stanley Cup, the Montreal Wanderers became the first team in hockey history not to record its victory at all.

Why did the Wanderers leave their name off the Cup? No one seems to know. The Hockey Hall of Fame could provide no answer. Current Stanley Cup trustee Brian O'Neill had no explanation. Several Stanley Cup biographers were unable to uncover any stories. The truth may be lost to history forever, but it seems the Wanderers must have lacked the initiative, or felt they lacked the proper authority—or perhaps they were simply not willing to pay—to make additions to the Stanley Cup.

Apparently, Ottawa (now known as the Senators) did not share whatever concern the Wanderers must have had. After the Senators won the trophy in 1909, a new base was built on below the original silver ring and a second silver ring was added, where the team recorded its victory. The Senators entertained two Stanley Cup challenges during the 1910 season, winning them both, but year's end saw the Wanderers win the Cup back from Ottawa. However, not only did the Montreal squad fail to take advantage of the new ring on the Stanley Cup to add their 1908 championship to the trophy, they also did not bother to record their victory for 1910. When Ottawa regained possession of the Cup in 1911, the Senators also left their name off the trophy. Again, no Stanley Cup authority has the answer, so it's only possible to speculate as to what happened.

One thing is certain: hockey, by 1910, had become big business. The formation of the National Hockey Association truly ushered in the era of professional competition for the Stanley Cup. The NHA was formed to confront the hockey powers of the day. The Montreal Wanderers had been frozen out of their old league, the Eastern Canada Hockey Association, when it was realigned as the Canadian Hockey Association. When Ambrose O'Brien, of Renfrew, Ontario, who had been trying to gain admittance for his team in the new league, was turned down by the CHA, he banded with the Wanderers instead.

Like the World Hockey Association versus the NHL in the 1970s, the upstart NHA and the establishment CHA went to war—except in 1910 the upstarts won and the National Hockey Association emerged as the new power in the game. M.J. O'Brien, father of Ambrose, and a multi-millionaire in mining and railroads, donated a new trophy, the O'Brien Cup, and it, the NHA executive decided, would be emblematic of hockey supremacy. It's possible, then, that as champions of the NHA, the 1910 Wanderers and the 1911 Senators would have felt no obligation to engrave their names on the Stanley Cup.

It seems like a good theory to explain why no team names exist on the Stanley Cup for those two seasons, but there are several reasons why it isn't practical. Every league that preceded the NHA had its own championship trophy. The Stanley Cup did not belong to any one league during this era. It was a challenge trophy symbolizing the top team in all of Canada. Also, the reason the O'Briens got involved in hockey in the first place was to try and bring the Stanley Cup to their hometown of Renfrew. As for the Wanderers and Senators, both teams displayed the Stanley Cup prominently in their team photos, even though they had not engraved their names on the Cup, and both teams continued to entertain Stanley Cup challenges from other leagues across Canada. Once again, as in 1908, the truth may be lost to history forever.

The Stanley Cup got back on track in 1912, but was in trouble again by 1915, albeit of a different kind. Between 1915 and 1918, the Ottawa Senators, Portland Rosebuds, and Vancouver Millionaires all put their names on the Cup, even though they had not officially won it. The Cup was no longer a challenge trophy by then. Its playoff had become a World Series-like showdown between the sport's two top pro leagues: the NHA and the Pacific Coast Hockey Association. All three of these teams had defeated the defending Stanley Cup champions to win their own league title, but then lost the Cup to the eventual winner in the NHA-PCHA playoff.

When the Vancouver Millionaires actually won the Stanley Cup in 1915, they placed the team name on the lower ring started by Ottawa in 1909, but also engraved the names of the players within the flutes on the inside of the original bowl. When Vancouver carved its 1918 PCHA title onto the lower ring it completed the space available there. When the Toronto Arenas (of the newly formed NHL), beat Vancouver in the playoffs that year, there was no room left on the Stanley Cup for them. Their name does not appear. In fact, no more names would be added to the Stanley Cup for six seasons. Why? Once again, no one knows. Only 1919 can be logically explained, in that no champion was declared that year. The series between the Montreal Canadiens and Seattle Metropolitans was called off, due to the Spanish Influenza epidemic that killed millions of people around the world, including Joe Hall of the Canadiens. Ottawa's Cup wins in 1920, 1921 and 1923, along with the Toronto St. Pats' victory in 1922, cannot be explained, other than that, perhaps like the Montreal Wanderers, these teams felt they lacked the authority—or the money—to make alterations to the Stanley Cup.

Finally, in 1924, when hockey's most prized trophy involved a three-league battle between the NHL, the PCHA, and the Western Canada Hockey League, a champion's name is once again found on the Stanley Cup. The Montreal Canadiens defeated Ottawa, Vancouver, and Calgary in two-straight games each and celebrated their victory with a gaudy silver band encircling the area between the original rings. Every player, as well as everyone else associated with the team that year, had their name engraved on the Stanley Cup, just as they have every season since.

And what about the teams from 1908, 1910, 1911, and 1918 to 1923? Well, it's true that they did not engrave their names on the trophy in their day, but it's not entirely accurate to say these teams cannot be found anywhere on the trophy. In 1948, when the NHL remodeled the Stanley Cup from a tall, narrow tube into the basic barrel-shape still seen today, the names of all Cup-winning teams were engraved on the newly created "shoulder" of the trophy where the collars met the barrel. So the Stanley Cup won't forget these missing teams, even if the teams didn't leave their mark on the trophy themselves.

CHAPTER 3

Stanley Cup Champions and Finalists

1893 – 1999

YEAR	WINNER	COACH	FINALIST	COACH
1999	Dallas Stars	Ken Hitchcock	Buffalo Sabres	Lindy Ruff
1998	Detroit Red Wings	Scotty Bowman	Washington Capitals	Ron Wilson
1997	Detroit Red Wings	Scotty Bowman	Philadelphia Flyers	Terry Murray
1996	Colorado Avalanche	Marc Crawford	Florida Panthers	Doug MacLean
1995	New Jersey Devils	Jacques Lemaire	Detroit Red Wings	Scotty Bowman
1994	New York Rangers	Mike Keenan	Vancouver Canucks	Pat Quinn
1993	Montreal Canadiens	Jacques Demers	Los Angeles Kings	Barry Melrose
1992	Pittsburgh Penguins	Scotty Bowman	Chicago Blackhawks	Mike Keenan
1991	Pittsburgh Penguins	Bob Johnson	Minnesota North Stars	Bob Gainey
1990	Edmonton Oilers	John Muckler	Boston Bruins	Mike Milbury
1989	Calgary Flames	Terry Crisp	Montreal Canadiens	Pat Burns
1988	Edmonton Oilers	Glen Sather	Boston Bruins	Terry O'Reilly
1987	Edmonton Oilers	Glen Sather	Philadelphia Flyers	Mike Keenan
1986	Montreal Canadiens	Jean Perron	Calgary Flames	Bob Johnson
1985	Edmonton Oilers	Glen Sather	Philadelphia Flyers	Mike Keenan
1984	Edmonton Oilers	Glen Sather	New York Islanders	Al Arbour
1983	New York Islanders	Al Arbour	Edmonton Oilers	Glen Sather
1982	New York Islanders	Al Arbour	Vancouver Canucks	Roger Neilson
1981	New York Islanders	Al Arbour	Minnesota North Stars	Glen Sonmor
1980	New York Islanders	Al Arbour	Philadelphia Flyers	Pat Quinn
1979	Montreal Canadiens	Scotty Bowman	New York Rangers	Fred Shero
1978	Montreal Canadiens	Scotty Bowman	Boston Bruins	Don Cherry
1977	Montreal Canadiens	Scotty Bowman	Boston Bruins	Don Cherry
1976	Montreal Canadiens	Scotty Bowman	Philadelphia Flyers	Fred Shero
1975	Philadelphia Flyers	Fred Shero	Buffalo Sabres	Floyd Smith
1974	Philadelphia Flyers	Fred Shero	Boston Bruins	Armand 'Bep' Guidolin
1973	Montreal Canadiens	Scotty Bowman	Chicago Black Hawks	Billy Reay
1972	Boston Bruins	Tom Johnson	New York Rangers	Emile Francis
1971	Montreal Canadiens	Al MacNeil	Chicago Black Hawks	Billy Reay
1970	Boston Bruins	Harry Sinden	St. Louis Blues	Scotty Bowman
1969	Montreal Canadiens	Claude Ruel	St. Louis Blues	Scotty Bowman
1968	Montreal Canadiens	Hector 'Toe' Blake	St. Louis Blues	Scotty Bowman
1967	Toronto Maple Leafs	George 'Punch' Imlach	Montreal Canadiens	Hector 'Toe' Blake
1966	Montreal Canadiens	Hector 'Toe' Blake	Detroit Red Wings	Sid Abel
1965	Montreal Canadiens	Hector 'Toe' Blake	Chicago Black Hawks	Billy Reay
1964	Toronto Maple Leafs	George 'Punch' Imlach	Detroit Red Wings	Sid Abel
1963	Toronto Maple Leafs	George 'Punch' Imlach	Detroit Red Wings	Sid Abel
1962	Toronto Maple Leafs	George 'Punch' Imlach	Chicago Black Hawks	Rudy Pilous
1961	Chicago Black Hawks	Rudy Pilous	Detroit Red Wings	Sid Abel
1960	Montreal Canadiens	Hector 'Toe' Blake	Toronto Maple Leafs	George 'Punch' Imlach
1959	Montreal Canadiens	Hector 'Toe' Blake	Toronto Maple Leafs	George 'Punch' Imlach
1958	Montreal Canadiens	Hector 'Toe' Blake	Boston Bruins	Milt Schmidt
1957	Montreal Canadiens	Hector 'Toe' Blake	Boston Bruins	Milt Schmidt
1956	Montreal Canadiens	Hector 'Toe' Blake	Detroit Red Wings	Jimmy Skinner
1955	Detroit Red Wings	Jimmy Skinner	Montreal Canadiens	Dick Irvin
1954	Detroit Red Wings	Tommy Ivan	Montreal Canadiens	Dick Irvin
1953	Montreal Canadiens	Dick Irvin	Boston Bruins	Lynn Patrick
1952	Detroit Red Wings	Tommy Ivan	Montreal Canadiens	Dick Irvin
1951	Toronto Maple Leafs	Joe Primeau	Montreal Canadiens	Dick Irvin
1950	Detroit Red Wings	Tommy Ivan	New York Rangers	Lynn Patrick
1949	Toronto Maple Leafs	Clarence 'Hap' Day	Detroit Red Wings	Tommy Ivan
1948	Toronto Maple Leafs	Clarence 'Hap' Day	Detroit Red Wings	Tommy Ivan
1947	Toronto Maple Leafs	Clarence 'Hap' Day	Montreal Canadiens	Dick Irvin
1946	Montreal Canadiens	Dick Irvin	Boston Bruins	Aubrey 'Dit' Clapper
1945	Toronto Maple Leafs	Clarence 'Hap' Day	Detroit Red Wings	Jack Adams
1944	Montreal Canadiens	Dick Irvin	Chicago Black Hawks	Paul Thompson
1943	Detroit Red Wings	Jack Adams	Boston Bruins	Art Ross
1942	Toronto Maple Leafs	Clarence 'Hap' Day	Detroit Red Wings	Jack Adams
1941	Boston Bruins	Ralph 'Cooney' Weiland	Detroit Red Wings	Ebbie Goodfellow
1940	New York Rangers	Frank Boucher	Toronto Maple Leafs	Dick Irvin
1939	Boston Bruins	Art Ross	Toronto Maple Leafs	Dick Irvin
1938	Chicago Black Hawks	Bill Stewart	Toronto Maple Leafs	Dick Irvin
1937	Detroit Red Wings	Jack Adams	New York Rangers	Lester Patrick
1936	Detroit Red Wings	Jack Adams	Toronto Maple Leafs	Dick Irvin
1935	Montreal Maroons	Tommy Gorman	Toronto Maple Leafs	Dick Irvin

YEAR	WINNER	COACH	FINALIST	COACH
1934	Chicago Black Hawks	Tommy Gorman	Detroit Red Wings	Herbie Lewis
1933	New York Rangers	Lester Patrick	Toronto Maple Leafs	Dick Irvin
1932	Toronto Maple Leafs	Dick Irvin	New York Rangers	Lester Patrick
1931	Montreal Canadiens	Cecil Hart	Chicago Black Hawks	Dick Irvin
1930	Montreal Canadiens	Cecil Hart	Boston Bruins	Art Ross
1929	Boston Bruins	Cy Denneny	New York Rangers	Lester Patrick
1928	New York Rangers	Lester Patrick	Montreal Maroons	Eddie Gerard
1927	Ottawa Senators	Dave Gill	Boston Bruins	Art Ross
	THE NATIONAL HOCKEY LEAGUE ASSUMED CONTROL OF STANLEY CUP COMPETITION AFTER 1926			
1926	Montreal Maroons	Eddie Gerard	Victoria Cougars	Lester Patrick
1925	Victoria Cougars	Lester Patrick	Montreal Canadiens	Leo Dandurand
1924	Montreal Canadiens	Leo Dandurand	Calgary Tigers	Eddie Oatman
			Vancouver Maroons	Art Duncan/Frank Patrick
1923	Ottawa Senators	Pete Green	Edmonton Eskimos	Ken McKenzie
			Vancouver Maroons	Lloyd Cook/Frank Patrick
1922	Toronto St. Pats	George O'Donoghue	Vancouver Millionaires	Lloyd Cook/Frank Patrick
1921	Ottawa Senators	Pete Green	Vancouver Millionaires	Lloyd Cook/Frank Patrick
1920	Ottawa Senators	Pete Green	Seattle Metropolitans	Pete Muldoon
1919	No decision	Series between Montreal and Seattle cancelled due to influenza epidemic		
1918	Toronto Arenas	Dick Carroll	Vancouver Millionaires	Frank Patrick
1917	Seattle Metropolitans	Pete Muldoon	Montreal Canadiens	Newsy Lalonde
1916	Montreal Canadiens	Newsy Lalonde	Portland Rosebuds	E.H. Savage (manager)
1915	Vancouver Millionaires	Frank Patrick	Ottawa Senators	Frank Shaughnessy (manager)
1914	Toronto Blueshirts	Scotty Davidson	Victoria Cougars	Lester Patrick
			Montreal Canadiens	Jimmy Gardner
1913	Quebec Bulldogs	Joe Malone (captain)	Sydney Miners	—
1912	Quebec Bulldogs	Mike Quinn	Moncton Victories	—
1911	Ottawa Senators	Bruce Stuart (captain)	Port Arthur Bearcats	—
			Galt	—
1910	Montreal Wanderers	Pud Glass (captain)	Berlin Union Jacks	—
	Ottawa Senators	Bruce Stuart (captain)	Edmonton Eskimos	—
			Galt	—
1909	Ottawa Senators	Bruce Stuart (captain)	(no challengers)	
1908	Montreal Wanderers	Cecil Blachford	Edmonton Eskimos	—
			Toronto Trolley Leaguers	—
			Winnipeg Maple Leafs	—
			Ottawa Victorias	—
1907	Montreal Wanderers	Cecil Blachford	Kenora Thistles	—
	Kenora Thistles	Tommy Phillips (captain)	Montreal Wanderers	—
1906	Montreal Wanderers	Cecil Blachford (captain)	New Glascow Cubs	—
			Ottawa Silver Seven	—
	Ottawa Silver Seven	A.T. Smith (manager)	Montreal Wanderers	—
			Smiths Falls	—
			Queen's University	—
1905	Ottawa Silver Seven	A.T. Smith (manager)	Rat Portage Thistles	—
			Dawson City Nuggets	—
1904	Ottawa Silver Seven	A.T. Smith (manager)	Brandon Wheat Kings	—
			Montreal Wanderers	—
			Toronto Marlboros	—
			Winnipeg Rowing Club	—
1903	Ottawa Silver Seven	A.T. Smith (manager)	Rat Portage Thistles	—
			Montreal Victorias	—
	Montreal AAA	Clare McKerrow	Winnipeg Victorias	—
1902	Montreal AAA	Clare McKerrow	Winnipeg Victorias	—
	Winnipeg Victorias	—	Toronto Wellingtons	—
1901	Winnipeg Victorias	Dan Bain (captain)	Montreal Shamrocks	—
1900	Montreal Shamrocks	Harry Trihey (captain)	Halifax Crescents	—
			Winnipeg Victorias	—
1899	Montreal Shamrocks	Harry Trihey (captain)	Queen's University	—
	Montreal Victorias	—	Winnipeg Victorias	—
1898	Montreal Victorias	Frank Richardson (mgr.)	(no challengers)	
1897	Montreal Victorias	Mike Grant (captain)	Ottawa Capitals	—
1896	Montreal Victorias	Mike Grant (captain)	Winnipeg Victorias	—
	Winnipeg Victorias	Jack Armytage (manager)	Montreal Victorias	—
1895	Montreal Victorias	Mike Grant (captain)	(no challengers)	
1894	Montreal AAA	—	Ottawa Generals	—
1893	Montreal AAA	—	(no challengers)	

CHAPTER 4

All-Time NHL Playoff Formats

1917-18 – The regular-season was split into two halves. The winners of both halves faced each other in a two-game, total-goals series for the NHL championship and the right to meet the Pacific Coast Hockey Association champion in the best-of-five Stanley Cup Finals.

1918-19 – Same as 1917-18, except that the NHL Finals were extended to a best-of-seven series.

1919-20 – Same as 1917-1918, except that Ottawa won both halves of the split regular-season schedule to earn an automatic berth into the best-of-five Stanley Cup Finals against the PCHA champions.

1921-22 – The top two teams at the conclusion of the regular-season faced each other in a two-game, total-goals series for the NHL championship. The NHL champion then moved on to play the winner of the PCHA-Western Canada Hockey League playoff series in the best-of-five Stanley Cup Finals.

1922-23 – The top two teams at the conclusion of the regular-season faced each other in a two-game, total-goals series for the NHL championship. The NHL champion then moved on to play the PCHA champion in the best-of-three Stanley Cup Semifinals, and the winner of the Semifinals played the WCHL champion, which had been given a bye, in the best-of-three Stanley Cup Finals.

1923-24 – The top two teams at the conclusion of the regular-season faced each other in a two-game, total-goals series for the NHL championship. The NHL champion then moved on to play the loser of the PCHA-WCHL playoff (the winner of the PCHA-WCHL playoff earned a bye into the Stanley Cup Finals) in the best-of-three Stanley Cup Semifinals. The winner of this series met the PCHA-WCHL playoff winner in the best-of-three Stanley Cup Finals.

1924-25 – The first place team (Hamilton) at the conclusion of the regular-season was scheduled to play the winner of a two-game, total goals series between the second (Toronto) and third (Montreal) place clubs. However, Hamilton refused to abide by this new format, demanding greater compensation than offered by the League. Thus, Toronto and Montreal played their two-game, total-goals series, and the winner (Montreal) earned the NHL title and then played the WCHL champion (Victoria) in the best-of-five Stanley Cup Finals.

1925-26 – The format which was intended for 1924-25 went into effect. The winner of the two-game, total-goals series between the second and third place teams squared off against the first place team in the two-game, total-goals NHL championship series. The NHL champion then moved on to play the Western Hockey League champion in the best-of-five Stanley Cup Finals.

After the 1925-26 season, the NHL was the only major professional hockey league still in existence and consequently took over sole control of the Stanley Cup competition.

1926-27 – The 10-team league was divided into two divisions – Canadian and American – of five teams apiece. In each division, the winner of the two-game, total-goals series between the second and third place teams faced the first place team in a two-game, total-goals series for the division title. The two division title winners then met in the best-of-five Stanley Cup Finals.

1928-29 – Both first place teams in the two divisions played each other in a best-of-five series. Both second place teams in the two divisions played each other in a two-game, total-goals series as did the two third place teams. The winners of these latter two series then played each other in a best-of-three series for the right to meet the winner of the series between the two first place clubs. This Stanley Cup Final was a best-of-three.

Series A: First in Canadian Division versus first in American (best-of-five)
Series B: Second in Canadian Division versus second in American (two-game, total-goals)
Series C: Third in Canadian Division versus third in American (two-game, total-goals)
Series D: Winner of Series B versus winner of Series C (best-of-three)
Series E: Winner of Series A versus winner of Series D (best of three) for Stanley Cup

1931-32 – Same as 1928-29, except that Series D was changed to a two-game, total-goals format and Series E was changed to best of five.

1936-37 – Same as 1931-32, except that Series B, C, and D were each best-of-three.

1938-39 – With the NHL reduced to seven teams, the two-division system was replaced by one seven-team league. Based on final regular-season standings, the following playoff format was adopted:

Series A: First versus Second (best-of-seven)
Series B: Third versus Fourth (best-of-three)
Series C: Fifth versus Sixth (best-of-three)
Series D: Winner of Series B versus winner of Series C (best-of-three)
Series E: Winner of Series A versus winner of Series D (best-of-seven)

1942-43 – With the NHL reduced to six teams (the "original six"), only the top four finishers qualified for playoff action. The best-of-seven Semifinals pitted Team #1 vs Team #3 and Team #2 vs Team #4. The winners of each Semifinal series met in the best-of-seven Stanley Cup Finals.

1967-68 – When it doubled in size from 6 to 12 teams, the NHL once again was divided into two divisions – East and West – of six teams apiece. The top four clubs in each division qualified for the playoffs (all series were best-of-seven):

Series A; Team #1 (East) vs Team #3 (East)
Series B: Team #2 (East) vs Team #4 (East)
Series C: Team #1 (West) vs Team #3 (West)
Series D: Team #2 (West) vs Team #4 (West)
Series E: Winner of Series A vs winner of Series B
Series F: Winner of Series C vs winner of Series D
Series G: Winner of Series E vs Winner of Series F

1970-71 – Same as 1967-68 except that Series E matched the winners of Series A and D, and Series F matched the winners of Series B and C.

1971-72 – Same as 1970-71, except that Series A and C matched Team #1 vs Team #4, and Series B and D matched Team #2 vs Team #3.

1974-75 – With the League now expanded to 18 teams in four divisions, a completely new playoff format was introduced. First, the #2 and #3 teams in each of the four divisions were pooled together in the Preliminary round. These eight (#2 and #3) clubs were ranked #1 to #8 based on regular-season record:

Series A: Team #1 vs Team #8 (best-of-three)
Series B: Team #2 vs Team #7 (best-of-three)
Series C: Team #3 vs Team #6 (best-of-three)
Series D: Team #4 vs Team #5 (best-of-three)

The winners of this Preliminary round then pooled together with the four division winners, which had received byes into this Quarterfinal round. These eight teams were again ranked #1 to #8 based on regular-season record:

Series E: Team #1 vs Team #8 (best-of-seven)
Series F: Team #2 vs Team #7 (best-of-seven)
Series G: Team #3 vs Team #6 (best-of-seven)
Series H: Team #4 vs Team #5 (best-of-seven)

The four Quarterfinals winners, which moved on to the Semifinals, were then ranked #1 to #4 based on regular season record:

Series I: Team #1 vs Team #4 (best-of-seven)
Series J: Team #2 vs Team #3 (best-of-seven)
Series K: Winner of Series I vs winner of Series J (best-of-seven)

1977-78 – Same as 1974-75, except that the Preliminary round consisted of the #2 teams in the four divisions and the next four teams based on regular-season record (not their standings within their divisions).

1979-80 – With the addition of four WHA franchises, the League expanded its playoff structure to include 16 of its 21 teams. The four first place teams in the four divisions automatically earned playoff berths. Among the 17 other clubs, the top 12, according to regular-season record, also earned berths. All 16 teams were then pooled together and ranked #1 to #16 based on regular-season record:

Series A: Team #1 vs Team #16 (best-of-five)
Series B: Team #2 vs Team #15 (best-of-five)
Series C: Team #3 vs Team #14 (best-of-five)
Series D: Team #4 vs Team #13 (best-of-five)
Series E: Team #5 vs Team #12 (best-of-five)
Series F: Team #6 vs Team #11 (best-of-five)
Series G: Team #7 vs Team #10 (best-of-five)
Series H: Team #8 vs Team #9 (best-of-five)

The eight Preliminary round winners, ranked #1 to #8 based on regular-season record, moved on to the Quarterfinals:

Series I: Team #1 vs Team #8 (best-of-seven)
Series J: Team #2 vs Team #7 (best-of-seven)
Series K: Team #3 vs Team #6 (best-of-seven)
Series L: Team #4 vs Team #5 (best-of-seven)

The eight Quarterfinals winners, ranked #1 to #4 based on regular-season record, moved on to the semifinals:

Series M: Team #1 vs Team #4 (best-of-seven)
Series N: Team #2 vs Team #3 (best-of-seven)
Series O: Winner of Series M vs winner of Series N (best-of-seven)

1981-82 – The first four teams in each division earned playoff berths. In each division, the first-place team opposed the fourth-place team and the second-place team opposed the third-place team in a best-of-five Division Semifinal (DSF) series. In each division, the two winners of the DSF met in a best-of-seven Division Final (DF) series. The two winners in each conference met in a best-of-seven Conference Final (CF) series. In the Prince of Wales Conference, the Adams Division winner opposed the Patrick Division winner; in the Clarence Campbell Conference, the Smythe Division winner opposed the Norris Division winner. The two CF winners met in a best-of-seven Stanley Cup Final (F) series.

1986-87 – Division Semifinal series changed from best-of-five to best-of-seven.

1993-94 – The NHL's playoff draw was conference-based rather than division-based. At the conclusion of the regular season, the top eight teams in each of the Eastern and Western Conferences qualified for the playoffs. The teams that finish in first place in each of the League's divisions were seeded first and second in each conference's playoff draw and were assured of home ice advantage in the first two playoff rounds.

The remaining teams were seeded based on their regular-season point totals. In each conference, the team seeded #1 played #8; #2 vs. #7; #3 vs. #6; and #4 vs. #5. All series were best-of-seven with home ice rotating on a 2-2-1-1-1 basis, with the exception of matchups between Central and Pacific Division teams. These matchups were played on a 2-3-2 basis to reduce travel. In a 2-3-2 series, the team with the most points could choose to start the series at home or on the road. The Eastern Conference champion faced the Western Conference champion in the Cup Final.

1994-95 – Same as 1993-94, except that in first, second or third-round playoff series involving Central and Pacific Division teams, the team with the better record had the choice of using either a 2-3-2 or a 2-2-1-1-1 format. When a 2-3-2 format was selected, the higher-ranked team also had the choice of playing games 1, 2, 6 and 7 at home or playing games 3, 4 and 5 at home. The format for the Stanley Cup Final remained 2-2-1-1-1.

1998-99 – The NHL's clubs were re-aligned into two conferences each consisting of three divisions. The number of teams qualifying for the Stanley Cup Playoffs remained unchanged at 16.

First-round playoff berths were awarded to the first-place team in each division as well as to the next five best teams based on regular-season point totals in each conference. The three division winners in each conference were seeded first through third for the playoffs and the next five best teams, in order of points, were seeded fourth through eighth. In each conference, the team seeded #1 played #8; #2 vs. #7; #3 vs. #6; and #4 vs. #5 in the quarterfinal round. Home-ice in the Conference Quarterfinals was granted to those teams seeded first through fourth in each conference.

In the Conference Semifinals and Conference Finals, teams were re-seeded according to the same criteria as the Conference Quarterfinals. Higher seeded teams gained home-ice advantage.

Home-ice advantage for the Stanley Cup Finals to be determined by points.

All series remain best-of-seven.

2000 Playoff Format

The National Hockey League's 28 clubs are aligned into two conferences, each consisting of three divisions (Eastern Conference: Atlantic, Northeast, Southeast; Western Conference: Central, Northwest, Pacific). The number of teams qualifying for the 2000 Stanley Cup Playoffs remains at 16.

First-round playoff berths will be awarded to the first-place team in each division, as well as to the next five best teams (based on regular-season point totals in each conference). The three division winners in each conference will be seeded first through third (in order of points) and the next five best teams (in order of points) will be seeded fourth through eighth. In each conference, the team seeded #1 will play the team seeded #8; #2 vs. #7; #3 vs. #6 and #4 vs. #5 in the Conference Quarterfinal round. Home-ice in the Conference Quarterfinals is granted to those teams seeded first through fourth in each conference.

In the Conference Semifinals and Conference Finals, teams will be re-seeded according to the same criteria as the Conference Quarterfinals (division leaders will be seeded first and granted home-ice advantage while the remaining teams will be seeded in order of regular-season points).

Home-ice advantage in the Stanley Cup series will be determined by points.

All series remain best-of-seven.

Tie-Breaking Procedure

In the event two or more clubs are tied in points at the conclusion of the regular season, the standing of the clubs in each conference will be determined in the following order:

1. The greater number of games won.
2. The greater number of points earned in games between the tied clubs. If two clubs are tied, and have not played an equal number of home games against each other, points earned in the first game played in the city that had the extra game shall not be included. If more than two clubs are tied, the higher percentage of available points earned in games among those clubs shall be used to determine the standing.
3. The greater differential between goals for and against for the entire regular season.

Conference Quarterfinals (Series A – H)

The six regular-season division champions will be ranked in the first three positions in their respective conferences, the clubs with the greatest number of points being ranked first in their respective conferences. The remaining five playoff clubs in each conference will be ranked based on regular-season points. Following are the matchups based on the rankings.

Eastern Conference

Series A #1 (Division winner) vs. #8
Series B #2 (Division winner) vs. #7
Series C #3 (Division winner) vs. #6
Series D #4 vs. #5

Western Conference

Series E #1 (Division winner) vs. #8
Series F #2 (Division winner) vs. #7
Series G #3 (Division winner) vs. #6
Series H #4 vs. #5

Conference Semifinals (Series I – L)

If one division winner is eliminated in the Conference Quarterfinals: The remaining division winners would be seeded first and second, followed by the two remaining clubs in order of regular-season points. The #1 seed would face the club with the fewest regular-season points, while the other two clubs would meet.

If two division winners are eliminated in the Conference Quarterfinals: The remaining division winner would be seeded first, followed by the three remaining clubs in order of regular-season points. The #1 seed would face the club with the fewest regular-season points, while the other two clubs would meet.

If all three division winners are eliminated in the Conference Quarterfinals: The remaining clubs would be ranked in order of regular-season points. The remaining team with the most regular-season points would be seeded first, followed by the three remaining teams. The #1 seed would face the #4 seed, while the #2 and #3 clubs would meet.

If a division winner meets a non-division winner that compiled more regular-season points: The division winner would receive home-ice advantage.

Conference Finals (Series M and N)

The same criteria used in the selection of order for the Conference Quarterfinals (Advancing division winners, followed by remaining clubs based on regular-season points) again will be in effect.

If a division winner meets a non-division winner that compiled more regular-season points: The division winner would receive home-ice advantage.

If Conference Semifinal series end early: Start dates for the Conference Finals may be moved up depending on a number of factors, including building availability and travel schedules.

Stanley Cup (Series O)

The Eastern Conference and Western Conference champion will meet in the Stanley Cup series. Home ice will be determined by the greater number of regular-season points, subject to the tie-breaking procedures outlined on the previous page. Games will be played on a 2-2-1-1-1 basis.

Stanley Cup Gallery

Usually viewed through champagne, the bottom of the bowl atop the Stanley Cup is engraved with the names of the Montreal Wanderers, winners of a two-game, total-goals final against the Kenora Thistles in March 1907. The second name from the bottom of the column on the left belongs to Lester Patrick, the future Pacific Coast hockey entrepreneur and, later, coach and manager of the New York Rangers. The engraved names of the 1915 Cup-winning Vancouver Millionaires —including Lester Patrick's brother Frank—can be found inside the fluting of the bowl to the right of the Wanderers.

1906
DEC 27-29 WANDERERS vs NEW GLASGOW
MONTREAL
1903

1906
DEC 27-29 WANDERERS vs NEW GLASGOW
MONTREAL
1903
OTTAWA
VANCOUVER
CALGARY
NEW YORK RANGERS PROFESSIONAL HOCKEY CLUB
WORLDS CHAMPIONS AND WINNERS OF THE
STANLEY CUP-1932-1933
TORONTO MAPLE LEAFS 1944-45
CANADIENS OF MONTREAL
1952-53
DETROIT RED WINGS
1954-55

TORONTO

The Changing Trophy

Lord Stanley, Canada's Governor-General, (opposite, top left) donated the squat silver bowl that soon bore his name. The custom of engraving the winners' names on the trophy forced it to grow as additional silver bands were added. By 1939 when the Bruins won (above), the trophy had become a slim cylinder that grew even taller by the time Toronto goaltender Turk Broda (opposite, bottom right) posed with the Cup in 1947. The silver bands from this cigar-shaped trophy were mounted on a wide barrel in 1948, forming the two-piece trophy displayed by Leaf captain Teeder Kennedy (right) and shown in an early publicity photo (opposite, bottom left.)

THE CANADIAN HOCKEY CLUB INCORPORATED
U.P. BOUCHER
DIDIER PITRE
COUPE STANLEY
LOUIS BERLINQUETTE
AMOS ARBOUR
JACK LAVIOLETTE
BERT. CORBEAU
GOLDIE PRODGERS
1915
1916
GEORGES VEZINA
A. OUIMET
THE STANLEY CUP HOLDERS
MONTREAL

Championship Teams

The Montreal Shamrocks (opposite, above) claimed the Stanley Cup as champions of the Canadian Amateur Hockey League in 1899 and 1900. The CAHL trophy is nearly twice as large, but is long since forgotten. The Quebec Bulldogs (opposite, below left) were members of the National Hockey Association when they won the Stanley Cup in 1912 and 1913. So were the Montreal Canadiens (opposite, below right) when they won their first of 24 Stanley Cup titles in 1916. The other trophy in both team pictures is the O'Brien Trophy, which later served as an NHL award until 1950. The New York Rangers (right) won the Stanley Cup for the third time in 13 seasons in 1940, but would have to wait 54 years to win it again. Detroit goaltender Harry Lumley celebrated a Stanley Cup triumph (below, center) surrounded by teammates Marty Pavelich, Sid Abel, Gerry Couture and George Gee on April 23, 1950. Three months later he was traded to Chicago to make room for Terry Sawchuk, who led the Red Wings to the Cup in 1952, 1954 and 1955.

Overtime Winner

Bill Barilko scored only five playoff goals in his career, but this one gave the Toronto Maple Leafs the Stanley Cup title in 1951 and remains one of the most famous moments in hockey history. The 1951 series marks the only time in Stanley Cup play that every game was decided in overtime. Barilko beat Gerry McNeil of the Canadiens at 2:53 of extended play in Game Five. It was the last goal he ever scored, as he lost his life in a plane crash while on a fishing trip that summer.

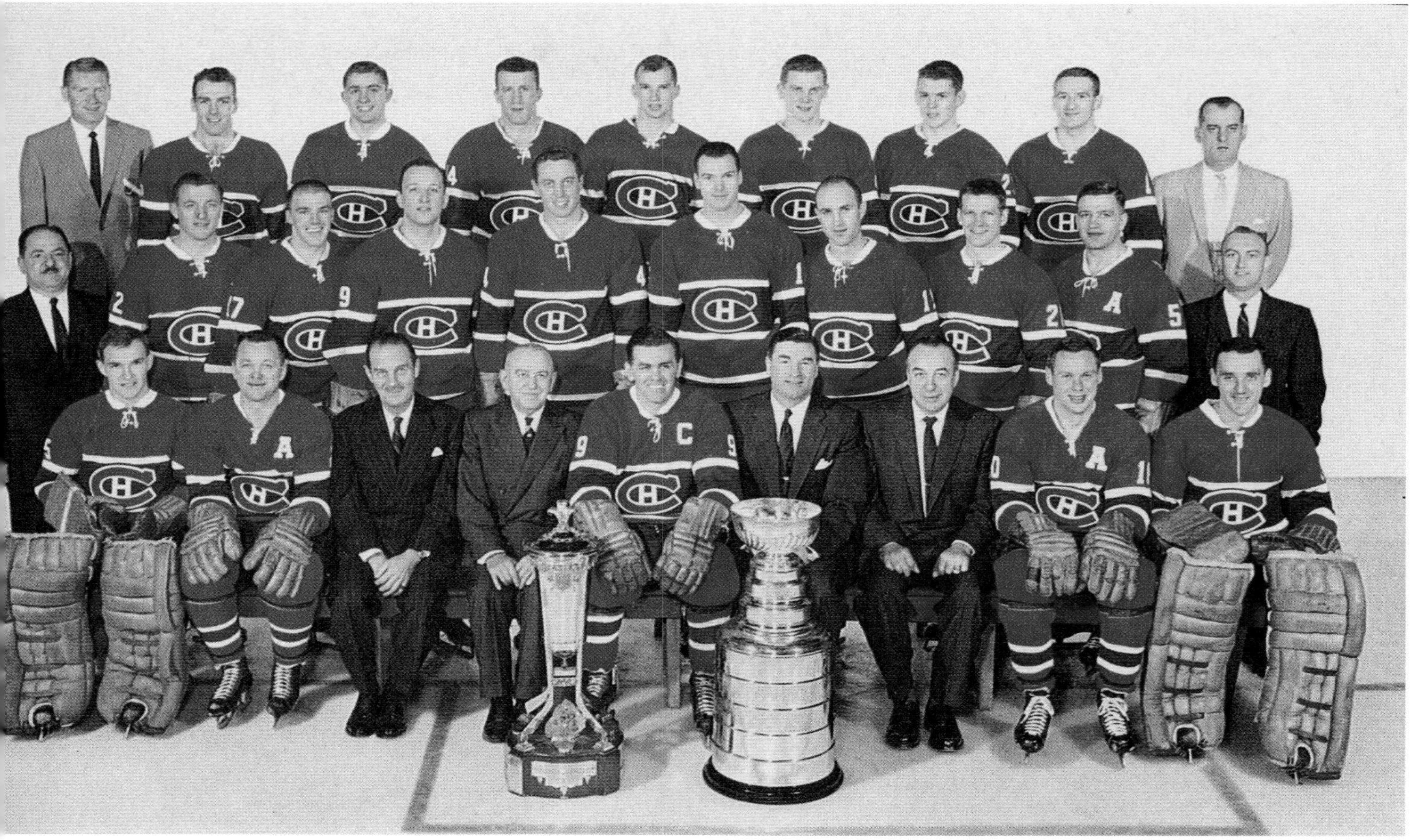

Triple Dynasty

Montreal hockey teams have dominated Stanley Cup competition from the very beginning, but none can match the overwhelming brilliance of les Canadiens. *The Montreal Canadiens of 1960 (above) capped a remarkable run of five straight Stanley Cup titles under captain Maurice Richard. Considering that the team also won the Stanley Cup in 1953 and lost a pair of seven-game series in 1954 and 1955, Montreal might have won eight straight championships with a bit of luck. Jean Beliveau (right) was a member of Montreal's five-time dynasty, and later captained the Canadiens to four Stanley Cup wins in a five-year span (1965 to 1969) before hoisting the silverware for a final time in 1971. Guy Lafleur (left) was a rookie with Montreal the following season. The heir apparent to Richard and Beliveau among the pantheon of Canadiens immortals, Lafleur won his third straight scoring title when the Canadiens won their third straight Stanley Cup championship in 1978. Montreal made it four in a row the following year.*

Bruins and Islanders

Though the Boston Bruins boasted superstars in Bobby Orr and Phil Esposito, and the Islanders had Mike Bossy, Bryan Trottier and Denis Potvin, both clubs were "lunch bucket" teams at heart. They beat their opponents with hustle and desire as much as with their superior talent. Bobby Orr's overtime goal (above, left) against St. Louis in 1970 brought Boston its first Stanley Cup title in 29 years. Bob Nystrom's goal against Philadelphia (below, right) in 1980 gave the Islanders a Cup victory after just eight seasons in the NHL. The Islanders went on to win four Stanley Cup titles in a row, and established a record by winning 19 straight playoff rounds before losing to Edmonton in 1984.

ISLANDERS
KOHO
LOUISVILLE

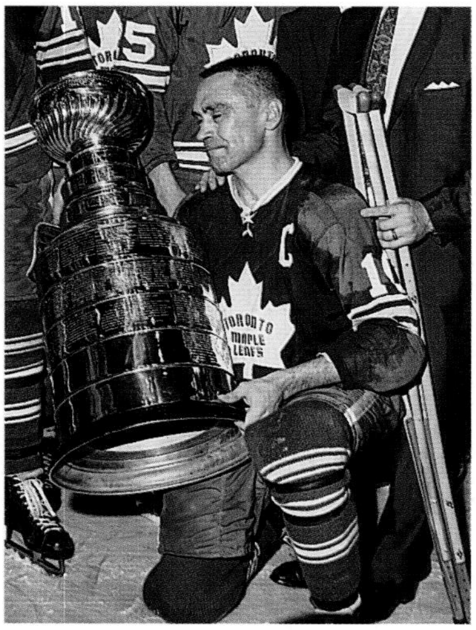

"C" is for Cup

The politics of a modern NHL franchise can involve a difficult balancing act between the agendas of a club owner, general manager, coach, players, and agents. A captain no longer serves as his teammates' voice in the affairs of management, but a good team captain can still set the tone in the dressing room. Whether it is through the quiet confidence of a Steve Yzerman (opposite) or George Armstrong (above, right), the on-ice brilliance of a Mario Lemieux (middle, right) or the fiery personalities of Rocket Richard (below) and Mark Messier (below, right), a team needs a true leader to succeed. Between them, the five men displayed on these pages have won the Stanley Cup 22 times. Richard leads the way with eight titles, four of them as captain of the Canadiens. Messier won the Cup five times in Edmonton, captaining them to their final victory in 1990 before serving as New York's inspirational on-ice leader in 1994. Armstrong captained the Leafs to four Stanley Cup titles in the 1960s. Lemieux led the Penguins to back-to-back championships in 1991 and 1992, while Yzerman did the same with Detroit in 1997 and 1998.

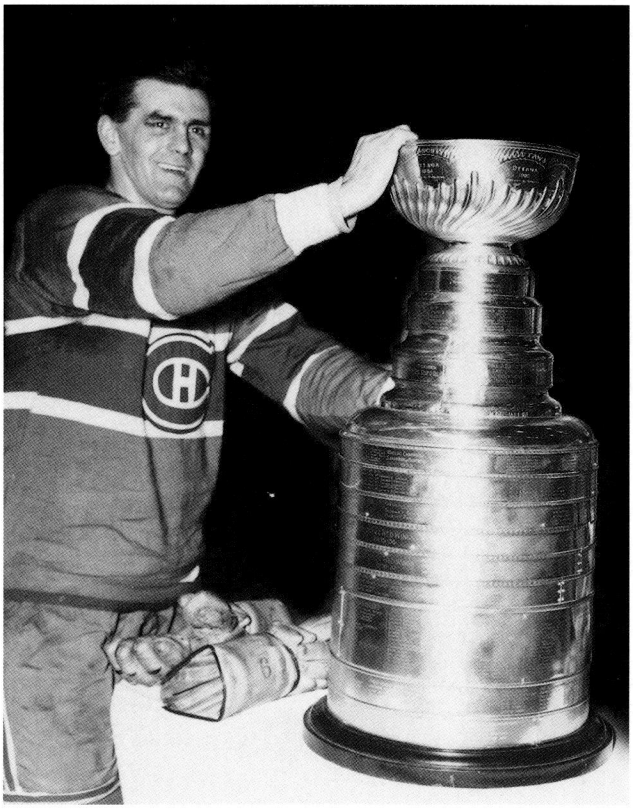

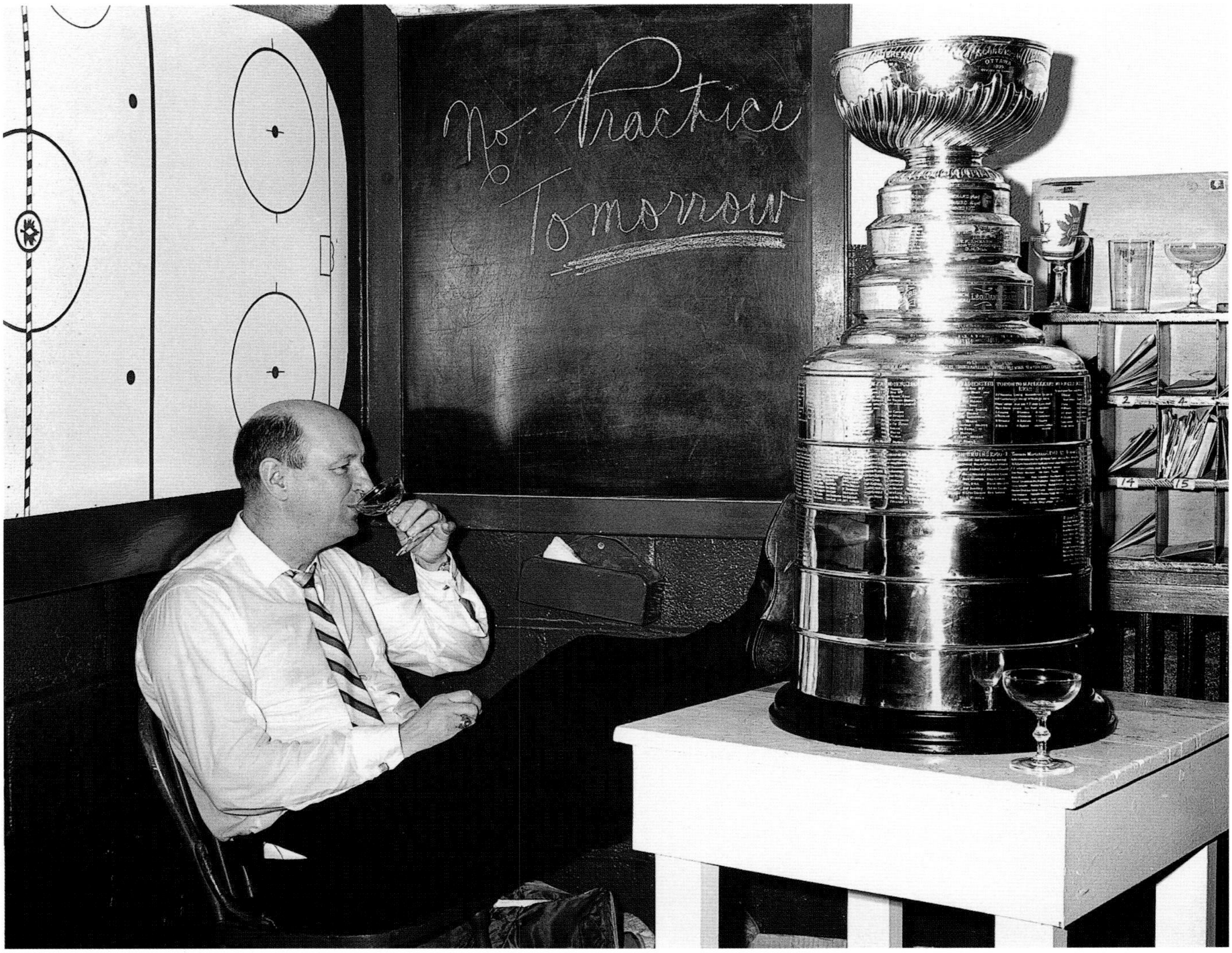

Bench Bosses

Though his dictatorial ways seldom sat well with his players, no one could argue that Punch Imlach (above) delivered results. His Toronto teams won the Stanley Cup three years in a row from 1962 to 1964 and added a fourth title in 1967. Likewise, Mike Keenan (left) would not win many popularity contests, but he did lead Philadelphia (1985 and 1987) and Chicago (1992) to the Finals before winning it all with the 1994 New York Rangers. Toe Blake (opposite, above) was a member of three Stanley Cup winners as a player. Here he celebrates his fourth win as a coach with Marcel Bonin in 1959. Blake's Canadiens made if five Cup titles in a row in 1960. He added three more before retiring in 1968. Scotty Bowman (opposite, below) equalled Blake's record when he coached his eighth Cup-winner with Detroit in 1998. Bowman began his Cup haul by winning five times with the Canadiens during the 1970s.

The Great One Fulfilled

There were many who doubted Wayne Gretzky would succeed when he entered the NHL as a skinny 18-year-old in 1979. Even as he set record after record, his critics would complain that he could not deliver the game's ultimate prize, particularly after the Oilers were swept by the Islanders in the 1983 Finals. Edmonton returned to the Finals one year later, and on May 19, 1984, Gretzky and the Oilers were Stanley Cup champions. They would win again three times in the next four years.

Photo Credits: Bruce Bennett Studios; CP Picture Archive – Brian Gavriloff; Dan Diamond and Associates; Hockey Hall of Fame file photo, Graphic Artists Collection and Imperial Oil Turofsky Collection.

CHAPTER 5

In the Beginning

From Amateur Challenge Trophy to Pro Hockey Supremacy

Eric Zweig

THE HISTORY OF THE STANLEY CUP prior to the formation of the NHL in 1917 tells the story of how hockey grew from a regionalized amateur pastime into a professional business. Like Darwin's theory of survival of the fittest, the Stanley Cup was able to evolve with the changing times.

When Lord Stanley proposed the idea of a championship trophy in 1892, the "modern" sport of hockey was less than 20 years old. First moved indoors off frozen lakes and rivers in Montreal in 1875, the game was still played most competitively in that city, as well as in nearby Ottawa and Quebec City. The Amateur Hockey Association of Canada, formed in 1886, comprised teams from those cities. Hockey also had a following in Kingston, where outdoor ice games had been played since at least the 1850s. The popularity of hockey in that city helped the game grow through southern Ontario, and in 1890 the Ontario Hockey Association was formed. By that year, the game had also spread to western Canada where it found a particularly fevered following in Winnipeg. Having been home to a variety of outdoor stick and ice games since the early 1800s, Canada's east coast had its own hockey following as well. All of these different areas of interest would eventually be brought together in the quest for Lord Stanley's Cup.

Originally called the Dominion Hockey Challenge Cup, Lord Stanley's trophy was first presented in 1893. It was awarded to the hockey club from the Montreal Amateur Athletic Association, who had won the league title in the Amateur Hockey Association which was recognized as the top league in Canada. But as Lord Stanley wanted his Cup to be truly representative of a national championship, he instructed his trustees, Philip Dansken Ross and Sheriff John Sweetland, to construct a set of terms that would allow teams from across the country to challenge for the trophy. The Stanley Cup, therefore, would not be the sole property of the AHA (or of any hockey league), but could be competed for by the senior champion of any recognized provincial association. However, once a team had won it the Stanley Cup belonged to them until someone defeated them. Defeating them did not necessarily entail issuing a challenge, for the trustees determined that the Stanley Cup could also change hands within a given league. For example, when the Montreal Victorias unseated the AAA for the AHA championship in 1895 they automatically became holders of Stanley Cup. But in order for the Manitoba Hockey League's Winnipeg Victorias to become champions in 1896, they had to issue a challenge to their Montreal counterparts. Once Winnipeg had won the Stanley Cup, it became property of them in the MHL and when the Montreal Vics successfully defended their AHA championship they had to challenge Winnipeg in order to win back the Stanley Cup.

Though the AHA was replaced by the Canadian Amateur Hockey League in 1899, the system of determining Stanley Cup winners that was devised in 1893 went on without a hitch until 1904 when the Ottawa Silver Seven threatened the status quo.

By defeating the defending champion Montreal AAA for the CAHL title in 1903, Ottawa had won the Stanley Cup, but trouble began the following season. On January 30, 1904, the Silver Seven were delayed en route to Montreal for a league game against the Victorias. As a result, the game was not yet over when the two teams agreed to leave the ice at midnight with Ottawa leading 4–1. CAHL officials refused to grant Ottawa the victory, and ordered that the game be replayed. The ensuing debate ended with the Silver Seven withdrawing from the league. CAHL officials hoped the Stanley Cup would then pass to their new league champion (Quebec), but the trustees ruled it would remain with Ottawa. Even though they were no longer a part of any established hockey league, the Silver Seven defeated the OHA champions from Toronto, then had a series with the Montreal Wanderers abandoned due to a scheduling conflict before defeating a team from Brandon, Manitoba that featured a young defenseman named Lester Patrick. Any further problems were resolved when the Silver Seven joined the Federal Amateur Hockey League in 1905. In 1906, the Ottawa club helped form the Eastern Canada Amateur Hockey Association (ECAHA), which replaced the CAHL as the top league in the country.

With a lineup that boasted future Hall of Famers Bouse Hutton, Harvey Pulford, Harry Westwick, Alf Smith, Billy Gilmour, and Frank McGee, the Silver Seven were the first legendary hockey team of the 20th century. Tough and talented, they remained Stanley Cup champions until finally relinquishing the trophy in 1906. During their championship run, the Silver Seven played off for the title ten times—far more than any other team during the Stanley Cup's challenge era.

From 1893 to 1906 the Winnipeg Victorias (1896 and 1901) were the only Stanley Cup winners from outside Montreal and Ottawa. In these early days of Stanley Cup competition, geography and climate played almost as important a role as skill in determining a champion. During this time period, the hockey season in leagues across Canada ran from January to early March—cold weather being a must in arenas that relied on natural ice. This being the case, a Stanley Cup challenge match might be scheduled in late December before the start of hockey season or in mid-March if weather still permitted, but the majority were scheduled in midseason during January and February. The Stanley Cup trustees could only accept as many challenges as time (ie the weather and regular-season schedules) would permit, and an arduous travel agenda didn't make an underdog's role any easier—as the Dawson City Nuggets discovered in 1905.

The most unusual challenge in Stanley Cup history was received by the trustees on September 9, 1904. Spearheaded by businessman and adventurer Joe Boyle, Dawson's Stanley Cup bid was officially sanctioned on December 10. Originally scheduled to be completed by January 10, 1905, the start of the series was pushed back to January 13 in order to accommodate an election that had been called in the Yukon Territory. The hockey players from Dawson City left town on December 18,

1904. Traveling 4,000 miles on foot and on dogsled, by bicycle, boat and by train, they arrived in Ottawa just one day before the start of the series. On the road for almost an entire month, they were in understandably poor condition. After a 9–2 Ottawa victory in the opener, the series concluded with Dawson City being defeated 23–2 on January 16, 1905. Frank McGee scored 14 goals for the Silver Seven that evening.

Ottawa's run as Stanley Cup champions ended when the team lost the ECAHA title to the Montreal Wanderers in March 1906. By November of that year, the Wanderers played a key role in ushering in a new era in Stanley Cup history. At the ECAHA annual meeting prior to the upcoming 1907 season, the Wanderers helped push through a resolution that allowed professional players to play alongside amateurs. The only stipulation was that teams would be required to declare which of their players were pros and which were amateurs, and that the status of these players would be published in the newspapers.

The issue of professionalism was a hot topic in Canada and around the sporting world during the late 19th century and into the 20th. Many people continued to cling to the British aristocratic tradition of sports for sports' sake, but the truth was that many hockey players had been paid to play almost from the beginning—though these payments were usually made in secret. The first openly professional hockey league was the International (Pro) Hockey League, which operated with teams in Pennsylvania, Michigan and northwestern Ontario from 1904 to 1907. Though the issue remained contentious, the Stanley Cup trustees (now P.D. Ross and William Foran) did not impose any moral judgements. If the top league in Canada voted to allow professionals to compete, than the Stanley Cup would be open to competition from professional teams. Once the decision was made, there was no turning back. By 1908, a new trophy (the Allan Cup) was introduced to recognize Canada's amateur champions. The Stanley Cup was now the emblem of professional hockey supremacy. Organizations like the Ontario Professional Hockey League and the Maritime Professional Hockey League would soon arise and send challengers to compete for the Stanley Cup.

In 1910, a new league emerged as the top hockey circuit in Canada. The National Hockey Association (forerunner of the NHL) introduced the Montreal Canadiens to the game during its inaugural season. In 1910–11 (the schedule was now beginning in December) the NHA changed the timing of hockey games from two 30-minute halves to three 20-minute periods. Prior to the 1911-12 season, the NHA eliminated the position of rover and introduced the six-man game. This year would also prove significant in that the Stanley Cup trustees declared that all challenge matches would now take place at the conclusion of the regular season.

Yet another change was introduced to hockey for the 1911–12 season. The Pacific Coast Hockey Association was formed by Frank and Lester Patrick. In addition to running the league, Frank would serve as a player, coach, general manager, and owner of the PCHA's Vancouver Millionaires. Lester held the same duties with the Victoria Aristocrats. (It was hoped the monied monikers would lend the league a touch of class.)

Using proceeds from the sale of their father's British Columbia lumber business, the Patrick brothers built Canada's first artificial ice rinks in Vancouver and Victoria in order to overcome the west coast's non-hockey climate. Using their hockey connections in the east, they raided talent from NHA rosters to stock their teams, as well as the PCHA's third franchise in New Westminster. Notable names like Newsy Lalonde, Tommy Dunderdale, and Moose Watson (Hockey Hall of Famers all) went west that first season, though the man who would give the PCHA the credibility it needed (as he had previously done for the NHA) did not come on board until the league's second season. Fred "Cyclone" Taylor was signed by the Vancouver Millionaires in 1912–13.

The Patricks were innovators, and while it was the NHA that would one day become the NHL it was the PCHA that truly modernized hockey. Though Frank and Lester stubbornly maintained the position of rover, they also painted blue lines on the ice to divide the playing surface into zones, legalized forward passing, and permitted goaltenders to leave their feet. In all, some 20 rules proposed by Frank Patrick would eventually find their way into NHL rule books.

Meanwhile, since its inception in 1910, no team from a rival league had been able to defeat the NHA's champion for the Stanley Cup. As such, the Stanley Cup was passed from the Montreal Wanderers in 1910 to the Ottawa Senators in 1911, to the Quebec Bulldogs in 1912 as the NHA found itself with a new league leader for three straight years. Quebec repeated as champions in 1913, but the Stanley Cup was claimed by the Toronto Blueshirts when they took the NHA title in 1914. That year, Victoria traveled east to take on Toronto for the Stanley Cup. The Aristocrats failed to submit an official request to play for the championship, leading to a statement from trustees Ross and Foran that this series was not regarded as a formal Cup challenge. Prior to the 1914–15 season, the NHA and PCHA simply agreed that their respective league champions would meet to determine the Stanley Cup winner. Because of the distances involved, all games in a given year would be played in one location, the site alternating yearly between the champions of east and west. The two leagues' differing sets of rules would be switched from game to game.

Another significant development in Stanley Cup history took place in the 1914–15 season. The PCHA's New Westminster Royals franchise left British Columbia for Oregon, where it became the Portland Rosebuds. (Portland is known as "The Rose City.") By admitting a United States city into a league that competed for the Stanley Cup, PCHA president Frank Patrick and the Stanley Cup trustees were recognizing that an American-based team might one day be playing for a trophy that had previously been emblematic of Canadian supremacy. In fact, the Rosebuds won the PCHA title in 1916, but they lost the Stanley Cup to the Montreal Canadiens, who won for the first time in franchise history. One year later, the Seattle Metropolitans beat the Canadiens in the NHA–PCHA "World Series" and the Stanley Cup headed south of the border.

Just 25 years after it had been presented, the Stanley Cup was no longer a challenge trophy, nor was it held by the champion team of the Dominion of Canada. These had been the preliminary conditions laid down by Lord Stanley. However, one of the original conditions had also provided that the Cup would be held or awarded by the trustees as they saw fit. By changing with the times, the trustees ensured that the Stanley Cup would always be the top prize in hockey.

CHAPTER 6

Playoff History, Current NHL Clubs

1918–1999

NOTE:

- Calgary totals include Atlanta, 1972-73 to 1979-80.
- Carolina totals include Hartford, 1979–80 to 1996-97
- Colorado totals include Quebec, 1979-80 to 1994-95.
- Dallas totals include Minnesota, 1967-68 to 1992-93.
- New Jersey totals include Kansas City, 1974-75 to 1975-76 and Colorado Rockies, 1976-77 to 1981-82.
- Phoenix totals include Winnipeg, 1979-80 to 1995-96.

ANAHEIM

All-Time Playoff Record vs. Other Clubs

	Series	W	L	GP	W	L	T	GF	GA	Last Mtg.	Round	Result
Detroit	2	0	2	8	0	8	0	14	30	1999	CQF	L 0-4
Phoenix	1	1	0	7	4	3	0	17	17	1997	CQF	W 4-3
Totals	**3**	**1**	**2**	**15**	**4**	**11**	**0**	**31**	**47**			

Playoff Results 1999-95

Year	Round	Opponent	Result	GF	GA
1999	CQF	Detroit	L 0-4	6	17
1997	CSF	Detroit	L 0-4	8	13
	CQF	Phoenix	W 4-3	17	17

Playoff Scoring Leaders

	Player	Years	GP	G	A	Pts.
1.	Paul Kariya	97-99	14	8	9	17
2.	Teemu Selanne	97-99	15	9	5	14
3.	Dmitri Mironov	97	11	1	10	11
4.	J.J. Daigneault	97	11	2	7	9
5.	Brian Bellows	97	11	2	4	6
6.	Steve Rucchin	97-99	12	1	5	6
7.	Jari Kurri	97	11	1	2	3
8.	Joe Sacco	97	11	2	0	2
9.	Marty MacInnis	99	4	2	0	2
10.	Dave Karpa	97	8	1	1	2
11.	Sean Pronger	97	9	0	2	2
12.	Darren Van Impe	97	9	0	2	2
13.	Warren Rychel	97	11	0	2	2
14.	Fredrik Olausson	99	4	0	2	2

Series Records vs. Other Clubs

Opponent	Year	Series	Winner	W	L	GF	GA
Phx.	1997	CQF	Ana.	4	3	17	17
Det.	1997	CSF	Det.	0	4	8	13
Det.	1999	CQF	Det.	0	4	6	17

BOSTON

All-Time Playoff Record vs. Other Clubs

	Series	W	L	GP	W	L	T	GF	GA	Last Mtg.	Round	Result
Buffalo	7	5	2	39	21	18	0	146	130	1999	CSF	L 2-4
Carolina	3	3	0	19	12	7	0	63	48	1999	CQF	W 4-2
Chicago	6	5	1	22	16	5	1	97	63	1978	QF	W 4-0
Colorado	2	1	1	11	6	5	0	37	36	1983	DSF	W 3-1
Dallas	1	0	1	3	0	3	0	13	20	1981	PR	L 0-3
Detroit	7	4	3	33	19	14	0	96	98	1957	SF	W 4-1
Edmonton	2	0	2	9	1	8	0	20	41	1990	F	L 1-4
Florida	1	0	1	5	1	4	0	16	22	1996	CQF	L 1-4
Los Angeles	2	2	0	13	8	5	0	56	38	1977	QF	W 4-2
Montreal	28	7	21	139	52	87	0	339	430	1994	CQF	W 4-3
New Jersey	3	1	2	18	7	11	0	52	55	1995	CQF	L 1-4
NY Islanders	2	0	2	11	3	8	0	35	49	1983	CF	L 2-4
NY Rangers	9	6	3	42	22	18	2	114	104	1973	QF	L 1-4
Philadelphia	4	2	2	20	11	9	0	60	57	1978	SF	W 4-1
Pittsburgh	4	2	2	19	9	10	0	62	67	1992	CF	L 0-4
St. Louis	2	2	0	8	8	0	0	48	15	1972	SF	W 4-0
Toronto	13	5	8	62	30	31	1	153	150	1974	QF	W 4-0
Washington	2	1	1	10	6	4	0	28	21	1998	CQF	L 2-4
Defunct	3	1	2	11	4	5	2	20	20			
Totals	**101**	**47**	**54**	**494**	**236**	**252**	**6**	**1448**	**1464**			

Playoff Results 1999-95

Year	Round	Opponent	Result	GF	GA
1999	CSF	Buffalo	L 2-4	14	17
	CQF	Carolina	W 4-2	16	10
1998	CQF	Washington	L 2-4	13	15
1996	CQF	Florida	L 1-4	16	22
1995	CQF	New Jersey	L 1-4	5	14

Playoff Scoring Leaders

	Player	Years	GP	G	A	Pts.
1.	Ray Bourque	80-99	180	36	125	161
2.	Phil Esposito	68-75	71	46	56	102
3.	Rick Middleton	77-88	111	45	55	100
4.	John Bucyk	58-77	109	40	60	100
5.	Bobby Orr	68-75	74	26	66	92
6.	Wayne Cashman	68-83	145	31	57	88
7.	Cam Neely	87-95	86	55	32	87
8.	Ken Hodge	68-76	86	34	47	81
9.	Brad Park	76-83	91	23	55	78
10.	Peter McNab	77-83	79	38	37	75

Series Records vs. Other Clubs

Opponent	Year	Series	Winner	W	L	T	GF	GA
Buf.	1982	DSF	Bos.	3	1		17	11
Buf.	1983	DF	Bos.	4	3		33	23
Buf.	1988	DSF	Bos.	4	2		28	22
Buf.	1989	DSF	Bos.	4	1		16	14
Buf.	1992	DSF	Bos.	4	3		19	24
Buf.	1993	DSF	Buf.	0	4		12	19
Buf.	1999	CSF	Buf.	2	4		14	17
Car.	1999	CQF	Bos.	4	2		16	10
Chi.	1927	QF*	Bos.	1	0	1	10	5
Chi.	1942	QF	Bos.	2	1		5	7
Chi.	1970	SF	Bos.	4	0		20	10
Chi.	1974	SF	Bos.	4	2		28	20
Chi.	1975	PRE	Chi.	1	2		15	12
Chi.	1978	QF	Bos.	4	0		19	9
Det.	1941	F	Bos.	4	0		12	6
Det.	1942	SF	Det.	0	2		5	9
Det.	1943	F	Det.	0	4		5	16
Det.	1945	SF	Det.	3	4		22	22
Det.	1946	SF	Bos.	4	1		16	10
Det.	1953	SF	Bos.	4	2		21	21
Det.	1957	SF	Bos.	4	1		15	14
Edm.	1988	F	Edm.	0	4		12	21
Edm.	1990	F	Edm.	1	4		8	20
Fla.	1996	CQF	Fla.	1	4		16	22
Hfd.	1990	DSF	Bos.	4	3		23	21
Hfd.	1991	DSF	Bos.	4	2		24	17
L.A.	1976	QF	Bos.	4	3		26	14
L.A.	1977	QF	Bos.	4	2		30	24
Min.	1981	PRE	Min.	0	3		13	20
Mtl.	1929	SF	Bos.	3	0		5	2
Mtl.	1930	F	Mtl.	0	2		3	7
Mtl.	1931	SF	Mtl.	2	3		13	13
Mtl.	1943	SF	Bos.	4	1		18	17
Mtl.	1946	F	Mtl.	1	4		13	19
Mtl.	1947	SF	Mtl.	1	4		10	16
Mtl.	1952	SF	Mtl.	3	4		12	18
Mtl.	1953	F	Mtl.	1	4		9	16
Mtl.	1954	SF	Mtl.	0	4		4	16
Mtl.	1955	SF	Mtl.	1	4		9	16
Mtl.	1957	F	Mtl.	1	4		6	15
Mtl.	1958	F	Mtl.	2	4		14	16
Mtl.	1968	QF	Mtl.	0	4		8	15
Mtl.	1969	SF	Mtl.	2	4		16	15
Mtl.	1971	QF	Mtl.	3	4		26	28
Mtl.	1977	F	Mtl.	0	4		6	16
Mtl.	1978	F	Mtl.	2	4		13	18
Mtl.	1979	SF	Mtl.	3	4		20	25
Mtl.	1984	DSF	Mtl.	0	3		2	10
Mtl.	1985	DSF	Mtl.	2	3		17	19
Mtl.	1986	DSF	Mtl.	0	3		6	10
Mtl.	1987	DSF	Mtl.	0	4		11	19
Mtl.	1988	DF	Bos.	4	1		15	10
Mtl.	1989	DF	Mtl.	1	4		13	16
Mtl.	1990	DF	Bos.	4	1		16	12
Mtl.	1991	DF	Bos.	4	3		18	18
Mtl.	1992	DF	Bos.	4	0		14	8
Mtl.	1994	CQF	Bos.	4	3		22	20
N.J.	1988	CF	Bos.	4	3		30	19
N.J.	1994	CSF	N.J.	2	4		17	22
N.J.	1995	CQF	N.J.	1	4		5	14
NYI	1980	QF	NYI	1	4		14	19
NYI	1983	CF	NYI	2	4		21	30
NYR	1927	SF*	Bos.	1	0	1	3	1
NYR	1928	SF*	NYR	0	1	1	2	5
NYR	1929	F	Bos.	2	0		4	1
NYR	1939	SF	Bos.	4	3		14	12
NYR	1940	SF	NYR	2	4		9	15
NYR	1958	SF	Bos.	4	2		28	16
NYR	1970	QF	Bos.	4	2		25	16
NYR	1972	F	Bos.	4	2		18	16
NYR	1973	QF	NYR	1	4		11	22
Phi.	1974	F	Phi.	2	4		13	15
Phi.	1976	SF	Phi.	1	4		12	19
Phi.	1977	SF	Bos.	4	0		14	8
Phi.	1978	QF	Bos.	4	1		21	15
Pit.	1979	QF	Bos.	4	0		16	7
Pit.	1980	PRE	Bos.	3	2		21	14
Pit.	1991	CF	Pit.	2	4		18	27
Pit.	1992	CF	Pit.	0	4		7	19
Que.	1982	DF	Que.	3	4		26	28
Que.	1983	DSF	Bos.	3	1		11	8
St.L.	1970	F	Bos.	4	0		20	7
St.L.	1972	SF	Bos.	4	0		28	8
Tor.	1933	SF	Tor.	2	3		27	9
Tor.	1935	SF	Tor.	1	3		2	7
Tor.	1936	QF*	Tor.	1	1		6	8
Tor.	1938	SF	Tor.	0	3		3	6
Tor.	1939	F	Bos.	4	1		12	6
Tor.	1941	SF	Bos.	4	3		15	17
Tor.	1948	SF	Tor.	1	4		13	20
Tor.	1949	SF	Tor.	1	4		10	16
Tor.	1951	SF	Tor.	1	4	1	5	17
Tor.	1959	SF	Tor.	3	4		21	20
Tor.	1969	QF	Bos.	4	0		24	5
Tor.	1970	QF	Bos.	4	1		18	10
Tor.	1974	QF	Bos.	4	0		17	9
Wsh.	1990	CF	Bos.	4	0		15	6
Wsh.	1998	CQF	Wsh.	2	4		13	15
Defunct Clubs								
Mtl.M	1930	SF	Bos.	3	1		11	5
Mtl.M	1937	QF	Mtl.M	1	2		6	8
Ott.	1927	F	Ott.	0	2	2	3	7

* Total-goals series

BUFFALO

All-Time Playoff Record vs. Other Clubs

	Series	W	L	GP	W	L	T	GF	GA	Last Mtg.	Round	Result
Boston	7	2	5	39	18	21	0	130	146	1999	CSF	W 4-2
Chicago	2	2	0	9	8	1	0	36	17	1980	QF	W 4-0
Colorado	2	0	2	8	2	6	0	27	35	1985	DSF	L 2-3
Dallas	3	1	2	13	5	8	0	37	39	1999	F	L 2-4
Montreal	7	3	4	35	17	18	0	111	124	1998	CSF	W 4-0
New Jersey	1	0	1	7	3	4	0	14	14	1994	CQF	L 3-4
NY Islanders	3	0	3	16	4	12	0	45	59	1980	SF	L 2-4
NY Rangers	1	1	0	3	2	1	0	11	6	1978	PR	W 2-1
Ottawa	2	2	0	11	8	3	0	26	19	1999	CQF	W 4-0
Philadelphia	5	1	4	26	9	17	0	67	83	1998	CQF	W 4-1
Pittsburgh	1	0	1	3	1	2	0	9	9	1979	PR	L 1-2
St. Louis	1	1	0	3	2	1	0	7	8	1976	PR	W 2-1
Toronto	1	1	0	5	4	1	0	21	16	1999	CF	W 4-1
Vancouver	2	2	0	7	6	1	0	28	14	1981	PR	W 3-0
Washington	1	0	1	6	2	4	0	11	13	1998	CF	L 2-4
Totals	**39**	**16**	**23**	**191**	**91**	**100**	**0**	**580**	**595**			

Playoff Results 1999-95

Year	Round	Opponent	Result	GF	GA
1999	F	Dallas	L 2-4	9	13
	CF	Toronto	W 4-1	21	16
	CSF	Boston	W 4-2	17	14
	CQF	Ottawa	W 4-0	12	6
1998	CF	Washington	L 2-4	11	13
	CSF	Montreal	W 4-0	17	10
	CQF	Philadelphia	W 4-1	18	9
1997	CSF	Philadelphia	L 1-4	13	21
	CQF	Ottawa	W 4-3	14	13
1995	CQF	Philadelphia	L 1-4	13	18

Playoff Scoring Leaders

	Player	Years	GP	G	A	Pts.
1.	Gilbert Perreault	73-85	90	33	70	103
2.	Richard Martin	73-80	62	24	29	53
3.	Craig Ramsay	73-85	89	17	31	48
4.	Danny Gare	75-81	57	23	21	44
5.	Rene Robert	73-79	47	22	17	39
6.	Don Luce	73-80	62	17	19	36
7.	Dale Hawerchuk	91-94	28	9	25	34
8.	Dave Andreychuk	83-92	41	12	20	32
9.	Alexander Mogilny	89-95	31	14	16	30
10.	Donald Audette	90-98	48	12	17	29
11.	Brian Holzinger	95-99	52	11	18	29

Series Records vs. Other Clubs

Opponent	Year	Series	Winner	W	L	GF	GA
Bos.	1982	DSF	Bos.	1	3	11	17
Bos.	1983	DF	Bos.	3	4	23	33
Bos.	1988	DSF	Bos.	2	4	22	28
Bos.	1989	DSF	Bos.	1	4	14	16
Bos.	1992	DSF	Bos.	3	4	24	19
Bos.	1993	DSF	Buf.	4	0	19	12
Bos.	1999	CSF	Buf.	4	2	17	14
Chi.	1975	QF	Buf.	4	1	20	10
Chi.	1980	QF	Buf.	4	0	16	7
Dal.	1999	F	Dal.	2	4	9	13
Min.	1977	PRE	Buf.	2	0	11	3
Min.	1981	QF	Min.	1	4	17	23
Mtl.	1973	QF	Mtl.	2	4	16	21
Mtl.	1975	SF	Buf.	4	2	21	29
Mtl.	1983	DSF	Buf.	3	0	8	2
Mtl.	1990	DSF	Mtl.	2	4	13	17
Mtl.	1991	DSF	Mtl.	2	4	24	29
Mtl.	1993	DF	Mtl.	0	4	12	16
Mtl.	1998	CSF	Buf.	4	0	17	10
N.J.	1994	CQF	N.J.	3	4	14	14
NYI	1976	QF	NYI	2	4	18	21
NYI	1977	QF	NYI	0	4	10	16
NYI	1980	SF	NYI	2	4	17	22
NYR	1978	PRE	Buf.	2	1	11	6
Ott.	1997	CQF	Buf.	4	3	14	13
Ott.	1999	CQF	Ott.	4	0	12	6
Phi.	1975	F	Phi.	2	4	12	19
Phi.	1978	QF	Phi.	1	4	11	16
Phi.	1995	CQF	Phi.	1	4	13	18
Phi.	1997	CSF	Phi.	1	4	13	21
Phi.	1998	CQF	Buf.	4	1	18	9
Pit.	1979	PRE	Pit.	1	2	9	9
Que.	1984	DSF	Que.	0	3	5	13
Que.	1985	DSF	Que.	2	3	22	22
St.L.	1976	PRE	Buf.	2	1	7	8
Tor.	1999	CF	Buf.	4	1	21	16
Van.	1980	PRE	Buf.	3	1	15	7
Van.	1981	PRE	Buf.	3	0	13	7
Wsh.	1998	CF	Wsh.	2	4	11	13

CALGARY

All-Time Playoff Record vs. Other Clubs

	Series	W	L	GP	W	L	T	GF	GA	Last Mtg.	Round	Result
Chicago	3	2	1	12	7	5	0	37	33	1996	CQF	L 0-4
Dallas	1	0	1	6	2	4	0	18	25	1981	SF	L 2-4
Detroit	1	0	1	2	0	2	0	5	8	1978	PR	L 0-2
Edmonton	5	1	4	30	11	19	0	96	132	1991	DSF	L 3-4
Los Angeles	6	2	4	26	13	13	0	102	105	1993	DSF	L 2-4
Montreal	2	1	1	11	5	6	0	32	31	1989	F	W 4-2
NY Rangers	1	0	1	4	1	3	0	8	14	1980	PR	L 1-3
Philadelphia	2	1	1	11	4	7	0	28	43	1981	QF	W 4-3
St. Louis	1	1	0	7	4	3	0	28	22	1986	CF	W 4-3
San Jose	1	0	1	7	3	4	0	35	26	1995	CQF	L 3-4
Toronto	1	0	1	2	0	2	0	5	9	1979	PR	L 0-2
Vancouver	5	3	2	25	13	12	0	82	80	1994	CQF	L 3-4
Winnipeg	3	1	2	13	6	7	0	43	45	1987	DSF	L 2-4
Totals	**32**	**12**	**20**	**156**	**69**	**87**	**0**	**529**	**590**			

Playoff Results 1999-95

Year	Round	Opponent	Result	GF	GA
1996	CQF	Chicago	L 0-4	7	16
1995	CQF	San Jose	L 3-4	35	26

Playoff Scoring Leaders

	Player	Years	GP	G	A	Pts.
1.	Al MacInnis	84-94	95	25	77	102
2.	Paul Reinhart	81-88	76	21	51	72
3.	Theoren Fleury	89-96	59	29	33	62
4.	Joel Otto	85-95	87	23	38	61
5.	Joe Nieuwendyk	87-95	66	32	28	60
6.	Joe Mullen	86-90	61	35	20	55
7.	Hakan Loob	84-89	73	26	28	54
8.	Lanny McDonald	82-89	72	24	23	47
9.	Jim Peplinski	81-89	99	15	31	46
10.	Gary Roberts	87-94	58	13	30	43

Series Records vs. Other Clubs

Note: Includes series played by Atlanta Flames, 1973-80.

Opponent	Year	Series	Winner	W	L	GF	GA
Chi.	1981	PRE	Cgy.	3	0	15	9
Chi.	1989	CF	Cgy.	4	1	15	8
Chi.	1996	CQF	Chi.	0	4	7	16
Det.	1978	PRE	Det.	0	2	5	8
Edm.	1983	DF	Edm.	1	4	13	35
Edm.	1984	DF	Edm.	3	4	27	33
Edm.	1986	DF	Cgy.	4	3	25	24
Edm.	1988	DF	Edm.	0	4	11	18
Edm.	1991	DSF	Edm.	3	4	20	22
L.A.	1976	PRE	L.A.	0	2	1	3
L.A.	1977	PRE	L.A.	1	2	7	11
L.A.	1988	DSF	Cgy.	4	1	30	18
L.A.	1989	DF	Cgy.	4	0	22	11
L.A.	1990	DSF	L.A.	2	4	24	29
L.A.	1993	DSF	L.A.	2	4	28	33
Min.	1981	SF	Min.	2	4	18	25
Mtl.	1986	F	Mtl.	1	4	13	15
Mtl.	1989	F	Cgy.	4	2	19	16
NYR	1980	PRE	NYR	1	3	8	14
Phi.	1974	QF	Phi.	0	4	6	17
Phi.	1981	QF	Cgy.	4	3	22	26
St.L.	1986	CF	Cgy.	4	3	28	22
S.J.	1995	CQF	S.J.	3	4	35	26
Tor.	1979	PRE	Tor.	0	2	5	9
Van.	1982	DSF	Van.	0	3	5	10
Van.	1983	DSF	Cgy.	3	1	17	14
Van.	1984	DSF	Cgy.	3	1	14	13
Van.	1989	DSF	Cgy.	4	3	26	20
Van.	1994	CQF	Van.	3	4	20	23
Wpg.	1985	DSF	Wpg.	1	3	13	15
Wpg.	1986	DSF	Cgy.	3	0	15	8
Wpg.	1987	DSF	Wpg.	2	4	15	22

CAROLINA

All-Time Playoff Record vs. Other Clubs

	Series	W	L	GP	W	L	T	GF	GA	Last Mtg.	Round	Result
Boston	3	0	3	19	7	12	0	48	63	1999	CQF	L 2-4
Colorado	2	1	1	9	5	4	0	35	34	1987	DSF	L 2-4
Montreal	5	0	5	27	8	19	0	70	96	1992	DSF	L 3-4
Totals	**10**	**1**	**9**	**55**	**20**	**35**	**0**	**157**	**194**			

Playoff Results 1999-95

Year	Round	Opponent	Result	GF	GA
1999	CQF	Boston	L 2-4	14	17

Playoff Scoring Leaders

	Player	Years	GP	G	A	Pts.
1.	Kevin Dineen	86-91, 99	44	17	14	31
2.	Dean Evason	86-91	38	8	15	23
3.	Ron Francis	86-90, 99	36	8	15	23
4.	Dave Babych	86-90	31	7	13	20
5.	Ray Ferraro	86-90	33	7	11	18
6.	John Anderson	86-89	20	6	11	17
7.	Stewart Gavin	86-88	22	8	7	15
8.	Paul MacDermid	86-89	26	5	8	13
9.	John Cullen	91-92	13	4	8	12
10.	Brad Shaw	89-92	19	4	8	12

Series Records vs. Other Clubs

Note: Includes series played by Hartford Whalers, 1980-92.

Opponent	Year	Series	Winner	W	L	GF	GA
Bos.	1990	DSF	Bos.	3	4	21	23
Bos.	1991	DSF	Bos.	2	4	17	24
Bos.	1999	CQF	Bos.	2	4	14	17
Mtl.	1980	PRE	Mtl.	0	3	8	18
Mtl.	1986	DF	Mtl.	3	4	13	16
Mtl.	1988	DSF	Mtl.	2	4	20	23
Mtl.	1989	DSF	Mtl.	0	4	11	18
Mtl.	1992	DSF	Mtl.	3	4	18	21
Que.	1986	DSF	Hfd.	3	0	16	7
Que.	1987	DSF	Que.	2	4	19	27

CHICAGO

All-Time Playoff Record vs. Other Clubs

	Series	W	L	GP	W	L	T	GF	GA	Last Mtg.	Round	Result
Boston	6	1	5	22	5	16	1	63	97	1978	QF	L 0-4
Buffalo	2	0	2	9	1	8	0	17	36	1980	QF	L 0-4
Calgary	3	1	2	12	5	7	0	33	37	1996	CQF	W 4-0
Colorado	2	0	2	12	4	8	0	28	49	1997	CQF	L 2-4
Dallas	6	4	2	33	19	14	0	119	119	1991	DSF	L 2-4
Detroit	14	8	6	69	38	31	0	210	190	1995	CF	L 1-4
Edmonton	4	1	3	20	8	12	0	77	102	1992	CF	W 4-0
Los Angeles	1	1	0	5	4	1	0	10	7	1974	QF	W 4-1
Montreal	17	5	12	81	29	50	2	185	261	1976	QF	L 0-4
NY Islanders	2	0	2	6	0	6	0	6	21	1979	QF	L 0-4
NY Rangers	5	4	1	24	14	10	0	66	54	1973	SF	W 4-1
Philadelphia	1	1	0	4	4	0	0	20	8	1971	QF	W 4-0
Pittsburgh	2	1	1	8	4	4	0	24	23	1992	F	L 0-4
St. Louis	9	7	2	45	27	18	0	166	129	1993	DSF	L 0-4
Toronto	9	3	6	38	15	22	1	89	111	1995	CQF	W 4-3
Vancouver	2	1	1	9	5	4	0	24	24	1995	CSF	W 4-0
Defunct	4	2	2	9	5	3	1	16	15			
Totals	**89**	**40**	**49**	**406**	**187**	**214**	**5**	**1153**	**1283**			

Playoff Results 1999-95

Year	Round	Opponent	Result	GF	GA
1997	CQF	Colorado	L 2-4	14	28
1996	CSF	Colorado	L 2-4	14	21
	CQF	Calgary	W 4-0	16	7
1995	CF	Detroit	L 1-4	12	13
	CSF	Vancouver	W 4-0	11	6
	CQF	Toronto	W 4-3	22	20

Playoff Scoring Leaders

	Player	Years	GP	G	A	Pts.
1.	Stan Mikita	60-78	155	59	91	150
2.	Denis Savard	81-90, 95-97	131	61	84	145
3.	Bobby Hull	59-72	116	62	67	129
4.	Steve Larmer	83-93	107	45	66	111
5.	Doug Wilson	78-91	95	19	61	80
6.	Jeremy Roenick	89-96	82	35	42	77
7.	Dennis Hull	65-77	104	33	34	67
8.	Pierre Pilote	59-68	82	8	52	60
9.	Tom Lysiak	79-86	67	23	33	56
10.	Bob Murray	77-90	112	19	37	56

Series Records vs. Other Clubs

Opponent	Year	Series	Winner	W	L	T	GF	GA
Bos.	1927	QF*	Bos.	0	1	1	5	10
Bos.	1942	QF	Bos.	1	2		7	5
Bos.	1970	SF	Bos.	0	4		10	20
Bos.	1974	SF	Bos.	2	4		20	28
Bos.	1975	PRE	Chi.	2	1		12	15
Bos.	1978	QF	Bos.	0	4		9	19
Buf.	1975	QF	Buf.	1	4		10	20
Buf.	1980	QF	Buf.	0	4		7	16
Cgy.	1981	PRE	Cgy.	0	3		9	15
Cgy.	1989	CF	Cgy.	1	4		8	15
Cgy.	1996	CQF	Chi.	4	0		16	7
Col.	1996	CSF	Col.	2	4		14	19
Col.	1997	CQF	Col.	2	4		14	28
Det.	1934	F	Chi.	3	1		9	7
Det.	1941	SF	Det.	0	2		2	5
Det.	1944	SF	Chi.	4	1		17	8
Det.	1961	F	Chi.	4	2		19	12
Det.	1963	SF	Det.	2	4		19	25
Det.	1964	SF	Det.	3	4		18	24
Det.	1965	SF	Chi.	4	3		23	19
Det.	1966	SF	Det.	2	4		10	22
Det.	1970	QF	Chi.	4	0		16	8
Det.	1985	DSF	Chi.	3	0		23	8
Det.	1987	DSF	Det.	0	4		6	15
Det.	1989	DSF	Chi.	4	2		25	18
Det.	1992	DF	Chi.	4	0		11	6
Det.	1995	CF	Det.	1	4		12	13
Edm.	1983	CF	Edm.	0	4		11	25
Edm.	1985	CF	Edm.	2	4		25	44
Edm.	1990	CF	Edm.	2	4		20	25
Edm.	1992	CF	Chi.	4	0		21	8
L.A.	1974	QF	Chi.	4	1		10	7
Min.	1982	DSF	Chi.	3	1		14	14
Min.	1983	DF	Chi.	4	1		22	17
Min.	1984	DSF	Min.	2	3		14	18
Min.	1985	DF	Chi.	4	2		32	29
Min.	1990	DSF	Chi.	4	3		21	18
Min.	1991	DSF	Min.	2	4		16	23
Mtl.	1930	QF*	Mtl.	0	1	1	2	3
Mtl.	1931	F	Mtl.	2	3		8	11
Mtl.	1934	QF*	Chi.	1	1		4	3
Mtl.	1938	QF	Chi.	2	1		11	8
Mtl.	1941	QF	Chi.	2	1		8	7
Mtl.	1944	F	Mtl.	0	4		8	16
Mtl.	1946	SF	Mtl.	0	4		7	26
Mtl.	1953	SF	Mtl.	3	4		14	18
Mtl.	1959	SF	Mtl.	2	4		16	21
Mtl.	1960	SF	Mtl.	0	4		6	14
Mtl.	1961	SF	Chi.	4	2		16	15
Mtl.	1962	SF	Chi.	4	2		19	13
Mtl.	1965	F	Mtl.	3	4		12	18
Mtl.	1968	SF	Mtl.	1	4		10	22
Mtl.	1971	F	Mtl.	3	4		18	20
Mtl.	1973	F	Mtl.	2	4		23	33
Mtl.	1976	QF	Mtl.	0	4		3	13
NYI	1977	PRE	NYI	0	2		3	7
NYI	1979	QF	NYI	0	4		3	14
NYR	1931	SF*	Chi.	2	0		3	0
NYR	1968	QF	Chi.	4	2		18	12
NYR	1971	SF	Chi.	4	3		21	14
NYR	1972	SF	NYR	0	4		9	17
NYR	1973	SF	Chi.	4	1		15	11
Phi.	1978	QF	Chi.	4	0		20	8
Pit.	1972	QF	Chi.	4	0		14	8
Pit.	1992	F	Pit.	0	4		10	15
St.L.	1973	QF	Chi.	4	1		22	9
St.L.	1980	PRE	Chi.	3	0		12	4
St.L.	1982	DF	Chi.	4	2		23	19
St.L.	1983	DSF	Chi.	3	1		16	10
St.L.	1988	DSF	St.L.	1	4		17	21
St.L.	1989	DF	Chi.	4	1		19	12
St.L.	1990	DF	Chi.	4	3		28	22
St.L.	1992	DSF	Chi.	4	2		23	19
St.L.	1993	DSF	St.L.	0	4		6	13
Tor.	1931	QF*	Chi.	1	0	1	4	3
Tor.	1932	QF*	Tor.	1	1		2	6
Tor.	1938	F	Chi.	3	1		10	8
Tor.	1940	QF	Tor.	0	2		3	5
Tor.	1962	F	Tor.	2	4		15	18
Tor.	1967	SF	Tor.	2	4		14	18
Tor.	1986	DSF	Tor.	0	3		9	18
Tor.	1994	CQF	Tor.	2	4		10	15
Tor.	1995	CQF	Chi.	4	3		22	20
Van.	1982	CF	Van.	1	4		13	18
Van.	1995	CSF	Chi.	4	0		11	6
Defunct Clubs								
Mtl.M	1934	SF*	Chi.	2	0		6	2
Mtl.M	1935	QF*	Mtl.M	0	1	1	0	1
NYA	1936	QF*	NYA	1	1		5	7
NYA	1938	SF	Chi.	2	1		5	5

* Total-goals series

COLORADO

All-Time Playoff Record vs. Other Clubs

	Series	W	L	GP	W	L	T	GF	GA	Last Mtg.	Round	Result
Boston	2	1	1	11	5	6	0	36	37	1983	DSF	L 1-3
Buffalo	2	2	0	8	6	2	0	35	27	1985	DSF	W 3-2
Chicago	2	2	0	12	8	4	0	49	28	1997	CQF	W 4-2
Dallas	1	0	1	7	3	4	0	16	23	1999	CF	L 3-4
Detroit	3	2	1	18	10	8	0	53	46	1999	CSF	W 4-2
Edmonton	2	1	1	12	7	5	0	35	30	1998	CQF	L 3-4
Florida	1	1	0	4	4	0	0	15	4	1996	F	W 4-0
Hartford	2	1	1	9	4	5	0	34	35	1987	DSF	W 4-2
Montreal	5	2	3	31	14	17	0	85	105	1993	DSF	L 2-4
NY Islanders	1	0	1	4	0	4	0	9	18	1982	CF	L 0-4
NY Rangers	1	0	1	6	2	4	0	19	25	1995	CQF	L 2-4
Philadelphia	2	0	2	11	4	7	0	29	39	1985	CF	L 2-4
San Jose	1	1	0	6	4	2	0	19	17	1999	CQF	W 4-2
Vancouver	1	1	0	6	4	2	0	24	17	1996	CQF	W 4-2
Totals	**26**	**14**	**12**	**145**	**75**	**70**	**0**	**458**	**451**			

Playoff Results 1999-95

Year	Round	Opponent	Result	GF	GA
1999	CF	Dallas	L 3-4	16	23
	CSF	Detroit	W 4-2	21	14
	CQF	San Jose	W 4-2	19	17
1998	CQF	Edmonton	L 3-4	16	19
1997	CF	Detroit	L 2-4	12	16
	CSF	Edmonton	W 4-1	19	11
	CQF	Chicago	W 4-2	28	14
1996	F	Florida	W 4-0	15	4
	CF	Detroit	W 4-2	20	16
	CSF	Chicago	W 4-2	21	14
	CQF	Vancouver	W 4-2	24	17
1995	CQF	NY Rangers	L 2-4	19	25

Playoff Scoring Leaders

	Player	Years	GP	G	A	Pts.
1.	Joe Sakic	93-99	76	41	53	94
2.	Peter Stastny	81-87	64	24	57	81
3.	Peter Forsberg	95-99	68	31	48	79
4.	Michel Goulet	80-87	66	34	30	64
5.	Valeri Kamensky	93-99	64	25	35	60
6.	Claude Lemieux	96-99	62	24	31	55
7.	Sandis Ozolinsh	96-99	65	13	42	55
8.	Anton Stastny	81-87	66	20	32	52
9.	Dale Hunter	81-87,99	86	17	29	46
10.	Adam Deadmarsh	95-99	71	18	23	41

Series Records vs. Other Clubs

Note: Includes series played by Quebec Nordiques, 1980-95.

Opponent	Year	Series	Winner	W	L	GF	GA
Bos.	1982	DF	Que.	4	3	28	26
Bos.	1983	DSF	Bos.	1	3	8	11
Buf.	1984	DF	Que.	3	0	13	5
Buf.	1985	DSF	Que.	3	2	22	22
Chi.	1996	CSF	Col.	4	2	19	14
Chi.	1997	CQF	Col.	4	2	28	14
Dal.	1999	CF	Dal.	3	4	16	23
Det.	1996	CF	Col.	4	2	20	16
Det.	1997	CF	Det.	2	4	12	16
Det.	1999	CSF	Col.	4	2	21	14
Edm.	1997	CSF	Col.	4	1	19	11
Edm.	1998	CQF	Edm.	3	4	16	19
Fla.	1996	F	Col.	4	0	15	4
Hfd.	1986	DSF	Hfd.	0	3	7	16
Hfd.	1987	DSF	Que.	4	2	27	19
Mtl.	1982	DSF	Que.	3	2	11	16
Mtl.	1984	DF	Mtl.	2	4	13	20
Mtl.	1985	DF	Que.	4	3	24	24
Mtl.	1987	DF	Mtl.	3	4	21	26
Mtl.	1993	DSF	Mtl.	2	4	16	19
NYI	1982	CF	NYI	0	4	9	18
NYR	1995	CQF	NYR	2	4	19	25
Phi.	1981	PRE	Phi.	2	3	17	22
Phi.	1985	CF	Phi.	2	4	12	17
S.J.	1999	CF	Col.	4	2	19	17
Van.	1996	CQF	Col.	4	2	24	17

DALLAS

All-Time Playoff Record vs. Other Clubs

	Series	W	L	GP	W	L	T	GF	GA	Last Mtg.	Round	Result
Boston	1	1	0	3	3	0	0	20	13	1981	PR	W 3-0
Buffalo	3	2	1	13	8	5	0	39	37	1999	F	W 4-2
Calgary	1	1	0	6	4	2	0	25	18	1981	SF	W 4-2
Chicago	6	2	4	33	14	19	0	119	119	1991	DSF	W 4-2
Colorado	1	1	0	7	4	3	0	23	16	1999	CF	W 4-3
Detroit	3	0	3	18	6	12	0	40	55	1998	CF	L 2-4
Edmonton	5	3	2	25	15	10	0	68	69	1999	CQF	W 4-0
Los Angeles	1	1	0	7	4	3	0	26	21	1968	QF	W 4-3
Montreal	2	1	1	13	6	7	0	37	48	1980	QF	W 4-3
NY Islanders	1	0	1	5	1	4	0	16	26	1981	F	L 1-4
Philadelphia	2	0	2	11	3	8	0	26	41	1980	SF	L 1-4
Pittsburgh	1	0	1	6	2	4	0	16	28	1991	F	L 2-4
St. Louis	11	6	5	62	34	28	0	191	174	1999	CSF	W 4-2
San Jose	1	1	0	6	4	2	0	16	12	1998	CQF	W 4-2
Toronto	2	2	0	7	6	1	0	35	26	1983	DSF	W 3-1
Vancouver	1	0	1	5	1	4	0	11	18	1994	CSF	L 1-4
Totals	**42**	**21**	**21**	**227**	**115**	**112**	**0**	**708**	**721**			

Playoff Results 1999-95

Year	Round	Opponent	Result	GF	GA
1999	F	Buffalo	W 4-2	13	9
	CF	Colorado	W 4-3	23	16
	CSF	St. Louis	W 4-2	17	12
	CQF	Edmonton	W 4-0	11	7
1998	CF	Detroit	L 2-4	11	15
	CSF	Edmonton	W 4-1	9	5
	CQF	San Jose	W 4-2	16	12
1997	CQF	Edmonton	L 3-4	18	21
1995	CQF	Detroit	L 1-4	10	17

Playoff Scoring Leaders

	Player	Years	GP	G	A	Pts.
1.	Brian Bellows	83-92	81	34	49	83
2.	Mike Modano	89-99	95	32	47	79
3.	Neal Broten	81-94, 97	115	28	51	79
4.	Bobby Smith	80-83, 91-92	77	26	50	76
5.	Steve Payne	80-85	71	35	35	70
6.	Dino Ciccarelli	81-86	62	28	23	51
7.	Brad Maxwell	80-84	58	10	39	49
8.	Dave Gagner	90-95	51	22	24	46
9.	Al MacAdam	80-84	63	20	24	44
10.	Craig Hartsburg	80-86	61	15	27	42

Series Records vs. Other Clubs

Note: Includes series played by Minnesota North Stars, 1968-92.

Opponent	Year	Series	Winner	W	L	GF	GA
Bos.	1981	PRE	Min.	3	0	20	13
Buf.	1977	PRE	Buf.	0	2	3	11
Buf.	1981	QF	Min.	4	1	23	17
Buf.	1999	F	Dal.	4	2	13	9
Cgy.	1981	SF	Min.	4	2	25	18
Chi.	1982	DSF	Chi.	1	3	14	14
Chi.	1983	DF	Chi.	1	4	17	22
Chi.	1984	DSF	Min.	3	2	18	14
Chi.	1985	DF	Chi.	2	4	29	32
Chi.	1990	DSF	Chi.	3	4	18	21
Chi.	1991	DSF	Min.	4	2	23	16
Col.	1999	CF	Dal..	4	3	23	16
Det.	1992	DSF	Det.	3	4	19	23
Det.	1995	CQF	Det.	1	4	10	17
Det.	1998	CF	Det.	2	4	11	15
Edm.	1984	CF	Edm.	0	4	10	22
Edm.	1991	CF	Min.	4	1	20	14
Edm.	1997	CQF	Edm.	3	4	18	21
Edm.	1998	CSF	Dal.	4	1	9	5
Edm.	1999	CQF	Dal.	4	0	11	7
L.A.	1968	QF	Min.	4	3	26	21
Mtl.	1971	SF	Mtl.	2	4	19	27
Mtl.	1980	QF	Min.	4	3	18	21
NYI	1981	F	NYI	1	4	16	26
Phi.	1973	QF	Phi.	2	4	12	14
Phi.	1980	SF	Phi.	1	4	14	27
Pit.	1991	F	Pit.	2	4	16	28
St.L.	1968	SF	St.L.	3	4	22	18

St.L.	1970	QF	St.L.	2	4	16	20
St.L.	1971	QF	Min.	4	2	16	15
St.L.	1972	QF	St.L.	3	4	19	19
St.L.	1984	DF	Min.	4	3	19	17
St.L.	1985	DSF	Min.	3	0	9	5
St.L.	1986	DSF	St.L.	2	3	20	18
St.L.	1989	DSF	St.L.	1	4	15	23
St.L.	1991	DF	Min.	4	2	22	17
St.L.	1994	CQF	Dal.	4	0	16	10
St.L.	1999	CSF	Dal.	4	2	17	12
S.J.	1998	CQF	Dal..	4	2	16	12
Tor.	1980	PRE	Min.	3	0	17	8
Tor.	1983	DSF	Min.	3	1	18	18
Van.	1994	CSF	Van.	1	4	11	18

DETROIT

All-Time Playoff Record vs. Other Clubs

	Series	W	L	GP	W	L	T	GF	GA	Last Mtg.	Round	Result
Anaheim	2	2	0	8	8	0	0	30	14	1999	CQF	W 4-0
Boston	7	3	4	33	14	19	0	98	96	1957	SF	L 1-4
Calgary	1	1	0	2	2	0	0	8	5	1978	PR	W 2-0
Chicago	14	6	8	69	31	38	0	190	210	1995	CF	W 4-1
Colorado	3	1	2	18	8	10	0	46	53	1999	CSF	L 2-4
Dallas	3	3	0	18	12	6	0	55	40	1998	CF	W 4-2
Edmonton	2	0	2	10	2	8	0	26	39	1988	CF	L 1-4
Montreal	12	7	5	62	29	33	0	149	161	1978	QF	L 1-4
New Jersey	1	0	1	4	0	4	0	7	16	1995	F	L 0-4
NY Rangers	5	4	1	23	13	10	0	57	49	1950	F	W 4-3
Philadelphia	1	1	0	4	4	0	0	16	6	1997	F	W 4-0
Phoenix	2	2	0	12	8	4	0	44	28	1998	CQF	W 4-2
St. Louis	6	4	2	35	20	15	0	111	92	1998	CSF	W 4-2
San Jose	2	1	1	11	7	4	0	51	27	1995	CSF	W 4-0
Toronto	23	11	12	117	59	58	0	321	311	1993	DSF	L 3-4
Washington	1	1	0	4	4	0	0	13	7	1998	F	W 4-0
Defunct	4	3	1	10	7	2	1	21	13			
Totals	**89**	**50**	**39**	**440**	**228**	**211**	**1**	**1243**	**1167**			

Playoff Results 1999-95

Year	Round	Opponent	Result	GF	GA
1999	CSF	Colorado	L 2-4	14	21
	CQF	Anaheim	W 4-0	17	6
1998	F	Washington	W 4-0	13	7
	CF	Dallas	W 4-2	15	11
	CSF	St. Louis	W 4-2	23	13
	CQF	Phoenix	W 4-2	24	18
1997	F	Philadelphia	W 4-0	16	6
	CF	Colorado	W 4-2	16	12
	CSF	Anaheim	W 4-0	13	8
	CQF	St. Louis	W 4-2	13	12
1996	CF	Colorado	L 2-4	16	20
	CSF	St. Louis	W 4-3	22	16
	CQF	Winnipeg	W 4-2	20	10
1995	F	New Jersey	L 0-4	7	16
	CF	Chicago	W 4-1	13	12
	CSF	San Jose	W 4-0	24	6
	CQF	Dallas	W 4-1	17	10

Playoff Scoring Leaders

	Player	Years	GP	G	A	Pts.
1.	Gordie Howe	47-70	154	67	91	158
2.	Steve Yzerman	84-99	145	61	87	148
3.	Sergei Fedorov	90-99	120	38	88	126
4.	Alex Delvecchio	52-70	121	35	69	104
5.	Ted Lindsay	45-57, 65	123	46	44	90
6.	Niklas Lidstrom	92-99	114	24	53	77
7.	Norm Ullman	56-66	80	27	47	74
8.	Vyacheslav Kozlov	93-99	100	36	35	71
9.	Sid Abel	39-52	93	28	28	56
10.	Paul Coffey	93-96	49	14	36	50

Series Records vs. Other Clubs

Opponent	Year	Series	Winner	W	L	T	GF	GA
Ana.	1997	CSF	Det.	4	0		13	8
Ana.	1999	CQF	Det.	4	0		17	6
Atl.	1978	PRE	Det.	2	0		8	5
Bos.	1941	F	Bos.	0	4		6	12
Bos.	1942	SF	Det.	2	0		9	5
Bos.	1943	F	Det.	4	0		16	5
Bos.	1945	SF	Det.	4	3		22	22
Bos.	1946	SF	Bos.	1	4		10	16
Bos.	1953	SF	Bos.	2	4		21	21
Bos.	1957	SF	Bos.	1	4		14	15
Chi.	1934	F	Chi.	1	3		7	9
Chi.	1941	SF	Det.	2	0		5	2
Chi.	1944	SF	Chi.	1	4		8	17
Chi.	1961	F	Chi.	2	4		12	19
Chi.	1963	SF	Det.	4	2		25	19
Chi.	1964	SF	Det.	4	3		24	18
Chi.	1965	SF	Chi.	3	4		19	23
Chi.	1966	SF	Det.	4	2		22	10
Chi.	1970	QF	Chi.	0	4		8	16
Chi.	1985	DSF	Chi.	0	3		8	23
Chi.	1987	DSF	Det.	4	0		15	6
Chi.	1989	DSF	Chi.	2	4		18	25
Chi.	1992	DF	Chi.	0	4		6	11
Chi.	1995	CF	Det.	4	1		13	12
Col.	1996	CF	Col.	4	2		16	20
Col.	1997	CF	Det.	4	2		16	12
Col.	1999	CSF	Col.	2	4		14	21
Dal.	1995	CQF	Det.	4	1		17	10
Dal.	1998	CF	Det.	4	2		15	11
Edm.	1987	CF	Edm.	1	4		10	16
Edm.	1988	CF	Edm.	1	4		16	23
Min.	1992	DSF	Det.	4	3		23	19
Mtl.	1937	SF	Det.	3	2		13	8
Mtl.	1939	QF	Det.	2	1		8	5
Mtl.	1942	QF	Det.	2	1		8	8
Mtl.	1949	SF	Det.	4	3		17	14
Mtl.	1951	SF	Mtl.	2	4		12	13
Mtl.	1952	F	Det.	4	0		11	2
Mtl.	1954	F	Det.	4	3		14	12
Mtl.	1955	F	Det.	4	3		27	20
Mtl.	1956	F	Mtl.	1	4		9	18
Mtl.	1958	SF	Mtl.	0	4		6	19
Mtl.	1966	F	Mtl.	2	4		14	18
Mtl.	1978	QF	Mtl.	1	4		10	24
N.J.	1995	F	N.J.	0	4		7	16
NYR	1933	SF*	NYR	0	2		3	6
NYR	1937	F	Det.	3	2		9	8
NYR	1941	QF	Det.	2	1		6	6
NYR	1948	SF	Det.	4	2		17	12
NYR	1950	F	Det.	4	3		22	17
Phi.	1997	F	Det.	4	0		16	6
Phx.	1998	CQF	Det.	4	2		24	18
St.L.	1984	DSF	St.L.	1	3		12	13
St.L.	1988	DF	Det.	4	1		21	14
St.L.	1991	DSF	St.L.	3	4		20	24
St.L.	1996	CSF	Det.	4	3		22	16
St.L.	1997	CQF	Det.	4	2		13	12
St.L.	1998	CSF	Det.	4	2		23	13
S.J.	1994	CQF	S.J.	3	4		27	21
S.J.	1995	CSF	Det.	4	0		24	6
Tor.	1929	QF*	Tor.	0	2		2	7
Tor.	1934	SF	Det.	3	2		11	12
Tor.	1936	F	Det.	3	1		18	11
Tor.	1939	SF	Tor.	1	2		8	10
Tor.	1940	SF	Tor.	0	2		2	5
Tor.	1942	F	Tor.	3	4		19	25
Tor.	1943	SF	Det.	4	2		20	17
Tor.	1945	F	Tor.	3	4		9	9
Tor.	1947	SF	Tor.	1	4		14	18
Tor.	1948	F	Tor.	0	4		7	18
Tor.	1949	F	Tor.	0	4		5	12
Tor.	1950	SF	Det.	4	3		10	11
Tor.	1952	SF	Det.	4	0		13	3
Tor.	1954	SF	Det.	4	1		15	8
Tor.	1955	SF	Det.	4	0		14	6
Tor.	1956	SF	Det.	4	1		14	10
Tor.	1960	SF	Tor.	2	4		16	20
Tor.	1961	SF	Det.	4	1		15	8
Tor.	1963	F	Tor.	1	4		10	17
Tor.	1964	F	Tor.	3	4		17	22
Tor.	1987	DF	Det.	4	3		20	18
Tor.	1988	DSF	Det.	4	2		32	20
Tor.	1993	DSF	Tor.	3	4		30	24
Wsh.	1998	F	Det.	4	0		13	7
Wpg.	1996	CQF	Det.	4	2		20	10
Defunct Clubs								
Mtl.M	1932	QF*	Mtl.M	0	1	1	1	3
Mtl.M	1933	QF*	Det.	2	0		5	2
Mtl.M	1936	SF	Det.	3	0		6	1
NYA	1940	QF	Det.	2	1		9	7

* Total-goals series

EDMONTON

All-Time Playoff Record vs. Other Clubs

	Series	W	L	GP	W	L	T	GF	GA	Last Mtg.	Round	Result
Boston	2	2	0	9	8	1	0	41	20	1990	F	W 4-1
Calgary	5	4	1	30	19	11	0	132	96	1991	DSF	W 4-3
Chicago	4	3	1	20	12	8	0	102	77	1992	CF	L 0-4
Colorado	2	1	1	12	5	7	0	30	35	1998	CQF	W 4-3
Dallas	5	2	3	25	10	15	0	69	68	1999	CQF	L 0-4
Detroit	2	2	0	10	8	2	0	39	26	1988	CF	W 4-1
Los Angeles	7	5	2	36	24	12	0	154	127	1992	DSF	W 4-2
Montreal	1	1	0	3	3	0	0	15	6	1981	PR	W 3-0
NY Islanders	3	1	2	15	6	9	0	47	58	1984	F	W 4-1
Philadelphia	3	2	1	15	8	7	0	49	44	1987	F	W 4-3
Vancouver	2	2	0	9	7	2	0	35	20	1992	DF	W 4-2
Winnipeg	6	6	0	26	22	4	0	120	75	1990	DSF	W 4-3
Totals	**42**	**31**	**11**	**210**	**132**	**78**	**0**	**833**	**652**			

Playoff Results 1999-95

Year	Round	Opponent	Result	GF	GA
1999	CQF	Dallas	L 0-4	7	11
1998	CSF	Dallas	L 1-4	5	9
	CQF	Colorado	W 4-3	19	16
1997	CSF	Colorado	L 1-4	11	19
	CQF	Dallas	W 4-3	21	18

Playoff Scoring Leaders

	Player	Years	GP	G	A	Pts.
1.	Wayne Gretzky	80-88	120	81	171	252
2.	Mark Messier	80-91	166	80	135	215
3.	Jari Kurri	81-90	146	92	110	202
4.	Glenn Anderson	81-91	164	81	102	183
5.	Paul Coffey	81-87	94	36	67	103
6.	Esa Tikkanen	85-92	114	51	46	97
7.	Charlie Huddy	82-91	138	16	61	77
8.	Craig Simpson	88-92	67	36	32	68
9.	Kevin Lowe	80-92, 97	171	9	43	52
10.	Randy Gregg	82-90	130	13	37	50

Series Records vs. Other Clubs

Opponent	Year	Series	Winner	W	L	GF	GA
Bos.	1988	F	Edm.	4	0	21	12
Bos.	1990	F	Edm.	4	1	20	8
Cgy.	1983	DF	Edm.	4	1	35	13
Cgy.	1984	DF	Edm.	4	3	33	27
Cgy.	1986	DF	Cgy.	3	4	24	25
Cgy.	1988	DF	Edm.	4	0	18	11
Cgy.	1991	DSF	Edm.	4	3	22	20
Chi.	1983	CF	Edm.	4	0	25	11
Chi.	1985	CF	Edm.	4	2	44	25
Chi.	1990	CF	Edm.	4	2	25	20
Chi.	1992	CF	Chi.	0	4	8	21
Col.	1997	CSF	Col.	1	4	11	19
Col.	1998	CQF	Edm.	4	3	19	16
Dal.	1997	CQF	Edm.	4	3	21	18
Dal.	1998	CSF	Dal.	1	4	5	9
Dal.	1999	CQF	Dal.	0	4	7	11
Det.	1987	CF	Edm.	4	1	16	10
Det.	1988	CF	Edm.	4	1	23	16
L.A.	1982	DSF	L.A.	2	3	23	27
L.A.	1985	DSF	Edm.	3	0	11	7
L.A.	1987	DSF	Edm.	4	1	32	20
L.A.	1989	DSF	L.A.	3	4	20	25
L.A.	1990	DF	Edm.	4	0	24	10
L.A.	1991	DF	Edm.	4	2	21	20
L.A.	1992	DSF	Edm.	4	2	23	18
Min.	1984	CF	Edm.	4	0	22	10
Min.	1991	CF	Min.	1	4	14	20
Mtl.	1981	PRE	Edm.	3	0	15	6
NYI	1981	QF	NYI	2	4	20	29
NYI	1983	F	NYI	0	4	6	17
NYI	1984	F	Edm.	4	1	21	12
Phi.	1980	PRE	Phi.	0	3	6	12
Phi.	1985	F	Edm.	4	1	21	14
Phi.	1987	F	Edm.	4	3	22	18
Van.	1986	DSF	Edm.	3	0	17	5
Van.	1992	DF	Edm.	4	2	18	15
Wpg.	1983	DSF	Edm.	3	0	14	9
Wpg.	1984	DSF	Edm.	3	0	18	7
Wpg.	1985	DF	Edm.	4	0	22	11
Wpg.	1987	DF	Edm.	4	0	17	9
Wpg.	1988	DSF	Edm.	4	1	25	17
Wpg.	1990	DSF	Edm.	4	3	24	22

FLORIDA

All-Time Playoff Record vs. Other Clubs

	Series	W	L	GP	W	L	T	GF	GA	Last Mtg.	Round	Result
Boston	1	1	0	5	4	1	0	22	16	1996	CQF	W 4-1
Colorado	1	0	1	4	0	4	0	4	15	1996	F	L 0-4
NY Rangers	1	0	1	5	1	4	0	10	13	1997	CQF	L 1-4
Philadelphia	1	1	0	6	4	2	0	15	11	1996	CSF	W 4-2
Pittsburgh	1	1	0	7	4	3	0	20	15	1996	CF	W4-3
Totals	**5**	**3**	**2**	**27**	**13**	**14**	**0**	**71**	**70**			

Playoff Results 1999-95

Year	Round	Opponent	Result	GF	GA
1997	CQF	NY Rangers	L 1-4	10	13
1996	F	Colorado	L 0-4	4	15
	CF	Pittsburgh	W 4-3	20	15
	CSF	Philadelphia	W 4-2	15	11
	CQF	Boston	W 4-1	22	16

Playoff Scoring Leaders

	Player	Years	GP	G	A	Pts.
1.	Ray Sheppard	96-97	26	10	8	18
2.	Dave Lowry	96-97	27	10	7	17
3.	Stu Barnes	96	22	6	10	16
4.	Bill Lindsay	96-97	25	5	6	11
5.	Rob Niedermayer	96-97	27	7	4	11
6.	Scott Mellanby	96-97	27	3	8	11
7.	Robert Svehla	96-97	27	1	10	11
8.	Tom Fitzgerald	96-97	27	4	5	9
9.	Paul Laus	96-97	26	2	7	9
10.	Ed Jovanovski	96-97	27	1	8	9

Series Records vs. Other Clubs

Opponent	Year	Series	Winner	W	L	GF	GA
Col.	1996	F	Col.	0	4	4	15
Bos.	1996	CQF	Fla.	4	1	22	16
NYR	1997	CQF	NYR	1	4	10	13
Phi.	1996	CSF	Fla.	4	2	15	11
Pit.	1996	CF	Fla.	4	3	20	15

LOS ANGELES

All-Time Playoff Record vs. Other Clubs

	Series	W	L	GP	W	L	T	GF	GA	Last Mtg.	Round	Result
Boston	2	0	2	13	5	8	0	38	56	1977	QF	L 2-4
Calgary	6	4	2	26	13	13	0	105	112	1993	DSF	W 4-2
Chicago	1	0	1	5	1	4	0	7	10	1974	QF	L 1-4
Dallas	1	0	1	7	3	4	0	21	26	1968	QF	L 3-4
Edmonton	7	2	5	36	12	24	0	127	154	1992	DSF	L 2-4
Montreal	1	0	1	5	1	4	0	12	15	1993	F	L 1-4
NY Islanders	1	0	1	4	1	3	0	10	21	1980	PR	L 1-3
NY Rangers	2	0	2	6	1	5	0	14	32	1981	PR	L 1-3
Oaklan d	1	1	0	7	4	3	0	23	25	1969	QF	W 4-3
St. Louis	2	0	2	8	0	8	0	13	32	1998	CQF	L 0-4
Toronto	3	1	2	12	5	7	0	31	41	1993	CF	W 4-3
Vancouver	3	2	1	17	9	8	0	66	60	1993	DF	W 4-2
Totals	**30**	**10**	**20**	**146**	**55**	**91**	**0**	**467**	**584**			

Playoff Results 1999-95

Year	Round	Opponent	Result	GF	GA
1998	CQF	St. Louis	L 0-4	8	16

Playoff Scoring Leaders

	Player	Years	GP	G	A	Pts.
1.	Wayne Gretzky	89-93	60	29	65	94
2.	Luc Robitaille	87-93, 98	77	35	43	78
3.	Dave Taylor	78-93	92	26	33	59
4.	Tomas Sandstrom	90-93	50	17	28	45
5.	Marcel Dionne	76-85	43	20	23	43
6.	Steve Duchesne	87-91	43	13	26	39
7.	Bernie Nicholls	82-89	34	16	21	37
8.	Tony Granato	90-93	52	13	24	37
9.	Mike Murphy	74-82	45	11	20	31
10.	Mike Donnelly	91-93	42	12	11	23

Series Records vs. Other Clubs

Opponent	Year	Series	Winner	W	L	GF	GA
Atl.	1976	PRE	L.A.	2	0	3	1
Atl.	1977	PRE	L.A.	2	1	11	7
Bos.	1976	QF	Bos.	3	4	14	26
Bos.	1977	QF	Bos.	2	4	24	30
Cgy.	1988	DSF	Cgy.	1	4	18	30
Cgy.	1989	DF	Cgy.	0	4	11	22
Cgy.	1990	DSF	L.A.	4	2	29	24
Cgy.	1993	DSF	L.A.	4	2	33	28
Chi.	1974	QF	Chi.	1	4	7	10
Edm.	1982	DSF	L.A.	3	2	27	23
Edm.	1985	DSF	Edm.	0	3	7	11
Edm.	1987	DSF	Edm.	1	4	20	32
Edm.	1989	DSF	L.A.	4	3	25	20
Edm.	1990	DF	Edm.	0	4	10	24
Edm.	1991	DF	Edm.	2	4	20	21
Edm.	1992	DSF	Edm.	2	4	18	23
Min.	1968	QF	Min.	3	4	21	26
Mtl.	1993	F	Mtl.	1	4	12	15
NYI	1980	PRE	NYI	1	3	10	21
NYR	1979	PRE	NYR	0	2	2	9
NYR	1981	PRE	NYR	1	3	12	23
Oak.	1969	QF	L.A.	4	3	23	25
St.L.	1969	SF	St.L.	0	4	5	16
St.L.	1998	CQF	St.L.	0	4	8	16
Tor.	1975	PRE	Tor.	1	2	6	7
Tor.	1978	PRE	Tor.	0	2	3	11
Tor.	1993	CF	L.A.	4	3	22	23
Van.	1982	DF	Van.	1	4	14	19
Van.	1991	DSF	L.A.	4	2	26	16
Van.	1993	DF	L.A.	4	2	26	25

MONTREAL

All-Time Playoff Record vs. Other Clubs

	Series	W	L	GP	W	L	T	GF	GA	Last Mtg.	Round	Result
Boston	28	21	7	139	87	52	0	430	339	1994	CQF	L 3-4
Buffalo	7	4	3	35	18	17	0	124	111	1998	CSF	L 0-4
Calgary	2	1	1	11	6	5	0	31	32	1989	F	L 2-4
Chicago	17	12	5	81	50	29	2	261	185	1976	QF	W 4-0
Colorado	5	3	2	31	17	14	0	105	85	1993	DSF	W 4-2
Dallas	2	1	1	13	7	6	0	48	37	1980	QF	L 3-4
Detroit	12	5	7	62	33	29	0	161	149	1978	QF	W 4-1
Edmonton	1	0	1	3	0	3	0	6	15	1981	PR	L 0-3
Hartford	5	5	0	27	19	8	0	96	70	1992	DSF	W 4-3
Los Angeles	1	1	0	5	4	1	0	15	12	1993	F	W 4-1
NY Islanders	4	3	1	22	14	8	0	64	55	1993	CF	W 4-1
NY Rangers	14	7	7	61	34	25	2	188	158	1996	CQF	L 2-4
New Jersey	1	0	1	5	1	4	0	11	22	1997	CQF	L 1-4
Philadelphia	4	3	1	21	14	7	0	72	52	1989	CF	W 4-2
Pittsburgh	1	1	0	6	4	2	0	18	15	1998	CQF	W 4-2
St. Louis	3	3	0	12	12	0	0	42	14	1977	QF	W 4-0
Toronto	15	8	7	71	42	29	0	215	160	1979	QF	W 4-0
Vancouver	1	1	0	5	4	1	0	20	9	1975	QF	W 4-1
Defunct	*11	6	4	28	15	9	4	70	71			
Totals	***134**	**85**	**48**	**638**	**381**	**249**	**8**	**1977**	**1591**			

* 1919 Final incomplete due to influenza epidemic.

Playoff Results 1999-95

Year	Round	Opponent	Result	GF	GA
1998	CSF	Buffalo	L 0-4	10	17
	CQF	Pittsburgh	W 4-2	18	15
1997	CQF	New Jersey	L 1-4	11	22
1996	CQF	NY Rangers	L 2-4	17	19

Playoff Scoring Leaders

	Player	Years	GP	G	A	Pts.
1.	Jean Beliveau	54-71	162	79	97	176
2.	Jacques Lemaire	68-79	145	61	78	139
3.	Larry Robinson	73-89	203	25	109	134
4.	Guy Lafleur	72-84	124	57	76	133
5.	Henri Richard	56-75	180	49	80	129
6.	Yvan Cournoyer	65-78	147	64	63	127
7.	Maurice Richard	44-60	133	82	44	126
8.	Bernie Geoffrion	51-64	127	56	59	115
9.	Steve Shutt	73-84	96	50	48	98
10.	Dickie Moore	52-63	112	38	56	94

Series Records vs. Other Clubs

Opponent	Year	Series	Winner	W	L	T	GF	GA
Bos.	1929	SF	Bos.	0	3		2	5
Bos.	1930	F	Mtl.	2	0		7	3
Bos.	1931	SF	Mtl.	3	2		13	13
Bos.	1943	SF	Bos.	1	4		17	18
Bos.	1946	F	Mtl.	4	1		19	13
Bos.	1947	SF	Mtl.	4	1		16	10
Bos.	1952	SF	Mtl.	4	3		18	12
Bos.	1953	F	Mtl.	4	1		16	9
Bos.	1954	SF	Mtl.	4	0		16	4
Bos.	1955	SF	Mtl.	4	1		16	9
Bos.	1957	F	Mtl.	4	1		15	6
Bos.	1958	F	Mtl.	4	2		16	14
Bos.	1968	QF	Mtl.	4	0		15	8
Bos.	1969	SF	Mtl.	4	2		15	16
Bos.	1971	QF	Mtl.	4	3		28	26
Bos.	1977	F	Mtl.	4	0		16	6
Bos.	1978	F	Mtl.	4	2		18	13
Bos.	1979	SF	Mtl.	4	3		25	20
Bos.	1984	DSF	Mtl.	3	0		10	2
Bos.	1985	DSF	Mtl.	3	2		19	17
Bos.	1986	DSF	Mtl.	3	0		10	6
Bos.	1987	DSF	Mtl.	4	0		19	11
Bos.	1988	DF	Bos.	1	4		10	15
Bos.	1989	DF	Mtl.	4	1		16	13
Bos.	1990	DF	Bos.	1	4		12	16
Bos.	1991	DF	Bos.	3	4		18	18
Bos.	1992	DF	Bos.	0	4		8	14
Bos.	1994	CQF	Bos.	3	4		20	22
Buf.	1973	QF	Mtl.	4	2		21	16
Buf.	1975	SF	Buf.	2	4		29	21
Buf.	1983	DSF	Buf.	0	3		2	8
Buf.	1990	DSF	Mtl.	4	2		17	13
Buf.	1991	DSF	Mtl.	4	2		29	24
Buf.	1993	DF	Mtl.	4	0		16	12
Buf.	1998	CSF	Buf.	0	4		10	17
Cgy.	1986	F	Mtl.	4	1		15	13
Cgy.	1989	F	Cgy.	2	4		16	19
Chi.	1930	QF*	Mtl.	1	0	1	3	2
Chi.	1931	F	Mtl.	3	2		11	8
Chi.	1934	QF*	Chi.	0	1	1	3	4
Chi.	1938	QF	Chi.	1	2		8	11
Chi.	1941	QF	Chi.	1	2		7	8
Chi.	1944	F	Mtl.	4	0		16	8
Chi.	1946	SF	Mtl.	4	0		26	7
Chi.	1953	SF	Mtl.	4	3		18	14
Chi.	1959	SF	Mtl.	4	2		21	16
Chi.	1960	SF	Mtl.	4	0		14	6
Chi.	1961	SF	Chi.	2	4		15	16
Chi.	1962	SF	Chi.	2	4		13	19
Chi.	1965	F	Mtl.	4	3		18	12
Chi.	1968	SF	Mtl.	4	1		22	10
Chi.	1971	F	Mtl.	4	3		20	18
Chi.	1973	F	Mtl.	4	2		33	23
Chi.	1976	QF	Mtl.	4	0		13	3
Det.	1937	SF	Det.	2	3		8	13
Det.	1939	QF	Det.	1	2		5	8
Det.	1942	QF	Det.	1	2		8	8
Det.	1949	SF	Det.	3	4		14	17
Det.	1951	SF	Mtl.	4	2		13	12
Det.	1952	F	Det.	0	4		2	11
Det.	1954	F	Det.	3	4		12	14
Det.	1955	F	Det.	3	4		20	27
Det.	1956	F	Mtl.	4	1		18	9
Det.	1958	SF	Mtl.	4	0		19	6
Det.	1966	F	Mtl.	4	2		18	14
Det.	1978	QF	Mtl.	4	1		24	10
Edm.	1981	PRE	Edm.	0	3		6	15
Hfd.	1980	PRE	Mtl.	3	0		18	8
Hfd.	1986	DF	Mtl.	4	3		16	13
Hfd.	1988	DSF	Mtl.	4	2		23	20
Hfd.	1989	DSF	Mtl.	4	0		18	11
Hfd.	1992	DSF	Mtl.	4	3		21	18
L.A.	1993	F	Mtl.	4	1		15	12
Min.	1971	SF	Mtl.	4	2		27	19
Min.	1980	QF	Min.	3	4		21	18
N.J.	1997	CQF	N.J.	1	4		11	22
NYI	1976	SF	Mtl.	4	1		17	14
NYI	1977	SF	Mtl.	4	2		19	13
NYI	1984	CF	NYI	2	4		12	17
NYI	1993	CF	Mtl.	4	1		16	11
NYR	1930	SF	Mtl.	2	0		4	1
NYR	1932	SF	NYR	1	3		9	13
NYR	1933	QF*	NYR	0	1	1	5	8
NYR	1935	QF*	NYR	0	1	1	5	6
NYR	1950	SF	NYR	1	4		7	15
NYR	1956	SF	Mtl.	4	1		24	9
NYR	1957	SF	Mtl.	4	1		22	12
NYR	1967	SF	Mtl.	4	0		14	8
NYR	1969	QF	Mtl.	4	0		16	7
NYR	1972	QF	NYR	2	4		14	19
NYR	1974	QF	NYR	2	4		17	21
NYR	1979	F	Mtl.	4	1		19	11
NYR	1986	CF	Mtl.	4	1		15	9
NYR	1996	CQF	NYR	2	4		14	19
Phi.	1973	SF	Mtl.	4	1		19	13
Phi.	1976	F	Mtl.	4	0		14	9
Phi.	1987	CF	Phi.	2	4		22	22

Phi.	1989	CF	Mtl.	4	2		17	8
Pit.	1998	CQF	Mtl.	4	2		18	15
Que.	1982	DSF	Que.	2	3		16	11
Que.	1984	DF	Mtl.	4	2		20	13
Que.	1985	DF	Que.	3	4		24	24
Que.	1987	DF	Mtl.	4	3		26	21
Que.	1993	DSF	Mtl.	4	2		19	16
St.L.	1968	F	Mtl.	4	0		11	7
St.L.	1969	F	Mtl.	4	0		12	3
St.L.	1977	QF	Mtl.	4	0		19	4
Tor.	1918	NHLF*	Tor.	1	1		7	10
Tor.	1925	NHLF*	Mtl.	2	0		5	2
Tor.	1944	SF	Mtl.	4	1		23	6
Tor.	1945	SF	Tor.	2	4		21	15
Tor.	1947	F	Tor.	2	4		13	13
Tor.	1951	F	Tor.	1	4		10	13
Tor.	1959	F	Mtl.	4	1		18	12
Tor.	1960	F	Mtl.	4	0		15	5
Tor.	1963	SF	Tor.	1	4		6	14
Tor.	1964	SF	Tor.	3	4		14	17
Tor.	1965	SF	Mtl.	4	2		17	14
Tor.	1966	SF	Mtl.	4	0		15	6
Tor.	1967	F	Tor.	2	4		16	17
Tor.	1978	SF	Mtl.	4	0		16	6
Tor.	1979	QF	Mtl.	4	0		19	10
Van.	1975	QF	Mtl.	4	1		20	9
Defunct Clubs								
Mtl.M	1927	QF*	Mtl.	1	0	1	2	1
Mtl.M	1928	SF	Mtl.M	0	1	1	2	3
Ott.	1919	NHLF	Mtl.	4	1		26	18
Ott.	1923	NHLF*	Ott.	1	1		2	3
Ott.	1924	NHLF*	Mtl.	2	0		5	2
Ott.	1927	SF *	Ott.	0	1	1	1	5
Seattle	1919	F**	–	2	2	1	10	19
Van/Cgy	1924	F	Mtl.	4	0		14	4

* Total-goals series
** No decision. Series suspended due to Spanish influenza epidemic.

NEW JERSEY

All-Time Playoff Record vs. Other Clubs

	Series	W	L	GP	W	L	T	GF	GA	Last Mtg.	Round	Result
Boston	3	2	1	18	11	7	0	55	52	1995	CQF	W 4-1
Buffalo	1	1	0	7	4	3	0	14	14	1994	CQF	W 4-3
Detroit	1	1	0	4	4	0	0	16	7	1995	F	W 4-0
Montreal	1	1	0	5	4	1	0	22	11	1997	CQF	W 4-1
NY Islanders	1	1	0	6	4	2	0	23	18	1988	DSF	W 4-2
NY Rangers	3	0	3	19	7	12	0	46	56	1997	CSF	L 1-4
Ottawa	1	0	1	6	2	4	0	12	13	1998	CQF	L 2-4
Philadelphia	2	1	1	8	4	4	0	23	20	1995	CF	W 4-2
Pittsburgh	4	1	3	24	11	13	0	65	77	1999	CQF	L 3-4
Washington	2	1	1	13	6	7	0	43	44	1990	DSF	L 2-4
Totals	**19**	**9**	**10**	**110**	**57**	**43**	**0**	**319**	**312**			

Playoff Results 1999-95

Year	Round	Opponent	Result	GF	GA
1999	CQF	Pittsburgh	L 3-4	18	21
1998	CQF	Ottawa	L 2-4	12	13
1997	CSF	NY Rangers	L 1-4	5	10
	CQF	Montreal	W 4-1	22	11
1995	F	Detroit	W 4-0	16	7
	CF	Philadelphia	W 4-2	20	14
	CSF	Pittsburgh	W 4-1	17	8
	CQF	Boston	W 4-1	14	5

Playoff Scoring Leaders

	Player	Years	GP	G	A	Pts.
1.	John MacLean	88-97	88	31	44	75
2.	Claude Lemieux	91-95	59	30	17	47
3.	Bruce Driver	88-95	82	10	32	42
4.	Stephane Richer	92-95	51	16	24	40
5.	Scott Stevens	92-99	75	10	24	34
6.	Scott Niedermayer	93-99	68	9	21	30
7.	Randy McKay	92-99	74	14	13	27
8.	Bobby Holik	93-99	67	7	18	25
9.	Peter Stastny	90-93	25	9	15	24
10.	Patrik Sundstrom	88-91	26	8	16	24

Series Records vs. Other Clubs

Note: Includes series played by Colorado Rockies, 1978.

Opponent	Year	Series	Winner	W	L	GF	GA
Bos.	1988	CF	Bos.	3	4	19	30
Bos.	1994	CSF	N.J.	4	2	22	17
Bos.	1995	CQF	N.J.	4	0	14	5
Buf.	1994	CQF	N.J.	4	3	14	14
NYI	1988	DSF	N.J.	4	2	23	18
Det.	1995	F	N.J.	4	0	16	7
Mtl.	1997	CQF	N.J.	4	1	22	11
NYR	1992	DSF	NYR	3	4	25	28
NYR	1994	CF	NYR	3	4	16	18
NYR	1997	CSF	NYR	1	4	5	10
Ott.	1998	CQF	Ott.	2	4	12	13
Phi.	1978	PRE	Phi.	0	2	3	6
Phi.	1995	CF	N.J.	4	2	20	14
Pit.	1991	DSF	Pit.	3	4	21	21
Pit.	1993	DSF	Pit.	1	4	13	23
Pit.	1995	CSF	N.J.	4	1	17	8
Pit.	1999	CQF	Pit.	3	4	18	21
Wsh.	1988	DF	N.J.	4	3	25	23
Wsh.	1990	DSF	Wsh.	2	4	18	21

NEW YORK ISLANDERS

All-Time Playoff Record vs. Other Clubs

	Series	W	L	GP	W	L	T	GF	GA	Last Mtg.	Round	Result
Boston	2	2	0	11	8	3	0	49	35	1983	CF	W 4-2
Buffalo	3	3	0	16	12	4	0	59	45	1980	SF	W 4-2
Chicago	2	2	0	6	6	0	0	21	6	1979	QF	W 4-0
Colorado	1	1	0	4	4	0	0	18	9	1982	CF	W 4-0
Dallas	1	1	0	5	4	1	0	26	16	1981	F	W 4-1
Edmonton	3	2	1	15	9	6	0	58	47	1984	F	L 1-4
Los Angeles	1	1	0	4	3	1	0	21	10	1980	PR	W 3-1
Montreal	4	1	3	22	8	14	0	55	64	1993	CF	L 1-4
New Jersey	1	0	1	6	2	4	0	18	23	1988	DSF	L 2-4
NY Rangers	8	5	3	39	20	19	0	129	132	1994	CQF	L 0-4
Philadelphia	4	1	3	25	11	14	0	69	83	1987	DF	L 3-4
Pittsburgh	3	3	0	19	11	8	0	67	58	1993	DF	W 4-3
Toronto	2	1	1	10	6	4	0	33	20	1981	PR	W 3-0
Vancouver	2	2	0	6	6	0	0	26	14	1982	F	W 4-0
Washington	6	5	1	30	18	12	0	99	88	1993	DSF	W 4-2
Totals	**43**	**30**	**13**	**218**	**128**	**90**	**0**	**748**	**650**			

Playoff Results 1999-95

Year	Round	Opponent	Result	GF	GA

(Last playoff appearance: 1994)

Playoff Scoring Leaders

	Player	Years	GP	G	A	Pts.
1.	Bryan Trottier	76-90	175	64	106	170
2.	Denis Potvin	78-88	185	56	108	164
3.	Mike Bossy	78-87	129	85	75	160
4.	Clark Gillies	75-86	159	47	46	93
5.	Bob Bourne	75-86	129	38	54	92
6.	Bob Nystrom	75-85	157	39	44	83
7.	John Tonelli	79-85	113	28	55	83
8.	Butch Goring	80-84	99	28	40	68
9.	Brent Sutter	82-90	88	24	35	59
10.	Stefan Persson	78-85	102	7	50	57

Series Records vs. Other Clubs

Opponent	Year	Series	Winner	W	L	GF	GA
Bos.	1980	QF	NYI	4	1	19	14
Bos.	1983	CF	NYI	4	2	30	21
Buf.	1976	QF	NYI	4	2	21	18
Buf.	1977	QF	NYI	4	0	16	10
Buf.	1980	SF	NYI	4	2	22	17
Chi.	1977	PRE	NYI	2	0	7	3
Chi.	1979	QF	NYI	4	0	14	3
Edm.	1981	QF	NYI	4	2	29	20
Edm.	1983	F	NYI	4	0	17	6
Edm.	1984	F	Edm.	1	4	12	21
L.A.	1980	PRE	NYI	3	1	21	10
Min.	1981	F	NYI	4	1	26	16
Mtl.	1976	SF	Mtl.	1	4	14	17
Mtl.	1977	SF	Mtl.	2	4	13	19
Mtl.	1984	CF	NYI	4	2	17	12
Mtl.	1993	CF	Mtl.	1	4	11	16
N.J.	1988	DSF	N.J.	2	4	18	23
NYR	1975	PRE	NYI	2	1	10	13
NYR	1979	SF	NYR	2	4	13	18
NYR	1981	SF	NYI	4	0	22	8
NYR	1982	DF	NYI	4	2	27	20
NYR	1983	DF	NYI	4	2	28	15
NYR	1984	DSF	NYI	3	2	13	14
NYR	1990	DSF	NYR	1	4	13	22
NYR	1994	CQF	NYR	0	4	3	22
Phi.	1975	SF	Phi.	3	4	16	19
Phi.	1980	F	NYI	4	2	26	25
Phi.	1985	DF	Phi.	1	4	11	16
Phi.	1987	DF	Phi.	3	4	16	23
Pit.	1975	QF	NYI	4	3	21	18
Pit.	1982	DSF	NYI	3	2	22	13
Pit.	1993	DF	NYI	4	3	24	27
Que.	1982	CF	NYI	4	0	18	9
Tor.	1978	QF	Tor.	3	4	13	16
Tor.	1981	PRE	NYI	3	0	20	4
Van.	1976	PRE	NYI	2	0	8	4
Van.	1982	F	NYI	4	0	18	10
Wsh.	1983	DSF	NYI	3	1	19	11
Wsh.	1984	DF	NYI	4	1	20	13
Wsh.	1985	DSF	NYI	3	2	14	12
Wsh.	1986	DSF	Wsh.	0	3	4	11
Wsh.	1987	DSF	NYI	4	3	19	19
Wsh.	1993	DSF	NYI	4	2	23	22

NEW YORK RANGERS

All-Time Playoff Record vs. Other Clubs

	Series	W	L	GP	W	L	T	GF	GA	Last Mtg.	Round	Result
Boston	9	3	6	42	18	22	2	104	114	1973	QF	W 4-1
Buffalo	1	0	1	3	1	2	0	6	11	1978	PR	L 1-2
Calgary	1	1	0	4	3	1	0	14	8	1980	PR	W 3-1
Chicago	5	1	4	24	10	14	0	54	66	1973	SF	L 1-4
Colorado	1	1	0	6	4	2	0	25	19	1995	CQF	W 4-2
Detroit	5	1	4	23	10	13	0	49	57	1950	F	L 3-4
Florida	1	1	0	5	4	1	0	13	10	1997	CQF	W 4-1
Los Angeles	2	2	0	6	5	1	0	32	14	1981	PR	W 3-1
Montreal	14	7	7	61	25	34	2	158	188	1996	CQF	W 4-2
New Jersey	3	3	0	19	12	7	0	56	46	1997	CSF	W 4-1
NY Islanders	8	3	5	39	19	20	0	132	129	1994	CQF	W 4-0
Philadelphia	10	4	6	47	20	27	0	153	157	1997	CF	L 1-4
Pittsburgh	3	0	3	15	3	12	0	45	65	1996	CSF	L 1-4
St. Louis	1	1	0	6	4	2	0	29	22	1981	QF	W 4-2
Toronto	8	5	3	35	19	16	0	86	86	1971	QF	W 4-2
Vancouver	1	1	0	7	4	3	0	21	19	1994	F	W 4-3
Washington	4	2	2	22	11	11	0	71	75	1994	CSF	W 4-1
Defunct	9	6	3	22	11	7	4	43	29			
Totals	**86**	**42**	**44**	**386**	**183**	**195**	**8**	**1091**	**1114**			

Playoff Results 1999-95

Year	Round	Opponent	Result	GF	GA
1997	CF	Philadelphia	L 1-4	13	20
	CSF	New Jersey	W 4-1	10	5
	CQF	Florida	W 4-1	13	10
1996	CSF	Pittsburgh	L 1-4	15	21
	CQF	Montreal	W 4-2	19	17
1995	CSF	Philadelphia	L 0-4	10	18
	CQF	Quebec	W 4-2	25	19

Playoff Scoring Leaders

	Player	Years	GP	G	A	Pts.
1.	Brian Leetch	88-97	82	28	61	89
2.	Mark Messier	92-97	70	29	51	80
3.	Rod Gilbert	62-75	79	34	33	67
4.	Don Maloney	79-87	85	22	35	57
5.	Walt Tkaczuk	69-80	93	19	32	51
6.	Steve Vickers	73-81	68	24	25	49
7.	Ron Greschner	75-90	84	17	32	49
8.	Ron Duguay	78-87	69	28	19	47
9.	Anders Hedberg	79-85	58	22	24	46
10.	Brad Park	69-75	64	12	32	44

Series Records vs. Other Clubs

Opponent	Year	Series	Winner	W	L	T	GF	GA
Atl.	1980	PRE	NYR	3	1		14	8
Bos.	1927	SF*	Bos.	0	1	1	1	3
Bos.	1928	SF*	NYR	1	0	1	5	2
Bos.	1929	F	Bos.	0	2		1	4
Bos.	1939	SF	Bos.	3	4		12	14
Bos.	1940	SF	NYR	4	2		15	9
Bos.	1958	SF	Bos.	2	4		16	28
Bos.	1970	QF	Bos.	2	4		16	25
Bos.	1972	F	Bos.	2	4		16	18
Bos.	1973	QF	NYR	4	1		22	11
Buf.	1978	PRE	Buf.	1	2		6	11
Chi.	1931	SF*	Chi.	0	2		0	3
Chi.	1968	QF	Chi.	2	4		12	18
Chi.	1971	SF	Chi.	3	4		14	21
Chi.	1972	SF	NYR	4	0		17	9
Chi.	1973	SF	Chi.	1	4		11	15
Det.	1933	SF*	NYR	2	0		6	3
Det.	1937	F	Det.	2	3		8	9

Det.	1941	QF	Det.	1	2		6	6
Det.	1948	SF	Det.	2	4		12	17
Det.	1950	F	Det.	3	4		17	22
Fla.	1997	CQF	NYR	4	1		13	10
L.A.	1979	PRE	NYR	2	0		9	2
L.A.	1981	PRE	NYR	3	1		23	12
Mtl.	1930	SF	Mtl.	0	2		1	4
Mtl.	1932	SF	NYR	3	1		13	9
Mtl.	1933	QF*	NYR	1	0	1	8	5
Mtl.	1935	QF*	NYR	1	0	1	6	5
Mtl.	1950	SF	NYR	4	1		15	7
Mtl.	1956	SF	Mtl.	1	4		9	24
Mtl.	1957	SF	Mtl.	1	4		12	22
Mtl.	1967	SF	Mtl.	0	4		8	14
Mtl.	1969	QF	Mtl.	0	4		7	16
Mtl.	1972	QF	NYR	4	2		19	14
Mtl.	1974	QF	NYR	4	2		21	17
Mtl.	1979	F	Mtl.	1	4		11	19
Mtl.	1986	CF	Mtl.	1	4		9	15
Mtl.	1996	CQF	NYR	4	2		19	14
N.J.	1992	DSF	NYR	4	3		28	25
N.J.	1994	CF	NYR	4	3		18	16
N.J.	1997	CSF	NYR	4	1		10	5
NYI	1975	PRE	NYI	1	2		13	10
NYI	1979	SF	NYR	4	2		18	13
NYI	1981	SF	NYI	0	4		8	22
NYI	1982	DF	NYI	2	4		20	27
NYI	1983	DF	NYI	2	4		15	28
NYI	1984	DSF	NYI	2	3		14	13
NYI	1990	DSF	NYR	4	1		22	13
NYI	1994	CQF	NYR	4	0		22	3
Phi.	1974	SF	Phi.	3	4		17	22
Phi.	1979	QF	NYR	4	1		28	8
Phi.	1980	QF	Phi.	1	4		7	14
Phi.	1982	DSF	NYR	3	1		19	15
Phi.	1983	DSF	NYR	3	0		18	9
Phi.	1985	DSF	Phi.	0	3		10	14
Phi.	1986	DSF	NYR	3	2		18	15
Phi.	1987	DSF	Phi.	2	4		13	22
Phi.	1995	CSF	Phi.	0	4		10	18
Phi.	1997	CF	Phi.	1	4		13	20
Pit.	1989	DSF	Pit.	0	4		11	19
Pit.	1992	DF	Pit.	2	4		19	24
Pit.	1996	CSF	Pit.	1	4		15	21
Que.	1995	CQF	NYR	4	2		25	19
St.L.	1981	QF	NYR	4	2		29	22
Tor.	1929	SF	NYR	2	0		3	1
Tor.	1932	F	Tor.	0	3		10	18
Tor.	1933	F	NYR	3	1		11	5
Tor.	1937	QF	NYR	2	0		5	1
Tor.	1940	F	NYR	4	2		14	11
Tor.	1942	SF	Tor.	2	4		12	13
Tor.	1962	SF	Tor.	2	4		15	22
Tor.	1971	QF	NYR	4	2		16	15
Van.	1994	F	NYR	4	3		21	19
Wsh.	1986	DF	NYR	4	2		20	25
Wsh.	1990	DF	Wsh.	1	4		15	22
Wsh.	1991	DSF	Wsh.	2	4		16	16
Wsh.	1994	CSF	NYR	4	1		20	12
Defunct Clubs								
Mtl.M	1928	F	NYR	3	2		5	6
Mtl.M	1931	QF*	NYR	2	0		8	1
Mtl.M	1934	QF*	Mtl.M	0	1	1	1	2
Mtl.M	1935	SF*	Mtl.M	1	1		4	5
Mtl.M	1937	SF	NYR	2	0		5	0
NYA	1929	QF*	NYR	1	0	1	1	0
NYA	1938	QF	NYA	1	2		7	8
Ott.	1930	QF*	NYR	1	0	1	6	3
Pit.P	1928	QF*	NYR	1	1		6	4

* Total-goals series

OTTAWA

All-Time Playoff Record vs. Other Clubs

	Series	W	L	GP	W	L	T	GF	GA	Last Mtg.	Round	Result
Buffalo	2	0	2	11	3	8	0	19	26	1999	CQF	L 0-4
New Jersey	1	1	0	6	4	2	0	13	12	1998	CQF	W 4-2
Washington	1	0	1	5	1	4	0	7	18	1998	CSF	L 4-1
Totals	**4**	**1**	**3**	**22**	**8**	**14**	**0**	**39**	**56**			

Playoff Results 1999-95

Year	Round	Opponent	Result	GF	GA
1999	CQF	Buffalo	L 0-4	6	12
1998	CSF	Washington	L 1-4	7	18
	CQF	New Jersey	W 4-2	13	12
1997	CQF	Buffalo	L 3-4	13	14

Playoff Scoring Leaders

	Player	Years	GP	G	A	Pts.
1.	Daniel Alfredsson	97-99	22	13	6	19
2.	Alexei Yashin	97-99	22	6	8	14
3.	Wade Redden	97-99	20	2	7	9
4.	Shawn McEachern	97-99	22	4	4	8
5.	Janne Laukkanen	97-99	22	2	3	5
6.	Igor Kravchuk	98-99	15	2	3	5
7.	Bruce Gardiner	97-99	21	1	4	5
8.	Steve Duchesne	97	7	1	4	5
9.	Andreas Dackell	97-99	22	2	2	4
10.	Jason York	97-99	18	2	2	4
11.	Nelson Emerson	99	4	1	3	4
12.	Sergei Zholtok	97-98	18	1	3	4

Series Records vs. Other Clubs

Opponent	Year	Series	Winner	W	L	GF	GA
Buf.	1997	CQF	Buf.	3	4	13	14
Buf.	1999	CQF	Buf.	0	4	6	12
N.J.	1998	CQF	Ott.	4	2	13	12
Wsh.	1998	CSF	Wsh.	1	4	7	18

PHILADELPHIA

All-Time Playoff Record vs. Other Clubs

	Series	W	L	GP	W	L	T	GF	GA	Last Mtg.	Round	Result
Boston	4	2	2	20	9	11	0	57	60	1978	QF	L 1-4
Buffalo	5	4	1	26	17	9	0	83	67	1998	CQF	L 1-4
Calgary	2	1	1	11	7	4	0	43	28	1981	QF	L 3-4
Chicago	1	0	1	4	0	4	0	8	20	1971	QF	L 0-4
Colorado	2	2	0	11	7	4	0	39	29	1985	CF	W 4-2
Dallas	2	2	0	11	8	3	0	41	26	1980	SF	W 4-1
Detroit	1	0	1	4	0	4	0	6	16	1997	F	L 0-4
Edmonton	3	1	2	15	7	8	0	44	49	1987	F	L 3-4
Florida	1	0	1	6	2	4	0	11	15	1996	CSF	L 2-4
Montreal	4	1	3	21	6	15	0	52	72	1989	CF	L 2-4
New Jersey	2	1	1	8	4	4	0	20	23	1995	CF	L 2-4
NY Islanders	4	3	1	25	14	11	0	83	69	1987	DF	W 4-3
NY Rangers	10	6	4	47	27	20	0	157	153	1997	CF	W 4-1
Pittsburgh	2	2	0	12	8	4	0	51	37	1997	CQF	W 4-1
St. Louis	2	0	2	11	3	8	0	20	34	1969	QF	L 0-4
Tampa Bay	1	1	0	6	4	2	0	26	13	1996	CQF	W 4-2
Toronto	4	3	1	23	14	9	0	78	56	1999	CQF	L 2-4
Vancouver	1	1	0	3	2	1	0	15	9	1979	PR	W 2-1
Washington	3	1	2	16	7	9	0	55	65	1989	DSF	W 4-2
Totals	**54**	**31**	**23**	**280**	**147**	**133**	**0**	**889**	**841**			

Playoff Results 1999-95

Year	Round	Opponent	Result	GF	GA
1999	CQF	Toronto	L 2-4	11	9
1998	CQF	Buffalo	L 1-4	9	18
1997	F	Detroit	L 0-4	6	16
	CF	NY Rangers	W 4-1	20	13
	CSF	Buffalo	W 4-1	21	13
	CQF	Pittsburgh	W 4-1	20	13
1996	CSF	Florida	L 2-4	11	15
	CQF	Tampa Bay	W 4-2	26	13
1995	CF	New Jersey	L 2-4	14	20
	CSF	NY Rangers	W 4-0	18	10
	CQF	Buffalo	W 4-1	18	13

Playoff Scoring Leaders

	Player	Years	GP	G	A	Pts.
1.	Bobby Clarke	71-84	136	42	77	119
2.	Brian Propp	80-89	116	52	60	112
3.	Bill Barber	73-83	129	53	55	108
4.	Rick MacLeish	71-81	108	53	52	105
5.	Tim Kerr	81-89	73	39	31	70
6.	Reggie Leach	75-81	91	47	22	69
7.	Eric Lindros	95-99	48	23	33	56
8.	Ken Linseman	79-82	41	11	42	53
9.	Mark Howe	83-89	82	8	45	53
10.	Rod Brind'Amour	95-99	57	24	27	51

Series Records vs. Other Clubs

Opponent	Year	Series	Winner	W	L	GF	GA
Atl.	1974	QF	Phi.	4	0	17	6
Bos.	1974	F	Phi.	4	2	15	13
Bos.	1976	SF	Phi.	4	1	19	12
Bos.	1977	SF	Bos.	0	4	8	14
Bos.	1978	QF	Bos.	1	4	15	21
Buf.	1975	F	Phi.	4	2	19	12
Buf.	1978	QF	Phi.	4	1	16	11
Buf.	1995	CQF	Phi.	4	1	18	13
Buf.	1997	CSF	Phi.	4	1	21	13
Buf.	1998	CQF	Buf.	1	4	9	18
Cgy.	1981	QF	Cgy.	3	4	26	22
Chi.	1971	QF	Chi.	0	4	8	20
Col.R	1978	PRE	Phi.	2	0	6	3
Det.	1997	F	Det.	0	4	6	16
Edm.	1980	PRE	Phi.	3	0	12	6
Edm.	1985	F	Edm.	1	4	14	21
Edm.	1987	F	Edm.	3	4	18	22
Fla.	1996	CSF	Fla.	2	4	11	15
Min.	1973	QF	Phi.	4	2	14	12
Min.	1980	SF	Phi.	4	1	27	14
Mtl.	1973	SF	Mtl.	1	4	13	19
Mtl.	1976	F	Mtl.	0	4	9	14
Mtl.	1987	CF	Phi.	4	2	22	22
Mtl.	1989	CF	Mtl.	2	4	8	17
N.J.	1995	CF	N.J.	2	4	14	20
NYI	1975	SF	Phi.	4	3	19	16
NYI	1980	F	NYI	2	4	25	26
NYI	1985	DF	Phi.	4	1	16	11
NYI	1987	DF	Phi.	4	3	23	16
NYR	1974	SF	Phi.	4	3	22	17
NYR	1979	QF	NYR	1	4	8	28
NYR	1980	QF	Phi.	4	1	14	7
NYR	1982	DSF	NYR	1	3	15	19
NYR	1983	DSF	NYR	0	3	9	18
NYR	1985	DSF	Phi.	3	0	14	10
NYR	1986	DSF	NYR	2	3	15	18
NYR	1987	DSF	Phi.	4	2	22	13
NYR	1995	CSF	Phi.	4	0	18	10
NYR	1997	CF	Phi.	4	1	20	13
Pit.	1989	DF	Phi.	4	3	31	24
Pit.	1997	CQF	Phi.	4	1	20	13
Que.	1981	PRE	Phi.	3	2	22	17
Que.	1985	CF	Phi.	4	2	17	12
St.L.	1968	QF	St.L.	3	4	17	17
St.L.	1969	QF	St.L.	0	4	3	17
Tor.	1975	QF	Phi.	4	0	15	6
Tor.	1976	QF	Phi.	4	3	33	23
Tor.	1977	QF	Phi.	4	2	19	18
Tor.	1999	CQF	Tor.	2	4	11	9
T.B.	1996	CQF	Phi.	4	2	26	13
Van.	1979	PRE	Phi.	2	1	15	9
Wsh.	1984	DSF	Wsh.	0	3	5	15
Wsh.	1988	DSF	Wsh.	3	4	25	31
Wsh.	1989	DSF	Phi.	4	2	25	19

PHOENIX

All-Time Playoff Record vs. Other Clubs

	Series	W	L	GP	W	L	T	GF	GA	Last Mtg.	Round	Result
Anaheim	1	0	1	7	3	4	0	17	17	1997	CQF	L 3-4
Calgary	3	2	1	13	7	6	0	45	43	1987	DSF	W 4-2
Detroit	2	0	2	12	4	8	0	28	44	1998	CQF	L 2-4
Edmonton	6	0	6	26	4	22	0	75	120	1990	DSF	L 3-4
St. Louis	2	0	2	11	4	7	0	29	39	1999	CQF	L 3-4
Vancouver	2	0	2	13	5	8	0	34	50	1993	DSF	L 2-4
Totals	**16**	**2**	**14**	**82**	**27**	**55**	**0**	**228**	**313**			

Playoff Results 1999-95

Year	Round	Opponent	Result	GF	GA
1999	CQF	St. Louis	L 3-4	16	19
1998	CQF	Detroit	L 2-4	18	24
1997	CQF	Anaheim	L 3-4	17	17
1996	CQF	Detroit	L 2-4	10	20

Playoff Scoring Leaders

	Player	Years	GP	G	A	Pts.
1.	Dale Hawerchuk	82-90	38	16	33	49
2.	Thomas Steen	82-93	56	12	32	44
3.	Keith Tkachuk	92-99	39	18	8	26
4.	Paul MacLean	82-88	35	16	10	26
5.	Dave Ellett	85-90	33	4	16	20
6.	Fredrik Olausson	87-93	35	4	13	17
7.	Randy Carlyle	84-92	31	3	14	17
8.	Brian Mullen	83-87	26	7	9	16
9.	Moe Mantha	82-90	16	5	10	15
10.	Laurie Boschman	83-90	34	5	10	15

Series Records vs. Other Clubs

Note: Includes series played by Winnipeg Jets, 1982-96

Opponent	Year	Series	Winner	W	L	GF	GA
Ana.	1997	CQF	Ana.	3	4	17	17
Cgy.	1985	DSF	Wpg.	3	1	15	13
Cgy.	1986	DSF	Cgy.	0	3	8	15
Cgy.	1987	DSF	Wpg.	4	2	22	15
Det.	1996	CQF	Det.	2	4	10	20
Det.	1998	CQF	Det.	2	4	18	24
Edm.	1983	DSF	Edm.	0	3	9	14
Edm.	1984	DSF	Edm.	0	3	7	18
Edm.	1985	DF	Edm.	0	4	11	22
Edm.	1987	DF	Edm.	0	4	9	17
Edm.	1988	DSF	Edm.	1	4	17	25
Edm.	1990	DSF	Edm.	3	4	22	24
St.L.	1982	DSF	St.L.	1	3	13	20
St.L.	1999	CQF	St.L.	3	4	16	29
Van.	1992	DSF	Van.	3	4	17	29
Van.	1993	DSF	Van.	2	4	17	21

PITTSBURGH

All-Time Playoff Record vs. Other Clubs

	Series	W	L	GP	W	L	T	GF	GA	Last Mtg.	Round	Result
Boston	4	2	2	19	10	9	0	67	62	1992	CF	W 4-0
Buffalo	1	1	0	3	2	1	0	9	9	1979	PR	W 2-1
Chicago	2	1	1	8	4	4	0	23	24	1992	F	W 4-0
Dallas	1	1	0	6	4	2	0	28	16	1991	F	W 4-2
Florida	1	0	1	7	3	4	0	15	20	1996	CF	L 3-4
Montreal	1	0	1	6	2	4	0	15	18	1998	CQF	L 2-4
New Jersey	4	3	1	24	13	11	0	77	65	1999	CQF	W 4-3
NY Islanders	3	0	3	19	8	11	0	58	67	1993	DF	L 3-4
NY Rangers	3	3	0	15	12	3	0	65	45	1996	CSF	W 4-1
Oakland	1	1	0	4	4	0	0	13	6	1970	QF	W 4-0
Philadelphia	2	0	2	12	4	8	0	37	51	1997	CQF	L 1-4
St. Louis	3	1	2	13	6	7	0	40	45	1981	PR	L 2-3
Toronto	3	0	3	12	4	8	0	27	39	1999	CSF	L 2-4
Washington	5	4	1	31	18	13	0	106	103	1996	CQF	W 4-2
Totals	**34**	**17**	**17**	**179**	**94**	**85**	**0**	**579**	**570**			

Playoff Results 1999-95

Year	Round	Opponent	Result	GF	GA
1999	CSF	Toronto	L 2-4	14	18
	CQF	New Jersey	W 4-3	21	18
1998	CQF	Montreal	L 2-4	15	18
1997	CQF	Philadelphia	L 1-4	13	20
1996	CF	Florida	L 3-4	15	20
	CSF	NY Rangers	W 4-1	21	15
	CQF	Washington	W 4-2	21	17
1995	CSF	New Jersey	L 1-4	8	17
	CQF	Washington	W 4-3	29	26

Playoff Scoring Leaders

	Player	Years	GP	G	A	Pts.
1.	Mario Lemieux	89-97	89	70	85	155
3.	Jaromir Jagr	91-99	113	55	64	119
2.	Kevin Stevens	89-95	86	43	57	100
4.	Ron Francis	91-98	97	32	68	100
5.	Larry Murphy	91-95	74	15	57	72
6.	Rick Tocchet	92-94	32	15	22	37
7.	Mark Recchi	91	24	10	24	34
8.	Joe Mullen	91-95, 97	62	16	15	31
9.	Paul Coffey	89-91	23	4	22	26
10.	Phil Bourque	89-92	56	13	12	25

Series Records vs. Other Clubs

Opponent	Year	Series	Winner	W	L	GF	GA
Bos.	1979	QF	Bos.	0	4	7	16
Bos.	1980	PRE	Bos.	2	3	14	21
Bos.	1991	CF	Pit.	4	2	27	18
Bos.	1992	CF	Pit.	4	0	19	7
Buf.	1979	PRE	Pit.	2	1	9	9
Chi.	1972	QF	Chi.	0	4	8	14
Chi.	1992	F	Pit.	4	0	15	10
Fla.	1996	CF	Fla.	3	4	15	20
Mtl.	1998	F	Mon.	2	4	15	18
Min.	1991	F	Pit.	4	2	28	16
N.J.	1991	DSF	Pit.	4	3	21	21
N.J.	1993	DSF	Pit.	4	1	23	13
N.J.	1995	CSF	N.J.	1	4	8	17
N.J.	1999	CQF	Pit.	4	3	21	18
NYI	1975	QF	NYI	3	4	18	21
NYI	1982	DSF	NYI	2	3	13	22
NYI	1993	DF	NYI	3	4	27	24
NYR	1989	DSF	Pit.	4	0	19	11
NYR	1992	DF	Pit.	4	2	24	19
NYR	1996	CSF	Pit.	4	1	21	15
Oak.	1970	QF	Pit.	4	0	13	6
Phi.	1989	DF	Phi.	3	4	24	31
Phi.	1997	CQF	Phi.	1	4	13	20
St.L.	1970	SF	St.L.	2	4	10	19
St.L.	1975	PRE	Pit.	2	0	9	6
St.L.	1981	PRE	St.L.	2	3	21	20
Tor.	1976	PRE	Tor.	1	2	3	8
Tor.	1977	PRE	Tor.	1	2	10	13
Tor.	1999	CSF	Tor.	2	4	14	18
Wsh.	1991	DF	Pit.	4	1	19	13
Wsh.	1992	DSF	Pit.	4	3	25	27
Wsh.	1994	CQF	Wsh.	2	4	12	20
Wsh.	1995	CQF	Pit.	4	3	29	26
Wsh.	1996	CQF	Pit.	4	2	21	15

ST. LOUIS

All-Time Playoff Record vs. Other Clubs

	Series	W	L	GP	W	L	T	GF	GA	Last Mtg.	Round	Result
Boston	2	0	2	8	0	8	0	15	48	1972	SF	L 0-4
Buffalo	1	0	1	3	1	2	0	8	7	1976	PR	L 1-2
Calgary	1	0	1	7	3	4	0	22	28	1986	CF	L 3-4
Chicago	9	2	7	45	18	27	0	129	166	1993	DSF	W 4-0
Dallas	11	5	6	62	28	34	0	174	191	1999	CSF	L 2-4
Detroit	6	2	4	35	15	20	0	92	111	1998	CQF	L 2-4
Los Angeles	2	2	0	8	8	0	0	32	13	1998	CSF	W 4-0
Montreal	3	0	3	12	0	12	0	14	42	1977	QF	L 0-4
NY Rangers	1	0	1	6	2	4	0	22	29	1981	QF	L 2-4
Philadelphia	2	2	0	11	8	3	0	34	20	1969	QF	W 4-0
Phoenix	2	2	0	11	7	4	0	39	29	1999	CQF	W 4-3
Pittsburgh	3	2	1	13	7	6	0	45	40	1981	PR	W 3-2
Toronto	5	3	2	31	17	14	0	88	90	1996	CQF	W 4-2
Vancouver	1	0	1	7	3	4	0	27	27	1995	CQF	L 3-4
Totals	**49**	**20**	**29**	**259**	**117**	**142**	**0**	**741**	**841**			

Playoff Results 1999-95

Year	Round	Opponent	Result	GF	GA
1999	CSF	Dallas	L 2-4	12	17
	CQF	Phoenix	W 4-3	19	16
1998	CSF	Detroit	L 2-4	13	23
	CQF	Los Angeles	W 4-0	16	8
1997	CQF	Detroit	L 2-4	12	13
1996	CSF	Detroit	L 3-4	16	22
	CQF	Toronto	W 4-2	21	15
1995	CQF	Vancouver	L 3-4	27	27

Playoff Scoring Leaders

	Player	Years	GP	G	A	Pts.
1.	Brett Hull	88-98	102	67	50	117
2.	Bernie Federko	77-89	91	35	66	101
3.	Doug Gilmour	84-88	49	17	38	55
4.	Frank St. Marseille	68-72	61	19	24	43
5.	Brian Sutter	77-88	65	21	21	42
6.	Jeff Brown	90-93	42	10	28	38
7.	Al MacInnis	95-99	47	11	25	36
8.	Adam Oates	90-91	25	9	25	34
9.	Red Berenson	68-77	55	21	12	33
10.	Gino Cavallini	86-91	67	14	19	33

Series Records vs. Other Clubs

Opponent	Year	Series	Winner	W	L	GF	GA
Bos.	1970	F	Bos.	0	4	7	20
Bos.	1972	SF	Bos.	0	4	8	28
Buf.	1978	PRE	Buf.	1	2	8	7
Cgy.	1986	CF	Cgy.	3	4	22	28
Chi.	1973	QF	Chi.	1	4	9	22
Chi.	1980	PRE	Chi.	0	3	4	12
Chi.	1982	DF	Chi.	2	4	19	23
Chi.	1983	DSF	Chi.	1	3	10	16
Chi.	1988	DSF	St.L.	4	1	21	17
Chi.	1989	DF	Chi.	1	4	12	19
Chi.	1990	DF	Chi.	3	4	22	28
Chi.	1992	DSF	Chi.	2	4	19	23
Chi.	1993	DSF	St.L.	4	0	13	6
Dal.	1994	CQF	Dal.	0	4	10	16
Dal.	1999	CSF	Dal.	2	4	12	17
Det.	1984	DSF	St.L.	3	1	13	12
Det.	1988	DF	Det.	1	4	14	21
Det.	1991	DSF	St.L.	4	3	24	20
Det.	1996	CSF	Det.	3	4	16	22
Det.	1997	CQF	Det.	2	4	12	13
Det.	1998	CSF	Det.	2	4	13	23
L.A.	1969	SF	St.L.	4	0	16	5
L.A.	1998	CQF	St.L.	4	0	16	8
Min.	1968	SF	St.L.	4	3	18	22
Min.	1970	QF	St.L.	4	2	20	16
Min.	1971	QF	Min.	2	4	15	16
Min.	1972	QF	St.L.	4	3	19	19
Min.	1984	DF	Min.	3	4	17	19
Min.	1985	DSF	Min.	0	3	5	9
Min.	1986	DSF	St.L.	3	2	18	20
Min.	1989	DSF	St.L.	4	1	23	15
Min.	1991	DF	Min.	2	4	17	22
Mtl.	1968	F	Mtl.	0	4	7	11
Mtl.	1969	F	Mtl.	0	4	3	12
Mtl.	1977	QF	Mtl.	0	4	4	19
NYR	1981	QF	NYR	2	4	22	29
Phi.	1968	QF	St.L.	4	3	17	17
Phi.	1969	QF	St.L.	4	0	17	3
Phx.	1999	CQF	St.L.	4	3	19	16
Pit.	1970	SF	St.L.	4	2	19	10
Pit.	1975	PRE	Pit,	0	2	6	9
Pit.	1981	PRE	St.L.	3	2	20	21
Tor.	1986	DF	St.L.	4	3	24	22
Tor.	1987	DSF	Tor.	2	4	12	15
Tor.	1990	DSF	St.L.	4	1	20	16
Tor.	1993	DF	Tor.	3	4	11	22
Tor.	1996	CQF	St.L.	4	2	21	15
Van.	1995	CQF	Van.	3	4	27	27
Wpg.	1982	DSF	St.L.	3	1	20	13

SAN JOSE

All-Time Playoff Record vs. Other Clubs

	Series	W	L	GP	W	L	T	GF	GA	Last Mtg.	Round	Result
Calgary	1	1	0	7	4	3	0	26	35	1995	CQF	W 4-3
Colorado	1	0	1	6	2	4	0	17	19	1999	CQF	L 2-4
Dallas	1	0	1	6	2	4	0	12	16	1998	CQF	L 2-4
Detroit	2	1	1	11	4	7	0	27	51	1995	CSF	L 0-4
Toronto	1	0	1	7	3	4	0	21	26	1994	CSF	L 3-4
Totals	**6**	**2**	**4**	**37**	**15**	**22**	**0**	**103**	**147**			

Playoff Results 1999-95

Year	Round	Opponent	Result	GF	GA
1999	CQF	Colorado	L 2-4	17	19
1998	CQF	Dallas	L 2-4	12	16
1995	CSF	Detroit	L 0-4	6	24
	CQF	Calgary	W 4-3	26	35

Playoff Scoring Leaders

	Player	Years	GP	G	A	Pts.
1.	Igor Larionov	94-95	25	6	21	27
2.	Ulf Dahlen	94-95	25	11	6	17
3.	Sergei Makarov	94-95	25	11	5	16
4.	Sandis Ozolinsh	94-95	25	3	12	15
5.	Jeff Norton	95, 99	20	1	12	13
6.	Ray Whitney	94-95	25	4	8	12
7.	Tom Pederson	94-95	24	1	11	12
8.	Jeff Friesen	94-99	23	3	8	11
9.	Todd Elik	94-95	14	5	5	10
10.	Johan Garpenlov	94	14	4	6	10

Series Records vs. Other Clubs

Opponent	Year	Series	Winner	W	L	GF	GA
Cgy.	1995	CQF	S.J.	4	3	26	35
Col.	1999	CQF	Col.	2	4	17	19
Dal.	1998	CQF	Dal.	2	4	12	16
Det.	1994	CQF	S.J.	4	3	21	27
Det.	1995	CSF	Det.	0	4	6	24
Tor.	1994	CSF	Tor.	3	4	21	26

TAMPA BAY

All-Time Playoff Record vs. Other Clubs

	Series	W	L	GP	W	L	T	GF	GA	Last Mtg.	Round	Result
Philadelphia	1	0	1	6	2	4	0	13	26	1996	CQF	L 2-4
Totals	**1**	**0**	**1**	**6**	**2**	**4**	**0**	**13**	**26**			

Playoff Results 1999-95

Year	Round	Opponent	Result	GF	GA
1996	CQF	Philadelphia	L 2-4	13	26

Playoff Scoring Leaders

	Player	Years	GP	G	A	Pts.
1.	John Cullen	96	5	3	3	6
2.	Rob Zamuner	96	6	2	3	5

3.	Alex. Selivanov	96	6	2	2	4
4.	Brian Bradley	96	5	0	3	3
5.	Petr Klima	96	4	2	0	2
6.	Brian Bellows	96	6	2	0	2
7.	Mikael Andersson	96	6	1	1	2
8.	Shawn Burr	96	6	0	2	2
9.	Chris Gratton	96	6	0	2	2
10.	Jason Wiemer	96	6	1	0	1
11.	Roman Hamrlik	96	5	0	1	1
12.	Bill Houlder	96	6	0	1	1
13.	Dave Shaw	96	6	0	1	1

Series Records vs. Other Clubs

Opponent	Year	Series	Winner	W	L	GF	GA
Phi.	1996	CQF	Phi.	2	4	13	26

TORONTO

All-Time Playoff Record vs. Other Clubs

	Series	W	L	GP	W	L	T	GF	GA	Last Mtg.	Round	Result
Boston	13	8	5	62	31	30	1	150	153	1974	QF	L 0-4
Buffalo	1	0	1	5	1	4	0	16	21	1999	CF	L 1-4
Calgary	1	1	0	2	2	0	0	9	5	1979	PR	W 2-0
Chicago	9	6	3	38	22	15	1	111	89	1995	CQF	L 3-4
Dallas	2	0	2	7	1	6	0	26	35	1983	DSF	L 1-3
Detroit	23	12	11	117	58	59	0	311	321	1993	DSF	W 4-3
Los Angeles	3	2	1	12	7	5	0	41	31	1993	CF	L 3-4
Montreal	15	7	8	71	29	42	0	160	215	1979	QF	L 0-4
NY Islanders	2	1	1	10	4	6	0	20	33	1981	PR	L 0-3
NY Rangers	8	3	5	35	16	19	0	86	86	1971	QF	L 2-4
Philadelphia	4	1	3	23	9	14	0	56	78	1999	CQF	W 4-2
Pittsburgh	3	3	0	12	8	4	0	39	27	1999	CSF	W 4-2
St. Louis	5	2	3	31	14	17	0	90	88	1996	CQF	L 2-4
San Jose	1	1	0	7	4	3	0	26	21	1994	CSF	W 4-3
Vancouver	1	0	1	5	1	4	0	9	16	1994	CF	L 1-4
Defunct	8	6	2	24	12	10	2	59	57			
Totals	**99**	**53**	**46**	**461**	**219**	**238**	**4**	**1209**	**1292**			

Playoff Results 1999-95

Year	Round	Opponent	Result	GF	GA
1999	CF	Buffalo	L 1-4	16	21
	CSF	Pittsburgh	W 4-2	18	14
	CQF	Philadelphia	W 4-2	9	11
1996	CQF	St. Louis	L 2-4	15	21
1995	CQF	Chicago	L 3-4	20	22

Playoff Scoring Leaders

	Player	Years	GP	G	A	Pts.
1.	Doug Gilmour	93-96	52	17	60	77
2.	Dave Keon	61-75	89	32	35	67
3.	Darryl Sittler	71-81	64	25	40	65
4.	Ted Kennedy	44-55	78	29	31	60
5.	George Armstrong	52-71	110	26	34	60
6.	Frank Mahovlich	59-67	84	24	36	60
7.	Wendel Clark	86-94, 96	73	33	26	59
8.	Red Kelly	60-67	70	17	38	55
9.	Syl Apps, Sr..	37-48	69	25	28	53
10.	Bob Pulford	59-69	89	25	26	51

Series Records vs. Other Clubs

Opponent	Year	Series	Winner	W	L	T	GF	GA
Atl.	1979	PRE	Tor.	2	0		9	5
Bos.	1933	SF	Tor.	3	2		9	7
Bos.	1935	SF	Tor.	3	1		7	2
Bos.	1936	QF*	Tor.	1	1		8	6
Bos.	1938	SF	Tor.	3	0		6	3
Bos.	1939	F	Bos.	1	4		6	12
Bos.	1941	SF	Bos.	3	4		17	15
Bos.	1948	SF	Tor.	4	1		20	13
Bos.	1949	SF	Tor.	4	1		16	10
Bos.	1951	SF	Tor.	4	1	1	17	5
Bos.	1959	SF	Tor.	4	3		20	21
Bos.	1969	QF	Bos.	0	4		5	24
Bos.	1972	QF	Bos.	1	4		10	18
Bos.	1974	QF	Bos.	0	4		9	17
Buf.	1999	CF	Buf.	1	4		16	21
Chi.	1931	QF*	Chi.	0	1	1	3	4
Chi.	1932	QF*	Tor.	1	1		6	2
Chi.	1938	F	Chi.	1	3		8	10
Chi.	1940	QF	Tor.	2	0		5	3
Chi.	1962	F	Tor.	4	2		18	15
Chi.	1967	SF	Tor.	4	2		18	14
Chi.	1986	DSF	Tor.	3	0		18	9
Chi.	1994	CQF	Tor.	4	2		15	10
Chi.	1995	CQF	Chi.	3	4		20	22
Det.	1929	QF*	Tor.	2	0		7	2
Det.	1934	SF	Det.	2	3		12	11
Det.	1936	F	Det.	1	3		11	18
Det.	1939	SF	Tor.	2	1		10	8
Det.	1940	SF	Tor.	2	0		5	2
Det.	1942	F	Tor.	4	3		25	19
Det.	1943	SF	Det.	2	4		17	10
Det.	1945	F	Tor.	4	3		9	9
Det.	1947	SF	Tor.	4	1		18	14
Det.	1948	F	Tor.	4	0		18	7
Det.	1949	F	Tor.	4	0		12	5
Det.	1950	SF	Det.	3	4		11	10
Det.	1952	SF	Det.	0	4		3	13
Det.	1954	SF	Det.	1	4		8	15
Det.	1955	SF	Det.	0	4		6	14
Det.	1956	SF	Det.	1	4		10	14
Det.	1960	SF	Tor.	4	2		20	16
Det.	1961	SF	Det.	1	4		8	15
Det.	1963	F	Tor.	4	1		17	10
Det.	1964	F	Tor.	4	3		22	17
Det.	1987	DF	Det.	3	4		18	20
Det.	1988	DSF	Det.	2	4		20	32
Det.	1993	DSF	Tor.	4	3		24	30
L.A.	1975	PRE	Tor.	2	1		7	6
L.A.	1978	PRE	Tor.	2	0		11	3
L.A.	1993	CF	L.A.	3	4		23	22
Min.	1980	PRE	Min.	0	3		8	17
Min.	1983	DSF	Min.	1	3		18	18
Mtl.	1918	NHLF*	Tor.	1	1		10	7
Mtl.	1925	NHLF*	Mtl.	0	2		2	5
Mtl.	1945	SF	Tor.	4	2		15	21
Mtl.	1944	SF	Mtl.	1	4		6	23
Mtl.	1947	F	Tor.	4	2		13	13
Mtl.	1951	F	Tor.	4	1		13	10
Mtl.	1959	F	Mtl.	1	4		12	18
Mtl.	1960	F	Mtl.	0	4		5	15
Mtl.	1963	SF	Tor.	4	1		14	6
Mtl.	1964	SF	Tor.	4	3		17	14
Mtl.	1965	SF	Mtl.	2	4		14	17
Mtl.	1966	SF	Mtl.	0	4		6	15
Mtl.	1967	F	Tor.	4	2		17	16
Mtl.	1978	SF	Mtl.	0	4		6	16
Mtl.	1979	QF	Mtl.	0	4		10	19
NYI	1978	QF	Tor.	4	3		16	13
NYI	1981	PRE	NYI	0	3		4	20
NYR	1929	SF	NYR	0	2		1	3
NYR	1932	F	Tor.	3	0		18	10
NYR	1933	F	NYR	1	3		5	11
NYR	1937	QF	NYR	0	2		1	5
NYR	1940	F	NYR	2	4		11	14
NYR	1942	SF	Tor.	4	2		13	12
NYR	1962	SF	Tor.	4	2		22	15
NYR	1971	QF	NYR	2	4		15	16
Phi.	1975	QF	Phi.	0	4		6	15
Phi.	1976	QF	Phi.	3	4		23	33
Phi.	1977	QF	Phi.	2	4		18	19
Phi.	1999	CQF	Tor.	4	2		9	11
Pit.	1976	PRE	Tor.	2	1		8	3
Pit.	1977	PRE	Tor.	2	1		13	10
Pit.	1999	CSF	Tor.	4	2		18	14
St.L.	1986	DF	St.L.	3	4		22	24
St.L.	1987	DSF	Tor.	4	2		15	12
St.L.	1990	DSF	St.L.	1	4		16	20
St.L.	1993	DF	Tor.	4	3		22	11
St.L.	1996	CQF	St.L.	2	4		15	21
S.J.	1994	CSF	Tor.	4	3		26	21
Van.	1994	CF	Van.	1	4		9	16

Defunct Clubs

Opponent	Year	Series	Winner	W	L	T	GF	GA
Mtl.M	1932	SF*	Tor.	1	0	1	4	3
Mtl.M	1935	F	Mtl.M	0	3		4	10
NYA	1936	SF	Tor.	2	1		6	3
NYA	1939	QF	Tor.	2	0		6	0
Ott.	1921	NHLF*	Ott.	0	2		0	7
Ott.	1922	NHLF*	Tor.	1	0	1	5	4
Van.M	1918	F	Tor.	3	2		18	21
Van.M	1922	F	Tor.	3	2		16	9

* Total-goals series

VANCOUVER

All-Time Playoff Record vs. Other Clubs

	Series	W	L	GP	W	L	T	GF	GA	Last Mtg.	Round	Result
Buffalo	2	0	2	7	1	6	0	14	28	1981	PR	L 0-3
Calgary	5	2	3	25	12	13	0	80	82	1994	CQF	W 4-3
Chicago	2	1	1	9	4	5	0	24	24	1995	CSF	L 0-4
Colorado	1	0	1	6	2	4	0	17	24	1996	CQF	L 2-4
Dallas	1	1	0	5	4	1	0	18	11	1994	CSF	W 4-1
Edmonton	2	0	2	9	2	7	0	20	35	1992	DF	L 2-4
Los Angeles	3	1	2	17	8	9	0	60	66	1993	DF	L 2-4
Montreal	1	0	1	5	1	4	0	9	20	1975	QF	L 1-4
NY Islanders	2	0	2	6	0	6	0	14	26	1982	F	L 0-4
NY Rangers	1	0	1	7	3	4	0	19	21	1994	F	L 3-4
Philadelphia	1	0	1	3	1	2	0	9	15	1979	PR	L 1-2
St. Louis	1	1	0	7	4	3	0	27	27	1995	CQF	W 4-3
Toronto	1	1	0	5	4	1	0	16	9	1994	CF	W 4-1
Winnipeg	2	2	0	13	8	5	0	50	34	1993	DSF	W 4-2
Totals	**25**	**9**	**16**	**124**	**54**	**70**	**0**	**377**	**422**			

Playoff Results 1999-95

Year	Round	Opponent	Result	GF	GA
1996	CQF	Colorado	L 2-4	17	24
1995	CSF	Chicago	L 0-4	6	11
	CQF	St. Louis	W 4-3	27	27

Playoff Scoring Leaders

	Player	Years	GP	G	A	Pts.
1.	Trevor Linden	89-96	79	30	50	80
2.	Pavel Bure	92-95	60	34	32	66
3.	Geoff Courtnall	91-95	65	26	35	61
4.	Cliff Ronning	91-95	66	24	32	56
5.	Jyrki Lumme	91-96	72	9	31	40
6.	Thomas Gradin	79-86	38	17	21	38
7.	Greg Adams	88-94	53	15	19	34
8.	Stan Smyl	79-89	41	16	17	33
9.	Dave Babych	92-95	60	9	18	27
10.	Murray Craven	93-94	34	8	15	23

Series Records vs. Other Clubs

Opponent	Year	Series	Winner	W	L	GF	GA
Buf.	1980	PRE	Buf.	1	3	7	15
Buf.	1981	PRE	Buf.	0	3	7	13
Cgy.	1982	DSF	Van.	3	0	10	5
Cgy.	1983	DSF	Cgy.	1	3	14	17
Cgy.	1984	DSF	Cgy.	1	3	13	14
Cgy.	1989	DSF	Cgy.	3	4	20	26
Cgy.	1994	CQF	Van.	4	3	23	20
Col.	1996	CQF	Col.	2	4	17	24
Chi.	1982	CF	Van.	4	1	18	13
Chi.	1995	CSF	Chi.	0	4	6	11
Dal.	1994	CSF	Van.	4	1	18	11
Edm.	1986	DSF	Edm.	0	3	5	17
Edm.	1992	DF	Edm.	2	4	15	18
L.A.	1982	DF	Van.	4	1	19	14
L.A.	1991	DSF	L.A.	2	4	16	26
L.A.	1993	DF	L.A.	2	4	25	26
Mtl.	1975	QF	Mtl.	1	4	9	20
NYI	1976	PRE	NYI	0	2	4	8
NYI	1982	F	NYI	0	4	10	18
NYR	1994	F	NYR	3	4	19	21
Phi.	1979	PRE	Phi.	1	2	9	15
St.L.	1995	CQF	Van.	4	3	27	27
Tor.	1994	CF	Van.	4	1	16	9
Wpg.	1992	DSF	Van.	4	3	29	17
Wpg.	1993	DSF	Van.	4	2	21	17

WASHINGTON

All-Time Playoff Record vs. Other Clubs

	Series	W	L	GP	W	L	T	GF	GA	Last Mtg.	Round	Result
Boston	2	1	1	10	4	6	0	15	13	1998	CQF	W 4-2
Buffalo	1	1	0	6	4	2	0	13	11	1998	CF	W 4-2
Detroit	1	0	1	4	0	4	0	7	13	1998	F	L 0-4
New Jersey	2	1	1	13	7	6	0	44	43	1990	DSF	W 4-2
NY Islanders	6	1	5	30	12	18	0	88	89	1993	DSF	L 2-4
NY Rangers	4	2	2	22	11	11	0	75	71	1994	CSF	L 1-4
Ottawa	1	1	0	5	4	1	0	18	7	1998	CSF	W 4-1
Philadelphia	3	2	1	16	9	7	0	65	55	1989	DSF	L 2-4
Pittsburgh	5	1	4	31	13	18	0	103	106	1996	CQF	L 2-4
Totals	**25**	**10**	**15**	**137**	**64**	**73**	**0**	**434**	**433**			

Playoff Results 1999-95

Year	Round	Opponent	Result	GF	GA
1998	F	Detroit	L 0-4	7	13
	CF	Buffalo	W 4-2	13	11
	CSF	Ottawa	W 4-1	18	7
	CQF	Boston	W 4-2	15	13
1996	CQF	Pittsburgh	L 2-4	17	21
1995	CQF	Pittsburgh	L 3-4	26	29

Playoff Scoring Leaders

	Player	Years	GP	G	A	Pts.
1.	Dale Hunter	88-98	100	25	47	72
2.	Mike Ridley	87-94	76	19	41	60
3.	Michal Pivonka	83-98	95	19	36	55
4.	Scott Stevens	83-90	67	9	44	53
5.	Kevin Hatcher	85-94	83	16	32	48
6.	Kelly Miller	87-98	100	17	30	47
7.	Calle Johansson	89-98	78	10	37	47
8.	Peter Bondra	91-98	56	23	23	46
9.	Mike Gartner	83-88	47	16	27	43
10.	Joe Juneau	94-98	44	13	28	41

Series Records vs. Other Clubs

Opponent	Year	Series	Winner	W	L	GF	GA
Bos.	1990	CF	Bos.	0	4	6	15
Bos.	1998	CQF	Wsh.	4	2	15	13
Buf.	1998	CF	Wsh.	4	2	13	11
Det.	1998	F	Det.	4	0	13	17
N.J.	1988	DF	N.J.	3	4	23	25
N.J.	1990	DSF	Wsh.	4	2	21	18
NYI	1983	DSF	NYI	1	3	11	19
NYI	1984	DF	NYI	1	4	13	20
NYI	1985	DSF	NYI	2	3	12	14
NYI	1986	DSF	Wsh.	3	0	11	4
NYI	1987	DSF	NYI	3	4	19	19
NYI	1993	DSF	NYI	2	4	22	23
NYR	1986	DF	NYR	2	4	25	20
NYR	1990	DF	Wsh.	4	1	22	15
NYR	1991	DSF	Wsh.	4	2	16	16
NYR	1994	CSF	NYR	1	4	12	20
Ott.	1998	CSF	Wsh.	4	1	18	7
Phi.	1984	DSF	Wsh.	3	0	15	5
Phi.	1988	DSF	Wsh.	4	3	31	25
Phi.	1989	DSF	Phi.	2	4	19	25
Pit.	1991	DF	Pit.	1	4	13	19
Pit.	1992	DSF	Pit.	3	4	27	25
Pit.	1994	CQF	Wsh.	4	2	20	12
Pit.	1995	CQF	Pit.	3	4	26	29
Pit.	1996	CQF	Pit.	2	4	15	21

NOTE:
Atlanta and Nashville
have not appeared in the playoffs.

Stanley Cup Standings, 1918-99

ranked by Cup wins

Teams	Cup Wins	Yrs.	Series	Wins	Losses	Games	Wins	Losses	Ties	Goals For	Goals Against	Winning %
Montreal	23 [1]	72	134 [2]	85	48	638	381	249	8	1977	1591	.603
Toronto	13 [3]	59	99	53	46	461	219	238	4	1209	1292	.479
Detroit	9	48	89	50	39	440	228	211	1	1243	1167	.519
Boston	5	59	101	47	54	494	236	252	6	1448	1464	.484
Edmonton	5	16	42	31	11	210	132	78	0	833	652	.629
NY Rangers	4	48	86	42	44	386	183	195	8	1091	1114	.484
NY Islanders	4	17	43	30	13	218	128	90	0	748	650	.587
Chicago	3	52	89	40	49	406	187	214	5	1171	1298	.467
Philadelphia	2	25	54	31	23	280	147	133	0	889	841	.525
Pittsburgh	2	19	34	17	17	179	94	85	0	579	570	.525
Dallas [4]	1	22	42	21	21	227	115	112	0	708	721	.507
Calgary [5]	1	21	32	12	20	156	69	87	0	529	573	.442
Colorado [6]	1	13	26	14	12	145	75	70	0	458	451	.517
New Jersey [7]	1	11	19	9	10	110	57	43	0	319	312	.518
St. Louis	0	29	49	20	29	259	117	142	0	741	841	.452
Buffalo	0	23	39	16	23	191	91	100	0	580	595	.476
Los Angeles	0	20	30	10	20	146	55	91	0	467	584	.377
Vancouver	0	16	25	9	16	124	54	70	0	377	422	.435
Washington	0	15	25	10	15	137	64	73	0	434	433	.467
Phoenix [8]	0	14	16	2	14	82	27	55	0	228	313	.329
Carolina [9]	0	9	10	1	9	55	20	35	0	157	194	.364
San Jose	0	4	6	2	4	37	15	22	0	103	147	.405
Ottawa	0	3	4	1	3	22	8	14	0	39	56	.364
Florida	0	2	5	3	2	27	13	14	0	71	70	.481
Anaheim	0	2	3	1	2	15	4	11	0	31	47	.267
Tampa Bay	0	1	1	0	1	6	2	4	0	13	26	.333

NOTES

1 Montreal also won the Stanley Cup in 1916.
2 1919 final incomplete due to influenza epidemic.
3 Toronto Blueshirts also won the Stanley Cup in 1914.
4 Includes totals of Minnesota North Stars 1967-93.
5 Includes totals of Atlanta Flames 1972-80.
6 Includes totals of Quebec Nordiques 1979-95.
7 Includes totals of Colorado Rockies 1976-82.
8 Includes totals of Winnipeg Jets 1979-96
9 Includes totals of Hartford Whalers 1979-97.

CHAPTER 7

All-Time Playoff Scoring Leaders

1918 – 1999

Goals

(40 or more goals)

Player	Teams	Yrs.	GP	G
Wayne Gretzky	Edm., L.A., St.L., NYR	16	208	122
Mark Messier	Edm., NYR	17	236	109
Jari Kurri	Edm., L.A., NYR, Ana., Col.	14	200	106
Glenn Anderson	Edm., Tor., NYR, St.L.	15	225	93
Mike Bossy	NYI	10	129	85
Maurice Richard	Mtl.	15	133	82
Jean Beliveau	Mtl.	17	162	79
Brett Hull	Cgy., St.L., Dal.	14	130	77
Claude Lemieux	Mtl., N.J., Col.	14	198	76
Dino Ciccarelli	Min., Wsh., Det.	14	141	73
Esa Tikkanen	Edm., NYR, St.L., Van., Wsh.	13	186	72
Bryan Trottier	NYI, Pit.	17	221	71
Mario Lemieux	Pit.	7	89	70
Gordie Howe	Det., Hfd.	20	157	68
Denis Savard	Chi., Mtl., T.B.	16	169	66
Yvan Cournoyer	Mtl.	12	147	64
Brian Propp	Phi., Bos., Min., Hfd.	13	160	64
Bobby Smith	Min., Mtl.	13	184	64
Bobby Hull	Chi., Wpg., Hfd.	14	119	62
Phil Esposito	Chi., Bos., NYR	15	130	61
Jacques Lemaire	Mtl.	11	145	61
Steve Yzerman	Det.	14	145	61
Joe Mullen	St.L., Cgy., Pit., Bos.	15	143	60
Stan Mikita	Chi.	18	155	59
Paul Coffey	Edm., Pit., L.A., Det., Phi., Car.	16	194	59
Guy Lafleur	Mtl., NYR, Que.	14	128	58
Bernie Geoffrion	Mtl., NYR	16	132	58
Cam Neely	Van., Bos.	9	93	57
Steve Larmer	Chi., NYR	13	140	56
Denis Potvin	NYI	14	185	56
Jaromir Jagr	Pit.	9	113	55
Rick MacLeish	Phi., Hfd., Pit., Det.	11	114	54
Doug Gilmour	St.L., Cgy., Tor., N.J.	14	152	54
Bill Barber	Phi.	11	129	53
Stephane Richer	Mtl., N.J.	11	128	52
Frank Mahovlich	Tor., Det., Mtl.	14	137	51
Brian Bellows	Min., Mtl., T.B., Ana., Wsh.	13	143	51
Steve Shutt	Mtl., L.A.	12	99	50
Henri Richard	Mtl.	18	180	49
Reggie Leach	Bos., Cal., Phi., Det.	8	94	47
Luc Robitaille	L.A., Pit., NYR	11	115	47
Rick Tocchet	Phi., Pit., Bos., Phx.	11	121	47
Ted Lindsay	Det., Chi.	16	133	47
Clark Gillies	NYI, Buf.	13	164	47
Joe Nieuwendyk	Cgy., Dal.	11	97	46
Dickie Moore	Mtl., Tor., St.L.	14	135	46
Rick Middleton	NYR, Bos.	12	114	45
Lanny McDonald	Tor., Col., Cgy.	13	117	44
Kevin Stevens	Pit.	6	86	43
Ken Linseman	Phi., Edm., Bos., Tor.	11	113	43
Mike Gartner	Wsh., Min., NYR, Tor., Phx.	15	122	43
Jeremy Roenick	Chi., Phx.	11	95	42
Bernie Nicholls	L.A., NYR, Edm., N.J., Chi., S.J.	13	118	42
Bobby Clarke	Phi.	13	136	42
Dale Hunter	Que., Wsh., Col.	18	186	42
Joe Sakic	Que., Col.	6	76	41
John Bucyk	Det., Bos.	14	124	41
Tim Kerr	Phi., NYR, Hfd.	10	81	40
Peter McNab	Buf., Bos., Van., N.J.	10	107	40
Ron Francis	Hfd., Pit., Car.	14	133	40
Bob Bourne	NYI, L.A.	13	139	40
John Tonelli	NYI, Cgy., L.A., Chi., Que.	13	172	40

Assists

(60 or more assists)

Player	Teams	Yrs.	GP	A
Wayne Gretzky	Edm., L.A., St.L., NYR	16	208	260
Mark Messier	Edm., NYR	17	236	186
Paul Coffey	Edm., Pit., L.A., Det., Phi., Car.	16	194	137
Jari Kurri	Edm., L.A., NYR, Ana., Col.	14	200	127
Ray Bourque	Bos.	19	180	125
Glenn Anderson	Edm., Tor., NYR, St.L.	15	225	121
Doug Gilmour	St.L., Cgy., Tor., N.J.	14	152	117
Larry Robinson	Mtl., L.A.	20	227	116
Bryan Trottier	NYI, Pit.	17	221	113
Larry Murphy	L.A., Wsh., Min., Pit., Tor., Det.	18	200	111
Denis Savard	Chi., Mtl., T.B.	16	169	109
Denis Potvin	NYI	14	185	108
Al MacInnis	Cgy., St.L.	15	142	102
Adam Oates	Det., St.L., Bos., Wsh.	11	126	100
Jean Beliveau	Mtl.	17	162	97
Bobby Smith	Min., Mtl.	13	184	96
Gordie Howe	Det., Hfd.	20	157	92
Chris Chelios	Mtl., Chi., Det.	15	173	92
Stan Mikita	Chi.	18	155	91
Brad Park	NYR, Bos., Det.	17	161	90
Sergei Fedorov	Det.	9	120	88
Steve Yzerman	Det.	14	145	87
Craig Janney	Bos., St.L., S.J., Wpg., Phx.	11	120	86
Mario Lemieux	Pit.	7	89	85
Brian Propp	Phi., Bos., Min., Hfd.	13	160	84
Ron Francis	Hfd., Pit., Car.	14	133	83
Henri Richard	Mtl.	18	180	80
Jacques Lemaire	Mtl.	11	145	78
Ken Linseman	Phi., Edm., Bos., Tor.	11	113	77
Bobby Clarke	Phi.	13	136	77
Guy Lafleur	Mtl., NYR, Que.	14	128	76
Phil Esposito	Chi., Bos., NYR	15	130	76
Dale Hunter	Que., Wsh., Col.	18	186	76
Mike Bossy	NYI	10	129	75
Steve Larmer	Chi., NYR	13	140	75
John Tonelli	NYI, Cgy., L.A., Chi., Que.	13	172	75
Peter Stastny	Que., N.J., St.L.	12	93	72
Bernie Nicholls	L.A., NYR, Edm., N.J., Chi., S.J.	13	118	72
Brian Bellows	Min., Mtl., T.B., Ana., Wsh.	13	143	71
Scott Stevens	Wsh., St.L., N.J.	16	155	71
Claude Lemieux	Mtl., N.J., Col.	14	198	71
Gilbert Perreault	Buf.	11	90	70
Geoff Courtnall	Bos., Edm., Wsh., Van., St.L.	15	156	70
Dale Hawerchuk	Wpg., Buf., St.L., Phi.	15	97	69
Alex Delvecchio	Det.	14	121	69
Bobby Hull	Chi., Wpg., Hfd.	14	119	67
Frank Mahovlich	Tor., Det., Mtl.	14	137	67
Bobby Orr	Bos., Chi.	8	74	66
Bernie Federko	St.L., Det.	11	91	66
Jean Ratelle	NYR, Bos.	15	123	66
Charlie Huddy	Edm., L.A., Buf., St.L.	14	183	66
Jaromir Jagr	Pit.	9	113	64
Dickie Moore	Mtl., Tor., St.L.	14	135	64
Doug Harvey	Mtl., NYR, Det., St.L.	15	137	64
Neal Broten	Min., Dal., N.J., L.A.	13	135	63
Yvan Cournoyer	Mtl.	12	147	63
John Bucyk	Det., Bos.	14	124	62
Brian Leetch	NYR	7	82	61
Doug Wilson	Chi., S.J.	12	95	61
Bernie Geoffrion	Mtl., NYR	16	132	60
Esa Tikkanen	Edm., NYR, St.L., Van., Wsh.	13	186	60

Points

(105 or more points)

Player	Teams	Yrs.	GP	G	A	Pts.
Wayne Gretzky	Edm., L.A., St.L., NYR	16	208	122	260	382
Mark Messier	Edm., NYR	17	236	109	186	295
Jari Kurri	Edm., L.A., NYR, Ana., Col.	14	200	106	127	233
Glenn Anderson	Edm., Tor., NYR, St.L.	15	225	93	121	214
Paul Coffey	Edm., Pit., L.A., Det., Phi., Car.	16	194	59	137	196
Bryan Trottier	NYI, Pit.	17	221	71	113	184
Jean Beliveau	Mtl.	17	162	79	97	176
Denis Savard	Chi., Mtl., T.B.	16	169	66	109	175
Doug Gilmour	St.L., Cgy., Tor., N.J.	14	152	54	117	171
Denis Potvin	NYI	14	185	56	108	164
Ray Bourque	Bos.	19	180	36	125	161
Mike Bossy	NYI	10	129	85	75	160
Gordie Howe	Det., Hfd.	20	157	68	92	160
Bobby Smith	Min., Mtl.	13	184	64	96	160
Mario Lemieux	Pit.	7	89	70	85	155
Stan Mikita	Chi.	18	155	59	91	150
Steve Yzerman	Det.	14	145	61	87	148
Brian Propp	Phi., Bos., Min., Hfd.	13	160	64	84	148
Claude Lemieux	Mtl., N.J., Col.	14	198	76	71	147
Larry Murphy	L.A., Wsh., Min., Pit., Tor., Det.	18	200	35	111	146
Larry Robinson	Mtl., L.A.	20	227	28	116	144
Jacques Lemaire	Mtl.	11	145	61	78	139
Adam Oates	Det., St.L., Bos., Wsh.	11	126	38	100	138
Al MacInnis	Cgy., St.L.	15	142	36	102	138
Phil Esposito	Chi., Bos., NYR	15	130	61	76	137
Brett Hull	Cgy., St.L., Dal.	14	130	77	58	135
Guy Lafleur	Mtl., NYR, Que.	14	128	58	76	134
Esa Tikkanen	Edm., NYR, St.L., Van.,Wsh.	13	186	72	60	132
Steve Larmer	Chi., NYR	13	140	56	75	131
Bobby Hull	Chi., Wpg., Hfd.	14	119	62	67	129
Henri Richard	Mtl.	18	180	49	80	129
Yvan Cournoyer	Mtl.	12	147	64	63	127
Sergei Fedorov	Det.	9	120	38	88	126
Maurice Richard	Mtl.	15	133	82	44	126
Brad Park	NYR, Bos., Det.	17	161	35	90	125
Ron Francis	Hfd., Pit., Car.	14	133	40	83	123
Brian Bellows	Min., Mtl., T.B., Ana., Wsh.	13	143	51	71	122
Ken Linseman	Phi., Edm., Bos., Tor.	11	113	43	77	120
Chris Chelios	Mtl., Chi.,Det.	15	173	28	92	120
Jaromir Jagr	Pit.	9	113	55	64	119
Bobby Clarke	Phi.	13	136	42	77	119
Bernie Geoffrion	Mtl., NYR	16	132	58	60	118
Frank Mahovlich	Tor., Det., Mtl.	14	137	51	67	118
Dino Ciccarelli	Min., Wsh., Det.	14	141	73	45	118
John Tonelli	NYI, Cgy., L.A., Chi., Que.	13	172	40	75	115
Dale Hunter	Que., Wsh., Col.	18	186	42	76	118
Bernie Nicholls	L.A., NYR, Edm., N.J., Chi., S.J.	13	118	42	72	114
Craig Janney	Bos., St.L., S.J., Wpg., Phx.	11	120	24	86	110
Dickie Moore	Mtl., Tor., St.L.	14	135	46	64	110
Geoff Courtnall	Bos., Edm., Wsh., Van., St.L.	15	156	39	70	109
Bill Barber	Phi.	11	129	53	55	108
Rick MacLeish	Phi., Hfd., Pit., Det.	11	114	54	53	107
Luc Robitaille	L.A., Pit., NYR	11	115	47	59	106
Joe Mullen	St.L., Cgy., Pit., Bos.	15	143	60	46	106
Peter Stastny	Que., N.J., St.L.	12	93	33	72	105

CHAPTER 8

Leading Playoff Scorers

1918 – 1999

Season	Player and Club	Games Played	Goals	Assists	Points
1998-99	Peter Forsberg, Colorado	19	8	16	24
1997-98	Steve Yzerman, Detroit	22	6	18	24
1996-97	Eric Lindros, Philadelphia	19	12	14	26
1995-96	Joe Sakic, Colorado	22	18	16	34
1994-95	Sergei Fedorov, Detroit	17	7	17	24
1993-94	Brian Leetch, NY Rangers	23	11	23	34
1992-93	Wayne Gretzky, Los Angeles	24	15	25	40
1991-92	Mario Lemieux, Pittsburgh	15	16	18	34
1990-91	Mario Lemieux, Pittsburgh	23	16	28	44
1989-90	Craig Simpson, Edmonton	22	16	15	31
	Mark Messier, Edmonton	22	9	22	31
1988-89	Al MacInnis, Calgary	22	7	24	31
1987-88	Wayne Gretzky, Edmonton	19	12	31	43
1986-87	Wayne Gretzky, Edmonton	21	5	29	34
1985-86	Doug Gilmour, St. Louis	19	9	12	21
	Bernie Federko, St. Louis	19	7	14	21
1984-85	Wayne Gretzky, Edmonton	18	17	30	47
1983-84	Wayne Gretzky, Edmonton	19	13	22	35
1982-83	Wayne Gretzky, Edmonton	16	12	26	38
1981-82	Bryan Trottier, NY Islanders	19	6	23	29
1980-81	Mike Bossy, NY Islanders	18	17	18	35
1979-80	Bryan Trottier, NY Islanders	21	12	17	29
1978-79	Jacques Lemaire, Montreal	16	11	12	23
	Guy Lafleur, Montreal	16	10	13	23
1977-78	Guy Lafleur, Montreal	15	10	11	21
	Larry Robinson, Montreal	15	4	17	21
1976-77	Guy Lafleur, Montreal	14	9	17	26
1975-76	Reggie Leach, Philadelphia	16	19	5	24
1974-75	Rick MacLeish, Philadelphia	17	11	9	20
1973-74	Rick MacLeish, Philadelphia	17	13	9	22
1972-73	Yvan Cournoyer, Montreal	17	15	10	25
1971-72	Phil Esposito, Boston	15	9	15	24
	Bobby Orr, Boston	15	5	19	24
1970-71	Frank Mahovlich, Montreal	20	14	13	27
1969-70	Phil Esposito, Boston	14	13	14	27
1968-69	Phil Esposito, Boston	10	8	10	18
1967-68	Bill Goldsworthy, Minnesota	14	8	7	15
1966-67	Jim Pappin, Toronto	12	7	8	15
1965-66	Norm Ullman, Detroit	12	6	9	15
1964-65	Bobby Hull, Chicago	14	10	7	17
1963-64	Gordie Howe, Detroit	14	9	10	19
1962-63	Gordie Howe, Detroit	11	7	9	16
	Norm Ullman, Detroit	11	4	12	16
1961-62	Stan Mikita, Chicago	12	6	15	21
1960-61	Gordie Howe, Detroit	11	4	11	15
	Pierre Pilote, Chicago	12	3	12	15
1959-60	Henri Richard, Montreal	8	3	9	12
	Bernie Geoffrion, Montreal	8	2	10	12
1958-59	Dickie Moore, Montreal	11	5	12	17
1957-58	Fleming Mackell, Boston	12	5	14	19
1956-57	Bernie Geoffrion, Montreal	11	11	7	18
1955-56	Jean Beliveau, Montreal	10	12	7	19
1954-55	Gordie Howe, Detroit	11	9	11	20
1953-54	Dickie Moore, Montreal	11	5	8	13
1952-53	Ed Sanford, Boston	11	8	3	11
1951-52	Ted Lindsay, Detroit	8	5	2	7
	Floyd Curry, Montreal	11	4	3	7
	Gordie Howe, Detroit	8	2	5	7
	Metro Prystai, Detroit	8	2	5	7
1950-51	Maurice Richard, Montreal	11	9	4	13
	Max Bentley, Toronto	11	2	11	13
1949-50	Pentti Lund, NY Rangers	12	6	5	11
1948-49	Gordie Howe, Detroit	11	8	3	11
1947-48	Ted Kennedy, Toronto	9	8	6	14
1946-47	Maurice Richard, Montreal	10	6	5	11
1945-46	Elmer Lach, Montreal	9	5	12	17
1944-45	Joe Carveth, Detroit	14	5	6	11
1943-44	Toe Blake, Montreal	9	7	11	18
1942-43	Carl Liscombe, Detroit	10	6	8	14
1941-42	Don Grosso, Detroit	12	8	6	14
1940-41	Milt Schmidt, Boston	11	5	6	11
1939-40	Phil Watson, NY Rangers	12	3	6	9
	Neil Colville, NY Rangers	12	2	7	9
1938-39	Bill Cowley, Boston	12	3	11	14
1937-38	Johnny Gottselig, Chicago	10	5	3	8
1936-37	Marty Barry, Detroit	10	4	7	11
1935-36	Frank Boll, Toronto	9	7	3	10
1934-35	Baldy Northcott, Mtl. Maroons	7	4	1	5
	Harvey Jackson, Toronto	7	3	2	5
	Cy Wentworth, Mtl. Maroons	7	3	2	5
1933-34	Larry Aurie, Detroit	9	3	7	10
1932-33	Cecil Dillon, NY Rangers	8	8	2	10
1931-32	Frank Boucher, NY Rangers	7	3	6	9
1930-31	Cooney Weiland, Boston	5	6	3	9
1929-30	Marty Barry, Boston	6	3	3	6
	Cooney Weiland, Boston	6	1	5	6
1928-29	Andy Blair, Toronto	4	3	0	3
	Butch Keeling, NY Rangers	6	3	0	3
	Ace Bailey, Toronto	4	1	2	3
1927-28	Frank Boucher, NY Rangers	9	7	1	8
1926-27	Harry Oliver, Boston	8	4	2	6
	Percy Galbraith, Boston	8	3	3	6
1925-26	Nels Stewart, Mtl. Maroons	8	6	3	9
1924-25	Howie Morenz, Montreal	6	7	1	8
1923-24	Howie Morenz, Montreal	6	7	3	10
1922-23	Punch Broadbent, Ottawa	8	6	1	7
1921-22	Babe Dye, Toronto	7	11	1	12
1920-21	Cy Denneny, Ottawa	7	4	2	6
1919-20	Frank Nighbor, Ottawa	5	6	1	7
	Jack Darragh, Ottawa	5	5	2	7
1918-19	Newsy Lalonde, Montreal	10	17	1	18
1917-18	Alf Skinner, Toronto	7	8	3	11

CHAPTER 9

Year-By-Year Highlights, Scores, and Rosters

1999 – 1893

1999

It had been five years since the NHL's best regular-season team had also been its playoff champion, but this year the Dallas Stars won the Stanley Cup after winning the Presidents' Trophy for the second year in a row. The Stars won the first Cup title in franchise history by beating the Buffalo Sabres in a hard-fought series that marked the first time since 1994 that the Stanley Cup final had not ended in a sweep. Dallas took the series in six games, with Brett Hull scoring the winning goal at 14:51 of the third overtime session. The second-longest game in the history of the Stanley Cup finals ended at 1:30 a.m. local time in Buffalo.

The Stars were led by Joe Nieuwendyk, who paced all playoff performers with 11 goals and won the Conn Smythe Trophy. Mike Modano's 18 assists were the best of the postseason, while Ed Belfour provided stellar goaltending, outperforming Buffalo's Dominik Hasek in the Stanley Cup finals after besting Colorado's Patrick Roy in the Western Conference final. The Stars had opened the playoffs with a four-game sweep of the Edmonton Oilers before downing the St. Louis Blues in a tight six-game series that saw four games decided in overtime.

CONN SMYTHE TROPHY
Joe Nieuwendyk - Center - Dallas Stars

CONFERENCE QUARTERFINALS

Apr.	22	Pittsburgh	1	at	New Jersey	3
Apr.	24	Pittsburgh	4	at	New Jersey	1
Apr.	25	New Jersey	2	at	Pittsburgh	4
Apr.	27	New Jersey	4	at	Pittsburgh	2
Apr.	30	Pittsburgh	3	at	New Jersey	4
May	2	New Jersey	2	at	Pittsburgh	3 OT
May	4	Pittsburgh	4	at	New Jersey	2

Pittsburgh won best-of-seven series 4-3

Apr.	21	Buffalo	2	at	Ottawa	1
Apr.	23	Buffalo	3	at	Ottawa	2 2OT
Apr.	25	Ottawa	0	at	Buffalo	3
Apr.	27	Ottawa	3	at	Buffalo	4

Buffalo won best-of-seven series 4-0

Apr.	22	Boston	2	at	Carolina	0
Apr.	24	Boston	2	at	Carolina	3 OT
Apr.	26	Carolina	3	at	Boston	2
Apr.	28	Carolina	1	at	Boston	4
Apr.	30	Boston	4	at	Carolina	3 2OT
May	2	Carolina	0	at	Boston	2

Boston won best-of-seven series 4-2

Apr.	22	Philadelphia	3	at	Toronto	1
Apr.	24	Philadelphia	1	at	Toronto	2
Apr.	26	Toronto	2	at	Philadelphia	1
Apr.	28	Toronto	2	at	Philadelphia	5
Apr.	30	Philadelphia	1	at	Toronto	2 OT
May	2	Toronto	1	at	Philadelphia	0

Toronto won best-of-seven series 4-2

Apr.	21	Edmonton	1	at	Dallas	2
Apr.	23	Edmonton	2	at	Dallas	3
Apr.	25	Dallas	3	at	Edmonton	2
Apr.	27	Dallas	3	at	Edmonton	2 3OT

Dallas won best-of-seven series 4-0

Apr.	24	Colorado	3	at	San Jose	1
Apr.	26	Colorado	2	at	San Jose	1 OT
Apr.	28	San Jose	4	at	Colorado	2
Apr.	30	San Jose	7	at	Colorado	3
May	1	San Jose	2	at	Colorado	6
May	3	Colorado	3	at	San Jose	2 OT

Colorado won best-of-seven series 4-2

Apr.	21	Anaheim	3	at	Detroit	5
Apr.	23	Anaheim	1	at	Detroit	5
Apr.	25	Detroit	4	at	Anaheim	2
Apr.	27	Detroit	3	at	Anaheim	0

Detroit won best-of-seven series 4-0

Apr.	22	St. Louis	3	at	Phoenix	1
Apr.	24	St. Louis	3	at	Phoenix	4 OT
Apr.	25	Phoenix	5	at	St. Louis	4
Apr.	27	Phoenix	2	at	St. Louis	1
Apr.	30	St. Louis	2	at	Phoenix	1 OT
May	2	Phoenix	3	at	St. Louis	5
May	4	St. Louis	1	at	Phoenix	0 OT

St. Louis won best-of-seven series 4-3

CONFERENCE SEMIFINALS

May	7	Pittsburgh	2	at	Toronto	0
May	9	Pittsburgh	2	at	Toronto	4
May	11	Toronto	3	at	Pittsburgh	4
May	13	Toronto	3	at	Pittsburgh	2 OT
May	15	Pittsburgh	1	at	Toronto	4
May	17	Toronto	4	at	Pittsburgh	3 OT

Toronto won best-of-seven series 4-2

May	6	Buffalo	2	at	Boston	4
May	9	Buffalo	3	at	Boston	1
May	12	Boston	2	at	Buffalo	3
May	14	Boston	0	at	Buffalo	3
May	16	Buffalo	3	at	Boston	5
May	18	Boston	2	at	Buffalo	3

Buffalo won best-of-seven series 4-2

May	6	St. Louis	0	at	Dallas	3
May	8	St. Louis	4	at	Dallas	5 OT
May	10	Dallas	2	at	St. Louis	3 OT
May	12	Dallas	2	at	St. Louis	3 OT
May	15	St. Louis	1	at	Dallas	3
May	17	Dallas	2	at	St. Louis	1 OT

Dallas won best-of-seven series 4-2

May	7	Detroit	3	at	Colorado	2 OT
May	9	Detroit	4	at	Colorado	0
May	11	Colorado	5	at	Detroit	3
May	13	Colorado	6	at	Detroit	2
May	16	Detroit	0	at	Colorado	3
May	18	Colorado	5	at	Detroit	2

Colorado won best-of-seven series 4-2

CONFERENCE FINALS

May	23	Buffalo	5	at	Toronto	4
May	25	Buffalo	3	at	Toronto	6
May	27	Toronto	2	at	Buffalo	1
May	29	Toronto	2	at	Buffalo	5
May	31	Buffalo	4	at	Toronto	2

Buffalo won best-of-seven series 4-1

May	22	Colorado	2	at	Dallas	1
May	24	Colorado	2	at	Dallas	4
May	26	Dallas	3	at	Colorado	0
May	28	Dallas	2	at	Colorado	3 OT
May	30	Colorado	7	at	Dallas	5
June	1	Dallas	4	at	Colorado	1
June	4	Colorado	1	at	Dallas	4

Dallas won best-of-seven series 4-3

FINALS

June	8	Buffalo	3	at	Dallas	2 OT
June	10	Buffalo	2	at	Dallas	4
June	12	Dallas	2	at	Buffalo	1
June	15	Dallas	1	at	Buffalo	2
June	17	Buffalo	0	at	Dallas	2
June	19	Dallas	2	at	Buffalo	1 3OT

Dallas won best-of-seven series 4-2

1998-99 – Dallas Stars – Derian Hatcher (Captain), Ed Belfour, Guy Carbonneau, Shawn Chambers, Benoit Hogue, Tony Hrkac, Brett Hull, Mike Keane, Jamie Langenbrunner, Jere Lehtinen, Craig Ludwig, Grant Marshall, Richard Matvichuk, Mike Modano, Joe Nieuwendyk, Derek Plante, Dave Reid, Jon Sim, Brian Skrudland, Blake Sloan, Darryl Sydor, Roman Turek, Pat Verbeek, Sergei Zubov, Thomas Hicks (Chairman of the Board and Owner), Jim Lites (President), Bob Gainey (Vice President, Hockey Operations and General Manager), Doug Armstrong (Assistant General Manager), Craig Button (Director of Player Personnel), Ken Hitchcock (Head Coach), Doug Jarvis (Assistant Coach), Rick Wilson (Assistant Coach), Rick McLaughlin (Vice President and Chief Financial Officer), Jeff Cogen (Vice President, Marketing and Promotion), Bill Strong (Vice President, Marketing and Broadcasting), Tim Bernhardt (Director of Amateur Scouting), Doug Overton (Director of Pro Scouting), Bob Gernander (Chief Scout), Stu MacGregor (Western Scout), Dave Suprenant (Medical Trainer), Dave Smith (Equipment Manager), Rich Matthews (Equipment Manager), J.J. McQueen (Strength and Conditioning Coach), Rick St. Croix (Goaltending Consultant), Dan Stuchal (Director of Team Services), Larry Kelly (Director of Public Relations).

1998

With a four-game sweep of the Washington Capitals, the Detroit Red Wings became the first team since the Pittsburgh Penguins to repeat as Stanley Cup champions (1991 and 1992). The Wings were led by Steve Yzerman, who became just the fifth player as captain of his team to receive the Conn Smythe Trophy as the most valuable player in the playoffs. Scotty Bowman equalled Toe Blake's NHL record of eight Stanley Cup coaching victories

Despite the four-game sweep in the finals, Detroit did not have a smooth road to the Cup, as they were forced to play six games in each of the three series leading up to the Stanley Cup. Overall, the team had equal success at home and on the road, posting identical 8–3 records. A total of ten Red Wing players contributed the 16 game-winning goals scored en route to the Stanley Cup.

The on-ice celebration produced one of the most emotional moments in NHL history, as injured teammate Vladimir Konstantinov participated in the post-game festivities from his wheelchair. Konstantinov had been a key part of Detroit's Stanley Cup championship in 1997, but nearly lost his life in a car accident one week after the victory.

CONN SMYTHE TROPHY
Steve Yzerman - Center - Detroit Red Wings

CONFERENCE QUARTERFINALS

Apr. 22	Ottawa	2	at	New Jersey	1 OT
Apr. 24	Ottawa	1	at	New Jersey	3
Apr. 26	New Jersey	1	at	Ottawa	2 OT
Apr. 28	New Jersey	3	at	Ottawa	4
Apr. 30	Ottawa	1	at	New Jersey	3
May 2	New Jersey	1	at	Ottawa	4

Ottawa won best-of-seven series 4-2

Apr. 23	Montreal	3	at	Pittsburgh	2 OT
Apr. 25	Montreal	1	at	Pittsburgh	4
Apr. 27	Pittsburgh	1	at	Montreal	3
Apr. 29	Pittsburgh	6	at	Montreal	3
May 1	Montreal	5	at	Pittsburgh	2
May 3	Pittsburgh	0	at	Montreal	3

Montreal won best-of-seven series 4-2

Apr. 22	Buffalo	3	at	Philadelphia	2
Apr. 24	Buffalo	2	at	Philadelphia	3
Apr. 27	Philadelphia	1	at	Buffalo	6
Apr. 29	Philadelphia	1	at	Buffalo	4
May 1	Buffalo	3	at	Philadelphia	2 OT

Buffalo won best-of-seven series 4-1

Apr. 22	Boston	1	at	Washington	3
Apr. 24	Boston	4	at	Washington	3 2OT
Apr. 26	Washington	3	at	Boston	2 2OT
Apr. 28	Washington	3	at	Boston	0
May 1	Boston	4	at	Washington	0
May 3	Washington	3	at	Boston	2 OT

Washington won best-of-seven series 4-2

Apr. 22	San Jose	1	at	Dallas	4
Apr. 24	San Jose	2	at	Dallas	5
Apr. 26	Dallas	1	at	San Jose	4
Apr. 28	Dallas	0	at	San Jose	1 OT
Apr. 30	San Jose	2	at	Dallas	3
May 2	Dallas	3	at	San Jose	2 OT

Dallas won best-of-seven series 4-2

Apr. 22	Edmonton	3	at	Colorado	2
Apr. 24	Edmonton	2	at	Colorado	5
Apr. 26	Colorado	5	at	Edmonton	4 OT
Apr. 28	Colorado	3	at	Edmonton	1
Apr. 30	Edmonton	3	at	Colorado	1
May 2	Colorado	0	at	Edmonton	2
May 4	Edmonton	4	at	Colorado	0

Edmonton won best-of-seven series 4-3

Apr. 22	Phoenix	3	at	Detroit	6
Apr. 24	Phoenix	7	at	Detroit	4
Apr. 26	Detroit	2	at	Phoenix	3
Apr. 28	Detroit	4	at	Phoenix	2
Apr. 30	Phoenix	1	at	Detroit	3
May 3	Detroit	5	at	Phoenix	2

Detroit won best-of-seven series 4-2

Apr. 22	Los Angeles	1	at	St. Louis	4
Apr. 24	Los Angeles	2	at	St. Louis	5
Apr. 26	St. Louis	1	at	Los Angeles	4
Apr. 30	St. Louis	2	at	Los Angeles	3

St. Louis won best-of-seven series 4-0

CONFERENCE SEMIFINALS

May 7	Ottawa	2	at	Washington	4
May 9	Ottawa	1	at	Washington	6
May 11	Washington	3	at	Ottawa	4
May 13	Washington	2	at	Ottawa	0
May 15	Ottawa	0	at	Washington	3

Washington won best-of-seven series 4-1

May 8	Montreal	2	at	Buffalo	3 OT
May 10	Montreal	3	at	Buffalo	6
May 12	Buffalo	5	at	Montreal	4 2OT
May 14	Buffalo	3	at	Montreal	1

Buffalo won best-of-seven series 4-0

May 7	Edmonton	1	at	Dallas	3
May 9	Edmonton	2	at	Dallas	0
May 11	Dallas	1	at	Edmonton	0 OT
May 13	Dallas	3	at	Edmonton	1
May 16	Edmonton	1	at	Dallas	2

Dallas won best-of-seven series 4-1

May 8	St. Louis	4	at	Detroit	2
May 10	St. Louis	1	at	Detroit	6
May 12	Detroit	3	at	St. Louis	2 2OT
May 14	Detroit	5	at	St. Louis	2
May 17	St. Louis	3	at	Detroit	1
May 19	Detroit	6	at	St. Louis	1

Detroit won best-of-seven series 4-2

CONFERENCE FINALS

May 23	Buffalo	2	at	Washington	0
May 25	Buffalo	2	at	Washington	3 OT
May 28	Washington	4	at	Buffalo	3 OT
May 30	Washington	2	at	Buffalo	0
June 2	Buffalo	2	at	Washington	1
June 4	Washington	3	at	Buffalo	2 OT

Washington won best-of-seven series 4-2

May 24	Detroit	2	at	Dallas	0
May 26	Detroit	1	at	Dallas	3
May 29	Dallas	3	at	Detroit	5
May 31	Dallas	2	at	Detroit	3
June 3	Detroit	2	at	Dallas	3 OT
June 5	Dallas	0	at	Detroit	2

Detroit won best-of-seven series 4-2

FINALS

June 9	Washington	1	at	Detroit	2
June 11	Washington	4	at	Detroit	5 OT
June 13	Detroit	2	at	Washington	1
June 16	Detroit	4	at	Washington	1

Detroit won best-of-seven series 4-0

1997-98 – Detroit Red Wings – Steve Yzerman (Captain), Doug Brown, Mathieu Dandenault, Kris Draper, Anders Eriksson, Sergei Fedorov, Viacheslav Fetisov, Brent Gilchrist, Kevin Hodson, Tomas Holmstrom, Michael Knuble, Joe Kocur, Vladimir Konstantinov, Vyacheslav Kozlov, Martin Lapointe, Igor Larionov, Nicklas Lidstrom, Jamie Macoun, Kirk Maltby, Darren McCarty, Dmitri Mironov, Larry Murphy, Chris Osgood, Bob Rouse, Brendan Shanahan, Aaron Ward, Mike Ilitch, (Owner/Chairman), Marian Ilitch (Owner), Atanas Ilitch (Vice President), Christopher Ilitch (Vice President), Denise Ilitch, Ronald Ilitch, Michael Ilitch Jr., Lisa Ilitch Murray, Carole Ilitch Trepeck, Jim Devellano (Senior Vice President), Scotty Bowman (Head Coach), Ken Holland (General Manager), Don Waddell (Assistant General Manager), Barry Smith (Associate Coach), Dave Lewis (Associate Coach), Jim Bedard (Goaltending Consultant), Jim Nill (Director of Player Development), Dan Belisle (Pro Scout), Mark Howe (Pro Scout), Hakan Andersson (Director of European Scouting), Mark Leach (USA Scout), Moe McDonnell (Eastern Scout), Bruce Haralson (Western Scout), John Wharton (Athletic Trainer), Paul Boyer (Equipment Manager), Tim Abbott (Assistant Equipment Manager), Bob Huddleston (Masseur), Sergei Mnatsakanov (Masseur), Wally Crossman (Dressing Room Assistant).

1997

The Detroit Red Wings won their first Stanley Cup title since 1955 with a four-game final-series sweep of the Philadelphia Flyers. The series opened at the CoreStates Center in Philadelphia in front of 20,291 fans, the largest crowd ever to witness a hockey game in the state of Pennsylvania. Goaltender Mike Vernon made 26 saves in a 4–2 Detroit win as unheralded Red Wings Kirk Maltby and Joe Kocur gave Detroit a 2-1 lead after the first period. Sergei Fedorov tallied the game-winner just after the midway point of the second. Maltby scored again in game two, breaking a 2–2 tie in the second period with what would prove to be the game-winning goal. Rod Brind'Amour scored both of the Flyers' goals in the game, connecting for two power-play markers 1:09 apart late in the first period.

The Red Wings returned home to a vocal and supportive home crowd for game three at Joe Louis Arena and responded with a 6–1 win to take a commanding 3–0 lead in the series. The Flyers opened the scoring on a first-period goal by John LeClair, but Detroit replied with three unanswered goals before the period ended. The win snapped Detroit's eight-game and 33-year home-ice losing streak in the Stanley Cup finals. Sergei Fedorov and Martin Lapointe each tallied twice to pace the Red Wings.

The Red Wings completed the series sweep by defeating the Flyers 2-1 in game four. Red Wings defenseman Nicklas Lidstrom's goal late in the first period gave Detroit a lead it would not relinquish and Darren McCarty scored the Stanley Cup-winning goal on a spectacular individual effort at 13:02 of the second period. Goaltender Mike Vernon was named the Conn Smythe Trophy winner as the MVP of the playoffs, finishing the postseason with a 16–4 record and 1.76 goals-against average. He allowed two goals or fewer in 17 of his 20 playoff games.

CONN SMYTHE TROPHY
Mike Vernon - Goaltender - Detroit Red Wings

CONFERENCE QUARTERFINALS

Apr. 17	Montreal	2	at	New Jersey	5
Apr. 19	Montreal	1	at	New Jersey	4
Apr. 22	New Jersey	6	at	Montreal	4
Apr. 24	New Jersey	3	at	Montreal	4 3OT
Apr. 26	Montreal	0	at	New Jersey	4

New Jersey won best-of-seven series 4-1

Apr. 17	Ottawa	1	at	Buffalo	3
Apr. 19	Ottawa	3	at	Buffalo	1
Apr. 21	Buffalo	3	at	Ottawa	2
Apr. 23	Buffalo	0	at	Ottawa	1 OT
Apr. 25	Ottawa	4	at	Buffalo	1
Apr. 27	Buffalo	3	at	Ottawa	0
Apr. 29	Ottawa	2	at	Buffalo	3 OT

Buffalo won best-of-seven series 4-3

Apr. 17	Pittsburgh	1	at	Philadelphia	5
Apr. 19	Pittsburgh	2	at	Philadelphia	3
Apr. 21	Philadelphia	5	at	Pittsburgh	3
Apr. 23	Philadelphia	1	at	Pittsburgh	4
Apr. 26	Pittsburgh	3	at	Philadelphia	6

Philadelphia won best-of-seven series 4-1

Apr. 17	NY Rangers	0	at	Florida	3
Apr. 20	NY Rangers	3	at	Florida	0
Apr. 22	Florida	3	at	NY Rangers	4 OT
Apr. 23	Florida	2	at	NY Rangers	3
Apr. 25	NY Rangers	3	at	Florida	2 OT

NY Rangers won best-of-seven series 4-1

Apr. 16	Chicago	0	at	Colorado	6
Apr. 18	Chicago	1	at	Colorado	3
Apr. 20	Colorado	3	at	Chicago	4 2OT
Apr. 22	Colorado	3	at	Chicago	6
Apr. 24	Chicago	0	at	Colorado	7
Apr. 26	Colorado	6	at	Chicago	3

Colorado won best-of-seven series 4-2

Apr. 16	Edmonton	3	at	Dallas	5
Apr. 18	Edmonton	4	at	Dallas	0
Apr. 20	Dallas	3	at	Edmonton	4 OT
Apr. 22	Dallas	4	at	Edmonton	3
Apr. 25	Edmonton	1	at	Dallas	0 2OT
Apr. 27	Dallas	3	at	Edmonton	2
Apr. 29	Edmonton	4	at	Dallas	3 OT

Edmonton won best-of-seven series 4-3

Apr. 16	St. Louis	2	at	Detroit	0
Apr. 18	St. Louis	1	at	Detroit	2
Apr. 20	Detroit	3	at	St. Louis	2
Apr. 22	Detroit	0	at	St. Louis	4
Apr. 25	St. Louis	2	at	Detroit	5
Apr. 27	Detroit	3	at	St. Louis	1

Detroit won best-of-seven series 4-2

Apr. 16	Phoenix	2	at	Anaheim	4
Apr. 18	Phoenix	2	at	Anaheim	4
Apr. 20	Anaheim	1	at	Phoenix	4
Apr. 22	Anaheim	0	at	Phoenix	2
Apr. 24	Phoenix	5	at	Anaheim	2
Apr. 27	Anaheim	3	at	Phoenix	2 OT
Apr. 29	Phoenix	0	at	Anaheim	3

Anaheim won best-of-seven series 4-3

CONFERENCE SEMIFINALS

May 2	NY Rangers	0	at	New Jersey	2
May 4	NY Rangers	2	at	New Jersey	0
May 6	New Jersey	2	at	NY Rangers	3
May 8	New Jersey	0	at	NY Rangers	3
May 11	NY Rangers	2	at	New Jersey	1 OT

NY Rangers won best-of-seven series 4-1

May 3	Philadelphia	5	at	Buffalo	3
May 5	Philadelphia	2	at	Buffalo	1
May 7	Buffalo	1	at	Philadelphia	4
May 9	Buffalo	5	at	Philadelphia	4 OT
May 11	Philadelphia	6	at	Buffalo	3

Philadelphia won best-of-seven series 4-1

May 2	Edmonton	1	at	Colorado	5
May 4	Edmonton	1	at	Colorado	4
May 7	Colorado	3	at	Edmonton	4
May 9	Colorado	3	at	Edmonton	2 OT
May 11	Edmonton	3	at	Colorado	4

Colorado won best-of-seven series 4-1

May 2	Anaheim	1	at	Detroit	2 OT
May 4	Anaheim	2	at	Detroit	3 3OT
May 6	Detroit	5	at	Anaheim	3
May 8	Detroit	3	at	Anaheim	2 2OT

Detroit won best-of-seven series 4-0

CONFERENCE FINALS

May 16	NY Rangers	1	at	Philadelphia	3
May 18	NY Rangers	5	at	Philadelphia	4
May 20	Philadelphia	6	at	NY Rangers	3
May 23	Philadelphia	3	at	NY Rangers	2
May 25	NY Rangers	2	at	Philadelphia	4

Philadelphia won best-of-seven series 4-1

May 15	Detroit	1	at	Colorado	2
May 17	Detroit	4	at	Colorado	2
May 19	Colorado	1	at	Detroit	2
May 22	Colorado	0	at	Detroit	6
May 24	Detroit	0	at	Colorado	6
May 26	Colorado	1	at	Detroit	3

Detroit won best-of-seven series 4-2

FINALS

May 31	Detroit	4	at	Philadelphia	2
June 3	Detroit	4	at	Philadelphia	2
June 5	Philadelphia	1	at	Detroit	6
June 7	Philadelphia	1	at	Detroit	2

Detroit won best-of-seven series 4-0

1996-97 – Detroit Red Wings – Steve Yzerman (Captain), Doug Brown, Mathieu Dandenault, Kris Draper, Sergei Fedorov, Viacheslav Fetisov, Kevin Hodson, Tomas Holmstrom, Joe Kocur, Vladimir Konstantinov, Vyacheslav Kozlov, Martin Lapointe, Igor Larionov, Nicklas Lidstrom, Kirk Maltby, Darren McCarty, Larry Murphy, Chris Osgood, Jamie Pushor, Bob Rouse, Tomas Sandstrom, Brendan Shanahan, Tim Taylor, Mike Vernon, Aaron Ward, Mike Ilitch (Owner/Chairman), Marian Ilitch (Owner), Atanas Ilitch (Vice President), Christopher Ilitch (Vice President), Denise Ilitch Lites, Ronald Ilitch, Michael Ilitch, Jr., Lisa Ilitch Murray, Carole Ilitch Trepeck, Jim Devellano (Senior Vice President), Scotty Bowman (Head Coach/Director of Player Personnel), Ken Holland (Assistant General Manager), Barry Smith (Associate Coach), Dave Lewis (Associate Coach), Mike Krushelnyski (Assistant Coach), Jim Nill (Director of Player Development), Dan Belisle (Pro Scout), Mark Howe (Pro Scout), Hakan Andersson (Director of European Scouting), John Wharton (Athletic Trainer), Paul Boyer (Equipment Manager), Tim Abbott (Assistant Equipment Manager), Sergei Mnatsakanov (Masseur).

1996

The Colorado Avalanche became Stanley Cup champions in their first season in the Mile High City after moving west from Quebec, sweeping the surprising Florida Panthers in the final series. Colorado was led by the scoring flash of Joe Sakic, Valeri Kamensky and Peter Forsberg, backed up by a solid defense and the stellar goaltending of Patrick Roy, but it was Uwe Krupp who scored the Cup-winning goal at 4:31 of the third overtime period in the longest 1-0 game in the history of the Stanley Cup finals.

Goaltending had been the story for Florida, as the Panthers, who had made the playoffs in just their third season, relied on the spectacular work of John Vanbiesbrouck to knock off the Boston Bruins, Philadelphia Flyers and Pittsburgh Penguins. Colorado advanced with victories over Vancouver and Chicago before defeating Detroit in the finals of the Western Conference.

Despite the final series sweep, the games were close (with the exception of Colorado's 8-1 win in game two), but the Avalanche clearly had the better of the play. Vanbiesbrouck's heroics gave the Panthers a chance, but ultimately Roy and Sakic, who established himself as a major NHL star, proved to be too much. Sakic led all playoff scorers with 18 goals and 34 points to earn the Conn Smythe Trophy as playof MVP.

CONN SMYTHE TROPHY
Joe Sakic - Center - Colorado Avalanche

CONFERENCE QUARTERFINALS

Apr. 16	Tampa Bay	3	at	Philadelphia	7
Apr. 18	Tampa Bay	2	at	Philadelphia	1 OT
Apr. 21	Philadelphia	4	at	Tampa Bay	5 OT
Apr. 23	Philadelphia	4	at	Tampa Bay	1
Apr. 25	Tampa Bay	1	at	Philadelphia	4
Apr. 27	Philadelphia	6	at	Tampa Bay	1

Philadelphia won best-of-seven series 4-2

Apr. 17	Washington	6	at	Pittsburgh	4
Apr. 19	Washington	5	at	Pittsburgh	3
Apr. 22	Pittsburgh	4	at	Washington	1
Apr. 24	Pittsburgh	3	at	Washington	2 4OT
Apr. 26	Washington	1	at	Pittsburgh	4
Apr. 28	Pittsburgh	3	at	Washington	2

Pittsburgh won best-of-seven series 4-2

Apr. 16	Montreal	3	at	NY Rangers	2 OT
Apr. 18	Montreal	5	at	NY Rangers	3
Apr. 21	NY Rangers	2	at	Montreal	1
Apr. 23	NY Rangers	4	at	Montreal	3
Apr. 26	Montreal	2	at	NY Rangers	3
Apr. 28	NY Rangers	5	at	Montreal	3

NY Rangers won best-of-seven series 4-2

Apr. 17	Boston	3	at	Florida	6
Apr. 22	Boston	2	at	Florida	6
Apr. 24	Florida	4	at	Boston	2
Apr. 25	Florida	2	at	Boston	6
Apr. 27	Boston	3	at	Florida	4

Florida won best-of-seven series 4-1

Apr. 17	Winnipeg	1	at	Detroit	4
Apr. 19	Winnipeg	0	at	Detroit	4
Apr. 21	Detroit	1	at	Winnipeg	4
Apr. 23	Detroit	6	at	Winnipeg	1
Apr. 26	Winnipeg	3	at	Detroit	1
Apr. 28	Detroit	4	at	Winnipeg	1

Detroit won best-of-seven series 4-2

Apr. 16	Vancouver	2	at	Colorado	5
Apr. 18	Vancouver	5	at	Colorado	4
Apr. 20	Colorado	4	at	Vancouver	0
Apr. 22	Colorado	3	at	Vancouver	4
Apr. 25	Vancouver	4	at	Colorado	5 OT
Apr. 27	Colorado	3	at	Vancouver	2

Colorado won best-of-seven series 4-2

Apr. 17	Calgary	1	at	Chicago	4
Apr. 19	Calgary	0	at	Chicago	3
Apr. 21	Chicago	7	at	Calgary	5
Apr. 23	Chicago	2	at	Calgary	1 3OT

Chicago won best-of-seven series 4-0

Apr. 16	St. Louis	3	at	Toronto	1
Apr. 18	St. Louis	4	at	Toronto	5 OT
Apr. 21	Toronto	2	at	St. Louis	3 OT
Apr. 23	Toronto	1	at	St. Louis	5
Apr. 25	St. Louis	4	at	Toronto	5 OT
Apr. 27	Toronto	1	at	St. Louis	2

St. Louis won best-of-seven series 4-2

CONFERENCE SEMIFINALS

May 2	Florida	2	at	Philadelphia	0
May 4	Florida	2	at	Philadelphia	3
May 7	Philadelphia	3	at	Florida	1
May 9	Philadelphia	3	at	Florida	4 OT
May 12	Florida	2	at	Philadelphia	1 2OT
May 14	Philadelphia	1	at	Florida	4

Florida won best-of-seven series 4-2

May 3	NY Rangers	3	at	Pittsburgh	4
May 5	NY Rangers	6	at	Pittsburgh	3
May 7	Pittsburgh	3	at	NY Rangers	2
May 9	Pittsburgh	4	at	NY Rangers	1
May 11	NY Rangers	3	at	Pittsburgh	7

Pittsburgh won best-of-seven series 4-1

May 3	St. Louis	2	at	Detroit	3
May 5	St. Louis	3	at	Detroit	8
May 8	Detroit	4	at	St. Louis	5 OT
May 10	Detroit	0	at	St. Louis	1
May 12	St. Louis	3	at	Detroit	2
May 14	Detroit	4	at	St. Louis	2
May 16	St. Louis	0	at	Detroit	1 2OT

Detroit won best-of-seven series 4-3

May 2	Chicago	3	at	Colorado	2 OT
May 4	Chicago	1	at	Colorado	5
May 6	Colorado	3	at	Chicago	4 OT
May 8	Colorado	3	at	Chicago	2 3OT
May 11	Chicago	1	at	Colorado	4
May 13	Colorado	4	at	Chicago	3 2OT

Colorado won best-of-seven series 4-2

CONFERENCE FINALS

May 18	Florida	5	at	Pittsburgh	1
May 20	Florida	2	at	Pittsburgh	3
May 24	Pittsburgh	2	at	Florida	5
May 26	Pittsburgh	2	at	Florida	1
May 28	Florida	0	at	Pittsburgh	3
May 30	Pittsburgh	3	at	Florida	4
June 1	Florida	3	at	Pittsburgh	1

Florida won best-of-seven series 4-3

May 19	Colorado	3	at	Detroit	2 OT
May 21	Colorado	3	at	Detroit	0
May 23	Detroit	6	at	Colorado	4
May 25	Detroit	2	at	Colorado	4
May 27	Colorado	2	at	Detroit	5
May 29	Detroit	1	at	Colorado	4

Colorado won best-of-seven series 4-2

FINALS

June 4	Florida	1	at	Colorado	3
June 6	Florida	1	at	Colorado	8
June 8	Colorado	3	at	Florida	2
June 10	Colorado	1	at	Florida	0 3OT

Colorado won best-of-seven series 4-0

1995-96 – Colorado Avalanche – Joe Sakic (Captain), Rene Corbet, Adam Deadmarsh, Stephane Fiset, Adam Foote, Peter Forsberg, Alexei Gusarov, Dave Hannan, Valeri Kamensky, Mike Keane, Jon Klemm, Uwe Krupp, Sylvain Lefebvre, Claude Lemieux, Curtis Leschyshyn, Troy Murray, Sandis Ozolinsh, Mike Ricci, Patrick Roy, Warren Rychel,

Chris Simon, Craig Wolanin, Stephane Yelle, Scott Young, Charlie Lyons (Chairman, CEO), Pierre Lacroix (Exec. V.P., G.M.), Marc Crawford (Head Coach), Joel Quenneville (Assistant Coach), Jacques Cloutier (Assistant Coach), Francois Giguere (Assistant General Manager), Michel Goulet (Director of Player Personnel), Dave Draper (Chief Scout), Jean Martineau (Director of Public Relations), Pat Karns (Trainer), Matthew Sokolowski (Assistant Trainer), Rob McLean (Equipment Manager), Mike Kramer (Assistant Equipment Manager), Brock Gibbins (Assistant Equipment Manager), Skip Allen (Strength and Conditioning Coach), Paul Fixter (Video Coordinator), Leo Vyssokov (Massage Therapist).

1995

After 21 seasons and two franchise relocations, the New Jersey Devils captured their first Stanley Cup title by downing the Detroit Red Wings in the championship final. Paced by the stellar goaltending of Martin Brodeur and the timely scoring of Claude Lemieux, the Devils upset the favored Red Wings in four straight games, outscoring, outshooting and outplaying Detroit in each encounter.

Both teams took similar routes to the finals. Detroit lost only two games in the opening three rounds, although they did need a trio of overtime victories to subdue Chicago in the Western Conference final. New Jersey dropped four games in the opening three rounds, including a pair to the Philadelphia Flyers in a stirring six-game Eastern Conference final.

New Jersey's Claude Lemieux, who scored only six times in the regular season, erupted for 13 goals in the postseason and was awarded the Conn Smythe Trophy. Neal Broten, a 14-year veteran acquired by New Jersey late in the season from Dallas, notched four game-winning goals for the champions. Devils coach Jacques Lemaire, who won eight Stanley Cup rings as a player, became the fourth individual to score a Stanley Cup-winning goal and coach a Stanley Cup-winning team.

CONN SMYTHE TROPHY
Claude Lemieux - RW - New Jersey Devils

CONFERENCE QUARTERFINALS

May 6	NY Rangers	4	at	Quebec	5
May 8	NY Rangers	8	at	Quebec	3
May 10	Quebec	3	at	NY Rangers	4
May 12	Quebec	2	at	NY Rangers	3 OT
May 14	NY Rangers	2	at	Quebec	4
May 16	Quebec	2	at	NY Rangers	4

NY Rangers won best-of-seven series 4-2

May 7	Buffalo	3	at	Philadelphia	4 OT
May 8	Buffalo	1	at	Philadelphia	3
May 10	Philadelphia	1	at	Buffalo	3
May 12	Philadelphia	4	at	Buffalo	2
May 14	Buffalo	4	at	Philadelphia	6

Philadelphia won best-of-seven series 4-1

May 6	Washington	5	at	Pittsburgh	4
May 8	Washington	3	at	Pittsburgh	5
May 10	Pittsburgh	2	at	Washington	6
May 12	Pittsburgh	2	at	Washington	6
May 14	Washington	5	at	Pittsburgh	6 OT
May 16	Pittsburgh	7	at	Washington	1
May 18	Washington	0	at	Pittsburgh	3

Pittsburgh won best-of-seven series 4-3

May 7	New Jersey	5	at	Boston	0
May 8	New Jersey	3	at	Boston	0
May 10	Boston	3	at	New Jersey	2
May 12	Boston	0	at	New Jersey	1 OT
May 14	New Jersey	3	at	Boston	2

New Jersey won best-of-seven series 4-1

May 7	Dallas	3	at	Detroit	4
May 9	Dallas	1	at	Detroit	4
May 11	Detroit	5	at	Dallas	1
May 14	Detroit	1	at	Dallas	4
May 15	Dallas	1	at	Detroit	3

Detroit won best-of-seven series 4-1

May 7	San Jose	5	at	Calgary	4
May 9	San Jose	5	at	Calgary	4 OT
May 11	Calgary	9	at	San Jose	2
May 13	Calgary	6	at	San Jose	4
May 15	San Jose	0	at	Calgary	5
May 17	Calgary	3	at	San Jose	5
May 19	San Jose	5	at	Calgary	4 2OT

San Jose won best-of-seven series 4-3

May 7	Vancouver	1	at	St. Louis	2
May 9	Vancouver	5	at	St. Louis	3
May 11	St. Louis	1	at	Vancouver	6
May 13	St. Louis	5	at	Vancouver	2
May 15	Vancouver	6	at	St. Louis	5 OT
May 17	St. Louis	8	at	Vancouver	2
May 19	Vancouver	5	at	St. Louis	3

Vancouver won best-of-seven series 4-3

May 7	Toronto	5	at	Chicago	3
May 9	Toronto	3	at	Chicago	0
May 11	Chicago	3	at	Toronto	2
May 13	Chicago	3	at	Toronto	1
May 15	Toronto	2	at	Chicago	4
May 17	Chicago	4	at	Toronto	5 OT
May 19	Toronto	2	at	Chicago	5

Chicago won best-of-seven series 4-3

CONFERENCE SEMIFINALS

May 21	NY Rangers	4	at	Philadelphia	5 OT
May 22	NY Rangers	3	at	Philadelphia	4 OT
May 24	Philadelphia	5	at	NY Rangers	2
May 26	Philadelphia	4	at	NY Rangers	1

Philadelphia won best-of-seven series 4-0

May 20	New Jersey	2	at	Pittsburgh	3
May 22	New Jersey	4	at	Pittsburgh	2
May 24	Pittsburgh	1	at	New Jersey	5
May 26	Pittsburgh	1	at	New Jersey	2 OT
May 28	New Jersey	4	at	Pittsburgh	1

New Jersey won best-of-seven series 4-1

May 21	San Jose	0	at	Detroit	6
May 23	San Jose	2	at	Detroit	6
May 25	Detroit	6	at	San Jose	2
May 27	Detroit	6	at	San Jose	2

Detroit won best-of-seven series 4-0

May 21	Vancouver	1	at	Chicago	2 OT
May 23	Vancouver	0	at	Chicago	2
May 25	Chicago	3	at	Vancouver	2 OT
May 27	Chicago	4	at	Vancouver	3 OT

Chicago won best-of-seven series 4-0

CONFERENCE FINALS

June 3	New Jersey	4	at	Philadelphia	1
June 5	New Jersey	5	at	Philadelphia	2
June 7	Philadelphia	3	at	New Jersey	2 OT
June 10	Philadelphia	4	at	New Jersey	2
June 11	New Jersey	3	at	Philadelphia	2
June 13	Philadelphia	2	at	New Jersey	4

New Jersey won best-of-seven series 4-2

June 1	Chicago	1	at	Detroit	2 OT
June 4	Chicago	2	at	Detroit	3
June 6	Detroit	4	at	Chicago	3 2OT
June 8	Detroit	2	at	Chicago	5
June 11	Chicago	1	at	Detroit	2 2OT

Detroit won best-of-seven series 4-1

FINALS

June 17	New Jersey	2	at	Detroit	1
June 20	New Jersey	4	at	Detroit	2
June 22	Detroit	2	at	New Jersey	5
June 24	Detroit	2	at	New Jersey	5

New Jersey won best-of-seven series 4-0

1994-95 – New Jersey Devils – Scott Stevens (Captain), Tommy Albelin, Martin Brodeur, Neil Broten, Sergei Brylin, Bob Carpenter, Shawn Chambers, Tom Chorske, Danton Cole, Ken Daneyko, Kevin Dean, Jim Dowd, Bruce Driver (Alternate Captain), Bill Guerin, Bobby Holik, Claude Lemieux, John MacLean (Alternate Captain), Chris McAlpine, Randy McKay, Scott Niedermayer, Mike Peluso, Stephane J.J. Richer, Brian Rolston, Chris Terreri, Valeri Zelepukin, Dr. John J. McMullen (Owner/Chairman), Peter S. McMullen (Owner), Lou Lamoriello (President/General Manager), Jacques Lemaire (Head Coach), Jacques Caron (Goaltender Coach), Dennis Gendron (Assistant Coach), Larry Robinson (Assistant Coach), Robbie Ftorek (AHL Coach), Alex Abasto (Assistant Equipment Manager), Bob Huddleston (Massage Therapist), David Nichols (Equipment Manager), Ted Schuch (Medical Trainer), Mike Vasalani (Strength Coach), David Conte (Director of Scouting), Claude Carrier (Scout), Milt Fisher (Scout), Dan Labraaten (Scout), Marcel Pronovost (Scout).

1994

The New York Rangers ended their 54-year Stanley Cup drought with a stirring, seven-game series win over the Vancouver Canucks. The Rangers jumped out to a 3–1 series lead, only to see the Canucks storm back to tie the series, forcing a deciding game at Madison Square Garden. Viewed by a record television audience worldwide, the Rangers earned a 3–2 win and the Stanley Cup.

Both the Rangers and Canucks followed a difficult route to the championship series. In the Eastern Conference final, the Rangers were stretched to the limit by the New Jersey Devils before prevailing four games to three with three games in the series decided in double overtime. The Canucks, meanwhile, had faced a 3–1 series deficit in their first-round series versus the Calgary Flames, but rallied to win the last three games in overtime.

Rangers defenseman Brian Leetch became the first U.S.-born player to capture the Conn Smythe Trophy as playoff MVP. Leetch led all players in scoring during the postseason with 34 points (11 goals, 23 assists) in 23 games. Head coach Mike Keenan, in his first season behind the Rangers bench, captured his first Stanley Cup victory. He had previously made championship series appearances with the Philadelphia Flyers (twice) and Chicago Blackhawks.

CONN SMYTHE TROPHY
Brian Leetch - Defense - NY Rangers

CONFERENCE QUARTERFINALS

Apr. 18	NY Islanders	0	at	NY Rangers	6
Apr. 17	NY Islanders	0	at	NY Rangers	6
Apr. 21	NY Rangers	5	at	NY Islanders	1
Apr. 24	NY Rangers	5	at	NY Islanders	2

NY Rangers won best-of-seven series 4-0

Apr. 17	Washington	5	at	Pittsburgh	3
Apr. 19	Washington	1	at	Pittsburgh	2
Apr. 21	Pittsburgh	0	at	Washington	2
Apr. 23	Pittsburgh	1	at	Washington	4
Apr. 25	Washington	2	at	Pittsburgh	3
Apr. 27	Pittsburgh	3	at	Washington	6

Washington won best-of-seven series 4-2

Apr. 17	Buffalo	2	at	New Jersey	0
Apr. 19	Buffalo	1	at	New Jersey	2
Apr. 21	New Jersey	2	at	Buffalo	1
Apr. 23	New Jersey	3	at	Buffalo	5
Apr. 25	Buffalo	3	at	New Jersey	5
Apr. 27	New Jersey	0	at	Buffalo	1 4OT

Apr.	29	Buffalo	1	at	New Jersey	2

New Jersey won best-of-seven series 4-3

Apr.	16	Montreal	2	at	Boston	3
Apr.	18	Montreal	3	at	Boston	2
Apr.	21	Boston	6	at	Montreal	3
Apr.	23	Boston	2	at	Montreal	5
Apr.	25	Montreal	2	at	Boston	1 OT
Apr.	27	Boston	3	at	Montreal	2
Apr.	29	Montreal	3	at	Boston	5

Boston won best-of-seven series 4-3

Apr.	18	San Jose	5	at	Detroit	4
Apr.	20	San Jose	0	at	Detroit	4
Apr.	22	Detroit	3	at	San Jose	2
Apr.	23	Detroit	3	at	San Jose	4
Apr.	26	Detroit	4	at	San Jose	6
Apr.	28	San Jose	1	at	Detroit	7
Apr.	30	San Jose	3	at	Detroit	2

San Jose won best-of-seven series 4-3

Apr.	18	Vancouver	5	at	Calgary	0
Apr.	20	Vancouver	5	at	Calgary	7
Apr.	22	Calgary	4	at	Vancouver	2
Apr.	24	Calgary	3	at	Vancouver	2
Apr.	26	Vancouver	2	at	Calgary	1 OT
Apr.	28	Calgary	2	at	Vancouver	3 OT
Apr.	30	Vancouver	4	at	Calgary	3 2OT

Vancouver won best-of-seven series 4-3

Apr.	18	Chicago	1	at	Toronto	5
Apr.	20	Chicago	0	at	Toronto	1 OT
Apr.	23	Toronto	4	at	Chicago	5
Apr.	24	Toronto	3	at	Chicago	4 OT
Apr.	26	Chicago	0	at	Toronto	1
Apr.	28	Toronto	1	at	Chicago	0

Toronto won best-of-seven series 4-2

Apr.	17	St. Louis	3	at	Dallas	5
Apr.	20	St. Louis	2	at	Dallas	4
Apr.	22	Dallas	5	at	St. Louis	4 OT
Apr.	24	Dallas	2	at	St. Louis	1

Dallas won best-of-seven series 4-0

CONFERENCE SEMIFINALS

May	1	Washington	3	at	NY Rangers	6
May	3	Washington	2	at	NY Rangers	5
May	5	NY Rangers	3	at	Washington	0
May	7	NY Rangers	2	at	Washington	4
May	9	Washington	3	at	NY Rangers	4

NY Rangers won best-of-seven series 4-1

May	1	Boston	2	at	New Jersey	1
May	3	Boston	6	at	New Jersey	5 OT
May	5	New Jersey	4	at	Boston	2
May	7	New Jersey	5	at	Boston	4 OT
May	9	Boston	0	at	New Jersey	2
May	11	New Jersey	5	at	Boston	3

New Jersey won best-of-seven series 4-2

May	2	San Jose	3	at	Toronto	2
May	4	San Jose	1	at	Toronto	5
May	6	Toronto	2	at	San Jose	5
May	8	Toronto	8	at	San Jose	3
May	10	Toronto	2	at	San Jose	5
May	12	San Jose	2	at	Toronto	3 OT
May	14	San Jose	2	at	Toronto	4

Toronto won best-of-seven series 4-3

May	2	Vancouver	6	at	Dallas	4
May	4	Vancouver	3	at	Dallas	0
May	6	Dallas	4	at	Vancouver	3
May	8	Dallas	1	at	Vancouver	2 OT
May	10	Dallas	2	at	Vancouver	4

Vancouver won best-of-seven series 4-1

CONFERENCE FINALS

May	15	New Jersey	4	at	NY Rangers	3 2OT
May	17	New Jersey	0	at	NY Rangers	4
May	19	NY Rangers	3	at	New Jersey	2 2OT
May	21	NY Rangers	1	at	New Jersey	3
May	23	New Jersey	4	at	NY Rangers	1
May	25	NY Rangers	4	at	New Jersey	2
May	27	New Jersey	1	at	NY Rangers	2 2OT

NY Rangers won best-of-seven series 4-3

May	16	Vancouver	2	at	Toronto	3 OT
May	18	Vancouver	4	at	Toronto	3
May	20	Toronto	0	at	Vancouver	4
May	22	Toronto	0	at	Vancouver	2
May	24	Toronto	3	at	Vancouver	4 2OT

Vancouver won best-of-seven series 4-1

FINALS

May	31	Vancouver	3	at	NY Rangers	2 OT
June	2	Vancouver	1	at	NY Rangers	3
June	4	NY Rangers	5	at	Vancouver	1
June	7	NY Rangers	4	at	Vancouver	2
June	9	Vancouver	6	at	NY Rangers	3
June	11	NY Rangers	1	at	Vancouver	4
June	14	Vancouver	2	at	NY Rangers	3

NY Rangers won best-of-seven series 4-3

1993-94 – New York Rangers – Mark Messier (Captain), Brian Leetch, Kevin Lowe, Adam Graves, Steve Larmer, Glenn Anderson, Jeff Beukeboom, Greg Gilbert, Mike Hartman, Glenn Healy, Mike Hudson, Alexander Karpovtsev, Joe Kocur, Alexei Kovalev, Nick Kypreos, Doug Lidster, Stephane Matteau, Craig MacTavish, Sergei Nemchinov, Brian Noonan, Ed Olczyk, Mike Richter, Esa Tikkanen, Jay Wells, Sergei Zubov, Neil Smith (President, General Manager and Governor), Robert Gutkowski, Stanley Jaffe, Kenneth Munoz (Governors), Larry Pleau (Assistant General Manager), Mike Keenan (Head Coach), Colin Campbell (Associate Coach), Dick Todd (Assistant Coach), Matthew Loughren (Manager, Team Operations), Barry Watkins (Director, Communications), Christer Rockstrom, Tony Feltrin, Martin Madden, Herb Hammond, Darwin Bennett (Scouts), Dave Smith, Joe Murphy, Mike Folga, Bruce Lifrieri (Trainers).

1993

The Montreal Canadiens claimed their 24th Stanley Cup title, defeating the Los Angeles Kings in an exciting five-game series. The Kings, led by playoff scoring leader Wayne Gretzky, were making their first appearance in the finals. After dropping the opening game of the series at home, Montreal responded with four straight wins, including three in overtime.

The overtime wins capped a record-setting performance for Montreal in extra time. After losing their first overtime game of the playoffs at Quebec in game one of the opening round, the club posted 10 straight wins in extra time, setting playoff records for most OT wins in one season and most consecutive OT wins. Of the 85 games played in the postseason this year, 28 were decided in overtime, smashing the previous playoff record of 16, set in 1982 and 1991.

Canadiens goaltender Patrick Roy was awarded the Conn Smythe Trophy as playoff MVP, posting a 16–4 record and 2.13 goals-against average in 20 games. Roy became the fifth multiple winner of the award, having previously won as a rookie in 1986.

CONN SMYTHE TROPHY
Patrick Roy - Goaltender - Montreal Canadiens

DIVISION SEMIFINALS

Apr.	18	Buffalo	5	at	Boston	4 OT
Apr.	20	Buffalo	4	at	Boston	0
Apr.	22	Boston	3	at	Buffalo	4 OT
Apr.	24	Boston	5	at	Buffalo	6 OT

Buffalo won best-of-seven series 4–0

Apr.	18	Montreal	2	at	Quebec	3 OT
Apr.	20	Montreal	1	at	Quebec	4
Apr.	22	Quebec	1	at	Montreal	2 OT
Apr.	24	Quebec	2	at	Montreal	3
Apr.	26	Montreal	5	at	Quebec	4 OT
Apr.	28	Quebec	2	at	Montreal	6

Montreal won best-of-seven series 4–2

Apr.	18	New Jersey	3	at	Pittsburgh	6
Apr.	20	New Jersey	0	at	Pittsburgh	7
Apr.	22	Pittsburgh	4	at	New Jersey	3
Apr.	25	Pittsburgh	1	at	New Jersey	4
Apr.	26	New Jersey	3	at	Pittsburgh	5

Pittsburgh won best-of-seven series 4–1

Apr.	18	NY Islanders	1	at	Washington	3
Apr.	20	NY Islanders	5	at	Washington	4 2OT
Apr.	22	Washington	3	at	NY Islanders	4 OT
Apr.	24	Washington	3	at	NY Islanders	4 2OT
Apr.	26	NY Islanders	4	at	Washington	6
Apr.	28	Washington	3	at	NY Islanders	5

Islanders won best-of-seven series 4–2

Apr.	18	St. Louis	4	at	Chicago	3
Apr.	21	St. Louis	2	at	Chicago	0
Apr.	23	Chicago	0	at	St. Louis	3
Apr.	25	Chicago	3	at	St. Louis	4 OT

St. Louis won best-of-seven series 4–0

Apr.	19	Toronto	3	at	Detroit	6
Apr.	21	Toronto	2	at	Detroit	6
Apr.	23	Detroit	2	at	Toronto	4
Apr.	25	Detroit	2	at	Toronto	3
Apr.	27	Toronto	5	at	Detroit	4 OT
Apr.	29	Detroit	7	at	Toronto	3
May	1	Toronto	4	at	Detroit	3 OT

Toronto won best-of-seven series 4–3

Apr.	19	Winnipeg	2	at	Vancouver	4
Apr.	21	Winnipeg	2	at	Vancouver	3
Apr.	23	Vancouver	4	at	Winnipeg	5
Apr.	25	Vancouver	3	at	Winnipeg	1
Apr.	27	Winnipeg	4	at	Vancouver	3 OT
Apr.	29	Vancouver	4	at	Winnipeg	3 OT

Vancouver won best-of-seven series 4–2

Apr.	18	Los Angeles	6	at	Calgary	3
Apr.	21	Los Angeles	4	at	Calgary	9
Apr.	23	Calgary	5	at	Los Angeles	2
Apr.	25	Calgary	1	at	Los Angeles	3
Apr.	27	Los Angeles	9	at	Calgary	4
Apr.	29	Calgary	6	at	Los Angeles	9

Los Angeles won best-of-seven series 4–2

DIVISION FINALS

May	2	Buffalo	3	at	Montreal	4
May	4	Buffalo	3	at	Montreal	4 OT
May	6	Montreal	4	at	Buffalo	3 OT
May	8	Montreal	4	at	Buffalo	3 OT

Montreal won best-of-seven series 4–0

May	2	NY Islanders	3	at	Pittsburgh	2
May	4	NY Islanders	0	at	Pittsburgh	3
May	6	Pittsburgh	3	at	NY Islanders	1
May	8	Pittsburgh	5	at	NY Islanders	6
May	10	NY Islanders	3	at	Pittsburgh	6
May	12	Pittsburgh	5	at	NY Islanders	7
May	14	NY Islanders	4	at	Pittsburgh	3 OT

Islanders won best-of-seven series 4–3

May	3	St. Louis	1	at	Toronto	2 2OT
May	5	St. Louis	2	at	Toronto	1 2OT
May	7	Toronto	3	at	St. Louis	4
May	9	Toronto	4	at	St. Louis	1
May	11	St. Louis	1	at	Toronto	5
May	13	Toronto	1	at	St. Louis	2
May	15	St. Louis	0	at	Toronto	6

Toronto won best-of-seven series 4–3

May	2	Los Angeles	2	at	Vancouver	5
May	5	Los Angeles	6	at	Vancouver	3
May	7	Vancouver	4	at	Los Angeles	7
May	9	Vancouver	7	at	Los Angeles	2
May	11	Los Angeles	4	at	Vancouver	3 2OT
May	13	Vancouver	3	at	Los Angeles	5

Los Angeles won best-of-seven series 4–2

CONFERENCE FINALS

May	16	NY Islanders	1	at	Montreal	4
May	18	NY Islanders	3	at	Montreal	4 2OT
May	20	Montreal	2	at	NY Islanders	1 OT

May	22	Montreal	1	at	NY Islanders	4
May	24	NY Islanders	2	at	Montreal	5

Montreal won best-of-seven series 4–1

May	17	Los Angeles	1	at	Toronto	4
May	19	Los Angeles	3	at	Toronto	2
May	21	Toronto	2	at	Los Angeles	4
May	23	Toronto	4	at	Los Angeles	2
May	25	Los Angeles	2	at	Toronto	3 OT
May	27	Toronto	4	at	Los Angeles	5 OT
May	29	Los Angeles	5	at	Toronto	4

Los Angeles won best-of-seven series 4–3

FINALS

June	1	Los Angeles	4	at	Montreal	1
June	3	Los Angeles	2	at	Montreal	3 OT
June	5	Montreal	4	at	Los Angeles	3 OT
June	7	Montreal	3	at	Los Angeles	2 OT
June	9	Los Angeles	1	at	Montreal	4

Montreal won best-of-seven series 4–1

1992-93 – Montreal Canadiens – Guy Carbonneau (Captain), Patrick Roy, Mike Keane, Eric Desjardins, Stephan Lebeau, Mathieu Schneider, Jean-Jacques Daigneault, Denis Savard, Lyle Odelein, Todd Ewen, Kirk Muller, John LeClair, Gilbert Dionne, Benoit Brunet, Patrice Brisebois, Paul Di Pietro, Andre Racicot, Donald Dufresne, Mario Roberge, Sean Hill, Ed Ronan, Kevin Haller, Vincent Damphousse, Brian Bellows, Gary Leeman, Rob Ramage, Ronald Corey (President), Serge Savard (Managing Director & Vice-President Hockey), Jacques Demers (Head Coach), Jacques Laperriere (Assistant Coach), Charles Thiffault (Assistant Coach), Francois Allaire (Goaltending Instructor), Jean Béliveau (Senior Vice-President, Corporate Affairs), Fred Steer (Vice-President, Finance & Adminstration), Aldo Giampaolo (Vice-President, Operations), Bernard Brisset (Vice-President, Marketing & Communications), André Boudrias (Assistant to the Managing Director & Director of Scouting), Jacques Lemaire (Assistant to the Managing Director), Gaeten Lefebvre (Athletic Trainer), John Shipman (Assistant to the Athletic Trainer), Eddy Palchak (Equipment Manager), Pierre Gervais (Assistant to the Equipment Manager), Robert Boulanger (Assistant to the Equipment Manager), Pierre Ouellete (Assistant to the Equipment Manager).

1992

The Penguins captured their second consecutive Stanley Cup title, winning the championship in four consecutive games from the Chicago Blackhawks, who were making their first appearance in the finals since 1973.

Both finalists established a new record for consecutive playoff wins with 11. The Blackhawks' victories spanned the first three rounds of the playoffs. The Penguins' 11 wins included their four-game final series sweep.

Mario Lemieux captured the Conn Smythe Trophy as playoff MVP for the second straight year, becoming just the second player in NHL history (Bernie Parent, 1974 and 1975) to accomplish the feat.

CONN SMYTHE TROPHY
Mario Lemieux - Center - Pittsburgh Penguins

DIVISION SEMIFINALS

Apr.	19	Hartford	0	at	Montreal	2
Apr.	21	Hartford	2	at	Montreal	5
Apr.	23	Montreal	2	at	Hartford	5
Apr.	25	Montreal	1	at	Hartford	3
Apr.	27	Hartford	4	at	Montreal	7
Apr.	29	Montreal	1	at	Hartford	2 OT
May 1		Hartford	2	at	Montreal	3 2OT

Montreal won best-of-seven series 4–3

Apr.	19	Buffalo	3	at	Boston	2
Apr.	21	Buffalo	2	at	Boston	3 OT
Apr.	23	Boston	3	at	Buffalo	2
Apr.	25	Boston	5	at	Buffalo	4 OT
Apr.	27	Buffalo	2	at	Boston	0
Apr.	29	Boston	3	at	Buffalo	9
May	1	Buffalo	2	at	Boston	3

Boston won best-of-seven series 4–3

Apr.	19	New Jersey	1	at	NY Rangers	2
Apr.	21	New Jersey	7	at	NY Rangers	3
Apr.	23	NY Rangers	1	at	New Jersey	3
Apr.	25	NY Rangers	3	at	New Jersey	0
Apr.	27	New Jersey	5	at	NY Rangers	6
Apr.	29	NY Rangers	3	at	New Jersey	5
May	1	New Jersey	4	at	NY Rangers	8

Rangers won best-of-seven series 4–3

Apr.	19	Pittsburgh	1	at	Washington	3
Apr.	21	Pittsburgh	2	at	Washington	6
Apr.	23	Washington	4	at	Pittsburgh	6
Apr.	25	Washington	7	at	Pittsburgh	2
Apr.	27	Pittsburgh	5	at	Washington	2
Apr.	29	Washington	4	at	Pittsburgh	6
May	1	Pittsburgh	3	at	Washington	1

Pittsburgh won best-of-seven series 4–3

Apr.	18	Minnesota	4	at	Detroit	3
Apr.	20	Minnesota	4	at	Detroit	2
Apr.	22	Detroit	5	at	Minnesota	4 OT
Apr.	24	Detroit	4	at	Minnesota	5
Apr.	26	Minnesota	0	at	Detroit	3
Apr.	28	Detroit	1	at	Minnesota	0 OT
Apr.	30	Minnesota	2	at	Detroit	5

Detroit won best-of-seven series 4–3

Apr.	18	St. Louis	1	at	Chicago	3
Apr.	20	St. Louis	5	at	Chicago	3
Apr.	22	Chicago	4	at	St. Louis	5 2OT
Apr.	24	Chicago	5	at	St. Louis	3
Apr.	26	St. Louis	4	at	Chicago	6
Apr.	28	Chicago	2	at	St. Louis	1

Chicago won best-of-seven series 4–2

Apr.	18	Winnipeg	3	at	Vancouver	2
Apr.	20	Winnipeg	2	at	Vancouver	3
Apr.	22	Vancouver	2	at	Winnipeg	4
Apr.	24	Vancouver	1	at	Winnipeg	3
Apr.	26	Winnipeg	2	at	Vancouver	8
Apr.	28	Vancouver	8	at	Winnipeg	3
Apr.	30	Winnipeg	0	at	Vancouver	5

Vancouver won best-of-seven series 4–3

Apr.	18	Edmonton	3	at	Los Angeles	1
Apr.	20	Edmonton	5	at	Los Angeles	8
Apr.	22	Los Angeles	3	at	Edmonton	4
Apr.	24	Los Angeles	4	at	Edmonton	3
Apr.	26	Edmonton	5	at	Los Angeles	2
Apr.	28	Los Angeles	0	at	Edmonton	3

Edmonton won best-of-seven series 4–2

DIVISION FINALS

May	3	Boston	6	at	Montreal	4
May	5	Boston	3	at	Montreal	2 OT
May	7	Montreal	2	at	Boston	3
May	9	Montreal	0	at	Boston	2

Boston won best-of-seven series 4–0

May	3	Pittsburgh	4	at	NY Rangers	2
May	5	Pittsburgh	2	at	NY Rangers	4
May	7	NY Rangers	6	at	Pittsburgh	5 OT
May	9	NY Rangers	4	at	Pittsburgh	5 OT
May	11	Pittsburgh	3	at	NY Rangers	2
May	13	NY Rangers	1	at	Pittsburgh	5

Pittsburgh won best-of-seven series 4–2

May	2	Chicago	2	at	Detroit	1
May	4	Chicago	3	at	Detroit	1
May	6	Detroit	4	at	Chicago	5
May	8	Detroit	0	at	Chicago	1

Chicago won best-of-seven series 4–0

May	3	Edmonton	4	at	Vancouver	3 OT
May	4	Edmonton	0	at	Vancouver	4
May	6	Vancouver	2	at	Edmonton	5
May	8	Vancouver	2	at	Edmonton	3
May	10	Edmonton	3	at	Vancouver	4
May	12	Vancouver	0	at	Edmonton	3

Edmonton won best-of-seven series 4–2

CONFERENCE FINALS

May	17	Boston	3	at	Pittsburgh	4 OT
May	19	Boston	2	at	Pittsburgh	5
May	21	Pittsburgh	5	at	Boston	1
May	23	Pittsburgh	5	at	Boston	1

Pittsburgh won best-of-seven series 4–0

May	16	Edmonton	2	at	Chicago	8
May	18	Edmonton	2	at	Chicago	4
May	20	Chicago	4	at	Edmonton	3 OT
May	22	Chicago	5	at	Edmonton	1

Chicago won best-of-seven series 4–0

FINALS

May	26	Chicago	4	at	Pittsburgh	5
May	28	Chicago	1	at	Pittsburgh	3
May	30	Pittsburgh	1	at	Chicago	0
June	1	Pittsburgh	6	at	Chicago	5

Pittsburgh won best-of-seven series 4–0

1991-92 – Pittsburgh Penguins – Mario Lemieux (Captain), Ron Francis, Bryan Trottier, Kevin Stevens, Bob Errey, Phil Bourque, Troy Loney, Rick Tocchet, Joe Mullen, Jaromir Jagr, Jiri Hrdina, Shawn McEachern, Ulf Samuelsson, Kjell Samuelsson, Larry Murphy, Gord Roberts, Jim Paek, Paul Stanton, Tom Barrasso, Ken Wregget, Jay Caufield, Jamie Leach, Wendell Young, Grant Jennings, Peter Taglianetti, Jock Callander, Dave Michayluk, Mike Needham, Jeff Chychrun, Ken Priestlay, Jeff Daniels, Howard Baldwin (Owner and President), Morris Belzberg (Owner), Thomas Ruta (Owner), Donn Patton (Executive Vice President and Chief Financial Officer), Paul Martha (Executive Vice President and General Counsel), Craig Patrick (Executive Vice President and General Manager), Bob Johnson (Coach), Scotty Bowman (Director of Player Development and Coach), Barry Smith, Rick Kehoe, Pierre McGuire, Gilles Meloche, Rick Paterson (Assistant Coaches), Steve Latin (Equipment Manager), Skip Thayer (Trainer), John Welday (Strength and Conditioning Coach), Greg Malone, Les Binkley, Charlie Hodge, John Gill, Ralph Cox (Scouts).

1991

The Penguins captured their first Stanley Cup championship, defeating the Minnesota North Stars in six games. The North Stars were making their second appearance in the finals.

Pittsburgh center Mario Lemieux, despite missing one game in the series due to a back injury, recorded 12 points (five goals, seven assists) in five games to lead all scorers. His overall playoff performance earned him Conn Smythe Trophy honors.

Penguins defenseman Larry Murphy tallied 10 points (one goal, nine assists) in six games, the second highest total for a defenseman in Stanley Cup finals history.

Four Pittsburgh players — Bryan Trottier, Paul Coffey, Joe Mullen and Jiri Hrdina — won a Stanley Cup championship with their second team. Trottier won four previous titles with the New York Islanders, Coffey captured three with Edmonton, while Mullen and Hrdina were members of the 1989 Stanley Cup-champion Calgary Flames.

CONN SMYTHE TROPHY
Mario Lemieux - Center - Pittsburgh Penguins

DIVISION SEMIFINALS

Apr.	3	Hartford	5	at	Boston	2
Apr.	5	Hartford	3	at	Boston	4
Apr.	7	Boston	6	at	Hartford	3
Apr.	9	Boston	3	at	Hartford	4
Apr.	11	Hartford	1	at	Boston	6
Apr.	13	Boston	3	at	Hartford	1

Boston won best-of-seven series 4–2

Apr.	3	Buffalo	5	at	Montreal	7
Apr.	5	Buffalo	4	at	Montreal	5
Apr.	7	Montreal	4	at	Buffalo	5
Apr.	9	Montreal	4	at	Buffalo	6
Apr.	11	Buffalo	3	at	Montreal	4 OT
Apr.	13	Montreal	5	at	Buffalo	1

Montreal won best-of-seven series 4–2

Apr.	3	New Jersey	3	at	Pittsburgh	1
Apr.	5	New Jersey	4	at	Pittsburgh	5 OT
Apr.	7	Pittsburgh	4	at	New Jersey	3
Apr.	9	Pittsburgh	1	at	New Jersey	4
Apr.	11	New Jersey	4	at	Pittsburgh	2
Apr.	13	Pittsburgh	4	at	New Jersey	3
Apr.	15	New Jersey	0	at	Pittsburgh	4

Pittsburgh won best-of-seven series 4–3

Apr.	3	Washington	1	at	NY Rangers	2
Apr.	5	Washington	3	at	NY Rangers	0
Apr.	7	NY Rangers	6	at	Washington	0
Apr.	9	NY Rangers	2	at	Washington	3
Apr.	11	Washington	5	at	NY Rangers	4 OT
Apr.	13	NY Rangers	2	at	Washington	4

Washington won best-of-seven series 4–2

Apr.	4	Minnesota	4	at	Chicago	3 OT
Apr.	6	Minnesota	2	at	Chicago	5
Apr.	8	Chicago	6	at	Minnesota	5
Apr.	10	Chicago	1	at	Minnesota	3
Apr.	12	Minnesota	6	at	Chicago	0
Apr.	14	Chicago	1	at	Minnesota	3

Minnesota won best-of-seven series 4–2

Apr.	4	Detroit	6	at	St. Louis	3
Apr.	6	Detroit	2	at	St. Louis	4
Apr.	8	St. Louis	2	at	Detroit	5
Apr.	10	St. Louis	3	at	Detroit	4
Apr.	12	Detroit	1	at	St. Louis	6
Apr.	14	St. Louis	3	at	Detroit	0
Apr.	16	Detroit	2	at	St. Louis	3

St. Louis won best-of-seven series 4–3

Apr.	4	Vancouver	6	at	Los Angeles	5
Apr.	6	Vancouver	2	at	Los Angeles	3 OT
Apr.	8	Los Angeles	1	at	Vancouver	2 OT
Apr.	10	Los Angeles	6	at	Vancouver	1
Apr.	12	Vancouver	4	at	Los Angeles	7
Apr.	14	Los Angeles	4	at	Vancouver	1

Los Angeles won best-of-seven series 4–2

Apr.	4	Edmonton	3	at	Calgary	1
Apr.	6	Edmonton	1	at	Calgary	3
Apr.	8	Calgary	3	at	Edmonton	4
Apr.	10	Calgary	2	at	Edmonton	5
Apr.	12	Edmonton	3	at	Calgary	5
Apr.	14	Calgary	2	at	Edmonton	1 OT
Apr.	16	Edmonton	5	at	Calgary	4 OT

Edmonton won best-of-seven series 4–3

DIVISION FINALS

Apr.	17	Montreal	1	at	Boston	2
Apr.	19	Montreal	4	at	Boston	3 OT
Apr.	21	Boston	3	at	Montreal	2
Apr	23	Boston	2	at	Montreal	6
Apr.	25	Montreal	1	at	Boston	4
Apr.	27	Boston	2	at	Montreal	3 OT
Apr.	29	Montreal	1	at	Boston	2

Boston won best-of-seven series 4–3

Apr.	17	Washington	4	at	Pittsburgh	2
Apr.	19	Washington	6	at	Pittsburgh	7 OT
Apr.	21	Pittsburgh	3	at	Washington	1
Apr.	23	Pittsburgh	3	at	Washington	1
Apr.	25	Washington	1	at	Pittsburgh	4

Pittsburgh won best-of-seven series 4–1

Apr.	18	Minnesota	2	at	St. Louis	1
Apr.	20	Minnesota	2	at	St. Louis	5
Apr.	22	St. Louis	1	at	Minnesota	5
Apr.	24	St. Louis	4	at	Minnesota	8
Apr.	26	Minnesota	2	at	St. Louis	4
Apr.	28	St. Louis	2	at	Minnesota	3

Minnesota won best-of-seven series 4–2

Apr.	18	Edmonton	3	at	Los Angeles	4 OT
Apr.	20	Edmonton	4	at	Los Angeles	3 2OT
Apr.	22	Los Angeles	3	at	Edmonton	4 2OT
Apr.	24	Los Angeles	2	at	Edmonton	4
Apr.	26	Edmonton	2	at	Los Angeles	5
Apr.	28	Los Angeles	3	at	Edmonton	4 OT

Edmonton won best-of-seven series 4–2

CONFERENCE FINALS

May	1	Pittsburgh	3	at	Boston	6
May	3	Pittsburgh	4	at	Boston	5 OT
May	5	Boston	1	at	Pittsburgh	4
May	7	Boston	1	at	Pittsburgh	4
May	9	Pittsburgh	7	at	Boston	2
May	11	Boston	3	at	Pittsburgh	5

Pittsburgh won best-of-seven series 4–2

May	2	MInnesota	3	at	Edmonton	1
May	4	Minnesota	2	at	Edmonton	7
May	6	Edmonton	3	at	Minnesota	7
May	8	Edmonton	1	at	Minnesota	5
May	10	Minnesota	3	at	Edmonton	2

Minnesota won best-of-seven series 4–1

FINALS

May	15	Minnesota	5	at	Pittsburgh	4
May	17	Minnesota	1	at	Pittsburgh	4
May	19	Pittsburgh	1	at	Minnesota	3
May	21	Pittsburgh	5	at	Minnesota	3
May	23	Minnesota	4	at	Pittsburgh	6
May	25	Pittsburgh	8	at	Minnesota	0

Pittsburgh won best-of-seven series 4–2

1990-91 – Pittsburgh Penguins – Mario Lemieux (Captain), Paul Coffey, Randy Hillier, Bob Errey, Tom Barrasso, Phil Bourque, Jay Caufield, Ron Francis, Randy Gilhen, Jiri Hrdina, Jaromir Jagr, Grant Jennings, Troy Loney, Joe Mullen, Larry Murphy, Jim Paek, Frank Pietrangelo, Barry Pederson, Mark Recchi, Gordie Roberts, Ulf Samuelsson, Paul Stanton, Kevin Stevens, Peter Taglianetti, Bryan Trottier, Scott Young, Wendell Young, Edward J. DeBartolo, Sr. (Owner), Marie D. DeBartolo York (President), Paul Martha (Vice-President & General Counsel), Craig Patrick (General Manager), Scotty Bowman (Director of Player Development & Recruitment), Bob Johnson (Coach), Rick Kehoe (Assistant Coach), Gilles Meloche (Goaltending Coach & Scout), Rick Paterson (Assistant Coach), Barry Smith (Assistant Coach), Steve Latin (Equipment Manager), Skip Thayer (Trainer), John Welday (Strength & Conditioning Coach), Greg Malone (Scout).

1990

The Oilers captured their fifth Stanley Cup title in seven years (and their first since trading Wayne Gretzky to Los Angeles in 1988), defeating Boston for their second Stanley Cup triumph over the Bruins in three seasons.

The two teams battled for 55:13 of overtime in game one at Boston Garden before Edmonton's Petr Klima ended the marathon encounter with the game-winner. It represented the longest game in Stanley Cup finals history, edging the previous mark of 53:50 set in game three of the 1931 series between Chicago and Montreal.

Edmonton goaltender Bill Ranford, who posted all 16 Oilers victories in the postseason, won the Conn Smythe Trophy as playoff MVP.

Seven players — Glenn Anderson, Grant Fuhr, Randy Gregg, Charlie Huddy, Jari Kurri, Kevin Lowe and Mark Messier — won their fifth Stanley Cup rings as members of the Oilers.

CONN SMYTHE TROPHY
Bill Ranford - Goaltender - Edmonton Oilers

DIVISION SEMIFINALS

Apr.	5	Hartford	4	at	Boston	3
Apr.	7	Hartford	1	at	Boston	3
Apr.	9	Boston	3	at	Hartford	5
Apr.	11	Boston	6	at	Hartford	5
Apr.	13	Hartford	2	at	Boston	3
Apr.	15	Boston	2	at	Hartford	3 OT
Apr.	17	Hartford	1	at	Boston	3

Boston won best-of-seven series 4–3

Apr.	5	Montreal	1	at	Buffalo	4
Apr.	7	Montreal	3	at	Buffalo	0
Apr.	9	Buffalo	1	at	Montreal	2 OT
Apr.	11	Buffalo	4	at	Montreal	2
Apr.	13	Montreal	4	at	Buffalo	2
Apr.	15	Buffalo	2	at	Montreal	5

Montreal won best-of-seven series 4–2

Apr.	5	NY Islanders	1	at	NY Rangers	2
Apr.	7	NY Islanders	2	at	NY Rangers	5
Apr.	9	NY Rangers	3	at	NY Islanders	4 2OT
Apr.	11	NY Rangers	6	at	NY Islanders	1
Apr.	13	NY Islanders	5	at	NY Rangers	6

Rangers won best-of-seven series 4–1

Apr.	5	Washington	5	at	New Jersey	4 OT
Apr.	7	Washington	5	at	New Jersey	6
Apr.	9	New Jersey	2	at	Washington	1
Apr.	11	New Jersey	1	at	Washington	3
Apr.	13	Washington	4	at	New Jersey	3
Apr.	15	New Jersey	2	at	Washington	3

Washington won best-of-seven series 4–2

Apr.	4	Minnesota	2	at	Chicago	1
Apr.	6	Minnesota	3	at	Chicago	5
Apr.	8	Chicago	2	at	Minnesota	1
Apr.	10	Chicago	0	at	Minnesota	4
Apr.	12	Minnesota	1	at	Chicago	5
Apr.	14	Chicago	3	at	Minnesota	5
Apr.	16	Minnesota	2	at	Chicago	5

Chicago won best-of-seven series 4–3

Apr.	4	Toronto	2	at	St. Louis	4
Apr.	6	Toronto	2	at	St. Louis	4
Apr.	8	St. Louis	6	at	Toronto	5 OT
Apr.	10	St. Louis	2	at	Toronto	4
Apr.	12	Toronto	3	at	St. Louis	4

St. Louis won best-of-seven series 4–1

Apr.	4	Los Angeles	5	at	Calgary	3
Apr.	6	Los Angeles	5	at	Calgary	8
Apr.	8	Calgary	1	at	Los Angeles	2 OT
Apr.	10	Calgary	4	at	Los Angeles	12
Apr.	12	Los Angeles	1	at	Calgary	5
Apr.	14	Calgary	3	at	Los Angeles	4 2OT

Los Angeles won best-of-seven series 4–2

Apr.	4	Winnipeg	7	at	Edmonton	5
Apr.	6	Winnipeg	2	at	Edmonton	3 OT
Apr.	8	Edmonton	1	at	Winnipeg	2
Apr.	10	Edmonton	3	at	Winnipeg	4 2OT
Apr.	12	Winnipeg	3	at	Edmonton	4
Apr.	14	Edmonton	4	at	Winnipeg	3
Apr.	16	Winnipeg	1	at	Edmonton	4

Edmonton won best-of-seven series 4–3

DIVISION FINALS

Apr.	19	Montreal	0	at	Boston	1
Apr.	21	Montreal	4	at	Boston	5 OT
Apr.	23	Boston	6	at	Montreal	3
Apr.	25	Boston	1	at	Montreal	4
Apr.	27	Montreal	1	at	Boston	3

Boston won best-of-seven series 4–1

Apr.	19	Washington	3	at	NY Rangers	7

Apr.	21	Washington	6	at	NY Rangers	3
Apr.	23	NY Rangers	1	at	Washington	7
Apr.	25	NY Rangers	3	at	Washington	4 OT
Apr.	27	Washington	2	at	NY Rangers	1 OT

Washington won best-of-seven series 4–1

Apr.	18	St. Louis	4	at	Chicago	3
Apr.	20	St. Louis	3	at	Chicago	5
Apr.	22	Chicago	4	at	St. Louis	5
Apr.	24	Chicago	3	at	St. Louis	2
Apr.	26	St. Louis	2	at	Chicago	3
Apr.	28	Chicago	2	at	St. Louis	4
Apr.	30	St. Louis	2	at	Chicago	8

Chicago won best-of-seven series 4–3

Apr.	18	Los Angeles	0	at	Edmonton	7
Apr.	20	Los Angeles	1	at	Edmonton	6
Apr.	22	Edmonton	5	at	Los Angeles	4
Apr.	24	Edmonton	6	at	Los Angeles	5 OT

Edmonton won best-of-seven series 4–0

CONFERENCE FINALS

May	3	Washington	3	at	Boston	5
May	5	Washington	0	at	Boston	3
May	7	Boston	4	at	Washington	1
May	9	Boston	3	at	Washington	2

Boston won best-of-seven series 4–0

May	2	Chicago	2	at	Edmonton	5
May	4	Chicago	4	at	Edmonton	3
May	6	Edmonton	1	at	Chicago	5
May	8	Edmonton	4	at	Chicago	2
May	10	Chicago	3	at	Edmonton	4
May	12	Edmonton	8	at	Chicago	4

Edmonton won best-of-seven series 4–2

FINALS

May	15	Edmonton	3	at	Boston	2 3OT
May	18	Edmonton	7	at	Boston	2
May	20	Boston	2	at	Edmonton	1
May	22	Boston	1	at	Edmonton	5
May	24	Edmonton	4	at	Boston	1

Edmonton won best-of-seven series 4–1

1989-90 – Edmonton Oilers – Kevin Lowe, Steve Smith, Jeff Beukeboom, Mark Lamb, Joe Murphy, Glenn Anderson, Mark Messier, Adam Graves, Craig MacTavish, Kelly Buchberger, Jari Kurri, Craig Simpson, Martin Gelinas, Randy Gregg, Charlie Huddy, Geoff Smith, Reijo Ruotsalainen, Craig Muni, Bill Ranford, Dave Brown, Pokey Reddick, Petr Klima, Esa Tikkanen, Grant Fuhr, Peter Pocklington (Owner), Glen Sather (President/General Manager), John Muckler (Coach), Ted Green (Co-Coach), Ron Low (Ass't Coach), Bruce MacGregor (Ass't General Manager), Barry Fraser (Director of Player Personnel), John Blackwell (Director of Operations, AHL), Ace Bailey, Ed Chadwick, Lorne Davis, Harry Howell, Matti Vaisanen and Albert Reeves (Scouts), Bill Tuele (Director of Public Relations), Werner Baum (Controller), Dr. Gordon Cameron (Medical Chief of Staff), Dr. David Reid (Team Physician), Barrie Stafford (Athletic Trainer), Ken Lowe (Athletic Therapist), Stuart Poirier (Massage Therapist), Lyle Kulchisky (Ass't Trainer).

1989

The Calgary Flames won their first Stanley Cup title with a 4–2 series victory over the Montreal Canadiens, who had defeated Calgary for the Stanley Cup in 1986. The Flames wrapped up the series with a 4–2 triumph over the Canadiens in game six, becoming the first visiting team to beat the Canadiens for the Stanley Cup on Montreal Forum ice.

Goaltender Mike Vernon tied an NHL playoff record by registering 16 wins during the postseason, tying the mark Edmonton's Grant Fuhr had set the previous year.

Al MacInnis became the fourth defenseman to win the Conn Smythe Trophy since the award was instituted in 1965. MacInnis joined Serge Savard (1969), Bobby Orr (1970 and 1972) and Larry Robinson (1978). MacInnis led the league in playoff scoring with 31 points (seven goals, 24 assists) and amassed a 17-game consecutive point-scoring streak, equaling the second longest in NHL playoff history and the longest ever by a defensemen.

CONN SMYTHE TROPHY
Al MacInnis - Defense - Calgary Flames

DIVISION SEMIFINALS

Apr.	5	Hartford	2	at	Montreal	6
Apr.	6	Hartford	2	at	Montreal	3
Apr.	8	Montreal	5	at	Hartford	4 OT
Apr.	9	Montreal	4	at	Hartford	3 OT

Montreal won best-of-seven series 4–0

Apr.	5	Buffalo	6	at	Boston	0
Apr.	6	Buffalo	3	at	Boston	5
Apr.	8	Boston	4	at	Buffalo	2
Apr.	9	Boston	3	at	Buffalo	2
Apr.	11	Buffalo	1	at	Boston	4

Boston won best-of-seven series 4–1

Apr.	5	Philadelphia	2	at	Washington	3
Apr.	6	Philadelphia	3	at	Washington	2
Apr.	8	Washington	4	at	Philadelphia	3 OT
Apr.	9	Washington	2	at	Philadelphia	5
Apr.	11	Philadelphia	8	at	Washington	5
Apr.	13	Washington	3	at	Philadelphia	4

Philadelphia won best-of-seven series 4–2

Apr.	5	NY Rangers	1	at	Pittsburgh	3
Apr.	6	NY Rangers	4	at	Pittsburgh	7
Apr.	8	Pittsburgh	5	at	NY Rangers	3
Apr.	9	Pittsburgh	4	at	NY Rangers	3

Pittsburgh won best-of-seven series 4–0

Apr.	5	Chicago	2	at	Detroit	3
Apr.	6	Chicago	5	at	Detroit	4 OT
Apr.	8	Detroit	2	at	Chicago	4
Apr.	9	Detroit	2	at	Chicago	3
Apr.	11	Chicago	4	at	Detroit	6
Apr.	13	Detroit	1	at	Chicago	7

Chicago won best-of-seven series 4–2

Apr.	5	Minnesota	3	at	St. Louis	4 OT
Apr.	6	Minnesota	3	at	St. Louis	4 OT
Apr.	8	St. Louis	5	at	Minnesota	3
Apr.	9	St. Louis	4	at	Minnesota	5
Apr.	11	Minnesota	1	at	St. Louis	6

St. Louis won best-of-seven series 4–1

Apr.	5	Vancouver	4	at	Calgary	3 OT
Apr.	6	Vancouver	2	at	Calgary	5
Apr.	8	Calgary	4	at	Vancouver	0
Apr.	9	Calgary	3	at	Vancouver	5
Apr.	11	Vancouver	0	at	Calgary	4
Apr.	13	Calgary	3	at	Vancouver	6
Apr.	15	Vancouver	3	at	Calgary	4 OT

Calgary won best-of-seven series 4–3

Apr.	5	Edmonton	4	at	Los Angeles	3
Apr.	6	Edmonton	2	at	Los Angeles	5
Apr.	8	Los Angeles	0	at	Edmonton	4
Apr.	9	Los Angeles	3	at	Edmonton	4
Apr.	11	Edmonton	2	at	Los Angeles	4
Apr.	13	Los Angeles	4	at	Edmonton	1
Apr.	15	Edmonton	3	at	Los Angeles	6

Los Angeles won best-of-seven series 4–3

DIVISION FINALS

Apr.	17	Boston	2	at	Montreal	3
Apr.	19	Boston	2	at	Montreal	3 OT
Apr.	21	Montreal	5	at	Boston	4
Apr.	23	Montreal	2	at	Boston	3
Apr.	25	Boston	2	at	Montreal	3

Montreal won best-of-seven series 4–1

Apr.	17	Philadelphia	3	at	Pittsburgh	4
Apr.	19	Philadelphia	4	at	Pittsburgh	2
Apr.	21	Pittsburgh	4	at	Philadelphia	3 OT
Apr.	23	Pittsburgh	1	at	Philadelphia	4
Apr.	25	Philadelphia	7	at	Pittsburgh	10
Apr.	27	Pittsburgh	2	at	Philadelphia	6
Apr.	29	Philadelphia	4	at	Pittsburgh	1

Philadelphia won best-of-seven series 4–3

Apr.	18	Chicago	3	at	St. Louis	1
Apr.	20	Chicago	4	at	St. Louis	5 2OT
Apr.	22	St. Louis	2	at	Chicago	5
Apr.	24	St. Louis	2	at	Chicago	3
Apr.	26	Chicago	4	at	St. Louis	2

Chicago won best-of-seven series 4–1

Apr.	18	Los Angeles	3	at	Calgary	4 OT
Apr.	20	Los Angeles	3	at	Calgary	8
Apr.	22	Calgary	5	at	Los Angeles	2
Apr.	24	Calgary	5	at	Los Angeles	3

Calgary won best-of-seven series 4–0

CONFERENCE FINALS

May	1	Philadelphia	3	at	Montreal	1
May	3	Philadelphia	0	at	Montreal	3
May	5	Montreal	5	at	Philadelphia	1
May	7	Montreal	3	at	Philadelphia	0
May	9	Philadelphia	2	at	Montreal	1 OT
May	11	Montreal	4	at	Philadelphia	2

Montreal won best-of-seven series 4–2

May	2	Chicago	0	at	Calgary	3
May	4	Chicago	4	at	Calgary	2
May	6	Calgary	5	at	Chicago	2
May	8	Calgary	2	at	Chicago	1 OT
May	10	Chicago	1	at	Calgary	3

Calgary won best-of-seven series 4–1

FINALS

May	14	Montreal	2	at	Calgary	3
May	17	Montreal	4	at	Calgary	2
May	19	Calgary	3	at	Montreal	4 2OT
May	21	Calgary	4	at	Montreal	2
May	23	Montreal	2	at	Calgary	3
May	25	Calgary	4	at	Montreal	2

Calgary won best-of-seven series 4–2

1988-89 – Calgary Flames – Mike Vernon, Rick Wamsley, Al MacInnis, Brad McCrimmon, Dana Murzyn, Ric Nattress, Joe Mullen, Lanny McDonald (Co-captain), Gary Roberts, Colin Patterson, Hakan Loob, Theoren Fleury, Jiri Hrdina, Tim Hunter (Ass't. captain), Gary Suter, Mark Hunter, Jim Peplinski (Co-captain), Joe Nieuwendyk, Brian MacLellan, Joel Otto, Jamie Macoun, Doug Gilmour, Rob Ramage. Norman Green, Harley Hotchkiss, Norman Kwong, Sonia Scurfield, B.J. Seaman, D.K. Seaman (Owners), Cliff Fletcher (President and General Manager), Al MacNeil (Ass't General Manager), Al Coates (Ass't to the President), Terry Crisp (Head Coach), Doug Risebrough, Tom Watt (Ass't Coaches), Glenn Hall (Goaltending Consultant), Jim Murray (Trainer), Bob Stewart (Equipment Manager), Al Murray (Ass't Trainer).

1988

The Edmonton Oilers won their fourth Stanley Cup title in five years with a 4–0 series victory over the Boston Bruins, who were making their first appearance in the Stanley Cup finals in 10 years.

For the first time since 1927, a Stanley Cup final game failed to determine a winner. During the fourth game of the series, a power failure at Boston Garden halted play at 16:37 of the second period with the teams tied 3–3. Under NHL bylaws, the match was suspended, to be made up in its entirety only in the event that a seventh and deciding game was necessary.

Thus the series shifted back to Edmonton where the Oilers, still holding a 3–0 series lead,

recorded a 6–3 victory to win the Cup. Wayne Gretzky was selected as the Conn Smythe Trophy winner for the second time in his career, establishing a Stanley Cup final series record of 13 points on three goals and ten assists.

CONN SMYTHE TROPHY
Wayne Gretzky - Center - Edmonton Oilers

DIVISION SEMIFINALS

Apr. 6	Hartford	3	at	Montreal	4
Apr. 7	Hartford	3	at	Montreal	7
Apr. 9	Montreal	4	at	Hartford	3
Apr. 10	Montreal	5	at	Hartford	7
Apr. 12	Hartford	3	at	Montreal	1
Apr. 14	Montreal	2	at	Hartford	1

Montreal won best-of-seven series 4–2

Apr. 6	Buffalo	3	at	Boston	7
Apr. 7	Buffalo	1	at	Boston	4
Apr. 9	Boston	2	at	Buffalo	6
Apr. 10	Boston	5	at	Buffalo	6 OT
Apr. 12	Buffalo	4	at	Boston	5
Apr. 14	Boston	5	at	Buffalo	2

Boston won best-of-seven series 4–2

Apr. 6	New Jersey	3	at	NY Islanders	4 OT
Apr. 7	New Jersey	3	at	NY Islanders	2
Apr. 9	NY Islanders	0	at	New Jersey	3
Apr. 10	NY Islanders	5	at	New Jersey	4 OT
Apr. 12	New Jersey	4	at	NY Islanders	2
Apr. 14	NY Islanders	5	at	New Jersey	6

New Jersey won best-of-seven series 4–2

Apr. 6	Philadelphia	4	at	Washington	2
Apr. 7	Philadelphia	4	at	Washington	5
Apr. 9	Washington	3	at	Philadelphia	4
Apr. 10	Washington	4	at	Philadelphia	5 OT
Apr. 12	Philadelphia	2	at	Washington	5
Apr. 14	Washington	7	at	Philadelphia	2
Apr. 16	Philadelphia	4	at	Washington	5 OT

Washington won best-of-seven series 4–3

Apr. 6	Toronto	6	at	Detroit	2
Apr. 7	Toronto	2	at	Detroit	6
Apr. 9	Detroit	6	at	Toronto	3
Apr. 10	Detroit	8	at	Toronto	0
Apr. 12	Toronto	6	at	Detroit	5 OT
Apr. 14	Detroit	5	at	Toronto	3

Detroit won best-of-seven series 4–2

Apr. 6	Chicago	1	at	St. Louis	5
Apr. 7	Chicago	2	at	St. Louis	3
Apr. 9	St. Louis	3	at	Chicago	6
Apr. 10	St. Louis	6	at	Chicago	5
Apr. 12	Chicago	3	at	St. Louis	5

St. Louis won best-of-seven series 4–1

Apr. 6	Los Angeles	2	at	Calgary	9
Apr. 7	Los Angeles	4	at	Calgary	6
Apr. 9	Calgary	2	at	Los Angeles	5
Apr. 10	Calgary	7	at	Los Angeles	3
Apr. 12	Los Angeles	4	at	Calgary	6

Calgary won best-of-seven series 4–1

Apr. 6	Winnipeg	4	at	Edmonton	7
Apr. 7	Winnipeg	2	at	Edmonton	3
Apr. 9	Edmonton	4	at	Winnipeg	6
Apr. 10	Edmonton	5	at	Winnipeg	3
Apr. 12	Winnipeg	2	at	Edmonton	6

Edmonton won best-of-seven series 4–1

DIVISION FINALS

Apr. 18	Boston	2	at	Montreal	5
Apr. 20	Boston	4	at	Montreal	3
Apr. 22	Montreal	1	at	Boston	3
Apr. 24	Montreal	0	at	Boston	2
Apr. 26	Boston	4	at	Montreal	1

Boston won best-of-seven series 4–1

Apr. 18	New Jersey	1	at	Washington	3
Apr. 20	New Jersey	5	at	Washington	2
Apr. 22	Washington	4	at	New Jersey	10
Apr. 24	Washington	4	at	New Jersey	1
Apr. 26	New Jersey	3	at	Washington	1
Apr. 28	Washington	7	at	New Jersey	2
Apr. 30	New Jersey	3	at	Washington	2

New Jersey won best-of-seven series 4–3

Apr. 19	St. Louis	4	at	Detroit	5
Apr. 21	St. Louis	0	at	Detroit	6
Apr. 23	Detroit	3	at	St. Louis	6
Apr. 25	Detroit	3	at	St. Louis	1
Apr. 27	St. Louis	3	at	Detroit	4

Detroit won best-of-seven series 4–1

Apr. 19	Edmonton	3	at	Calgary	1
Apr. 21	Edmonton	5	at	Calgary	4 OT
Apr. 23	Calgary	2	at	Edmonton	4
Apr. 25	Calgary	4	at	Edmonton	6

Edmonton won best-of-seven series 4–0

CONFERENCE FINALS

May 2	New Jersey	3	at	Boston	5
May 4	New Jersey	3	at	Boston	2 OT
May 6	Boston	6	at	New Jersey	1
May 8	Boston	1	at	New Jersey	3
May 10	New Jersey	1	at	Boston	7
May 12	Boston	3	at	New Jersey	6
May 14	New Jersey	2	at	Boston	6

Boston won best-of-seven series 4–3

May 3	Detroit	1	at	Edmonton	4
May 5	Detroit	3	at	Edmonton	5
May 7	Edmonton	2	at	Detroit	5
May 9	Edmonton	4	at	Detroit	3 OT
May 11	Detroit	4	at	Edmonton	8

Edmonton won best-of-seven series 4–1

FINALS

May 18	Boston	1	at	Edmonton	2
May 20	Boston	2	at	Edmonton	4
May 22	Edmonton	6	at	Boston	3
May 24	Edmonton	3	at	Boston	3 *
May 26	Boston	3	at	Edmonton	6

** Game suspended at 16:37 of second period due to power failure.*

Edmonton won best-of-seven series 4–0

1987-88 – Edmonton Oilers – Keith Acton, Glenn Anderson, Jeff Beukeboom, Geoff Courtnall, Grant Fuhr, Randy Gregg, Wayne Gretzky, Dave Hannan, Charlie Huddy, Mike Krushelnyski, Jari Kurri, Normand Lacombe, Kevin Lowe, Craig MacTavish, Kevin McClelland, Marty McSorley, Mark Messier, Craig Muni, Bill Ranford, Craig Simpson, Steve Smith, Esa Tikkanen, Peter Pocklington (Owner), Glen Sather (General Manager/Coach), John Muckler (Co-Coach), Ted Green (Ass't Coach), Bruce MacGregor (Ass't General Manager), Barry Fraser (Director of Player Personnel), Bill Tuele (Director of Public Relations), Dr. Gordon Cameron (Team Physician), Peter Millar (Athletic Therapist), Barrie Stafford (Trainer), Juergen Mers (Massage Therapist), Lyle Kulchisky (Ass't Trainer).

1987

After a year's absence, the Edmonton Oilers returned to the finals and captured their third Stanley Cup title in four seasons.

Edmonton and Philadelphia carried the championship series to a full seven games for the first time since the Montreal Canadiens — Chicago Blackhawks series in 1971. Philadelphia goaltender Ron Hextall received the Conn Smythe Trophy, joining Roger Crozier (1966 Detroit Red Wings), Glenn Hall (1968 St. Louis Blues) and Reg Leach (1976 Philadelphia Flyers) as the only players on a losing club to be so honored.

CONN SMYTHE TROPHY
Ron Hextall - Goaltender - Philadelphia Flyers

DIVISION SEMIFINALS

Apr. 8	Quebec	2	at	Hartford	3 OT
Apr. 9	Quebec	4	at	Hartford	5
Apr. 11	Hartford	1	at	Quebec	5
Apr. 12	Hartford	1	at	Quebec	4
Apr. 14	Quebec	7	at	Hartford	5
Apr. 16	Hartford	4	at	Quebec	5 OT

Quebec won best-of-seven series 4–2

Apr. 8	Boston	2	at	Montreal	6
Apr. 9	Boston	3	at	Montreal	4 OT
Apr. 11	Montreal	5	at	Boston	4
Apr. 12	Montreal	4	at	Boston	2

Montreal won best-of-seven series 4–0

Apr. 8	NY Rangers	3	at	Philadelphia	0
Apr. 9	NY Rangers	3	at	Philadelphia	8
Apr. 11	Philadelphia	3	at	NY Rangers	0
Apr. 12	Philadelphia	3	at	NY Rangers	6
Apr. 14	NY Rangers	1	at	Philadelphia	3
Apr. 16	Philadelphia	5	at	NY Rangers	0

Philadelphia won best-of-seven series 4–2

Apr. 8	NY Islanders	3	at	Washington	4
Apr. 9	NY Islanders	3	at	Washington	1
Apr. 11	Washington	2	at	NY Islanders	0
Apr. 12	Washington	4	at	NY Islanders	1
Apr. 14	NY Islanders	4	at	Washington	2
Apr. 16	Washington	4	at	NY Islanders	5
Apr. 18	NY Islanders	3	at	Washington	2 4OT

Islanders won best-of-seven series 4–3

Apr. 8	Toronto	1	at	St. Louis	3
Apr. 9	Toronto	3	at	St. Louis	2 OT
Apr. 11	St. Louis	5	at	Toronto	3
Apr. 12	St. Louis	1	at	Toronto	2
Apr. 14	Toronto	2	at	St. Louis	1
Apr. 16	St. Louis	0	at	Toronto	4

Toronto won best-of-seven series 4–2

Apr. 8	Chicago	1	at	Detroit	3
Apr. 9	Chicago	1	at	Detroit	5
Apr. 11	Detroit	4	at	Chicago	3 OT
Apr. 12	Detroit	3	at	Chicago	1

Detroit won best-of-seven series 4–0

Apr. 8	Los Angeles	5	at	Edmonton	2
Apr. 9	Los Angeles	3	at	Edmonton	13
Apr. 11	Edmonton	6	at	Los Angeles	5
Apr. 12	Edmonton	6	at	Los Angeles	3
Apr. 14	Los Angeles	4	at	Edmonton	5

Edmonton won best-of-seven series 4–1

Apr. 8	Winnipeg	4	at	Calgary	2
Apr. 9	Winnipeg	3	at	Calgary	2
Apr. 11	Calgary	3	at	Winnipeg	2 OT
Apr. 12	Calgary	3	at	Winnipeg	4
Apr. 14	Winnipeg	3	at	Calgary	4
Apr. 16	Calgary	1	at	Winnipeg	6

Winnipeg won best-of-seven series 4–2

DIVISION FINALS

Apr. 20	Quebec	7	at	Montreal	5
Apr. 22	Quebec	2	at	Montreal	1
Apr. 24	Montreal	7	at	Quebec	2
Apr. 26	Montreal	3	at	Quebec	2 OT
Apr. 28	Quebec	2	at	Montreal	3
Apr. 30	Montreal	2	at	Quebec	3
May 2	Quebec	3	at	Montreal	5

Montreal won best-of-seven series 4–3

Apr. 20	NY Islanders	2	at	Philadelphia	4
Apr. 22	NY Islanders	2	at	Philadelphia	1
Apr. 24	Philadelphia	4	at	NY Islanders	1
Apr. 26	Philadelphia	6	at	NY Islanders	4
Apr. 28	NY Islanders	2	at	Philadelphia	1
Apr. 30	Philadelphia	2	at	NY Islanders	4
May 2	NY Islanders	1	at	Philadelphia	5

Philadelphia won best-of-seven series 4–3

Apr. 21	Toronto	4	at	Detroit	2
Apr. 23	Toronto	7	at	Detroit	2
Apr. 25	Detroit	4	at	Toronto	2

Apr.	27	Detroit	2	at	Toronto	3 OT
Apr.	29	Toronto	0	at	Detroit	3
May	1	Detroit	4	at	Toronto	2
May	3	Toronto	0	at	Detroit	3

Detroit won best-of-seven series 4–3

Apr.	21	Winnipeg	2	at	Edmonton	3 OT
Apr.	23	Winnipeg	3	at	Edmonton	5
Apr.	25	Edmonton	5	at	Winnipeg	2
Apr.	27	Edmonton	4	at	Winnipeg	2

Edmonton won best-of-seven series 4–0

CONFERENCE FINALS

May	4	Montreal	3	at	Philadelphia	4 OT
May	6	Montreal	5	at	Philadelphia	2
May	8	Philadelphia	4	at	Montreal	3
May	10	Philadelphia	6	at	Montreal	3
May	12	Montreal	5	at	Philadelphia	2
May	14	Philadelphia	4	at	Montreal	3

Philadelphia won best-of-seven series 4–2

May	5	Detroit	3	at	Edmonton	1
May	7	Detroit	1	at	Edmonton	4
May	9	Edmonton	2	at	Detroit	1
May	11	Edmonton	3	at	Detroit	2
May	13	Detroit	3	at	Edmonton	6

Edmonton won best-of-seven series 4–1

FINALS

May	17	Philadelphia	2	at	Edmonton	4
May	20	Philadelphia	2	at	Edmonton	3 OT
May	22	Edmonton	3	at	Philadelphia	5
May	24	Edmonton	4	at	Philadelphia	1
May	26	Philadelphia	4	at	Edmonton	3
May	28	Edmonton	2	at	Philadelphia	3
May	31	Philadelphia	1	at	Edmonton	3

Edmonton won best-of-seven series 4–3

1986-87 – Edmonton Oilers – Glenn Anderson, Jeff Beukeboom, Kelly Buchberger, Paul Coffey, Grant Fuhr, Randy Gregg, Wayne Gretzky, Charlie Huddy, Dave Hunter, Mike Krushelnyski, Jari Kurri, Moe Lemay, Kevin Lowe, Craig MacTavish, Kevin McClelland, Marty McSorley, Mark Messier, Andy Moog, Craig Muni, Kent Nilsson, Jaroslav Pouzar, Reijo Ruotsalainen, Steve Smith, Esa Tikkanen, Peter Pocklington (Owner), Glen Sather (General Manager/Coach), John Muckler (Co-Coach), Ted Green (Ass't. Coach), Ron Low (Ass't. Coach), Bruce MacGregor (Ass't. General Manager), Barry Fraser (Director of Player Personnel), Peter Millar (Athletic Therapist), Barrie Stafford (Trainer), Lyle Kulchisky (Ass't Trainer).

1986

The Montreal Canadiens set a new professional record for championships, winning their 23rd Stanley Cup title. Montreal had been tied with the New York Yankees, who had amassed 22 World Series titles to that point in their history. The series between the Canadiens and the Calgary Flames marked the first All-Canadian final since Montreal and Toronto faced each other in 1967.

Brian Skrudland scored nine seconds into overtime in game two to set a new record for the fastest overtime goal in playoff history, eclipsing the old mark of 11 seconds set by J.P. Parise of the NY Islanders on April 11, 1975.

Twenty-year-old goaltender Patrick Roy became the youngest player to earn the Conn Smythe Trophy in the 22-year history of the award. Roy posted a record-tying 15 playoff wins (15–5) and a 1.92 average in 20 postseason games.

CONN SMYTHE TROPHY
Patrick Roy - Goaltender - Montreal Canadiens

DIVISION SEMIFINALS

Apr.	9	Hartford	3	at	Quebec	2 OT
Apr.	10	Hartford	4	at	Quebec	1
Apr.	12	Quebec	4	at	Hartford	9

Hartford won best-of-five series 3–0

Apr.	9	Boston	1	at	Montreal	3
Apr.	10	Boston	2	at	Montreal	3
Apr.	12	Montreal	4	at	Boston	3

Montreal won best-of-five series 3–0

Apr.	9	NY Rangers	6	at	Philadelphia	2
Apr.	10	NY Rangers	1	at	Philadelphia	2
Apr.	12	Philadelphia	2	at	NY Rangers	5
Apr.	13	Philadelphia	7	at	NY Rangers	1
Apr.	15	NY Rangers	5	at	Philadelphia	2

Rangers won best-of-five series 3–2

Apr.	9	NY Islanders	1	at	Washington	3
Apr.	10	NY Islanders	2	at	Washington	5
Apr.	12	Washington	3	at	NY Islanders	1

Washington won best-of-five series 3–0

Apr.	9	Toronto	5	at	Chicago	3
Apr.	10	Toronto	6	at	Chicago	4
Apr.	12	Chicago	2	at	Toronto	7

Toronto won best-of-five series 3–0

Apr.	9	St. Louis	2	at	Minnesota	1
Apr.	10	St. Louis	2	at	Minnesota	6
Apr.	12	Minnesota	3	at	St. Louis	4
Apr.	13	Minnesota	7	at	St. Louis	4
Apr.	15	St. Louis	6	at	Minnesota	3

St. Louis won best-of-five series 3–2

Apr.	9	Vancouver	3	at	Edmonton	7
Apr.	10	Vancouver	1	at	Edmonton	5
Apr.	12	Edmonton	5	at	Vancouver	1

Edmonton won best-of-five series 3–0

Apr.	9	Winnipeg	1	at	Calgary	5
Apr.	10	Winnipeg	4	at	Calgary	6
Apr.	12	Calgary	4	at	Winnipeg	3 OT

Calgary won best-of-five series 3–0

DIVISION FINALS

Apr.	17	Hartford	4	at	Montreal	1
Apr.	19	Hartford	1	at	Montreal	3
Apr.	21	Montreal	4	at	Hartford	1
Apr.	23	Montreal	1	at	Hartford	2 OT
Apr.	25	Hartford	3	at	Montreal	5
Apr.	27	Montreal	0	at	Hartford	1
Apr.	29	Hartford	1	at	Montreal	2 OT

Montreal won best-of-seven series 4–3

Apr.	17	NY Rangers	4	at	Washington	3 OT
Apr.	19	NY Rangers	1	at	Washington	8
Apr.	21	Washington	6	at	NY Rangers	3
Apr.	23	Washington	5	at	NY Rangers	6 OT
Apr.	25	NY Rangers	4	at	Washington	2
Apr.	27	Washington	1	at	NY Rangers	2

Rangers won best-of-seven series 4–2

Apr.	18	Toronto	1	at	St. Louis	6
Apr.	20	Toronto	3	at	St. Louis	0
Apr.	22	St. Louis	2	at	Toronto	5
Apr.	24	St. Louis	7	at	Toronto	4
Apr.	26	Toronto	3	at	St. Louis	4 OT
Apr.	28	St. Louis	3	at	Toronto	5
Apr.	30	Toronto	1	at	St. Louis	2

St. Louis won best-of-seven series 4–3

Apr.	18	Calgary	4	at	Edmonton	1
Apr.	20	Calgary	5	at	Edmonton	6 OT
Apr.	22	Edmonton	2	at	Calgary	3
Apr.	24	Edmonton	7	at	Calgary	4
Apr.	26	Calgary	4	at	Edmonton	1
Apr.	28	Edmonton	5	at	Calgary	2
Apr.	30	Calgary	3	at	Edmonton	2

Calgary won best-of-seven series 4–3

CONFERENCE FINALS

May	1	NY Rangers	1	at	Montreal	2
May	3	NY Rangers	2	at	Montreal	6
May	5	Montreal	4	at	NY Rangers	3 OT
May	7	Montreal	0	at	NY Rangers	2
May	9	NY Rangers	1	at	Montreal	3

Montreal won best-of-seven series 4–1

May	2	St. Louis	3	at	Calgary	2
May	4	St. Louis	2	at	Calgary	8
May	6	Calgary	5	at	St. Louis	3
May	8	Calgary	2	at	St. Louis	5
May	10	St. Louis	2	at	Calgary	4
May	12	Calgary	5	at	St. Louis	6 OT
May	14	St. Louis	1	at	Calgary	2

Calgary won best-of-seven series 4–3

FINALS

May	16	Montreal	2	at	Calgary	5
May	18	Montreal	3	at	Calgary	2 OT
May	20	Calgary	3	at	Montreal	5
May	22	Calgary	0	at	Montreal	1
May	24	Montreal	4	at	Calgary	3

Montreal won best-of-seven series 4–1

1985-86 – Montreal Canadiens – Bob Gainey, Doug Soetaert, Patrick Roy, Rick Green, David Maley, Ryan Walter, Serge Boisvert, Mario Tremblay, Bobby Smith, Craig Ludwig, Tom Kurvers, Kjell Dahlin, Larry Robinson, Guy Carbonneau, Chris Chelios, Petr Svoboda, Mats Naslund, Lucien DeBlois, Steve Rooney, Gaston Gingras, Mike Lalor, Chris Nilan, John Kordic, Claude Lemieux, Mike McPhee, Brian Skrudland, Stephane Richer, Ronald Corey (President), Serge Savard (General Manager), Jean Perron (Coach), Jacques Laperrière (Ass't. Coach), Jean Béliveau (Vice President), Francois-Xavier Seigneur (Vice President), Fred Steer (Vice President), Jacques Lemaire (Ass't. General Manager), André Boudrias (Ass't. General Manager), Claude Ruel (Scouting), Yves Belanger (Athletic Therapist), Gaetan Lefebvre (Ass't. Athletic Therapist), Eddy Palchak (Trainer), Sylvain Toupin (Ass't. Trainer).

1985

In the 1985 playoffs, Wayne Gretzky set new records for assists (30) and points (47) in one playoff year. Gretzky also tied the modern record shared by Montreal's Jean Beliveau (1956) and Mike Bossy (1982) for most goals in the Stanley Cup Finals with seven in five games. Jari Kurri scored 19 goals in 18 games to tie the record for goals in one playoff year. Kurri also broke teammate Mark Messier's record for most hat tricks in a playoff year with four, including one four-goal game. Paul Coffey, who registered 12 goals and 25 assists in 18 games, shattered the one-year playoff records for goals, assists and points by a defenseman. Coffey broke Boston Bruin Bobby Orr's records for goals (nine in 1970) and assists (19 in 1972), and New York Islander Denis Potvin's record for points (25 in 1981). Edmonton's Grant Fuhr tied New York Islanders' goaltender Billy Smith for most wins, 15, in a playoff year. Fuhr posted a 15–3 record in 18 games. Smith amassed 15 wins in both 1980 and 1982. For the first time in the finals, two penalty shots were awarded in the same series. Both were stopped by Fuhr.

CONN SMYTHE TROPHY
Wayne Gretzky - Center - Edmonton Oilers

DIVISION SEMIFINALS

Apr.	10	Boston	5	at	Montreal	3
Apr.	11	Boston	3	at	Montreal	5
Apr.	13	Montreal	4	at	Boston	2
Apr.	14	Montreal	6	at	Boston	7
Apr.	16	Boston	0	at	Montreal	1

Montreal won best-of-five series 3–2

Apr.	10	Buffalo	2	at	Quebec	5

Apr. 11	Buffalo	2	at	Quebec	3
Apr. 13	Quebec	4	at	Buffalo	6
Apr. 14	Quebec	4	at	Buffalo	7
Apr. 16	Buffalo	5	at	Quebec	6

Quebec won best-of-five series 3–2

Apr. 10	NY Rangers	4	at	Philadelphia	5 OT
Apr. 11	NY Rangers	1	at	Philadelphia	3
Apr. 13	Philadelphia	6	at	NY Rangers	5

Philadelphia won best-of-five series 3–0

Apr. 10	NY Islanders	3	at	Washington	4 OT
Apr. 11	NY Islanders	1	at	Washington	2 2OT
Apr. 13	Washington	1	at	NY Islanders	2
Apr. 14	Washington	4	at	NY Islanders	6
Apr. 16	NY Islanders	2	at	Washington	1

Islanders won best-of-five series 3–2

Apr. 10	Minnesota	3	at	St. Louis	2
Apr. 11	Minnesota	4	at	St. Louis	3
Apr. 13	St. Louis	0	at	Minnesota	2

Minnesota won best-of-five series 3–0

Apr. 10	Detroit	5	at	Chicago	9
Apr. 11	Detroit	1	at	Chicago	6
Apr. 13	Chicago	8	at	Detroit	2

Chicago won best-of-five series 3–0

Apr. 10	Los Angeles	2	at	Edmonton	3 OT
Apr. 11	Los Angeles	2	at	Edmonton	4
Apr. 13	Edmonton	4	at	Los Angeles	3 OT

Edmonton won best-of-five series 3–0

Apr. 10	Calgary	4	at	Winnipeg	5 OT
Apr. 11	Calgary	2	at	Winnipeg	5
Apr. 13	Winnipeg	0	at	Calgary	4
Apr. 14	Winnipeg	5	at	Calgary	3

Winnipeg won best-of-five series 3–1

DIVISION FINALS

Apr. 18	Quebec	2	at	Montreal	1 OT
Apr. 21	Quebec	4	at	Montreal	6
Apr. 23	Montreal	6	at	Quebec	7 OT
Apr. 25	Montreal	3	at	Quebec	1
Apr. 27	Quebec	5	at	Montreal	1
Apr. 30	Montreal	5	at	Quebec	2
May 2	Quebec	3	at	Montreal	2 OT

Quebec won best-of-seven series 4–3

Apr. 18	NY Islanders	0	at	Philadelphia	3
Apr. 21	NY Islanders	2	at	Philadelphia	5
Apr. 23	Philadelphia	5	at	NY Islanders	3
Apr. 25	Philadelphia	2	at	NY Islanders	6
Apr. 28	NY Islanders	0	at	Philadelphia	1

Philadelphia won best-of-seven series 4–1

Apr. 18	Minnesota	8	at	Chicago	5
Apr. 21	Minnesota	2	at	Chicago	6
Apr. 23	Chicago	5	at	Minnesota	3
Apr. 25	Chicago	7	at	Minnesota	6 2OT
Apr. 28	Minnesota	5	at	Chicago	4 OT
Apr. 30	Chicago	6	at	Minnesota	5 OT

Chicago won best-of-seven series 4–2

Apr. 18	Winnipeg	2	at	Edmonton	4
Apr. 20	Winnipeg	2	at	Edmonton	5
Apr. 23	Edmonton	5	at	Winnipeg	4
Apr. 25	Edmonton	8	at	Winnipeg	3

Edmonton won best-of-seven series 4–0

CONFERENCE FINALS

May 5	Philadelphia	1	at	Quebec	2 OT
May 7	Philadelphia	4	at	Quebec	2
May 9	Quebec	2	at	Philadelphia	4
May 12	Quebec	5	at	Philadelphia	3
May 14	Philadelphia	2	at	Quebec	1
May 16	Quebec	0	at	Philadelphia	3

Philadelphia won best-of-seven series 4–2

May 4	Chicago	2	at	Edmonton	11
May 7	Chicago	3	at	Edmonton	7
May 9	Edmonton	2	at	Chicago	5
May 12	Edmonton	6	at	Chicago	8
May 14	Chicago	5	at	Edmonton	10
May 16	Edmonton	8	at	Chicago	2

Edmonton won best-of-seven series 4–2

FINALS

May 21	Edmonton	1	at	Philadelphia	4
May 23	Edmonton	3	at	Philadelphia	1
May 25	Philadelphia	3	at	Edmonton	4
May 28	Philadelphia	3	at	Edmonton	5
May 30	Philadelphia	3	at	Edmonton	8

Edmonton won best-of-seven series 4–1

1984-85 – Edmonton Oilers – Glenn Anderson, Bill Carroll, Paul Coffey, Lee Fogolin, Grant Fuhr, Randy Gregg, Wayne Gretzky, Charlie Huddy, Pat Hughes, Dave Hunter, Don Jackson, Mike Krushelnyski, Jari Kurri, Willy Lindstrom, Kevin Lowe, Dave Lumley, Kevin McClelland, Larry Melnyk, Mark Messier, Andy Moog, Mark Napier, Jaroslav Pouzar, Dave Semenko, Esa Tikkanen, Peter Pocklington (Owner), Glen Sather (General Manager/Coach), John Muckler (Ass't. Coach), Ted Green (Ass't. Coach), Bruce MacGregor (Ass't. General Manager), Barry Fraser (Director of Player Personnel/Chief Scout), Peter Millar (Athletic Therapist), Barrie Stafford, Lyle Kulchisky (Trainers)

1984

The Edmonton Oilers, who joined the NHL in 1979–80 with the Hartford Whalers, Quebec Nordiques and Winnipeg Jets, became the first of the four former World Hockey Association clubs to win the Stanley Cup.

In his first championship game, Oilers' goalie Grant Fuhr posted a shutout to hand the defending champion New York Islanders their first loss in 10 final series games.

Four different Oilers — Kevin McClelland, Glenn Anderson, Mark Messier and Ken Linseman — scored game-winning goals.

Messier won the Conn Smythe Trophy with eight goals and 18 assists for 26 points in 19 games.

CONN SMYTHE TROPHY
Mark Messier - Center - Edmonton Oilers

DIVISION SEMIFINALS

Apr. 4	Montreal	2	at	Boston	1
Apr. 5	Montreal	3	at	Boston	1
Apr. 7	Boston	0	at	Montreal	5

Montreal won best-of-five series 3–0

Apr. 4	Quebec	3	at	Buffalo	2
Apr. 5	Quebec	6	at	Buffalo	2
Apr. 7	Buffalo	1	at	Quebec	4

Quebec won best-of-five series 3–0

Apr. 4	NY Rangers	1	at	NY Islanders	4
Apr. 5	NY Rangers	3	at	NY Islanders	0
Apr. 7	NY Islanders	2	at	NY Rangers	7
Apr. 8	NY Islanders	4	at	NY Rangers	1
Apr. 10	NY Rangers	2	at	NY Islanders	3 OT

Islanders won best-of-five series 3–2

Apr. 4	Philadelphia	2	at	Washington	4
Apr. 5	Philadelphia	2	at	Washington	6
Apr. 7	Washington	5	at	Philadelphia	1

Washington won best-of-five series 3–0

Apr. 4	Chicago	3	at	Minnesota	1
Apr. 5	Chicago	5	at	Minnesota	6
Apr. 7	Minnesota	4	at	Chicago	1
Apr. 8	Minnesota	3	at	Chicago	4
Apr. 10	Chicago	1	at	Minnesota	4

Minnesota won best-of-five series 3–2

Apr. 4	Detroit	2	at	St. Louis	3
Apr. 5	Detroit	5	at	St. Louis	3
Apr. 7	St. Louis	4	at	Detroit	3 2OT
Apr. 8	St. Louis	3	at	Detroit	2 OT

St. Louis won best-of-five series 3–1

Apr. 4	Winnipeg	2	at	Edmonton	9
Apr. 5	Winnipeg	4	at	Edmonton	5 OT
Apr. 7	Edmonton	4	at	Winnipeg	1

Edmonton won best-of-five series 3–0

Apr. 4	Vancouver	3	at	Calgary	5
Apr. 5	Vancouver	2	at	Calgary	4
Apr. 7	Calgary	0	at	Vancouver	7
Apr. 8	Calgary	5	at	Vancouver	1

Calgary won best-of-five series 3–1

DIVISION FINALS

Apr. 12	Montreal	2	at	Quebec	4
Apr. 13	Montreal	4	at	Quebec	1
Apr. 15	Quebec	1	at	Montreal	2
Apr. 16	Quebec	4	at	Montreal	3 OT
Apr. 18	Montreal	4	at	Quebec	0
Apr. 20	Quebec	3	at	Montreal	5

Montreal won best-of-seven series 4–2

Apr. 12	Washington	3	at	NY Islanders	2
Apr. 13	Washington	4	at	NY Islanders	5 OT
Apr. 15	NY Islanders	3	at	Washington	1
Apr. 16	NY Islanders	5	at	Washington	2
Apr. 18	Washington	3	at	NY Islanders	5

Islanders won best-of-seven series 4–1

Apr. 12	St. Louis	1	at	Minnesota	2
Apr. 13	St. Louis	4	at	Minnesota	3 OT
Apr. 15	Minnesota	1	at	St. Louis	3
Apr. 16	Minnesota	3	at	St. Louis	2
Apr. 18	St. Louis	0	at	Minnesota	6
Apr. 20	Minnesota	0	at	St. Louis	4
Apr. 22	St. Louis	3	at	Minnesota	4 OT

Minnesota won best-of-seven series 4–3

Apr. 12	Calgary	2	at	Edmonton	5
Apr. 13	Calgary	6	at	Edmonton	5 OT
Apr. 15	Edmonton	3	at	Calgary	2
Apr. 16	Edmonton	5	at	Calgary	3
Apr. 18	Calgary	5	at	Edmonton	4
Apr. 20	Edmonton	4	at	Calgary	5 OT
Apr. 22	Calgary	4	at	Edmonton	7

Edmonton won best-of-seven series 4–3

CONFERENCE FINALS

Apr. 24	NY Islanders	0	at	Montreal	3
Apr. 26	NY Islanders	2	at	Montreal	4
Apr. 28	Montreal	2	at	NY Islanders	5
May 1	Montreal	1	at	NY Islanders	3
May 3	NY Islanders	3	at	Montreal	1
May 5	Montreal	1	at	NY Islanders	4

Islanders won best-of-seven series 4–2

Apr. 24	Minnesota	1	at	Edmonton	7
Apr. 26	Minnesota	3	at	Edmonton	4
Apr. 28	Edmonton	8	at	Minnesota	5
May 1	Edmonton	3	at	Minnesota	1

Edmonton won best-of-seven series 4–0

FINALS

May 10	Edmonton	1	at	NY Islanders	0
May 12	Edmonton	1	at	NY Islanders	6
May 15	NY Islanders	2	at	Edmonton	7
May 17	NY Islanders	2	at	Edmonton	7
May 19	NY Islanders	2	at	Edmonton	5

Edmonton won best-of-seven series 4–1

1983-84 – Edmonton Oilers – Glenn Anderson, Paul Coffey, Pat Conacher, Lee Fogolin, Grant Fuhr, Randy Gregg, Wayne Gretzky, Charlie Huddy, Pat Hughes, Dave Hunter, Don Jackson, Jari Kurri, Willy Lindstrom, Ken Linseman, Kevin Lowe, Dave Lumley, Kevin McClelland, Mark Messier, Andy Moog, Jaroslav Pouzar, Dave Semenko, Peter Pocklington (Owner), Glen Sather (General Manager/Coach), John Muckler (Ass't. Coach), Ted Green (Ass't. Coach), Bruce MacGregor (Ass't. General Manager), Barry Fraser (Director of Player Personnel/Chief Scout), Peter Millar (Athletic Therapist), Barrie Stafford (Trainer)

1983

The New York Islanders won their fourth straight Stanley Cup title to become only the second NHL franchise in history to amass that many championships in a row. The Montreal Canadiens own the all-time record with five consecutive Cup wins from 1956 to 1960. The Canadiens also won four in a row between 1976 and 1979.

Goaltender Billy Smith won the Conn Smythe Trophy after limiting the Edmonton Oilers to just six goals in four games and shutting out the Campbell Conference champions in seven of 12 periods of play.

In his first appearance in the finals, Wayne Gretzky tallied four assists on the Oilers' six goals.

CONN SMYTHE TROPHY
Billy Smith - Goaltender - New York Islanders

DIVISION SEMIFINALS

Apr.	5	Quebec	3	at	Boston	4 OT
Apr.	7	Quebec	2	at	Boston	4
Apr.	9	Boston	1	at	Quebec	2
Apr.	10	Boston	2	at	Quebec	1

Boston won best-of-five series 3–1

Apr.	6	Buffalo	1	at	Montreal	0
Apr.	7	Buffalo	3	at	Montreal	0
Apr.	9	Montreal	2	at	Buffalo	4

Buffalo won best-of-five series 3–0

Apr.	5	NY Rangers	5	at	Philadelphia	3
Apr.	7	NY Rangers	4	at	Philadelphia	3
Apr.	9	Philadelphia	3	at	NY Rangers	9

Rangers won best-of-five series 3–0

Apr.	6	Washington	2	at	NY Islanders	5
Apr.	7	Washington	4	at	NY Islanders	2
Apr.	9	NY Islanders	6	at	Washington	2
Apr.	10	NY Islanders	6	at	Washington	3

Islanders won best-of-five series 3–1

Apr.	6	St. Louis	4	at	Chicago	2
Apr.	7	St. Louis	2	at	Chicago	7
Apr.	9	Chicago	2	at	St. Louis	1
Apr.	10	Chicago	5	at	St. Louis	3

Chicago won best-of-five series 3–1

Apr.	6	Toronto	4	at	Minnesota	5
Apr.	7	Toronto	4	at	Minnesota	5 OT
Apr.	9	Minnesota	3	at	Toronto	6
Apr.	10	Minnesota	5	at	Toronto	4 OT

Minnesota won best-of-five series 3–1

Apr.	6	Winnipeg	3	at	Edmonton	6
Apr.	7	Winnipeg	3	at	Edmonton	4
Apr.	9	Edmonton	4	at	Winnipeg	3

Edmonton won best-of-five series 3–0

Apr.	6	Vancouver	3	at	Calgary	4 OT
Apr.	7	Vancouver	3	at	Calgary	5
Apr.	9	Calgary	4	at	Vancouver	5
Apr.	10	Calgary	4	at	Vancouver	3 OT

Calgary won best-of-five series 3–1

DIVISION FINALS

Apr.	14	Buffalo	7	at	Boston	4
Apr.	15	Buffalo	3	at	Boston	5
Apr.	17	Boston	3	at	Buffalo	4
Apr.	18	Boston	6	at	Buffalo	2
Apr.	20	Buffalo	0	at	Boston	9
Apr.	22	Boston	3	at	Buffalo	5
Apr.	24	Buffalo	2	at	Boston	3 OT

Boston won best-of-seven series 4–3

Apr.	14	NY Rangers	1	at	NY Islanders	4
Apr.	15	NY Rangers	0	at	NY Islanders	5
Apr.	17	NY Islanders	6	at	NY Rangers	7
Apr.	18	NY Islanders	1	at	NY Rangers	3
Apr.	20	NY Rangers	2	at	NY Islanders	7
Apr.	22	NY Islanders	5	at	NY Rangers	2

Islanders won best-of-seven series 4–2

Apr.	14	Minnesota	2	at	Chicago	5
Apr.	15	Minnesota	4	at	Chicago	7
Apr.	17	Chicago	1	at	Minnesota	5
Apr.	18	Chicago	4	at	Minnesota	3 OT
Apr.	20	Minnesota	2	at	Chicago	5

Chicago won best-of-seven series 4–1

Apr.	14	Calgary	3	at	Edmonton	6
Apr.	15	Calgary	1	at	Edmonton	5
Apr.	17	Edmonton	10	at	Calgary	2
Apr.	18	Edmonton	5	at	Calgary	6
Apr.	20	Calgary	1	at	Edmonton	9

Edmonton won best-of-seven series 4–1

CONFERENCE FINALS

Apr.	26	NY Islanders	5	at	Boston	2
Apr.	28	NY Islanders	1	at	Boston	4
Apr.	30	Boston	3	at	NY Islanders	7
May	3	Boston	3	at	NY Islanders	8
May	5	NY Islanders	1	at	Boston	5
May	7	Boston	4	at	NY Islanders	8

Islanders won best-of-seven series 4–2

Apr.	24	Chicago	4	at	Edmonton	8
Apr.	26	Chicago	2	at	Edmonton	8
May	1	Edmonton	3	at	Chicago	2
May	3	Edmonton	6	at	Chicago	3

Edmonton won best-of-seven series 4–0

FINALS

May	10	NY Islanders	2	at	Edmonton	0
May	12	NY Islanders	6	at	Edmonton	3
May	14	Edmonton	1	at	NY Islanders	5
May	17	Edmonton	2	at	NY Islanders	4

Islanders won best-of-seven series 4–0

1982-83 – New York Islanders – Mike Bossy, Bob Bourne, Paul Boutilier, Billy Carroll, Greg Gilbert, Clark Gillies, Butch Goring, Mats Hallin, Tomas Jonsson, Anders Kallur, Gord Lane, Dave Langevin, Mike McEwen, Rollie Melanson, Wayne Merrick, Ken Morrow, Bob Nystrom, Stefan Persson, Denis Potvin, Billy Smith, Brent Sutter, Duane Sutter, John Tonelli, Bryan Trottier, Al Arbour (coach), Lorne Henning (ass't coach), Bill Torrey (general manager), Ron Waske, Jim Pickard (trainers)

1982

The Islanders distinguished themselves as the first U.S.-based team in history to win three consecutive Stanley Cup championships with a sweep of the Vancouver Canucks.

The Canucks, meanwhile, became the first Vancouver team since the 1924 Maroons of the Western Canada Hockey League to appear in the Stanley Cup finals.

Mike Bossy won the Conn Smythe Trophy after scoring seven goals in the four-game series, tying the modern record for most goals in the finals set by Jean Beliveau in 1956.

Bryan Trottier tallied 32 playoff assists in 19 games to set a new record, while goalie Billy Smith amassed a 15–4–0 mark to equal his own record for playoff wins.

CONN SMYTHE TROPHY
Mike Bossy - Right Wing - New York Islanders

DIVISION SEMIFINALS

Apr.	7	Quebec	1	at	Montreal	5
Apr.	8	Quebec	3	at	Montreal	2
Apr.	10	Montreal	1	at	Quebec	2
Apr.	11	Montreal	6	at	Quebec	2
Apr.	13	Quebec	3	at	Montreal	2 OT

Quebec won best-of-five series 3–2

Apr.	7	Buffalo	1	at	Boston	3
Apr.	8	Buffalo	3	at	Boston	7
Apr.	10	Boston	2	at	Buffalo	5
Apr.	11	Boston	5	at	Buffalo	2

Boston won best-of-five series 3–1

Apr.	7	Chicago	3	at	Minnesota	2 OT
Apr.	8	Chicago	5	at	Minnesota	3
Apr.	10	Minnesota	7	at	Chicago	1
Apr.	11	Minnesota	2	at	Chicago	5

Chicago won best-of-five series 3–1

Apr.	7	St. Louis	4	at	Winnipeg	3
Apr.	8	St. Louis	2	at	Winnipeg	5
Apr.	10	Winnipeg	3	at	St. Louis	6
Apr.	11	Winnipeg	2	at	St. Louis	8

St. Louis won best-of-five series 3–1

Apr.	7	Pittsburgh	1	at	NY Islanders	8
Apr.	8	Pittsburgh	2	at	NY Islanders	7
Apr.	10	NY Islanders	1	at	Pittsburgh	2 OT
Apr.	11	NY Islanders	2	at	Pittsburgh	5
Apr.	13	Pittsburgh	3	at	NY Islanders	4 OT

Islanders won best-of-five series 3–2

Apr.	7	Philadelphia	4	at	NY Rangers	1
Apr.	8	Philadelphia	3	at	NY Rangers	7
Apr.	10	NY Rangers	4	at	Philadelphia	3
Apr.	11	NY Rangers	7	at	Philadelphia	5

Rangers won best-of-five series 3–1

Apr.	7	Los Angeles	10	at	Edmonton	8
Apr.	8	Los Angeles	2	at	Edmonton	3 OT
Apr.	10	Edmonton	5	at	Los Angeles	6 OT
Apr.	12	Edmonton	3	at	Los Angeles	2
Apr.	13	Los Angeles	7	at	Edmonton	4

Los Angeles won best-of-five series 3–2

Apr.	7	Calgary	3	at	Vancouver	5
Apr.	8	Calgary	1	at	Vancouver	2 OT
Apr.	10	Vancouver	3	at	Calgary	1

Vancouver won best-of-five series 3–0

DIVISION FINALS

Apr.	15	Quebec	3	at	Boston	4
Apr.	16	Quebec	4	at	Boston	8
Apr.	18	Boston	2	at	Quebec	3 OT
Apr.	19	Boston	2	at	Quebec	7
Apr.	21	Quebec	4	at	Boston	3
Apr.	23	Boston	6	at	Quebec	5 OT
Apr.	25	Quebec	2	at	Boston	1

Quebec won best-of-seven series 4–3

Apr.	15	Chicago	5	at	St. Louis	4
Apr.	16	Chicago	1	at	St. Louis	3
Apr.	18	St. Louis	5	at	Chicago	6
Apr.	19	St. Louis	4	at	Chicago	7
Apr.	21	Chicago	2	at	St. Louis	3 OT
Apr.	23	St. Louis	0	at	Chicago	2

Chicago won best-of-seven series 4–2

Apr.	15	NY Rangers	5	at	NY Islanders	4
Apr.	16	NY Rangers	2	at	NY Islanders	7
Apr.	18	NY Islanders	4	at	NY Rangers	3 OT
Apr.	19	NY Islanders	5	at	NY Rangers	3
Apr.	21	NY Rangers	4	at	NY Islanders	2
Apr.	23	NY Islanders	5	at	NY Rangers	3

Islanders won best-of-seven series 4–2

Apr.	15	Los Angeles	2	at	Vancouver	3
Apr.	16	Los Angeles	3	at	Vancouver	2 OT
Apr.	18	Vancouver	4	at	Los Angeles	3 OT
Apr.	19	Vancouver	5	at	Los Angeles	4
Apr.	21	Los Angeles	2	at	Vancouver	5

Vancouver won best-of-seven series 4–1

CONFERENCE FINALS

Apr.	27	Quebec	1	at	NY Islanders	4
Apr.	29	Quebec	2	at	NY Islanders	5
May	1	NY Islanders	5	at	Quebec	4 OT
May	4	NY Islanders	4	at	Quebec	2

Islanders won best-of-seven series 4–0

Apr.	27	Vancouver	2	at	Chicago	1 2OT
Apr.	29	Vancouver	1	at	Chicago	4
May	1	Chicago	3	at	Vancouver	4

May 4	Chicago	3	at	Vancouver	5
May 6	Vancouver	6	at	Chicago	2

Vancouver won best-of-seven series 4–1

FINALS

May 8	Vancouver	5	at	NY Islanders	6 OT
May 11	Vancouver	4	at	NY Islanders	6
May 13	NY Islanders	3	at	Vancouver	0
May 16	NY Islanders	3	at	Vancouver	1

Islanders won best-of-seven series 4–0

1981-82 – New York Islanders – Mike Bossy, Bob Bourne, Billy Carroll, Butch Goring, Greg Gilbert, Clark Gillies, Tomas Jonsson, Anders Kallur, Gord Lane, Dave Langevin, Hector Marini, Mike McEwen, Rollie Melanson, Wayne Merrick, Ken Morrow, Bob Nystrom, Stefan Persson, Denis Potvin, Billy Smith, Brent Sutter, Duane Sutter, John Tonelli, Bryan Trottier, Al Arbour (coach), Lorne Henning (ass't coach), Bill Torrey (general manager), Jim Devellano (ass't. general manager/dir. of scouting), Ron Waske, Jim Pickard (trainers)

1981

The New York Islanders captured a second consecutive Stanley Cup championship, needing five games to defeat the Minnesota North Stars. For Minnesota, it marked the club's first trip to the finals since joining the NHL in 1967–68.

With 17 goals and 18 assists, New York's Mike Bossy shattered playoff records for points (35) and power-play goals (nine) in his 18 postseason outings.

Dino Ciccarelli of Minnesota broke Don Maloney's rookie scoring record with 21 playoff points and Steve Christoff's rookie mark for playoff goals with 14.

CONN SMYTHE TROPHY
Butch Goring - Center - New York Islanders

PRELIMINARY ROUND

Apr. 8	Toronto	2	at	NY Islanders	9
Apr. 9	Toronto	1	at	NY Islanders	5
Apr. 11	NY Islanders	6	at	Toronto	1

Islanders won best-of-five series 3–0

Apr. 8	Pittsburgh	2	at	St. Louis	4
Apr. 9	Pittsburgh	6	at	St. Louis	4
Apr. 11	St. Louis	5	at	Pittsburgh	4
Apr. 12	St. Louis	3	at	Pittsburgh	6
Apr. 14	Pittsburgh	3	at	St. Louis	4 2OT

St. Louis won best-of-five series 3–2

Apr. 8	Edmonton	6	at	Montreal	3
Apr. 9	Edmonton	3	at	Montreal	1
Apr. 11	Montreal	2	at	Edmonton	6

Edmonton won best-of-five series 3–0

Apr. 8	NY Rangers	3	at	Los Angeles	1
Apr. 9	NY Rangers	4	at	Los Angeles	5
Apr. 11	Los Angeles	3	at	NY Rangers	10
Apr. 12	Los Angeles	3	at	NY Rangers	6

Rangers won best-of-five series 3–1

Apr. 8	Vancouver	2	at	Buffalo	3 OT
Apr. 9	Vancouver	2	at	Buffalo	5
Apr. 11	Buffalo	5	at	Vancouver	3

Buffalo won best-of-five series 3–0

Apr. 8	Quebec	4	at	Philadelphia	6
Apr. 9	Quebec	5	at	Philadelphia	8
Apr. 11	Philadelphia	0	at	Quebec	2
Apr. 12	Philadelphia	3	at	Quebec	4 OT
Apr. 14	Quebec	2	at	Philadelphia	5

Philadelphia won best-of-five series 3–2

Apr. 8	Chicago	3	at	Calgary	4
Apr. 9	Chicago	2	at	Calgary	6
Apr. 11	Calgary	5	at	Chicago	4 2OT

Calgary won best-of-five series 3–0

Apr. 8	Minnesota	5	at	Boston	4 OT
Apr. 9	Minnesota	9	at	Boston	6
Apr. 11	Boston	3	at	Minnesota	6

Minnesota won best-of-five series 3–0

QUARTERFINALS

Apr. 16	Edmonton	2	at	NY Islanders	8
Apr. 17	Edmonton	3	at	NY Islanders	6
Apr. 19	NY Islanders	2	at	Edmonton	5
Apr. 20	NY Islanders	5	at	Edmonton	4 OT
Apr. 22	Edmonton	4	at	NY Islanders	3
Apr. 24	NY Islanders	5	at	Edmonton	2

Islanders won best-of-seven series 4–2

Apr. 16	NY Rangers	3	at	St. Louis	6
Apr. 17	NY Rangers	6	at	St. Louis	4
Apr. 19	St. Louis	3	at	NY Rangers	6
Apr. 20	St. Louis	1	at	NY Rangers	4
Apr. 22	NY Rangers	3	at	St. Louis	4
Apr. 24	St. Louis	4	at	NY Rangers	7

Rangers won best-of-seven series 4–2

Apr. 16	Minnesota	4	at	Buffalo	3 OT
Apr. 17	Minnesota	5	at	Buffalo	2
Apr. 19	Buffalo	4	at	Minnesota	6
Apr. 20	Buffalo	5	at	Minnesota	4 OT
Apr. 22	Minnesota	4	at	Buffalo	3

Minnesota won best-of-seven series 4–1

Apr. 16	Calgary	0	at	Philadelphia	4
Apr. 17	Calgary	5	at	Philadelphia	4
Apr. 19	Philadelphia	1	at	Calgary	2
Apr. 20	Philadelphia	4	at	Calgary	5
Apr. 22	Calgary	4	at	Philadelphia	9
Apr. 24	Philadelphia	3	at	Calgary	2
Apr. 26	Calgary	4	at	Philadelphia	1

Calgary won best-of-seven series 4–3

SEMIFINALS

Apr. 28	NY Rangers	2	at	NY Islanders	5
Apr. 30	NY Rangers	3	at	NY Islanders	7
May 2	NY Islanders	5	at	NY Rangers	1
May 5	NY Islanders	5	at	NY Rangers	2

Islanders won best-of-seven series 4–0

Apr. 28	Minnesota	4	at	Calgary	1
Apr. 30	Minnesota	2	at	Calgary	3
May 3	Calgary	4	at	Minnesota	6
May 5	Calgary	4	at	Minnesota	7
May 7	Minnesota	1	at	Calgary	3
May 9	Calgary	3	at	Minnesota	5

Minnesota won best-of-seven series 4–2

FINALS

May 12	Minnesota	3	at	NY Islanders	6
May 14	Minnesota	3	at	NY Islanders	6
May 17	NY Islanders	7	at	Minnesota	5
May 19	NY Islanders	2	at	Minnesota	4
May 21	Minnesota	1	at	NY Islanders	5

Islanders won best-of-seven series 4–1

1980-81 – New York Islanders – Denis Potvin, Mike McEwen, Ken Morrow, Gord Lane, Bob Lorimer, Stefan Persson, Dave Langevin, Mike Bossy, Bryan Trottier, Butch Goring, Wayne Merrick, Clark Gillies, John Tonelli, Bob Nystrom, Bill Carroll, Bob Bourne, Hector Marini, Anders Kallur, Duane Sutter, Garry Howatt, Lorne Henning, Billy Smith, Rollie Melanson, Al Arbour (coach), Bill Torrey (general manager), Jim Devellano (chief scout), Ron Waske, Jim Pickard (trainers).

1980

In their eighth NHL season, the New York Islanders became the second expansion team to win the Stanley Cup. Two players, Billy Smith and Bob Nystrom, had been with the team since its inception in 1972.

In game one, Denis Potvin recorded the first power-play goal ever scored in overtime in Stanley Cup history. The Flyers' Jimmy Watson went off at the 2:08 mark, and Potvin scored 1:59 later to end the game and give the Islanders their first win in the finals. Nystrom also scored an overtime goal, the Cup-winner in game six, to raise his career total to four playoff overtime goals. Maurice "Rocket" Richard, who scored six overtime goals in the playoffs, owns the all-time record.

CONN SMYTHE TROPHY
Bryan Trottier - Center - New York Islanders

PRELIMINARY ROUND

Apr. 8	Edmonton	3	at	Philadelphia	4 OT
Apr. 9	Edmonton	1	at	Philadelphia	5
Apr. 11	Philadelphia	3	at	Edmonton	2 2OT

Philadelphia won best-of-five series 3–0

Apr. 8	Vancouver	1	at	Buffalo	2
Apr. 9	Vancouver	0	at	Buffalo	6
Apr. 11	Buffalo	4	at	Vancouver	5
Apr. 12	Buffalo	3	at	Vancouver	1

Buffalo won best-of-five series 3–1

Apr. 8	Hartford	1	at	Montreal	6
Apr. 9	Hartford	4	at	Montreal	8
Apr. 11	Montreal	4	at	Hartford	3 OT

Montreal won best-of-five series 3–0

Apr. 8	Pittsburgh	4	at	Boston	2
Apr. 10	Pittsburgh	1	at	Boston	4
Apr. 12	Boston	1	at	Pittsburgh	4
Apr. 13	Boston	8	at	Pittsburgh	3
Apr. 14	Pittsburgh	2	at	Boston	6

Boston won best-of-five series 3–2

Apr. 8	Los Angeles	1	at	NY Islanders	8
Apr. 9	Los Angeles	6	at	NY Islanders	3
Apr. 11	NY Islanders	4	at	Los Angeles	3 OT
Apr. 12	NY Islanders	6	at	Los Angeles	0

Islanders won best-of-five series 3–1

Apr. 8	Toronto	3	at	Minnesota	6
Apr. 9	Toronto	2	at	Minnesota	7
Apr. 11	Minnesota	4	at	Toronto	3 OT

Minnesota won best-of-five series 3–0

Apr. 8	St. Louis	2	at	Chicago	3 OT
Apr. 9	St. Louis	1	at	Chicago	5
Apr. 11	Chicago	4	at	St. Louis	1

Chicago won best-of-five series 3–0

Apr. 8	Atlanta	1	at	NY Rangers	2 OT
Apr. 9	Atlanta	1	at	NY Rangers	5
Apr. 11	NY Rangers	2	at	Atlanta	4
Apr. 12	NY Rangers	5	at	Atlanta	2

Rangers won best-of-five series 3–1

QUARTERFINALS

Apr. 16	NY Rangers	1	at	Philadelphia	2
Apr. 17	NY Rangers	1	at	Philadelphia	4
Apr. 19	Philadelphia	3	at	NY Rangers	0
Apr. 20	Philadelphia	3	at	NY Rangers	4
Apr. 22	NY Rangers	1	at	Philadelphia	3

Philadelphia won best-of-seven series 4–1

Apr. 16	Chicago	0	at	Buffalo	5
Apr. 17	Chicago	4	at	Buffalo	6
Apr. 19	Buffalo	2	at	Chicago	1
Apr. 20	Buffalo	3	at	Chicago	2

Buffalo won best-of-seven series 4–0

Apr. 16	Minnesota	3	at	Montreal	0
Apr. 17	Minnesota	4	at	Montreal	1
Apr. 19	Montreal	5	at	Minnesota	0
Apr. 20	Montreal	5	at	Minnesota	1
Apr. 22	Minnesota	2	at	Montreal	6
Apr. 24	Montreal	2	at	Minnesota	5
Apr. 27	Minnesota	3	at	Montreal	2

Minnesota won best-of-seven series 4–3

Apr. 16	NY Islanders	2	at	Boston	1 OT
Apr. 17	NY Islanders	5	at	Boston	4 OT
Apr. 19	Boston	3	at	NY Islanders	5

Apr. 21	Boston	4	at	NY Islanders	3 OT
Apr. 22	NY Islanders	4	at	Boston	2

Islanders won best-of-seven series 4–1

SEMIFINALS

Apr. 29	Minnesota	6	at	Philadelphia	5
May 1	Minnesota	0	at	Philadelphia	7
May 4	Philadelphia	5	at	Minnesota	3
May 6	Philadelphia	3	at	Minnesota	2
May 8	Minnesota	3	at	Philadelphia	7

Philadelphia won best-of-seven series 4–1

Apr. 29	NY Islanders	4	at	Buffalo	1
May 1	NY Islanders	2	at	Buffalo	1 2OT
May 3	Buffalo	4	at	NY Islanders	7
May 6	Buffalo	7	at	NY Islanders	4
May 8	NY Islanders	0	at	Buffalo	2
May 10	Buffalo	2	at	NY Islanders	5

Islanders won best-of-seven series 4–2

FINALS

May 13	NY Islanders	4	at	Philadelphia	3 OT
May 15	NY Islanders	3	at	Philadelphia	8
May 17	Philadelphia	2	at	NY Islanders	6
May 19	Philadelphia	2	at	NY Islanders	5
May 22	NY Islanders	3	at	Philadelphia	6
May 24	Philadelphia	4	at	NY Islanders	5 OT

Islanders won best-of-seven series 4–2

1979-80 – New York Islanders – Gord Lane, Jean Potvin, Bob Lorimer, Denis Potvin, Stefan Persson, Ken Morrow, Dave Langevin, Duane Sutter, Garry Howatt, Clark Gillies, Lorne Henning, Wayne Merrick, Bob Bourne, Steve Tambellini, Bryan Trottier, Mike Bossy, Bob Nystrom, John Tonelli, Anders Kallur, Butch Goring, Alex McKendry, Glenn Resch, Billy Smith, Al Arbour (coach), Bill Torrey (general manager), Jim Devellano (chief scout), Ron Waske, Jim Pickard (trainers).

1979

The Montreal Canadiens captured their fourth straight Stanley Cup championship to record the second longest streak of championships in NHL history. Only the Canadiens' five-year stronghold on the Cup from 1956 to 1960 lasted longer.

Montreal's game five series-winning effort also marked the first time since 1968 that the Canadiens won the Cup on home ice. At the conclusion of the series, Jacques Lemaire, Yvan Cournoyer and Ken Dryden retired from the NHL. The trio left the game with a combined total of 24 Cup victories among them. Scotty Bowman, who had amassed his fifth Cup title in seven seasons behind the Canadiens bench, also made his farewell appearance with the team as he joined the Buffalo Sabres the following season.

CONN SMYTHE TROPHY
Bob Gainey - Left Wing - Montreal Canadiens

PRELIMINARY ROUND

Apr. 10	Vancouver	3	at	Philadelphia	2
Apr. 12	Philadelphia	6	at	Vancouver	4
Apr. 14	Vancouver	2	at	Philadelphia	7

Philadelphia won best-of-three series 2–1

Apr. 10	Los Angeles	1	at	NY Rangers	7
Apr. 12	NY Rangers	2	at	Los Angeles	1 OT

Rangers won best-of-three series 2–0

Apr. 10	Toronto	2	at	Atlanta	1
Apr. 12	Atlanta	4	at	Toronto	7

Toronto won best-of-three series 2–0

Apr. 10	Pittsburgh	4	at	Buffalo	3
Apr. 12	Buffalo	3	at	Pittsburgh	1
Apr. 14	Pittsburgh	4	at	Buffalo	3 OT

Pittsburgh won best-of-three series 2–1

QUARTERFINALS

Apr. 16	Chicago	2	at	NY Islanders	6
Apr. 18	Chicago	0	at	NY Islanders	1 OT
Apr. 20	NY Islanders	4	at	Chicago	0
Apr. 22	NY Islanders	3	at	Chicago	1

Islanders won best-of-seven series 4–0

Apr. 16	Toronto	2	at	Montreal	5
Apr. 18	Toronto	1	at	Montreal	5
Apr. 21	Montreal	4	at	Toronto	3 2OT
Apr. 22	Montreal	5	at	Toronto	4 OT

Montreal won best-of-seven series 4–0

Apr. 16	Pittsburgh	2	at	Boston	6
Apr. 18	Pittsburgh	3	at	Boston	4
Apr. 21	Boston	2	at	Pittsburgh	1
Apr. 22	Boston	4	at	Pittsburgh	1

Boston won best-of-seven series 4–0

Apr. 16	NY Rangers	2	at	Philadelphia	3 OT
Apr. 18	NY Rangers	7	at	Philadelphia	1
Apr. 20	Philadelphia	1	at	NY Rangers	5
Apr. 22	Philadelphia	0	at	NY Rangers	6
Apr. 24	NY Rangers	8	at	Philadelphia	3

Rangers won best-of-seven series 4–1

SEMIFINALS

Apr. 26	NY Rangers	4	at	NY Islanders	1
Apr. 28	NY Rangers	3	at	NY Islanders	4 OT
May 1	NY Islanders	1	at	NY Rangers	3
May 3	NY Islanders	3	at	NY Rangers	2 OT
May 5	NY Rangers	4	at	NY Islanders	3
May 8	NY Islanders	1	at	NY Rangers	2

Rangers won best-of-seven series 4–2

Apr. 26	Boston	2	at	Montreal	4
Apr. 28	Boston	2	at	Montreal	5
May 1	Montreal	1	at	Boston	2
May 3	Montreal	3	at	Boston	4 OT
May 5	Boston	1	at	Montreal	5
May 8	Montreal	2	at	Boston	5
May 10	Boston	4	at	Montreal	5 OT

Montreal won best-of-seven series 4–3

FINALS

May 13	NY Rangers	4	at	Montreal	1
May 15	NY Rangers	2	at	Montreal	6
May 17	Montreal	4	at	NY Rangers	1
May 19	Montreal	4	at	NY Rangers	3 OT
May 21	NY Rangers	1	at	Montreal	4

Montreal won best-of-seven series 4–1

1978-79 – Montreal Canadiens – Ken Dryden, Larry Robinson, Serge Savard, Guy Lapointe, Brian Engblom, Gilles Lupien, Rick Chartraw, Guy Lafleur, Steve Shutt, Jacques Lemaire, Yvan Cournoyer, Réjean Houle, Pierre Mondou, Bob Gainey, Doug Jarvis, Yvon Lambert, Doug Risebrough, Pierre Larouche, Mario Tremblay, Cam Connor, Pat Hughes, Rod Langway, Mark Napier, Michel Larocque, Richard Sévigny, Scotty Bowman (coach), Irving Grundman (managing director), Eddy Palchak, Pierre Meilleur (trainers).

1978

The Montreal Canadiens lost just ten regular-season games in 1977–78 and were favored in the postseason. The Habs needed nine games to reach the finals, where they again met Boston in a rematch of the 1977 series. The Bruins also needed just nine games to advance, winning three overtime games en route to a berth in the final round of the playoffs.

Conn Smythe Trophy winner Larry Robinson led all playoff performers with 17 assists and tied teammate Guy Lafleur (10–11–21) for the overall playoff scoring lead with 21 points. Robinson was one of three Canadiens, including Doug Jarvis and Steve Shutt, to appear in all 95 games during the course of the season.

CONN SMYTHE TROPHY
Larry Robinson - Defense - Montreal Canadiens

PRELIMINARY ROUND

Apr. 11	Colorado	2	at	Philadelphia	3 OT
Apr. 13	Philadelphia	3	at	Colorado	1

Colorado won best-of-three series 2–0

Apr. 11	NY Rangers	1	at	Buffalo	4
Apr. 13	Buffalo	3	at	NY Rangers	4 OT
Apr. 15	NY Rangers	1	at	Buffalo	4

Buffalo won best-of-three series 2–1

Apr. 11	Los Angeles	3	at	Toronto	7
Apr. 13	Toronto	4	at	Los Angeles	0

Toronto won best-of-three series 2–0

Apr. 11	Detroit	5	at	Atlanta	3
Apr. 13	Atlanta	2	at	Detroit	3

Detroit won best-of-three series 2–0

QUARTERFINALS

Apr. 17	Detroit	2	at	Montreal	6
Apr. 19	Detroit	4	at	Montreal	2
Apr. 21	Montreal	4	at	Detroit	2
Apr. 23	Montreal	8	at	Detroit	0
Apr. 25	Detroit	2	at	Montreal	4

Montreal won best-of-seven series 4–1

Apr. 17	Chicago	1	at	Boston	6
Apr. 19	Chicago	3	at	Boston	4 OT
Apr. 21	Boston	4	at	Chicago	3 OT
Apr. 23	Boston	5	at	Chicago	2

Boston won best-of-seven series 4–0

Apr. 17	Toronto	1	at	NY Islanders	4
Apr. 19	Toronto	2	at	NY Islanders	3 OT
Apr. 21	NY Islanders	0	at	Toronto	2
Apr. 23	NY Islanders	1	at	Toronto	3
Apr. 25	Toronto	1	at	NY Islanders	2 OT
Apr. 27	NY Islanders	2	at	Toronto	5
Apr. 29	Toronto	2	at	NY Islanders	1 OT

Toronto won best-of-seven series 4–3

Apr. 17	Buffalo	1	at	Philadelphia	4
Apr. 19	Buffalo	2	at	Philadelphia	3
Apr. 22	Philadelphia	1	at	Buffalo	4
Apr. 23	Philadelphia	4	at	Buffalo	2
Apr. 25	Buffalo	2	at	Philadelphia	4

Philadelphia won best-of-seven series 4–1

SEMIFINALS

May 2	Toronto	3	at	Montreal	5
May 4	Toronto	2	at	Montreal	3
May 6	Montreal	6	at	Toronto	1
May 9	Montreal	2	at	Toronto	0

Montreal won best-of-seven series 4–0

May 2	Philadelphia	2	at	Boston	3 OT
May 4	Philadelphia	5	at	Boston	7
May 7	Boston	1	at	Philadelphia	3
May 9	Boston	4	at	Philadelphia	2
May 11	Philadelphia	3	at	Boston	6

Boston won best-of-seven series 4–1

FINALS

May 13	Boston	1	at	Montreal	4
May 16	Boston	2	at	Montreal	3 OT
May 18	Montreal	0	at	Boston	4
May 21	Montreal	3	at	Boston	4 OT
May 23	Boston	1	at	Montreal	4
May 25	Montreal	4	at	Boston	1

Montreal won best-of-seven series 4–2

1977-78 – Montreal Canadiens – Ken Dryden, Larry Robinson, Serge Savard, Guy Lapointe, Bill Nyrop, Pierre Bouchard, Brian Engblom, Gilles Lupien, Rick Chartraw, Guy Lafleur, Steve Shutt, Jacques Lemaire, Yvan Cournoyer, Réjean Houle, Pierre Mondou, Bob Gainey, Doug Jarvis, Yvon Lambert, Doug Risebrough, Pierre Larouche, Mario Tremblay, Michel Larocque, Murray Wilson, Scotty Bowman (coach), Sam Pollock (general manager), Eddy Palchak, Pierre Meilleur (trainers).

1977

Winning their second consecutive Stanley Cup championship, the Canadiens extended their undefeated streak against Boston in the finals to six straight series.

Jacques Lemaire, who scored three of Montreal's game-winning goals including the Cup-winner in overtime, joined Maurice Richard (3) and Don Raleigh (2) as the only players to record more than one overtime goal in Stanley Cup final series play. Lemaire first scored in overtime against the St. Louis Blues in the 1968 final, and duplicated the feat in the finale of this latest series. In game two, Ken Dryden posted his fourth shutout of the playoffs to tie the record shared by six goaltenders.

Guy Lafleur won the Conn Smythe Trophy with nine goals and 17 assists for 26 points in 14 playoff games.

CONN SMYTHE TROPHY
Guy Lafleur - Right Wing - Montreal Canadiens

PRELIMINARY ROUND

Apr.	5	Chicago	2	at	NY Islanders	5
Apr.	7	Chicago	1	at	NY Islanders	2

Islanders won best-of-three series 2–0

Apr.	5	Minnesota	2	at	Buffalo	4
Apr.	7	Buffalo	7	at	Minnesota	1

Buffalo won best-of-three series 2–0

Apr.	5	Atlanta	2	at	Los Angeles	5
Apr.	7	Los Angeles	2	at	Atlanta	3
Apr.	9	Atlanta	2	at	Los Angeles	4

Los Angeles won best-of-three series 2–1

Apr.	5	Toronto	4	at	Pittsburgh	2
Apr.	7	Pittsburgh	6	at	Toronto	4
Apr.	9	Toronto	5	at	Pittsburgh	2

Toronto won best-of-three series 2–1

QUARTERFINALS

Apr.	11	St. Louis	2	at	Montreal	7
Apr.	13	St. Louis	0	at	Montreal	3
Apr.	16	Montreal	5	at	St. Louis	1
Apr.	17	Montreal	4	at	St. Louis	1

Montreal won best-of-seven series 4–0

Apr.	11	Toronto	3	at	Philadelphia	2
Apr.	13	Toronto	4	at	Philadelphia	1
Apr.	15	Philadelphia	4	at	Toronto	3 OT
Apr.	17	Philadelphia	6	at	Toronto	5 OT
Apr.	19	Toronto	0	at	Philadelphia	2
Apr.	21	Philadelphia	4	at	Toronto	3

Philadelphia won best-of-seven series 4–2

Apr.	11	Los Angeles	3	at	Boston	8
Apr.	13	Los Angeles	2	at	Boston	6
Apr.	15	Boston	7	at	Los Angeles	6
Apr.	17	Boston	4	at	Los Angeles	7
Apr.	19	Los Angeles	3	at	Boston	1
Apr.	21	Boston	4	at	Los Angeles	3

Boston won best-of-seven series 4–2

Apr.	11	Buffalo	2	at	NY Islanders	4
Apr.	13	Buffalo	2	at	NY Islanders	4
Apr.	15	NY Islanders	4	at	Buffalo	3
Apr.	17	NY Islanders	4	at	Buffalo	3

Islanders won best-of-seven series 4–0

SEMIFINALS

Apr.	23	NY Islanders	3	at	Montreal	4
Apr.	26	NY Islanders	0	at	Montreal	3
Apr.	28	Montreal	3	at	NY Islanders	5
Apr.	30	Montreal	4	at	NY Islanders	0
May	3	NY Islanders	4	at	Montreal	3 OT
May	5	Montreal	2	at	NY Islanders	1

Montreal won best-of-seven series 4–2

Apr.	24	Boston	4	at	Philadelphia	3 OT
Apr.	26	Boston	5	at	Philadelphia	4 2OT
Apr.	28	Philadelphia	1	at	Boston	2
May	1	Philadelphia	0	at	Boston	3

Boston won best-of-seven series 4–0

FINALS

May	7	Boston	3	at	Montreal	7
May	10	Boston	0	at	Montreal	3
May	12	Montreal	4	at	Boston	2
May	14	Montreal	2	at	Boston	1 OT

Montreal won best-of-seven series 4–0

1976-77 – Montreal Canadiens – Ken Dryden, Guy Lapointe, Larry Robinson, Serge Savard, Jimmy Roberts, Rick Chartraw, Bill Nyrop, Pierre Bouchard, Brian Engblom, Yvan Cournoyer, Guy Lafleur, Jacques Lemaire, Steve Shutt, Pete Mahovlich, Murray Wilson, Doug Jarvis, Yvon Lambert, Bob Gainey, Doug Risebrough, Mario Tremblay, Rejean Houle, Pierre Mondou, Mike Polich, Michel Larocque, Scotty Bowman (coach), Sam Pollock (general manager), Eddy Palchak, Pierre Meilleur (trainers).

1976

The Montreal Canadiens returned to the Stanley Cup finals after a two-year absence. Guy Lafleur scored his first two goals in the finals and both proved to be game winners as the Canadiens swept Philadelphia to end the Flyers' two-year reign as champions.

Philadelphia's Reggie Leach scored four times in the series to finish the playoffs with the all-time record of 19 postseason goals. Leach became the third player on a Stanley Cup loser to earn the Conn Smythe Trophy.

CONN SMYTHE TROPHY
Reggie Leach - RW - Philadelphia Flyers

PRELIMINARY ROUND

Apr.	6	Buffalo	2	at	St. Louis	5
Apr.	8	St. Louis	2	at	Buffalo	3 OT
Apr.	9	St. Louis	1	at	Buffalo	2 OT

Buffalo won best-of-three series 2–1

Apr.	6	Vancouver	3	at	NY Islanders	5
Apr.	8	NY Islanders	3	at	Vancouver	1

Islanders won best-of-three series 2–0

Apr.	6	Atlanta	2	at	Los Angeles	1
Apr.	8	Los Angeles	1	at	Atlanta	0

Los Angeles won best-of-three series 2–0

Apr.	6	Pittsburgh	1	at	Toronto	4
Apr.	8	Toronto	0	at	Pittsburgh	2
Apr.	9	Pittsburgh	0	at	Toronto	4

Toronto won best-of-three series 2–1

QUARTERFINALS

Apr.	11	Chicago	0	at	Montreal	4
Apr.	13	Chicago	1	at	Montreal	3
Apr.	15	Montreal	2	at	Chicago	1
Apr.	18	Montreal	4	at	Chicago	1

Montreal won best-of-seven series 4–0

Apr.	12	Toronto	1	at	Philadelphia	4
Apr.	13	Toronto	1	at	Philadelphia	3
Apr.	15	Philadelphia	4	at	Toronto	5
Apr.	17	Philadelphia	3	at	Toronto	4
Apr.	20	Toronto	1	at	Philadelphia	7
Apr.	22	Philadelphia	5	at	Toronto	8
Apr.	25	Toronto	3	at	Philadelphia	7

Philadelphia won best-of-seven series 4–3

Apr.	11	Los Angeles	0	at	Boston	4
Apr.	13	Los Angeles	3	at	Boston	2 OT
Apr.	15	Boston	4	at	Los Angeles	6
Apr.	17	Boston	3	at	Los Angeles	0
Apr.	20	Los Angeles	1	at	Boston	7
Apr.	22	Boston	3	at	Los Angeles	4 OT
Apr.	25	Los Angeles	0	at	Boston	3

Boston won best-of-seven series 4–3

Apr.	11	NY Islanders	3	at	Buffalo	5
Apr.	13	NY Islanders	2	at	Buffalo	3 OT
Apr.	15	Buffalo	3	at	NY Islanders	5
Apr.	17	Buffalo	2	at	NY Islanders	4
Apr.	20	NY Islanders	4	at	Buffalo	3
Apr.	22	Buffalo	2	at	NY Islanders	3

Islanders won best-of-seven series 4–2

SEMIFINALS

Apr.	27	NY Islanders	2	at	Montreal	3
Apr.	29	NY Islanders	3	at	Montreal	4
May	1	Montreal	3	at	NY Islanders	2
May	4	Montreal	2	at	NY Islanders	5
May	6	NY Islanders	2	at	Montreal	5

Montreal won best-of-seven series 4–1

Apr.	27	Boston	4	at	Philadelphia	2
Apr.	29	Boston	1	at	Philadelphia	2 OT
May	2	Philadelphia	5	at	Boston	2
May	4	Philadelphia	4	at	Boston	2
May	6	Boston	3	at	Philadelphia	6

Philadelphia won best-of-seven series 4–1

FINALS

May	9	Philadelphia	3	at	Montreal	4
May	11	Philadelphia	1	at	Montreal	2
May	13	Montreal	3	at	Philadelphia	2
May	16	Montreal	5	at	Philadelphia	3

Montreal won best-of-seven series 4–0

1975-76 – Montreal Canadiens – Ken Dryden, Serge Savard, Guy Lapointe, Larry Robinson, Bill Nyrop, Pierre Bouchard, Jimmy Roberts, Guy Lafleur, Steve Shutt, Pete Mahovlich, Yvan Cournoyer, Jacques Lemaire, Yvon Lambert, Bob Gainey, Doug Jarvis, Doug Risebrough, Murray Wilson, Mario Tremblay, Rick Chartraw, Michel Larocque, Scotty Bowman (coach), Sam Pollock (general manager), Eddy Palchak, Pierre Meilleur (trainers).

1975

Two modern-era expansion teams met in the Stanley Cup finals for the time in 1975, as the Philadelphia Flyers defeated the Buffalo Sabres in six games. The Sabres had reached the championship series in just their fifth year in the NHL.

Bernie Parent's netminding highlighted the series as he allowed only 12 goals in six games and clinched the Cup with a shutout for the second straight year, defeating the Buffalo Sabres. Parent became the first player to win the Conn Smythe Trophy in consecutive years and joined Boston's Bobby Orr as the only players to have won the award twice.

CONN SMYTHE TROPHY
Bernie Parent - Goaltender - Philadelphia Flyers

PRELIMINARY ROUND

Apr.	8	Toronto	2	at	Los Angeles	3 OT
Apr.	10	Los Angeles	2	at	Toronto	3 OT
Apr.	11	Toronto	2	at	Los Angeles	1

Toronto won best-of-three series 2–1

Apr.	8	Chicago	2	at	Boston	8
Apr.	10	Boston	3	at	Chicago	4 OT
Apr.	11	Chicago	6	at	Boston	4

Chicago won best-of-three series 2–1

Apr.	8	St. Louis	3	at	Pittsburgh	4
Apr.	10	Pittsburgh	5	at	St. Louis	3

Pittsburgh won best-of-three series 2–0

Apr.	8	NY Islanders	3	at	NY Rangers	2
Apr.	10	NY Rangers	8	at	NY Islanders	3
Apr.	11	NY Islanders	4	at	NY Rangers	3 OT

Islanders won best-of-three series 2–1

QUARTERFINALS

Apr.	13	Toronto	3	at	Philadelphia	6
Apr.	15	Toronto	0	at	Philadelphia	3

Apr.	17	Philadelphia	2	at	Toronto	0
Apr.	19	Philadelphia	4	at	Toronto	3 OT

Philadelphia won best-of-seven series 4–0

Apr.	13	Chicago	1	at	Buffalo	4
Apr.	15	Chicago	1	at	Buffalo	3
Apr.	17	Buffalo	4	at	Chicago	5 OT
Apr.	20	Buffalo	6	at	Chicago	2
Apr.	22	Chicago	1	at	Buffalo	3

Buffalo won best-of-seven series 4–1

Apr.	13	Vancouver	2	at	Montreal	6
Apr.	15	Vancouver	2	at	Montreal	1
Apr.	17	Montreal	4	at	Vancouver	1
Apr.	19	Montreal	4	at	Vancouver	0
Apr.	22	Vancouver	4	at	Montreal	5 OT

Montreal won best-of-seven series 4–1

Apr.	13	NY Islanders	4	at	Pittsburgh	5
Apr.	15	NY Islanders	1	at	Pittsburgh	3
Apr.	17	Pittsburgh	6	at	NY Islanders	4
Apr.	20	Pittsburgh	1	at	NY Islanders	3
Apr.	22	NY Islanders	4	at	Pittsburgh	2
Apr.	24	Pittsburgh	1	at	NY Islanders	4
Apr.	26	NY Islanders	1	at	Pittsburgh	0

Islanders won best-of-seven series 4–3

SEMIFINALS

Apr.	29	NY Islanders	0	at	Philadelphia	4
May	1	NY Islanders	4	at	Philadelphia	5 OT
May	4	Philadelphia	1	at	NY Islanders	0
May	7	Philadelphia	3	at	NY Islanders	4 OT
May	8	NY Islanders	5	at	Philadelphia	1
May	11	Philadelphia	1	at	NY Islanders	2
May	13	NY Islanders	1	at	Philadelphia	4

Philadelphia won best-of-seven series 4–3

Apr.	27	Montreal	5	at	Buffalo	6 OT
Apr.	29	Montreal	2	at	Buffalo	4
May	1	Buffalo	0	at	Montreal	7
May	3	Buffalo	2	at	Montreal	8
May	6	Montreal	4	at	Buffalo	5 OT
May	8	Buffalo	4	at	Montreal	3

Buffalo won best-of-seven series 4–2

FINALS

May	15	Buffalo	1	at	Philadelphia	4
May	18	Buffalo	1	at	Philadelphia	2
May	20	Philadelphia	4	at	Buffalo	5 OT
May	22	Philadelphia	2	at	Buffalo	4
May	25	Buffalo	1	at	Philadelphia	5
May	27	Philadelphia	2	at	Buffalo	0

Philadelphia won best-of-seven series 4–2

1974-75 – Philadelphia Flyers – Bernie Parent, Wayne Stephenson, Ed Van Impe, Tom Bladon, André Dupont, Joe Watson, Jimmy Watson, Ted Harris, Larry Goodenough, Rick MacLeish, Bobby Clarke, Bill Barber, Reggie Leach, Gary Dornhoefer, Ross Lonsberry, Bob Kelly, Terry Crisp, Don Saleski, Dave Schultz, Orest Kindrachuk, Bill Clement, Fred Shero (coach), Keith Allen (general manager), Frank Lewis, Jim McKenzie (trainers).

1974

Owning a 17–0–2 record in their previous 19 outings at home against Philadelphia, Boston was a heavy favorite with home-ice advantage coming into the Stanley Cup finals.

Flyers' captain Bobby Clarke ended his team's drought at the Garden in game two by scoring two goals, the second in sudden-death, and adding one assist to overcome an early 2–0 deficit.

Goaltender Bernie Parent limited the Bruins to three goals in his three remaining wins, including a sixth game shutout as the Flyers became the first expansion team to win the Stanley Cup, after only seven years in the NHL.

Parent earned the Conn Smythe Trophy with a 12–5–0 record and 2.02 average in 17 games

CONN SMYTHE TROPHY
Bernie Parent - Goaltender - Philadelphia Flyers

QUARTERFINALS

Apr.	10	Toronto	0	at	Boston	1
Apr.	11	Toronto	3	at	Boston	6
Apr.	13	Boston	6	at	Toronto	3
Apr.	14	Boston	4	at	Toronto	3 OT

Boston won best-of-seven series 4–0

Apr.	10	NY Rangers	4	at	Montreal	1
Apr.	11	NY Rangers	1	at	Montreal	4
Apr.	13	Montreal	4	at	NY Rangers	2
Apr.	14	Montreal	4	at	NY Rangers	6
Apr.	16	NY Rangers	3	at	Montreal	2 OT
Apr.	18	Montreal	2	at	NY Rangers	5

Rangers won best-of-seven series 4–2

Apr.	9	Atlanta	1	at	Philadelphia	4
Apr.	11	Atlanta	1	at	Philadelphia	5
Apr.	12	Philadelphia	4	at	Atlanta	1
Apr.	14	Philadelphia	4	at	Atlanta	3 OT

Philadelphia won best-of-seven series 4–0

Apr.	10	Los Angeles	1	at	Chicago	3
Apr.	11	Los Angeles	1	at	Chicago	4
Apr.	13	Chicago	1	at	Los Angeles	0
Apr.	14	Chicago	1	at	Los Angeles	5
Apr.	16	Los Angeles	0	at	Chicago	1

Chicago won best-of-seven series 4–1

SEMIFINALS

Apr.	18	Chicago	4	at	Boston	2
Apr.	21	Chicago	6	at	Boston	8
Apr.	23	Boston	3	at	Chicago	4 OT
Apr.	25	Boston	5	at	Chicago	2
Apr.	28	Chicago	2	at	Boston	6
Apr.	30	Boston	4	at	Chicago	2

Boston won best-of-seven series 4–2

Apr.	20	NY Rangers	0	at	Philadelphia	4
Apr.	23	NY Rangers	2	at	Philadelphia	5
Apr.	25	Philadelphia	3	at	NY Rangers	5
Apr.	28	Philadelphia	1	at	NY Rangers	2 OT
Apr.	30	NY Rangers	1	at	Philadelphia	4
May	2	Philadelphia	1	at	NY Rangers	4
May	5	NY Rangers	3	at	Philadelphia	4

Philadelphia won best-of-seven series 4–3

FINALS

May	7	Philadelphia	2	at	Boston	3
May	9	Philadelphia	3	at	Boston	2 OT
May	12	Boston	1	at	Philadelphia	4
May	14	Boston	2	at	Philadelphia	4
May	16	Philadelphia	1	at	Boston	5
May	19	Boston	0	at	Philadelphia	1

Philadelphia won best-of-seven series 4–2

1973-74 – Philadelphia Flyers – Bernie Parent, Ed Van Impe, Tom Bladon, André Dupont, Joe Watson, Jimmy Watson, Barry Ashbee, Bill Barber, Dave Schultz, Don Saleski, Gary Dornhoefer, Terry Crisp, Bobby Clarke, Simon Nolet, Ross Lonsberry, Rick MacLeish, Bill Flett, Orest Kindrachuk, Bill Clement, Bob Kelly, Bruce Cowick, Al MacAdam, Bobby Taylor, Fred Shero (coach), Keith Allen (general manager), Frank Lewis, Jim McKenzie (trainers).

1973

The Canadiens and Black Hawks met in a rematch of the 1971 final. Chicago's Tony Esposito and Montreal's Ken Dryden, teammates in the noted 1972 Summit Series against the Soviet Union prior to the start of the season, now faced each other at opposite ends of the ice. Yvan Cournoyer, who recorded the game-winning goals in the second and sixth contests, closed out the playoffs setting a modern record of 15 tallies en route to winning the Conn Smythe Trophy. Cournoyer (6–6–12) and Jacques Lemaire (3–9–12) both tied Gordie Howe's record for points in the finals, while the latter also set a new record for assists in the finals with nine. Henri Richard became the first player to play for 11 Stanley Cup champions and tied the overall record held by Toe Blake, who played on three and coached eight more before retiring in 1968. After coaching the St. Louis Blues to three successive finals from 1968 to 1970, Montreal's Scotty Bowman earned his first Stanley Cup championship.

CONN SMYTHE TROPHY
Yvan Cournoyer - RW - Montreal Canadiens

QUARTERFINALS

Apr.	4	Buffalo	1	at	Montreal	2
Apr.	5	Buffalo	3	at	Montreal	7
Apr.	7	Montreal	5	at	Buffalo	2
Apr.	8	Montreal	1	at	Buffalo	5
Apr.	10	Buffalo	3	at	Montreal	2 OT
Apr.	12	Montreal	4	at	Buffalo	2

Montreal won best-of-seven series 4–2

Apr.	4	NY Rangers	6	at	Boston	2
Apr.	5	NY Rangers	4	at	Boston	2
Apr.	7	Boston	4	at	NY Rangers	2
Apr.	8	Boston	0	at	NY Rangers	4
Apr.	10	NY Rangers	6	at	Boston	3

Rangers won best-of-seven series 4–1

Apr.	4	St. Louis	1	at	Chicago	7
Apr.	5	St. Louis	0	at	Chicago	1
Apr.	7	Chicago	5	at	St. Louis	2
Apr.	8	Chicago	3	at	St. Louis	5
Apr.	10	St. Louis	1	at	Chicago	6

Chicago won best-of-seven series 4–1

Apr.	4	Minnesota	3	at	Philadelphia	0
Apr.	5	Minnesota	1	at	Philadelphia	4
Apr.	7	Philadelphia	0	at	Minnesota	5
Apr.	8	Philadelphia	3	at	Minnesota	0
Apr.	10	Minnesota	2	at	Philadelphia	3 OT
Apr.	12	Philadelphia	4	at	Minnesota	1

Philadelphia won best-of-seven series 4–2

SEMIFINALS

Apr.	14	Philadelphia	5	at	Montreal	4 OT
Apr.	17	Philadelphia	3	at	Montreal	4 OT
Apr.	19	Montreal	2	at	Philadelphia	1
Apr.	22	Montreal	4	at	Philadelphia	1
Apr.	24	Philadelphia	3	at	Montreal	5

Montreal won best-of-seven series 4–1

Apr.	12	NY Rangers	4	at	Chicago	1
Apr.	15	NY Rangers	4	at	Chicago	5
Apr.	17	Chicago	2	at	NY Rangers	1
Apr.	19	Chicago	3	at	NY Rangers	1
Apr.	24	NY Rangers	1	at	Chicago	4

Chicago won best-of-seven series 4–1

FINALS

Apr.	29	Chicago	3	at	Montreal	8
May	1	Chicago	1	at	Montreal	4
May	3	Montreal	4	at	Chicago	7
May	6	Montreal	4	at	Chicago	0
May	8	Chicago	8	at	Montreal	7
May	10	Montreal	6	at	Chicago	4

Montreal won best-of-seven series 4–2

1972-73 – Montreal Canadiens – Ken Dryden, Guy Lapointe, Serge Savard, Larry Robinson, Jacques Laperrière, Bob Murdoch, Pierre Bouchard, Jimmy Roberts, Yvan Cournoyer, Frank Mahovlich, Jacques Lemaire, Pete Mahovlich, Marc Tardif, Henri Richard, Réjean Houle, Guy Lafleur, Chuck Lefley, Claude Larose, Murray Wilson, Steve Shutt, Michel Plasse, Scotty Bowman (coach), Sam Pollock (general manager), Ed Palchak, Bob Williams (trainers).

1972

After 43 years of waiting, the New York Rangers finally got a chance to avenge their 1929 loss to the Boston Bruins in the Stanley Cup finals. However, history would repeat itself as the Bruins defeated the Rangers in this six-game confrontation.

Bobby Orr, who scored his second Cup-winning goal in three years, became the first two-time winner of the Conn Smythe Trophy. With four goals and four assists in the finals, Orr raised his playoff totals to five goals and 19 assists, breaking Jean Beliveau's assist mark set in 1971.

CONN SMYTHE TROPHY
Bobby Orr - Defense - Boston Bruins

QUARTERFINALS

Apr.	5	Toronto	0	at	Boston	5
Apr.	6	Toronto	4	at	Boston	3 OT
Apr.	8	Boston	2	at	Toronto	0
Apr.	9	Boston	5	at	Toronto	4
Apr.	11	Toronto	2	at	Boston	3

Boston won best-of-seven series 4–1

Apr.	5	Montreal	2	at	NY Rangers	3
Apr.	6	Montreal	2	at	NY Rangers	5
Apr.	8	NY Rangers	1	at	Montreal	2
Apr.	9	NY Rangers	6	at	Montreal	4
Apr.	11	Montreal	2	at	NY Rangers	1
Apr	13	NY Rangers	3	at	Montreal	2

Rangers won best-of-seven series 4–2

Apr.	5	Pittsburgh	1	at	Chicago	3
Apr.	6	Pittsburgh	2	at	Chicago	3
Apr.	8	Chicago	2	at	Pittsburgh	0
Apr.	9	Chicago	6	at	Pittsburgh	5 OT

Chicago won best-of-seven series 4–0

Apr.	5	St. Louis	0	at	Minnesota	3
Apr.	6	St. Louis	5	at	Minnesota	6 OT
Apr.	8	Minnesota	1	at	St. Louis	2
Apr.	9	Minnesota	2	at	St. Louis	3
Apr.	11	St. Louis	3	at	Minnesota	4
Apr.	13	Minnesota	2	at	St. Louis	4
Apr.	16	St. Louis	2	at	Minnesota	1 OT

St. Louis won best-of-seven series 4–2

SEMIFINALS

Apr.	18	St. Louis	1	at	Boston	6
Apr.	20	St. Louis	2	at	Boston	10
Apr.	23	Boston	7	at	St. Louis	2
Apr.	25	Boston	5	at	St. Louis	3

Boston won best-of-seven series 4–0

Apr.	16	NY Rangers	3	at	Chicago	2
Apr.	18	NY Rangers	5	at	Chicago	3
Apr.	20	Chicago	2	at	NY Rangers	3
Apr	23	Chicago	2	at	NY Rangers	6

Rangers won best-of-seven series 4–0

FINALS

Apr.	30	NY Rangers	5	at	Boston	6
May	2	NY Rangers	1	at	Boston	2
May	4	Boston	2	at	NY Rangers	5
May	7	Boston	3	at	NY Rangers	2
May	9	NY Rangers	3	at	Boston	2
May	11	Boston	3	at	NY Rangers	0

Boston won best-of-seven series 4–2

1971-72 – Boston Bruins – Gerry Cheevers, Eddie Johnston, Bobby Orr, Ted Green, Carol Vadnais, Dallas Smith, Don Awrey, Phil Esposito, Ken Hodge, John Bucyk, Mike Walton, Wayne Cashman, Garnet Bailey, Derek Sanderson, Fred Stanfield, Ed Westfall, John McKenzie, Don Marcotte, Garry Peters, Chris Hayes, Tom Johnson (coach), Milt Schmidt (general manager), Dan Canney, John Forristall (trainers).

1971

After missing the playoffs for the first time in 22 years in 1970, the Canadiens rebounded in 1971 to win their 16th Stanley Cup title. Brothers Frank and Peter Mahovlich were reunited in mid-season, and the two responded with a total of nine goals in the seven-game final. Frank also set a modern playoff record with 14 goals and tied Phil Esposito's record 27-point performance of 1970. After Chicago went ahead 2–0 in game seven, Henri Richard scored the tying and winning goals to seal the victory. The hero of the playoffs was rookie goaltender Ken Dryden, who appeared in all 20 postseason games after only six starts during the regular season. Dryden's performance, which included a 12–8 record and 3.00 average, earned him the Conn Smythe Trophy. While the series heralded the beginning of Dryden's career, it also marked the conclusion of Jean Beliveau's playing days. Beliveau, who finished the playoffs with six goals and a record 16 assists, left the sport as the all-time leader in playoff assists (97) and points (176) and temporarily shared first place with Henri Richard in Stanley Cup titles won as a player at 10.

CONN SMYTHE TROPHY
Ken Dryden - Goaltender - Montreal Canadiens

QUARTERFINALS

Apr.	7	Montreal	1	at	Boston	3
Apr.	8	Montreal	7	at	Boston	5
Apr.	10	Boston	1	at	Montreal	3
Apr.	11	Boston	5	at	Montreal	2
Apr.	13	Montreal	3	at	Boston	7
Apr.	15	Boston	3	at	Montreal	8
Apr.	18	Montreal	4	at	Boston	2

Montreal won best-of-seven series 4–3

Apr.	7	Toronto	4	at	NY Rangers	5
Apr.	8	Toronto	4	at	NY Rangers	1
Apr.	10	NY Rangers	1	at	Toronto	3
Apr.	11	NY Rangers	4	at	Toronto	2
Apr.	13	Toronto	1	at	NY Rangers	3
Apr.	15	NY Rangers	2	at	Toronto	1 OT

Rangers won best-of-seven series 4–2

Apr.	7	Philadelphia	2	at	Chicago	5
Apr.	8	Philadelphia	2	at	Chicago	6
Apr.	10	Chicago	3	at	Philadelphia	2
Apr.	11	Chicago	6	at	Philadelphia	2

Chicago won best-of-seven series 4–0

Apr.	7	Minnesota	3	at	St. Louis	2
Apr.	8	Minnesota	2	at	St. Louis	4
Apr.	10	St. Louis	3	at	Minnesota	0
Apr.	11	St. Louis	1	at	Minnesota	2
Apr.	13	Minnesota	4	at	St. Louis	3
Apr.	15	St. Louis	2	at	Minnesota	5

Minnesota won best-of-seven series 4–2

SEMIFINALS

Apr.	20	Minnesota	2	at	Montreal	7
Apr.	22	Minnesota	6	at	Montreal	3
Apr.	24	Montreal	6	at	Minnesota	3
Apr.	25	Montreal	2	at	Minnesota	5
Apr.	27	Minnesota	1	at	Montreal	6
Apr.	29	Montreal	3	at	Minnesota	2

Montreal won best-of-seven series 4–2

Apr.	18	NY Rangers	2	at	Chicago	1 OT
Apr.	20	NY Rangers	0	at	Chicago	3
Apr.	22	Chicago	1	at	NY Rangers	4
Apr.	25	Chicago	7	at	NY Rangers	1
Apr.	27	NY Rangers	2	at	Chicago	3 OT
Apr.	29	Chicago	2	at	NY Rangers	3 3OT
May	2	NY Rangers	2	at	Chicago	4

Chicago won best-of-seven series 4–3

FINALS

May	4	Montreal	1	at	Chicago	2 OT
May	6	Montreal	3	at	Chicago	5
May	9	Chicago	2	at	Montreal	4
May	11	Chicago	2	at	Montreal	5
May	13	Montreal	0	at	Chicago	2
May	16	Chicago	3	at	Montreal	4
May	18	Montreal	3	at	Chicago	2

Montreal won best-of-seven series 4–3

1970-71 – Montreal Canadiens – Ken Dryden, Rogie Vachon, Jacques Laperrière, J.C. Tremblay, Guy Lapointe, Terry Harper, Pierre Bouchard, Jean Béliveau, Marc Tardif, Yvan Cournoyer, Réjean Houle, Claude Larose, Henri Richard, Phil Roberto, Pete Mahovlich, Leon Rochefort, John Ferguson, Bobby Sheehan, Jacques Lemaire, Frank Mahovlich, Bob Murdoch, Chuck Lefley, Al MacNeil (coach), Sam Pollock (general manager), Yvon Belanger, Ed Palchak (trainers).

1970

For the third straight year, the St. Louis Blues qualified for the finals but faced new rivals in the Boston Bruins, who featured the first 100-point defenseman in NHL history in Norris Trophy recipient Bobby Orr.

After winning the first three by margins of five, four and three goals, respectively, the Bruins were extended into overtime in the fourth game. Conn Smythe Trophy winner Orr quickly ended the affair at the 40 second mark of overtime with his first goal of the series. With Orr literally flying through the air on the play, his winning tally has become one of the most memorable images in hockey history.

The series victory marked the Bruins' first Stanley Cup title in 29 years.

CONN SMYTHE TROPHY
Bobby Orr - Defense - Boston Bruins

QUARTERFINALS

Apr.	8	Detroit	2	at	Chicago	4
Apr.	9	Detroit	2	at	Chicago	4
Apr.	11	Chicago	4	at	Detroit	2
Apr.	12	Chicago	4	at	Detroit	2

Chicago won best-of-seven series 4–0

Apr.	8	NY Rangers	2	at	Boston	8
Apr.	9	NY Rangers	3	at	Boston	5
Apr.	11	Boston	3	at	NY Rangers	4
Apr.	12	Boston	2	at	NY Rangers	4
Apr.	14	NY Rangers	2	at	Boston	3
Apr.	16	Boston	4	at	NY Rangers	1

Boston won best-of-seven series 4–2

Apr.	8	Minnesota	2	at	St. Louis	6
Apr.	9	Minnesota	1	at	St. Louis	2
Apr.	11	St. Louis	2	at	Minnesota	4
Apr.	12	St. Louis	0	at	Minnesota	4
Apr.	14	Minnesota	3	at	St. Louis	6
Apr.	16	St. Louis	4	at	Minnesota	2

St. Louis won best-of-seven series 4–2

Apr.	8	Oakland	1	at	Pittsburgh	2
Apr.	9	Oakland	1	at	Pittsburgh	3
Apr.	11	Pittsburgh	5	at	Oakland	2
Apr.	12	Pittsburgh	3	at	Oakland	2 OT

Pittsburgh won best-of-seven series 4–0

SEMIFINALS

Apr.	19	Boston	6	at	Chicago	3
Apr.	21	Boston	4	at	Chicago	1
Apr.	23	Chicago	2	at	Boston	5
Apr.	26	Chicago	4	at	Boston	5

Boston won best-of-seven series 4–0

Apr.	19	Pittsburgh	1	at	St. Louis	3
Apr.	21	Pittsburgh	1	at	St. Louis	4

Apr. 23	St. Louis	2	at	Pittsburgh	3
Apr. 26	St. Louis	1	at	Pittsburgh	2
Apr. 28	Pittsburgh	0	at	St. Louis	5
Apr. 30	St. Louis	4	at	Pittsburgh	3

St. Louis won best-of-seven series 4–2

FINALS

May 3	Boston	6	at	St. Louis	1
May 5	Boston	6	at	St. Louis	2
May 7	St. Louis	1	at	Boston	4
May 10	St. Louis	3	at	Boston	4 OT

Boston won best-of-seven series 4–0

1969-70 – Boston Bruins – Gerry Cheevers, Eddie Johnston, Bobby Orr, Rick Smith, Dallas Smith, Bill Speer, Gary Doak, Don Awrey, Phil Esposito, Ken Hodge, John Bucyk, Wayne Carleton, Wayne Cashman, Derek Sanderson, Fred Stanfield, Ed Westfall, John McKenzie, Jim Lorentz, Don Marcotte, Bill Lesuk, Dan Schock, Harry Sinden (coach), Milt Schmidt (general manager), Dan Canney, John Forristall (trainers).

1969

Following in his predecessor's footsteps, Claude Ruel won the Stanley Cup in his first season behind the Canadiens' bench and became the 11th rookie coach in NHL history to go the distance with his team.

Goaltender Rogie Vachon limited St. Louis to three goals in four outings and registered his first career playoff and Stanley Cup shutout in the third game.

Serge Savard became the first defenseman to win the Conn Smythe Trophy.

CONN SMYTHE TROPHY
Serge Savard - Defense - Montreal Canadiens

QUARTERFINALS

Apr. 2	NY Rangers	1	at	Montreal	3
Apr. 3	NY Rangers	2	at	Montreal	5
Apr. 5	Montreal	4	at	NY Rangers	1
Apr. 6	Montreal	4	at	NY Rangers	3

Montreal won best-of-seven series 4–0

Apr. 2	Toronto	0	at	Boston	10
Apr. 3	Toronto	0	at	Boston	7
Apr. 5	Boston	4	at	Toronto	3
Apr. 6	Boston	3	at	Toronto	2

Boston won best-of-seven series 4–0

Apr. 2	Philadelphia	2	at	St. Louis	5
Apr. 3	Philadelphia	0	at	St. Louis	5
Apr. 5	St. Louis	3	at	Philadelphia	0
Apr. 6	St. Louis	4	at	Philadelphia	1

St. Louis won best-of-seven series 4–0

Apr. 2	Los Angeles	5	at	Oakland	4 OT
Apr. 3	Los Angeles	2	at	Oakland	4
Apr. 5	Oakland	5	at	Los Angeles	2
Apr. 6	Oakland	2	at	Los Angeles	4
Apr. 9	Los Angeles	1	at	Oakland	4
Apr. 10	Oakland	3	at	Los Angeles	4
Apr. 13	Los Angeles	5	at	Oakland	3

Los Angeles won best-of-seven series 4–3

SEMIFINALS

Apr. 10	Boston	2	at	Montreal	3 OT
Apr. 13	Boston	3	at	Montreal	4 OT
Apr. 17	Montreal	0	at	Boston	5
Apr. 20	Montreal	2	at	Boston	3
Apr. 22	Boston	2	at	Montreal	4
Apr. 24	Montreal	2	at	Boston	1 2OT

Montreal won best-of-seven series 4–2

Apr. 15	Los Angeles	0	at	St. Louis	4
Apr. 17	Los Angeles	2	at	St. Louis	3
Apr. 19	St. Louis	5	at	Los Angeles	2
Apr. 20	St. Louis	4	at	Los Angeles	1

St. Louis won best-of-seven series 4–0

FINALS

Apr. 27	St. Louis	1	at	Montreal	3
Apr. 29	St. Louis	1	at	Montreal	3
May 1	Montreal	4	at	St. Louis	0
May 4	Montreal	2	at	St. Louis	1

Montreal won best-of-seven series 4–0

1968-69 – Montreal Canadiens – Gump Worsley, Rogie Vachon, Jacques Laperrière, J.C. Tremblay, Ted Harris, Serge Savard, Terry Harper, Larry Hillman, Jean Béliveau, Ralph Backstrom, Dick Duff, Yvan Cournoyer, Claude Provost, Bobby Rousseau, Henri Richard, John Ferguson, Christian Bordeleau, Mickey Redmond, Jacques Lemaire, Lucien Grenier, Tony Esposito, Claude Ruel (coach), Sam Pollock (general manager), Larry Aubut, Eddy Palchak (trainers).

1968

The NHL doubled in size with the addition of six expansion teams which comprised one of two new divisions. In the playoffs, Montreal won the East Division, and St. Louis won the West to earn a chance at the Stanley Cup. The Blues lineup boasted several aging superstars, including two-time Vezina Trophy winner Glenn Hall, two-time Art Ross Trophy winner Dickie Moore and seven-time Norris Trophy recipient Doug Harvey. The three were no strangers to playoff action with 40 years of postseason experience among them. Rookie defenseman Serge Savard, who would amass seven Stanley Cup rings in his career, scored his first two career playoff goals while shorthanded in games two and three to tie a final series record. Toe Blake retired after capturing his eighth Stanley Cup in 13 years as coach of the Canadiens and set a record as the first person to win a total of 11 Stanley Cup championships in a career. Blake also played on championship teams with the Montreal Maroons in 1935 and the Canadiens in 1944 and 1946.

CONN SMYTHE TROPHY
Glenn Hall - Goaltender - St. Louis Blues

QUARTERFINALS

Apr. 4	Boston	1	at	Montreal	2
Apr. 6	Boston	3	at	Montreal	5
Apr. 9	Montreal	5	at	Boston	2
Apr. 11	Montreal	3	at	Boston	2

Montreal won best-of-seven series 4–0

Apr. 4	Chicago	1	at	NY Rangers	3
Apr. 9	Chicago	1	at	NY Rangers	2
Apr. 11	NY Rangers	4	at	Chicago	7
Apr. 13	NY Rangers	1	at	Chicago	3
Apr. 14	Chicago	2	at	NY Rangers	1
Apr. 16	NY Rangers	1	at	Chicago	4

Chicago won best-of-seven series 4–2

Apr. 4	St. Louis	1	at	Philadelphia	0
Apr. 6	St. Louis	3	at	Philadelphia	4
Apr. 10	Philadelphia	2	at	St. Louis	3 2OT
Apr. 11	Philadelphia	2	at	St. Louis	5
Apr. 13	St. Louis	1	at	Philadelphia	6
Apr. 16	Philadephia	2	at	St. Louis	1 2OT
Apr. 18	St. Louis	3	at	Philadelphia	1

St. Louis won best-of-seven series 4–3

Apr. 4	Minnesota	1	at	Los Angeles	2
Apr. 6	Minnesota	0	at	Los Angeles	2
Apr. 9	Los Angeles	5	at	Minnesota	7
Apr. 11	Los Angeles	2	at	Minnesota	3
Apr. 13	Minnesota	2	at	Los Angeles	3
Apr. 16	Los Angeles	3	at	Minnesota	4 OT
Apr. 18	Minnesota	9	at	Los Angeles	4

Minnesota won best-of-seven series 4–3

SEMIFINALS

Apr. 18	Chicago	2	at	Montreal	9
Apr. 20	Chicago	1	at	Montreal	4
Apr. 23	Montreal	4	at	Chicago	2
Apr. 25	Montreal	1	at	Chicago	2
Apr. 28	Chicago	3	at	Montreal	4 OT

Montreal won best-of-seven series 4–1

Apr. 21	Minnesota	3	at	St. Louis	5
Apr. 22	St. Louis	2	at	Minnesota	3 OT
Apr. 25	Minnesota	5	at	St. Louis	1
Apr. 27	Minnesota	3	at	St. Louis	4 OT
Apr. 29	Minnesota	2	at	St. Louis	3 OT
May 1	St. Louis	1	at	Minnesota	5
May 3	Minnesota	1	at	St. Louis	2 2OT

St. Louis won best-of-seven series 4–3

FINALS

May 5	Montreal	3	at	St. Louis	2 OT
May 7	Montreal	1	at	St. Louis	0
May 9	St. Louis	3	at	Montreal	4 OT
May 11	St. Louis	2	at	Montreal	3

Montreal won best-of-seven series 4–0

1967-68 – Montreal Canadiens – Gump Worsley, Rogie Vachon, Jacques Laperrière, J.C. Tremblay, Ted Harris, Serge Savard, Terry Harper, Carol Vadnais, Jean Béliveau, Gilles Tremblay, Ralph Backstrom, Dick Duff, Claude Larose, Yvan Cournoyer, Claude Provost, Bobby Rousseau, Henri Richard, John Ferguson, Danny Grant, Jacques Lemaire, Mickey Redmond, Toe Blake (coach), Sam Pollock (general manager), Larry Aubut, Eddy Palchak (trainers).

1967

With an average age of 31, the Toronto Maple Leafs sported the oldest lineup ever to win the Stanley Cup. Goaltender Johnny Bower (42) and defenseman Allan Stanley (41) were the senior citizens of the squad, which included seven players over 35 and 12 members over 30.

Dave Keon, a 27-year-old "youngster" who scored a goal and assist in the series, captured the Conn Smythe Trophy on the basis of an outstanding defensive performance.

CONN SMYTHE TROPHY
Dave Keon - Center - Toronto Maple Leafs

SEMIFINALS

Apr. 6	Toronto	2	at	Chicago	5
Apr. 9	Toronto	3	at	Chicago	1
Apr. 11	Chicago	1	at	Toronto	3
Apr. 13	Chicago	4	at	Toronto	3
Apr. 15	Toronto	4	at	Chicago	2
Apr. 18	Chicago	1	at	Toronto	3

Toronto won best-of-seven series 4–2

Apr. 6	NY Rangers	4	at	Montreal	6
Apr. 8	NY Rangers	1	at	Montreal	3
Apr. 11	Montreal	3	at	NY Rangers	2
Apr. 13	Montreal	2	at	NY Rangers	1 OT

Montreal won best-of-seven series 4–0

FINALS

Apr. 20	Toronto	2	at	Montreal	6
Apr. 22	Toronto	3	at	Montreal	0
Apr. 25	Montreal	2	at	Toronto	3 2OT
Apr. 27	Montreal	6	at	Toronto	2
Apr. 29	Toronto	4	at	Montreal	1
May 2	Montreal	1	at	Toronto	3

Toronto won best-of-seven series 4–2

1966-67 – Toronto Maple Leafs – Johnny Bower, Terry Sawchuk, Larry Hillman, Marcel Pronovost, Tim Horton, Bob Baun, Aut Erickson, Allan Stanley, Red Kelly, Ron Ellis, George Armstrong, Pete Stemkowski, Dave Keon, Mike Walton, Jim Pappin, Bob Pulford, Brian Conacher, Eddie Shack, Frank Mahovlich, Milan Marcetta, Larry Jeffrey, Bruce Gamble, Punch Imlach (manager-coach), Bob Haggart (trainer).

1966

The Canadiens repeated as champions to give coach Toe Blake his seventh title in 11 years behind the Montreal bench. Henri Richard, a member of each of those seven Stanley Cup teams, scored the game-winner in overtime in game six, marking the ninth time in history that a series-winning goal had been scored in overtime.

Despite his team's loss in the finals, goaltender Roger Crozier received the Conn Smythe Trophy after posting a 2.17 average and one shutout in 12 playoff games.

CONN SMYTHE TROPHY
Roger Crozier - Goaltender - Detroit Red Wings

SEMIFINALS

Apr.	7	Toronto	3	at	Montreal	4
Apr.	9	Toronto	0	at	Montreal	2
Apr.	12	Montreal	5	at	Toronto	2
Apr.	14	Montreal	4	at	Toronto	1

Toronto won best-of-seven series 4–2

Apr.	7	Detroit	1	at	Chicago	2
Apr.	10	Detroit	7	at	Chicago	0
Apr.	12	Chicago	2	at	Detroit	1
Apr.	14	Chicago	1	at	Detroit	5
Apr.	17	Detroit	5	at	Chicago	3
Apr.	19	Chicago	2	at	Detroit	3

Detroit won best-of-seven series 4–2

FINALS

Apr.	24	Detroit	3	at	Montreal	2
Apr.	26	Detroit	5	at	Montreal	2
Apr.	28	Montreal	4	at	Detroit	2
May	1	Montreal	2	at	Detroit	1
May	3	Detroit	1	at	Montreal	5
May	5	Montreal	3	at	Detroit	2 OT

Montreal won best-of-seven series 4–2

1965-66 – Montreal Canadiens – Gump Worsley, Charlie Hodge, Jean-Claude Tremblay, Ted Harris, Jean-Guy Talbot, Terry Harper, Jacques Laperrière, Noel Price, Jean Béliveau, Ralph Backstrom, Dick Duff, Gilles Tremblay, Claude Larose, Yvan Cournoyer, Claude Provost, Bobby Rousseau, Henri Richard, Dave Balon, John Ferguson, Leon Rochefort, Jim Roberts, Toe Blake (coach), Sam Pollock (general manager), Larry Aubut, Andy Galley (trainers).

1965

Repeating the feat accomplished in 1955, the home team won every game in the finals. With the extra game at the Montreal Forum, the Canadiens treated their fans to four victories.

Lorne "Gump" Worsley, appearing in his first Stanley Cup series after 12 seasons in the NHL, recorded two shutouts in four starts, including one in game seven.

Jean Beliveau captured the inaugural Conn Smythe Trophy as the most valuable player for his team in the playoffs after amassing eight goals and eight assists in 13 games.

CONN SMYTHE TROPHY
Jean Beliveau - Center - Montreal Canadiens

SEMIFINALS

Apr.	1	Chicago	3	at	Detroit	4
Apr.	4	Chicago	3	at	Detroit	6
Apr.	6	Detroit	2	at	Chicago	5
Apr.	8	Detroit	1	at	Chicago	2
Apr.	11	Chicago	2	at	Detroit	4
Apr.	13	Detroit	0	at	Chicago	4
Apr.	15	Chicago	4	at	Detroit	2

Chicago won best-of-seven series 4–3

Apr.	1	Toronto	2	at	Montreal	3
Apr.	3	Toronto	1	at	Montreal	3
Apr.	6	Montreal	2	at	Toronto	3 OT
Apr.	8	Montreal	2	at	Toronto	4
Apr.	10	Toronto	1	at	Montreal	3
Apr.	13	Montreal	4	at	Toronto	3 OT

Montreal won best-of-seven series 4–2

FINALS

Apr.	17	Chicago	2	at	Montreal	3
Apr.	20	Chicago	0	at	Montreal	2
Apr.	22	Montreal	1	at	Chicago	3
Apr.	25	Montreal	1	at	Chicago	5
Apr.	27	Chicago	0	at	Montreal	6
Apr.	29	Montreal	1	at	Chicago	2
May	1	Chicago	0	at	Montreal	4

Montreal won best-of-seven series 4–3

1964-65 – Montreal Canadiens – Gump Worsley, Charlie Hodge, Jean-Claude Tremblay, Ted Harris, Jean-Guy Talbot, Terry Harper, Jacques Laperrière, Jean Gauthier, Noel Picard, Jean Béliveau, Ralph Backstrom, Dick Duff, Claude Larose, Yvan Cournoyer, Claude Provost, Bobby Rousseau, Henri Richard, Dave Balon, John Ferguson, Red Berenson, Jim Roberts, Toe Blake (coach), Sam Pollock (general manager), Larry Aubut, Andy Galley (trainers).

1964

Tying their club record set from 1947 to 1949, Toronto captured the Stanley Cup for a third consecutive season.

The Maple Leafs advanced by defeating the Canadiens in seven games. In the Finals, the Leafs lost games 2, 3 and 5 by one-goal margins to trail the Detroit Red Wings three games to two.

With the score tied 3–3 late in game six, Maple Leafs defenseman Bob Baun took a Gordie Howe slapshot on his skate and dropped to the ice in pain. After freezing and taping the injury, he returned for overtime and scored the winning goal at 2:43 of the extra period. On crutches for the next two days, Baun would later suit up for the series finale and never miss a shift as Toronto won the Cup. The following day, x-rays confirmed what Baun had known all along, that the ankle was in fact broken. The Leafs blueliner spent two more months on crutches.

SEMIFINALS

Mar.	26	Toronto	0	at	Montreal	2
Mar.	28	Toronto	2	at	Montreal	1
Mar.	31	Montreal	3	at	Toronto	2
Apr.	2	Montreal	3	at	Toronto	5
Apr.	4	Toronto	2	at	Montreal	4
Apr.	7	Montreal	0	at	Toronto	3
Apr.	9	Toronto	3	at	Montreal	1

Toronto won best-of-seven series 4–3

Mar.	26	Detroit	1	at	Chicago	4
Mar.	29	Detroit	5	at	Chicago	4
Mar.	31	Chicago	0	at	Detroit	3
Apr.	2	Chicago	3	at	Detroit	2 OT
Apr.	5	Detroit	2	at	Chicago	3
Apr.	7	Chicago	2	at	Detroit	7
Apr.	9	Detroit	4	at	Chicago	2

Detroit won best-of-seven series 4–3

FINALS

Apr.	11	Detroit	2	at	Toronto	3
Apr.	14	Detroit	4	at	Toronto	3 OT
Apr.	16	Toronto	3	at	Detroit	4
Apr.	18	Toronto	4	at	Detroit	2
Apr.	21	Detroit	2	at	Toronto	1
Apr.	23	Toronto	4	at	Detroit	3 OT
Apr.	25	Detroit	0	at	Toronto	4

Toronto won best-of-seven series 4–3

1963-64 – Toronto Maple Leafs – Johnny Bower, Don Simmons, Carl Brewer, Tim Horton, Bob Baun, Allan Stanley, Larry Hillman, Al Arbour, Red Kelly, Gerry Ehman, Andy Bathgate, George Armstrong, Ron Stewart, Dave Keon, Billy Harris, Don McKenney, Jim Pappin, Bob Pulford, Eddie Shack, Frank Mahovlich, Ed Litzenberger, Punch Imlach (manager-coach), Bob Haggert (trainer).

1963

Five different Maple Leafs — Bob Nevin, Dick Duff, Ron Stewart, Red Kelly and Dave Keon — recorded multiple-goal performances in Toronto's four victories, and 38-year-old goaltender Johnny Bower limited Detroit to 10 goals in five games.

Keon scored twice in game five with Toronto players in the penalty box, establishing a new playoff record for shorthanded goals in one game.

SEMIFINALS

Mar.	26	Montreal	1	at	Toronto	3
Mar.	28	Montreal	2	at	Toronto	3
Mar.	30	Toronto	2	at	Montreal	0
Apr.	2	Toronto	1	at	Montreal	3
Apr.	4	Montreal	0	at	Toronto	5

Toronto won best-of-seven series 4–1

Mar.	26	Detroit	4	at	Chicago	5
Mar.	28	Detroit	2	at	Chicago	5
Mar.	31	Chicago	2	at	Detroit	4
Apr.	2	Chicago	1	at	Detroit	4
Apr.	4	Detroit	4	at	Chicago	2
Apr.	7	Chicago	4	at	Detroit	7

Detroit won best-of-seven series 4–2

FINALS

Apr.	9	Detroit	2	at	Toronto	4
Apr.	11	Detroit	2	at	Toronto	4
Apr.	14	Toronto	2	at	Detroit	3
Apr.	16	Toronto	4	at	Detroit	2
Apr.	18	Detroit	1	at	Toronto	3

Toronto won best-of-seven series 4–1

1962-63 – Toronto Maple Leafs – Johnny Bower, Don Simmons, Carl Brewer, Tim Horton, Kent Douglas, Allan Stanley, Bob Baun, Larry Hillman, Red Kelly, Dick Duff, George Armstrong, Bob Nevin, Ron Stewart, Dave Keon, Billy Harris, Bob Pulford, Eddie Shack, Ed Litzenberger, Frank Mahovlich, John MacMillan, Punch Imlach (manager-coach), Bob Haggert (trainer).

1962

The Maple Leafs regained the Stanley Cup after 11 years, putting an end to the club's longest period without a championship in its 45-year NHL history through 1962.

In his Stanley Cup debut, 22-year-old Dave Keon scored a goal and added an assist.

Stan Mikita tallied two assists in game five to set new playoff records for assists (15) and points (21). The latter broke Gordie Howe's mark of 20 points set in the 1955 playoffs.

SEMIFINALS

Mar.	27	Chicago	1	at	Montreal	2
Mar.	29	Chicago	3	at	Montreal	4
Apr.	1	Montreal	1	at	Chicago	4
Apr.	3	Montreal	3	at	Chicago	5
Apr.	5	Chicago	4	at	Montreal	3
Apr.	8	Montreal	0	at	Chicago	2

Chicago won best-of-seven series 4–2

Mar.	27	NY Rangers	2	at	Toronto	4
Mar.	29	NY Rangers	1	at	Toronto	2
Apr.	1	Toronto	4	at	NY Rangers	5
Apr.	3	Toronto	2	at	NY Rangers	4
Apr.	5	NY Rangers	2	at	Toronto	3 2OT
Apr.	7	NY Rangers	1	at	Toronto	7

Toronto won best-of-seven series 4–2

FINALS

Apr.	10	Chicago	1	at	Toronto	4

Apr.	12	Chicago	2	at	Toronto	3
Apr.	15	Toronto	0	at	Chicago	3
Apr.	17	Toronto	1	at	Chicago	4
Apr.	19	Chicago	4	at	Toronto	8
Apr.	22	Toronto	2	at	Chicago	1

Toronto won best-of-seven series 4–2

1961-62 – Toronto Maple Leafs – Johnny Bower, Don Simmons, Carl Brewer, Tim Horton, Bob Baun, Allan Stanley, Al Arbour, Larry Hillman, Red Kelly, Dick Duff, George Armstrong, Frank Mahovlich, Bob Nevin, Ron Stewart, Billy Harris, Bert Olmstead, Bob Pulford, Eddie Shack, Dave Keon, Ed Litzenberger, John MacMillan, Punch Imlach (manager-coach), Bob Haggert (trainer).

1961

The Chicago Black Hawks captured their first Stanley Cup title since 1938, clinching their third championship overall since joining the NHL in 1926-27.

Two of the greatest athletes in Chicago sports history — Bobby Hull and Stan Mikita — made their premier Stanley Cup appearances, and both figured prominently in the outcome. "The Golden Jet" sparkled in game one with his first two Stanley Cup goals, including the game-winner, while Mikita scored the winner in game five.

SEMIFINALS

Mar.	21	Chicago	2	at	Montreal	6
Mar.	23	Chicago	4	at	Montreal	3
Mar.	26	Montreal	1	at	Chicago	2 2OT
Mar.	28	Montreal	5	at	Chicago	2
Apr.	1	Chicago	3	at	Montreal	0
Apr.	4	Montreal	0	at	Chicago	3

Chicago won best-of-seven series 4–2

Mar.	22	Detroit	2	at	Toronto	3 2OT
Mar.	25	Detroit	4	at	Toronto	2
Mar.	26	Toronto	0	at	Detroit	2
Mar.	28	Toronto	1	at	Detroit	4
Apr.	1	Detroit	3	at	Toronto	2

Detroit won best-of-seven series 4–1

FINALS

Apr.	6	Detroit	2	at	Chicago	3
Apr.	8	Chicago	1	at	Detroit	3
Apr.	10	Detroit	1	at	Chicago	3
Apr.	12	Chicago	1	at	Detroit	2
Apr.	14	Detroit	3	at	Chicago	6
Apr.	16	Chicago	5	at	Detroit	1

Chicago won best-of-seven series 4–2

1960-61 – Chicago Black Hawks – Glenn Hall, Al Arbour, Pierre Pilote, Elmer Vasko, Jack Evans, Dollard St-Laurent, Reggie Fleming, Tod Sloan, Ron Murphy, Ed Litzenberger, Bill Hay, Bobby Hull, Ab McDonald, Eric Nesterenko, Kenny Wharram, Earl Balfour, Stan Mikita, Murray Balfour, Chico Maki, Wayne Hicks, Tommy Ivan (manager), Rudy Pilous (coach), Nick Garen (trainer).

1960

The Canadiens retained the Stanley Cup for an unprecedented fifth straight season. No team has since matched this record-setting achievement.

Jacques Plante, who had introduced the goalie mask to the hockey world on November 1, 1959, in New York, sparkled with his self-designed face guard. His Stanley Cup performance, which included just five goals allowed in four games, played a large role in the acceptance of the mask by goaltenders worldwide.

Maurice Richard played in the last four games of his career. In game three, "The Rocket" scored his 34th goal in the finals, still an all-time record.

SEMIFINALS

Mar.	24	Chicago	3	at	Montreal	4
Mar.	26	Chicago	3	at	Montreal	4 OT
Mar.	29	Montreal	4	at	Chicago	0
Mar.	31	Montreal	2	at	Chicago	0

Montreal won best-of-seven series 4–0

Mar.	23	Detroit	2	at	Toronto	1
Mar.	26	Detroit	2	at	Toronto	4
Mar.	27	Toronto	5	at	Detroit	4 3OT
Mar.	29	Toronto	1	at	Detroit	2 OT
Apr.	2	Detroit	4	at	Toronto	5
Apr.	3	Toronto	4	at	Detroit	2

Toronto won best-of-seven series 4–2

FINALS

Apr.	7	Toronto	2	at	Montreal	4
Apr.	9	Toronto	1	at	Montreal	2
Apr.	12	Montreal	5	at	Toronto	2
Apr.	14	Montreal	4	at	Toronto	0

Montreal won best-of-seven series 4–0

1959-60 – Montreal Canadiens – Jacques Plante, Charlie Hodge, Doug Harvey, Tom Johnson, Bob Turner, Jean-Guy Talbot, Albert Langlois, Ralph Backstrom, Jean Béliveau, Marcel Bonin, Bernie Geoffrion, Phil Goyette, Bill Hicke, Don Marshall, Ab McDonald, Dickie Moore, André Pronovost, Claude Provost, Henri Richard, Maurice Richard, Frank Selke (manager), Toe Blake (coach), Hector Dubois, Larry Aubut (trainers).

1959

The Canadiens skated to a fourth consecutive championship, breaking the record of three they had shared with Toronto (1947 to 1949). Maurice Richard was held off the scoresheet during the playoffs for the first time in his career. Injuries had restricted his participation to just four games.

Led by newly appointed general manager Punch Imlach, the Toronto Maple Leafs made their first appearance in the Stanley Cup finals since 1951, rebounding from a last-place finish in 1957-58. The Leafs had a perfect record of three wins and no losses in overtime games in this postseason.

SEMIFINALS

Mar.	24	Chicago	2	at	Montreal	4
Mar.	26	Chicago	1	at	Montreal	5
Mar.	28	Montreal	2	at	Chicago	4
Mar.	31	Montreal	1	at	Chicago	3
Apr.	2	Chicago	2	at	Montreal	4
Apr.	4	Montreal	5	at	Chicago	4

Montreal won best-of-seven series 4–2

Mar.	24	Toronto	1	at	Boston	5
Mar.	26	Toronto	2	at	Boston	4
Mar.	28	Boston	2	at	Toronto	3 OT
Mar.	31	Boston	2	at	Toronto	3 OT
Apr.	2	Toronto	4	at	Boston	1
Apr.	4	Boston	5	at	Toronto	4
Apr.	7	Toronto	3	at	Boston	2

Toronto won best-of-seven series 4–3

FINALS

Apr.	9	Toronto	3	at	Montreal	5
Apr.	11	Toronto	1	at	Montreal	3
Apr.	14	Montreal	2	at	Toronto	3 OT
Apr.	16	Montreal	3	at	Toronto	2
Apr.	18	Toronto	3	at	Montreal	5

Montreal won best-of-seven series 4–1

1958-59 – Montreal Canadiens – Jacques Plante, Charlie Hodge, Doug Harvey, Tom Johnson, Bob Turner, Jean-Guy Talbot, Albert Langlois, Bernie Geoffrion, Ralph Backstrom, Bill Hicke, Maurice Richard, Dickie Moore, Claude Provost, Ab McDonald, Henri Richard, Marcel Bonin, Phil Goyette, Don Marshall, André Pronovost, Jean Béliveau, Frank Selke (manager), Toe Blake (coach), Hector Dubois, Larry Aubut (trainers).

1958

The Canadiens and Bruins met for a second consecutive year in the Stanley Cup finals. Once again, Boston had been an upset winner in the semifinals, eliminating the New York Rangers in a high-scoring six-game series.

In the finals, the Habs won the Stanley Cup in six games. The Canadiens' third straight Stanley Cup title equalled the NHL record set by the Toronto Maple Leafs from 1947 to 1949.

Maurice Richard was the top overall playoff goal-scorer with 11. In game five of the finals, he notched the third final series overtime goal of his career and his sixth overtime goal in playoff competiton, setting all-time records in each category.

SEMIFINALS

Mar.	25	Detroit	1	at	Montreal	8
Mar.	27	Detroit	1	at	Montreal	5
Mar.	30	Montreal	2	at	Detroit	1 OT
Apr.	1	Montreal	4	at	Detroit	3

Montreal won best-of-seven series 4–0

Mar.	25	Boston	3	at	NY Rangers	5
Mar.	27	Boston	4	at	NY Rangers	3 OT
Mar.	29	NY Rangers	0	at	Boston	5
Apr.	1	NY Rangers	5	at	Boston	2
Apr.	3	NY Rangers	1	at	Boston	6
Apr.	5	NY Rangers	2	at	Boston	8

Boston won best-of-seven series 4–2

FINALS

Apr.	8	Boston	1	at	Montreal	2
Apr.	10	Boston	5	at	Montreal	2
Apr.	13	Montreal	3	at	Boston	0
Apr.	15	Montreal	1	at	Boston	3
Apr.	17	Boston	2	at	Montreal	3 OT
Apr.	20	Montreal	5	at	Boston	3

Montreal won best-of-seven series 4–2

1957-58 – Montreal Canadiens – Jacques Plante, Gerry McNeil, Doug Harvey, Tom Johnson, Bob Turner, Dollard St-Laurent, Jean-Guy Talbot, Albert Langlois, Jean Béliveau, Bernie Geoffrion, Maurice Richard, Dickie Moore, Claude Provost, Floyd Curry, Bert Olmstead, Henri Richard, Marcel Bonin, Phil Goyette, Don Marshall, André Pronovost, Connie Broden, Frank Selke (manager), Toe Blake (coach), Hector Dubois, Larry Aubut (trainers).

1957

The Boston Bruins were surprise finalists in 1957, eliminating the regular-season champion Detroit Red Wings in five games. Maurice "Rocket" Richard scored four times in game one, including three goals in the second period, to equal Ted Lindsay's modern Stanley Cup record for goals in a game.

Jacques Plante held the Bruins to six goals in five games as Montreal won its second consecutive Stanley Cup championship. Fleming Mackell had four of Boston's six goals.

SEMIFINALS

Mar.	26	Boston	3	at	Detroit	1
Mar.	28	Boston	2	at	Detroit	7
Mar.	31	Detroit	3	at	Boston	4
Apr.	2	Detroit	0	at	Boston	2
Apr.	4	Boston	4	at	Detroit	3

Boston won best-of-seven series 4–1

Mar.	26	Montreal	4	at	NY Rangers	1
Mar.	28	Montreal	3	at	NY Rangers	4 OT
Mar.	30	NY Rangers	3	at	Montreal	8
Apr.	2	NY Rangers	1	at	Montreal	3
Apr.	4	NY Rangers	3	at	Montreal	4 OT

Montreal won best-of-seven series 4–1

FINALS

Apr.	6	Boston	1	at	Montreal	5

Apr.	9	Boston	0	at Montreal	1
Apr.	11	Montreal	4	at Boston	2
Apr.	14	Montreal	0	at Boston	2
Apr.	16	Boston	1	at Montreal	5

Montreal won best-of-seven series 4–1

1956-57 – Montreal Canadiens – Jacques Plante, Gerry McNeil, Doug Harvey, Tom Johnson, Bob Turner, Dollard St-Laurent, Jean-Guy Talbot, Jean Béliveau, Bernie Geoffrion, Floyd Curry, Dickie Moore, Maurice Richard, Claude Provost, Bert Olmstead, Henri Richard, Phil Goyette, Don Marshall, André Pronovost, Connie Broden, Frank Selke (manager), Toe Blake (coach), Hector Dubois, Larry Aubut (trainers).

1956

Two rookies played integral roles on this first of five consecutive Stanley Cup championship teams for the Montreal Canadiens. Former playing star Toe Blake took over for Dick Irvin behind the Canadiens' bench as coach, while rookie center Henri Richard joined his famous brother Maurice on the ice. Blake, who would become the 10th rookie coach in NHL history to win the Cup, won his first game in the finals as a coach, and young Richard notched his first Stanley Cup goal.

Jean Beliveau scored seven times in the series, including at least one in each game, to set a modern record for goals in the finals and tie Maurice Richard's overall NHL playoff record of 12 goals set in 1944.

SEMIFINALS

Mar.	20	NY Rangers	1	at Montreal	7
Mar.	22	NY Rangers	4	at Montreal	2
Mar.	24	Montreal	3	at NY Rangers	1
Mar.	25	Montreal	5	at NY Rangers	3
Mar.	27	NY Rangers	0	at Montreal	7

Montreal won best-of-seven series 4–1

Mar.	20	Toronto	2	at Detroit	3
Mar.	22	Toronto	1	at Detroit	3
Mar.	24	Detroit	5	at Toronto	4 OT
Mar.	27	Detroit	0	at Toronto	2
Mar.	29	Toronto	1	at Detroit	3

Detroit won best-of-seven series 4–1

FINALS

Mar.	31	Detroit	4	at Montreal	6
Apr.	3	Detroit	1	at Montreal	5
Apr.	5	Montreal	1	at Detroit	3
Apr.	8	Montreal	3	at Detroit	0
Apr.	10	Detroit	1	at Montreal	3

Montreal won best-of-seven series 4–1

1955-56 – Montreal Canadiens – Jacques Plante, Doug Harvey, Butch Bouchard, Bob Turner, Tom Johnson, Jean-Guy Talbot, Dollard St-Laurent, Jean Béliveau, Bernie Geoffrion, Bert Olmstead, Floyd Curry, Jackie Leclair, Maurice Richard, Dickie Moore, Henri Richard, Kenny Mosdell, Don Marshall, Claude Provost, Frank Selke (manager), Toe Blake (coach), Hector Dubois (trainer).

1955

On March 17, Maurice Richard had been suspended for the remainder of the regular-season and playoffs for punching a linesman. The high-scoring right-winger's absence was sorely felt by the Canadiens.

In game two of the finals, Detroit's Ted Lindsay scored four times to set a modern record for goals in a championship game, and the Red Wings won their 15th consecutive contest to establish another NHL record. Lindsay then tallied one assist, his last of the series, in game four to tie Elmer Lach's record of 12 playoff assists set in 1946.

Gordie Howe set two records in the series. He amassed 12 points in the finals (five goals, seven assists) to establish a new mark, and snapped Toe Blake's overall playoff record with 20 points (nine goals, 11 assists) in 11 games.

For the first time in a best-of-seven final, the home team won all seven games.

SEMIFINALS

Mar.	22	Toronto	4	at Detroit	7
Mar.	24	Toronto	1	at Detroit	2
Mar.	26	Detroit	2	at Toronto	1
Mar.	29	Detroit	3	at Toronto	0

Detroit won best-of-seven series 4–0

Mar.	22	Boston	0	at Montreal	2
Mar.	24	Boston	1	at Montreal	3
Mar.	27	Montreal	2	at Boston	4
Mar.	29	Montreal	4	at Boston	3 OT
Mar.	31	Boston	1	at Montreal	5

Montreal won best-of-seven series 4–1

FINALS

Apr.	3	Montreal	2	at Detroit	4
Apr.	5	Montreal	1	at Detroit	7
Apr.	7	Detroit	2	at Montreal	4
Apr.	9	Detroit	3	at Montreal	5
Apr.	10	Montreal	1	at Detroit	5
Apr.	12	Detroit	3	at Montreal	6
Apr.	14	Montreal	1	at Detroit	3

Detroit won best-of-seven series 4–3

1954-55 – Detroit Red Wings – Terry Sawchuk, Red Kelly, Bob Goldham, Marcel Pronovost, Benny Woit, Jim Hay, Larry Hillman, Ted Lindsay, Tony Leswick, Gordie Howe, Alex Delvecchio, Marty Pavelich, Glen Skov, Earl Reibel, John Wilson, Bill Dineen, Vic Stasiuk, Marcel Bonin, Jack Adams (manager), Jimmy Skinner (coach), Carl Mattson (trainer).

1954

Tony Leswick's Cup-winning tally was only the second goal ever scored in overtime during the seventh and deciding game of a Stanley Cup final series. Leswick, who notched the winner at 4:29 of the first extra period, matched the feat first accomplished by former Red Wing Pete Babando in 1950.

Marguerite Norris, president of the Detroit club, was presented with the Stanley Cup by NHL President Clarence Campbell at the conclusion of the series. She became the first woman in history to have her name engraved on the Stanley Cup.

SEMIFINALS

Mar.	23	Toronto	0	at Detroit	5
Mar.	25	Toronto	3	at Detroit	1
Mar.	27	Detroit	3	at Toronto	1
Mar.	30	Detroit	2	at Toronto	1
Apr.	1	Toronto	3	at Detroit	4 2OT

Detroit won best-of-seven series 4–1

Mar.	23	Boston	0	at Montreal	2
Mar.	25	Boston	1	at Montreal	8
Mar.	28	Montreal	4	at Boston	3
Mar.	30	Montreal	2	at Boston	0

Montreal won best-of-seven series 4–0

FINALS

Apr.	4	Montreal	1	at Detroit	3
Apr.	6	Montreal	3	at Detroit	1
Apr.	8	Detroit	5	at Montreal	2
Apr.	10	Detroit	2	at Montreal	0
Apr.	11	Montreal	1	at Detroit	0 OT
Apr.	13	Detroit	1	at Montreal	4
Apr.	16	Montreal	1	at Detroit	2 OT

Detroit won best-of-seven series 4–3

1953-54 – Detroit Red Wings – Terry Sawchuk, Red Kelly, Bob Goldham, Benny Woit, Marcel Pronovost, Al Arbour, Keith Allen, Ted Lindsay, Tony Leswick, Gordie Howe, Marty Pavelich, Alex Delvecchio, Metro Prystai, Glen Skov, Johnny Wilson, Bill Dineen, Jimmy Peters Sr., Earl Reibel, Vic Stasiuk, Jack Adams (manager), Tommy Ivan (coach), Carl Mattson (trainer).

1953

After goaltender Jacques Plante recorded a split decision in the first two games he ever played in the Stanley Cup finals, Canadiens coach Dick Irvin sent Gerry McNeil into the nets. The move resulted in two shutouts in the final three games as Montreal regained the Cup for the first time in seven years.

Elmer Lach scored the series-winning goal at 1:22 of overtime in the fifth and final game.

SEMIFINALS

Mar.	24	Boston	0	at Detroit	7
Mar.	26	Boston	5	at Detroit	3
Mar.	29	Detroit	1	at Boston	2 OT
Mar.	31	Detroit	2	at Boston	6
Apr.	2	Boston	4	at Detroit	6
Apr.	5	Detroit	2	at Boston	4

Boston won best-of-seven series 4–2

Mar.	24	Chicago	1	at Montreal	3
Mar.	26	Chicago	3	at Montreal	4
Mar.	29	Montreal	1	at Chicago	2 OT
Mar.	31	Montreal	1	at Chicago	3
Apr.	2	Chicago	4	at Montreal	2
Apr.	4	Montreal	3	at Chicago	0
Apr.	7	Chicago	1	at Montreal	4

Montreal won best-of-seven series 4–3

FINALS

Apr.	9	Boston	2	at Montreal	4
Apr.	11	Boston	4	at Montreal	1
Apr.	12	Montreal	3	at Boston	0
Apr.	14	Montreal	7	at Boston	3
Apr.	16	Boston	0	at Montreal	1 OT

Montreal won best-of-seven series 4–1

1952-53 – Montreal Canadiens – Gerry McNeil, Jacques Plante, Doug Harvey, Butch Bouchard, Tom Johnson, Dollard St-Laurent, Bud MacPherson, Maurice Richard, Elmer Lach, Bert Olmstead, Bernie Geoffrion, Floyd Curry, Paul Masnick, Billy Reay, Dickie Moore, Kenny Mosdell, Dick Gamble, Johnny McCormack, Lorne Davis, Calum MacKay, Eddie Mazur, Frank Selke (manager), Dick Irvin (coach), Hector Dubois (trainer).

1952

Terry Sawchuk made his debut in the Cup finals and rose to the occasion, recording two shutouts and limiting Montreal to just two goals during the four-game series. Meanwhile, Gordie Howe contributed his first two career goals in a Stanley Cup championship series.

The Red Wings set an NHL record by winning all eight postseason games, including a four-game sweep over Toronto in the first round.

SEMIFINALS

Mar.	25	Toronto	0	at Detroit	3
Mar.	27	Toronto	0	at Detroit	1
Mar.	29	Detroit	6	at Toronto	2
Apr.	1	Detroit	3	at Toronto	1

Detroit won best-of-seven series 4–0

Mar.	25	Boston	1	at Montreal	5
Mar.	27	Boston	0	at Montreal	4
Mar.	30	Montreal	1	at Boston	4
Apr.	1	Montreal	2	at Boston	3
Apr.	3	Boston	1	at Montreal	0
Apr.	6	Montreal	3	at Boston	2 2OT
Apr.	8	Boston	1	at Montreal	3

Montreal won best-of-seven series 4–3

FINALS

Apr.	10	Detroit	3	at	Montreal	1
Apr.	12	Detroit	2	at	Montreal	1
Apr.	13	Montreal	0	at	Detroit	3
Apr.	15	Montreal	0	at	Detroit	3

Detroit won best-of-seven series 4–0

1951-52 – Detroit Red Wings – Terry Sawchuk, Bob Goldham, Benny Woit, Red Kelly, Leo Reise Jr., Marcel Pronovost, Ted Lindsay, Tony Leswick, Gordie Howe, Metro Prystai, Marty Pavelich, Sid Abel, Glen Skov, Alex Delvecchio, John Wilson, Vic Stasiuk, Larry Zeidel, Jack Adams (manager), Tommy Ivan (coach), Carl Mattson (trainer).

1951

The 1951 series distinguished itself as the only Stanley Cup final in which every game ended in overtime. Sid Smith, Ted Kennedy, Harry Watson and Bill Barilko notched the overtime winners for Toronto, while Maurice "Rocket" Richard, who scored goals in all five contests, netted one in Montreal's lone victory.

Richard's overtime tally was his second in a final series and the fourth of his playoff career, breaking the record of three set by Boston's Mel Hill in 1939.

For Barilko, his overtime goal would be his last as the rugged defenseman died tragically in a plane crash during the summer.

SEMIFINALS

Mar.	27	Montreal	3	at	Detroit	2 4OT
Mar.	29	Montreal	1	at	Detroit	0 3OT
Mar.	31	Detroit	2	at	Montreal	0
Apr.	3	Detroit	4	at	Montreal	1
Apr.	5	Montreal	5	at	Detroit	2
Apr.	7	Detroit	2	at	Montreal	3

Montreal won best-of-seven series 4–2

Mar.	28	Boston	2	at	Toronto	0
Mar.	31	Boston	1	at	Toronto	1 OT*
Apr.	1	Toronto	3	at	Boston	0
Apr.	3	Toronto	3	at	Boston	1
Apr.	7	Boston	1	at	Toronto	4
Apr.	8	Toronto	6	at	Boston	0

* game called after one overtime period due to curfew.

Toronto won best-of-seven series 4–1

FINALS

Apr.	11	Montreal	2	at	Toronto	3 OT
Apr.	14	Montreal	3	at	Toronto	2 OT
Apr.	17	Toronto	2	at	Montreal	1 OT
Apr.	19	Toronto	3	at	Montreal	2 OT
Apr.	21	Montreal	2	at	Toronto	3 OT

Toronto won best-of-seven series 4–1

1950-51 – Toronto Maple Leafs – Turk Broda, Al Rollins, Jim Thomson, Gus Mortson, Bill Barilko, Bill Juzda, Fern Flaman, Hugh Bolton, Ted Kennedy, Sid Smith, Tod Sloan, Cal Gardner, Howie Meeker, Harry Watson, Max Bentley, Joe Klukay, Danny Lewicki, Ray Timgren, Fleming Mackell, Johnny McCormack, Bob Hassard, Conn Smythe (manager), Joe Primeau (coach), Tim Daly (trainer).

1950

Bumped from Madison Square Garden by the circus, the Rangers opted to play games two and three in Toronto.

Gordie Howe failed to appear for the winners in this series as a result of a serious head injury sustained in the first game of the playoffs. After sliding head first into the boards, Howe required surgery to repair a fractured nose and cheekbone. Despite the seriousness of the injury, he resumed his career the following season.

Even without Howe, Detroit managed to capture the Cup in seven games, but not without a fight. New York battled Detroit to a 3–3 tie at the end of regulation in game seven, which the Red Wings' Pete Babando ultimately ended at the 28:31 mark of overtime. Babando's goal was the first sudden-death tally ever scored in the seventh game of a final series.

New York's Don Raleigh set a record that would remain unmatched until 1993 when he scored two overtime goals in one Stanley Cup final series.

SEMIFINALS

Mar.	28	Toronto	5	at	Detroit	0
Mar.	30	Toronto	1	at	Detroit	3
Apr.	1	Detroit	0	at	Toronto	2
Apr.	4	Detroit	2	at	Toronto	1 2OT
Apr.	6	Toronto	2	at	Detroit	0
Apr.	8	Detroit	4	at	Toronto	0
Apr.	9	Toronto	0	at	Detroit	1 OT

Detroit won best-of-seven series 4–3

Mar.	29	Montreal	1	at	NY Rangers	3
Apr.	1	NY Rangers	3	at	Montreal	2
Apr.	2	Montreal	1	at	NY Rangers	4
Apr.	4	NY Rangers	2	at	Montreal	3 OT
Apr.	6	NY Rangers	3	at	Montreal	0

Rangers won best-of-seven series 4–1

FINALS

Apr.	11	NY Rangers	1	at	Detroit	4
Apr.	13	Detroit	1	vs.	NY Rangers	3 *
Apr.	15	Detroit	4	vs.	NY Rangers	0 *
Apr.	18	NY Rangers	4	at	Detroit	3 OT
Apr.	20	NY Rangers	2	at	Detroit	1 OT
Apr.	22	NY Rangers	4	at	Detroit	5
Apr.	23	NY Rangers	3	at	Detroit	4 2OT

* played in Toronto

Detroit won best-of-seven series 4–3

1949-50 – Detroit Red Wings – Harry Lumley, Jack Stewart, Leo Reise Jr., Clare Martin, Al Dewsbury, Lee Fogolin, Marcel Pronovost, Red Kelly, Ted Lindsay, Sid Abel, Gordie Howe, George Gee, Jimmy Peters Sr., Marty Pavelich, Jim McFadden, Pete Babando, Max McNab, Gerry Couture, Joe Carveth, Steve Black, John Wilson, Larry Wilson, Jack Adams (manager), Tommy Ivan (coach), Carl Mattson (trainer).

1949

The Toronto Maple Leafs established two NHL records in this 1949 series. Most significantly, they captured their third straight Stanley Cup title, a feat last accomplished 44 years earlier by the Ottawa Silver Seven. They had also won an unprecedented ninth straight game in the finals dating back to April 19, 1947.

SEMIFINALS

Mar.	22	Montreal	1	at	Detroit	2 3OT
Mar.	24	Montreal	4	at	Detroit	3 OT
Mar.	26	Detroit	2	at	Montreal	3
Mar.	29	Detroit	3	at	Montreal	1
Mar.	31	Montreal	1	at	Detroit	3
Apr.	2	Detroit	1	at	Montreal	3
Apr.	5	Montreal	1	at	Detroit	3

Detroit won best-of-seven series 4–3

Mar.	22	Toronto	3	at	Boston	0
Mar.	24	Toronto	3	at	Boston	2
Mar.	26	Boston	5	at	Toronto	4 OT
Mar.	29	Boston	1	at	Toronto	3
Mar.	30	Toronto	3	at	Boston	2

Toronto won best-of-seven series 4–1

FINALS

Apr.	8	Toronto	3	at	Detroit	2 OT
Apr.	10	Toronto	3	at	Detroit	1
Apr.	13	Detroit	1	at	Toronto	3
Apr.	16	Detroit	1	at	Toronto	3

Toronto won best-of-seven series 4–0

1948-49 – Toronto Maple Leafs – Turk Broda, Jim Thomson, Gus Mortson, Bill Barilko, Garth Boesch, Bill Juzda, Ted Kennedy, Howie Meeker, Vic Lynn, Harry Watson, Bill Ezinicki, Cal Gardner, Max Bentley, Joe Klukay, Sid Smith, Don Metz, Ray Timgren, Fleming Mackell, Harry Taylor, Bob Dawes, Tod Sloan, Conn Smythe (manager), Hap Day (coach), Tim Daly (trainer).

1948

The series marked the beginning and end of two great Stanley Cup careers. For Detroit's Gordie Howe, it was an introduction to the rigors of championship competition. For Toronto's Syl Apps, who scored one goal in game four, it meant the conclusion of a Hall-of-Fame career.

Toronto became the fourth NHL team to repeat as Stanley Cup champions, joining the Ottawa Senators (1920-1921), Montreal Canadiens (1930-1931) and Detroit Red Wings (1936-1937).

SEMIFINALS

Mar.	24	Boston	4	at	Toronto	5 OT
Mar.	27	Boston	3	at	Toronto	5
Mar.	30	Toronto	5	at	Boston	1
Apr.	1	Toronto	2	at	Boston	3
Apr.	3	Boston	2	at	Toronto	3

Toronto won best-of-seven series 4–1

Mar.	24	NY Rangers	1	at	Detroit	2
Mar.	26	NY Rangers	2	at	Detroit	5
Mar.	28	Detroit	2	at	NY Rangers	3
Mar.	30	Detroit	1	at	NY Rangers	3
Apr.	1	NY Rangers	1	at	Detroit	3
Apr.	4	Detroit	4	at	NY Rangers	2

Detroit won best-of-seven series 4–2

FINALS

Apr.	7	Detroit	3	at	Toronto	5
Apr.	10	Detroit	2	at	Toronto	4
Apr.	11	Toronto	2	at	Detroit	0
Apr.	14	Toronto	7	at	Detroit	2

Toronto won best-of-seven series 4–0

1947-48 – Toronto Maple Leafs – Turk Broda, Jim Thomson, Wally Stanowski, Garth Boesch, Bill Barilko, Gus Mortson, Phil Samis, Syl Apps Sr., Bill Ezinicki, Harry Watson, Ted Kennedy, Howie Meeker, Vic Lynn, Nick Metz, Max Bentley, Joe Klukay, Les Costello, Don Metz, Sid Smith, Conn Smythe (manager), Hap Day (coach), Tim Daly (trainer).

1947

The Toronto Maple Leafs were a "new look" club in 1946–47. Young players like Calder Trophy-winner Howie Meeker, Bill Barilko and Bill Ezinicki were new performers in the Leafs' overhauled lineup.

In the first all-Canadian final in 12 years, the Maple Leafs defeated the Canadiens in six games. Toronto's "Teeder" Kennedy potted three goals in the series, including the Cup-winner in the closing match-up. The Leafs were the youngest NHL team to win the Stanley Cup.

SEMIFINALS

Mar.	25	Boston	1	at	Montreal	3
Mar.	27	Boston	1	at	Montreal	2 OT
Mar.	29	Montreal	2	at	Boston	4
Apr.	1	Montreal	5	at	Boston	1
Apr.	3	Boston	3	at	Montreal	4 2OT

Montreal won best-of-seven series 4–1

Mar.	26	Detroit	2	at	Toronto	3 OT
Mar.	29	Detroit	9	at	Toronto	1
Apr.	1	Toronto	4	at	Detroit	1
Apr.	3	Toronto	4	at	Detroit	1
Apr.	5	Detroit	1	at	Toronto	6

Toronto won best-of-seven series 4–1

FINALS

Apr. 8	Toronto	0	at	Montreal	6
Apr. 10	Toronto	4	at	Montreal	0
Apr. 12	Montreal	2	at	Toronto	4
Apr. 15	Montreal	1	at	Toronto	2 OT
Apr. 17	Toronto	1	at	Montreal	3
Apr. 19	Montreal	1	at	Toronto	2

Toronto won best-of-seven series 4–2

1946-47 – Toronto Maple Leafs – Turk Broda, Garth Boesch, Gus Mortson, Jim Thomson, Wally Stanowski, Bill Barilko, Harry Watson, Bud Poile, Ted Kennedy, Syl Apps Sr., Don Metz, Nick Metz, Bill Ezinicki, Vic Lynn, Howie Meeker, Gaye Stewart, Joe Klukay, Gus Bodnar, Bob Goldham, Conn Smythe (manager), Hap Day (coach), Tim Daly (trainer).

1946

Two high-scoring forward units met in the NHL's first post-World War II Stanley Cup final. Boston was led by the Kraut Line of Bobby Bauer, Milt Schmidt and Woody Dumart. The Canadiens featured the Punch Line of Maurice Richard, Elmer Lach and Toe Blake. In game one, Richard scored the first of a record six overtime goals in his playoff career and the first of his record three career overtime tallies in the finals.

The Canadiens won a close, hard-fought series in five games, with three contests requiring overtime.

SEMIFINALS

Mar. 19	Chicago	2	at	Montreal	6
Mar. 21	Chicago	1	at	Montreal	5
Mar. 24	Montreal	8	at	Chicago	2
Mar. 26	Montreal	7	at	Chicago	2

Montreal won best-of-seven series 4–0

Mar. 19	Detroit	1	at	Boston	3
Mar. 21	Detroit	3	at	Boston	0
Mar. 24	Boston	5	at	Detroit	2
Mar. 26	Boston	4	at	Detroit	1
Mar. 28	Detroit	3	at	Boston	4 OT

Boston won best-of-seven series 4–1

FINALS

Mar. 30	Boston	3	at	Montreal	4 OT
Apr. 2	Boston	2	at	Montreal	3 OT
Apr. 4	Montreal	4	at	Boston	2
Apr. 7	Montreal	2	at	Boston	3 OT
Apr. 9	Boston	3	at	Montreal	6

Montreal won best-of-seven series 4–1

1945-46 – Montreal Canadiens – Elmer Lach, Toe Blake, Maurice Richard, Bob Fillion, Dutch Hiller, Murph Chamberlain, Kenny Mosdell, Buddy O'Connor, Glen Harmon, Jimmy Peters Sr., Butch Bouchard, Billy Reay, Ken Reardon, Leo Lamoureux, Frank Eddolls, Gerry Plamondon, Bill Durnan, Tommy Gorman (manager), Dick Irvin (coach), Ernie Cook (trainer).

1945

Two rookie goaltenders — Toronto's Frank McCool and Detroit's Harry Lumley — manned the opposing nets in the Stanley Cup finals for the first time. McCool, who never played in another final series, posted shutouts in the each of the first three games to set a new Stanley Cup record, while Lumley rebounded with two of his own in games five and six to knot the series at three games apiece.

SEMIFINALS

Mar. 20	Toronto	1	at	Montreal	0
Mar. 22	Toronto	3	at	Montreal	2
Mar. 24	Montreal	4	at	Toronto	1
Mar. 27	Montreal	3	at	Toronto	4 OT
Mar. 29	Toronto	3	at	Montreal	10
Mar. 31	Montreal	2	at	Toronto	3

Toronto won best-of-seven series 4–2

Mar. 20	Boston	4	at	Detroit	3
Mar. 22	Boston	4	at	Detroit	2
Mar. 25	Detroit	3	at	Boston	2
Mar. 27	Detroit	3	at	Boston	2
Mar. 29	Boston	2	at	Detroit	3 OT
Apr. 1	Detroit	3	at	Boston	5
Apr. 3	Boston	3	at	Detroit	5

Detroit won best-of-seven series 4–3

FINALS

Apr. 6	Toronto	1	at	Detroit	0
Apr. 8	Toronto	2	at	Detroit	0
Apr. 12	Detroit	0	at	Toronto	1
Apr. 14	Detroit	5	at	Toronto	3
Apr. 19	Toronto	0	at	Detroit	2
Apr. 21	Detroit	1	at	Toronto	0 OT
Apr. 22	Toronto	2	at	Detroit	1

Toronto won best-of-seven series 4–3

1944-45 – Toronto Maple Leafs – Don Metz, Frank McCool, Wally Stanowski, Reg Hamilton, Elwyn Morris, Johnny McCreedy, Tommy O'Neill, Ted Kennedy, Babe Pratt, Gus Bodnar, Art Jackson, Jack McLean, Mel Hill, Nick Metz, Bob Davidson, Sweeney Schriner, Lorne Carr, Conn Smythe (manager), Frank Selke (business manager), Hap Day (coach), Tim Daly (trainer).

1944

Making his Stanley Cup debut, Maurice "Rocket" Richard scored five goals, including the first of his NHL-record three career hat tricks in the finals in game two. In total, the Punch Line of Elmer Lach, Toe Blake and Richard combined for 10 of the Canadiens' 16 goals in the series, including all five Montreal scores in the finale. Blake netted the Cup-winning goal at 9:12 of the first overtime period in game four, marking the fourth time an NHL player had clinched the Cup with a sudden-death tally.

In that final overtime contest, Canadiens goaltender Bill Durnan stonewalled Chicago's Virgil Johnson on the first penalty shot ever awarded in a Stanley Cup final.

The victory gave the Canadiens their first Stanley Cup championship since 1931.

SEMIFINALS

Mar. 21	Toronto	3	at	Montreal	1
Mar. 23	Toronto	1	at	Montreal	5
Mar. 25	Montreal	2	at	Toronto	1
Mar. 28	Montreal	4	at	Toronto	1
Mar. 30	Toronto	0	at	Montreal	11

Montreal won best-of-seven series 4–1

Mar. 21	Chicago	2	at	Detroit	1
Mar. 23	Chicago	1	at	Detroit	4
Mar. 26	Detroit	0	at	Chicago	2
Mar. 28	Detroit	1	at	Chicago	7
Mar. 30	Chicago	5	at	Detroit	2

Chicago won best-of-seven series 4–1

FINALS

Apr. 4	Chicago	1	at	Montreal	5
Apr. 6	Montreal	3	at	Chicago	1
Apr. 9	Montreal	3	at	Chicago	2
Apr. 13	Chicago	4	at	Montreal	5 OT

Montreal won best-of-seven series 4–0

1943-44 – Montreal Canadiens – Toe Blake, Maurice Richard, Elmer Lach, Ray Getliffe, Murph Chamberlain, Phil Watson, Butch Bouchard, Glen Harmon, Buddy O'Connor, Jerry Heffernan, Mike McMahon Sr., Leo Lamoureux, Fernand Majeau, Bob Fillion, Bill Durnan, Tommy Gorman (manager), Dick Irvin (coach), Ernie Cook (trainer).

1943

A new era in hockey history was ushered in with the 1942–43 season. The departure of the New York Americans franchise left the NHL with just the New York Rangers, Boston Bruins, Chicago Black Hawks, Detroit Red Wings, Toronto Maple Leafs and Montreal Canadiens — the so-called "Original Six."

After losing the Stanley Cup in 1941 and 1942, the Red Wings' third straight trip to the finals proved to be the charm as they swept the Bruins, avenging the similar treatment they had received from Boston two years before. Goaltender Johnny Mowers blanked the Bruins at Boston Garden in the last two games to ice the championship.

SEMIFINALS

Mar. 21	Toronto	2	at	Detroit	4
Mar. 23	Toronto	3	at	Detroit	2 4OT
Mar. 25	Detroit	4	at	Toronto	2
Mar. 27	Detroit	3	at	Toronto	6
Mar. 28	Toronto	2	at	Detroit	4
Mar. 30	Detroit	3	at	Toronto	2 OT

Detroit won best-of-seven series 4–2

Mar. 21	Montreal	4	at	Boston	5 OT
Mar. 23	Montreal	3	at	Boston	5
Mar. 25	Boston	3	at	Montreal	2 OT
Mar. 27	Boston	0	at	Montreal	4
Mar. 30	Montreal	4	at	Boston	5 OT

Boston won best-of-seven series 4–1

FINALS

Apr. 1	Boston	2	at	Detroit	6
Apr. 4	Boston	3	at	Detroit	4
Apr. 7	Detroit	4	at	Boston	0
Apr. 8	Detroit	2	at	Boston	0

Detroit won best-of-seven series 4–0

1942-43 – Detroit Red Wings – Jack Stewart, Jimmy Orlando, Sid Abel, Alex Motter, Harry Watson, Joe Carveth, Mud Bruneteau, Eddie Wares, Johnny Mowers, Cully Simon, Don Grosso, Carl Liscombe, Connie Brown, Syd Howe, Les Douglas, Hal Jackson, Joe Fisher, Jack Adams (manager), Ebbie Goodfellow (playing-coach), Honey Walker (trainer).

1942

In the most remarkable comeback in Stanley Cup history, Toronto rebounded from a 3–0 deficit to win the series in seven games. The feat has never been duplicated in the finals.

The Maple Leafs hosted the first crowd of over 16,000 in Canada in game seven.

SERIES A - SEMIFINALS

Mar. 21	NY Rangers	1	at	Toronto	3
Mar. 22	Toronto	4	at	NY Rangers	2
Mar. 24	Toronto	0	at	NY Rangers	3
Mar. 28	NY Rangers	1	at	Toronto	2
Mar. 29	Toronto	1	at	NY Rangers	3
Mar. 31	NY Rangers	2	at	Toronto	3

Toronto won best-of-seven series 4–2

SERIES B AND C - QUARTERFINALS

Mar. 22	Boston	2	at	Chicago	1 OT
Mar. 24	Chicago	4	at	Boston	0
Mar. 26	Chicago	2	at	Boston	3

Boston won best-of-three series 2–1

Mar. 22	Montreal	1	at	Detroit	2
Mar. 24	Detroit	0	at	Montreal	5
Mar. 26	Montreal	2	at	Detroit	6

Detroit won best-of-three series 2–1

SERIES D - SEMIFINALS

Mar. 29	Detroit	6	at	Boston	4
Mar. 31	Boston	1	at	Detroit	3

Detroit won best-of-three series 2–0

FINALS

Apr. 4	Detroit	3	at	Toronto	2
Apr. 7	Detroit	4	at	Toronto	2
Apr. 9	Toronto	2	at	Detroit	5
Apr. 12	Toronto	4	at	Detroit	3
Apr. 14	Detroit	3	at	Toronto	9
Apr. 16	Toronto	3	at	Detroit	0
Apr. 18	Detroit	1	at	Toronto	3

Toronto won best-of-seven series 4–3

1941-42 – Toronto Maple Leafs – Wally Stanowski, Syl Apps Sr., Bob Goldham, Gordie Drillon, Hank Goldup, Ernie Dickens, Sweeney Schriner, Bucko McDonald, Bob Davidson, Nick Metz, Bingo Kampman, Don Metz, Gaye Stewart, Turk Broda, Johnny McCreedy, Lorne Carr, Pete Langelle, Billy Taylor, Conn Smythe (manager), Hap Day (coach), Frank Selke (business manager), Tim Daly (trainer).

1941

In the third best-of-seven series ever played in the Stanley Cup finals, Boston became the first to win in four straight games. Since the National Hockey League was formed in 1917, only four teams — the 1929 Boston Bruins and 1930 Montreal Canadiens in two straight and the 1932 Toronto Maple Leafs and 1935 Montreal Maroons in three straight — had ever won the Cup in the fewest possible games.

SERIES A - SEMIFINALS

Mar. 20	Toronto	0	at	Boston	3
Mar. 22	Toronto	5	at	Boston	3
Mar. 25	Boston	2	at	Toronto	7
Mar. 27	Boston	2	at	Toronto	1
Mar. 29	Toronto	2	at	Boston	1 OT
Apr. 1	Boston	2	at	Toronto	1
Apr. 3	Toronto	1	at	Boston	2

Boston won best-of-seven series 4–3

SERIES B AND C - QUARTERFINALS

Mar. 20	NY Rangers	1	at	Detroit	2 OT
Mar. 23	Detroit	1	at	NY Rangers	3
Mar. 25	NY Rangers	2	at	Detroit	3

Detroit won best-of-three series 2–1

Mar. 20	Montreal	1	at	Chicago	2
Mar. 22	Chicago	3	at	Montreal	4 2OT
Mar. 25	Montreal	2	at	Chicago	3

Chicago won best-of-three series 2–1

SERIES D - SEMIFINALS

Mar. 27	Chicago	1	at	Detroit	3
Mar. 30	Detroit	2	at	Chicago	1 OT

Detroit won best-of-three series 2–0

FINALS

Apr. 6	Detroit	2	at	Boston	3
Apr. 8	Detroit	1	at	Boston	2
Apr. 10	Boston	4	at	Detroit	2
Apr. 12	Boston	3	at	Detroit	1

Boston won best-of-seven series 4–0

1940-41 – Boston Bruins – Bill Cowley, Des Smith, Dit Clapper, Frank Brimsek, Flash Hollett, John Crawford, Bobby Bauer, Pat McReavy, Herb Cain, Mel Hill, Milt Schmidt, Woody Dumart, Roy Conacher, Terry Reardon, Art Jackson, Eddie Wiseman, Art Ross (manager), Cooney Weiland (coach), Win Green (trainer).

1940

With the circus heading towards New York, the Rangers were forced to play the first two games of the finals on consecutive nights before vacating Madison Square Garden for the rest of the series.

Three of the Rangers' four game-winning goals were scored in overtime, including the Cup-winner by Bryan Hextall in game six. It marked the third time in NHL history that the last goal of the season had been tallied in sudden-death.

Lynn and Murray Patrick skated for the winners to become the third and fourth members of the Patrick family, joining father (and Rangers manager) Lester and uncle Frank, to have their names engraved on the Stanley Cup.

SERIES A - SEMIFINALS

Mar. 19	Boston	0	at	NY Rangers	4
Mar. 21	NY Rangers	2	at	Boston	4
Mar. 24	NY Rangers	3	at	Boston	4
Mar. 26	Boston	0	at	NY Rangers	1
Mar. 28	NY Rangers	1	at	Boston	0
Mar. 30	Boston	1	at	NY Rangers	4

Rangers won best-of-seven series 4–2

SERIES B AND C - QUARTERFINALS

Mar. 19	Chicago	2	at	Toronto	3 OT
Mar. 21	Toronto	2	at	Chicago	1

Toronto won best-of-three series 2–0

Mar. 19	NY Americans	1	at	Detroit	2 OT
Mar. 22	Detroit	4	at	NY Americans	5
Mar. 24	NY Americans	1	at	Detroit	3

Detroit won best-of-three series 2–1

SERIES D - SEMIFINALS

Mar. 26	Detroit	1	at	Toronto	2
Mar. 28	Toronto	3	at	Detroit	1

Toronto won best-of-three series 2–0

FINALS

Apr. 2	Toronto	1	at	NY Rangers	2 OT
Apr. 3	Toronto	2	at	NY Rangers	6
Apr. 6	NY Rangers	1	at	Toronto	2
Apr. 9	NY Rangers	0	at	Toronto	3
Apr. 11	NY Rangers	2	at	Toronto	1 2OT
Apr. 13	NY Rangers	3	at	Toronto	2 OT

Rangers won best-of-seven series 4–2

1939-40 – New York Rangers – Dave Kerr, Art Coulter, Ott Heller, Alex Shibicky, Mac Colville, Neil Colville, Phil Watson, Lynn Patrick, Clint Smith, Muzz Patrick, Babe Pratt, Bryan Hextall Sr., Kilby Macdonald, Dutch Hiller, Alf Pike, Sanford Smith, Lester Patrick (manager), Frank Boucher (coach), Harry Westerby (trainer).

1939

The NHL expanded the Stanley Cup finals to a best-of-seven format, though it took the Bruins only five games to defeat the Maple Leafs.

Boston goaltender Frank Brimsek held Toronto to just six goals in five games as the Bruins took the Cup for the first time in 10 seasons.

Mel Hill of Boston, who earlier set an NHL record with three overtime goals in the first round of the playoffs, scored twice in the series, and Bill Cowley led all playoff scorers with 11 assists and 14 points, setting modern-era playoff records in both categories.

SERIES A - SEMIFINALS

Mar. 21	Boston	2	at	NY Rangers	1 3OT
Mar. 23	NY Rangers	2	at	Boston	3 OT
Mar. 26	NY Rangers	1	at	Boston	4
Mar. 28	Boston	1	at	NY Rangers	2
Mar. 30	NY Rangers	2	at	Boston	1 OT
Apr. 1	Boston	1	at	NY Rangers	3
Apr. 2	NY Rangers	1	at	Boston	2 3OT

Boston won best-of-seven series 4–3

SERIES B AND C - QUARTERFINALS

Mar. 21	NY Americans	0	at	Toronto	4
Mar. 23	Toronto	2	at	NY Americans	0

Toronto won best-of-three series 2–0

Mar. 21	Detroit	0	at	Montreal	2
Mar. 23	Montreal	3	at	Detroit	7
Mar. 26	Montreal	0	at	Detroit	1 OT

Detroit won best-of-three series 2–1

SERIES D - SEMIFINALS

Mar. 28	Detroit	1	at	Toronto	4
Mar. 30	Toronto	1	at	Detroit	3
Apr. 1	Detroit	4	at	Toronto	5 OT

Toronto won best-of-three series 2–1

FINALS

Apr. 6	Toronto	1	at	Boston	2
Apr. 9	Toronto	3	at	Boston	2 OT
Apr. 11	Boston	3	at	Toronto	1
Apr. 13	Boston	2	at	Toronto	0
Apr. 16	Toronto	1	at	Boston	3

Boston won best-of-seven series 4–1

1938-39 – Boston Bruins – Bobby Bauer, Mel Hill, Flash Hollett, Roy Conacher, Gord Pettinger, Milt Schmidt, Woody Dumart, Jack Crawford, Ray Getliffe, Frank Brimsek, Eddie Shore, Dit Clapper, Bill Cowley, Jack Portland, Red Hamill, Cooney Weiland, Art Ross (manager-coach), Win Green (trainer).

1938

The Black Hawks faced the start of the Stanley Cup finals without top goaltender Mike Karakas, who had played every game during the season but broke his big toe on April 3. Chicago was forced to sign journeyman netminder Alfie Moore, who played game one and posted a win in his only Cup appearance.

Following the victory, NHL President Frank Calder ruled Moore ineligible for further play, and Chicago had to call on minor-league goalie Paul Goodman, who lost his first NHL start in game two.

Karakas finally returned with a steel-capped boot to protect his toe and won both starts, while teammate Doc Romnes wore a football helmet to guard a broken nose and scored the winning goal in game three before a record crowd of 18,497.

Eight American-born players — Karakas, Romnes, Alex Levinsky, Carl Voss, Carl Dahlstrom, Roger Jenkins, Louis Trudel and Virgil Johnson — skated for the Black Hawks to set a record (not broken until 1995) for U.S. talent on a Cup winner.

SERIES A - SEMIFINALS

Mar. 24	Boston	0	at	Toronto	1 2OT
Mar. 26	Boston	1	at	Toronto	2
Mar. 29	Toronto	3	at	Boston	2 OT

Toronto won best-of-five series 3–0

SERIES B AND C - QUARTERFINALS

Mar. 22	NY Americans	2	at	NY Rangers	1 2OT
Mar. 24	NY Rangers	4	at	NY Americans	3
Mar. 27	NY Americans	3	at	NY Rangers	2 4OT

Americans won best-of-three series 2–1

Mar. 22	Chicago	4	at	Montreal	6
Mar. 24	Montreal	0	at	Chicago	4
Mar. 26	Chicago	3	at	Montreal	2 OT

Chicago won best-of-three series 2–1

SERIES D - SEMIFINALS

Mar. 29	Chicago	1	at	NY Americans	3
Mar. 31	NY Americans	0	at	Chicago	1 2OT
Apr. 3	Chicago	3	at	NY Americans	2

Chicago won best-of-three series 2–1

FINALS

Apr. 5	Chicago	3	at	Toronto	1
Apr. 7	Chicago	1	at	Toronto	5
Apr. 10	Toronto	1	at	Chicago	2
Apr. 12	Toronto	1	at	Chicago	4

Chicago won best-of-five series 3–1

1937-38 – Chicago Black Hawks – Art Wiebe, Carl Voss, Hal Jackson, Mike Karakas, Mush March, Jack Shill, Earl Seibert, Cully Dahlstrom, Alex Levinsky, Johnny Gottselig, Louis Trudel, Pete Palangio, Bill MacKenzie, Doc Romnes, Paul Thompson, Roger Jenkins, Alfie Moore, Bert Connolly, Virgil Johnson, Paul Goodman, Bill Stewart (manager-coach), Eddie Froelich (trainer).

1937

The Rangers, turned away from Madison Square Garden once again by the incoming circus after game one, agreed to play the remainder of the series on Detroit's home ice.

First-year goaltender Earl Robertson, who would never play a regular-season game for the Red Wings during his career, became the first rookie netminder to post two shutouts in the finals, blanking the Rangers in the last two games of the series.

With their second straight Stanley Cup title, Detroit became the first U.S.-based squad to repeat as champions.

SERIES A - SEMIFINALS

Mar.	23	Montreal	0	at	Detroit	4
Mar.	25	Montreal	1	at	Detroit	5
Mar.	27	Detroit	1	at	Montreal	3
Mar.	30	Detroit	1	at	Montreal	3
Apr.	1	Detroit	2	at	Montreal	1 3OT

Detroit won best-of-five series 3–2

SERIES B AND C - QUARTERFINALS

Mar.	23	Boston	1	at	Mtl Maroons	4
Mar.	25	Mtl Maroons	0	at	Boston	4
Mar.	28	Mtl Maroons	4	at	Boston	1

Maroons won best-of-three series 2–1

Mar.	23	NY Rangers	3	at	Toronto	0
Mar.	25	Toronto	1	at	NY Rangers	2 OT

Rangers won best-of-three series 2–0

SERIES D - SEMIFINALS

Apr.	1	Mtl Maroons	0	at	NY Rangers	1
Apr.	3	NY Rangers	4	at	Mtl Maroons	0

Rangers won best-of-three series 2–0

FINALS

Apr.	6	Detroit	1	at	NY Rangers	5
Apr.	8	NY Rangers	2	at	Detroit	4
Apr.	11	NY Rangers	1	at	Detroit	0
Apr.	13	NY Rangers	0	at	Detroit	1
Apr.	15	NY Rangers	0	at	Detroit	3

Detroit won best-of-five series 3–2

1936-37 – Detroit Red Wings – Norman Smith, Pete Kelly, Larry Aurie, Herbie Lewis, Hec Kilrea, Mud Bruneteau, Syd Howe, Wally Kilrea, Jimmy Franks, Bucko McDonald, Gord Pettinger, Ebbie Goodfellow, John Gallagher, Ralph Bowman, John Sorrell, Marty Barry, Earl Robertson, John Sherf, Howard Mackie, Jack Adams (manager-coach), Honey Walker (trainer).

1936

Under the coaching guidance of Jack Adams, the Detroit Red Wings captured their first Stanley Cup championship after 10 NHL seasons.

The series marked Frank "King" Clancy's sixth and final appearance as a player in the finals. However, it would not be his last Stanley Cup series, for Clancy went on to earn prominence as an NHL referee, working 20 Stanley Cup games in that capacity.

SERIES A - SEMIFINALS

Mar.	24	Detroit	1	at	Mtl Maroons	0 6OT
Mar.	26	Detroit	3	at	Mtl Maroons	0
Mar.	28	Mtl Maroons	1	at	Detroit	2

Detroit vwon best-of-five series 3–0

SERIES B AND C - QUARTERFINALS

Mar.	24	Toronto	0	at	Boston	3
Mar.	26	Boston	3	at	Toronto	8

Toronto won total-goals series 8–6

Mar.	24	Chicago	0	at	NY Americans	3
Mar.	26	NY Americans	4	at	Chicago	5

Americans won total-goals series 7–5

SERIES D - SEMIFINALS

Mar.	28	NY Americans	1	at	Toronto	3
Mar.	31	Toronto	0	at	NY Americans	1
Apr.	2	NY Americans	1	at	Toronto	3

Toronto won best-of-three series 2-1

FINALS

Apr.	5	Toronto	1	at	Detroit	3
Apr.	7	Toronto	4	at	Detroit	9
Apr.	9	Detroit	3	at	Toronto	4 OT
Apr.	11	Detroit	3	at	Toronto	2

Detroit won best-of-five series 3–1

1935-36 – Detroit Red Wings – John Sorrell, Syd Howe, Marty Barry, Herbie Lewis, Mud Bruneteau, Wally Kilrea, Hec Kilrea, Gord Pettinger, Bucko McDonald, Ralph Bowman, Pete Kelly, Doug Young, Ebbie Goodfellow, Norman Smith, Jack Adams (manager-coach), Honey Walker (trainer).

1935

In the first All-Canadian final since the Montreal Maroons beat Victoria in 1926, the Montreal team battled to its second Stanley Cup championship with a three-game sweep of Toronto. Maroons netminder Alex Connell allowed just four goals in three games.

Winning coach Tommy Gorman became the first and only coach to win successive Stanley Cup titles with two different teams. He had directed the Chicago Black Hawks to the championship a year earlier. Gorman currently ranks as one of three NHL coaches (Dick Irvin and Scotty Bowman are the others) to have led more than one team to the Stanley Cup.

SERIES A - SEMIFINALS

Mar.	23	Toronto	0	at	Boston	1 2OT
Mar.	26	Toronto	2	at	Boston	0
Mar.	28	Boston	0	at	Toronto	3
Mar.	30	Boston	1	at	Toronto	2 OT

Toronto won best-of-five series 3–1

SERIES B AND C - QUARTERFINALS

Mar.	23	Chicago	0	at	Mtl Maroons	0
Mar.	26	Mtl Maroons	1	at	Chicago	0 OT

Maroons won total-goals series 1–0

Mar.	24	Montreal	1	at	NY Rangers	2
Mar.	26	NY Rangers	4	at	Montreal	4

Rangers won total-goals series 6–5

SERIES D - SEMIFINALS

Mar.	28	Mtl Maroons	2	at	NY Rangers	1
Mar.	30	NY Rangers	3	at	Mtl Maroons	3

Maroons won total-goals series 5–4

FINALS

Apr.	4	Mtl Maroons	3	at	Toronto	2 OT
Apr.	6	Mtl Maroons	3	at	Toronto	1
Apr.	9	Toronto	1	at	Mtl Maroons	4

Maroons won best-of-five series 3–0

1934-35 – Montreal Maroons – Lionel Conacher, Cy Wentworth, Alex Connell, Toe Blake, Stewart Evans, Earl Robinson, Bill Miller, Dave Trottier, Jimmy Ward, Larry Northcott, Hooley Smith, Russ Blinco, Allan Shields, Sammy McManus, Gus Marker, Bob Gracie, Herb Cain, Tommy Gorman (manager-coach), Bill O'Brien (trainer).

1934

For the second year in a row, the Stanley Cup-winning goal was scored in overtime. When Chicago's Harold "Mush" March netted the series-winner at 30:05 of overtime, the Black Hawks captured their first Cup victory.

Chicago's Chuck Gardiner limited Detroit to two goals in his club's three victories, while Detroit goaltender Wilf Cude led the Red Wings to their only win of the series in game three despite suffering a broken nose midway through the contest. Cude stopped 52 of 53 Detroit shots in the deciding game, while Gardiner turned aside all 40 Black Hawk blasts. Gardiner had been plagued by severe headaches all year. Two months after the Stanley Cup series he died of a brain hemorrhage.

SERIES A - SEMIFINALS

Mar.	22	Detroit	2	at	Toronto	1 OT
Mar.	24	Detroit	6	at	Toronto	3
Mar.	26	Toronto	3	at	Detroit	1
Mar.	28	Toronto	5	at	Detroit	1
Mar.	30	Toronto	0	at	Detroit	1

Detroit won best-of-five series 3–2

SERIES B AND C - QUARTERFINALS

Mar.	22	Chicago	3	at	Montreal	2
Mar.	25	Montreal	1	at	Chicago	1 OT

Chicago won total-goals series 4–3

Mar.	20	NY Rangers	0	at	Mtl Maroons	0
Mar.	25	Mtl Maroons	2	at	NY Rangers	1

Maroons won total-goals series 2–1

SERIES D - SEMIFINALS

Mar.	28	Chicago	3	at	Mtl Maroons	0
Apr.	1	Mtl Maroons	2	at	Chicago	3

Chicago won total-goals series 6–2

FINALS

Apr.	3	Chicago	2	at	Detroit	1 2OT
Apr.	5	Chicago	4	at	Detroit	1
Apr.	8	Detroit	5	at	Chicago	2
Apr.	10	Detroit	0	at	Chicago	1 2OT

Chicago won best-of-five series 3–1

1933-34 – Chicago Black Hawks – Clarence Abel, Rosie Couture, Louis Trudel, Lionel Conacher, Paul Thompson, Leroy Goldsworthy, Art Coulter, Roger Jenkins, Don McFayden, Tom Cook, Doc Romnes, Johnny Gottselig, Mush March, Johnny Sheppard, Chuck Gardiner (captain), Bill Kendall, Tommy Gorman (manager-coach), Eddie Froelich (trainer).

1933

Again the circus forced the Rangers out of New York, with all but game one contested on Toronto's home ice. However, this year the Rangers would not be denied

In the final match, New York's Bill Cook became the first of 13 NHL players to register a Stanley Cup-winning goal in overtime when he snapped a scoreless tie at 7:33 of the fourth period. Goalie Andy Aitkenhead posted the fourth shutout by an NHL rookie in the finals.

SERIES A - SEMIFINALS

Mar.	25	Toronto	1	at	Boston	2 OT
Mar.	28	Toronto	1	at	Boston	0 OT
Mar.	30	Boston	2	at	Toronto	1 OT
Apr.	1	Boston	3	at	Toronto	5
Apr.	3	Boston	0	at	Toronto	1 6OT

Toronto won best-of-five series 3–2

SERIES B AND C - QUARTERFINALS

Mar.	25	Detroit	2	at	Mtl Maroons	0
Mar.	28	Mtl Maroons	2	at	Detroit	3

Detroit won total-goals series 5–2

Mar.	26	Montreal	2	at	NY Rangers	5
Mar.	28	NY Rangers	3	at	Montreal	3

Rangers won total-goals series 8–5

SERIES D - SEMIFINALS

Mar.	30	Detroit	0	at	NY Rangers	2
Apr.	2	NY Rangers	4	at	Detroit	3

Rangers won total-goals series 6–3

FINALS

Apr.	4	Toronto	1	at	NY Rangers	5
Apr.	8	NY Rangers	3	at	Toronto	1
Apr.	11	NY Rangers	2	at	Toronto	3
Apr.	13	NY Rangers	1	at	Toronto	0 OT

Rangers won best-of-five series 3–1

1932-33 – New York Rangers – Ching Johnson, Butch Keeling, Frank Boucher, Art Somers, Babe Siebert, Bun Cook, Andy Aitkenhead, Ott Heller, Oscar Asmundson, Gord Pettinger, Doug Brennan, Cecil Dillon, Bill Cook (captain), Murray Murdoch, Earl Seibert, Lester Patrick (manager-coach), Harry Westerby (trainer).

1932

After losing to Toronto in game one, the Rangers also lost the home-ice advantage because the circus had once again invaded Madison Square Garden. Game two, originally set for New York, was moved to Boston.

Toronto's famed Kid Line of Harvey "Busher" Jackson, Charlie Conacher and Joe Primeau made its Stanley Cup debut, combining for eight goals in the three-game sweep.

The Leafs' Dick Irvin, who lost in the 1931 finals with the Chicago Black Hawks, earned his first title as a coach.

SERIES A - SEMIFINALS

Mar.	24	NY Rangers	3	at	Montreal	4
Mar.	26	NY Rangers	4	at	Montreal	3 3OT
Mar.	27	Montreal	0	at	NY Rangers	1
Mar.	29	Montreal	2	at	NY Rangers	5

Rangers won best-of-five series 3–1

SERIES B AND C - QUARTERFINALS

Mar.	27	Toronto	0	at	Chicago	1
Mar.	29	Chicago	1	at	Toronto	6

Toronto won total-goals series 6–2

Mar.	27	Mtl Maroons	1	at	Detroit	1
Mar.	29	Detroit	0	at	Mtl Maroons	2

Maroons won total-goals series 3–1

SERIES D - SEMIFINALS

Mar.	31	Toronto	1	at	Mtl Maroons	1
Apr.	2	Mtl Maroons	2	at	Toronto	3 OT

Toronto won total-goals series 4–3

FINALS

Apr.	5	Toronto	6	at	NY Rangers	4
Apr.	7	Toronto	6	vs	NY Rangers	2 *
Apr.	9	NY Rangers	4	at	Toronto	6

* played in Boston

Toronto won best-of-five series 3–0

1931-32 – Toronto Maple Leafs – Charlie Conacher, Harvey Jackson, King Clancy, Andy Blair, Red Horner, Lorne Chabot, Alex Levinsky, Joe Primeau, Hal Darragh, Hal Cotton, Frank Finnigan, Hap Day, Ace Bailey, Bob Gracie, Fred Robertson, Earl Miller, Conn Smythe (manager), Dick Irvin (coach), Tim Daly (trainer).

1931

The Montreal Canadiens became the second NHL team to repeat as Stanley Cup champions, duplicating the feat accomplished by the Ottawa Senators in 1920 and 1921. Chicago's Dick Irvin made his coaching debut in the finals against the team which he would later lead to three Stanley Cup titles.

Over 18,000 fans packed Chicago Stadium for game two to set a new record for the largest attendance in hockey history.

SEMIFINALS

Mar.	24	Montreal	4	at	Boston	5 OT
Mar.	26	Montreal	1	at	Boston	0
Mar.	28	Boston	3	at	Montreal	4 OT
Mar.	30	Boston	3	at	Montreal	1
Apr.	1	Boston	2	at	Montreal	3 OT

Montreal won best-of-five series 3–2

SERIES B AND C - QUARTERFINALS

Mar.	24	Chicago	2	at	Toronto	2
Mar.	26	Toronto	1	at	Chicago	2 OT

Chicago won total-goals series 4–3

Mar.	24	Mtl Maroons	1	at	NY Rangers	5
Mar.	26	NY Rangers	3	at	Mtl Maroons	0

Rangers won total-goals series 8–1

SERIES D - SEMIFINALS

Mar.	29	NY Rangers	0	at	Chicago	2
Mar.	31	Chicago	1	at	NY Rangers	0

Chicago won total-goals series 3–0

FINALS

Apr.	3	Montreal	2	at	Chicago	1
Apr.	5	Montreal	1	at	Chicago	2 2OT
Apr.	9	Chicago	3	at	Montreal	2 3OT
Apr.	11	Chicago	2	at	Montreal	4
Apr.	14	Chicago	0	at	Montreal	2

Montreal won best-of-five series 3–2

1930-31 – Montreal Canadiens – George Hainsworth, Wildor Larochelle, Marty Burke, Sylvio Mantha, Howie Morenz, Johnny Gagnon, Aurel Joliat, Armand Mondou, Pit Lepine, Albert Leduc, Georges Mantha, Art Lesieur, Nick Wasnie, Bert McCaffrey, Gus Rivers, Jean Pusie, Léo Dandurand (manager), Cecil Hart (coach), Ed Dufour (trainer).

1930

The defending champion Boston Bruins had skated to the NHL's top regular-season record in 1929–30. The Bruins' 38–5–1 record translates into an .875 winning percentage that is still the best in NHL history. The team did not lose back-to-back games all season until being swept by the Canadiens in the best-of-three Stanley Cup series. Boston's surprising defeat prompted the NHL to lengthen the finals to a best-of-five in the future.

The Canadiens, who had lost all four of their regular-season meetings with the Bruins, were led by captain Sylvio Mantha who tallied a goal in both final series games.

SERIES A - SEMIFINALS

Mar.	20	Boston	2	at	Mtl Maroons	1 3OT
Mar.	22	Boston	4	at	Mtl Maroons	2
Mar.	25	Mtl Maroons	1	at	Boston	0 2OT
Mar.	27	Mtl Maroons	1	at	Boston	5

Boston won best-of-five series 3–1

SERIES B AND C - QUARTERFINALS

Mar.	23	Montreal	1	at	Chicago	0
Mar.	26	Chicago	2	at	Montreal	2 3OT

Montreal won total-goals series 3–2

Mar.	20	NY Rangers	1	at	Ottawa	1
Mar.	23	Ottawa	2	at	NY Rangers	5

Rangers won total-goals series 6–3

SERIES D - SEMIFINALS

Mar.	28	NY Rangers	1	at	Montreal	2 4OT
Mar.	30	Montreal	2	at	NY Rangers	0

Montreal won best-of-three series 2–0

FINALS

Apr.	1	Montreal	3	at	Boston	0
Apr.	3	Boston	3	at	Montreal	4

Montreal won best-of-three series 2–0

1929-30 – Montreal Canadiens – George Hainsworth, Marty Burke, Sylvio Mantha, Howie Morenz, Bert McCaffrey, Aurel Joliat, Albert Leduc, Pit Lepine, Wildor Larochelle, Nick Wasnie, Gerald Carson, Armand Mondou, Georges Mantha, Gus Rivers, Léo Dandurand (manager), Cecil Hart (coach), Ed Dufour (trainer).

1929

When the Bruins met the Rangers in this series, it marked the first time in Stanley Cup history that two American teams clashed head-on for the prized trophy.

Goalie Cecil "Tiny" Thompson backstopped the Bruins to consecutive wins, allowing just one goal in the two games and posting the third Stanley Cup shutout ever by an NHL rookie as Boston captured its first Cup.

Dit Clapper and Harry Oliver scored the two game-winning goals.

SERIES A - SEMIFINALS

Mar.	19	Montreal	0	at	Boston	1
Mar.	21	Montreal	0	at	Boston	1
Mar.	23	Boston	3	at	Montreal	2

Boston won best-of-five series 3–0

SERIES B AND C - QUARTERFINALS

Mar.	19	NY Rangers	0	at	NY Americans	0
Mar.	21	NY Americans	0	at	NY Rangers	1 2OT

Rangers won total-goals series 1–0

Mar.	19	Toronto	3	at	Detroit	1
Mar.	21	Detroit	1	at	Toronto	4

Toronto won total-goals series 7–2

SERIES D - SEMIFINALS

Mar.	24	Toronto	0	at	NY Rangers	1
Mar.	26	NY Rangers	2	at	Toronto	1 OT

Rangers won best-of-three series 2–0

FINALS

Mar.	28	NY Rangers	0	at	Boston	2
Mar.	29	Boston	2	at	NY Rangers	1

Boston won best-of-three series 2–0

1928-29 – Boston Bruins – Tiny Thompson, Eddie Shore, Lionel Hitchman, Perk Galbraith, Eric Pettinger, Frank Fredrickson, Mickey Mackay, Red Green, Dutch Gainor, Harry Oliver, Eddie Rodden, Dit Clapper, Cooney Weiland, Lloyd Klein, Cy Denneny, Bill Carson, George Owen, Myles Lane, Art Ross (manager-coach), Win Green (trainer).

1928

Though the Rangers moved into the finals, the circus moved into New York's Madison Square Garden and took priority over the hockey team. As a result, club management decided to play the entire series in Montreal.

After losing goalie Lorne Chabot to an eye injury midway through game two, 44-year-old Rangers coach and early era star player Lester Patrick took over between the pipes, inspiring the New Yorkers to a 2–1 overtime victory. The following day the Rangers signed New York Americans netminder Joe Miller, who responded with two wins including the second shutout by an NHL rookie in Stanley Cup history.

In only their second NHL season, the Rangers captured their first Stanley Cup title and became only the second American team in history, joining the 1917 Seattle Metropolitans of the PCHA, to possess the trophy.

QUARTERFINALS

Mar.	27	Mtl Maroons	1	at	Ottawa	0
Mar.	29	Ottawa	1	at	Mtl Maroons	2

Maroons won total-goals series 3–1

Mar.	27	Pittsburgh	0	at	NY Rangers	4
Mar.	29	Pittsburgh	4	at	NY Rangers	2

Rangers won total-goals series 6–4

SEMIFINALS

Mar.	31	Montreal	2	at	Mtl Maroons	2
Apr.	3	Mtl Maroons	1	at	Montreal	0 OT

Maroons won total-goals series 3–2

Mar.	31	Boston	1	at	NY Rangers	1

Apr.	3	NY Rangers	4	at	Boston	1

Rangers won total-goals series 5–2

FINALS

Apr.	5	NY Rangers	0	at	Mtl Maroons	2
Apr.	7	NY Rangers	2	at	Mtl Maroons	1 OT
Apr.	10	NY Rangers	0	at	Mtl Maroons	2
Apr.	12	NY Rangers	1	at	Mtl Maroons	0
Apr.	14	NY Rangers	2	at	Mtl Maroons	1

Rangers won best-of-five series 3–2

1927-28 – New York Rangers – Lorne Chabot, Clarence Abel, Leon Bourgault, Ching Johnson, Bill Cook, Bun Cook, Frank Boucher, Bill Boyd, Murray Murdoch, Paul Thompson, Alex Gray, Joe Miller, Patsy Callighen, Lester Patrick (manager-coach), Harry Westerby (trainer).

1927

With the collapse of major professional hockey in the west, the Stanley Cup became sole property of the NHL in 1927. The American Division champion Boston Bruins met the Canadian champion Ottawa Senators in what became the first Stanley Cup of a new era.

Cy Denneny led the Senators with four of the team's seven total goals, including the game-winners in both victories.

QUARTERFINALS

Mar.	29	Montreal	1	at	Mtl Maroons	1
Mar.	31	Mtl Maroons	0	at	Montreal	1 OT

Montreal won total-goals series 2–1

Mar.	29	Boston	6	vs	Chicago	1 *
Mar.	31	Chicago	4	at	Boston	4

* at New York

Boston won total-goals series 10–5

SEMIFINALS

Apr.	2	Ottawa	4	at	Montreal	0
Apr.	4	Montreal	1	at	Ottawa	1

Ottawa won total-goals series 5–1

Apr.	2	NY Rangers	0	at	Boston	0
Apr.	4	Boston	3	at	NY Rangers	1

Boston won total-goals series 3–1

FINALS

Apr.	7	Ottawa	0	at	Boston	0 OT
Apr.	9	Ottawa	3	at	Boston	1
Apr.	11	Boston	1	at	Ottawa	1 OT
Apr.	13	Boston	1	at	Ottawa	3

Ottawa won best-of-five series 2-0-2

1926-27 – Ottawa Senators – Alex Connell, King Clancy, George Boucher, Ed Gorman, Frank Finnigan, Alex Smith, Hec Kilrea, Hooley Smith, Cy Denneny, Frank Nighbor, Jack Adams, Milt Halliday, Dave Gill (manager-coach).

1926

The Montreal Maroons became NHL champions in just their second season in the league and hosted the first Stanley Cup series to be played at the Montreal Forum.

Playing in his first career Stanley Cup series, Nels Stewart scored six of Montreal's 10 goals, and goaltender Clint Benedict recorded an unprecedented three shutouts en route to the Maroons' Stanley Cup triumph versus the Victoria Cougars.

With the NHL taking full control of the Stanley Cup following the Western Hockey League's demise soon after this series, the 1926 championship marked the finale of one of the most dynamic eras in Stanley Cup history. Since 1893, Cup play had grown from an amateur challenge in eastern Canada to a professional competition involving teams from across the continent.

SCORES

Mar.	30	Victoria Cougars	0	at	Mtl Maroons	3
Apr.	1	Victoria Cougars	0	at	Mtl Maroons	3
Apr.	3	Victoria Cougars	3	at	Mtl Maroons	2
Apr.	6	Victoria Cougars	0	at	Mtl Maroons	2

1925-26 – Montreal Maroons – Clint Benedict, Reg Noble, Frank Carson, Dunc Munro, Nels Stewart, Harry Broadbent, Babe Siebert, Chuck Dinsmore, Bill Phillips, Hobie Kitchen, Sam Rothschield, Albert Holway, George Horne, Bernie Brophy, Eddie Gerard (manager-coach), Bill O'Brien (trainer).

1925

The Victoria Cougars, who joined the Western Canada Hockey league with the Vancouver Maroons after the Pacific Coast Hockey Association folded, became the last non-NHL team to win the Stanley Cup and only the third west coast club to capture the trophy, joining the 1915 Vancouver Millionaires and the 1917 Seattle Metropolitans as champions.

All eight Montreal goals in the series came from the Canadiens' top line of Howie Morenz, Aurel Joliat and Billy Boucher, but Victoria posted a more balanced attack with eight different skaters combining for 16 goals.

SCORES

Mar.	21	Montreal	2	at	Victoria Cougars	5
Mar.	23	Montreal	1	vs	Victoria Cougars	3 *
Mar.	27	Montreal	4	at	Victoria Cougars	2
Mar.	30	Montreal	1	at	Victoria Cougars	6

* played in Vancouver

1924-25 – Victoria Cougars – Harry Holmes, Clem Loughlin, Gord Fraser, Frank Fredrickson, Jack Walker, Wilf Hart, Harold Halderson, Frank Foyston, Wally Elmer, Harry Meeking, Jocko Anderson, Lester Patrick (manager-coach).

1924

As in 1922, the PCHA champions (Vancouver Maroons) and the winners of the WCHL (Calgary Tigers) met in a postseason playoff, only this year it would determine which team got a bye into the Stanley Cup finals against the NHL champion. The series was played in Vancouver, Calgary and Winnipeg as the teams traveled east, and was won by the Tigers two games to one.

Billy Boucher scored three of the Canadiens' five goals in Montreal's series with the Maroons, including both game-winning tallies, to lift Montreal over Vancouver, which lost its chance at the Stanley Cup for the third straight year.

After defeating the PCHA champs, Montreal took on the Tigers in the Stanley Cup final. A 21-year-old rookie forward named Howie Morenz paced the Canadiens with a hat trick in game one and a goal in game two as Montreal rolled past Calgary to complete a sweep of both 1924 series.

Morenz, Aurel Joliat and Sylvio Mantha all made their first appearances on a Stanley Cup winner.

SCORES

Mar.	18	Vancouver	2	at	Montreal	3
Mar.	20	Vancouver	1	at	Montreal	2
Mar.	22	Calgary Tigers	1	at	Montreal	6
Mar.	25	Calgary Tigers	0	vs	Montreal	3 *

* Game transferred to Ottawa to benefit from artificial ice.

1923-24 – Montreal Canadiens – Georges Vezina, Sprague Cleghorn, Billy Coutu, Howie Morenz, Aurel Joliat, Billy Boucher, Odie Cleghorn, Sylvio Mantha, Bobby Boucher, Billy Bell, Billy Cameron, Joe Malone, Charles Fortier, Leo Dandurand (manager-coach).

1923

For the first time in Stanley Cup history, brothers opposed each other in the finals. In fact, two sets of brothers — Cy and Corb Denneny and George and Frank Boucher — stood on opposite sides of the center line for the opening face-off. Cy and George skated with Ottawa, while Corb and Frank suited up for Vancouver (who were now known as the Maroons). Each of the Boucher brothers scored twice in the series.

Ottawa's Harry "Punch" Broadbent, who posted the only goal in game one, scored five in the series to lead the Senators, whom Vancouver coach Frank Patrick called the greatest team he had ever seen.

The WCHL-PCHA playoff format was abandoned, but the WCHL champions were given the opportunity to compete directly for the Stanley Cup in a best-of-three series. The Eskimos gave the weary Senators a difficult time, but Ottawa came through with a pair of one-goal victories. Cy Denneny and Harry Broadbent scored the game-winning goals.

SCORES

Mar.	16	Ott. Senators	1	at	Vancouver	0
Mar.	19	Ott. Senators	1	at	Vancouver	4
Mar.	23	Ott. Senators	3	at	Vancouver	2
Mar.	26	Ott. Senators	5	at	Vancouver	1
Mar.	29	Ott. Senators	2	vs	Edmonton	1 OT*
Mar.	31	Ott. Senators	1	vs	Edmonton	0 *

* played in Vancouver

1922-23 – Ottawa Senators – George Boucher, Lionel Hitchman, Frank Nighbor, King Clancy, Harry Helman, Clint Benedict, Jack Darragh, Eddie Gerard, Cy Denneny, Harry Broadbent, Tommy Gorman (manager), Pete Green (coach), F. Dolan (trainer).

1922

With the inception of the Western Canada Hockey League (WCHL) in 1921-22, a new playoff structure was designed to match the champions of the two western leagues against each other with the winner to meet the NHL champions for the Stanley Cup. After defeating the WCHL's Regina Capitals in the preliminary series, the PCHA's Vancouver Millionaires set out for Toronto, where the NHL champion St. Pats awaited their arrival.

Cecil "Babe" Dye notched nine of his club's 16 goals, including two game-winners, and goaltender John Ross Roach, who recorded the first Stanley Cup shutout by an NHL rookie, posted a 1.80 goals-against average as Toronto won its second Stanley Cup championship.

Jack Adams, who had been lured away from Toronto by Vancouver in 1920, returned in impressive fashion, scoring six goals in the series.

SCORES

Mar.	17	Vancouver	4	at	Toronto St. Pats	3
Mar.	20	Vancouver	1	at	Toronto St. Pats	2 OT
Mar.	23	Vancouver	3	at	Toronto St. Pats	0
Mar.	25	Vancouver	0	at	Toronto St. Pats	6
Mar.	28	Vancouver	1	at	Toronto St. Pats	5

1921-22 – Toronto St. Pats – Ted Stackhouse, Corb Denneny, Rod Smylie, Lloyd Andrews, John Ross Roach, Harry Cameron, Billy Stuart, Babe Dye, Ken Randall, Reg Noble, Eddie Gerard (borrowed for one game from Ottawa), Stan Jackson, Nolan Mitchell, Charlie Querrie (manager), George O'Donoghue (coach).

1921

A gathering of 11,000 fans, the largest crowd ever to see a hockey game anywhere in the world at the time, jammed the Vancouver arena for the first game

of this series, and an estimated record of 51,000 tickets were sold for the entire five-game series.

Jack Darragh was the hero for the second straight year, scoring both Ottawa goals in the finale as the Senators became the first NHL club to capture back-to-back Stanley Cup titles and the first team since the Quebec Bulldogs of 1912 and 1913 to repeat as champions.

SCORES

Mar.	21	Ott. Senators	1	at	Vancouver	3
Mar.	24	Ott. Senators	4	at	Vancouver	3
Mar.	28	Ott. Senators	3	at	Vancouver	2
Mar.	31	Ott. Senators	2	at	Vancouver	3
Apr.	4	Ott. Senators	2	at	Vancouver	1

1920-21 – Ottawa Senators – Jack McKell, Jack Darragh, Morley Bruce, George Boucher, Eddie Gerard, Clint Benedict, Sprague Cleghorn, Frank Nighbor, Harry Broadbent, Cy Denneny, Leth Graham, Tommy Gorman (manager), Pete Green (coach), F. Dolan (trainer).

1920

When the Mets arrived in Ottawa, it became apparent that their red, white and green barber pole uniforms were all too similar to the Senators' red, white and black pattern. Ottawa agreed to play in white jerseys.

Poor ice conditions marred the first three games, and the series was subsequently shifted to the artificial surface at Toronto's Mutual Street Arena. Jack Darragh, who had tallied the winning marker in game one, lifted Ottawa to the championship with a hat trick in the decisive game.

Pete Green became the second rookie coach in the NHL to win the Cup, joining Dick Carroll of the 1918 Toronto Arenas.

SCORES

Mar.	22	Seattle Mets	2	at	Ott. Senators	3
Mar.	24	Seattle Mets	0	at	Ott. Senators	3
Mar.	27	Seattle Mets	3	at	Ott. Senators	1
Mar.	30	Seattle Mets	5	vs	Ott. Senators	2 *
Apr.	1	Seattle Mets	1	vs	Ott. Senators	6 *

* played in Toronto

1919-20 – Ottawa Senators – Jack McKell, Jack Darragh, Morley Bruce, Horrace Merrill, George Boucher, Eddie Gerard, Clint Benedict, Sprague Cleghorn, Frank Nighbor, Harry Broadbent, Cy Denneny, Tommy Gorman (manager), Pete Green (coach).

1919

Seattle's Frank Foyston and Montreal's Newsy Lalonde, two of the greatest scorers of the early 20th century, were at their best in this series. Foyston notched nine goals and Lalonde six as the two clubs stood even at two wins and one tie apiece after five games.

Several of the players became seriously ill with the flu, which had reached epidemic proportions throughout North America and the world in 1918 and 1919. So many Montreal players were sick, health officials were forced to cancel the deciding game and the series was abandoned with no winner declared. Canadiens defenseman Joe Hall, hospitalized with a severe case of Spanish Influenza, died on April 5, 1919, in Seattle.

SCORES

Mar.	19	Montreal	0	at	Seattle Mets	7
Mar.	22	Montreal	4	at	Seattle Mets	2
Mar.	24	Montreal	2	at	Seattle Mets	7
Mar.	26	Montreal	0	at	Seattle Mets	0 OT
Mar.	30	Montreal	4	at	Seattle Mets	3 OT

SERIES CANCELLED DUE TO INFLUENZA EPIDEMIC

1918-19 – No decision – Series halted by Spanish influenza epidemic, illness of several players and death of Joe Hall of Montreal Canadiens from flu. Five games had been played when the series was halted, each team having won two and tied one. Final scores are listed above.

1918

Prior to the start of the 1917-18 campaign, the National Hockey Association dissolved and the NHL took its place. The new league started out with four teams — the Montreal Canadiens and Wanderers, Ottawa and Toronto — but the Wanderers withdrew after the Montreal Arena burned down.

After capturing the first NHL title, Toronto played host to Vancouver in the Stanley Cup finals which meant that eastern rules would be used in games one, three and five. Because neither club seemed comfortable playing an unfamiliar style, Toronto won the series with the advantage of playing the final game under eastern rules.

Alf Skinner led the Arenas with eight goals in five games, while Fred "Cyclone" Taylor paced Vancouver with nine. Rookie coach Dick Carroll steered his team to the NHL's first Stanley Cup championship.

SCORES

Mar.	20	Vancouver	3	at	Toronto Arenas	5
Mar.	23	Vancouver	6	at	Toronto Arenas	4
Mar.	26	Vancouver	3	at	Toronto Arenas	6
Mar.	28	Vancouver	8	at	Toronto Arenas	1
Mar.	30	Vancouver	1	at	Toronto Arenas	2

1917-18 – Toronto Arenas – Rusty Crawford, Harry Meeking, Ken Randall, Corb Denneny, Harry Cameron, Jack Adams, Alf Skinner, Harry Mummery, Harry Holmes, Reg Noble, Sammy Hebert, Jack Marks, Jack Coughlin, Charlie Querrie (manager), Dick Carroll (coach), Frank Carroll (trainer).

1917

In only their second season, the Seattle Metropolitans skated to the PCHA title and distinguished themselves as the first U.S. team to host a Stanley Cup series. They also became the first American squad to capture the coveted trophy. Consequently, one of Lord Stanley's original conditions — that the trophy be held by the champion of the Dominion of Canada — had been eradicated.

Seattle's Bernie Morris, who finished second in the PCHA scoring race with 37 goals in 24 games, scored a team-high 14 times against Montreal, including six in the finale, to lead the Mets over the Canadiens.

SCORES

Mar.	17	Montreal	8	at	Seattle Mets	4
Mar.	20	Montreal	1	at	Seattle Mets	6
Mar.	23	Montreal	1	at	Seattle Mets	4
Mar.	25	Montreal	1	at	Seattle Mets	9

1916-17 – Seattle Metropolitans – Harry Holmes, Ed Carpenter, Cully Wilson, Jack Walker, Bernie Morris, Frank Foyston, Roy Rickey, Jim Riley, Bobby Rowe (captain), Peter Muldoon (manager).

1916

The PCHA had become the first Canadian league to place a team in the United States in 1915 when the New Westminster Royals moved to Oregon and became the Portland Rosebuds. One year later, Portland became the first American-based team to play for the Stanley Cup

For the first time, the Stanley Cup series came down to a fifth and final game after both participants split the first four games. Portland's Tommy Dunderdale put the Rosebuds ahead early, but the Canadiens bounced back. Skene Ronan tied the game, and Goldie Prodgers netted the Cup-winner.

In his first Stanley Cup appearance, goaltender Georges Vezina backed the Canadiens with a 2.60 average in five games en route to the club's first championship.

SCORES

Mar.	20	Portland	2	at	Montreal	0
Mar.	22	Portland	1	at	Montreal	2
Mar.	25	Portland	3	at	Montreal	6
Mar.	28	Portland	6	at	Montreal	5
Mar.	30	Portland	1	at	Montreal	2

1915-16 – Montreal Canadiens – Georges Vezina, Bert Corbeau, Jack Laviolette, Newsy Lalonde, Louis Berlinguette, Goldie Prodgers, Howard McNamara, Didier Pitre, Skene Ronan, Amos Arbour, Georges Poulin, Jacques Fournier, George Kennedy (manager).

1915

An informal agreement was reached between the NHA and PCHA in 1915 that called for the two league's respective champions to meet each year to determine the Stanley Cup winner. The arrangement stated that the series would be played alternately in the east and west, and that the different rules of the two leagues would alternate game by game. (The PCHA still employed the rover, though it had introduced more modern passing rules.)

Deadlocked with 14–6–0 records at the conclusion of the NHA season, the Ottawa Senators and Montreal Wanderers played a two-game total goals series for the league title and the right to face the PCHA champions. The Senators outscored the Canadiens 4–1 and packed up for the first Stanley Cup series to be played west of Winnipeg.

Fred "Cyclone" Taylor notched six goals in three games, and Barney Stanley scored four in the third, to lead the Millionaires to a one-sided sweep of the best-of-five series.

SCORES

Mar.	22	Ott. Senators	2	at	Vancouver	6
Mar.	24	Ott. Senators	3	at	Vancouver	8
Mar.	26	Ott. Senators	3	at	Vancouver	12

1914-15 – Vancouver Millionaires – Kenny Mallen, Frank Nighbor, Fred (Cyclone) Taylor, Hughie Lehman, Lloyd Cook, Mickey MacKay, Barney Stanley, Jim Seaborn, Si Griffis (captain), Jean Matz, Frank Patrick (playing manager).

1914

The Montreal Canadiens, making their first appearance in a Stanley Cup series, faced the Toronto Blueshirts in a two-game showdown for the NHA title and possession of the Cup.

Although each team posted a shutout on its home ice, the Blueshirts, who later became the NHL's Maple Leafs, outscored the Canadiens overall.

Game two in Toronto was the first Stanley Cup matchup ever played on artificial ice.

Three days after the conclusion of the series between the Blueshirts and Canadiens, Victoria of the Pacific Coast Hockey Association came east to play in Toronto. In the first of what would prove to be 13 consecutive east-west confrontations for the Stanley Cup, Victoria overlooked the formality of submitting a challenge, and thus the trustees did not regard the series as legitimate which might have led to quite a dispute if the Aristocrats had won. As it was though, Toronto swept the first best-of-five series in Stanley Cup history. Frank Foyston led the balanced Blueshirts attack with three goals, including the Cup-winner in game three.

SCORES

Mar. 7	Tor. Blueshirts	0	at	Mtl. Canadiens	2
Mar. 11	Mtl. Canadiens	0	at	Tor. Blueshirts	6
Total Goals:					
	Tor. Blueshirts	6		Mtl. Canadiens	2
Mar. 14	Victoria Aristocrats	2	at	Tor. Blueshirts	5
Mar. 17	Victoria Aristocrats	5	at	Tor. Blueshirts	6 OT
Mar. 19	Victoria Aristocrats	1	at	Tor. Blueshirts	2

1913-14 – Toronto Blueshirts – Con Corbeau, F. Roy McGiffen, Jack Walker, George McNamara, Cully Wilson, Frank Foyston, Harry Cameron, Harry Holmes, Alan M. Davidson (captain), Harriston, Jack Marshall (playing-manager), Frank and Dick Carroll (trainers).

1913

Quebec repeated as NHA champs and faced the Sydney Miners or "Millionaires", the top Maritime club, in defense of the Stanley Cup. "Phantom" Joe Malone poured in nine goals in the first game. He was not put in the lineup for the second, and the result was closer. Joe Hall scored three times in game two.

After the Sydney series, Victoria challenged Quebec but the Bulldogs refused to put the Stanley Cup in competition so the two teams played an exhibition series with Victoria winning two games to one by scores of 7-5, 3-6, 6-1. It was the first meeting between the Eastern champions and the Western champions from the Pacific Coast Hockey Association. The following year, and until the Western Hockey League disbanded after the 1926 playoffs, the Cup went to the winner of the series between East and West.

SCORES

Mar. 8	Sydney Miners	3	at	Quebec Bulldogs	14
Mar. 10	Sydney Miners	2	at	Quebec Bulldogs	6

1912-13 – Quebec Bulldogs – Joe Malone, Joe Hall, Paddy Moran, Harry Mummery, Tommy Smith, Jack Marks, Rusty Crawford, Billy Creighton, Jeff Malone, Rocket Power, M.J. Quinn (manager), D. Beland (trainer).

1912

Two major rule changes were introduced at the outset of 1912. The NHA required teams to play for the first time with six men per side instead of seven (abandoning the position of rover), and the Cup trustees declared that all Stanley Cup challenges had to take place after the regular season.

The Quebec Bulldogs, who posted a league-high 10–8–0 record, successfully defended their newly acquired trophy against Moncton of the Maritime Professional Hockey League. Jack MacDonald contributed nine goals while Joe Malone scored in Quebec's sweep of the best-of-three series.

Although the famed Patrick brothers, Frank and Lester, had started the Pacific Coast Hockey Association, not one of the three original PCHA teams challenged for the Stanley Cup. The Patricks introduced the first artificial ice surfaces in Canada at their new 10,000-seat Arena in Vancouver and in a smaller Victoria facility.

SCORES

Mar. 11	Moncton	3	at	Quebec Bulldogs	9
Mar. 13	Moncton	0	at	Quebec Bulldogs	8

1911-12 – Quebec Bulldogs – Goldie Prodgers, Joe Hall, Walter Rooney, Paddy Moran, Jack Marks, Jack MacDonald, Eddie Oatman, George Leonard, Joe Malone (captain), C. Nolan (coach), M.J. Quinn (manager), D. Beland (trainer).

1911

Prior to 1912, teams could challenge the Stanley Cup champions for the title at any time, thus there was more than one Championship Series played in most of the seasons between 1894 and 1911. After defeating Waterloo for the Ontario Professional Hockey League crown, Galt downed Port Hope, champions of the Eastern Professional Hockey League, in what became the second of two playoff series leading up to a challenge for the Stanley Cup.

The NHA champion Senators (13–3–0) had claimed the Cup from the Wanderers before defeaing Galt 7-4. Marty Walsh, who had first appeared in Stanley Cup competition with Queen's University in 1906, notched a hat trick for the winning Ottawa side.

Three days after defeating Galt, Ottawa took on the Port Arthur Bearcats, champions of the New (Northern) Ontario Hockey Association who had beaten the Saskatchewan champions from Prince Albert to earn the challenge.

In the one-game confrontation, the Senators' Marty Walsh scored 10 goals to fall four short of the record set by Frank McGee in 1905.

SCORES

Mar. 13	Galt	4	at	Ott. Senators	7
Mar. 16	Port Arthur	4	at	Ott. Senators	14

1910-11 – Ottawa Senators – Hamby Shore, Percy LeSueur, Jack Darragh, Bruce Stuart, Marty Walsh, Bruce Ridpath, Fred Lake, Albert (Dubby) Kerr, Alex Currie, Horace Gaul.

1910 March

When the Senators joined the National Hockey Association they brought the Stanley Cup into what was now unquestionably Canada's top hockey league. By winning the 1910 NHA title, the Montreal Wanderers took possession of the Stanley Cup from Ottawa and accepted a challenge from Berlin, 1910 champions of the OPHL. The Wanderers held on to their trophy in a one-game affair, with Ernie Russell (4) and Harry Hyland (3) scoring all seven goals for the winners.

SCORES

Mar. 12	Berlin	3	at	Mtl. Wanderers	7

1909-10 – Montreal Wanderers – Cecil W. Blachford, Ernie (Moose) Johnson, Ernie Russell, Riley Hern, Harry Hyland, Jack Marshall, Frank (Pud) Glass (captain), Jimmy Gardner, R.R. Boon (manager).

1910 January

The Eastern Canada Hockey Association became the Canadian Hockey Association in 1910 in order to freeze out the Montreal Wanderers. The Wanderers then helped to form the NHA, which introduced the Montreal Canadiens, who would eventually become hockey's most prolific champions.

Concerned by the number of "ringers" imported by Cup contestants, the trustees ruled that only players who had skated with their teams during the regular-season could be eligible for the Stanley Cup competition.

The Ottawa Senators were still members of the CHA when the 1910 season began. As holders of the Stanley Cup they defended the trophy against Galt, the 1909 champions of the Ontario Professional Hockey League (OPHL). Marty Walsh scored six goals in the first game en route to a sweep over the challengers.

The Senators had abandoned the CHA for the NHA when they took time out from the regular-season schedule for another Stanley Cup challenge. Edmonton had come east again for what was expected to be a close series, but Ottawa was too strong. The two-game set saw the Senators' Bruce Stuart and Gordie Roberts scored seven goals apiece, while Fred Whitcroft notched five for Edmonton.

SCORES

Jan. 5	Galt	3	at	Ottawa Senators	12
Jan. 7	Galt	1	at	Ottawa Senators	3
Total Goals:					
	Ottawa Senators	15		Galt	4
Jan. 18	Edmonton	4	at	Ottawa Senators	8
Jan. 20	Edmonton	7	at	Ottawa Senators	13
Total Goals:					
	Ottawa Senators	21		Edmonton	11

1909-10 – Ottawa Senators – Albert (Dubbie) Kerr, Fred Lake, Percy Lesueur, Ken Mallen, Bruce Ridpath, Gordie Roberts, Hamby Shore, Bruce Stuart, Marty Walsh.

1909

Prior to the 1909 season Montreal's AAA and Victoria clubs, who were the last amateur teams in the ECAHA, dropped out of the league. Consequently, the league was renamed the Eastern Canada Hockey Association with "Amateur" dropped from the title.

The Ottawa Senators, formerly the Silver Seven, posted a 10–2–0 record to capture the first all-pro, ECHA championship. Ottawa, as champions of the ECHA, took over the Stanley Cup in 1909 and, although a challenge was accepted by the Cup trustees from the Winnipeg Shamrocks, games could not be arranged because of the lateness of the season. No other challenges were made in 1909.

Fred "Cyclone" Taylor, who tallied eight goals in 11 games, made his debut on a Stanley Cup championship team with the Senators.

1908-09 – Ottawa Senators – Fred Lake, Percy LeSueur, Fred (Cyclone) Taylor, H.L. (Billy) Gilmour, Albert (Dubbie) Kerr, Edgar Dey, Marty Walsh, Bruce Stuart (captain).

1908 December

As champions of the Alberta Hockey League, the Edmonton Eskimos earned the right to play a challenge series against the defending champions, the Montreal Wanderers.

With six of its seven players brought in especially to face the Wanderers, Edmonton established a new record for ringers on a Cup challenger. Only rover Fred Whitcroft was legitimate. Lester Patrick, Tom Phillips and Didier Pitre headlined the cast of imports.

After dropping the first game, Edmonton replaced two of its ringers with two regulars, Harold Deeton and Jack Miller, who had made the trip to Montreal. They responded, scoring three and two goals, respectively. It marked the Wanderers' first Stanley Cup loss in seven games.

Harry Smith scored six goals, including five in the first game, as the Wanderers successfully defended the Cup on total goals despite splitting the series.

SCORES

Dec. 28	Edmonton	3	at	Mtl. Wanderers	7
Dec. 30	Edmonton	7	at	Mtl. Wanderers	6
Total Goals:					
	Mtl. Wanderers	13		Edmonton	10

1907-08 – Montreal Wanderers – Riley Hern, Art Ross, Walter Smaill, Frank (Pud) Glass, Bruce Stuart, Ernie Russell, Ernie (Moose) Johnson, Cecil Blachford (captain), Tom Hooper, Larry Gilmour, Ernie Liffiton, R.R. Boon (manager).

1908 March

After retaining the Eastern Canada Amateur Hockey Association crown with an 8–2–0 record, the Wanderers faced the Winnipeg Maple Leafs, champions of the Manitoba Hockey League.

For the first time in Stanley Cup play, every man on the winning team except the goalie scored at least once as the Wanderers took the first game. In the second game, Bruce Stuart and Ernie Johnson each registered four goals.

The Toronto "Trolley Leaguers", champions of the OPHL, the first entirely pro hockey league ever formed in Canada, played the Wanderers in a one-game, sudden-death affair.

The see-saw battle included four ties until Ernie Johnson scored the Wanderers' game-winning goal and Bruce Stuart tallied an insurance marker.

In his premier Stanley Cup appearance, Newsy Lalonde scored twice for Toronto.

SCORES

Mar.	10	Wpg. Maple Leafs	5	at	Mtl. Wanderers	11
Mar.	12	Wpg. Maple Leafs	3	at	Mtl. Wanderers	9
Total Goals:						
		Mtl. Wanderers	20		Wpg. Maple Leafs	8
Mar.	14	Toronto	4	at	Mtl. Wanderers	6

1908 January

The Ottawa Victorias, the latest cast of challengers, had actually finished third in the Federal Amateur Hockey League in 1907, but were awarded the league championship when the first and second place clubs — Montagnards and Cornwall — withdrew from competition. Nevertheless, Ottawa's challenge was accepted by the Cup trustees.

Ernie Russell netted 10 goals in two games, including six in the second, as Montreal easily defended the trophy.

SCORES

Jan.	9	Ottawa Victorias	3	at	Mtl. Wanderers	9
Jan.	13	Ottawa Victorias	1	at	Mtl. Wanderers	13
Total Goals:						
		Mtl. Wanderers	22		Ottawa Victorias	4

1907 March

Immediately after capturing the ECAHA league title with a perfect record of 10–0–0, the Wanderers submitted a challenge to the Cup trustees, who accepted the bid.

After the departure of Art Ross, Kenora imported two more players, Alf Smith and Harry Westwick of Ottawa, to face the Wanderers. Although Smith scored in each game, Montreal's Ernie Russell led a winning attack with four goals in the first game and added a single in the second. Though Kenora won the second game, the Wanderers still took the total-goals series.

Both games were played in Winnipeg as a result of unsatisfactory rink conditions in Kenora.

SCORES

Mar.	23	Mtl. Wanderers	7	vs	Kenora Thistles	2 *
Mar.	25	Mtl. Wanderers	5	vs	Kenora Thistles	6 *

* played in Winnipeg

Total Goals:

Mtl. Wanderers	12	Kenora Thistles	8

1906-07 – (Mar.) – Montreal Wanderers – W.S. (Billy) Strachan, Riley Hern, Lester Patrick, Hod Stuart, Frank (Pud) Glass, Ernie Russell, Cecil Blachford (captain), Ernie (Moose) Johnson, Rod Kennedy, Jack Marshall, R.R. Boon (manager).

1907 January

Because no ice had been available after the Wanderers took the Stanley Cup title from Ottawa in 1906, this east-west confrontation had to be delayed until the start of the 1907 schedule.

The Kenora Thistles, formerly the Rat Portage Thistles, brought in Art Ross and Roxy Beaudro as ringers in an effort to beef up the lineup which had failed to win its Cup challenges in 1903 and 1905.

Tom Phillips scored seven times in the two games, including all four Thistles goals in the first contest, as Kenora (with its population of 4,000 people) became the smallest town ever to win a Stanley Cup championship.

SCORES

Jan.	17	Kenora Thistles	4	at	Mtl. Wanderers	2
Jan.	21	Kenora Thistles	8	at	Mtl. Wanderers	6
Total Goals:						
		Kenora Thistles	12		Mtl. Wanderers	8

1906-07 – (Jan.) – Kenora Thistles – Eddie Geroux, Art Ross, Si Griffis, Tom Hooper, Billy McGimsie, Roxy Beaudro, Tom Phillips.

1906 December

A new ruling allowed professionals to play with the amateurs in the ECAHA, and the Wanderers were quick to give contracts to Riley Hern, "Pud" Glass, Hod Stuart, Ernie Johnson and Jack Marshall — who officially became the first five pros in Stanley Cup competition. Players like Cecil Blachford and Ernie Russell chose to remain amateur. The challenging New Glasgow squad was strictly amateur.

Amidst the partially pro lineup, it was amateur rover Lester Patrick who led Montreal over New Glasgow with a hat trick in each game.

SCORES

Dec.	27	New Glasgow	3	at	Mtl. Wanderers	10
Dec.	29	New Glasgow	2	at	Mtl. Wanderers	7
Total Goals:						
		Mtl. Wanderers	17		New Glasgow	5

1905-06 – Montreal Wanderers – Henri Menard, Billy Strachan, Rod Kennedy, Lester Patrick, Frank (Pud) Glass, Ernie Russell, Ernie (Moose) Johnson, Cecil Blachford (captain), Josh Arnold, R.R. Boon (manager).

1906 March

Late in the ECAHA season, the Cup trustees decided that Ottawa should defend the Cup against Smiths Falls, champions of the reconstituted FAHL. Frank McGee notched nine goals in the two games, which would be the last of Ottawa's nine straight successful Cup defenses.

It is interesting to note that the title "Silver Seven" was given only to the team and not to any particular seven players. Ottawa's line-up included a total of 16 players during its Stanley Cup reign that spanned from 1903 to 1906.

Ottawa and Montreal each concluded the regular-season at 9–1–0, leading to a two-game, total-goals series for the ECAHA championship and possession of the Stanley Cup.

In his Stanley Cup debut, Ernie Russell scored four goals to lift Montreal over Ottawa 9–1 in the first game, which left the defending champs with the task of outscoring the Wanderers by a minimum of nine goals in the second in order to retain the trophy.

Ottawa unveiled Smiths Falls goalie Percy Lesueur in goal for the second game, and after he gave up an early goal, Ottawa stormed to a 9–1 lead on the strength of Harry Smith's five-goal effort to tie the series. However, Montreal rover Lester Patrick scored two late goals for the Wanderers to lock up the club's first Stanley Cup title.

SCORES

Mar.	6	Smiths Falls	5	at	Silver Seven	6
Mar.	8	Smiths Falls	2	at	Silver Seven	8
Mar	14	Silver Seven	1	at	Mtl. Wanderers	9
Mar	17	Mtl. Wanderers	3	at	Silver Seven	9
Total Goals:						
		Mtl. Wanderers	12		Silver Seven	10

1906 February

Ottawa was among several Federal Amateur and Canadian Amateur Hockey League teams that banded together to form the new Eastern Canada Amateur Hockey Association in 1906. During the ECAHA season, the Silver Seven took time out to host Queen's University, which had challenged for the Stanley Cup for the third time.

Alf and Harry Smith, the best of seven brothers to have tried out for the Ottawa squad, led the Silver Seven to victory. Alf scored five goals in the first game, and Harry duplicated the feat in the second.

SCORES

Feb.	27	Queen's U.	7	at	Silver Seven	16
Feb.	28	Queen's U.	7	at	Silver Seven	12

1905-06 – (Feb.) – Ottawa Silver Seven – Harvey Pulford (captain), Arthur Moore, Harry Westwick, Frank McGee, Alf Smith (playing coach), Billy Gilmour, Billy Hague, Percy LeSueur, Harry Smith, Tommy Smith, Dion, Ebbs.

1905 March

Having edged out the Montreal Wanderers for the FAHL title, Ottawa retained the Stanley Cup and faced a challenge from the team in Rat Portage (later known as Kenora, Ontario).

Ottawa had lost Frank McGee for the series opener, and the fleet-footed Thistles skated to victory. Tom Phillips put on a show for the fans with the first five-goal performance in a Stanley Cup game by a player other than the high-scoring McGee.

Ottawa's rink crew flooded the ice in the remaining two games, and the move greatly slowed the Thistles' fast-paced attack. McGee returned to score three goals in both games, including the Cup-winner in the finale.

SCORES

Mar.	7	Rat Portage	9	at	Silver Seven	3
Mar.	9	Rat Portage	2	at	Silver Seven	4
Mar.	11	Rat Portage	4	at	Silver Seven	5

1904-05 – Ottawa Silver Seven – Dave Finnie, Harvey Pulford (captain), Arthur Moore, Harry Westwick, Frank McGee, Alf Smith (playing coach), Billy Gilmour, Frank White, Horace Gaul, Hamby Shore, Bones Allen.

1905 January

Now a member of the FAHL, Ottawa took on Dawson City in a midseason challenge for the Stanley Cup. The Nuggets, backed by Yukon prospector Colonel Joe Boyle, departed from Dawson City on December 19 to meet the famed Silver Seven nearly a month later. The 4,000-mile excursion included travel by dogsled, boat and train and set the club back by over $3,000.

Wearied from the long trek, the challengers were overwhelmed. In the second game, Ottawa set Stanley Cup scoring records of every variety, including an unparalleled 14-goals from Frank McGee.

SCORES

Jan.	13	Dawson City	2	at	Silver Seven	9
Jan.	16	Dawson City	2	at	Silver Seven	23

1904 March

The Montreal Wanderers, who had stripped the cross-city rival AAA club of its best players, skated to the inaugural Federal Amateur Hockey League (FAHL) championship with a perfect 6–0–0 record. As such, they were granted a two-game, total-goals challenge for the Stanley Cup.

Following the first game, which ended with a 5–5 tie, a new two-game series was scheduled to be played in Ottawa. However, the Wanderers refused to play unless one of the games would be staged in Montreal. As defenders of the Cup, the Silver Seven did not have to yield to such a demand, and the series was awarded to Ottawa.

Ottawa faced Brandon, the champions of the Manitoba/Northwestern Hockey League, in their fourth Stanley Cup challenge of the season and won in consecutive games. Frank McGee scored eight goals in the two games, including five in the first to tie his own Stanley Cup record set earlier in the year. A 21-year-old Lester Patrick starred for Brandon in his Cup debut.

SCORES

Mar.	2	Silver Seven	5	at	Mtl. Wanderers	5
Mar.	9	Brandon	3	at	Silver Seven	6
Mar.	11	Brandon	3	at	Silver Seven	9

1903-04 – Ottawa Silver Seven – S.C. (Suddy) Gilmour, Arthur Moore, Frank McGee, J.B. (Bouse) Hutton, H.L. (Billy) Gilmour, Jim McGee, Harry Westwick, E.H. (Harvey) Pulford (captain), Scott, Alf Smith (playing coach).

1904 February

On February 8, Ottawa pulled out of the Canadian Amateur Hockey League over a dispute involving a make-up game with the Montreal Vics. As a result, the Quebec Bulldogs, who had won the league title, petitioned the trustees to strip the Silver Seven of the Cup and award it to them. The request would be denied, but while the debate continued, Ottawa faced a new challenger, the Toronto Marlboros of the Ontario Hockey Association.

Frank McGee led the Silver Seven with three goals in the first game and the first five-goal performance ever recorded in Stanley Cup competition in the second to insure the sweep.

SCORES

Feb.	23	Tor. Marlboros	3	at	Silver Seven	6
Feb.	25	Tor. Marlboros	2	at	Silver Seven	11

1904 January

Before beginning the new CAHL season, the Ottawa Silver Seven successfully defended the Cup against a new Winnipeg team. Ottawa's "One-eyed" Frank McGee registered a hat trick in the first game, but captain Bill Breen rallied the challengers with two goals in the second. In the finale, goalie Bouse Hutton shut down Winnipeg completely, with McGee scoring the game-winner.

Prior to the opening contest, both teams agreed to paint what essentially became the first "goal line" in hockey history. A red line was drawn from goalpost to goalpost in order to aid the referee.

Joe Hall made his Stanley Cup debut with the underdog Rowing Club.

SCORES

Dec.	30	Winnipeg R.C.	1	at	Silver Seven	9
Jan.	1	Winnipeg R.C.	6	at	Silver Seven	2
Jan.	4	Winnipeg R.C.	0	at	Silver Seven	2

1903 March

The 1903 CAHL season ended with both Ottawa and the Montreal Victorias finishing ahead of the defending champion Montreal AAA. As both Ottawa and the Vics had identical records of 6–2–0, a two-game total-goals playoff was arranged to determine both the new CAHL and Stanley Cup champion.

After a tie in game one, Ottawa's famed Gilmour brothers — Billy, Dave and Suddy — combined for five goals and Frank McGee added a hat trick en route to a convincing victory. After winning the Stanley Cup, the Ottawa team became known as the Silver Seven.

The Rat Portage Thistles, playing with only one man over the age of 20, journeyed from northwestern Ontario to Ottawa to meet the Silver Seven. The game proved to be a springboard for the Ottawa club, which successfully defended the Cup for the first of nine straight times.

Billy and Dave Gilmour combined with Frank McGee for all 10 Ottawa goals in the series.

SCORES

Mar.	7	Ottawa	1	at	Mtl. Victorias	1
Mar.	10	Mtl. Victorias	0	at	Ottawa	8
Total Goals:						
		Ottawa	9		Mtl. Victorias	1
Mar	12	Rat Portage	2	at	Silver Seven	6
Mar	14	Rat Portage	2	at	Silver Seven	4

1902-03 – (Mar.) – Ottawa Silver Seven – S.C. (Suddy) Gilmour, P.T. (Percy) Sims, J.B. (Bouse) Hutton, D.J. (Dave) Gilmour, H.L. (Billy) Gilmour, Harry Westwick, Frank McGee, F.H. Wood, A.A. Fraser, Charles D. Spittal, E.H. (Harvey) Pulford (captain), Arthur Moore, Alf Smith (coach.)

1903 February

The Montreal AAA took time out from the CAHL schedule to face a challenge from the Winnipeg Victorias in a much-discussed series. The first game was a lopsided contest won by the AAA, but the Vics bounced back in the second. With the score tied 2–2 at midnight after 27 minutes of overtime in this Saturday night affair, the Mayor of Westmount refused to allow the game to continue into the Sabbath. The Cup trustees first decided to resume the overtime the following Monday, but later realized it would be impossible to sell tickets to a game which might end after a few minutes or even a few seconds. Consequently, the game was replayed.

Tom Phillips, one of the greatest players of the early era, made his Stanley Cup debut with three goals in four games for Montreal. The Winnipeg players all wore tube skates, the first time an entire team had appeared in the east so equipped.

SCORES

Jan.	29	Wpg. Victorias	1	at	Mtl. AAA	8
Jan.	31	Wpg. Victorias	2	at	Mtl. AAA	2 OT
Feb.	2	Wpg. Victorias	4	at	Mtl. AAA	2
Feb.	4	Wpg. Victorias	1	at	Mtl. AAA	4

1902-03 – (Feb.) – Montreal AAA – Tom Hodge, R.R. (Dickie) Boon, W.C. (Billy) Nicholson, Tom Phillips, Art Hooper, W.J. (Billy) Bellingham, Charles A. Liffiton, Jack Marshall, Jim Gardner, Cecil Blachford, George Smith.

1902 March

Montreal, having won the championship of the CAHL, challenged Winnipeg, and a best-of-three Stanley Cup series was arranged. Over 4,000 fans packed the Winnipeg Arena for game one, paying as much as $25 for $5 and $10 seats for this battle of the giants. Even larger crowds attended the subsequent games.

After the rival teams split the first two games, Montreal's Art Hooper and Jack Marshall scored early in the third game to give the AAA a 2–0 lead. However, it was a stubborn defense which lifted the Montrealers to victory and earned them the moniker "Little Men of Iron", a nickname which became commonly associated with the Montreal Wanderers who later employed most of the AAA's star players.

SCORES

Mar.	13	Mtl. AAA	0	at	Wpg. Victorias	1
Mar.	15	Mtl. AAA	5	at	Wpg. Victorias	0
Mar.	17	Mtl. AAA	2	at	Wpg. Victorias	1

1901-02 – (Mar.) – Montreal AAA – Tom Hodge, R.R. (Dickie) Boon, William C. (Billy) Nicholson, Archie Hooper, W.J. (Billy) Bellingham, Charles A. Liffiton, Jack Marshall, Roland Elliott, Jim Gardner.

1902 January

The Cup trustees accepted a challenge from the Toronto Wellingtons of the Ontario Hockey Association, and the Vics easily won the Cup in two games. For unknown reasons, Toronto wore Winnipeg uniforms in the first match and their own in the second.

SCORES

Jan.	21	Tor. Wellingtons	3	at	Wpg. Victorias	5
Jan.	23	Tor. Wellingtons	3	at	Wpg. Victorias	5

1901-02 – (Jan.) – Winnipeg Victorias – Burke Wood, A.B. (Tony) Gingras, Charles W. Johnstone, R.M. (Rod) Flett, Magnus L. Flett, Dan Bain (captain), Fred Scanlon, F. Cadham, G. Brown.

1901

After a five-year hiatus, the Winnipeg Vics regained the Stanley Cup from the defending champion Shamrocks in consecutive victories. Forward Dan Bain, who scored the Cup-winning goal four minutes into overtime in game two, played both games with a mask as the Vics continued to surprise Montrealers with new innovations from the west.

Winnipeg's victory over the Shamrocks meant the Stanley Cup passed out of the CAHL, so that when Ottawa unseated the Montreal team for the league title their was no Cup to claim. Due to the lateness of the season (March) and the travel to Winnipeg that would be involved, Ottawa declined to issue a Stanley Cup challenge.

SCORES

Jan.	29	Wpg. Victorias	4	at	Mtl. Shamrocks	3
Jan.	31	Wpg. Victorias	2	at	Mtl. Shamrocks	1 OT

1900-01 – Winnipeg Victorias – Burke Wood, Jack Marshall, A.B. (Tony) Gingras, Charles W. Johnstone, R.M. (Rod) Flett, Magnus L. Flett, Dan Bain (captain), G. Brown.

1900 March

The end of the 1900 season saw the Montreal Shamrocks finish atop the CAHL standings again. Having thus retained their Stanley Cup title, the Shamrocks soundly turned back an attempt by the Halifax Crescents of the Maritime Hockey League to take the Cup. Montreal's Arthur Farrell established a new Stanley Cup record with four goals in each game to lead the champs.

SCORES

Mar.	5	Halifax	2	at	Mtl. Shamrocks	10
Mar.	7	Halifax	0	at	Mtl. Shamrocks	11

1899-1900 – Montreal Shamrocks – Joe McKenna, Frank Tansey, Frank Wall, Art Farrell, Fred Scanlon, Harry Trihey (captain), Jack Brannen.

1900 February

In mid-season, the Shamrocks faced Winnipeg in the first best-of-three challenge to go the limit. The series was evenly played with only one goal separating the teams in each contest. Harry Trihey was the

offensive star again with seven goals in three games, including three in the finale.

The Winnipeg club, which had become noted for its innovations, introduced a new hockey stick which had the upper edge of the blade tapered, making it much lighter and considerably more modern.

SCORES

Feb.	12	Wpg. Victorias	4	at	Mtl. Shamrocks	3
Feb.	14	Wpg. Victorias	2	at	Mtl. Shamrocks	3
Feb.	16	Wpg. Victorias	4	at	Mtl. Shamrocks	5

1899 March

The Montreal Shamrocks, formerly the Crystals, captured the 1899 CAHL title. The key game was a 1–0 victory over the Montreal Victorias in front of 8,000 fans in the brand new Montreal (Westmount) Arena. Harry Trihey scored the lone goal, which gave the Shamrocks a 7–1–0 record on the season to the Victorias' mark of 6–2–0. By defeating the defending champions for their own league title, the Shamrocks won the Stanley Cup, which they successfully defended against Queen's University. Trihey of the Irish netted a hat trick, and Arthur Farrell posted two more in the 6–2 victory.

SCORES

Mar.	14	Queen's U.	2	at	Mtl. Shamrocks	6

1898-99 – (Mar.) – Montreal Shamrocks – Jim McKenna, Frank Tansey, Frank Wall, Harry Trihey (captain), Art Farrell, Fred Scanlon, Jack Brannen, John Dobby, Charles Hoerner.

1899 February

The Amateur Hockey Asociation had dissolved prior to the start of the season with the Canadian Amateur Hockey League (CAHL) taking its place as the top hockey league in the country. The five former AHA franchises now comprised the new league.

The Montreal Vics successfully defended the Cup against their perennial rivals from Winnipeg in a series marred by controversy. After narrowly winning the first game of the set, Montreal's Bob McDougall slashed and injured Winnipeg's Tony Gingras, and the referee imposed a two-minute penalty, which Winnipeg protested was too lenient. The westerners were so incensed, they left the ice.

Insulted by the incident, the referee left the arena. He did reappear over an hour after play had stopped, and gave Winnipeg five minutes to resume play. Upon their failure to return, the game was awarded to Montreal.

SCORES

Feb.	15	Wpg. Victorias	1	at	Mtl. Victorias	2
Feb.	18	Wpg. Victorias	2	at	Mtl. Victorias	3

1898-99 – (Feb.) – Montreal Victorias – Gordon Lewis, Mike Grant, Graham Drinkwater, Cam Davidson, Bob McDougall, Ernie McLea, Frank Richardson, Jack Ewing, Russell Bowie, Douglas Acer, Fred McRobie.

1898

The Montreal Victorias claimed their fourth consecutive AHA title, romping to the championship with a perfect record of 8–0–0. Vics forward Cam Davidson headlined the cast of scoring leaders with 14 goals in seven regular-season games. As champions of the AHA, the Montreal team retained the Stanley Cup and was not called upon to defend it.

1897-98 – Montreal Victorias – Gordon Lewis, Hartland McDougall, Mike Grant, Graham Drinkwater, Cam Davidson, Bob McDougall, Ernie McLea, Frank Richardson (captain), Jack Ewing.

1897

The Montreal Victorias were champions of the AHA for a third straight season in 1897 (again with a 7–1–0 record), and accepted a challenge from the Ottawa Capitals, winners of the Central Canada Hockey Association title. The challenge was scheduled for December, which would place it just before the beginning of the next hockey season. Although this Stanley Cup confrontation was originally set as a best-of-three series, the trustees ended the affair after one game because the two teams were unevenly matched.

SCORES

Dec.	27	Ottawa	2	at	Mtl. Victorias	14

1896-97 – Montreal Victorias – Gordon Lewis, Harold Henderson, Mike Grant (captain), Cam Davidson, Graham Drinkwater, Robert McDougall, Ernie McLea, Shirley Davidson, Hartland McDougall, Jack Ewing, Percy Molson, David Gillilan, McLellan.

1896 December

Immediately after winning the AHA championship with a 7–1–0 record, the recently dethroned Cup champion Montreal Vics wasted no time in requesting a challenge against the Winnipeg Vics, but satisfactory ice could not be ensured and the game was put off until the following winter.

The long-awaited rematch was described at the time as the greatest sporting event in Winnipeg history. Throngs of fans jammed the arena, with many paying as much as $12 per seat. Back in Montreal, the *Daily Star* newspaper arranged a public gathering whereby fans received up-to-the-minute game reports via telegraph.

The Montrealers overcame a 4–2 halftime deficit to tie the game 5–5, before Ernie McLea, who posted the first Stanley Cup hat trick, rifled his third goal of the night past goalie George "Whitey" Merritt to win the game in the closing seconds.

SCORES

Dec.	30	Mtl. Victorias	6	at	Wpg. Victorias	5

1895-96 – (Dec.) – Montreal Victorias – Harold Henderson, Mike Grant (captain), Robert McDougall, Graham Drinkwater, Shirley Davidson, Ernie McLea, Robert Jones, Cam Davidson, David Gillian, Stanley Willett, W. Wallace.

1896 February

The first east-west confrontation in Stanley Cup history pitted the defending Montreal Victorias against the Winnipeg Victorias, champions of the Manitoba Hockey League (MHL).

"Whitey" Merritt, the Winnipeg netminder, introduced the first set of goalie pads in Stanley Cup history to the Montrealers when he skated onto to the ice with a pair of white cricket pads and proceeded to register a shutout. Dan Bain scored the Cup-winning goal midway through the game, and C.J. Campbell added the other.

SCORES

Feb.	14	Wpg. Victorias	2	at	Mtl. Victorias	0

1895-96 – (Feb.) – Winnipeg Victorias – G.H. Merritt, Rod Flett, Fred Higginbotham, Jack Armitage (captain), C.J. (Tote) Campbell, Dan Bain, Charles Johnstone, H. Howard.

1895

The Montreal Victorias wrapped up the AHA title on March 8, and, having unseated the Montreal AAA, were prepared to defend the Stanley Cup as league champions. However, trustees Sweetland and Ross had already agreed to a challenge match between the 1894 champion AAA club and Queen's University with the game set for March 9.

In what remains one of the most unusual Stanley Cup situations ever, Sweetland and Ross maintained that if the AAA defeated Queen's, the Vics would be declared champions, but if Queen's won, the trophy would pass out of the AHA for the first time and go to the university squad. The first challenge match in Stanley Cup history turned out to be a one-sided affair as the AAA won the game, and the Vics were awarded the trophy.

Clarence McKerrow, playing in place of the injured Billy Barlow, became the first "ringer" in Stanley Cup history and scored once for the AAA in a winning effort.

SCORES

Mar.	9	Queen's U.	1	at	Mtl. AAA	5

1894-95 – Montreal Victorias – Robert Jones, Harold Henderson, Mike Grant (captain), Shirley Davidson, Bob McDougall, Norman Rankin, Graham Drinkwater, Roland Elliot, William Pullan, Hartland McDougall, Jim Fenwick, A. McDougall.

1894

The 1894 AHA season ended precariously. Four of the five competing clubs — the Montreal AAA, Montreal Victorias, Ottawa Capitals and Quebec — finished with 5–3–0 records and shares of first place. The determination of a champion, and thus the winner of the Stanley Cup, created many problems for the league's governors who simply could not come to terms on a solution suitable to all involved. With two of the four finalists from Montreal, home-ice advantage became the major issue of contention. After Quebec ultimately withdrew, it was decided that all playoff games would be staged in Montreal and that Ottawa would be given a bye into the finals since it was the sole "road" team.

In what must be termed the first Stanley Cup playoff game ever, the two Montreal clubs battled to a 3–2 decision in favor of the defending champions, who then downed Ottawa in the finale.

Forward Billy Barlow, who finished third overall with eight goals in eight regular-season games, scored twice in each postseason contest as the AAA successfully defended its title.

SCORES

Mar.	17	Mtl. Victorias	2	at	Mtl. AAA	3
Mar.	22	Ottawa	1	at	Mtl. AAA	3

1893-94 – Montreal AAA – Herbert Collins, Allan Cameron, George James, Billy Barlow, Clare Mussen, Archie Hodgson, E. O'Brien, Haviland Routh, Alex Irving, James Stewart, A.C. (Toad) Wand, A.B. Kingan, E. O'Brien.

1893

In accordance with Lord Stanley's terms, the Montreal AAA Hockey Club captured the inaugural Stanley Cup championship as a result of winning Canada's Amateur Hockey Association (AHA) title. The AAA squad skated to a 7–1–0 record to beat out the 6–2–0 Ottawa Generals, who had handed the Montrealers their lone defeat of the season on opening day. Harvie Routh led the newly crowned champs with a league-high 12 goals in seven games.

Formed in 1886, the AHA was considered the top hockey league in all of Canada. By 1893, its schedule consisted of 20 games played among it five club members, which included three Montreal teams — the AAA, Victorias and Crystals — as well as Ottawa and Quebec.

Once the AAA had been declared holders of the Cup, any Canadian hockey team deemed acceptable by the trustees could challenge for the trophy, but none would for two years.

1892-93 – Montreal AAA – Tom Paton, James Stewart, Allan Cameron, Haviland Routh, Archie Hodgson, Billy Barlow, A.B. Kingan, G.S. Lowe.

CHAPTER 10

Stanley Cup Playoffs Record Book

Team and Individual Records, 1918 –1999

Team Records

GAMES PLAYED

MOST GAMES PLAYED BY ALL TEAMS, ONE PLAYOFF YEAR:

92 – 1991. There were 51 DSF, 24 DF, 11 CF and 6 F games.
90 – 1994. There were 48 CQF, 23 CSF, 12 CF and 7 F games.
87 – 1987. There were 44 DSF, 25 DF, 11 CF and 7 F games.

MOST GAMES PLAYED, ONE TEAM, ONE PLAYOFF YEAR:

26 – Philadelphia Flyers, 1987. Won DSF 4-2 against NY Rangers, DF 4-3 against NY Islanders, CF 4-2 against Montreal, and lost F 4-3 against Edmonton.
24 – Pittsburgh Penguins, 1991. Won DSF 4-3 against New Jersey, DF 4-1 against Washington, CF 4-2 against Boston, and F 4-2 against Minnesota.
– Los Angeles Kings, 1993. Won DSF 4-2 against Calgary, DF 4-2 against Vancouver, CF 4-3 against Toronto, and lost F 4-1 against Montreal.
– Vancouver Canucks, 1994. Won CQF 4-3 against Calgary, CSF 4-1 against Dallas, CF 4-1 against Toronto, and lost F 4-3 against NY Rangers.

PLAYOFF APPEARANCES

MOST STANLEY CUP CHAMPIONSHIPS:

23 – Montreal Canadiens 1924-30-31-44-46-53-56-57-58-59-60-65-66-68-69-71-73-76-77-78-79-86-93
13 – Toronto Maple Leafs 1918-22-32-42-45-47-48-49-51-62-63-64-67
9 – Detroit Red Wings 1936-37-43-50-52-54-55-97-98

MOST CONSECUTIVE STANLEY CUP CHAMPIONSHIPS:

5 – Montreal Canadiens (1956-57-58-59-60)
4 – Montreal Canadiens (1976-77-78-79)
– NY Islanders (1980-81-82-83)

MOST FINAL SERIES APPEARANCES:

32 – Montreal Canadiens in 82-year history.
21 – Toronto Maple Leafs in 82-year history.
– Detroit Red Wings in 72-year history.

MOST CONSECUTIVE FINAL SERIES APPEARANCES:

10 – Montreal Canadiens, (1951-60, inclusive)
5 – Montreal Canadiens, (1965-69, inclusive)
– NY Islanders, (1980-84, inclusive)

MOST YEARS IN PLAYOFFS:

72 – Montreal Canadiens in 82-year history.
59 – Toronto Maple Leafs in 82-year history.
– Boston Bruins in 75-year history.

MOST CONSECUTIVE PLAYOFF APPEARANCES:

29 – Boston Bruins (1968-96, inclusive)
28 – Chicago Blackhawks (1970-97, inclusive)
24 – Montreal Canadiens (1971-94, inclusive)
21 – Montreal Canadiens (1949-69, inclusive)
20 – Detroit Red Wings (1939-58, inclusive)
– St. Louis Blues (1980-99, inclusive)

TEAM WINS

MOST HOME WINS, ONE TEAM, ONE PLAYOFF YEAR:

11 – Edmonton Oilers, 1988 in 11 home games.
10 – Edmonton Oilers, 1985 in 10 home games.
– Montreal Canadiens, 1986 in 11 home games.
– Montreal Canadiens, 1993 in 11 home games.

MOST ROAD WINS, ONE TEAM, ONE PLAYOFF YEAR:

10 – New Jersey Devils, 1995. Won three at Boston in CQF; two at Pittsburgh in CSF; three at Philadelphia in CF; and two at Detroit in F series.
8 – NY Islanders, 1980. Won two at Los Angeles in PR; three at Boston in QF; two at Buffalo in SF; and one at Philadelphia in F series.
– Philadelphia Flyers, 1987. Won two at NY Rangers in DSF; two at NY Islanders in DF; three at Montreal in CF; and one at Edmonton in F series.
– Edmonton Oilers, 1990. Won one at Winnipeg in DSF; two at Los Angeles in DF; two at Chicago in CF and three at Boston in F series.
– Pittsburgh Penguins, 1992. Won two at Washington in DSF; two at NY Rangers in DF; two at Boston in CF; and two at Chicago in F series.
– Vancouver Canucks, 1994. Won three at Calgary in CQF; two at Dallas in CSF; one at Toronto in CF; and two at NY Rangers in F series.
– Colorado Avalanche, 1996. Won two at Vancouver in CQF; two at Chicago in CSF; two at Detroit in CF; and two at Florida in F series.
– Detroit Red Wings, 1998. Won two at Phoenix in CQF; three at St. Louis in CSF; one at Dallas in CF; and two at Washington in F series.
– Colorado Avalanche, 1999. Won three at San Jose in CQF; three at Detroit in CSF; and two at Dallas in CF series.

MOST ROAD WINS, ALL TEAMS, ONE PLAYOFF YEAR:

46 – 1987. Of 87 games played, road teams won 46 (22 DSF, 14 DF, 8 CF and 2 in F series).

MOST OVERTIME WINS, ONE TEAM, ONE PLAYOFF YEAR:

10 – Montreal Canadiens, 1993. Two against Quebec in DSF; three against Buffalo in DF; two against NY Islanders in CF; and three against Los Angeles in F series. Montreal played 20 games.
6 – NY Islanders, 1980. One against Los Angeles in PR; two against Boston in QF; one against Buffalo in SF; and two against Philadelphia in F series. Islanders played 21 games.
– Vancouver Canucks, 1994. Three against Calgary in CQF; one against Dallas in CSF; one against Toronto in CF; and one against NY Rangers in F series. Vancouver played 24 games.

MOST OVERTIME WINS AT HOME, ONE TEAM, ONE PLAYOFF YEAR:

4 – St. Louis Blues, 1968. Won one vs. Philadelphia in QF and three vs. Minnesota in SF.
– Montreal Canadiens, 1993. Won one vs. Quebec in DSF, one vs. Buffalo in DF, one vs. NY Islanders in CF and one vs. Los Angeles in F series.

MOST OVERTIME WINS ON THE ROAD, ONE TEAM, ONE PLAYOFF YEAR:

6 – Montreal Canadiens, 1993. Won one vs. Quebec in DSF, two vs. Buffalo in DF, one vs. NY Islanders in CF and two vs. Los Angeles in F series.

TEAM LOSSES

MOST LOSSES, ONE TEAM, ONE PLAYOFF YEAR:

11 – Philadelphia Flyers, 1987. Lost two vs. NY Rangers in DSF; three vs. NY Islanders in DF; two vs. Montreal in CF; and four vs. Edmonton in F series.

MOST HOME LOSSES, ONE TEAM, ONE PLAYOFF YEAR:

6 – Philadelphia Flyers, 1987. Lost one vs. NY Rangers in DSF; two vs. NY Islanders in DF; two vs. Montreal in CF; and one vs. Edmonton in F series.
– Washington Capitals, 1998. Lost two vs. Boston in CQF; two vs. Buffalo in CF; and two vs. Detroit in F series.
– Colorado Avalanche, 1999. Lost two vs. San Jose in CQF; two vs. Detroit in CSF; and two vs. Dallas in CF series.

MOST ROAD LOSSES, ONE TEAM, ONE PLAYOFF YEAR:

6 – St. Louis Blues, 1968. Lost two at Philadelphia in QF; two at Minnesota in SF; and two at Montreal in F series.
– St. Louis Blues, 1970. Lost two at Minnesota in QF; two at Pittsburgh in SF; and two at Boston in F series.
– NY Islanders, 1984. Lost one at NY Rangers in DSF; two at Montreal in CF; and three at Edmonton in F series.
– Los Angeles Kings, 1993. Lost one at Calgary in DSF; one at Vancouver in DF; two at Toronto in CF; and two at Montreal in F series.

MOST OVERTIME LOSSES, ONE TEAM, ONE PLAYOFF YEAR:

4 – Montreal Canadiens, 1951. Lost four vs. Toronto in F series.
– St. Louis Blues, 1968. Lost one vs. Philadelphia in QF; one vs. Minnesota in SF; and two vs. Montreal in F series.
– Los Angeles Kings, 1991. Lost one vs. Vancouver in DSF; and three vs. Edmonton in DF series.
– Los Angeles Kings, 1993. Lost one vs. Toronto in CF; and three vs. Montreal in F series.
– Philadelphia Flyers, 1996. Lost two vs. Tampa Bay in CQF; and two vs. Florida in CSF series.

MOST OVERTIME LOSSES AT HOME, ONE TEAM, ONE PLAYOFF YEAR:

2 – Two overtime losses at home by one team in one playoff year has occurred 39 times. The Pittsburgh Penguins are the most recent team to equal this mark when they lost twice in overtime at home to the Toronto Maple Leafs in the 1999 Stanley Cup CSF series.

MOST OVERTIME LOSSES ON THE ROAD, ONE TEAM, ONE PLAYOFF YEAR:

3 – Los Angeles Kings, 1991. Lost one at Vancouver in DSF; and two at Edmonton in DF series.
– St. Louis Blues, 1996. Lost two at Toronto in CQF; and one at Detroit in CSF series.
– Dallas Stars, 1999. Lost two at St. Louis in CSF; and one at Colorado in CF series.

PLAYOFF WINNING STREAKS

LONGEST PLAYOFF WINNING STREAK:

14 – Pittsburgh Penguins. Streak started May 9, 1992, at Pittsburgh with a 5-4 win in fourth game of DF series against NY Rangers, won by Pittsburgh 4-2. Continued with a four-game win over Boston in 1992 CF and a four-game sweep of Chicago in 1992 F. Pittsburgh then won the first three games of 1993 DSF versus New Jersey. New Jersey ended the streak April 25, 1993, at New Jersey with a 4-1 win.
12 – Edmonton Oilers. Streak started May 15, 1984, at Edmonton with a 7-2 win in third game of F series against NY Islanders won by Edmonton 4-1. Continued with a three-game sweep of Los Angeles in 1985 DSF and a four-game sweep of Winnipeg in 1985 DF, Edmonton then

won the first two games of 1985 CF versus Chicago. Chicago ended the streak May 9, 1985, at Chicago with a 5-2 win.

MOST CONSECUTIVE WINS, ONE TEAM, ONE PLAYOFF YEAR:

11 – Chicago Blackhawks in 1992. Chicago won last three games of DSF against St. Louis to win series 4-2 and then defeated Detroit 4-0 in DF and Edmonton 4-0 in CF.

– Pittsburgh Penguins in 1992. Pittsburgh won last three games of DF against NY Rangers to win series 4-2 and then defeated Boston 4-0 in CF and Chicago 4-0 in F.

– Montreal Canadiens in 1993. Montreal won last four games of DSF against Quebec to win series 4-2, defeated Buffalo 4-0 in DF and won first three games of CF against NY Islanders.

PLAYOFF LOSING STREAKS

LONGEST PLAYOFF LOSING STREAK:

16 – Chicago Black Hawks. Streak started on April 21, 1975 as Chicago lost last two games in a QF series against Buffalo. Then Chicago lost four games to Montreal in 1976 QF; two games to NY Islanders in 1977 PR; four games to Boston in 1978 QF and four games to NY Islanders in 1979 QF. Chicago ended the streak with a 3-2 win against St. Louis in the opening game of a 1980 PR series..

12 – Toronto Maple Leafs. Streak started on April 16, 1979 as Toronto lost four straight games in a QF series against Montreal. Continued with three-game PR defeats versus Philadelphia and NY Islanders in 1980 and 1981 respectively. Toronto failed to qualify for the 1982 playoffs and lost the first two games of a 1983 DSF against Minnesota. Toronto ended the streak with a 6-3 win against Minnesota on April 9, 1983.

MOST GOALS IN A SERIES, ONE TEAM

MOST GOALS, ONE TEAM, ONE PLAYOFF SERIES:

44 – Edmonton Oilers in 1985 CF. Edmonton won best-of-seven series 4-2, outscoring Chicago 44-25.

35 – Edmonton Oilers in 1983 DF. Edmonton won best-of-seven series 4-1, outscoring Calgary 35-13.

– Calgary Flames in 1995 CQF. Calgary lost best-of-seven series 3-4, outscoring San Jose 35-26.

MOST GOALS, ONE TEAM, TWO-GAME SERIES:

11 – Buffalo Sabres in 1977 PR. Buffalo won best-of-three series 2-0, outscoring Minnesota 11-3.

– Toronto Maple Leafs in 1978 PR. Toronto won best-of-three series 2-0, outscoring Los Angeles 11-3.

10 – Boston Bruins in 1927 QF. Boston won two-game total-goals series 10-5.

MOST GOALS, ONE TEAM, THREE-GAME SERIES:

23 – Chicago Black Hawks in 1985 DSF. Chicago won best-of-five series 3-0, outscoring Detroit 23-8.

20 – Minnesota North Stars in 1981 PR. Minnesota won best-of-five series 3-0, outscoring Boston 20-13.

– NY Islanders in 1981 PR. New York won best-of-five series 3-0, outscoring Toronto 20-4.

MOST GOALS, ONE TEAM, FOUR-GAME SERIES:

28 – Boston Bruins in 1972 SF. Boston won best-of-seven series 4-0, outscoring St. Louis 28-8.

MOST GOALS, ONE TEAM, FIVE-GAME SERIES:

35 – Edmonton Oilers in 1983 DF. Edmonton won best-of-seven series 4-1, outscoring Calgary 35-13.

32 – Edmonton Oilers in 1987 DSF. Edmonton won best-of-seven series 4-1, outscoring Los Angeles 32-20.

28 – NY Rangers in 1979 QF. NY Rangers won best-of-seven series 4-1, outscoring Philadelphia 28-8.

27 – Philadelphia Flyers in 1980 SF. Philadelphia won best-of-seven series 4-1, outscoring Minnesota 27-14.

– Los Angeles Kings, in 1982 DSF. Los Angeles won best-of-five series 3-2, outscoring Edmonton 27-23.

MOST GOALS, ONE TEAM, SIX-GAME SERIES:

44 – Edmonton Oilers in 1985 CF. Edmonton won best-of-seven series 4-2, outscoring Chicago 44-25.

33 – Montreal Canadiens in 1973 F. Montreal won best-of-seven series 4-2, outscoring Chicago 33-23.

– Chicago Black Hawks in 1985 DF. Chicago won best-of-seven series 4-2, outscoring Minnesota 33-29.

– Los Angeles Kings in 1993 DSF. Los Angeles won best-of-seven series 4-2, outscoring Calgary 33-28.

MOST GOALS, ONE TEAM, SEVEN-GAME SERIES:

35 – Calgary Flames in 1995 CQF. Calgary lost best-of-seven series 3-4, outscoring San Jose 35-26.

33 – Philadelphia Flyers in 1976 QF. Philadelphia won best-of-seven series 4-3, outscoring Toronto 33-23.

– Boston Bruins in 1983 DF. Boston won best-of-seven series 4-3, outscoring Buffalo 33-23.

– Edmonton Oilers in 1984 DF. Edmonton won best-of-seven series 4-3, outscoring Calgary 33-27.

FEWEST GOALS IN A SERIES, ONE TEAM

FEWEST GOALS, ONE TEAM, TWO-GAME SERIES:

0 – NY Americans in 1929 SF. Lost two-game total-goals series 1-0 against NY Rangers.

– Chicago Black Hawks in 1935 SF. Lost two-game total-goals series 1-0 against Mtl. Maroons.

– Mtl. Maroons in 1937 SF. Lost best-of-three series 2-0 to NY Rangers while being outscored 5-0.

– NY Americans in 1939 QF. Lost best-of-three series 2-0 to Toronto while being outscored 6-0.

FEWEST GOALS, ONE TEAM, THREE-GAME SERIES:

1 – Mtl. Maroons in 1936 SF. Lost best-of-five series 3-0 to Detroit and were outscored 6-1.

FEWEST GOALS, ONE TEAM, FOUR-GAME SERIES:

2 – Boston Bruins in 1935 SF. Lost best-of-five series 3-1 to Toronto while being outscored 7-2.

– Montreal Canadiens in 1952 F. Lost best-of-seven series 4-0 to Detroit while being outscored 11-2.

FEWEST GOALS, ONE TEAM, FIVE-GAME SERIES:

5 – NY Rangers in 1928 F. NY Rangers won best-of-five series 3-2, while being outscored by Mtl. Maroons 6-5.

– Boston Bruins in 1995 CQF. New Jersey won best-of-seven series 4-1, while outscoring Boston 14-5.

– New Jersey Devils in 1997 CSF. NY Rangers won best-of-seven series 4-1, while outscoring New Jersey 10-5.

FEWEST GOALS, ONE TEAM, SIX-GAME SERIES:

5 – Boston Bruins in 1951 SF. Toronto won best-of-seven series 4-1 with 1 tie, outscoring Boston 17-5.

FEWEST GOALS, ONE TEAM, SEVEN-GAME SERIES:

9 – Toronto Maple Leafs, in 1945 F. Toronto won best-of-seven series 4-3; teams tied in scoring 9-9.

– Detroit Red Wings, in 1945 F. Toronto won best-of-seven series 4-3; teams tied in scoring 9-9.

MOST GOALS IN A SERIES, BOTH TEAMS

MOST GOALS, BOTH TEAMS, ONE PLAYOFF SERIES:

69 – Edmonton Oilers, Chicago Black Hawks in 1985 CF. Edmonton won best-of-seven series 4-2, outscoring Chicago 44-25.

62 – Chicago Black Hawks, Minnesota North Stars in 1985 DF. Chicago won best-of-seven series 4-2, outscoring Minnesota 33-29.

61 – Los Angeles Kings, Calgary Flames in 1993 DSF. Los Angeles won best-of-seven series 4-2, outscoring Calgary 33-28.

– San Jose Sharks, Calgary Flames in 1995 CQF. San Jose won best-of-seven series 4-3, while being outscored 35-26.

MOST GOALS, BOTH TEAMS, TWO-GAME SERIES:

17 – Toronto St. Patricks, Montreal Canadiens in 1918 NHL F. Toronto won two-game total-goals series 10-7.

15 – Boston Bruins, Chicago Black Hawks in 1927 QF. Boston won two-game total-goals series 10-5.

– Pittsburgh Penguins, St. Louis Blues in 1975 PR. Pittsburgh won best-of-three series 2-0, outscoring St. Louis 9-6.

MOST GOALS, BOTH TEAMS, THREE-GAME SERIES:

33 – Minnesota North Stars, Boston Bruins in 1981 PR. Minnesota won best-of-five series 3-0, outscoring Boston 20-13.

31 – Chicago Black Hawks, Detroit Red Wings in 1985 DSF. Chicago won best-of-five series 3-0, outscoring Detroit 23-8.

28 – Toronto Maple Leafs, NY Rangers in 1932 F. Toronto won best-of-five series 3-0, outscoring New York 18-10.

MOST GOALS, BOTH TEAMS, FOUR-GAME SERIES:

36 – Boston Bruins, St. Louis Blues in 1972 SF. Boston won best-of-seven series 4-0, outscoring St. Louis 28-8.

– Minnesota North Stars, Toronto Maple Leafs in 1983 DSF. Minnesota won best-of-five series 3-1; teams tied in scoring 18-18.

– Edmonton Oilers, Chicago Black Hawks in 1983 CF. Edmonton won best-of-seven series 4-0, outscoring Chicago 25-11.

35 – NY Rangers, Los Angeles Kings in 1981 PR. NY Rangers won best-of-five series 3-1, outscoring Los Angeles 23-12.

MOST GOALS, BOTH TEAMS, FIVE-GAME SERIES:

52 – Edmonton Oilers, Los Angeles Kings in 1987 DSF. Edmonton won best-of-seven series 4-1, outscoring Los Angeles 32-20.

50 – Los Angeles Kings, Edmonton Oilers in 1982 DSF. Los Angeles won best-of-five series 3-2, outscoring Edmonton 27-23.

48 – Edmonton Oilers, Calgary Flames in 1983 DF. Edmonton won best-of-seven series 4-1, outscoring Calgary 35-13.

– Calgary Flames, Los Angeles Kings in 1988 DSF. Calgary won best-of-seven series 4-1, outscoring Los Angeles 30-18.

MOST GOALS, BOTH TEAMS, SIX-GAME SERIES:

69 – Edmonton Oilers, Chicago Black Hawks in 1985 CF. Edmonton won best-of-seven series 4-2, outscoring Chicago 44-25.

62 – Chicago Black Hawks, Minnesota North Stars in 1985 DF. Chicago won best-of-seven series 4-2, outscoring Minnesota 33-29.

61 – Los Angeles Kings, Calgary Flames in 1993 DSF. Los Angeles won best-of-seven series 4-2, outscoring Calgary 33-28.

MOST GOALS, BOTH TEAMS, SEVEN-GAME SERIES:

61 – San Jose Sharks, Calgary Flames in 1995 CQF. San Jose won best-of-seven series 4-3, while being outscored 35-26.

60 – Edmonton Oilers, Calgary Flames in 1984 DF. Edmonton won best-of-seven series 4-3, outscoring Calgary 33-27.

FEWEST GOALS IN A SERIES, BOTH TEAMS

FEWEST GOALS, BOTH TEAMS, TWO-GAME SERIES:

1 – NY Rangers, NY Americans, in 1929 SF. NY Rangers defeated NY Americans 1-0 in two-game, total-goals series.

– Mtl. Maroons, Chicago Black Hawks in 1935 SF. Mtl. Maroons defeated Chicago 1-0 in two-game, total-goals series.

FEWEST GOALS, BOTH TEAMS, THREE-GAME SERIES:

7 – **Boston Bruins, Montreal Canadiens** in 1929 SF. Boston won best-of-five series 3-0, outscoring Montreal 5-2.
– **Detroit Red Wings, Mtl. Maroons** in 1936 SF. Detroit won best-of-five series 3-0, outscoring Mtl. Maroons 6-1.

FEWEST GOALS, BOTH TEAMS, FOUR-GAME SERIES:

9 – **Toronto Maple Leafs, Boston Bruins** in 1935 SF. Toronto won best-of-five series 3-1, outscoring Boston 7-2.

FEWEST GOALS, BOTH TEAMS, FIVE-GAME SERIES:

11 – **NY Rangers, Mtl. Maroons** in 1928 F. NY Rangers won best-of-five series 3-2, being outscored by Mtl. Maroons 6-5.

FEWEST GOALS, BOTH TEAMS, SIX-GAME SERIES:

20 – **Toronto Maple Leafs, Philadelphia Flyers** in 1999 CQF. Toronto won best-of-seven series 4-2, being outscored by Philadelphia 11-9.

FEWEST GOALS, BOTH TEAMS, SEVEN-GAME SERIES:

18 – **Toronto Maple Leafs, Detroit Red Wings** in 1945 F. Toronto won best-of-seven series 4-3; teams tied in scoring 9-9.

MOST GOALS IN A GAME OR PERIOD

MOST GOALS, ONE TEAM, ONE GAME:

13 – **Edmonton Oilers** at Edmonton, April 9, 1987. Edmonton 13, Los Angeles 3. Edmonton won best-of-seven DSF 4-1.
12 – Los Angeles Kings at Los Angeles, April 10, 1990. Los Angeles 12, Calgary 4. Los Angeles won best-of-seven DSF 4-2.
11 – Montreal Canadiens at Montreal, March 30, 1944. Montreal 11, Toronto 0. Montreal won best-of-seven SF 4-1.
– Edmonton Oilers at Edmonton, May 4, 1985. Edmonton 11, Chicago 2. Edmonton won best-of-seven CF 4-2.

MOST GOALS, ONE TEAM, ONE PERIOD:

7 – **Montreal Canadiens**, March 30, 1944, at Montreal in third period, during 11-0 win against Toronto.

MOST GOALS, BOTH TEAMS, ONE GAME:

18 – **Los Angeles Kings, Edmonton Oilers** at Edmonton, April 7, 1982. Los Angeles 10, Edmonton 8. Los Angeles won best-of-five DSF 3-2.
17 – Pittsburgh Penguins, Philadelphia Flyers at Pittsburgh, April 25, 1989. Pittsburgh 10, Philadelphia 7. Philadelphia won best-of-seven DF 4-3.
16 – Edmonton Oilers, Los Angeles Kings at Edmonton, April 9, 1987. Edmonton 13, Los Angeles 3. Edmonton won best-of-seven DSF 4-1.
– Los Angeles Kings, Calgary Flames at Los Angeles, April 10, 1990. Los Angeles 12, Calgary 4. Los Angeles won best-of-seven DF 4-2.

MOST GOALS, BOTH TEAMS, ONE PERIOD:

9 – **NY Rangers, Philadelphia Flyers,** April 24, 1979, at Philadelphia, third period. NY Rangers won 8-3, scoring six of nine third-period goals.
– **Los Angeles Kings, Calgary Flames**, at Los Angeles, April 10, 1990, second period. Los Angeles won 12-4, scoring five of nine second-period goals.
8 – Chicago Black Hawks, Montreal Canadiens, at Montreal, May 8, 1973, second period. Chicago won 8-7, scoring five of eight second-period goals.
– Chicago Black Hawks, Edmonton Oilers, at Chicago, May 12, 1985, first period. Chicago won 8-6, scoring five of eight first-period goals.
– Edmonton Oilers, Winnipeg Jets, at Edmonton, April 6, 1988, third period. Edmonton won 7-4, scoring six of eight third period goals.
– Hartford Whalers, Montreal Canadiens, at Hartford, April 10, 1988, third period. Hartford won 7-5, scoring five of eight third period goals.
– Vancouver Canucks, NY Rangers, at New York, June 9, 1994, third period. Vancouver won 6-3, scoring five of eight third period goals.

TEAM POWER-PLAY GOALS

MOST POWER-PLAY GOALS BY ALL TEAMS, ONE PLAYOFF YEAR:

199 – **1988** in 83 games.

MOST POWER-PLAY GOALS, ONE TEAM, ONE PLAYOFF YEAR:

35 – **Minnesota North Stars,** 1991 in 23 games.
32 – Edmonton Oilers, 1988 in 18 games.
31 – NY Islanders, 1981, in 18 games.

MOST POWER-PLAY GOALS, ONE TEAM, ONE SERIES:

15 – **NY Islanders** in 1980 F against Philadelphia. NY Islanders won series 4-2.
– **Minnesota North Stars** in 1991 DSF against Chicago. Minnesota won series 4-2.
13 – NY Islanders in 1981 QF against Edmonton. NY Islanders won series 4-2.
– Calgary Flames in 1986 CF against St. Louis. Calgary won series 4-3.
12 – Toronto Maple Leafs in 1976 QF series won by Philadelphia 4-3.

MOST POWER-PLAY GOALS, BOTH TEAMS, ONE SERIES:

21 – **NY Islanders, Philadelphia Flyers** in 1980 F, won by NY Islanders 4-2. NY Islanders had 15 and Flyers 6.
– **NY Islanders, Edmonton Oilers** in 1981 QF, won by NY Islanders 4-2. NY Islanders had 13 and Edmonton 8.
– **Philadelphia Flyers, Pittsburgh Penguins** in 1989 DF, won by Philadelphia 4-3. Philadelphia had 11 and Pittsburgh 10.
– **Minnesota North Stars, Chicago Blackhawks** in 1991 DSF, won by Minnesota 4-2. Minnesota had 15 and Chicago 6.
20 – Toronto Maple Leafs, Philadelphia Flyers in 1976 QF series won by Philadelphia 4-3. Toronto had 12 and Philadelphia 8.

MOST POWER-PLAY GOALS, ONE TEAM, ONE GAME:

6 – **Boston Bruins,** April 2, 1969, at Boston against Toronto. Boston won 10-0.

MOST POWER-PLAY GOALS, BOTH TEAMS, ONE GAME:

8 – **Minnesota North Stars, St. Louis Blues,** April 24, 1991 at Minnesota. Minnesota had 4, St. Louis 4. Minnesota won 8-4.
7 – Minnesota North Stars, Edmonton Oilers, April 28, 1984 at Minnesota. Minnesota had 4, Edmonton 3. Edmonton won 8-5.
– Philadelphia Flyers, NY Rangers, April 13, 1985 at New York. Philadelphia had 4, NY Rangers 3. Philadelphia won 6-5.
– Edmonton Oilers, Chicago Black Hawks, May 14, 1985 at Edmonton. Chicago had 5, Edmonton 2. Edmonton won 10-5.
– Edmonton Oilers, Los Angeles Kings, April 9, 1987 at Edmonton. Edmonton had 5, Los Angeles 2. Edmonton won 13-3.
– Vancouver Canucks, Calgary Flames, April 9, 1989 at Vancouver. Vancouver had 4, Calgary 3. Vancouver won 5-3.

MOST POWER-PLAY GOALS, ONE TEAM, ONE PERIOD:

4 – **Toronto Maple Leafs,** March 26, 1936, second period against Boston at Toronto. Toronto won 8-3.
– **Minnesota North Stars,** April 28, 1984, second period against Edmonton at Minnesota. Edmonton won 8-5.
– **Boston Bruins,** April 11, 1991, third period against Hartford at Boston. Boston won 6-1.
– **Minnesota North Stars,** April 24, 1991, second period against St. Louis at Minnesota. Minnesota won 8-4.
– **St. Louis Blues,** April 27, 1998, third period at Los Angeles. St. Louis won 4-3.

MOST POWER-PLAY GOALS, BOTH TEAMS, ONE PERIOD:

5 – **Minnesota North Stars, Edmonton Oilers,** April 28, 1984, second period, at Minnesota. Minnesota had 4 and Edmonton 1. Edmonton won 8-5.
– **Vancouver Canucks, Calgary Flames,** April 9, 1989, third period at Vancouver. Vancouver had 3 and Calgary 2. Vancouver won 5-3.
– **Minnesota North Stars, St. Louis Blues,** April 24, 1991, second period, at Minnesota. Minnesota had 4 and St. Louis 1. Minnesota won 8-4.

TEAM SHORTHAND GOALS

MOST SHORTHAND GOALS BY ALL TEAMS, ONE PLAYOFF YEAR:

33 – **1988,** in 83 games.

MOST SHORTHAND GOALS, ONE TEAM, ONE PLAYOFF YEAR:

10 – **Edmonton Oilers,** 1983, in 16 games.
9 – NY Islanders, 1981, in 19 games.
8 – Philadelphia Flyers, 1989, in 19 games.

MOST SHORTHAND GOALS, ONE TEAM, ONE SERIES:

6 – **Calgary Flames** in 1995 against San Jose in best-of-seven CQF won by San Jose 4-3.
– **Vancouver Canucks** in 1995 against St. Louis in best-of-seven CQF won by Vancouver 4-3.
5 – NY Rangers in 1979 against Philadelphia in best-of-seven QF, won by NY Rangers 4-1.
– Edmonton Oilers in 1983 against Calgary in best-of-seven DF won by Edmonton 4-1.

MOST SHORTHAND GOALS, BOTH TEAMS, ONE SERIES:

7 – **Boston Bruins (4), NY Rangers (3),** in 1958 SF won by Boston 4-2.
– **Edmonton Oilers (5), Calgary Flames (2),** in 1983 DF won by Edmonton 4-1.
– **Vancouver Canucks (6), St. Louis Blues (1),** in 1995 CQF won by Vancouver 4-3.

MOST SHORTHAND GOALS, ONE TEAM, ONE GAME:

3 – **Boston Bruins,** April 11, 1981, at Minnesota. Minnesota won 6-3.
– **NY Islanders,** April 17, 1983, at NY Rangers. NY Rangers won 7-6.
– **Toronto Maple Leafs,** May 8, 1994, at San Jose. Toronto won 8-3.

MOST SHORTHAND GOALS, BOTH TEAMS, ONE GAME:

4 – **NY Islanders, NY Rangers,** April 17, 1983, at NY Rangers. NY Islanders had 3 shorthand goals, NY Rangers 1. NY Rangers won 7-6.
– **Boston Bruins, Minnesota North Stars,** April 11, 1981, at Minnesota. Boston had 3 shorthand goals, Minnesota 1. Minnesota won 6-3.
– **San Jose Sharks, Toronto Maple Leafs,** May 8, 1994, at San Jose. Toronto had 3 shorthand goals, San Jose 1. Toronto won 8-3.
3 – Toronto Maple Leafs, Detroit Red Wings, April 5, 1947, at Toronto. Toronto had 2 shorthand goals, Detroit 1. Toronto won 6-1.
– NY Rangers, Boston Bruins, April 1, 1958, at Boston. NY Rangers had 2 shorthand goals, Boston 1. NY Rangers won 5-2.
– Minnesota North Stars, Philadelphia Flyers, May 4, 1980, at Minnesota. Minnesota had 2 shorthand goals, Philadelphia 1. Philadelphia won 5-3.
– Edmonton Oilers, Winnipeg Jets, April 9, 1988, at Winnipeg. Winnipeg had 2 shorthand goals, Edmonton 1. Winnipeg won 6-4.
– New Jersey Devils, NY Islanders, April 14, 1988, at New Jersey. NY Islanders had 2 shorthand goals, New Jersey 1. New Jersey won 6-5.
– Montreal Canadiens, New Jersey Devils, April 17, 1997, at New Jersey. Montreal had 2 shorthand goals, New Jersey 1. New Jersey won 5-2

MOST SHORTHAND GOALS, ONE TEAM, ONE PERIOD:

2 – **Toronto Maple Leafs,** April 5, 1947, at Toronto against Detroit, first period. Toronto won 6-1.
– **Toronto Maple Leafs,** April 13, 1965, at Toronto against Montreal, first period. Montreal won 4-3.
– **Boston Bruins,** April 20, 1969, at Boston against Montreal, first period. Boston won 3-2.

- **Boston Bruins,** April 8, 1970, at Boston against NY Rangers, second period. Boston won 8-2.
- **Boston Bruins,** April 30, 1972, at Boston against NY Rangers, first period. Boston won 6-5.
- **Chicago Black Hawks,** May 3, 1973, at Chicago against Montreal, first period. Chicago won 7-4.
- **Montreal Canadiens,** April 23, 1978, at Detroit, first period. Montreal won 8-0.
- **NY Islanders,** April 8, 1980, at New York against Los Angeles, second period. NY Islanders won 8-1.
- **Los Angeles Kings,** April 9, 1980, at NY Islanders, first period. Los Angeles won 6-3.
- **Boston Bruins,** April 13, 1980, at Pittsburgh, second period. Boston won 8-3.
- **Minnesota North Stars,** May 4, 1980, at Minnesota against Philadelphia, second period. Philadelphia won 5-3.
- **Boston Bruins,** April 11, 1981, at Minnesota, third period. Minnesota won 6-3.
- **NY Islanders,** May 12, 1981, at New York against Minnesota, first period. NY Islanders won 6-3.
- **Montreal Canadiens,** April 7, 1982, at Montreal against Quebec, third period. Montreal won 5-1.
- **Edmonton Oilers,** April 24, 1983, at Edmonton against Chicago, third period. Edmonton won 8-4.
- **Winnipeg Jets,** April 14, 1985, at Calgary, second period. Winnipeg won 5-3.
- **Boston Bruins,** April 6, 1988, at Boston against Buffalo, first period. Boston won 7-3.
- **NY Islanders,** April 14, 1988, at New Jersey, third period. New Jersey won 6-5.
- **Detroit Red Wings,** April 29, 1993, at Toronto, second period. Detroit won 7-3.
- **Toronto Maple Leafs,** May 8, 1994, at San Jose, third period. Toronto won 8-3.
- **Calgary Flames,** May 11, 1995, at San Jose, first period. Calgary won 9-2.
- **Vancouver Canucks,** May 15, 1995 at St. Louis, second period. Vancouver won 6-5.
- **Montreal Canadiens,** April 17, 1997, at New Jersey, second period. New Jersey won 5-2.
- **Philadelphia Flyers,** April 26, 1997, at Philadelphia against Pittsburgh, first period. Philadelphia won 6-3.
- **Phoenix Coyotes,** April 24, 1998, at Detroit, second period. Phoenix won 7-4.
- **Buffalo Sabres,** April 27, 1998, at Buffalo against Philadelphia, second period. Buffalo won 6-1.
- **San Jose Sharks,** April 30, 1999, at Colorado, third period. San Jose won 7-3.

MOST SHORTHAND GOALS, BOTH TEAMS, ONE PERIOD:

3 – Toronto Maple Leafs, Detroit Red Wings, April 5, 1947, at Toronto, first period. Toronto had 2 shorthand goals, Detroit 1. Toronto won 6-1.
- **Toronto Maple Leafs, San Jose Sharks,** May 8, 1994, at San Jose, third period. Toronto had 2 shorthand goals, San Jose 1. Toronto won 8-3.

FASTEST GOALS

FASTEST FIVE GOALS, BOTH TEAMS:

3:06 – Chicago Black Hawks, Minnesota North Stars, at Chicago April 21, 1985. Keith Brown scored for Chicago at 1:12, second period; Ken Yaremchuk, Chicago, 1:27; Dino Ciccarelli, Minnesota, 2:48; Tony McKegney, Minnesota, 4:07; and Curt Fraser, Chicago, 4:18. Chicago won 6-2 and best-of-seven DF 4-2.

3:20 – Minnesota North Stars, Philadelphia Flyers, at Philadelphia, April 29, 1980. Paul Shmyr scored for Minnesota at 13:20, first period; Steve Christoff, Minnesota, 13:59; Ken Linseman, Philadelphia, 14:54; Tom Gorence, Philadelphia, 15:36; and Linseman, 16:40. Minnesota won 6-5. Philadelphia won best-of-seven SF 4-1.

4:19 – Toronto Maple Leafs, NY Rangers at Toronto, April 9, 1932. Ace Bailey scored for Toronto at 15:07, third period; Fred Cook, NY Rangers, 16:32; Bob Gracie, Toronto, 17:36; Frank Boucher, NY Rangers, 18:26 and 19:26. Toronto won 6-4 and best-of-five F 3-0.

FASTEST FIVE GOALS, ONE TEAM:

3:36 – Montreal Canadiens at Montreal, March 30, 1944, against Toronto. Toe Blake scored at 7:58 and 8:37 of third period; Maurice Richard, 9:17; Ray Getliffe, 10:33; and Buddy O'Connor, 11:34. Canadiens won 11-0 and best-of-seven SF 4-1.

FASTEST FOUR GOALS, BOTH TEAMS:

1:33 – Philadelphia Flyers, Toronto Maple Leafs at Philadelphia, April 20, 1976. Don Saleski of Philadelphia scored at 10:04 of second period; Bob Neely, Toronto, 10:42; Gary Dornhoefer, Philadelphia, 11:24; and Don Saleski, 11:37. Philadelphia won 7-1 and best-of-seven QF series 4-3.

1:34 – Montreal Canadiens, Calgary Flames at Montreal, May 20, 1986. Joel Otto of Calgary scored at 17:59 of first period; Bobby Smith, Montreal, 18:25; Mats Naslund, Montreal, 19:17; and Bob Gainey, Montreal, 19:33. Montreal won 5-3 and best-of-seven F series 4-1.

1:38 – Boston Bruins, Philadelphia Flyers at Philadelphia, April 26, 1977. Gregg Sheppard of Boston scored at 14:01 of second period; Mike Milbury, Boston, 15:01; Gary Dornhoefer, Philadelphia, 15:16; and Jean Ratelle, Boston, 15:39. Boston won 5-4 and best-of-seven SF series 4-0.

FASTEST FOUR GOALS, ONE TEAM:

2:35 – Montreal Canadiens at Montreal, March 30, 1944, against Toronto. Toe Blake scored at 7:58 and 8:37 of third period; Maurice Richard, 9:17; Ray Getliffe, 10:33. Montreal won 11-0 and best-of-seven SF 4-1.

FASTEST THREE GOALS, BOTH TEAMS:

0:21 – Edmonton Oilers, Chicago Black Hawks at Edmonton, May 7, 1985. Behn Wilson scored for Chicago at 19:22 of third period, Jari Kurri at 19:36 and Glenn Anderson at 19:43 for Edmonton. Edmonton won 7-3 and best-of-seven CF 4-2.

0:27 – Phoenix Coyotes, Detroit Red Wings at Detroit, April 24, 1998. Jeremy Roenick scored for Phoenix at 13:24 of second period. Mathieu Dandenault scored for Detroit at 13:32, and Keith Tkachuk scored for Phoenix at 13:51. Phoenix won 7-4, Detroit won the best-of-seven CQF 4-2.

0:30 – Chicago Black Hawks, Pittsburgh Penguins at Chicago, June 1, 1992. Dirk Graham scored for Chicago at 6:21 of first period, Kevin Stevens for Pittsburgh at 6:33 and Dirk Graham at 6:51. Pittsburgh won 6-5 and best-of-seven F 4-0.

FASTEST THREE GOALS, ONE TEAM:

0:23 – Toronto Maple Leafs at Toronto, April 12, 1979, against Atlanta. Darryl Sittler scored at 4:04 and 4:16 of first period; Ron Ellis, 4:27. Leafs won 7-4 and best-of-three PR 2-0.

0:38 – NY Rangers at New York, April 12, 1986 against Philadelphia. Jim Wiemer scored at 12:29 of third period; Bob Brooke, 12:43; Ron Greschner, 13:07. NY Rangers won 5-2 and best-of-five DSF 3-2.

0:56 – Montreal Canadiens at Detroit, April 6, 1954. Dickie Moore scored at 15:03 of first period; Maurice Richard, 15:28 and 15:59. Montreal won 3-1. Detroit won best-of-seven F 4-3.

FASTEST TWO GOALS, BOTH TEAMS:

0:05 – Pittsburgh Penguins, Buffalo Sabres at Buffalo, April 14, 1979. Gilbert Perreault scored for Buffalo at 12:59 and Jim Hamilton for Pittsburgh at 13:04 of first period. Pittsburgh won 4-3 and best-of-three PR 2-1.

0:08 – Minnesota North Stars, St. Louis Blues at Minnesota, April 9, 1989. Bernie Federko scored for St. Louis at 2:28 of third period and Perry Berezan at 2:36 for Minnesota. Minnesota won 5-4. St. Louis won best-of-seven DSF 4-1.
- Phoenix Coyotes, Detroit Red Wings, at Detroit, April 24, 1998. Jeremy Roenick scored for Phoenix at 13:24 of the second period and Mathieu Dandenault scored for Detroit at 13:32. Phoenix won 7-4, Detroit won the best-of-seven CQF 4-2.

0:09 – NY Islanders, Washington Capitals at Washington, April 10, 1986. Bryan Trottier scored for NY Islanders at 18:26 of second period and Scott Stevens at 18:35 for Washington. Washington won 5-2, and best-of-five DSF 3-0.
- Buffalo Sabres, Toronto Maple Leafs at Toronto, May 23, 1999. Vaclav Varada scored at 4:23 of first period for Buffalo and Mats Sundin scored at 4:32 for Toronto. Buffalo won 5-4, and best of seven CF 4-1.

FASTEST TWO GOALS, ONE TEAM:

0:05 – Detroit Red Wings at Detroit, April 11, 1965, against Chicago. Norm Ullman scored at 17:35 and 17:40, second period. Detroit won 4-2. Chicago won best-of-seven SF 4-3.

OVERTIME

SHORTEST OVERTIME:

0:09 – Montreal Canadiens, Calgary Flames, at Calgary, May 18, 1986. Montreal won 3-2 on Brian Skrudland's goal and captured the best-of-seven F 4-1.

0:11 – NY Islanders, NY Rangers, at NY Rangers, April 11, 1975. NY Islanders won 4-3 on Jean-Paul Parise's goal and captured the best-of-three PR 2-1.

LONGEST OVERTIME:

116:30 – Detroit Red Wings, Mtl. Maroons at Montreal, March 24, 25, 1936. Detroit 1, Mtl. Maroons 0. Mud Bruneteau scored, assisted by Hec Kilrea, at 16:30 of sixth overtime period, or after 176 minutes, 30 seconds from start of game, which ended at 2:25 a.m. Detroit won best-of-five SF 3-0.

MOST OVERTIME GAMES, ONE PLAYOFF YEAR:

28 – 1993. 85 games played.
21 – 1999. 86 games played.
19 – 1996. 86 games played.
– 1998. 82 games played.
18 – 1994. 90 games played.
– 1995. 81 games played.

FEWEST OVERTIME GAMES, ONE PLAYOFF YEAR:

0 – 1963. None of the 16 games went into overtime, the only year since 1926 that no overtime was required in any playoff series.

MOST OVERTIME GAMES, ONE SERIES:

5 – Toronto Maple Leafs, Montreal Canadiens in 1951. Toronto won best-of-seven F 4-1.
4 – Toronto Maple Leafs, Boston Bruins in 1933. Toronto won best-of-five SF 3-2.
- Boston Bruins, NY Rangers in 1939. Boston won best-of-seven SF 4-3.
- St. Louis Blues, Minnesota North Stars in 1968. St. Louis won best-of-seven SF 4-3.
- Dallas Stars, St. Louis Blues in 1999. Dallas won best-of-seven CSF 4-2.

THREE-OR-MORE GOAL GAMES

MOST THREE-OR-MORE GOAL GAMES BY ALL TEAMS, ONE PLAYOFF YEAR:

12 – 1983 in 66 games.
– 1988 in 83 games.
11 – 1985 in 70 games.
– 1992 in 86 games.

MOST THREE-OR-MORE GOAL GAMES, ONE TEAM, ONE PLAYOFF YEAR:

6 – Edmonton Oilers in 16 games, 1983.
– Edmonton Oilers in 18 games, 1985.

SHUTOUTS

MOST SHUTOUTS, ONE PLAYOFF YEAR, ALL TEAMS:

18 – 1997. Of 82 games played, Colorado and NY Rangers had 3 each, Edmonton, New Jersey, and St. Louis had 2. Anaheim, Buffalo, Detroit, Florida, Ottawa and Phoenix had 1.

16 – 1994. Of 90 games played, NY Rangers and Vancouver had 4 each, Toronto had 3, Buffalo had 2. Washington, Detroit and New Jersey had 1.

FEWEST SHUTOUTS, ONE PLAYOFF YEAR, ALL TEAMS:

0 – 1959. 18 games played.

MOST SHUTOUTS, BOTH TEAMS, ONE SERIES:

5 – 1945 F, Toronto Maple Leafs, Detroit Red Wings. Toronto had 3 shutouts, Detroit 2.

Toronto won best-of-seven series 4-3.
– **1950 SF, Toronto Maple Leafs, Detroit Red Wings.** Toronto had 3 shutouts, Detroit 2. Detroit won best-of-seven series 4-3.

TEAM PENALTIES

FEWEST PENALTIES, BOTH TEAMS, BEST-OF-SEVEN SERIES:
19 – Detroit Red Wings, Toronto Maple Leafs in 1945 F, won by Toronto 4-3. Detroit received 10 minors, Toronto had 9 minors.

FEWEST PENALTIES, ONE TEAM, BEST-OF-SEVEN SERIES:
9 – Toronto Maple Leafs in 1945 F, won by Toronto 4-3 against Detroit.

MOST PENALTIES, BOTH TEAMS, ONE SERIES:
219 – New Jersey Devils, Washington Capitals in 1988 DF won by New Jersey 4-3. New Jersey received 98 minors, 11 majors, 9 misconducts and 1 match penalty. Washington received 80 minors, 11 majors, 8 misconducts and 1 match penalty.

MOST PENALTY MINUTES, BOTH TEAMS, ONE SERIES:
656 – New Jersey Devils, Washington Capitals in 1988 DF won by New Jersey 4-3. New Jersey had 351 minutes; Washington 305.

MOST PENALTIES, ONE TEAM, ONE SERIES:
119 – New Jersey Devils in 1988 DF versus Washington. New Jersey received 98 minors, 11 majors, 9 misconducts and 1 match penalty.

MOST PENALTY MINUTES, ONE TEAM, ONE SERIES:
351 – New Jersey Devils in 1988 DF versus Washington. Series won by New Jersey 4-3.

MOST PENALTIES, BOTH TEAMS, ONE GAME:
66 – Detroit Red Wings, St. Louis Blues, at St. Louis, April 12, 1991. Detroit received 33 penalties; St. Louis 33. St. Louis won 6-1.
62 – New Jersey Devils, Washington Capitals, at New Jersey, April 22, 1988. New Jersey received 32 penalties; Washington 30. New Jersey won 10-4.

MOST PENALTY MINUTES, BOTH TEAMS, ONE GAME:
298 Minutes – Detroit Red Wings, St. Louis Blues, at St. Louis, April 12, 1991. Detroit received 33 penalties for 152 minutes; St. Louis 33 penalties for 146 minutes. St. Louis won 6-1.
267 Minutes – NY Rangers, Los Angeles Kings, at Los Angeles, April 9, 1981. NY Rangers received 31 penalties for 142 minutes; Los Angeles 28 penalties for 125 minutes. Los Angeles won 5-4.

MOST PENALTIES, ONE TEAM, ONE GAME:
33 – Detroit Red Wings, at St. Louis, April 12,1991. St. Louis won 6-1.
– St. Louis Blues, at St. Louis, April 12, 1991. St. Louis won 6-1.
32 – New Jersey Devils, at Washington, April 22,1988. New Jersey won 10-4.
31 – NY Rangers, at Los Angeles, April 9, 1981. Los Angeles won 5-4.
30 – Philadelphia Flyers, at Toronto, April 15, 1976. Toronto won 5-4.

MOST PENALTY MINUTES, ONE TEAM, ONE GAME:
152 – Detroit Red Wings, at St. Louis, April 12, 1991. St. Louis won 6-1.
146 – St. Louis Blues, at St. Louis, April 12, 1991. St. Louis won 6-1.
142 – NY Rangers, at Los Angeles, April 9, 1981. Los Angeles won 5-4.

MOST PENALTIES, BOTH TEAMS, ONE PERIOD:
43 – NY Rangers, Los Angeles Kings, at Los Angeles, April 9, 1981, first period. NY Rangers had 24 penalties; Los Angeles 19. Los Angeles won 5-4.

MOST PENALTY MINUTES, BOTH TEAMS, ONE PERIOD:
248 – NY Islanders, Boston Bruins, at Boston, April 17, 1980, first period. Each team received 124 minutes. Islanders won 5-4.

MOST PENALTIES, ONE TEAM, ONE PERIOD:
24 – NY Rangers, at Los Angeles, April 9, 1981, first period. Los Angeles won 5-4.

MOST PENALTY MINUTES, ONE TEAM, ONE PERIOD:
125 – NY Rangers, at Los Angeles, April 9, 1981, first period. Los Angeles won 5-4.

Individual Records

GAMES PLAYED

MOST YEARS IN PLAYOFFS:
20 – Gordie Howe, Detroit, Hartford (1947-58, inclusive; 60-61; 63-66, inclusive; 70 & 80)
– Larry Robinson, Montreal, Los Angeles (1973-92 inclusive)
19 – Red Kelly, Detroit, Toronto
– Ray Bourque, Boston

MOST CONSECUTIVE YEARS IN PLAYOFFS:
20 – Larry Robinson, Montreal, Los Angeles (1973-1992, inclusive).
17 – Brad Park, NY Rangers, Boston, Detroit (1969-1985, inclusive).
– Ray Bourque, Boston (1980-96, inclusive).
16 – Jean Beliveau, Montreal (1954-69, inclusive).
– Bob Gainey, Montreal (1974-89, inclusive).
– Dale Hunter, Quebec, Washington (1981-96, inclusive)

MOST PLAYOFF GAMES:
236 – Mark Messier, Edmonton, NY Rangers
227 – Larry Robinson, Montreal, Los Angeles
225 – Glenn Anderson, Edmonton, Toronto, NY Rangers, St. Louis
221 – Bryan Trottier, NY Islanders, Pittsburgh
214 – Kevin Lowe, Edmonton, NY Rangers

GOALS

MOST GOALS IN PLAYOFFS (CAREER):
122 – Wayne Gretzky, Edmonton, Los Angeles, St. Louis, NY Rangers
109 – Mark Messier, Edmonton, NY Rangers
106 – Jari Kurri, Edmonton, Los Angeles, NY Rangers, Anaheim
93 – Glenn Anderson, Edmonton, Toronto, NY Rangers, St. Louis
85 – Mike Bossy, NY Islanders

MOST GOALS, ONE PLAYOFF YEAR:
19 – Reggie Leach, Philadelphia, 1976. 16 games.
– Jari Kurri, Edmonton, 1985. 18 games.
18 – Joe Sakic, Colorado, 1996. 22 games.
17 – Newsy Lalonde, Montreal, 1919. 10 games.
– Mike Bossy, NY Islanders, 1981. 18 games.
– Steve Payne, Minnesota, 1981. 19 games.
– Mike Bossy, NY Islanders, 1982. 19 games.
– Mike Bossy, NY Islanders, 1983. 19 games
– Wayne Gretzky, Edmonton, 1985. 18 games.
– Kevin Stevens, Pittsburgh, 1991. 24 games.

MOST GOALS IN ONE SERIES (OTHER THAN FINAL):
12 – Jari Kurri, Edmonton, in 1985 CF, 6 games vs. Chicago.
11 – Newsy Lalonde, Montreal, in 1919 NHL F, 5 games vs. Ottawa.
10 – Tim Kerr, Philadelphia, in 1989 DF, 7 games vs. Pittsburgh.
9 – Reggie Leach, Philadelphia, in 1976 SF, 5 games vs. Boston.
– Bill Barber, Philadelphia, in 1980 SF, 5 games vs. Minnesota.
– Mike Bossy, NY Islanders, in 1983 CF, 6 games vs. Boston.
– Mario Lemieux, Pittsburgh, in 1989 DF, 7 games vs. Philadelphia.

MOST GOALS IN FINAL SERIES (NHL ONLY):
9 – Babe Dye, Toronto, in 1922, 5 games vs. Van. Millionaires.
8 – Alf Skinner, Toronto, in 1918, 5 games vs. Van. Millionaires.
7 – Jean Beliveau, Montreal, in 1956, 5 games vs. Detroit.
– Mike Bossy, NY Islanders, in 1982, 4 games vs. Vancouver.
– Wayne Gretzky, Edmonton, in 1985, 5 games vs. Philadelphia.

MOST GOALS, ONE GAME:
5 – Newsy Lalonde, Montreal, March 1, 1919, at Montreal. Final score: Montreal 6, Ottawa 3.
– Maurice Richard, Montreal, March 23, 1944, at Montreal. Final score: Montreal 5, Toronto 1.
– Darryl Sittler, Toronto, April 22, 1976, at Toronto. Final score: Toronto 8, Philadelphia 5.
– Reggie Leach, Philadelphia, May 6, 1976, at Philadelphia. Final score: Philadelphia 6, Boston 3.
– Mario Lemieux, Pittsburgh, April 25, 1989, at Pittsburgh. Final score: Pittsburgh 10, Philadelphia 7.

MOST GOALS, ONE PERIOD:
4 – Tim Kerr, Philadelphia, April 13, 1985, at New York vs. NY Rangers, second period. Final score: Philadelphia 6, NY Rangers 5.
– Mario Lemieux, Pittsburgh, April 25, 1989, at Pittsburgh vs. Philadelphia, first period. Final score: Pittsburgh 10, Philadelphia 7.

ASSISTS

MOST ASSISTS IN PLAYOFFS (CAREER):
260 – Wayne Gretzky, Edmonton, Los Angeles, St. Louis, NY Rangers
186 – Mark Messier, Edmonton, NY Rangers
137 – Paul Coffey, Edmonton, Pittsburgh, Los Angeles, Detroit, Philadelphia, Carolina
127 – Jari Kurri, Edmonton, Los Angeles, NY Rangers, Anaheim
125 – Ray Bourque, Boston

MOST ASSISTS, ONE PLAYOFF YEAR:
31 – Wayne Gretzky, Edmonton, 1988. 19 games.
30 – Wayne Gretzky, Edmonton, 1985. 18 games.
29 – Wayne Gretzky, Edmonton, 1987. 21 games.
28 – Mario Lemieux, Pittsburgh, 1991. 23 games.
26 – Wayne Gretzky, Edmonton, 1983. 16 games.

MOST ASSISTS IN ONE SERIES (OTHER THAN FINAL):
14 – Rick Middleton, Boston, in 1983 DF, 7 games vs. Buffalo.
– Wayne Gretzky, Edmonton, in 1985 CF, 6 games vs. Chicago.
13 – Wayne Gretzky, Edmonton, in 1987 DSF, 5 games vs. Los Angeles.
– Doug Gilmour, Toronto, in 1994 CSF, 7 games vs. San Jose.
11 – Al MacInnis, Calgary, in 1984 DF, 7 games vs. Edmonton.
– Mark Messier, Edmonton, in 1989 DSF, 7 games vs. Los Angeles.
– Mike Ridley, Washington, in 1992 DSF, 7 games vs. Pittsburgh.
– Ron Francis, Pittsburgh, in 1995 CQF, 7 games vs. Washington.
10 – Fleming Mackell, Boston, in 1958 SF, 6 games vs. NY Rangers.
– Stan Mikita, Chicago, in 1962 SF, 6 games vs. Montreal.
– Bob Bourne, NY Islanders, in 1983 DF, 6 games vs. NY Rangers.
– Wayne Gretzky, Edmonton, in 1988 DSF, 5 games vs. Winnipeg.
– Mario Lemieux, Pittsburgh, in 1992 DSF, 6 games vs. Washington.

MOST ASSISTS IN FINAL SERIES:
10 – Wayne Gretzky, Edmonton, in 1988, 4 games plus suspended game vs. Boston.
9 – Jacques Lemaire, Montreal, in 1973, 6 games vs. Chicago.
– Wayne Gretzky, Edmonton, in 1987, 7 games vs. Philadelphia.
– Larry Murphy, Pittsburgh, in 1991, 6 games vs. Minnesota.

MOST ASSISTS, ONE GAME:
6 – Mikko Leinonen, NY Rangers, April 8, 1982, at New York. Final score: NY Rangers 7, Philadelphia 3.
– Wayne Gretzky, Edmonton, April 9, 1987, at Edmonton. Final score: Edmonton 13, Los Angeles 3.
5 – Toe Blake, Montreal, March 23, 1944, at Montreal. Final score: Montreal 5, Toronto 1.
– Maurice Richard, Montreal, March 27, 1956, at Montreal. Final score: Montreal 7, NY Rangers 0.
– Bert Olmstead, Montreal, March 30, 1957, at Montreal. Final score: Montreal 8, NY Rangers 3.

- Don McKenney, Boston, April 5, 1958, at Boston. Final score: Boston 8, NY Rangers 2.
- Stan Mikita, Chicago, April 4, 1973, at Chicago. Final score: Chicago 7, St. Louis 1.
- Wayne Gretzky, Edmonton, April 8, 1981, at Montreal. Final score: Edmonton 6, Montreal 3.
- Paul Coffey, Edmonton, May 14, 1985, at Edmonton. Final score: Edmonton 10, Chicago 5.
- Doug Gilmour, St. Louis, April 15, 1986, at Minnesota. Final score: St. Louis 6, Minnesota 3.
- Risto Siltanen, Quebec, April 14, 1987, at Hartford. Final score: Quebec 7, Hartford 5.
- Patrik Sundstrom, New Jersey, April 22, 1988, at New Jersey. Final score: New Jersey 10, Washington 4.
- Geoff Courtnall, St. Louis Blues, April 23, 1998, at St. Louis. Final score: St. Louis 8, Los Angeles 3.

MOST ASSISTS, ONE PERIOD:

3 – Three assists by one player in one period of a playoff game has been recorded on 71 occasions. Mike Ricci of the San Jose Sharks is the most recent to equal this mark with 3 assists in the third period at Colorado, April 28, 1999. Final score: San Jose 4, Colorado 3.
– Wayne Gretzky has had 3 assists in one period 5 times; Ray Bourque, 3 times; Toe Blake, Jean Beliveau, Doug Harvey and Bobby Orr, twice. Nick Metz of Toronto was the first player to be credited with 3 assists in one period of a playoff game Mar. 21, 1941 at Toronto vs. Boston.

POINTS

MOST POINTS IN PLAYOFFS (CAREER):

382 – Wayne Gretzky, Edmonton, Los Angeles, St. Louis, NY Rangers, 122 goals, 260 assists
295 – Mark Messier, Edmonton, NY Rangers, 109 goals, 186 assists
233 – Jari Kurri, Edmonton, Los Angeles, NY Rangers, Anaheim, 106 goals, 127 assists
214 – Glenn Anderson, Edmonton, Toronto, NY Rangers, St. Louis, 93 goals, 121 assists
196 – Paul Coffey, Edmonton, Pittsburgh, Los Angeles, Detroit, Philadelphia, Carolina, 59 goals, 137 assists

MOST POINTS, ONE PLAYOFF YEAR:

47 – Wayne Gretzky, Edmonton, in 1985. 17 goals, 30 assists in 18 games.
44 – Mario Lemieux, Pittsburgh, in 1991. 16 goals, 28 assists in 23 games.
43 – Wayne Gretzky, Edmonton, in 1988. 12 goals, 31 assists in 19 games.
40 – Wayne Gretzky, Los Angeles, in 1993. 15 goals, 25 assists in 24 games.
38 – Wayne Gretzky, Edmonton, in 1983. 12 goals, 26 assists in 16 games.

MOST POINTS IN ONE SERIES (OTHER THAN FINAL):

19 – Rick Middleton, Boston, in 1983 DF, 7 games vs. Buffalo. 5 goals, 14 assists.
18 – Wayne Gretzky, Edmonton, in 1985 CF, 6 games vs. Chicago. 4 goals, 14 assists.
17 – Mario Lemieux, Pittsburgh, in 1992 DSF, 6 games vs. Washington. 7 goals, 10 assists.
16 – Barry Pederson, Boston, in 1983 DF, 7 games vs. Buffalo. 7 goals, 9 assists.
– Doug Gilmour, Toronto, in 1994 CSF, 7 games vs. San Jose. 3 goals, 13 assists.
15 – Jari Kurri, Edmonton, in 1985 CF, 6 games vs. Chicago. 12 goals, 3 assists.
– Wayne Gretzky, Edmonton, in 1987 DSF, 5 games vs. Los Angeles. 2 goals, 13 assists.
– Tim Kerr, Philadelphia, in 1989 DF, 7 games vs. Pittsburgh. 10 goals, 5 assists.
– Mario Lemieux, Pittsburgh, in 1991 CF, 6 games vs. Boston. 6 goals, 9 assists.

MOST POINTS IN FINAL SERIES:

13 – Wayne Gretzky, Edmonton, in 1988, 4 games plus suspended game vs. Boston. 3 goals, 10 assists.
12 – Gordie Howe, Detroit, in 1955, 7 games vs. Montreal. 5 goals, 7 assists.
– Yvan Cournoyer, Montreal, in 1973, 6 games vs. Chicago. 6 goals, 6 assists.
– Jacques Lemaire, Montreal, in 1973, 6 games vs. Chicago. 3 goals, 9 assists.
– Mario Lemieux, Pittsburgh, in 1991, 5 games vs. Minnesota. 5 goals, 7 assists.

MOST POINTS, ONE GAME:

8 – Patrik Sundstrom, New Jersey, April 22, 1988 at New Jersey during 10-4 win over Washington. Sundstrom had 3 goals, 5 assists.
– Mario Lemieux, Pittsburgh, April 25, 1989 at Pittsburgh during 10-7 win over Philadelphia. Lemieux had 5 goals, 3 assists.
7 – Wayne Gretzky, Edmonton, April 17, 1983 at Calgary during 10-2 win. Gretzky had 4 goals, 3 assists.
– Wayne Gretzky, Edmonton, April 25,1985 at Winnipeg during 8-3 win. Gretzky had 3 goals, 4 assists.
– Wayne Gretzky, Edmonton, April 9, 1987, at Edmonton during 13-3 win over Los Angeles. Gretzky had 1 goal, 6 assists.
6 – Dickie Moore, Montreal, March 25, 1954, at Montreal during 8-1 win over Boston. Moore had 2 goals, 4 assists.
– Phil Esposito, Boston, April 2, 1969, at Boston during 10-0 win over Toronto. Esposito had 4 goals, 2 assists.
– Darryl Sittler, Toronto, April 22, 1976, at Toronto during 8-5 win over Philadelphia. Sittler had 5 goals, 1 assist.
– Guy Lafleur, Montreal, April 11, 1977, at Montreal during 7-2 win over St. Louis. Lafleur had 3 goals, 3 assists.
– Mikko Leinonen, NY Rangers, April 8, 1982, at New York during 7-3 win over Philadelphia. Leinonen had 6 assists.
– Paul Coffey, Edmonton, May 14, 1985 at Edmonton during 10-5 win over Chicago. Coffey had 1 goal, 5 assists.
– John Anderson, Hartford, April 12, 1986 at Hartford during 9-4 win over Quebec. Anderson had 2 goals, 4 assists.
– Mario Lemieux, Pittsburgh, April 23, 1992 at Pittsburgh during 6-4 win over Washington. Lemieux had 3 goals, 3 assists.
– Geoff Courtnall, St. Louis Blues, April 23, 1998 at St. Louis during 8-3 win over Los Angeles. Courtnall had 1 goal, 5 assists.

MOST POINTS, ONE PERIOD:

4 – Maurice Richard, Montreal, March 29, 1945, at Montreal vs. Toronto. Third period, 3 goals, 1 assist. Final score: Montreal 10, Toronto 3.
– Dickie Moore, Montreal, March 25, 1954, at Montreal vs. Boston. First period, 2 goals, 2 assists. Final score: Montreal 8, Boston 1.
– Barry Pederson, Boston, April 8, 1982, at Boston vs. Buffalo. Second period, 3 goals, 1 assist. Final score: Boston 7, Buffalo 3.
– Peter McNab, Boston, April 11, 1982, at Buffalo. Second period, 1 goal, 3 assists. Final score: Boston 5, Buffalo 2.
– Tim Kerr, Philadelphia, April 13, 1985 at New York. Second period, 4 goals. Final score: Philadelphia 6, Rangers 5.
– Ken Linseman, Boston, April 14, 1985 at Boston vs. Montreal. Second period, 2 goals, 2 assists. Final score: Boston 7, Montreal 6.
– Wayne Gretzky, Edmonton, April 12, 1987, at Los Angeles. Third period, 1 goal, 3 assists. Final score: Edmonton 6, Los Angeles 3.
– Glenn Anderson, Edmonton, April 6, 1988, at Edmonton vs. Winnipeg. Third period, 3 goals, 1 assist. Final score: Edmonton 7, Winnipeg 4.
– Mario Lemieux, Pittsburgh, April 25, 1989, at Pittsburgh vs. Philadelphia. First period, 4 goals. Final score: Pittsburgh 10, Philadelphia 7.
– Dave Gagner, Minnesota, April 8, 1991, at Minnesota vs. Chicago. First period, 2 goals, 2 assists. Final score: Chicago 6, Minnesota 5.
– Mario Lemieux, Pittsburgh, April 23, 1992, at Pittsburgh vs. Washington. Second period, 2 goals, 2 assists. Final score: Pittsburgh 6, Washington 4.

POWER-PLAY GOALS

MOST POWER-PLAY GOALS IN PLAYOFFS (CAREER):

35 – Mike Bossy, NY Islanders
34 – Dino Ciccarelli, Minnesota, Washington, Detroit
– Wayne Gretzky, Edmonton, Los Angeles, St. Louis, NY Rangers
28 – Mario Lemieux, Pittsburgh
27 – Denis Potvin, NY Islanders

MOST POWER-PLAY GOALS, ONE PLAYOFF YEAR:

9 – Mike Bossy, NY Islanders, 1981. 18 games against Toronto, Edmonton, NY Rangers and Minnesota.
– Cam Neely, Boston, 1991. 19 games against Hartford, Montreal and Pittsburgh.
8 – Tim Kerr, Philadelphia, 1989. 19 games.
– John Druce, Washington, 1990. 15 games.
– Brian Propp, Minnesota, 1991. 23 games.
– Mario Lemieux, Pittsburgh, 1992. 15 games.

MOST POWER-PLAY GOALS, ONE PLAYOFF SERIES:

6 – Chris Kontos, Los Angeles, 1989, DSF vs. Edmonton, won by Los Angeles 4-3.
5 – Andy Bathgate, Detroit, 1966, SF vs. Chicago, won by Detroit 4-2.
– Denis Potvin, NY Islanders, 1981, QF vs. Edmonton, won by NY Islanders 4-2.
– Ken Houston, Calgary, 1981, QF vs. Philadelphia, won by Calgary 4-3.
– Rick Vaive, Chicago, 1988, DSF vs. St. Louis, won by St. Louis 4-1.
– Tim Kerr, Philadelphia, 1989, DF vs. Pittsburgh, won by Philadelphia 4-3.
– Mario Lemieux, Pittsburgh, 1989, DF vs. Philadelphia won by Philadelphia 4-3.
– John Druce, Washington, 1990, DF vs. NY Rangers won by Washington 4-1.
– Pat LaFontaine, Buffalo, 1992, DSF vs. Boston won by Boston 4-3.
– Adam Graves, NY Rangers, 1996, CQF vs Montreal, won by NY Rangers 4-2.

MOST POWER-PLAY GOALS, ONE GAME:

3 – Syd Howe, Detroit, March 23, 1939, at Detroit vs. Montreal. Detroit won 7-3.
– Sid Smith, Toronto, April 10, 1949, at Detroit. Toronto won 3-1.
– Phil Esposito, Boston, April 2, 1969, at Boston vs. Toronto. Boston won 10-0.
– John Bucyk, Boston, April 21, 1974, at Boston vs. Chicago. Boston won 8-6.
– Denis Potvin, NY Islanders, April 17, 1981, at New York vs. Edmonton. NY Islanders won 6-3.
– Tim Kerr, Philadelphia, April 13, 1985, at NY Rangers. Philadelphia won 6-5.
– Jari Kurri, Edmonton, April 9, 1987, at Edmonton vs. Los Angeles. Edmonton won 13-3.
– Mark Johnson, New Jersey, April 22, 1988, at New Jersey vs. Washington. New Jersey won 10-4.
– Dino Ciccarelli, Detroit, April 29, 1993, at Toronto. Detroit won 7-3.
– Dino Ciccarelli, Detroit, May 11, 1995, at Dallas. Detroit won 5-1.
– Valeri Kamensky, Colorado, April 24, 1997, at Colorado vs. Chicago. Colorado won 7-0.

MOST POWER-PLAY GOALS, ONE PERIOD:

3 – Tim Kerr, Philadelphia, April 13, 1985 at New York, second period in 6-5 win vs. NY Rangers.
2 – Two power-play goals have been scored by one player in one period on 53 occasions. Charlie Conacher of Toronto was the first to score two power-play goals in one period, setting the mark on March 26, 1936. Brendan Shanahan of the Detroit Red Wings is the most recent to equal this mark with two power-play goals in the first period at Phoenix, May 3, 1998. Final score: Detroit 5, Phoenix 2.

SHORTHAND GOALS

MOST SHORTHAND GOALS IN PLAYOFFS (CAREER):

14 – Mark Messier, Edmonton, NY Rangers
11 – Wayne Gretzky, Edmonton, Los Angeles, St. Louis
10 – Jari Kurri, Edmonton, Los Angeles, NY Rangers
8 – Ed Westfall, Boston, NY Islanders
– Hakan Loob, Calgary

MOST SHORTHAND GOALS, ONE PLAYOFF YEAR:

3 – Derek Sanderson, Boston, 1969. 1 against Toronto in QF, won by Boston 4-0; 2 against Montreal in SF, won by Montreal, 4-2.

- **Bill Barber,** Philadelphia, 1980. All against Minnesota in SF, won by Philadelphia 4-1.
- **Lorne Henning,** NY Islanders, 1980. 1 against Boston in QF, won by NY Islanders 4-1; 1 against Buffalo in SF, won by NY Islanders 4-2, 1 against Philadelphia in F, won by NY Islanders 4-2.
- **Wayne Gretzky,** Edmonton, 1983. 2 against Winnipeg in DSF, won by Edmonton 3-0; 1 against Calgary in DF, won by Edmonton 4-1.
- **Wayne Presley,** Chicago, 1989. All against Detroit in DSF, won by Chicago 4-2.
- **Todd Marchant,** Edmonton, 1997. 1 against Dallas in CQF, won by Edmonton 4-3; 2 against Colorado in CSF, won by Colorado 4-1.

MOST SHORTHAND GOALS, ONE PLAYOFF SERIES:

3 – Bill Barber, Philadelphia, 1980, SF vs. Minnesota, won by Philadelphia 4-1.
- **Wayne Presley,** Chicago, 1989, DSF vs. Detroit, won by Chicago 4-2.

2 – Mac Colville, NY Rangers, 1940, SF vs. Boston, won by NY Rangers 4-2.
- Jerry Toppazzini, Boston, 1958, SF vs. NY Rangers, won by Boston 4-2.
- Dave Keon, Toronto, 1963, F vs. Detroit, won by Toronto 4-1.
- Bob Pulford, Toronto, 1964, F vs. Detroit, won by Toronto 4-3.
- Serge Savard, Montreal, 1968, F vs. St. Louis, won by Montreal 4-0.
- Derek Sanderson, Boston, 1969, SF vs. Montreal, won by Montreal 4-2.
- Bryan Trottier, NY Islanders, 1980, PR vs. Los Angeles, won by NY Islanders 3-1.
- Bobby Lalonde, Boston, 1981, PR vs. Minnesota, won by Minnesota 3-0.
- Butch Goring, NY Islanders, 1981, SF vs. NY Rangers, won by NY Islanders 4-0.
- Wayne Gretzky, Edmonton, 1983, DSF vs. Winnipeg, won by Edmonton 3-0.
- Mark Messier, Edmonton, 1983, DF vs. Calgary, won by Edmonton 4-1.
- Jari Kurri, Edmonton, 1983, CF vs. Chicago, won by Edmonton 4-0.
- Wayne Gretzky, Edmonton, 1985, DF vs. Winnipeg, won by Edmonton 4-0.
- Kevin Lowe, Edmonton, 1987, F vs. Philadelphia, won by Edmonton 4-3.
- Bob Gould, Washington, 1988, DSF vs. Philadelphia, won by Washington 4-3.
- Dave Poulin, Philadelphia, 1989, DF vs. Pittsburgh, won by Philadelphia 4-3.
- Russ Courtnall, Montreal, 1991, DF vs. Boston, won by Boston 4-3.
- Sergei Fedorov, Detroit, 1992, DSF vs. Minnesota, won by Detroit 4-3.
- Mark Messier, NY Rangers, 1992, DSF vs. New Jersey, won by NY Rangers 4-3.
- Tom Fitzgerald, NY Islanders, 1993, DF vs. Pittsburgh, won by NY Islanders 4-3.
- Mark Osborne, Toronto, 1994, CSF vs. San Jose, won by Toronto 4-3.
- Tony Amonte, Chicago, 1997, CQF vs. Colorado, won by Colorado 4-2.
- Brian Rolston, New Jersey, 1997, CQF vs. Montreal, won by New Jersey 4-1.
- Rod Brind'Amour, Philadelphia, 1997, CQF vs. Pittsburgh, won by Philadelphia 4-1.
- Todd Marchant, Edmonton, 1997, CSF vs. Colorado, won by Colorado 4-1.
- Jeremy Roenick, Phoenix, 1998, CQF vs. Detroit, won by Detroit 4-2.
- Vincent Damphousse, San Jose, 1999, CQF vs. Colorado, won by Colorado 4-2.
- Dixon Ward, Buffalo, 1999, CF vs. Toronto, won by Buffalo 4-1.

MOST SHORTHAND GOALS, ONE GAME:

2 – Dave Keon, Toronto, April 18, 1963, at Toronto, in 3-1 win vs. Detroit.
- **Bryan Trottier,** NY Islanders, April 8, 1980 at New York, in 8-1 win vs. Los Angeles.
- **Bobby Lalonde,** Boston, April 11, 1981 at Minnesota, in 6-3 win by Minnesota.
- **Wayne Gretzky,** Edmonton, April 6, 1983 at Edmonton, in 6-3 win vs. Winnipeg.
- **Jari Kurri,** Edmonton, April 24, 1983, at Edmonton, in 8-3 win vs. Chicago.
- **Mark Messier,** NY Rangers, April 21, 1992, at New York, in 7-3 loss vs. New Jersey.
- **Tom Fitzgerald,** NY Islanders, May 8, 1993, at New York, in 6-5 win vs. Pittsburgh.
- **Rod Brind'Amour,** Philadelphia, April 26, 1997, at Philadelphia, in 6-3 win vs. Pittsburgh.
- **Jeremy Roenick,** Phoenix, April 24, 1998, at Detroit, in 7-4 win by Phoenix.
- **Vincent Damphousse,** San Jose, April 30, 1999, at Colorado, in 7-3 win by San Jose.

MOST SHORTHAND GOALS, ONE PERIOD:

2 – Bryan Trottier, NY Islanders, April 8, 1980, second period at New York in 8-1 win vs. Los Angeles.
- **Bobby Lalonde,** Boston, April 11, 1981, third period at Minnesota, in 6-3 win by Minnesota.
- **Jari Kurri,** Edmonton, April 24, 1983, third period at Edmonton, in 8-4 win vs. Chicago.
- **Rod Brind'Amour,** Philadelphia, April 26, 1997, first period at Philadelphia, in 6-3 win vs. Pittsburgh.
- **Jeremy Roenick,** Phoenix, April 24, 1998, second period at Detroit, in 7-4 win by Phoenix.
- **Vincent Damphousse,** San Jose, April 30, 1999, third period at Colorado, in 7-3 win by San Jose.

GAME-WINNING GOALS

MOST GAME-WINNING GOALS IN PLAYOFFS (CAREER):

24 – Wayne Gretzky, Edmonton, Los Angeles, St. Louis, NY Rangers
19 – Claude Lemieux, Montreal, New Jersey, Colorado
18 – Maurice Richard, Montreal
17 – Mike Bossy, NY Islanders
- Glenn Anderson, Edmonton, Toronto, NY Rangers, St. Louis

MOST GAME-WINNING GOALS, ONE PLAYOFF YEAR:

6 – Joe Sakic, Colorado, 1996. 22 games.
- **Joe Nieuwendyk,** Dallas, 1999. 23 games.

5 – Mike Bossy, NY Islanders, 1983. 19 games.
- Jari Kurri, Edmonton, 1987. 21 games.
- Bobby Smith, Minnesota, 1991. 23 games.
- Mario Lemieux, Pittsburgh, 1992. 15 games.

MOST GAME-WINNING GOALS, ONE PLAYOFF SERIES:

4 – Mike Bossy, NY Islanders, 1983, CF vs. Boston, won by NY Islanders 4-2.

OVERTIME GOALS

MOST OVERTIME GOALS IN PLAYOFFS (CAREER):

6 – Maurice Richard, Montreal (1 in 1946; 3 in 1951; 1 in 1957; 1 in 1958.)
5 – Glenn Anderson, Edmonton, Toronto, NY Rangers, St. Louis
4 – Bob Nystrom, NY Islanders
- Dale Hunter, Quebec, Washington
- Wayne Gretzky, Edmonton, Los Angeles
- Stephane Richer, Montreal, New Jersey
- Joe Murphy, Edmonton, Chicago
- Esa Tikkanen, Edmonton, NY Rangers

3 – Mel Hill, Boston
- Rene Robert, Buffalo
- Danny Gare, Buffalo
- Jacques Lemaire, Montreal
- Bobby Clarke, Philadelphia
- Terry O'Reilly, Boston
- Mike Bossy, NY Islanders
- Steve Payne, Minnesota
- Ken Morrow, NY Islanders
- Lanny McDonald, Toronto, Calgary
- Peter Stastny, Quebec
- Dino Ciccarelli, Minnesota, Washington
- Russ Courtnall, Montreal
- Kirk Muller, Montreal
- Doug Gilmour, St. Louis, Calgary, Toronto
- Greg Adams, Vancouver
- Claude Lemieux, Montreal, Colorado
- Mike Gartner, Washington, Toronto
- Jeremy Roenick, Chicago, Phoenix

MOST OVERTIME GOALS, ONE PLAYOFF YEAR:

3 – Mel Hill, Boston, 1939. All against NY Rangers in best-of-seven SF, won by Boston 4-3.
- **Maurice Richard,** Montreal, 1951. 2 against Detroit in best-of-seven SF, won by Montreal 4-2; 1 against Toronto best-of-seven F, won by Toronto 4-1.

MOST OVERTIME GOALS, ONE PLAYOFF SERIES:

3 – Mel Hill, Boston, 1939, SF vs. NY Rangers, won by Boston 4-3. Hill scored at 59:25 of overtime March 21 for a 2-1 win; at 8:24, March 23 for a 3-2 win; and at 48:00, April 2 for a 2-1 win.

SCORING BY A DEFENSEMAN

MOST GOALS BY A DEFENSEMAN, ONE PLAYOFF YEAR:

12 – Paul Coffey, Edmonton, 1985. 18 games.
11 – Brian Leetch, NY Rangers, 1994. 23 games.
9 – Bobby Orr, Boston, 1970. 14 games.
- Brad Park, Boston, 1978. 15 games.

8 – Denis Potvin, NY Islanders, 1981. 18 games.
- Ray Bourque, Boston, 1983. 17 games.
- Denis Potvin, NY Islanders, 1983. 20 games.
- Paul Coffey, Edmonton, 1984. 19 games.

MOST GOALS BY A DEFENSEMAN, ONE GAME:

3 – Bobby Orr, Boston, April 11, 1971 at Montreal. Final score: Boston 5, Montreal 2.
- **Dick Redmond,** Chicago, April 4, 1973 at Chicago. Final score: Chicago 7, St. Louis 1.
- **Denis Potvin,** NY Islanders, April 17, 1981 at New York. Final score: NY Islanders 6, Edmonton 3.
- **Paul Reinhart,** Calgary, April 14, 1983 at Edmonton. Final score: Edmonton 6, Calgary 3.
- **Doug Halward,** Vancouver, April 7, 1984 at Vancouver. Final score: Vancouver 7, Calgary 0.
- **Paul Reinhart,** Calgary, April 8, 1984 at Vancouver. Final score: Calgary 5, Vancouver 1.
- **Al Iafrate,** Washington, April 26, 1993 at Washington. Final score: Washington 6, NY Islanders 4.
- **Eric Desjardins,** Montreal, June 3, 1993 at Montreal. Final score: Montreal 3, Los Angeles 2.
- **Gary Suter,** Chicago, April 24, 1994, at Chicago. Final score: Chicago 4, Toronto 3.
- **Brian Leetch,** NY Rangers, May 22, 1995 at Philadelphia. Final score: Philadelphia 4, NY Rangers 3.

MOST ASSISTS BY A DEFENSEMAN, ONE PLAYOFF YEAR:

25 – Paul Coffey, Edmonton, 1985. 18 games.
24 – Al MacInnis, Calgary, 1989. 22 games.
23 – Brian Leetch, NY Rangers, 1994. 23 games.
19 – Bobby Orr, Boston, 1972. 15 games.
18 – Ray Bourque, Boston, 1988. 23 games.
- Ray Bourque, Boston, 1991. 19 games.
- Larry Murphy, Pittsburgh, 1991. 23 games.

MOST ASSISTS BY A DEFENSEMAN, ONE GAME:

5 – Paul Coffey, Edmonton, May 14, 1985 at Edmonton vs. Chicago. Edmonton won 10-5.
- **Risto Siltanen,** Quebec, April 14, 1987 at Hartford. Quebec won 7-5.

MOST POINTS BY A DEFENSEMAN, ONE PLAYOFF YEAR:

37 – Paul Coffey, Edmonton, in 1985. 12 goals, 25 assists in 18 games.
34 – Brian Leetch, NY Rangers, in 1994. 11 goals, 23 assists in 23 games.
31 – Al MacInnis, Calgary, in 1989. 7 goals, 24 assists in 22 games.
25 – Denis Potvin, NY Islanders, in 1981. 8 goals, 17 assists in 18 games.
- Ray Bourque, Boston, in 1991. 7 goals, 18 assists in 19 games.

MOST POINTS BY A DEFENSEMAN, ONE GAME:

6 – Paul Coffey, Edmonton, May 14, 1985 at Edmonton vs. Chicago. 1 goal, 5 assists. Edmonton won 10-5.
5 – Eddie Bush, Detroit, April 9, 1942, at Detroit vs. Toronto. 1 goal, 4 assists. Detroit won 5-2.
- Bob Dailey, Philadelphia, May 1, 1980, at Philadelphia vs. Minnesota. 1 goal, 4 assists. Philadelphia won 7-0.
- Denis Potvin, NY Islanders, April 17, 1981, at New York vs. Edmonton. 3 goals, 2 assists. NY Islanders won 6-3.
- Risto Siltanen, Quebec, April 14, 1987, at Hartford. 5 assists. Quebec won 7-5.

SCORING BY A ROOKIE

MOST GOALS BY A ROOKIE, ONE PLAYOFF YEAR:

14 – Dino Ciccarelli, Minnesota, 1981. 19 games.
11 – Jeremy Roenick, Chicago, 1990. 20 games.
10 – Claude Lemieux, Montreal, 1986. 20 games.
9 – Pat Flatley, NY Islanders, 1984. 21 games
8 – Steve Christoff, Minnesota, 1980. 14 games.
– Brad Palmer, Minnesota, 1981. 19 games.
– Mike Krushelnyski, Boston, 1983. 17 games.
– Bob Joyce, Boston, 1988. 23 games.

MOST POINTS BY A ROOKIE, ONE PLAYOFF YEAR:

21 – Dino Ciccarelli, Minnesota, in 1981. 14 goals, 7 assists in 19 games.
20 – Don Maloney, NY Rangers, in 1979. 7 goals, 13 assists in 18 games.

THREE-OR-MORE-GOAL GAMES

MOST THREE-OR-MORE-GOAL GAMES IN PLAYOFFS (CAREER):

10 – Wayne Gretzky, Edmonton, Los Angeles, St. Louis, NY Rangers. 8 three-goal games; 2 four-goal games.
7 – Maurice Richard, Montreal. 4 three-goal games; 2 four-goal games; 1 five-goal game.
– Jari Kurri, Edmonton, Los Angeles, NY Rangers. 6 three-goal games; 1 four-goal game.
6 – Dino Ciccarelli, Minnesota, Washington, Detroit. 5 three-goal games; 1 four-goal game.
5 – Mike Bossy, NY Islanders. 4 three-goal games; 1 four-goal game.

MOST THREE-OR-MORE-GOAL GAMES, ONE PLAYOFF YEAR:

4 – Jari Kurri, Edmonton, 1985. 1 four-goal game, 3 three-goal games.
3 – Mark Messier, Edmonton, 1983. 3 three-goal games.
– Mike Bossy, NY Islanders, 1983. 1 four-goal game, 2 three-goal games
2 – Newsy Lalonde, Montreal, 1919. 1 five-goal game, 1 four-goal game.
– Maurice Richard, Montreal, 1944. 1 five-goal game; 1 three-goal game.
– Doug Bentley, Chicago, 1944. 2 three-goal games.
– Norm Ullman, Detroit, 1964. 2 three-goal games.
– Phil Esposito, Boston, 1970. 2 three-goal games.
– Pit Martin, Chicago, 1973. 2 three-goal games.
– Rick MacLeish, Philadelphia, 1975. 2 three-goal games.
– Lanny McDonald, Toronto, 1977. 1 three-goal game; 1 four-goal game.
– Wayne Gretzky, Edmonton, 1981. 2 three-goal games.
– Wayne Gretzky, Edmonton, 1983. 2 four-goal games.
– Wayne Gretzky, Edmonton, 1985. 2 three-goal games.
– Petr Klima, Detroit, 1988. 2 three-goal games.
– Cam Neely, Boston, 1991. 2 three-goal games.
– Wayne Gretzky, NY Rangers, 1997. 2 three-goal games.
– Daniel Alfredsson, Ottawa, 1998. 2 three-goal games.

MOST THREE-OR-MORE-GOAL GAMES, ONE PLAYOFF SERIES:

3 – Jari Kurri, Edmonton 1985, CF vs. Chicago won by Edmonton 4-2. Kurri scored 3 goals May 7 at Edmonton in 7-3 win, 3 goals May 14 at Edmonton in 10-5 win and 4 goals May 16 at Chicago in 8-2 win.
2 – Doug Bentley, Chicago, 1944, SF vs. Detroit, won by Chicago 4-1. Bentley scored 3 goals Mar. 28 at Chicago in 7-1 win and 3 goals Mar. 30 at Detroit in 5-2 win.
– Norm Ullman, Detroit, 1964, SF vs. Chicago, won by Detroit 4-3. Ullman scored 3 goals Mar. 29 at Chicago in 7-1 win and 3 goals April 7 at Detroit in 7-2 win.
– Mark Messier, Edmonton, 1983, DF vs. Calgary won by Edmonton 4-1. Messier scored 4 goals April 14 at Edmonton in 6-3 win and 3 goals April 17 at Calgary in 10-2 win.
– Mike Bossy, NY Islanders, 1983, CF vs. Boston won by NY Islanders 4-2. Bossy scored 3 goals May 3 at New York in 8-3 win and 4 goals May 7 at New York in 8-4 win.

SCORING STREAKS

LONGEST CONSECUTIVE GOAL-SCORING STREAK, ONE PLAYOFF YEAR:

10 Games – Reggie Leach, Philadelphia, 1976. Streak started April 17 at Toronto and ended May 9 at Montreal. He scored one goal in each of eight games; two in one game; and five in another; a total of 15 goals.

LONGEST CONSECUTIVE POINT-SCORING STREAK, ONE PLAYOFF YEAR:

18 games – Bryan Trottier, NY Islanders, 1981. 11 goals, 18 assists, 29 points.
17 games – Wayne Gretzky, Edmonton, 1988. 12 goals, 29 assists, 41 points.
– Al MacInnis, Calgary, 1989. 7 goals, 19 assists, 26 points.

LONGEST CONSECUTIVE POINT-SCORING STREAK, MORE THAN ONE PLAYOFF YEAR:

27 games – Bryan Trottier, NY Islanders, 1980, 1981 and 1982. 7 games in 1980 (3 goals, 5 assists, 8 points), 18 games in 1981 (11 goals, 18 assists, 29 points), and two games in 1982 (2 goals, 3 assists, 5 points). Total points, 42.
19 games – Wayne Gretzky, Edmonton, Los Angeles, 1988 and 1989. 17 games in 1988 (12 goals, 29 assists, 41 points with Edmonton), 2 games in 1989 (1 goal, 2 assists, 3 points with Los Angeles). Total points, 44.

FASTEST GOALS

FASTEST GOAL FROM START OF GAME:

0:06 – Don Kozak, Los Angeles, April 17, 1977, at Los Angeles vs. Boston and goaltender Gerry Cheevers. Los Angeles won 7-4.
0:07 – Bob Gainey, Montreal, May 5, 1977, at New York vs. NY Islanders and goaltender Glenn Resch. Montreal won 2-1.
– Terry Murray, Philadelphia, April 12, 1981, at Quebec vs. goaltender Dan Bouchard. Quebec won 4-3 in overtime.
0:08 – Stan Smyl, Vancouver, April 7, 1982, at Vancouver vs. Calgary and goaltender Pat Riggin. Vancouver won 5-3.

FASTEST GOAL FROM START OF PERIOD (OTHER THAN FIRST):

0:06 – Pelle Eklund, Philadelphia, April 25, 1989, at Pittsburgh vs. goaltender Tom Barrasso, second period. Pittsburgh won 10-7.
0:09 – Bill Collins, Minnesota, April 9, 1968, at Minnesota vs. Los Angeles and goaltender Wayne Rutledge, third period. Minnesota won 7-5.
– Dave Balon, Minnesota, April 25, 1968, at St. Louis vs. goaltender Glenn Hall, third period. Minnesota won 5-1.
– Murray Oliver, Minnesota, April 8, 1971, at St. Louis vs. goaltender Ernie Wakely, third period. St. Louis won 4-2.
– Clark Gillies, NY Islanders, April 15, 1977, at Buffalo vs. goaltender Don Edwards, third period. NY Islanders won 4-3.
– Eric Vail, Atlanta, April 11, 1978, at Atlanta vs. Detroit and goaltender Ron Low, third period. Detroit won 5-3.
– Stan Smyl, Vancouver, April 10, 1979, at Philadelphia vs. goaltender Wayne Stephenson, third period. Vancouver won 3-2.
– Wayne Gretzky, Edmonton, April 6, 1983, at Edmonton vs. Winnipeg and goaltender Brian Hayward, second period. Edmonton won 6-3.
– Mark Messier, Edmonton, April 16, 1984, at Calgary vs. goaltender Don Edwards, third period. Edmonton won 5-3.
– Brian Skrudland, Montreal, May 18, 1986 at Calgary vs. goaltender Mike Vernon, overtime. Montreal won 3-2.

FASTEST TWO GOALS:

0:05 – Norm Ullman, Detroit, at Detroit, April 11, 1965, vs. Chicago and goaltender Glenn Hall. Ullman scored at 17:35 and 17:40 of second period. Detroit won 4-2.

FASTEST TWO GOALS FROM START OF A GAME:

1:08 – Dick Duff, Toronto, April 9, 1963 at Toronto vs. Detroit and goaltender Terry Sawchuk. Duff scored at 49 seconds and 1:08. Final score: Toronto 4, Detroit 2.

FASTEST TWO GOALS FROM START OF A PERIOD:

0:35 – Pat LaFontaine, NY Islanders, May 19, 1984 at Edmonton vs. goaltender Andy Moog. LaFontaine scored at 13 and 35 seconds of third period. Final score: Edmonton 5, NY Islanders 2.

PENALTIES

MOST PENALTY MINUTES IN PLAYOFFS (CAREER):

729 – Dale Hunter, Quebec, Washington, Colorado
541 – Chris Nilan, Montreal, NY Rangers, Boston
489 – Claude Lemieux, Montreal, New Jersey, Colorado
466 – Willi Plett, Atlanta, Calgary, Minnesota, Boston
455 – Dave Williams, Toronto, Vancouver, Los Angeles

MOST PENALTIES, ONE GAME:

8 – Forbes Kennedy, Toronto, April 2, 1969, at Boston. Four minors, 2 majors, 1 10-minute misconduct, 1 game misconduct. Final score: Boston 10, Toronto 0.
– Kim Clackson, Pittsburgh, April 14, 1980, at Boston. Five minors, 2 majors, 1 10-minute misconduct. Final score: Boston 6, Pittsburgh 2

MOST PENALTY MINUTES, ONE GAME:

42 – Dave Schultz, Philadelphia, April 22, 1976, at Toronto. One minor, 2 majors, 1 10-minute misconduct and 2 game-misconducts. Final score: Toronto 8, Philadelphia 5.

MOST PENALTIES, ONE PERIOD AND MOST PENALTY MINUTES, ONE PERIOD:

6 Penalties; 39 Minutes – Ed Hospodar, NY Rangers, April 9, 1981, at Los Angeles, first period. Two minors, 1 major, 1 10-minute misconduct, 2 game misconducts. Final score: Los Angeles 5, NY Rangers 4.

GOALTENDING

MOST PLAYOFF GAMES APPEARED IN BY A GOALTENDER (CAREER):

179 – Patrick Roy, Montreal, Colorado
150 – Grant Fuhr, Edmonton, Toronto, Buffalo, Los Angeles, St. Louis
134 – Mike Vernon, Calgary, Detroit, San Jose
132 – Bill Smith, Los Angeles, NY Islanders
– Andy Moog, Edmonton, Boston, Dallas, Montreal

MOST MINUTES PLAYED BY A GOALTENDER (CAREER):

11,055 – Patrick Roy, Montreal, Colorado
8,834 – Grant Fuhr, Edmonton, Toronto, Buffalo, Los Angeles, St. Louis
7,977 – Mike Vernon, Calgary, Detroit, San Jose
7,645 – Bill Smith, Los Angeles, NY Islanders
7,452 – Andy Moog, Edmonton, Boston, Dallas, Montreal

MOST MINUTES PLAYED BY A GOALTENDER, ONE PLAYOFF YEAR:

1,544 – Kirk McLean, Vancouver, 1994. 24 games.
– Ed Belfour, Dallas, 1999. 23 games.
1,540 – Ron Hextall, Philadelphia, 1987. 26 games.
1,477 – Mike Richter, NY Rangers, 1994. 23 games.
1,454 – Pfatrick Roy, Colorado, 1996. 22 games.

MOST SHUTOUTS IN PLAYOFFS (CAREER):

15 – Clint Benedict, Ottawa, Mtl. Maroons
14 – Jacques Plante, Montreal, St. Louis
13 – Turk Broda, Toronto
12 – Terry Sawchuk, Detroit, Los Angeles
– Patrick Roy, Montreal, Colorado

MOST SHUTOUTS, ONE PLAYOFF YEAR:

4 – Clint Benedict, Mtl. Maroons, 1926. 8 games.
– Clint Benedict, Mtl. Maroons, 1928. 9 games.
– Dave Kerr, NY Rangers, 1937. 9 games.
– Frank McCool, Toronto, 1945. 13 games.
– Terry Sawchuk, Detroit, 1952. 8 games.
– Bernie Parent, Philadelphia, 1975. 17 games.
– Ken Dryden, Montreal, 1977. 14 games.

- **Mike Richter**, NY Rangers, 1994. 23 games.
- **Kirk McLean,** Vancouver, 1994. 24 games.
- **Olaf Kolzig,** Washington, 1998. 21 games.

MOST SHUTOUTS, ONE PLAYOFF SERIES:

3 – Dave Kerr, NY Rangers, in 1940 SF, 6 games vs. Boston.
- **Frank McCool,** Toronto, in 1945 F, 7 games vs. Detroit.
- **Turk Broda,** Toronto, in 1950 SF, 7 games vs. Detroit.
- **Felix Potvin,** Toronto, in 1994 CQF, 6 games vs. Chicago.
- **Martin Brodeur,** New Jersey, in 1995 CQF, 5 games vs. Boston.

MOST WINS BY A GOALTENDER, (CAREER):

110 – Patrick Roy, Montreal, Colorado
92 – Grant Fuhr, Edmonton, Buffalo, St. Louis
88 – Bill Smith, Los Angeles, NY Islanders
80 – Ken Dryden, Montreal

MOST WINS BY A GOALTENDER, ONE PLAYOFF YEAR:

16 – Grant Fuhr, Edmonton, 1988. 19 games.
- **Mike Vernon,** Calgary, 1989. 22 games.
- **Bill Ranford,** Edmonton, 1990. 22 games
- **Tom Barrasso,** Pittsburgh, 1992. 21 games.
- **Patrick Roy,** Montreal, 1993. 20 games.
- **Mike Richter,** NY Rangers, 1994. 23 games.
- **Martin Brodeur,** New Jersey, 1995. 20 games.
- **Patrick Roy,** Colorado, 1996. 22 games.
- **Mike Vernon,** Detroit, 1997. 20 games.
- **Chris Osgood,** Detroit, 1998. 22 games.
- **Ed Belfour,** Dallas, 1999. 23 games.

MOST CONSECUTIVE WINS BY A GOALTENDER, MORE THAN ONE PLAYOFF YEAR:

14 – Tom Barrasso, Pittsburgh, 1992, 1993; 3 wins against NY Rangers in 1992 DF, won by Pittsburgh 4-2; 4 wins against Boston in 1992 CF, won by Pittsburgh 4-0; 4 wins against Chicago in 1992 F, won by Pittsburgh 4-0; 3 wins against New Jersey in 1993 DSF, won by Pittsburgh 4-1.

MOST CONSECUTIVE WINS BY A GOALTENDER, ONE PLAYOFF YEAR:

11 – Ed Belfour, Chicago, 1992. 3 wins against St. Louis in DSF, won by Chicago 4-2; 4 wins against Detroit in DF, won by Chicago 4-0; and 4 wins against Edmonton in CF, won by Chicago 4-0.
- **Tom Barrasso,** Pittsburgh, 1992. 3 wins against NY Rangers in DF, won by Pittsburgh 4-2; 4 wins against Boston in CF, won by Pittsburgh 4-0; and 4 wins against Chicago in F, won by Pittsburgh 4-0.
- **Patrick Roy,** Montreal, 1993. 4 wins against Quebec in DSF, won by Montreal 4-2; 4 wins against Buffalo in DF, won by Montreal 4-0; and 3 wins against NY Islanders in CF, won by Montreal 4-1.

LONGEST SHUTOUT SEQUENCE:

248:32– Norman Smith, Detroit, 1936. In best-of-five SF, Smith shut out Mtl. Maroons 1-0, March 24, in 116:30 overtime; shut out Maroons 3-0 in second game, March 26; and was scored against at 12:02 of first period, March 29, by Gus Marker. Detroit won SF 3-0.

MOST CONSECUTIVE SHUTOUTS:

3 – Clint Benedict, Mtl. Maroons, 1926. Benedict shut out Ottawa 1-0, Mar. 27; he then shut out Victoria twice, 3-0, Mar. 30; 3-0, Apr. 1. Mtl. Maroons won NHL F vs. Ottawa 2 goals to 1 and won the best-of-five F vs. Victoria 3-1.
- **John Ross Roach,** NY Rangers, 1929. Roach shut out NY Americans twice, 0-0, Mar. 19; 1-0, Mar. 21; he then shut out Toronto 1-0, Mar. 24. NY Rangers won QF vs. NY Americans 1 goal to 0 and won the best-of-three SF vs. Toronto 2-0.
- **Frank McCool,** Toronto, 1945. McCool shut out Detroit 1-0, April 6; 2-0, April 8; 1-0, April 12. Toronto won the best-of-seven F 4-3.

Playoff Coaching

Minimum 65 Games Coached

Coach	Team	Games Coached	W	L	T	Winning Percentage	Playoff Years	Cups	Career
Scotty Bowman	St.L.	52	26	26	0	.500	4		
	Mtl	98	70	28	0	.714	8	5	
	Buf	36	18	18	0	.500	5		
	Pit	33	23	10	0	.697	2	1	
	Det	96	63	33	0	.656	6	2	
	Total	**315**	**200**	**115**	**0**	**.635**	**25**	**8**	**1967-99**
Al Arbour	St.L.	11	4	7	0	.364	1		
	NYI	198	119	79	0	.601	15	4	
	Total	**209**	**123**	**86**	**0**	**.589**	**16**	**4**	**1970-94**
Dick Irvin	Chi	9	5	3	1	.611	1		
	Tor	66	33	32	1	.508	9	1	
	Mtl	115	62	53	0	.539	14	3	
	Total	**190**	**100**	**88**	**2**	**.532**	**24**	**4**	**1930-56**
Mike Keenan	Phi	57	32	25	0	.561	4		
	Chi	60	33	27	0	.550	4		
	NYR	23	16	7	0	.696	1	1	
	St.L.	20	10	10	0	.500	2		
	Total	**160**	**91**	**69**	**0**	**.569**	**11**	**1**	**1984-98**
Glen Sather	**Edm**	**127**	**89**	**37**	**1**	**.705**	**10**	**4**	**1979-94**
Pat Quinn	Phi	39	22	17	0	.564	3		
	L.A.	3	0	3	0	.000	1		
	Van	61	31	30	0	.508	5		
	Tor	17	9	8	0	.529	1		
	Total	**120**	**62**	**58**	**0**	**.517**	**10**		**1978-99**
Pat Burns	Mtl	56	30	26	0	.536	4		
	Tor	46	23	23	0	.500	3		
	Bos	18	8	10	0	.333	2		
	Total	**120**	**61**	**59**	**0**	**.508**	**9**		**1988-99**
Toe Blake	**Mtl**	**119**	**82**	**37**	**0**	**.689**	**13**	**8**	**1955-68**
Billy Reay	**Chi**	**116**	**56**	**60**	**0**	**.483**	**12**		**1957-77**
Fred Shero	Phi	83	48	35	0	.578	6	2	
	NYR	27	15	12	0	.444	3		
	Total	**110**	**63**	**47**	**0**	**.573**	**8**	**2**	**1971-81**
Jack Adams	**Det**	**105**	**52**	**52**	**1**	**.500**	**15**	**3**	**1922-47**
Jacques Demers	St.L.	33	16	17	0	.485	3		
	Det	38	20	18	0	.526	3		
	Mtl	27	19	8	0	.704	2	1	
	Total	**98**	**55**	**43**	**0**	**.561**	**8**	**1**	**1979-98**

Coach	Team	Games Coached	W	L	T	Winning Percentage	Playoff Years	Cups	Career
Punch Imlach	**Tor**	**92**	**44**	**48**	**0**	**.478**	**11**	**4**	**1958-80**
Emile Francis	NYR	75	34	41	0	.453	9		
	St.L.	14	5	0	9	.357	2		
	Total	**89**	**39**	**50**	**0**	**.438**	**11**		**1965-83**
Roger Neilson	Tor	19	8	11	0	.421	2		
	Buf	8	4	4	0	.500	1		
	Van	21	12	9	0	.571	2		
	NYR	29	13	16	0	.448	3		
	Phi	11	3	8	0	.273	1		
	Total	**88**	**40**	**48**	**0**	**.455**	**10**		**1977-99**
Terry Murray	Wsh	39	18	21	0	.462	4		
	Phi	46	28	18	0	.609	3		
	Total	**85**	**46**	**39**	**0**	**.541**	**7**		**1989-97**
Jacques Lemaire	Mtl	27	15	12	0	.556	2		
	N.J.	56	34	22	0	.607	4	1	
	Total	**83**	**49**	**34**	**0**	**.590**	**6**	**1**	**1983-98**
Hap Day	**Tor**	**80**	**49**	**31**	**0**	**.613**	**9**	**5**	**1940-50**
Bryan Murray	Wsh	53	24	29	0	.453	7		
	Det	25	10	15	0	.400	3		
	Total	**78**	**34**	**44**	**0**	**.436**	**10**		**1981-99**
Sid Abel	Chi	7	3	4	0	.429	1		
	Det	69	29	40	0	.420	8		
	Total	**76**	**32**	**44**	**0**	**.421**	**9**	**0**	**1952-76**
Bob Johnson	Cgy	52	25	27	0	.481	5		
	Pit	24	16	8	0	.667	1	1	
	Total	**76**	**41**	**35**	**0**	**.539**	**6**	**1**	**1982-91**
Bob Pulford	L.A.	26	10	16	0	.385	4		
	Chi	50	18	32	0	.360	7		
	Total	**76**	**28**	**48**	**0**	**.368**	**11**		**1972-88**
Michel Bergeron	**Que**	**68**	**31**	**37**	**0**	**.456**	**7**		**1980-90**
Tommy Ivan	**Det**	**67**	**36**	**31**	**0**	**.537**	**7**	**3**	**1947-58**
John Muckler	Edm	40	25	15	0	.625	2	1	
	Buf	27	11	16	0	.407	4		
	Total	**67**	**36**	**31**	**0**	**.537**	**6**	**1**	**1968-99**
Lester Patrick	**NYR**	**65**	**32**	**26**	**7**	**.546**	**12**	**2**	**1926-39**
Art Ross	**Bos**	**65**	**27**	**33**	**5**	**.454**	**11**	**1**	**1917-45**

CHAPTER 11

Stanley Cup-Winning Goal Scorers

1918 – 1999

Year	Player, Team	Time of Goal	Period	Score	Series
1999	Brett Hull, Dallas	54:51	OT	3-2	4-2
1998	Martin Lapointe, Detroit	2:26	2nd	4-1	4-0
1997	Darren McCarty, Detroit	13:02	2nd	2-1	4-0
1996	Uwe Krupp, Colorado	44:31	OT	1-0	4-0
1995	Neal Broten, New Jersey	7:56	2nd	5-2	4-0
1994	Mark Messier, NY Rangers	13:29	2nd	3-2	4-3
1993	Kirk Muller, Montreal	3:51	2nd	4-1	4-1
1992	Ron Francis, Pittsburgh	7:59	3rd	6-5	4-0
1991	Ulf Samuelsson, Pittsburgh	2:00	1st	8-0	4-2
1990	Craig Simpson, Edmonton	9:31	2nd	4-1	4-1
1989	Doug Gilmour, Calgary	11:02	3rd	4-2	4-2
1988	Wayne Gretzky, Edmonton	9:44	2nd	6-3	4-0
1987	Jari Kurri, Edmonton	14:59	2nd	3-1	4-3
1986	Bobby Smith, Montreal	10:30	3rd	4-3	4-1
1985	Paul Coffey, Edmonton	17:57	1st	8-3	4-1
1984	Ken Linseman, Edmonton	0:38	2nd	5-2	4-1
1983	Mike Bossy, NY Islanders	12:39	1st	4-2	4-0
1982	Mike Bossy, NY Islanders	5:00	2nd	3-1	4-0
1981	Wayne Merrick, NY Islanders	5:37	1st	5-1	4-1
1980	Bob Nystrom, NY Islanders	7:11	OT	5-4	4-2
1979	Yvon Lambert, Montreal	1:02	2nd	4-1	4-1
1978	Mario Tremblay, Montreal	9:20	1st	4-1	4-2
1977	Jacques Lemaire, Montreal	4:32	OT	2-1	4-1
1976	Guy Lafleur, Montreal	14:18	3rd	5-3	4-0
1975	Bob Kelly, Philadelphia	0:11	3rd	2-0	4-2
1974	Rick MacLeish, Philadelphia	14:48	1st	1-0	4-2
1973	Yvan Cournoyer, Montreal	8:13	3rd	6-4	4-2
1972	Bobby Orr, Boston	11:18	1st	3-0	4-2
1971	Henri Richard, Montreal	2:34	3rd	3-2	4-3
1970	Bobby Orr, Boston	0:40	OT	4-3	4-0
1969	John Ferguson, Montreal	3:02	3rd	2-1	4-1
1968	J.C. Tremblay, Montreal	11:40	3rd	3-2	4-0
1967	Jim Pappin, Toronto	19:24	2nd	3-1	4-2
1966	Henri Richard, Montreal	2:20	OT	3-2	4-2
1965	Jean Beliveau, Montreal	0:14	1st	4-0	4-3
1964	Andy Bathgate, Toronto	3:04	1st	4-0	4-3
1963	Eddie Shack, Toronto	13:28	3rd	3-1	4-1
1962	Dick Duff, Toronto	14:14	3rd	2-1	4-2
1961	Ab McDonald, Chicago	18:49	2nd	5-1	4-2
1960	Jean Beliveau, Montreal	8:16	1st	4-0	4-0
1959	Marcel Bonin, Montreal	9:55	2nd	5-3	4-1
1958	Bernie Geoffrion, Montreal	19:26	2nd	5-3	4-2
1957	Dickie Moore, Montreal	0:14	2nd	5-1	4-1
1956	Maurice Richard, Montreal	15:08	2nd	3-1	4-1
1955	Gordie Howe, Detroit	19:49	2nd	3-1	4-3
1954	Tony Leswick, Detroit	4:20	OT	2-1	4-3
1953	Elmer Lach, Montreal	1:22	OT	1-0	4-1
1952	Metro Prystai, Detroit	6:50	1st	3-0	4-0
1951	Bill Barilko, Toronto	2:53	OT	3-2	4-1
1950	Pete Babando, Detroit	28:31	OT	4-3	4-3
1949	Cal Gardner, Toronto	19:45	2nd	3-1	4-0
1948	Harry Watson, Toronto	11:13	1st	7-2	4-0
1947	Ted Kennedy, Toronto	14:39	3rd	2-1	4-2
1946	Toe Blake, Montreal	11:06	3rd	6-3	4-1
1945	Babe Pratt, Toronto	12:14	3rd	2-1	4-3
1944	Toe Blake, Montreal	9:12	OT	5-4	4-0
1943	Joe Carveth, Detroit	12:09	1st	2-0	4-0
1942	Pete Langelle, Toronto	9:48	3rd	3-1	4-3
1941	Bobby Bauer, Boston	8:43	2nd	3-1	4-0
1940	Bryan Hextall, NY Rangers	2:07	OT	3-2	4-2
1939	Roy Conacher, Boston	17:54	2nd	3-1	4-1
1938	Carl Voss, Chicago	16:45	2nd	4-3	3-1
1937	Marty Barry, Detroit	19:22	1st	3-0	3-2
1936	Pete Kelly, Detroit	9:45	3rd	3-2	3-1
1935	Baldy Northcott, Mtl. Maroons	16:18	2nd	4-1	3-0
1934	Mush March, Chicago	30:05	OT	1-0	3-1
1933	Bill Cook, NY Rangers	7:34	OT	1-0	3-1
1932	Ace Bailey, Toronto	15:07	3rd	6-4	3-0
1931	Johnny Gagnon, Montreal	9:59	2nd	2-0	3-2
1930	Howie Morenz, Montreal	1:00	2nd	4-3	2-0
1929	Bill Carson, Boston	18:02	3rd	2-1	2-0
1928	Frank Boucher, NY Rangers	3:35	3rd	2-1	3-2
1927	Cy Denneny, Ottawa	7:30	2nd	3-1	2-0
1926	Nels Stewart, Mtl. Maroons	2:50	2nd	2-0	3-1
1925	Gizzy Hart, Victoria	2:35	2nd	6-1	3-1
1924	Billy Boucher, Montreal	14:00	3rd	2-1	2-0
	Howie Morenz. Montreal	4:55	1st	3-0	2-0
1923	Eddie Gerard, Ottawa	17:25	1st	5-1	3-1
	Punch Broadbent, Ottawa	11:23	1st	1-0	2-0
1922	Babe Dye, Toronto	4:20	1st	5-1	3-2
1921	Jack Darragh, Ottawa	9:40	2nd	2-1	3-2
1920	Jack Darragh, Ottawa	5:00	3rd	6-1	3-2
1919	— no decision —				
1918	Corb Denneny, Toronto	10:30	3rd	2-1	3-2

CHAPTER 12

Three-Or-More-Goal Games, Playoffs

1918 – 1999

Player	Team	Date	City	Total Goals	Opposing Goaltender	Score	
Wayne Gretzky (10)	Edm.	Apr. 11/81	Edm.	3	Richard Sevigny	Edm. 6	Mtl. 2
		Apr. 19/81	Edm.	3	Billy Smith	Edm. 5	NYI 2
		Apr. 6/83	Edm.	4	Brian Hayward	Edm. 6	Wpg. 3
		Apr. 17/83	Cgy.	4	Rejean Lemelin	Edm.10	Cgy. 2
		Apr. 25/85	Wpg.	3	Bryan Hayward (2)		
					Marc Behrend (1)	Edm. 8	Wpg. 3
		May 25/85	Edm.	3	Pelle Lindbergh	Edm. 4	Phi. 3
		Apr. 24/86	Cgy.	3	Mike Vernon	Edm. 7	Cgy. 4
	L.A.	May 29/93	Tor.	3	Felix Potvin	L.A. 5	Tor. 4
	NYR	Apr. 23/97	NYR	3	John Vanbiesbrouck	NYR 3	Fla. 2
		May 18/97	Phi.	3	Garth Snow	NYR 5	Phi. 4
Maurice Richard (7)	Mtl.	Mar. 23/44	Mtl.	5	Paul Bibeault	Mtl. 5	Tor. 1
		Apr. 7/44	Chi.	3	Mike Karakas	Mtl. 3	Chi. 1
		Mar. 29/45	Mtl.	4	Frank McCool	Mtl. 10	Tor. 3
		Apr. 14/53	Bos.	3	Gord Henry	Mtl. 7	Bos. 3
		Mar. 20/56	Mtl.	3	Gump Worsley	Mtl. 7	NYR 1
		Apr. 6/57	Mtl.	4	Don Simmons	Mtl. 5	Bos. 1
		Apr. 1/58	Det.	3	Terry Sawchuk	Mtl. 4	Det. 3
Jari Kurri (7)	Edm.	Apr. 4/84	Edm.	3	Doug Soetaert (1)		
					Mike Veisor (2)	Edm. 9	Wpg. 2
		Apr. 25/85	Wpg.	3	Bryan Hayward (2)		
					Marc Behrend (1)	Edm. 8	Wpg. 3
		May 7/85	Edm.	3	Murray Bannerman	Edm. 7	Chi. 3
		May 14/85	Edm.	3	Murray Bannerman	Edm.10	Chi. 5
		May 16/85	Chi.	4	Murray Bannerman	Edm. 8	Chi. 2
		Apr. 9/87	Edm.	4	Rollie Melanson (2)		
					Daren Eliot (2)	Edm.13	L.A. 3
		May 18/90	Bos.	3	Andy Moog (2)		
					Rejean Lemelin (1)	Edm. 7	Bos. 2
Dino Ciccarelli (6)	Min.	May 5/81	Min.	3	Pat Riggin	Min. 7	Cgy. 4
		Apr. 10/82	Min.	3	Murray Bannerman	Min. 7	Chi. 1
	Wsh.	Apr. 5/90	N.J.	3	Sean Burke	Wsh. 5	N.J. 4
		Apr. 25/92	Pit.	4	Tom Barrasso (1)		
					Ken Wregget (3)	Wsh. 7	Pit. 2
	Det.	Apr. 29/93	Tor.	3	Felix Potvin (2)		
					Daren Puppa (1)	Det. 7	Tor. 3
		May 11/95	Dal.	3	Andy Moog (2)		
					Darcy Wakaluk (1)	Det. 5	Dal. 1
Mike Bossy (5)	NYI	Apr. 16/79	NYI	3	Tony Esposito	NYI 6	Chi. 2
		May 8/82	NYI	3	Richard Brodeur	NYI 6	Van. 5
		Apr. 10/83	Wsh.	3	Al Jensen	NYI 6	Wsh. 3
		May 3/83	NYI	3	Pete Peeters	NYI 8	Bos. 3
		May 7/83	NYI	4	Pete Peeters	NYI 8	Bos. 4
Phil Esposito (4)	Bos.	Apr. 2/69	Bos.	4	Bruce Gamble	Bos.10	Tor. 0
		Apr. 8/70	Bos.	3	Ed Giacomin	Bos. 8	NYR 2
		Apr. 19/70	Chi.	3	Tony Esposito	Bos. 6	Chi. 3
		Apr. 8/75	Bos.	3	Tony Esposito (2)		
					Michel Dumas (1)	Bos. 8	Chi. 2
Mark Messier (4)	Edm.	Apr. 14/83	Edm.	4	Rejean Lemelin	Edm. 6	Cgy. 3
		Apr. 17/83	Cgy.	3	Rejean Lemelin (1)	Edm.10	Cgy. 2
					Don Edwards (2)		
		Apr. 26/83	Edm.	3	Murray Bannerman	Edm. 8	Chi. 2
	NYR	May 25/94	N.J.	3	Martin Brodeur (2)	NYR 4	N.J. 2
					ENG (1)		
Steve Yzerman (4)	Det.	Apr. 6/89	Det.	3	Alain Chevrier	Chi. 5	Det. 4
		Apr. 4/91	St.L.	3	Vincent Riendeau (2)	Det. 6	St.L. 3
		May 8/96	St.L.	3	Jon Casey	St.L. 5	Det. 4
		Apr. 21/99	Det.	3	Guy Hebert (2)	Det. 5	Ana. 3
					Pat Jablonski (1)		
Bernie Geoffrion (3)	Mtl.	Mar. 27/52	Mtl.	3	Jim Henry	Mtl. 4	Bos. 0
		Apr. 7/55	Mtl.	3	Terry Sawchuk	Mtl. 4	Det. 2
		Mar. 30/57	Mtl.	3	Gump Worsley	Mtl. 8	NYR 3
Norm Ullman (3)	Det.	Mar. 29/64	Chi.	3	Glenn Hall	Det. 5	Chi. 4
		Apr. 7/64	Det.	3	Glenn Hall (2)		
					Denis DeJordy (1)	Det. 7	Chi. 2
		Apr. 11/65	Det.	3	Glenn Hall	Det. 4	Chi. 2
John Bucyk (3)	Bos.	May 3/70	St.L.	3	Jacques Plante (1)		
					Ernie Wakely (2)	Bos. 6	St.L. 1
		Apr. 20/72	Bos.	3	Jacques Caron (1)		
					Ernie Wakely (2)	Bos.10	St.L. 2
		Apr. 21/74	Bos.	3	Tony Esposito	Bos. 8	Chi. 6
Rick MacLeish (3)	Phi.	Apr. 11/74	Phi.	3	Phil Myre	Phi. 5	Atl. 1
		Apr. 13/75	Phi.	3	Gord McRae	Phi. 6	Tor. 3
		May 13/75	Phi.	3	Glenn Resch	Phi. 4	NYI 1

Player	Team	Date	City	Total Goals	Opposing Goaltender	Score	
Denis Savard (3)	Chi.	Apr. 19/82	Chi.	3	Mike Liut	Chi. 7	St.L. 4
		Apr. 10/86	Chi.	4	Ken Wregget	Tor. 6	Chi. 4
		Apr. 9/88	St.L.	3	Greg Millen	Chi. 6	St.L. 3
Tim Kerr (3)	Phi.	Apr. 13/85	NYR	4	Glen Hanlon	Phi. 6	NYR 5
		Apr. 20/87	Phi.	3	Kelly Hrudey	Phi. 4	NYI 2
		Apr. 19/89	Pit.	3	Tom Barrasso	Phi. 4	Pit. 2
Cam Neely (3)	Bos.	Apr. 9/87	Mtl.	3	Patrick Roy	Mtl. 4	Bos. 3
		Apr. 5/91	Bos.	3	Peter Sidorkiewicz	Bos. 4	Hfd. 3
		Apr. 25/91	Bos.	3	Patrick Roy	Bos. 4	Mtl. 1
Petr Klima (3)	Det.	Apr. 7/88	Tor.	3	Alan Bester (2)		
					Ken Wregett (1)	Det. 6	Tor. 2
		Apr. 21/88	St.L.	3	Greg Millen	Det. 6	St.L. 0
	Edm.	May 4/91	Edm.	3	Jon Casey	Edm. 7	Min. 2
Esa Tikkanen (3)	Edm.	May 22/88	Edm.	3	Rejean Lemelin	Edm. 6	Bos. 3
		Apr. 16/91	Cgy.	3	Mike Vernon	Edm. 5	Cgy. 4
		Apr. 26/92	L.A.	3	Kelly Hrudey	Edm. 5	L.A. 2
					Tom Askey (1)		
Mario Lemieux (3)	Pit.	Apr. 25/89	Pit.	5	Ron Hextall	Pit. 10	Phi. 7
		Apr. 23/92	Pit.	3	Don Beaupre	Pit. 6	Wsh. 4
		May 11/96	Pit.	3	Mike Richter	Pit. 7	NYR 3
Mike Gartner (3)	NYR	Apr. 13/90	NYR	3	Mark Fitzpatrick		
					Glenn Healy (1)	NYR 6	NYI 5
		Apr. 27/92	NYR	3	Chris Terreri	NYR 8	N.J. 5
	Tor.	Apr. 25/96	Tor.	3	Jon Casey	Tor. 5	St.L. 4
Newsy Lalonde (2)	Mtl.	Mar. 1/19	Mtl.	5	Clint Benedict	Mtl. 6	Ott. 3
		Mar. 22/19	Sea.	4	Harry Holmes	Mtl. 4	Sea. 2
Howie Morenz (2)	Mtl.	Mar. 22/24	Mtl.	3	Charles Reid	Mtl. 6	Cgy.T.1
		Mar. 27/25	Mtl.	3	Harry Holmes	Mtl. 4	Vic. 2
Toe Blake (2)	Mtl.	Mar. 22/38	Mtl.	3	Mike Karakas	Mtl. 6	Chi. 4
		Mar. 26/46	Chi.	3	Mike Karakas	Mtl. 7	Chi. 2
Doug Bentley (2)	Chi.	Mar. 28/44	Chi.	3	Connie Dion	Chi. 7	Det. 1
		Mar. 30/44	Det.	3	Connie Dion	Chi. 5	Det. 2
Ted Kennedy (2)	Tor.	Apr. 14/45	Tor.	3	Harry Lumley	Det. 5	Tor. 3
		Mar. 27/48	Tor.	4	Frank Brimsek	Tor. 5	Bos. 3
Bobby Hull (2)	Chi.	Apr. 7/63	Det.	3	Terry Sawchuk	Det. 7	Chi. 4
		Apr. 9/72	Pit.	3	Jim Rutherford	Chi. 6	Pit. 5
F. St. Marseille (2)	St.L.	Apr. 28/70	St.L.	3	Al Smith	St.L. 5	Pit. 0
		Apr. 6/72	Min.	3	Cesare Maniago	Min. 6	St.L. 5
Pit Martin (2)	Chi.	Apr. 4/73	Chi.	3	Wayne Stephenson	Chi. 7	St.L. 1
		May 10/73	Chi.	3	Ken Dryden	Mtl. 6	Chi. 4
Yvan Cournoyer (2)	Mtl.	Apr. 5/73	Mtl.	3	Dave Dryden	Mtl. 7	Buf. 3
		Apr. 11/74	Mtl.	3	Ed Giacomin	Mtl. 4	NYR 1
Guy Lafleur (2)	Mtl.	May 1/75	Mtl.	3	Roger Crozier (1)		
					Gerry Desjardins (2)	Mtl. 7	Buf. 0
		Apr. 11/77	Mtl.	3	Ed Staniowski	Mtl. 7	St.L. 2
Lanny McDonald (2)	Tor.	Apr. 9/77	Pit.	3	Denis Herron	Tor. 5	Pit. 2
		Apr. 17/77	Tor.	4	Wayne Stephenson	Phi. 6	Tor. 5
Butch Goring (2)	L.A.	Apr. 9/77	L.A.	3	Phil Myre	L.A. 4	Atl. 2
	NYI	May 17/81	Min.	3	Gilles Meloche	NYI 7	Min. 5
Bryan Trottier (2)	NYI	Apr. 8/80	NYI	3	Doug Keans	NYI 8	L.A. 1
		Apr. 9/81	NYI	3	Michel Larocque	NYI 5	Tor. 1
Bill Barber (2)	Phi.	May 4/80	Min.	4	Gilles Meloche	Phi. 5	Min. 3
		Apr. 9/81	Phi.	3	Dan Bouchard	Phi. 8	Que. 5
Brian Propp (2)	Phi.	Apr. 22/81	Phi.	3	Pat Riggin	Phi. 9	Cgy. 4
		Apr. 21/85	Phi.	3	Billy Smith	Phi. 5	NYI 2
Paul Reinhart (2)	Cgy	Apr. 14/83	Edm.	3	Andy Moog	Edm. 6	Cgy. 3
		Apr. 8/84	Van	3	Richard Brodeur	Cgy. 5	Van. 1
Peter Stastny (2)	Que.	Apr. 5/83	Bos.	3	Pete Peeters	Bos. 4	Que. 3
		Apr. 11/87	Que.	3	Mike Liut (2)		
					Steve Weeks (1)	Que. 5	Hfd. 1
Glenn Anderson (2)	Edm.	Apr. 26/83	Edm.	4	Murray Bannerman	Edm. 8	Chi. 2
		Apr. 6/88	Wpg.	3	Daniel Berthiaume	Edm. 7	Wpg. 4
Michel Goulet (2)	Que.	Apr. 23/85	Que.	3	Steve Penney	Que. 7	Mtl. 6
		Apr. 12/87	Que.	3	Mike Liut	Que. 4	Hfd. 1
Peter Zezel (2)	Phi.	Apr. 13/86	NYR	3	John Vanbiesbrouck	Phi. 7	NYR 1
	St.L.	Apr. 11/89	St.L.	3	Jon Casey (2)		
					Kari Takko (1)	St.L. 6	Min. 1
Geoff Courtnall (2)	Van.	Apr. 4/91	L.A.	3	Kelly Hrudey	Van. 6	L.A. 5
		Apr. 30/92	Van.	3	Rick Tabaracci	Van. 5	Win. 0
Joe Sakic (2)	Que.	May 6/95	Que.	3	Mike Richter	Que. 5	NYR 4
	Col.	Apr. 25/96	Col.	3	Corey Hirsch	Col. 5	Van. 4
Daniel Alfredsson (2)	Ott.	Apr. 28/98	Ott.	3	Martin Brodeur	Ott. 4	N.J. 3
		May 11/98	Ott.	3	Olaf Kolzig	Ott. 4	Wsh. 3
Harry Meeking	Tor.	Mar. 11/18	Tor.	3	Georges Vezina	Tor. 7	Mtl. 3

Player	Team	Date	City	Total Goals	Opposing Goaltender	Score	
Alf Skinner	Tor.	Mar.23/18	Tor.	3	Hugh Lehman	Van.M. 6	Tor. 4
Joe Malone	Mtl.	Feb.23/19	Mtl.	3	Clint Benedict	Mtl. 8	Ott. 4
Odie Cleghorn	Mtl.	Feb.27/19	Ott.	3	Clint Benedict	Mtl. 5	Ott. 3
Jack Darragh	Ott.	Apr. 1/20	Tor.	3	Harry Holmes	Ott. 6	Sea. 1
George Boucher	Ott.	Mar. 10/21	Ott.	3	Jake Forbes	Ott. 5	Tor. 0
Babe Dye	Tor.	Mar.28/22	Tor.	4	Hugh Lehman	Tor. 5	Van.M. 1
Percy Galbraith	Bos.	Mar.31/27	Bos.	3	Hugh Lehman	Bos. 4	Chi. 4
Harvey Jackson	Tor.	Apr. 5/32	NYR	3	John Ross Roach	Tor. 6	NYR 4
Frank Boucher	NYR	Apr. 9/32	Tor.	3	Lorne Chabot	Tor. 6	NYR 4
Charlie Conacher	Tor.	Mar.26/36	Tor.	3	Tiny Thompson	Tor. 8	Bos. 3
Syd Howe	Det.	Mar.23/39	Det.	3	Claude Bourque	Det. 7	Mtl. 3
Bryan Hextall Sr.	NYR	Apr. 3/40	NYR	3	Turk Broda	NYR 6	Tor. 2
Joe Benoit	Mtl.	Mar.22/41	Mtl.	3	Sam LoPresti	Mtl. 4	Chi. 3
Syl Apps Sr.	Tor.	Mar.25/41	Tor.	3	Frank Brimsek	Tor. 7	Bos. 2
Jack McGill	Bos.	Mar.29/42	Bos.	3	Johnny Mowers	Det. 6	Bos. 4
Don Metz	Tor.	Apr. 14/42	Tor.	3	Johnny Mowers	Tor. 9	Det. 3
Mud Bruneteau	Det.	Apr. 1/43	Det.	3	Frank Brimsek	Det. 6	Bos. 2
Don Grosso	Det.	Apr. 7/43	Bos.	3	Frank Brimsek	Det. 4	Bos. 0
Carl Liscombe	Det.	Apr. 3/45	Bos.	4	Paul Bibeault	Det. 5	Bos. 3
Billy Reay	Mtl.	Apr. 1/47	Bos.	4	Frank Brimsek	Mtl. 5	Bos. 1
Gerry Plamondon	Mtl.	Mar.24/49	Det.	3	Harry Lumley	Mtl. 4	Det. 3
Sid Smith	Tor.	Apr. 10/49	Det.	3	Harry Lumley	Tor. 3	Det. 1
Pentti Lund	NYR	Apr. 2/50	NYR	3	Bill Durnan	NYR 4	Mtl. 1
Ted Lindsay	Det.	Apr. 5/55	Det.	4	Charlie Hodge (1)		
					Jacques Plante (3)	Det. 7	Mtl. 1
Gordie Howe	Det.	Apr. 10/55	Det.	3	Jacques Plante	Det. 5	Mtl. 1
Phil Goyette	Mtl.	Mar.25/58	Mtl.	3	Terry Sawchuk	Mtl. 8	Det. 1
Jerry Toppazzini	Bos.	Apr. 5/58	Bos.	3	Gump Worsley	Bos. 8	NYR 2
Bob Pulford	Tor.	Apr. 19/62	Tor.	3	Glenn Hall	Tor. 8	Chi. 4
Dave Keon	Tor.	Apr. 9/64	Mtl.	3	Charlie Hodge	Tor. 3	Mtl. 1
Henri Richard	Mtl.	Apr. 20/67	Mtl.	3	Terry Sawchuk (2)		
					Johnny Bower (1)	Mtl. 6	Tor. 2
Rosaire Paiement	Phi.	Apr. 13/68	Phi.	3	Glenn Hall (1)		
					Seth Martin (2)	Phi. 6	St.L. 1
Jean Beliveau	Mtl.	Apr. 20/68	Mtl.	3	Denis DeJordy	Mtl. 4	Chi. 1
Red Berenson	St.L.	Apr. 15/69	St.L.	3	Gerry Desjardins	St.L. 4	L.A. 0
Ken Schinkel	Pit.	Apr. 10/70	Oak.	3	Gary Smith	Pit. 5	Oak. 2
Jim Pappin	Chi.	Apr. 10/71	Phi.	3	Bruce Gamble	Chi. 6	Phi. 2
Bobby Orr	Bos.	Apr. 10/71	Mtl.	3	Ken Dryden	Bos. 5	Mtl. 2
Jacques Lemaire	Mtl.	Apr. 20/71	Mtl.	3	Gump Worsley	Mtl. 7	Min. 2
Vic Hadfield	NYR	Apr. 22/71	NYR	3	Tony Esposito	NYR 4	Chi. 1
Fred Stanfield	Bos.	Apr. 18/72	Bos.	3	Jacques Caron	Bos. 6	St.L. 1
Ken Hodge	Bos.	Apr. 30/72	Bos.	3	Eddie Giacomin	Bos. 6	NYR 5
Steve Vickers	NYR	Apr. 10/73	Bos.	3	Ross Brooks (2)		
					Eddie Johnston (1)	NYR 6	Bos. 3
Dick Redmond	Chi.	Apr. 4/73	Chi.	3	Wayne Stephenson	Chi. 7	St.L. 1
Tom Williams	L.A.	Apr. 14/74	L.A.	3	Mike Veisor	L.A. 5	Chi. 1
Marcel Dionne	L.A.	Apr. 15/76	L.A.	3	Gilles Gilbert	L.A. 6	Bos. 4
Don Saleski	Phi.	Apr. 20/76	Phi.	3	Wayne Thomas	Phi. 7	Tor. 1
Darryl Sittler	Tor.	Apr. 22/76	Tor.	5	Bernie Parent	Tor. 8	Phi. 5
Reggie Leach	Phi.	May 6/76	Phi.	5	Gilles Gilbert	Phi. 6	Bos. 3
Jim Lorentz	Buf.	Apr. 7/77	Min.	3	Pete LoPresti (2)		
					Gary Smith (1)	Buf. 7	Min. 1
Bobby Schmautz	Bos.	Apr. 11/77	Bos.	3	Rogie Vachon	Bos. 8	L.A. 3
Billy Harris	NYI	Apr. 23/77	Mtl.	3	Ken Dryden	Mtl. 4	NYI 3
George Ferguson	Tor.	Apr. 11/78	Tor.	3	Rogie Vachon	Tor. 7	L.A. 3
Jean Ratelle	Bos.	May 3/79	Bos.	3	Ken Dryden	Bos. 4	Mtl. 3
Stan Jonathan	Bos.	May 8/79	Bos.	3	Ken Dryden	Bos. 5	Mtl. 2
Ron Duguay	NYR	Apr. 20/80	NYR	3	Pete Peeters	NYR 4	Phi. 2
Steve Shutt	Mtl.	Apr. 22/80	Mtl.	3	Gilles Meloche	Mtl. 6	Min. 2
Gilbert Perreault	Buf.	May 6/80	NYI	3	Billy Smith (2)		
					ENG (1)	Buf. 7	NYI 4
Paul Holmgren	Phi.	May 15/80	Phil	3	Billy Smith	Phi. 8	NYI 3
Steve Payne	Min.	Apr. 8/81	Bos.	3	Rogie Vachon	Min. 5	Bos. 4
Denis Potvin	NYI	Apr. 17/81	NYI	3	Andy Moog	NYI 6	Edm. 3
Barry Pederson	Bos.	Apr. 9/82	Bos.	3	Don Edwards	Bos. 7	Buf. 3
Duane Sutter	NYI	Apr. 15/83	NYI	3	Glen Hanlon	NYI 5	NYR 0
Doug Halward	Van.	Apr. 7/84	Van.	3	Rejean Lemelin (2)		
					Don Edwards (1)	Van. 7	Cgy. 0
Jorgen Pettersson	St.L.	Apr. 8/84	Det.	3	Eddie Mio	St.L. 3	Det. 2
Clark Gillies	NYI	May 12/84	NYI	3	Grant Fuhr	NYI 6	Edm. 1
Ken Linseman	Bos.	Apr. 14/85	Bos.	3	Steve Penney	Bos. 7	Mtl. 6
Dave Andreychuk	Buf.	Apr. 14/85	Buf.	3	Dan Bouchard	Buf. 7	Que. 4
Greg Paslawski	St.L.	Apr. 15/86	Min.	3	Don Beaupre	St.L. 6	Min. 3
Doug Risebrough	Cgy.	May 4/86	Cgy.	3	Rick Wamsley	Cgy. 8	St.L. 2
Mike McPhee	Mtl.	Apr. 11/87	Bos.	3	Doug Keans	Mtl. 5	Bos. 4
John Ogrodnick	Que.	Apr. 14/87	Hfd.	3	Mike Liut	Que. 7	Hfd. 5
Pelle Eklund	Phi.	May 10/87	Mtl.	3	Patrick Roy (1)		
					Bryan Hayward (2)	Phi. 6	Mtl. 3
John Tucker	Buf.	Apr. 9/88	Bos.	4	Andy Moog	Buf. 6	Bos. 2
Tony Hrkac	St.L.	Apr. 10/88	St.L.	4	Darren Pang	St.L. 6	Chi. 5
Hakan Loob	Cgy.	Apr. 10/88	Cgy.	3	Glenn Healy	Cgy. 7	L.A. 3
Ed Olczyk	Tor.	Apr. 12/88	Tor.	3	Greg Stefan (2)		
					Glen Hanlon (1)	Tor. 6	Det. 5
Aaron Broten	N.J.	Apr. 20/88	N.J.	3	Pete Peeters	N.J. 5	Wsh. 2
Mark Johnson	N.J.	Apr. 22/88	Wsh.	4	Pete Peeters	N.J. 10	Wsh. 4
Patrik Sundstrom	N.J.	Apr. 22/88	Wsh.	3	Pete Peeters (2)		
					Clint Malarchuk (1)	N.J. 10	Wsh. 4
Bob Brooke	Min.	Apr. 5/89	St.L.	3	Greg Millen	St.L. 4	Min. 3
Chris Kontos	L.A.	Apr. 6/89	L.A.	3	Grant Fuhr	L.A. 5	Edm. 2
Wayne Presley	Chi.	Apr. 13/89	Chi.	3	Greg Stefan (1)		
					Glen Hanlon (2)	Chi. 7	Det. 1
Tony Granato	L.A.	Apr. 10/90	L.A.	3	Mike Vernon (1)		
					Rick Wamsley (2)	L.A. 12	Cgy. 4
Tomas Sandstrom	L.A.	Apr. 10/90	L.A.	3	Mike Vernon (1)		
					Rick Wamsley (2)	L.A. 12	Cgy. 4
Dave Taylor	L.A.	Apr. 10/90	L.A.	3	Mike Vernon (1)		
					Rick Wamsley (2)	L.A. 12	Cgy. 4
Bernie Nicholls	NYR	Apr. 19/90	NYR	3	Mike Liut	NYR 7	Wsh. 3
John Druce	Wsh.	Apr. 21/90	NYR	3	John Vanbiesbrouck	Wsh. 6	NYR 3
Adam Oates	St.L.	Apr. 12/91	St.L.	3	Tim Chevaldae	St.L. 6	Det. 1
Luc Robitaille	L.A.	Apr. 26/91	L.A.	3	Grant Fuhr	L.A. 5	Edm. 2
Ron Francis	Pit.	May 9/92	Pit.	3	Mike Richter (2)		
					John V'brouck (1)	Pit. 5	NYR. 4
Dirk Graham	Chi.	June 1/92	Chi.	3	Tom Barrasso	Pit. 5	Chi. 2
Joe Murphy	Edm.	May 6/92	Edm.	3	Kirk McLean	Edm. 5	Van. 2
Ray Sheppard	Det.	Apr. 24/92	Min.	3	Jon Casey	Min. 5	Det. 2
Kevin Stevens	Pit.	May 21/92	Bos.	4	Andy Moog	Pit. 5	Bos. 2
Pavel Bure	Van.	Apr. 28/92	Wpg.	3	Rick Tabaracci	Van. 8	Wpg. 3
Brian Noonan	Chi.	Apr. 18/93	Chi.	3	Curtis Joseph	St.L. 4	Chi. 3
Dale Hunter	Wsh.	Apr. 20/93	Wsh.	3	Glenn Healy	NYI 5	Wsh. 4
Teemu Selanne	Wpg.	Apr. 23/93	Wpg.	3	Kirk McLean	Wpg. 5	Van. 4
Ray Ferraro	NYI	Apr. 26/93	Wsh.	4	Don Beaupre	Wsh. 6	NYI 4
Al Iafrate	Wsh.	Apr. 26/93	Wsh.	3	Glenn Healy (2)		
					Mark Fitzpatrick (1)	Wsh. 6	NYI 4
Paul Di Pietro	Mtl.	Apr. 28/93	Mtl.	3	Ron Hextall	Mtl. 6	Que. 2
Wendel Clark	Tor.	May 27/93	L.A.	3	Kelly Hrudey	L.A. 5	Tor. 4
Eric Desjardins	Mtl.	Jun. 3/93	Mtl.	3	Kelly Hrudey	Mtl. 3	L.A. 2
Tony Amonte	Chi.	Apr. 23/94	Chi.	4	Felix Potvin	Chi. 5	Tor. 4
Gary Suter	Chi.	Apr. 24/94	Chi.	3	Felix Potvin	Chi. 4	Tor. 3
Ulf Dahlen	S.J.	May 6/94	S.J.	3	Felix Potvin	S.J. 5	Tor. 2
Mike Sullivan	Cgy.	May 11/95	S.J.	3	Arturs Irbe (2)		
					Wade Flaherty (1)	Cgy. 9	S.J. 2
Theoren Fleury	Cgy.	May 13/95	S.J.	4	Arturs Irbe (3)		
					ENG (1)	Cgy. 6	S.J. 4
Brendan Shanahan	St.L.	May 13/95	Van.	3	Kirk McLean	St.L. 5	Van. 2
John LeClair	Phi.	May 21/95	Phi.	3	Mike Richter	Phi. 5	NYR 4
Brian Leetch	NYR	May 22/95	Phi.	3	Ron Hextall	Phi. 4	NYR 3
Trevor Linden	Van.	Apr. 25/96	Col.	3	Patrick Roy	Col. 5	Van. 4
Jaromir Jagr	Pit.	May 11/96	Pit.	3	Mike Richter	Pit. 7	NYR 3
Peter Forsberg	Col.	Jun. 6/96	Col.	3	John Vanbiesbrouck	Col. 8	Fla. 1
Valeri Zelepukin	N.J.	Apr. 22/97	Mtl.	3	Jocelyn Thibault	N.J. 6	Mtl. 4
Valeri Kamensky	Col.	Apr. 24/97	Col.	3	Jeff Hackett (2)		
					Chris Terreri (1)	Col. 7	Chi. 0
Eric Lindros	Phi.	May 20/97	NYR	3	Mike Richter	Phi. 6	NYR 3
Matthew Barnaby	Buf.	May 10/98	Buf.	3	Andy Moog (2)		
					ENG (1)	Buf. 6	Mtl. 3
Martin Straka	Pit.	Apr. 25/99	Pit.	3	Martin Brodeur	Pit. 4	N.J. 2

CHAPTER 13

Overtime

1918 – 1999

Overtime Record of Current Teams

(Listed by number of OT games played)

	Overall				Home					Road				
Team	GP	W	L	T	GP	W	L	T	Last OT Game	GP	W	L	T	Last OT Game
Montreal	120	69	49	2	55	36	18	1	May 12/98	65	33	31	1	May 8/98
Boston	98	38	57	3	45	20	24	1	May 3/98	53	18	33	2	Apr. 30/99
Toronto	92	48	43	1	58	31	26	1	Apr. 30/99	34	17	17	0	May 13/99
NY Rangers	63	30	33	0	27	12	15	0	Apr. 22/97	36	18	18	0	May 11/97
Chicago	62	30	30	2	30	16	13	1	Apr. 20/97	32	14	17	1	May 2/96
Detroit	63	31	32	0	38	16	22	0	Jun. 11/98	25	15	10	0	Jun. 3/98
Philadelphia	45	22	23	0	20	11	9	0	May 1/98	25	11	14	0	Apr. 30/99
NY Islanders	38	29	9	0	17	14	3	0	May 20/93	21	15	6	0	May 18/93
St. Louis	44	24	20	0	22	17	5	0	May 12/99	22	7	15	0	May 8/99
Dallas [1]	42	18	24	0	19	7	12	0	Jun. 8/99	23	11	12	0	Jun. 19/99
Buffalo	40	21	19	0	22	13	9	0	Jun. 19/99	18	8	10	0	Jun. 8/99
Edmonton	34	20	14	0	19	10	9	0	Apr. 27/99	15	10	5	0	Apr. 29/97
Colorado [2]	32	20	12	0	14	8	6	0	May 28/99	18	12	6	0	May 3/99
Los Angeles	30	12	18	0	16	8	8	0	Jun. 7/93	14	4	10	0	Jun. 3/93
Calgary [3]	30	11	19	0	14	4	10	0	Apr. 23/96	16	7	9	0	Apr. 28/94
Vancouver	29	13	16	0	12	5	7	0	May 27/95	17	8	9	0	Apr. 25/96
Washington	26	13	13	0	10	5	5	0	May 25/98	16	8	8	0	Jun. 11/98
Pittsburgh	20	11	9	0	12	7	5	0	May 13/99	8	4	4	0	Apr. 24/96
New Jersey [4]	20	5	15	0	9	2	7	0	Apr. 22/98	11	3	8	0	May 2/99
Carolina [5]	13	6	7	0	9	5	4	0	Apr. 30/99	4	1	3	0	May 1/92
Phoenix [6]	12	5	7	0	8	3	5	0	May 4/99	4	2	2	0	Apr. 27/93
Florida	5	2	3	0	3	1	2	0	Apr. 25/97	2	1	1	0	Apr. 22/97
Anaheim	4	1	3	0	1	0	1	0	May 8/97	3	1	2	0	May 4/97
San Jose	7	3	4	0	4	1	3	0	May 3/99	3	2	1	0	May 19/95
Tampa Bay	2	2	0	0	1	1	0	0	Apr. 21/96	1	1	0	0	Apr. 18/96
Ottawa	3	2	1	0	2	1	1	0	Apr. 23/99	1	1	0	0	Apr. 22/98

[1] Totals include those of Minnesota 1967-93.
[2] Totals include those of Quebec 1979-95.
[3] Totals include those of Atlanta 1972-80.
[4] Totals include those of Kansas City and Colorado 1974-82
[5] Totals include those of Hartford 1979-97.
[6] Totals include those of Winnipeg 1979-96.

Overtime Games since 1918

Abbreviations: Teams/Cities: Ana. - Anaheim; Atl. - Atlanta; Bos. - Boston; Buf. - Buffalo; Cgy. - Calgary; Cgy. T. - Calgary Tigers (Western Canada Hockey League); Chi. - Chicago; Col. - Colorado; Dal. - Dallas; Det. - Detroit; Edm. - Edmonton; Edm. E. - Edmonton Eskimos (WCHL); Fla. - Florida; Hfd. - Hartford; K.C. - Kansas City; L.A. - Los Angeles; Min. - Minnesota; Mtl. - Montreal; Mtl.M. - Montreal Maroons; N.J. - New Jersey; NYA - NY Americans; NYI - New York Islanders; NYR - New York Rangers; Oak. - Oakland; Ott. - Ottawa; Phi. - Philadelphia; Phx. - Phoenix; Pit. - Pittsburgh; Que. - Quebec; St.L. - St.Louis; Sea. - Seattle Metropolitans (Pacific Coast Hockey Association); S.J. - San Jose; T.B. - Tampa Bay; Tor. - Toronto; Van. - Vancouver; Van. M - Vancouver Millionaires (PCHA); Vic. - Victoria Cougars (WCHL); Wpg. - Winnipeg; Wsh. - Washington.

SERIES CF - conference final; CSF - conference semi-final; CQF - conference quarter-final; DF - division final; DSF - division semi-final; F - final; PR - preliminary round; QF - quarter final; SF - semi-final.

Date	City	Series	Score		Scorer	Time	Series Winner
Mar. 26/19	Sea.	F	Mtl. 0	Sea. 0	no scorer	20:00	
Mar. 30/19	Sea.	F	Mtl. 4	Sea. 3	Odie Cleghorn	15:57	
Mar. 20/22	Tor.	F	Tor 2	Van.M. 1	Babe Dye	4:50	Tor.
Mar. 29/23	Van.	F	Ott. 2	Edm.E. 1	Cy Denneny	2:08	Ott.
Mar. 31/27	Mtl.	QF	Mtl. 1	Mtl. M. 0	Howie Morenz	12:05	Mtl.
Apr. 7/27	Bos.	F	Ott. 0	Bos. 0	no scorer	20:00	Ott.
Apr. 11/27	Ott.	F	Bos. 1	Ott. 1	no scorer	20:00	Ott.
Apr. 3/28	Mtl.	QF	Mtl. M. 1	Mtl. 0	Russ Oatman	8:20	Mtl.M.
Apr. 7/28	Mtl.	F	NYR 2	Mtl. M. 1	Frank Boucher	7:05	NYR
Mar. 21/29	NY	QF	NYR 1	NYA 0	Butch Keeling	29:50	NYR
Mar. 26/29	Tor.	SF	NYR 2	Tor. 1	Frank Boucher	2:03	NYR
Mar. 20/30	Mtl.	SF	Bos. 2	Mtl. M. 1	Harry Oliver	45:35	Bos.
Mar. 25/30	Bos.	SF	Mtl. M. 1	Bos. 0	Archie Wilcox	26:27	Bos.
Mar. 26/30	Mtl.	QF	Chi. 2	Mtl. 2	Howie Morenz (Mtl.)	51:43	Mtl.
Mar. 28/30	Mtl.	SF	Mtl. 2	NYR 1	Gus Rivers	68:52	Mtl.
Mar. 24/31	Bos.	SF	Bos. 5	Mtl. 4	Cooney Weiland	18:56	Mtl.
Mar. 26/31	Chi.	QF	Chi. 2	Tor. 1	Stew Adams	19:20	Chi.
Mar. 28/31	Mtl.	SF	Mtl. 4	Bos. 3	Georges Mantha	5:10	Mtl.
Apr. 1/31	Mtl.	SF	Mtl. 3	Bos. 2	Wildor Larochelle	19:00	Mtl.
Apr. 5/31	Chi.	F	Chi. 2	Mtl. 1	Johnny Gottselig	24:50	Mtl.
Apr. 9/31	Mtl.	F	Chi. 3	Mtl. 2	Cy Wentworth	53:50	Mtl.
Mar. 26/32	Mtl.	SF	NYR 4	Mtl. 3	Fred Cook	59:32	NYR
Apr. 2/32	Tor.	SF	Tor. 3	Mtl. M. 2	Bob Gracie	17:59	Tor.
Mar. 25/33	Bos.	SF	Bos. 2	Tor. 1	Marty Barry	14:14	Tor.
Mar. 28/33	Bos.	SF	Tor. 1	Bos. 0	Busher Jackson	15:03	Tor.
Mar. 30/33	Tor.	SF	Bos. 2	Tor. 1	Eddie Shore	4:23	Tor.
Apr. 3/33	Tor.	SF	Tor. 1	Bos. 0	Ken Doraty	104:46	Tor.
Apr. 13/33	Tor.	F	NYR 1	Tor. 0	Bill Cook	7:33	NYR
Mar. 22/34	Tor.	SF	Det. 2	Tor. 1	Herbie Lewis	1:33	Det.
Mar. 25/34	Chi.	QF	Chi. 1	Mtl. 1	Mush March (Chi.)	11:05	Chi.
Apr. 3/34	Det.	F	Chi. 2	Det. 1	Paul Thompson	21:10	Chi.
Apr. 10/34	Chi.	F	Chi. 1	Det. 0	Mush March	30:05	Chi.
Mar. 23/35	Bos.	SF	Bos. 1	Tor. 0	Dit Clapper	33:26	Tor.
Mar. 26/35	Chi.	QF	Mtl. M. 1	Chi. 0	Baldy Northcott	4:02	Mtl.M.
Mar. 30/35	Tor.	SF	Tor. 2	Bos. 1	Pep Kelly	1:36	Tor.
Apr. 4/35	Tor.	F	Mtl. M. 3	Tor. 2	Dave Trottier	5:28	Mtl.M.
Mar. 24/36	Mtl.	SF	Det. 1	Mtl. M. 0	Mud Bruneteau	116:30	Det.
Apr. 9/36	Tor.	F	Tor. 4	Det. 3	Buzz Boll	0:31	Det.
Mar. 25/37	NYR	QF	NYR 2	Tor. 1	Babe Pratt	13:05	NYR
Apr. 1/37	Mtl.	SF	Det. 2	Mtl. 1	Hec Kilrea	51:49	Det.
Mar. 22/38	NY	QF	NYA 2	NYR 1	Johnny Sorrell	21:25	NYA
Mar. 24/38	Tor.	SF	Tor. 1	Bos. 0	George Parsons	21:31	Tor.
Mar. 26/38	Mtl.	QF	Chi. 3	Mtl. 2	Paul Thompson	11:49	Chi.
Mar. 27/38	NY	QF	NYA 3	NYR 2	Lorne Carr	60:40	NYA
Mar. 29/38	Bos.	SF	Tor. 3	Bos. 2	Gordie Drillon	10:04	Tor.
Mar. 31/38	Chi.	SF	Chi. 1	NYA 0	Cully Dahlstrom	33:01	Chi.
Mar. 21/39	NYR	SF	Bos. 2	NYR 1	Mel Hill	59:25	Bos.
Mar. 23/39	Bos.	SF	Bos. 3	NYR 2	Mel Hill	8:24	Bos.
Mar. 26/39	Det.	QF	Det. 1	Mtl. 0	Marty Barry	7:47	Det.
Mar. 30/39	Bos.	SF	NYR 2	Bos. 1	Clint Smith	17:19	Bos.
Apr. 1/39	Tor.	SF	Tor. 5	Det. 4	Gordie Drillon	5:42	Tor.
Apr. 2/39	Bos.	SF	Bos. 2	NYR 1	Mel Hill	48:00	Bos.
Apr. 9/39	Bos.	F	Tor. 3	Bos. 2	Doc Romnes	10:38	Bos.
Mar. 19/40	Det.	QF	Det. 2	NYA 1	Syd Howe	0:25	Det.
Mar. 19/40	Tor.	QF	Tor. 3	Chi. 2	Syl Apps, Sr.	6:35	Tor.
Apr. 2/40	NYR	F	NYR 2	Tor. 1	Alf Pike	15:30	NYR
Apr. 11/40	Tor.	F	NYR 2	Tor. 1	Muzz Patrick	31:43	NYR
Apr. 13/40	Tor.	F	NYR 3	Tor. 2	Bryan Hextall, Sr.	2:07	NYR
Mar. 20/41	Det.	QF	Det. 2	NYR 1	Gus Giesebrecht	12:01	Det.
Mar. 22/41	Mtl.	QF	Mtl. 4	Chi. 3	Charlie Sands	34:04	Chi.
Mar. 29/41	Bos.	SF	Tor. 2	Bos. 1	Pete Langelle	17:31	Bos.
Mar. 30/41	Chi.	SF	Det. 2	Chi. 1	Gus Giesebrecht	9:15	Det.
Mar. 22/42	Chi.	QF	Bos. 2	Chi. 1	Des Smith	6:51	Bos.
Mar. 21/43	Bos.	SF	Bos. 5	Mtl. 4	Don Gallinger	12:30	Bos.
Mar. 23/43	Det.	SF	Tor. 3	Det. 2	Jack McLean	70:18	Det.
Mar. 25/43	Mtl.	SF	Bos. 3	Mtl. 2	Harvey Jackson	3:20	Bos.
Mar. 30/43	Tor.	SF	Det. 3	Tor. 2	Adam Brown	9:21	Det.
Mar. 30/43	Bos.	SF	Bos. 5	Mtl. 4	Ab DeMarco	3:41	Bos.
Apr. 13/44	Mtl.	F	Mtl. 5	Chi. 4	Toe Blake	9:12	Mtl.
Mar. 27/45	Tor.	SF	Tor. 4	Mtl. 3	Gus Bodnar	12:36	Tor.
Mar. 29/45	Det.	SF	Det. 3	Bos. 2	Mud Bruneteau	17:12	Det.
Apr. 21/45	Tor.	F	Det. 1	Tor. 0	Ed Bruneteau	14:16	Tor.
Mar. 28/46	Bos.	SF	Bos. 4	Det. 3	Don Gallinger	9:51	Bos.
Mar. 30/46	Mtl.	F	Mtl. 4	Bos. 3	Maurice Richard	9:08	Mtl.
Apr. 2/46	Mtl.	F	Mtl. 3	Bos. 2	Jim Peters	16:55	Mtl.
Apr. 7/46	Bos.	F	Bos. 3	Mtl. 2	Terry Reardon	15:13	Mtl.
Mar. 26/47	Tor.	SF	Tor. 3	Det. 2	Howie Meeker	3:05	Tor.
Mar. 27/47	Mtl.	SF	Mtl. 2	Bos. 1	Kenny Mosdell	5:38	Mtl.
Apr. 3/47	Mtl.	SF	Mtl. 4	Bos. 3	John Quilty	36:40	Mtl.
Apr. 15/47	Tor.	F	Tor. 2	Mtl. 1	Syl Apps, Sr.	16:36	Tor.
Mar. 24/48	Tor.	SF	Tor. 5	Bos. 4	Nick Metz	17:03	Tor.
Mar. 22/49	Det.	SF	Det. 2	Mtl. 1	Max McNab	44:52	Det.
Mar. 24/49	Det.	SF	Mtl. 4	Det. 3	Gerry Plamondon	2:59	Det.
Mar. 26/49	Tor.	SF	Bos. 5	Tor. 4	Woody Dumart	16:14	Tor.
Apr. 8/49	Det.	F	Tor. 3	Det. 2	Joe Klukay	17:31	Tor.
Apr. 4/50	Tor.	SF	Det. 2	Tor. 1	Leo Reise, Sr.	20:38	Det.
Apr. 4/50	Mtl.	SF	Mtl. 3	NYR 2	Elmer Lach	15:19	NYR
Apr. 9/50	Det.	SF	Det. 1	Tor. 0	Leo Reise	8:39	Det.
Apr. 18/50	Det.	F	NYR 4	Det. 3	Don Raleigh	8:34	Det.
Apr. 20/50	Det.	F	NYR 2	Det. 1	Don Raleigh	1:38	Det.
Apr. 23/50	Det.	F	Det. 4	NYR 3	Pete Babando	28:31	Det.
Mar. 27/51	Det.	SF	Mtl. 3	Det. 2	Maurice Richard	61:09	Mtl.
Mar. 29/51	Det.	SF	Mtl. 1	Det. 0	Maurice Richard	42:20	Mtl.
Mar. 31/51	Tor.	SF	Bos. 1	Tor. 1	no scorer	20:00	Tor.
Apr. 11/51	Tor.	F	Tor. 3	Mtl. 2	Sid Smith	5:51	Tor.
Apr. 14/51	Tor.	F	Mtl. 3	Tor. 2	Maurice Richard	2:55	Tor.
Apr. 17/51	Mtl.	F	Tor. 2	Mtl. 1	Ted Kennedy	4:47	Tor.
Apr. 19/51	Mtl.	F	Tor. 3	Mtl. 2	Harry Watson	5:15	Tor.
Apr. 21/51	Tor.	F	Tor. 3	Mtl. 2	Bill Barilko	2:53	Tor.

Date	City	Series	Score		Scorer	Time	Series Winner
Apr. 6/52	Bos.	SF	Mtl. 3	Bos. 2	Paul Masnick	27:49	Mtl.
Mar. 29/53	Bos.	SF	Bos. 2	Det. 1	Jack McIntyre	12:29	Bos.
Mar. 29/53	Chi.	SF	Chi. 2	Mtl. 1	Al Dewsbury	5:18	Mtl.
Apr. 16/53	Mtl.	F	Mtl. 1	Bos. 0	Elmer Lach	1:22	Mtl.
Apr. 1/54	Det.	SF	Det. 4	Tor. 3	Ted Lindsay	21:01	Det.
Apr. 11/54	Det.	F	Mtl. 1	Det. 0	Kenny Mosdell	5:45	Det.
Apr. 16/54	Det.	F	Det. 2	Mtl. 1	Tony Leswick	4:29	Det.
Mar. 29/55	Bos.	SF	Mtl. 4	Bos. 3	Don Marshall	3:05	Mtl.
Mar. 24/56	Tor.	SF	Det. 5	Tor. 4	Ted Lindsay	4:22	Det.
Mar. 28/57	NYR	SF	NYR 4	Mtl. 3	Andy Hebenton	13:38	Mtl.
Apr. 4/57	Mtl.	SF	Mtl. 4	NYR 3	Maurice Richard	1:11	Mtl.
Mar. 27/58	NYR	SF	Bos. 4	NYR 3	Jerry Toppazzini	4:46	Bos.
Mar. 30/58	Det.	SF	Mtl. 2	Det. 1	André Pronovost	11:52	Mtl.
Apr. 17/58	Mtl.	F	Mtl. 3	Bos. 2	Maurice Richard	5:45	Mtl.
Mar. 28/59	Tor.	SF	Tor. 3	Bos. 2	Gerry Ehman	5:02	Tor.
Mar. 31/59	Tor.	SF	Tor. 3	Bos. 2	Frank Mahovlich	11:21	Tor.
Apr. 14/59	Tor.	F	Tor. 3	Mtl. 2	Dick Duff	10:06	Mtl.
Mar. 26/60	Mtl.	SF	Mtl. 4	Chi. 3	Doug Harvey	8:38	Mtl.
Mar. 27/60	Det.	SF	Tor. 5	Det. 4	Frank Mahovlich	43:00	Tor.
Mar. 29/60	Det.	SF	Det. 2	Tor. 1	Gerry Melnyk	1:54	Tor.
Mar. 22/61	Tor.	SF	Tor. 3	Det. 2	George Armstrong	24:51	Det.
Mar. 26/61	Chi.	SF	Chi. 2	Mtl. 1	Murray Balfour	52:12	Chi.
Apr. 5/62	Tor.	SF	Tor. 3	NYR 2	Red Kelly	24:23	Tor.
Apr. 2/64	Det.	SF	Chi. 3	Det. 2	Murray Balfour	8:21	Det.
Apr. 14/64	Tor.	F	Det. 4	Tor. 3	Larry Jeffrey	7:52	Tor.
Apr. 23/64	Det.	F	Tor. 4	Det. 3	Bob Baun	1:43	Tor.
Apr. 6/65	Tor.	SF	Tor. 3	Mtl. 2	Dave Keon	4:17	Mtl.
Apr. 13/65	Tor.	SF	Mtl. 4	Tor. 3	Claude Provost	16:33	Mtl.
May 5/66	Det.	F	Mtl. 3	Det. 2	Henri Richard	2:20	Mtl.
Apr. 13/67	NYR	SF	Mtl. 2	NYR 1	John Ferguson	6:28	Mtl.
Apr. 25/67	Tor.	F	Tor. 3	Mtl. 2	Bob Pulford	28:26	Tor.
Apr. 10/68	St.L.	QF	St.L. 3	Phi. 2	Larry Keenan	24:10	St.L.
Apr. 16/68	St.L.	QF	Phi. 2	St.L. 1	Don Blackburn	31:18	St.L.
Apr. 16/68	Min.	QF	Min. 4	L.A. 3	Milan Marcetta	9:11	Min.
Apr. 22/68	Min.	SF	Min. 3	St.L. 2	Parker MacDonald	3:41	St.L.
Apr. 27/68	St.L.	SF	St.L. 4	Min. 3	Gary Sabourin	1:32	St.L.
Apr. 28/68	Mtl.	SF	Mtl. 4	Chi. 3	Jacques Lemaire	2:14	Mtl.
Apr. 29/68	St.L.	SF	St.L. 3	Min. 2	Bill McCreary	17:27	St.L.
May 3/68	St.L.	SF	St.L. 2	Min. 1	Ron Schock	22:50	St.L.
May 5/68	St.L.	F	Mtl. 3	St.L. 2	Jacques Lemaire	1:41	Mtl.
May 9/68	Mtl.	F	Mtl. 4	St.L. 3	Bobby Rousseau	1:13	Mtl.
Apr. 2/69	Oak.	QF	L.A. 5	Oak. 4	Ted Irvine	0:19	L.A.
Apr. 10/69	Mtl.	SF	Mtl. 3	Bos. 2	Ralph Backstrom	0:42	Mtl.
Apr. 13/69	Mtl.	SF	Mtl. 4	Bos. 3	Mickey Redmond	4:55	Mtl.
Apr. 24/69	Bos.	SF	Mtl. 2	Bos. 1	Jean Béliveau	31:28	Mtl.
Apr. 12/70	Oak.	QF	Pit. 3	Oak. 2	Michel Briere	8:28	Pit.
May 10/70	Bos.	F	Bos. 4	St.L. 3	Bobby Orr	0:40	Bos.
Apr. 15/71	Tor.	QF	NYR 2	Tor. 1	Bob Nevin	9:07	NYR
Apr. 18/71	Chi.	SF	NYR 2	Chi. 1	Pete Stemkowski	1:37	Chi.
Apr. 27/71	Chi.	SF	Chi. 3	NYR 2	Bobby Hull	6:35	Chi.
Apr. 29/71	NYR	SF	NYR 3	Chi. 2	Pete Stemkowski	41:29	Chi.
May 4/71	Chi.	F	Chi. 2	Mtl. 1	Jim Pappin	21:11	Mtl.
Apr. 6/72	Bos.	QF	Tor. 4	Bos. 3	Jim Harrison	2:58	Bos.
Apr. 6/72	Min.	QF	Min. 6	St.L. 5	Bill Goldsworthy	1:36	St.L.
Apr. 9/72	Pit.	QF	Chi. 6	Pit. 5	Pit Martin	0:12	Chi.
Apr. 16/72	Min.	QF	St.L. 2	Min. 1	Kevin O'Shea	10:07	St.L.
Apr. 1/73	Mtl.	QF	Buf. 3	Mtl. 2	René Robert	9:18	Mtl.
Apr. 10/73	Phi.	QF	Phi. 3	Min. 2	Gary Dornhoefer	8:35	Phi.
Apr. 14/73	Mtl.	SF	Phi. 5	Mtl. 4	Rick MacLeish	2:56	Mtl.
Apr. 17/73	Mtl.	SF	Mtl. 4	Phi. 3	Larry Robinson	6:45	Mtl.
Apr. 14/74	Tor.	QF	Bos. 4	Tor. 3	Ken Hodge	1:27	Bos.
Apr. 14/74	Atl.	QF	Phi. 4	Atl. 3	Dave Schultz	5:40	Phi.
Apr. 16/74	Mtl.	QF	NYR 3	Mtl. 2	Ron Harris	4:07	NYR
Apr. 23/74	Chi.	SF	Chi. 4	Bos. 3	Jim Pappin	3:48	Bos.
Apr. 28/74	NYR	SF	NYR 2	Phi. 1	Rod Gilbert	4:20	Phi.
May 9/74	Bos.	F	Phi. 3	Bos. 2	Bobby Clarke	12:01	Phi.
Apr. 8/75	L.A.	PR	L.A. 3	Tor. 2	Mike Murphy	8:53	Tor.
Apr. 10/75	Tor.	PR	Tor. 3	L.A. 2	Blaine Stoughton	10:19	Tor.
Apr. 10/75	Chi.	PR	Chi. 4	Bos. 3	Ivan Boldirev	7:33	Chi.
Apr. 11/75	NYR	PR	NYI 4	NYR 3	Jean-Paul Parise	0:11	NYI
Apr. 19/75	Tor.	QF	Phi. 4	Tor. 3	André Dupont	1:45	Phi.
Apr. 17/75	Chi.	QF	Chi. 5	Buf. 4	Stan Mikita	2:31	Buf.
Apr. 22/75	Mtl.	QF	Mtl. 5	Van. 4	Guy Lafleur	17:06	Mtl.
May 1/75	Phi.	SF	Phi. 5	NYI 4	Bobby Clarke	2:56	Phi.
May 7/75	NYI	SF	NYI 4	Phi. 3	Jude Drouin	1:53	Phi.
Apr. 27/75	Buf.	SF	Buf. 6	Mtl. 5	Danny Gare	4:42	Buf.
May 6/75	Buf.	SF	Buf. 5	Mtl. 4	René Robert	5:56	Buf.
May 20/75	Buf.	F	Buf. 5	Phi. 4	René Robert	18:29	Phi.
Apr. 8/76	Buf.	PR	Buf. 3	St.L. 2	Danny Gare	11:43	Buf.
Apr. 9/76	Buf.	PR	Buf. 2	St.L. 1	Don Luce	14:27	Buf.
Apr. 13/76	Bos.	QF	L.A. 3	Bos. 2	Butch Goring	0:27	Bos.
Apr. 13/76	Buf.	QF	Buf. 3	NYI 2	Danny Gare	14:04	NYI
Apr. 22/76	L.A.	QF	L.A. 4	Bos. 3	Butch Goring	18:28	Bos.
Apr. 29/76	Phi.	SF	Phi. 2	Bos. 1	Reggie Leach	13:38	Phi.
Apr. 15/77	Tor.	QF	Phi. 4	Tor. 3	Rick MacLeish	2:55	Phi.
Apr. 17/77	Tor.	QF	Phi. 6	Tor. 5	Reggie Leach	19:10	Phi.
Apr. 24/77	Phi.	SF	Bos. 4	Phi. 3	Rick Middleton	2:57	Bos.
Apr. 26/77	Phi.	SF	Bos. 5	Phi. 4	Terry O'Reilly	30:07	Bos.
May 3/77	Mtl.	SF	NYI 4	Mtl. 3	Billy Harris	3:58	Mtl.
May 14/77	Bos.	F	Mtl. 2	Bos. 1	Jacques Lemaire	4:32	Mtl.
Apr. 11/78	Phi.	PR	Phi. 3	Col. 2	Mel Bridgman	0:23	Phi.
Apr. 13/78	NYR	PR	NYR 4	Buf. 3	Don Murdoch	1:37	Buf.
Apr. 19/78	Bos.	QF	Bos. 4	Chi. 3	Terry O'Reilly	1:50	Bos.
Apr. 19/78	NYI	QF	NYI 3	Tor. 2	Mike Bossy	2:50	Tor.
Apr. 21/78	Chi.	QF	Bos. 4	Chi. 3	Peter McNab	10:17	Bos.
Apr. 25/78	NYI	QF	NYI 2	Tor. 1	Bob Nystrom	8:02	Tor.
Apr. 29/78	NYI	QF	Tor. 2	NYI 1	Lanny McDonald	4:13	Tor.
May 2/78	Bos.	SF	Bos. 3	Phi. 2	Rick Middleton	1:43	Bos.
May 16/78	Mtl.	F	Mtl. 3	Bos. 2	Guy Lafleur	13:09	Mtl.
May 21/78	Bos.	F	Bos. 4	Mtl. 3	Bobby Schmautz	6:22	Mtl.
Apr. 12/79	L.A.	PR	NYR 2	L.A. 1	Phil Esposito	6:11	NYR
Apr. 14/79	Buf.	PR	Pit. 4	Buf. 3	George Ferguson	0:47	Pit.
Apr. 16/79	Phi.	QF	Phi. 3	NYR 2	Ken Linseman	0:44	NYR
Apr. 18/79	NYI	QF	NYI 1	Chi. 0	Mike Bossy	2:31	NYI
Apr. 21/79	Tor.	QF	Mtl. 4	Tor. 3	Cam Connor	25:25	Mtl.
Apr. 22/79	Tor.	QF	Mtl. 5	Tor. 4	Larry Robinson	4:14	Mtl.
Apr. 28/79	NYI	SF	NYI 4	NYR 3	Denis Potvin	8:02	NYR
May 3/79	NYR	SF	NYI 3	NYR 2	Bob Nystrom	3:40	NYR
May 3/79	Bos.	SF	Bos. 4	Mtl. 3	Jean Ratelle	3:46	Mtl.
May 10/79	Mtl.	SF	Mtl. 5	Bos. 4	Yvon Lambert	9:33	Mtl.
May 19/79	NYR	F	Mtl. 4	NYR 3	Serge Savard	7:25	Mtl.
Apr. 8/80	NYR	PR	NYR 2	Atl. 1	Steve Vickers	0:33	NYR
Apr. 8/80	Phi.	PR	Phi. 4	Edm. 3	Bobby Clarke	8:06	Phi.
Apr. 8/80	Chi.	PR	Chi. 3	St.L. 2	Doug Lecuyer	12:34	Chi.
Apr. 11/80	Hfd.	PR	Mtl. 4	Hfd. 3	Yvon Lambert	0:29	Mtl.
Apr. 11/80	Tor.	PR	Min. 4	Tor. 3	Al MacAdam	0:32	Min.
Apr. 11/80	L.A.	PR	NYI 4	L.A. 3	Ken Morrow	6:55	NYI
Apr. 11/80	Edm.	PR	Phi. 3	Edm. 2	Ken Linseman	23:56	Phi.
Apr. 16/80	Bos.	QF	NYI 2	Bos. 1	Clark Gillies	1:02	NYI
Apr. 17/80	Bos.	QF	NYI 5	Bos. 4	Bob Bourne	1:24	NYI
Apr. 21/80	NYI	QF	Bos. 4	NYI 3	Terry O'Reilly	17:13	NYI
May 1/80	Buf.	SF	NYI 2	Buf. 1	Bob Nystrom	21:20	NYI
May 13/80	Phi.	F	NYI 4	Phi. 3	Denis Potvin	4:07	NYI
May 24/80	NYI	F	NYI 5	Phi. 4	Bob Nystrom	7:11	NYI
Apr. 8/81	Buf.	PR	Buf. 3	Van. 2	Alan Haworth	5:00	Buf.
Apr. 8/81	Bos.	PR	Min. 5	Bos. 4	Steve Payne	3:34	Min.
Apr. 11/81	Chi.	PR	Cgy. 5	Chi. 4	Willi Plett	35:17	Cgy.
Apr. 12/81	Que.	PR	Que. 4	Phi. 3	Dale Hunter	0:37	Phi.
Apr. 14/81	St.L.	PR	St.L. 4	Pit. 3	Mike Crombeen	25:16	St.L.
Apr. 16/81	Buf.	QF	Min. 4	Buf. 3	Steve Payne	0:22	Min.
Apr. 20/81	Min.	QF	Buf. 5	Min. 4	Craig Ramsay	16:32	Min.
Apr. 20/81	Edm.	QF	NYI 5	Edm. 4	Ken Morrow	5:41	NYI
Apr. 7/82	Min.	DSF	Chi. 3	Min. 2	Greg Fox	3:34	Chi.
Apr. 8/82	Edm.	DSF	Edm. 3	L.A. 2	Wayne Gretzky	6:20	L.A.
Apr. 8/82	Van.	DSF	Van. 2	Cgy. 1	Dave Williams	14:20	Van.
Apr. 10/82	Pit.	DSF	Pit. 2	NYI 1	Rick Kehoe	4:14	NYI
Apr. 10/82	L.A.	DSF	L.A. 6	Edm. 5	Daryl Evans	2:35	L.A.
Apr. 13/82	Mtl.	DSF	Que. 3	Mtl. 2	Dale Hunter	0:22	Que.
Apr. 13/82	NYI	DSF	NYI 4	Pit. 3	John Tonelli	6:19	NYI
Apr. 16/82	Van.	DF	L.A. 3	Van. 2	Steve Bozek	4:33	Van.
Apr. 18/82	Que.	DF	Que. 3	Bos. 2	Wilf Paiement	11:44	Que.
Apr. 18/82	NYR	DF	NYI 4	NYR 3	Bryan Trottier	3:00	NYI
Apr. 18/82	L.A.	DF	Van. 4	L.A. 3	Colin Campbell	1:23	Van.
Apr. 21/82	St.L.	DF	St.L. 3	Chi. 2	Bernie Federko	3:28	Chi.
Apr. 23/82	Que.	DF	Bos. 6	Que. 5	Peter McNab	10:54	Que.
Apr. 27/82	Chi.	CF	Van. 2	Chi. 1	Jim Nill	28:58	Van.
May 1/82	Que.	CF	NYI 5	Que. 4	Wayne Merrick	16:52	NYI
May 8/82	NYI	F	NYI 6	Van. 5	Mike Bossy	19:58	NYI
Apr. 5/83	Bos.	DSF	Bos. 4	Que. 3	Barry Pederson	1:46	Bos.
Apr. 6/83	Cgy.	DSF	Cgy. 4	Van. 3	Eddy Beers	12:27	Cgy.
Apr. 7/83	Min.	DSF	Min. 5	Tor. 4	Bobby Smith	5:03	Min.
Apr. 10/83	Tor.	DSF	Min. 5	Tor. 4	Dino Ciccarelli	8:05	Min.
Apr. 10/83	Van.	DSF	Cgy. 4	Van. 3	Greg Meredith	1:06	Cgy.
Apr. 18/83	Min.	DF	Chi. 4	Min. 3	Rich Preston	10:34	Chi.
Apr. 24/83	Bos.	DF	Bos. 3	Buf. 2	Brad Park	1:52	Bos.
Apr. 5/84	Edm.	DSF	Edm. 5	Wpg. 4	Randy Gregg	0:21	Edm.
Apr. 7/84	Det.	DSF	St.L. 4	Det. 3	Mark Reeds	37:07	St.L.
Apr. 8/84	Det.	DSF	St.L. 3	Det. 2	Jorgen Pettersson	2:42	St.L.
Apr. 10/84	NYI	DSF	NYI 3	NYR 2	Ken Morrow	8:56	NYI
Apr. 13/84	Min.	DF	St.L. 4	Min. 3	Doug Gilmour	16:16	Min.
Apr. 13/84	Edm.	DF	Cgy. 6	Edm. 5	Carey Wilson	3:42	Edm.
Apr. 13/84	NYI	DF	NYI 5	Wsh. 4	Anders Kallur	7:35	NYI
Apr. 16/84	Mtl.	DF	Que. 4	Mtl. 3	Bo Berglund	3:00	Mtl.
Apr. 20/84	Cgy.	DF	Cgy. 5	Edm. 4	Lanny McDonald	1:04	Edm.
Apr. 22/84	Min.	DF	Min. 4	St.L. 3	Steve Payne	6:00	Min.
Apr. 10/85	Phi.	DSF	Phi. 5	NYR 4	Mark Howe	8:01	Phi.
Apr. 10/85	Wsh.	DSF	Wsh. 4	NYI 3	Alan Haworth	2:28	NYI
Apr. 10/85	Edm.	DSF	Edm. 3	L.A. 2	Lee Fogolin	3:01	Edm.
Apr. 10/85	Wpg.	DSF	Wpg. 5	Cgy. 4	Brian Mullen	7:56	Wpg.
Apr. 11/85	Wsh.	DSF	Wsh. 2	NYI 1	Mike Gartner	21:23	NYI
Apr. 13/85	L.A.	DSF	Edm. 4	L.A. 3	Glenn Anderson	0:46	Edm.
Apr. 18/85	Mtl.	DF	Que. 2	Mtl. 1	Mark Kumpel	12:23	Que.

Date	City	Series	Score		Scorer	Time	Series Winner
Apr. 23/85	Que.	DF	Que. 7	Mtl. 6	Dale Hunter	18:36	Que.
May 2/85	Mtl.	DF	Que. 3	Mtl. 2	Peter Stastny	2:22	Que.
Apr. 25/85	Min.	DF	Chi. 7	Min. 6	Darryl Sutter	21:57	Chi.
Apr. 28/85	Chi.	DF	Min. 5	Chi. 4	Dennis Maruk	1:14	Chi.
Apr. 30/85	Min.	DF	Chi. 6	Min. 5	Darryl Sutter	15:41	Chi.
May 5/85	Que.	CF	Que. 2	Phi. 1	Peter Stastny	6:20	Phi.
Apr. 9/86	Que.	DSF	Hfd. 3	Que. 2	Sylvain Turgeon	2:36	Hfd.
Apr. 12/86	Wpg.	DSF	Cgy. 4	Wpg. 3	Lanny McDonald	8:25	Cgy.
Apr. 17/86	Wsh.	DF	NYR 4	Wsh. 3	Brian MacLellan	1:16	NYR
Apr. 20/86	Edm.	DF	Edm. 6	Cgy. 5	Glenn Anderson	1:04	Cgy.
Apr. 23/86	Hfd.	DF	Hfd. 2	Mtl. 1	Kevin Dineen	1:07	Mtl.
Apr. 23/86	NYR	DF	NYR 6	Wsh. 5	Bob Brooke	2:40	NYR
Apr. 26/86	St L.	DF	St L. 4	Tor. 3	Mark Reeds	7:11	StL.
Apr. 29/86	Mtl.	DF	Mtl. 2	Hfd. 1	Claude Lemieux	5:55	Mtl.
May 5/86	NYR	CF	Mtl. 4	NYR 3	Claude Lemieux	9:41	Mtl.
May 12/86	St L.	CF	St L. 6	Cgy. 5	Doug Wickenheiser	7:30	Cgy.
May 18/86	Cgy.	F	Mtl. 3	Cgy. 2	Brian Skrudland	0:09	Mtl.
Apr. 8/87	Hfd.	DSF	Hfd. 3	Que. 2	Paul MacDermid	2:20	Que.
Apr. 9/87	Mtl.	DSF	Mtl. 4	Bos. 3	Mats Naslund	2:38	Mtl.
Apr. 9/87	St.L.	DSF	Tor. 3	St.L. 2	Rick Lanz	10:17	Tor.
Apr. 11/87	Wpg.	DSF	Cgy. 3	Wpg. 2	Mike Bullard	3:53	Wpg.
Apr. 11/87	Chi.	DSF	Det. 4	Chi. 3	Shawn Burr	4:51	Det.
Apr. 16/87	Que.	DSF	Que. 5	Hfd. 4	Peter Stastny	6:05	Que.
Apr. 18/87	Wsh.	DSF	NYI 3	Wsh. 2	Pat LaFontaine	68:47	NYI
Apr. 21/87	Edm.	DF	Edm. 3	Wpg. 2	Glenn Anderson	0:36	Edm.
Apr. 26/87	Que.	DF	Mtl. 3	Que. 2	Mats Naslund	5:30	Mtl.
Apr. 27/87	Tor.	DF	Tor. 3	Det. 2	Mike Allison	9:31	Det.
May 4/87	Phi.	CF	Phi. 4	Mtl. 3	Ilkka Sinislao	9:11	Phi.
May 20/87	Edm.	F	Edm. 3	Phi. 2	Jari Kurri	6:50	Edm.
Apr. 6/88	NYI	DSF	NYI 4	N.J. 3	Pat LaFontaine	6:11	N.J.
Apr. 10/88	Phi.	DSF	Phi. 5	Wsh. 4	Murray Craven	1:18	Wsh.
Apr. 10/88	N.J.	DSF	NYI 5	N.J. 4	Brent Sutter	15:07	N.J.
Apr. 10/88	Buf.	DSF	Buf. 6	Bos. 5	John Tucker	5:32	Bos.
Apr. 12/88	Det.	DSF	Tor. 6	Det. 5	Ed Olczyk	0:34	Det.
Apr. 16/88	Wsh.	DSF	Wsh. 5	Phi. 4	Dale Hunter	5:57	Wsh.
Apr. 21/88	Cgy.	DF	Edm. 5	Cgy. 4	Wayne Gretzky	7:54	Edm.
May 4/88	Bos.	CF	N.J. 3	Bos. 2	Doug Brown	17:46	Bos.
May 9/88	Det.	CF	Edm. 4	Det. 3	Jari Kurri	11:02	Edm.
Apr. 5/89	St.L.	DSF	St.L. 4	Min. 3	Brett Hull	11:55	St.L.
Apr. 5/89	Cgy.	DSF	Van. 4	Cgy. 3	Paul Reinhart	2:47	Cgy.
Apr. 6/89	St.L.	DSF	St.L. 4	Min. 3	Rick Meagher	5:30	St.L.
Apr. 6/89	Det.	DSF	Chi. 5	Det. 4	Duane Sutter	14:36	Chi.
Apr. 8/89	Hfd.	DSF	Mtl. 5	Hfd. 4	Stephane Richer	5:01	Mtl.
Apr. 8/89	Phi.	DSF	Wsh. 4	Phi. 3	Kelly Miller	0:51	Phi.
Apr. 9/89	Hfd.	DSF	Mtl. 4	Hfd. 3	Russ Courtnall	15:12	Mtl.
Apr. 15/89	Cgy.	DSF	Cgy. 4	Van. 3	Joel Otto	19:21	Cgy.
Apr. 18/89	Cgy.	DF	Cgy. 4	L.A. 3	Doug Gilmour	7:47	Cgy.
Apr. 19/89	Mtl.	DF	Mtl. 3	Bos. 2	Bobby Smith	12:24	Mtl.
Apr. 20/89	St.L.	DF	St.L. 5	Chi. 4	Tony Hrkac	33:49	Chi.
Apr. 21/89	Phi.	DF	Pit. 4	Phi. 3	Phil Bourque	12:08	Phi.
May 8/89	Chi.	CF	Cgy. 2	Chi. 1	Al MacInnis	15:05	Cgy.
May 9/89	Mtl.	CF	Phi. 2	Mtl. 1	Dave Poulin	5:02	Mtl.
May 19/89	Mtl.	F	Mtl. 4	Cgy. 3	Ryan Walter	38:08	Cgy.
Apr. 5/90	N.J.	DSF	Wsh. 5	N.J. 4	Dino Ciccarelli	5:34	Wsh.
Apr. 6/90	Edm.	DSF	Edm. 3	Wpg. 2	Mark Lamb	4:21	Edm.
Apr. 8/90	Tor.	DSF	St.L. 6	Tor. 5	Sergio Momesso	6:04	St.L.
Apr. 8/90	L.A.	DSF	L.A. 2	Cgy. 1	Tony Granato	8:37	L.A.
Apr. 9/90	Mtl.	DSF	Mtl. 2	Buf. 1	Brian Skrudland	12:35	Mtl.
Apr. 9/90	NYI	DSF	NYI 4	NYR 3	Brent Sutter	20:59	NYR
Apr. 10/90	Wpg.	DSF	Wpg. 4	Edm. 3	Dave Ellett	21:08	Edm.
Apr. 14/90	L.A.	DSF	L.A. 4	Cgy. 3	Mike Krushelnyski	23:14	L.A.
Apr. 15/90	Hfd.	DSF	Hfd. 3	Bos. 2	Kevin Dineen	12:30	Bos.
Apr. 21/90	Bos.	DF	Bos. 5	Mtl. 4	Garry Galley	3:42	Bos.
Apr. 24/90	L.A.	DF	Edm. 6	L.A. 5	Joe Murphy	4:42	Edm.
Apr. 25/90	Wsh.	DF	Wsh. 4	NYR 3	Rod Langway	0:34	Wsh.
Apr. 27/90	NYR	DF	Wsh. 2	NYR 1	John Druce	6:48	Wsh.
May 15/90	Bos.	F	Edm. 3	Bos. 2	Petr Klima	55:13	Edm.
Apr. 4/91	Chi.	DSF	Min. 4	Chi. 3	Brian Propp	4:14	Min.
Apr. 5/91	Pit.	DSF	Pit. 5	N.J. 4	Jaromir Jagr	8:52	Pit.
Apr. 6/91	L.A.	DSF	L.A. 3	Van. 2	Wayne Gretzky	11:08	L.A.
Apr. 8/91	Van.	DSF	Van. 2	L.A. 1	Cliff Ronning	3:12	L.A.
Apr. 11/91	NYR	DSF	Wsh. 5	NYR 4	Dino Ciccarelli	6:44	Wsh.
Apr. 11/91	Mtl.	DSF	Mtl. 4	Buf. 3	Russ Courtnall	5:56	Mtl.
Apr. 14/91	Edm.	DSF	Cgy. 2	Edm. 1	Theoren Fleury	4:40	Edm.
Apr. 16/91	Cgy.	DSF	Edm. 5	Cgy. 4	Esa Tikkanen	6:58	Edm.
Apr. 18/91	L.A.	DF	L.A. 4	Edm. 3	Luc Robitaille	2:13	Edm.
Apr. 19/91	Bos.	DF	Mtl. 4	Bos. 3	Stephane Richer	0:27	Bos.
Apr. 19/91	Pit.	DF	Pit. 7	Wsh. 6	Kevin Stevens	8:10	Pit.
Apr. 20/91	L.A.	DF	Edm. 4	L.A. 3	Petr Klima	24:48	Edm.
Apr. 22/91	Edm.	DF	Edm. 4	L.A. 3	Esa Tikkanen	20:48	Edm.
Apr. 27/91	Mtl.	DF	Mtl. 3	Bos. 2	Shayne Corson	17:47	Bos.
Apr. 28/91	Edm.	DF	Edm. 4	L.A. 3	Craig MacTavish	16:57	Edm.
May 3/91	Bos.	CF	Bos. 5	Pit. 4	Vladimir Ruzicka	8:14	Pit.
Apr. 21/92	Bos.	DSF	Bos. 3	Buf. 2	Adam Oates	11:14	Bos.
Apr. 22/92	Min.	DSF	Det. 5	Min. 4	Yves Racine	1:15	Det.
Apr. 22/92	St.L.	DSF	St.L. 5	Chi. 4	Brett Hull	23:33	Chi.

Date	City	Series	Score		Scorer	Time	Series Winner
Apr. 25/92	Buf.	DSF	Bos. 5	Buf. 4	Ted Donato	2:08	Bos.
Apr. 28/92	Min.	DSF	Det. 1	Min. 0	Sergei Fedorov	16:13	Det.
Apr. 29/92	Hfd.	DSF	Hfd. 2	Mtl. 1	Yvon Corriveau	0:24	Mtl.
May 1/92	Mtl.	DSF	Mtl. 3	Hfd. 2	Russ Courtnall	25:26	Mtl.
May 3/92	Van.	DF	Edm. 4	Van. 3	Joe Murphy	8:36	Edm.
May 5/92	Mtl.	DF	Bos. 3	Mtl. 2	Peter Douris	3:12	Bos.
May 7/92	Pit.	DF	NYR 6	Pit. 5	Kris King	1:29	Pit.
May 9/92	Pit.	DF	Pit. 5	NYR 4	Ron Francis	2:47	Pit.
May 17/92	Pit.	CF	Pit. 4	Bos. 3	Jaromir Jagr	9:44	Pit.
May 20/92	Edm.	CF	Chi. 4	Edm. 3	Jeremy Roenick	2:45	Chi.
Apr. 18/93	Bos.	DSF	Buf. 5	Bos. 4	Bob Sweeney	11:03	Buf.
Apr. 18/93	Que.	DSF	Que. 3	Mtl. 2	Scott Young	16:49	Mtl.
Apr. 20/93	Wsh.	DSF	NYI 5	Wsh. 4	Brian Mullen	34:50	NYI
Apr. 22/93	Mtl.	DSF	Mtl. 2	Que. 1	Vincent Damphousse	10:30	Mtl.
Apr. 22/93	Buf.	DSF	Buf. 4	Bos. 3	Yuri Khmylev	1:05	Buf.
Apr. 22/93	NYI	DSF	NYI 4	Wsh. 3	Ray Ferraro	4:46	NYI
Apr. 24/93	Buf.	DSF	Buf. 6	Bos. 5	Brad May	4:48	Buf.
Apr. 24/93	NYI	DSF	NYI 4	Wsh. 3	Ray Ferraro	25:40	NYI
Apr. 25/93	St.L.	DSF	St.L. 4	Chi. 3	Craig Janney	10:43	St.L.
Apr. 26/93	Que.	DSF	Mtl. 5	Que. 4	Kirk Muller	8:17	Mtl.
Apr. 27/93	Det.	DSF	Tor. 5	Det. 4	Mike Foligno	2:05	Tor.
Apr. 27/93	Van.	DSF	Wpg. 4	Van. 3	Teemu Selanne	6:18	Van.
Apr. 29/93	Wpg.	DSF	Van. 4	Wpg. 3	Greg Adams	4:30	Van.
May 1/93	Det.	DSF	Tor. 4	Det. 3	Nik. Borschevsky	2:35	Tor.
May 3/93	Tor.	DF	Tor. 2	St.L. 1	Doug Gilmour	23:16	Tor.
May 4/93	Mtl.	DF	Mtl. 4	Buf. 3	Guy Carbonneau	2:50	Mtl.
May 5/93	Tor.	DF	St.L. 2	Tor. 1	Jeff Brown	23:03	Tor.
May 6/93	Buf.	DF	Mtl. 4	Buf. 3	Gilbert Dionne	8:28	Mtl.
May 8/93	Buf.	DF	Mtl. 4	Buf. 3	Kirk Muller	11:37	Mtl.
May 11/93	Van.	DF	L.A. 4	Van. 3	Gary Shuchuk	26:31	L.A.
May 14/93	Pit.	DF	NYI 4	Pit. 3	Dave Volek	5:16	NYI
May 18/93	Mtl.	CF	Mtl. 4	NYI 3	Stephan Lebeau	26:21	Mtl.
May 20/93	NYI	CF	Mtl. 2	NYI 1	Guy Carbonneau	12:34	Mtl.
May 25/93	Tor.	CF	Tor. 3	L.A. 2	Glenn Anderson	19:20	L.A.
May 27/93	L.A.	CF	L.A. 5	Tor. 4	Wayne Gretzky	1:41	L.A.
Jun. 3/93	Mtl.	F	Mtl. 3	L.A. 2	Eric Desjardins	0:51	Mtl.
Jun. 5/93	L.A.	F	Mtl. 4	L.A. 3	John LeClair	0:34	Mtl.
Jun. 7/93	L.A.	F	Mtl. 3	L.A. 2	John LeClair	14:37	Mtl.
Apr. 20/94	Tor.	CQF	Tor. 1	Chi. 0	Todd Gill	2:15	Tor.
Apr. 22/94	St.L.	CQF	Dal. 5	St.L. 4	Paul Cavallini	8:34	Dal.
Apr. 24/94	Chi.	CQF	Chi. 4	Tor. 3	Jeremy Roenick	1:23	Tor.
Apr. 25/94	Bos.	CQF	Mtl. 2	Bos. 1	Kirk Muller	17:18	Bos.
Apr. 26/94	Cgy.	CQF	Van. 2	Cgy. 1	Geoff Courtnall	7:15	Van.
Apr. 27/94	Buf.	CQF	Buf. 1	N.J. 0	Dave Hannan	65:43	N.J.
Apr. 28/94	Van.	CQF	Van. 3	Cgy. 2	Trevor Linden	16:43	Van.
Apr. 30/94	Cgy.	CQF	Van. 4	Cgy. 3	Pavel Bure	22:20	Van.
May 3/94	N.J.	CSF	Bos. 6	N.J. 5	Don Sweeney	9:08	N.J.
May 7/94	Bos.	CSF	N.J. 5	Bos. 4	Stephane Richer	14:19	N.J.
May 8/94	Van.	CSF	Van. 2	Dal. 1	Sergio Momesso	11:01	Van.
May 12/94	Tor.	CSF	Tor. 3	S.J. 2	Mike Gartner	8:53	Tor.
May 15/94	NYR	CF	N.J. 4	NYR 3	Stephane Richer	35:23	NYR
May 16/94	Tor.	CF	Tor. 3	Van. 2	Peter Zezel	16:55	Van.
May 19/94	N.J.	CF	NYR 3	N.J. 2	Stephane Matteau	26:13	NYR
May 24/94	Van.	CF	Van. 4	Tor. 3	Greg Adams	20:14	Van.
May 27/94	NYR	CF	NYR 2	N.J. 1	Stephane Matteau	24:24	NYR
May 31/94	NYR	F	Van. 3	NYR 2	Greg Adams	19:26	NYR
May 7/95	Phi.	CQF	Phi. 4	Buf. 3	Karl Dykhuis	10:06	Phi.
May 9/95	Cgy.	CQF	S.J. 5	Cgy. 4	Ulf Dahlen	12:21	S.J.
May 12/95	NYR	CQF	NYR 3	Que. 2	Steve Larmer	8:09	NYR
May 12/95	N.J.	CQF	N.J. 1	Bos. 0	Randy McKay	8:51	N.J.
May 14/95	Pit.	CQF	Pit. 6	Wsh. 5	Luc Robitaille	4:30	Pit.
May 15/95	St.L.	CQF	Van. 6	St.L. 5	Cliff Ronning	1:48	Van.
May 17/95	Tor.	CQF	Tor. 5	Chi. 4	Randy Wood	10:00	Chi.
May 19/95	Cgy.	CQF	S.J. 5	Cgy. 4	Ray Whitney	21:54	S.J.
May 21/95	Phi.	CSF	Phi. 5	NYR 4	Eric Desjardins	7:03	Phi.
May 21/95	Chi.	CSF	Chi. 2	Van. 1	Joe Murphy	9:04	Chi.
May 22/95	Phi.	CSF	Phi. 4	NYR 3	Kevin Haller	0:25	Phi.
May 25/95	Van.	CSF	Chi. 3	Van. 2	Chris Chelios	6:22	Chi.
May 26/95	N.J.	CSF	N.J. 2	Pit. 1	Neal Broten	18:36	N.J.
May 27/95	Van.	CSF	Chi. 4	Van. 3	Chris Chelios	5:35	Chi.
Jun. 1/95	Det.	CF	Det. 2	Chi. 1	Nicklas Lidstrom	1:01	Det.
Jun. 6/95	Chi.	CF	Det. 4	Chi. 3	Vladimir Konstantinov	29:25	Det.
Jun. 7/95	N.J.	CF	Phi. 3	N.J. 2	Eric Lindros	4:19	N.J.
Jun. 11/95	Det.	CF	Det. 2	Chi. 1	Vyacheslav Kozlov	22:25	Det.
Apr. 16/96	NYR	CQF	Mtl. 3	NYR 2	Vincent Damphousse	5:04	NYR
Apr. 18/96	Tor.	CQF	Tor. 5	St.L. 4	Mats Sundin	4:02	St.L.
Apr. 18/96	Phi.	CQF	T.B. 2	Phi. 1	Brian Bellows	9:05	Phi.
Apr. 21/96	St.L.	CQF	St.L. 3	Tor. 2	Glenn Anderson	1:24	St.L.
Apr. 21/96	T.B.	CQF	T.B. 5	Phi. 4	Alexander Selivanov	2:04	Phi.
Apr. 23/96	Cgy.	CQF	Chi. 2	Cgy. 1	Joe Murphy	50:02	Chi.
Apr. 24/96	Wsh.	CQF	Pit. 3	Wsh. 2	Petr Nedved	79:15	Pit.
Apr. 25/96	Col.	CQF	Col. 5	Van. 4	Joe Sakic	0:51	Col.
Apr. 25/96	Tor.	CQF	Tor. 5	St.L. 4	Mike Gartner	7:31	St.L.
May 2/96	Col.	CSF	Chi. 3	Col. 2	Jeremy Roenick	6:29	Col.
May 6/96	Chi.	CSF	Chi. 4	Col. 3	Sergei Krivokrasov	0:46	Col.
May 8/96	St.L.	CSF	St.L. 5	Det. 4	Igor Kravchuk	3:23	Det.

Date	City	Series	Score		Scorer	Time	Series Winner
May 8/96	Chi.	CSF	Col. 3	Chi. 2	Joe Sakic	44:33	Col.
May 9/96	Fla.	CSF	Fla. 4	Phi. 3	Dave Lowry	4:06	Fla.
May 12/96	Phi.	CSF	Fla. 2	Phi. 1	Mike Hough	28:05	Fla.
May 13/96	Chi.	CSF	Col. 4	Chi. 3	Sandis Ozolinsh	25:18	Col.
May 16/96	Det.	CSF	Det. 1	St.L. 0	Steve Yzerman	21:15	Det.
May 19/96	Det.	CF	Col. 3	Det. 2	Mike Keane	17:31	Col.
Jun. 10/96	Fla.	F	Col. 1	Fla. 0	Uwe Krupp	44:31	Col.
Apr. 20/97	Chi.	CQF	Chi. 4	Col. 3	Sergei Krivokrasov	31:03	Col.
Apr. 20/97	Edm.	CQF	Edm. 4	Dal. 3	Kelly Buchberger	9:15	Edm.
Apr. 22/97	NYR	CQF	NYR 4	Fla. 3	Esa Tikkanen	16:29	NYR
Apr. 23/97	Ott.	CQF	Ott. 1	Buf. 0	Daniel Alfredsson	2:34	Buf.
Apr. 24/97	Mtl.	CQF	Mtl. 4	N.J. 3	Patrice Brisebois	47:37	N.J.
Apr. 25/97	Fla.	CQF	NYR 3	Fla. 2	Esa Tikkanen	12:02	NYR
Apr. 25/97	Dal.	CQF	Edm. 1	Dal. 0	Ryan Smyth	20:22	Edm.
Apr. 27/97	Phx.	CQF	Ana. 3	Phx. 2	Paul Kariya	7:29	Ana.
Apr. 29/97	Buf.	CQF	Buf. 3	Ott. 2	Derek Plante	5:24	Buf.
Apr. 29/97	Dal.	CQF	Edm. 4	Dal. 3	Todd Marchant	12:26	Edm.
May 2/97	Det.	CSF	Det. 2	Ana. 1	Martin Lapointe	0:59	Det.
May 4/97	Det.	CSF	Det. 3	Ana. 2	Vyacheslav Kozlov	41:31	Det.
May 8/97	Ana.	CSF	Det. 3	Ana. 2	Brendan Shanahan	37:03	Det.
May 9/97	Phi.	CSF	Buf. 5	Phi. 4	Ed Ronan	6:24	Phi.
May 9/97	Edm.	CSF	Col. 3	Edm. 2	Claude Lemieux	8:35	Col.
May 11/97	N.J.	CSF	NYR 2	N.J. 1	Adam Graves	14:08	NYR
Apr. 22/98	N.J.	CQF	OTT. 2	N.J. 1	Bruce Gardiner	5:58	Ott.
Apr. 23/98	Pit.	CQF	Mtl. 3	Pit. 2	Benoit Brunet	18:43	Mtl.
Apr. 24/98	Wsh.	CQF	Bos. 4	Wsh. 3	Darren Van Impe	20:54	Wsh.
Apr. 26/98	Ott.	CQF	Ott. 2	N.J. 1	Alexei Yashin	2:47	Ott.
Apr. 26/98	Bos.	CQF	Wsh. 3	Bos. 2	Joe Juneau	26:31	Wsh.
Apr. 26/98	Edm.	CQF	Col. 5	Edm. 4	Joe Sakic	15:25	Edm.
Apr. 28/98	S.J.	CQF	S.J. 1	Dal. 0	Andrei Zyuzin	6:31	Dal.
May 1/98	Phi.	CQF	Buf. 3	Phi. 2	Michal Grosek	5:40	Buf.
May 2/98	S.J.	CQF	Dal. 3	S.J. 2	Mike Keane	3:43	Dal.
May 3/98	Bos.	CQF	Wsh. 3	Bos. 2	Brian Bellows	15:24	Wsh.
May 3/98	Buf.	CSF	Buf. 3	Mtl. 2	Geoff Sanderson	2:37	Buf.
May 11/98	Edm.	CSF	Dal. 1	Edm. 0	Benoit Hogue	13:07	Dal.
May 12/98	Mtl.	CSF	Buf. 5	Mtl. 4	Michael Peca	21:24	Buf.
May 12/98	St.L.	CSF	Det. 3	St.L. 2	Brendan Shanahan	31:12	Det.
May 25/98	Wsh.	CF	Wsh. 3	Buf. 2	Todd Krygier	3:01	Wsh.
May 28/98	Buf.	CF	Wsh. 4	Buf. 3	Peter Bondra	9:37	Wsh.
Jun. 3/98	Dal.	CF	Dal. 3	Det. 2	Jamie Langenbrunner	0:46	Det.
Jun. 4/98	Buf.	CF	Wsh. 3	Buf. 2	Joe Juneau	6:24	Wsh.
Jun. 11/98	Det.	F	Det. 5	Wsh. 4	Kris Draper	15:24	Det.
Apr. 23/99	Ott.	CQF	Buf. 3	Ott. 2	Miroslav Satan	30:35	Buf.
Apr. 24/99	Car.	CQF	Car. 3	Bos. 2	Ray Sheppard	17:05	Bos.
Apr. 24/99	Phx.	CQF	Phx. 4	St.L. 3	Shane Doan	8:58	St.L.
Apr. 26/99	S.J.	CQF	Col. 2	S.J. 1	Milan Hejduk	7:53	Col.
Apr. 27/99	Edm.	CQF	Dal. 3	Edm. 2	Joe Nieuwendyk	57:34	Dal.
Apr. 30/99	Tor.	CQF	Tor. 2	Phi. 1	Yanic Perreault	11:51	Tor.
Apr. 30/99	Car.	CQF	Bos. 4	Car. 3	Anson Carter	34:45	Bos.
May 2/99	Pit.	CQF	Pit. 3	N.J. 2	Jaromir Jagr	8:59	Pit.
May 3/99	S.J.	CQF	Col. 3	S.J. 2	Milan Hejduk	13:12	Col.
May 4/99	Phx.	CQF	St.L. 1	Phx. 0	Pierre Turgeon	17:59	St.L.
May 7/99	Col.	CSF	Det. 3	Col. 2	Kirk Maltby	4:18	Col.
May 8/99	Dal.	CSF	Dal. 5	St.L. 4	Joe Nieuwendyk	8:22	Dal.
May 10/99	St.L.	CSF	St.L. 3	Dal. 2	Pavol Demitra	2:43	Dal.
May 12/99	St.L.	CSF	St.L. 3	Dal. 2	Pierre Turgeon	5:52	Dal.
May 13/99	Pit.	CSF	Tor. 3	Pit. 2	Sergei Berezin	2:18	Tor.
May 17/99	Pit.	CSF	Tor. 4	Pit. 3	Garry Valk	1:57	Tor.
May 17/99	St.L.	CSF	Dal. 2	St.L. 1	Mike Mondano	2:21	Dal.
May 28/99	Col.	CF	Col. 3	Dal. 2	Chris Drury	19:29	Dal.
Jun. 8/99	Dal.	F	Buf. 3	Dal. 2	Jason Woolley	15:30	Dal.
Jun. 19/99	Buf.	F	Dal. 2	Buf. 1	Brett Hull	54:51	Dal.

Ten Longest Overtime Games

Date	City	Series	Score		Scorer	Time	Series Win
Mar. 24/36	Mtl.	SF	Det. 1	Mtl. M. 0	Mud Bruneteau	116:30	Det.
Apr. 3/33	Tor.	SF	Tor. 1	Bos. 0	Ken Doraty	104:46	Tor.
Apr. 24/96	Wsh.	CQF	Pit. 3	Wsh. 2	Petr Nedved	79:15	Pit.
Mar. 23/43	Det.	SF	Tor. 3	Det. 2	Jack McLean	70:18	Det.
Mar. 28/30	Mtl.	SF	Mtl. 2	NYR 1	Gus Rivers	68:52	Mtl.
Apr. 18/87	Wsh.	DSF	NYI 3	Wsh. 2	Pat LaFontaine	68:47	NYI
Apr. 27/94	Buf.	CQF	Buf. 1	N.J. 0	Dave Hannan	65:43	N.J.
Mar. 27/51	Det.	SF	Mtl. 3	Det. 2	Maurice Richard	61:09	Mtl.
Mar. 27/38	NY	QF	NYA 3	NYR 2	Lorne Carr	60:40	NYA
Mar. 26/32	Mtl.	SF	NYR 4	Mtl. 3	Fred Cook	59:32	NYR

Playoff Penalty Shots

Date	Player	Goaltender	Scored	Final Score					Series
3/25/37	Lionel Conacher, MtlM	Tiny Thompson, Bos.	N	MtlM	0	at	Bos	4	QF
4/15/37	Alex Shibicky, NYR	Earl Robertson, Det.	N	NYR	0	at	Det	3	F
4/13/44	Virgil Johnson, Chi	Bill Durnan, Mtl. *	N	Chi	4	at	Mtl	5	F
4/9/68	Wayne Connelly, Min	Terry Sawchuk, L.A.	Y	LA	5	at	Min	7	QF
4/27/68	Jim Roberts, StL	Cesare Maniago, Min.	N	StL	4	at	Min	3	SF
5/16/71	Frank Mahovlich, Mtl	Tony Esposito, Chi.	N	Chi	3	at	Mtl	4	F
5/7/75	Bill Barber, Phi	Glenn Resch, NYI *	N	Phi	3	at	NYI	4	SF
4/20/79	Mike Walton, Chi	Glenn Resch, NYI	N	NYI	4	at	Chi	0	QF
4/9/81	Peter McNab, Bos	Don Beaupre, Min. *	N	Min	5	at	Bos	4	PR
4/17/81	Anders Hedberg, NYR	Mike Liut, St.L.	Y	NYR	6	at	StL	4	QF
4/9/83	Denis Potvin, NYI	Pat Riggin, Wsh.	N	NYI	6	at	Wsh	2	DSF
4/28/84	Wayne Gretzky, Edm	Don Beaupre, Min.	Y	Edm	8	at	Min	5	CF
5/1/84	Mats Naslund, Mtl	Bill Smith, NYI	N	Mtl	1	at	NYI	3	CF
4/14/85	Bob Carpenter, Wsh	Bill Smith, NYI	N	Wsh	4	at	NYI	6	DF
5/28/85	Ron Sutter, Phi	Grant Fuhr, Edm.	N	Phi	3	at	Edm	5	F
5/30/85	Dave Poulin, Phi	Grant Fuhr, Edm.	N	Phi	3	at	Edm	8	F
4/9/88	John Tucker, Buf	Andy Moog, Bos.	Y	Bos	2	at	Buf	6	DSF
4/9/88	Petr Klima, Det	Allan Bester, Tor.	Y	Det	6	at	Tor	3	DSF
4/8/89	Neal Broten, Min	Greg Millen, St.L.	Y	StL	5	at	Min	3	DSF
4/4/90	Al MacInnis, Cgy	Kelly Hrudey, L.A.	Y	LA	5	at	Cgy	3	DSF
4/5/90	Randy Wood, NYI	Mike Richter, NYR	N	NYI	1	at	NYR	2	DSF
5/3/90	Kelly Miller, Wsh	Andy Moog, Bos.	N	Wsh	3	at	Bos	5	CF
5/18/90	Petr Klima, Edm	Rejean Lemelin, Bos.	N	Edm.	7	at	Bos	2	F
4/6/91	Basil McRae, Min	Ed Belfour, Chi.	Y	Min	2	at	Chi	5	DSF
4/10/91	Steve Duchesne, LA	Kirk McLean, Van.	Y	LA	6	at	Van	1	DSF
5/11/92	Jaromir Jagr, Pit	J. Vanbiesbrouck, NYR	Y	Pit	3	at	NYR	2	DF
5/13/92	Shawn McEachern, Pit	J. Vanbiesbrouck, NYR	N	NYR	1	at	Pit	2	DF
6/7/94	Pavel Bure, Van	Mike Richter, NYR	N	NYR	4	at	Van	2	F
5/9/95	Patrick Poulin, Chi	Felix Potvin, Tor.	N	Tor	3	at	Chi	0	CQF
5/10/95	Michal Pivonka, Wsh	Tom Barrasso, Pit.	N	Pit	2	at	Wsh	6	CQF
4/24/96	Joe Juneau, Wsh	Ken Wregget, Pit.**	N	Pit	3	at	Wsh	2	CQF
5/11/97	Eric Lindros, Phi	Steve Shields, Buf.	Y	Phi	6	at	Buf	3	CSF
4/23/98	Alexei Morozov, Pit	Andy Moog, Mtl.***	N	Mtl	3	at	Pit	2	CQF
4/22/99	Mats Sundin, Tor	J. Vanbiesbrouck, Phi.	N	Phi	3	at	Tor	0	CQF
5/29/99	Mats Sundin, Tor	Dominik Hasek, Buf.	Y	Tor	2	at	Buf	5	CF

* The game was decided in overtime, but the shot was taken during regulation time.
** Joe Juneau's penalty shot April 24, 1996 was the first attempted in overtime.
*** Shot taken in overtime.

Conn Smythe Trophy Update

A total of 30 different players have won the Conn Smythe Trophy, awarded to the most valuable player to his team in the playoffs. The trophy was first awarded in 1965. Five players have won the award twice: Bobby Orr, Bernie Parent, Wayne Gretzky, Mario Lemieux and Patrick Roy.

Four players have won the Conn Smythe Trophy as members of teams that have lost teams in the Stanley Cup Finals: Roger Crozier (1966, Detroit Red Wings), Glenn Hall (1968, St. Louis Blues), Reggie Leach (1976, Philadelphia Flyers) and Ron Hextall (1987, Philadelphia Flyers).

Twenty-year-old Patrick Roy of the 1986 Montreal Canadiens was the youngest player ever to win the Conn Smythe Trophy.

The Conn Smythe Trophy is voted upon by the Professional Hockey Writers Association (PHWA) at the conclusion of the final game of the Stanley Cup. A complete listing of Conn Smythe winners follows:

1999	Joe Nieuwendyk, C, Dal.
1998	Steve Yzerman, C, Det.
1997	Mike Vernon, G, Det.
1996	Joe Sakic, C, Col.
1995	Claude Lemieux, RW, N.J.
1994	Brian Leetch, D, NYR
1993	Patrick Roy, G, Mtl.
1992	Mario Lemieux, C, Pit.
1991	Mario Lemieux, C. Pit.
1990	Bill Ranford, G, Edm.
1989	Al MacInnis, D, Cgy.
1988	Wayne Gretzky, C, Edm.
1987	Ron Hextall, G, Phi.
1986	Patrick Roy, G, Mtl.
1985	Wayne Gretzky, C, Edm.
1984	Mark Messier, C, Edm.
1983	Billy Smith, G, NYI
1982	Mike Bossy, RW, NYI
1981	Butch Goring, C, NYI
1980	Bryan Trottier, C, NYI
1979	Bob Gainey, LW, Mtl.
1978	Larry Robinson, D, Mtl.
1977	Guy Lafleur, RW, Mtl.
1976	Reggie Leach, RW, Phi.
1975	Bernie Parent, G, Phi.
1974	Bernie Parent, G, Phi.
1973	Yvan Cournoyer, RW, Mtl.
1972	Bobby Orr, D, Bos.
1971	Ken Dryden, G, Mtl.
1970	Bobby Orr, D, Bos.
1969	Serge Savard, D, Mtl.
1968	Glenn Hall, G, St.L.
1967	Dave Keon, C, Tor.
1966	Roger Crozier, G, Det.
1965	Jean Beliveau, C, Mtl.

CHAPTER 14

This Date in Stanley Cup History

December

Dec. 27, 1897 • In the only Stanley Cup challenge of the season, the defending champion Montreal Victorias turned back the Ottawa Capitals 15-2 to retain their champion status.

Dec. 27, 1906 • Riley Hern, "Pud" Glass, "Hod" Stuart, Ernie Johnson and Jack Marshall of the Montreal Wanderers officially became the first professionals to compete for the Stanley Cup. Glass scored four goals as the defending champion Montreal club downed the challenging New Glasgow Cubs 10-3 in the first game of a two-game, total-goals series.

Dec. 30, 1896 • Ernie McLea notched the first hat trick in Stanley Cup history as the Montreal Victorias regained possession of the coveted trophy with a 6-5 win versus the defending champion Winnipeg Victorias. Winnipeg had won the Cup earlier in the year, defeating the Montreal Vics 2-0 on February 14, 1896.

Dec. 30, 1904 • In the first game of a best-of-three challenge between the Winnipeg Rowing Club and the defending champion Ottawa Silver Seven, a red line was drawn between each set of goalposts to aid the referee in awarding goals. These lines became the first known "Goal Lines" in hockey history.

January

Jan. 16, 1905 • "One-Eyed" Frank McGee netted an all-time Stanley Cup record 14 goals in the Ottawa Silver Seven's 23-2 win over the Dawson City Nuggets, who had trekked over 4,000 miles by dogsled, boat and train to challenge for the Cup.

Jan. 31, 1901 • The Stanley Cup was won in overtime for the first time when Dan Bain of the Winnipeg Victorias scored four minutes into the extra session for a 2-1 victory over the Montreal Shamrocks. Winnipeg swept the best-of-three series.

February

Feb. 14, 1896 • Winnipeg Victorias goaltender G.H. Merritt, credited as the first netminder to wear goalie pads, posted a 2-0 shutout to capture the Stanley Cup from the reigning champion Montreal Victorias. The game marked the first successful challenge in Stanley Cup history.

Feb. 25, 1904 • Ottawa Silver Seven sniper Frank McGee registered the first five-goal performance in Stanley Cup history in an 11-2 win over the challenging Toronto Marlboros.

March

Mar. 5, 1900 • Defending champion Montreal Shamrocks forward Arthur Farrell led his club to a 10-2 victory against the challenging Halifax Crescents with an unprecedented four-goal Stanley Cup performance.

Mar. 9, 1893 • Upon defeating the Montreal Crystals 2-1, the Montreal Amateur Athletic Association (MAAA) captured the 1893 Amateur Hockey Association (AHA) title and the first Stanley Cup championship. The MAAA lineup consisted of nine players: Billy Barlow (forward), Allan Cameron (defense), Archie Hodgson (forward), Alex Irving (forward), A. Kingan (forward), J. Lowe (forward), T. Paton (goaltender), Harvie Routh (forward) and James Stewart (defense).

Mar. 9, 1895 • In the first official challenge for the Stanley Cup, the defending champion Montreal AAA team retained possession of the trophy with a 5-1 triumph over the Queen's University Golden Gaels.

Mar. 11, 1914 • The Toronto Blueshirts (later renamed the Maple Leafs) captured their first Stanley Cup title with a 6-0 home-ice shutout against the Montreal Canadiens in a playoff to determine the NHA champion. The game marked the first Stanley Cup contest ever played on an artificial ice surface.

Mar. 14, 1908 • Making his Stanley Cup debut, "Newsy" Lalonde scored twice, but still the Montreal Wanderers scored a 6-4 win over Lalonde's Toronto Trolley Leaguers for a successful defense of their championship title .

Mar. 16, 1911 • Ottawa Senators forward Marty Walsh scored 10 goals—second in Stanley Cup history only to Frank McGee's 14-goal total (January 16, 1905)—en route to a 13-4 win over the Port Arthur Bearcats.

Mar. 16, 1923 • For the first time in Stanley Cup history, two brothers opposed each other in the Finals. In fact, two sets of brothers—Cy and Corb Denneny, and George and Frank Boucher—lined up on opposite sides of the ice. Cy and George skated for the Ottawa Senators, while Corb and Frank played for Vancouver Maroons. None of the four scored in this opening game, won by Ottawa 1-0.

Mar. 18, 1892 • At a dinner of the Ottawa Amateur Athletic Association, Lord Kilcoursie, a player on the Ottawa Rebels hockey club, read the following message on behalf of Lord Stanley of Preston, the Governor-General of Canada,:"It would be a good thing if there were a challenge cup which should be held from year to year by the champion hockey team in the Dominion (of Canada)....I am willing to give a cup which shall be held...by the winning team." That cup eventually became the Stanley Cup, which has been presented annually since 1893.

Mar. 21, 1921 • More than 11,000 fans jammed the Vancouver Arena for the first game of this best-of-five Stanley Cup series between the hometown Millionaires and the visiting Ottawa Senators. It marked the largest crowd ever to witness a hockey game anywhere in the world up until this date. Vancouver downed Ottawa 2-1.

Mar. 22, 1894 • Forward Billy Barlow netted two goals as the Montreal AAA downed the Ottawa Generals 3-1 in this one-game battle for the 1894 Stanley Cup.

Mar. 22, 1919 • Montreal center "Newsy" Lalonde became the first NHL player ever to score four goals in one Finals game, spurring the Canadiens to a 4-2 win against the PCHA's Seattle Metropolitans. Only "Babe" Dye of the Toronto St. Pats (March 28, 1922), Detroit's Ted Lindsay (April 5, 1955) and Montreal's Maurice "Rocket" Richard (April 6, 1957) have since matched Lalonde's four-goal feat.

Mar. 23, 1918 • Alf Skinner of the Toronto Arenas registered the first hat trick by an NHL player in a Stanley Cup Finals game. The PCHA's Vancouver Millionaires downed Toronto 6-4 in Game Two of the 1918 Finals, the first Stanley Cup series involving an NHL franchise.

Mar. 25, 1917 • The Seattle Metropolitans of the Pacific Coast Hockey Association (PCHA) distinguished themselves as the first United States team to win the Stanley Cup. Seattle's Bernie Morris scored six times en route to a 9-1 triumph over the Montreal Canadiens.

Mar. 25, 1922 • Toronto goaltender John Ross Roach blanked the Vancouver Millionaires 6-0, recording the first Stanley Cup shutout by a goaltender in NHL play.

Mar. 26, 1919 • In the longest game to that point in Finals history, the Montreal Canadiens and Seattle Metropolitans (PCHA) played for 80 minutes (60 minutes of regulation time and 20 minutes of overtime) without scoring a goal. Georges Vezina and Harry Holmes dominated the first scoreless tie in Stanley Cup history with a display of superior goaltending.

Mar. 27, 1925 • Howie Morenz led the Montreal Canadiens to a 4-2 win

over the PCHA's Victoria Cougars with the second three-goal output of his Stanley Cup Finals career, setting an NHL record in the process. Maurice "Rocket" Richard later surpassed Morenz's mark with three hat tricks, including one four-goal and two three-goal performances.

Mar. 28, 1922 • "Babe" Dye scores four goals to lead the Toronto St. Pats to a 5-1 win over the Vancouver Millionaires and a three games to one victory in their Stanley Cup series. Dye joined "Newsy Lalonde" (March 22, 1919) as the second player in NHL history to score four goals in a Stanley Cup game.

Mar. 28, 1929 • For the first time in history, two American teams—the Boston Bruins and New York Rangers—clashed in the Finals. The Bruins' "Dit" Clapper and "Dutch" Gainor scored goals, and "Tiny" Thompson posted the third Stanley Cup shutout ever by an NHL rookie to give Boston a 2-0 win in Game One. The Bruins won 2-1 the following night to capture their first championship title.

Mar. 29, 1929 • Harry Oliver scored a goal and an assist, and Bill Carson netted the game-winning tally as the Boston Bruins earned their first Stanley Cup title with a 2-1 win versus the New York Rangers. The victory completed a two-game sweep by Boston in the best-of-three Finals.

Mar. 30, 1916 • In the fifth and final game for the 1916 Stanley Cup title, the Montreal Canadiens downed the PCHA's Portland Rosebuds 2-1 on goals by Skene Ronan and Goldie Prodgers, who netted the winning tally. The victory marked the first of Montreal's 24 championships, a record surpassed only by the New York Yankees in professional sports history.

Mar. 30, 1918 • In the fifth and final game of the 1918 Finals, Alf Skinner and Corb Denneny engineered a successful comeback with unanswered goals in a 2-1 win over the PCHA's Vancouver Millionaires. Denneny notched the game-winner as the Toronto Arenas became the first NHL team to capture Lord Stanley's Cup.

Mar. 30, 1919 • Montreal Canadiens right winger Odie Cleghorn scored the first overtime goal by an NHL player in the Finals, snapping a 3-3 tie at 15:57 of the overtime period. The game knotted the 1919 Finals between Montreal and the Seattle Metropolitans at 2-2-1 after five outings. However, the series never resumed because players from both squads suffered the consequences of a raging flu epidemic. Montreal's Joe Hall, who had been become ill during this fifth game, died on April 5, 1919, as a result of the sickness.

Mar. 30, 1925 • The Victoria Cougars of the Western Canada Hockey League downed the Montreal Canadiens 6-1 to become the last non-NHL team to capture the Stanley Cup. The win gave Victoria a 3-1 margin over Montreal in the best-of-five championship series.

Mar. 30, 1946 • In Game One, right winger Maurice "Rocket" Richard registered the first of his record three overtime goals in Finals action, snapping a 3-3 tie at 9:08 of the extra period. The goal gave the Montreal Canadiens the first of their four victories versus the Boston Bruins en route to the 1946 Stanley Cup.

April 1 - 10

April 1, 1920 • The Ottawa Senators downed the PCHA's Seattle Metropolitans 6–1 in the fifth and final game in their best-of-five Stanley Cup series. Games Four and Five of the series were played on artificial ice in Toronto because of mild weather in Ottawa. One year later, the Senators would become the first NHL team to win back-to-back Stanley Cup championships.

April 3, 1930 • The Canadiens downed the Bruins 4-3 to complete a two-game sweep of the 1930 Finals. For the defending Stanley Cup champion Boston Bruins, who had posted the NHL's best regular-season record in 1929-30 with a 38-5-1 mark, the games marked their first back-to-back losses of the year.

April 4, 1921 • The Ottawa Senators defeated the Vancouver Millionaires 2-1 in the decisive fifth game of the 1921 Stanley Cup series. Jack Darragh scored both goals for the Senators, who became the first NHL team to capture back-to-back Stanley Cup titles.

April 4, 1944 • Montreal Canadiens rookie right winger Maurice "Rocket" Richard made his Stanley Cup debut, tallying an assist on linemate "Toe" Blake's game-winning goal in this 5-1 victory against the Chicago Black Hawks in Game One of the 1944 Finals. Richard continued to play a key role in Montreal's drive towards the title, scoring four more goals in the remaining three games of the Canadiens' four-game sweep against Chicago.

April 5, 1931 • Over 18,000 fans jammed Chicago Stadium for Game Two of the 1931 championship series, setting a new record for the largest attendance for one game in hockey history. Black Hawks left winger Johnny Gottselig thrilled the hometown fans with the game-winning goal in double overtime as Chicago downed the Montreal Canadiens 2-1. The Canadiens later won the Stanley Cup series three games to two.

April 5, 1955 • Detroit Red Wings left winger Ted Lindsay became the third player in NHL history to score four goals in one Stanley Cup game and tied a Finals record with three goals in one period. Joining "Newsy" Lalonde (March 22, 1919) and "Babe" Dye (March 28, 1922) in achieving the four-goal feat, Lindsay scored the game-winning tally as Detroit downed Montreal 7-1.

April 6, 1926 • Goaltender Clint Benedict backstopped the Montreal Maroons to their first Stanley Cup title, blanking the Victoria Cougars 2-0 to win the best-of-five confrontation 3-1. The shutout was Benedict's third of the series, establishing a new Stanley Cup record for one year.

April 6, 1937 • When regular netminder Normie Smith left Game One of the Finals with an elbow injury, the Detroit Red Wings placed minor leaguer Earl Robertson of the International League's Pittsburgh Hornets into the nets to finish the series. After a 5-1 loss to the New York Rangers in the opener, Robertson, who had never before played an NHL game, backstopped the Red Wings to three wins in their next four outings to capture the 1937 Stanley Cup.

April 6, 1944 • Rookie right winger Maurice "Rocket" Richard registered the first of his NHL record three Stanley Cup hat tricks as Montreal won Game Two 3-1 over Chicago. The victory was the second of four straight by the Canadiens versus the Black Hawks en route to the 1944 title.

April 6, 1945 • For the first time in Stanley Cup history, two rookie goaltenders—Toronto's Frank McCool and Detroit's Harry Lumley—opposed each other in the Finals. On the strength of Dave "Sweeney" Schriner's first-period goal, McCool and the Leafs blanked the Wings 1-0 to open the best-of-seven series. For McCool, it was the first of a record three straight Stanley Cup shutouts and four victories en route to winning the 1945 title.

April 6, 1954 • Dickie Moore and Maurice "Rocket" Richard of the Montreal Canadiens combined for the fastest three goals by an NHL team in Finals history, scoring three times within 56 seconds. Moore scored at 15:03 of the first period, followed by Richard at 15:28 and 15:59. The Canadiens downed the Red Wings 3-2 in Detroit.

April 6, 1957 • Right winger Maurice "Rocket" Richard tied "Newsy" Lalonde, "Babe" Dye and Ted Lindsay for the NHL record with four goals in one Stanley Cup game, leading Montreal to a 5-1 triumph over the Boston Bruins in Game One of the 1957 Finals. The four-goal effort also distinguished Richard as the only NHL player to record three hat tricks in a Stanley Cup career. Montreal went on to win the best-of-seven series four games to one.

April 6, 1961 • In their Stanley Cup debuts, Bobby Hull (2-0-2) and Stan Mikita (0-2-2) led the Chicago Black Hawks to a 3-2 win against the Detroit Red Wings in Game One of the 1961 Finals. Hull netted the winning tally at 13:15 of the first period. Chicago went on to defeat Detroit four games to two in the best-of-seven series.

April 7, 1927 • The American Division champion Boston Bruins battled the Canadian Division champion Ottawa Senators to a 0-0 overtime tie in the first all-NHL Stanley Cup game. The best-of-five series, eventually won by Ottawa 2-0-2 over Boston, marked the dawn of the modern Stanley Cup era.

April 7, 1928 • After losing starting goaltender Lorne Chabot to an eye injury midway through Game Two, 44-year-old New York Rangers coach and former star player Lester Patrick took over between the

pipes and inspired his club to a 2-1 overtime victory in Game Two of the 1928 Finals. After signing New York Americans rookie netminder Joe Miller the following day, the Rangers skated to two wins in their next three outings to win the best-of-five championship series 3-2.

April 7, 1948 • 20-year-old right winger Gordie Howe of Detroit made his Stanley Cup debut in Game One of the 1948 Finals but failed to register a point as the Toronto Maple Leafs downed the Red Wings 5-3. The Leafs later went on to sweep Detroit in four straight games to capture the best-of-seven series and the Stanley Cup. Howe did not score in the series.

April 7, 1960 • In Game One of the 1960 Finals, Montreal right winger Maurice "Rocket" Richard extended his all-time record of Stanley Cup series appearances to 12, while Toronto's Bert Olmstead and Montreal's Doug Harvey, Bernie "Boom Boom" Geoffrion and Tom Johnson extended their records for consecutive Finals appearances to 10. Montreal defeated Toronto 4-2.

April 7, 1982 • The Edmonton Oilers and Los Angeles Kings combined for 18 goals, setting an NHL record for the highest scoring playoff game. Edmonton won the game 10-8 in Game One of their best-of-five Smythe Division Semifinal. Los Angeles won the series 3-2.

April 8, 1934 • Detroit Red Wings goaltender Wilf Cude suffered a broken nose midway through Game Three but remained in nets until the final buzzer sounded, inspiring his team to a 5-2 upset win against the Black Hawks in Chicago. It was Detroit's only victory during the best-of-five Finals won by Chicago, three games to one.

April 8, 1937 • Referee Clarence Campbell officiated his first Stanley Cup contest in Game Two of the 1937 Finals, a 4-2 win for the Detroit Red Wings over the New York Rangers. Campbell, who later became the third League President in NHL history in 1946, doled out three penalties during the affair.

April 8, 1943 • After blanking Boston 4-0 the previous night, Detroit goalie Johnny Mowers shut out the Bruins 2-0, completing a four-game sweep in the 1943 Finals. Joe Carveth of the Red Wings registered the winning tally at 12:09 of the first period, and teammate Carl Liscombe added an insurance marker to lock up the title.

April 8, 1980 • Gordie Howe established an NHL record for most years in the playoffs (20) by appearing for the Hartford Whalers in Game One of their best-of-three Preliminary round series against Montreal. Howe, making his first NHL playoff appearance since the 1969-70 season, passed former Detroit and Toronto defenseman Red Kelly, who had played in 19 playoff seasons.

April 8, 1982 • Mikko Leinonen of the New York Rangers became the first NHL player to record six assists in a playoff game, helping his club to a 7-3 win over Philadelphia in Game Two of their Patrick Division Final. Leinonen's mark was equalled by Edmonton's Wayne Gretzky during the 1987 playoffs

April 9, 1932 • The Toronto Maple Leafs defeated the New York Rangers 6-4 to complete a three-game sweep of the 1932 Finals. The series marked the Stanley Cup debut of the Leafs' famed "Kid Line" of Harvey "Busher" Jackson, Charlie Conacher and Joe Primeau, who combined for eight goals in Toronto's three victories.

April 9, 1935 • After winning the first two games of the 1935 Finals in Toronto, the Montreal Maroons completed a three-game sweep of the Maple Leafs with a 4-1 win in the best-of-five Stanley Cup series.

April 9, 1942 • Eddie Bush of the Detroit Red Wings established a new NHL record with five points (1-4-5) by a defenseman in one Stanley Cup Finals game. Bush, who never scored another point in his NHL career, led Detroit to a 5-2 victory over the Toronto Maple Leafs.

April 9, 1946 • In Game Five of the 1946 Finals, Montreal center Elmer Lach scored a goal and two assists in a 6-3 win against the Boston Bruins. The victory gave the Canadiens their second Stanley Cup title in three years.

April 9, 1987 • The Edmonton Oilers established an NHL record for most goals in a playoff game, recording a 13-3 win over Los Angeles in Game Two of their Smythe Division Semifinal. Edmonton went on to win the best-of-seven series 4-1.

April 10, 1934 • The Chicago Black Hawks earned their first Stanley Cup title with a 1-0 overtime victory versus the Detroit Red Wings in Game Four of the best-of-five championship. Harold "Mush" March potted the series-winner at 10:05 of the second overtime period.

April 10, 1949 • Toronto left winger Sid Smith set a new NHL record with three power-play goals in one Finals game. Toronto defeated Detroit 3-1.

April 10, 1956 • Center Jean Beliveau notched a goal and two assists as the Montreal Canadiens took Game Five (3-1) and the 1956 Stanley Cup title from the Detroit Red Wings. The goal gave Beliveau seven versus Detroit, establishing a modern record for one Final series. New York Islanders right winger Mike Bossy (1982) and Edmonton Oilers center Wayne Gretzky (1985) have since tied Beliveau's Stanley Cup mark.

April 10, 1982 • The Los Angeles Kings scored five third-period goals and added the game-winner in overtime to defeat the Edmonton Oilers 6-5 in Game Three of the 1982 Smythe Division Semifinal in one of the greatest comebacks in NHL playoff history. Trailing 5-0 entering the third period, Los Angeles forward Steve Bozek scored the tying goal with just five seconds remaining and Daryl Evans capped the furious Kings rally by adding the overtime winner at 2:35. Los Angeles went on to win the best-of-five series 3-2.

April 10, 1985 • Detroit Red Wings defenseman Brad Park set an NHL record by appearing in postseason play for the 17th consecutive season. Park, marking his second playoff year in a Red Wings uniform, played in all three games of Detroit's Norris Division Semifinal series against Chicago, which the Black Hawks won 3-0. He had previously made playoff appearances for the New York Rangers (seven seasons) and Boston Bruins (eight seasons).

April 11 – 20

April 11, 1936 • Detroit coach Jack Adams steered the Red Wings to their first Stanley Cup championship with a 3-2 victory over the Toronto Maple Leafs in Game Four of the best-of-five Stanley Cup confrontation. The Wings, who had entered the NHL in 1926-27, became the last of the League's "Original Six" teams to win the Cup.

April 11, 1965 • Detroit Red Wings center Norm Ullman set NHL individual and team playoff records by scoring two goals just five seconds apart in Game Five of their Semifinal series against Chicago. Ullman scored at 17:35 and 17:40 of the second period. Chicago won the best-of-seven series 4-3.

April 11, 1971 • Boston Bruins defenseman Bobby Orr became the first defenseman to score three goals in a playoff game during a 5-2 win over the Montreal Canadiens. Since then, seven other defensemen have equalled Orr's mark. (See April 24, 1994 for list.)

April 11, 1980 • Montreal's Yvon Lambert scored at 0:29 of overtime to give the Canadiens a 4-3 victory over Hartford and a sweep of the best-of-five series. The game marked the final NHL appearance of two Hall-of-Famers, as Hartford's Gordie Howe and Bobby Hull retired following the Whalers' elimination from the playoffs.

April 11, 1981 • The Boston Bruins set a new playoff record by scoring three shorthanded goals against the Minnesota North Stars in Game Three of their Quarterfinal series. The three shorthanded goals were not enough as Minnesota won the game 6-3 and swept the best-of-five series.

April 11, 1989 • Philadelphia's Ron Hextall was the first goaltender to score a goal in the playoffs with an empty-net goal against the Washington Capitals. The Flyers won the game 8-5.

April 12, 1938 • The Chicago Black Hawks captured the 1938 Stanley Cup title with a 4-1 victory against the Toronto Maple Leafs in Game Four of the best-of-five title series. Eight American-born players—Carl Dahlstrom, Roger Jenkins, Virgil Johnson, Mike Karakas, Alex Levinsky, Elwin "Doc" Romnes, Louis Trudel and Carl Voss—skated for Chicago in the Finals to set a new Stanley Cup record for United States talent on a championship team.

April 12, 1941 • For the first time since the NHL adopted the best-of-

seven Finals format in 1939, a team won the Stanley Cup in straight games. The Boston Bruins topped the Detroit Red Wings 3-1 to complete their four-game sweep of the 1941 series.

April 12, 1945 • Maple Leafs rookie netminder Frank McCool set a new record with his third consecutive Stanley Cup shutout, 1-0 against the Red Wings, as Toronto moved to within one game of sweeping Detroit in the Finals. The Leafs later won the championship series in seven games.

April 12, 1960 • Right winger Maurice "Rocket" Richard scored his all-time record 34th and final Stanley Cup goal, helping the Montreal Canadiens to a 5-2 win over the Toronto Maple Leafs in Game Three of the 1960 Finals. The Canadiens' victory was the third in a four-game sweep against the Leafs.

April 12, 1979 • The Toronto Maple Leafs set a playoff record for the fastest three goals by one team during a 7-4 victory over the Atlanta Flames in Game Two of their Preliminary round series. Darryl Sittler scored at 4:04 and 4:16 and Ron Ellis at 4:27 of the first period. Toronto went on to win the best-of-three series 2-0.

April 13, 1985 • Philadelphia Flyers center Tim Kerr set a new playoff record by scoring four goals in one period, eclipsing the mark of three held by many players. Kerr scored the four goals in the second period of a 6-5 win over the New York Rangers. Three of Kerr's goals were scored on the power-play, also setting a new record.

April 13, 1933 • Bill Cook snapped a scoreless tie at 7:33 of overtime to give the New York Rangers a 1-0 victory against the Toronto Maple Leafs. Rangers rookie goaltender Andy Aitkenhead posted the shutout as New York captured the best-of-five series in four games.

April 13, 1940 • Frank Boucher, who played on New York's first two Stanley Cup championship teams in 1928 and 1933, coached the Rangers to a third title with a 3-2 overtime win in Game Six of the best-of-seven series. Among Boucher's players on the team were brothers Lynn and "Muzz" Patrick, the third and fourth members of the legendary Patrick family (including their father Lester and uncle Frank) to have their names engraved on the Cup. Bryan Hextall scored the winning goal.

April 13, 1944 • Montreal's famed Punch Line—left winger "Toe" Blake, center Elmer Lach and right winger Maurice "Rocket" Richard—powered the Canadiens to a 5-4 series-clinching comeback victory versus the Chicago Black Hawks in Game Four of the 1944 Finals. After Chicago had taken a 4-1 lead through two periods, Lach scored at 10:02 of the third, followed by Richard's back-to-back tallies at 16:05 and 17:20 to tie the game at four goals apiece after regulation time. Blake then ended the game and the season with a blast past netminder Mike Karakas at 9:12 of overtime. The win gave the Canadiens their first Stanley Cup title since 1931, ending their longest period without a championship from their first season in the National Hockey Association (NHA), 1909-1910, to the present.

April 13, 1952 • Right winger Gordie Howe registered his first two Stanley Cup goals and goaltender Terry Sawchuk posted a shutout to lead the Detroit Red Wings past the Montreal Canadiens 3-0 in Game Three of the 1952 Finals. The win was Detroit's third straight en route to a four-game sweep of Montreal in the best-of-seven season finale.

April 14, 1928 • In only their second season as an NHL franchise, the New York Rangers captured the 1928 Stanley Cup with a 2-1 triumph over the Montreal Maroons in the final game of the best-of-five title series. The Rangers became only the second American team in history to win the Stanley Cup, joining the 1917 champion Seattle Metropolitans of the Pacific Coast Hockey Association.

April 14, 1931 • Goaltender George Hainsworth blanked the Chicago Black Hawks 2-0 as the Montreal Canadiens became the second NHL team to win Stanley Cup championships in two consecutive seasons. The Ottawa Senators first accomplished the feat in 1920 and 1921.

April 14, 1942 • Brothers Don Metz (3-2-5) and Nick Metz (1-2-3) led the Toronto Maple Leafs to a record-tying 9-3 victory against the Detroit Red Wings in the 1942 Finals. The Leafs' nine-goal outburst matched the Finals scoring mark for an NHL team set by Detroit on April 7, 1936, in a 9-4 win against Toronto.

April 14, 1948 • The Toronto Maple Leafs repeated as Stanley Cup champions with a 7-2 win against the Detroit Red Wings, thus completing a four-game sweep of the 1948 Finals. The game spelled the end of a career for Toronto captain Syl Apps, who punctuated his stint in the NHL with a goal in this series-ending victory.

April 14, 1953 • Maurice "Rocket" Richard became the second NHL player to register two hat tricks in Finals history, joining Howie Morenz in achieving the feat. Richard, who led Montreal to a 7-3 win against Boston, later added a four-goal performance to his record on April 6, 1957.

April 14, 1955 • Right winger Gordie Howe scored the winning goal in Game Seven of the 1955 Stanley Cup Finals to lead the Detroit Red Wings past the Montreal Canadiens 3-1. The goal gave Howe a 5-7-12 scoring mark in the series, setting a new individual mark for Finals competition.

April 14, 1960 • Goaltender Jacques Plante blanked the Toronto Maple Leafs 4-0 as the Montreal Canadiens captured their record-setting fifth straight Stanley Cup championship. The victory marked the end of a career for Maurice "Rocket" Richard, the NHL's all-time leader with 34 goals in Stanley Cup play.

April 15, 1937 • In Game Five of the 1937 Stanley Cup series, referee Mickey Ion awarded Rangers right winger Alex Shibicky the first penalty shot in Finals history. Red Wings rookie goaltender Earl Robertson stopped Shibicky's shot and posted his second straight shutout, 3-0 against New York, as Detroit became the first American team to repeat as Cup champions.

April 15, 1952 • In his fourth shutout in eight postseason games, Detroit Red Wings goalie Terry Sawchuk blanked the Montreal Canadiens 3-0 to complete a four-game sweep of the 1952 Finals. The Wings, who had also swept the Toronto Maple Leafs in the Semifinals, distinguished themselves as the first NHL team to win every postseason game in one year.

April 16, 1939 • Goaltender Frank Brimsek, alias "Mr. Zero", allowed only one goal, his sixth in five Stanley Cup games against Toronto, to lead the Boston Bruins past the Maple Leafs 3-1 to win the 1939 championship.

April 16, 1949 • The Toronto Maple Leafs swept the Detroit Red Wings to become the first NHL team to win three consecutive Stanley Cup titles (1947-49). The 3-1 series-ending victory also marked the Leafs' ninth straight win in Finals action.

April 16, 1953 • Assisted by linemate Maurice "Rocket" Richard, Elmer Lach scored the only goal in Game Five at 1:22 of overtime, and goalie Gerry McNeil blanked the Boston Bruins for the second time in three outings as the Montreal Canadiens earned the 1953 Stanley Cup championship.

April 16, 1954 • Tony Leswick's Stanley Cup-winning tally was the second overtime goal ever scored in the seventh game of a Final series. Leswick, who notched the decisive goal at 4:29 of overtime in Detroit's 2-1 victory over the Montreal Canadiens in Game Seven, matched the feat first accomplished by former Red Wings left winger Pete Babando in 1950.

April 16, 1961 • The Chicago Black Hawks earned their first Stanley Cup championship since 1938 and their third title since joining the NHL in 1926-27. The Black Hawks downed Detroit 5-1 to take the best-of-seven Finals four games to two.

April 16, 1994 • The Boston Bruins opened their Eastern Conference Quarterfinal series against the Montreal Canadiens, extending their NHL record for most consecutive playoff appearances to 27 years.

April 16, 1997 • The Mighty Ducks of Anaheim, making their first playoff appearance, were led by Paul Kariya (2-1-3) and Teemu Selanne (2-1-3) in a 4-2 home win over the Phoenix Coyotes in Game One of their Western Conference Quarterfinal. The win extended the Mighty Ducks home undefeated streak, including regular season, to 15 games (11-0-4).

April 17, 1958 • Right winger Maurice "Rocket" Richard led the Montreal Canadiens to a 3-2 win against the Boston Bruins in Game Five with a goal at 5:45 of overtime. The overtime goal was Richard's

third in a Stanley Cup game and sixth in a playoff game, extending his record in each category. The Canadiens went on to win the best-of-seven series in six games.

April 17, 1977 • Don Kozak of the Los Angeles Kings scored the fastest goal from the start of an NHL playoff game, tallying just six seconds into his club's 7-4 win over the Boston Bruins in Game Four of their Quarterfinal series.

April 17, 1997 • The Ottawa Se1nators made their first playoff appearance since joining the NHL in 1992-93, dropping a 3-1 decision to the Buffalo Sabres at Marine Midland Arena in Game One of their Eastern Conference Quarterfinal.

April 17, 1997 • New Jersey Devils goaltender Martin Brodeur became just the second goaltender in NHL playoff history to score a goal, coming in a 5-2 win over the Montreal Canadiens in Game One of their Eastern Conference Quarterfinal. Philadelphia's Ron Hextall was the first goaltender to score a goal in the playoffs, on April 11, 1989 versus the Washington Capitals.

April 18, 1942 • The Toronto Maple Leafs completed the greatest comeback in Stanley Cup history with their fourth straight victory after losing the first three games of the Finals to the Detroit Red Wings. Leafs goaltender Turk Broda provided the heroics, allowing the Red Wings only seven goals in the last four games, including this 3-1 series-ending victory.

April 18, 1959 • Montreal Canadiens left winger Marcel Bonin scored the Stanley Cup-winning goal at 9:55 of the second period en route to a 5-3 win over the Toronto Maple Leafs in Game Six. This victory ended the series and gave Montreal the fourth of its record five straight Stanley Cup titles.

April 18, 1963 • In Game Five of the 1963 Finals, Toronto Maple Leafs center Dave Keon scored two shorthanded goals against the Detroit Red Wings, setting a single-game playoff record. Keon's heroics led Toronto to a 3-1 Cup-winning triumph over Detroit. It marked the second of three straight Stanley Cups for the Leafs.

April 18, 1987 • Pat LaFontaine scored the dramatic game-winning goal at 8:42 of the fourth overtime period in Game Seven of the Patrick Division Final versus Washington.

April 18, 1994 • The San Jose Sharks defeated the Detroit Red Wings 5-4 at Joe Louis Arena in Detroit in Game One of their Western Conference Quarterfinal series to become the first club since the 1975 New York Islanders to win the first Stanley Cup playoff game in franchise history. Since the Islanders defeated the New York Rangers 3-2 on April 8, 1975, seven clubs had lost their playoff debuts prior to San Jose's win.

April 18, 1994 • The New York Rangers posted their second consecutive 6-0 shutout to open the Stanley Cup playoffs against the New York Islanders. The Rangers became the first club to open the postseason with consecutive shutouts since the Buffalo Sabres defeated Montreal 1-0 and 3-0 in 1983.

April 19, 1947 • After assisting on defenseman Vic Lynn's goal at 5:39 of the second period to tie the game at one goal apiece, Toronto Maple Leafs center Ted "Teeder" Kennedy scored the Cup-winner at 14:39 of the third period to defeat the Montreal Canadiens 2-1 in Game Six. The series-ending victory earned Toronto its third Stanley Cup title in six seasons.

April 20, 1950 • New York center Don Raleigh set a Stanley Cup record with his second overtime goal in as many games as the Rangers downed the Detroit Red Wings 4-3 in Game Five of the 1950 Finals. The win proved to be the Rangers' last of the series as Detroit went on to win the final two games and the Stanley Cup.

April 20, 1967 • In Game One of the 1967 Finals, a 6-2 win for the Montreal Canadiens, defenseman Leonard "Red" Kelly skated in the 12th Stanley Cup series of his career, tying Maurice "Rocket" Richard for the all-time record. Montreal's Henri Richard and Jean Beliveau, both of whom played in the game, would later tie the mark as well.

April 20, 1997 • Chicago Blackhawks forward Sergei Krivokrasov scored at 11:03 of the second overtime period in a 4-3 win over the Colorado Avalanche in Game Three of their Western Conference Quarterfinal at the United Center. The goal stopped Avalanche goaltender Patrick Roy's overtime shutout streak at 162 minutes and 56 seconds, the longest streak in NHL playoff history.

April 20, 1997 • The Edmonton Oilers staged a game-tying, three-goal flurry in the last four minutes of the third period versus the Dallas Stars en route to a 4-3 overtime win in Game Three at Edmonton. It marked the first time since the NHL took exclusive control of the Stanley Cup in 1926-27 that a club had won a playoff game after trailing by three goals with less than five minutes to play. With Dallas leading 3-0 in the third period, Edmonton got goals from Doug Weight (16:00), Andrei Kovalenko (17:44) and Mike Grier (17:56) to tie the game, with Kelly Buchberger adding the game-winner at 9:15 of overtime. Edmonton took a 2-1 lead in the series.

April 20, 1993 • The Pittsburgh Penguins set an NHL playoff record with their 13th consecutive postseason win, a 7-0 decision over the New Jersey Devils in Game Two of their Patrick Division Semifinal. The Penguins passed the previous mark of 12, set by the Edmonton Oilers in the 1984 and 1985 playoff seasons. The Penguins extended their record to 14 games before dropping Game Four to the Devils, ending the streak.

April 21 – 30

April 21, 1951 • Toronto Maple Leafs defenseman Bill Barilko scored the Cup-winning goal at 2:53 of overtime to defeat the Montreal Canadiens 3-2 in Game Five of the 1951 Finals. It was the only Stanley Cup series in which every game had ended in overtime. Toronto's Sid Smith, Ted Kennedy, Harry Watson, Barilko and Montreal's Maurice "Rocket" Richard each netted overtime winners during the five-game matchup. Barilko died in an off-season plane crash in the summer of 1951, though his remains would not be discovered until 1962.

April 22, 1945 • At 12:14 of the third period, Maple Leafs defenseman Walter "Babe" Pratt scored the Cup-winning goal to give Toronto a 2-1 victory over the Detroit Red Wings in Game Seven of the Finals. Leafs rookie goaltender Frank McCool, who allowed only nine goals in seven starts, limited the Wings to one goal or less for the fifth time in the series.

April 22, 1962 • Toronto's Bob Nevin and Dick Duff notched third-period goals to defeat the Chicago Black Hawks 2-1 in Game Six of the 1962 Finals. The win propelled the Maple Leafs to their first of three straight Stanley Cup championships.

April 22, 1976 • Toronto center Darryl Sittler equalled Maurice Richard's 32-year-old record for most goals in one playoff game by scoring five goals in the Maple Leafs' 8-5 Quarterfinal series win over the Philadelphia Flyers. Philadelphia's Reg Leach joined Richard and Sittler just days later, as Leach scored five of his playoff-record 19 goals on May 6, 1976, in a 6-3 win over the Boston Bruins.

April 22, 1988 • Patrik Sundstrom set an NHL record by recording eight points (3-5-8) in New Jersey's 10-4 win over Washington in Game Three of the Patrick Division Final.

April 23, 1950 • In the first Game Seven overtime in Finals history, left winger Pete Babando, assisted by center George Gee at 8:31 of the second overtime period, gave the Detroit Red Wings a 4-3 win and the 1950 Stanley Cup title. Four years later, another Detroit left winger, Tony Leswick, repeated Babando's overtime feat in Game Seven of the 1954 Finals. Since then, no player has scored the Cup-winning goal in overtime in the seventh and deciding game of the Finals.

April 23, 1996 • The Tampa Bay Lightning established an all-time NHL attendance record as 28,183 fans filled the ThunderDome for Game Four of Tampa Bay's Eastern Conference Quarterfinal series with the Philadelphia Flyers. The Flyers won 4-1, tying the series at two wins apiece. They went on to win the series in six.

April 23, 1997 • Wayne Gretzky scored a natural hat trick in the second period to lead the New York Rangers to a 3-2 victory over the Florida Panthers at Madison Square Garden, opening up a 3-1 series lead. Gretzky scored three goals in a 6:23 span to give the Rangers a

3-1 lead. The hat trick was his ninth in the postseason, extending his playoff record.

April 24, 1994 • Chicago Blackhawks defenseman Gary Suter tallied three goals in a 4-3 overtime win over the Toronto Maple Leafs in Game Four of their Western Conference Quarterfinal series. Suter became the eighth defenseman in Stanley Cup playoffs history to post a hat trick, joining Bobby Orr, Dick Redmond, Denis Potvin, Doug Halward, Paul Reinhart (twice), Al Iafrate and Eric Desjardins.

April 24, 1996 • Petr Nedved of the Penguins scored at the 19:15 mark of the fourth overtime period to give Pittsburgh a 3-2 win over Washington in the third-longest game in NHL history. Washington's Joe Juneau was stopped by Ken Wregget on the first penalty shot ever taken in overtime of a Stanley Cup playoff game.

April 24, 1997 • The Colorado Avalanche shut out the Chicago Blackhawks 7-0 to gain a 3-2 series lead. It marked the 89th playoff win of Patrick Roy's career, an NHL record.

April 24, 1999 • Colorado Avalanche goaltender Patrick Roy, the NHL's all-time leader for postseason victories, earned his 100th career playoff win as the Avalanche defeated San Jose 3–1 to take a 1-0 lead in their opening-round series.

April 25, 1964 • Toronto goalie Johnny Bower blanked the Detroit Red Wings 4-0 to propel the Maple Leafs to their third straight Stanley Cup title. Four different scorers provided the offensive support for Bower, the Leafs' "China Wall."

April 26, 1975 • Goaltender Glenn Resch and the New York Islanders blanked the Pittsburgh Penguins 1-0 to win Game Seven and capture their 1975 Quarterfinal series. The Islanders became just the second team in NHL history to win a best-of-seven series after losing the first three games, joining the 1942 Toronto Maple Leafs. The Islanders nearly repeated the feat in the Semifinals against Philadelphia. The Islanders again lost the first three games of the series only to bounce back and win the next three. Their bid for an unprecedented second straight 0-3 comeback was stopped as they lost Game Seven, 4-1.

April 26, 1997 • Playing in his final NHL game, Pittsburgh's Mario Lemieux registered a goal and an assist but it wasn't enough as the Philadelphia Flyers defeated the Penguins 6-3, capturing the series 4-1. The sellout crowd at Philadelphia's CoreStates Center acknowledged Lemieux's outstanding career with a rousing standing ovation following the game.

April 27, 1980 • Minnesota's Al MacAdam scored the series-winning goal late in the third period to give the visiting North Stars a 3-2 win over the Montreal Canadiens in Game Seven of the 1980 Quarterfinal series. The Minnesota win stopped the Canadiens' bid for a record-tying fifth consecutive Stanley Cup, a mark that had been set by Montreal from 1956-60.

April 27, 1994 • Buffalo Sabres center Dave Hannan scored at 5:43 of the fourth overtime period in a 1-0 home win over the New Jersey Devils in Game Six of their Eastern Conference Quarterfinal series. This game was the sixth longest in NHL history, beginning at 7:39 p.m. and concluding at 1:51 a.m.—six hours and 12 minutes later. Sabres goaltender Dominik Hasek turned aside all 70 of the shots he faced, while New Jersey netminder Martin Brodeur made 49 saves on 50 shots.

April 27, 1998 • The St. Louis Blues tallied four power-play goals in a span of 3:07 during the third period of a 4-3 win over Los Angeles in Game Three of their Western Conference Quarterfinal. The four fastest power-play goals by one team in NHL history were scored by Pascal Rheaume (9:59), Brett Hull (11:03) Pierre Turgeon (11:59) and Terry Yake (13:06).

April 28, 1996 • A sold-out crowd at the Winnipeg Arena said good-bye to the Winnipeg Jets following a 4-1 loss to the Detroit Red Wings in Game Six of their Western Conference Quarterfinal series. It marked the final game for the Jets before moving to Phoenix and becoming the Coyotes.

April 29, 1973 • Tony Esposito of the Chicago Black Hawks and Ken Dryden of the Montreal Canadiens, who had been Team Canada's goaltending duo in the 1972 Summit Series versus the Soviet Union, faced each other on opposite sides of the ice in Game One of the 1973 Finals. Dryden and the Canadiens won the contest 8-3 and went on to win the title series in six games. Montreal's Henri Richard tied brother Maurice and Leonard "Red" Kelly for the all-time record for Finals appearances with the 12th of his career.

April 30, 1972 • The New York Rangers made their first appearance in a Stanley Cup finals series game since 1950, losing to the Boston Bruins 6-5 in the opening contest. The 1972 championship clash between New York and Boston marked the first time in 43 years that the two had met in the Finals. Boston won the best-of-seven series in six games.

May 1 - 10

May 1, 1965 • Montreal captain Jean Beliveau notched the winning goal and added one assist to lead the Canadiens past the Chicago Black Hawks in Game Seven of the 1965 Finals. Beliveau, who posted a 5-5-10 scoring total in the seven-game Stanley Cup series, received a new NHL award, the Conn Smythe Trophy, as the most valuable player to his team in the playoffs.

May 2, 1967 • With the oldest lineup in Finals history, the Toronto Maple Leafs defeated the Montreal Canadiens 3-1 in Game Six to win the 1967 Stanley Cup. The Leafs' roster included 42-year-old goalie Johnny Bower and 41-year-old defenseman Allan Stanley as well as seven others at least 30 years old. Toronto defenseman Leonard "Red" Kelly played his 65th game in Finals competition, setting a Stanley Cup record later tied by Montreal's Henri Richard.

May 4, 1969 • With a 2-1 win in Game Four of the 1969 Stanley Cup, the Montreal Canadiens swept the St. Louis Blues in the Finals for the second straight season. The Conn Smythe Trophy was presented to Serge Savard, the first defenseman to receive the award.

May 4, 1972 • New York Rangers defenseman Brad Park registered two power-play goals in the first period of a 5-2 win against the Boston Bruins to tie a Stanley Cup Finals record for one period. Park joined Sid Smith (April 10, 1949) of Toronto and Maurice "Rocket" Richard (April 6, 1954) and Bernie "Boom Boom" Geoffrion (April 7, 1955) in accomplishing this power-play feat.

May 4, 1998 • Curtis Joseph of the Edmonton Oilers blanked the Colorado Avalanche 4-0 to become just the second goaltender in NHL playoff history to post back-to-back shutouts in Games Six and Seven of a playoff series. Joseph and the Oilers recorded a 2-0 win over the Avalanche in Game Six.

May 5, 1966 • At 2:30 of overtime in Game Six, Montreal Canadiens center Henri Richard became the ninth player in NHL history to record a Stanley Cup-winning goal in sudden-death. Richard's overtime goal gave Montreal a 3-2 win versus the Detroit Red Wings. Detroit goaltender Roger Crozier, who amassed a 2.17 average and one shutout in 12 playoff games, earned the Conn Smythe Trophy as the most valuable player to his team in postseason competition. Crozier was the first Conn Smythe winner from a losing team.

May 7, 1995 • The Boston Bruins made their 1995 Stanley Cup Playoffs debut, dropping a 5-0 home decision to the New Jersey Devils. The Bruins extended their NHL record by appearing in the playoffs for the 28th consecutive year.

May 8, 1973 • The Chicago Black Hawks and Montreal Canadiens combined to set an NHL record with 15 goals in one Finals game. Led by Stan Mikita's two-goal, two-assist performance, the Black Hawks edged the Canadiens 8-7 in Game Five at the Montreal Forum. Montreal went on to win the series four games to two.

May 8, 1982 • The Vancouver Canucks became the first team since the 1924 Vancouver Maroons of the Western Canada Hockey League (WCHL) to represent that city in the Stanley Cup Finals. The Canucks lost this opening game 6-5 in overtime to the New York Islanders, who went on to take the series in four straight games.

May 8, 1995 • New York Rangers center Mark Messier scored the 100th goal of his playoff career in an 8-3 win over the Quebec Nordiques in Game Two of their Eastern Conference Quarterfinal. He

became just the third player in NHL history to reach the milestone, joining former Oiler teammates Wayne Gretzky (110 career playoff goals) and Jari Kurri (102).

May 9, 1999 • With Detroit's 4-0 win over Colorado in Game Two of their Conference Semifinal series, Red Wings head coach Scotty Bowman recorded his 200th career playoff victory.

May 10, 1970 • Bobby Orr, who had distinguished himself in 1969-70 as the first defenseman in NHL history to record 100 points (33-87-120) in a season, scored just 40 seconds into overtime to give the Boston Bruins a 4-3 win and a four-game sweep versus the St. Louis Blues in the 1970 Finals. For Orr, the Conn Smythe Trophy winner, the goal was his first of the series.

May 10, 1973 • In Montreal's 6-4 series-ending victory in Game Six, Yvan Cournoyer (6-6-12) and Jacques Lemaire (5-7-12) tallied 1-2-3 and 0-2-2 scoring totals, respectively, to tie Gordie Howe's record of 12 points in one Final series. Meanwhile, Montreal's Henri Richard tied Leonard "Red" Kelly's all-time record for Stanley Cup games with the 65th of his career.

May 11 - 20

May 11, 1968 • The Montreal Canadiens swept the St. Louis Blues in straight games with a 3-2 win in Game Four of the 1968 Finals. For Montreal coach "Toe" Blake, it was his 11th Stanley Cup title, setting an all-time record for one individual. Blake, who had won three championships as a player and eight as a coach, retired following the series. Canadiens center Henri Richard later tied Blake's mark with his 11th Stanley Cup in 1973.

May 11, 1972 • For the second time in three seasons, defenseman Bobby Orr scored the Stanley Cup-winning goal as the Boston Bruins blanked the New York Rangers 3-0 in Game Six. The goal gave Orr, who won the Conn Smythe Trophy, a 5-19-24 scoring total in 15 playoff games.

May 11, 1995 • Detroit Red Wings right wing Dino Ciccarelli tallied three power-play goals in a 5-1 win over the Dallas Stars in Game Three of their Western Conference Quarterfinal to tie an NHL playoff record for most power-play goals in one game. Nine players, including Ciccarelli, had previously shared the record. Ciccarelli was the last player to accomplish the feat, on April 29, 1993 versus Toronto, and became the first player in NHL history to post three power-play goals in a playoff game on separate occasions.

May 11, 1996 • Colorado Avalanche goaltender Patrick Roy became the NHL's all-time playoff leader in minutes played by a goaltender, passing former New York Islanders standout Bill Smith. Colorado defeated Chicago 4-1 to take a 3-2 series lead.

May 12, 1995 • New Jersey Devils goaltender Martin Brodeur became just the fifth goaltender since the NHL introduced the best-of-seven format in 1939 to register three shutouts in one playoff series, following a 1-0 overtime win over the Boston Bruins in Game Four of their Conference Quarterfinal series. Brodeur joined Dave Kerr of the New York Rangers (1940), and three Toronto Maple Leafs goaltenders—Frank McCool (1945), Turk Broda (1950) and Felix Potvin (1994)—in this select club.

May 14, 1977 • Montreal Canadiens center Jacques Lemaire scored his third game-winning goal of the 1977 Finals and his second career overtime tally in a Stanley Cup game, leading the Montreal Canadiens to a 2-1 series-clinching win against the Boston Bruins. Only Maurice "Rocket" Richard of the Canadiens (3) and Don "Bones" Raleigh of the Rangers (2) have ever posted more than one career overtime goal in Finals history.

May 14, 1993 • The New York Islanders defeated the Pittsburgh Penguins 4-3 in overtime to win their Patrick Division Final in seven games. For Islanders coach Al Arbour, it represented his 30th career playoff series win as a coach, moving him into a tie for the all-time lead with Penguins coach Scott Bowman. The win was also Arbour's 200th postseason game.

May 15, 1990 • Edmonton's Petr Klima scored 15:13 into the third overtime period to lead the Oilers to a 3-2 triumph over the Boston Bruins in Game One of the 1990 Finals at Boston Garden. The 55:13 overtime was the longest in Finals history, 1:23 longer than the 53:50 of overtime played in Game Three of the 1931 Finals between Chicago and Montreal.

May 15, 1995 • The Vancouver Canucks tallied two shorthanded goals in 17 seconds during the second period of their 6-5 win over the St. Louis Blues in Game Five of their Conference Quarterfinal series to set an NHL playoff record for the fastest two shorthanded goals by one team. The Canucks passed the old mark of 24 seconds set by the 1978 Montreal Canadiens versus Detroit on April 23, 1978. Christian Ruuttu scored for Vancouver at 4:31 of the second period, followed by Geoff Courtnall at 4:48.

May 16, 1971 • Center Jean Beliveau tallied two assists, the final two points of his NHL career, as the Montreal Canadiens downed the Chicago Black Hawks 4-3 in Game Six of the 1971 Finals. Beliveau, the all-time leader in Finals history with a 30-31-61 scoring total, helped his club win the Stanley Cup two days later in Game Seven.

May 16, 1976 • In Game Four of the 1976 Finals, Philadelphia Flyers right winger Reggie Leach scored his 19th goal of the playoffs, extending his NHL record in that category. Although the Flyers lost the game 5-3 and the series 4-0 to the Montreal Canadiens, Leach won the Conn Smythe Trophy as the most valuable player to his team in the playoffs.

May 16, 1982 • Right winger Mike Bossy scored twice, including the series-winning goal, to lead the New York Islanders to their third straight Stanley Cup championship. The 3-1 victory gave New York a four-game sweep against the Vancouver Canucks.

May 16, 1993 • Montreal Canadiens goaltender Patrick Roy recorded his 60th career playoff win in the Canadiens' 4-1 win in Game One of the Wales Conference Final, becoming just the fifth goaltender in NHL history to reach the plateau. Other goaltenders with 60-or-more postseason wins are Grant Fuhr (92), Billy Smith (88), Ken Dryden (80) and Jacques Plante (71).

May 16, 1996 • The Detroit Red Wings defeated the St. Louis Blues 1-0 in a classic seventh and deciding game of their Western Conference Semifinal series at Joe Louis Arena. Steve Yzerman notched the series-winning goal at 1:15 of the second overtime period as Detroit rallied from three straight losses after opening the series with a pair of wins.

May 17, 1981 • In Game Three of the 1981 Finals, Minnesota North Stars right wing Dino Ciccarelli broke Don Maloney's one-year rookie playoff scoring record (20 points in 1979) with his 21st point, a goal against the New York Islanders. The Islanders won the game 7-5 and later took the series 4-1.

May 17, 1983 • The New York Islanders beat the Edmonton Oilers 4-2 to complete a four-game sweep of the 1983 Finals. It was the Islanders' fourth straight Stanley Cup, one short of the NHL record for consecutive championships set by the Montreal Canadiens from 1956 to 1960).

May 18, 1971 • The Montreal Canadiens, who had missed the playoffs in 1970, won the 1971 Stanley Cup with a 3-2 triumph over the Chicago Black Hawks in Game Seven. 23-year-old rookie goalie Ken Dryden took the Conn Smythe Trophy with a 12-8 record and a 3.00 average in the playoffs.

May 18, 1986 • Montreal center Brian Skrudland notched the fastest overtime goal in playoff history, scoring just nine seconds into overtime to give the Canadiens a 3-2 victory over the Calgary Flames in Game Two of the 1986 Finals. The win was the first of four straight for Montreal en route to the team's 23rd Stanley Cup title.

May 19, 1974 • The Philadelphia Flyers, who had entered the NHL in 1967-68, became the first expansion team to win the Stanley Cup, downing the Boston Bruins 1-0 in Game Six of the 1974 Finals. Left winger Rick MacLeish scored the game's only goal, while goaltender Bernie Parent, who won the Conn Smythe Trophy as playoff MVP, recorded the shutout.

May 19, 1984 • The Edmonton Oilers, one of four former WHA teams which joined the League in 1979-80, won their first Stanley Cup title.

Oilers center Mark Messier, who registered an 8-18-26 scoring mark in 19 playoff games, won the Conn Smythe Trophy.

May 20, 1986 • In the first period of Game Three, Montreal and Calgary combined for the fastest four goals by two teams in a Finals game. Calgary's Joel Otto (17:59) and Montreal's Bobby Smith (18:25), Mats Naslund (19:17) and Bob Gainey (19:33) posted goals within one minute and 34 seconds to set the mark. The Canadiens defeated the Flames 5-3.

May 20, 1993 • The Montreal Canadiens won their seventh overtime game in the postseason, a 2-1 win over the New York Islanders, to set a new playoff record. The Canadiens passed the previous mark of six, set by the Islanders in 1980.

May 21 - 31

May 21, 1979 • Center Jacques Lemaire scored twice, including his second career Stanley Cup-winning goal, to power the Montreal Canadiens past the New York Rangers 4-1 in Game Five. The win gave Montreal its fourth straight Stanley Cup, one short of the record (5) set by the same team, 1956-60.

May 21, 1981 • New York Islanders center Butch Goring notched two goals to help defeat the Minnesota North Stars 5-1 in the fifth and final game of the 1981 Finals. Goring, who assisted the winning goal in Game Two and scored the winner in Game Three, earned the Conn Smythe Trophy.

May 22, 1987 • In Game Three of the 1987 Finals, Edmonton Oilers center Mark Messier set a new playoff record with his eighth career shorthanded goal. Edmonton lost the game 5-3 loss to the Philadelphia Flyers but went on to win the series in seven games.

May 22, 1999 • The Colorado Avalanche defeated the Dallas Stars 2-1 in the opening game of the Western Conference Final, tying a playoff record for consecutive road victories (seven). The Avalanche equalled a mark previously set by the 1980 and 1982 New York Islanders and the 1995 New Jersey Devils. Dallas went on to defeat Colorado in seven games.

May 24, 1980 • Right winger Bob Nystrom scored at 7:11 of overtime as the New York Islanders defeated the Philadelphia Flyers 5-4 and captured the 1980 Stanley Cup in six games. Nystrom's goal was the fourth and final overtime tally of his playoff career and moved him into second place on the all-time list behind Maurice "Rocket" Richard (6).

May 24, 1986 • The Montreal Canadiens defeated the Calgary Flames 4-3 in Game Five en route to their 23rd Stanley Cup title, a new professional record for the most championship seasons. Montreal had been tied with Major League Baseball's New York Yankees, winners of 22 World Series.

May 24, 1990 • The Edmonton Oilers won their fifth Stanley Cup in seven years with a 4-1 win over the Boston Bruins in Game Five of the 1990 Finals at Boston Garden. Edmonton goaltender Bill Ranford, who registered all 16 wins for the Oilers in the postseason, captured the Conn Smythe Trophy as playoff MVP. Seven Oilers players—Glenn Anderson, Grant Fuhr, Randy Gregg, Charlie Huddy, Jari Kurri, Kevin Lowe and Mark Messier—were members of all five championship clubs.

May 24, 1994 • Greg Adams of the Vancouver Canucks scored at 14 seconds of the second overtime period to give his team a 4-3 win over the Toronto Maple Leafs in Game Five of the Western Conference Final at Pacific Coliseum. The win clinched the series for the Canucks and earned them a berth in the Stanley Cup Championship for the first time since 1982.

May 24, 1995 • New York Rangers center Mark Messier's goal in the second period of a 5-2 loss to the Philadelphia Flyers in Game Three of their Conference Semifinal was the 102nd of his playoff career, tying Jari Kurri for second place on the all-time list.

May 25, 1978 • Conn Smythe Trophy winner Larry Robinson assisted Mario Tremblay's Stanley Cup-winning goal to lead the Montreal Canadiens past the Boston Bruins 4-1 in Game Six. Robinson was one of three Canadiens, including Doug Jarvis and Steve Shutt, who appeared in all 95 games during the 1977-78 season.

May 25, 1985 • Edmonton Oilers center Wayne Gretzky notched three goals in the first period of a 4-3 win against the Philadelphia Flyers to tie a an NHL record for one Finals period. Three players—Toronto's Harvey "Busher" Jackson (April 5, 1932), Detroit's Ted Lindsay (April 5, 1955) and Montreal's Maurice "Rocket" Richard (April 6, 1957)—previously shared the mark.

May 25, 1989 • The Calgary Flames captured their first Stanley Cup title with a 4-2 win over the Montreal Canadiens in Game Six of the 1989 Stanley Cup Championship. Goaltender Mike Vernon recorded his 16th victory of the postseason, tying an NHL playoff record set by Edmonton's Grant Fuhr the previous year, and defenseman Al MacInnis won the Conn Smythe Trophy after leading all playoff scorers with totals of 7-24-31 in 22 games.

May 27, 1975 • Philadelphia goaltender Bernie Parent blanked the Buffalo Sabres 2-0 in Game Six en route to the Flyers' second straight Stanley Cup title. Parent earned the Conn Smythe Trophy to become the first back-to-back winner of the award and the second player, after Bobby Orr, to win it twice. Edmonton's Wayne Gretzky collected his second career Conn Smythe Trophy in 1988, Mario Lemieux of the Penguins won the award in 1991 and 1992 and Patrick Roy of Montreal won in 1986 and 1993.

May 27, 1994 • Stephane Matteau of the New York Rangers scored at 4:24 of the second overtime period to give his team a 2-1 win over the New Jersey Devils in the seventh and deciding game of the Eastern Conference Final at Madison Square Garden. A record three games in the series were decided in double overtime, with Matteau scoring the winner in two of them. The win earned the Rangers a berth in the Stanley Cup Championship for the first time since 1979.

May 27, 1995 • Detroit Red Wings defenseman Paul Coffey became the all-time leading scorer for defensemen in Stanley Cup playoff history, tallying two points (1-1-2) in Detroit's 6-2 win over the San Jose Sharks in Game Four of their Conference Semifinal. The Red Wings clinched the series in four straight games. Coffey's first-period goal was his 165th point in the postseason (51-114-165 in 146 games), moving him past former New York Islanders rearguard and Hockey Hall of Famer Denis Potvin. Potvin registered 164 points (56-108-164) in 185 career playoff games.

May 30, 1985 • The Edmonton Oilers downed the Philadelphia Flyers 8-3 in Game Five to take the 1985 Stanley Cup and their second straight championship title. Conn Smythe Trophy winner Wayne Gretzky scored a goal and assisted on three others to set playoff records for assists (30) and points (47) in a single postseason, and Jari Kurri tied Reg Leach's record with his 19th goal of the playoffs.

May 30, 1998 • Washington Capitals goaltender Olaf Kolzig became the 10th goaltender in NHL history to record four shutouts in one playoff year, blanking the Buffalo Sabres 2-0 in Game Four of the Eastern Conference Final. Washington went on to win the series in six games and reach the Stanley Cup Finals for the first time.

May 31, 1987 • Right winger Jari Kurri scored the Cup-winning goal at 14:59 of the second period as the Edmonton Oilers beat the Philadelphia Flyers 3-1 in Game Seven of the 1987 Finals. The win marked the third Cup title in four seasons for Edmonton.

May 31, 1997 • The 1997 Stanley Cup Finals opened at the CoreStates Center in Philadelphia in front of 20,291 fans, the largest crowd ever to witness a hockey game in the state of Pennsylvania. The Detroit Red Wings won Game One of the series as goaltender Mike Vernon made 26 saves in a 4-2 win. Unheralded Red Wings Kirk Maltby and Joe Kocur gave Detroit a 2-1 lead after the first period and Sergei Fedorov tallied the game-winner just after the midway point of the second period.

June

June 1, 1992 • In the first NHL game ever played in the month of June, the Pittsburgh Penguins captured their second consecutive Stanley Cup championship with a 6-5 win over the Chicago Blackhawks at Chicago Stadium. The Penguins, who won the best-of-seven series

4-0, tied an NHL playoff record by winning their 11th straight game in the postseason. Mario Lemieux led all playoff scorers and joined Philadelphia goaltender Bernie Parent as just the second player ever to earn back-to-back Conn Smythe Trophy honors.

June 3, 1993 • Montreal Canadiens defenseman Eric Desjardins became the first defenseman in NHL history to record a hat trick in the Stanley Cup Finals. Desjardins tallied a game-tying power-play goal late in the third period and added the overtime winner in a 4-3 win. The tying goal came as a result of a stick measurement requested by Canadiens coach Jacques Demers. The stick used by Los Angeles defenseman Marty McSorley was found to have a curve that exceeded the allowable limit, resulting in a two-minute penalty to McSorley at 18:15 of the third period. Desjardins scored 32 seconds later. His winning goal was scored after just 51 seconds of overtime.

June 4, 1996 • The 1996 Stanley Cup finals opened with the Colorado Avalanche defeating the Florida Panthers 3-1 at McNichols Sports Arena in Denver. For the first time in NHL history, the two competing teams were each making their inaugural appearance in the Stanley Cup finals.

June 5, 1997 • The Detroit Red Wings opened a commanding three-games-to-none lead in the Stanley Cup finals with a 6-1 win over Philadelphia in Game Three at Joe Louis Arena. After the Flyers' John LeClair had opened the scoring at 7:03 of the first period, Detroit replied with three unanswered goals in the opening period. The win broke an eight-game Red Wings home losing streak in the final round of the Stanley Cup dating back to 1964. Detroit forwards Sergei Fedorov and Martin Lapointe each tallied two goals to pace the Red Wings over the Flyers. With the loss, Philadelphia's record dropped to nine wins and two losses when scoring first in the 1997 playoffs.

June 7, 1993 • John LeClair posted his second overtime goal in as many games to lead the Canadiens to a 3-2 win at Los Angeles to take a 3-1 series lead in the Finals. LeClair became the second player in NHL history, after Don Raleigh of the New York Rangers in 1950 versus Detroit, to tally overtime goals in consecutive games in the Finals.

June 8, 1996 • A Stanley Cup game is played in Florida for the first time as the visiting Colorado Avalanche rally to defeat the Florida Panthers 3-2 at the Miami Arena and take a commanding 3-0 lead in the series.

June 9, 1993 • The Montreal Canadiens captured their 24th Stanley Cup championship, defeating the Los Angeles Kings 4-1 to win the Stanley Cup Final series in five games. Canadiens goaltender Patrick Roy was awarded the Conn Smythe Trophy as playoff MVP, posting a 16-4 record and an average of 2.13 in 20 games.

June 10, 1996 • Uwe Krupp scored the Stanley Cup-winning goal at 4:31 of the third overtime period, giving the Colorado Avalanche a 1-0 victory over the Florida Panthers in the third-longest game ever played in the Stanley Cup Final. In sweeping the series, the Avalanche, who had relocated to Denver from Quebec, became the first NHL club to win the Stanley Cup after its first season in a new city.

June 14, 1994 • The New York Rangers defeated the Vancouver Canucks 3-2 at Madison Square Garden in Game Seven of the Stanley Cup Finals. This was the first seven-game Final series since 1987 and just the third since 1967. Rangers defenseman Brian Leetch captured the Conn Smythe Trophy as playoff MVP, leading all postseason scorers with 34 points (11-23-34) in 23 games.

June 16, 1998 • The Detroit Red Wings captured their second straight Stanley Cup title, sweeping the Washington Capitals with a 4-1 victory. Scotty Bowman's eighth Stanley Cup win as a coach tied Toe Blake's NHL record.

June 17, 1995 • The 1995 Stanley Cup Championship series opened at Joe Louis Arena and the New Jersey Devils captured Game One with a 2-1 win. Right wing Claude Lemieux scored the game-winning goal early in the third period, his third game-winner of the playoffs and 14th of his career in the postseason. The Devils improved their road record in the playoffs to 9-1, setting a new NHL record for most road wins by one team in the playoffs.

June 19, 1999 • The Dallas Stars captured their first Stanley Cup title in franchise history with a 2-1 win over Buffalo in Game Six of the Finals. Brett Hull scored at 14:51 of the third overtime, ending the second longest game in finals history. The longest was played on May 15, 1990.

June 20, 1995 • The New Jersey Devils defeated the Detroit Red Wings 4-2 at Joe Louis Arena to take a two games to none series lead in the Stanley Cup Championship. New Jersey extended its playoff record by winning its 10th game on the road and tied another playoff record by winning their seventh straight road game.

STANLEY CUP NOTEBOOK

First-Game Winners Hold Decisive Edge

Since the NHL implemented the best-of-seven Stanley Cup Championship format in 1939, the following winning trends have developed:

- Teams winning Game 1 have won the Cup 48 of 61 times (79%).
- Teams winning both Games 1 and 2 have won the Cup 37 of 40 times (93%).
- Teams winning Games 1, 2 and 3 have won the Cup 24 of 25 times (96%).
- Teams winning Game 3 after splitting the first two games have won the Cup 18 of 21 times (86%).
- Teams holding a 2-1 series lead have won the Cup 31 of 36 times (86%).
- Teams winning Game 5 after splitting the first four games have won the Cup 13 of 16 times (81%).
- Teams holding a 3-2 series lead have won the Cup 22 of 26 times (85%).

Stanley Before Calder

Tony Esposito, Danny Grant and Ken Dryden all won the Stanley Cup one year before they captured the Calder Trophy as the NHL's top rookie.

Grant was a member of the 1968 Cup-winning Montreal Canadiens before winning the Calder in 1969 with Minnesota. Tony Esposito won the Cup with the Canadiens in 1969 and the Calder the following season with the Chicago Black Hawks. Dryden won the Cup with the Canadiens in 1971, in addition to claiming the Conn Smythe Trophy as the postseason's MVP. He received the Calder in 1972.

Sub-.500 Teams in the Stanley Cup Final

Fifteen teams have advanced to the Stanley Cup Final after posting regular-season records below the .500 mark.

The complete list follows with Cup winners shown in bold.

Year	Team	Regular-Season Record
1991	Minnesota North Stars	27-39-14
1982	Vancouver Canucks	30-33-17
1968	St. Louis Blues	27-31-16
1961	Detroit Red Wings	25-29-16
1959	Toronto Maple Leafs	27-32-11
1958	Boston Bruins	27-28-15
1953	Boston Bruins	28-29-13
1951	Montreal Canadiens	25-30-15
1950	New York Rangers	28-31-11
1949	**Toronto Maple Leafs**	22-25-13
1944	Chicago Black Hawks	22-23-5
1942	Detroit Red Wings	19-25-4
1939	Toronto Maple Leafs	19-20-9
1938	**Chicago Black Hawks**	14-25-9
1937	New York Rangers	19-20-9

Crease Captain on the Cup

Charlie Gardiner, captain of the Chicago Black Hawks in 1934, is the only goaltender to have his name appear on the Cup as the captain of a Cup-winning team.

CHAPTER 15

Final Series History, Team by Team

1918 – 99

Overall Final Series Record

1918-99

TEAM	SERIES	W	L	GP	W	L	GF	GA
Anaheim	–	–	–	–	–	–	–	–
Atlanta	–	–	–	–	–	–	–	–
Boston [1]	17	5	12	77	28	47	168	219
Buffalo	2	0	2	12	4	8	21	32
Calgary ('20s)	1	0	1	2	0	2	1	9
Calgary	2	1	1	11	5	6	32	31
Chicago	10	3	7	53	22	31	132	158
Colorado	1	1	0	4	4	0	15	4
Dallas [2]	3	1	2	17	7	10	45	63
Detroit	21	9	12	109	50	59	268	283
Edmonton ('20s) [3]	1	0	1	2	0	2	1	3
Edmonton	6	5	1	30	20	10	108	78
Florida	1	0	1	4	0	4	4	11
Hartford	–	–	–	–	–	–	–	–
Los Angeles	1	0	1	5	1	4	12	15
Montreal [4]	32	23	8	163	105	57	481	381
Mtl. Maroons	3	2	1	12	8	4	26	12
New Jersey	1	1	0	4	4	0	16	7
Ottawa ('20s) [1,5]	4	4	0	20	13	5	47	33
Ottawa	–	–	–	–	–	–	–	–
Nashville	–	–	–	–	–	–	–	–
NY Islanders	5	4	1	24	17	7	99	78
NY Rangers	10	4	6	50	22	28	115	130
Philadelphia	7	2	5	38	14	24	106	124
Phoenix	–	–	–	–	–	–	–	–
Pittsburgh	2	2	0	10	8	2	43	26
St. Louis	3	0	3	12	0	12	24	63
San Jose	–	–	–	–	–	–	–	–
Seattle [4,6]	1	0	0	5	2	2	19	10
Tampa Bay	–	–	–	–	–	–	–	–
Toronto [7]	21	13	8	105	56	49	278	269
Vancouver ('20s) [8]	5	0	5	21	7	14	52	61
Vancouver	2	0	2	11	3	8	29	39
Victoria [9]	2	1	1	8	4	4	19	18
Washington	1	0	1	4	0	4	7	13

1 Ottawa played two tie games against Boston in 1927.
2 Includes appearances by Minnesota North Stars in 1981 and 1991.
3 An Edmonton team also played for the Stanley Cup in 1908 and 1910.
4 No decision in 1919 Finals, interrupted by flu epidemic. Seattle and Montreal had each won two games. One game was tied.
Note: Montreal also won the Stanley Cup in 1916 for 24 titles overall.
5 Ottawa franchise was also Stanley Cup champion in 1903, 1904, 1905, 1909 and 1911.
6 Seattle Metropolitans of the PCHA won the Stanley Cup in 1917.
7 Toronto Blueshirts won the Stanley Cup in 1914, giving the franchise 14 victories in all. Total also include Toronto Arenas (1918) and Toronto St. Pats (1922).
8 Vancouver of the PCHA won the Stanley Cup in 1915.
9 Victoria of the PCHA also played for the Stanley Cup in 1914 (Victoria represented the WCHL in 1925 and the WHL in 1926).

BOSTON 1925-99

All-Time Final Series Record

Versus	Series	W	L	GP	W	L	GF	GA
Detroit	2	1	1	8	4	4	17	22
Edmonton	2	0	2	9	1	8	17	38
Montreal	7	0	7	33	7	26	64	107
NY Rangers	2	2	0	8	6	2	22	17
Ottawa* ('20s)	1	0	1	4	0	2	3	7
Philadelphia	1	0	1	6	2	4	13	15
St. Louis	1	1	0	4	4	0	20	7
Toronto	1	1	0	5	4	1	12	6
TOTALS	**17**	**5**	**12**	**77**	**28**	**47**	**168**	**219**

Final Series Appearances

Versus	Year	Winner	W	L	GF	GA
Ottawa*	1927	Ottawa	0	2	3	7
NY Rangers	1929	Boston	2	0	4	1
Montreal	1930	Montreal	0	2	3	7
Toronto	1939	Boston	4	1	12	6
Detroit	1941	Boston	4	0	12	6
Detroit	1943	Detroit	0	4	5	16
Montreal	1946	Montreal	1	4	13	19
Montreal	1953	Montreal	1	4	9	16
Montreal	1957	Montreal	1	4	6	15
Montreal	1958	Montreal	2	4	14	16
St. Louis	1970	Boston	4	0	20	7
NY Rangers	1972	Boston	4	2	18	16
Philadelphia	1974	Philadelphia	2	4	13	15
Montreal	1977	Montreal	0	4	6	16
Montreal	1978	Montreal	2	4	13	18
Edmonton	1988	Edmonton	0	4	9	18
Edmonton	1990	Edmonton	1	4	8	20

* includes two ties

Top Five Final Series Scorers

Player	GP	G	A	TP	PIM
Bobby Orr	16	8	12	20	31
Phil Esposito	16	4	15	19	28
Ken Hodge	16	6	10	16	27
Milt Schmidt	18	6	8	14	4
John Bucyk	16	8	5	13	4

BUFFALO 1971-99

All-Time Final Series Record

Versus	Series	W	L	GP	W	L	GF	GA
Dallas	1	0	1	6	2	4	9	13
Philadelphia	1	0	1	6	2	4	12	19
TOTALS	**2**	**0**	**2**	**12**	**4**	**8**	**21**	**32**

Final Series Appearances

Versus	Year	Winner	W	L	GF	GA
Philadelphia	1975	Philadelphia	2	4	12	19
Dallas	1999	Dallas	2	4	9	13

Top Five Final Series Scorers

Player	GP	G	A	TP	PIM
Rick Martin	6	2	4	6	6
Don Luce	6	2	3	5	12
Stu Barnes	6	3	0	3	0
Danny Gare	6	2	1	3	4
Jerry Korab	6	2	1	3	6
Jim Lorentz	6	1	2	3	2
Alexei Zhitnik	6	1	2	3	18
Richard Smehlik	6	0	3	3	2

CALGARY 1922-26

All-Time Final Series Record

Versus	Series	W	L	GP	W	L	GF	GA
Montreal	1	0	1	2	0	2	1	9
TOTALS	**1**	**0**	**1**	**2**	**0**	**2**	**1**	**9**

Final Series Appearances

Versus	Year	Winner	W	L	GF	GA
Montreal	1924	Montreal	0	2	1	9

Top Two Final Series Scorers

Player	GP	G	A	TP	PIM
Herb Gardiner	2	1	0	1	0
Bernie Morris	2	0	1	1	0

CALGARY 1973-99

All-Time Final Series Record

Versus	Series	W	L	GP	W	L	GF	GA
Montreal	2	1	1	11	5	6	32	31
TOTALS	**2**	**1**	**1**	**11**	**5**	**6**	**32**	**31**

Final Series Appearances

Versus	Year	Winner	W	L	GF	GA
Montreal	1986	Montreal	1	4	13	15
Montreal	1989	Calgary	4	2	19	16

Top Five Final Series Scorers

Player	GP	G	A	TP	PIM
Al MacInnis	11	5	8	13	26
Joe Mullen	10	7	4	11	8
Joel Otto	11	3	8	11	14
Doug Gilmour	6	4	3	7	6
Jim Peplinski	9	1	5	6	47

CHICAGO 1927-99

All-Time Final Series Record

Versus	Series	W	L	GP	W	L	GF	GA
Detroit	2	2	0	10	7	3	28	19
Montreal	5	0	5	29	10	19	69	98
Pittsburgh	1	0	1	4	0	4	10	15
Toronto	2	1	1	10	5	5	25	26
TOTALS	**10**	**3**	**7**	**53**	**22**	**31**	**132**	**158**

Final Series Appearances

Versus	Year	Winner	W	L	GF	GA
Montreal	1931	Montreal	2	3	8	11
Detroit	1934	Chicago	3	1	9	7
Toronto	1938	Chicago	3	1	10	8
Montreal	1944	Montreal	0	4	8	16
Detroit	1961	Chicago	4	2	19	12
Toronto	1962	Toronto	2	4	15	18
Montreal	1965	Montreal	3	4	12	18
Montreal	1971	Montreal	3	4	18	20
Montreal	1973	Montreal	2	4	23	33
Pittsburgh	1992	Pittsburgh	0	4	10	15

Top Five Final Series Scorers

Player	GP	G	A	TP	PIM
Stan Mikita	31	10	21	31	58
Bobby Hull	26	11	17	28	26
Pierre Pilote	17	2	13	15	22
Jim Pappin	13	7	4	11	18
Johnny Gottselig	13	6	5	11	6

COLORADO 1980-99

All-Time Final Series Record

Versus	Series	W	L	GP	W	L	GF	GA
Florida	1	1	0	4	4	0	15	5
TOTALS	**1**	**1**	**0**	**4**	**4**	**0**	**15**	**4**

Final Series Appearances

Versus	Year	Winner	W	L	GF	GA
Florida	1996	Colorado	4	0	15	4

Top Five Final Series Scorers

Player	GP	G	A	TP	PIM
Peter Forsberg	4	3	2	5	0
Joe Sakic	4	1	4	5	2
Adam Deadmarsh	4	0	4	4	4
Uwe Krupp	4	2	1	3	2
Rene Corbet	4	2	1	3	0

DALLAS 1968-99

All-Time Final Series Record*

Versus	Series	W	L	GP	W	L	GF	GA
Buffalo	1	1	0	6	4	2	13	9
NY Islanders	1	0	1	5	1	4	16	26
Pittsburgh	1	0	1	6	2	4	16	28
TOTALS	**3**	**1**	**2**	**17**	**7**	**10**	**45**	**63**

* Includes final series appearances by Minnesota in 1981 and 1991.

Final Series Appearances

Versus	Year	Winner	W	L	GF	GA
NY Islanders	1981	NY Islanders	1	4	16	26
Pittsburgh	1991	Pittsburgh	2	4	16	28
Buffalo	1999	Dallas	4	2	13	9

Top Five Final Series Scorers

Player	GP	G	A	TP	PIM
Bobby Smith	11	4	5	9	8
Steve Payne	5	5	2	7	2
Mike Modano	6	0	7	7	8
Dave Gagner	6	4	2	6	14
Dino Ciccarelli	5	3	2	5	19
Neal Broten	11	3	2	5	4
Jere Lehtinen	6	2	3	5	0

DETROIT 1927-99

All-Time Final Series Record

Versus	Series	W	L	GP	W	L	GF	GA
Boston	2	1	1	8	4	4	22	17
Chicago	2	0	2	10	3	7	19	28
Montreal	5	3	2	29	15	14	75	70
New Jersey	1	0	1	4	0	4	7	16
NY Rangers	2	2	0	12	7	5	31	25
Philadelphia	1	1	0	4	4	0	16	6
Toronto	7	1	6	38	13	25	85	114
Washington	1	1	0	4	4	0	13	7
TOTALS	**21**	**9**	**12**	**109**	**50**	**59**	**268**	**283**

Final Series Appearances

Versus	Year	Winner	W	L	GF	GA
Chicago	1934	Chicago	1	3	7	9
Toronto	1936	Detroit	3	1	18	11
NY Rangers	1937	Detroit	3	2	9	8
Boston	1941	Boston	0	4	6	12
Toronto	1942	Toronto	3	4	19	25
Boston	1943	Detroit	4	0	16	5
Toronto	1945	Toronto	3	4	9	9
Toronto	1948	Toronto	0	4	7	18
Toronto	1949	Toronto	0	4	5	12
NY Rangers	1950	Detroit	4	3	22	17
Montreal	1952	Detroit	4	0	11	2
Montreal	1954	Detroit	4	3	14	12
Montreal	1955	Detroit	4	3	27	20
Montreal	1956	Montreal	1	4	9	18
Chicago	1961	Chicago	2	4	12	19
Toronto	1963	Toronto	1	4	10	17
Toronto	1964	Toronto	3	4	17	22
Montreal	1966	Montreal	2	4	14	18
New Jersey	1995	New Jersey	0	4	7	16
Philadelphia	1997	Detroit	4	0	16	6
Washington	1998	Detroit	4	0	13	7

Top Five Final Series Scorers

Player	GP	G	A	TP	PIM
Gordie Howe	55	18	32	50	94
Alex Delvecchio	47	16	22	38	2
Ted Lindsay	44	19	15	34	48
Sid Abel	34	9	11	20	25
Syd Howe	28	8	12	20	4

EDMONTON 1922-26

All-Time Final Series Record

Versus	Series	W	L	GP	W	L	GF	GA
Ottawa	1	0	1	2	0	2	1	3
TOTALS	**1**	**0**	**1**	**2**	**0**	**2**	**1**	**3**

Final Series Appearances*

Versus	Year	Winner	W	L	GF	GA
Ottawa	1923	Ottawa	0	2	1	3

Top Two Final Series Scorers

Player	GP	G	A	TP	PIM
Crutchy Morrison	2	1	0	1	0
Joe Simpson	2	0	1	1	0

EDMONTON 1980-99

All-Time Final Series Record

Versus	Series	W	L	GP	W	L	GF	GA
Boston	2	2	0	9	8	1	38	17
NY Islanders	2	1	1	9	4	5	27	29
Philadelphia	2	2	0	12	8	4	43	32
TOTALS	**6**	**5**	**1**	**30**	**20**	**10**	**108**	**78**

Final Series Appearances

Versus	Year	Winner	W	L	GF	GA
NY Islanders	1983	NY Islanders	0	4	6	17
NY Islanders	1984	Edmonton	4	1	21	12
Philadelphia	1985	Edmonton	4	1	21	14
Philadelphia	1987	Edmonton	4	3	22	18
Boston	1988	Edmonton	4	0	18	9
Boston	1990	Edmonton	4	1	20	8

Top Five Final Series Scorers

Player	GP	G	A	TP	PIM
Wayne Gretzky	26	16	30	46	6
Jari Kurri	31	14	24	38	14
Glenn Anderson	31	14	12	26	55
Mark Messier	31	9	15	24	35
Paul Coffey	21	7	15	22	24

FLORIDA 1994-99

All-Time Final Series Record

Versus	Series	W	L	GP	W	L	GF	GA
Colorado	1	0	1	4	0	4	4	15
TOTALS	**1**	**0**	**1**	**4**	**0**	**4**	**4**	**15**

Final Series Appearances

Versus	Year	Winner	W	L	GF	GA
Colorado	1996	Colorado	0	4	4	15

Top Five Final Series Scorers

Player	GP	G	A	TP	PIM
Ed Jovanovski	4	0	2	2	11
Stu Barnes	4	1	0	1	2
Tom Fitzgerald	4	1	0	1	0
Rob Niedermayer	4	1	0	1	2
Ray Sheppard	4	1	0	1	0
Johan Garpenlov	4	0	1	1	2
Bill Lindsay	4	0	1	1	4
Dave Lowry	4	0	1	1	2
Scott Mellanby	4	0	1	1	4
Martin Straka	4	0	1	1	0

LOS ANGELES 1968-99

All-Time Final Series Record

Versus	Series	W	L	GP	W	L	GF	GA
Montreal	1	0	1	5	1	4	12	15
TOTALS	**1**	**0**	**1**	**5**	**1**	**4**	**12**	**15**

Final Series Appearances

Versus	Year	Winner	W	L	GF	GA
Montreal	1993	Montreal	1	4	12	15

Top Five Final Series Scorers

Player	GP	G	A	TP	PIM
Wayne Gretzky	5	2	5	7	2
Luc Robitaille	5	3	2	5	4
Tony Granato	5	1	3	4	10
Marty McSorley	5	2	0	2	16
Dave Taylor	3	1	1	2	6
Mike Donnelly	5	1	1	2	0
Tomas Sandstrom	5	0	2	2	4

MONTREAL 1918-99

All-Time Final Series Record

Versus	Series	W	L	GP	W	L	GF	GA
Boston	7	7	0	33	26	7	107	64
Calgary	2	1	1	11	6	5	31	32
Chicago	5	5	0	29	19	10	98	69
Detroit	5	2	3	29	14	15	70	75
Los Angeles	1	1	0	5	4	1	15	12
NY Rangers	1	1	0	5	4	1	19	11
Philadelphia	1	1	0	4	4	0	14	9
St. Louis	2	2	0	8	8	0	23	10
Toronto	5	2	3	26	13	13	72	60
Defunct Teams	*3	1	1	13	7	5	32	39
TOTALS	***32**	**23**	**8**	**163**	**105**	**57**	**481**	**381**

Final Series Appearances*

Versus	Year	Winner	W	L	GF	GA
Seattle	1919	no decision	2	2	10	19
Van/Cgy	1924	Montreal	4	0	14	4
Victoria	1925	Victoria	1	3	8	16
Boston	1930	Montreal	2	0	7	3
Chicago	1931	Montreal	3	2	11	8
Chicago	1944	Montreal	4	0	16	8
Boston	1946	Montreal	4	1	19	13
Toronto	1947	Toronto	2	4	13	13
Toronto	1951	Toronto	1	4	10	13
Detroit	1952	Detroit	0	4	2	11
Boston	1953	Montreal	4	1	16	9
Detroit	1954	Detroit	3	4	12	14
Detroit	1955	Detroit	3	4	20	27
Detroit	1956	Montreal	4	1	18	9
Boston	1957	Montreal	4	1	15	6
Boston	1958	Montreal	4	2	16	14
Toronto	1959	Montreal	4	1	18	12
Toronto	1960	Montreal	4	0	15	5
Chicago	1965	Montreal	4	3	18	12
Detroit	1966	Montreal	4	2	18	14
Toronto	1967	Toronto	2	4	16	17
St. Louis	1968	Montreal	4	0	11	7
St. Louis	1969	Montreal	4	0	12	3
Chicago	1971	Montreal	4	3	20	18
Chicago	1973	Montreal	4	2	33	23
Philadelphia	1976	Montreal	4	0	14	9
Boston	1977	Montreal	4	0	16	6
Boston	1978	Montreal	4	2	18	13
NY Rangers	1979	Montreal	4	1	19	11
Calgary	1986	Montreal	4	1	15	13
Calgary	1989	Calgary	2	4	16	19
Los Angeles	1993	Montreal	4	1	15	12

* No decision in 1919 Finals, interrupted by flu epidemic. Seattle and Montreal had each won two games. One game was tied.
NOTE: Montreal defeated the Portland Rosebuds for the Stanley Cup in 1916, prior to the formation of the NHL, giving the franchise 24 championships in total.

Top Five Final Series Scorers

Player	GP	G	A	TP	PIM
Jean Beliveau	64	30	32	62	78
Henri Richard	65	21	26	47	68
Maurice Richard	59	34	12	46	83
Bernie Geoffrion	53	24	22	46	32
Yvan Cournoyer	50	21	19	40	18

MTL. MAROONS 1925-38

All-Time Final Series Record

Versus	Series	W	L	GP	W	L	GF	GA
NY Rangers	1	0	1	5	2	3	6	5
Toronto	1	1	0	3	3	0	10	4
Victoria	1	1	0	4	3	1	10	3
TOTALS	**3**	**2**	**1**	**12**	**8**	**4**	**26**	**12**

Final Series Appearances

Versus	Year	Winner	W	L	GF	GA
Victoria	1926	Mtl. Maroons	3	1	10	3
NY Rangers	1928	NY Rangers	2	3	6	5
Toronto	1935	Mtl. Maroons	3	0	10	4

Top Five Final Series Scorers

Player	GP	G	A	TP	PIM
Nels Stewart	9	8	1	9	22
Babe Siebert	8	2	3	5	12
Bill Phillips	9	3	1	4	2
Cy Wentworth	3	2	2	4	0
Earl Robinson	3	2	1	3	0
Baldy Northcott	3	2	1	3	0

NEW JERSEY 1975-99

All-Time Final Series Record

Versus	Series	W	L	GP	W	L	GF	GA
Detroit	1	1	0	4	4	0	16	7
TOTALS	**1**	**1**	**0**	**4**	**4**	**0**	**16**	**7**

Final Series Appearances

Versus	Year	Winner	W	L	GF	GA
Detroit	1995	New Jersey	4	0	16	7

Top Five Final Series Scorers

Player	GP	G	A	TP	PIM
Neal Broten	4	3	3	6	4
John MacLean	4	1	4	5	0
Stephane Richer	4	2	2	4	0
Scott Niedermayer	4	1	3	4	0
Bill Guerin	4	0	4	4	12

NY ISLANDERS 1973-99

All-Time Final Series Record

Versus	Series	W	L	GP	W	L	GF	GA
Edmonton	2	1	1	9	5	4	29	27
Minnesota	1	1	0	5	4	1	26	16
Philadelphia	1	1	0	6	4	2	26	25
Vancouver	1	1	0	4	4	0	18	10
TOTALS	**5**	**4**	**1**	**24**	**17**	**7**	**99**	**78**

Final Series Appearances

Versus	Year	Winner	W	L	GF	GA
Philadelphia	1980	NY Islanders	4	2	26	25
Minnesota	1981	NY Islanders	4	1	26	16
Vancouver	1982	NY Islanders	4	0	18	10
Edmonton	1983	NY Islanders	4	0	17	6
Edmonton	1984	Edmonton	1	4	12	21

Top Five Final Series Scorers

Player	GP	G	A	TP	PIM
Mike Bossy	23	17	17	34	4
Bryan Trottier	24	10	20	30	30
Denis Potvin	24	8	18	26	28
Clark Gillies	24	9	14	23	35
Butch Goring	24	9	7	16	2

NY RANGERS 1927-99

All-Time Final Series Record

Versus	Series	W	L	GP	W	L	GF	GA
Boston	2	0	2	8	2	6	17	22
Detroit	2	0	2	12	5	7	25	31
Montreal	1	0	1	5	1	4	11	19
Mtl. Maroons	1	1	0	5	3	2	5	6
Toronto	3	2	1	13	7	6	35	34
Vancouver	1	1	0	7	4	3	21	19
TOTALS	**10**	**4**	**6**	**50**	**22**	**28**	**114**	**131**

Final Series Appearances

Versus	Year	Winner	W	L	GF	GA
Mtl. Maroons	1928	NY Rangers	3	2	6	5
Boston	1929	Boston	0	2	1	4

Toronto	1932	Toronto	0	3	10	18
Toronto	1933	NY Rangers	3	1	11	5
Detroit	1937	Detroit	2	3	8	9
Toronto	1940	NY Rangers	4	2	14	11
Detroit	1950	Detroit	3	4	17	22
Boston	1972	Boston	2	4	16	18
Montreal	1979	Montreal	1	4	11	19
Vancouver	1994	NY Rangers	4	3	21	19

Top Five Final Series Scorers

Player	GP	G	A	TP	PIM
Frank Boucher	19	8	6	14	6
Brian Leetch	7	5	6	11	4
Bill Cook	14	3	5	8	24
Fred "Bun" Cook	14	5	2	7	18
Rod Gilbert	6	4	3	7	11
Alexei Kovalev	7	4	3	7	2
Mark Messier	6	2	5	7	17

OTTAWA 1918-34

All-Time Final Series Record

Versus	Series	W	L	GP	W	L	GF	GA
Boston*	1	1	0	4	2	0	7	3
Defunct Teams	3	3	0	16	11	5	40	30
TOTALS	****4**	****4**	**0**	**20**	**13**	**5**	**47**	**33**

Final Series Appearances

Versus	Year	Winner	W	L	GF	GA
Seattle	1920	Ottawa	3	2	15	11
Vancouver	1921	Ottawa	3	2	12	11
Van./Edm.	1923	Ottawa	5	1	13	8
Boston*	1927	Ottawa	2	0	7	3

* includes two ties ** Ottawa won five Cup titles prior to 1918.

Top Five Final Series Scorers

Player	GP	G	A	TP	PIM
Jack Darragh	10	10	2	12	13
Cy Denneny	20	7	4	11	13
Frank Nighbor	17	7	3	10	0
Punch Broadbent	11	8	0	8	0
George Boucher	20	6	0	6	39

PHILADELPHIA 1968-99

All-Time Final Series Record

Versus	Series	W	L	GP	W	L	GF	GA
Boston	1	1	0	6	4	2	15	13
Buffalo	1	1	0	6	4	2	19	12
Detroit	1	0	1	4	0	4	6	16
Edmonton	2	0	2	12	4	8	32	43
Montreal	1	0	1	4	0	4	9	14
NY Islanders	1	0	1	6	2	4	25	26
TOTALS	**7**	**2**	**5**	**38**	**14**	**24**	**106**	**124**

Final Series Appearances

Versus	Year	Winner	W	L	GF	GA
Boston	1974	Philadelphia	4	2	15	13
Buffalo	1975	Philadelphia	4	2	19	12
Montreal	1976	Montreal	0	4	9	14
NY Islanders	1980	NY Islanders	2	4	25	26
Edmonton	1985	Edmonton	1	4	14	21
Edmonton	1987	Edmonton	3	4	18	22
Detroit	1997	Detroit	4	0	6	16

Top Five Final Series Scorers

Player	GP	G	A	TP	PIM
Bobby Clarke	22	9	12	21	22
Brian Propp	18	9	9	18	4
Rick MacLeish	18	6	9	15	8
Bill Barber	22	5	10	15	17
Reg Leach	16	8	5	13	0

PITTSBURGH 1968-99

All-Time Final Series Record

Versus	Series	W	L	GP	W	L	GF	GA
Chicago	1	1	0	4	4	0	15	10
Minnesota	1	1	0	6	4	2	18	16
TOTALS	**2**	**2**	**0**	**10**	**8**	**2**	**43**	**26**

Final Series Appearances

Versus	Year	Winner	W	L	GF	GA
Minnesota	1991	Pittsburgh	4	2	28	16
Chicago	1992	Pittsburgh	4	0	15	10

Top Five Final Series Scorers

Player	GP	G	A	TP	PIM
Mario Lemieux	9	10	10	20	6
Larry Murphy	10	2	11	13	8
Kevin Stevens	10	6	6	12	27
Ron Francis	10	4	5	9	6
Joe Mullen	6	3	5	8	0
Rick Tocchet	4	2	6	8	2

ST. LOUIS 1968-99

All-Time Final Series Record

Versus	Series	W	L	GP	W	L	GF	GA
Boston	1	0	1	4	0	4	7	20
Montreal	2	0	2	8	0	8	17	43
TOTALS	**3**	**0**	**3**	**12**	**0**	**12**	**24**	**63**

Final Series Appearances

Versus	Year	Winner	W	L	GF	GA
Montreal	1968	Montreal	0	4	7	11
Montreal	1969	Montreal	0	4	3	12
Boston	1970	Boston	0	4	7	20

Top Five Final Series Scorers

Player	GP	G	A	TP	PIM
Frank St. Marseille	12	4	3	7	4
G.'Red' Berenson	12	3	1	4	15
Barclay Plager	9	1	2	3	6
Jim Roberts	12	1	2	3	10
Noel Picard	12	0	3	3	28

TORONTO 1918-99

All-Time Final Series Record

Versus	Series	W	L	GP	W	L	GF	GA
Boston	1	0	1	5	1	4	6	12
Chicago	2	1	1	10	5	5	26	25
Detroit	7	6	1	38	25	13	114	85
Montreal	5	3	2	26	13	13	60	72
NY Rangers	3	1	2	13	6	7	34	35
Defunct Teams	3	2	1	13	6	7	38	40
TOTALS	***21**	**13**	**8**	**105**	**56**	**49**	**278**	**269**

Final Series Appearances*

Versus	Year	Winner	W	L	GF	GA
Vancouver	1918	Toronto	3	2	18	21
Vancouver	1922	Toronto	3	2	16	9
NY Rangers	1932	Toronto	3	0	18	10
NY Rangers	1933	NY Rangers	1	3	5	11
Mtl. Maroons	1935	Mtl. Maroons	0	3	4	10
Detroit	1936	Detroit	1	3	11	18
Chicago	1938	Chicago	1	3	8	10
Boston	1939	Boston	1	4	6	12
NY Rangers	1940	NY Rangers	2	4	11	14
Detroit	1942	Toronto	4	3	25	19
Detroit	1945	Toronto	4	3	9	9
Montreal	1947	Toronto	4	2	13	13
Detroit	1948	Toronto	4	0	18	7
Detroit	1949	Toronto	4	0	12	5
Montreal	1951	Toronto	4	1	13	10
Montreal	1959	Montreal	1	4	12	18
Montreal	1960	Montreal	0	4	5	15
Chicago	1962	Toronto	4	2	18	15
Detroit	1963	Toronto	4	1	17	10
Detroit	1964	Toronto	4	3	22	17
Montreal	1967	Toronto	4	2	17	16

* Toronto Blueshirts won the NHA title in 1914 and defeated Victoria Aristocrats for the Stanley Cup, giving the franchise 14 championships in all

Top Five Final Series Scorers

Player	GP	G	A	TP	PIM
Ted Kennedy	26	12	11	23	8
George Armstrong	33	9	13	22	22
Frank Mahovlich	32	7	15	22	39
Syl Apps	32	10	11	21	6
Bob Pulford	33	8	13	21	44

SEATTLE 1918-24

All-Time Final Series Record

Versus	Series	W	L	GP	W	L	GF	GA
Montreal	1	0	0	5	2	2	19	10
TOTALS	***1**	***0**	**0**	**5**	**2**	**2**	**19**	**10**

Final Series Appearances

Versus	Year	Winner	W	L	GF	GA
Montreal	1919	No Decision*	2	2	19	10

* No decision in 1919 Finals, interrupted by flu epidemic. Seattle and Montreal had each won two games. One game was tied. Seattle won the Stanley Cup in 1917.

Top Five Final Series Scorers

Player	GP	G	A	TP	PIM
Frank Foyston	5	9	1	10	0
Cully Wilson	5	1	3	4	6
Muzz Murray	5	3	0	3	3
Jack Walker	5	3	0	3	9
Roy Rickey	5	1	2	3	0

VANCOUVER 1918-26

All-Time Final Series Record

Versus	Series	W	L	GP	W	L	GF	GA
Montreal	1	0	1	2	0	2	3	5
Ottawa	2	0	2	9	3	6	19	22
Toronto	2	0	2	10	4	6	30	34
TOTALS	***5**	**0**	**5**	**21**	**7**	**14**	**52**	**61**

Final Series Appearances*

Versus	Year	Winner	W	L	GF	GA
Toronto	1918	Toronto	2	3	21	18
Ottawa	1921	Ottawa	2	3	12	12
Toronto	1922	Toronto	2	3	9	16
Ottawa	1923	Ottawa	1	3	7	10
Montreal	1924	Montreal	0	2	3	5

* Vancouver Millionaires won the Stanley Cup in 1915

Top Five Final Series Scorers

Player	GP	G	A	TP	PIM
Mickey MacKay	21	7	6	13	16
Cyclone Taylor	10	9	1	10	15
Jack Adams	10	8	2	10	6
Art Duncan	16	4	4	8	10
Lloyd Cook	21	5	2	7	38
Alf Skinner	13	5	2	7	16

VANCOUVER 1971-99

All-Time Final Series Record

Versus	Series	W	L	GP	W	L	GF	GA
NY Islanders	1	0	1	4	0	4	10	18
NY Rangers	1	0	1	7	3	4	19	21
TOTALS	**2**	**0**	**2**	**11**	**3**	**8**	**29**	**39**

Final Series Appearances

Versus	Year	Winner	W	L	GF	GA
NY Islanders	1982	NY Islanders	0	4	10	18
NY Rangers	1994	NY Rangers	3	4	19	21

Top Five Final Series Scorers

Player	GP	G	A	TP	PIM
Pavel Bure	7	3	5	8	15
Cliff Ronning	7	1	6	7	6
Geoff Courtnall	7	4	1	5	11
Thomas Gradin	4	3	2	5	2
Trevor Linden	7	3	2	5	6

VICTORIA 1918-26

All-Time Final Series Record

Versus	Series	W	L	GP	W	L	GF	GA
Montreal	1	1	0	4	3	1	16	8
Mtl. Maroons	1	0	1	4	1	3	3	10
TOTALS	***2**	**1**	**1**	**8**	**4**	**4**	**19**	**18**

Final Series Appearances*

Versus	Year	Winner	W	L	GF	GA
Montreal	1925	Victoria	3	1	16	8
Mtl. Maroons	1926	Mtl. Maroons	1	3	3	10

* Victoria also played for the Stanley Cup in 1914 prior to the formation of the NHL.

Top Five Final Series Scorers

Player	GP	G	A	TP	PIM
Frank Fredrickson	8	4	4	8	16
Jack Walker	8	4	2	6	0
Slim Halderson	8	3	1	4	16
Gord Fraser	8	2	1	3	14
Gizzy Hart	8	2	1	3	2

WASHINGTON 1971-99

All-Time Final Series Record

Versus	Series	W	L	GP	W	L	GF	GA
Detroit	1	0	1	4	0	4	7	13
TOTALS	**1**	**0**	**1**	**4**	**0**	**4**	**7**	**13**

Final Series Appearances

Versus	Year	Winner	W	L	GF	GA
Detroit	1998	Detroit	0	4	7	13

Top Five Final Series Scorers

Player	GP	G	A	TP	PIM
Joey Juneau	4	1	3	4	0
Brian Bellows	4	2	1	3	0
Adams Oates	4	1	2	3	0
Peter Bondra	4	1	1	2	4
Jeff Brown	2	0	2	2	0
Andrei Nikolishin	4	0	2	2	2

These current NHL clubs have not appeared in the Stanley Cup Finals:

Mighty Ducks of Anaheim, Atlanta Thrashers, Carolina Hurricanes, Nashville Predators, Ottawa Senators, Phoenix Coyotes, San Jose Sharks, Tampa Bay Lightning

CHAPTER 16

Final Series Record Book

Team and Individual Records, 1918 –1999

Team Records

Note: Statistics from the suspended game in 1988 Final have not been included in the compilation of categories in the Team Records section, but are included in the Individual Records section.

MOST STANLEY CUP CHAMPIONSHIPS (1893-1999)

24 – Montreal Canadiens (1916-24-30-31-44-46-53-56-57-58-59-60-65-66-68-69-71-73-76-77-78-79-86-93)

14 – Toronto Maple Leafs (1914-18-22-32-42-45-47-48-49-51-62-63-64-67)

9 – Detroit Red Wings (1936-37-43-50-52-54-55-97-98)

NOTE: Montreal Canadiens totals include 1916 victory prior to formation of the NHL. Toronto Maple Leaf totals include those of the pre-NHL Toronto Blueshirts (1914), as well as the Toronto Arenas (1918) and Toronto St. Pats (1922).

MOST CONSECUTIVE STANLEY CUP CHAMPIONSHIPS

5 – Montreal Canadiens (1956-57-58-59-60)

4 – NY Islanders (1980-81-82-83)

– Montreal Canadiens (1976-77-78-79)

MOST YEARS IN THE FINALS (1893-1999)

35 – Montreal Canadiens

22 – Toronto Maple Leafs

21 – Detroit Red Wings

NOTE: Montreal Canadiens totals include 1916 victory prior to formation of the NHL. Toronto Maple Leaf totals include those of the pre-NHL Toronto Blueshirts (1914), as well as the Toronto Arenas (1918) and Toronto St. Pats (1922).

MOST CONSECUTIVE YEARS IN THE FINALS

10 – Montreal Canadiens (1951-60, inclusive)

5 – Montreal Canadiens (1965-69, inclusive)

– NY Islanders (1980-84, inclusive)

MOST GOALS, BOTH TEAMS, ONE SERIES

56 – Montreal Canadiens, Chicago Black Hawks in 1973. Montreal won series 4-2, outscoring Chicago 33-23.

51 – NY Islanders, Philadelphia Flyers in 1980. New York won series 4-2, outscoring Philadelphia 26-25.

MOST GOALS, ONE TEAM, ONE SERIES

33 – Montreal Canadiens in 1973. Montreal won best-of-seven series 4-2, outscoring Chicago 33-23.

28 – Pittsburgh Penguins in 1991. Pittsburgh won best-of-seven series 4-2,outscoring Minnesota 28-16.

MOST GOALS, BOTH TEAMS, FOUR-GAME SERIES

29 – Detroit Red Wings, Toronto Maple Leafs in 1936. Detroit won series 3-1, outscoring Toronto 18-11.

28 – NY Islanders, Vancouver Canucks in 1982. New York won series 4-0, outscoring Vancouver 18-10.

MOST GOALS, ONE TEAM, FOUR-GAME SERIES

20 – Boston Bruins in 1970. Boston won best-of-seven series 4-0, outscoring St. Louis 20-7.

18 – Detroit Red Wings in 1936. Detroit won best-of-five series 3-1, outscoring Toronto 18-11.

– Toronto Maple Leafs in 1948. Toronto won best-of-seven series 4-0, outscoring Detroit 18-7.

– NY Islanders in 1982. New York won best-of-seven series 4-0, outscoring Vancouver 18-10.

– Edmonton Oilers in 1988. Edmonton won best-of-seven series 4-0, outscoring Boston 18-9.

MOST GOALS, BOTH TEAMS, FIVE-GAME SERIES

42 – NY Islanders, Minnesota North Stars in 1981. New York won series 4-1, outscoring Minnesota 26-16.

39 – Vancouver Millionaires, Toronto Arenas in 1918. Toronto won series 3-2, but was outscored by Vancouver 21-18

35 – Edmonton Oilers, Philadelphia Flyers in 1985. Edmonton won series 4-1, outscoring Philadelphia 21-14.

MOST GOALS, ONE TEAM, FIVE-GAME SERIES

26 – NY Islanders in 1981. New York won best-of-seven series 4-1, outscoring Minnesota 26-16.

21 – Vancouver Millionaires in 1918. Vancouver lost best-of-five series 3-2, outscoring Toronto Arenas 21-18

– Edmonton Oilers in 1984. Edmonton won best-of-seven series 4-1, outscoring NY Islanders 21-12.

– Edmonton Oilers in 1985. Edmonton won best-of-seven series 4-1, outscoring Philadelphia 21-14.

MOST GOALS, BOTH TEAMS, SIX-GAME SERIES

56 – Montreal Canadiens, Chicago Black Hawks in 1973. Montreal won series 4-2, outscoring Chicago 33-23.

51 – NY Islanders, Philadelphia Flyers in 1980. New York won series 4-2, outscoring Philadelphia. 26-25.

MOST GOALS, ONE TEAM, SIX-GAME SERIES

33 – Montreal Canadiens in 1973. Montreal won best-of-seven series 4-2, outscoring Chicago 33-23.

28 – Pittsburgh Penguins in 1991. Pittsburgh won best-of-seven series 4-2, outscoring Minnesota 28-16.

MOST GOALS, BOTH TEAMS, SEVEN-GAME SERIES

47 – Detroit Red Wings, Montreal Canadiens in 1955. Detroit won series 4-3, outscoring Montreal 27-20.

44 – Toronto Maple Leafs, Detroit Red Wings in 1942. Toronto won series 4-3, outscoring Detroit 25-19.

MOST GOALS, ONE TEAM, SEVEN-GAME SERIES

27 – Detroit Red Wings in 1955. Detroit won best-of-seven series 4-3, outscoring Montreal 27-20.

25 – Toronto Maple Leafs in 1942. Toronto won best-of-seven series 4-3, outscoring Detroit 25-19.

FEWEST GOALS, BOTH TEAMS, FOUR-GAME SERIES

10 – Ottawa Senators, Boston Bruins in 1927. Ottawa won best-of-five 2-0-2, outscoring Boston 7-3.

13 – Montreal Maroons, Victoria Cougars in 1926. Maroons won series 3-1, outscoring Victoria 10-3.

– Detroit Red Wings, Montreal Canadiens in 1952. Detroit won series 4-0, outscoring Montreal 11-2.

FEWEST GOALS, ONE TEAM, FOUR-GAME SERIES

2 – Montreal Canadiens in 1952. Detroit won best-of-seven series 4-0, outscoring Montreal 11-2.

3 – Victoria Cougars in 1926. Montreal Maroons won best-of-five series 3-1, outscoring Victoria 10-3.

– Boston Bruins in 1927. Ottawa Senators won best-of-five series 2-0-2, outscoring Boston 7-3.

– St. Louis Blues in 1969. Montreal won best-of-seven series 4-0, outscoring St. Louis 12-3.

FEWEST GOALS, BOTH TEAMS, FIVE-GAME SERIES

11 – NY Rangers, Montreal Maroons in 1928. New York won best-of-five series 3-2, but were outscored by Montreal 6-5.

17 – Detroit Red Wings, NY Rangers in 1937. Detroit won best-of-five 3-2, outscoring New York 9-8.

FEWEST GOALS, ONE TEAM, FIVE-GAME SERIES

5 – NY Rangers in 1928. NY Rangers won best-of-five series 3-2, but were outscored by Montreal 6-5.

6 – Montreal Maroons in 1928. New York won best-of-five series 3-2, but were outscored by Montreal 6-5.

– Toronto Maple Leafs in 1939. Boston won best-of-seven series 4-1, outscoring Toronto 12-6.

– Boston Bruins in 1957. Montreal won best-of-seven series 4-1, outscoring Boston 15-6.

FEWEST GOALS, BOTH TEAMS, SIX-GAME SERIES

22 – Dallas Stars, Buffalo Sabres in 1999. Dallas won best-of-seven series 4-2, outscoring Buffalo 13-9.

25 – NY Rangers, Toronto Maple Leafs in 1940. New York won best-of-seven series 4-2, outscoring Toronto 14-11.

FEWEST GOALS, ONE TEAM, SIX-GAME SERIES

9 – Buffalo Sabres in 1999. Dallas won best-of-seven series 4-2, outscoring Buffalo 13-9.

11 – Toronto Maple Leafs in 1940. NY Rangers won best-of-seven series 4-2, outscoring Toronto 14-11.

FEWEST GOALS, BOTH TEAMS, SEVEN-GAME SERIES

18 – Toronto Maple Leafs, Detroit Red Wings in 1945. Toronto won series 4-3, teams even in scoring 9-9.

26 – Detroit Red Wings, Montreal Canadiens in 1954. Detroit won series 4-3, outscoring Montreal 14-12.

FEWEST GOALS, ONE TEAM, SEVEN-GAME SERIES

9 – Detroit Red Wings in 1945. Toronto won best-of-seven series 4-3, teams even in scoring 9-9.

– Toronto Maple Leafs in 1945. Toronto won best-of-seven series 4-3, teams even in scoring 9-9.

12 – Montreal Canadiens in 1954. Detroit won best-of-seven series 4-3, outscoring Montreal 14-12.

– Chicago Black Hawks in 1965. Montreal won best-of-seven series 4-3, outscoring Chicago 18-12.

MOST GOALS, BOTH TEAMS, ONE GAME

15 – Chicago Black Hawks 8 at Montreal Canadiens 7, in Game 5, May 8, 1973. Montreal won series 4-2.

13 – Toronto Maple Leafs 4 at Detroit Red Wings 9, in Game 2, April 7, 1936. Detroit won series 3-1.

MOST GOALS, ONE TEAM, ONE GAME

9 – Detroit Red Wings, in Game 2, April 7, 1936. Toronto 4 at Detroit 9. Detroit won series 3-1.

– Toronto Maple Leafs in Game 5, April 14, 1942. Detroit 3 at Toronto 9. Toronto won series 4-3.

MOST GOALS, BOTH TEAMS, ONE PERIOD

8 – Chicago Black Hawks (5), Montreal Canadiens (3) in 2nd period of Game 5, May 8, 1973. Chicago 8 at Montreal 7. Montreal won best-of-seven series 4-2.

– Vancouver Canucks (5), NY Rangers (3) in 3rd period of Game 5, June 9, 1994. Vancouver 6 at NY Rangers 3. NY Rangers won best-of-seven series 4-3.

6 – Toronto Maple Leafs (3), NY Rangers (3) in 3rd period of Game 3, April 9, 1932. New York 4 at Toronto 6. Toronto won best-of-five series 3-0.

– Montreal Canadiens (4), Calgary Flames (2) in 1st period of Game 3, May 20, 1986. Calgary 3 at Montreal 5. Montreal won best-of-seven series 4-1.
– Pittsburgh Penguins (3), Chicago Blackhawks (3) in 1st period of Game 4, June 1, 1992. Pittsburgh 6 at Chicago 5. Pittsburgh won best-of-seven series 4-0.

MOST GOALS, ONE TEAM, ONE PERIOD
5 – Toronto Maple Leafs, in 2nd period of Game 5, April 14, 1942. Detroit 3 at Toronto 9. Toronto won best-of-seven series 4-3.
– Chicago Black Hawks, in 2nd period of Game 5, May 8, 1973. Chicago 8 at Montreal 7. Montreal won best-of-seven series 4-2.
– Vancouver Canucks, in 3rd period of Game 5, June 9, 1994. Vancouver 6 at NY Rangers 3. Rangers won best-of-seven series 4-3.

LONGEST OVERTIME
55:13 – Edmonton Oilers 3 at Boston Bruins 2 in Game 1, May 15, 1990. Edmonton's Petr Klima, assisted by Jari Kurri and Craig MacTavish, scored at 15:13 of the 3rd overtime period, 115:13 from start of game. Edmonton won best-of-seven series 4-1.
54:51 – Dallas Stars 2 at Buffalo Sabres 1 in Game 6, June 19, 1999. Brett Hull of Dallas, assisted by Jere Lehtinen and Mike Modano, scored at 14:41 of the 3rd overtime period, 114:51 from the start of game. Dallas won best-of-seven series 4-2.
53:50 – Chicago Black Hawks 3 at Montreal Canadiens 2 in Game 3, April 9, 1931. Chicago's Marvin "Cy" Wentworth, assisted by Stewart Adams, scored at 13:50 of the 3rd overtime period, 113:50 from start of game. Montreal won best-of-five series 3-2.

SHORTEST OVERTIME
0:09 – Montreal Canadiens 3 at Calgary Flames 2 in Game 2, May 18, 1986. Montreal's Brian Skrudland, assisted by Mike McPhee and Claude Lemieux, scored nine seconds into overtime. Montreal won best-of-seven series 4-1.
0:31 – Detroit Red Wings 3 at Toronto Maple Leafs 4, April 9, 1936. Toronto's Frank "Buzz" Boll, assisted by Reg "Red" Horner and Art Jackson, scored 31 seconds into overtime. Detroit won best-of-five series 3-1.

MOST OVERTIME GAMES, ONE SERIES
5 – 1951. Of the five games played in the series, all went into overtime. Toronto Maple Leafs won four of the five games to defeat Montreal Canadiens 4-1 in best-of-seven series. Sid Smith, Ted "Teeder" Kennedy, Harry Watson and Bill Barilko scored the overtime winners for Toronto, while Maurice Richard replied for Montreal.

MOST OVERTIME VICTORIES, ONE TEAM, ONE SERIES
4 – Toronto Maple Leafs in 1951. Sid Smith, Ted "Teeder" Kennedy, Harry Watson and Bill Barilko scored the overtime winners in Games 1,3,4,5, respectively, for Toronto, who defeated Montreal 4-1 in best-of-seven series.

MOST HOME VICTORIES, BOTH TEAMS, ONE SERIES
7 – **Detroit Red Wings (4), Montreal Canadiens (3)** in 1955. Detroit won Games 1,2,5,7 at home and Montreal won Games 3,4,6 at home. Detroit won best-of-seven series 4-3.
– Montreal Canadiens (4), Chicago Black Hawks (3) in 1965. Montreal won Games 1,2,5,7 at home and Chicago won Games 3,4,6 at home. Montreal won best-of-seven series 4-3.

MOST HOME VICTORIES, ONE TEAM, ONE SERIES
4 – Detroit Red Wings in 1955. Detroit defeated Montreal Canadiens 4-3 in best-of-seven series, winning Games 1,2,5,7 in Detroit.
– Montreal Canadiens in 1965. Montreal defeated Chicago Black Hawks 4-3 in best-of-seven series, winning Games 1,2,5,7 in Montreal.

MOST ROAD VICTORIES, BOTH TEAMS, ONE SERIES
5 – Toronto Maple Leafs (3), Detroit Red Wings (2) in 1945. Toronto won Games 1,2,7 in Detroit and Detroit won Games 4,6 in Toronto. Toronto won best-of-seven series 4-3.
– Montreal Canadiens (3), Detroit Red Wings (2) in 1966. Montreal won Games 3,4,6 in Detroit and Detroit won Games 1,2 in Montreal. Montreal won best-of-seven series 4-2.

MOST ROAD VICTORIES, ONE TEAM, ONE SERIES
3 – Ottawa Senators in 1921. Ottawa defeated Vancouver Millionaires 3–2 in best-of-five, winning Games 2,3,5 in Vancouver. All five games were played in Vancouver as per the agreement between the NHL and PCHA.
– NY Rangers in 1928. New York defeated Montreal Maroons 3-2 in best-of-five, winning Games 2,4,5 in Montreal. All five games were played in Montreal as the circus occupied Madison Square Garden.
– Toronto Maple Leafs in 1945. Toronto defeated Detroit Red Wings 4-3 in best-of-seven, winning Games 1,2,7 in Detroit.
– Montreal Canadiens in 1966. Montreal defeated Detroit Red Wings 4-2 in best-of-seven, winning Games 3,4,6 in Detroit.
– Edmonton Oilers in 1990. Edmonton defeated Boston Bruins 4-1 in best-of-seven, winning Games 1,2,5 in Boston.

MOST CONSECUTIVE FINAL SERIES GAME VICTORIES
10 – Montreal Canadiens. Streak began May 9, 1976, at Montreal with a 4-3 win over Philadelphia in Game 1 and ended May 18, 1978, at Boston with a 4-0 loss in Game 3. Included in the streak were 4 wins over Philadelphia in 1976, 4 over Boston in 1977 and 2 more over Boston in 1978.
9 – Toronto Maple Leafs. Streak began April 19, 1947, at Toronto with a 2-1 win over Montreal in Game 6 and ended when the team failed to advance to 1950 Finals. Included in the streak were 1 win over Montreal in 1947, 4 over Detroit in 1948 and 4 more over Detroit in 1949.
– NY Islanders. Streak began May 21, 1981, at New York with a 5-1 win over Minnesota in Game 5 and ended May 10, 1984, at New York with a 1-0 loss to Edmonton in Game 1. Included in the streak were 1 win over Minnesota in 1981, 4 over Vancouver in 1982 and 4 over Edmonton in 1983.

MOST SHUTOUTS, BOTH TEAMS, ONE SERIES
5 – Toronto Maple Leafs (3), Detroit Red Wings (2) in 1945. Toronto won best-of-seven series 4-3.
3 – Montreal Maroons (3), Victoria Cougars (0) in 1926. Maroons won best-of-five series 3-1.
– Montreal Maroons (2), NY Rangers (1) in 1928. New York won best-of-five series 3-2.
– Detroit Red Wings (2), NY Rangers (1) in 1937. Detroit won best-of-five series 3-2.
– Montreal Canadiens (3), Chicago Black Hawks (0) in 1965. Montreal won best-of-seven series 4-3.

MOST SHUTOUTS, ONE TEAM, ONE SERIES
3 – Montreal Maroons in 1926. Maroons defeated Victoria Cougars 3-1 in best-of-five series
– Toronto Maple Leafs in 1945. Toronto defeated Detroit 4-3 in best-of-seven series.
– Montreal Canadiens in 1965. Montreal defeated Chicago 4-3 in best-of-seven series.

MOST PENALTIES, BOTH TEAMS, ONE SERIES
142 – Philadelphia Flyers (75), Boston Bruins (67) in 1974. Philadelphia defeated Boston in series 4-2.
128 – Philadelphia Flyers (72), NY Islanders (56) in 1980. NY Islanders won best-of-seven series 4-2.

MOST PENALTIES, ONE TEAM, ONE SERIES
75 – Philadelphia Flyers in 1974. Philadelphia defeated Boston in best-of-seven series 4-2.
72 – Philadelphia Flyers in 1980. NY Islanders won best-of-seven series 4-2.

MOST PENALTY MINUTES, BOTH TEAMS, ONE SERIES
511 – Calgary Flames (256), Montreal Canadiens (255) in 1986. Montreal won best-of-seven series 4-1.
395 – Philadelphia Flyers (219), NY Islanders (176) in 1980. New York won best-of-seven series 4-2.

MOST PENALTY MINUTES, ONE TEAM, ONE SERIES
256 – Calgary Flames in 1986. Montreal won best-of-seven series 4-1.
255 – Montreal Canadiens in 1986. Montreal defeated Calgary in best-of-seven series 4-1.

MOST PENALTIES, BOTH TEAMS, ONE GAME
43 – Philadelphia Flyers (22) at Boston Bruins (21) in Game 5, May 16, 1974. Boston 5, Philadelphia 1. Philadelphia won best-of-seven series 4-2.
37 – Boston Bruins (22) at Montreal Canadiens (15) in Game 5, May 23, 1978. Montreal 4, Boston 1. Montreal won best-of-seven series 4-2.

MOST PENALTIES, ONE TEAM, ONE GAME
22 – Philadelphia Flyers in Game 5, May 16, 1974. Philadelphia 1 at Boston 5. Philadelphia won best-of-seven series 4-2.
21 – Boston Bruins in Game 5, May 16, 1974. Philadelphia 1 at Boston 5. Philadelphia won series 4-2.

MOST PENALTY MINUTES, BOTH TEAMS, ONE GAME
176 – Calgary Flames (86) at Montreal Canadiens (90) in Game 4, May 22, 1986. Montreal 1, Calgary 0. Montreal won series 4-1.
135 – Philadelphia Flyers (67) at Boston Bruins (68) in Game 5, May 16, 1974. Boston 5, Philadelphia 1. Philadelphia won best-of-seven series 4-2.

MOST PENALTY MINUTES, ONE TEAM, ONE GAME
90 – Montreal Canadiens in Game 4, May 22, 1986. Calgary 0 at Montreal 1. Montreal won series 4-1.
86 – Calgary Flames in Game 4, May 22, 1986. Calgary 0 at Montreal 1. Montreal won series 4-1.

MOST PENALTIES, BOTH TEAMS, ONE PERIOD
21 – Boston Bruins (11) at Philadelphia Flyers (10) in 1st period of Game 4, May 14, 1974. Philadelphia 4, Boston 2. Philadelphia won series 4-2.
20 – Philadelphia Flyers (10) at NY Islanders (10) in 2nd period of Game 3, May 17, 1980. NY Islanders 6, Philadelphia 2. NY Islanders won series 4-2.
– Calgary Flames (10) at Montreal Canadiens (10) in 3rd period of Game 4, May 22, 1986. Montreal 1, Calgary 0. Montreal won series 4-1.

MOST PENALTIES, ONE TEAM, ONE PERIOD
11 – Boston Bruins in 1st period of Game 4, May 14, 1974. Boston 2 at Philadelphia 4. Philadelphia won series 4-2.
10 – several teams tied.

MOST PENALTY MINUTES, BOTH TEAMS, ONE PERIOD
152 – Calgary Flames (72) at Montreal Canadiens (80) in 3rd period of Game 4, May 22, 1986. Montreal 1, Calgary 0. Montreal won series 4-1.
104 – Vancouver Canucks (52) at NY Islanders (52) in 2nd period of Game 1, May 8, 1982. NY Islanders 6, Vancouver 5 (OT). NY Islanders won series 4-0.

MOST PENALTY MINUTES, ONE TEAM, ONE PERIOD
80 – Montreal Canadiens in 3rd period of Game 4, May 22, 1986. Montreal 1, Calgary 0. Montreal won series 4-1.
72 – Calgary Flames in 3rd period of Game 4, May 22, 1986. Montreal 1, Calgary 0. Montreal won series 4-1.

FEWEST PENALTIES, BOTH TEAMS, ONE SERIES
19 – Detroit Red Wings (10), Toronto Maple Leafs (9) in 1945. Toronto won best-of-seven series 4-3.

FEWEST PENALTIES, ONE TEAM, ONE SERIES
9 – Toronto Maple Leafs in 1945. Toronto defeated Detroit in best-of-seven series 4-3.
10 – Detroit Red Wings in 1945. Toronto defeated Detroit in best-of-seven series 4-3.

FEWEST PENALTY MINUTES, BOTH TEAMS, ONE SERIES
41 – Toronto Maple Leafs (21), Detroit Red Wings (20) in 1945. Toronto won best-of-seven series 4-3.

FEWEST PENALTY MINUTES, ONE TEAM, ONE SERIES

21 – Toronto Maple Leafs in 1945. Toronto defeated Detroit in best-of-seven series 4-3.
20 – Detroit Red Wings in 1945. Toronto defeated Detroit in best-of-seven series 4-3.

FEWEST PENALTIES AND PENALTY MINUTES, BOTH TEAMS, ONE GAME

0 – Toronto Maple Leafs 1 at Detroit Red Wings 0 in Game 6, April 16, 1942. Toronto won series 4-3.

FEWEST PENALTIES AND PENALTY MINUTES, ONE TEAM, ONE GAME

0 – Toronto Maple Leafs in Game 6, April 16, 1942. Toronto 1 at Detroit 0. Toronto won series 4-3.
– Detroit Red Wings in Game 6, April 16, 1942. Toronto 1 at Detroit 0. Toronto won series 4-3.
– Detroit Red Wings in Game 2, April 8, 1945. Detroit 0 at Toronto 2. Toronto won series 4-3.
– Toronto Maple Leafs in Game 3, April 12, 1945. Detroit 0 at Toronto 1. Toronto won series 4-3.
– NY Rangers in Game 2, April 13, 1950. NY Rangers 3, Detroit 1 (at Toronto). Detroit won series 4-3.
– Boston Bruins in Game 5, April 16, 1953. Boston 0 at Montreal 1 (OT). Montreal won series 4-1.

MOST POWER-PLAY GOALS, BOTH TEAMS, ONE SERIES

21 – NY Islanders (15), Philadelphia Flyers (6) in 1980. New York won best-of-seven series 4-2.
14 – Montreal Canadiens (10), Chicago Black Hawks (4) in 1965. Montreal won best-of-seven series 4-3.

MOST POWER-PLAY GOALS, ONE TEAM, ONE SERIES

15 – NY Islanders in 1980. New York defeated Philadelphia in best-of-seven series 4-2.
10 – Montreal Canadiens in 1965. Montreal defeated Chicago in best-of-seven series 4-3.

MOST POWER-PLAY GOALS, BOTH TEAMS, ONE GAME

5 – seven times.

MOST POWER-PLAY GOALS, ONE TEAM, ONE GAME

5 – NY Islanders, May 17, 1980, in Game 3 at New York. NY Islanders 6, Philadelphia 2. New York won best-of-seven series 4-2.
4 – Toronto Maple Leafs, April 10, 1947, in Game 2 at Montreal. Toronto 4, Montreal 0. Toronto won best-of-seven series 4-2.
– Montreal Canadiens, April 27, 1965, in Game 5 at Montreal. Montreal 6, Chicago 0. Montreal won best-of-seven series 4-3.
– Edmonton Oilers, May 28, 1985, in Game 4 at Edmonton. Edmonton 5, Philadelphia 3. Edmonton won best-of-seven series 4-1.
– Colorado Avalanche, June 6, 1996 in Game 2 at Colorado. Colorado 8, Florida 1. Colorado won best-of-seven series 4-0.

MOST POWER-PLAY GOALS, BOTH TEAMS, ONE PERIOD

4 – Florida Panthers (1) at Colorado Avalanche (3), in 1st period of Game 2, June 6, 1996. Colorado 8, Florida 1. Colorado won best-of-seven series 4-0.

MOST POWER-PLAY GOALS, ONE TEAM, ONE PERIOD

3 – Montreal Canadiens, April 6, 1954, in 1st period of Game 2 at Detroit. Montreal 3, Detroit 1. Detroit won best-of-seven series 4-3.
– NY Rangers, May 4, 1972, in 1st period of Game 3 at New York. NY Rangers 5, Boston 2. Boston won best-of-seven series 4-2.
– Montreal Canadiens, May 12, 1977, in 1st period of Game 3 at Boston. Montreal 4, Boston 2. Montreal won best-of-seven series 4-0.
– NY Islanders, May 17, 1980, in 1st period of Game 3 at New York. NY Islanders 7, Philadelphia 5. New York won best-of-seven series 4-2.
– Colorado Avalanche, June 6, 1996, in 1st period of Game 2 at Colorado. Colorado 8, Florida 1. Colorado won best-of-seven series 4-0.

MOST SHORTHAND GOALS, BOTH TEAMS, ONE SERIES

6 – Pittsburgh Penguins (3), Minnesota North Stars (3) in 1991. Pittsburgh won best-of-seven series 4-2.
4 – NY Rangers (4), Toronto Maple Leafs (0) in 1933. NY Rangers won best-of-five series 3-1.

MOST SHORTHAND GOALS, ONE TEAM, ONE SERIES

4 – NY Rangers in 1933. NY Rangers defeated Toronto in best-of-five series 3-1.
3 – Detroit Red Wings in 1955. Detroit defeated Montreal in best-of-seven series 4-3.
– Toronto Maple Leafs in 1963. Toronto defeated Detroit in best-of-seven series 4-1.
– Boston Bruins in 1972. Boston defeated NY Rangers in best-of-seven series 4-2.
– Edmonton Oilers in 1987. Edmonton defeated Philadelphia in best-of-seven series 4-3.
– Pittsburgh Penguins in 1991. Pittsburgh defeated Minnesota in best-of-seven series 4-2.
– Minnesota North Stars in 1991. Pittsburgh defeated Minnesota in best-of-seven series 4-2.

MOST SHORTHAND GOALS, BOTH TEAMS, ONE GAME

2 – nine times.

MOST SHORTHAND GOALS, ONE TEAM, ONE GAME

2 – seven times.

MOST SHORTHAND GOALS, BOTH TEAMS, ONE PERIOD

2 – NY Rangers (0) at Boston Bruins (2), in 1st period of Game 1, April 30, 1972. Boston 6, NY Rangers 5. Boston won series 4-2.
– Montreal Canadiens (0) at Chicago Black Hawks (2), in 1st period of Game 3, May 3, 1973. Chicago 7, Montreal 4. Montreal won series 4-2.
– Minnesota North Stars (0), NY Islanders (2), in 1st period of Game 1, May 12, 1981. NY Islanders 6, Minnesota 3. New York won series 4-1.
– Minnesota North Stars (1), Pittsburgh Penguins (1), in 2nd period of Game 1, May 15, 1991. Minnesota 5, Pittsburgh 4. Pittsburgh won series 4-2.

MOST SHORTHAND GOALS, ONE TEAM, ONE PERIOD

2 – Boston Bruins in 1st period of Game 1, April 30, 1972. Boston 6, NY Rangers 5. Boston won best-of-seven series 4-2.
– Chicago Black Hawks in 1st period of Game 3, May 3, 1973. Chicago 7, Montreal 4. Montreal won best-of-seven series 4-2.
– NY Islanders in 1st period of Game 1, May 12, 1981. NY Islanders 6, Minnesota 3. NY Islanders won series 4-1.

FASTEST TWO GOALS, BOTH TEAMS

0:10 – Toronto Maple Leafs at Detroit Red Wings in Game 1, April 5, 1936. Detroit's Wally Kilrea and Toronto's Frank "Buzz" Boll scored at 12:05 and 12:15 of 1st period, respectively. Detroit 3, Toronto 1. Detroit won best-of-five series 3-1.
– Montreal Canadiens at Toronto Maple Leafs in Game 3, April 12, 1947. Toronto's Vic Lynn and Montreal's Leo Gravelle scored at 12:23 and 12:33 of 2nd period, respectively. Toronto 4, Montreal 2. Toronto won best-of-seven series 4-2.
0:13 – Detroit Red Wings at Toronto Maple Leafs in Game 1, April 11, 1964. Detroit's Bruce MacGregor and Toronto's George Armstrong scored at 4:31 and 4:44 of 1st period, respectively. Toronto 3, Detroit 2. Toronto won best-of-seven series 4-3.

FASTEST TWO GOALS, ONE TEAM

0:12 – Montreal Maroons, April 9, 1935, in Game 3 at Montreal. Montreal 4, Toronto 1. Lawrence "Baldy" Northcott and Marvin "Cy" Wentworth scored at 16:18 and 16:30 of 2nd period, respectively. Montreal won best-of-five series 3-0.
– Montreal Canadiens, April 7, 1955 in Game 3 at Montreal. Montreal 4, Detroit 2. Bernie "Boom Boom" Geoffrion scored at 8:30 and 8:42 of first period. Detroit won best-of-seven series 4-3.
0:15 – Edmonton Oilers, May 25, 1985, in Game 3 at Edmonton. Edmonton 4, Philadelphia 3. Wayne Gretzky scored at 1:10 and 1:25 of 1st period. Edmonton won best-of-seven series 4-1.

FASTEST THREE GOALS, BOTH TEAMS

0:30 – Pittsburgh Penguins 6 at Chicago Blackhawks 5 in Game 4, June 1, 1992. Chicago's Dirk Graham scored at 6:21 of 1st period, Pittsburgh's Kevin Stevens scored at 6:33 and Graham scored at 6:51. Pittsburgh won best-of-seven series 4-0.
0:31 – Philadelphia Flyers 3 at Edmonton Oilers 4 in Game 3, May 25, 1985. Edmonton's Wayne Gretzky scored at 1:10 and 1:25 of first period and Philadelphia's Derrick Smith scored at 1:41. Edmonton won series 4-1.
1:18 – Calgary Flames 3 at Montreal Canadiens 5 in Game 3, May 20, 1986. Calgary's Joel Otto scored at 17:59 of first period, and Montreal's Bobby Smith at 18:25 and Mats Naslund at 19:17. Montreal won best-of-seven series 4-1.

FASTEST THREE GOALS, ONE TEAM

0:56 – Montreal Canadiens, April 6, 1954, in Game 2 at Detroit. Montreal 3, Detroit 1. Dickie Moore scored at 15:03 of first period, and Maurice "Rocket" Richard scored at 15:28 and again at 15:59. Detroit won best-of-seven series 4-3.
1:08 – Montreal Canadiens, May 20, 1986, in Game 3 at Montreal. Montreal 5, Calgary 3. Bobby Smith scored at 18:25, Mats Naslund at 19:17 and Bob Gainey at 19:33 of 1st period. Montreal won series 4-1.

FASTEST FOUR GOALS, BOTH TEAMS

1:34 – Calgary Flames 3 at Montreal Canadiens 5 in Game 3, May 20, 1986. Calgary's Joel Otto scored at 17:59 of 1st period, followed by Montreal's Bobby Smith at 18:25, Mats Naslund at 19:17 and Bob Gainey at 19:33. Montreal won best-of-seven series 4-1.
2:54 – NY Rangers 4 at Toronto Maple Leafs 6 in Game 3, April 9, 1932. New York's Fred "Bun" Cook scored at 16:32 of 3rd period, followed by Toronto's Bob Gracie at 17:36 and New York's Frank Boucher at 18:26 and again at 19:26. Toronto won best-of-five series 3-0.

FASTEST FOUR GOALS, ONE TEAM

5:29 – Montreal Canadiens, March 31, 1956, in Game 1 at Montreal. Montreal 6, Detroit 4. Jack LeClair, Bernie "Boom Boom" Geoffrion, Jean Beliveau and Claude Provost scored at 5:20, 6:20, 7:31 and 10:49 of 3rd period, respectively. Montreal won best-of-seven series 4-1.
5:57 – Montreal Canadiens, April 29, 1973, in Game 1 at Montreal. Montreal 8, Chicago 3. Jacques Lemaire, Peter Mahovlich, Frank Mahovlich and Chuck Lefley scored at 8:38, 12:36, 13:34 and 14:35 of 3rd period, respectively. Montreal won best-of-seven series 4-2.

FASTEST FIVE GOALS, BOTH TEAMS

4:20 – NY Rangers 4 at Toronto Maple Leafs 6 in Game 3, April 9, 1932. Toronto's Irvine "Ace" Bailey scored at 15:07 of 1st period, followed by New York's Fred "Bun" Cook at 16:34, Toronto's Bob Gracie at 17:36 and New York's Frank Boucher at 18:24 and again at 19:27. Toronto won best-of-five series 3-0.
6:32 – Chicago Black Hawks 8 at Montreal Canadiens 7 in Game 5, May 8, 1973. Montreal's Claude Larose scored at 0:37 of the 2nd period, followed by Chicago's Dave Kryskow at 3:10, Larose again at 4:23, Chicago's Stan Mikita at 6:21 and Montreal's Yvan Cournoyer at 7:09. Montreal won best-of-seven series 4-2.

FASTEST FIVE GOALS, ONE TEAM

10:29 – Edmonton Oilers, May 15, 1984, in Game 3 at Edmonton. Edmonton 7, NY Islanders 2. Glenn Anderson scored at 19:12 of 2nd period, followed by Paul Coffey at 19:29, Mark Messier at 5:32 of 3rd period and Dave Semenko at 5:52. Edmonton won series 4-1.
14:20 – NY Islanders, May 12, 1983, in Game 2 at Edmonton. NY Islanders 6, Edmonton 3. Tomas Jonsson scored at 14:21 of 2nd period, followed by Bob Nystrom at 17:55, Mike Bossy at 19:17, Bob Bourne at 8:03 of 3rd period, and Brent Sutter at 8:41. New York won series 4-0.

Individual Records

Note: Statistics from the suspended game in 1988 Final have not been included in the compilation of categories in the Team Records section, but are included in the Individual Records section.

MOST YEARS IN FINALS

12 – **Maurice Richard,** Montreal (1944-46-47-51-52-53-54-56-57-58-59-60)
– **Leonard "Red" Kelly,** Detroit (1948-49-50-52-54-55-56) and Toronto (1960-62-63-64-67)
– **Jean Beliveau,** Montreal (1954-55-56-57-58-60-65-66-67-68-69-71)
– **Henri Richard,** Montreal (1956-57-58-59-60-65-66-67-68-69-71-73)
11 – Bert Olmstead, Montreal (1951-52-53-54-55-56-57-58) and Toronto (1959-60-62)
– Doug Harvey, Montreal (1951-52-53-54-55-56-57-58-59-60) and St. Louis (1968)
– Jean-Guy Talbot, Montreal (1956-57-58-59-60-65-66-67) and St. Louis (1968-69-70)
10 – Gordie Howe, Detroit (1948-49-52-54-55-56-61-63-64-66)
– Claude Provost, Montreal (1956-57-58-59-60-65-66-67-68-69)
– Yvan Cournoyer, Montreal (1965-66-67-68-69-71-73-76-77-78)

MOST CONSECUTIVE YEARS IN FINALS

10 – **Bernie Geoffrion,** Montreal (1951-60 inclusive)
– **Doug Harvey,** Montreal (1951-60 inclusive)
– **Tom Johnson,** Montreal (1951-60 inclusive)
– **Bert Olmstead**, Montreal (1951-58, inclusive) and Toronto (1959-60)
9 – Dickie Moore, Montreal (1952-60 inclusive)
8 – Floyd Curry, Montreal (1951-58 inclusive)
7 – Dollard St. Laurent, Montreal (1952-58 inclusive)

MOST GAMES PLAYED IN FINALS

65 – **Leonard "Red" Kelly,** Detroit (37) and Toronto (28)
– **Henri Richard,** Montreal
64 – Jean Beliveau, Montreal
59 – Maurice Richard, Montreal
56 – Bert Olmstead, Montreal (43) and Toronto (13)
55 – Gordie Howe, Detroit
– Jean-Guy Talbot, Montreal (43) and St. Louis (12)
54 – Emile "Butch" Bouchard, Montreal
– Yvan Cournoyer, Montreal
– Doug Harvey, Montreal (52) and St. Louis (2).

MOST CONSECUTIVE GAMES IN FINALS

53 – **Bernie Geoffrion,** Montreal (Game 1 in 1951 through Game 4 in 1960)
48 – Dickie Moore, Montreal (Game 1 in 1952 through Game 4 in 1960)
41 – Floyd Curry, Montreal (Game 1 in 1951 through Game 3 in 1958)
40 – Bert Olmstead, Montreal (Game 1 in 1951 through Game 2 in 1958)
38 – Tom Johnson, Montreal (Game 1 in 1951 through Game 5 in 1957)
36 – Doug Harvey, Montreal (Game 4 in 1954 through Game 4 in 1960)

MOST CAREER POINTS IN FINALS

62 – **Jean Beliveau,** Montreal (30-32-62 in 64 games)
53 – Wayne Gretzky, Edmonton (16-30-46 in 26 games), Los Angeles (2-5-7 in 5 games) (18-35-53 in 31 games overall)
50 – Gordie Howe, Detroit (18-32-50 in 55 games)
47 – Henri Richard, Montreal (21-26-47 in 65 games)
46 – Maurice Richard, Montreal (34-12-46 in 59 games)
– Bernie Geoffrion, Montreal (24-22-46 in 53 games)
41 – Frank Mahovlich, Toronto (7-15-22 in 32 games) and Montreal (9-10-19 in 13 games) (16-25-41 in 45 games overall)
40 – Yvan Cournoyer, Montreal (21-19-40 in 50 games)
39 – Jari Kurri, Edmonton (14-24-38 in 31 games), Los Angeles 1-0-1 in 5 games) (15-24-39 in 36 games overall)
38 – Alex Delvecchio, Detroit (16-22-38 in 47 games)
37 – Jacques Lemaire, Montreal (19-18-37 in 40 games)
35 – Dick Duff, Toronto (5-7-12 in 20 games) and Montreal (10-13-23 in 27 games) (15-20-35 in 47 games overall)
– Doug Harvey, Montreal (4-30-34 in 52 games) and St.Louis (0-1-1 in 2 games) (4-31-35 in 54 games overall)

MOST CAREER GOALS IN FINALS

34 – **Maurice Richard,** Montreal (34-12-46 in 59 games)
30 – Jean Beliveau, Montreal (30-32-62 in 65 games)
24 – Bernie Geoffrion, Montreal (24-22-46 in 53 games)
21 – Yvan Cournoyer, Montreal (21-19-40 in 50 games)
– Henri Richard, Montreal (21-26-47 in 65 games)
19 – Jacques Lemaire, Montreal (19-18-37 in 40 games)
18 – Gordie Howe, Detroit (18-32-50 in 55 games)
– Ted Lindsay, Detroit (19-14-34 in 44 games)
– Wayne Gretzky, Edmonton (16-30-46 in 26 games), Los Angeles (2-5-7 in 5 games) (18-35-53 in 31 games overall)
17 – Mike Bossy, NY Islanders (17-17-34 in 23 games)
16 – Frank Foyston, Seattle (15-2-17 in 10 games) and Victoria (1-0-1 in 8 games) (16-2-18 in 18 games overall)
– Frank Mahovlich, Toronto (7-15-22 in 32 games) and Montreal (9-10-19 in 13 games) (16-25-41 in 45 games overall)
– Glenn Anderson, Edmonton (14-12-26 in 31 games) and NY Rangers (2-1-3 in 7 games) (16-13-29 in 38 games overall)

MOST CAREER ASSISTS IN FINALS

35 – **Wayne Gretzky,** Edmonton (16-30-46 in 26 games), Los Angeles (2-5-7 in 5 games) (18-35-53 in 31 games overall)
32 – Jean Beliveau, Montreal (30-32-62 in 64 games)
– Gordie Howe, Detroit (18-32-50 in 55 games)
31 – Doug Harvey, Montreal (4-30-34 in 52 games) and St.Louis (0-1-1 in 2 games) (4-31-35 in 54 games overall)
26 – Henri Richard, Montreal (21-26-47 in 65 games)
25 – Frank Mahovlich, Toronto (7-15-22 in 32 games) and Montreal (9-10-19 in 13 games) (16-25-41 in 45 games overall)
24 – Jari Kurri, Edmonton (14-24-38 in 31 games), Los Angeles (1-01- in 5 games) (15-24-39 in 36 games overall)
22 – Bernie Geoffrion, Montreal (24-22-46 in 53 games)
– Alex Delvecchio, Detroit (16-22-38 in 47 games)
20 – Dick Duff, Toronto (5-7-12 in 20 games) and Montreal (10-13-23 in 27 games) (15-20-35 in 47 games)
– Leonard "Red" Kelly, Detroit (6-7-13 in 37 games) and Toronto (5-13-18 in 28 games) (11-20-31 in 65 games)
– Mark Messier, Edmonton (9-15-24 in 31 games) and NY Rangers (2-5-7 in 7 games) (11-20-31 in 38 games overall)

MOST CAREER GAME-WINNING GOALS IN FINALS

9 – **Jean Beliveau,** Montreal
8 – Maurice Richard, Montreal
6 – Yvan Cournoyer, Montreal
– Bernie Geoffrion, Montreal

MOST CAREER OVERTIME GOALS IN FINALS

3 – **Maurice Richard,** Montreal (1 in 1946, 1 in 1951, 1 in 1958)
2 – Don Raleigh, NY Rangers (2 in 1950)
– Jacques Lemaire, Montreal (1 in 1968; 1 in 1977)
– John LeClair, Montreal (2 in 1993)

MOST CAREER OVERTIME ASSISTS IN FINALS

2 – **Elwin "Doc" Romnes,** Chicago (2 in 1934)
– **Emile "Butch" Bouchard,** Montreal (1 in 1944, 1 in 1946)
– **Ed Slowinski,** NY Rangers (2 in 1950)
– **Tod Sloan,** Toronto (2 in 1951)
– **Guy Lafleur,** Montreal (1 in 1977, 1 in 1979)
– **John Tonelli,** NY Islanders (2 in 1980)
– **Harry Watson,** Toronto Maple Leafs (1 in 1947, 1 in 1951)

MOST CAREER OVERTIME POINTS IN FINALS

4 – **Maurice Richard,** Montreal (3-1-4)
3 – Elwin "Doc" Romnes, Chicago (0-2-2) and Toronto (1-0-1) (1-2-3 overall)
– Guy Lafleur, Montreal (1-2-3)
– Harry Watson, Toronto (1-2-3)

MOST CAREER POWER-PLAY GOALS IN FINALS

11 – **Jean Beliveau,** Montreal
10 – Bernie Geoffrion, Montreal
8 – Mike Bossy, NY Islanders
– Yvan Cournoyer, Montreal
7 – Alex Delvecchio, Detroit

MOST CAREER POWER-PLAY ASSISTS IN FINALS

16 – **Jean Beliveau,** Montreal
14 – Gordie Howe, Detroit
– Wayne Gretzky, Edmonton (11), Los Angeles (3)
12 – Doug Harvey, Montreal (11), St. Louis (1)
– Denis Potvin, NY Islanders
11 – Mike Bossy, NY Islanders

MOST CAREER POWER-PLAY POINTS IN FINALS

27 – **Jean Beliveau,** Montreal (11-16-27)
19 – Mike Bossy, NY Islanders (8-11-19)
– Wayne Gretzky, Edmonton (5-11-16), Los Angeles (0-3-3)
18 – Bernie Geoffrion, Montreal (10-8-18)
– Yvan Cournoyer, Montreal (8-10-18)
– Denis Potvin, NY Islanders (6-12-18)
– Gordie Howe, Detroit (4-14-18)
16 – Alex Delvecchio, Detroit (7-9-16)
15 – Bryan Trottier, NY Islanders (4-11-15)

MOST CAREER SHORTHAND GOALS IN FINALS

2 – **Cecil Dillon,** NY Rangers (2 in 1933)
– **Dave Keon,** Toronto (2 in 1963)
– **Bob Pulford,** Toronto (2 in 1964)
– **Marcel Pronovost,** Detroit (1 in 1955) and Toronto (1 in 1967)
– **Serge Savard,** Montreal (2 in 1968)
– **Derek Sanderson,** Boston (1 in 1970, 1 in 1972)
– **Peter Mahovlich,** Montreal (1 in 1971, 1 in 1973)
– **Kevin Lowe,** Edmonton (2 in 1987)
– **Mario Lemieux,** Pittsburgh (2 in 1991)

MOST CAREER SHORTHAND ASSISTS IN FINALS

4 – **Bobby Orr,** Boston (2 in 1970, 1 in 1972, 1 in 1974)
2 – George Armstrong, Toronto (2 in 1963)
– Allan Stanley, Toronto (1 in 1963, 1 in 1964)
– Claude Provost, Montreal (1 in 1968, 1 in 1969)
– Bob Bourne, NY Islanders (1 in 1980, 1 in 1982)
– Wayne Gretzky, Edmonton (2 in 1987)

MOST CAREER SHORTHAND POINTS IN FINALS

4 – **Bobby Orr,** Boston (0-4-4)
2 – several players tied.

MOST CAREER PENALTY MINUTES IN FINALS

94 – **Gordie Howe,** Detroit (in 55 games)
87 – Kevin McClelland, Edmonton (in 22 games)
86 – Duane Sutter, NY Islanders (in 24 games)
83 – Maurice Richard, Montreal (in 59 games)
79 – Wayne Cashman, Boston (in 26 games)
78 – Jean Beliveau, Montreal (in 64 games)

MOST PENALTY MINUTES, ONE GAME

29 – **Kevin McClelland,** Edmonton, in Game 5, May 30, 1985. Philadelphia 3 at Edmonton 8. McClelland was assessed 2 minors, 1 major, 1 misconduct and 1 game misconduct.
27 – Claude Lemieux, Montreal, in Game 4, May 22, 1986. Calgary 0 at Montreal 1. Lemieux was assessed 1 minor, 1 major, 1 misconduct and 1 game misconduct.

MOST PENALTY MINUTES, ONE PERIOD

25 – **Kevin McClelland,** Edmonton, in third period of Game 5, May 30, 1985. Philadelphia 3 at Edmonton 8. McClelland was assessed 1 major, 1 misconduct and 1 game misconduct.
– **Claude Lemieux,** Montreal, in third period of Game 4, May 22, 1986. Calgary 0 at Montreal 1. Lemieux was assessed 1 major, 1 misconduct and 1 game misconduct.

MOST CAREER SHUTOUTS IN FINALS

8 – **Clint Benedict,** Ottawa, (1 in 1920, 2 in 1921, 1 in 1923) and Montreal Maroons (3 in 1926, 1 in 1928)
4 – Walter "Turk" Broda, Toronto (1 in 1940, 1 in 1942, 1 in 1947, 1 in 1948)
– Jacques Plante, Montreal (1 in 1956, 1 in 1957, 1 in 1958, 1 in 1960)
3 – Harry Lumley, Detroit (2 in 1945, 1 in 1950)
– Frank McCool, Toronto (3 in 1945)
– Gerry McNeil, Montreal (2 in 1953, 1 in 1954)
– Terry Sawchuk, Detroit (2 in 1952, 1 in 1954)
– Lorne "Gump" Worsley, Montreal (2 in 1965, 1 in 1968)

MOST CAREER GAMES PLAYED BY A GOALTENDER IN FINALS

41 – **Jacques Plante,** Montreal (38) and St.Louis (3)
38 – Walter "Turk" Broda, Toronto
37 – Terry Sawchuk, Detroit (33) and Toronto (4)
32 – Ken Dryden, Montreal
– Glenn Hall, Detroit (5), Chicago (19) and St. Louis (8)

MOST CAREER MINUTES PLAYED BY A GOALTENDER IN FINALS

2,423 – **Jacques Plante,** Montreal (2,279) and St. Louis (164)
2,369 – Walter "Turk" Broda, Toronto
2,185 – Terry Sawchuk, Detroit (1,960) and Toronto (225)
1,947 – Ken Dryden, Montreal
1,844 – Glenn Hall, Detroit (300), Chicago (1,060), St. Louis (484)

MOST YEARS BY A GOALTENDER IN FINALS

10 – **Jacques Plante,** Montreal (8) and St. Louis (2)
8 – Walter "Turk" Broda, Toronto
7 – Terry Sawchuk, Detroit (6) and Toronto (1)
– Glenn Hall, Detroit (1), Chicago (3) and St. Louis (3)
6 – Johnny Bower, Toronto
– Ken Dryden, Montreal

MOST CONSECUTIVE YEARS BY A GOALTENDER IN FINALS

8 – **Jacques Plante,** Montreal (1953-60, inclusive)
5 – Billy Smith, NY Islanders (1980-84, inclusive)

MOST CAREER WINS BY A GOALTENDER IN FINALS

25 – **Jacques Plante,** Montreal
24 – Ken Dryden, Montreal
21 – Walter "Turk" Broda, Toronto
19 – Terry Sawchuk, Detroit (17) and Toronto (2)
17 – Billy Smith, NY Islanders

MOST CONSECUTIVE WINS BY A GOALTENDER IN FINALS

10 – **Ken Dryden,** Montreal. Streak began May 9, 1976, at Montreal with a 4-3 win over Philadelphia in Game 1 and ended May 18, 1978, at Boston with a 4-0 loss in Game 3. Included were four wins over Philadelphia in 1976, four over Boston in 1977 and two more over Boston in 1978.
9 – Walter "Turk" Broda, Toronto. Streak began April 19, 1947, at Toronto with a 2-1 win over Montreal in Game 6 and ended when the team failed to advance to the 1950 Finals. Included were one win over Montreal in 1947, four over Detroit in 1948 and four over Detroit in 1949.
– Billy Smith, NY Islanders. Streak began May 21, 1981, at New York with a 5-1 win over Minnesota in Game 5 and ended May 10, 1984, at New York with a 1-0 loss to Edmonton in Game 1. Included were one win over Minnesota in 1981, four over Vancouver in 1982 and four over Edmonton in 1983.

LOWEST CAREER GOALS-AGAINST AVERAGE (MINIMUM 15 GAMES PLAYED)

1.55 – **Clint Benedict,** Ottawa, Mtl. Maroons (25 games)
1.82 – Lorne "Gump" Worsley, Montreal (16 games)
1.86 – Gerry McNeil, Montreal (15 games)
2:04 – Patrick Roy, Montreal, Colorado (20 games)
2:11 – Bill Durnan, Montreal (15 games)
2:15 – Walter "Turk" Broda, Toronto (38 games)

HIGHEST CAREER WINNING PERCENTAGE, (MINIMUM 15 GAMES PLAYED)

.750 – **Ken Dryden,** Montreal (24-8)
.739 – Billy Smith, NY Islanders (17-6)
.737 – Grant Fuhr, Edmonton (14-5)
.733 – Lorne "Gump" Worsley, Montreal (11-4)
.700 – Patrick Roy, Montreal, Colorado (14-6)
.667 – Bill Durnan, Montreal (10-5)

MOST POINTS, ONE SERIES

13 – **Wayne Gretzky,** Edmonton (3-10-13 in 4 games plus suspended game), in 1988.
12 – Gordie Howe, Detroit, (5-7-12 in 7 games), in 1955.
– Yvan Cournoyer, Montreal (6-6-12 in 6 games), in 1973.
– Jacques Lemaire, Montreal (3-9-12 in 6 games) in 1973.
– Mario Lemieux, Pittsburgh (6-6-12 in 6 games), in 1991.
11 – Ted Lindsay, Detroit (5-6-11 in 7 games), in 1955.
– Frank Mahovlich, Montreal (5-6-11 in 6 games), in 1973.
– Mike Bossy, NY Islanders (4-7-11 in 6 games), in 1980.
– Wayne Gretzky, Edmonton (7-4-11 in 5 games), in 1985.
– Paul Coffey, Edmonton (3-8-11 in 5 games), in 1985.
– Wayne Gretzky, Edmonton (2-9-11 in 7 games), in 1987.
– Brian Leetch, NY Rangers (5-6-11 in 7 games), in 1994.

MOST POINTS, FOUR-GAME SERIES

13 – **Wayne Gretzky,** Edmonton (3-10-13), in 1988. (includes suspended game)
9 – Guy Lafleur, Montreal (2-7-9), in 1977.
– Denis Potvin, NY Islanders (2-7-9), in 1982.
8 – Hector "Toe" Blake, Montreal (3-5-8), in 1944.
– Henri Richard, Montreal, (3-5-8), in 1960.
– Phil Esposito, Boston (2-6-8), in 1970.
– Mike Bossy, NY Islanders (7-1-8), in 1982.
– Rick Tocchet, Pittsburgh (2-6-8), in 1992.

MOST POINTS, FIVE-GAME SERIES

11 – **Wayne Gretzky,** Edmonton (7-4-11), in 1985.
– **Paul Coffey,** Edmonton (3-8-11), in 1985.
10 – Alf Skinner, Toronto Arenas (8-2-10), in 1918
– Mickey Mackay, Vancouver Millionaires (5-5-10), in 1918
– Frank Foyston, Seattle Metropolitans, (9-1-10), in 1919
– Babe Dye, Toronto St. Pats, (9-1-10), in 1922
– Jean Beliveau, Montreal (7-3-10), in 1956.

MOST POINTS, SIX-GAME SERIES

12 – **Yvan Cournoyer,** Montreal (6-6-12), in 1973.
– **Jacques Lemaire**, Montreal (3-9-12) in 1973.
– **Mario Lemieux,** Pittsburgh (5-7-12), in 1991.
11 – Frank Mahovlich, Montreal (5-6-11), in 1973.
– Mike Bossy, NY Islanders (4-7-11), in 1980.

MOST POINTS, SEVEN-GAME SERIES

12 – **Gordie Howe,** Detroit, (5-7-12 in 7 games), in 1955.
11 – Ted Lindsay, Detroit (5-6-11 in 7 games), in 1955.
– Wayne Gretzky, Edmonton (2-9-11 in 7 games), in 1987.
– Brian Leetch, NY Rangers 5-6-11 in 7 games), in 1994.

MOST POINTS BY A DEFENSEMAN, ONE SERIES

11 – **Paul Coffey,** Edmonton, (3-8-11 in 5 games), in 1985.
– **Brian Leetch,** NY Rangers, (5-6-11 in 7 games), in 1994.
10 – Larry Murphy, Pittsburgh, (1-9-10 in 6 games), in 1991.
9 – Denis Potvin, NY Islanders, (5-4-9 in 6 games), in 1980.
– Denis Potvin, NY Islanders, (2-7-9 in 4 games), in 1982.
– Al MacInnis, Calgary, (5-4-9 in 6 games), in 1989.
8 – Pierre Pilote, Chicago, (2-6-8 in 6 games), in 1961.
– Bobby Orr, Boston, (4-4-8 in 6 games), in 1972.
– Pat Stapleton, Chicago, (0-8-8 in 6 games), in 1973.

MOST POINTS BY A ROOKIE, ONE SERIES

7 – **Roy Conacher,** Boston, (5-2-7 in 5 games), in 1939.
– **Ralph Backstrom,** Montreal, (3-4-7 in 5 games), in 1959.
6 – Johnny Gagnon, Montreal, (4-2-6 in 5 games), in 1931.
– Brian Propp, Philadelphia, (3-3-6 in 6 games), in 1980.

MOST GOALS, ONE SERIES

9 – **Cyclone Taylor,** Vancouver Millionaires (in 5 games), in 1918
– **Frank Foyston,** Seattle Metropolitans (in 5 games), in 1919
– **Babe Dye,** Toronto St. Pats, (in 5 games), in 1922
8 – Alf Skinner, Toronto Arenas, (in 5 games), in 1918
7 – Jean Beliveau, Montreal (in 5 games), in 1956.
– Mike Bossy, NY Islanders (in 4 games), in 1982.
– Wayne Gretzky, Edmonton (in 5 games), in 1985.
6 – Frank Nighbor, Ottawa (in 5 games), in 1920
– Frank Foyston, Seattle, (in 5 games), in 1920
– Jack Adams, Vancouver, (in 5 games) in 1922
– Nels Stewart, Mtl. Maroons (in 4 games), in 1926
– Alex Delvecchio, Detroit (in 7 games), in 1955.
– Bernie Geoffrion, Montreal (in 7 games), in 1955.
– John Bucyk, Boston (in 4 games), in 1970.
– Yvan Cournoyer, Montreal (in 6 games), in 1973.
– Esa Tikkanen, Edmonton (in 4 games plus suspended game), in 1988.

MOST GOALS, FOUR-GAME SERIES

7 – **Mike Bossy,** NY Islanders, in 1982.
6 – Nels Stewart, Mtl. Maroons, in 1926
– John Bucyk, Boston, in 1970.
– Esa Tikkanen, Edmonton, in 1988.

MOST GOALS, FIVE-GAME SERIES

9 – **Cyclone Taylor,** Vancouver Millionaires, in 1918.
– **Frank Foyston,** Seattle Metropolitans, in 1919.
– **Babe Dye,** Toronto St. Pats, in 1922.
8 – Alf Skinner, Toronto Arenas, in 1918.
7 – Jean Beliveau, Montreal, in 1956.
– Wayne Gretzky, Edmonton, in 1985.
6 – Frank Nighbor, Ottawa, in 1920

MOST GOALS, SIX-GAME SERIES

6 – **Yvan Cournoyer,** Montreal, in 1973.
5 – Bernie Geoffrion, Montreal, in 1958.
– Ken Hodge, Boston, in 1972.
– Pit Martin, Chicago, in 1973.
– Frank Mahovlich, Montreal, in 1973.
– Denis Potvin, NY Islanders, in 1980.
– Al MacInnis, Calgary, in 1989.
– Joe Mullen, Calgary, in 1989.

MOST GOALS, SEVEN-GAME SERIES

6 – **Alex Delvecchio,** Detroit, in 1955.
– **Bernie Geoffrion,** Montreal, in 1955.
5 – 9 players tied.

MOST GOALS BY A DEFENSEMAN, ONE SERIES

5 – **Denis Potvin** (in 6 games), NY Islanders, in 1980.
– **Al MacInnis** (in 6 games), Calgary, in 1989.
– **Brian Leetch** (in 7 games), NY Rangers, in 1994.
4 – Bobby Orr (in 6 games), Boston, in 1972.
– Brad Park (in 6 games), Boston, in 1978.

MOST GOALS BY A ROOKIE, ONE SERIES

5 – **Roy Conacher** (in 5 games), Boston, in 1939.
4 – Johnny Gagnon (in 5 games), Montreal, in 1931.

MOST ASSISTS, ONE SERIES

10 – **Wayne Gretzky,** Edmonton (in 4 games plus suspended game), in 1988.
9 – Jacques Lemaire, Montreal (in 6 games), in 1973.
– Wayne Gretzky, Edmonton (in 7 games), in 1987.
– Larry Murphy, Pittsburgh (in 6 games), in 1991.
8 – Billy Taylor, Toronto (in 7 games), in 1942.
– Bert Olmstead, Montreal (in 5 games), in 1956.
– Phil Esposito, Boston (in 6 games), in 1972.
– Pat Stapleton, Chicago (in 6 games), in 1973.
– Paul Coffey, Edmonton (in 5 games), in 1985.

MOST ASSISTS, FOUR-GAME SERIES

10 – **Wayne Gretzky,** Edmonton, in 1988.
7 – Guy Lafleur, Montreal, in 1977.
– Denis Potvin, NY Islanders, in 1982.
6 – Bernie Geoffrion, Montreal, in 1960.
– Phil Esposito, Boston, in 1970.
– Rick Tocchet, Pittsburgh, in 1992.

MOST ASSISTS, FIVE-GAME SERIES

8 – **Bert Olmstead,** Montreal, in 1956.
– **Paul Coffey,** Edmonton, in 1985.
7 – Bill Cowley, Boston, in 1939.

MOST ASSISTS, SIX-GAME SERIES

9 – **Jacques Lemaire,** Montreal, in 1973.
– **Larry Murphy,** Pittsburgh, in 1991.
8 – Phil Esposito, Boston, in 1972.
– Pat Stapleton, Chicago, in 1973.

MOST ASSISTS, SEVEN-GAME SERIES

9 – **Wayne Gretzky,** Edmonton, in 1987.
8 – Billy Taylor, Toronto, in 1942.

MOST ASSISTS BY A DEFENSEMAN, ONE SERIES

9 – **Larry Murphy** (in 6 games), Pittsburgh, in 1991.
8 – Pat Stapleton (in 6 games), Chicago, in 1973.
– Paul Coffey (in 5 games), Edmonton, in 1985.
7 – Denis Potvin (in 4 games), NY Islanders, in 1982.

MOST ASSISTS BY A ROOKIE, ONE SERIES

5 – **Jaromir Jagr** (in 6 games), Pittsburgh, in 1991.
4 – Ralph Backstrom (in 5 games), Montreal, in 1959.
– Lars Molin (in 4 games), Vancouver, in 1982.
– Derrick Smith (in 5 games), Philadelphia, in 1985.
3 – Brian Propp (in 6 games), Philadelphia, in 1980.

– Dino Ciccarelli (in 5 games), Minnesota, in 1981.
– Billy Carroll (in 5 games), NY Islanders, in 1981.
– Pat Flatley (in 5 games), NY Islanders, in 1984.
– Janne Niinimaa (in 4 games), Philadelphia Flyers, in 1997.

MOST OVERTIME GOALS, ONE SERIES
2 – Don Raleigh, NY Rangers (in 7 games), in 1950.
– John LeClair, Montreal Canadiens (in 5 games), in 1993.

MOST POWER-PLAY GOALS, ONE SERIES
4 – Jean Beliveau, Montreal Canadiens (in 7 games), in 1965.
– Mike Bossy, NY Islanders (in 6 games), in 1980.
3 – Bernie Geoffrion, Montreal (in 7 games), in 1955.
– Dick Duff, Montreal (in 4 games), in 1969.
– Steve Shutt, Montreal (in 4 games), in 1976.
– Denis Potvin, NY Islanders (in 6 games), in 1980.
– Mike Bossy, NY Islanders (in 4 games), in 1982.
– Clark Gillies, NY Islanders (in 5 games), in 1984.
– Joe Mullen, Calgary (in 6 games), in 1989.

MOST POWER-PLAY ASSISTS, ONE SERIES
6 – Mike Bossy, NY Islanders (in 6 games), in 1980.
– Wayne Gretzky, Edmonton (in 4 games plus suspended game), in 1988.
4 – eight players tied.

MOST SHORTHAND GOALS, ONE SERIES
2 – Cecil Dillon, NY Rangers (in 4 games), in 1933.
– Dave Keon, Toronto (in 5 games), in 1963.
– Bob Pulford, Toronto (in 7 games), in 1964.
– Serge Savard, Montreal (in 4 games), in 1968.
– Kevin Lowe, Edmonton (in 7 games), in 1987.

MOST PENALTY MINUTES, ONE SERIES
53 – Mel Bridgman, Philadelphia (in 6 games), in 1980.
49 – Chris Nilan, Montreal (in 3 games), in 1986.
44 – Eddie Gerard, Ottawa (in 2 games), in 1921
43 – Brad Marsh, Philadelphia (in 5 games), in 1985.
– Tim Hunter, Calgary (in 5 games), in 1986.
41 – Jimmy Orlando, Detroit (in 7 games), in 1942.
– Wayne Cashman, Boston (in 6 games), in 1974.

MOST SHUTOUTS BY A GOALTENDER, ONE SERIES
3 – Clint Benedict, Montreal Maroons (in 4 games), in 1926
– Frank McCool, Toronto (in 7 games), in 1945.
2 – seven goaltenders tied.

MOST MINUTES PLAYED BY A GOALTENDER, ONE SERIES
459 – Harry Lumley, Detroit (in 7 games), in 1950.
– Chuck Rayner, NY Rangers (in 7 games), in 1950.
441 – Ken Dryden, Montreal (in 7 games), in 1971.
– Tony Esposito, Chicago (in 7 games), in 1971.

LONGEST SHUTOUT SEQUENCE BY A GOALTENDER
188:35 – Frank McCool, Toronto, in 1945. McCool posted shutouts in each of the first three games against Detroit and did not allow a goal until 8:35 of the first period in Game 4.
161:23 – Terry Sawchuk, Detroit, in 1952. Sawchuk did not allow a Montreal goal from 18:37 of the first period in Game 2 through the end of Game 4, the concluding match of the series.

FEWEST GOALS ALLOWED BY A GOALTENDER, ONE SERIES (MINIMUM 4 GAMES PLAYED)
2 – Terry Sawchuk, Detroit (in 4 games), in 1952.
3 – Clint Benedict, Montreal Maroons (in 4 games), in 1926
– Alex Connell, Ottawa (in 4 games), in 1927
– Rogie Vachon, Montreal (in 4 games), in 1969.

MOST GOALS ALLOWED BY A GOALTENDER, ONE SERIES
32 – Tony Esposito, Chicago (in 6 games), in 1973.
25 – Johnny Mowers, Detroit (in 7 games), in 1942.

MOST GOALS, ONE GAME
4 – Newsy Lalonde, Montreal, in Game 2, March 22, 1919. Montreal 4 at Seattle 2.
– Babe Dye, Toronto, in Game 5. March 28, 1922. Vancouver 1 at Toronto 5.
Ted Lindsay, Detroit, in Game 2, April 5, 1955. Montreal 1 at Detroit 7.
– Maurice Richard, Montreal, in Game 1, April 6, 1957. Boston 1 at Montreal 5.
3 – 26 players tied.

MOST ASSISTS, ONE GAME
4 – Eddie Bush, Detroit, in Game 3, April 9, 1942. Toronto 2 at Detroit 5.
– Sid Abel, Detroit, in Game 1, April 1, 1943. Boston 2 at Detroit 6.
– Hector "Toe" Blake, Montreal, in Game 4, April 13, 1944. Chicago 4 at Montreal 5.
– Earl "Dutch" Reibel, Detroit, in Game 2, April 5, 1955. Montreal 1 at Detroit 7.
– Brad Maxwell, Minnesota, in Game 4, May 19, 1981. NY Islanders 2 at Minnesota 4.
– Brian Propp, Philadelphia, in Game 5, May 26, 1987. Philadelphia 4 at Edmonton 3.
– Wayne Gretzky, Edmonton, in Game 3, May 22, 1988. Edmonton 6 at Boston 3.
– Larry Murphy, Pittsburgh, in Game 5, May 23, 1991. Minnesota 4 at Pittsburgh 6.
– Joe Sakic, Colorado, in Game 2, June 6, 1996. Florida 1 at Colorado 8.

MOST POINTS, ONE GAME
5 – Eddie Bush (1-4-5), Detroit, in Game 3, April 9, 1942. Toronto 2 at Detroit 5.
– Syl Apps (2-3-5), Toronto, in Game 5, April 14, 1942. Detroit 3 at Toronto 9.
– Don Metz (3-2-5), Toronto, in Game 5, April 14, 1942. Detroit 3 at Toronto 9.
– Sid Abel (1-4-5), Detroit, in Game 1, April 1, 1943. Boston 2 at Detroit 6.
– Hector "Toe" Blake (1-4-5), Montreal, in Game 4, April 13, 1944. Chicago 4 at Montreal 5.
– Jari Kurri (3-2-5), Edmonton, in Game 2, May 17, 1990. Edmonton 7 at Boston 2.

MOST POWER-PLAY GOALS, ONE GAME
3 – Sid Smith, Toronto, in Game 2, April 10, 1949. Detroit 1 at Toronto 3.
2 – several players tied.

MOST GOALS, ONE PERIOD
3 – Harvey "Busher" Jackson, Toronto, in second period of Game 1, April 5, 1932. Toronto 6 at NY Rangers 4.
– Ted Lindsay, Detroit, in 2nd period of Game 2, April 5, 1955. Montreal 4 at Detroit 7.
– Maurice Richard, Montreal, in 2nd period of Game 1, April 6, 1957. Boston 1 at Montreal 5.
– Wayne Gretzky, Edmonton, in 1st period of Game 3, May 25, 1985. Philadelphia 3 at Edmonton 4.
– Dirk Graham, Chicago, in 1st period of Game 4, June 1, 1992. Pittsburgh 6 at Chicago 5.
– Peter Forsberg, Colorado, in 1st period of Game 2, June 6, 1996. Florida 1 at Colorado 8.

MOST ASSISTS, ONE PERIOD
3 – Joe Primeau, Toronto, in 3rd period of Game 2, April 7, 1932. Toronto 6 at NY Rangers 2.
– Hector "Toe" Blake, Montreal, in 3rd period of Game 4, April 13, 1944. Chicago 4 at Montreal 5 (OT).
– Doug Harvey, Montreal, in 2nd period of Game 1, April 6, 1957. Boston 1 at Montreal 5.
– Henri Richard, Montreal, in 1st period of Game 1, April 7, 1960. Toronto 2 at Montreal 4.
– Bobby Rousseau, Montreal, in 1st period of Game 7, May 1, 1965. Chicago 0 at Montreal 4.
– Pat Stapleton, Chicago, in 1st period of Game 1, April 29, 1973. Chicago 3 at Montreal 8.
– Paul Coffey, Edmonton, in 1st period of Game 3, May 25, 1985. Philadelphia 3 at Edmonton 4.
– Larry Murphy, Pittsburgh, in 1st period of Game 5, May 23, 1991. Minnesota 4 at Pittsburgh 6.
– Joe Sakic, Colorado, in 1st period of Game 2, June 6, 1996. Florida 1 at Colorado 8.

MOST POINTS, ONE PERIOD
3 – 34 players tied.

MOST POWER-PLAY GOALS, ONE PERIOD
2 – Sid Smith, Toronto, in 1st period of Game 2, April 10, 1949. Detroit 1 at Toronto 3.
– Maurice Richard, Montreal, in 1st of Game 2, April 6, 1954. Montreal 3 at Detroit 1.
– Bernie Geoffrion, Montreal, in 1st period of Game 3, April 7, 1955. Detroit 2 at Montreal 4.
– Brad Park, NY Rangers, in 1st period of Game 3, May 4, 1972. Boston 2 at NY Rangers 5.
– Peter Forsberg, Colorado Avalanche, in 1st period of Game 2, June 6, 1996. Florida 1 at Colorado 8.

MOST SHORTHAND GOALS, ONE PERIOD
1 – several players tied.

FASTEST TWO GOALS
0:12 – Bernie Geoffrion, Montreal, in Game 3, April 7, 1955. Detroit 2 at Montreal 5. Geoffrion scored at 8:30 and 8:42 of 1st period.
0:15 – Wayne Gretzky, Edmonton, in Game 3, May 25, 1985. Philadelphia 3 at Edmonton 4. Gretzky scored at 1:10 and 1:25 of 1st period.

FASTEST GOAL FROM START OF GAME
0:10 – Glenn Anderson, Edmonton, in suspended game, May 24, 1988. Edmonton 3 at Boston 3.
– John Byce, Boston, in Game 3, May 20, 1990. Boston 2 at Edmonton 1.

FASTEST GOAL FROM START OF PERIOD
0:09 – Brian Skrudland, Montreal, in 1st overtime of Game 2, May 18, 1986. Montreal 3 at Calgary 2 (OT).
0:10 – Glenn Anderson, Edmonton, in 1st period of suspended game, May 24, 1988. Edmonton 3 at Boston 3.
– John Byce, Boston, in 1st period of Game 3, May 20, 1990. Boston 2 at Edmonton 1.

FASTEST OVERTIME GOAL
0:09 – Brian Skrudland, Montreal, in Game 2, May 18, 1986. Montreal 3 at Calgary 2 (OT).
0:31 – Frank "Buzz" Boll, Toronto, in Game 3, April 9, 1936. Detroit 3 at Toronto 4 (OT).

FASTEST TWO GOALS FROM START OF GAME
1:08 – Dick Duff, Toronto, in Game 1, April 9, 1963. Detroit 2 at Toronto 4. Duff scored at 0:49 and 1:08 of 1st period.

FASTEST TWO GOALS FROM START OF PERIOD
0:35 – Pat LaFontaine, NY Islanders, in Game 5, May 19, 1984. NY Islanders 2 at Edmonton 5. LaFontaine scored at 0:13 and 0:35 of 3rd period.

Coaching

MOST STANLEY CUP CHAMPIONSHIPS BY A COACH

8 – Hector "Toe" Blake, Montreal (1956-57-58-59-60-65-66-68)
– Scotty Bowman, Montreal (1973-76-77-78-79), Pittsburgh (1992) and Detroit (1997-98)
5 – Clarence "Hap" Day, Toronto (1942-45-47-48-49)
4 – Dick Irvin, Toronto (1932) and Montreal (1944-46-53)
– George "Punch" Imlach, Toronto (1962-63-64-67)
– Al Arbour, NY Islanders (1980-81-82-83)
– Glen Sather, Edmonton (1984-85-87-88)
3 – Pete Green, Ottawa (1920-21-23)
– Lester Patrick, Victoria (1925) and NY Rangers (1928-33)
– Jack Adams, Detroit (1936-37-43)
– Tommy Ivan, Detroit (1950-52-54)

MOST YEARS IN THE FINALS BY A COACH

16 – Dick Irvin, Chicago (1931), Toronto (1932-33-35-36-38-39-40) and Montreal (1944-46-47-51-52-53-54-55)
12 – Scotty Bowman, St. Louis (1968-69-70), Montreal (1973-76-77-78-79), Pittsburgh (1992) and Detroit (1995-97-98)
9 – Hector "Toe" Blake, Montreal (1956-57-58-59-60-65-66-67-68)
* 8 – Lester Patrick, Victoria (1914-25-26) and NY Rangers (1928-29-32-33-37)
6 – George "Punch" Imlach, Toronto (1959-60-62-63-64-67)
5 – Jack Adams, Detroit (1936-37-42-43-45)
– Clarence "Hap" Day, Toronto (1942-45-47-48-49)
– Tommy Ivan, Detroit (1948-49-50-52-54)
– Al Arbour, NY Islanders (1980-81-82-83-84)
– Glen Sather, Edmonton (1983-84-85-87-88)

MOST GAMES BY A COACH

77 – Dick Irvin, Chicago (5), Toronto (29) and Montreal (43)
53 – Scott Bowman, St. Louis (12), Montreal (25), Pittsburgh (4) and Detroit (12)
48 – Hector "Toe" Blake, Montreal
33 – George "Punch" Imlach, Toronto
* 30 – Lester Patrick, Victoria (11) and NY Rangers (19)
28 – Clarence "Hap" Day, Toronto
26 – Tommy Ivan, Detroit

MOST WINS BY A COACH

34 – Hector "Toe" Blake, Montreal
32 – Dick Irvin, Chicago (2), Toronto (9) and Montreal (21)
– Scotty Bowman, St. Louis (0), Montreal (20), Pittsburgh (4) and Detroit (8)
20 – Clarence "Hap" Day, Toronto
17 – George "Punch" Imlach, Toronto
– Al Arbour, NY Islanders
16 – Glen Sather, Edmonton

BEST WINNING PERCENTAGE BY A COACH (MINIMUM 15 GAMES)

.714 – Clarence "Hap" Day, Toronto (20-8 in 28 games)
.708 – Hector "Toe" Blake, Montreal (34-14 in 48 games)
.708 – Al Arbour, NY Islanders (17-7 in 24 games)
.640 – Glen Sather, Edmonton (16-9 in 25 games)
.604 – Scott Bowman, St. Louis (0-12 in 12 games), Montreal (20-5 in 25 games), Pittsburgh (4-0 in 4 games) and Detroit (8-4 in 12 games); 32-21 in 53 games overall)
.522 – Jack Adams, Detroit (12-11 in 23 games)
.515 – George "Punch" Imlach, Toronto (17-16 in 33 games)

* Lester Patrick's total includes the 1914 Victoria Aristocrats of the Pacific Coast Hockey Association, prior to the formation of the NHL.

Officiating

MOST GAMES OFFICIATED BY A REFEREE

42 – Bill Chadwick (1941 through 1955)
35 – Andy vanHellemond (1977 through 1996)
24 – Frank Udvari (1956 through 1966)
20 – Frank "King" Clancy (1940 through 1949)
17 – Art Skov (1964 through 1975)
15 – Eddie Powers (1957 through 1962)
– Don Koharski (1986 through 1999)
14 – Ag Smith (1933 through 1940)
– John Ashley (1964 through 1972)
13 – Bobby Hewitson (1929 through 1934)

MOST GAMES OFFICIATED BY A LINESMAN

56 – Matt Pavelich (1957 through 1979)
54 – George Hayes (1948 through 1964)
52 – John D'Amico (1965 through 1987)
48 – Neil Armstrong (1960 through 1977)
45 – Ray Scapinello (1980 through 1999)
40 – Sam Babcock (1942 through 1956)
34 – Bill Morrison (1951 through 1965)
– Ron Finn (1979 through 1990)
28 – Kevin Collins (1987 through 1999)
27 – Claude Bechard (1969 through 1979)
15 – Leon Stickle (1977 through 1985)

Early Playoff Records

1893-1918

Team Records

MOST GOALS, BOTH TEAMS, ONE GAME:
25 – Ottawa Silver Seven, Dawson City at Ottawa, Jan. 16, 1905. Ottawa 23, Dawson City 2. Ottawa won best-of-three series 2-0.

MOST GOALS, ONE TEAM, ONE GAME:
23 – Ottawa Silver Seven at Ottawa, Jan. 16, 1905. Ottawa defeated Dawson City 23-2.

MOST GOALS, BOTH TEAMS, BEST-OF-THREE SERIES:
42 – Ottawa Silver Seven, Queen's University at Ottawa, 1906. Ottawa defeated Queen's 16-7, Feb. 27, and 12-7, Feb. 28.

MOST GOALS, ONE TEAM, BEST-OF-THREE SERIES:
32 – Ottawa Silver Seven in 1905 at Ottawa. Defeated Dawson City 9-2, Jan. 13, and 23-2, Jan. 16.

MOST GOALS, BOTH TEAMS, BEST-OF-FIVE SERIES:
39 – Toronto Arenas, Vancouver Millionaires at Toronto, 1918. Toronto won 5-3, Mar. 20; 6-3, Mar. 26; 2-1, Mar. 30. Vancouver won 6-4, Mar. 23, and 8-1, Mar. 28. Toronto scored 18 goals; Vancouver 21.

MOST GOALS, ONE TEAM, BEST-OF-FIVE SERIES:
26 – Vancouver Millionaires in 1915 at Vancouver. Defeated Ottawa Senators 6-2, Mar. 22; 8-3, Mar. 24; and 12-3 Mar. 26.

Individual Records

MOST GOALS IN PLAYOFFS:
63 – Frank McGee, Ottawa Silver Seven, in 22 playoff games. Seven goals in four games, 1903; 21 goals in eight games, 1904; 18 goals in four games, 1905; 17 goals in six games, 1906.

MOST GOALS, ONE PLAYOFF SERIES:
15 – Frank McGee, Ottawa Silver Seven, in two games in 1905 at Ottawa. Scored one goal, Jan. 13, in 9-2 victory over Dawson City and 14 goals, Jan. 16, in 23-2 victory.

MOST GOALS, ONE PLAYOFF GAME:
14 – Frank McGee, Ottawa Silver Seven, Jan. 16, 1905 at Ottawa in 23-2 victory over Dawson City.

FASTEST THREE GOALS:
0:40 – Marty Walsh, Ottawa Senators, at Ottawa, March 16, 1911, at 3:00, 3:10, and 3:40 of third period. Ottawa defeated Port Arthur 13-4.

CHAPTER 17

Final Series Scoring, Year-By-Year

1918 – 1999

1918

TORONTO	GP	G	A	PTS	PIM
Alf Skinner	5	8	2	10	18
Harry Mummery	5	0	6	6	21
Harry Cameron	5	3	1	4	12
Corb Denneny	5	3	1	4	0
Reg Noble	5	2	1	3	12
Harry Meeking	5	1	2	3	18
Ken Randall	5	1	0	1	21

GOALTENDER	GP	W	L	MIN	GA	SO	AVG
Hap Holmes	5	3	2	300	21	0	4.20

VANCOUVER	GP	G	A	PTS	PIM
D.'Mickey' MacKay	5	5	5	10	12
F.'Cyclone' Taylor	5	9	0	9	15
Ran MacDonald	5	2	2	4	9
Lloyd Cook	5	2	0	2	12
Barney Stanley	5	2	0	2	6
Si Griffis	5	1	0	1	9
Leo Cook	5	0	0	0	6
Speed Moynes	5	0	0	0	0

GOALTENDER	GP	W	L	MIN	GA	SO	AVG
Hugh Lehman	5	2	3	300	18	0	3.60

1919

MONTREAL	GP	G	A	PTS	PIM
E. 'Newsy' Lalonde	5	6	0	6	3
Didier Pitre	5	0	3	3	0
Odie Cleghorn	5	2	0	2	9
Louis Berlinquette	5	1	1	2	0
Jack MacDonald	5	1	1	2	3
Bert Corbeau	5	0	1	1	3
Billy Couture	5	0	1	1	0
Joe Hall	5	0	0	0	6

GOALTENDER	GP	W	L	T	MIN	GA	SO	AVG
Georges Vezina	5	2	2	1	336	19	1	3.39

SEATTLE	GP	G	A	PTS	PIM
Frank Foyston	5	9	1	10	0
C. 'Cully' Wilson	5	1	3	4	6
Muzz Murray	5	3	0	3	3
Jack Walker	5	3	0	3	9
Roy Rickey	5	1	2	3	0
Ran McDonald	5	1	1	2	3
Bobby Rowe	5	1	0	1	6

GOALTENDER	GP	W	L	T	MIN	GA	SO	AVG
Hap Holmes	5	2	2	1	336	10	2	1.79

1920

OTTAWA	GP	G	A	PTS	PIM
Frank Nighbor	5	6	1	7	2
Jack Darragh	5	5	2	7	3
Eddie Gerard	2	2	1	3	3
George Boucher	5	2	0	2	3
Cy Denneny	5	0	2	2	3
Sprague Cleghorn	5	0	1	1	4
H.'Punch' Broadbent	4	0	0	0	0
Jack McKell	5	0	0	0	0
Morley Bruce	5	0	0	0	0

GOALTENDER	GP	W	L	MIN	GA	SO	AVG
Clint Benedict	5	3	2	300	11	1	2.20

SEATTLE	GP	G	A	PTS	PIM
Frank Foyston	5	6	1	7	7
Jack Walker	5	1	3	4	0
Roy Rickey	2	2	1	3	0
Bobby Rowe	5	2	0	2	13
Bernie Morris	2	0	2	2	0
Jim Riley	5	0	1	1	0
Muzz Murray	5	0	0	0	5
Charlie Tobin	5	0	0	0	0
Sibby Nicholls	5	0	0	0	0

GOALTENDER	GP	W	L	MIN	GA	SO	AVG
Hap Holmes	5	2	3	300	15	0	3.00

1921

OTTAWA	GP	G	A	PTS	PIM
Jack Darragh	5	5	0	5	7
Cy Denneny	5	2	2	4	10
George Boucher	5	2	0	2	9
H.'Punch' Broadbent	5	2	0	2	0
Sprague Cleghorn	5	1	1	2	36
Frank Nighbor	2	0	1	1	0
Eddie Gerard	2	0	0	0	44
Jack McKell	4	0	0	0	0

GOALTENDER	GP	W	L	MIN	GA	SO	AVG
Clint Benedict	5	3	2	300	12	2	2.40

VANCOUVER	GP	G	A	PTS	PIM
Alf Skinner	3	4	0	4	12
Jack Adams	5	2	1	3	6
Lloyd Cook	5	2	1	3	20
Art Duncan	5	2	1	3	6
T.'Smokey' Harris	5	2	1	3	8
D.'Mickey' MacKay	5	0	1	1	0
F.'Cyclone' Taylor	5	0	1	1	0
Bill Adams	4	0	0	0	0
Syd Desireau	5	0	0	0	0

GOALTENDER	GP	W	L	MIN	GA	SO	AVG
Hugh Lehman	5	2	3	300	12	1	2.40

1922

TORONTO	GP	G	A	PTS	PIM
C.'Babe' Dye	5	9	1	10	3
Corb Denneny	5	3	2	5	2
Rod Smylie	5	1	3	4	0
Lloyd Andrews	5	2	0	2	3
B.'Red' Stuart	5	0	2	2	6
Harry Cameron	4	0	2	2	11
Ken Randall	4	1	0	1	19
Reg Noble	5	0	1	1	9
Eddie Gerard	1	0	0	0	0
Ted Stackhouse	4	0	0	0	0

GOALTENDER	GP	W	L	MIN	GA	SO	AVG
John Ross Roach	5	3	2	305	9	1	1.77

VANCOUVER	GP	G	A	PTS	PIM
Jack Adams	5	6	1	7	-
Ernie Parkes	5	0	3	3	-
Lloyd Cook	5	1	0	1	-
D.'Mickey' MacKay	5	1	0	1	-
Eddie Oatman	5	1	0	1	-
Art Duncan	5	0	1	1	-
Alf Skinner	5	0	1	1	-
Charlie Tobin	5	0	0	0	-
Syd Desireau	1	0	0	0	-

GOALTENDER	GP	W	L	MIN	GA	SO	AVG
Hugh Lehman	5	2	3	305	16	1	3.15

1923

OTTAWA	GP	G	A	PTS	PIM
Punch Broadbent	6	6	1	7	12
George Boucher	6	2	1	3	6
Cy Denneny	6	1	1	2	8
Frank Nighbor	6	1	1	2	10
Lionel Hitchman	5	1	0	1	4
F.'King' Clancy	6	1	0	1	4
Eddie Gerard	6	1	0	1	4
Clint Benedict	6	0	0	0	2
Harry Helman	2	0	0	0	0

GOALTENDER	GP	W	L	MIN	GA	SO	AVG
Clint Benedict	6	5	1	360	8	1	1.33
F.'King' Clancy	1	0	0	2	0	0	0.00

VANCOUVER	GP	G	A	PTS	PIM
Art Duncan	4	2	2	4	0
Frank Boucher	4	2	0	2	0
Alf Skinner	3	1	1	2	4
Ernie Parkes	4	0	2	2	2
D.'Mickey' MacKay	4	1	0	1	4
T.'Smokey' Harris	4	1	0	1	8
Lloyd Cook	4	0	1	1	4
Charlie Cotch	2	0	0	0	0
Corb Denneny	3	0	0	0	0

GOALTENDER	GP	W	L	MIN	GA	SO	AVG
Hugh Lehman	4	1	3	240	10	0	2.50

EDMONTON	GP	G	A	PTS	PIM
J.'Crutchy' Morrison	2	1	0	1	0
Joe Simpson	2	0	1	1	0
Johnny Sheppard	1	0	0	0	0
Helge Bostrom	1	0	0	0	0
Art Gagne	2	0	0	0	2
G.'Duke' Keats	2	0	0	0	4
Bob Trapp	2	0	0	0	2
E.'Ty' Arbour	2	0	0	0	0
E.'Spiff' Campbell	2	0	0	0	0

GOALTENDER	GP	W	L	MIN	GA	SO	AVG
Hal Winkler	2	0	2	122	3	0	1.46

1924

MONTREAL	GP	G	A	PTS	PIM
Billy Boucher	4	5	1	6	6
Howie Morenz	4	4	2	6	4
Aurel Joliat	4	3	1	4	6
Sprague Cleghorn	4	2	2	4	2
Odie Cleghorn	4	0	1	1	0
Bobby Boucher	3	0	0	0	0
Billy Bell	3	0	0	0	0
Billy Coutu	4	0	0	0	0
Billy Cameron	4	0	0	0	0
Sylvio Mantha	4	0	0	0	0

GOALTENDER	GP	W	L	MIN	GA	SO	AVG
Georges Vezina	4	4	0	240	4	1	1.00

VANCOUVER	GP	G	A	PTS	PIM
Frank Boucher	2	1	1	2	2
Helge Bostrum	2	1	0	1	0
Joe Matte	2	1	0	1	2
Lloyd Cook	2	0	0	0	2
Art Duncan	2	0	0	0	4
D.'Mickey' MacKay	2	0	0	0	0
Charlie Cotch	1	0	0	0	0
Ernie Parkes	2	0	0	0	0
Alf Skinner	2	0	0	0	0

GOALTENDER	GP	W	L	MIN	GA	SO	AVG
Hugh Lehman	2	0	2	120	5	0	2.50

CALGARY	GP	G	A	PTS	PIM
Herb Gardiner	2	1	0	1	0
Bernie Morris	2	0	1	1	0
Ernie Anderson	2	0	0	0	2
Bobby Benson	2	0	0	0	0
Rusty Crawford	2	0	0	0	0
M.'Red' Dutton	2	0	0	0	4
Eddie Oatman	2	0	0	0	0
Harry Oliver	2	0	0	0	0
C.'Cully' Wilson	2	0	0	0	2

GOALTENDER	GP	W	L	MIN	GA	SO	AVG
Charlie Reid	2	0	2	120	9	0	4.50

1925

VICTORIA	GP	G	A	PTS	PIM
Jack Walker	4	4	2	6	0
Frank Fredrickson	4	3	3	6	6
Gord Fraser	4	2	1	3	6
W.'Gizzy' Hart	4	2	1	3	0
H.'Slim' Halderson	4	2	1	3	8
Clem Loughlin	4	1	0	1	4
Frank Foyston	4	1	0	1	0
Jocko Anderson	4	1	0	1	10
Harry Meeking	4	0	1	1	2
Wally Elmer	2	0	0	0	0

GOALTENDER	GP	W	L	MIN	GA	SO	AVG
Hap Holmes	4	3	1	240	8	0	2.00

MONTREAL	GP	G	A	PTS	PIM
Howie Morenz	4	4	0	4	4
Aurel Joliat	4	2	0	2	16
Billy Boucher	4	1	1	2	13
Billy Coutu	4	1	0	1	10
Sprague Cleghorn	4	0	0	0	2
John Matz	4	0	0	0	2
Odie Cleghorn	4	0	0	0	0
F.'Curly' Headley	4	0	0	0	0
Sylvio Mantha	4	0	0	0	2

GOALTENDER	GP	W	L	MIN	GA	SO	AVG
Georges Vezina	4	1	3	240	16	0	4.00

1926

MTL MAROONS	GP	G	A	PTS	PIM
Nels Stewart	4	6	1	7	14
A.'Babe' Siebert	4	1	2	3	2
Bill Phillips	4	1	1	2	0
H.'Punch' Broadbent	4	1	0	1	22
Dunc Munro	4	1	0	1	6
Reg Noble	4	0	0	0	4
Chuck Dinsmore	4	0	0	0	2
Frank Carson	4	0	0	0	0
Sammy Rothschild	4	0	0	0	0
A.'Toots' Holway	2	0	0	0	0

GOALTENDER	GP	W	L	MIN	GA	SO	AVG
Clint Benedict	4	3	1	240	3	3	0.75

VICTORIA	GP	G	A	PTS	PIM
Frank Fredrickson	4	1	1	2	10
H.'Slim' Halderson	4	1	0	1	8
Clem Loughlin	4	1	0	1	8
Jack Walker	4	0	0	0	0
Gordon Fraser	4	0	0	0	14
Russell Oatman	4	0	0	0	10
W.'Gizzy' Hart	4	0	0	0	2
Frank Foyston	4	0	0	0	2
Harry Meeking	4	0	0	0	6
Jocko Anderson	1	0	0	0	0

GOALTENDER	GP	W	L	MIN	GA	SO	AVG
Hap Holmes	4	1	3	240	10	0	2.50

1927

OTTAWA	GP	G	A	PTS	PIM
Cy Denneny	4	4	0	4	0
Frank Finnigan	4	2	0	2	0
F.'King' Clancy	4	1	1	2	4
Frank Nighbor	4	0	1	1	0
Hec Kilrea	4	0	1	1	2
R.'Hooley' Smith	4	0	1	1	12
Milt Halliday	4	0	0	0	0
Ed Gorman	4	0	0	0	0
Jack Adams	4	0	0	0	2
Alex Smith	4	0	0	0	8
George Boucher	4	0	0	0	27

GOALTENDER	GP	W	L	T	MIN	GA	SO	AVG
Alex Connell	4	2	0	2	240	3	1	0.75

BOSTON	GP	G	A	PTS	PIM
Harry Oliver	4	2	1	3	2
Jimmy Herberts	4	1	0	1	18
Harry Meeking	4	0	0	0	0
Percy Galbraith	4	0	0	0	0
Bill Stuart	4	0	0	0	0
Billy Boucher	4	0	0	0	0
Billy Coutu	4	0	0	0	2
Sprague Cleghorn	4	0	0	0	4
Frank Fredrickson	4	0	0	0	16
Lionel Hitchman	4	0	0	0	17
Eddie Shore	4	0	0	0	20

GOALTENDER	GP	W	L	T	MIN	GA	SO	AVG
Hal Winkler	4	0	2	2	240	7	1	1.75

1928

MTL MAROONS	GP	G	A	PTS	PIM
Bill Phillips	5	2	0	2	2
Nels Stewart	5	2	0	2	8
A.'Babe' Siebert	4	1	1	2	10
M.'Red' Dutton	5	1	1	2	13
R.'Hooley' Smith	5	0	2	2	13
Dunc Munro	5	0	1	1	2
Joe Lamb	4	0	0	0	21
Frank Carson	5	0	0	0	0
Fred Brown	5	0	0	0	0
Jimmy Ward	5	0	0	0	2
Russell Oatman	5	0	0	0	12

GOALTENDER	GP	W	L	MIN	GA	SO	AVG
Clint Benedict	5	2	3	307	5	1	0.98

NY RANGERS	GP	G	A	PTS	PIM
Frank Boucher	5	4	0	4	2
Bill Cook	5	1	2	3	16
I.'Ching' Johnson	5	0	2	2	26
F.'Bun' Cook	5	0	1	1	4
C.'Taffy' Abel	5	0	1	1	10
Paul Thompson	3	0	0	0	19
Pat Callighen	5	0	0	0	0
Alex Gray	5	0	0	0	0
Bill Boyd	5	0	0	0	2
Leo Bourgeault	5	0	0	0	6
Murray Murdoch	5	0	0	0	10

GOALTENDERS	GP	W	L	MIN	GA	SO	AVG
Joe Miller	3	2	1	180	3	1	1.00
Lester Patrick	1	1	0	47	1	0	1.28
Lorne Chabot	2	0	1	80	2	0	1.50

1929

NY RANGERS	GP	G	A	PTS	PIM
M.'Butch' Keeling	2	1	0	1	0
Russell Oatman	1	0	0	0	0
Gerald Carson	1	0	0	0	0
Bill Boyd	1	0	0	0	0
Leroy Goldsworthy	1	0	0	0	0
Ralph Taylor	1	0	0	0	0
Frank Boucher	2	0	0	0	0
Murray Murdoch	2	0	0	0	0
M.'Sparky' Vail	2	0	0	0	0
Leo Bourgeault	2	0	0	0	0
I.'Ching' Johnson	2	0	0	0	2
Bill Cook	2	0	0	0	4
F.'Bun' Cook	2	0	0	0	4
Paul Thompson	2	0	0	0	4
C.'Taffy' Abel	2	0	0	0	4

GOALTENDER	GP	W	L	MIN	GA	SO	AVG
John Roach	2	0	2	120	4	0	2.00

BOSTON	GP	G	A	PTS	PIM
Harry Oliver	2	1	1	2	2
A.'Dit' Clapper	2	1	0	1	0
N.'Dutch' Gainor	2	1	0	1	0
Bill Carson	2	1	0	1	2
Red Green	1	0	0	0	0
Ernie Rodden	1	0	0	0	0
Cy Denneny	1	0	0	0	0
Lloyd Klein	1	0	0	0	0
R.'Cooney' Weiland	2	0	0	0	0
D.'Mickey' MacKay	2	0	0	0	0
George Owen	2	0	0	0	0
Miles Lane	2	0	0	0	0
Percy Galbraith	2	0	0	0	2
Eddie Shore	2	0	0	0	8
Lionel Hitchman	2	0	0	0	10

GOALTENDER	GP	W	L	MIN	GA	SO	AVG
'Tiny' Thompson	2	2	0	120	1	1	0.50

1930

MONTREAL	GP	G	A	PTS	PIM
Albert Leduc	2	1	2	3	0
Sylvio Mantha	2	2	0	2	2
A.'Pit' Lepine	2	1	1	2	0
Nick Wasnie	2	1	1	2	6
Bert McCaffrey	2	1	0	1	0
Howie Morenz	2	1	0	1	6
Marty Burke	2	0	1	1	0
Aurel Joliat	2	0	1	1	0
Georges Mantha	2	0	0	0	0
Gerald Carson	2	0	0	0	0
Gus Rivers	2	0	0	0	0
Armand Mondou	2	0	0	0	2
Wildor Larochelle	2	0	0	0	8

GOALTENDER	GP	W	L	MIN	GA	SO	AVG
Geo. Hainsworth	2	2	0	120	3	1	1.50

BOSTON	GP	G	A	PTS	PIM
A.'Dit' Clapper	2	1	0	1	0
Percy Galbraith	2	1	0	1	2
Eddie Shore	2	1	0	1	8
R.'Cooney' Weiland	2	0	1	1	0
Harry Oliver	2	0	1	1	2
N.'Dutch' Gainor	1	0	0	0	0
Bill Carson	2	0	0	0	0
Harry Connor	2	0	0	0	0
Miles Lane	2	0	0	0	0
D.'Mickey' MacKay	2	0	0	0	2
George Owen	2	0	0	0	2
Lionel Hitchman	2	0	0	0	4
Marty Barry	2	0	0	0	6

GOALTENDER	GP	W	L	MIN	GA	SO	AVG
'Tiny' Thompson	2	0	2	120	7	0	3.50

1931

MONTREAL	GP	G	A	PTS	PIM
Johnny Gagnon	5	4	2	6	2
A.'Pit' Lepine	5	3	1	4	4
Georges Mantha	5	2	1	3	4
Aurel Joliat	5	0	2	2	2
Nick Wasnie	5	1	1	2	2
Howie Morenz	5	1	0	1	6
Albert Leduc	2	0	1	1	2
Marty Burke	5	0	1	1	2
Wildor Larochelle	5	0	1	1	6
Armand Mondou	3	0	0	0	0
Jean Pusie	3	0	0	0	0
Gus Rivers	5	0	0	0	0
Art Lesieur	5	0	0	0	4
Sylvio Mantha	5	0	0	0	16

GOALTENDER	GP	W	L	MIN	GA	SO	AVG
Geo. Hainsworth	5	3	2	379	8	1	1.27

CHICAGO	GP	G	A	PTS	PIM
Johnny Gottselig	5	2	2	4	2
Stewart Adams	5	2	1	3	2
Vic Ripley	5	1	1	2	2
E.'Ty' Arbour	5	1	0	1	0
H.'Mush' March	5	1	0	1	6
M.'Cy' Wentworth	5	1	0	1	8
R.'Lolo' Couture	5	0	1	1	2
Frank Ingram	5	0	1	1	2
Tom Cook	5	0	1	1	7
Art Somers	5	0	0	0	0
Vic Desjardins	5	0	0	0	0
E.'Doc' Romnes	5	0	0	0	2
C.'Taffy' Abel	5	0	0	0	6
Helge Bostrum	5	0	0	0	8
Ted Graham	5	0	0	0	10

GOALTENDER	GP	W	L	MIN	GA	SO	AVG
Chuck Gardiner	5	2	3	379	11	0	1.74

1932

TORONTO	GP	G	A	PTS	PIM
H.'Busher' Jackson	3	5	2	7	9
Charlie Conacher	3	3	2	5	2
C.'Happy' Day	3	1	3	4	4
Joe Primeau	3	0	4	4	0
Andy Blair	3	2	0	2	2
F.'King' Clancy	3	2	0	2	8
Bob Gracie	3	1	1	2	0
R.'Red' Horner	3	1	1	2	6
Frank Finnigan	3	1	1	2	8
H.'Baldy' Cotton	3	1	1	2	10
I.'Ace' Bailey	3	1	0	1	0
Earl Miller	2	0	0	0	0
Harry Darragh	3	0	0	0	0
Fred Robertson	3	0	0	0	0
Alex Levinsky	3	0	0	0	2

GOALTENDER	GP	W	L	MIN	GA	SO	AVG
Lorne Chabot	3	3	0	180	10	0	3.33

NY RANGERS	GP	G	A	PTS	PIM
Frank Boucher	3	3	3	6	0
F.'Bun' Cook	3	4	1	5	6
Bill Cook	3	0	2	2	0
Cecil Dillon	3	1	0	1	4
Doug Brennan	3	1	0	1	4
I.'Ching' Johnson	3	1	0	1	10
Murray Murdoch	3	0	1	1	0
Ott Heller	3	0	1	1	2
Hib Milks	3	0	0	0	0
Vic Desjardins	3	0	0	0	0
N.'Dutch' Gainor	3	0	0	0	2
Art Somers	3	0	0	0	4
Earl Seibert	3	0	0	0	6
M.'Butch' Keeling	3	0	0	0	10

GOALTENDER	GP	W	L	MIN	GA	SO	AVG
John Roach	3	0	3	180	18	0	6.00

1933

NY RANGERS	GP	G	A	PTS	PIM
Cecil Dillon	4	3	1	4	4
Bill Cook	4	2	1	3	4
Art Somers	4	0	3	3	4
Ott Heller	4	2	0	2	4
Murray Murdoch	4	1	1	2	2

M.'Butch' Keeling	4	1	1	2	6
Earl Seibert	4	1	0	1	2
Fred 'Bun' Cook	4	1	0	1	4
Ossie Asmundson	4	0	1	1	2
Frank Boucher	4	0	1	1	4
Gord Pettinger	4	0	0	0	0
Doug Brennan	4	0	0	0	2
I.'Ching' Johnson	4	0	0	0	8
A.'Babe' Siebert	4	0	0	0	10

GOALTENDER	GP	W	L	MIN	GA	SO	AVG
Andy Aitkenhead	4	3	1	248	5	1	1.21

TORONTO	GP	G	A	PTS	PIM
Ken Doraty	4	3	0	3	2
F.'King' Clancy	4	0	2	2	6
Alex Levinsky	4	1	0	1	6
R.'Red' Horner	4	1	0	1	8
Charlie Sands	4	0	1	1	0
Bob Gracie	4	0	1	1	0
H.'Baldy' Cotton	4	0	1	1	2
Joe Primeau	4	0	1	1	4
F.'Buzz' Boll	1	0	0	0	0
Andy Blair	4	0	0	0	0
I.'Ace' Bailey	4	0	0	0	2
H.'Busher' Jackson	4	0	0	0	2
Bill Thoms	4	0	0	0	2
Charlie Conacher	4	0	0	0	6
C.'Happy' Day	4	0	0	0	6

GOALTENDER	GP	W	L	MIN	GA	SO	AVG
Lorne Chabot	4	1	3	248	11	0	2.66

1934

CHICAGO	GP	G	A	PTS	PIM
E.'Doc' Romnes	4	1	3	4	0
Paul Thompson	4	2	1	3	0
Johnny Gottselig	4	2	1	3	4
H.'Mush' March	4	1	1	2	2
R.'Lolo' Couture	4	1	1	2	2
Lionel Conacher	4	1	0	1	2
Art Coulter	4	1	0	1	4
Don McFayden	4	0	1	1	2
Bill Kendall	1	0	0	0	0
John Sheppard	3	0	0	0	0
Roger Jenkins	4	0	0	0	0
Leroy Goldsworthy	4	0	0	0	0
Tom Cook	4	0	0	0	0
Louis Trudel	4	0	0	0	0
C.'Taffy' Abel	4	0	0	0	2

GOALTENDER	GP	W	L	MIN	GA	SO	AVG
Chuck Gardiner	4	3	1	291	7	1	1.44

DETROIT	GP	G	A	PTS	PIM
Larry Aurie	4	2	2	4	0
Herbie Lewis	4	2	1	3	2
R.'Cooney' Weiland	4	1	1	2	2
Gord Pettinger	3	1	0	1	0
Doug Young	4	1	0	1	2
Frank Carson	2	0	1	1	0
Wilf Starr	3	0	1	1	2
Walter Buswell	4	0	1	1	2
Ted Graham	4	0	1	1	4
Ron Moffatt	2	0	0	0	0
Burr Williams	2	0	0	0	0
Eddie Wiseman	3	0	0	0	0
Gene Carrigan	3	0	0	0	0
Leighton Emms	3	0	0	0	2
Gus Marker	3	0	0	0	2
John Sorrell	4	0	0	0	0
Ebbie Goodfellow	4	0	0	0	6

GOALTENDER	GP	W	L	MIN	GA	SO	AVG
Wilf Cude	4	1	3	291	9	0	1.86

1935

MTL MAROONS	GP	G	A	PTS	PIM
M.'Cy' Wentworth	3	2	2	4	0
Earl Robinson	3	2	1	3	0
L.'Baldy' Northcott	3	2	1	3	0
Jimmy Ward	3	1	1	2	0
Russ Blinco	3	1	1	2	0
Gus Marker	3	1	0	1	0
Dave Trottier	3	1	0	1	4
Allan Shields	3	0	1	1	2
Herb Cain	3	0	0	0	0
Bob Gracie	3	0	0	0	0
Bill Miller	3	0	0	0	0
Stewart Evans	3	0	0	0	4
R.'Hooley' Smith	3	0	0	0	4
Lionel Conacher	3	0	0	0	8

GOALTENDER	GP	W	L	MIN	GA	SO	AVG
Alex Connell	3	3	0	185	4	0	1.30

TORONTO	GP	G	A	PTS	PIM
Frank Finnigan	3	1	1	2	0
H.'Busher' Jackson	3	1	0	1	0
Bill Thoms	3	1	0	1	0
F.'King' Clancy	3	1	0	1	4
Nick Metz	3	0	1	1	0
Ken Doraty	1	0	0	0	0
Andy Blair	1	0	0	0	2
Frank 'Buzz' Boll	2	0	0	0	0
Hec Kilrea	2	0	0	0	2
B.'Flash' Hollett	3	0	0	0	0
C.'Happy' Day	3	0	0	0	0
H.'Baldy' Cotton	3	0	0	0	0
Joe Primeau	3	0	0	0	0
R.'Pep' Kelly	3	0	0	0	0
Charlie Conacher	3	0	0	0	4
R.'Red' Horner	3	0	0	0	4

GOALTENDER	GP	W	L	MIN	GA	SO	AVG
Geo. Hainsworth	3	0	3	185	10	0	3.24

1936

DETROIT	GP	G	A	PTS	PIM
John Sorrell	4	2	3	5	0
Syd Howe	4	2	3	5	2
Gord Pettinger	4	2	2	4	0
Marty Barry	4	2	2	4	2
W.'Bucko' McDonald	4	3	0	3	4
Wally Kilrea	4	2	1	3	0
M.'Mud' Bruneteau	4	1	2	3	0
Herbie Lewis	4	1	2	3	0
Pete Kelly	4	1	1	2	0
R.'Scotty' Bowman	4	1	1	2	2
Doug Young	4	0	2	2	0
Hec Kilrea	4	0	2	2	0
Ebbie Goodfellow	4	1	0	1	2
Larry Aurie	4	0	1	1	2

GOALTENDER	GP	W	L	MIN	GA	SO	AVG
Norman Smith	4	3	1	241	11	0	2.74

TORONTO	GP	G	A	PTS	PIM
Frank 'Buzz' Boll	4	3	1	4	0
Joe Primeau	4	3	1	4	0
Bill Thoms	4	2	2	4	0
Bob Davidson	4	1	2	3	2
Reg 'Pep' Kelly	4	2	0	2	0
Frank Finnigan	4	0	2	2	0
H.'Busher' Jackson	4	0	2	2	2
R.'Red' Horner	4	0	2	2	8
Art Jackson	4	0	1	1	0
Charlie Conacher	4	0	1	1	2
Jack Shill	4	0	1	1	4
Andy Blair	4	0	0	0	2
F.'King' Clancy	4	0	0	0	2
C.'Happy' Day	4	0	0	0	4

GOALTENDER	GP	W	L	MIN	GA	SO	AVG
Geo. Hainsworth	4	1	3	241	18	0	4.48

1937

NY RANGERS	GP	G	A	PTS	PIM
M.'Butch' Keeling	5	2	1	3	0
Frank Boucher	5	1	2	3	0
Joe Cooper	5	1	2	3	12
Lynn Patrick	5	2	0	2	2
Neil Colville	5	1	1	2	0
W.'Babe' Pratt	5	1	1	2	9
Cecil Dillon	5	0	2	2	0
Art Coulter	5	0	2	2	6
Murray Murdoch	5	0	1	1	0
Mac Colville	5	0	1	1	0
Alex Shibicky	5	0	0	0	0
I.'Ching' Johnson	5	0	0	0	2
Phil Watson	5	0	0	0	4
Ott Heller	5	0	0	0	5

GOALTENDER	GP	W	L	MIN	GA	SO	AVG
Dave Kerr	5	2	3	300	9	1	1.80

DETROIT	GP	G	A	PTS	PIM
Syd Howe	5	1	4	5	0
Marty Barry	5	3	1	4	0
John Sorrell	5	2	2	4	2
Ebbie Goodfellow	4	0	2	2	12
M.'Mud' Bruneteau	5	1	0	1	2
Herbie Lewis	5	1	0	1	4
John Gallagher	5	1	0	1	8
Hec Kilrea	5	0	1	1	0
Gord Pettinger	5	0	1	1	2
John Sherf	5	0	1	1	2
Wally Kilrea	5	0	1	1	4
Pete Kelly	3	0	0	0	0
Howie Mackie	3	0	0	0	0
W.'Bucko' McDonald	5	0	0	0	0
R.'Scotty' Bowman	5	0	0	0	2

GOALTENDERS	GP	W	L	MIN	GA	SO	AVG
Earl Robertson	5	2	2	280	8	2	1.71
Norman Smith	1	1	0	20	0	0	0.00

1938

CHICAGO	GP	G	A	PTS	PIM
Johnny Gottselig	4	2	2	4	0
Paul Thompson	4	1	2	3	2
Elwin 'Doc' Romnes	4	1	2	3	2
Carl Voss	4	2	0	2	0
H.'Mush' March	3	1	1	2	6
C.'Cully' Dahlstrom	4	1	1	2	0
Jack Shill	4	1	1	2	4
Earl Seibert	4	1	1	2	8
Roger Jenkins	4	0	2	2	6
Louis Trudel	4	0	1	1	0
Virgil Johnson	2	0	0	0	0
Pete Palangio	3	0	0	0	0
Alex Levinsky	4	0	0	0	0
Art Wiebe	4	0	0	0	2
Bill MacKenzie	4	0	0	0	9

GOALTENDERS	GP	W	L	MIN	GA	SO	AVG
Mike Karakas	2	2	0	120	2	0	1.00
Alfie Moore	1	1	0	60	1	0	1.00
Paul Goodman	1	0	1	60	5	0	5.00

TORONTO	GP	G	A	PTS	PIM
Gordie Drillon	4	4	1	5	2
Syl Apps	4	1	2	3	0
George Parsons	3	2	0	2	11
Jimmy Fowler	4	0	2	2	0
R.'Pep' Kelly	4	0	2	2	0
Bill Thoms	4	0	2	2	0
Bob Davidson	4	0	2	2	4
H.'Busher' Jackson	4	1	0	1	8
Reg Hamilton	4	0	1	1	2
R.'Red' Horner	4	0	1	1	8
Murray Armstrong	2	0	0	0	0
E.'Murph' Chamberlain	2	0	0	0	2
Nick Metz	4	0	0	0	0
Frank 'Buzz' Boll	4	0	0	0	2
R.'Bingo' Kampman	4	0	0	0	6

GOALTENDER	GP	W	L	MIN	GA	SO	AVG
W.'Turk' Broda	4	1	3	240	10	0	2.50

1939

BOSTON	GP	G	A	PTS	PIM
Roy Conacher	5	5	2	7	6
Bill Cowley	5	0	7	7	2
Mel Hill	5	2	2	4	4
Bobby Bauer	5	2	1	3	0
Eddie Shore	5	0	3	3	6
Jack Crawford	5	1	1	2	4
Milt Schmidt	5	0	2	2	0
B.'Flash' Hollett	5	1	0	1	0
Woody Dumart	5	1	0	1	2
A.'Dit' Clapper	5	0	0	0	0
R.'Cooney' Weiland	5	0	0	0	0
Gord Pettinger	5	0	0	0	0
Ray Getliffe	5	0	0	0	2
R.'Red' Hamill	5	0	0	0	2
Jack Portland	5	0	0	0	2

GOALTENDER	GP	W	L	MIN	GA	SO	AVG
Frank Brimsek	5	4	1	311	6	1	1.16

TORONTO	GP	G	A	PTS	PIM
E.'Doc' Romnes	5	1	3	4	0
Gus Marker	5	1	2	3	0
R.'Bingo' Kampman	5	1	1	2	12
Gordie Drillon	5	0	2	2	4
E.'Murph' Chamberlain	5	1	0	1	0
Syl Apps	5	1	0	1	2
R.'Red' Horner	5	1	0	1	6
H.'Busher' Jackson	3	0	1	1	2
Nick Metz	5	0	1	1	2
Jack Church	1	0	0	0	0
Don Metz	2	0	0	0	0
Robert 'Red' Heron	2	0	0	0	4
Jimmy Fowler	4	0	0	0	0
Pete Langelle	4	0	0	0	0
R.'Pep' Kelly	4	0	0	0	0

	GP	G	A	PTS	PIM
Bob Davidson	5	0	0	0	0
W.'Bucko' McDonald	5	0	0	0	0
Reg Hamilton	5	0	0	0	4

GOALTENDER	GP	W	L	MIN	GA	SO	AVG
W.'Turk' Broda	5	1	4	311	12	0	2.32

1940

NY RANGERS	GP	G	A	PTS	PIM
Bryan Hextall	6	4	1	5	7
Neil Colville	6	2	3	5	12
Phil Watson	6	1	4	5	8
W.'Dutch' Hiller	6	1	2	3	0
Alf Pike	6	2	0	2	4
Lynn Patrick	6	1	1	2	0
W.'Babe' Pratt	6	1	1	2	6
Alex Shibicky	5	0	2	2	2
Ott Heller	6	0	2	2	8
M.'Muzz' Patrick	6	1	0	1	6
Art Coulter	6	1	0	1	8
Clint Smith	6	0	1	1	2
Mac Colville	6	0	1	1	6
Stan Smith	1	0	0	0	0
Bert Gardiner	2	0	0	0	0
Kilby MacDonald	6	0	0	0	4

GOALTENDER	GP	W	L	MIN	GA	SO	AVG
Dave Kerr	6	4	2	394	11	0	1.68

TORONTO	GP	G	A	PTS	PIM
Syl Apps	6	2	2	4	2
Hank Goldup	6	2	1	3	0
D.'Sweeney' Schriner	5	0	3	3	2
Gordie Drillon	6	2	0	2	0
Nick Metz	5	1	1	2	9
Gus Marker	6	1	1	2	2
R.'Red' Horner	5	0	2	2	14
Pete Langelle	6	0	2	2	0
Billy Taylor	2	1	0	1	0
R.'Red' Heron	6	1	0	1	0
Wally Stanowski	6	1	0	1	2
Jack Church	2	0	1	1	2
Bob Davidson	6	0	1	1	11
Reg Hamilton	1	0	0	0	0
W.'Bucko' McDonald	1	0	0	0	0
R.'Pep' Kelly	2	0	0	0	0
Don Metz	2	0	0	0	0
E.'Murph' Chamberlain	3	0	0	0	2
R.'Bingo' Kampman	6	0	0	0	19

GOALTENDER	GP	W	L	MIN	GA	SO	AVG
W.'Turk' Broda	6	2	4	394	14	1	2.13

1941

BOSTON	GP	G	A	PTS	PIM
Milt Schmidt	4	3	4	7	0
Eddie Wiseman	4	3	0	3	0
Roy Conacher	4	1	2	3	0
Woody Dumart	4	0	3	3	2
Bobby Bauer	4	1	1	2	0
Terry Reardon	4	1	1	2	2
B.'Flash' Hollett	4	1	1	2	4
Pat McReavy	4	1	1	2	5
Jack Crawford	4	0	2	2	0
A.'Dit' Clapper	4	0	2	2	2
Des Smith	4	0	2	2	2
Art Jackson	4	1	0	1	0
Herb Cain	4	0	1	1	0
Mel Hill	4	0	0	0	0

GOALTENDER	GP	W	L	MIN	GA	SO	AVG
Frank Brimsek	4	4	0	240	6	0	1.50

DETROIT	GP	G	A	PTS	PIM
Carl Liscombe	4	2	1	3	5
Syd Howe	4	1	2	3	0
Bill Jennings	4	1	1	2	0
Sid Abel	4	1	1	2	2
Connie Brown	3	0	2	2	0
M.'Mud' Bruneteau	4	1	0	1	0
R.'Gus' Giesebrecht	4	0	1	1	0
Don Grosso	4	0	1	1	0
J.'Black Jack' Stewart	4	0	1	1	2
Jimmy Orlando	4	0	1	1	6
Eddie Bruneteau	2	0	0	0	0
Ken Kilrea	2	0	0	0	0
Eddie Wares	3	0	0	0	0
Hal Jackson	4	0	0	0	0
Bob Whitelaw	4	0	0	0	0
Alex Motter	4	0	0	0	2

GOALTENDER	GP	W	L	MIN	GA	SO	AVG
Johnny Mowers	4	0	4	240	12	0	3.00

1942

TORONTO	GP	G	A	PTS	PIM
Billy Taylor	7	1	8	9	2
D.'Sweeney' Schriner	7	5	3	8	4
Don Metz	4	4	3	7	0
Syl Apps	7	3	4	7	2
Wally Stanowski	7	2	5	7	0
Lorne Carr	7	3	2	5	6
Nick Metz	7	2	3	5	4
Bob Goldham	7	2	2	4	22
John McCreedy	7	1	2	3	6
Pete Langelle	7	1	1	2	0
Bob Davidson	7	1	1	2	14
R.'Bingo' Kampman	7	0	2	2	8
Hank Goldup	3	0	0	0	0
W.'Bucko' McDonald	3	0	0	0	0
Gordie Drillon	3	0	0	0	0
Gaye Stewart	3	0	0	0	0
Ernie Dickens	5	0	0	0	4

GOALTENDER	GP	W	L	MIN	GA	SO	AVG
W.'Turk' Broda	7	4	3	420	19	1	2.71

DETROIT	GP	G	A	PTS	PIM
Don Grosso	7	4	4	8	14
Syd Howe	7	3	3	6	0
Carl Liscombe	7	2	4	6	2
Eddie Bush	6	1	5	6	16
M.'Mud' Bruneteau	7	2	1	3	4
Sid Abel	7	2	1	3	4
Eddie Wares	7	0	3	3	20
Jerry Brown	7	2	0	2	4
Pat McReavy	6	1	1	2	2
Alex Motter	7	1	1	2	6
Jimmy Orlando	7	0	2	2	41
Joe Carveth	7	1	0	1	0
Adam Brown	5	0	1	1	4
J.'Black Jack' Stewart	7	0	1	1	6
R.'Gus' Giesebrecht	2	0	0	0	0
Doug McCaig	2	0	0	0	6

GOALTENDER	GP	W	L	MIN	GA	SO	AVG
Johnny Mowers	7	3	4	420	25	0	3.57

1943

DETROIT	GP	G	A	PTS	PIM
Sid Abel	4	1	5	6	2
Carl Liscombe	4	2	3	5	2
M.'Mud' Bruneteau	3	3	0	3	0
Joe Carveth	4	3	0	3	2
Don Grosso	4	3	0	3	4
Les Douglas	4	2	1	3	2
Eddie Wares	4	0	3	3	2
J.'Black Jack' Stewart	4	1	1	2	8
Jimmy Orlando	4	0	2	2	6
Syd Howe	3	1	0	1	0
Alex Motter	1	0	1	1	0
Hal Jackson	4	0	1	1	4
Harry Watson	1	0	0	0	0
Joe Fisher	1	0	0	0	0
John Simon	3	0	0	0	0
Adam Brown	4	0	0	0	2

GOALTENDER	GP	W	L	MIN	GA	SO	AVG
Johnny Mowers	4	4	0	240	5	2	1.25

BOSTON	GP	G	A	PTS	PIM
Art Jackson	4	3	0	3	7
Herb Cain	2	0	2	2	0
Bill Cowley	4	0	2	2	2
Jack Crawford	3	1	0	1	2
Ab DeMarco	4	1	0	1	0
B.'Flash' Hollett	4	0	1	1	0
Don Gallinger	4	0	1	1	4
E.'Murph' Chamberlain	4	0	1	1	6
A.'Bep' Guidolin	4	0	1	1	8
Ossie Aubuchon	1	0	0	0	0
Jackie Schmidt	2	0	0	0	0
A.'Dit' Clapper	4	0	0	0	2
I.'Yank' Boyd	4	0	0	0	2
H.'Busher' Jackson	4	0	0	0	2
Jack Shewchuk	4	0	0	0	4

GOALTENDER	GP	W	L	MIN	GA	SO	AVG
Frank Brimsek	4	0	4	240	16	0	4.00

1944

MONTREAL	GP	G	A	PTS	PIM
H.'Toe' Blake	4	3	5	8	2
Maurice Richard	4	5	2	7	4
Elmer Lach	4	2	3	5	0
Ray Getliffe	4	2	1	3	4
Phil Watson	4	2	1	3	6
E.'Butch' Bouchard	4	0	3	3	0
E.'Murph' Chamberlain	4	1	0	1	2
Mike McMahon	4	1	0	1	12
Jerry Heffernan	2	0	1	1	0
H.'Buddy' O'Connor	3	0	1	1	2
Leo Lamoureux	4	0	1	1	2
Fern Majeau	1	0	0	0	0
Bob Fillion	2	0	0	0	2
Glen Harmon	4	0	0	0	0

GOALTENDER	GP	W	L	MIN	GA	SO	AVG
Bill Durnan	4	4	0	249	8	0	1.93

CHICAGO	GP	G	A	PTS	PIM
George Allen	4	3	2	5	4
Clint Smith	4	1	3	4	0
John Harms	4	3	0	3	2
Doug Bentley	4	1	2	3	2
C.'Cully' Dahlstrom	4	0	2	2	2
Virgil Johnson	4	0	1	1	2
Bill Mosienko	4	0	1	1	2
Art Wiebe	4	0	1	1	4
George Gregor	1	0	0	0	0
Jack Toupin	1	0	0	0	0
Johnny Gottselig	2	0	0	0	0
Earl Seibert	4	0	0	0	0
Cliff Purpur	4	0	0	0	0
Joe Cooper	4	0	0	0	6

GOALTENDER	GP	W	L	MIN	GA	SO	AVG
Mike Karakas	4	0	4	249	16	0	3.86

1945

TORONTO	GP	G	A	PTS	PIM
T.'Teeder' Kennedy	7	4	1	5	2
Mel Hill	7	1	2	3	4
W.'Babe' Pratt	7	1	1	2	4
Gus Bodnar	7	1	0	1	2
E.'Moe' Morris	7	1	0	1	2
D.'Sweeney' Schriner	7	1	0	1	2
Nick Metz	3	0	1	1	0
Wally Stanowski	7	0	1	1	0
Bob Davidson	7	0	1	1	0
John McCreedy	4	0	0	0	0
Reg Hamilton	7	0	0	0	0
Art Jackson	7	0	0	0	0
Don Metz	7	0	0	0	0
Lorne Carr	7	0	0	0	5

GOALTENDER	GP	W	L	MIN	GA	SO	AVG
Frank McCool	7	4	3	434	9	3	1.24

DETROIT	GP	G	A	PTS	PIM
B.'Flash' Hollett	7	2	2	4	0
Joe Carveth	7	2	1	3	0
Eddie Bruneteau	7	2	1	3	0
Murray Armstrong	7	2	0	2	0
Ted Lindsay	7	1	0	1	4
M.'Mud' Bruneteau	7	0	1	1	2
Bill Quackenbush	7	0	1	1	2
Tony Bukovich	1	0	0	0	0
Steve Wojciechowski	2	0	0	0	0
Cliff Purpur	4	0	0	0	4
Syd Howe	5	0	0	0	2
Carl Liscombe	7	0	0	0	0
J.'Jud' McAtee	7	0	0	0	0
Earl Seibert	7	0	0	0	2
Hal Jackson	7	0	0	0	4

GOALTENDER	GP	W	L	MIN	GA	SO	AVG
Harry Lumley	7	3	4	434	9	2	1.24

1946

MONTREAL	GP	G	A	PTS	PIM
Elmer Lach	5	3	4	7	0
Maurice Richard	5	3	2	5	0
E.'Murph' Chamberlain	5	2	1	3	0
W.'Dutch' Hiller	5	2	1	3	0
E.'Butch' Bouchard	5	2	1	3	4
Glen Harmon	5	1	2	3	0
Bob Fillion	5	2	0	2	2
Ken Mosdell	5	2	0	2	2
Frank Eddolls	4	0	1	1	0
Jim Peters	5	1	0	1	4

H.'Toe' Blake	5	1	0	1	5
Gerry Plamondon	1	0	0	0	0
H.'Buddy' O'Connor	5	0	0	0	0
Leo Lamoureux	5	0	0	0	2
Billy Reay	5	0	0	0	2
Kenny Reardon	5	0	0	0	4

GOALTENDER	GP	W	L	MIN	GA	SO	AVG
Bill Durnan	5	4	1	341	13	0	2.29

BOSTON	GP	G	A	PTS	PIM
A.'Bep' Guidolin	5	2	1	3	9
Don Gallinger	5	1	2	3	0
Bill Cowley	5	1	2	3	2
Milt Schmidt	5	1	2	3	2
Bobby Bauer	5	2	0	2	2
Terry Reardon	5	2	0	2	2
Woody Dumart	5	1	1	2	0
Ken Smith	5	0	2	2	0
Herb Cain	5	0	2	2	2
Murray Henderson	5	1	0	1	0
Jack Crawford	5	1	0	1	0
Pat Egan	5	1	0	1	4
Bill Shill	3	0	1	1	2
Roy Conacher	1	0	0	0	0
A.'Dit' Clapper	1	0	0	0	0
Jack McGill	5	0	0	0	0
Jack Church	5	0	0	0	2

GOALTENDER	GP	W	L	MIN	GA	SO	AVG
Frank Brimsek	5	1	4	341	19	0	3.34

1947

TORONTO	GP	G	A	PTS	PIM
T.'Teeder' Kennedy	6	3	2	5	2
Vic Lynn	6	3	1	4	12
Harry Watson	6	2	1	3	0
Gaye Stewart	6	1	2	3	6
Howie Meeker	6	0	3	3	6
N.'Bud' Poile	5	2	0	2	2
Syl Apps	6	1	1	2	0
Gus Mortson	6	1	1	2	6
Don Metz	6	0	2	2	4
Bill Barilko	6	0	2	2	6
Gus Bodnar	1	0	0	0	0
Nick Metz	1	0	0	0	0
Wally Stanowski	5	0	0	0	0
Joe Klukay	6	0	0	0	0
Garth Boesch	6	0	0	0	6
Jimmy Thomson	6	0	0	0	12
Bill Ezinicki	6	0	0	0	16

GOALTENDER	GP	W	L	MIN	GA	SO	AVG
W.'Turk' Broda	6	4	2	377	13	1	2.07

MONTREAL	GP	G	A	PTS	PIM
H.'Buddy' O'Connor	6	3	3	6	0
H.'Toe' Blake	6	0	4	4	0
Maurice Richard	5	3	0	3	25
E.'Butch' Bouchard	6	0	3	3	14
Leo Gravelle	4	2	0	2	2
Billy Reay	6	2	0	2	2
Glen Harmon	6	1	1	2	0
George Allen	6	1	1	2	6
Roger Leger	6	0	2	2	6
E.'Murph' Chamberlain	6	1	0	1	6
John Quilty	2	0	1	1	2
Jim Peters	6	0	1	1	4
Leo Lamoureux	2	0	0	0	4
Hub Macey	3	0	0	0	0
Kenny Reardon	4	0	0	0	16
Bob Fillion	5	0	0	0	0
Frank Eddolls	5	0	0	0	2
Murdo McKay	6	0	0	0	0

GOALTENDER	GP	W	L	MIN	GA	SO	AVG
Bill Durnan	6	2	4	377	13	1	2.07

1948

TORONTO	GP	G	A	PTS	PIM
Harry Watson	4	5	1	6	4
Max Bentley	4	2	4	6	0
T.'Teeder' Kennedy	4	2	2	4	0
Syl Apps	4	2	2	4	0
Les Costello	4	1	2	3	0
Gus Mortson	1	1	1	2	0
Joe Klukay	4	1	1	2	2
Bill Ezinicki	4	1	1	2	4
Vic Lynn	4	1	1	2	18
Garth Boesch	4	1	0	1	0
Howie Meeker	4	1	0	1	7
Phil Samis	3	0	1	1	2
Wally Stanowski	4	0	1	1	0
Jim Thomson	4	0	1	1	5
Nick Metz	4	0	0	0	2
Bill Barilko	4	0	0	0	13

GOALTENDER	GP	W	L	MIN	GA	SO	AVG
W.'Turk' Broda	4	4	0	240	7	1	1.75

DETROIT	GP	G	A	PTS	PIM
Pete Horeck	4	2	2	4	8
Jim McFadden	4	1	1	2	0
Jim Conacher	4	1	0	1	0
Ted Lindsay	4	1	0	1	2
Leo Reise	4	1	0	1	4
Fern Gauthier	4	1	0	1	5
Pat Lundy	1	0	1	1	0
Lee Fogolin Sr.	2	0	1	1	6
Bill Quackenbush	4	0	1	1	0
Marty Pavelich	4	0	1	1	2
Sid Abel	4	0	1	1	9
Enio Sclisizzi	1	0	0	0	0
Al Dewsbury	1	0	0	0	0
Rod Morrison	1	0	0	0	0
A.'Bep' Guidolin	1	0	0	0	2
J.'Black Jack' Stewart	3	0	0	0	0
Eddie Bruneteau	3	0	0	0	0
Max McNab	3	0	0	0	2
L.'Red' Kelly	4	0	0	0	0
Gordie Howe	4	0	0	0	9

GOALTENDER	GP	W	L	MIN	GA	SO	AVG
Harry Lumley	4	0	4	240	18	0	4.50

1949

TORONTO	GP	G	A	PTS	PIM
Sid Smith	4	3	1	4	0
Max Bentley	4	2	2	4	0
Ray Timgren	4	1	3	4	0
Jim Thomson	4	1	3	4	4
Joe Klukay	4	1	2	3	2
T.'Teeder' Kennedy	4	1	2	3	2
Fleming Mackell	4	0	3	3	2
Cal Gardner	4	1	1	2	0
Bill Ezinicki	4	1	1	2	10
Gus Mortson	4	1	0	1	2
Harry Watson	4	0	1	1	2
Garth Boesch	4	0	1	1	4
Bill Barilko	4	0	1	1	8
Vic Lynn	4	0	0	0	0
Bob Dawes	4	0	0	0	2
Bill Juzda	4	0	0	0	4

GOALTENDER	GP	W	L	MIN	GA	SO	AVG
W.'Turk' Broda	4	4	0	258	5	0	1.16

DETROIT	GP	G	A	PTS	PIM
Ted Lindsay	4	1	2	3	6
George Gee	4	1	2	3	14
Pete Horeck	4	1	1	2	4
J.'Black Jack' Stewart	4	1	1	2	8
Gordie Howe	4	0	2	2	2
Bill Quackenbush	4	1	0	1	0
Jim McFadden	4	0	1	1	4
Fred Glover	2	0	0	0	0
Jerry Reid	2	0	0	0	2
Marty Pavelich	2	0	0	0	4
Gerry Couture	3	0	0	0	0
N.'Bud' Poile	3	0	0	0	0
Lee Fogolin Sr.	3	0	0	0	0
Nels Podolsky	3	0	0	0	0
Enio Sclisizzi	3	0	0	0	2
Max McNab	3	0	0	0	2
L.'Red' Kelly	4	0	0	0	0
Leo Reise	4	0	0	0	2
Sid Abel	4	0	0	0	4

GOALTENDER	GP	W	L	MIN	GA	SO	AVG
Harry Lumley	4	0	4	258	12	0	2.79

1950

DETROIT	GP	G	A	PTS	PIM
Sid Abel	7	5	2	7	2
Ted Lindsay	6	4	2	6	6
Gerry Couture	7	4	2	6	0
George Gee	7	2	3	5	0
Pete Babando	5	2	2	4	2
Joe Carveth	7	1	3	4	4
Jim McFadden	7	2	1	3	2
Marty Pavelich	7	2	1	3	6
Al Dewsbury	5	0	3	3	8
L.'Red' Kelly	7	0	3	3	2
J.'Black Jack' Stewart	7	0	3	3	10
Jim Peters	5	0	2	2	0
Johnny Wilson	5	0	1	1	0
Marcel Pronovost	6	0	1	1	4
Doug McKay	1	0	0	0	0
Larry Wilson	2	0	0	0	0
Clare Martin	3	0	0	0	0
Max McNab	4	0	0	0	0
Lee Fogolin Sr.	4	0	0	0	2
Steve Black	6	0	0	0	0
Leo Reise	7	0	0	0	8

GOALTENDER	GP	W	L	MIN	GA	SO	AVG
Harry Lumley	7	4	3	459	17	1	2.22

NY RANGERS	GP	G	A	PTS	PIM
Edgar Laprade	7	3	3	6	2
Tony Leswick	7	2	4	6	2
H.'Buddy' O'Connor	7	3	1	4	2
Dunc Fisher	7	2	2	4	12
Nick Mickoski	7	0	4	4	0
Allan Stanley	7	2	1	3	6
Alex Kaleta	7	0	3	3	0
Ed Slowinski	7	0	3	3	4
Don Raleigh	7	2	0	2	0
Pentti Lund	7	1	1	2	0
Pat Egan	7	1	1	2	4
Gus Kyle	7	1	0	1	14
Jack Gordon	4	0	1	1	2
Jack Lancien	2	0	0	0	0
Fred Shero	4	0	0	0	0
Jack McLeod	5	0	0	0	0
Frank Eddolls	7	0	0	0	2

GOALTENDER	GP	W	L	MIN	GA	SO	AVG
Chuck Rayner	7	3	4	459	22	0	2.88

1951

TORONTO	GP	G	A	PTS	PIM
Tod Sloan	5	3	4	7	7
Sid Smith	5	5	1	6	0
T.'Teeder' Kennedy	5	2	4	6	2
Max Bentley	5	0	4	4	2
Harry Watson	5	1	2	3	4
Howie Meeker	5	1	1	2	10
Bill Barilko	5	1	0	1	6
Gus Mortson	5	0	1	1	0
Danny Lewicki	3	0	0	0	0
Fern Flaman	3	0	0	0	6
Ray Timgren	5	0	0	0	0
Joe Klukay	5	0	0	0	0
Cal Gardner	5	0	0	0	0
Bill Juzda	5	0	0	0	2
Fleming Mackell	5	0	0	0	2
Jim Thomson	5	0	0	0	4

GOALTENDERS	GP	W	L	MIN	GA	SO	AVG
Al Rollins	3	3	0	193	5	0	1.55
W.'Turk' Broda	2	1	1	129	5	0	2.33

MONTREAL	GP	G	A	PTS	PIM
Maurice Richard	5	5	2	7	4
Billy Reay	5	1	2	3	10
Doug Harvey	5	0	3	3	2
Paul Masnick	5	2	0	2	4
Paul Meger	5	1	1	2	2
Bert Olmstead	5	0	2	2	7
Elmer Lach	5	1	0	1	2
E.'Butch' Bouchard	5	0	1	1	0
J.'Bud' MacPherson	5	0	1	1	4
Ross Lowe	1	0	0	0	0
Bob Dawes	1	0	0	0	2
Eddie Mazur	2	0	0	0	0
Calum MacKay	5	0	0	0	0
Tom Johnson	5	0	0	0	2
Kenny Mosdell	5	0	0	0	2
Floyd Curry	5	0	0	0	2
Bernie Geoffrion	5	0	0	0	4

GOALTENDER	GP	W	L	MIN	GA	SO	AVG
Gerry McNeil	5	1	4	322	13	0	2.42

1952

DETROIT	GP	G	A	PTS	PIM
Ted Lindsay	4	3	0	3	4
Metro Prystai	4	2	1	3	0
Gordie Howe	4	2	1	3	2
Tony Leswick	4	2	1	3	14
Marty Pavelich	4	1	2	3	2
Glen Skov	4	1	2	3	12
Vic Stasiuk	3	0	1	1	0
Johnny Wilson	4	0	1	1	0
Alex Delvecchio	4	0	1	1	2

	GP	G	A	PTS	PIM
Sid Abel	4	0	1	1	2
Leo Reise	2	0	0	0	0
L.'Red' Kelly	3	0	0	0	0
Larry Zeidel	3	0	0	0	0
Benny Woit	4	0	0	0	2
Marcel Pronovost	4	0	0	0	2
Bob Goldham	4	0	0	0	4

GOALTENDER	GP	W	L	MIN	GA	SO	AVG
Terry Sawchuk	4	4	0	240	2	2	0.50

MONTREAL	GP	G	A	PTS	PIM
Tom Johnson	4	1	0	1	0
Elmer Lach	4	1	0	1	4
Bernie Geoffrion	4	0	1	1	0
Floyd Curry	4	0	1	1	0
Bert Olmstead	4	0	1	1	2
Stan Long	2	0	0	0	0
Dollard St. Laurent	2	0	0	0	0
Dick Gamble	2	0	0	0	0
Billy Reay	3	0	0	0	0
Eddie Mazur	3	0	0	0	4
Paul Meger	4	0	0	0	0
J.'Bud' MacPherson	4	0	0	0	0
Maurice Richard	4	0	0	0	4
E.'Butch' Bouchard	4	0	0	0	6
Doug Harvey	4	0	0	0	6
Paul Masnick	4	0	0	0	6
Dickie Moore	4	0	0	0	12

GOALTENDER	GP	W	L	MIN	GA	SO	AVG
Gerry McNeil	4	0	4	240	10	0	2.50

1953

MONTREAL	GP	G	A	PTS	PIM
Maurice Richard	5	4	1	5	0
Kenny Mosdell	5	2	2	4	4
Calum MacKay	5	1	2	3	6
Dickie Moore	5	2	0	2	9
Floyd Curry	5	1	1	2	0
Elmer Lach	5	1	1	2	0
Bert Olmstead	5	1	1	2	2
Dollard St. Laurent	5	0	2	2	2
Doug Harvey	5	0	2	2	4
Paul Masnick	3	1	0	1	0
Bernie Geoffrion	5	1	0	1	0
Lorne Davis	5	1	0	1	2
Tom Johnson	5	1	0	1	4
E.'Butch' Bouchard	5	0	1	1	2
Eddie Mazur	5	0	1	1	11
Paul Meger	1	0	0	0	0
John McCormack	2	0	0	0	0
Billy Reay	4	0	0	0	0

GOALTENDERS	GP	W	L	MIN	GA	SO	AVG
Gerry McNeil	3	3	0	181	3	2	0.99
Jacques Plante	2	1	1	120	6	0	3.00

BOSTON	GP	G	A	PTS	PIM
Ed Sandford	5	2	1	3	5
Fleming Mackell	5	0	3	3	2
Milt Schmidt	4	2	0	2	2
Dave Creighton	5	1	1	2	0
Leo Labine	5	1	1	2	4
Woody Dumart	5	0	2	2	0
Jack McIntyre	4	1	0	1	0
John Peirson	5	1	0	1	2
Bob Armstrong	5	1	0	1	6
Bill Quackenbush	5	0	1	1	2
Frank Martin	5	0	1	1	2
Real Chevrefils	5	0	1	1	6
Joe Klukay	5	0	1	1	7
Hal Laycoe	5	0	1	1	10
Warren Godfrey	5	0	0	0	0
Jerry Toppazzini	5	0	0	0	4

GOALTENDERS	GP	W	L	MIN	GA	SO	AVG
Gord Henry	3	1	2	163	10	0	3.68
'Sugar' Jim Henry	3	0	2	138	5	0	2.17

1954

DETROIT	GP	G	A	PTS	PIM
Alex Delvecchio	7	2	4	6	0
L.'Red' Kelly	7	3	1	4	0
Metro Prystai	7	2	2	4	0
Ted Lindsay	7	2	2	4	14
Gordie Howe	7	1	2	3	23
Johnny Wilson	7	2	0	2	0
Earl Reibel	4	1	1	2	0
Tony Leswick	7	1	1	2	8
Bob Goldham	7	0	1	1	0
Benny Woit	7	0	1	1	4
Marty Pavelich	7	0	1	1	4
Marcel Pronovost	7	0	0	0	8
Glen Skov	7	0	1	1	10
Gilles Dube	2	0	0	0	0
Keith Allen	3	0	0	0	0
Jim Peters	6	0	0	0	0
Bill Dineen	7	0	0	0	0

GOALTENDER	GP	W	L	MIN	GA	SO	AVG
Terry Sawchuk	7	4	3	430	12	1	1.67

MONTREAL	GP	G	A	PTS	PIM
Floyd Curry	7	3	0	3	2
Maurice Richard	7	3	0	3	20
Bernie Geoffrion	7	2	1	3	16
Dickie Moore	7	1	2	3	8
Paul Masnick	6	0	3	3	4
Elmer Lach	4	0	2	2	0
Jean Beliveau	6	0	2	2	2
Dollard St. Laurent	6	1	0	1	6
Kenny Mosdell	7	1	0	1	2
Tom Johnson	7	1	0	1	8
Calum MacKay	3	0	1	1	0
Doug Harvey	6	0	1	1	4
Eddie Mazur	7	0	1	1	0
Bert Olmstead	7	0	1	1	8
Paul Meger	2	0	0	0	2
J.'Bud' MacPherson	2	0	0	0	4
Gaye Stewart	3	0	0	0	0
John McCormack	4	0	0	0	0
E.'Butch' Bouchard	7	0	0	0	4
Lorne Davis	7	0	0	0	6

GOALTENDERS	GP	W	L	MIN	GA	SO	AVG
Gerry McNeil	3	2	1	190	3	1	0.95
Jacques Plante	4	1	3	240	10	0	2.50

1955

DETROIT	GP	G	A	PTS	PIM
Gordie Howe	7	5	7	12	24
Ted Lindsay	7	5	6	11	6
Alex Delvecchio	7	6	4	10	0
Earl Reibel	7	2	5	7	2
Vic Stasiuk	7	3	3	6	2
L.'Red' Kelly	7	2	3	5	17
Marcel Pronovost	7	1	2	3	2
Marty Pavelich	7	1	2	3	12
Bob Goldham	7	0	2	2	2
Jim Hay	5	1	0	1	0
Glen Skov	7	1	0	1	4
Marcel Bonin	7	0	1	1	4
Tony Leswick	7	0	1	1	10
Johnny Wilson	7	0	0	0	0
Bill Dineen	7	0	0	0	2
Benny Woit	7	0	0	0	4

GOALTENDER	GP	W	L	MIN	GA	SO	AVG
Terry Sawchuk	7	4	3	420	20	0	2.86

MONTREAL	GP	G	A	PTS	PIM
Bernie Geoffrion	7	6	2	8	2
Jean Beliveau	7	3	5	8	12
Floyd Curry	7	5	1	6	2
Calum MacKay	7	2	4	6	2
Kenny Mosdell	7	1	4	5	6
Doug Harvey	7	0	5	5	4
Jack LeClair	7	2	0	2	2
Dickie Moore	7	0	2	2	16
Tom Johnson	7	1	0	1	16
Dollard St. Laurent	7	0	1	1	10
Bert Olmstead	7	0	1	1	14
E.'Butch' Bouchard	7	0	1	1	31
Jim Bartlett	2	0	0	0	0
Paul Ronty	2	0	0	0	2
Dick Gamble	2	0	0	0	2
George McAvoy	3	0	0	0	0
Don Marshall	7	0	0	0	2

GOALTENDERS	GP	W	L	MIN	GA	SO	AVG
Jacques Plante	7	3	3	403	24	0	3.57
Charlie Hodge	1	0	1	17	3	0	10.59

1956

MONTREAL	GP	G	A	PTS	PIM
Jean Beliveau	5	7	3	10	8
Bert Olmstead	5	0	8	8	4
Bernie Geoffrion	5	3	3	6	2
Maurice Richard	5	2	2	4	12
Floyd Curry	5	1	3	4	4
Henri Richard	5	2	1	3	11
Claude Provost	5	1	2	3	2
Dickie Moore	5	0	3	3	6
Doug Harvey	5	0	3	3	6
Jack LeClair	5	1	1	2	4
Don Marshall	5	1	0	1	0
Kenny Mosdell	4	0	1	1	0
Jean-Guy Talbot	4	0	1	1	2
E.'Butch' Bouchard	1	0	0	0	0
Dollard St. Laurent	3	0	0	0	2
Bob Turner	5	0	0	0	4
Tom Johnson	5	0	0	0	8

GOALTENDER	GP	W	L	MIN	GA	SO	AVG
Jacques Plante	5	4	1	300	9	1	1.80

DETROIT	GP	G	A	PTS	PIM
Gordie Howe	5	1	5	6	4
Ted Lindsay	5	2	3	5	6
Alex Delvecchio	5	3	1	4	0
Norm Ullman	5	1	1	2	11
L.'Red' Kelly	5	1	0	1	2
Bill Dineen	5	1	0	1	4
Al Arbour	4	0	1	1	0
Earl Reibel	5	0	1	1	2
John Bucyk	5	0	1	1	4
Lorne Ferguson	5	0	1	1	8
Marty Pavelich	5	0	1	1	8
Cummy Burton	1	0	0	0	0
Murray Costello	2	0	0	0	0
Gord Hollingworth	2	0	0	0	2
Gerry Melnyk	4	0	0	0	0
Metro Prystai	4	0	0	0	4
Bob Goldham	5	0	0	0	2
Marcel Pronovost	5	0	0	0	2
Larry Hillman	5	0	0	0	2

GOALTENDER	GP	W	L	MIN	GA	SO	AVG
Glenn Hall	5	1	4	300	18	0	3.60

1957

MONTREAL	GP	G	A	PTS	PIM
Bernie Geoffrion	5	4	2	6	2
Doug Harvey	5	0	5	5	6
Maurice Richard	5	4	0	4	2
Floyd Curry	5	2	2	4	0
Dickie Moore	5	1	3	4	2
Don Marshall	5	1	2	3	2
Phil Goyette	5	1	1	2	2
Jean Beliveau	5	1	1	2	6
Tom Johnson	5	0	2	2	2
Henri Richard	5	0	2	2	8
Bert Olmstead	5	0	2	2	9
Andre Pronovost	3	1	0	1	0
Connie Braden	4	0	1	1	0
Claude Provost	5	0	1	1	2
Dollard St. Laurent	5	0	1	1	9
Bob Turner	2	0	0	0	0
Jean-Guy Talbot	5	0	0	0	6

GOALTENDER	GP	W	L	MIN	GA	SO	AVG
Jacques Plante	5	4	1	300	5	1	1.00

BOSTON	GP	G	A	PTS	PIM
Fleming Mackell	5	4	0	4	2
Don McKenney	5	1	1	2	0
Leo Labine	5	1	1	2	12
Larry Regan	5	0	2	2	4
Doug Mohns	5	0	1	1	0
Bob Armstrong	5	0	1	1	2
Jerry Toppazzini	5	0	1	1	2
Leo Boivin	5	0	1	1	4
Fern Flaman	5	0	1	1	13
Cal Gardner	5	0	0	0	0
Jack Caffery	5	0	0	0	0
Vic Stasiuk	5	0	0	0	2
Real Chevrefils	5	0	0	0	2
Jack Bionda	5	0	0	0	6
Carl Boone	5	0	0	0	10
John Peirson	5	0	0	0	12

GOALTENDER	GP	W	L	MIN	GA	SO	AVG
Don Simmons	5	1	4	300	15	1	3.00

1958

MONTREAL	GP	G	A	PTS	PIM
Bernie Geoffrion	6	5	3	8	0
Doug Harvey	6	2	5	7	8
Jean Beliveau	6	2	4	6	8
Dickie Moore	6	1	5	6	2
Maurice Richard	6	4	1	5	8
Henri Richard	6	1	2	3	9
Claude Provost	6	1	0	1	2
Bert Olmstead	5	0	1	1	0
Marcel Bonin	5	0	1	1	10

	GP	G	A	PTS	PIM
Don Marshall	6	0	1	1	0
Connie Braden	1	0	0	0	0
Ab McDonald	1	0	0	0	2
Tom Johnson	2	0	0	0	0
Al Langlois	3	0	0	0	0
Floyd Curry	3	0	0	0	0
Dollard St. Laurent	4	0	0	0	8
Bob Turner	6	0	0	0	2
Phil Goyette	6	0	0	0	2
Jean-Guy Talbot	6	0	0	0	6
Andre Pronovost	6	0	0	0	10

GOALTENDER	GP	W	L	MIN	GA	SO	AVG
Jacques Plante	6	4	2	366	14	1	2.30

BOSTON	GP	G	A	PTS	PIM
Larry Regan	6	2	4	6	2
Don McKenney	6	4	1	5	0
Fleming Mackell	6	1	4	5	6
Bronco Horvath	6	3	1	4	4
Allan Stanley	6	1	2	3	4
Vic Stasiuk	6	0	3	3	0
Norm Johnson	6	2	0	2	4
Jerry Toppazzini	6	1	1	2	2
Doug Mohns	6	0	2	2	8
Leo Labine	6	0	2	2	8
Carl Boone	6	0	1	1	4
Fern Flaman	6	0	1	1	4
Leo Boivin	6	0	1	1	9
John Peirson	2	0	0	0	0
Larry Hillman	5	0	0	0	2
John Bucyk	6	0	0	0	6

GOALTENDER	GP	W	L	MIN	GA	SO	AVG
Don Simmons	6	2	4	366	15	0	2.46

1959

MONTREAL	GP	G	A	PTS	PIM
Bernie Geoffrion	5	3	4	7	6
Ralph Backstrom	5	3	4	7	8
Henri Richard	5	1	5	6	5
Doug Harvey	5	0	6	6	10
Marcel Bonin	5	3	2	5	2
Dickie Moore	5	2	3	5	8
Claude Provost	5	2	2	4	2
Tom Johnson	5	2	1	3	2
Ab McDonald	5	1	1	2	0
Phil Goyette	5	0	2	2	0
Andre Pronovost	5	1	0	1	0
Don Marshall	5	0	1	1	0
Jean-Guy Talbot	5	0	1	1	6
Bob Turner	5	0	1	1	8
Bill Hicke	1	0	0	0	0
Al Langlois	4	0	0	0	2
Maurice Richard	4	0	0	0	2

GOALTENDER	GP	W	L	MIN	GA	SO	AVG
Jacques Plante	5	4	1	310	12	0	2.32

TORONTO	GP	G	A	PTS	PIM
Billy Harris	5	3	1	4	14
Frank Mahovlich	5	2	2	4	6
Gerry Ehman	5	0	4	4	4
Ron Stewart	5	2	1	3	2
Dick Duff	5	2	1	3	4
Bert Olmstead	5	2	1	3	6
Bob Pulford	5	1	2	3	4
George Armstrong	5	0	2	2	6
Carl Brewer	5	0	2	2	18
Dave Creighton	5	0	1	1	0
Tim Horton	5	0	1	1	2
Allan Stanley	5	0	1	1	2
Barry Cullen	1	0	0	0	0
Noel Price	2	0	0	0	2
Larry Regan	3	0	0	0	0
Brian Cullen	3	0	0	0	0
Marc Reaume	4	0	0	0	0
Bob Baun	5	0	0	0	11

GOALTENDER	GP	W	L	MIN	GA	SO	AVG
Johnny Bower	5	1	4	310	18	0	3.48

1960

MONTREAL	GP	G	A	PTS	PIM
Henri Richard	4	3	5	8	9
Bernie Geoffrion	4	0	6	6	0
Dickie Moore	4	2	3	5	2
Jean Beliveau	4	4	0	4	4
Maurice Richard	4	1	2	3	2
Phil Goyette	4	2	0	2	2
Doug Harvey	4	2	0	2	6
Marcel Bonin	4	0	2	2	6
Al Langlois	4	0	2	2	12
Don Marshall	4	1	0	1	0
Bill Hicke	4	0	1	1	0
Jean-Guy Talbot	4	0	1	1	4
Claude Provost	4	0	1	1	0
Andre Pronovost	4	0	1	1	0
Bob Turner	4	0	0	0	0
Ralph Backstrom	4	0	0	0	2
Tom Johnson	4	0	0	0	2

GOALTENDER	GP	W	L	MIN	GA	SO	AVG
Jacques Plante	4	4	0	240	5	1	1.25

TORONTO	GP	G	A	PTS	PIM
Bert Olmstead	4	2	0	2	0
Larry Regan	4	1	1	2	0
L.'Red' Kelly	4	0	2	2	2
George Armstrong	4	0	2	2	2
Johnny Wilson	4	1	0	1	2
Bob Baun	4	1	0	1	17
Billy Harris	3	0	1	1	0
Tim Horton	4	0	1	1	0
Dick Duff	4	0	1	1	2
Gary Edmundson	4	0	1	1	2
Carl Brewer	4	0	1	1	6
Gerry Ehman	3	0	0	0	2
Allan Stanley	4	0	0	0	0
Jerry James	4	0	0	0	0
Ron Stewart	4	0	0	0	0
Frank Mahovlich	4	0	0	0	0
Bob Pulford	4	0	0	0	8

GOALTENDER	GP	W	L	MIN	GA	SO	AVG
Johnny Bower	4	0	4	240	15	0	3.75

1961

CHICAGO	GP	G	A	PTS	PIM
Pierre Pilote	6	2	6	8	2
Stan Mikita	6	3	4	7	2
Bobby Hull	6	2	5	7	2
Murray Balfour	5	3	3	6	4
Bill Hay	6	1	3	4	8
Ron Murphy	6	2	1	3	0
Ken Wharram	6	2	1	3	10
Ab McDonald	6	1	1	2	0
Eric Nesterenko	6	1	1	2	2
Reg Fleming	6	1	0	1	2
Jack Evans	6	1	0	1	10
Ed Litzenberger	4	0	1	1	0
Dollard St. Laurent	5	0	1	1	2
Tod Sloan	6	0	1	1	6
Elmer Vasko	6	0	1	1	6
Chico Maki	1	0	0	0	0
Wayne Hillman	1	0	0	0	0
Wayne Hicks	1	0	0	0	2
Al Arbour	3	0	0	0	2
Earl Balfour	6	0	0	0	0

GOALTENDER	GP	W	L	MIN	GA	SO	AVG
Glenn Hall	6	4	2	360	12	0	2.00

DETROIT	GP	G	A	PTS	PIM
Gordie Howe	6	1	7	8	8
Alex Delvecchio	6	3	3	6	0
Allan Johnson	6	1	2	3	0
Vic Stasiuk	6	1	2	3	4
Bruce MacGregor	6	1	2	3	6
Howie Young	6	1	1	2	18
Norm Ullman	5	0	2	2	2
Val Fonteyne	6	0	2	2	0
Len Lunde	5	1	0	1	0
Parker MacDonald	6	1	0	1	0
Leo Labine	6	1	0	1	0
Howie Glover	6	1	0	1	0
Marcel Pronovost	4	0	1	1	0
Warren Godfrey	6	0	1	1	10
Gerry Melnyk	6	0	0	0	0
Gerry Odrowski	6	0	0	0	4
Pete Goegan	6	0	0	0	14

GOALTENDERS	GP	W	L	MIN	GA	SO	AVG
Hank Bassen	4	1	2	220	9	0	2.45
Terry Sawchuk	3	1	2	140	10	0	4.29

1962

TORONTO	GP	G	A	PTS	PIM
Frank Mahovlich	6	4	3	7	21
George Armstrong	6	3	4	7	0
Tim Horton	6	1	6	7	12
Dick Duff	6	1	4	5	16
Ron Stewart	6	0	5	5	2
Bob Pulford	6	3	0	3	14
Billy Harris	6	2	1	3	0
Dave Keon	6	2	1	3	0
L.'Red' Kelly	6	1	2	3	0
Bob Baun	6	0	3	3	15
Bob Nevin	6	1	1	2	4
Bert Olmstead	4	0	1	1	0
Allan Stanley	6	0	1	1	2
Carl Brewer	6	0	1	1	18
Al Arbour	2	0	0	0	0
Ed Litzenberger	4	0	0	0	2
Eddie Shack	5	0	0	0	12

GOALTENDERS	GP	W	L	MIN	GA	SO	AVG
Johnny Bower	4	2	1	195	7	0	2.15
Don Simmons	3	2	1	165	8	0	2.91

CHICAGO	GP	G	A	PTS	PIM
Bobby Hull	6	4	4	8	6
Stan Mikita	6	3	5	8	15
Ab McDonald	6	3	2	5	0
Bill Hay	6	0	4	4	4
Pierre Pilote	6	0	4	4	6
Eric Nesterenko	6	0	4	4	14
Reg Fleming	6	2	0	2	18
Bronco Horvath	6	1	1	2	2
Murray Balfour	6	1	1	2	11
Bob Turner	6	1	0	1	0
Ken Wharram	6	0	1	1	4
Dollard St. Laurent	6	0	1	1	8
Merv Kuryluk	2	0	0	0	0
Gerry Melnyk	5	0	0	0	2
Elmer Vasko	6	0	0	0	0
Jack Evans	6	0	0	0	12

GOALTENDER	GP	W	L	MIN	GA	SO	AVG
Glenn Hall	6	2	4	360	18	1	3.00

1963

TORONTO	GP	G	A	PTS	PIM
Dave Keon	5	4	2	6	0
L.'Red' Kelly	5	2	2	4	2
Tim Horton	5	1	3	4	4
Allan Stanley	5	0	4	4	4
Bob Nevin	5	3	0	3	0
Dick Duff	5	2	1	3	2
George Armstrong	5	1	2	3	0
Ed Litzenberger	5	1	2	3	4
Bob Pulford	5	0	3	3	8
Ron Stewart	5	2	0	2	2
Eddie Shack	5	1	1	2	4
Frank Mahovlich	4	0	1	1	4
Billy Harris	5	0	1	1	0
Kent Douglas	5	0	1	1	2
Carl Brewer	5	0	1	1	4
Bob Baun	5	0	1	1	6
John MacMillan	1	0	0	0	0

GOALTENDER	GP	W	L	MIN	GA	SO	AVG
Johnny Bower	5	4	1	300	10	0	2.00

DETROIT	GP	G	A	PTS	PIM
Gordie Howe	5	3	3	6	8
Marcel Pronovost	5	0	4	4	0
Norm Ullman	5	0	4	4	2
Larry Jeffrey	5	2	1	3	4
Alex Delvecchio	5	1	2	3	0
Alex Faulkner	5	2	0	2	2
Floyd Smith	5	0	2	2	4
Vic Stasiuk	4	1	0	1	0
Eddie Joyal	5	1	0	1	0
Bruce MacGregor	5	0	1	1	0
Andre Pronovost	5	0	1	1	0
Parker MacDonald	5	0	1	1	2
Bob Dillabough	1	0	0	0	0
Howie Young	2	0	0	0	0
Gerry Odrowski	2	0	0	0	2
Val Fonteyne	5	0	0	0	0
Pete Goegan	5	0	0	0	2
Doug Barkley	5	0	0	0	6
Bill Gadsby	5	0	0	0	12

GOALTENDER	GP	W	L	MIN	GA	SO	AVG
Terry Sawchuk	5	1	4	300	17	0	3.40

1964

TORONTO	GP	G	A	PTS	PIM
Frank Mahovlich	7	1	7	8	0
George Armstrong	7	4	3	7	10
L.'Red' Kelly	7	2	4	6	2
Don McKenney	5	1	5	6	0
Dave Keon	7	4	1	5	0
Bob Pulford	7	3	2	5	10

	GP	G	A	PTS	PIM
Andy Bathgate	7	3	2	5	12
Allan Stanley	7	1	3	4	12
Bob Baun	7	1	2	3	16
Ron Stewart	7	0	3	3	2
Billy Harris	7	1	1	2	4
Tim Horton	7	0	2	2	12
Gerry Ehman	7	1	0	1	2
Carl Brewer	5	0	1	1	10
Al Arbour	1	0	0	0	0
Ed Litzenberger	1	0	0	0	10
Larry Hillman	6	0	0	0	2
Jim Pappin	7	0	0	0	0
Eddie Shack	7	0	0	0	4

GOALTENDER	GP	W	L	MIN	GA	SO	AVG
Johnny Bower	7	4	3	430	17	1	2.37

DETROIT	GP	G	A	PTS	PIM
Gordie Howe	7	4	4	8	8
Alex Delvecchio	7	1	4	5	0
Norm Ullman	7	1	3	4	2
Floyd Smith	7	3	0	3	0
Bruce MacGregor	7	3	0	3	4
Doug Barkley	7	0	3	3	8
Eddie Joyal	7	2	1	3	6
Larry Jeffrey	7	1	2	3	4
Pit Martin	7	1	2	3	10
Andre Pronovost	7	0	2	2	8
Bill Gadsby	7	0	2	2	14
Paul Henderson	7	1	0	1	4
John MacMillan	4	0	1	1	2
Parker MacDonald	7	0	1	1	0
Alex Faulkner	1	0	0	0	0
Bob Dillabough	1	0	0	0	0
Irv Spencer	7	0	0	0	0
Al Langlois	7	0	0	0	8
Marcel Pronovost	7	0	0	0	8

GOALTENDER	GP	W	L	MIN	GA	SO	AVG
Terry Sawchuk	7	3	4	430	22	0	3.07

1965

MONTREAL	GP	G	A	PTS	PIM
Jean Beliveau	7	5	5	10	18
Dick Duff	7	3	5	8	5
Bobby Rousseau	7	1	5	6	4
J.C. Tremblay	7	1	5	6	14
Henri Richard	7	3	0	3	20
John Ferguson	7	2	1	3	13
Ted Harris	7	0	3	3	34
Yvan Cournoyer	7	2	0	2	0
Ralph Backstrom	7	1	1	2	4
Claude Provost	7	0	2	2	12
Noel Picard	3	0	1	1	0
G.'Red' Berenson	7	0	1	1	2
Jean Lanthier	2	0	0	0	4
Dave Balon	5	0	0	0	0
Claude Larose	7	0	0	0	4
Jim Roberts	7	0	0	0	14
Jean-Guy Talbot	7	0	0	0	18
Terry Harper	7	0	0	0	19

GOALTENDERS	GP	W	L	MIN	GA	SO	AVG
L.'Gump' Worsley	4	3	1	240	5	2	1.25
Charlie Hodge	3	1	2	180	7	1	2.33

CHICAGO	GP	G	A	PTS	PIM
Bobby Hull	7	2	2	4	10
Chico Maki	7	1	3	4	8
Pierre Pilote	5	0	3	3	14
Stan Mikita	7	0	3	3	35
Fred Stanfield	7	1	1	2	0
Matt Ravlich	7	1	1	2	8
Phil Esposito	7	1	1	2	8
Elmer Vasko	7	1	1	2	12
Doug Mohns	7	1	1	2	15
Ken Wharram	5	1	0	1	2
Bill Hay	7	1	0	1	0
Camille Henry	7	1	0	1	2
Doug Jarrett	7	1	0	1	10
Dennis Hull	1	0	0	0	0
John McKenzie	4	0	0	0	0
Gerry Melnyk	6	0	0	0	0
Eric Nesterenko	7	0	0	0	6
Al MacNeil	7	0	0	0	12

GOALTENDERS	GP	W	L	MIN	GA	SO	AVG
Glenn Hall	7	3	4	400	15	0	2.25
Denis DeJordy	1	0	0	20	3	0	9.00

1966

MONTREAL	GP	G	A	PTS	PIM
J.C. Tremblay	6	1	5	6	0
Jean Beliveau	6	3	2	5	0
Henri Richard	6	1	4	5	2
Gilles Tremblay	6	2	2	4	0
Ralph Backstrom	6	2	2	4	2
Dave Balon	6	2	2	4	16
Dick Duff	6	1	3	4	2
Yvan Cournoyer	6	2	1	3	0
Bobby Rousseau	6	1	2	3	4
Terry Harper	6	1	2	3	4
Leon Rochefort	4	1	1	2	4
Claude Provost	6	1	1	2	2
Noel Price	1	0	1	1	0
Jean-Guy Talbot	6	0	1	1	8
Jim Roberts	6	0	1	1	10
Claude Larose	2	0	0	0	0
Ted Harris	6	0	0	0	4
John Ferguson	6	0	0	0	8

GOALTENDER	GP	W	L	MIN	GA	SO	AVG
L.'Gump' Worsley	6	4	2	362	14	0	2.32

DETROIT	GP	G	A	PTS	PIM
Norm Ullman	6	4	2	6	6
Floyd Smith	6	3	1	4	0
Paul Henderson	6	1	3	4	4
Andy Bathgate	6	1	3	4	4
Ab McDonald	4	1	2	3	2
Alex Delvecchio	6	0	3	3	0
Dean Prentice	6	1	1	2	2
Bill Gadsby	6	1	1	2	2
Bruce MacGregor	6	1	1	2	2
Gordie Howe	6	1	1	2	6
Bert Marshall	6	0	2	2	8
Gary Bergman	6	0	1	1	4
Warren Godfrey	1	0	0	0	0
Irv Spencer	1	0	0	0	0
Murray Hall	1	0	0	0	0
Bob Wall	4	0	0	0	2
Val Fonteyne	6	0	0	0	0
Parker MacDonald	6	0	0	0	2
Leo Boivin	6	0	0	0	6
Bryan Watson	6	0	0	0	12

GOALTENDERS	GP	W	L	MIN	GA	SO	AVG
Roger Crozier	6	2	3	308	16	0	3.12
Hank Bassen	1	0	1	54	2	0	2.22

1967

TORONTO	GP	G	A	PTS	PIM
Jim Pappin	6	4	4	8	6
Bob Pulford	6	1	6	7	0
Pete Stemkowski	6	2	4	6	4
Tim Horton	6	2	3	5	8
Mike Walton	6	2	1	3	0
L.'Red' Kelly	6	0	3	3	2
Larry Hillman	6	1	1	2	0
Dave Keon	6	1	1	2	0
Ron Ellis	6	1	1	2	4
Brian Conacher	6	1	1	2	19
Frank Mahovlich	6	0	2	2	8
Marcel Pronovost	6	1	0	1	4
George Armstrong	6	1	0	1	4
Allan Stanley	6	0	1	1	6
Aut Erickson	1	0	0	0	2
Milan Marcetta	2	0	0	0	0
Eddie Shack	4	0	0	0	8
Bob Baun	5	0	0	0	2

GOALTENDERS	GP	W	L	MIN	GA	SO	AVG
Johnny Bower	3	2	0	163	3	1	1.10
Terry Sawchuk	4	2	2	225	12	0	3.20

MONTREAL	GP	G	A	PTS	PIM
Henri Richard	6	4	3	7	0
Jean Beliveau	6	4	2	6	10
Yvan Cournoyer	6	2	2	4	4
Bobby Rousseau	6	0	4	4	2
Dick Duff	6	1	2	3	4
Ralph Backstrom	6	2	0	2	2
Leon Rochefort	6	1	1	2	2
John Ferguson	6	1	1	2	16
Dave Balon	5	0	2	2	2
J.C. Tremblay	6	0	2	2	0
Jim Roberts	3	1	0	1	0
Gilles Tremblay	6	0	1	1	0
Ted Harris	6	0	1	1	12
Claude Larose	6	0	1	1	15
Claude Provost	4	0	0	0	0
Jean-Guy Talbot	6	0	0	0	0
Jacques Laperriere	6	0	0	0	2
Terry Harper	6	0	0	0	6

GOALTENDERS	GP	W	L	MIN	GA	SO	AVG
Rogie Vachon	5	2	3	308	14	0	2.73
L.'Gump' Worsley	2	0	1	80	2	0	1.50

1968

MONTREAL	GP	G	A	PTS	PIM
Yvan Cournoyer	4	2	2	4	2
Henri Richard	4	2	1	3	0
John Ferguson	4	0	3	3	4
Serge Savard	4	2	0	2	0
J.C. Tremblay	4	1	1	2	0
Ralph Backstrom	4	1	1	2	0
Dick Duff	4	1	1	2	2
Jacques Lemaire	4	1	1	2	4
Bobby Rousseau	4	1	0	1	6
Claude Larose	4	0	1	1	0
Claude Provost	4	0	1	1	2
Ted Harris	4	0	1	1	6
Jean Beliveau	1	0	0	0	0
Carol Vadnais	1	0	0	0	2
Mickey Redmond	2	0	0	0	0
Danny Grant	4	0	0	0	0
Terry Harper	4	0	0	0	4
Jacques Laperriere	4	0	0	0	6

GOALTENDER	GP	W	L	MIN	GA	SO	AVG
L.'Gump' Worsley	4	4	0	243	7	1	1.73

ST. LOUIS	GP	G	A	PTS	PIM
G.'Red' Berenson	4	2	1	3	7
Frank St. Marseille	4	1	1	2	0
Barclay Plager	4	1	1	2	6
Craig Cameron	1	1	0	1	0
Gary Sabourin	4	1	0	1	2
Dickie Moore	4	1	0	1	4
Doug Harvey	2	0	1	1	4
Gary Veneruzzo	3	0	1	1	0
Al Arbour	4	0	1	1	0
Tim Ecclestone	4	0	1	1	2
Jean-Guy Talbot	4	0	1	1	4
Noel Picard	4	0	1	1	6
Bill McCreary	3	0	0	0	0
Gerry Melnyk	3	0	0	0	0
Ron Schock	4	0	0	0	0
Larry Keenan	4	0	0	0	0
Terry Crisp	4	0	0	0	0
Jim Roberts	4	0	0	0	2
Bob Plager	4	0	0	0	20

GOALTENDER	GP	W	L	MIN	GA	SO	AVG
Glenn Hall	4	0	4	243	11	0	2.72

1969

MONTREAL	GP	G	A	PTS	PIM
Dick Duff	4	4	2	6	2
Jean Beliveau	4	0	5	5	4
Yvan Cournoyer	4	1	3	4	0
John Ferguson	4	2	0	2	20
Ralph Backstrom	4	1	1	2	4
Serge Savard	4	1	1	2	8
J.C. Tremblay	4	0	2	2	6
Bobby Rousseau	4	1	0	1	2
Jacques Lemaire	4	1	0	1	4
Ted Harris	4	1	0	1	6
Claude Provost	3	0	1	1	0
Mickey Redmond	4	0	1	1	0
Henri Richard	4	0	1	1	2
Christian Bordeleau	3	0	0	0	0
Terry Harper	4	0	0	0	4
Jacques Laperriere	4	0	0	0	22

GOALTENDER	GP	W	L	MIN	GA	SO	AVG
Rogie Vachon	4	4	0	240	3	1	0.75

ST. LOUIS	GP	G	A	PTS	PIM
Frank St. Marseille	4	1	1	2	2
Terry Gray	3	1	0	1	8
Larry Keenan	4	1	0	1	8
Barclay Plager	4	0	1	1	0
Terry Crisp	4	0	1	1	2
Jim Roberts	4	0	1	1	4
Bill McCreary	4	0	1	1	4
Noel Picard	4	0	1	1	8
Camille Henry	2	0	0	0	0
Craig Cameron	2	0	0	0	0
Bob Plager	2	0	0	0	2
Bill Plager	3	0	0	0	4
Jean-Guy Talbot	4	0	0	0	2

	GP	G	A	PTS	PIM
Ron Schock	4	0	0	0	2
Al Arbour	4	0	0	0	4
G.'Red' Berenson	4	0	0	0	4
Gary Sabourin	4	0	0	0	4
Ab McDonald	4	0	0	0	4
Tim Ecclestone	4	0	0	0	10

GOALTENDERS	GP	W	L	MIN	GA	SO	AVG
Glenn Hall	2	0	2	120	5	0	2.50
Jacques Plante	2	0	2	120	6	0	3.00

1970

BOSTON	GP	G	A	PTS	PIM
Phil Esposito	4	2	6	8	4
John Bucyk	4	6	0	6	0
Derek Sanderson	4	3	3	6	8
Bobby Orr	4	1	4	5	6
John McKenzie	4	1	4	5	14
Ed Westfall	4	2	1	3	0
Rick Smith	4	1	3	4	2
Fred Stanfield	4	1	3	4	4
Ken Hodge	4	0	3	3	2
Wayne Cashman	4	2	0	2	8
Wayne Carleton	4	1	1	2	0
Dallas Smith	4	0	1	1	6
Don Awrey	4	0	1	1	12
Bill Speer	1	0	0	0	0
Bill Lesuk	2	0	0	0	0
Jim Lorentz	4	0	0	0	0
Don Marcotte	4	0	0	0	0
Gary Doak	4	0	0	0	2

GOALTENDER	GP	W	L	MIN	GA	SO	AVG
Gerry Cheevers	4	4	0	241	7	0	1.74

ST. LOUIS	GP	G	A	PTS	PIM
Frank St. Marseille	4	2	1	3	2
Jim Roberts	4	1	1	2	4
Phil Goyette	4	0	2	2	2
Gary Sabourin	4	1	0	1	0
Terry Gray	4	1	0	1	0
Larry Keenan	4	1	0	1	0
G.'Red' Berenson	4	1	0	1	4
Bill McCreary	3	0	1	1	0
Ab McDonald	4	0	1	1	0
Tim Ecclestone	4	0	1	1	6
Bob Plager	4	0	1	1	6
Noel Picard	4	0	1	1	14
Barclay Plager	1	0	0	0	0
Ron Anderson	1	0	0	0	2
Norm Dennis	1	0	0	0	2
Bill Plager	2	0	0	0	0
Al Arbour	2	0	0	0	0
Andre Boudrias	3	0	0	0	2
Ray Fortin	3	0	0	0	6
Jean-Guy Talbot	4	0	0	0	0
Terry Crisp	4	0	0	0	0

GOALTENDERS	GP	W	L	MIN	GA	SO	AVG
Jacques Plante	1	0	0	24	1	0	2.50
Glenn Hall	2	0	2	121	8	0	3.97
Ernie Wakely	2	0	2	96	11	0	6.87

1971

MONTREAL	GP	G	A	PTS	PIM
Frank Mahovlich	7	4	4	8	4
Pete Mahovlich	7	5	2	7	16
Yvan Cournoyer	7	4	2	6	6
Jacques Lemaire	7	3	1	4	11
Jean Beliveau	7	1	3	4	6
Henri Richard	7	2	1	3	2
Guy Lapointe	7	1	2	3	19
Jacques Laperriere	7	0	3	3	2
J.C. Tremblay	7	0	3	3	7
Rejean Houle	7	0	3	3	10
Terry Harper	7	0	2	2	10
John Ferguson	6	0	1	1	8
Claude Larose	2	0	0	0	0
Bob Murdoch	2	0	0	0	0
Pierre Bouchard	3	0	0	0	2
Phil Roberto	5	0	0	0	12
Leon Rochefort	6	0	0	0	6
Marc Tardif	7	0	0	0	19

GOALTENDER	GP	W	L	MIN	GA	SO	AVG
Ken Dryden	7	4	3	441	18	0	2.45

CHICAGO	GP	G	A	PTS	PIM
Bobby Hull	7	3	6	9	8
Jim Pappin	7	4	2	6	8
Cliff Koroll	7	2	3	5	4
Stan Mikita	7	1	4	5	6
Dennis Hull	7	3	1	4	2
Lou Angotti	7	2	2	4	9
Chico Maki	7	2	1	3	4
Danny O'Shea	7	1	1	2	12
Pit Martin	6	0	2	2	4
Pat Stapleton	7	0	2	2	0
Bill White	7	0	2	2	10
Rick Foley	4	0	1	1	4
Doug Jarrett	7	0	1	1	2
Dan Maloney	2	0	0	0	4
Jerry Korab	2	0	0	0	14
Paul Shmyr	3	0	0	0	17
Gerry Pinder	5	0	0	0	2
Eric Nesterenko	7	0	0	0	8
Keith Magnuson	7	0	0	0	36

GOALTENDER	GP	W	L	MIN	GA	SO	AVG
Tony Esposito	7	3	4	441	20	1	2.72

1972

BOSTON	GP	G	A	PTS	PIM
Ken Hodge	6	5	3	8	19
Bobby Orr	6	4	4	8	17
Phil Esposito	6	0	8	8	14
Mike Walton	6	1	4	5	6
Wayne Cashman	6	3	1	4	15
Fred Stanfield	6	1	2	3	0
John Bucyk	6	1	2	3	2
Ed Westfall	6	0	2	2	10
John McKenzie	6	0	2	2	25
Don Marcotte	5	1	0	1	6
Garnet 'Ace' Bailey	6	1	0	1	14
Derek Sanderson	6	1	0	1	26
Dallas Smith	6	0	1	1	10
Carol Vadnais	6	0	1	1	13
Ted Green	4	0	0	0	0
Don Awrey	6	0	0	0	21

GOALTENDERS	GP	W	L	MIN	GA	SO	AVG
Ed Johnston	3	2	1	180	6	0	2.00
Gerry Cheevers	3	2	1	180	10	1	3.33

NY RANGERS	GP	G	A	PTS	PIM
Rod Gilbert	6	4	3	7	11
Brad Park	6	2	4	6	11
Ted Irvine	6	1	4	5	10
Bobby Rousseau	6	2	2	4	5
Pete Stemkowski	6	1	3	4	8
Vic Hadfield	6	1	3	4	16
Bruce MacGregor	6	1	2	3	2
Walt Tkaczuk	6	1	2	3	17
Dale Rolfe	6	2	0	2	10
Rod Seiling	6	1	1	2	6
Bill Fairbairn	6	0	2	2	0
Jim Neilson	3	0	1	1	2
Jean Ratelle	6	0	1	1	0
Ron Stewart	1	0	0	0	0
Jim Dorey	1	0	0	0	0
Ab DeMarco	1	0	0	0	0
Phil Goyette	3	0	0	0	0
Gary Doak	5	0	0	0	34
Gene Carr	6	0	0	0	9
Glen Sather	6	0	0	0	11

GOALTENDERS	GP	W	L	MIN	GA	SO	AVG
Gilles Villemure	3	1	2	180	7	0	2.33
Ed Giacomin	3	1	2	180	11	0	3.67

1973

MONTREAL	GP	G	A	PTS	PIM
Yvan Cournoyer	6	6	6	12	0
Jacques Lemaire	6	3	9	12	0
Frank Mahovlich	6	5	6	11	0
Pete Mahovlich	6	3	5	8	12
Claude Larose	6	3	4	7	2
Chuck Lefley	6	3	3	6	2
Marc Tardif	6	3	3	6	4
Guy Lapointe	6	1	3	4	8
Henri Richard	6	2	1	3	0
Rejean Houle	6	1	2	3	0
Jacques Laperriere	2	1	1	2	0
Guy Lafleur	6	0	2	2	0
Larry Robinson	6	0	2	2	2
Murray Wilson	6	0	2	2	2
Pierre Bouchard	6	1	0	1	4
Serge Savard	6	1	0	1	6
Bob Murdoch	4	0	0	0	2
Jim Roberts	6	0	0	0	6

GOALTENDER	GP	W	L	MIN	GA	SO	AVG
Ken Dryden	6	4	2	360	21	1	3.50

CHICAGO	GP	G	A	PTS	PIM
Stan Mikita	5	3	5	8	0
Pat Stapleton	6	0	8	8	4
Dennis Hull	6	3	4	7	4
Pit Martin	6	5	0	5	4
Jim Pappin	6	3	2	5	10
Ralph Backstrom	6	1	3	4	0
Bill White	6	1	3	4	2
Cliff Koroll	6	1	2	3	2
Dave Kryskow	3	2	0	2	0
Len Frig	4	1	1	2	0
Lou Angotti	6	1	1	2	0
John Marks	6	1	1	2	2
Chico Maki	6	0	2	2	0
J.P. Bordeleau	6	1	0	1	4
Dick Redmond	4	0	1	1	0
Doug Jarrett	6	0	1	1	0
Phil Russell	6	0	1	1	16
Jerry Korab	5	0	0	0	6

GOALTENDERS	GP	W	L	MIN	GA	SO	AVG
Tony Esposito	6	2	4	355	32	0	5.41
Gary Smith	1	0	0	5	0	0	0.00

1974

PHILADELPHIA	GP	G	A	PTS	PIM
Bobby Clarke	6	3	3	6	14
Rick MacLeish	6	2	3	5	4
Andre Dupont	6	2	1	3	33
Dave Schultz	6	1	2	3	38
Bill Flett	6	0	3	3	4
Don Saleski	6	0	3	3	6
Orest Kindrachuk	6	2	0	2	11
Bill Barber	6	1	1	2	2
Ross Lonsberry	6	1	1	2	2
Terry Crisp	6	1	1	2	2
Tom Bladon	6	1	1	2	21
Ed Van Impe	6	0	2	2	13
Joe Watson	6	0	2	2	16
Bill Clement	3	1	0	1	2
Simon Nolet	6	0	1	1	0
Jimmy Watson	6	0	1	1	30
Gary Dornhoefer	3	0	0	0	0
Bruce Cowick	6	0	0	0	7

GOALTENDER	GP	W	L	MIN	GA	SO	AVG
Bernie Parent	6	4	2	372	13	1	2.10

BOSTON	GP	G	A	PTS	PIM
Bobby Orr	6	3	4	7	8
Gregg Sheppard	6	2	3	5	2
Ken Hodge	6	1	4	5	6
Wayne Cashman	6	2	2	4	41
John Bucyk	6	1	3	4	2
Phil Esposito	6	2	1	3	10
Carol Vadnais	6	0	3	3	22
Andre Savard	6	1	1	2	20
Dallas Smith	6	0	2	2	8
Don Marcotte	6	1	0	1	2
Dave Forbes	6	0	1	1	2
Terry O'Reilly	6	0	1	1	25
Rich Leduc	5	0	0	0	9
Darryl Edestrand	6	0	0	0	2
Al Sims	6	0	0	0	4
Bobby Schmautz	6	0	0	0	18

GOALTENDER	GP	W	L	MIN	GA	SO	AVG
Gilles Gilbert	6	2	4	372	15	0	2.42

1975

PHILADELPHIA	GP	G	A	PTS	PIM
Bill Barber	6	2	4	6	0
Bobby Clarke	6	2	3	5	2
Reggie Leach	6	3	1	4	0
Bob Kelly	5	2	2	4	7
Rick MacLeish	6	1	3	4	2
Terry Crisp	4	0	4	4	0
Ross Lonsberry	6	2	1	3	2
Dave Schultz	6	2	0	2	13
Gary Dornhoefer	6	2	0	2	14
Don Saleski	6	1	1	2	8
Larry Goodenough	2	0	2	2	2
Orest Kindrachuk	5	0	2	2	2
Jimmy Watson	6	0	2	2	0
Ted Harris	6	0	2	2	2
Ed Van Impe	6	0	2	2	8
Bill Clement	5	1	0	1	2
Andre Dupont	6	1	0	1	10
Tom Bladon	4	0	1	1	8
Joe Watson	6	0	0	0	2

GOALTENDER	GP	W	L	MIN	GA	SO	AVG
Bernie Parent	6	4	2	378	20	1	3.17

BUFFALO	GP	G	A	PTS	PIM
Rick Martin	6	2	4	6	6
Don Luce	6	2	3	5	12
Danny Gare	6	2	1	3	4
Jerry Korab	6	2	1	3	6
Jim Lorentz	6	1	2	3	2
Rene Robert	6	1	2	3	6
Gilbert Perreault	6	1	1	2	6
Craig Ramsay	6	0	2	2	0
Jim Schoenfeld	6	0	2	2	11
Bill Hajt	6	1	0	1	2
Rick Dudley	4	0	1	1	9
Brian Spencer	6	0	1	1	4
Jocelyn Guevremont	6	0	1	1	8
Lee Fogolin Jr.	4	0	0	0	0
Peter McNab	6	0	0	0	0
Fred Stanfield	6	0	0	0	0
Larry Carriere	6	0	0	0	4

GOALTENDERS	GP	W	L	MIN	GA	SO	AVG
Roger Crozier	2	1	1	118	3	0	1.53
Gerry Desjardins	5	1	3	260	16	0	3.69

1976

MONTREAL	GP	G	A	PTS	PIM
Guy Lafleur	4	2	5	7	2
Steve Shutt	4	3	3	6	0
Pete Mahovlich	4	1	4	5	4
Pierre Bouchard	4	2	0	2	2
Jacques Lemaire	4	2	0	2	2
Yvan Cournoyer	4	1	1	2	0
Larry Robinson	4	1	1	2	4
Doug Risebrough	4	0	2	2	2
Jim Roberts	4	1	0	1	0
Guy Lapointe	4	1	0	1	8
Murray Wilson	3	0	1	1	0
Bill Nyrop	4	0	1	1	2
Bob Gainey	4	0	1	1	12
Rick Chartraw	2	0	0	0	0
Mario Tremblay	2	0	0	0	7
Yvon Lambert	3	0	0	0	4
Doug Jarvis	4	0	0	0	0
Serge Savard	4	0	0	0	2

GOALTENDER	GP	W	L	MIN	GA	SO	AVG
Ken Dryden	4	4	0	240	9	0	2.25

PHILADELPHIA	GP	G	A	PTS	PIM
Reggie Leach	4	4	0	4	0
Tom Bladon	4	0	3	3	2
Bobby Clarke	4	0	3	3	4
Larry Goodenough	4	1	1	2	2
Bill Barber	4	1	1	2	6
Andre Dupont	4	1	1	2	7
Mel Bridgman	4	0	2	2	4
Ross Lonsberry	4	1	0	1	0
Dave Schultz	4	1	0	1	10
Jack McIlhargey	4	0	1	1	4
Gary Dornhoefer	4	0	1	1	6
Terry Crisp	1	0	0	0	0
Terry Murray	2	0	0	0	0
Orest Kindrachuk	4	0	0	0	0
Bob Kelly	4	0	0	0	2
Joe Watson	4	0	0	0	2
Don Saleski	4	0	0	0	4
Jimmy Watson	4	0	0	0	4

GOALTENDER	GP	W	L	MIN	GA	SO	AVG
Wayne Stephenson	4	0	4	240	14	0	3.50

1977

MONTREAL	GP	G	A	PTS	PIM
Guy Lafleur	4	2	7	9	4
Jacques Lemaire	4	4	2	6	2
Steve Shutt	4	2	3	5	0
Yvon Lambert	4	2	2	4	6
Pete Mahovlich	4	1	3	4	4
Guy Lapointe	4	0	4	4	0
Doug Risebrough	2	2	1	3	2
Larry Robinson	4	0	3	3	6
Mario Tremblay	4	2	0	2	5
Serge Savard	4	0	2	2	0
Rick Chartraw	4	1	0	1	4
Doug Jarvis	4	0	1	1	0
Murray Wilson	4	0	1	1	6
Pierre Bouchard	4	0	1	1	6
Bill Nyrop	1	0	0	0	0
Mike Polich	1	0	0	0	0
Pierre Mondou	2	0	0	0	0
Jim Roberts	4	0	0	0	4
Bob Gainey	4	0	0	0	12

GOALTENDER	GP	W	L	MIN	GA	SO	AVG
Ken Dryden	4	4	0	240	6	1	1.50

BOSTON	GP	G	A	PTS	PIM
Brad Park	4	1	4	5	2
Bobby Schmautz	4	2	0	2	0
Rick Middleton	4	0	2	2	0
Peter McNab	4	1	0	1	2
Gregg Sheppard	4	1	0	1	6
Terry O'Reilly	4	1	0	1	8
Jean Ratelle	4	0	1	1	0
Wayne Cashman	4	0	1	1	13
Matti Hagman	1	0	0	0	0
Earl Anderson	2	0	0	0	0
Darryl Edestrand	2	0	0	0	0
John Bucyk	2	0	0	0	0
Al Sims	2	0	0	0	0
John Wensink	3	0	0	0	4
Mike Milbury	3	0	0	0	20
Dave Forbes	4	0	0	0	0
Gary Doak	4	0	0	0	4
Stan Jonathan	4	0	0	0	4
Don Marcotte	4	0	0	0	4
Rick Smith	4	0	0	0	6

GOALTENDER	GP	W	L	MIN	GA	SO	AVG
Gerry Cheevers	4	0	4	240	16	0	4.00

1978

MONTREAL	GP	G	A	PTS	PIM
Larry Robinson	6	2	4	6	4
Guy Lafleur	6	3	2	5	8
Steve Shutt	6	3	1	4	2
Pierre Mondou	6	1	3	4	4
Mario Tremblay	3	2	1	3	14
Yvon Lambert	6	1	2	3	2
Yvan Cournoyer	6	1	2	3	6
Jacques Lemaire	6	1	2	3	6
Serge Savard	6	0	3	3	4
Doug Jarvis	6	0	3	3	10
Rejean Houle	6	1	1	2	4
Bob Gainey	6	1	1	2	10
Bill Nyrop	5	0	2	2	6
Guy Lapointe	6	0	2	2	5
Pierre Larouche	2	1	0	1	0
Doug Risebrough	6	1	0	1	7
Brian Engblom	1	0	0	0	0
Gilles Lupien	2	0	0	0	17
Rick Chartraw	3	0	0	0	0
Pierre Bouchard	4	0	0	0	5

GOALTENDER	GP	W	L	MIN	GA	SO	AVG
Ken Dryden	6	4	2	379	13	0	2.06

BOSTON	GP	G	A	PTS	PIM
Brad Park	6	4	1	5	8
Peter McNab	6	2	3	5	2
Gregg Sheppard	6	1	3	4	2
Don Marcotte	6	1	2	3	4
Bobby Schmautz	6	1	2	3	11
Terry O'Reilly	6	1	2	3	16
Jean Ratelle	6	0	3	3	0
Mike Milbury	6	0	3	3	10
Wayne Cashman	6	0	2	2	2
Rick Middleton	6	1	0	1	0
Gary Doak	6	1	0	1	4
Rick Smith	6	1	0	1	10
Bob Miller	6	0	1	1	9
Al Sims	3	0	0	0	0
Dennis O'Brien	5	0	0	0	6
Stan Jonathan	6	0	0	0	20
John Wensink	6	0	0	0	24

GOALTENDERS	GP	W	L	MIN	GA	SO	AVG
Gerry Cheevers	6	2	4	359	18	1	3.01
Ron Grahame	1	0	0	20	0	0	0.00

1979

MONTREAL	GP	G	A	PTS	PIM
Jacques Lemaire	5	4	3	7	2
Steve Shutt	5	2	4	6	2
Yvon Lambert	5	2	4	6	4
Bob Gainey	5	3	2	5	6
Rejean Houle	5	1	4	5	2
Guy Lafleur	5	2	1	3	0
Serge Savard	5	1	2	3	2
Doug Risebrough	5	1	2	3	12
Mario Tremblay	5	1	1	2	4
Rick Chartraw	5	1	1	2	12
Doug Jarvis	5	0	2	2	2
Mark Napier	5	1	0	1	2
Larry Robinson	5	0	1	1	0
Pierre Larouche	1	0	0	0	0
Gilles Lupien	4	0	0	0	2
Brian Engblom	5	0	0	0	0
Pierre Mondou	5	0	0	0	2
Rod Langway	5	0	0	0	12

GOALTENDERS	GP	W	L	MIN	GA	SO	AVG
Ken Dryden	5	4	1	287	11	0	2.30
Michel Larocque	1	0	0	20	0	0	0.00

NY RANGERS	GP	G	A	PTS	PIM
Phil Esposito	5	2	1	3	10
Pat Hickey	5	1	2	3	0
Anders Hedberg	5	1	2	3	2
Dave Maloney	5	1	2	3	10
Ron Duguay	5	2	0	2	4
Steve Vickers	5	1	1	2	0
Don Murdoch	5	1	1	2	2
Mike McEwen	5	0	2	2	4
Carol Vadnais	5	1	0	1	0
Ron Greschner	5	1	0	1	8
Bobby Sheehan	5	0	1	1	0
Walt Tkaczuk	5	0	1	1	4
Don Maloney	5	0	1	1	6
Dave Farrish	1	0	0	0	0
Lucien DeBlois	2	0	0	0	0
Ulf Nilsson	2	0	0	0	2
Pierre Plante	5	0	0	0	0
Ed Johnstone	5	0	0	0	2
Mario Marois	5	0	0	0	4

GOALTENDER	GP	W	L	MIN	GA	SO	AVG
John Davidson	5	1	4	307	19	0	3.17

1980

NY ISLANDERS	GP	G	A	PTS	PIM
Mike Bossy	6	4	7	11	4
Denis Potvin	6	5	4	9	6
Bryan Trottier	6	4	4	8	0
Clark Gillies	6	2	6	8	13
Stefan Persson	6	3	4	7	10
Butch Goring	6	3	3	6	0
Bob Nystrom	6	3	1	4	30
Duane Sutter	6	1	3	4	28
Bob Bourne	6	0	4	4	2
John Tonelli	6	0	3	3	4
Lorne Henning	6	1	1	2	0
Garry Howatt	6	0	1	1	21
Wayne Merrick	6	0	0	0	0
Bob Lorimer	6	0	0	0	6
Ken Morrow	6	0	0	0	6
Dave Langevin	6	0	0	0	9
Gord Lane	6	0	0	0	28

GOALTENDERS	GP	W	L	MIN	GA	SO	AVG
Billy Smith	6	4	2	351	23	0	3.93
G.'Chico' Resch	1	0	0	20	2	0	6.00

PHILADELPHIA	GP	G	A	PTS	PIM
Paul Holmgren	5	4	4	8	15
Ken Linseman	6	1	7	8	16
Bobby Clarke	6	4	3	7	2
Rick MacLeish	6	3	3	6	2
Brian Propp	6	3	3	6	4
Reggie Leach	6	1	4	5	0
Bill Barber	6	1	4	5	9
Bob Dailey	6	1	3	4	4
Mel Bridgman	6	1	3	4	53
Behn Wilson	6	0	4	4	28
Mike Busniuk	6	2	1	3	7
Tom Gorence	5	1	1	2	16
John Paddock	2	2	0	2	0
Bob Kelly	6	1	0	1	9
Jimmy Watson	5	0	1	1	9
Andre Dupont	6	0	1	1	14
Norm Barnes	1	0	0	0	4
Al Hill	6	0	0	0	2
Jack McIlhargey	6	0	0	0	25

GOALTENDERS	GP	W	L	MIN	GA	SO	AVG
Pete Peeters	5	2	3	311	20	0	3.86
Phil Myre	1	0	1	60	6	0	6.00

1981

NY ISLANDERS	GP	G	A	PTS	PIM
Mike Bossy	5	4	4	8	0
Wayne Merrick	5	3	5	8	0
Butch Goring	5	5	2	7	0

Bryan Trottier	5	2	5	7	14
Denis Potvin	5	2	4	6	8
John Tonelli	5	0	5	5	8
Anders Kallur	5	2	2	4	4
Bob Nystrom	5	2	2	4	10
Billy Carroll	5	1	3	4	0
Mike McEwen	5	2	1	3	2
Bob Bourne	5	1	2	3	12
Clark Gillies	5	0	3	3	8
Dave Langevin	5	0	2	2	10
Ken Morrow	5	1	0	1	2
Gord Lane	5	1	0	1	18
Duane Sutter	5	0	1	1	0
Bob Lorimer	5	0	0	0	9

GOALTENDER	GP	W	L	MIN	GA	SO	AVG
Billy Smith	5	4	1	300	16	0	3.20

MINNESOTA	GP	G	A	PTS	PIM
Steve Payne	5	5	2	7	2
Dino Ciccarelli	5	3	2	5	19
Bobby Smith	5	2	3	5	2
Craig Hartsburg	5	1	4	5	2
Steve Christoff	5	2	2	4	0
Al MacAdam	5	1	3	4	2
Brad Maxwell	4	0	4	4	9
Tim Young	2	0	3	3	0
Tom McCarthy	3	0	3	3	2
Kent-Erik Andersson	5	1	0	1	0
Brad Palmer	5	1	0	1	4
Neal Broten	5	0	1	1	2
Gordie Roberts	5	0	1	1	2
Greg Smith	5	0	1	1	6
Ken Solheim	1	0	0	0	0
Jack Carlson	2	0	0	0	0
Paul Shmyr	2	0	0	0	2
Kevin Maxwell	2	0	0	0	4
Mike Polich	3	0	0	0	0
Tom Younghans	3	0	0	0	4
Fred Barrett	3	0	0	0	6
Curt Giles	5	0	0	0	2

GOALTENDERS	GP	W	L	MIN	GA	SO	AVG
Don Beaupre	3	1	2	180	13	0	4.33
Gilles Meloche	2	0	2	120	12	0	6.00

1982

NY ISLANDERS	GP	G	A	PTS	PIM
Denis Potvin	4	2	7	9	4
Mike Bossy	4	7	1	8	0
Bryan Trottier	4	1	6	7	10
Stefan Persson	4	0	5	5	4
Clark Gillies	4	2	1	3	8
Butch Goring	4	1	2	3	2
Bob Nystrom	4	2	0	2	21
Billy Carroll	4	1	1	2	2
Bob Bourne	4	1	1	2	17
Brent Sutter	4	0	2	2	0
John Tonelli	4	0	2	2	4
Duane Sutter	4	1	0	1	32
Tomas Jonsson	2	0	1	1	2
Wayne Merrick	4	0	1	1	0
Mike McEwen	2	0	0	0	0
Anders Kallur	4	0	0	0	0
Ken Morrow	4	0	0	0	0
Dave Langevin	4	0	0	0	2
Gord Lane	4	0	0	0	22

GOALTENDER	GP	W	L	MIN	GA	SO	AVG
Billy Smith	4	4	0	260	10	1	2.31

VANCOUVER	GP	G	A	PTS	PIM
Thomas Gradin	4	3	2	5	2
Lars Molin	4	0	4	4	0
Gerry Minor	4	1	2	3	0
Dave Williams	4	0	3	3	14
Curt Fraser	4	0	3	3	28
Ivan Boldirev	4	2	0	2	2
Stan Smyl	4	2	0	2	19
Lars Lindgren	4	1	0	1	2
Jim Nill	3	1	0	1	6
Doug Halward	4	0	1	1	4
Colin Campbell	4	0	1	1	26
Per-Olov Brasar	1	0	0	0	0
Garth Butcher	1	0	0	0	0
Blair MacDonald	1	0	0	0	0
Ivan Hlinka	2	0	0	0	0
Gary Lupul	2	0	0	0	0
Marc Crawford	3	0	0	0	0
Anders Eldebrink	3	0	0	0	2
Ron Delorme	4	0	0	0	4
Neil Belland	4	0	0	0	4
Harold Snepsts	4	0	0	0	16
Darcy Rota	4	0	0	0	19

GOALTENDER	GP	W	L	MIN	GA	SO	AVG
Richard Brodeur	4	0	4	260	17	0	3.92

1983

NY ISLANDERS	GP	G	A	PTS	PIM
Duane Sutter	4	2	5	7	0
Ken Morrow	4	3	2	5	2
Brent Sutter	4	3	2	5	10
Mike Bossy	3	2	2	4	0
Bob Bourne	4	2	2	4	6
Bryan Trottier	4	1	3	4	4
Denis Potvin	4	0	3	3	4
Bob Nystrom	4	1	1	2	2
Anders Kallur	4	1	1	2	4
Tomas Jonsson	4	1	1	2	8
Stefan Persson	4	0	2	2	4
John Tonelli	4	1	0	1	0
Dave Langevin	4	0	1	1	0
Clark Gillies	4	0	1	1	6
Greg Gilbert	1	0	0	0	0
Butch Goring	4	0	0	0	0
Billy Carroll	4	0	0	0	0
Wayne Merrick	4	0	0	0	0
Gord Lane	4	0	0	0	2

GOALTENDER	GP	W	L	MIN	GA	SO	AVG
Billy Smith	4	4	0	240	6	1	1.50

EDMONTON	GP	G	A	PTS	PIM
Wayne Gretzky	4	0	4	4	0
Jari Kurri	4	3	0	3	2
Glenn Anderson	4	1	1	2	11
Lee Fogolin Jr.	4	0	2	2	0
Mark Messier	4	1	0	1	2
Dave Semenko	4	1	0	1	0
Charlie Huddy	4	0	1	1	0
Tom Roulston	4	0	1	1	0
Paul Coffey	4	0	1	1	4
Ray Cote	4	0	0	0	0
Willy Lindstrom	4	0	0	0	0
Randy Gregg	4	0	0	0	0
Pat Hughes	4	0	0	0	2
Kevin Lowe	4	0	0	0	2
Don Jackson	4	0	0	0	4
Ken Linseman	4	0	0	0	4
Dave Hunter	4	0	0	0	8
Dave Lumley	4	0	0	0	9

GOALTENDER	GP	W	L	MIN	GA	SO	AVG
Andy Moog	4	0	4	240	15	0	3.75

1984

EDMONTON	GP	G	A	PTS	PIM
Wayne Gretzky	5	4	3	7	4
Jari Kurri	5	1	5	6	2
Mark Messier	5	3	1	4	7
Paul Coffey	5	2	2	4	0
Kevin McClelland	5	2	2	4	16
Glenn Anderson	5	1	3	4	8
Willy Lindstrom	5	2	1	3	0
Dave Semenko	5	1	2	3	4
Charlie Huddy	5	0	3	3	4
Pat Hughes	5	0	3	3	4
Dave Lumley	5	1	1	2	17
Ken Linseman	5	1	1	2	26
Pat Conacher	2	1	0	1	0
Randy Gregg	5	1	0	1	2
Kevin Lowe	5	1	0	1	4
Dave Hunter	3	0	1	1	6
Lee Fogolin Jr.	5	0	1	1	6
Jaroslav Pouzar	5	0	0	0	6
Don Jackson	5	0	0	0	13

GOALTENDERS	GP	W	L	MIN	GA	SO	AVG
Andy Moog	3	2	0	128	4	0	1.88
Grant Fuhr	3	2	1	172	8	1	2.79

NY ISLANDERS	GP	G	A	PTS	PIM
Clark Gillies	5	5	3	8	0
Pat Flatley	5	1	3	4	8
Bryan Trottier	5	2	2	4	2
Pat LaFontaine	5	2	1	3	0
Brent Sutter	5	1	2	3	6
Mike Bossy	5	0	3	3	0
Greg Gilbert	5	1	1	2	26
Stefan Persson	4	0	2	2	2
Paul Boutilier	5	0	2	2	0
Anders Kallur	5	0	1	1	0
Ken Morrow	5	0	1	1	4
Denis Potvin	5	0	1	1	6
Billy Carroll	1	0	0	0	0
Mats Hallin	2	0	0	0	0
Bob Nystrom	2	0	0	0	4
Dave Langevin	2	0	0	0	5
Gord Dineen	3	0	0	0	24
Butch Goring	5	0	0	0	0
John Tonelli	5	0	0	0	4
Tomas Jonsson	5	0	0	0	8
Duane Sutter	5	0	0	0	26

GOALTENDERS	GP	W	L	MIN	GA	SO	AVG
Billy Smith	5	1	3	245	17	0	4.16
Roland Melanson	3	0	1	55	3	0	3.27

1985

EDMONTON	GP	G	A	PTS	PIM
Wayne Gretzky	5	7	4	11	0
Paul Coffey	5	3	8	11	6
Jari Kurri	5	1	6	7	0
Mark Messier	5	2	4	6	6
Charlie Huddy	5	1	5	6	6
Mike Krushelnyski	5	2	2	4	4
Willy Lindstrom	5	3	0	3	2
Glenn Anderson	5	1	1	2	12
Dave Hunter	5	1	0	1	25
Randy Gregg	4	0	1	1	2
Kevin McClelland	5	0	1	1	41
Jaroslav Pouzar	1	0	0	0	0
Larry Melnyk	1	0	0	0	0
Dave Lumley	1	0	0	0	2
Billy Carroll	2	0	0	0	0
Esa Tikkanen	3	0	0	0	4
Pat Hughes	4	0	0	0	2
Dave Semenko	4	0	0	0	14
Mark Napier	5	0	0	0	0
Kevin Lowe	5	0	0	0	4
Lee Fogolin Jr.	5	0	0	0	8
Don Jackson	5	0	0	0	35

GOALTENDER	GP	W	L	MIN	GA	SO	AVG
Grant Fuhr	5	4	1	300	13	0	2.60

PHILADELPHIA	GP	G	A	PTS	PIM
Derrick Smith	5	1	4	5	0
Dave Poulin	5	1	3	4	4
Rich Sutter	3	3	0	3	4
Brian Propp	5	2	1	3	0
Tim Kerr	3	2	1	3	9
Murray Craven	5	1	2	3	4
Ron Sutter	5	1	2	3	6
Todd Bergen	4	1	1	2	0
Mark Howe	5	1	1	2	0
Lindsay Carson	3	0	2	2	2
Doug Crossman	5	0	2	2	12
Rick Tocchet	5	0	2	2	14
Ilkka Sinisalo	5	1	0	1	0
Peter Zezel	5	0	1	1	4
Brad Marsh	5	0	1	1	43
Len Hachborn	1	0	0	0	0
Ray Allison	1	0	0	0	2
Dave Brown	1	0	0	0	19
Thomas Eriksson	4	0	0	0	0
Miroslav Dvorak	5	0	0	0	2
Joe Paterson	5	0	0	0	19
Ed Hospodar	5	0	0	0	34

GOALTENDERS	GP	W	L	MIN	GA	SO	AVG
Pelle Lindbergh	4	1	3	185	11	0	3.57
Bob Froese	3	0	1	115	9	0	4.70

1986

MONTREAL	GP	G	A	PTS	PIM
Mats Naslund	5	3	4	7	0
Bobby Smith	5	2	2	4	8
Chris Chelios	5	1	3	4	19
Gaston Gingras	4	2	1	3	0
David Maley	5	1	2	3	2
Claude Lemieux	5	1	2	3	31
Larry Robinson	5	0	3	3	15
Guy Carbonneau	5	0	3	3	23
Brian Skrudland	5	2	0	2	32
Mike Lalor	5	0	2	2	19
Mike McPhee	5	0	2	2	24
Kjell Dahlin	4	1	0	1	0
Rick Green	5	1	0	1	0
Bob Gainey	5	1	0	1	2
Ryan Walter	5	0	1	1	2
Stephane Richer	1	0	0	0	0
Steve Rooney	1	0	0	0	0
Serge Boisvert	2	0	0	0	0
Chris Nilan	3	0	0	0	49

	GP	G	A	PTS	PIM
Craig Ludwig	5	0	0	0	14
John Kordic	5	0	0	0	15

GOALTENDER	GP	W	L	MIN	GA	SO	AVG
Patrick Roy	5	4	1	301	12	1	2.39

CALGARY	GP	G	A	PTS	PIM
Dan Quinn	5	1	4	5	4
Jim Peplinski	5	1	3	4	37
Al MacInnis	5	0	4	4	8
Joe Mullen	4	2	1	3	4
Lanny McDonald	5	2	1	3	6
Joel Otto	5	1	2	3	12
Steve Bozek	4	2	0	2	19
John Tonelli	5	2	0	2	15
Paul Reinhart	5	1	1	2	2
Hakan Loob	5	0	2	2	2
Doug Risebrough	5	1	0	1	12
Nick Fotiu	2	0	1	1	10
Paul Baxter	4	0	1	1	17
Jamie Macoun	5	0	1	1	4
Tim Hunter	5	0	1	1	43
Brian Bradley	1	0	0	0	0
Yves Courteau	1	0	0	0	0
Brett Hull	2	0	0	0	0
Colin Patterson	2	0	0	0	0
Mike Eaves	2	0	0	0	2
Perry Berezan	2	0	0	0	4
Terry Johnson	2	0	0	0	12
Robin Bartel	4	0	0	0	12
Neil Sheehy	5	0	0	0	31

GOALTENDERS	GP	W	L	MIN	GA	SO	AVG
Mike Vernon	5	1	4	260	14	0	3.23
Rejean Lemelin	1	0	0	41	1	0	1.46

1987

EDMONTON	GP	G	A	PTS	PIM
Wayne Gretzky	7	2	9	11	2
Jari Kurri	7	5	4	9	4
Paul Coffey	7	2	4	6	14
Glenn Anderson	7	4	1	5	14
Mark Mesier	7	2	3	5	10
Kevin Lowe	7	2	1	3	4
Randy Gregg	7	1	2	3	0
Mike Krushelnyski	7	1	1	2	6
Craig MacTavish	7	0	2	2	6
Charlie Huddy	7	0	2	2	10
Kevin McClelland	7	1	0	1	4
Marty McSorley	7	1	0	1	10
Jaroslav Pouzar	3	0	1	1	2
Craig Muni	5	0	1	1	0
Kent Nilsson	7	0	1	1	0
Dave Hunter	7	0	1	1	4
Kelly Buchberger	3	0	0	0	5
Steve Smith	3	0	0	0	6
Reijo Ruotsalainen	7	0	0	0	4
Esa Tikkanen	7	0	0	0	6

GOALTENDER	GP	W	L	MIN	GA	SO	AVG
Grant Fuhr	7	4	3	427	17	0	2.39

PHILADELPHIA	GP	G	A	PTS	PIM
Brian Propp	7	4	5	9	0
Pelle Eklund	7	1	7	8	0
Rick Tocchet	7	3	4	7	24
Ron Sutter	7	0	4	4	6
Brad McCrimmon	7	2	1	3	10
Scott Mellanby	7	1	2	3	4
Doug Crossman	7	1	2	3	6
Murray Craven	6	2	0	2	2
Peter Zezel	7	1	1	2	2
Brad Marsh	7	0	2	2	2
J.J. Daigneault	5	1	0	1	0
Lindsay Carson	6	1	0	1	0
Derrick Smith	7	1	0	1	10
Mark Howe	7	0	1	1	0
Kjell Samuelsson	7	0	1	1	10
Dave Brown	7	0	1	1	11
Tim Tookey	1	0	0	0	0
Don Nachbaur	1	0	0	0	0
Daryl Stanley	4	0	0	0	2
Ilkka Sinisalo	5	0	0	0	2
Dave Poulin	7	0	0	0	8

GOALTENDER	GP	W	L	MIN	GA	SO	AVG
Ron Hextall	7	3	4	427	22	0	3.09

1988

Includes suspended game, May 24, 1988

EDMONTON	GP	G	A	PTS	PIM
Wayne Gretzky	5	3	10	13	0
Esa Tikkanen	5	6	3	9	18
Glenn Anderson	5	3	3	6	4
Jari Kurri	5	1	4	5	4
Craig Simpson	5	3	1	4	10
Steve Smith	5	0	4	4	2
Mike Krushelnyski	5	1	2	3	6
Kevin McClelland	5	1	2	3	26
Mark Messier	5	1	2	3	4
Randy Gregg	5	0	3	3	4
Kevin Lowe	5	0	2	2	4
Craig Muni	5	0	2	2	0
Keith Acton	5	1	0	1	0
Normand Lacombe	5	1	0	1	4
Charlie Huddy	1	0	0	0	0
Jeff Beukeboom	4	0	0	0	0
Geoff Courtnall	5	0	0	0	0
Craig MacTavish	5	0	0	0	2
Marty McSorley	5	0	0	0	4

GOALTENDER	GP	W	L	MIN	GA	SO	AVG
Grant Fuhr	5	4	0	277	12	0	2.60

BOSTON	GP	G	A	PTS	PIM
Ken Linseman	5	2	2	4	6
Glen Wesley	5	2	2	4	0
Cam Neely	5	2	1	3	4
Ray Bourque	5	0	3	3	6
Steve Kasper	5	2	0	2	2
Randy Burridge	5	1	1	2	2
Bob Joyce	5	1	1	2	0
Moe Lemay	5	1	1	2	6
Craig Janney	5	0	2	2	0
Bob Sweeney	5	0	2	2	2
Greg Hawgood	2	1	0	1	0
Greg Johnston	1	0	1	1	0
Keith Crowder	5	0	1	1	10
Gord Kluzak	5	0	1	1	4
Rick Middleton	5	0	1	1	0
Nevin Markwart	1	0	0	0	2
Tom McCarthy	1	0	0	0	0
Willi Plett	2	0	0	0	4
Reed Larson	2	0	0	0	2
Jay Miller	3	0	0	0	24
Allen Pedersen	4	0	0	0	6
Michael Thelven	4	0	0	0	6
Bill O'Dwyer	5	0	0	0	0

GOALTENDERS	GP	W	L	MIN	GA	SO	AVG
Andy Moog	3	0	2	157	11	0	4.20
Rejean Lemelin	2	0	2	120	8	0	4.00

1989

CALGARY	GP	G	A	PTS	PIM
Al MacInnis	6	5	4	9	18
Joe Mullen	6	5	3	8	4
Joel Otto	6	2	6	8	2
Doug Gilmour	6	4	3	7	6
Theoren Fleury	6	1	1	2	2
Joe Nieuwendyk	6	1	1	2	2
Colin Patterson	6	1	1	2	16
Tim Hunter	4	0	2	2	6
Jim Peplinski	4	0	2	2	10
Jamie Macoun	6	0	2	2	8
Rob Ramage	6	0	2	2	10
Lanny McDonald	3	1	0	1	2
Mark Hunter	4	0	1	1	12
Hakan Loob	6	0	1	1	0
Brian MacLellan	6	0	1	1	4
Brad McCrimmon	6	0	1	1	6
Dana Murzyn	6	0	1	1	8
Jiri Hrdina	3	0	0	0	0
Ric Nattress	6	0	0	0	12
Gary Roberts	6	0	0	0	8

GOALTENDER	GP	W	L	MIN	GA	SO	AVG
Mike Vernon	6	4	2	397	16	0	2.42

MONTREAL	GP	G	A	PTS	PIM
Chris Chelios	6	1	6	7	10
Bobby Smith	6	3	2	5	20
Mike McPhee	6	1	3	4	4
Claude Lemieux	4	2	1	3	18
Larry Robinson	6	2	1	3	4
Mike Keane	6	1	2	3	4
Mats Naslund	6	1	2	3	4
Brian Skrudland	6	0	3	3	18
Petr Svoboda	6	0	3	3	8
Russ Courtnall	6	2	0	2	12
Stephane Richer	6	1	1	2	10
Rick Green	6	1	0	1	2
Ryan Walter	6	1	0	1	4
Shayne Corson	6	0	1	1	18
Bob Gainey	6	0	1	1	4
Brent Gilchrist	2	0	0	0	4
Guy Carbonneau	6	0	0	0	6
Eric Desjardins	6	0	0	0	2
Craig Ludwig	6	0	0	0	8

GOALTENDER	GP	W	L	MIN	GA	SO	AVG
Patrick Roy	6	2	4	395	17	0	2.58

1990

EDMONTON	GP	G	A	PTS	PIM
Craig Simpson	5	4	4	8	6
Jari Kurri	5	3	5	8	2
Glenn Anderson	5	4	3	7	6
Esa Tikkanen	5	3	2	5	10
Mark Messier	5	0	5	5	6
Joe Murphy	5	2	2	4	4
Steve Smith	5	1	2	3	13
Mark Lamb	5	0	3	3	2
Adam Graves	5	2	0	2	0
Craig MacTavish	5	0	2	2	2
Reijo Ruotsalainen	5	0	2	2	2
Petr Klima	5	1	0	1	0
Martin Gelinas	5	0	1	1	2
Randy Gregg	5	0	1	1	0
Kelly Buchberger	5	0	0	0	2
Charlie Huddy	5	0	0	0	4
Kevin Lowe	5	0	0	0	0
Craig Muni	5	0	0	0	2

GOALTENDER	GP	W	L	MIN	GA	SO	AVG
Bill Ranford	5	4	1	355	8	0	1.35

BOSTON	GP	G	A	PTS	PIM
Ray Bourque	5	3	2	5	6
Cam Neely	5	0	4	4	10
Greg Hawgood	5	1	2	3	4
Randy Burridge	5	0	2	2	2
Lyndon Byers	2	1	0	1	0
John Byce	3	1	0	1	0
Greg Johnston	4	1	0	1	4
John Carter	5	1	0	1	19
Bob Sweeney	5	0	1	1	7
Don Sweeney	5	0	1	1	6
Peter Douris	1	0	0	0	0
Andy Brickley	2	0	0	0	0
Dave Poulin	2	0	0	0	0
Jim Wiemer	2	0	0	0	0
Bob Gould	4	0	0	0	0
Bob Carpenter	5	0	0	0	2
Dave Christian	5	0	0	0	0
Garry Galley	5	0	0	0	4
Craig Janney	5	0	0	0	0
Allen Pedersen	5	0	0	0	2
Brian Propp	5	0	0	0	0
Glen Wesley	5	0	0	0	2

GOALTENDERS	GP	W	L	MIN	GA	SO	AVG
Andy Moog	5	1	4	319	16	0	3.01
Rejean Lemelin	1	0	0	36	4	0	6.67

1991

PITTSBURGH	GP	G	A	PTS	PIM
Mario Lemieux	5	5	7	12	6
Larry Murphy	6	1	9	10	6
Joe Mullen	6	3	5	8	0
Kevin Stevens	6	4	3	7	27
Ron Francis	6	3	3	6	6
Jaromir Jagr	6	0	5	5	0
Phil Bourque	6	2	2	4	4
Bob Errey	6	2	1	3	8
Mark Recchi	6	2	1	3	8
Ulf Samuelsson	6	2	1	3	12
Bryan Trottier	6	1	2	3	14
Peter Taglianetti	5	0	3	3	8
Scott Young	1	1	1	2	0
Paul Coffey	5	0	2	2	0
Jim Paek	5	1	0	1	2
Troy Loney	6	1	0	1	26
Jiri Hrdina	2	0	0	0	0
Grant Jennings	2	0	0	0	2
Randy Gilhen	5	0	0	0	12
Gordie Roberts	6	0	0	0	23
Paul Stanton	6	0	0	0	8

GOALTENDERS	GP	W	L	MIN	GA	SO	AVG
Tom Barrasso	6	3	2	319	13	1	2.45
Frank Pietrangelo	1	1	0	40	3	0	4.50

MINNESOTA	GP	G	A	PTS	PIM
Dave Gagner	6	4	2	6	14
Neal Broten	6	3	1	4	2
Ulf Dahlen	6	2	2	4	0

Mike Modano	6	2	2	4	6
Bobby Smith	6	1	3	4	4
Brian Propp	6	1	3	4	4
Stewart Gavin	6	0	3	3	2
Gaetan Duchesne	6	1	1	2	6
Brian Bellows	6	0	2	2	16
Shawn Chambers	6	0	2	2	6
Marc Bureau	6	1	0	1	8
Chris Dahlquist	6	0	1	1	4
Jim Johnson	6	0	1	1	10
Mark Tinordi	6	0	1	1	15
Perry Berezan	1	0	0	0	0
Doug Smail	1	0	0	0	0
Shane Churla	5	0	0	0	4
Basil McRae	5	0	0	0	26
Brian Glynn	6	0	0	0	6
Neil Wilkinson	6	0	0	0	2

GOALTENDERS	GP	W	L	MIN	GA	SO	AVG
Jon Casey	6	2	3	290	21	0	4.34
Brian Hayward	2	0	1	67	6	0	5.37

1992

PITTSBURGH	GP	G	A	PTS	PIM
Rick Tocchet	4	2	6	8	2
Mario Lemieux	4	5	2	7	0
Kevin Stevens	4	2	3	5	0
Ron Francis	4	1	2	3	0
Larry Murphy	4	1	2	3	2
Jim Paek	4	0	3	3	2
Jaromir Jagr	4	2	0	2	2
Shawn McEachern	4	0	2	2	0
Bob Errey	3	1	0	1	0
Phil Bourque	4	1	0	1	0
Troy Loney	4	0	1	1	0
Kjell Samuelsson	4	0	1	1	2
Paul Stanton	4	0	1	1	20
Dave Michayluk	1	0	0	0	0
Jiri Hrdina	3	0	0	0	0
Jock Callender	4	0	0	0	0
Gordie Roberts	4	0	0	0	8
Ulf Samuelsson	4	0	0	0	2
Bryan Trottier	4	0	0	0	2

GOALTENDER	GP	W	L	MIN	GA	SO	AVG
Tom Barrasso	4	4	0	240	10	1	2.50

CHICAGO	GP	G	A	PTS	PIM
Chris Chelios	4	1	4	5	19
Dirk Graham	4	4	0	4	0
Brian Noonan	4	0	3	3	2
Jeremy Roenick	4	2	0	2	0
Brent Sutter	4	1	1	2	0
Greg Gilbert	3	0	2	2	10
Michel Goulet	4	1	0	1	2
Bryan Marchment	4	1	0	1	2
Stu Grimson	2	0	1	1	0
Rod Buskas	3	0	1	1	0
Steve Larmer	4	0	1	1	2
Jocelyn Lemieux	4	0	1	1	0
Stephane Matteau	4	0	1	1	0
Cam Russell	1	0	0	0	0
Rob Brown	3	0	0	0	2
Mike Peluso	3	0	0	0	4
Mike Hudson	4	0	0	0	2
Frantisek Kucera	4	0	0	0	0
Steve Smith	4	0	0	0	4
Igor Kravchuk	4	0	0	0	2

GOALTENDERS	GP	W	L	MIN	GA	SO	AVG
Ed Belfour	4	0	3	187	11	0	3.53
Dominik Hasek	1	0	1	53	4	0	4.53

1993

MONTREAL	GP	G	A	PTS	PIM
Eric Desjardins	5	3	1	4	6
John LeClair	5	2	2	4	0
Kirk Muller	5	2	2	4	6
Vincent Damphousse	5	1	3	4	8
Stephan Lebeau	5	1	2	3	4
Mike Keane	4	0	3	3	2
Paul DiPietro	5	2	0	2	0
Gilbert Dionne	5	1	1	2	4
Brian Bellows	5	1	1	2	4
Ed Ronan	5	1	1	2	6
Mathieu Schneider	5	1	1	2	8
Lyle Odelein	5	0	2	2	6
Kevin Haller	3	0	1	1	0
Benoit Brunet	5	0	1	1	2
Guy Carbonneau	5	0	1	1	0
Gary Leeman	5	0	1	1	2
Donald Dufresne	1	0	0	0	0
Sean Hill	1	0	0	0	0
Denis Savard	1	0	0	0	0
Patrice Brisebois	5	0	0	0	8
J.J. Daigneault	5	0	0	0	6

GOALTENDER	GP	W	L	MIN	GA	SO	AVG
Patrick Roy	5	4	1	315	11	0	2.10

LOS ANGELES	GP	G	A	PTS	PIM
Wayne Gretzky	5	2	5	7	2
Luc Robitaille	5	3	2	5	4
Tony Granato	5	1	3	4	10
Marty McSorley	5	2	0	2	16
Dave Taylor	3	1	1	2	6
Mike Donnelly	5	1	1	2	0
Tomas Sandstrom	5	0	2	2	4
Pat Conacher	5	1	0	1	2
Jari Kurri	5	1	0	1	2
Jimmy Carson	2	0	1	1	0
Mark Hardy	4	0	1	1	4
Rob Blake	5	0	1	1	18
Alexei Zhitnik	5	0	1	1	4
Lonnie Loach	1	0	0	0	0
Charlie Huddy	4	0	0	0	4
Corey Millen	5	0	0	0	2
Warren Rychel	5	0	0	0	2
Gary Shuchuk	5	0	0	0	0
Darryl Sydor	5	0	0	0	4
Tim Watters	5	0	0	0	4

GOALTENDER	GP	W	L	MIN	GA	SO	GAA
Kelly Hrudey	5	1	4	316	15	0	2.85

1994

NY RANGERS	GP	G	A	PTS	PIM
Brian Leetch	7	5	6	11	4
Alexei Kovalev	7	4	3	7	2
Mark Messier	7	2	5	7	17
Sergei Zubov	6	1	5	6	0
Steve Larmer	7	4	0	4	2
Adam Graves	7	1	3	4	4
Glenn Anderson	7	2	1	3	4
Doug Lidster	7	2	0	2	10
Jeff Beukeboom	7	0	2	2	25
Sergei Nemchinov	7	0	2	2	2
Greg Gilbert	7	0	1	1	2
Craig MacTavish	7	0	1	1	6
Stephane Matteau	7	0	1	1	6
Brian Noonan	7	0	1	1	0
Esa Tikkanen	7	0	1	1	12
Nick Kypreos	1	0	0	0	0
Alex. Karpovtsev	2	0	0	0	0
Joe Kocur	6	0	0	0	2
Kevin Lowe	6	0	0	0	6
Jay Wells	7	0	0	0	8

GOALTENDER	GP	W	L	MIN	GA	SO	AVG
Mike Richter	7	4	3	439	19	0	2.60

VANCOUVER	GP	G	A	PTS	PIM
Pavel Bure	7	3	5	8	15
Cliff Ronning	7	1	6	7	6
Geoff Courtnall	7	4	1	5	11
Trevor Linden	7	3	2	5	6
Jeff Brown	7	3	1	4	8
Bret Hedican	7	1	3	4	4
Jyrki Lumme	7	0	4	4	6
Greg Adams	7	1	2	3	2
Nathan Lafayette	7	0	3	3	0
Sergio Momesso	7	1	1	2	17
Murray Craven	7	0	2	2	4
Dave Babych	7	1	0	1	2
Martin Gelinas	7	1	0	1	4
Shawn Antoski	7	0	1	1	8
Gerald Diduck	7	0	1	1	6
Brian Glynn	7	0	1	1	0
Tim Hunter	7	0	0	0	18
John McIntyre	7	0	0	0	6

GOALTENDER	GP	W	L	MIN	GA	SO	AVG
Kirk McLean	7	3	4	437	20	0	2.75

1995

NEW JERSEY	GP	G	A	PTS	PIM
Neal Broten	4	3	3	6	4
John MacLean	4	1	4	5	0
Stephane Richer	4	2	2	4	0
Scott Niedermayer	4	1	3	4	0
Bill Guerin	4	0	4	4	12
Shawn Chambers	4	2	1	3	0
Bruce Driver	4	1	2	3	0
Claude Lemieux	4	2	0	2	4
Jim Dowd	1	1	1	2	2
Sergei Brylin	3	1	1	2	4
Bobby Holik	4	1	1	2	8
Tom Chorske	3	0	2	2	0
Tommy Albelin	4	0	2	2	2
Scott Stevens	4	0	2	2	4
Randy McKay	4	1	0	1	0
Brian Rolston	2	0	1	1	0
Bob Carpenter	4	0	1	1	2
Valeri Zelepukin	3	0	0	0	4
Mike Peluso	4	0	0	0	0
Ken Daneyko	4	0	0	0	6

GOALTENDER	GP	W	L	MIN	GA	SO	AVG
Martin Brodeur	4	4	0	206	7	0	1.75

DETROIT	GP	G	A	PTS	PIM
Sergei Fedorov	4	3	2	5	0
Doug Brown	4	0	3	3	2
Viacheslav Fetisov	4	0	3	3	0
Dino Ciccarelli	4	1	1	2	6
Paul Coffey	4	1	1	2	0
Nicklas Lidstrom	4	0	2	2	0
Steve Yzerman	4	1	0	1	0
Vyacheslav Kozlov	4	1	0	1	0
Martin Lapointe	2	0	1	1	8
Ray Sheppard	3	0	1	1	0
Kris Draper	4	0	0	0	4
Bob Errey	4	0	0	0	4
Bob Rouse	4	0	0	0	0
Vladimir Konstantinov	4	0	0	0	8
Darren McCarty	4	0	0	0	4
Shawn Burr	2	0	0	0	0
Stu Grimson	2	0	0	0	2
Mark Howe	2	0	0	0	0
Mike Krushelnyski	2	0	0	0	0
Mike Ramsey	2	0	0	0	0
Tim Taylor	2	0	0	0	2
Keith Primeau	3	0	0	0	8

GOALTENDERS	GP	W	L	MIN	GA	SO	AVG
Mike Vernon	4	0	4	240	14	0	4.08
Chris Osgood	1	0	0	32	1	0	1.88

1996

COLORADO	GP	G	A	PTS	PIM
Peter Forsberg	4	3	2	5	0
Joe Sakic	4	1	4	5	2
Adam Deadmarsh	4	0	4	4	4
Uwe Krupp	4	2	1	3	2
Rene Corbet	4	2	1	3	0
Valeri Kamensky	4	1	2	3	8
Jon Klemm	4	2	0	2	0
Mike Keane	4	1	1	2	0
Scott Young	4	1	1	2	0
Alexei Gusarov	4	0	2	2	2
Sandis Ozolinsh	4	0	2	2	4
Claude Lemieux	2	1	0	1	4
Mike Ricci	4	1	0	1	6
Adam Foote	4	0	1	1	4
Sylvain Lefebvre	4	0	1	1	2
Curtis Leschyshyn	4	0	1	1	4
Dave Hannan	3	0	0	0	0
Warren Rychel	3	0	0	0	19

GOALTENDER	GP	W	L	MIN	GA	SO	AVG
Patrick Roy	4	4	0	285	4	1	0.84

FLORIDA	GP	G	A	PTS	PIM
Ed Jovanovski	4	0	2	2	11
Stu Barnes	4	1	0	1	2
Tom Fitzgerald	4	1	0	1	0
Rob Niedermayer	4	1	0	1	2
Ray Sheppard	4	1	0	1	0
Johan Garpenlov	4	0	1	1	2
Bill Lindsay	4	0	1	1	4
Dave Lowery	4	0	1	1	2
Scott Mellanby	4	0	1	1	4
Martin Straka	4	0	1	1	0
Radek Dvorak	1	0	0	0	0
Jody Hull	2	0	0	0	0
Jason Woolley	2	0	0	0	0
Rhett Warrener	3	0	0	0	0
Terry Carkner	4	0	0	0	4
Mike Hough	4	0	0	0	0
Paul Laus	4	0	0	0	2
Gord Murphy	4	0	0	0	0
Brian Skrudland	4	0	0	0	4
Robert Svehla	4	0	0	0	2

GOALTENDERS	GP	W	L	MIN	GA	SO	AVG
John Vanbiesbrouck	4	0	4	245	11	0	2.69
Mark Fitzpatrick	1	0	0	40	4	0	6.00

1997

DETROIT	GP	G	A	PTS	PIM
Sergei Fedorov	4	3	3	6	2
Steve Yzerman	4	3	1	4	0
Brendan Shanahan	4	3	1	4	0
Kirk Maltby	4	2	1	3	2
Martin Lapointe	4	2	1	3	6
Darren McCarty	4	1	2	3	4
Larry Murphy	4	0	3	3	0
Joe Kocur	4	1	1	2	2
Viacheslav Fetisov	4	0	2	2	10
Vyacheslav Kozlov	4	0	2	2	0
Nicklas Lidstrom	4	1	0	1	0
Kris Draper	4	0	1	1	2
Doug Brown	4	0	1	1	2
Tomas Sandstrom	4	0	1	1	4
Mike Vernon	4	0	1	1	0
Igor Larionov	4	0	0	0	4
Vladimir Konstantinov	4	0	0	0	2
Bob Rouse	4	0	0	0	0
Aaron Ward	4	0	0	0	0

GOALTENDER	GP	W	L	MIN	GA	SO	AVG
Mike Vernon	4	4	0	240	6	0	1.50

PHILADELPHIA	GP	G	A	PTS	PIM
Rod Brind'Amour	4	3	1	4	0
John LeClair	4	2	1	3	4
Eric Lindros	4	1	2	3	8
Janne Niinimaa	4	0	3	3	0
Eric Desjardins	4	0	2	2	2
Mikael Renberg	4	0	1	1	0
John Druce	4	0	0	0	0
Joel Otto	4	0	0	0	0
Kjell Samuelsson	4	0	0	0	2
Trent Klatt	4	0	0	0	6
Shjon Podein	4	0	0	0	2
Chris Therien	4	0	0	0	0
Dainius Zubrus	4	0	0	0	0
Dale Hawerchuk	3	0	0	0	0
Karl Dykhuis	3	0	0	0	2
Pat Falloon	3	0	0	0	2
Colin Forbes	3	0	0	0	0
Paul Coffey	2	0	0	0	6
Dan Lacroix	2	0	0	0	2
Michel Petit	2	0	0	0	2
Petr Svoboda	1	0	0	0	2
Dan Kordic	1	0	0	0	0

GOALTENDERS	GP	W	L	MIN	GA	SO	AVG
Ron Hextall	3	0	3	178	12	0	4.04
Garth Snow	1	0	1	58	4	0	4.11

1998

DETROIT	GP	G	A	PTS	PIM
Doug Brown	4	3	2	5	0
Tomas Holmstrom	4	1	4	5	2
Steve Yzerman	4	2	2	4	2
Martin Lapointe	4	2	1	3	6
Sergei Fedorov	4	1	2	3	0
Vacheslav Fetisov	4	0	3	3	2
Nicklas Lidstrom	4	1	1	2	2
Larry Murphy	4	1	1	2	0
Igor Larionov	4	0	2	2	4
Darren McCarty	4	0	2	2	2
Kris Draper	4	1	0	1	2
Joey Kocur	4	1	0	1	4
Anders Eriksson	4	0	1	1	4
Vyacheslav Kozlov	4	0	1	1	0
Bob Rouse	4	0	1	1	2
Brendan Shanahan	4	0	1	1	0
Jamie Macoun	4	0	0	0	0
Kirk Maltby	4	0	0	0	6

GOALTENDER	GP	W	L	MIN	GA	SO	AVG
Chris Osgood	4	4	0	254	7	0	1.65

WASHINGTON	GP	G	A	PTS	PIM
Joe Juneau	4	1	3	4	0
Brian Bellows	4	2	1	3	0
Adams Oates	4	1	2	3	0
Peter Bondra	4	1	1	2	4
Jeff Brown	2	0	2	2	0
Andrei Nikolishin	4	0	2	2	2
Chris Simon	4	1	0	1	6
Richard Zednik	4	1	0	1	4
Sergei Gonchar	4	0	1	1	4
Dale Hunter	4	0	1	1	2
Calle Johansson	4	0	1	1	2
Craig Berube	4	0	0	0	0
Phil Housley	4	0	0	0	2
Joe Reekie	4	0	0	0	2
Esa Tikkanen	4	0	0	0	4
Mark Tinordi	4	0	0	0	6
Kelly Miller	3	0	0	0	0
Mike Eagles	2	0	0	0	0
Ken Klee	2	0	0	0	0
Todd Krygier	2	0	0	0	2
Jeff Toms	1	0	0	0	0

GOALTENDER	GP	W	L	MIN	GA	SO	AVG
Olaf Kolzig	4	0	4	251	13	0	3.11

1999

DALLAS	GP	G	A	PTS	PIM
Mike Modano	6	0	7	7	8
Jere Lehtinen	6	2	3	5	0
Brett Hull	5	3	0	3	0
Joe Nieuwendyk	6	2	1	3	9
Jamie Langenbrunner	6	1	2	3	4
Sergei Zubov	6	0	3	3	2
Derian Hatcher	6	1	1	2	10
Craig Ludwig	6	1	1	2	10
Richard Matvichuk	6	0	2	2	6
Dave Reid	6	0	2	2	2
Darryl Sydor	6	1	0	1	8
Pat Verbeek	6	1	0	1	4
Shawn Chambers	6	0	1	1	2
Mike Keane	6	0	1	1	0
Brian Skrudland	6	0	1	1	8
Tony Hrkac	3	0	1	1	2
Guy Carbonneau	6	0	0	0	0
Blake Sloan	6	0	0	0	0
Benoit Hogue	2	0	0	0	2
Jonathan Sim	2	0	0	0	0

GOALTENDER	GP	W	L	MIN	GA	SO	AVG
Ed Belfour	6	4	2	429	9	1	1.26

BUFFALO	GP	G	A	PTS	PIM
Stu Barnes	6	3	0	3	0
Alexei Zhitnik	6	1	2	3	18
Richard Smehlik	6	0	3	3	2
Wayne Primeau	6	1	1	2	4
Jason Woolley	6	1	1	2	6
Michael Peca	6	1	0	1	2
Geoff Sanderson	6	1	0	1	4
Dixon Ward	6	1	0	1	8
Curtis Brown	6	0	1	1	2
Brian Holzinger	6	0	1	1	9
Joe Juneau	6	0	1	1	0
Miroslav Satan	6	0	1	1	2
Dominik Hasek	6	0	0	0	2
Jay McKee	6	0	0	0	2
James Patrick	6	0	0	0	4
Erik Rasmussen	6	0	0	0	2
Vaclav Varada	6	0	0	0	6
Rhett Warrener	5	0	0	0	6
Michal Grosek	1	0	0	0	0
Paul Kruse	1	0	0	0	0
Rob Ray	1	0	0	0	0

GOALTENDER	GP	W	L	MIN	GA	SO	AVG
Dominik Hasek	6	2	4	428	12	0	1.68

Stanley Cup Notebook

Eye in the Sky

For the first time in NHL history, a playoff result was determined by a video replay during the 1992 Division Semifinals between the Detroit Red Wings and Minnesota North Stars.

Sergei Fedorov's overtime shot appeared to hit the crossbar. After a stop in play, referee Rob Shick consulted the supervisor of officials and video-replay official Wally Harris, who determined that the puck had entered the net, giving the Wings a 1-0 victory.

Gold Medalist and Stanley Cup Champion

New York Islanders' defenseman Ken Morrow is the only player in hockey history to win both an Olympic Gold Medal and a Stanley Cup in the same year.

After helping the United States Olympic team win the gold medal at the 1980 Winter Games in Lake Placid, Morrow joined the New York Islanders and helped them win the first of their four consecutive Stanley Cup championships.

Right Place at the Right Time

Doug McKay played one game in his NHL career, but that was during the 1950 Stanley Cup Finals as a member of the Detroit Red Wings. McKay is the only player to make his sole NHL appearance with a Cup-winning team in the Stanley Cup Finals.

Stanley Cup Bookends

Claude Provost, a 15-year veteran of the Montreal Canadiens, and Cooney Weiland, who played 11 years for Boston, Detroit and Ottawa, are the only players to spend at least a decade in the NHL and win the Stanley Cup in both their first and last seasons in the league.

Mario's Magic

Mario Lemieux tied three NHL records on April 25, 1989, in a game against the Philadelphia Flyers. Lemieux's eight-point evening tied a record for most points in a post-season game, his four goals in the opening stanza tied a record for most goals in one period and his five goals matched the mark for most goals in a playoff game.

CHAPTER 18

Players on Stanley Cup-Winning Teams

1893 – 1999

A TOTAL OF 976 PLAYERS HAVE SKATED FOR Stanley Cup championship teams since the trophy was first awarded to the Montreal Amateur Athletic Association (MAAA) hockey club in 1893. Of the 976 winners, 521 (53.4%) have won one Cup title, while 455 (46.6%) have won on two or more occasions.

Cup wins	**1**	**2**	**3**	**4**	**5**	**6**	**7**	**8**	**9**	**10**	**11**
Players	521	250	73	77	30	16	2	3	1	2	1
Pct.	53.4	25.6	7.5	7.9	3.1	1.6					

Henri Richard holds the record for playing on the most Stanley Cup champions, winning 11 times in his career. During Richard's 20 years with the Montreal Canadiens from 1955-56 to 1974-75, "The Pocket Rocket" never played more than four consecutive seasons without earning a new Stanley Cup ring.

Jean Beliveau and Yvan Cournoyer of the Canadiens share second place behind Richard with 10 Cup wins apiece, and Montreal's Claude Provost ranks third with nine. Red Kelly, Maurice Richard and Jacques Lemaire are tied with eight, while Serge Savard and Jean-Guy Talbot have seven each. Kelly is the only player to rank among these all-time Stanley Cup winners without ever playing for the Canadiens. He won the Cup four times with Detroit in the 1950s and four times with Toronto in the '60s.

Kelly, Dick Duff, Frank Mahovlich, Bob Goldham, Bryan Trottier and Larry Murphy are the only players in history to win multiple Stanley Cup titles with two different teams. Of the 452 players to win more than one Stanley Cup championship, 343 won with the same team every time. Another 100 players won with two teams, while eight won with three and one won with four.

Jack Marshall owns the record for playing with four different teams to win the Stanley Cup. Marshall played on championship teams with the 1901 Winnipeg Vics, 1902 Montreal AAA, 1907 and 1910 Montreal Wanderers and 1914 Toronto Blueshirts.

Eight players have skated for three different Stanley Cup winning franchises in their careers. Frank Foyston, Jack Walker, Claude Lemieux (still active) and Mike Keane (still active) had Cup wins with three different clubs, while Larry Hillman, Harry Holmes, Al Arbour and Gordon Pettinger won four Cup titles with three separate teams.

A

Abel, Clarence 'Taffy'	NY Rangers 28; Chicago 34
Abel, Sid	Detroit 43,50,52
Acton, Keith	Edmonton 88
Adams, Jack	Toronto 18; Ottawa 27
Aitkenhead, Andy	NY Rangers 33
Albelin, Tommy	New Jersey 95
Allen, 'Bones'	Ottawa 05
Allen, Keith	Detroit 54
Anderson, Doug	Montreal 53
Anderson, Glenn	Edmonton 84,85,87,88,90; NY Rangers 94
Anderson, Jocko	Victoria 25
Andrews, Lloyd	Toronto 22
Apps, Syl	Toronto 42,47,48
Arbour, Al	Detroit 54, Chicago 61; Toronto 62,64
Arbour, Amos	Montreal 16
Armitage, Jack	Winnipeg Vics 1896
Armstrong, George	Toronto 62,63,64,67
Arnold, Josh	Mtl Wanderers 06
Ashbee, Barry	Philadelphia 74
Asmundson, Ossie	NY Rangers 33
Aurie, Larry	Detroit 36,37
Awrey, Don	Boston 70,72

B

Babando, Pete	Detroit 50
Backor, Peter	Toronto 45
Backstrom, Ralph	Montreal 59,60,65,66,68,69
Bailey, Garnet 'Ace'	Boston 72
Bailey, Irvine 'Ace'	Toronto 32
Bain, Dan	Winnipeg Vics 1896, 01
Balfour, Earl	Chicago 61
Balfour, Murray	Chicago 61
Balon, Dave	Montreal 65,66
Barber, Bill	Philadelphia 74,75
Barilko, Bill	Toronto 47,48,49,51
Barlow, Billy	Mtl AAA 1893,94
Barrasso, Tom	Pittsburgh 91,92
Barry, Marty	Detroit 36,37
Bathgate, Andy	Toronto 64
Bauer, Bobby	Boston 39,41
Baun, Bob	Toronto 62,63,64,67
Beaudro, Roxy	Kenora 07
Belfour, Ed	Dallas 99
Beliveau, Jean	Montreal 56,57,58,59,60,65, 66,68,69,71
Bell, Billy	Montreal 24
Bellingham, Billy	Mtl AAA 02
Bellows, Brian	Montreal 93
Benedict, Clint	Ottawa 20,21,23; Mtl Maroons 26
Benoit, Joe	Montreal 46
Bentley, Max	Toronto 48,49,51
Berenson, Gordon 'Red'	Montreal 65,66
Berlinquette, Louis	Montreal 16

Beukeboom, Jeff	Edmonton 87,88,90; NY Rangers 94
Blachford, Cecil	Mtl Wanderers 06,07,08,10
Black, Steve	Detroit 50
Bladon, Tom	Philadelphia 74,75
Blair, Andy	Toronto 32
Blake, Hector 'Toe'	Mtl Maroons 35; Montreal 44,46
Blinco, Russ	Mtl Maroons 35
Bodnar, Gus	Toronto 45,47
Boesch, Garth	Toronto 47,48,49
Boisvert, Serge	Montreal 86
Bonin, Marcel	Detroit 55; Montreal 58,59,60
Boon, Dick	Mtl AAA 02
Bordeleau, Christian	Montreal 69
Bossy, Mike	NY Islanders 80,81,82,83
Bouchard, Emile 'Butch'	Montreal 44,46,53,56
Bouchard, Pierre	Montreal 71,73,76,77,78
Boucher, Billy	Montreal 24
Boucher, Bobby	Montreal 24
Boucher, Frank	NY Rangers 28,33
Boucher, George	Ottawa 20,21,23,27
Bourgeault, Leo	NY Rangers 28
Bourne, Bob	NY Islanders 80,81,82,83
Bourque, Phil	Pittsburgh 91,92
Boutilier, Paul	NY Islanders 83
Bower, Johnny	Toronto 62,63,64,67
Bowman, Ralph 'Scotty'	Detroit 36,37
Boyd, Bill	NY Rangers 28
Brannen, Jack	Mtl Shamrocks 1899,1900
Brennan, Doug	NY Rangers 33
Brewer, Carl	Toronto 62,63,64
Brimsek, Frank	Boston 39,41
Brisebois, Patrice	Montreal 93
Broadbent, Harry	Ottawa 20,21,23; Mtl Maroons 26
Broda, Walter 'Turk'	Toronto 42,47,48,49,51
Broden, Connie	Montreal 57,58
Brodeur, Martin	New Jersey 95
Brophy, Bernie	Mtl Maroons 26
Broten, Neal	New Jersey 95
Brown, Adam	Detroit 43
Brown, Dave	Edmonton 90
Brown, Doug	Detroit 97, 98
Brown, G.	Winnipeg Vics 01
Brown, Pat	Detroit 43
Bruce, Morley	Ottawa 20,21
Brunet, Benoit	Montreal 93
Bruneteau, Moderre 'Mud'	Detroit 36,37,43
Brylin, Sergei	New Jersey 95
Buchberger, Kelly	Edmonton 87,90
Bucyk, Johnny	Boston 70,72
Burke, Marty	Montreal 30,31

C

Cain, Herb	Mtl Maroons 35; Boston 41
Callender, Jock	Pittsburgh 92
Callighen, Pat	NY Rangers 28
Cameron, Allan	Mtl AAA 1893,94
Cameron, Billy	Montreal 24
Cameron, Harry	Toronto 14,18,22
Campbell, C.J.	Winnipeg Vics 1896
Carbonneau, Guy	Montreal 86, 93; Dallas 99
Carleton, Wayne	Boston 70
Carpenter, Bob	New Jersey 95
Carpenter, Ed	Seattle 17
Carr, Lorne	Toronto 42,45
Carroll, Billy	NY Islanders 81,82,83; Edmonton 85
Carson, Bill	Boston 29
Carson, Frank	Mtl Maroons 26
Carson, Gerald	Montreal 30
Carveth, Joe	Detroit 43,50
Cashman, Wayne	Boston 70,72
Caufield, Jay	Pittsburgh 91,92
Chabot, Lorne	NY Rangers 28; Toronto 32
Chamberlain, Erwin 'Murph'	Montreal 44,46
Chambers, Shawn	New Jersey 95; Dallas 99
Chartraw, Rick	Montreal 76,77,78,79
Cheevers, Gerry	Boston 70,72
Chelios, Chris	Montreal 86
Chorske, Tom	New Jersey 95
Chychrun, Jeff	Pittsburgh 92
Clancy, Frank 'King'	Ottawa 23,27; Toronto 32
Clapper, Aubrey 'Dit'	Boston 29,39,41
Clarke, Bobby	Philadelphia 74,75
Cleghorn, Odie	Montreal 24
Cleghorn, Sprague	Ottawa 20,21; Montreal 24
Clement, Bill	Philadelphia 74,75
Coffey, Paul	Edmonton 84,85,87; Pittsburgh 91
Cole, Danton	New Jersey 95
Collins, Herb	Mtl AAA 1894
Colville, Mac	NY Rangers 40
Colville, Neil	NY Rangers 40
Conacher, Brian	Toronto 67
Conacher, Charlie	Toronto 32
Conacher, Lionel	Chicago 34; Mtl Maroons 35
Conacher, Pat	Edmonton 84
Conacher, Roy	Boston 39,41
Connell, Alex	Ottawa 27; Mtl Maroons 35
Connolly, Bert	Chicago 38
Connor, Cam	Montreal 79
Cook, Bill	NY Rangers 28,33
Cook, Fred 'Bun'	NY Rangers 28,33
Cook, Lloyd	Vancouver 15
Cook, Tom	Chicago 34
Corbeau, Bert	Montreal 16
Corbeau, Con	Toronto 14
Corbet, Rene	Colorado 96
Costello, Les	Toronto 48
Cotton, Harold 'Baldy'	Toronto 32
Coughlin, Jack	Toronto 18
Coulter, Art	Chicago 34; NY Rangers 40
Cournoyer, Yvan	Montreal 65,66,68,69,71,73, 76,77,78,79
Courtnall, Geoff	Edmonton 88
Coutu, Billy	Montreal 24
Couture, Gerald 'Doc'	Detroit 50
Cowick, Bruce	Philadelphia 74
Cowley, Bill	Boston 39,41
Crawford, Jack	Boston 39,41
Crawford, Russell 'Rusty'	Quebec 13; Toronto 18
Creighton, Billy	Quebec 13
Crisp, Terry	Philadelphia 74,75
Currie, Alex	Ottawa 11
Curry, Floyd	Montreal 53,56,57,58

D

Dahlin, Kjell	Montreal 86
Dahlstrom, Carl 'Cully'	Chicago 38
Daigneault, J.J.	Montreal 93
Damphousse, Vincent	Montreal 93
Daneyko, Ken	New Jersey 95
Daniels, Jeff	Pittsburgh 92
Dandenault, Mathieu	Detroit 97, 98
Darragh, Harold	Toronto 32
Darragh, Jack	Ottawa 11,20,21,23
Davidson, Bob	Toronto 42,45
Davidson, Cam	Mtl Victorias 1896,97,98
Davidson, Shirley	Mtl Victorias 1895,96,97
Davis, Lorne	Montreal 53
Dawes, Robert	Toronto 49
Day, Clarence 'Hap'	Toronto 32
Deadmarsh, Adam	Colorado 96
Dean, Kevin	New Jersey 95
DeBlois, Lucien	Montreal 86
Delvecchio, Alex	Detroit 52,54,55
Denneny, Corb	Toronto 18,22
Denneny, Cy	Ottawa 20,21,23,27; Boston 29
Desjardins, Eric	Montreal 93
Dewsbury, Al	Detroit 50
Dey, Edgar	Ottawa 09
Dickens, Ernie	Toronto 42
Dillon, Cecil	NY Rangers 33
Dineen, Bill	Detroit 54,55
Dinsmore, Chuck	Mtl Maroons 26
Dionne, Gilbert	Montreal 93
DiPietro, Paul	Montreal 93
Doak, Gary	Boston 70
Dobby, John	Mtl Shamrocks 1899
Dornhoefer, Gary	Philadelphia 74,75
Douglas, Kent	Toronto 63
Douglas, Les	Detroit 43
Dowd, Jim	New Jersey 95
Draper, Kris	Detroit 97, 98
Drillon, Gordie	Toronto 42
Drinkwater, Graham	Mtl Victorias 1895,96,97,98
Driver, Bruce	New Jersey 95
Dryden, Ken	Montreal 71,73,76,77,78,79
Dube, Gilles	Detroit 54
Dufresne, Donald	Montreal 93
Duff, Dick	Toronto 62,63; Montreal 65,66,68,69
Dumart, Woody	Boston 39, 41
Dupont, Andre 'Moose'	Philadelphia 74,75
Durnan, Bill	Montreal 44,46
Dye, Cecil 'Babe'	Toronto 22

E

Eddolls, Frank	Montreal 46
Ehman, Gerry	Toronto 64
Elliot, Roland	Mtl Victorias 1895; Mtl AAA 02
Ellis, Ron	Toronto 67
Elmer, Wally	Victoria 25
Engblom, Brian	Montreal 77,78,79
Erickson, Aut	Toronto 67
Eriksson, Anders	Detroit 98
Errey, Bob	Pittsburgh 91,92
Esposito, Phil	Boston 70,72
Esposito, Tony	Montreal 69
Evans, Jack	Chicago 61
Evans, Stewart	Mtl Maroons 35
Ewen, Todd	Montreal 93
Ewing, Jack	Mtl Victorias 1897,98
Ezinicki, Bill	Toronto 47,48,49

F

Farrell, Art	Mtl Shamrocks 1899,1900
Fedorov, Sergei	Detroit 97, 98
Fenwick, Art	Mtl Victorias 1895
Ferguson, John	Montreal 65,66,68,69,71
Fetisov, Viacheslav	Detroit 97, 98
Fillion, Bob	Montreal 44,46
Finnie, Dave	Ottawa 05
Finnigan, Frank	Ottawa 27; Toronto 32
Fiset, Stephane	Colorado 96
Fisher, Joe	Detroit 43
Flaman, Fern	Toronto 51
Fleming, Reg	Chicago 61
Flett, Bill	Philadelphia 74
Flett, Magnus	Winnipeg Vics 01
Flett, Rod	Winnipeg Vics 1896, 01
Fleury, Theoren	Calgary 89
Fogolin, Sr., Lee	Detroit 50
Fogolin, Jr,. Lee	Edmonton 84,85
Foote, Adam	Colorado 96
Forsberg, Peter	Colorado 96
Fortier, Charles	Montreal 24
Fournier, Jack	Montreal 16
Foyston, Frank	Toronto 14; Seattle 17; Victoria 25
Francis, Ron	Pittsburgh 91,92
Franks, Jim	Detroit 37
Fraser, A.A.	Ottawa 03
Fraser, Gordon	Victoria 25
Fredrickson, Frank	Victoria 25; Boston 29
Fuhr, Grant	Edmonton 84,85,87,88,90

G

Gagnon, Johnny	Montreal 31
Gainey, Bob	Montreal 76,77,78,79,86
Gainor, Norman 'Dutch'	Boston 29; Montreal 44
Galbraith, Percy 'Perk'	Boston 29
Gallagher, John	Detroit 37
Gamble, Bruce	Toronto 67
Gamble, Dick	Montreal 53,56
Gardiner, Chuck	Chicago 34
Gardner, Cal	Toronto 49,51
Gardner, Jimmy	Mtl AAA 02; Mtl Wanderers 10
Gaul, Horace	Ottawa 05,11
Gauthier, Jean	Montreal 65
Gee, George	Detroit 50
Gelinas, Martin	Edmonton 90
Geoffrion, Bernie	Montreal 53,56,57,58,59,60
Gerard, Eddie	Ottawa 20,21,23; Toronto 22
Geroux, Eddie	Kenora 07
Getliffe, Ray	Boston 39; Montreal 44
Gilbert, Greg	NY Islanders 82,83; NY Rangers 94
Gilchrist, Brent	Detroit 98
Gillelan, David.	Mtl Victorias 1896,1897
Gillies, Clark	NY Islanders 80,81,82,83
Gilhen, Randy	Pittsburgh 91
Gilmour, Billy	Ottawa 03,04,05,09
Gilmour, Dave	Ottawa 03

Gilmour, Doug	Calgary 89
Gilmour, Larry	Mtl Wanderers 08
Gilmour, Suddy	Ottawa 03,04
Gingras, Gaston	Montreal 86
Gingras, Tony	Winnipeg Vics 01
Glass, Frank 'Pud'	Mtl Wanderers 06,07,08,10
Goldham, Bob	Toronto 42, 47; Detroit 52,54,55
Goldsworthy, Leroy	Chicago 34
Goldup, Hank	Toronto 42
Goodenough, Larry	Philadelphia 75
Goodfellow, Ebbie	Detroit 36,37,43
Goodman, Paul	Chicago 38
Goring, Butch	NY Islanders 80,81,82,83
Gorman, Ed	Ottawa 27
Gottselig, Johnny	Chicago 34,38
Goyette, Phil	Montreal 57,58,59,60
Gracie, Bob	Toronto 32; Mtl Maroons 35
Graham, Leth	Ottawa 21
Grant, Danny	Montreal 68
Grant, Mike	Mtl Victorias 1895,96,97,98
Graves, Adam	Edmonton 90; NY Rangers 94
Gray, Alex	NY Rangers 28
Green, Red	Boston 29
Green, Rick	Montreal 86
Green, Ted	Boston 72
Gregg, Randy	Edmonton 84,85,87,88,90
Grenier, Lucien	Montreal 69
Gretzky, Wayne	Edmonton 84,85,87,88
Griffis, Si	Kenora 07; Vancouver 15
Grosso, Don	Detroit 43
Guerin, Bill	New Jersey 95
Gusarov, Alexei	Colorado 96

H

Haidy, Gordon	Detroit 50
Hainsworth, George	Montreal 30,31
Halderson, Harold 'Slim'	Victoria 25
Hall, Glenn	Chicago 61
Hall, Joe	Quebec 12,13
Haller, Kevin	Montreal 93
Halliday, Milt	Ottawa 27
Hallin, Mats	NY Islanders 83
Hamill, Robert 'Red'	Boston 39
Hamilton, Reg	Toronto 42,45
Hannan, Dave	Edmonton 88; Colorado 96
Harmon, Glen	Montreal 44,46
Harper, Terry	Montreal 65,66,68,69,71
Harris, Ted	Montreal 65,66,68,69; Philadelphia 75
Harris, Billy	Toronto 62,63,64
Harriston	Toronto 14
Hart, Harold 'Gizzy'	Victoria 25
Hartman, Mike	NY Rangers 94
Harvey, Doug	Montreal 53,56,57,58,59,60
Hatcher, Derian	Dallas 99
Hay, Jim	Detroit 55
Hay, Bill	Chicago 61
Hayes, Chris	Boston 72
Healy, Glenn	NY Rangers 94
Hebert, Sammy	Toronto 18
Heffernan, Gerry	Montreal 44
Heller, Ott	NY Rangers 33,40
Helman, Harry	Ottawa 23
Henderson, Harold	Mtl Victorias 1895,96,97
Henning, Lorne	NY Islanders 80,81
Hern, Riley	Mtl Wanderers 07,08,10
Hextall, Sr., Bryan	NY Rangers 40
Hicke, Bill	Montreal 59,60
Hicks, Wayne	Chicago 61
Higginbotham, Fred	Winnipeg Vics 1896
Hill, Mel	Boston 39,41; Toronto 45
Hill, Sean	Montreal 93
Hiller, Wilbert 'Dutch'	NY Rangers 40; Montreal 46
Hillier, Randy	Pittsburgh 91
Hillman, Larry	Detroit 55; Toronto 64,67; Montreal 69
Hillman, Wayne	Chicago 61
Hitchman, Lionel	Ottawa 23; Boston 29
Hodge, Charlie	Montreal 59,60,65,66
Hodge, Ken	Boston 70,72
Hodge, Tom	Mtl AAA 02
Hodgson, Archie	Mtl AAA 1893,94
Hodson, Kevin	Detroit 97, 98
Hoerner, Charles	Mtl Shamrocks 1899
Hogue, Benoit	Dallas 99
Holik, Bobby	New Jersey 95
Hollett, Bill 'Flash'	Boston 39, 41
Holmes, Harry	Toronto 14,18; Seattle 17; Victoria 25
Holmstrom, Tomas	Detroit 97, 98
Holway, Albert 'Toots'	Mtl Maroons 26
Hooper, Art	Mtl AAA 02
Hooper, Tom	Kenora 07; Mtl Wanderers 08
Horne, George 'Shorty'	Mtl Maroons 26
Horner, Reginald 'Red'	Toronto 32
Horton, Tim	Toronto 62,63,64,67
Houle, Rejean	Montreal 71,73,77,78,79
Howard, H.	Winnipeg Vics 1896
Howatt, Garry	NY Islanders 80,81
Howe, Gordie	Detroit 50,52,54,55
Howe, Syd	Detroit 36,37,43
Hrkac, Tony	Dallas 99
Hrdina, Jiri	Calgary 89, Pittsburgh 91,92
Huddy, Charlie	Edmonton 84,85,87,88,90
Hudson, Mike	NY Rangers 94
Hughes, Pat	Montreal 79; Edmonton 84,85
Hull, Bobby	Chicago 61
Hull, Brett	Dallas 99
Hunter, Dave	Edmonton 84,85,87
Hunter, Mark	Calgary 89
Hunter, Tim	Calgary 89
Hutton, Bouse	Ottawa 03,04
Hyland, Harry	Mtl Wanderers 10

I-J

Irving, Alex	Mtl AAA 1893, 94
Jackson, Art	Boston 41; Toronto 45
Jackson, Don	Edmonton 84,85
Jackson, Harold	Chicago 38; Detroit 43
Jackson, Harvey 'Busher'	Toronto 32
Jackson, Stan	Toronto 22
Jagr, Jaromir	Pittsburgh 91,92
James, George	Mtl AAA 1894
Jarvis, Doug	Montreal 76,77,78,79
Jeffrey, Larry	Toronto 67
Jenkins, Roger	Chicago 34,38
Jennings, Grant	Pittsburgh 91,92
Johnson, Ernie 'Moose'	Mtl Wanderers 06,07,08,10
Johnson, Ivan 'Ching'	NY Rangers 28,33
Johnson, Tom	Montreal 53,56,57,58,59,60
Johnson, Virgil	Chicago 38
Johnston, Ed	Boston 70,72
Johnstone, Charles	Winnipeg Vics 1896, 01
Johnstone, Ross	Toronto 45
Joliat, Aurel	Montreal 24,30,31
Jones, Robert	Mtl Victorias 1895,96
Jonsson, Tomas	NY Islanders 82,83
Juzda, Bill	Toronto 51

K

Kallur, Anders	NY Islanders 80,81,82,83
Kamensky, Valeri	Colorado 96
Kampman, Rudolph 'Bingo'	Toronto 42
Karakas, Mike	Chicago 38
Karpovtsev, Alexander	NY Rangers 94
Keane, Mike	Montreal 93; Colorado 96; Dallas 99
Keeling, Mel 'Butch'	NY Rangers 33
Kelly, Bob	Philadelphia 74,75
Kelly, Leonard 'Red'	Detroit 50,52,54,55; Toronto 62,63,64,67
Kelly, Pete	Detroit 36,37
Kendall, Bill	Chicago 34
Kennedy, Rod	Mtl Wanderers 06,07
Kennedy, Ted 'Teeder'	Toronto 45,47,48,49,51
Keon, Dave	Toronto 62,63,64,67
Kerr, Albert 'Dubbie'	Ottawa 09,11
Kerr, Dave	NY Rangers 40
Kilrea, Hec	Ottawa 27; Detroit 36,37
Kindrachuk, Orest	Philadelphia 74,75
Kingan, A.B.	Mtl AAA 1893,94
Kitchen, Chapman 'Hobey'	Mtl Maroons 26
Klein, Lloyd	Boston 29
Klemm, Jon	Colorado 96
Klima, Petr	Edmonton 90
Klukay, Joe	Toronto 47,48,49,51
Knuble, Michael	Detroit 98
Kocur, Joe	NY Rangers 94, Detroit 97, 98
Konstantinov, Vladimir	Detroit 97
Kordic, John	Montreal 86
Kovalev, Alexei	NY Rangers 94
Kozlov, Vyacheslav	Detroit 97, 98
Krupp, Uwe	Colorado 96
Krushelnyski, Mike	Edmonton 85,87,88
Kurri, Jari	Edmonton 84,85,87,88,90
Kurvers, Tom	Montreal 86
Kypreos, Nick	NY Rangers 94

L

Lach, Elmer	Montreal 44,46,53
Lacombe, Normand	Edmonton 88
Lafleur, Guy	Montreal 73,76,77,78,79
Lake, Fred	Ottawa 09,11
Lalonde, Edouard 'Newsy'	Montreal 16
Lalor, Mike	Montreal 86
Lamb, Mark	Edmonton 90
Lambert, Yvon	Montreal 76,77,78,79
Lamoureux, Leo	Montreal 44,46
Lane, Gord	NY Islanders 80,81,82,83
Lane, Myles	Boston 29
Langelle, Pete	Toronto 42
Langenbrunner, Jamie	Dallas 99
Langevin, Dave	NY Islanders 80,81,82,83
Langlois, Al	Montreal 58,59,60
Langway, Rod	Montreal 79
Laperriere, Jacques	Montreal 65,66,68,69,71,73
Lapointe, Guy	Montreal 71,73,76,77,78,79
Lapointe, Martin	Detroit 97, 98
Larionov, Igor	Detroit 97, 98
Larmer, Steve	NY Rangers 94
Larochelle, Wildor	Montreal 30,31
Larocque, Michel 'Bunny'	Montreal 76,77,78,79
Larose, Claude	Montreal 65,66,68,71,73
Larouche, Pierre	Montreal 78,79
Laviolette, Jack	Montreal 16
Leach, Jamie	Pittsburgh 92
Leach, Reg	Philadelphia 75
Lebeau, Stephan	Montreal 93
LeClair, Jack	Montreal 56
LeClair, John	Montreal 93
Leduc, Albert	Montreal 30,31
Leetch, Brian	NY Rangers 94
Leeman, Gary	Montreal 93
Lefebvre, Sylvain	Colorado 96
Lehtinen, Jere	Dallas 99
Lefley, Chuck	Montreal 71,73
Lehman, Hugh	Vancouver 15
Lemaire, Jacques	Montreal 68,69,71,73,76, 77,78,79
Lemay, Moe	Edmonton 87
Lemieux, Claude	Montreal 86; New Jersey 95; Colorado 96
Lemieux, Mario	Pittsburgh 91,92
Leonard	Quebec 12
Lepine, Alfred 'Pit'	Montreal 30,31
Leschyshyn, Curtis	Colorado 96
Lesieur, Art	Montreal 31
LeSueur, Percy	Ottawa 09,11
Lesuk, Bill	Boston 70
Leswick, Jack	Chicago 34
Leswick, Tony	Detroit 52,54,55
Levinsky, Alex	Toronto 32; Chicago 38
Lewicki, Dan	Toronto 51
Lewis, Gordon	Mtl Victorias 1896,97,98
Lewis, Herbie	Detroit 36,37
Lidster, Doug	NY Rangers 94
Liffiton, Charles	Mtl AAA 02; Mtl Wanderers 08
Lindsay, Ted	Detroit 50,52,54,55
Lidstrom, Nicklas	Detroit 97, 98
Lindstrom, Willy	Edmonton 84,85
Linseman, Ken	Edmonton 84
Liscombe, Carl	Detroit 43
Litzenberger, Eddie	Chicago 61; Toronto 62,63,64
Loney, Troy	Pittsburgh 91,92
Lonsberry, Ross	Philadelphia 74,75
Loob, Hakan	Calgary 89
Lorentz, Jim	Boston 70
Lorimer, Bob	NY Islanders 80,81
Loughlin, Clem	Victoria 25
Lowe, Jim	Mtl AAA 1893
Lowe, Kevin	Edmonton 84,85,87,88,90; NY Rangers 94
Lowery, Fred 'Frock'	Mtl Maroons 26
Ludwig, Craig	Montreal 86; Dallas 99
Lumley, Dave	Edmonton 84,85
Lumley, Harry	Detroit 50
Lupien, Gilles	Montreal 78,79
Lynn, Vic	Toronto 47,48,49

M

MacAdam, Al	Philadelphia 74
MacDonald, Kilby	NY Rangers 40
MacInnis, Al	Calgary 89
MacKay, Calum 'Baldy'	Montreal 53
MacKay, Duncan 'Mickey'	Vancouver 15; Boston 29
MacKenzie, Bill	Chicago 38
Mackie, Howie	Detroit 37
Mackell, Fleming	Toronto 49,51
MacLean, John	New Jersey 95
MacLeish, Rick	Philadelphia 74,75
MacLellan, Brian	Calgary 89
MacMillan, John	Toronto 62,63
Macoun, Jamie	Calgary 89; Detroit 98
MacPherson, James 'Bud'	Montreal 53
MacTavish, Craig	Edmonton 87,88,90; NY Rangers 94
Mahovlich, Frank	Toronto 62,63,64,67; Montreal 71,73
Mahovlich, Peter	Montreal 71,73,76,77
Majeau, Fern	Montreal 44
Maki, Ronald 'Chico'	Chicago 61
Maley, David	Montreal 86
Mallen, Ken	Vancouver 15
Malone, Jeff	Quebec 13
Malone, Joe	Quebec 12,13; Montreal 24
Maltby, Kirk	Detroit 97, 98
Mantha, Georges	Montreal 30,31
Mantha, Sylvio	Montreal 24,30,31
Marcetta, Milan	Toronto 67
March, Harold 'Mush'	Chicago 34,38
Marcotte, Don	Boston 70,72
Marini, Hector	NY Islanders 81,82
Marker, Gus	Mtl Maroons 35
Marks, Jack	Quebec 12,13; Toronto 18
Marshall, Don	Montreal 56,57,58,59,60
Marshall, Grant	Dallas 99
Marshall, Jack	Winnipeg Vics 01; Mtl AAA 02; Mtl Wanderers 07,10; Toronto 14
Martin, Clare	Detroit 50
Masnick, Paul	Montreal 53
Matteau, Stephane	NY Rangers 94
Matvichuk, Richard	Dallas 99
Matz, Johnny	Vancouver 15
Mazur, Eddie	Montreal 53
McAlpine, Chris	New Jersey 95
McCaffrey, Bert	Montreal 30,31
McCarty, Darren	Detroit 97, 98
McClelland, Kevin	Edmonton 84,85,87,88
McCool, Frank	Toronto 45
McCormack, John	Toronto 51; Montreal 53
McCreedy, John	Toronto 42,45
McCrimmon, Brad	Calgary 89
McDonald, Ab	Montreal 58,59,60; Chicago 61
McDonald, Jack	Quebec 12
McDonald, Lanny	Calgary 89
McDonald, Wilfrid 'Bucko'	Detroit 36,37; Toronto 42
McDougall, A.	Mtl Victorias 1895
McDougall, Bob	Mtl Victorias 1895,96,97,98
McDougall, Hartland	Mtl Victorias 1895,96,97,98
McEachern, Shawn	Pittsburgh 92
McEwen, Mike	NY Islanders 81,82,83
McFadden, Jim	Detroit 50
McFadyen, Don	Chicago 34
McGee, Frank	Ottawa 03,04,05
McGee, Jim	Ottawa 04
McGiffen, Roy 'Minnie'	Toronto 14
McGimsie, Billy	Kenora 07
McKay, Doug	Detroit 50
McKay, Randy	New Jersey 95
McKell, Jack	Ottawa 21
McKendry, Alex	NY Islanders 80
McKenna, Joe	Mtl Shamrocks 1899,1900
McKenney, Don	Toronto 64
McKenzie, John	Boston 70,72
McLea, Ernest	Mtl Victorias 1896,97,98
McLean, Jack	Toronto 45
McLellan	Mtl Victorias 1897
McMahon, Mike	Montreal 44
McManus, Sam	Mtl Maroons 35
McNab, Max	Detroit 50
McNamara, George	Toronto 14
McNamara, Howard	Montreal 16
McNeil, Gerry	Montreal 53,57,58
McPhee, Mike	Montreal 86
McReavy, Pat	Boston 41
McSorley, Marty	Edmonton 87,88
Meeker, Howie	Toronto 47,48,51
Meeking, Harry	Toronto 18; Victoria 25
Meger, Paul	Montreal 53
Melanson, Roland	NY Islanders 81,82,83
Melnyk, Larry	Edmonton 85
Menard, Henri	Mtl Wanderers 06
Merrick, Wayne	NY Islanders 80,81,82,83
Merrill, Horace	Ottawa 20
Merritt, G.H.	Winnipeg Vics 1896
Messier, Mark	Edmonton 84,85,87,88,90; NY Rangers 94
Metz, Don	Toronto 42,45,47,48,49
Metz, Nick	Toronto 42,45,47,48
Michayluk, Dave	Pittsburgh 92
Mikita, Stan	Chicago 61
Miller, Bill	Mtl Maroons 35
Miller, Earl	Toronto 32
Mironov, Dmitri	Detroit 98
Mitchell, Ivan	Toronto 22
Modano, Mike	Dallas 99
Molson, Percy	Mtl Victorias 1897
Mondou, Armand	Montreal 30,31
Mondou, Pierre	Montreal 77,78,79
Moog, Andy	Edmonton 84,85,87
Moore, Alfie	Chicago 38
Moore, Art	Ottawa 03,04,05
Moore, Dickie	Montreal 53,56,57,58,59,60
Moran, Paddy	Quebec 12,13
Morenz, Howie	Montreal 24,30,31
Morris, Bernie	Seattle 17
Morris, Elwin 'Moe'	Toronto 45
Morrow, Ken	NY Islanders 80,81,82,83
Mortson, Gus	Toronto 47,48,49,51
Mosdell, Kenny	Montreal 46,53,56,59
Motter, Alex	Detroit 43
Mowers, Johnny	Detroit 43
Mullen, Joe	Calgary 89, Pittsburgh 91,92
Muller, Kirk	Montreal 93
Mummery, Harry	Quebec 13; Toronto 18
Muni, Craig	Edmonton 87,88,90
Munro, Dunc	Mtl Maroons 26
Murdoch, Bob	Montreal 71,73
Murdoch, Murray	NY Rangers 28,33
Murphy, Joe	Edmonton 90
Murphy, Larry	Pittsburgh 91,92, Detroit 97, 98
Murphy, Ron	Chicago 61
Murray, Troy	Colorado 96
Murzyn, Dana	Calgary 89
Mussen, Clare	Mtl AAA 1894

N

Napier, Mark	Montreal 79; Edmonton 85
Naslund, Mats	Montreal 86
Nattress, Ric	Calgary 89
Needham, Mike	Pittsburgh 92
Nemchinov, Sergei	NY Rangers 94
Nesterenko, Eric	Chicago 61
Neville, Mike	Toronto 18
Nevin, Bob	Toronto 62,63
Nicholson, Billy	Mtl AAA 02
Niedermayer, Scott	New Jersey 95
Nieuwendyk, Joe	Calgary 89; Dallas 99
Nighbor, Frank	Vancouver 15; Ottawa 20,21,23,27
Nilan, Chris	Montreal 86
Nilsson, Kent	Edmonton 87
Noble, Reg	Toronto 18,22; Mtl Maroons 26
Nolan, Pat	Toronto 22
Nolet, Simon	Philadelphia 74
Noonan, Brian	NY Rangers 94
Northcott, Lawrence 'Baldy'	Mtl Maroons 35
Nyrop, Bill	Montreal 76,77,78
Nystrom, Bob	NY Islanders 80,81,82,83

O

Oatman, Eddie	Quebec 12
O'Brien, E.	Mtl AAA 1894
O'Connor, Herbert 'Buddy'	Montreal 44,46
Odelein, Lyle	Montreal 93
Olczyk, Ed	NY Rangers 94
Oliver, Harry	Boston 29
Olmstead, Bert	Montreal 53,56,57,58; Toronto 62
O'Neill, Tom	Toronto 45
Orlando, Jimmy	Detroit 43
Orr, Bobby	Boston 70,72
Osgood, Chris	Detroit 97, 98
Otto, Joel	Calgary 89
Owen, George	Boston 29
Ozolinsh, Sandis	Colorado 96

P

Paek, Jim	Pittsburgh 91,92
Palangio, Pete	Chicago 38
Pappin, Jim	Toronto 64,67
Parent, Bernie	Philadelphia 74,75
Paton, Tom	Mtl AAA 1893
Patrick, Frank	Vancouver 15
Patrick, Lester	Mtl Wanderers 06,07; NY Rangers 28
Patrick, Lynn	NY Rangers 40
Patrick, Murray 'Muzz'	NY Rangers 40
Patterson, Colin	Calgary 89
Pavelich, Marty	Detroit 50,52,54,55
Pederson, Barry	Pittsburgh 91
Peluso, Mike	New Jersey 95
Peplinski, Jim	Calgary 89
Persson, Stefan	NY Islanders 80,81,82,83
Peters, Garry	Boston 72
Peters, Jim	Montreal 46; Detroit 50,54
Pettinger, Gordon	NY Rangers 33; Detroit 36,37; Boston 39
Phillips, Bill	Mtl Maroons 26
Phillips, Tom	Kenora 07
Picard, Noel	Montreal 65
Pietrangelo, Frank	Pittsburgh 91
Pike, Alf	NY Rangers 40
Pilote, Pierre	Chicago 61
Pitre, Didier 'Pit'	Montreal 16
Plamondon, Gerry	Montreal 46
Plante, Derek	Dallas 99
Plante, Jacques	Montreal 53,56,57,58,59,60
Plasse, Michel	Montreal 73
Poile, Norman 'Bud'	Toronto 47
Polich, Mike	Montreal 77
Portland, Jack	Boston 39
Potvin, Denis	NY Islanders 80,81,82,83
Potvin, Jean	NY Islanders 80
Poulin, 'Skinner'	Montreal 16
Pouzar, Jaroslav	Edmonton 84,85,87
Power, 'Rocket'	Quebec 13
Pratt, Walter 'Babe'	NY Rangers 40; Toronto 45
Price, Noel	Montreal 66
Priestlay, Ken	Pittsburgh 92
Primeau, Joe	Toronto 32
Prodgers, George 'Goldie'	Quebec 12; Montreal 16
Pronovost, Andre	Montreal 57,58,59,60
Pronovost, Marcel	Detroit 50,52,54,55; Toronto 67
Provost, Claude	Montreal 56,57,58,59,60,65, 66,68,69
Prystai, Metro	Detroit 52,54
Pulford, Bob	Toronto 62,63,64,67
Pulford, Harvey	Ottawa 03,04,05
Pullan, William	Mtl Victorias 1895
Pusie, Jean	Montreal 31
Pushor, Jamie	Detroit 97

R

Racicot, Andre	Montreal 93
Ramage, Rob	Calgary 89, Montreal 93
Randall, Ken	Toronto 18,22
Ranford, Bill	Edmonton 88,90
Rankin, Norman	Mtl Victorias 1895
Reardon, Kenny	Montreal 46
Reardon, Terry	Boston 41
Reay, Billy	Montreal 46,53
Recchi, Mark	Pittsburgh 91
Reddick, Eldon	Edmonton 90
Redmond, Mickey	Montreal 68,69
Reibel, Earl 'Dutch'	Detroit 54,55
Reid, Dave	Dallas 99
Reise, Jr., Leo	Detroit 50,52
Resch, Glenn 'Chico'	NY Islanders 80
Ricci, Mike	Colorado 96
Richard, Henri	Montreal 56,57,58,59,60,65, 66,68,69,71,73
Richard, Maurice 'Rocket'	Montreal 44,46,53,56,57, 58,59,60
Richardson, Frank	Mtl Victorias 1898
Richer, Stephane	Montreal 86; New Jersey 95

Richter, Mike	NY Rangers 94
Rickey, Roy	Seattle 17
Ridpath, Bruce	Ottawa 11
Riley, Jim	Seattle 17
Risebrough, Doug	Montreal 76,77,78,79
Rivers, Gus	Montreal 30,31
Roach, John	Toronto 22
Roberge, Mario	Montreal 93
Roberto, Phil	Montreal 71
Roberts, Gary	Calgary 89
Roberts, Gord	Pittsburgh 91,92
Roberts, Jimmy	Montreal 65,66,73,76,77
Robertson, Earl	Detroit 37
Robertson, Fred	Toronto 32
Robinson, Earl	Mtl Maroons 35
Robinson, Larry	Montreal 73,76,77,78,79,86
Rochefort, Leon	Montreal 66,71
Rodden, Eddie	Boston 29
Rollins, Al	Toronto 51
Rolston, Brian	New Jersey 95
Romnes, Elwin 'Doc'	Chicago 34,38
Ronan, Ed	Montreal 93
Ronan, Skene	Montreal 16
Rooney, Steve	Montreal 86
Rooney, Walter	Quebec 12
Ross, Art	Kenora 07; Mtl Wanderers 08
Rothschild, Sam	Mtl Maroons 26
Roulston, William 'Rolly'	Detroit 37
Rouse, Bob	Detroit 97, 98
Rousseau, Bobby	Montreal 65,66,68,69
Routh, Harvie	Mtl AAA 1893,94
Rowe, Bob	Seattle 17
Roy, Patrick	Montreal 86, 93; Colorado 96
Ruotsalainen, Reijo	Edmonton 87,90
Russell, Ernie	Mtl Wanderers 06,07,08,10
Rychel, Warren	Colorado 96

S

St. Laurent, Dollard	Montreal 53,56,57,58; Chicago 61
Sakic, Joe	Colorado 96
Saleski, Don	Philadelphia 74,75
Samis, Phil	Toronto 48
Samuelsson, Kjell	Pittsburgh 92
Samuelsson, Ulf	Pittsburgh 91,92
Sanderson, Derek	Boston 70,72
Sands, Charlie	Boston 39
Sandstrom, Tomas	Detroit 97
Savard, Denis	Montreal 93
Savard, Serge	Montreal 68,69,73,76, 77,78,79
Sawchuk, Terry	Detroit 52,54,55; Toronto 67
Scanlon, Fred	Mtl Shamrocks 1899,1900
Schmidt, Milt	Boston 39,41
Schneider, Mathieu	Montreal 93
Schriner, David	Toronto 42,45
Schultz, Dave	Philadelphia 74,75
Scott	Ottawa 04
Scott, Laurie	NY Rangers 28
Seaborn, Jimmy	Vancouver 15
Seibert, Earl	NY Rangers 33; Chicago 38
Semenko, Dave	Edmonton 84,85
Sevigny, Richard	Montreal 79
Shack, Edward	Toronto 62,63,64,67
Shanahan, Brendan	Detroit 97, 98
Sheehan, Bobby	Montreal 71
Sheppard, John	Chicago 34
Sherf, John	Detroit 37
Shewchuk, Jack	Boston 41
Shibicky, Alex	NY Rangers 40
Shields, Allan	Mtl Maroons 35
Shill, Jack	Chicago 38
Schock, Dan	Boston 70
Shore, Eddie	Boston 29,39
Shore, Hamby	Ottawa 05,11
Shutt, Steve	Montreal 73,76,77,78,79
Siebert, Albert 'Babe'	Mtl Maroons 26; NY Rangers 33
Sim, Jonathan	Dallas 99
Simmons, Donald	Toronto 62,63,64
Simms, Percy	Ottawa 03
Simon, Chris	Colorado 96
Simon, John	Detroit 43
Simpson, Craig	Edmonton 88,90
Skinner, Alf	Toronto 18
Skov, Glen	Detroit 52,54,55
Skrudland, Brian	Montreal 86; Dallas 99
Sloan, Blake	Dallas 99
Sloan, Tod	Toronto 51; Chicago 61
Smail, Wally	Mtl Wanderers 08
Smith, Alex	Ottawa 27
Smith, Alf	Ottawa 04,05
Smith, Billy	NY Islanders 80,81,82,83
Smith, Bobby	Montreal 86
Smith, Clint	NY Rangers 40
Smith, Dallas	Boston 70,72
Smith, Des	Boston 41
Smith, Geoff	Edmonton 90
Smith, Normie	Detroit 36,37
Smith, Reginald 'Hooley'	Ottawa 27; Mtl Maroons 35
Smith, Rick	Boston 70
Smith, Sid	Toronto 48,49,51
Smith, Stan	NY Rangers 40
Smith, Steve	Edmonton 87,88,90
Smylie, Rod	Toronto 22
Soetaert, Doug	Montreal 86
Somers, Art	NY Rangers 33
Sorrell, John	Detroit 36,37
Speer, Bill	Boston 70
Spittal, Charles	Ottawa 23
Stackhouse, Ted	Toronto 22
Stanfield, Fred	Boston 70,72
Stanley, Allan	Toronto 62,63,64,67
Stanley, Russell 'Barney'	Vancouver 15
Stanowski, Wally	Toronto 42,45,47,48
Stanton, Paul	Pittsburgh 91,92
Starr, Wilf	Detroit 36
Stasiuk, Vic	Detroit 52,55
Stemkowski, Peter	Toronto 67
Stephenson, Wayne	Philadelphia 75
Stevens, Kevin	Pittsburgh 91,92
Stevens, Scott	New Jersey 95
Stewart, Gaye	Toronto 42,47
Stewart, John ''Black Jack'	Detroit 43,50
Stewart, James	Mtl AAA 1893,94
Stewart, Nels	Mtl Maroons 26
Stewart, Ron	Toronto 62,63,64
Strachan, Billy	Mtl Wanderers 06,07
Stuart, Bill	Toronto 22
Stuart, Bruce	Mtl Wanderers 08; Ottawa 09,11
Stuart, Hod	Mtl Wanderers 07
Suter, Gary	Calgary 89
Sutter, Brent	NY Islanders 82,83
Sutter, Duane	NY Islanders 80,81,82,83
Svoboda, Petr	Montreal 86
Sydor, Darryl	Dallas 99

T

Taglianetti, Peter	Pittsburgh 91,92
Talbot, Jean-Guy	Montreal 56,57,58,59, 60,65,66
Tambellini, Steve	NY Islanders 80
Tansey, Frank	Mtl Shamrocks 1899,1900
Tardif, Marc	Montreal 71,73
Taylor, Billy	Toronto 42
Taylor, Bobby	Philadelphia 74
Taylor, Fred 'Cyclone'	Ottawa 09; Vancouver 15
Taylor, Harry	Toronto 49
Taylor, Tim	Detroit 97
Terreri, Chris	New Jersey 95
Thompson, Cecil 'Tiny'	Boston 29
Thompson, Paul	NY Rangers 28; Chicago 34,38
Thomson, Jimmy	Toronto 47,48,49,51
Tikkanen, Esa	Edmonton 85,87,88,90; NY Rangers 94
Timgren, Ray	Toronto 49,51
Tocchet, Rick	Pittsburgh 92
Tonelli, John	NY Islanders 80,81,82,83
Tremblay, Gilles	Montreal 66,68
Tremblay, J.C.	Montreal 65,66,68,69,71
Tremblay, Mario	Montreal 76,77,78,79,86
Trihey, Harry	Mtl Shamrocks 1899,1900
Trottier, Bryan	NY Islanders 80,81,82,83 Pittsburgh 91,92
Trottier, Dave	Mtl Maroons 35
Trudel, Louis	Chicago 34,38
Turek, Roman	Dallas 99
Turner, Bob	Montreal 56,57,58,59,60

V

Vachon, Rogie	Montreal 68,69,71
Vadnais, Carol	Montreal 68; Boston 72
Van Impe, Ed	Philadelphia 74,75
Vasko, Elmer	Chicago 61
Verbeek, Pat	Dallas 99
Vernon, Mike	Calgary 89, Detroit 97
Vezina, Georges	Montreal 16,24
Voss, Carl	Chicago 38

W

Walker, Jack	Toronto 14; Seattle 17; Victoria 25
Wall, Frank	Mtl Shamrocks 1899,1900
Wallace, W.	Mtl Victorias 1896
Walsh, Marty	Ottawa 09,11
Walter, Ryan	Montreal 86
Walton, Mike	Toronto 67; Boston 72
Wamsley, Rick	Calgary 89
Wand, A.C. 'Toad'	Mtl AAA 1894
Ward, Aaron	Detroit 97, 98
Ward, Jimmy	Mtl Maroons 35
Wares, Eddie	Detroit 43
Wasnie, Nick	Montreal 30,31
Watson, Harry	Detroit 43; Toronto 47,48,49,51
Watson, Jimmy	Philadelphia 74,75
Watson, Joe	Philadelphia 74,75
Watson, Phil	NY Rangers 40; Montreal 44
Weiland, Ralph 'Cooney'	Boston 29,39
Wells, Jay	NY Rangers 94
Wentworth, Marvin 'Cy'	Mtl Maroons 35
Westfall, Ed	Boston 70,72
Westwick, Harry	Ottawa 03,04,05
Wharram, Ken	Chicago 61
White, Frank	Ottawa 05
Wiebe, Art	Chicago 38
Willett, Stanley	Mtl Victorias 1896
Wilson, Carol 'Cully'	Toronto 14; Seattle 17
Wilson, Johnny	Detroit 50,52,54,55
Wilson, Larry	Detroit 50
Wilson, Murray	Montreal 73,76,77
Wiseman, Eddie	Boston 41
Woit, Benny	Detroit 52,54,55
Wolanin, Craig	Colorado 96
Wood, Burke	Winnipeg Vics 01
Wood, F.H.	Ottawa 03
Worsley, Lorne 'Gump'	Montreal 65,66,68,69
Wregget, Ken	Pittsburgh 92

Y-Z

Yelle, Stephane	Colorado 96
Young, Doug	Detroit 36,37
Young, Scott	Pittsburgh 91, Colorado 96
Young, Wendell	Pittsburgh 91,92
Yzerman, Steve	Detroit 97, 98
Zeidel, Larry	Detroit 52
Zelepukin, Valeri	New Jersey 95
Zubov, Sergei	NY Rangers 94; Dallas 99

CHAPTER 19

Final Series Scoring Register

1918 – 1999

A

PLAYER	YRS	GP	G	A	TP	PIM
Clarence 'Taffy' Abel	4	16	0	1	1	22
Sid Abel	7	34	9	11	20	25
Keith Acton	1	5	1	0	1	0
Bill Adams	1	4	0	0	0	0
Greg Adams	1	7	1	2	3	2
Jack Adams	3	14	8	2	10	8
Stewart Adams	1	5	2	1	3	2
Tommy Albelin	1	4	0	2	2	2
George Allen	2	10	4	3	7	10
Keith Allen	1	3	0	0	0	0
Ray Allison	1	1	0	0	0	2
Earl Anderson	1	2	0	0	0	0
Ernie Anderson	1	2	0	0	0	2
Glenn Anderson	7	38	16	13	29	59
Jocko Anderson	2	5	1	0	1	10
Ron Anderson	1	1	0	0	0	2
Kent-Erik Andersson	1	5	1	0	1	0
Lloyd Andrews	1	5	2	0	2	3
Lou Angotti	2	13	3	3	6	9
Shawn Antoski	1	7	0	1	1	8
Syl Apps	6	32	10	11	21	6
Al Arbour	7	20	0	2	2	6
Ernest 'Ty' Arbour	2	7	1	0	1	0
Bob Armstrong	2	10	1	1	2	8
George Armstrong	6	33	9	13	22	22
Murray Armstrong	2	9	2	0	2	0
Ossie Asmundson	1	4	0	1	1	2
Ossie Aubuchon	1	1	0	0	0	0
Larry Aurie	2	8	2	3	5	2
Don Awrey	2	10	0	1	1	33

B

PLAYER	YRS	GP	G	A	TP	PIM
Pete Babando	1	5	2	2	4	2
Dave Babych	1	7	1	0	1	2
Ralph Backstrom	8	42	11	12	23	22
Garnet 'Ace' Bailey	1	6	1	0	1	14
Irvine 'Ace' Bailey	1	7	1	0	1	2
Earl Balfour	1	6	0	0	0	0
Murray Balfour	2	11	4	4	8	15
Dave Balon	3	16	2	4	6	18
Bill Barber	4	22	5	10	15	17
Bill Barilko	4	19	1	3	4	33
Doug Barkley	2	12	0	3	3	14
Norm Barnes	1	1	0	0	0	4
Stu Barnes	2	10	4	0	4	2
Fred Barrett	1	3	0	0	0	6
Marty Barry	3	11	5	3	8	8
Robin Bartel	1	4	0	0	0	12
Jim Bartlett	1	2	0	0	0	0
Andy Bathgate	2	13	4	5	9	16
Bobby Bauer	3	19	5	2	7	2
Bob Baun	6	32	2	6	8	67
Paul Baxter	1	4	0	1	1	17
Jean Beliveau	12	64	30	32	62	78
Billy Bell	1	3	0	0	0	0
Neil Belland	1	4	0	0	0	4
Brian Bellows	3	15	3	4	7	20
Clint Benedict	1	6	0	0	0	2
Bobby Benson	1	2	0	0	0	0
Doug Bentley	1	4	1	2	3	2
Max Bentley	3	13	4	10	14	2
Gordon 'Red' Berenson	4	19	3	2	5	17
Perry Berezan	2	3	0	0	0	4
Todd Bergen	1	4	1	1	2	0
Gary Bergman	1	6	0	1	1	4
Louis Berlinquette	*1	5	1	1	2	0
Craig Berube	1	4	0	0	0	0
Jeff Beukeboom	2	11	0	2	2	25
Jack Bionda	1	5	0	0	0	6
Steve Black	1	6	0	0	0	0
Tom Bladon	3	14	1	5	6	31
Andy Blair	4	12	2	0	2	6
Hector 'Toe' Blake	3	15	4	9	13	7
Rob Blake	1	5	0	1	1	18
Russ Blinco	1	3	1	1	2	0
Gus Bodnar	2	8	1	0	1	2
Garth Boesch	3	14	1	0	1	10
Serge Boisvert	1	2	0	0	0	0
Leo Boivin	3	17	0	2	2	19
Ivan Boldirev	1	4	2	0	2	2
Frank 'Buzz' Boll	4	11	3	1	4	2
Peter Bondra	1	4	1	1	2	4
Marcel Bonin	4	21	3	6	9	22
Carl Boone	2	11	0	1	1	14
Christian Bordeleau	1	3	0	0	0	0
J.P. Bordeleau	1	6	1	0	1	4
Mike Bossy	5	23	17	17	34	4
Helge Bostrum	3	8	1	0	1	8
Emile 'Butch' Bouchard	9	44	2	10	12	61
Pierre Bouchard	5	21	3	1	4	19
Billy Boucher	1	4	0	0	0	0
Bobby Boucher	3	11	6	2	8	19
Frank Boucher	7	25	11	7	18	8
George Boucher	*4	20	6	1	7	45
Andre Boudrias	1	3	0	0	0	2
Leo Bourgeault	2	7	0	0	0	6
Bob Bourne	4	19	4	9	13	37
Phil Bourque	2	10	3	2	5	4
Raymond Bourque	2	10	3	5	8	12
Paul Boutilier	1	5	0	2	2	0
Ralph 'Scotty' Bowman	2	9	1	1	2	4
Bill Boyd	2	6	0	0	0	2
Irwin 'Yank' Boyd	1	4	0	0	0	2
Steve Bozek	1	4	2	0	2	19
Connie Braden	2	5	0	1	1	0
Brian Bradley	1	1	0	0	0	0
Per-Olov Brasar	1	1	0	0	0	0
Doug Brennan	2	7	1	0	1	6
Carl Brewer	5	25	0	6	6	56
Andy Brickley	1	2	0	0	0	0
Mel Bridgman	2	10	1	5	6	57
Rod Brind'Amour	1	4	3	1	4	0
Patrice Brisebois	1	5	0	0	0	8
H.'Punch' Broadbent	*4	19	9	1	10	34
Neal Broten	3	15	6	5	11	4
Adam Brown	2	9	0	1	1	6
Connie Brown	1	3	0	2	2	0
Curtis Brown	1	6	0	1	1	2
Dave Brown	2	8	0	1	1	30
Doug Brown	3	12	3	6	9	4
Fred Brown	1	5	0	0	0	0
Jeff Brown	2	9	3	3	6	8
Jerry Brown	1	7	2	0	2	4
Rob Brown	1	3	0	0	0	2
Morley Bruce	1	5	0	0	0	0
Eddie Bruneteau	3	12	2	1	3	0
Benoit Brunet	1	5	0	1	1	2
Moderre 'Mud' Bruneteau	6	30	8	4	12	8
Sergei Brylin	1	3	1	1	2	4
Kelly Buchberger	2	8	0	0	0	7
John Bucyk	6	29	8	6	14	14
Tony Bukovich	1	1	0	0	0	0
Pavel Bure	1	7	3	5	8	15
Marc Bureau	1	6	1	0	1	8
Marty Burke	2	7	0	2	2	2
Shawn Burr	1	2	0	0	0	0
Randy Burridge	2	10	1	3	4	4
Cummy Burton	1	1	0	0	0	0
Eddie Bush	1	6	1	5	6	16
Rod Buskas	1	3	0	1	1	0
Mike Busniuk	1	6	2	1	3	7
Walter Buswell	1	4	0	1	1	2
Garth Butcher	1	1	0	0	0	0
John Byce	1	3	1	0	1	0
Lyndon Byers	1	2	1	0	1	0

C

PLAYER	YRS	GP	G	A	TP	PIM
Jack Caffery	1	5	0	0	0	0
Herb Cain	4	14	0	5	5	2
Jock Callender	1	4	0	0	0	0
Pat Callighen	1	5	0	0	0	0
Billy Cameron	1	4	0	0	0	0
Craig Cameron	2	3	1	0	1	0
Harry Cameron	*2	9	3	3	6	23
Colin Campbell	1	4	0	1	1	26
'Spiff' Campbell	1	2	0	0	0	0
Guy Carbonneau	4	22	0	4	4	29
Terry Carkner	1	4	0	0	0	4
Wayne Carleton	1	4	1	1	2	0
Jack Carlson	1	2	0	0	0	0
Bob Carpenter	2	9	0	1	1	4
Gene Carr	1	6	0	0	0	9
Lorne Carr	2	14	3	2	5	11
Larry Carriere	1	6	0	0	0	4
Gene Carrigan	1	3	0	0	0	0
Billy Carroll	5	16	2	4	6	2
Bill Carson	2	4	1	0	1	2
Frank Carson	3	11	0	1	1	0
Gerald Carson	2	3	0	0	0	0
Jimmy Carson	1	2	0	1	1	0
Lindsay Carson	2	9	1	2	3	2
John Carter	1	5	1	0	1	19
Joe Carveth	4	25	7	4	11	6
Wayne Cashman	5	26	7	6	13	79
E.'Murph' Chamberlain	7	29	5	2	7	18
Shawn Chambers	3	16	2	4	6	8
Rick Chartraw	4	14	2	1	3	16
Chris Chelios	3	15	3	13	16	48
Real Chevrefils	2	10	0	1	1	8
Tom Chorske	1	3	0	2	2	0
Dave Christian	1	5	0	0	0	0
Steve Christoff	1	5	2	2	4	0
Jack Church	3	8	0	1	1	4
Shane Churla	1	5	0	0	0	4
Dino Ciccarelli	2	9	4	3	7	25
Frank 'King' Clancy	6	24	5	3	8	28
Aubrey 'Dit' Clapper	6	18	2	2	4	2
Bobby Clarke	4	22	9	12	21	22
Odie Cleghorn	3	13	2	1	3	9
Sprague Cleghorn	5	22	3	4	7	48
Bill Clement	2	8	2	0	2	4
Paul Coffey	7	33	8	18	26	30
Mac Colville	2	11	0	2	2	6
Neil Colville	2	11	3	4	7	12
Brian Conacher	1	6	1	1	2	19
Charlie Conacher	4	14	3	3	6	14
Jim Conacher	4	4	1	0	1	0
Lionel Conacher	2	7	1	0	1	10
Pat Conacher	2	7	2	0	2	2
Roy Conacher	3	10	6	4	10	6
Harry Connor	1	2	0	0	0	0
Bill Cook	4	14	3	5	8	24
Fred 'Bun' Cook	4	14	5	2	7	18
Leo Cook	1	5	0	0	0	6
Lloyd Cook	*5	21	5	2	7	38
Tom Cook	2	9	0	1	1	7
Joe Cooper	2	9	1	2	3	18
Bert Corbeau	*1	5	0	1	1	3
Rene Corbet	1	4	2	1	3	0
Shayne Corson	1	6	0	1	1	18
Les Costello	1	4	1	2	3	0
Murray Costello	1	2	0	0	0	0
Charlie Cotch	2	3	0	0	0	0
Ray Cote	1	4	0	0	0	0
Harold 'Baldy' Cotton	3	10	1	2	3	12
Art Coulter	3	15	2	2	4	18
Yvan Cournoyer	9	50	21	19	40	18
Yves Courteau	1	1	0	0	0	0
Geoff Courtnall	2	12	4	1	5	11

PLAYER	YRS	GP	G	A	TP	PIM
Russ Courtnall	1	6	2	0	2	12
Billy Coutu	*4	17	1	1	2	12
Gerry Couture	2	10	4	2	6	0
Rosie 'Lolo' Couture	2	9	1	2	3	4
Bruce Cowick	1	6	0	0	0	7
Bill Cowley	3	14	1	11	12	6
Murray Craven	3	18	3	4	7	10
Jack Crawford	4	17	3	3	6	6
Marc Crawford	1	3	0	0	0	0
Russell 'Rusty' Crawford	*1	2	0	0	0	0
Dave Creighton	2	10	1	2	3	0
Terry Crisp	6	23	1	6	7	4
Doug Crossman	2	12	1	4	5	18
Keith Crowder	1	5	0	1	1	10
Barry Cullen	1	1	0	0	0	0
Brian Cullen	1	3	0	0	0	0
Floyd Curry	8	41	12	8	20	10

D

PLAYER	YRS	GP	G	A	TP	PIM
Ulf Dahlen	1	6	2	2	4	0
Kjell Dahlin	1	4	1	0	1	0
Chris Dahlquist	1	6	0	1	1	4
Carl 'Cully' Dahlstrom	2	8	1	3	4	2
J.J. Daigneault	2	10	1	0	1	6
Bob Dailey	1	6	1	3	4	4
Vincent Damphousse	1	5	1	3	4	8
Ken Daneyko	1	4	0	0	0	6
Harry Darragh	1	3	0	0	0	0
Jack Darragh	*2	10	10	2	12	10
Bob Davidson	6	33	2	7	9	31
Lorne Davis	2	12	1	0	1	8
Bob Dawes	2	5	0	0	0	4
Clarence 'Hap' Day	4	14	1	3	4	14
Adam Deadmarsh	1	4	0	4	4	4
Lucien DeBlois	1	2	0	0	0	0
Ron Delorme	1	4	0	0	0	4
Alex Delvecchio	8	47	16	22	38	2
Ab DeMarco	2	5	1	0	1	0
Corb Denneny	3	13	6	3	9	2
Cy Denneny	5	21	7	5	12	21
Norm Dennis	1	1	0	0	0	2
Syd Desireau	2	6	0	0	0	0
Eric Desjardins	4	15	3	3	6	108
Vic Desjardins	2	8	0	0	0	0
Al Dewsbury	2	6	0	3	3	8
Ernie Dickens	1	5	0	0	0	4
Gerald Diduck	1	7	0	1	1	6
Bob Dillabough	2	2	0	0	0	0
Cecil Dillon	3	12	4	3	7	8
Bill Dineen	3	19	1	0	1	6
Gord Dineen	1	3	0	0	0	24
Chuck Dinsmore	1	4	0	0	0	2
Gilbert Dionne	1	5	1	1	2	4
Paul DiPietro	1	5	2	0	2	0
Gary Doak	4	19	1	0	1	44
Mike Donnelly	1	5	1	1	2	0
Ken Doraty	2	5	3	0	3	2
Jim Dorey	1	1	0	0	0	0
Gary Dornhoefer	3	13	2	1	3	20
Kent Douglas	1	5	0	1	1	2
Les Douglas	1	4	2	1	3	2
Peter Douris	1	1	0	0	0	0
Jim Dowd	1	1	1	1	2	2
Kris Draper	3	12	1	1	2	8
Gordie Drillon	4	20	6	3	9	6
Bruce Driver	1	4	1	2	3	0
John Druce	1	4	0	0	0	0
Gilles Dube	1	2	0	0	0	0
Gaetan Duchesne	1	6	1	1	2	6
Rick Dudley	1	4	0	1	1	9
Dick Duff	9	47	15	20	35	39
Donald Dufresne	1	1	0	0	0	0
Ron Duguay	1	5	2	0	2	4
Woody Dumart	4	19	2	6	8	4
Art Duncan	4	16	4	4	8	10
Andre 'Moose' Dupont	4	22	4	3	7	64
Mervyn 'Red' Dutton	2	2	1	1	2	17
Miroslav Dvorak	1	5	0	0	0	2
Radek Dvorak	1	1	0	0	0	0
Cecil 'Babe' Dye	1	5	9	1	10	3
Karl Dykhuis	1	3	0	0	0	2

E

PLAYER	YRS	GP	G	A	TP	PIM
Mike Eagles	1	2	0	0	0	0
Mike Eaves	1	2	0	0	0	2
Tim Ecclestone	3	12	0	2	2	18
Frank Eddolls	3	16	0	1	1	4
Darryl Edestrand	2	8	0	0	0	2
Gary Edmundson	1	4	0	1	1	2
Pat Egan	2	12	2	1	3	8
Gerry Ehman	3	15	1	4	5	8
Pelle Eklund	1	7	1	7	8	0
Anders Eldebrink	1	3	0	0	0	2
Ron Ellis	1	6	1	1	2	4
Wally Elmer	1	2	0	0	0	0
Leighton 'Hap' Emms	1	3	0	0	0	2
Brian Engblom	2	6	0	0	0	0
Aut Erickson	1	1	0	0	0	2
Anders Eriksson	1	4	0	1	1	4
Thomas Eriksson	1	4	0	0	0	0
Bob Errey	3	13	3	1	4	12
Phil Esposito	5	28	7	17	24	46
Jack Evans	2	12	1	0	1	22
Stewart Evans	1	3	0	0	0	4
Bill Ezinicki	3	14	2	2	4	30

F

PLAYER	YRS	GP	G	A	TP	PIM
Bill Fairbairn	1	6	0	2	2	0
Pat Falloon	1	3	0	0	0	2
Dave Farrish	1	1	0	0	0	0
Alex Faulkner	2	6	2	0	2	2
Sergei Fedorov	3	12	7	7	14	2
John Ferguson	6	33	5	6	11	69
Lorne Ferguson	1	5	0	1	1	8
Viacheslav Fetisov	3	12	0	8	8	12
Bob Fillion	3	12	2	0	2	4
Frank Finnigan	4	14	4	4	8	8
Dunc Fisher	1	7	2	2	4	12
Joe Fisher	1	1	0	0	0	0
Tom Fitzgerald	1	4	1	0	1	0
Fern Flaman	3	14	0	2	2	23
Patrick Flatley	1	5	1	3	4	8
Reg Fleming	2	12	3	0	3	20
Bill Flett	1	6	0	3	3	4
Theoren Fleury	1	6	1	1	2	2
Lee Fogolin, Jr.	4	18	0	3	3	14
Lee Fogolin, Sr.	3	9	0	1	1	8
Rick Foley	1	4	0	1	1	4
Val Fonteyne	3	17	0	2	2	0
Adam Foote	1	4	0	1	1	4
Colin Forbes	1	3	0	0	0	0
Dave Forbes	2	10	0	1	1	2
Peter Forsberg	1	4	3	2	5	0
Ray Fortin	1	3	0	0	0	6
Nick Fotiu	1	2	0	1	1	10
Jimmy Fowler	2	8	0	2	2	0
Frank Foyston	*4	18	16	2	18	9
Ron Francis	2	10	4	5	9	6
Curt Fraser	1	4	0	3	3	28
Gord Fraser	2	8	2	1	3	20
Frank Fredrickson	3	12	4	4	8	32
Len Frig	1	4	1	1	2	0

G

PLAYER	YRS	GP	G	A	TP	PIM
Bill Gadsby	3	18	1	3	4	28
Art Gagne	1	2	0	0	0	2
Dave Gagner	1	6	4	2	6	14
Johnny Gagnon	1	5	4	2	6	2
Bob Gainey	6	30	5	5	10	46
Norman 'Dutch' Gainor	3	6	1	0	1	2
Percy Galbraith	3	8	1	0	1	4
John Gallagher	1	5	1	0	1	8
Don Gallinger	2	9	1	3	4	4
Garry Galley	1	5	0	0	0	4
Dick Gamble	2	4	0	0	0	2
Bert Gardiner	1	2	0	0	0	0
Herb Gardiner	1	2	1	0	1	0
Cal Gardner	3	14	1	1	2	0
Danny Gare	1	6	2	1	3	4
Johan Garpenlov	1	4	0	1	1	2
Fern Gauthier	1	4	1	0	1	5
Stewart Gavin	1	6	0	3	3	2
George Gee	2	11	3	5	8	14
Martin Gelinas	2	12	1	1	2	6
Bernie Geoffrion	10	53	24	22	46	32
Eddie Gerard	*4	11	3	1	4	51
Ray Getliffe	2	9	2	1	3	6
Roy 'Gus' Giesebrecht	2	6	0	1	1	0
Greg Gilbert	4	16	1	4	5	38
Rod Gilbert	1	6	4	3	7	11
Brent Gilchrist	1	2	0	0	0	4
Curt Giles	1	5	0	0	0	2
Randy Gilhen	1	5	0	0	0	12
Clark Gillies	5	24	9	14	23	35
Doug Gilmour	1	6	4	3	7	6
Gaston Gingras	1	4	2	1	3	0
Fred Glover	1	2	0	0	0	0
Howie Glover	1	6	1	0	1	0
Brian Glynn	2	13	9	1	1	6
Warren Godfrey	3	12	0	1	1	10
Pete Goegan	2	11	0	0	0	16
Bob Goldham	5	30	2	5	7	30
Leroy Goldsworthy	2	5	0	0	0	0
Hank Goldup	2	9	2	1	3	0
Sergei Gonchar	1	4	0	1	1	4
Larry Goodenough	2	6	1	3	4	4
Ebbie Goodfellow	3	12	1	2	3	20
Jack Gordon	1	4	0	1	1	2
Tom Gorence	1	5	1	1	2	16
Butch Goring	5	24	9	7	16	2
Ed Gorman	1	4	0	0	0	0
Johnny Gottselig	4	15	6	5	11	6
Bob Gould	1	4	0	0	0	0
Michel Goulet	1	4	1	0	1	2
Phil Goyette	6	27	3	5	8	8
Bob Gracie	3	10	1	2	3	0
Thomas Gradin	1	4	3	2	5	2
Dirk Graham	1	4	4	0	4	0
Ted Graham	2	9	0	1	1	14
Tony Granato	1	5	1	3	4	10
Danny Grant	1	4	0	0	0	0
Leo Gravelle	1	4	2	0	2	2
Adam Graves	2	12	3	3	6	4
Alex Gray	1	5	0	0	0	0
Terry Gray	2	7	2	0	2	8
Red Green	1	1	0	0	0	0
Rick Green	2	11	2	0	2	2
Ted Green	1	4	0	0	0	0
Randy Gregg	6	31	2	7	9	8
George Gregor	1	1	0	0	0	0
Ron Greschner	1	5	1	0	1	8
Wayne Gretzky	6	31	18	35	53	8
Si Griffis	*1	5	1	0	1	9
Stu Grimson	2	4	0	1	1	2
Michal Grosek	1	1	0	0	0	0
Don Grosso	3	15	7	5	12	14
Bill Guerin	1	4	0	4	4	12
Jocelyn Guevremont	1	6	0	1	1	8
Armand 'Bep' Guidolin	3	10	2	2	4	19
Alexei Gusarov	1	4	0	2	2	2

H

PLAYER	YRS	GP	G	A	TP	PIM
Len Hachborn	1	1	0	0	0	0
Vic Hadfield	1	6	1	3	4	16
Matti Hagman	1	1	0	0	0	0
Bill Hajt	1	6	1	0	1	2
Harold 'Slim' Halderson	2	8	3	1	4	16
Joe Hall	*1	5	0	0	0	6
Murray Hall	1	1	0	0	0	0
Kevin Haller	1	3	0	1	1	0
Milt Halliday	1	4	0	0	0	0
Mats Hallin	1	2	0	0	0	0
Doug Halward	1	4	0	1	1	4
Robert 'Red' Hamill	1	5	0	0	0	2
Reg Hamilton	4	17	0	1	1	6
Dave Hannan	1	3	0	0	0	0
Mark Hardy	1	4	0	1	1	4
Glen Harmon	3	15	2	3	5	0
John Harms	1	4	3	0	3	2
Terry Harper	6	34	1	4	5	47
Billy Harris	5	26	6	5	11	18
Ted Harris	6	33	1	7	8	64
T. 'Smokey' Harris	*2	9	3	1	4	16
Wilfrid 'Gizzy' Hart	2	8	5	2	7	18
Dominik Hasek	6	0	0	0	0	2
Derian Hatcher	1	6	1	1	2	10
Craig Hartsburg	1	5	1	4	5	2
Doug Harvey	11	54	4	31	35	60
Dale Hawerchuk	1	3	0	0	0	0
Greg Hawgood	2	7	2	2	4	4
Bill Hay	3	19	2	7	9	12
Jim Hay	1	5	1	0	1	0
Fern 'Curly' Headly	1	4	0	0	0	0
Anders Hedberg	1	5	1	2	3	2
Bret Hedican	1	7	1	3	4	4
Jerry Heffernan	1	2	0	1	1	0

Ott Heller	4	18	2	3	5	19
Harry Helman	1	2	0	0	0	0
Murray Henderson	1	5	1	0	1	0
Paul Henderson	2	13	2	3	5	8
Lorne Henning	1	6	1	1	2	0
Camille Henry	2	9	1	0	1	2
Jimmy Herberts	1	4	1	0	1	18
Robert 'Red' Heron	2	8	1	0	1	4
Bryan Hextall	1	6	4	1	5	7
Bill Hicke	2	5	0	1	1	0
Pat Hickey	1	5	1	2	3	0
Wayne Hicks	1	1	0	0	0	2
Al Hill	1	6	0	0	0	2
Mel Hill	3	16	3	4	7	8
Sean Hill	1	1	0	0	0	0
Wilbert 'Dutch' Hiller	2	11	3	3	6	0
Larry Hillman	4	22	1	1	2	6
Wayne Hillman	1	1	0	0	0	0
Lionel Hitchman	4	13	1	0	1	35
Ivan Hlinka	1	2	0	0	0	0
Ken Hodge	3	16	6	10	16	27
Benoit Hogue	1	2	0	0	0	2
Bobby Holik	1	4	1	1	2	8
Bill 'Flash' Hollett	5	23	4	4	8	4
Gord Hollingworth	1	2	0	0	0	2
Paul Holmgren	1	5	4	4	8	15
Tomas Holmstrom	1	4	1	4	5	2
Albert 'Toots' Holway	1	2	0	0	0	0
Brian Holzinger	1	6	0	1	1	9
Pete Horeck	2	8	3	3	6	12
Reginald 'Red' Horner	7	28	3	6	9	54
Tim Horton	6	33	4	16	20	38
Bronco Horvath	2	12	4	2	6	6
Ed Hospodar	1	5	0	0	0	34
Mike Hough	1	4	0	0	0	0
Rejean Houle	4	24	3	10	13	16
Phil Housley	1	4	0	0	0	2
Garry Howatt	1	6	0	1	1	21
Gordie Howe	10	55	18	32	50	94
Mark Howe	3	14	1	2	3	0
Syd Howe	6	28	8	12	20	4
Jiri Hrdina	3	8	0	0	0	0
Tony Hrkac	1	3	0	1	1	2
Charlie Huddy	7	31	1	11	12	28
Mike Hudson	1	4	0	0	0	2
Pat Hughes	3	13	0	3	3	8
Bobby Hull	4	26	11	17	28	26
Brett Hull	2	7	3	0	3	0
Dennis Hull	3	14	6	5	11	6
Jody Hull	1	2	0	0	0	0
Dale Hunter	1	4	0	1	1	2
Dave Hunter	4	19	1	2	3	43
Mark Hunter	1	4	0	1	1	12
Tim Hunter	3	16	0	3	3	67

I-J

PLAYER	YRS	GP	G	A	TP	PIM
Frank Ingram	1	5	0	1	1	2
Ted Irvine	1	6	1	4	5	10
Art Jackson	4	19	4	1	5	7
Don Jackson	3	14	0	0	0	52
Hal Jackson	3	15	0	1	1	8
Harvey 'Busher' Jackson	7	25	7	5	12	25
Jaromir Jagr	2	10	2	5	7	2
Jerry James	1	4	0	0	0	0
Craig Janney	2	10	0	2	2	0
Doug Jarrett	3	20	1	2	3	12
Doug Jarvis	4	19	0	6	6	12
Larry Jeffrey	2	12	3	3	6	8
Roger Jenkins	2	8	0	2	2	6
Bill Jennings	1	4	1	1	2	0
Grant Jennings	1	2	0	0	0	2
Calle Johansson	1	4	0	1	1	2
Allan Johnson	1	6	1	2	3	0
Ivan 'Ching' Johnson	5	19	1	2	3	48
Jim Johnson	1	6	0	1	1	10
Norm Johnson	1	6	2	0	2	4
Terry Johnson	1	2	0	0	0	12
Tom Johnson	10	49	6	3	9	44
Virgil Johnson	2	6	0	1	1	2
Greg Johnston	2	5	1	1	2	4
Ed Johnstone	1	5	0	0	0	2
Aurel Joliat	4	15	5	4	9	24
Stan Jonathan	2	10	0	0	0	24
Tomas Jonsson	3	11	1	2	3	18
Ed Jovanovski	1	4	0	2	2	11
Eddie Joyal	2	12	3	1	4	6
Bob Joyce	1	5	1	1	2	0
Joe Juneau	2	10	1	4	5	0
Bill Juzda	2	9	0	0	0	6

K

PLAYER	YRS	GP	G	A	TP	PIM
Alex Kaleta	1	7	0	3	3	0
Anders Kallur	4	18	3	4	7	8
Valeri Kamensky	1	4	1	2	3	8
Rudolph 'Bingo' Kampman	4	22	1	3	4	45
Alexander Karpovtsev	1	2	0	0	0	0
Steve Kasper	1	5	2	0	2	2
Mike Keane	4	20	2	7	9	6
Gordon 'Duke' Keats	1	2	0	0	0	4
Mel 'Butch' Keeling	4	14	4	2	6	16
Larry Keenan	3	12	2	0	2	8
Bob Kelly	3	15	3	2	5	18
Leonard 'Red' Kelly	12	65	11	20	31	29
Pete Kelly	2	7	1	1	2	0
Reginald 'Pep' Kelly	5	17	2	2	4	0
Bill Kendall	1	1	0	0	0	0
Ted 'Teeder' Kennedy	5	26	12	11	23	8
Dave Keon	4	24	11	5	16	0
Tim Kerr	1	3	2	1	3	9
Hec Kilrea	4	15	0	4	4	4
Ken Kilrea	1	2	0	0	0	0
Wally Kilrea	2	9	2	2	4	4
Orest Kindrachuk	3	15	2	2	4	13
Trent Klatt	1	4	0	0	0	6
Ken Klee	1	2	0	0	0	0
Jon Klemm	1	4	2	0	2	0
Lloyd Klein	1	1	0	0	0	0
Petr Klima	1	5	1	0	1	0
Joe Klukay	5	24	2	4	6	11
Gord Kluzak	1	5	0	1	1	4
Joe Kocur	3	14	2	1	3	6
Vladimir Konstantinov	2	8	0	0	0	10
Jerry Korab	3	11	2	1	3	26
Dan Kordic	1	1	0	0	0	0
John Kordic	1	5	0	0	0	15
Cliff Koroll	2	13	3	5	8	6
Alexei Kovalev	1	7	4	3	7	2
Vyacheslav Kozlov	3	12	1	3	4	0
Igor Kravchuk	1	4	0	0	0	2
Uwe Krupp	1	4	2	1	3	2
Paul Kruse	1	0	0	0	0	0
Mike Krushelnyski	4	19	4	5	9	16
Todd Krygier	1	2	0	0	0	2
Dave Kryskow	1	3	2	0	2	0
Frantisek Kucera	1	4	0	0	0	0
Jari Kurri	7	36	15	24	39	16
Merv Kuryluk	1	2	0	0	0	0
Gus Kyle	1	7	1	0	1	14
Nick Kypreos	1	1	0	0	0	0

L

PLAYER	YRS	GP	G	A	TP	PIM
Leo Labine	4	22	3	4	7	24
Elmer Lach	6	27	8	10	18	6
Normand Lacombe	1	5	1	0	1	4
Dan Lacroix	1	2	0	0	0	2
Nathan Lafayette	1	7	0	3	3	0
Guy Lafleur	5	25	9	17	26	14
Pat LaFontaine	1	5	2	1	3	0
E.'Newsy' Lalonde	*1	5	6	0	6	3
Mike Lalor	1	5	0	2	2	19
Joe Lamb	1	4	0	0	0	21
Mark Lamb	1	5	0	3	3	2
Yvon Lambert	4	18	5	8	13	16
Leo Lamoureux	3	11	0	1	1	8
Jack Lancien	1	2	0	0	0	0
Gord Lane	4	19	1	0	1	70
Miles Lane	2	4	0	0	0	0
Pete Langelle	3	17	1	3	4	0
Jamie Langenbrunner	1	6	1	2	3	4
Dave Langevin	5	21	0	3	3	26
Al Langlois	4	18	0	2	2	22
Rod Langway	1	5	0	0	0	12
Jean Lanthier	1	2	0	0	0	4
Jacques Laperriere	5	23	1	4	5	32
Guy Lapointe	5	27	3	11	14	40
Martin Lapointe	3	10	4	3	7	20
Edgar Laprade	1	7	3	3	6	2
Igor Larionov	2	8	0	2	2	8
Steve Larmer	2	11	4	1	5	4
Wildor Larochelle	2	7	0	1	1	14
Claude Larose	6	27	3	6	9	21
Pierre Larouche	2	3	1	0	1	0
Reed Larson	1	2	0	0	0	2
Paul Laus	1	4	0	0	0	2
Hal Laycoe	1	5	0	1	1	10
Reggie Leach	3	16	8	5	13	0
Stephan Lebeau	1	5	1	2	3	4
Jack LeClair	2	12	3	1	4	6
John LeClair	2	9	4	3	7	4
Albert Leduc	2	4	1	3	4	2
Richie Leduc	1	5	0	0	0	9
Brian Leetch	1	7	5	6	11	4
Gary Leeman	1	5	0	1	1	2
Sylvain Lefebvre	1	4	0	1	1	2
Chuck Lefley	1	6	3	3	6	2
Roger Leger	1	6	0	2	2	6
Jere Lehtinen	1	6	2	3	5	0
Jacques Lemaire	8	40	19	18	37	31
Moe Lemay	1	5	1	1	2	6
Claude Lemieux	4	15	6	3	9	57
Jocelyn Lemieux	1	4	0	1	1	0
Mario Lemieux	2	9	10	9	19	6
Alfred 'Pit' Lepine	2	7	4	2	6	4
Curtis Leschyshyn	1	4	0	1	1	4
Art Lesieur	1	5	0	0	0	4
Bill Lesuk	1	2	0	0	0	0
Tony Leswick	4	25	5	7	12	34
Alex Levinsky	3	11	1	0	1	8
Danny Lewicki	1	3	0	0	0	0
Herbie Lewis	3	13	4	3	7	6
Doug Lidster	1	7	2	0	2	10
Nicklas Lidstrom	3	12	2	3	5	2
Trevor Linden	1	7	3	2	5	6
Eric Lindros	1	4	1	2	3	8
Lars Lindgren	1	4	1	0	1	2
Bill Lindsay	1	4	0	1	1	4
Ted Lindsay	8	44	19	15	34	48
Willy Lindstrom	3	14	5	1	6	2
Ken Linseman	4	20	4	10	14	52
Carl Liscombe	4	22	6	8	14	9
Ed Litzenberger	4	14	1	3	4	16
Lonnie Loach	1	1	0	0	0	0
Troy Loney	2	10	1	1	2	26
Stan Long	1	2	0	0	0	0
Ross Lonsberry	3	16	4	2	6	4
Hakan Loob	2	11	0	3	3	2
Jim Lorentz	2	10	1	2	3	2
Bob Lorimer	2	11	0	0	0	15
Clem Loughlin	2	8	2	0	2	12
Kevin Lowe	7	37	3	3	6	24
Ross Lowe	1	1	0	0	0	0
Dave Lowery	1	4	0	1	1	2
Don Luce	1	6	2	3	5	12
Craig Ludwig	3	17	1	1	2	32
Dave Lumley	3	10	1	1	2	28
Jyrki Lumme	1	7	0	4	4	6
Pentti Lund	1	7	1	1	2	0
Len Lunde	1	5	1	0	1	0
Pat Lundy	1	1	0	1	1	0
Gilles Lupien	2	6	0	0	0	19
Gary Lupul	1	2	0	0	0	0
Vic Lynn	3	14	4	2	6	30

M

PLAYER	YRS	GP	G	A	TP	PIM
Al MacAdam	1	5	1	3	4	2
Blair MacDonald	1	1	0	0	0	0
Jack MacDonald	*1	5	1	1	2	3
Kilby MacDonald	1	6	0	0	0	4
Parker MacDonald	4	24	3	1	4	14
Ran MacDonald	2	10	3	3	6	12
Hub Macey	1	3	0	0	0	0
Bruce MacGregor	5	30	6	6	12	14
Al MacInnis	2	11	5	8	13	26
Calum MacKay	4	20	3	7	10	8
D. 'Mickey' MacKay	*7	25	7	6	13	18
Fleming Mackell	5	25	5	10	15	14
Bill MacKenzie	1	4	0	0	0	9
Howie Mackie	1	3	0	0	0	0
John MacLean	1	4	1	4	5	0
Rick MacLeish	3	18	6	9	15	8
Brian MacLellan	1	6	0	1	1	4
John MacMillan	2	5	0	1	1	2
Al MacNeil	1	7	0	0	0	12
Jamie Macoun	3	15	0	3	3	12
James 'Bud' MacPherson	3	11	0	1	1	8
Craig MacTavish	4	24	0	5	5	16

Keith Magnuson	1	7	0	0	0	36
Frank Mahovlich	8	45	16	25	41	43
Peter Mahovlich	4	21	10	14	24	36
Fern Majeau	1	1	0	0	0	0
Chico Maki	4	21	3	6	9	12
David Maley	1	5	1	2	3	2
Dan Maloney	1	2	0	0	0	4
Dave Maloney	1	5	1	2	3	10
Don Maloney	1	5	0	1	1	6
Kirk Maltby	2	8	2	1	3	8
Georges Mantha	2	7	2	1	3	4
Sylvio Mantha	4	15	2	0	2	20
Milan Marcetta	1	2	0	0	0	0
Harold 'Mush' March	3	12	3	2	5	14
Bryan Marchment	1	4	1	0	1	2
Don Marcotte	5	25	3	2	5	16
Gus Marker	4	17	3	3	6	4
John Marks	1	6	1	1	2	2
Nevin Markwart	1	1	0	0	0	2
Mario Marois	1	5	0	0	0	4
Brad Marsh	2	12	0	3	3	45
Bert Marshall	1	6	0	2	2	8
Don Marshall	6	32	3	4	7	4
Clare Martin	1	3	0	0	0	0
Frank Martin	1	5	0	1	1	2
Hubert 'Pit' Martin	3	19	6	4	10	18
Rick Martin	1	6	2	4	6	6
Paul Masnick	4	18	3	3	6	14
Joe Matte	1	2	1	0	1	2
Stephane Matteau	2	11	0	2	2	6
Richard Matvichuk	1	6	0	2	2	6
John Matz	1	4	0	0	0	2
Brad Maxwell	1	4	0	4	4	9
Kevin Maxwell	1	2	0	0	0	4
Eddie Mazur	4	17	0	2	2	15
Jerome 'Jud' McAtee	1	7	0	0	0	0
George McAvoy	1	3	0	0	0	0
Bert McCaffrey	1	2	1	0	1	0
Doug McCaig	1	2	0	0	0	6
Darren McCarty	3	12	1	4	5	10
Tom McCarthy	2	4	0	3	3	2
Kevin McClelland	4	22	4	5	9	87
John McCormack	2	6	0	0	0	0
Bill McCreary	3	10	0	2	2	4
John McCreedy	2	11	1	2	3	6
Brad McCrimmon	2	13	2	2	4	16
Ab McDonald	7	30	6	7	13	8
Lanny McDonald	2	8	3	1	4	8
Wilfrid 'Bucko' McDonald	5	18	3	0	3	4
Shawn McEachern	1	4	0	2	2	0
Mike McEwen	3	12	2	3	5	6
Jim McFadden	3	15	3	3	6	6
Don McFayden	1	4	0	1	1	2
Jack McGill	1	5	0	0	0	0
Jack McIlhargey	2	10	0	1	1	29
Jack McIntyre	1	4	1	0	1	0
Doug McKay	1	1	0	0	0	0
Murdo McKay	1	6	0	0	0	0
Randy McKay	1	4	1	0	1	0
Jay McKee	1	6	0	0	0	2
Jack McKell	2	9	0	0	0	0
Don McKenney	3	16	6	7	13	0
John McKenzie	3	14	1	6	7	39
Jack McLeod	1	5	0	0	0	0
Mike McMahon	1	4	1	0	1	12
Max McNab	3	10	0	0	0	4
Peter McNab	3	16	3	3	6	4
Mike McPhee	2	11	1	5	6	28
Basil McRae	1	5	0	0	0	26
Pat McReavy	2	10	2	2	4	7
Marty McSorley	3	17	3	0	3	30
Howie Meeker	3	15	2	4	6	23
Harry Meeking	4	20	1	3	4	26
Paul Meger	4	12	1	1	2	4
Scott Mellanby	2	11	1	3	4	84
Gerry Melnyk	5	24	0	0	0	2
Larry Melnyk	1	1	0	0	0	0
Wayne Merrick	4	19	3	6	9	0
Mark Messier	7	38	11	20	31	52
Don Metz	5	21	4	5	9	4
Nick Metz	8	32	3	7	10	17
Dave Michayluk	1	1	0	0	0	0
Nick Mickoski	1	7	0	4	4	0
Rick Middleton	3	15	1	3	4	0
Stan Mikita	5	31	10	21	31	58
Mike Milbury	2	9	0	3	3	30
Hubert 'Hib' Milks	1	3	0	0	0	0
Corey Millen	1	5	0	0	0	2
Bill Miller	1	3	0	0	0	0
Bob Miller	1	6	0	1	1	9
Earl Miller	1	2	0	0	0	0
Jay Miller	1	3	0	0	0	24
Kelly Miller	1	3	0	0	0	0
Gerry Minor	1	4	1	2	3	0
Mike Modano	2	12	2	9	11	14
Ron Moffatt	1	2	0	0	0	0
Doug Mohns	3	18	1	4	5	23
Lars Molin	1	4	0	4	4	0
Sergio Momesso	1	7	1	1	2	17
Armand Mondou	2	5	0	0	0	2
Pierre Mondou	3	13	1	3	4	6
Dickie Moore	10	52	10	21	31	69
Howie Morenz	4	15	10	2	12	20
Bernie Morris	*2	4	0	3	3	0
Elwin 'Moe' Morris	1	7	1	0	1	2
John 'Crutchy' Morrison	1	2	1	0	1	0
Rod Morrison	1	1	0	0	0	0
Ken Morrow	5	24	4	3	7	14
Gus Mortson	4	16	3	3	6	8
Kenny Mosdell	6	33	6	7	13	16
Bill Mosienko	1	4	0	1	1	2
Alex Motter	3	12	1	2	3	8
'Speed' Moynes	1	5	0	0	0	0
Joe Mullen	3	16	10	9	19	8
Kirk Muller	1	5	2	2	4	6
Harry Mummery	*1	5	0	6	6	21
Craig Muni	3	15	0	3	3	2
Dunc Munro	2	9	1	1	2	8
Bob Murdoch	2	6	0	0	0	2
Don Murdoch	1	5	1	1	2	2
Murray Murdoch	5	19	1	3	4	12
Gord Murphy	1	4	0	0	0	0
Joe Murphy	1	5	2	2	4	4
Larry Murphy	4	18	3	15	18	8
Ron Murphy	1	6	2	1	3	0
Hugh 'Muzz' Murray	2	10	3	0	3	8
Terry Murray	1	2	0	0	0	0
Dana Murzyn	1	6	0	1	1	8

N

PLAYER	YRS	GP	G	A	TP	PIM
Don Nachbaur	1	1	0	0	0	0
Mark Napier	2	10	1	0	1	2
Mats Naslund	2	11	4	6	10	4
Ric Nattress	1	6	0	0	0	12
Cam Neely	2	10	2	5	7	14
Jim Neilson	1	3	0	1	1	2
Sergei Nemchinov	1	7	0	2	2	2
Eric Nesterenko	4	26	1	5	6	30
Bob Nevin	2	11	4	1	5	4
Rob Niedermayer	1	4	1	0	1	2
Scott Niedermayer	1	4	1	3	4	0
Joe Nieuwendyk	2	12	3	2	5	11
'Sibby' Nicholls	1	5	0	0	0	0
Frank Nighbor	*4	17	7	4	11	12
Janne Niinimaa	1	4	0	3	3	0
Andrei Nikolishin	1	4	0	2	2	2
Chris Nilan	1	3	0	0	0	49
Jim Nill	1	3	1	0	1	6
Kent Nilsson	1	7	0	1	1	0
Ulf Nilsson	1	2	0	0	0	2
Reg Noble	3	14	2	2	4	25
Simon Nolet	1	6	0	1	1	0
Brian Noonan	2	11	0	4	4	2
Larry 'Baldy' Northcott	1	3	2	1	3	0
Bill Nyrop	3	10	0	3	3	8
Bob Nystrom	5	21	8	4	12	67

O

PLAYER	YRS	GP	G	A	TP	PIM
Adam Oates	1	4	1	2	3	0
Eddie Oatman	*2	7	1	0	1	0
Russell Oatman	3	10	0	0	0	22
Dennis O'Brien	1	5	0	0	0	6
H. 'Buddy' O'Connor	4	21	6	5	11	4
Lyle Odelein	1	5	0	2	2	6
Gerry Odrowski	2	8	0	0	0	6
Bill O'Dwyer	1	5	0	0	0	0
Harry Oliver	4	10	3	3	6	6
Bert Olmstead	11	56	5	19	24	52
Terry O'Reilly	3	16	2	3	5	49
Jimmy Orlando	3	15	0	5	5	53
Bobby Orr	3	16	8	12	20	31
Danny O'Shea	1	7	1	1	2	12
Joel Otto	3	15	3	8	11	14
George Owen	2	4	0	0	0	2
Sandis Ozolinsh	1	4	0	2	2	4

P-Q

PLAYER	YRS	GP	G	A	TP	PIM
John Paddock	1	2	2	0	2	0
Jim Paek	2	9	1	3	4	4
Pete Palangio	1	3	0	0	0	0
Brad Palmer	1	5	1	0	1	4
Jim Pappin	4	26	11	8	19	24
Brad Park	3	16	7	9	16	21
Ernie Parkes	3	11	0	5	5	2
George Parsons	1	3	2	0	2	11
Joe Paterson	1	5	0	0	0	19
James Patrick	1	6	0	0	0	4
Lynn Patrick	2	11	3	1	4	2
Murray 'Muzz' Patrick	1	6	1	0	1	6
Colin Patterson	2	8	1	1	2	16
Marty Pavelich	7	36	4	8	12	38
Steve Payne	1	5	5	2	7	2
Michael Peca	1	6	1	0	1	2
Allen Pedersen	2	9	0	0	0	8
John Peirson	3	12	1	0	1	14
Mike Peluso	2	7	0	0	0	4
Jim Peplinski	2	9	1	5	6	47
Gilbert Perreault	1	6	1	1	2	6
Stefan Persson	4	18	3	13	16	20
Jim Peters	4	22	1	3	4	8
Michel Petit	1	2	0	0	0	2
Gord Pettinger	5	21	3	3	6	2
Meryn 'Bill' Phillips	2	9	3	1	4	2
Noel Picard	4	15	0	4	4	28
Alf Pike	1	6	2	0	2	4
Pierre Pilote	3	17	2	13	15	22
Gerry Pinder	1	5	0	0	0	2
Didier Pitre	*1	5	0	3	3	0
Barclay Plager	3	9	1	2	3	6
Bill Plager	2	5	0	0	0	4
Bob Plager	3	10	0	1	1	28
Gerry Plamondon	1	1	0	0	0	0
Pierre Plante	1	5	0	0	0	0
Willi Plett	1	2	0	0	0	4
Shjon Podein	1	4	0	0	0	2
Nels Podolsky	1	3	0	0	0	0
Norman 'Bud' Poile	2	8	2	0	2	2
Mike Polich	2	4	0	0	0	0
Jack Portland	1	5	0	0	0	2
Denis Potvin	5	24	9	19	28	28
Dave Poulin	3	14	1	3	4	12
Jaroslav Pouzar	3	9	0	1	1	8
Walter 'Babe' Pratt	3	18	3	3	6	19
Dean Prentice	1	6	1	1	2	2
Noel Price	2	3	0	1	1	2
Joe Primeau	4	14	3	6	9	4
Keith Primeau	1	3	0	0	0	8
Wayne Primeau	1	6	1	1	2	4
Andre Pronovost	6	30	2	4	6	18
Marcel Pronovost	9	51	2	8	10	30
Brian Propp	5	29	10	12	22	8
Claude Provost	10	49	5	11	16	24
Metro Prystai	3	15	4	3	7	4
Bob Pulford	6	33	8	13	21	44
Cliff Purpur	2	8	0	0	0	4
Jean Pusie	1	3	0	0	0	0
Bill Quackenbush	4	20	1	3	4	4
John Quilty	1	2	0	1	1	2
Dan Quinn	1	5	1	4	5	4

R

PLAYER	YRS	GP	G	A	TP	PIM
Don Raleigh	1	7	2	0	2	0
Rob Ramage	1	6	0	2	2	10
Craig Ramsay	1	6	0	2	2	0
Mike Ramsey	1	2	0	0	0	0
Ken Randall	*2	9	2	0	2	40
Erik Rasmussen	1	6	0	0	0	2
Jean Ratelle	3	16	0	5	5	0
Matt Ravlich	1	7	1	1	2	8
Rob Ray	1	1	0	0	0	0
Kenny Reardon	2	9	0	0	0	20
Terry Reardon	2	9	3	1	4	4
Marc Reaume	1	4	0	0	0	0
Billy Reay	5	23	3	2	5	14

Mark Recchi	1	6	2	1	3	8
Dick Redmond	1	4	0	1	1	0
Mickey Redmond	2	6	0	1	1	0
Joe Reekie	1	4	0	0	0	2
Larry Regan	4	18	3	7	10	6
Earl Reibel	3	16	3	7	10	4
Dave Reid	1	6	0	2	2	2
Jerry Reid	1	2	0	0	0	2
Leo Reise	4	17	1	0	1	14
Paul Reinhart	1	5	1	1	2	2
Mikael Renberg	1	4	0	1	1	0
Mike Ricci	1	4	1	0	1	6
Henri Richard	12	65	21	26	47	68
Maurice 'Rocket' Richard	12	59	34	12	46	83
Roy Rickey	*2	7	3	3	6	0
Jim Riley	1	5	0	1	1	0
Vic Ripley	1	5	1	1	2	2
Doug Risebrough	5	22	5	5	10	35
Gus Rivers	2	7	0	0	0	0
Rene Robert	1	6	1	2	3	6
Phil Roberto	1	5	0	0	0	12
Gary Roberts	1	6	0	0	0	8
Gordie Roberts	3	15	0	1	1	33
Jim Roberts	9	42	3	3	6	44
Fred Robertson	1	3	0	0	0	0
Earl Robinson	1	3	2	1	3	0
Larry Robinson	7	36	5	15	20	35
Luc Robitaille	1	5	3	2	5	4
Leon Rochefort	3	16	2	2	4	12
Ernie Rodden	1	1	0	0	0	0
Jeremy Roenick	1	4	2	0	2	0
Dale Rolfe	1	6	2	0	2	10
Brian Rolston	1	2	0	1	1	0
Elwin 'Doc' Romnes	4	18	3	8	11	4
Ed Ronan	1	5	1	1	2	6
Paul Ronty	1	2	0	0	0	2
Steve Rooney	1	1	0	0	0	0
Darcy Rota	1	4	0	0	0	19
Sammy Rothschild	1	4	0	0	0	0
Tom Roulston	1	4	0	1	1	0
Bob Rouse	3	12	0	1	1	2
Bobby Rousseau	6	33	6	13	19	23
Bobby Rowe	*2	10	3	0	3	19
Reijo Ruotsalainen	2	12	0	2	2	6
Cam Russell	1	1	0	0	0	0
Phil Russell	1	6	0	1	1	16
Warren Rychel	2	8	0	0	0	21

S

PLAYER	YRS	GP	G	A	TP	PIM
Gary Sabourin	3	12	2	0	2	6
Joe Sakic	1	4	1	4	5	2
Dollard St. Laurent	9	43	1	6	7	47
Frank St. Marseille	3	12	4	3	7	4
Don Saleski	3	16	1	4	5	18
Kjell Samuelsson	3	15	0	2	2	14
Ulf Samuelsson	2	10	2	1	3	14
Phil Samis	1	3	0	1	1	2
Derek Sanderson	2	10	4	3	7	34
Geoff Sanderson	1	6	1	0	1	4
Ed Sandford	1	5	2	1	3	5
Charlie Sands	1	4	0	1	1	0
Tomas Sandstrom	2	9	0	3	3	8
Miroslav Satan	1	6	0	1	1	2
Glen Sather	1	6	0	0	0	11
Andre Savard	1	6	1	1	2	20
Denis Savard	1	1	0	0	0	0
Serge Savard	7	33	5	8	13	22
Bobby Schmautz	3	16	3	2	5	29
Jackie Schmidt	1	2	0	0	0	0
Milt Schmidt	4	18	6	8	14	4
Mathieu Schneider	1	5	1	1	2	8
Ron Schock	2	8	0	0	0	2
Jim Schoenfeld	1	6	0	2	2	11
Dave 'Sweeney' Schriner	3	19	6	6	12	8
Dave Schultz	3	16	4	2	6	61
Enio Sclisizzi	2	4	0	0	0	2
Earl Seibert	5	22	2	1	3	18
Rod Seiling	1	6	1	1	2	6
Dave Semenko	3	13	2	2	4	18
Eddie Shack	4	21	1	1	2	28
Brendan Shanahan	2	8	3	2	5	0
Bobby Sheehan	1	5	0	1	1	0
Neil Sheehy	1	5	0	0	0	31
Gregg Sheppard	3	16	4	6	10	10
John Sheppard	2	4	0	0	0	0
Ray Sheppard	2	7	1	1	2	0
John Sherf	1	5	0	1	1	2
Fred Shero	1	4	0	0	0	0
Jack Shewchuk	1	4	0	0	0	4
Alex Shibicky	2	10	0	2	2	2
Allan Shields	1	3	0	1	1	2
Bill Shill	1	3	0	1	1	2
Jack Shill	2	8	1	2	3	8
Paul Shmyr	2	5	0	0	0	19
Eddie Shore	4	13	1	3	4	42
Gary Shuchuk	1	5	0	0	0	0
Steve Shutt	4	19	10	11	21	4
Albert 'Babe' Siebert	3	12	2	3	5	22
Jonathan Sim	1	2	0	0	0	0
Chris Simon	1	4	1	0	1	6
John Simon	1	3	0	0	0	0
Craig Simpson	2	10	7	5	12	16
Joe Simpson	1	2	0	1	1	0
Al Sims	3	11	0	0	0	4
Ilkka Sinisalo	2	10	1	0	1	2
Alf Skinner	5	18	13	3	17	34
Glen Skov	3	18	2	3	5	26
Brian Skrudland	4	21	2	4	6	62
Blake Sloan	1	6	0	0	0	0
Tod Sloan	2	11	3	5	8	13
Ed Slowinski	1	7	0	3	3	4
Doug Smail	1	1	0	0	0	0
Richard Smehlik	1	6	0	3	3	2
Alex Smith	1	4	0	0	0	8
Bobby Smith	4	22	8	10	18	34
Clint Smith	2	10	1	4	5	2
Dallas Smith	3	16	0	4	4	24
Derrick Smith	2	12	2	4	6	10
Des Smith	1	4	0	2	2	2
Floyd Smith	3	18	6	3	9	4
Greg Smith	1	5	0	1	1	6
Ken Smith	1	5	0	2	2	0
Reginald 'Hooley' Smith	3	12	0	3	3	29
Rick Smith	3	14	2	3	5	18
Sid Smith	2	9	8	2	10	0
Stan Smith	1	1	0	0	0	0
Steve Smith	4	17	1	6	7	25
Stan Smyl	1	4	2	0	2	19
Rod Smylie	1	5	1	3	4	0
Harold Snepsts	1	4	0	0	0	16
Ken Solheim	1	1	0	0	0	0
Art Somers	3	12	0	3	3	8
John Sorrell	3	13	4	5	9	2
Bill Speer	1	1	0	0	0	0
Brian Spencer	1	6	0	1	1	4
Irv Spencer	2	8	0	0	0	0
Ted Stackhouse	1	4	0	0	0	0
Fred Stanfield	4	23	3	6	9	4
Allan Stanley	8	46	4	13	17	36
Daryl Stanley	1	4	0	0	0	2
Russell 'Barney' Stanley	*1	5	2	0	2	6
Wally Stanowski	5	29	3	7	10	2
Paul Stanton	2	10	0	1	1	28
Pat Stapleton	2	13	0	10	10	4
Wilf Starr	1	3	0	1	1	2
Vic Stasiuk	6	31	5	9	14	8
Peter Stemkowski	2	12	3	7	10	12
Kevin Stevens	2	10	6	6	12	27
Scott Stevens	1	4	0	2	2	4
Gaye Stewart	3	12	1	2	3	6
John 'Black Jack' Stewart	6	29	2	7	9	34
Nels Stewart	2	9	8	1	9	22
Ron Stewart	6	28	4	9	13	8
Martin Straka	1	4	0	1	1	0
Billy 'Red' Stuart	2	9	0	2	2	6
Brent Sutter	4	17	5	7	12	16
Duane Sutter	5	24	4	9	13	86
Rich Sutter	1	3	3	0	3	4
Ron Sutter	2	12	1	6	7	12
Robert Svehla	1	4	0	0	0	2
Petr Svoboda	2	7	0	3	3	10
Bob Sweeney	2	10	0	3	3	9
Don Sweeney	1	5	0	1	1	6
Darryl Sydor	2	11	1	0	1	12

T

PLAYER	YRS	GP	G	A	TP	PIM
Peter Taglianetti	1	5	0	3	3	8
Jean-Guy Talbot	11	55	0	5	5	56
Marc Tardif	2	13	3	3	6	23
Billy Taylor	2	9	2	8	10	2
Dave Taylor	1	3	1	1	2	6
Fred 'Cyclone' Taylor	*2	10	9	1	10	15
Ralph Taylor	1	1	0	0	0	0
Tim Taylor	1	2	0	0	0	2
Michael Thelven	1	4	0	0	0	6
Chris Therien	1	4	0	0	0	0
Jimmy Thomson	1	6	0	0	0	12
Paul Thompson	4	13	3	3	6	25
Bill Thoms	4	15	3	4	7	2
Jim Thomson	3	13	1	4	5	13
Esa Tikkanen	6	31	9	6	15	54
Ray Timgren	2	9	1	3	4	21
Mark Tinordi	2	10	0	1	1	21
Walt Tkaczuk	2	11	1	3	4	0
Charlie Tobin	*2	10	0	0	0	0
Rick Tocchet	3	16	5	12	17	40
John Tonelli	6	29	3	10	13	35
Tim Tookey	1	1	0	0	0	0
Jeff Toms	1	1	0	0	0	0
Jerry Toppazzini	3	16	1	2	3	8
Jack Toupin	1	1	0	0	0	0
Bob Trapp	1	2	0	0	0	2
Gilles Tremblay	2	12	2	3	5	0
J.C. Tremblay	6	34	3	18	21	27
Mario Tremblay	4	14	5	2	7	30
Dave Trottier	1	3	1	0	1	4
Bryan Trottier	7	34	11	22	33	46
Louis Trudel	2	8	0	1	1	0
Bob Turner	6	28	1	1	2	14

U-V

PLAYER	YRS	GP	G	A	TP	PIM
Norm Ullman	5	28	6	12	18	23
Carol Vadnais	4	18	1	4	5	37
Mel 'Sparky' Vail	1	2	0	0	0	0
Ed Van Impe	2	12	0	4	4	21
Vaclav Varada	1	6	0	0	0	6
Elmer Vasko	3	19	1	2	3	18
Gary Veneruzzo	1	3	0	1	1	0
Pat Verbeek	1	6	1	0	1	4
Mike Vernon	3	13	0	1	1	0
Steve Vickers	1	5	1	1	2	0
Carl Voss	1	4	2	0	2	0

W

PLAYER	YRS	GP	G	A	TP	PIM
Jack Walker	*4	18	8	5	13	9
Bob Wall	1	4	0	0	0	2
Ryan Walter	2	11	1	1	2	6
Mike Walton	2	12	3	5	8	6
Aaron Ward	1	4	0	0	0	0
Dixon Ward	1	6	1	0	1	8
Jimmy Ward	2	8	1	1	2	2
Eddie Wares	3	14	0	6	6	22
Rhett Warrener	2	8	0	0	0	6
Nick Wasnie	2	7	2	2	4	8
Bryan Watson	1	6	0	0	0	12
Harry Watson	5	20	8	5	13	10
Jimmy Watson	4	21	0	4	4	43
Joe Watson	3	16	0	2	2	20
Phil Watson	3	15	3	5	8	18
Tim Watters	1	5	0	0	0	4
Ralph 'Cooney' Weiland	4	13	1	2	3	2
Jay Wells	1	7	0	0	0	8
John Wensink	2	9	0	0	0	28
Marvin 'Cy' Wentworth	2	8	3	2	5	8
Glen Wesley	2	10	2	2	4	2
Ed Westfall	2	10	2	3	5	10
Ken Wharram	3	17	3	2	5	16
Bill White	2	13	1	5	6	12
Bob Whitelaw	1	4	0	0	0	0
Art Wiebe	2	8	0	1	1	6
Jim Wiemer	1	2	0	0	0	0
Neil Wilkinson	1	6	0	0	0	2
Burr Williams	1	2	0	0	0	0
Dave 'Tiger' Williams	1	4	0	3	3	14
Behn Wilson	1	6	0	4	4	28
Carol 'Cully' Wilson	*2	7	1	3	4	8
Johnny Wilson	5	27	3	2	5	2
Larry Wilson	1	2	0	0	0	0
Murray Wilson	3	13	0	4	4	8
Eddie Wiseman	2	7	3	0	3	0
Steve Wochy	1	2	0	0	0	0
Benny Woit	3	18	0	1	1	10
Jason Woolley	2	8	1	1	2	6

Y-Z

PLAYER	YRS	GP	G	A	TP	PIM
Doug Young	2	8	1	2	3	2
Howie Young	2	8	1	1	2	18
Scott Young	2	5	2	2	4	0
Tim Young	1	2	0	3	3	0
Tom Younghans	1	3	0	0	0	4
Steve Yzerman	3	12	6	3	9	2
Richard Zednik	1	4	1	0	1	4
Larry Zeidel	1	3	0	0	0	0
Valeri Zelepukin	1	3	0	0	0	4
Peter Zezel	2	12	1	2	3	6
Alexei Zhitnik	2	11	1	3	4	22
Sergei Zubov	2	12	1	8	9	2
Dainius Zubrus	1	4	0	0	0	0

* Note: Totals do not include appearances before 1918.

Final Series Goaltending Register

GOALTENDER	YRS	GP	W	L	MIN	GA	SO	AVG
Andy Aitkenhead	1	4	3	1	248	5	1	1.21
Tom Barrasso	2	10	7	2	559	23	2	2.47
Hank Bassen	2	5	1	3	274	11	0	2.41
Don Beaupre	1	3	1	2	180	13	0	4.33
Ed Belfour	2	10	4	5	616	20	1	1.95
Clint Benedict [1,2]	4	25	16	9	1507	39	8	1.55
Johnny Bower	6	28	13	13	1638	70	2	2.56
Frank Brimsek	4	18	9	9	1132	47	1	2.49
Walter 'Turk' Broda	8	38	21	17	2369	85	4	2.15
Martin Brodeur	1	4	4	0	206	7	0	1.75
Richard Brodeur	1	4	0	4	260	17	0	3.92
Jon Casey	1	6	2	3	290	21	0	4.34
Lorne Chabot	3	9	4	4	508	23	0	2.72
Gerry Cheevers	4	17	8	9	1020	51	2	3.00
King Clancy [2]	1	1	0	0	2	0	0	0.00
Alex Connell [3]	2	7	5	0	425	7	1	0.99
Roger Crozier	2	8	3	4	426	19	0	2.68
Wilf Cude	1	4	1	3	291	9	0	1.86
John Davidson	1	5	1	4	307	19	0	3.17
Denis DeJordy	1	1	0	0	20	3	0	9.00
Gerry Desjardins	1	5	1	3	260	16	0	3.69
Ken Dryden	6	32	24	8	1947	78	2	2.40
Bill Durnan	3	15	10	5	967	34	1	2.11
Tony Esposito	2	13	5	8	796	52	1	3.92
Mark Fitzpatrick	1	1	0	0	40	4	0	6.00
Bob Froese	1	3	0	1	115	9	0	4.70
Grant Fuhr	4	20	14	5	1176	50	1	2.55
Chuck Gardiner	2	9	5	4	670	18	1	1.61
Ed Giacomin	1	3	1	2	180	11	0	3.67
Gilles Gilbert	1	6	2	4	372	15	0	2.42
Paul Goodman	1	1	0	1	60	5	0	5.00
Ron Grahame	1	1	0	0	20	0	0	0.00
George Hainsworth	4	14	6	8	925	39	2	2.53
Glenn Hall	7	32	10	22	1904	87	1	2.74
Dominik Hasek	2	7	2	5	481	16	0	2.00
Brian Hayward	1	2	0	1	67	6	0	5.37
Gordie Henry	1	3	1	2	163	10	0	3.68
'Sugar' Jim Henry	1	3	0	2	138	5	0	2.17
Ron Hextall	2	10	3	7	605	34	0	3.37
Charlie Hodge	2	4	1	3	197	10	1	3.05
Hap Holmes [1,4]	5	23	11	11	1416	64	2	2.71
Kelly Hrudey	1	5	1	4	316	15	0	2.85
Ed Johnston	1	3	2	1	180	6	0	2.00
Mike Karakas	2	6	2	4	369	18	0	2.93
Dave Kerr	2	11	6	5	694	20	1	1.73
Olaf Kolzig	1	4	0	4	251	13	0	3.11
Michel Larocque	1	1	0	0	20	0	0	0.00
Hugh Lehman [1]	5	21	7	14	1265	61	2	2.89
Rejean Lemelin	3	4	0	2	197	13	0	3.96
Pelle Lindbergh	1	4	1	3	185	11	0	3.57
Harry Lumley	4	22	7	15	1391	56	3	2.42
Frank McCool	1	7	4	3	434	9	3	1.24
Kirk McLean	1	7	3	4	437	20	0	2.75
Gerry McNeil	4	15	6	9	933	29	3	1.86
Roland Melanson	1	3	0	1	55	3	0	3.27
Gilles Meloche	1	2	0	2	120	12	0	6.00
Joe Miller	1	3	2	1	180	3	1	1.00
Andy Moog	4	15	3	10	844	46	0	3.27
Alfie Moore	1	1	1	0	60	1	0	1.00
Johnny Mowers	3	15	7	8	900	42	2	2.80
Phil Myre	1	1	0	1	60	6	0	6.00
Chris Osgood	2	5	4	0	286	8	0	1.68
Bernie Parent	2	12	8	4	750	33	2	2.64
Lester Patrick	1	1	1	0	47	1	0	1.28
Pete Peeters	1	5	2	3	311	20	0	3.86
Frank Pietrangelo	1	1	1	0	40	3	0	4.50
Jacques Plante	10	41	25	14	2423	92	4	2.28
Bill Ranford	1	5	4	1	355	8	0	1.35
Chuck Rayner	1	7	3	4	459	22	0	2.88
Charlie Reid	1	2	0	2	120	9	0	4.50
Glenn 'Chico' Resch	1	1	0	0	20	2	0	6.00
Mike Richter	1	7	4	3	439	19	0	2.60
John Ross Roach	3	10	3	7	605	31	1	3.07
Earl Robertson	1	5	2	2	280	8	2	1.71
Al Rollins	1	3	3	0	193	5	0	1.55
Patrick Roy	4	20	14	6	1296	44	2	2.04
Terry Sawchuk	7	37	19	18	2185	95	3	2.61
Don Simmons	3	14	5	9	831	38	1	2.74
Billy Smith	5	24	17	6	1396	72	2	3.09
Gary Smith	1	1	0	0	5	0	0	0.00
Normie Smith	2	5	4	1	261	11	0	2.53
Garth Snow	1	1	0	1	58	4	0	4.11
Wayne Stephenson	1	4	0	4	240	14	0	3.50
Cecil 'Tiny' Thompson	2	4	2	2	240	8	1	2.00
Jon Vanbiesbrouck	1	4	0	4	245	11	0	2.69
Rogie Vachon	2	9	6	3	548	17	1	1.86
Mike Vernon	4	19	9	10	1137	50	0	2.64
Georges Vezina [1,4]	3	13	7	5	816	39	2	2.87
Gilles Villemure	1	3	1	2	180	7	0	2.33
Ernie Wakely	1	2	0	2	96	11	0	6.87
Hal Winkler [3]	2	6	0	4	362	10	1	1.66
Lorne 'Gump' Worsley	4	16	11	5	925	28	3	1.82

[1] Note: Totals do not include appearances before 1918.
[2] Clancy replaced Clint Benedict in goal while Benedict served a two-minute penalty on March 31, 1923.
[3] also recorded two ties in the 1927 Finals.
[4] also recorded a tie in the 1919 Finals.

Final Series Coaching Register

COACH	YRS	CUPS	GC	W	L	PCT
Sid Abel	4	0	24	8	16	.333
Jack Adams	5	3	23	12	11	.522
Al Arbour	5	4	24	17	7	.708
Toe Blake	9	8	48	34	14	.708
Frank Boucher	1	1	6	4	2	.667
Scotty Bowman	11	7	53	32	21	.604
Pat Burns	1	0	6	2	4	.333
Dick Carroll	1	1	5	3	2	.600
Don Cherry	2	0	10	2	8	.200
Dit Clapper	1	0	5	1	4	.200
Lloyd Cook [1]	3	0	14	5	9	.357
Marc Crawford	1	1	4	4	0	1.000
Terry Crisp	1	1	6	4	2	.667
Leo Dandurand	2	1	8	5	3	.625
Hap Day	5	5	28	20	8	.714
Jacques Demers	1	1	5	4	1	.800
Cy Denneny	1	1	2	2	0	1.000
Art Duncan [1]	1	0	2	0	2	.000
Emile Francis	1	0	6	2	4	.333
Bob Gainey	1	0	6	2	4	.333
Eddie Gerard	2	1	9	5	4	.555
Dave Gill [2]	1	1	4	2	0	.750
Ebbie Goodfellow	1	0	4	0	4	.000
Tommy Gorman	2	2	7	6	1	.857
Pete Green	3	3	16	11	5	.688
Bep Guidolin	1	0	6	2	4	.333
Cecil Hart	2	2	7	5	2	.714
Ken Hitchcock	1	1	6	4	2	.667
Punch Imlach	6	4	33	17	16	.515
Dick Irvin	16	4	77	32	45	.416
Tommy Ivan	5	3	26	12	14	.462
Bob Johnson	2	1	11	5	6	.455
Tom Johnson	1	1	6	4	2	.667
Mike Keenan	4	1	23	8	15	.348
Newsy Lalonde [3,4]	2	1	10	5	4	.550
Jacques Lemaire	1	1	4	4	0	1.000
Herbie Lewis	1	0	4	1	3	.250
Doug MacLean	1	0	4	0	4	.000
Al MacNeil	1	1	7	4	3	.571
Ken McKenzie	1	0	2	0	2	.000
Barry Melrose	1	0	4	1	4	.200
Mike Milbury	1	0	5	1	4	.200
John Muckler	1	1	5	4	1	.800
Pete Muldoon [3,4]	3	1	14	7	6	.536
Terry Murray	1	1	4	0	4	.000
Roger Neilson	1	0	4	0	4	.000
Eddie Oatman	1	0	2	0	2	.000
Terry O'Reilly	1	0	4	0	4	.000
Frank Patrick [4]	2	1	8	5	3	.625
Lester Patrick [4]	8	3	30	12	18	.400
Lynn Patrick	2	0	12	4	8	.333
Jean Perron	1	1	5	4	1	.800
Rudy Pilous	2	1	12	6	6	.500
Joe Primeau	1	1	5	4	1	.800
Pat Quinn	2	0	13	5	8	.385
Billy Reay	3	0	20	8	12	.400
Lindy Ruff	1	0	6	2	4	.333
Art Ross [2]	4	1	15	4	9	.333
Claude Ruel	1	1	4	4	0	1.000
Glen Sather	5	4	25	16	9	.640
Fred Shero	4	2	21	9	12	.429
Jimmy Skinner	2	1	12	5	7	.417
Milt Schmidt	2	0	11	3	8	.273
Harry Sinden	1	1	4	4	0	1.000
Floyd Smith	1	0	6	2	4	.333
Glen Sonmor	1	0	5	1	4	.200
Bill Stewart	1	1	4	3	1	.750
Paul Thompson	1	0	4	0	4	.000
Cooney Weiland	1	1	4	4	0	1.000
Ron Wilson	1	0	4	0	4	.000

[1] served as player/coach under manager Frank Patrick.
[2] also recorded two ties in the 1927 Finals.
[3] also recorded a tie in the 1919 Finals.
[4] also includes totals prior to 1918 (Newsy Lalonde 3-2 in 1916, Pete Muldoon 3-1 in 1917, Frank Patrick 3-0 in 1915, Lester Patrick 0-3 in 1914).

Stanley Cup Notebook

Penalty Shots in the Stanley Cup Finals

A total of seven penalty shots have been awarded to players in the Stanley Cup Finals. None of the seven has been successful.

Date	Shooter	Goalie
April 15, 1937	Alex Shibicky (NYR)	Earl Robertson (Det)
April 13, 1944	Virgil Johnson (Chi)	Bill Durnan (Mtl)
May 16, 1971	Frank Mahovlich (Mtl)	Tony Esposito (Chi)
May 28, 1985	Ron Sutter (Phi)	Grant Fuhr (Edm)
May 30, 1985	Dave Poulin (Phi)	Grant Fuhr (Edm)
May 18, 1990	Petr Klima (Edm)	Rejean Lemelin (Bos)
June 7, 1994	Pavel Bure (Van)	Mike Richter (NYR)

Finals Relocate

The 1950 Stanley Cup Finals between the Detroit Red Wings and the New York Rangers featured the last games in the finals to ever be relocated to a neutral site venue. Games 2 and 3 were moved from Madison Square Garden to Maple Leaf Gardens in Toronto to accommodate a circus appearance in New York. The two games were split, as the Rangers won 3-1 on April 13, and Detroit posted a 4-0 victory on April 15. Detroit won the best-of-seven series 4-3.

CHAPTER 20

The Post-War Dynasties

Eight Benchmark Championship Teams

THE MODERN ECONOMICS OF SPORTS have made it almost impossible to keep a championship team together year after year. For example, eight different teams won the Stanley Cup between 1990 and 1999 for a diversity of titlist not seen since the first decade after the NHL assumed control of the trophy in 1926–27. The Edmonton Oilers' Stanley Cup triumph of 1990 may well have marked the end of an era of hockey dynasties dating back to the days after World War II.

The dynasty teams of the Post-War era also include legendary clubs like the Detroit Red Wings of the early 1950s, the Toronto Maple Leafs of the 1960s, three different Montreal Canadiens teams, and the New York Islanders of the early 1980s.

Although the definition of a sports "dynasty" can be debated, the following criteria have been used here:

a) Three-or-more consecutive Stanley Cup wins
b) Five or six consecutive playoff appearances including four Stanley Cup wins
c) Seven consecutive playoff appearances including five Stanley Cup wins

Eight teams fit this definition of a dynasty:

1) Toronto 1947-1951
2) Detroit 1950-1955
3) Montreal 1956-1960
4) Toronto 1962-1964
5) Montreal 1965-1969
6) Montreal 1976-1979
7) NY Islanders 1980-1983
8) Edmonton 1984-1990

Post-War NHL Dynasty Teams

Toronto 1947-51

STANDINGS

	Regular Season					Playoffs			
	GP	W	L	T	PCT	GP	W	L	PCT
*1946-47	60	31	19	10	.600	11	8	3	.727
*1947-48	60	32	15	13	.642	9	8	1	.889
*1948-49	60	22	25	13	.475	9	8	1	.889
1949-50	70	31	27	12	.529	7	3	4	.429
•*1950-51	70	41	16	13	.679	11	8	2	.733
	320	**157**	**102**	**61**	**.586**	**47**	**35**	**11**	**.755**

• Suspended game vs. Boston counted as a tie

PLAYERS ON ALL STANLEY CUP TEAMS

Bill Barilko, Turk Broda, Ted Kennedy, Joe Klukay, Howie Meeker, Gus Mortson, Jim Thomson, Harry Watson

ALL-STAR SELECTIONS

Turk Broda	G	1st (1948)
Gus Mortson	D	1st (1950)
Ted Kennedy	C	2nd (1950, 1951)
Jim Thomson	D	2nd (1951)
Sid Smith	LW	2nd (1951)

INDIVIDUAL HONORS

Howie Meeker, Calder, 1947
Turk Broda, Vezina, 1948
Al Rollins, Vezina, 1951

Detroit 1950-55

STANDINGS

	Regular Season					Playoffs			
	GP	W	L	T	PCT	GP	W	L	PCT
*1949-50	70	37	19	14	.629	14	8	6	.571
1950-51	70	44	13	13	.721	6	2	4	.333
*1951-52	70	44	14	12	.714	8	8	0	1.000
1952-53	70	36	16	18	.643	6	2	4	.333
*1953-54	70	37	19	14	.629	12	8	4	.667
*1954-55	70	42	17	11	.679	11	8	3	.727
	420	**240**	**98**	**82**	**.659**	**57**	**36**	**21**	**.632**

PLAYERS ON ALL STANLEY CUP TEAMS

Gordie Howe, Red Kelly, Ted Lindsay, Marty Pavelich, Marcel Pronovost, Johnny Wilson

ALL-STAR SELECTIONS

Sid Abel	C	1st (1950), 2nd (1951)
Ted Lindsay	LW	1st (1950, 1951, 1952 1953, 1954)
Leo Reise	D	2nd (1950, 1951)
Red Kelly	D	1st (1951, 1952, 1953, 1954, 1955), 2nd (1951)
Gordie Howe	RW	1st (1951, 1952, 1953, 1954), 2nd (1950)
Terry Sawchuk	G	1st (1951, 1952, 1953) 2nd (1954, 1955)
Alex Delvecchio	C	2nd (1953)
Bob Goldham	D	2nd (1955)

INDIVIDUAL HONORS

Ted Lindsay, Art Ross, 1950
Gordie Howe, Art Ross, 1951, 1952, 1953, 1964; Hart, 1952, 1953
Red Kelly, Norris, 1954; Lady Byng, 1951, 1953, 1954
Terry Sawchuk, Calder, 1951; Vezina, 1952, 1953, 1955

Montreal 1956-60

STANDINGS

	Regular Season					Playoffs			
	GP	W	L	T	PCT	GP	W	L	PCT
*1955-56	70	45	15	10	.714	10	8	2	.800
*1956-57	70	35	23	12	.586	10	8	2	.800
*1957-58	70	43	17	10	.686	10	8	2	.800
*1958-59	70	39	18	13	.650	11	8	3	.727
*1959-60	70	40	18	12.	.657	8	8	0	1.000
	350	**202**	**91**	**57**	**.659**	**49**	**40**	**9**	**.816**

PLAYERS ON ALL STANLEY CUP TEAMS

Jean Beliveau, Bernie Geoffrion, Doug Harvey, Tom Johnson, Don Marshall, Dickie Moore, Jacques Plante, Claude Provost, Henri Richard, Maurice Richard, Jean-Guy Talbot, Bob Turner

ALL-STAR SELECTIONS

Jacques Plante	G	1st (1956, 1969), 2nd (1957, 1958, 1960)
Doug Harvey	D	1st (1956, 1957, 1958. 1960), 2nd (1959)
Jean Beliveau	C	1st (1956, 1957, 1959, 1960), 2nd (1958)
Maurice Richard	RW	1st (1956), 2nd (1957)
Tom Johnson	D	1st (1959), 2nd (1956)
Bert Olmstead	LW	2nd (1956)
Dickie Moore	LW	1st (1958, 1959)
Bernie Geoffrion	RW	2nd (1960)

INDIVIDUAL HONORS

Jean Beliveau, Art Ross, 1956; Hart, 1956
Doug Harvey, Norris, 1956, 1957, 1958, 1968
Jacques Plante, Vezina, 1956, 1957, 1958, 1959, 1960
Dickie Moore, Art Ross, 1958, 1959
Tom Johnson, Norris, 1959
Ralph Backstrom, Calder, 1959

* Stanley Cup winner

Post-War NHL Dynasty Teams

continued

Toronto 1962-64

Standings

	Regular Season					Playoffs			
	GP	W	L	T	PCT	GP	W	L	PCT
*1961-62	70	37	22	11	.607	12	8	4	.667
*1962-63	70	35	23	12	.586	10	8	2	.800
*1963-64	70	33	25	12	.557	14	8	6	.571
	210	**105**	**70**	**35**	**.583**	**36**	**24**	**12**	**.667**

Players on All Stanley Cup Teams

George Armstrong, Bob Baun, Johnny Bower, Carl Brewer, Billy Harris, Tim Horton, Red Kelly, Dave Keon, Frank Mahovlich, Bob Pulford, Ed Shack, Don Simmons, Allan Stanley, Ron Stewart

All-Star Selections

Carl Brewer	D	1st (1963), 2nd (1962)
Frank Mahovlich	LW	1st (1963), 2nd (1962, 1964)
Dave Keon	C	2nd (1962)
Tim Horton	D	1st (1964), 2nd (1963)

Individual Honors

Dave Keon, Lady Byng, 1962, 1963
Kent Douglas, Calder, 1963

Montreal 1965-69

Standings

	Regular Season					Playoffs			
	GP	W	L	T	PCT	GP	W	L	PCT
*1964-65	70	36	23	11	.593	13	8	5	.615
*1965-66	70	41	21	8	.643	10	8	2	.800
1966-67	70	32	25	13	.550	10	6	4	.600
*1967-68	74	42	22	10	.635	13	12	1	.923
*1968-69	76	46	19	11	.678	14	12	2	.857
	360	**197**	**110**	**53**	**.621**	**58**	**48**	**10**	**.767**

Players on All Stanley Cup Teams

Ralph Backstrom, Jean Beliveau, Yvan Cournoyer, Dick Duff, John Ferguson, Terry Harper, Ted Harris, Jacques Laperriere, Claude Provost, Henri Richard, Bobby Rousseau, J.C. Tremblay, Gump Worsley

All-Star Selections

Jacques Laperriere	D	1st (1965, 1966)
Claude Provost	RW	1st (1965)
Charlie Hodge	G	2nd (1965)
Gump Worsley	G	1st (1968), 2nd (1966)
Jean Beliveau	C	2nd (1966, 1969)
Bobby Rousseau	RW	2nd (1966)
J.C. Tremblay	D	2nd (1968)
Ted Harris	D	2nd (1969)
Yvan Cournoyer	RW	2nd (1969)

Individual Honors

Jean Beliveau, Conn Smythe, 1965
Jacques Laperriere, Norris, 1966
Gump Worsley, Vezina, 1966, 1968
Charlie Hodge, Vezina, 1966
Rogie Vachon, Vezina, 1968
Claude Provost, Masterton, 1968
Serge Savard, Conn Smythe, 1969

Montreal 1976-79

Standings

	Regular Season					Playoffs			
	GP	W	L	T	PCT	GP	W	L	PCT
*1975-76	80	58	11	11	.794	13	12	1	.923
*1976-77	80	60	8	12	.825	14	12	2	.857
*1977-78	80	59	10	11	.806	15	12	3	.800
*1978-79	80	52	17	11	.719	16	12	4	.750
	320	**229**	**46**	**45**	**.786**	**58**	**48**	**10**	**.828**

Players on All Stanley Cup Teams

Rick Chartraw, Yvan Cournoyer, Ken Dryden, Bob Gainey, Doug Jarvis, Guy Lafleur, Yvon Lambert, Michel Laroque, Jacques Lemaire, Doug Risbrough, Steve Shutt, Mario Trembaly

All-Star Selections

Ken Dryden	G	1st (1976, 1977, 1978, 1979)
Guy Lafleur	RW	1st (1976, 1977, 1978, 1979)
Guy Lapointe	D	2nd (1976, 1977)
Larry Robinson	D	1st (1977, 1979) 2nd (1978)
Steve Shutt	LW	1st (1977), 2nd (1978)
Serge Savard	D	2nd (1979)

Individual Honors

Guy Lafleur, Art Ross, 1976, 1977, 1978; Hart, 1977, 1978; Conn Smythe, 1977
Ken Dryden, Vezina 1976,1977, 1978, 1979
Michel Laroque, Vezina, 1977, 1978, 1979
Larry Robinson, Norris, 1977; Conn Smythe, 1978
Bob Gainey, Selke, 1978, 1979; Conn Smythe, 1979
Serge Savard, Masterton, 1979

NY Islanders 1980-83

Standings

	Regular Season					Playoffs			
	GP	W	L	T	PCT	GP	W	L	PCT
*1979-80	80	39	28	13	.569	21	15	6	.714
*1980-81	80	48	18	14	.688	18	15	3	.833
*1981-82	80	54	16	10	.738	19	15	4	.789
*1982-83	80	42	26	12	.600	20	15	5	.769
	320	**183**	**88**	**49**	**.648**	**78**	**60**	**18**	**.769**

Players on All Stanley Cup Teams

Mike Bossy, Bob Bourne, Clark Gillies, Butch Goring, Anders Kallur, Gord Lane, Dave Langevin, Wayne Merrick, Ken Morrow, Bob Nystrom, Stefan Persson, Denis Potvin, Billy Smith, Duane Sutter, John Tonelli, Bryan Trottier

All-Star Selections

Denis Potvin	D	1st (1981)
Mike Bossy	RW	1st (1981, 1982, 1983, 1984)
Billy Smith	G	1st (1982)
Bryan Trottier	C	2nd (1982)
John Tonelli	LW	2nd (1982)
Roland Melanson	G	2nd (1983)

Individual Honors

Bryan Trottier, Conn Smythe, 1980
Butch Goring, Conn Smythe, 1981
Billy Smith, Vezina, 1982; Jennings, 1983; Conn Smythe, 1983
Mike Bossy, Conn Smythe, 1982; Lady Byng, 1983
Roland Melanson, Jennings, 1983

Edmonton 1984-90

Standings

	Regular Season					Playoffs			
	GP	W	L	T	PCT	GP	W	L	PCT
*1983-84	80	57	18	5	.744	19	15	4	.789
*1984-85	80	49	20	11	.681	18	15	3	.833
1985-86	80	56	17	7	.744	10	6	4	.600
*1986-87	80	50	24	6	.663	21	16	5	.762
*1987-88	80	44	25	11	.619	18	16	2	.889
1988-89	80	38	34	8	.525	7	3	4	.429
*1989-90	80	38	28	14	.563	22	16	6	.727
	560	**332**	**166**	**62**	**.648**	**115**	**87**	**28**	**.757**

Players on All Stanley Cup Teams

Glenn Anderson, Grant Fuhr, Randy Gregg, Charlie Huddy, Jari Kurri, Kevin Lowe, Mark Messier

All-Star Selections

Wayne Gretzky	C	1st (1984, 1985, 1986, 1987), 2nd (1988)
Paul Coffey	D	1st (1985, 1986) 2nd (1984)
Jari Kurri	RW	1st (1985, 1987) 2nd (1984, 1986, 1989)
Mark Messier	C	1st (1990)
	LW	2nd (1984)
Grant Fuhr	G	1st (1988)

Individual Honors

Wayne Gretzky, Art Ross, 1984, 1985, 1986, 1987; Hart, 1984, 1985, 1986, 1987; Conn Smythe, 1985, 1988
Mark Messier, Conn Smythe, 1984 Hart, 1990;
Jari Kurri, Lady Byng, 1985
Paul Coffey, Norris, 1985, 1986
Grant Fuhr, Vezina, 1988
Bill Ranford, Conn Smythe, 1990

* Stanley Cup winner

CHAPTER 21

Final Series Game Summaries

1990 – 1999

1990

EDMONTON OILERS - BOSTON BRUINS

GAME #1 - May 15, 1990 - Boston Garden - Edmonton 3, Boston 2 (3 OT)

EDMONTON: Glenn Anderson, Kelly Buchberger, Martin Gelinas, Adam Graves, Randy Gregg, Charlie Huddy, Petr Klima, Jari Kurri, Mark Lamb, Kevin Lowe, Craig MacTavish, Mark Messier, Craig Muni, Joe Murphy, Bill Ranford, Eldon Reddick, Reijo Ruotsalainen, Craig Simpson, Steve Smith, Esa Tikkanen.

BOSTON: Raymond Bourque, Randy Burridge, Lyndon Byers, Bob Carpenter, John Carter, Dave Christian, Garry Galley, Bob Gould, Greg Hawgood, Craig Janney, Rejean Lemelin, Andy Moog, Cam Neely, Allen Pedersen, Dave Poulin, Brian Propp, Bob Sweeney, Don Sweeney, Glen Wesley, Jim Wiemer.

First Period

1. EDMONTON GRAVES (MURPHY, SIMPSON) 9:46

Penalties: Anderson (Edm) (crosschecking) 3:05; Neely (Bos) (interference) 4:41; Messier (Edm) (tripping) 12:24; Carter (Bos) (roughing) 15:53.

Second Period

2. EDMONTON ANDERSON (MESSIER, RUOTSALAINEN) 13:00

Penalties: Tikkanen (Edm) (holding) 9:44; Huddy (Edm) (hooking) 14:38.

Third Period

3. BOSTON BOURQUE (HAWGOOD, NEELY) 3:43
4. BOSTON BOURQUE (NEELY, HAWGOOD) 18:31

Penalties: None.

First Overtime

No scoring.
Penalties: None.

Second Overtime

No scoring.
Penalties: None.

Third Overtime

5. EDMONTON KLIMA (KURRI, MacTAVISH) 15:13 (GWG)

Penalties: Neely (Bos) (roughing) 2:41; Smith (Edm) (roughing) 2:41; Moog (Bos) (slashing) 13:48; Tikkanen (Edm) (slashing) 13:48.

Goalies: Ranford (Edm), Moog (Bos)

Shots:								
	Edm	6 -	4 -	6 -	7 -	5 -	3	31
	Bos	10 -	6 -	15 -	6 -	7 -	8	52

Referee: Don Koharski
Linesmen: Ray Scapinello, Swede Knox

GAME #2 - May 18, 1990 - Boston Garden - Edmonton 7, Boston 2

EDMONTON: Glenn Anderson, Kelly Buchberger, Martin Gelinas, Adam Graves, Randy Gregg, Charlie Huddy, Petr Klima, Jari Kurri, Mark Lamb, Kevin Lowe, Craig MacTavish, Mark Messier, Craig Muni, Joe Murphy, Bill Ranford, Eldon Reddick, Reijo Ruotsalainen, Craig Simpson, Steve Smith, Esa Tikkanen.

BOSTON: Raymond Bourque, Randy Burridge, Bob Carpenter, John Carter, Dave Christian, Garry Galley, Bob Gould, Greg Hawgood, Craig Janney, Greg Johnston, Rejean Lemelin, Andy Moog, Cam Neely, Allen Pedersen, Dave Poulin, Brian Propp, Bob Sweeney, Don Sweeney, Glen Wesley, Jim Wiemer.

First Period

1. EDMONTON GRAVES (MURPHY, GREGG) 8:38
2. EDMONTON KURRI (TIKKANEN) 10:53 (PPG)
3. BOSTON BOURQUE (NEELY) 19:07

Penalties: Messier (Edm) (roughing) 0:49; Anderson (Edm) (tripping) 4:45; Carter (Bos) (highsticking major, game misconduct) 6:20; Smith (Edm) (hooking) 6:45; D. Sweeney (Bos) (elbowing) 12:55; Buchberger (Edm) (unsportsmanlike conduct) 12:55; Lamb (Edm) (tripping) 14:56.

Second Period

4. BOSTON HAWGOOD (BOURQUE, BURRIDGE) 2:56 (PPG)
5. EDMONTON KURRI (TIKKANEN) 4:21
6. EDMONTON SIMPSON (KURRI) 15:28
7. EDMONTON TIKKANEN (KURRI) 17:10
8. EDMONTON MURPHY (SMITH) 19:12

Penalties: Tikkanen (Edm) (holding) 1:14; Neely (Bos) (roughing) 2:27; Smith (Edm) (roughing) 2:27; Tikkanen (Edm) (roughing) 11:00; Hawgood (Bos) (roughing) 11:00; Ranford (Edm) (delay of game) 11:14.

Third Period

9. EDMONTON KURRI (RUOTSALAINEN, LAMB) 7:27

Penalties: B. Sweeney (Bos) (holding) 5:30; Johnston (Bos) (double minor, roughing) 12:50; Murphy (Edm) (roughing, unsportsmanlike conduct) 12:50.

Goalies: Ranford (Edm), Moog, Lemelin (Bos),

Shots:					
	Edm	2 -	9 -	11	22
	Bos	10 -	12 -	5	27

Referee: Kerry Fraser
Linesmen: Ron Finn, Wayne Bonney

(NOTE: Edmonton's Petr Klima was awarded a penalty shot at 19:00 of the second period. He was unsuccessful against Boston's Rejean Lemelin).

GAME #3 - May 20, 1990 - Northlands Coliseum - Boston 2, Edmonton 1

EDMONTON: Glenn Anderson, Kelly Buchberger, Martin Gelinas, Adam Graves, Randy Gregg, Charlie Huddy, Petr Klima, Jari Kurri, Mark Lamb, Kevin Lowe, Craig MacTavish, Mark Messier, Craig Muni, Joe Murphy, Bill Ranford, Eldon Reddick, Reijo Ruotsalainen, Craig Simpson, Steve Smith, Esa Tikkanen.

BOSTON: Raymond Bourque, Andy Brickley, Randy Burridge, John Byce, Bob Carpenter, John Carter, Dave Christian, Garry Galley, Bob Gould, Greg Hawgood, Craig Janney, Greg Johnston, Rejean Lemelin, Andy Moog, Cam Neely, Allen Pedersen, Brian Propp, Bob Sweeney, Don Sweeney, Glen Wesley.

First Period

1. BOSTON BYCE (NEELY) 0:10
2. BOSTON JOHNSTON (BURRIDGE, B. SWEENEY) 16:18

Penalties: D. Sweeney (Bos) (holding) 3:16; Gelinas (Edm) (hooking) 6:32; MacTavish (Edm) (tripping) 12:18; Kurri (Edm) (interference) 17:17.

Second Period

No scoring.
Penalties: Simpson (Edm) (interference) 12:28; Pedersen (Bos) (holding) 15:37.

Third Period

3. EDMONTON TIKKANEN (KURRI, SMITH) 5:54 (PPG)

Penalties: D. Sweeney (Bos) (holding) 1:30; Galley (Bos) (holding) 5:32; Bourque (Bos) (holding) 6:01; Smith (Edm) (interference) 6:33.

Goalies: Ranford (Edm), Moog (Bos)

Shots:					
	Bos	13 -	7 -	2	22
	Edm	11 -	4 -	14	29

Referee: Andy vanHellemond
Linesmen: Ray Scapinello, Swede Knox

GAME #4 - May 22, 1990 - Northlands Coliseum - Edmonton 5, Boston 1

EDMONTON: Glenn Anderson, Kelly Buchberger, Martin Gelinas, Adam Graves, Randy Gregg, Charlie Huddy, Petr Klima, Jari Kurri, Mark Lamb, Kevin Lowe, Craig MacTavish, Mark Messier, Craig Muni, Joe Murphy, Bill Ranford, Eldon Reddick, Reijo Ruotsalainen, Craig Simpson, Steve Smith, Esa Tikkanen.

BOSTON: Raymond Bourque, Andy Brickley, Randy Burridge, John Byce, Bob Carpenter, John Carter, Dave Christian, Peter Douris, Garry Galley, Greg Hawgood, Craig Janney, Greg Johnston, Rejean Lemelin, Andy Moog, Cam Neely, Allen Pedersen, Brian Propp, Bob Sweeney, Don Sweeney, Glen Wesley.

First Period

1. EDMONTON ANDERSON (SIMPSON, LAMB) 2:13 (PPG)
2. EDMONTON ANDERSON (MESSIER, SIMPSON) 16:27

Penalties: Carpenter (Bos) (interference) 0:24; Neely (Bos) (roughing) 3:16; Muni (Edm) (roughing) 3:16; Messier (Edm) (boarding) 13:33; Carter (Bos) (unsportsmanlike conduct) 16:11; Ruotsalainen (Edm) (unsportsmanlike conduct) 16:11; Hawgood (Bos) (slashing) 18:52.

Second Period

3. EDMONTON SIMPSON (MESSIER, ANDERSON) 1:00
4. EDMONTON TIKKANEN (KURRI, MacTAVISH) 19:15

Penalties: Wesley (Bos) (hooking) 6:20; Simpson (Edm) (tripping) 12:39; Anderson (Edm) (tripping) 19:50.

Third Period

5. BOSTON CARTER (unassisted) 15:02
6. EDMONTON SIMPSON (ANDERSON, MESSIER) 18:36

Penalties: Simpson (Edm) (elbowing) 5:04; Burridge (Bos) (slashing) 12:14; Neely (Bos) (highsticking) 15:14; B. Sweeney (Bos) (fighting) 17:06; Smith (Edm) (fighting) 17:06.

Goalies: Ranford (Edm), Moog (Bos)

Shots:					
	Bos	7 -	11 -	7	25
	Edm	12 -	10 -	11	33

Referee: Don Koharski
Linesmen: Ron Finn, Wayne Bonney

GAME #5 - May 24, 1990 - Boston Garden - Edmonton 4, Boston 1

EDMONTON: Glenn Anderson, Kelly Buchberger, Martin Gelinas, Adam Graves, Randy Gregg, Charlie Huddy, Petr Klima, Jari Kurri, Mark Lamb, Kevin Lowe, Craig MacTavish, Mark Messier, Craig Muni, Joe Murphy, Bill Ranford, Eldon Reddick, Reijo Ruotsalainen, Craig Simpson, Steve Smith, Esa Tikkanen.

BOSTON: Raymond Bourque, Randy Burridge, John Byce, Lyndon Byers, Bob Carpenter, John Carter, Dave Christian, Garry Galley, Bob Gould, Greg Hawgood, Craig Janney, Greg Johnston, Rejean Lemelin, Andy Moog, Cam Neely, Allen Pedersen, Brian Propp, Bob Sweeney, Don Sweeney, Glen Wesley.

First Period

No scoring.

Penalties: Bourque (Bos) (crosschecking) 2:56; Tikkanen (Edm) (holding) 4:32; Galley (Bos) (holding) 4:45.

Second Period

1.	EDMONTON	ANDERSON (unassisted)	1:17	
2.	EDMONTON	SIMPSON (ANDERSON)	9:31	(GWG)

Penalties: None.

Third Period

3.	EDMONTON	SMITH (MESSIER, SIMPSON)	6:09
4.	EDMONTON	MURPHY (LAMB, GELINAS)	14:53
5.	BOSTON	BYERS (B. SWEENEY, BOURQUE)	16:30

Penalties: Huddy (Edm) (hooking) 7:09; Bourque (Bos) (holding) 11:46.

Goalies: Ranford (Edm), Moog (Bos)

Shots:					
	Edm	10	5	7	22
	Bos	10	10	10	30

Referee: Andy vanHellemond

Linesmen: Ray Scapinello, Swede Knox

1991

PITTSBURGH PENGUINS - MINNESOTA NORTH STARS

GAME #1 - May 15, 1991 - Civic Arena - Minnesota 5, Pittsburgh 4

PITTSBURGH: Tom Barrasso, Phil Bourque, Bob Errey, Ron Francis, Jiri Hrdina, Jaromir Jagr, Grant Jennings, Mario Lemieux, Troy Loney, Joe Mullen, Larry Murphy, Frank Pietrangelo, Mark Recchi, Gordie Roberts, Ulf Samuelsson, Paul Stanton, Kevin Stevens, Peter Taglianetti, Bryan Trottier, Scott Young.

MINNESOTA: Brian Bellows, Neal Broten, Marc Bureau, Jon Casey, Shawn Chambers, Shane Churla, Ulf Dahlen, Chris Dahlquist, Gaetan Duchesne, Dave Gagner, Stewart Gavin, Brian Glynn, Brian Hayward, Jim Johnson, Basil McRae, Mike Modano, Brian Propp, Bobby Smith, Mark Tinordi, Neil Wilkinson.

First Period

1.	PITTSBURGH	SAMUELSSON (FRANCIS)	3:45
2.	MINNESOTA	BROTEN (unassisted)	6:32
3.	MINNESOTA	DAHLEN (SMITH, CHAMBERS)	9:49

Penalties: Propp (Min) (slashing), 4:17; Loney (Pit) (roughing), 7:45; Chambers (Min) (hooking), 12:32; Tinordi (Min) (highsticking), 13:45; Recchi (Pit) (interference), 15:02; McRae (Min) (unsportsmanlike conduct), 18:13; Bureau (Min) (boarding), 19:39.

Second Period

4.	PITTSBURGH	LEMIEUX (FRANCIS)	3:54	(SHG)
5.	MINNESOTA	BUREAU (GAVIN)	6:53	(SHG)
6.	PITTSBURGH	YOUNG (MURPHY, JAGR)	7:43	(PPG)
7.	MINNESOTA	BROTEN (MODANO)	17:01	

Penalties: Roberts (Pit) (interference), 2:01; Johnson (Min) (slashing), 5:58; Bureau (Min) (holding), 10:25; Stanton (Pit) (hooking), 19:11.

Third Period

8.	MINNESOTA	SMITH (DAHLEN)	1:39	(GWG)
9.	PITTSBURGH	MULLEN (JAGR, YOUNG)	10:35	

Penalties: Jennings (Pit) (crosschecking), 4:08; Casey (Min) (slashing), 8:25.

Goalies: Casey (Min), Barrasso (Pit)

Shots:					
	Min	9	12	8	29
	Pit	17	11	10	38

Referee: Don Koharski

Linesmen: Ray Scapinello, Wayne Bonney

GAME #2 - May 17, 1991 - Civic Arena - Pittsburgh 4, Minnesota 1

PITTSBURGH: Tom Barrasso, Phil Bourque, Paul Coffey, Bob Errey, Ron Francis, Randy Gilhen, Jaromir Jagr, Mario Lemieux, Troy Loney, Joe Mullen, Larry Murphy, Jim Paek, Frank Pietrangelo, Mark Recchi, Gordie Roberts, Ulf Samuelsson, Paul Stanton, Kevin Stevens, Peter Taglianetti, Bryan Trottier.

MINNESOTA: Brian Bellows, Perry Berezan, Neal Broten, Marc Bureau, Jon Casey, Shawn Chambers, Ulf Dahlen, Chris Dahlquist, Gaetan Duchesne, Dave Gagner, Stewart Gavin, Brian Glynn, Brian Hayward, Jim Johnson, Mike Modano, Brian Propp, Doug Smail, Bobby Smith, Mark Tinordi, Neil Wilkinson.

First Period

1.	PITTSBURGH	ERREY (TAGLIANETTI)	14:26	(SHG)
2.	PITTSBURGH	STEVENS (LEMIEUX, MURPHY)	19:10	(PPG,GWG)

Penalties: Francis (Pit) (hooking) 1:07; Errey (Pit) (boarding), 9:08; Recchi (Pit) (crosschecking), 13:06; Samuelsson (Pit) (hold), 15:12; Bellows (Min) (hooking), 16:36; Chambers (Min) (interference), 18:59; Pit bench (too many men, served by Stevens), 20:00.

Second Period

3.	MINNESOTA	MODANO (CHAMBERS, CASEY)	0:55	(PPG)
4.	PITTSBURGH	LEMIEUX (BOURQUE)	15:04	
5.	PITTSBURGH	STEVENS (MULLEN, MURPHY)	16:32	

Penalties: Duchesne (Min) (holding) 6:22; Murphy (Pit) (hooking), 6:37; Smith (Min) (interference), 9:30; Glynn (Min) (roughing), 17:27; Wilkinson (Min) (roughing), 19:58; Bureau (Min) (roughing), Loney (Pit) (roughing, fighting major), Tinordi (Min) (fighting major), 20:00.

Third Period

No scoring.

Penalties: Modano (Min) (highsticking), 5:29; Duchesne (Min) (hooking), 10:39; Samuelsson (Pit) (holding), 12:58; Bureau (Min) (roughing), Stevens (Pit) (roughing), Trottier (Pit) (misconduct), 16:20; Gagner (Min), Stanton (Pit) (roughing), 17:03; Roberts (Pit) (holding, spearing major, game misconduct), 17:34; Min bench (too many men, served by Modano), 19:41; Francis (Pit) (holding), 20:00.

Goalies: Casey (Min), Barrasso (Pit)

Shots:					
	Min	12	12	16	40
	Pit	14	12	5	31

Referee: Andy vanHellemond

Linesmen: Kevin Collins, Gord Broseker

GAME #3 - May 19, 1991 - Met Center - Minnesota 3, Pittsburgh 1

PITTSBURGH: Tom Barrasso, Phil Bourque, Paul Coffey, Bob Errey, Ron Francis, Randy Gilhen, Jiri Hrdina, Jaromir Jagr, Troy Loney, Joe Mullen, Larry Murphy, Jim Paek, Frank Pietrangelo, Mark Recchi, Gordie Roberts, Ulf Samuelsson, Paul Stanton, Kevin Stevens, Peter Taglianetti, Bryan Trottier.

MINNESOTA: Brian Bellows, Neal Broten, Marc Bureau, Jon Casey, Shawn Chambers, Shane Churla, Ulf Dahlen, Chris Dahlquist, Gaetan Duchesne, Dave Gagner, Stewart Gavin, Brian Glynn, Brian Hayward, Jim Johnson, Basil McRae, Mike Modano, Brian Propp, Bobby Smith, Mark Tinordi, Neil Wilkinson.

First Period

No scoring.

Penalties: Errey (Pit) (charging), 9:08; Francis (Pit) (holding) 13:44; Smith (Min) (interference), 16:21.

Second Period

1.	MINNESOTA	GAGNER (MODANO, JOHNSON)	7:21	
2.	MINNESOTA	SMITH (BELLOWS, DAHLQUIST)	7:54	(GWG)

Penalties: McRae (Min) (boarding), 4:08; Recchi (Pit), Chambers (Min) (unsportsmanlike conduct), 5:23; Duchesne (Min) (holding), 8:38; Taglianetti (Pit) (highsticking), 12:36; Loney (Pit), Johnson (Min) (roughing), 17:28.

Third Period

3.	PITTSBURGH	BOURQUE (JAGR, TROTTIER)	1:23
4.	MINNESOTA	DUCHESNE (GAVIN, BROTEN)	2:09

Penalties: Johnson (Min) (highsticking), Bourque (Pit) (slashing), 7:20; Stanton (Pit), Bellows (Min) (roughing), 8:09; Gilhen (Pit) (holding), Gagner (Min) (roughing), 8:13; Samuelsson (Pit) (elbowing), 8:53; Dahlquist (Min) (tripping), 13:34; Stevens (Pit) (spearing major, game misconduct), 18:47; Barrasso (Pit) (slashing, served by Mullen), 19:21; Gilhen (Pit), Bellows (Min) (misconduct), 19:53; Errey (Pit) (charging), Smith (Min) (highsticking), 20:00.

Goalies: Casey (Min), Barrasso (Pit)

Shots:					
	Pit	7	8	15	30
	Min	12	8	13	33

Referee: Kerry Fraser

Linesmen: Ray Scapinello, Wayne Bonney

GAME #4 - May 21, 1991 - Met Center - Pittsburgh 5, Minnesota 3

PITTSBURGH: Tom Barrasso, Phil Bourque, Paul Coffey, Bob Errey, Ron Francis, Randy Gilhen, Jaromir Jagr, Grant Jennings, Mario Lemieux, Troy Loney, Joe Mullen, Larry Murphy, Jim Paek, Frank Pietrangelo, Mark Recchi, Gordie Roberts, Ulf Samuelsson, Paul Stanton, Kevin Stevens, Bryan Trottier.

MINNESOTA: Brian Bellows, Neal Broten, Marc Bureau, Jon Casey, Shawn Chambers, Shane Churla, Ulf Dahlen, Chris Dahlquist, Gaetan Duchesne, Dave Gagner, Stewart Gavin, Brian Glynn, Brian Hayward, Jim Johnson, Basil McRae, Mike Modano, Brian Propp, Bobby Smith, Mark Tinordi, Neil Wilkinson.

First Period

1.	PITTSBURGH	STEVENS (unassisted)	0:58
2.	PITTSBURGH	FRANCIS (STEVENS, MULLEN)	2:36
3.	PITTSBURGH	LEMIEUX (RECCHI, MURPHY)	2:58
4.	MINNESOTA	GAGNER (BELLOWS, DAHLEN)	18:22

Penalties: Samuelsson (Pit) (charging), 7:27; Stanton (Pit), Propp (Min) (highsticking), 7:44; Johnson (Min) (holding), 14:45; Samuelsson (Pit) (holding), 18:38.

Second Period

5.	PITTSBURGH	TROTTIER (ERREY, JAGR)	9:55	(GWG)
6.	MINNESOTA	PROPP (GAGNER)	13:10	(PPG)
7.	MINNESOTA	MODANO (PROPP, GAGNER)	18:25	(PPG)

Penalties: Modano (Min) (slashing) 4:28; Murphy (Pit), McRae (Min) (roughing), 11:22; Stevens (Pit) (holding), 11:49; Lemieux (Pit) (interference), Bellows (Min) (roughing), 12:34; Lemieux (Pit) (roughing), 13:10; Murphy (Pit) (roughing), 16:59; Errey (Pit) (highsticking), 18:06; Gagner (Min) (roughing), 18:50.

Third Period

8.	PITTSBURGH	BOURQUE (MULLEN, LEMIEUX)	19:45	(ENG)

Penalties: Loney (Pit) (highsticking major, game misconduct), 13:03; Casey (Min) (interference, served by Propp), 16:52.

Goalies: Casey (Min), Barrasso (Pit)

Shots:				
Pit	13	5	6	24
Min	14	17	7	38

Referee: Andy vanHellemond
Linesmen: Kevin Collins, Gord Broseker

GAME #5 - May 23, 1991 - Civic Arena - Pittsburgh 6, Minnesota 4

PITTSBURGH: Tom Barrasso, Phil Bourque, Paul Coffey, Bob Errey, Ron Francis, Randy Gilhen, Jaromir Jagr, Mario Lemieux, Troy Loney, Joe Mullen, Larry Murphy, Jim Paek, Frank Pietrangelo, Mark Recchi, Gordie Roberts, Ulf Samuelsson, Paul Stanton, Kevin Stevens, Peter Taglianetti, Bryan Trottier.

MINNESOTA: Brian Bellows, Neal Broten, Marc Bureau, Jon Casey, Shawn Chambers, Shane Churla, Ulf Dahlen, Chris Dahlquist, Gaetan Duchesne, Dave Gagner, Stewart Gavin, Brian Glynn, Brian Hayward, Jim Johnson, Basil McRae, Mike Modano, Brian Propp, Bobby Smith, Mark Tinordi, Neil Wilkinson.

First Period

1.	PITTSBURGH	LEMIEUX (MURPHY, COFFEY)	5:36	(PPG)
2.	PITTSBURGH	STEVENS (COFFEY, MURPHY)	10:08	(PPG)
3.	PITTSBURGH	RECCHI (LEMIEUX, BOURQUE)	11:45	
4.	PITTSBURGH	RECCHI (LEMIEUX, MURPHY)	13:41	
5.	MINNESOTA	BROTEN (TINORDI)	14:52	(SHG)

Penalties: Glynn (Min) (crosschecking), 3:38; Trottier (Pit) (crosschecking), 7:07; Tinordi (Min) (hooking), 9:54; McRae (Min) (charging, roughing, unsportsmanlike conduct), Churla (Min) (roughing), Paek (Pit) (roughing), Stevens (Pit) (roughing), 14:26.

Second Period

6.	MINNESOTA	GAGNER (PROPP)	6:54	(SHG)
7.	PITTSBURGH	FRANCIS (MULLEN)	16:26	(GWG)

Penalties: Dahlquist (Min) (hooking), 5:23; Trottier (Pit) (tripping), 10:46; Gagner (Min) (interference), Taglianetti (Pit) (holding), 14:53; Bourque (Pit) (illegal stick), 17:20.

Third Period

8.	MINNESOTA	DAHLEN (SMITH, DUCHESNE)	1:36
9.	MINNESOTA	GAGNER (PROPP, GAVIN)	7:41
10.	PITTSBURGH	LONEY (MURPHY,FRANCIS)	18:21

Penalties: Taglianetti (Pit) (crosschecking), 8:40; Gagner (Min) (tripping), 9:49; Glynn (Min) (crosschecking), 10:05; Tinordi (Min), Stevens (Pit) (roughing), 12:00; Gagner (Min), Lemieux (Pit) (roughing), 19:02.

Goalies: Casey, Hayward (Min), Barrasso, Pietrangelo (Pit)

Shots:				
Min	7	9	9	25
Pit	18	5	8	31

Referee: Kerry Fraser
Linesmen: Ray Scapinello, Wayne Bonney

GAME #6 - May 25, 1991 - Met Center - Pittsburgh 8, Minnesota 0

PITTSBURGH: Tom Barrasso, Phil Bourque, Paul Coffey, Bob Errey, Ron Francis, Randy Gilhen, Jaromir Jagr, Mario Lemieux, Troy Loney, Joe Mullen, Larry Murphy, Jim Paek, Frank Pietrangelo, Mark Recchi, Gordie Roberts, Ulf Samuelsson, Paul Stanton, Kevin Stevens, Peter Taglianetti, Bryan Trottier.

MINNESOTA: Brian Bellows, Neal Broten, Marc Bureau, Jon Casey, Shawn Chambers, Shane Churla, Ulf Dahlen, Chris Dahlquist, Gaetan Duchesne, Dave Gagner, Stewart Gavin, Brian Glynn, Brian Hayward, Jim Johnson, Basil McRae, Mike Modano, Brian Propp, Bobby Smith, Mark Tinordi, Neil Wilkinson.

First Period

1.	PITTSBURGH	SAMUELSSON (TAGLIANETTI, TROTTIER)	2:00 (PPG,GWG)
2.	PITTSBURGH	LEMIEUX (MURPHY)	12:19 (SHG)
3.	PITTSBURGH	MULLEN (STEVENS, TAGLIANETTI)	13:14 (PPG)

Penalties: Broten (Min) (interference), 0:09; Johnson (Min) (highsticking), 6:20; Stevens (Pit) (holding), 10:25; Roberts (Pit) (roughing), 10:59; Modano (Min) (interference), 11:17; Roberts (Pit) (interference), 13:58; Taglianetti (Pit) (tripping), 17:35.

Second Period

4.	PITTSBURGH	ERREY (JAGR, LEMIEUX)	13:15
5.	PITTSBURGH	FRANCIS (MULLEN)	14:28
6.	PITTSBURGH	MULLEN (STEVENS, SAMUELSSON)	18:44

Penalties: Samuelsson (Pit) (roughing), Recchi (Pit) (roughing), Tinordi (Min) (double minor, roughing), Churla (Min) (roughing), McRae (Min) (misconduct), 8:03; Gagner (Min) (roughing), 15:18.

Third Period

7.	PITTSBURGH	PAEK (LEMIEUX)	1:19
8.	PITTSBURGH	MURPHY (LEMIEUX)	13:45 (PPG)

Penalties: McRae (Min) (slashing), 12:27; Stevens (Pit), Gavin (Min) (slashing), 13:03.

Goalies: Casey, Hayward (Min), Barrasso (Pit)

Shots:				
Pit	11	9	8	28
Min	16	7	16	39

Referee: Don Koharski
Linesmen: Kevin Collins, Gord Broseker

1992

PITTSBURGH PENGUINS - CHICAGO BLACKHAWKS

GAME #1 - May 26, 1992 - Civic Arena - Pittsburgh 5, Chicago 4

PITTSBURGH: Tom Barrasso, Phil Bourque, Jock Callander, Bob Errey, Ron Francis, Jiri Hrdina, Jaromir Jagr, Mario Lemieux, Troy Loney, Shawn McEachern, Larry Murphy, Jim Paek, Gord Roberts, Kjell Samuelsson, Ulf Samuelsson, Paul Stanton, Kevin Stevens, Rick Tocchet, Bryan Trottier, Ken Wregget.

CHICAGO: Ed Belfour, Rob Brown, Chris Chelios, Michel Goulet, Dirk Graham, Dominik Hasek, Mike Hudson, Igor Kravchuk, Frantisek Kucera, Steve Larmer, Jocelyn Lemieux, Bryan Marchment, Stephane Matteau, Brian Noonan, Mike Peluso, Jeremy Roenick, Cam Russell, Steve Smith, Brent Sutter.

First Period

1.	CHICAGO	CHELIOS (SUTTER)	6:34	(PPG)
2.	CHICAGO	GOULET (unassisted)	13:17	
3.	CHICAGO	GRAHAM (CHELIOS)	13:43	
4.	PITTSBURGH	BOURQUE (TOCCHET, FRANCIS)	17:26	(PPG)

Penalties: Hudson (Chi) (interference) 2:07; Roberts (Pit) (holding) 6:27; Peluso (Chi) (hooking) 9:34; Kravchuk (Chi) (holding) 15:44; Trottier (Pit) (interference) 18:39.

Second Period

5.	CHICAGO	SUTTER (LARMER, CHELIOS)	11:36
6.	PITTSBURGH	TOCCHET (STANTON, McEACHERN)	15:24
7.	PITTSBURGH	LEMIEUX (STEVENS)	16:23

Penalties: Brown (Chi) (elbowing) 2:17; Chicago bench (too many men) 13:21.

Third Period

8.	PITTSBURGH	JAGR (unassisted)	15:05	
9.	PITTSBURGH	LEMIEUX (MURPHY, FRANCIS)	19:47	(PPG,GWG)

Penalties: Stanton (Pit) (hooking) 1:24; Murphy (Pit) (hooking) 17:39; Smith (Chi) (hooking) 19:42.

Goalies: Belfour (Chi), Barrasso (Pit)

Shots:				
Chi	11	11	12	34
Pit	15	10	14	39

Referee: Andy vanHellemond
Linesmen: Kevin Collins, Gerard Gauthier.

GAME #2 - May 28, 1992 - Civic Arena - Pittsburgh 3, Chicago 1

PITTSBURGH: Tom Barrasso, Phil Bourque, Jock Callander, Bob Errey, Ron Francis, Jiri Hrdina, Jaromir Jagr, Mario Lemieux, Troy Loney, Shawn McEachern, Larry Murphy, Jim Paek, Gord Roberts, Kjell Samuelsson, Ulf Samuelsson, Paul Stanton, Kevin Stevens, Rick Tocchet, Bryan Trottier, Ken Wregget.

CHICAGO: Ed Belfour, Rod Buskas, Chris Chelios, Greg Gilbert, Michel Goulet, Dirk Graham, Stu Grimson, Dominik Hasek, Mike Hudson, Igor Kravchuk, Frantisek Kucera, Steve Larmer, Jocelyn Lemieux, Bryan Marchment, Stephane Matteau, Brian Noonan, Mike Peluso, Jeremy Roenick, Steve Smith, Brent Sutter.

First Period

1.	PITTSBURGH	ERREY (PAEK)	9:52	(SHG)

Penalties: Peluso (Chi) (roughing) 2:07; Stanton (Pit) (delay of game, tripping) 7:38; Smith (Chi) (interference) 11:05; Noonan (Chi) (crosschecking) 18:36.

Second Period

2.	CHICAGO	MARCHMENT (NOONAN, GILBERT)	10:24	
3.	PITTSBURGH	LEMIEUX (TOCCHET)	12:55	(PPG,GWG)
4.	PITTSBURGH	LEMIEUX (TOCCHET, K. SAMUELSSON)	15:23	

Penalties: Marchment (Chi) (elbowing) 12:12; Chicago bench (too many men) 19:43.

Third Period

No scoring.

Penalties: Roberts (Pit) (holding) 5:09.

Goalies: Belfour (Chi), Barrasso (Pit)

Shots:				
Chi	11	4	4	19
Pit	8	11	6	25

Referee: Terry Gregson
Linesmen: Swede Knox, Ray Scapinello.

GAME #3 - May 30, 1992 - Chicago Stadium - Pittsburgh 1, Chicago 0

PITTSBURGH: Tom Barrasso, Phil Bourque, Jock Callander, Ron Francis, Jiri Hrdina, Jaromir Jagr, Mario Lemieux, Troy Loney, Shawn McEachern, Dave Michayluk, Larry Murphy, Jim Paek, Gord Roberts, Kjell Samuelsson, Ulf Samuelsson, Paul Stanton, Kevin Stevens, Rick Tocchet, Bryan Trottier, Ken Wregget.

CHICAGO: Ed Belfour, Rob Brown, Rod Buskas, Chris Chelios, Greg Gilbert, Michel Goulet, Dirk Graham, Dominik Hasek, Mike Hudson, Igor Kravchuk, Frantisek Kucera, Steve Larmer, Jocelyn Lemieux, Bryan Marchment, Stephane Matteau, Brian Noonan, Mike Peluso, Jeremy Roenick, Steve Smith, Brent Sutter.

First Period

1.	PITTSBURGH	STEVENS (PAEK, TOCCHET)	15:26	(GWG)

Penalties: K. Samuelsson (Pit) (highsticking) 5:43; Roberts (Pit) (tripping) 11:50; Goulet (Chi) (holding) 16:47, Jagr (Pit) (holding) 19:14.

Second Period

No scoring.

Penalties: Larmer (Chi) (crosschecking) 4:38; Stanton (Pit) (holding) 7:04; Chelios (Chi) (slashing) 10:56.

Third Period
No scoring.
Penalties: Paek (Pit) (interference) 10:05; Chelios (Chi) (fighting major, game misconduct) 19:29.

Goalies: Belfour (Chi), Barrasso (Pit)

Shots:					
Pit	6	- 8	- 6	20
Chi	13	- 6	- 8	27

Referee: Don Koharski
Linesmen: Kevin Collins, Gerard Gauthier

GAME #4 - June 1, 1992 - Chicago Stadium - Pittsburgh 6, Chicago 5

PITTSBURGH: Tom Barrasso, Phil Bourque, Jock Callander, Bob Errey, Ron Francis, Jiri Hrdina, Jaromir Jagr, Mario Lemieux, Troy Loney, Shawn McEachern, Larry Murphy, Jim Paek, Gord Roberts, Kjell Samuelsson, Ulf Samuelsson, Paul Stanton, Kevin Stevens, Rick Tocchet, Bryan Trottier, Ken Wregget.

CHICAGO: Ed Belfour, Rob Brown, Rod Buskas, Chris Chelios, Greg Gilbert, Michel Goulet, Dirk Graham, Stu Grimson, Dominik Hasek, Mike Hudson, Igor Kravchuk, Frantisek Kucera, Steve Larmer, Jocelyn Lemieux, Bryan Marchment, Stephane Matteau, Brian Noonan, Jeremy Roenick, Steve Smith, Brent Sutter.

First Period

1.	PITTSBURGH	JAGR (LONEY)	1:37	
2.	CHICAGO	GRAHAM (MATTEAU, CHELIOS)	6:21	
3.	PITTSBURGH	STEVENS (LEMIEUX, TOCCHET)	6:33	
4.	CHICAGO	GRAHAM (CHELIOS)	6:51	
5.	PITTSBURGH	LEMIEUX (MURPHY, STEVENS)	10:13	(PPG)
6.	CHICAGO	GRAHAM (LEMIEUX, NOONAN)	16:18	

Penalties: U. Samuelsson (Pit) (interference), Stanton (Pit) (misconduct), Gilbert (Chi) (misconduct) 7:28; Chelios (Chi) (elbowing) 8:17; Roberts (Pit) (roughing) 12:44.

Second Period

7.	PITTSBURGH	TOCCHET (LEMIEUX, STEVENS)	0:58	
8.	CHICAGO	ROENICK (NOONAN, GILBERT)	15:40	

Penalties: Stanton (Pit) (hooking) 2:21; Tocchet (Pit) (holding) 5:41.

Third Period

9.	PITTSBURGH	MURPHY (TOCCHET)	4:51	
10.	PITTSBURGH	FRANCIS (McEACHERN, PAEK)	7:59	(GWG)
11.	CHICAGO	ROENICK (GRIMSON, BUSKAS)	11:18	

Penalties: none.

Goalies: Belfour, Hasek (Chi), Barrasso (Pit)

Shots:				
Pit	12	- 9	- 8	29
Chi	8	- 14	- 7	29

Referee: Andy vanHellemond
Linesmen: Swede Knox, Ray Scapinello

1993

MONTREAL CANADIENS – LOS ANGELES KINGS

GAME #1 - June 1, 1993 - Montreal Forum - Los Angeles 4, Montreal 1

LOS ANGELES: Rob Blake, Pat Conacher, Gord Donnelly, Tony Granato, Wayne Gretzky, Mark Hardy, Kelly Hrudey, Charlie Huddy, Jari Kurri, Marty McSorley, Corey Millen, Luc Robitaille, Warren Rychel, Tomas Sandstrom, Dave Taylor, Tim Watters, Gary Shuchuk, Darryl Sydor, Alexei Zhitnik.

MONTREAL: Brian Bellows, Benoit Brunet, Patrice Brisebois, Guy Carbonneau, J.J. Daigneault, Vincent Damphousse, Eric Desjardins, Gilbert Dionne, Paul DiPietro, Sean Hill, John LeClair, Stephan Lebeau, Gary Leeman, Kirk Muller, Lyle Odelein, Ed Ronan, Patrick Roy, Denis Savard, Mathieu Schneider.

First Period

1.	LOS ANGELES	ROBITAILLE (ZHITNIK, GRETZKY)	3:30	(PPG)
2.	MONTREAL	RONAN (unassisted)	18:09	

Penalties: Odelein (Mtl) (holding) 2:42, Dionne (Mtl) (highsticking) 6:12, McSorley (LA) (delay of game) 11:03, Kurri (LA) (holding) 15:54.

Second Period

3.	LOS ANGELES	ROBITAILLE (BLAKE, GRETZKY)	17:41	(PPG, GWG)

Penalties: Granato (LA) (goaltender interference) 5:08, Taylor (LA) Muller (Mtl) (roughing) 6:23, McSorley (LA) Odelein (Mtl) (unsportsmanlike conduct) 7:16, Damphousse (Mtl) (slashing) 10:23, Millen (LA) Desjardins (Mtl) (highsticking) Brisebois (Mtl) (delay of game) 18:33, Gretzky (LA) (hooking) 19:32.

Third Period

4.	LOS ANGELES	KURRI (GRETZKY, GRANATO)	1:51	
5.	LOS ANGELES	GRETZKY (SANDSTROM)	18:02	(ENG)

Penalties: Huddy (LA) (hooking) 6:41, Daigneault (Mtl) (cross-checking) 18:41.

Goalies: Hrudey (LA), Roy (Montreal)

Shots:				
LA	11	- 20	- 7	38
Mtl	11	- 10	- 11	32

Referee: Andy vanHellemond
Linesmen: Gerard Gauthier, Ray Scapinello.

GAME #2 - June 3, 1993 - Montreal Forum - Montreal 3, Los Angeles 2 (OT)

LOS ANGELES: Rob Blake, Pat Conacher, Gord Donnelly, Tony Granato, Wayne Gretzky, Kelly Hrudey, Charlie Huddy, Marty McSorley, Corey Millen, Luc Robitaille, Warren Rychel, Tomas Sandstrom, Gary Shuchuk, Darryl Sydor, Dave Taylor, Tim Watters, Alexei Zhitnik.

MONTREAL: Brian Bellows, Benoit Brunet, Patrice Brisebois, Guy Carbonneau, J.J. Daigneault, Vincent Damphousse, Eric Desjardins, Paul DiPietro, Gilbert Dionne, Kevin Haller, Mike Keane, John LeClair, Stephan Lebeau, Gary Leeman, Kirk Muller, Lyle Odelein, Ed Ronan, Patrick Roy, Mathieu Schneider.

First Period

1.	MONTREAL	DESJARDINS (DAMPHOUSSE LEBEAU)	18:31	

Penalties: Odelein (Mtl) (roughing) 5:57, Robitaille (LA) (hooking) 6:40, Brisebois (Mtl) (interference) 7:05, Blake (LA) (tripping) 10:25, Roy (Mtl) (highsticking) 10:38, Watters (LA) (holding) Muller (Mtl) (tripping) 13:01, Sydor (LA) (holding) 14:44, Schneider (Mtl) (highsticking) 17:02, Granato (LA) (holding) 17:53.

Second Period

2.	LOS ANGELES	TAYLOR (unassisted)	5:12	(SHG)

Penalties: Muller (Mtl) (cross-checking) 0:35, Huddy (LA) (cross-checking) 4:20, McSorley (LA) Damphousse (Mtl) (roughing) 9:43, Robitaille (LA) Dionne (Mtl) (roughing) 16:02.

Third Period

3.	LOS ANGELES	CONACHER (TAYLOR, GRANATO)	8:32	
4.	MONTREAL	DESJARDINS (DAMPHOUSSE, SCHNEIDER)	18:47	(PPG)

Penalties: Brunet (Mtl) (slashing) 1:31, Damphousse (Mtl) (cross-checking) 2:30, Zhitnik (LA) (tripping) 4:17, Taylor (LA) (goaltender interference) 11:56, Brisebois (Mtl) (cross-checking) 13:16, McSorley (LA) (illegal stick) 18:15).

Overtime

5.	MONTREAL	DESJARDINS (BRUNET, RONAN)	0:51	(GWG)

Penalties: Blake (LA) (misconduct) 0:51.

Goalies: Hrudey (LA), Roy (Montreal)

Shots:					
LA	5	- 9	- 9	- 1	24
Mtl	16	- 12	- 11	- 2	41

Referee: Kerry Fraser
Linesmen: Kevin Collins, Ray Scapinello.

GAME #3 - June 5, 1993 - Great Western Forum - Montreal 4, Los Angeles 3 (OT)

MONTREAL: Brian Bellows, Benoit Brunet, Patrice Brisebois, Guy Carbonneau, J.J. Daigneault, Vincent Damphousse, Eric Desjardins, Paul DiPietro, Gilbert Dionne, Kevin Haller, Mike Keane, John LeClair, Stephan Lebeau, Gary Leeman, Kirk Muller, Lyle Odelein, Ed Ronan, Patrick Roy, Mathieu Schneider.

LOS ANGELES: Rob Blake, Pat Conacher, Gord Donnelly, Tony Granato, Wayne Gretzky, Mark Hardy, Kelly Hrudey, Charlie Huddy, Marty McSorley, Corey Millen, Luc Robitaille, Warren Rychel, Tomas Sandstrom, Gary Shuchuk, Darryl Sydor, Dave Taylor, Tim Watters, Alexei Zhitnik.

First Period

1.	MONTREAL	BELLOWS (HALLER, MULLER)	10:26	(PPG)

Penalties: Zhitnik (LA) (tripping) 4:23, Bellows (Mtl) (cross-checking) 5:21, Desjardins (Mtl) (interference) 7:40, Watters (LA) (tripping) 10:21, Ronan (Mtl) (goaltender interference) 13:09, Lebeau (Mtl) (slashing) 16:37, Blake (LA) (roughing) 19:59.

Second Period

2.	MONTREAL	DIONNE (KEANE, LEBEAU)	2:41
3.	MONTREAL	SCHNEIDER (CARBONNEAU)	3:02
4.	LOS ANGELES	ROBITAILLE (GRETZKY, SANDSTROM)	7:52
5.	LOS ANGELES	GRANATO (unassisted)	11:02
6.	LOS ANGELES	GRETZKY (DONNELLY, HARDY)	17:07

Penalties: Ronan (Mtl) Taylor (LA) (slashing) 11:42.

Third Period
No scoring.
Penalties: Lebeau (Mtl) (holding) 6:48, Sandstrom (LA) (goaltender interference) 10:50.

Overtime

7.	MONTREAL	LeCLAIR (MULLER, BELLOWS)	0:34	(GWG)

Penalties: none.

Goalies: Roy (Montreal), Hrudey (LA)

Shots:					
Mtl	12	- 9	- 12	- 3	36
LA	10	- 13	- 10	- 0	33

Referee: Terry Gregson
Linesmen: Wayne Bonney, Ray Scapinello.

GAME #4 - June 7, 1993 - Great Western Forum - Montreal 3, Los Angeles 2 (OT)

MONTREAL: Brian Bellows, Benoit Brunet, Patrice Brisebois, Guy Carbonneau, J.J. Daigneault, Vincent Damphousse, Eric Desjardins, Paul DiPietro, Gilbert Dionne, Kevin Haller, Mike Keane, John LeClair, Stephan Lebeau, Gary Leeman, Kirk Muller, Lyle Odelein, Ed Ronan, Patrick Roy, Mathieu Schneider.

LOS ANGELES: Rob Blake, Pat Conacher, Gord Donnelly, Tony Granato, Wayne Gretzky, Mark Hardy, Kelly Hrudey, Jari Kurri, Lonnie Loach, Marty McSorley, Corey Millen, Luc Robitaille, Warren Rychel, Tomas Sandstrom, Gary Shuchuk, Darryl Sydor, Tim Watters, Alexei Zhitnik.

First Period

1.	MONTREAL	MULLER (unassisted)	10:57

Penalties: Conacher (LA).(cross-checking) 1:53, Desjardins (Mtl) (highsticking) Granato (LA) (roughing) 4:24, Schneider (Mtl) (elbowing) 16:50.

Second Period
2. MONTREAL DAMPHOUSSE (KEANE, DESJARDINS) 5:24 (PPG)
3. LOS ANGELES DONNELLY (GRANATO) 6:33
4. LOS ANGELES McSORLEY (GRETZKY, ROBITAILLE) 19:55 (PPG)
Penalties: Hardy (LA) (holding) 3:32, McSorley (LA) (misconduct) 5:24, Daigneault (Mtl) (roughing) Rychel (LA) (goaltender interference) 7:37, Brisebois (Mtl) Blake (LA) (roughing) 12:09, Sydor (LA) (interference) 15:58, Bellows (Mtl) (hooking) 19:10.

Third Period
No scoring.
Penalties: Daigneault (Mtl) (cross-checking) 2:42, Schneider (Mtl) Granato (LA) (roughing) 19:30.

Overtime
5. MONTREAL LeCLAIR (unassisted) 14:37 (GWG)
Penalties: none.

Goalies: Roy (Montreal), Hrudey (LA)

Shots:	Mtl	13	- 7	- 12	- 7	39
	LA	6	- 11	- 15	- 10	42

Referee: Andy vanHellemond
Linesmen: Kevin Collins, Gerard Gauthier

GAME #5 - June 9, 1993 - Montreal Forum - Montreal 4, Los Angeles 1

LOS ANGELES: Rob Blake, Jimmy Carson, Pat Conacher, Gord Donnelly, Tony Granato, Wayne Gretzky, Mark Hardy, Kelly Hrudey, Charlie Huddy, Jari Kurri, Marty McSorley, Corey Millen, Luc Robitaille, Warren Rychel, Tomas Sandstrom, Gary Shuchuk, Darryl Sydor, Tim Watters, Alexei Zhitnik.

MONTREAL: Brian Bellows, Benoit Brunet, Patrice Brisebois, Guy Carbonneau, J.J. Daigneault, Vincent Damphousse, Eric Desjardins, Paul DiPietro, Gilbert Dionne, Donald Dufresne, Mike Keane, John LeClair, Stephan Lebeau, Gary Leeman, Kirk Muller, Lyle Odelein, Ed Ronan, Patrick Roy, Mathieu Schneider.

First Period
1. MONTREAL DiPIETRO (LEEMAN, LeCLAIR) 15:10
Penalties: Schneider (Mtl) (tripping) 4:35, Keane (Mtl) (charging) 10:46, Granato (LA) (tripping) 12:49, Blake (LA) Sandstrom (LA) Ronan (Mtl) 19:23.

Second Period
2. LOS ANGELES McSORLEY (CARSON, ROBITAILLE) 2:40
3. MONTREAL MULLER (DAMPHOUSSE, ODELEIN) 3:51 (GWG)
4. MONTREAL LEBEAU (KEANE, LeCLAIR) 11:31 (PPG)
Penalties: Leeman (Mtl) (tripping) 5:52, Damphousse (Mtl) (elbowing) 7:40, Hardy (LA) (holding) 10:29.

Third Period
5. MONTREAL DiPIETRO (DIONNE, ODELEIN) 12:06
Penalties: none

Goalies: Hrudey (LA), Roy (Montreal)

Shots:	LA	7	- 7	- 5	19
	Mtl	10	- 12	- 7	29

Referee: Terry Gregson
Linesmen: Wayne Bonney, Ray Scapinello

1994

NEW YORK RANGERS – VANCOUVER CANUCKS

GAME #1 - May 31, 1994 - Madison Square Garden - Vancouver 3, NY Rangers 2 (OT)

VANCOUVER: Greg Adams, Shawn Antoski, Dave Babych, Jeff Brown, Pavel Bure, Geoff Courtnall, Murray Craven, Gerald Diduck, Martin Gelinas, Brian Glynn, Bret Hedican, Tim Hunter, Nathan Lafayette, Jyrki Lumme, Trevor Linden, John McIntyre, Kirk McLean, Sergio Momesso, Cliff Ronning, Kay Whitmore.

NY RANGERS Glenn Anderson, Jeff Beukeboom, Greg Gilbert, Adam Graves, Glenn Healy, Joe Kocur, Alexei Kovalev, Steve Larmer, Brian Leetch, Doug Lidster, Kevin Lowe, Craig MacTavish, Stephane Matteau, Mark Messier, Sergei Nemchinov, Brian Noonan, Mike Richter, Esa Tikkanen, Jay Wells, Sergei Zubov.

First Period
1. NY RANGERS LARMER (KOVALEV, LEETCH) 3:32
Penalties: Wells (NYR) (cross-checking) 1:47, Linden (Van) (tripping) 2:27, McIntyre (Van) (roughing) 8:50, Craven (Van) (slashing) 10:35, Beukeboom (NYR) (interference) 15:54.

Second Period
No scoring
Penalties: Messier (NYR) (hooking) 0:20, Lidster (NYR) (tripping) 8:49, Lowe (NYR) (roughing) 8:50, Courtnall (Van) (interference) 13:18, Momesso (Van) (goaltender interference) 16:15, Beukeboom (NYR) (highsticking) 19:34.

Third Period
2. VANCOUVER HEDICAN (ADAMS, LUMME) 5:45
3. NY RANGERS KOVALEV (LEETCH, ZUBOV) 8:29
4. VANCOUVER GELINAS (RONNING, MOMESSO) 19:00
Penalties: none.

Overtime
5. VANCOUVER ADAMS (RONNING, BURE) 19:26 (GWG)
Penalties: Momesso (Van), Gilbert (NYR) (roughing) 9:31.

Goalies: McLean (Vancouver), Richter (NY Rangers)

Shots:	Van	10	- 5	- 7	- 9	31
	NYR	15	- 9	- 13	- 17	54

Referee: Terry Gregson
Linesmen: Randy Mitton, Ray Scapinello

GAME #2 - June 2, 1994 - Madison Square Garden - NY Rangers 3, Vancouver 1

VANCOUVER: Greg Adams, Shawn Antoski, Dave Babych, Jeff Brown, Pavel Bure, Geoff Courtnall, Murray Craven, Gerald Diduck, Martin Gelinas, Brian Glynn, Bret Hedican, Tim Hunter, Nathan Lafayette, Jyrki Lumme, Trevor Linden, John McIntyre, Kirk McLean, Sergio Momesso, Cliff Ronning, Kay Whitmore.

NY RANGERS: Glenn Anderson, Jeff Beukeboom, Greg Gilbert, Adam Graves, Glenn Healy, Alexander Karpovtsev, Joe Kocur, Alexei Kovalev, Steve Larmer, Brian Leetch, Doug Lidster, Craig MacTavish, Stephane Matteau, Mark Messier, Sergei Nemchinov, Brian Noonan, Mike Richter, Esa Tikkanen, Jay Wells, Sergei Zubov.

First Period
1. NY RANGERS LIDSTER (unassisted) 6:22
2. VANCOUVER MOMESSO (Ronning, Hedican) 14:04
Penalties: Craven (Van) (tripping) 2:03, Lidster (NYR) (interference) 7:44, Hunter (Van) (roughing) 10:21, Hunter (Van) (misconduct) 15:26, Anderson (NYR) (interference) 16:55.

Second Period
3. NY RANGERS ANDERSON (Messier) 11:42 (SHG, GWG)
Penalties: Brown (Van) (hooking) 4:27, Matteau (NYR) (holding) 6:12, Graves (NYR) (tripping) 10:35, Antoski (Van) (roughing) 13:58, Tikkanen (NYR) (goaltender interference) 17:08.

Third Period
4. NY RANGERS LEETCH (unassisted) 19:55 (ENG)
Penalties: Lidster (NYR) (interference) 1:43, Diduck (Van), Kovalev (NYR) (highsticking) 4:32, Brown (Van), Matteau (NYR) (roughing) 15:29.

Goalies: McLean (Vancouver), Richter (NY Rangers)

Shots:	Van	10	- 6	- 13	29
	NYR	14	- 13	- 13	40

Referee: Bill McCreary
Linesmen: Kevin Collins, Gerard Gauthier

GAME #3 - June 4, 1994 - Pacific Coliseum - NY Rangers 5, Vancouver 1

NY RANGERS: Glenn Anderson, Jeff Beukeboom, Greg Gilbert, Adam Graves, Glenn Healy, Alexander Karpovtsev, Joe Kocur, Alexei Kovalev, Steve Larmer, Brian Leetch, Doug Lidster, Kevin Lowe, Craig MacTavish, Stephane Matteau, Mark Messier, Sergei Nemchinov, Brian Noonan, Mike Richter, Esa Tikkanen, Jay Wells.

VANCOUVER: Greg Adams, Shawn Antoski, Dave Babych, Jeff Brown, Pavel Bure, Geoff Courtnall, Murray Craven, Gerald Diduck, Martin Gelinas, Brian Glynn, Bret Hedican, Tim Hunter, Nathan Lafayette, Jyrki Lumme, Trevor Linden, John McIntyre, Kirk McLean, Sergio Momesso, Cliff Ronning, Kay Whitmore.

First Period
1. VANCOUVER BURE (LINDEN, ADAMS) 1:03
2. NY RANGERS LEETCH (unassisted) 13:39
3. NY RANGERS ANDERSON (NEMCHINOV, BEUKEBOOM) 19:19 (GWG)
Penalties: Wells (NYR) (tripping) 2:54, Anderson (NYR) (roughing), Hunter (Van) (charging) 5:42, Lumme (Van) (holding) 9:57, MacTavish (NYR) (holding) 15:04, Leetch (NYR) (tripping) 17:56, Lowe (NYR), Ronning (Van) (highsticking), Messier (NYR), Momesso (Van) (roughing), Bure (Van) (highsticking major, game misconduct) 18:12.

Second Period
4. NY RANGERS LEETCH (TIKKANEN, BEUKEBOOM) 18:32
Penalties: Lowe (NYR) (roughing) 5:34, Messier (NYR), Antoski (Van) (roughing) 16:28.

Third Period
5. NY RANGERS LARMER (unassisted) 0:25
6. NY RANGERS KOVALEV (GRAVES, MESSIER) 13:03 (PPG)
Penalties: Tikkanen (NYR) (hooking) 3:13, Hedican (Van) (holding) 5:34, McIntyre (Van) (holding) 7:58, MacTavish (NYR) (holding) 9:46, Momesso (Van) (crosschecking) 11:42, Gelinas (Van) (roughing) 16:35, Antoski (Van) (crosschecking, roughing) 19:19.

Goalies: Richter (NY Rangers), McLean (Vancouver)

Shots:	NYR	11	- 5	- 9	25
	Van	9	- 10	- 6	25

Referee: Andy Van Hellemond
Linesmen: Randy Mitton, Ray Scapinello

GAME #4 - June 7, 1994 - Pacific Coliseum - NY Rangers 4, Vancouver 2

NY RANGERS: Glenn Anderson, Jeff Beukeboom, Greg Gilbert, Adam Graves, Glenn Healy, Joe Kocur, Alexei Kovalev, Steve Larmer, Brian Leetch, Doug Lidster, Kevin Lowe, Craig MacTavish, Stephane Matteau, Mark Messier, Sergei Nemchinov, Brian Noonan, Mike Richter, Esa Tikkanen, Jay Wells, Sergei Zubov.

VANCOUVER: Greg Adams, Shawn Antoski, Dave Babych, Jeff Brown, Pavel Bure, Geoff Courtnall, Murray Craven, Gerald Diduck, Martin Gelinas, Brian Glynn, Bret Hedican, Tim Hunter, Nathan Lafayette, Jyrki Lumme, Trevor Linden, John McIntyre, Kirk McLean, Sergio Momesso, Cliff Ronning, Kay Whitmore.

First Period

1.	VANCOUVER	LINDEN (LUMME, BROWN)	13:25 (PPG)
2.	VANCOUVER	RONNING (BURE, CRAVEN)	16:19

Penalties: Courtnall (Van) (elbowing) 3:11, Beukeboom (NYR) (highsticking) 6:35, Graves (NYR) (holding) 13:02, Messier (NYR) (boarding major) 14:17, Linden (Van) (holding stick) 15:07, Courtnall (Van) (interference) 17:54, Tikkanen (NYR) (roughing) 18:45.

Second Period

3.	NY RANGERS	LEETCH (MacTAVISH, GILBERT)	4:03
4.	NY RANGERS	ZUBOV (MESSIER, LEETCH)	19:44 (PPG)

Penalties: Lidster (NYR) (holding) 1:13, Brown (Van) (tripping) 7:19, Lidster (NYR) (holding) 16:58, Adams (Van) (boarding) 18:55.

Third Period

5.	NY RANGERS	KOVALEV (LEETCH, ZUBOV)	15:05 (PPG, GWG)
6.	NY RANGERS	LARMER (ZUBOV, LEETCH)	17:56

Penalties: NYR bench (too many men) 3:53, Lumme (Van) (holding) 4:48, Tikkanen (NYR), Diduck (Van) (roughing) 10:42, Messier (NYR) (slashing) 11:29, Gelinas (Van) (roughing) 14:31.

Goalies: Richter (NY Rangers), McLean (Vancouver)

Shots:				
NYR	8 -	8 -	11	27
Van	8 -	12 -	10	30

Referee: Terry Gregson
Linesmen: Kevin Collins, Gerard Gauthier

(NOTE: Vancouver's Pavel Bure was awarded a penalty shot at 6:31 of the second period. He was unsuccessful against NY Ranger's goaltender Mike Richter.)

GAME #5 - June 9, 1994 - Madison Square Garden - Vancouver 6, NY Rangers 3

VANCOUVER: Greg Adams, Shawn Antoski, Dave Babych, Jeff Brown, Pavel Bure, Geoff Courtnall, Murray Craven, Gerald Diduck, Martin Gelinas, Brian Glynn, Bret Hedican, Tim Hunter, Nathan Lafayette, Jyrki Lumme, Trevor Linden, John McIntyre, Kirk McLean, Sergio Momesso, Cliff Ronning, Kay Whitmore.

NY RANGERS: Glenn Anderson, Jeff Beukeboom, Greg Gilbert, Adam Graves, Glenn Healy, Joe Kocur, Alexei Kovalev, Steve Larmer, Brian Leetch, Doug Lidster, Kevin Lowe, Craig MacTavish, Stephane Matteau, Mark Messier, Sergei Nemchinov, Brian Noonan, Mike Richter, Esa Tikkanen, Jay Wells, Sergei Zubov.

First Period

No scoring.

Penalties: Hunter (Van) (elbowing) 0:49, Momesso (Van) (slashing, fighting major), Ronning (Van), Matteau (NYR) (roughing), Beukeboom (NYR) (instigator, fighting major, game misconduct), Wells (NYR) (highsticking) 12:06, Hunter (Van), Wells (NYR) (roughing) 13:20, Ronning (Van), Larmer (NYR) (holding) 17:20, Nemchinov (NYR) (elbowing) 19:32.

Second Period

1.	VANCOUVER	BROWN (RONNING, ANTOSKI)	8:10

Penalties: Courtnall (Van) (elbowing major) 10:13, Messier (NYR) (hooking) 18:19.

Third Period

2.	VANCOUVER	COURTNALL (LAFAYETTE, HEDICAN)	0:26
3.	VANCOUVER	BURE (CRAVEN)	2:48
4.	NY RANGERS	LIDSTER (KOVALEV)	3:27
5.	NY RANGERS	LARMER (MATTEAU, NEMCHINOV)	6:20
6.	NY RANGERS	MESSIER (ANDERSON, GRAVES)	9:02
7.	VANCOUVER	BABYCH (BURE)	9:31 (GWG)
8.	VANCOUVER	COURTNALL (LAFAYETTE, LUMME)	12:20
9.	VANCOUVER	BURE (RONNING, HEDICAN)	13:04

Penalties: Kocur (NYR) (slashing) 18:41.

Goalies: McLean (Vancouver), Richter (NY Rangers)

Shots:				
Van	12 -	8 -	17	37
NYR	10 -	13 -	15	38

Referee: Andy Van Hellemond
Linesmen: Randy Mitton, Ray Scapinello

GAME #6 - June 11, 1994 - Pacific Coliseum - Vancouver 4, NY Rangers 1

NY RANGERS: Glenn Anderson, Jeff Beukeboom, Greg Gilbert, Adam Graves, Glenn Healy, Joe Kocur, Alexei Kovalev, Steve Larmer, Brian Leetch, Doug Lidster, Kevin Lowe, Craig MacTavish, Stephane Matteau, Mark Messier, Sergei Nemchinov, Brian Noonan, Mike Richter, Esa Tikkanen, Jay Wells, Sergei Zubov.

VANCOUVER: Greg Adams, Shawn Antoski, Dave Babych, Jeff Brown, Pavel Bure, Geoff Courtnall, Murray Craven, Gerald Diduck, Martin Gelinas, Brian Glynn, Bret Hedican, Tim Hunter, Nathan Lafayette, Jyrki Lumme, Trevor Linden, John McIntyre, Kirk McLean, Sergio Momesso, Cliff Ronning, Kay Whitmore.

First Period

1.	VANCOUVER	BROWN (LINDEN)	9:42 (PPG)

Penalties: Beukeboom (NYR) (elbowing) 3:02, Leetch (NYR) (interference) 9:39.

Second Period

2.	VANCOUVER	COURTNALL (LUMME, BURE)	12:29 (GWG)
3.	NY RANGERS	KOVALEV (MESSIER, LEETCH)	14:42 (PPG)

Penalties: Momesso (Van) (interference) 2:26, Diduck (Van) (tripping) 7:27, McIntyre (Van) (interference) 13:23.

Third Period

4.	VANCOUVER	BROWN (unassisted)	8:35
5.	VANCOUVER	COURTNALL (LAFAYETTE, DIDUCK)	18:28

Penalties: none.

Goalies: Richter (NY Rangers), McLean (Vancouver)

Shots:				
NYR	7 -	12 -	10	29
Van	16 -	8 -	7	31

Referee: Bill McCreary
Linesmen: Kevin Collins, Gerard Gauthier

GAME #7 - June 14, 1994 - Madison Square Garden - NY Rangers 3, Vancouver 2

VANCOUVER: Greg Adams, Shawn Antoski, Dave Babych, Jeff Brown, Pavel Bure, Geoff Courtnall, Murray Craven, Gerald Diduck, Martin Gelinas, Brian Glynn, Bret Hedican, Tim Hunter, Nathan Lafayette, Jyrki Lumme, Trevor Linden, John McIntyre, Kirk McLean, Sergio Momesso, Cliff Ronning, Kay Whitmore.

NY RANGERS: Glenn Anderson, Jeff Beukeboom, Greg Gilbert, Adam Graves, Glenn Healy, Joe Kocur, Alexei Kovalev, Steve Larmer, Brian Leetch, Doug Lidster, Kevin Lowe, Craig MacTavish, Stephane Matteau, Mark Messier, Sergei Nemchinov, Brian Noonan, Mike Richter, Esa Tikkanen, Jay Wells, Sergei Zubov.

First Period

1.	NY RANGERS	LEETCH (ZUBOV, MESSIER)	11:02
2.	NY RANGERS	GRAVES (KOVALEV, ZUBOV)	14:45 (PPG)

Penalties: Lumme (Van) (crosschecking) 14:03, Hedican (Van), Tikkanen (NYR) (roughing) 18:50.

Second Period

3.	VANCOUVER	LINDEN (GLYNN, BURE)	5:21 (SHG)
4.	NY RANGERS	MESSIER (GRAVES, NOONAN)	13:29 (PPG,GWG)

Penalties: Brown (Van) (interference) 4:38, Babych (Van) (tripping) 12:36, Messier (NYR) (hooking) 16:39.

Third Period

5.	VANCOUVER	LINDEN (COURTNALL, RONNING)	4:50 (PPG)

Penalties: Tikkanen (NYR) (hooking) 4:16, Linden (Van), MacTavish (NYR) (roughing) 10:55.

Goalies: McLean (Vancouver), Richter (NY Rangers)

Shots:				
Van	9 -	12 -	9	30
NYR	12 -	14 -	9	35

Referee: Terry Gregson
Linesmen: Kevin Collins, Ray Scapinello

1995

NEW JERSEY DEVILS - DETROIT RED WINGS

GAME #1 - June 17, 1995 - Joe Louis Arena - New Jersey 2, Detroit 1

NEW JERSEY: Tommy Albelin, Martin Brodeur, Neal Broten, Sergei Brylin, Bobby Carpenter, Tom Chorske, Sean Chambers, Ken Daneyko, Bruce Driver, Bill Guerin, Bobby Holik, Claude Lemieux, Randy McKay, John MacLean, Scott Niedermayer, Mike Peluso, Stephane Richer, Scott Stevens, Chris Terreri, Valeri Zelepukin.

DETROIT: Doug Brown, Shawn Burr, Dino Ciccarelli, Paul Coffey, Kris Draper, Bob Errey, Sergei Fedorov, Viacheslav Fetisov, Stu Grimson, Mark Howe, Vladimir Konstantinov, Nicklas Lidstrom, Darren McCarty, Chris Osgood, Keith Primeau, Bob Rouse, Ray Sheppard, Mike Vernon, Steve Yzerman, Vyacheslav Kozlov.

First Period

No Scoring

Penalties: Guerin (NJ) (holding) 6:47; Konstantinov (Det) (holding stick) 11:05.

Second Period

1.	NEW JERSEY	RICHER (ALBELIN, BROTEN)	9:41 (PPG)
2.	DETROIT	CICCARELLI (LIDSTROM, COFFEY)	13:08 (PPG)

Penalties: Draper (Det) (roughing), 9:35; Holik (NJ) (highsticking) 11:37; Lemieux (NJ) (hooking) 13:41; Daneyko (NJ) (roughing), Ciccarelli (Det) (roughing) 15:54.

Third Period

3.	NEW JERSEY	LEMIEUX (MacLEAN, CHORSKE)	3:17 (GWG)

Penalties: Brown (Det) (tripping) 4:48.

Goalies: Brodeur (NJ), Vernon (Det)

Shots:				
NJ	9 -	10 -	9	28
Det	7 -	5 -	5	17

Referee: Bill McCreary
Linesmen: Brian Murphy, Kevin Collins

GAME #2 - June 20, 1995 - Joe Louis Arena - New Jersey 4, Detroit 2

NEW JERSEY: Tommy Albelin, Martin Brodeur, Neal Broten, Bobby Carpenter, Sean Chambers, Ken Daneyko, Jim Dowd, Bruce Driver, Bill Guerin, Bobby Holik, Claude Lemieux, Randy McKay, John MacLean, Scott Niedermayer, Mike Peluso, Stephane Richer, Brian Rolston, Scott Stevens, Chris Terreri, Valeri Zelepukin.

DETROIT: Doug Brown, Shawn Burr, Dino Ciccarelli, Paul Coffey, Kris Draper, Bob Errey, Sergei Fedorov, Viacheslav Fetisov, Mark Howe, Vladimir Konstantinov, Vyacheslav Kozlov, Mike Krushelnyski, Nicklas Lidstrom, Darren McCarty, Chris Osgood, Bob Rouse, Ray Sheppard, Tim Taylor, Mike Vernon, Steve Yzerman.

First Period

No Scoring

Penalties: Stevens (NJ) (roughing) 0:37; Ciccarelli (Det) (slashing) 5:57; McCarty (Det) (roughing) 8:49; Broten (NJ) (highsticking) 9:27.

Second Period

1.	DETROIT	KOZLOV (CICCARELLI, FEDOROV)	7:17 (PPG)
2.	NEW JERSEY	MacLEAN (NIEDERMAYER,BROTEN)	9:40

Penalties: Brodeur (NJ) (delay of game) 6:56; Guerin (NJ) (slashing), McCarty (Det) (slashing) 8:58; Errey (Det) (charging) 16:01; Dowd (NJ) (interference) 18:30.

Third Period

3.	DETROIT	FEDOROV (BROWN, FETISOV)	1:36
4.	NEW JERSEY	NIEDERMAYER (DOWD)	9:47
5.	NEW JERSEY	DOWD (CHAMBERS, ALBELIN)	18:36 (GWG)
6.	NEW JERSEY	RICHER (NIEDERMAYER)	19:36 (ENG)

Penalties: Holik (NJ) (boarding) 4;58.

Goalies: Brodeur (NJ), Vernon (Det)

Shots:				
NJ	3	9	11	23
Det	7	6	5	18

Referee: Terry Gregson

Linemen: Ray Scapinello, Wayne Bonney

GAME #3 - June 22, 1995 - Meadowlands Arena - New Jersey 5, Detroit 2

DETROIT: Doug Brown, Dino Ciccarelli, Paul Coffey, Kris Draper, Bob Errey, Sergei Fedorov, Viacheslav Fetisov, Vladimir Konstantinov, Vyacheslav Kozlov, Martin Lapointe, Nicklas Lidstrom, Darren McCarty, Chris Osgood, Keith Primeau, Mike Ramsey, Bob Rouse, Ray Sheppard, Tim Taylor, Mike Vernon, Steve Yzerman.

NEW JERSEY: Tommy Albelin, Martin Brodeur, Neal Broten, Sergei Brylin, Bobby Carpenter, Sean Chambers, Tom Chorske, Ken Daneyko, Bruce Driver, Bill Guerin, Bobby Holik, Claude Lemieux, Randy McKay, John MacLean, Scott Niedermayer, Mike Peluso, Stephane Richer, Scott Stevens, Chris Terreri, Valeri Zelepukin.

First Period

1.	NEW JERSEY	DRIVER (BROTEN, MacLEAN)	10:30 (PPG)
2.	NEW JERSEY	LEMIEUX (CARPENTER, STEVENS)	16:52

Penalties: Primeau (Det) (slashing), Lemieux (NJ) (roughing) 1:09; Konstantinov (Det) (holding the stick) 8:56; Holik (NJ) (tripping) 10:58; Lapointe (Det) (unsportsmanlike conduct), Guerin (NJ) (unsportsmanlike conduct) 16:58.

Second Period

3.	NEW JERSEY	BROTEN (STEVENS, MacLEAN)	6:59 (GWG)
4.	NEW JERSEY	McKAY (HOLIK, DRIVER)	8:20

Penalties: Broten (NJ) (holding the stick) 11:01; Primeau (Det) (tripping) 16:03; Carpenter (NJ) (cross-checking) 19:47.

Third Period

5.	NEW JERSEY	HOLIK (GUERIN, RICHER)	8:14 (PPG)
6.	DETROIT	FEDOROV (FETISOV, BROWN)	16:57 (PPG)
7.	DETROIT	YZERMAN (SHEPPARD, LIDSTROM)	18:27 (PPG)

Third Period: Albelin (NJ) (highsticking) 2:30; Konstantinov (Det) (highsticking) 4:25; Draper (Det) (highsticking) 5:17; Primeau (Det) (cross-checking) 6:31; Holik (Det) (interference) 8:44; Richer (NJ) (hooking) 12:28; Ciccarelli (Det) (roughing), Taylor (Det) (roughing), Lapointe (Det) (double roughing minor), Zelepukin (NJ) (double roughing minor), Guerin (NJ) (boarding, roughing), Brylin (NJ) (highsticking, roughing) 15:37.

Goalies: Vernon, Osgood (Det), Brodeur (NJ)

Shots:				
Det	7	5	12	24
NJ	15	8	8	31

Referee: Kerry Fraser Linesmen: Kevin Collins, Brian Murphy

GAME #4 - June 24, 1995 - Meadowlands Arena - New Jersey 5, Detroit 2

DETROIT: Doug Brown, Dino Ciccarelli, Paul Coffey, Kris Draper, Bob Errey, Sergei Fedorov, Viacheslav Fetisov, Stu Grimson, Vladimir Konstantinov, Vyacheslav Kozlov, Mike Krushelnyski, Martin Lapointe, Nicklas Lidstrom, Darren McCarty, Chris Osgood, Keith Primeau, Mike Ramsey, Bob Rouse, Mike Vernon, Steve Yzerman.

NEW JERSEY: Tommy Albelin, Martin Brodeur, Neal Broten, Sergei Brylin, Bobby Carpenter, Sean Chambers, Tom Chorske, Ken Daneyko, Bruce Driver, Bill Guerin, Bobby Holik, Claude Lemieux, Randy McKay, John MacLean, Scott Niedermayer, Mike Peluso, Stephane Richer, Brian Rolston, Scott Stevens, Chris Terreri.

First Period

1.	NEW JERSEY	BROTEN (RICHER, CHORSKE)	1:08
2.	DETROIT	FEDOROV (LAPOINTE, FETISOV)	2:03
3.	DETROIT	COFFEY (BROWN, FEDOROV)	13:01 (SHG)
4.	NEW JERSEY	CHAMBERS (DRIVER, MacLEAN)	17:45

Penalties: Errey (Det) (hooking) 11:03; Daneyko (NJ) (roughing) 13:36; Primeau (Det) (goaltender interference) 15:35.

Second Period

5.	NEW JERSEY	BROTEN (NIEDERMAYER, GUERIN)	7:56 (GWG)

Penalties: Daneyko (NJ) (slashing) 0:30; Lapointe (Det) (roughing), Stevens (NJ) (roughing) 10:09; Guerin (NJ) (interference) 12:43; Konstantinov (Det) (hooking) 19:12.

Third Period

6.	NEW JERSEY	BRYLIN (ROLSTON, GUERIN)	7:46
7.	NEW JERSEY	CHAMBERS (BRYLIN, GUERIN)	12:32

Penalties: Grimson (Det) (roughing) 10:24.

Goalies: Vernon (Det), Brodeur (NJ)

Shots:				
Det	8	7	1	16
NJ	8	8	10	26

Referee: Bill McCreary Linesmen: Wayne Bonney, Ray Scapinello

1996

COLORADO AVALANCHE – FLORIDA PANTHERS

GAME #1 - June 4, 1996 - McNichols Sports Arena - Colorado 3, Florida 1

COLORADO: Rene Corbet, Adam Deadmarsh, Stephane Fiset, Adam Foote, Peter Forsberg, Alexei Gusarov, Dave Hannan, Valeri Kamensky, Mike Keane, Jon Klemm, Uwe Krupp, Sylvain Lefebvre, Curtis Leschyshyn, Sandis Ozolinsh, Mike Ricci, Patrick Roy, Warren Rychel, Joe Sakic, Stephane Yelle, Scott Young.

FLORIDA: Stu Barnes, Terry Carkner, Tom Fitzgerald, Mark Fitzpatrick, Johan Garpenlov, Mike Hough, Jody Hull, Ed Jovanovski, Paul Laus, Bill Lindsay, Dave Lowry, Scott Mellanby, Gord Murphy, Rob Niedermayer, Ray Sheppard, Brian Skrudland, Martin Straka, Robert Svehla, John Vanbiesbrouck, Rhett Warrener.

First Period

1.	FLORIDA	FITZGERALD (LINDSAY)	16:51

Penalties: Mellanby (Fla) (roughing) 9:12; Skrudland (Fla) (roughing) 9:21; Krupp (Col) (high sticking) 13:46; Gusarov (Col) (holding) 18:15.

Second Period

2.	COLORADO	YOUNG (DEADMARSH, LEFEBVRE)	10:32	
3.	COLORADO	RICCI (OZOLINSH, KEANE)	12:21	(GWG)
4.	COLORADO	KRUPP (KAMENSKY, FORSBERG)	14:21	

Penalties: Svehla (Fla) (interference) :41; Lindsay (Fla) (roughing) 7:56; Ricci (Col) (roughing) 15:31; Svehla (Fla) (roughing) 17:39; Ricci (Col) (goaltender interference) 18:30.

Third Period

No scoring

Penalties: Sakic (Col) (holding) 3:35; Carkner (Fla) (slashing) 7:51; Vanbiesbrouck (Fla) (slashing) 9:55; Jovanovski (Fla) (roughing) 19:42.

Goalies: Roy (Col), Vanbiesbrouck (Fla)

Shots:				
Col	6	15	9	30
Fla	12	6	8	26

Referee: Bill McCreary Linesmen: Ray Scapinello, Brian Murphy

GAME #2 - June 6, 1996 - McNichols Sports Arena - Colorado 8, Florida 1

COLORADO: Rene Corbet, Adam Deadmarsh, Stephane Fiset, Adam Foote, Peter Forsberg, Alexei Gusarov, Dave Hannan, Valeri Kamensky, Mike Keane, Jon Klemm, Uwe Krupp, Sylvain Lefebvre, Curtis Leschyshyn, Sandis Ozolinsh, Mike Ricci, Patrick Roy, Warren Rychel, Joe Sakic, Stephane Yelle, Scott Young.

FLORIDA: Stu Barnes, Terry Carkner, Tom Fitzgerald, Mark Fitzpatrick, Johan Garpenlov, Mike Hough, Jody Hull, Ed Jovanovski, Paul Laus, Bill Lindsay, Dave Lowry, Scott Mellanby, Gord Murphy, Rob Niedermayer, Ray Sheppard, Brian Skrudland, Martin Straka, Robert Svehla, John Vanbiesbrouck, Rhett Warrener.

First Period

1.	COLORADO	FORSBERG (unassisted)	4:11	
2.	FLORIDA	BARNES (LOWRY, JOVANOVSKI)	7:52	(PPG)
3.	COLORADO	CORBET (YOUNG, SAKIC)	10:43	(PPG, GWG)
4.	COLORADO	FORSBERG (SAKIC, OZOLINSH)	13:46	(PPG)
5.	COLORADO	FORSBERG (SAKIC, DEADMARSH)	15:05	(PPG)

Penalties: Deadmarsh (Col) (roughing) 5:53; Lindsay (Fla) (slashing) 8:55; Carkner (Fla) (roughing) 12:51; Vanbiesbrouck (Fla) (interference) 14:50.

Second Period

6.	COLORADO	CORBET (unassisted)	4:37
7.	COLORADO	KAMENSKY (GUSAROV, DEADMARSH)	5:08
8.	COLORADO	KLEMM (CORBET, KRUPP)	10:03

Penalties: Lefebvre (Col) (holding) 6:26; Rychel (Col) (roughing) 17:01.

Third Period

9.	COLORADO	KLEMM (SAKIC)	17:28	(PPG)

Penalties: Kamensky (Col) (double high sticking minor) 3:11; Jovanovski (Fla), Kamensky (Col) (roughing), Leschyshyn (Col) (charging) 7:28; Jovanovski (Fla) (fighting major), Rychel (Col) (instigator, fighting major, game misconduct) 9:39; Laus (Fla) (goaltender interference) 11:42; Mellanby (Fla) (roughing) 16:09.

Goalies: Roy (Col), Vanbiesbrouck, Fitzpatrick (Fla)

Shots:				
Col	11	12	7	30
Fla	8	15	5	28

Referee: Don Koharski Linesmen: Kevin Collins, Gerard Gauthier

GAME #3 - June 8, 1996 - Miami Arena - Colorado 3, Florida 2

COLORADO: Rene Corbet, Adam Deadmarsh, Stephane Fiset, Adam Foote, Peter Forsberg, Alexei Gusarov, Dave Hannan, Valeri Kamensky, Mike Keane, Jon Klemm, Uwe Krupp, Sylvain Lefebvre, Claude Lemieux, Curtis Leschyshyn, Sandis Ozolinsh, Mike Ricci, Patrick Roy, Joe Sakic, Stephane Yelle, Scott Young.

FLORIDA: Stu Barnes, Terry Carkner, Tom Fitzgerald, Mark Fitzpatrick, Johan Garpenlov, Mike Hough, Ed Jovanovski, Paul Laus, Bill Lindsay, Dave Lowry, Scott Mellanby, Gord Murphy, Rob

Niedermayer, Ray Sheppard, Brian Skrudland, Martin Straka, Robert Svehla, John Vanbiesbrouck, Rhett Warrener, Jason Woolley.

First Period

1.	COLORADO	LEMIEUX (KAMENSKY, FORSBERG)	2:44	
2.	FLORIDA	SHEPPARD (STRAKA, JOVANOVSKI)	9:14	(PPG)
3.	FLORIDA	NIEDERMAYER (MELLANBY, GARPENLOV)	11:19	

Penalties: Deadmarsh (Col) (hooking) 7:40; Foote (Col), Lowry (Fla) (roughing) 12:49.

Second Period

4.	COLORADO	KEANE (FOOTE, GUSAROV)	1:38	
5.	COLORADO	SAKIC (DEADMARSH, LESCHYSHYN)	3:00	(GWG)

Penalties: None

Third Period

No scoring

Penalties: None

Goalies: Roy (Col), Vanbiesbrouck (Fla)

Shots:					
	Col	6	10	6	22
	Fla	16	13	5	34

Referee: Andy Van Hellemond

Linesmen: Ray Scapinello, Brian Murphy

GAME #4 - June 10, 1996 - Miami Arena - Colorado 1, Florida 0 (3 OT)

COLORADO: Rene Corbet, Adam Deadmarsh, Stephane Fiset, Adam Foote, Peter Forsberg, Alexei Gusarov, Valeri Kamensky, Mike Keane, Jon Klemm, Uwe Krupp, Sylvain Lefebvre, Claude Lemieux, Curtis Leschyshyn, Sandis Ozolinsh, Mike Ricci, Patrick Roy, Warren Rychel, Joe Sakic, Stephane Yelle, Scott Young.

FLORIDA: Stu Barnes, Terry Carkner, Radek Dvorak, Tom Fitzgerald, Mark Fitzpatrick, Johan Garpenlov, Mike Hough, Ed Jovanovski, Paul Laus, Bill Lindsay, Dave Lowry, Scott Mellanby, Gord Murphy, Rob Niedermayer, Ray Sheppard, Brian Skrudland, Martin Straka, Robert Svehla, John Vanbiesbrouck, Jason Woolley.

First Period

No scoring

Penalties: Svehla (Fla) (roughing) 18:51.

Second Period

No scoring

Penalties: Kamensky (Col) (hooking), Ozolinsh (Col), Niedermayer (Fla) (roughing) 5:21; Foote (Col) (roughing) 9:28; Jovanovski (Fla) (cross-checking) 12:27; Leschyshyn (Col) (hooking) 15:33; Ricci (Col), Barnes (Fla) (roughing) 18:05.

Third Period

No scoring

Penalties: Vanbiesbrouck (Fla) (interference) 5:15; Lemieux (Col) (high sticking) 6:29.

First Overtime

No scoring

Penalties: Ozolinsh (Col), Garpenlov (Fla) (roughing) 13:04.

Second Overtime

No scoring

Penalties: Lemieux (Col) (roughing), Skrudland (Fla) (slashing) 9:57.

Third Overtime

1.	COLORADO	KRUPP (unassisted)	4:31	(GWG)

Penalties: None

Goalies: Roy (Col), Vanbiesbrouck (Fla)

Shots:									
	Col	9	10	10	11	12	4	56
	Fla	10	17	8	7	18	3	63

Referee: Bill McCreary

Linesmen: Kevin Collins, Gerard Gauthier

1997

DETROIT RED WINGS - PHILADELPHIA FLYERS

GAME #1 - May 31, 1997 - CoreStates Center - Detroit 4, Philadelphia 2

DETROIT: Doug Brown, Kris Draper, Sergei Fedorov, Viacheslav Fetisov, Joe Kocur, Vladimir Konstantinov, Vyacheslav Kozlov, Martin Lapointe, Igor Larionov, Nicklas Lidstrom, Kirk Maltby, Darren McCarty, Larry Murphy, Bob Rouse, Tomas Sandstrom, Brendan Shanahan, Aaron Ward, Steve Yzerman.

Philadelphia: Rod Brind'Amour, Paul Coffey, Eric Desjardins, John Druce, Dale Hawerchuk, Trent Klatt, Dan Kordic, Dan Lacroix, John LeClair, Eric Lindros, Janne Niinimaa, Joel Otto, Shjon Podein, Mikael Renberg, Kjell Samuelsson, Petr Svoboda, Chris Therien, Dainius Zubrus.

First Period

1.	DETROIT	MALTBY (DRAPER)	6:38	(SH)
2.	PHILADELPHIA	BRIND'AMOUR (LINDROS, NIINIMAA)	7:37	(PPG)
3.	DETROIT	KOCUR	15:56	

Penalties: Sandstrom (Det) (high sticking) 5:50; Fetisov (Det) (interference) 11:26; Klatt (Phi) (interference) 17:09; Kocur (Det) (interference) 19:42.

Second Period

4.	DETROIT	FEDOROV (MURPHY, MCCARTY)	11:41	(GWG)
5.	PHILADELPHIA	LeCLAIR (RENBERG, LINDROS)	17:11	

Penalties: Lacroix (Phi) (interference) 5:48; Fedorov (Det) (tripping) 7:08; Fetisov (Det) (interference) 15:07; Klatt (Phi) (charging) 17:45.

Third Period

6.	DETROIT	YZERMAN (MURPHY)	0:56

Penalties: Svoboda (Phi) (cross checking) 6:27; Lindros (Phi) (roughing) 17:48.

Goalies: Vernon (Det), Hextall (Phi)

Shots:					
	Det	8	12	10	30
	Phi	10	9	9	28

Referee: Bill McCreary

Linesmen: Ray Scapinello, Dan Schachte

GAME #2 - June 3, 1997 - CoreStates Center - Detroit 4, Philadelphia 2

DETROIT: Doug Brown, Kris Draper, Sergei Fedorov, Viacheslav Fetisov, Joe Kocur, Vladimir Konstantinov, Vyacheslav Kozlov, Martin Lapointe, Igor Larionov, Nicklas Lidstrom, Kirk Maltby, Darren McCarty, Larry Murphy, Bob Rouse, Tomas Sandstrom, Brendan Shanahan, Aaron Ward, Steve Yzerman.

PHILADELPHIA: Rod Brind'Amour, Paul Coffey, Eric Desjardins, John Druce, Karl Dykhuis, Pat Falloon, Colin Forbes, Dale Hawerchuk, Trent Klatt, John LeClair, Eric Lindros, Janne Niinimaa, Joel Otto, Shjon Podein, Mikael Renberg, Kjell Samuelsson, Chris Therien, Dainius Zubrus.

First Period

1.	DETROIT	SHANAHAN	1:37	
2.	DETROIT	YZERMAN (MURPHY, FETISOV)	9:22	(PPG)
3.	PHILADELPHIA	BRIND'AMOUR (NIINIMAA)	17:42	(PPG)
4.	PHILADELPHIA	BRIND'AMOUR (NIINIMAA, LeCLAIR)	18:51	(PPG)

Penalties: Coffey (Phi) (holding) 4:29; Coffey (Phi) (hooking) 7:24; Lapointe (Det) (charging) 10:21; Fetisov (Det) (high sticking) 17:09; Larionov (Det) (hooking) 18:37.

Second Period

5.	DETROIT	MALTBY (KOCUR)	2:39	(GWG)

Penalties: Maltby (Det) (roughing), Coffey (Phi) (roughing) 6:54; Bench (Det) (too many men) 9:03; LeClair (Phi) (elbowing) 12:13.

Third Period

6.	DETROIT	SHANAHAN (LAPOINTE, FEDOROV)	9:56

Penalties: Lapointe (Det) (roughing), Dykhuis (Phi) (roughing) 10:27.

Goalies: Vernon (Det), Snow (Phi)

Shots:					
	Det	14	9	5	28
	Phi	14	9	8	31

Referee: Terry Gregson

Linesmen: Wayne Bonney, Gord Broseker

GAME #3 - June 5, 1997 - Joe Louis Arena - Detroit 6, Philadelphia 1

DETROIT: Doug Brown, Kris Draper, Sergei Fedorov, Viacheslav Fetisov, Joe Kocur, Vladimir Konstantinov, Vyacheslav Kozlov, Martin Lapointe, Igor Larionov, Nicklas Lidstrom, Kirk Maltby, Darren McCarty, Larry Murphy, Bob Rouse, Tomas Sandstrom, Brendan Shanahan, Aaron Ward, Steve Yzerman.

PHILADELPHIA: Rod Brind'Amour, Eric Desjardins, John Druce, Karl Dykhuis, Pat Falloon, Colin Forbes, Dale Hawerchuk, Trent Klatt, John LeClair, Eric Lindros, Janne Niinimaa, Joel Otto, Michel Petit, Shjon Podein, Mikael Renberg, Kjell Samuelsson, Chris Therien, Dainius Zubrus.

First Period

1.	PHILADELPHIA	LeCLAIR (DESJARDINS, BRIND'AMOUR)	7:03	(PPG)
2.	DETROIT	YZERMAN (KOZLOV)	9:03	(PPG)
3.	DETROIT	FEDOROV	11:05	(GWG)
4.	DETROIT	LAPOINTE (BROWN, FEDOROV)	19:00	

Penalties: McCarty (Det) (ob.-interference) 6:10; Desjardins (Phi) (ob.-holding) 8:44; Fetisov (Det) (ob.-interference) 12:14; Sandstrom (Det) (ob.-holding) 12:54; Lapointe (Det) (tripping) 16:43.

Second Period

5.	DETROIT	FEDOROV (KOZLOV, SHANAHAN)	3:12	(PPG)
6.	DETROIT	SHANAHAN (MCCARTY, FETISOV)	19:17	

Penalties: Klatt (Phi) (ob.-hooking) 2:24; Petit (Phi) (holding) 10:14.

Third Period

7.	DETROIT	LAPOINTE (FEDOROV, VERNON)	1:08	(PPG)

Penalties: Lindros (Phi) (cross checking) 0:46; Lindros (Phi) (elbowing) 8:12; McCarty (Det) (ob.-interference) 8:39; Fetisov (Det) (slashing) 13:02; Brown (Det) (slashing) 19:41.

Goalies: Hextall (Phi), Vernon (Det)

Shots:					
	Phi	8	7	7	22
	Det	10	12	7	29

Referee: Kerry Fraser

Linesmen: Dan Schachte, Ray Scapinello

GAME #4 - June 7, 1997 - Joe Louis Arena - Detroit 2, Philadelphia 1

DETROIT: Doug Brown, Kris Draper, Sergei Fedorov, Viacheslav Fetisov, Joe Kocur, Vladimir Konstantinov, Vyacheslav Kozlov, Martin Lapointe, Igor Larionov, Nicklas Lidstrom, Kirk Maltby, Darren McCarty, Larry Murphy, Bob Rouse, Tomas Sandstrom, Brendan Shanahan, Aaron Ward, Steve Yzerman.

PHILADELPHIA: Rod Brind'Amour, Eric Desjardins, John Druce, Karl Dykhuis, Pat Falloon, Colin Forbes, Trent Klatt, Dan Lacroix, John LeClair, Eric Lindros, Janne Niinimaa, Joel Otto, Michel Petit, Shjon Podein, Mikael Renberg, Kjell Samuelsson, Chris Therien, Dainius Zubrus.

First Period

1.	DETROIT	LIDSTROM (MALTBY)	19:27

Penalties: LeClair (Phi) (ob.-holding) 3:23; Larionov (Det) (ob.-interference) 4:31; Lindros (Phi)

(ob.-interference) 9:22; Falloon (Phi) (holding stick) 13:21.

Second Period

2. DETROIT McCARTY (SANDSTROM, YZERMAN) 13:02 (GWG)

Penalties: Konstantinov (Det) (ob.-interference) 9:27.

Third Period

3. PHILADELPHIA LINDROS (DESJARDINS) 19:45

Penalties: Samuelsson (Phi) (high sticking) 1:32; Podein (Phi) (high sticking) 11:54; Draper (Det) (slashing) 14:39.

Goalies: Hextall (Phi), Vernon (Det)

Shots:					
	Phi	8	12	7	27
	Det	9	10	9	28

Referee: Bill McCreary

Linesmen: Wayne Bonney, Gord Broseker

1998

DETROIT RED WINGS - WASHINGTON CAPITALS

Game #1 - June 9, 1998 - Joe Louis Arena - Detroit 2, Washington 1

WASHINGTON: Brian Bellows, Craig Berube, Peter Bondra, Jeff Brown, Mike Eagles, Sergei Gonchar, Phil Housley, Dale Hunter, Calle Johansson, Joe Juneau, Olaf Kolzig, Kelly Miller, Andrei Nikolishin, Adam Oates, Bill Ranford, Joe Reekie, Chris Simon, Esa Tikkanen, Mark Tinordi, Richard Zednik.

DETROIT: Doug Brown, Kris Draper, Anders Eriksson, Sergei Fedorov, Viacheslav Fetisov, Kevin Hodson, Tomas Holmstrom, Joey Kocur, Vyacheslav Kozlov, Igor Larionov, Martin Lapointe, Nicklas Lidstrom, Jamie Macoun, Kirk Maltby, Darren McCarty, Larry Murphy, Chris Osgood, Bob Rouse, Brendan Shanahan, Steve Yzerman.

First Period

1. DETROIT KOCUR (BROWN, HOLMSTROM) 14:04
2. DETROIT LIDSTROM (YZERMAN, HOLMSTROM) 16:18 (GWG)

Penalties: Lapointe (Det) (tripping) 4:21, Tinordi (Wsh) (interference) 17:22.

Second Period

3. WASHINGTON ZEDNIK (NIKOLISHIN, BONDRA) 15:57

Penalties: Detroit (too many men – bench) 5:48, Yzerman (Det) (slashing) 8:51, Simon (Wsh) (roughing) 18:06.

Third Period

No Scoring.

Penalties: Nikolishin (Wsh) (interference) 0:38, Kocur (Det) (roughing) 4:19.

Goalies: Kolzig (Wsh), Osgood (Det)

Shots:					
	Wsh	6	4	7	17
	Det	10	9	12	31

Referee: Bill McCreary

Linesmen: Ray Scapinello, Dan Schachte

Game #2 - June 11, 1998 -Joe Louis Arena - Detroit 5, Washington 4 (OT)

WASHINGTON: Brian Bellows, Craig Berube, Peter Bondra, Jeff Brown, Mike Eagles, Sergei Gonchar, Phil Housley, Dale Hunter, Calle Johansson, Joe Juneau, Olaf Kolzig, Todd Krygier, Andrei Nikolishin, Adam Oates, Bill Ranford, Joe Reekie, Chris Simon, Esa Tikkanen, Mark Tinordi, Richard Zednik.

DETROIT: Doug Brown, Kris Draper, Anders Eriksson, Sergei Fedorov, Viacheslav Fetisov, Kevin Hodson, Tomas Holmstrom, Joey Kocur, Vyacheslav Kozlov, Igor Larionov, Martin Lapointe, Nicklas Lidstrom, Jamie Macoun, Kirk Maltby, Darren McCarty, Larry Murphy, Chris Osgood, Bob Rouse, Brendan Shanahan, Steve Yzerman.

First Period

1. DETROIT YZERMAN (HOLMSTROM, LIDSTROM) 7:49

Penalties: Reekie (Wsh) (holding-obstruction) 13:05, Bondra (Wsh) hooking 15:22.

Second Period

2. WASHINGTON BONDRA (NIKOLISHIN, BROWN) 1:51
3. WASHINGTON SIMON (BROWN, HUNTER) 6:11
4. WASHINGTON OATES (JUNEAU, JOHANSSON) 11:03

Penalties: Maltby (Det) (high sticking) 3:09, Zednik (Wsh) (hooking-obstruction) 7:12, Simon (Wsh) (roughing) 14:11, Osgood (Det) (unsportsmanlike conduct) 14:11, Maltby (Det) (slashing) 16:20.

Third Period

5. DETROIT YZERMAN (FETISOV, McCARTY) 6:37
6. WASHINGTON JUNEAU (GONCHAR, BELLOWS) 7:05 (PPG)
7. DETROIT LAPOINTE (LARIONOV, FETISOV) 8:08
8. DETROIT BROWN (unassisted) 15:46

Penalties: Lidstrom (Det) (interference) 6:23, Zednik (Wsh) (cross checking) 10:18), Lapointe (Det) (interference) 11:40.

Overtime

9. DETROIT DRAPER (LAPOINTE, SHANAHAN) 15:24 (GWG)

Penalties Tikkanen (Wsh) (roughing) 5:24, Kocur (Det) (roughing) 5:24.

Goalies: Kolzig (Wsh), Osgood (Det)

Shots:						
	Wsh	8	15	7	3	33
	Det	14	14	20	12	60

Referee: Don Koharski

Linesmen: Gord Broseker, Kevin Collins

Game #3 - June 13, 1998 - MCI Center - Detroit 2, Washington 1

DETROIT: Doug Brown, Kris Draper, Anders Eriksson, Sergei Fedorov, Viacheslav Fetisov, Kevin Hodson, Tomas Holmstrom, Joey Kocur, Vyacheslav Kozlov, Igor Larionov, Martin Lapointe, Nicklas Lidstrom, Jamie Macoun, Kirk Maltby, Darren McCarty, Larry Murphy, Chris Osgood, Bob Rouse, Brendan Shanahan, Steve Yzerman.

WASHINGTON: Brian Bellows, Craig Berube, Peter Bondra, Sergei Gonchar, Phil Housley, Dale Hunter, Calle Johansson, Joe Juneau, Ken Klee, Olaf Kolzig, Kelly Miller, Andrei Nikolishin, Adam Oates, Bill Ranford, Joe Reekie, Chris Simon, Esa Tikkanen, Mark Tinordi, Jeff Toms, Richard Zednik.

First Period

1. DETROIT HOLMSTROM (YZERMAN, McCARTY) 0:35

Penalties: Simon (Wsh) (slashing) 2:48, Hunter (Wsh) (charging) 8:10, Housley (Wsh) (elbowing) 12:29, Holmstrom (Det) (interference on the goaltender) 13:11, Lapointe (Det) (interference) 17:01.

Second Period

No Scoring.

Penalties: Krygier (Wsh) (roughing) 2:05, Eriksson (Det) (ob-holding) 7:29, Larionov (Det) (ob-tripping) 10:17, Draper (Det) (roughing) 15:23, Gonchar (Wsh) (roughing) 15:23.

Third Period

2. WASHINGTON BELLOWS (OATES, JUNEAU) 10:35 (PPG)
3. DETROIT FEDOROV (BROWN, FETISOV) 15:09 (GWG)

Penalties: Gonchar (Wsh) (roughing) 5:50, McCarty (Det) (tripping) 9:22.

Goalies: Osgood (Det). Kolzig (Wsh).

Shots:					
	Det	13	11	10	34
	Wsh	1	12	5	18

Referee: Terry Gregson

Linesmen: Ray Scapinello, Dan Schachte

Game #4 - June 16, 1998 - MCI Center - Detroit 4, Washington 1

DETROIT: Doug Brown, Kris Draper, Anders Eriksson, Sergei Fedorov, Viacheslav Fetisov, Kevin Hodson, Tomas Holmstrom, Joey Kocur, Vyacheslav Kozlov, Igor Larionov, Martin Lapointe, Nicklas Lidstrom, Jamie Macoun, Kirk Maltby, Darren McCarty, Larry Murphy, Chris Osgood, Bob Rouse, Brendan Shanahan, Steve Yzerman.

WASHINGTON: Brian Bellows, Craig Berube, Peter Bondra, Sergei Gonchar, Phil Housley, Dale Hunter, Calle Johansson, Joe Juneau, Ken Klee, Olaf Kolzig, Todd, Krygier, Kelly Miller, Andrei Nikolishin, Adam Oates, Bill Ranford, Joe Reekie, Chris Simon, Esa Tikkanen, Mark Tinordi, Richard Zednik.

First Period

1. DETROIT BROWN (FEDOROV, MURPHY) 10:30 (PPG)

Penalties: Eriksson (Det) (interference) 7:17, Bondra (Wsh) (interference) 9:12, Johansson (Wsh) (roughing) 11:01.

Second Period

2. DETROIT LAPOINTE (LARIONOV, ROUSE) 2:26 (GWG)
3. WASHINGTON BELLOWS (OATES, JUNEAU) 7:49
4. DETROIT MURPHY (HOLMSTROM, FEDOROV) 11:46 (PPG)

Penalties: Tinordi (Wsh) (roughing) 9:13, Maltby (Det) (roughing) 9:13, Tikkanen (Wsh) (interference on the goaltender) 11:02, Larionov (Det) (hooking) 12:41, Rouse (Det) (high sticking) 16:07, Tinordi (Wsh) (slashing) 19:53.

Third Period

5. DETROIT BROWN (KOZLOV, ERIKSSON) 1:32 (PPG)

Penalties: Fetisov(Det) (interference) 13:08.

Goalies: Osgood (Det), Kolzig (Wsh).

Shots:					
	Det	14	12	12	38
	Wsh	6	14	11	31

Referee: Bill McCreary

Linesmen: Gord Broseker, Kevin Collins

1999

DALLAS STARS - BUFFALO SABRES

Game #1 - June 8, 1999 - Dr Pepper Star Center - Buffalo 3, Dallas 2 (OT)

BUFFALO: Stu Barnes, Curtis Brown, Michal Grosek, Dominik Hasek, Brian Holzinger, Joe Juneau, Jay McKee, James Patrick, Michael Peca, Wayne Primeau, Erik Rasmussen, Dwayne Roloson, Geoff Sanderson, Miroslav Satan, Richard Smehlik, Vaclav Varada, Dixon Ward, Rhett Warrener, Jason Woolley, Alexei Zhitnik

DALLAS: Ed Belfour, Guy Carbonneau, Shawn Chambers, Derian Hatcher, Brett Hull, Mike Keane, Jamie Langenbrunner, Jere Lehtinen, Craig Ludwig, Richard Matvichuk, Mike Modano, Joe Nieuwendyk, Dave Reid, Jonathan Sim, Brian Skrudland, Blake Sloan, Darryl Sydor, Roman Turek, Pat Verbeek, Sergei Zubov.

First Period

1. DALLAS HULL (MODANO, LEHTINEN) 10:17 (PPG)

Penalties: Zubov (Dal) (roughing) 6:36, Satan (Buf) (boarding) 8:18, Patrick (Buf) (high sticking - double minor) 12:46, Ward (Buf) (interference) 19:11.

Second Period

No Scoring.

Penalties: Varada (Buf) (goaltender interference) 4:53, Zhitnik (Buf) (interference) 7:07, Ward (Buf) (roughing) 9:34, Ludwig (Dal) (hooking) 12:21, Matvichuk (Dal) (interference) 16:33.

Third Period

2. BUFFALO BARNES (JUNEAU, SMEHLIK) 8:33
3. BUFFALO PRIMEAU (ZHITNIK, SMEHLIK) 13:37 (PPG)
4. DALLAS LEHTINEN (MODANO, ZUBOV) 19:11

Penalties: Sydor (Dal) (ob-tripping) 12:10, McKee (Buf) (charging) 14:17.

Overtime

5. BUFFALO WOOLLEY (BROWN) 15:30 (GWG)

Penalties: Zhitnik (Buf) (hooking) 6:41, Sanderson (Buf) (boarding) 9:06.

Goalies: Hasek (Buf), Belfour (Dal).

Shots:						
	Buf	5	4	10	5	24
	Dal	11	13	6	7	37

Referee: Terry Gregson, Bill McCreary

Linesmen: Ray Scapinello, Jay Sharrers

Game #2 - June 10, 1999 - Dr Pepper Star Center - Dallas 4, Buffalo 2

BUFFALO: Stu Barnes, Curtis Brown, Dominik Hasek, Brian Holzinger, Joe Juneau, Paul Kruse, Jay McKee, James Patrick, Michael Peca, Wayne Primeau, Erik Rasmussen, Dwayne Roloson, Geoff Sanderson, Miroslav Satan, Richard Smehlik, Vaclav Varada, Dixon Ward, Rhett Warrener, Jason Woolley, Alexei Zhitnik

DALLAS: Ed Belfour, Guy Carbonneau, Shawn Chambers, Derian Hatcher, Tony Hrkac, Brett Hull, Mike Keane, Jamie Langenbrunner, Jere Lehtinen, Craig Ludwig, Richard Matvichuk, Mike Modano, Joe Nieuwendyk, Dave Reid, Brian Skrudland, Blake Sloan, Darryl Sydor, Roman Turek, Pat Verbeek, Sergei Zubov.

First Period

No Scoring.

Penalties: Skrudland (Dal) (charging) 12:25, Zhitnik (Buf) (boarding) 15:31, Smehlik (Buf) (roughing) 20:00, Hatcher (Buf) (roughing) 20:00, Zhitnik (Buf) (cross checking) 20:00, Holzinger (Buf) (fighting major) 20:00, Nieuwendyk (Dal) (fighting major) 20:00, Modano (Dal) (tripping) 20:00.

Second Period

1. BUFFALO PECA (WOOLLEY, SATAN) 7:27 (PPG)
2. DALLAS LANGENBRUNNER (MATVICHUK, NIEUWENDYK) 18:26

Penalties: Sydor (Dal) (hooking) 5:41, Woolley (Buf) (interference) 9:19, Varada (Buf) (ob-tripping) 13:14, Zhitnik (Buf) (tripping) 20:00.

Third Period

3. DALLAS LUDWIG (SKRUDLAND) 4:25
4. BUFFALO ZHITNIK (unassisted) 5:36 (PPG)
5. DALLAS HULL (HRKAC, CHAMBERS) 17:10 (GWG)
6. DALLAS HATCHER (ZUBOV, KEANE) 19:34 (ENG)

Penalties: Sydor (Dal) (high sticking) 4:50, Varada (Buf) (high sticking) 10:32, Zhitnik (Buf) (hooking) 11:48, Hatcher (Dal) (high sticking) 17:31.

Goalies: Hasek (Buf), Belfour (Dal).

Shots:					
	Buf	7	10	4	21
	Dal	5	7	19	31

Referee: Kerry Fraser, Dan Marouelli

Linesmen: Kevin Collins, Gord Broseker

Game #3 - June 12, 1999 - Marine Midland Arena - Dallas 2, Buffalo 1

DALLAS: Ed Belfour, Guy Carbonneau, Shawn Chambers, Derian Hatcher, Tony Hrkac, Brett Hull, Mike Keane, Jamie Langenbrunner, Jere Lehtinen, Craig Ludwig, Richard Matvichuk, Mike Modano, Joe Nieuwendyk, Dave Reid, Brian Skrudland, Blake Sloan, Darryl Sydor, Roman Turek, Pat Verbeek, Sergei Zubov.

BUFFALO: Stu Barnes, Curtis Brown, Dominik Hasek, Brian Holzinger, Joe Juneau, Jay McKee, James Patrick, Michael Peca, Wayne Primeau, Erik Rasmussen, Rob Ray, Dwayne Roloson, Geoff Sanderson, Miroslav Satan, Richard Smehlik, Vaclav Varada, Dixon Ward, Rhett Warrener, Jason Woolley, Alexei Zhitnik

First Period

No Scoring.

Penalties: Chambers (Dal) (roughing) 7:45, Rasmussen (Buf) (roughing) 7:45, Ludwig (Dal) (interference) 7:45, Matvichuk (Dal) (roughing) 9:43, Skrudland (Dal) (slashing) 18:13, Hatcher (Dal) (roughing) 18:46.

Second Period

1. BUFFALO BARNES (SMEHLIK, HOLZINGER) 7:51
2. DALLAS NIEUWENDYK (REID, LANGENBRUNNER) 15:33

Penalties: Zhitnik (Buf) (interference) 3:38, Modano (Dal) (tripping), 9:54, Modano (Dal) (slashing) 12:21, Holzinger (Buf) (high sticking) 19:09, Modano (Dal) (interference) 19:23.

Third Period

3. DALLAS NIEUWENDYK (LANGENBRUNNER, REID) 9:35 (GWG)

Penalties: Hrkac (Dal) (tripping) 17:38.

Goalies: Belfour (Dal), Hasek (Buf).

Shots:					
	Dal	8	13	8	29
	Buf	3	6	3	12

Referee: Terry Gregson, Don Koharski

Linesmen: Ray Scapinello, Jay Sharrers

Game #4 - June 15, 1999 - Marine Midland Arena - Buffalo 2, Dallas 1

DALLAS: Ed Belfour, Guy Carbonneau, Shawn Chambers, Derian Hatcher, Tony Hrkac, Mike Keane, Jamie Langenbrunner, Jere Lehtinen, Craig Ludwig, Richard Matvichuk, Mike Modano, Joe Nieuwendyk, Dave Reid, Jonathan Sim, Brian Skrudland, Blake Sloan, Darryl Sydor, Roman Turek, Pat Verbeek, Sergei Zubov.

BUFFALO: Stu Barnes, Curtis Brown, Randy Cunneyworth, Dominik Hasek, Brian Holzinger, Joe Juneau, Jay McKee, James Patrick, Michael Peca, Wayne Primeau, Erik Rasmussen, Dwayne Roloson, Geoff Sanderson, Miroslav Satan, Richard Smehlik, Vaclav Varada, Dixon Ward, Rhett Warrener, Jason Woolley, Alexei Zhitnik

First Period

1. BUFFALO SANDERSON (unassisted) 8:09
2. DALLAS LEHTINEN (MODANO, HATCHER) 10:14 (PPG)

Penalties: Matvichuk (Dal) (roughing), 3:48, Primeau (Buf) (charging), 9:32, Woolley (Buf) (holding) 19:05.

Second Period

3. BUFFALO WARD (unassisted) 7:37 (GWG)

Penalties: Verbeek (Dal) (interference) 0:21, Ludwig (Dal) (interference) 11:07, Skrudland (Dal) (roughing) 14:49, Holzinger (Buf) (boarding) 16:44, Verbeek (Dal) (roughing) 20:00, Hatcher (Dal) (roughing) 20:00, Hasek (Buf) (roughing) 20:00, Zhitnik (Buf) (roughing) 20:00.

Third Period

No Scoring.

Penalties: Nieuwendyk (Dal) (hooking) 1:06), Reid (Dal) (roughing) 20:00, Warrener (Buf) (roughing) 20:00, Langenbrunner (Dal) (slashing) 20:00, Ward (Buf) (roughing - double minor) 20:00.

Goalies: Belfour (Dal), Hasek (Buf).

Shots:					
	Dal	9	9	13	31
	Buf	7	9	2	18

Referee: Bill McCreary, Dan Marouelli

Linesmen: Kevin Collins, Gord Broseker

Game #5 - June 17, 1999 - Dr Pepper StarCenter - Dallas 2, Buffalo 0

BUFFALO: Stu Barnes, Curtis Brown, Randy Cunneyworth, Dominik Hasek, Brian Holzinger, Joe Juneau, Jay McKee, James Patrick, Michael Peca, Wayne Primeau, Erik Rasmussen, Dwayne Roloson, Geoff Sanderson, Miroslav Satan, Richard Smehlik, Vaclav Varada, Dixon Ward, Rhett Warrener, Jason Woolley, Alexei Zhitnik

DALLAS: Ed Belfour, Guy Carbonneau, Shawn Chambers, Derian Hatcher, Benoit Hogue, Brett Hull, Mike Keane, Jamie Langenbrunner, Jere Lehtinen, Craig Ludwig, Richard Matvichuk, Mike Modano, Joe Nieuwendyk, Dave Reid, Brian Skrudland, Blake Sloan, Darryl Sydor, Roman Turek, Pat Verbeek, Sergei Zubov.

First Period

No Scoring.

Penalties: Ludwig (Dal) (ob-tripping) 2:08.

Second Period

1. DALLAS SYDOR (MODANO, ZUBOV) 2:23 (GWG)

Penalties: Brown (Buf) (interference) 1:42 Woolley. (Buf) (ob-holding) 3:31, Langenbrunner (Dal) (roughing) 7:44

Third Period

2. DALLAS VERBEEK (MATVICHUK, MODANO) 15:21

Penalties: Primeau (Buf) (roughing) 8:21, Sydor (Dal) (roughing) 8:21, Warrener (Buf) (slashing) 16:31, Zhitnik (Buf) (elbowing) 17:27, Nieuwendyk (Dal) (roughing) 17:27, Skrudland (Dal) (ob-tripping) 19:29, Warrener (Buf) (roughing) 20:00, Hatcher (Dal) (roughing) 20:00.

Goalies: Hasek (Buf), Belfour (Dal).

Shots:					
	Buf	9	5	9	23
	Dal	8	7	6	21

Referee: Don Koharski, Kerry Fraser

Linesmen: Ray Scapinello, Jay Sharrers

Game #6 - June 19, 1999 - Marine Midland Arena - Dallas 2, Buffalo 1 (3 OT)

DALLAS: Ed Belfour, Guy Carbonneau, Shawn Chambers, Derian Hatcher, Benoit Hogue, Brett Hull, Mike Keane, Jamie Langenbrunner, Jere Lehtinen, Craig Ludwig, Richard Matvichuk, Mike Modano, Joe Nieuwendyk, Dave Reid, Brian Skrudland, Blake Sloan, Darryl Sydor, Roman Turek, Pat Verbeek, Sergei Zubov.

BUFFALO: Stu Barnes, Curtis Brown, Randy Cunneyworth, Dominik Hasek, Brian Holzinger, Joe Juneau, Jay McKee, James Patrick, Michael Peca, Wayne Primeau, Erik Rasmussen, Dwayne Roloson, Geoff Sanderson, Miroslav Satan, Darryl Shannon, Richard Smehlik, Vaclav Varada, Dixon Ward, Jason Woolley, Alexei Zhitnik

First Period

1. DALLAS LEHTINEN (MODANO, LUDWIG) 8:09

Penalties: None.

Second Period

2. BUFFALO BARNES (PRIMEAU, ZHITNIK) 18:21

Penalties: Sanderson (Buf) (interference) 5:19, Ludwig (Dal) (interference) 10:49, Hogue (Dal) (tripping) 14:28, Peca (Buf) (slashing) 19:27.

Third Period

No Scoring.

Penalties: None.

First Overtime

No Scoring.

Penalties: None.

Second Overtime

No Scoring.

Penalties: None.

Third Overtime

3. DALLAS HULL (LEHTINEN, MODANO) 14:51 (GWG)

Penalties: None

Goalies: Belfour (Dal), Hasek (Buf) .

Shots:								
	Dal	5	11	10	4	13	7	50
	Buf	11	15	6	6	12	4	54

Referee: Terry Gregson, Bill McCreary

Linesmen: Kevin Collins, Gord Broseker

CHAPTER 22

Stranger Than Fiction

Odd and Unusual Moments in Stanley Cup History

James Duplacey

1905: The Ottawa Silver Seven felt it necessary to see if one could kick the Cup across Ottawa's Rideau Canal. One of them lined it up and gave it a boot, drop-kick style. It didn't make it. The Stanley Cup landed in the canal, which, fortunately, happened to be frozen at the time. The boys went on their merry way, and the Cup stayed on the Canal until the next day when sober heads prevailed and Lord Stanley's mug was rescued.

1906: The Montreal Wanderers won the Cup this year, dethroning the Silver Seven who had held the trophy since 1903. But when the Montreal players asked to see their prize, the Cup was no where to be found. Someone, somehow remembered that Harry Smith had the Mug at his home and after a quick search, sure enough there it was. It was retrieved and presented to the victorious Wanderers.

1907: The injustices of the Cup continued. The Wanderers quickly forgot the valuable lesson of the previous year and left the Cup at the home of the photographer they hired to document their trophy win. A young fellow happened by and grabbed the Cup, hoping to extract a small ransom for its return. However, no one was interested, so he returned it to the photographer's home, where an astute lady decided it would make a wonderful flower pot. It served that purpose for a few months until the the Wanderers brass remembered it and rescued it from its earthly grave.

1923: After returning home from the west coast with the Stanley Cup, rookie Frank "King" Clancy asked Ottawa Senator executives if he could bring the Cup home to show his father, a well-known amateur athlete and the original "King." The following season, NHL president Frank Calder asked the Senators for the Cup, but they couldn't find it. It was then that that Clancy admitted it was at home, sitting on his mantlepiece.

1924: The Montreal Canadiens wanted to celebrate their Cup win by drinking champagne from the Silver Mug. To this end they headed to owner Leo Dandurand's home to swill the bubbly. As fate would have it, they suffered a flat tire along the way and the boys bolted from the car, leaving Lord Stanley on the curb while they tended to the flat. When they arrived at Dandurand's and prepared to serve the victory wine, they discovered they'd left the Grail behind, on the streets of Montreal. Back into the car (a Tin Lizzie, no less) they rumbled and found the Cup where they had left it, on the sidewalk.

1962: The Cup was given much better care over the ensuing years, but it found itself in danger one year after the Chicago Black Hawks had the nerve to pluck the Cup from the grasp of the Montreal Canadiens, who had won it five times in succession through 1960. With the Habs losing in the semi-finals to the Hawks for the second year in a row in 1962, an unhappy fan went into the lobby of the Chicago Stadium where the trophy was displayed in a glass case. The loyal fan broke the glass and made a beeline to freedom with his prize. However, he was quickly caught and the Mug apprehended. His only excuse was that he couldn't stand seeing the Windy City win the coveted silverware.

1970: After the Toronto Maple Leafs won the Cup in 1963, the original collar beneath the Stanley Cup bowl was retired to the Hockey Hall of Fame. In January 1970, the collar was stolen. Later, an anonymous phone call told police to check the backroom of a Toronto cleaning store for a very important piece of history. The police weren't sure what they would find, but there, wrapped like a Christmas present was the original collar of the Stanley Cup.

1975: One of the more unusual events in Stanley Cup history took place during the 1975 final between the Philadelphia Flyers and Buffalo Sabres. Game three of the series was played on May 20 on a humid night in Buffalo. Fog inside the old Memorial Auditorium became so thick that the game had to be delayed. Players skated around the ice, waving towels to move the mist away. Suddenly, a bat flew down from the rafters and flew in circles just above the playing surface. The crowd cheered as all the players scattered—except Buffalo's Jim Lorentz, who dispatched the winged creature with a swipe of his hockey stick. The Sabres went on to win the game 3–2 in overtime, but dropped the series in six.

1977: The current Stanley Cup was almost stolen in 1977, but a keen-eyed employee of the Hall of Fame thwarted the attempt. Seven men, with a large gym bag and tools, were seen near the Cup. When spotted, they dashed outside. In their car, police found a series of photos detailing the Hall and the necessary equipment to pull off the heist.

1979: After the Montreal Canadiens won their fourth straight Stanley Cup championship in 1979, Guy Lafleur took the Cup home to Thurso, Quebec, and invited all his neighbors and friends to come over and see it. He held a barbecue to thank everyone for their support and gave them a chance to have their pictures taken with the Cup. Lafleur returned the trophy to Montreal the next day, much to the relief of the Canadiens front office. (Lafleur hadn't mentioned his plan to borrow the Cup for the day.) Though the Lafleur story was unusual, players on winning teams have had access to the Cup since the early 1970s. In 1994, the NHL took a more active role in the scheduling of players' visits with the Stanley Cup. In recent years, a security person has been sent by the NHL and/or the Hockey Hall of Fame to monitor the Stanley Cup's appearances.

1984: When the Edmonton Oilers won the Stanley Cup for the first time in 1984, Peter Pocklington included the name of his father, Basil Pocklington, on the trophy. As Basil had no con-

nection with the team, the name was crossed out with a row of X's that still remain on the Cup. The X's do not appear on the Hockey Hall of Fame's replica Cup.

1987: The Philadelphia Flyers trailed the Edmonton Oilers three games to one in the finals. Flyers coach Mike Keenan used the Cup as a motivational tool, bringing it into the dressing room to charge up his players. The Flyer won Game 5, so Keenan repeated the process before Game 6 which Philadelphia won as well. When he attempted to display the Cup before Game 7 in Edmonton, it could not be found. The Oilers won and, miraculously, there was the Cup for presentation. The story that emerged had Edmonton general manager Glen Sather instruct team trainer Sparky Kulchisky to stash the Cup in the trunk of his car when the Flyers came calling.

1988: The Edmonton Oilers won the Stanley Cup for the fourth time this year, and took it on a tour of Edmonton to celebrate. One stop on this tour was an establishment where the entertainers address by undress, and the Mug was proudly placed on display as an "entertainment" item along side the ladies. By methods unknown, or undisclosed, the Cup was slightly bent in various places, so it was taken to a local automotive shop and repaired. It returned to its home at the Hall of Fame in Toronto a little worse for wear, but a quick trip to the silversmith returned the venerable mug as good as new.

Stanley Cup Notebook

Spelling: A number of players have their names spelled incorrectly on the Stanley Cup, and so to do the Toronto Maple Leafs and the Montreal Canadiens. When Toronto won the Stanley Cup in 1964, the word "Leafs" was engraved as "Leaes." Montreal's 1966 winner is spelled "Canadiene." When the team won its first Stanley Cup title in 1916 it is identified merely as "Canadian." Among the players with errors are "Gave" Stewart in 1947 an Ted "Kennedyy" in 1951. When Detroit won the Stanley Cup in 1952, coach Tommy Ivan's name was misspelled as "Nivan" and Alex Delvecchio was recorded as "Belvecchio." Even non-playing personnel can have their names misspelled: "G. Bettex" is listed with the 1956 Montreal Canadiens. The correct name is Gaston Bettez, the assistant trainer of the Canadiens.

Names on Twice: Cy Denneny has his name on the Cup twice in 1929, one as a player and once as a coach, although his name is spelled wrong the second time (Dennenny). Journeyman Pete Palangio played three games for the Black Hawks in the 1938 playoffs but got his name on the Cup twice, once spelled correctly and once, he is listed merely as "Palagio".

Don Simmons played an important role in the Maple Leafs' 1962 Stanley Cup victory, winning games five and six to give Toronto the championship. Although he never appeared in a postseason game again, his name is on the Cup in 1963 and 1964. The Maple Leafs put Stafford Smythe's name on the Cup in 1932 as the team's mascot. In 1942, Hughie Smythe was named the team's mascot and in 1945, Kerry Day gets the nod. The Leafs are the only team to ever give their "mascot" a spot on the Cup. They were also the first team to include the names of team doctors on the Cup, adding the medics and dropping the mascot in 1948.

Marguerite Norris was the first woman to have her name engraved on the Stanley Cup. She was president of the Detroit Red Wings when they won the NHL title in 1955. Sonia Scurfield was co-owner of the Calgary Flames in 1989 and Marie Denise DeBartolo York was president of the Pittsburgh Penguins in 1991. The number of women on the Stanley Cup more than doubled in 1997 with the names of Marian Ilitch, Denise Ilitch Lites, Lisa Ilitch Murray and Carole Ilitch Trepeck included as members of the front office of the Detroit Red Wings. These four women got their names on the Cup again in 1998.

Tie games used to be a part of the NHL playoffs until the practice of two-game total-goals series was abandoned for the 1936–37 postseason. Since then, only two NHL playoff games have ended before a winner was declared, and both involved the Boston Bruins. On Saturday, March 31, 1951, the Bruins and Leafs were tied 1–1 after one period of overtime when the game was halted. At that time, the city of Toronto did not allow sports to be played on Sunday and the clock was just about to strike midnight. On May 24, 1988, a power failure at the Boston Garden stopped a Stanley Cup game between the Bruins and Edmonton Oilers. The game was postponed, and was never replayed as the Oilers went on to defeat the Bruins in four straight games.

U.S.-Based Teams: The 1916 Portland Rosebuds were the first team based in the United States to participate in a Stanley Cup championship. The 1917 Seattle Metropolitans were the first U.S. team to win the Cup. There has since been ten different U.S. clubs who have been Cup-winners. The Detroit Red Wings have won nine Stanley Cup titles, more than any other U.S.-based team, and were the first to win back-to-back titles in 1936 and 1937. (They duplicated this feat on two other occassions: 1954 and 1955 and 1997 and 1998.

The New York Islanders are the only U.S.-based club to have captured more than two consecutive Stanley Cup titles. Winning from 1980 through 1983, the Islanders became only the second franchise in NHL history to win four consecutive titles, joining the Montreal Canadiens (1956-60; 1976-79).

Back-to-Back Winners: Many players have won consecutive championships in their careers, but few have ever accomplished the feat with two different teams. One player, Eddie Gerard, won the Cup with the 1921 Ottawa Senators, 1922 Toronto St. Pats and again in 1923 with the Senators. A total of 10 players have won consecutive Stanley Cups with different clubs.

Player	First Champion	Second Champion
Jack Marshall	1901 Winnipeg	1902 Montreal
Art Ross	1907 Kenora	1908 Montreal
Bruce Stuart	1908 Montreal	1909 Ottawa
Harry Holmes	1917 Seattle	1918 Toronto
Eddie Gerard	1921 Ottawa	1922 Toronto
Eddie Gerard	1922 Toronto	1923 Ottawa
Lionel Conacher	1934 Chicago	1935 Montreal
Ab McDonald	1960 Montreal	1961 Chicago
Al Arbour	1961 Chicago	1962 Toronto
Ed Litzenberger	1961 Chicago	1962 Toronto
Claude Lemieux	1995 New Jersey	1996 Colorado

CHAPTER 23

Player Register

Career NHL Playoff Records, 1918–1999

Abbreviations: A – assists; **G** – goals; **GP** – games played; **GW** – game-winning goals; **PIM** – penalties in minutes; **PP** – powerplay goals; **Pts** – points; **SH** – shorthand goals; ***** – league-leading total; ♦ – member of Stanley Cup winning team.
Goaltender Register begins on page 208.

Season	Club	GP	G	A	Pts	PIM	PP	SH	GW
AALTO, Antti	Center								
1999	Anaheim	4	0	0	0	2	0	0	0
Playoff Totals		**4**	**0**	**0**	**0**	**2**	**0**	**0**	**0**
ABBOTT, Reg *No playoffs*	Center								
ABEL, Clarence	Defense								
1927	NY Rangers	2	0	1	1	8	....	....	....
1928♦	NY Rangers	9	1	0	1	14	....	....	....
1929	NY Rangers	6	0	0	0	8	....	....	....
1930	Chicago	2	0	0	0	10	....	....	....
1931	Chicago	9	0	0	0	8	....	....	....
1932	Chicago	2	0	0	0	2	....	....	....
1934♦	Chicago	8	0	0	0	8	....	....	....
Playoff Totals		**38**	**1**	**1**	**2**	**58**	....	....	....
ABEL, Gerry *No playoffs*	Left wing								
ABEL, Sid	Center								
1939	Detroit	6	1	1	2	2	....	....	....
1940	Detroit	5	0	3	3	21	....	....	....
1941	Detroit	9	2	2	4	2	....	....	....
1942	Detroit	12	4	2	6	8	....	....	....
1943♦	Detroit	10	5	8	13	4	....	....	....
1946	Detroit	3	0	0	0	0	....	....	....
1947	Detroit	3	1	1	2	2	....	....	....
1948	Detroit	10	0	3	3	16	....	....	....
1949	Detroit	11	3	3	6	6	....	....	....
1950♦	Detroit	14	*6	2	8	6	....	....	....
1951	Detroit	6	4	3	7	0	....	....	....
1952♦	Detroit	7	2	2	4	12	....	....	....
1953	Chicago	1	0	0	0	0	....	....	....
Playoff Totals		**97**	**28**	**30**	**58**	**79**	....	....	....
ABGRALL, Dennis *No playoffs*	Right wing								
ABRAHAMSSON, Thommy *No playoffs*	Defense								
ACHTYMICHUK, Gene *No playoffs*	Center								
ACOMB, Doug *No playoffs*	Center								
ACTON, Keith	Center								
1981	Montreal	2	0	0	0	6	0	0	0
1982	Montreal	5	0	4	4	16	0	0	0
1983	Montreal	3	0	0	0	0	0	0	0
1984	Minnesota	15	4	7	11	12	1	0	1
1985	Minnesota	9	4	4	8	6	1	0	2
1986	Minnesota	5	0	3	3	6	0	0	0
1988♦	Edmonton	7	2	0	2	16	0	0	2
1989	Philadelphia	16	2	3	5	18	0	0	0
1994	NY Islanders	4	0	0	0	8	0	0	0
Playoff Totals		**66**	**12**	**21**	**33**	**88**	**2**	**0**	**5**
ADAM, Douglas *No playoffs*	Left wing								
ADAM, Russ *No playoffs*	Center								
ADAMS, Greg	Left wing								
1989	Vancouver	7	2	3	5	2	0	0	0
1991	Vancouver	5	0	0	0	2	0	0	0
1992	Vancouver	6	0	2	2	4	0	0	0
1993	Vancouver	12	7	6	13	6	5	0	1
1994	Vancouver	23	6	8	14	2	2	0	2
1995	Dallas	5	2	0	2	0	0	0	0
1997	Dallas	3	0	1	1	0	0	0	0
1998	Dallas	12	2	2	4	0	0	0	2
1999	Phoenix	3	0	1	1	0	0	0	0
Playoff Totals		**76**	**19**	**23**	**42**	**16**	**7**	**0**	**5**
ADAMS, Greg	Left wing								
1984	Washington	1	0	0	0	0	0	0	0
1985	Washington	5	0	0	0	9	0	0	0
1986	Washington	9	1	3	4	27	0	0	0
1987	Washington	7	1	3	4	38	1	0	0
1988	Washington	14	0	5	5	58	0	0	0
1989	Vancouver	7	0	0	0	21	0	0	0
Playoff Totals		**43**	**2**	**11**	**13**	**153**	**1**	**0**	**0**
ADAMS, Jack	Center								
1918♦	Toronto	2	0	0	0	0	....	....	....
1925	Toronto	2	1	0	1	7	....	....	....
1927♦	Ottawa	6	0	0	0	0	....	....	....
Playoff Totals		**10**	**1**	**0**	**1**	**7**	....	....	....
ADAMS, John	Left wing								
1941	Montreal	3	0	0	0	0	....	....	....
Playoff Totals		**3**	**0**	**0**	**0**	**0**	....	....	....
ADAMS, Kevyn	Center								
1999	Toronto	7	0	2	2	14	0	0	0
Playoff Totals		**7**	**0**	**2**	**2**	**14**	**0**	**0**	**0**
ADAMS, Stew	Left wing								
1930	Chicago	2	0	0	0	6	....	....	....
1931	Chicago	9	3	3	6	8	....	....	....
Playoff Totals		**11**	**3**	**3**	**6**	**14**	....	....	....
ADDUONO, Rick *No playoffs*	Center								
AFFLECK, Bruce	Defense								
1975	St. Louis	1	0	0	0	0	0	0	0
1976	St. Louis	3	0	0	0	0	0	0	0
1977	St. Louis	4	0	0	0	0	0	0	0
Playoff Totals		**8**	**0**	**0**	**0**	**0**	**0**	**0**	**0**
AFINOGENOV, Maxim *No playoffs*	Right wing								
AGNEW, Jim	Defense								
1992	Vancouver	4	0	0	0	6	0	0	0
Playoff Totals		**4**	**0**	**0**	**0**	**6**	**0**	**0**	**0**
AHERN, Fred	Right wing								
1978	Colorado	2	0	1	1	2	0	0	0
Playoff Totals		**2**	**0**	**1**	**1**	**2**	**0**	**0**	**0**
AHLIN, Tony *No playoffs*	Left wing								
AHOLA, Peter	Defense								
1992	Los Angeles	6	0	0	0	2	0	0	0
Playoff Totals		**6**	**0**	**0**	**0**	**2**	**0**	**0**	**0**
AHRENS, Chris	Defense								
1973	Minnesota	1	0	0	0	0	0	0	0
Playoff Totals		**1**	**0**	**0**	**0**	**0**	**0**	**0**	**0**
AILSBY, Lloyd *No playoffs*	Defense								
AITKEN, Brad *No playoffs*	Left wing								
AIVAZOFF, Micah *No playoffs*	Center								
ALATALO, Mika *No playoffs*	Left wing								
ALBELIN, Tommy	Defense								
1991	New Jersey	3	0	1	1	2	0	0	0
1992	New Jersey	1	1	1	2	0	0	0	0
1993	New Jersey	5	2	0	2	0	1	0	1
1994	New Jersey	20	2	5	7	14	1	0	1
1995♦	New Jersey	20	1	7	8	2	0	0	0
1996	Calgary	4	0	0	0	0	0	0	0
Playoff Totals		**53**	**6**	**14**	**20**	**18**	**2**	**0**	**2**
ALBRIGHT, Clint *No playoffs*	Center								
ALDCORN, Gary	Left wing								
1960	Detroit	6	1	2	3	4	0	0	0
Playoff Totals		**6**	**1**	**2**	**3**	**4**	**0**	**0**	**0**
ALDRIDGE, Keith *No playoffs*	Defense								
ALEXANDER, Claire	Defense								
1975	Toronto	7	0	0	0	0	0	0	0
1976	Toronto	9	2	4	6	4	1	0	0
Playoff Totals		**16**	**2**	**4**	**6**	**4**	**1**	**0**	**0**
ALEXANDRE, Art	Left wing								
1932	Mtl. Canadiens	4	0	0	0	0	0	0	0
Playoff Totals		**4**	**0**	**0**	**0**	**0**	**0**	**0**	**0**
ALFREDSSON, Daniel	Right wing								
1997	Ottawa	7	5	2	7	6	3	0	2
1998	Ottawa	11	7	2	9	20	2	1	1
1999	Ottawa	4	1	2	3	4	1	0	0
Playoff Totals		**22**	**13**	**6**	**19**	**30**	**6**	**1**	**3**
ALLAN, Jeff *No playoffs*	Defense								
ALLEN, Chris *No playoffs*	Defense								
ALLEN, George	Left wing/defense								
1939	NY Rangers	7	0	0	0	4	....	....	....
1940	Chicago	2	0	0	0	0	....	....	....
1941	Chicago	5	2	2	4	10	....	....	....
1942	Chicago	3	1	1	2	0	....	....	....
1944	Chicago	9	5	4	9	8	....	....	....
1946	Chicago	4	0	0	0	4	....	....	....
1947	Montreal	11	1	3	4	6	....	....	....
Playoff Totals		**41**	**9**	**10**	**19**	**32**	....	....	....
ALLEN, Keith	Defense								
1954♦	Detroit	5	0	0	0	0	0	0	0
Playoff Totals		**5**	**0**	**0**	**0**	**0**	**0**	**0**	**0**
ALLEN, Peter *No playoffs*	Defense								
ALLEN, Viv *No playoffs*	Right wing								
ALLEY, Steve	Left wing								
1980	Hartford	3	0	1	1	0	0	0	0
Playoff Totals		**3**	**0**	**1**	**1**	**0**	**0**	**0**	**0**
ALLISON, Dave *No playoffs*	Defense								
ALLISON, Jamie *No playoffs*	Defense								
ALLISON, Jason	Center								
1998	Boston	6	2	6	8	4	1	0	0
1999	Boston	12	2	9	11	6	1	0	0
Playoff Totals		**18**	**4**	**15**	**19**	**10**	**2**	**0**	**0**
ALLISON, Mike	Left wing								
1981	NY Rangers	14	3	1	4	20	1	0	2
1982	NY Rangers	10	1	3	4	18	0	0	0
1983	NY Rangers	8	0	5	5	10	0	0	0
1984	NY Rangers	5	0	1	1	6	0	0	0
1986	NY Rangers	16	0	2	2	38	0	0	0
1987	Toronto	13	3	5	8	15	1	0	2
1988	Los Angeles	5	0	0	0	16	0	0	0
1989	Los Angeles	7	1	0	1	10	0	0	0
1990	Los Angeles	4	1	0	1	2	0	1	0
Playoff Totals		**82**	**9**	**17**	**26**	**135**	**2**	**1**	**4**
ALLISON, Ray	Right wing								
1980	Hartford	2	0	1	1	0	0	0	0
1982	Philadelphia	3	2	0	2	2	2	0	0
1983	Philadelphia	3	0	1	1	12	0	0	0
1984	Philadelphia	3	0	1	1	4	0	0	0
1985	Philadelphia	1	0	0	0	2	0	0	0
Playoff Totals		**12**	**2**	**3**	**5**	**20**	**2**	**0**	**0**
ALLUM, Bill *No playoffs*	Defense								
AMADIO, Dave	Defense								
1968	Los Angeles	7	0	2	2	8	0	0	0
1969	Los Angeles	9	1	0	1	10	0	0	0
Playoff Totals		**16**	**1**	**2**	**3**	**18**	**0**	**0**	**0**
AMBROZIAK, Peter *No playoffs*	Left wing								
AMODEO, Mike *No playoffs*	Defense								
AMONTE, Tony	Right wing								
1991	NY Rangers	2	0	2	2	2	0	0	0
1992	NY Rangers	13	3	6	9	2	2	0	0
1994	Chicago	6	4	2	6	4	1	0	1
1995	Chicago	16	3	3	6	10	0	0	0
1996	Chicago	7	2	4	6	6	1	0	0
1997	Chicago	6	4	2	6	8	0	0	0
Playoff Totals		**50**	**16**	**19**	**35**	**32**	**4**	**0**	**1**
ANDERSON, Bill	Defense								
1943	Boston	1	0	0	0	0	0	0	0
Playoff Totals		**1**	**0**	**0**	**0**	**0**	**0**	**0**	**0**
ANDERSON, Dale	Defense								
1957	Detroit	2	0	0	0	0	0	0	0
Playoff Totals		**2**	**0**	**0**	**0**	**0**	**0**	**0**	**0**
ANDERSON, Doug	Center								
1953♦	Montreal	2	0	0	0	0	0	0	0
Playoff Totals		**2**	**0**	**0**	**0**	**0**	**0**	**0**	**0**
ANDERSON, Earl	Right wing								
1975	Boston	3	0	1	1	0	0	0	0
1977	Boston	2	0	0	0	0	0	0	0
Playoff Totals		**5**	**0**	**1**	**1**	**0**	**0**	**0**	**0**

Season	Club	GP	G	A	Pts	PIM	PP	SH	GW
ANDERSON, Glenn									Right wing
1981	Edmonton	9	5	7	12	12	3	0	0
1982	Edmonton	5	2	5	7	8	0	0	1
1983	Edmonton	16	10	10	20	32	1	0	2
1984◆	Edmonton	19	6	11	17	33	1	0	1
1985◆	Edmonton	18	10	16	26	38	2	0	1
1986	Edmonton	10	8	3	11	14	1	0	2
1987◆	Edmonton	21	14	13	27	59	4	0	2
1988◆	Edmonton	19	9	16	25	49	4	0	1
1989	Edmonton	7	1	2	3	8	1	0	0
1990◆	Edmonton	22	10	12	22	20	2	0	2
1991	Edmonton	18	6	7	13	41	3	0	0
1993	Toronto	21	7	11	18	31	0	0	2
1994◆	NY Rangers	23	3	3	6	42	0	1	2
1995	St. Louis	6	1	1	2	*49	0	0	0
1996	St. Louis	11	1	4	5	6	0	0	1
Playoff Totals		**225**	**93**	**121**	**214**	**442**	**22**	**1**	**17**
ANDERSON, Jim *No playoffs*									Left wing
ANDERSON, John									Right wing
1978	Toronto	2	0	0	0	0	0	0	0
1979	Toronto	6	0	2	2	0	0	0	0
1980	Toronto	3	1	1	2	0	0	0	0
1981	Toronto	2	0	0	0	0	0	0	0
1983	Toronto	4	2	4	6	0	1	0	0
1986	Hartford	10	5	8	13	0	3	0	0
1987	Hartford	6	1	2	3	0	1	0	0
1989	Hartford	4	0	1	1	2	0	0	0
Playoff Totals		**37**	**9**	**18**	**27**	**2**	**5**	**0**	**0**
ANDERSON, Murray *No playoffs*									Defense
ANDERSON, Perry									Left wing
1982	St. Louis	10	2	0	2	4	1	0	0
1984	St. Louis	9	0	0	0	27	0	0	0
1985	St. Louis	3	0	0	0	7	0	0	0
1988	New Jersey	10	0	0	0	113	0	0	0
1991	New Jersey	4	0	1	1	10	0	0	0
Playoff Totals		**36**	**2**	**1**	**3**	**161**	**1**	**0**	**0**
ANDERSON, Ron *No playoffs*									Right wing
ANDERSON, Ron									Right wing
1969	Los Angeles	4	0	0	0	2	0	0	0
1970	St. Louis	1	0	0	0	2	0	0	0
Playoff Totals		**5**	**0**	**0**	**0**	**4**	**0**	**0**	**0**
ANDERSON, Russ									Defense
1977	Pittsburgh	3	0	1	1	14	0	0	0
1979	Pittsburgh	2	0	0	0	0	0	0	0
1980	Pittsburgh	5	0	2	2	14	0	0	0
Playoff Totals		**10**	**0**	**3**	**3**	**28**	**0**	**0**	**0**
ANDERSON, Shawn									Defense
1989	Buffalo	5	0	1	1	4	0	0	0
1993	Washington	6	0	0	0	0	0	0	0
1994	Washington	8	1	0	1	12	0	0	0
Playoff Totals		**19**	**1**	**1**	**2**	**16**	**0**	**0**	**0**
ANDERSON, Tom									Left wing/defense
1936	NY Americans	5	0	0	0	6	....	....	....
1938	NY Americans	6	1	4	5	2	....	....	....
1939	NY Americans	2	0	0	0	0	....	....	....
1940	NY Americans	3	1	3	4	0	....	....	....
Playoff Totals		**16**	**2**	**7**	**9**	**8**	....	....	....
ANDERSSON, Erik *No playoffs*									Center
ANDERSSON, Kent-Erik									Right wing
1980	Minnesota	13	2	4	6	2	0	0	1
1981	Minnesota	19	2	4	6	2	0	0	0
1982	Minnesota	4	0	2	2	0	0	0	0
1983	NY Rangers	9	0	0	0	0	0	0	0
1984	NY Rangers	5	0	1	1	0	0	0	0
Playoff Totals		**50**	**4**	**11**	**15**	**4**	**0**	**0**	**1**
ANDERSSON, Mikael									Left wing
1988	Buffalo	1	1	0	1	0	0	0	0
1990	Hartford	5	0	3	3	2	0	0	0
1992	Hartford	7	0	2	2	6	0	0	0
1996	Tampa Bay	6	1	1	2	0	0	0	0
1999	Philadelphia	6	0	1	1	2	0	0	0
Playoff Totals		**25**	**2**	**7**	**9**	**10**	**0**	**0**	**0**
ANDERSSON, Niklas *No playoffs*									Left wing
ANDERSSON, Peter									Defense
1984	Washington	3	0	1	1	2	0	0	0
1985	Washington	2	0	0	0	0	0	0	0
1986	Quebec	2	0	1	1	0	0	0	0
Playoff Totals		**7**	**0**	**2**	**2**	**2**	**0**	**0**	**0**
ANDERSSON, Peter *No playoffs*									Defense
ANDRASCIK, Steve									Right wing
1972	NY Rangers	1	0	0	0	0	0	0	0
Playoff Totals		**1**	**0**	**0**	**0**	**0**	**0**	**0**	**0**
ANDREA, Paul *No playoffs*									Right wing
ANDREWS, Lloyd									Left wing
1922◆	Toronto	7	2	0	2	5	....	....	....
Playoff Totals		**7**	**2**	**0**	**2**	**5**	....	....	....

Season	Club	GP	G	A	Pts	PIM	PP	SH	GW
ANDREYCHUK, Dave									Left wing
1983	Buffalo	4	1	0	1	4	0	0	0
1984	Buffalo	2	0	1	1	2	0	0	0
1985	Buffalo	5	4	2	6	4	0	0	2
1988	Buffalo	6	2	4	6	0	1	0	0
1989	Buffalo	5	0	3	3	0	0	0	0
1990	Buffalo	6	2	5	7	2	1	0	0
1991	Buffalo	6	2	2	4	8	1	0	0
1992	Buffalo	7	1	3	4	12	0	0	0
1993	Toronto	21	12	7	19	35	4	0	3
1994	Toronto	18	5	5	10	16	3	1	0
1995	Toronto	7	3	2	5	25	2	0	0
1997	New Jersey	1	0	0	0	0	0	0	0
1998	New Jersey	6	1	0	1	4	1	0	0
1999	New Jersey	4	2	0	2	4	0	0	0
Playoff Totals		**98**	**35**	**34**	**69**	**116**	**13**	**1**	**5**
ANDRIEVSKI, Alexander *No playoffs*									Right wing
ANDRUFF, Ron									Center
1978	Colorado	2	0	0	0	0	0	0	0
Playoff Totals		**2**	**0**	**0**	**0**	**0**	**0**	**0**	**0**
ANDRUSAK, Greg									Defense
1999	Pittsburgh	12	1	0	1	6	0	0	1
Playoff Totals		**12**	**1**	**0**	**1**	**6**	**0**	**0**	**1**
ANGOTTI, Lou									Center/right wing
1966	Chicago	6	0	0	0	2	0	0	0
1967	Chicago	6	2	1	3	2	0	0	0
1968	Philadelphia	7	0	0	0	2	0	0	0
1970	Chicago	8	0	0	0	0	0	0	0
1971	Chicago	16	3	3	6	9	0	0	1
1972	Chicago	6	0	0	0	0	0	0	0
1973	Chicago	16	3	4	7	2	0	0	2
Playoff Totals		**65**	**8**	**8**	**16**	**17**	**0**	**0**	**3**
ANHOLT, Darrel *No playoffs*									Defense
ANSLOW, Bert *No playoffs*									Center
ANTONOVICH, Mike *No playoffs*									Center
ANTOSKI, Shawn									Left wing
1994	Vancouver	16	0	1	1	36	0	0	0
1995	Philadelphia	13	0	1	1	10	0	0	0
1996	Philadelphia	7	1	1	2	28	0	0	1
Playoff Totals		**36**	**1**	**3**	**4**	**74**	**0**	**0**	**1**
ANTROPOV, Nikolai *No playoffs*									Center
APPS Jr., Syl									Center
1972	Pittsburgh	4	1	0	1	2	0	0	0
1975	Pittsburgh	9	2	3	5	9	1	0	1
1976	Pittsburgh	3	0	1	1	0	0	0	0
1977	Pittsburgh	3	1	0	1	12	1	0	0
1978	Los Angeles	2	0	1	1	0	0	0	0
1979	Los Angeles	2	1	0	1	0	1	0	0
Playoff Totals		**23**	**5**	**5**	**10**	**23**	**3**	**0**	**1**
APPS Sr., Syl									Center
1937	Toronto	2	0	1	1	0	....	....	....
1938	Toronto	7	1	4	5	0	....	....	....
1939	Toronto	10	2	6	8	2	....	....	....
1940	Toronto	10	*5	2	7	2	....	....	....
1941	Toronto	7	3	2	5	2	....	....	....
1942◆	Toronto	13	5	*9	*14	2	....	....	....
1947◆	Toronto	11	5	1	6	0	....	....	....
1948◆	Toronto	9	4	4	8	0	....	....	....
Playoff Totals		**69**	**25**	**29**	**54**	**8**	....	....	....
ARBOUR, Al									Defense
1956	Detroit	4	0	1	1	0	0	0	0
1957	Detroit	5	0	0	0	6	0	0	0
1958	Detroit	4	0	1	1	4	0	0	0
1959	Chicago	6	1	2	3	26	0	0	0
1960	Chicago	4	0	0	0	4	0	0	0
1961◆	Chicago	7	0	0	0	2	0	0	0
1962◆	Toronto	8	0	0	0	6	0	0	0
1964◆	Toronto	1	0	0	0	0	0	0	0
1965	Toronto	1	0	0	0	2	0	0	0
1968	St. Louis	14	0	3	3	10	0	0	0
1969	St. Louis	12	0	0	0	10	0	0	0
1970	St. Louis	14	0	1	1	16	0	0	0
1971	St. Louis	6	0	0	0	6	0	0	0
Playoff Totals		**86**	**1**	**8**	**9**	**92**	**0**	**0**	**0**
ARBOUR, Amos *No playoffs*									Left wing
ARBOUR, Jack *No playoffs*									Defense
ARBOUR, John									Defense
1971	St. Louis	5	0	0	0	0	0	0	0
Playoff Totals		**5**	**0**	**0**	**0**	**0**	**0**	**0**	**0**
ARBOUR, Ty									Left wing
1930	Chicago	2	1	0	1	0	....	....	....
1931	Chicago	9	1	0	1	6	....	....	....
Playoff Totals		**11**	**2**	**0**	**2**	**6**	....	....	....
ARCHAMBAULT, Michel *No playoffs*									Left wing
ARCHIBALD, Dave									Center/Left wing
1989	Minnesota	5	0	1	1	0	0	0	0
Playoff Totals		**5**	**0**	**1**	**1**	**0**	**0**	**0**	**0**
ARCHIBALD, Jim *No playoffs*									Right wing
ARESHENKOFF, Ron *No playoffs*									Center

Season	Club	GP	G	A	Pts	PIM	PP	SH	GW
ARMSTRONG, Bill *No playoffs*									Center
ARMSTRONG, Bob									Defense
1952	Boston	5	0	0	0	2	....	....	....
1953	Boston	11	1	1	2	10	....	....	....
1954	Boston	4	0	1	1	0	....	....	....
1955	Boston	5	0	0	0	2	....	....	....
1957	Boston	10	0	3	3	10	....	....	....
1959	Boston	7	0	2	2	4	....	....	....
Playoff Totals		**42**	**1**	**7**	**8**	**28**	....	....	....
ARMSTRONG, Derek *No playoffs*									Center
ARMSTRONG, George									Center/Right Wing
1952	Toronto	4	0	0	0	2	....	....	....
1954	Toronto	5	1	0	1	2	....	....	....
1955	Toronto	4	1	0	1	4	....	....	....
1956	Toronto	5	4	2	6	0	....	....	....
1959	Toronto	12	0	4	4	10	....	....	....
1960	Toronto	10	1	4	5	4	....	....	....
1961	Toronto	5	1	1	2	0	....	....	....
1962◆	Toronto	12	7	5	12	2	....	....	....
1963◆	Toronto	10	3	6	9	4	....	....	....
1964◆	Toronto	14	5	8	13	10	....	....	....
1965	Toronto	6	1	0	1	4	....	....	....
1966	Toronto	4	0	1	1	4	....	....	....
1967◆	Toronto	9	2	1	3	6	....	....	....
1969	Toronto	4	0	0	0	0	0	0	0
1971	Toronto	6	0	2	2	0	0	0	0
Playoff Totals		**110**	**26**	**34**	**60**	**52**	....	....	....
ARMSTRONG, Murray									Center
1938	Toronto	3	0	0	0	0	....	....	....
1940	NY Americans	3	0	0	0	0	....	....	....
1944	Detroit	8	6	*16	*22	6	....	....	....
1945	Detroit	14	4	2	6	2	....	....	....
1946	Detroit	5	0	2	2	0	....	....	....
Playoff Totals		**33**	**10**	**20**	**30**	**8**	....	....	....
ARMSTRONG, Norm *No playoffs*									Defense
ARMSTRONG, Tim *No playoffs*									Center
ARNASON, Chuck									Right wing
1975	Pittsburgh	9	2	4	6	4	1	0	0
Playoff Totals		**9**	**2**	**4**	**6**	**4**	**1**	**0**	**0**
ARNIEL, Scott									Left wing
1982	Winnipeg	3	0	0	0	0	0	0	0
1983	Winnipeg	2	0	0	0	0	0	0	0
1984	Winnipeg	2	0	0	0	5	0	0	0
1985	Winnipeg	8	1	2	3	9	0	0	1
1986	Winnipeg	3	0	0	0	12	0	0	0
1988	Buffalo	6	0	1	1	5	0	0	0
1989	Buffalo	5	1	0	1	4	0	1	0
1990	Buffalo	5	1	0	1	4	0	0	0
Playoff Totals		**34**	**3**	**3**	**6**	**39**	**0**	**1**	**1**
ARNOTT, Jason									Center
1997	Edmonton	12	3	6	9	18	1	0	0
1998	New Jersey	5	0	2	2	0	0	0	0
1999	New Jersey	7	2	2	4	4	1	0	0
Playoff Totals		**24**	**5**	**10**	**15**	**22**	**2**	**0**	**0**
ARTHUR, Fred									Defense
1982	Philadelphia	4	0	0	0	2	0	0	0
Playoff Totals		**4**	**0**	**0**	**0**	**2**	**0**	**0**	**0**
ARUNDEL, John *No playoffs*									Defense
ARVEDSON, Magnus									Center
1998	Ottawa	11	0	1	1	6	0	0	0
1999	Ottawa	3	0	1	1	2	0	0	0
Playoff Totals		**14**	**0**	**2**	**2**	**8**	**0**	**0**	**0**
ASHAM, Arron *No playoffs*									Right wing
ASHBEE, Barry									Defense
1973	Philadelphia	11	0	4	4	20	0	0	0
1974◆	Philadelphia	6	0	0	0	2	0	0	0
Playoff Totals		**17**	**0**	**4**	**4**	**22**	**0**	**0**	**0**
ASHBY, Don									Center
1977	Toronto	9	1	0	1	4	0	0	0
1980	Edmonton	3	0	0	0	0	0	0	0
Playoff Totals		**12**	**1**	**0**	**1**	**4**	**0**	**0**	**0**
ASHTON, Brent									Left wing
1980	Vancouver	4	1	0	1	6	0	0	0
1981	Vancouver	3	0	0	0	0	0	0	0
1984	Minnesota	12	1	2	3	22	0	0	0
1985	Quebec	18	6	4	10	13	1	1	1
1986	Quebec	3	2	1	3	9	0	1	0
1987	Detroit	16	4	9	13	6	2	0	0
1988	Detroit	16	7	5	12	10	2	1	0
1990	Winnipeg	7	3	1	4	2	2	0	1
1993	Calgary	6	0	3	3	2	0	0	0
Playoff Totals		**85**	**24**	**25**	**49**	**70**	**7**	**3**	**2**
ASHWORTH, Frank *No playoffs*									Center
ASMUNDSON, Oscar									Center
1933◆	NY Rangers	8	0	2	2	4	0	0	0
1934	NY Rangers	1	0	0	0	0	0	0	0
Playoff Totals		**9**	**0**	**2**	**2**	**4**	**0**	**0**	**0**

Season	Club	GP	G	A	Pts	PIM	PP	SH	GW
ASTLEY, Mark	Defense								
1995	Buffalo	2	0	0	0	0	0	0	0
Playoff Totals		**2**	**0**	**0**	**0**	**0**	**0**	**0**	**0**
ATANAS, Walt	*No playoffs* Right wing								
ATCHEYNUM, Blair	Right wing								
1998	St. Louis	10	0	0	0	2	0	0	0
1999	St. Louis	13	1	3	4	6	0	0	0
Playoff Totals		**23**	**1**	**3**	**4**	**8**	**0**	**0**	**0**
ATKINSON, Steve	Right wing								
1973	Buffalo	1	0	0	0	0	0	0	0
Playoff Totals		**1**	**0**	**0**	**0**	**0**	**0**	**0**	**0**
ATTWELL, Bob	*No playoffs* Right wing								
ATTWELL, Ron	*No playoffs* Right wing								
AUBIN, Norm	Center								
1983	Toronto	1	0	0	0	0	0	0	0
Playoff Totals		**1**	**0**	**0**	**0**	**0**	**0**	**0**	**0**
AUBIN, Serge	*No playoffs* Center								
AUBRY, Pierre	Left wing								
1982	Quebec	15	1	1	2	30	0	0	1
1983	Quebec	2	0	0	0	0	0	0	0
1984	Detroit	3	0	0	0	2	0	0	0
Playoff Totals		**20**	**1**	**1**	**2**	**32**	**0**	**0**	**1**
AUBUCHON, Ossie	Left wing								
1943	Boston	6	1	0	1	0	....	....	....
Playoff Totals		**6**	**1**	**0**	**1**	**0**	....	....	....
AUCOIN, Adrian	Defense								
1995	Vancouver	4	1	0	1	0	1	0	0
1996	Vancouver	6	0	0	0	2	0	0	0
Playoff Totals		**10**	**1**	**0**	**1**	**2**	**1**	**0**	**0**
AUDET, Philippe	*No playoffs* Left wing								
AUDETTE, Donald	Right wing								
1990	Buffalo	2	0	0	0	0	0	0	0
1993	Buffalo	8	2	2	4	6	0	0	0
1994	Buffalo	7	0	1	1	6	0	0	0
1995	Buffalo	5	1	1	2	4	1	0	0
1997	Buffalo	11	4	5	9	6	0	0	0
1998	Buffalo	15	5	8	13	10	3	0	2
Playoff Totals		**48**	**12**	**17**	**29**	**32**	**4**	**0**	**2**
AUGE, Les	*No playoffs* Defense								
AUGUSTA, Patrik	*No playoffs* Right wing								
AURIE, Larry	Right wing								
1929	Detroit	2	1	0	1	2	....	....	....
1932	Detroit	2	0	0	0	0	....	....	....
1933	Detroit	4	1	0	1	4	....	....	....
1934	Detroit	9	3	*7	*10	2	....	....	....
1936◆	Detroit	7	1	2	3	2	....	....	....
Playoff Totals		**24**	**6**	**9**	**15**	**10**	....	....	....
AWREY, Don	Defense								
1968	Boston	4	0	1	1	4	0	0	0
1969	Boston	10	0	1	1	28	0	0	0
1970◆	Boston	14	0	5	5	32	0	0	0
1971	Boston	7	0	0	0	17	0	0	0
1972◆	Boston	15	0	4	4	45	0	0	0
1973	Boston	4	0	0	0	6	0	0	0
1975	Montreal	11	0	6	6	12	0	0	0
1977	Pittsburgh	3	0	1	1	0	0	0	0
1978	NY Rangers	3	0	0	0	6	0	0	0
Playoff Totals		**71**	**0**	**18**	**18**	**150**	**0**	**0**	**0**
AXELSSON, Per-Johan	Left wing								
1998	Boston	6	1	0	1	0	0	0	0
1999	Boston	12	1	1	2	4	0	0	0
Playoff Totals		**18**	**2**	**1**	**3**	**4**	**0**	**0**	**0**
AYRES, Vern	*No playoffs* Defense								
BABANDO, Pete	Left wing								
1948	Boston	5	1	1	2	2	....	....	....
1949	Boston	4	0	0	0	2	....	....	....
1950	Detroit	8	2	2	4	2	....	....	....
Playoff Totals		**17**	**3**	**3**	**6**	**6**	....	....	....
BABCOCK, Bobby	*No playoffs* Defense								
BABE, Warren	Left wing								
1989	Minnesota	2	0	0	0	0	0	0	0
Playoff Totals		**2**	**0**	**0**	**0**	**0**	**0**	**0**	**0**
BABIN, Mitch	*No playoffs* Center								
BABY, John	*No playoffs* Defense								
BABYCH, Dave	Defense								
1982	Winnipeg	4	1	2	3	29	1	0	0
1983	Winnipeg	3	0	0	0	0	0	0	0
1984	Winnipeg	3	1	1	2	0	1	0	0
1985	Winnipeg	8	2	7	9	6	2	0	0
1986	Hartford	8	1	3	4	14	0	0	0
1987	Hartford	6	1	1	2	14	1	0	0
1988	Hartford	6	3	2	5	2	0	0	0
1989	Hartford	4	1	5	6	2	0	0	0
1990	Hartford	7	1	2	3	0	0	0	0
1992	Vancouver	13	2	6	8	10	1	0	1
1993	Vancouver	12	2	5	7	6	1	0	0
1994	Vancouver	24	3	5	8	12	0	0	1
1995	Vancouver	11	2	2	4	14	1	1	0
1998	Philadelphia	5	1	0	1	4	1	0	0
Playoff Totals		**114**	**21**	**41**	**62**	**113**	**9**	**1**	**2**
BABYCH, Wayne	Right wing								
1980	St. Louis	3	1	2	3	2	0	0	0
1981	St. Louis	11	2	0	2	8	1	0	0
1982	St. Louis	7	3	2	5	8	0	0	1
1984	St. Louis	10	1	4	5	4	0	0	0
1986	Hartford	10	0	1	1	2	0	0	0
Playoff Totals		**41**	**7**	**9**	**16**	**24**	**1**	**0**	**1**
BACA, Jergus	*No playoffs* Defense								
BACKMAN, Mike	Right wing								
1982	NY Rangers	1	0	0	0	2	0	0	0
1983	NY Rangers	9	2	2	4	0	0	0	1
Playoff Totals		**10**	**2**	**2**	**4**	**2**	**0**	**0**	**1**
BACKOR, Pete	*No playoffs* Defense								
BACKSTROM, Ralph	Center								
1959◆	Montreal	11	3	5	8	12	....	....	....
1960◆	Montreal	7	0	3	3	2	....	....	....
1961	Montreal	5	0	0	0	4	....	....	....
1962	Montreal	5	0	1	1	6	....	....	....
1963	Montreal	5	0	0	0	2	....	....	....
1964	Montreal	7	2	1	3	8	....	....	....
1965◆	Montreal	13	2	3	5	10	....	....	....
1966◆	Montreal	10	3	4	7	4	....	....	....
1967	Montreal	10	5	2	7	6	....	....	....
1968◆	Montreal	13	4	3	7	4	0	0	2
1969◆	Montreal	14	3	4	7	10	0	1	1
1973	Chicago	16	5	6	11	0	0	1	0
Playoff Totals		**116**	**27**	**32**	**59**	**68**	....	....	....
BAILEY, Ace	Right wing								
1929	Toronto	4	1	*2	*3	4	....	....	....
1931	Toronto	2	1	1	2	0	....	....	....
1932◆	Toronto	7	1	0	1	4	....	....	....
1933	Toronto	8	0	1	1	4	....	....	....
Playoff Totals		**21**	**3**	**4**	**7**	**12**	....	....	....
BAILEY, Bob	Right wing								
1954	Toronto	5	0	2	2	4	0	0	0
1955	Toronto	1	0	0	0	0	0	0	0
1957	Detroit	5	0	2	2	2	0	0	0
1958	Detroit	4	0	0	0	16	0	0	0
Playoff Totals		**15**	**0**	**4**	**4**	**22**	**0**	**0**	**0**
BAILEY, Garnet	Left wing								
1969	Boston	1	0	0	0	2	0	0	0
1971	Boston	1	0	0	0	10	0	0	0
1972◆	Boston	13	2	4	6	16	0	0	1
Playoff Totals		**15**	**2**	**4**	**6**	**28**	**0**	**0**	**1**
BAILEY, Reid	Defense								
1981	Philadelphia	12	0	2	2	23	0	0	0
1982	Philadelphia	2	0	0	0	0	0	0	0
1983	Toronto	2	0	0	0	2	0	0	0
Playoff Totals		**16**	**0**	**2**	**2**	**25**	**0**	**0**	**0**
BAILLARGEON, Joel	*No playoffs* Left wing								
BAIRD, Ken	*No playoffs* Defense								
BAKER, Bill	Defense								
1982	St. Louis	4	0	0	0	0	0	0	0
1983	NY Rangers	2	0	0	0	0	0	0	0
Playoff Totals		**6**	**0**	**0**	**0**	**0**	**0**	**0**	**0**
BAKER, Jamie	Center								
1994	San Jose	14	3	2	5	30	0	0	1
1995	San Jose	11	2	2	4	12	0	0	1
Playoff Totals		**25**	**5**	**4**	**9**	**42**	**0**	**0**	**2**
BAKOVIC, Peter	*No playoffs* Right wing								
BALDERIS, Helmut	*No playoffs* Right wing								
BALDWIN, Doug	*No playoffs* Defense								
BALFOUR, Earl	Left wing								
1952	Toronto	1	0	0	0	0	0	0	0
1956	Toronto	3	0	1	1	2	0	0	0
1959	Chicago	6	0	2	2	0	0	0	0
1960	Chicago	4	0	0	0	0	0	0	0
1961◆	Chicago	12	0	0	0	2	0	0	0
Playoff Totals		**26**	**0**	**3**	**3**	**4**	**0**	**0**	**0**
BALFOUR, Murray	Right wing								
1960	Chicago	4	1	0	1	0	....	....	....
1961◆	Chicago	11	5	5	10	14	....	....	....
1962	Chicago	12	1	1	2	15	....	....	....
1963	Chicago	6	0	2	2	12	....	....	....
1964	Chicago	7	2	2	4	4	....	....	....
Playoff Totals		**40**	**9**	**10**	**19**	**45**	....	....	....
BALL, Terry	*No playoffs* Defense								
BALMOCHNYKH, Maxim	*No playoffs* Left wing								
BALON, Dave	Left wing								
1962	NY Rangers	6	2	3	5	2	0	0	2
1964	Montreal	7	1	1	2	25	0	0	0
1965◆	Montreal	10	0	0	0	10	0	0	0
1966◆	Montreal	9	2	3	5	16	0	0	0
1967	Montreal	9	0	2	2	6	0	0	0
1968	Minnesota	14	4	*9	13	14	1	0	1
1969	NY Rangers	4	1	0	1	0	0	0	0
1970	NY Rangers	6	1	1	2	32	0	1	0
1971	NY Rangers	13	3	2	5	4	2	0	1
Playoff Totals		**78**	**14**	**21**	**35**	**109**	**3**	**1**	**4**
BALTIMORE, Bryon	*No playoffs* Defense								
BALUIK, Stan	*No playoffs* Center								
BANCROFT, Steve	*No playoffs* Defense								
BANDURA, Jeff	*No playoffs* Defense								
BANHAM, Frank	*No playoffs* Right wing								
BANKS, Darren	*No playoffs* Left wing								
BANNISTER, Drew	Defense								
1997	Edmonton	12	0	0	0	30	0	0	0
Playoff Totals		**12**	**0**	**0**	**0**	**30**	**0**	**0**	**0**
BARAHONA, Ralph	*No playoffs* Center								
BARBE, Andy	*No playoffs* Right wing								
BARBER, Bill	Left wing								
1973	Philadelphia	11	3	2	5	22	0	0	0
1974◆	Philadelphia	17	3	6	9	18	0	0	1
1975◆	Philadelphia	17	6	9	15	8	0	0	0
1976	Philadelphia	16	6	7	13	18	3	0	0
1977	Philadelphia	10	1	4	5	2	0	0	0
1978	Philadelphia	12	6	3	9	2	1	0	0
1979	Philadelphia	8	3	4	7	10	0	0	0
1980	Philadelphia	19	12	9	21	23	1	3	4
1981	Philadelphia	12	11	5	16	0	3	1	1
1982	Philadelphia	4	1	5	6	4	0	1	0
1983	Philadelphia	3	1	1	2	2	1	0	0
Playoff Totals		**129**	**53**	**55**	**108**	**109**	**9**	**5**	**6**
BARBER, Don	Right/Left wing								
1989	Minnesota	4	1	1	2	2	0	0	1
1990	Minnesota	7	3	3	6	8	2	0	1
Playoff Totals		**11**	**4**	**4**	**8**	**10**	**2**	**0**	**2**
BARILKO, Bill	Defense								
1947◆	Toronto	11	0	3	3	18	....	....	....
1948◆	Toronto	9	1	0	1	17	....	....	....
1949◆	Toronto	9	0	1	1	20	....	....	....
1950	Toronto	7	1	1	2	18	....	....	....
1951◆	Toronto	11	3	2	5	31	....	....	....
Playoff Totals		**47**	**5**	**7**	**12**	**104**	....	....	....
BARKLEY, Doug	Defense								
1963	Detroit	11	0	3	3	16	0	0	0
1964	Detroit	14	0	5	5	33	0	0	0
1965	Detroit	5	0	1	1	14	0	0	0
Playoff Totals		**30**	**0**	**9**	**9**	**63**	**0**	**0**	**0**
BARLOW, Bob	Left wing								
1970	Minnesota	6	2	2	4	6	1	0	0
Playoff Totals		**6**	**2**	**2**	**4**	**6**	**1**	**0**	**0**
BARNABY, Matthew	Right wing								
1993	Buffalo	1	0	1	1	4	0	0	0
1994	Buffalo	3	0	0	0	17	0	0	0
1997	Buffalo	8	0	4	4	36	0	0	0
1998	Buffalo	15	7	6	13	22	3	0	1
1999	Pittsburgh	13	0	0	0	35	0	0	0
Playoff Totals		**40**	**7**	**11**	**18**	**114**	**3**	**0**	**1**
BARNES, Blair	*No playoffs* Right wing								
BARNES, Norm	Defense								
1979	Philadelphia	2	0	0	0	0	0	0	0
1980	Philadelphia	10	0	0	0	8	0	0	0
Playoff Totals		**12**	**0**	**0**	**0**	**8**	**0**	**0**	**0**
BARNES, Stu	Center								
1993	Winnipeg	6	1	3	4	2	0	0	0
1996	Florida	22	6	10	16	4	2	0	2
1997	Pittsburgh	5	0	1	1	0	0	0	0
1998	Pittsburgh	6	3	3	6	2	0	0	1
1999	Buffalo	21	7	3	10	6	4	0	1
Playoff Totals		**60**	**17**	**20**	**37**	**14**	**6**	**0**	**4**

Season	Club	GP	G	A	Pts	PIM	PP	SH	GW
BARON, Murray	Defense								
1992	St. Louis	2	0	0	0	2	0	0	0
1993	St. Louis	11	0	0	0	12	0	0	0
1994	St. Louis	4	0	0	0	10	0	0	0
1995	St. Louis	7	1	1	2	2	0	0	0
1996	St. Louis	13	1	0	1	20	0	1	0
1997	Phoenix	1	0	0	0	0	0	0	0
1998	Phoenix	6	0	2	2	6	0	0	0
Playoff Totals		**44**	**2**	**3**	**5**	**52**	**0**	**1**	**0**
BARON, Normand	Left wing								
1984	Montreal	3	0	0	0	22	0	0	0
Playoff Totals		**3**	**0**	**0**	**0**	**22**	**0**	**0**	**0**
BARR, Dave	Right wing								
1982	Boston	5	1	0	1	0	0	0	0
1983	Boston	10	0	0	0	2	0	0	0
1985	St. Louis	2	0	0	0	2	0	0	0
1986	St. Louis	11	1	1	2	14	1	0	0
1987	Detroit	13	1	0	1	14	0	0	0
1988	Detroit	16	5	7	12	22	2	0	0
1989	Detroit	6	3	1	4	6	1	0	1
1993	New Jersey	5	1	0	1	6	0	0	0
1994	Dallas	3	0	1	1	4	0	0	0
Playoff Totals		**71**	**12**	**10**	**22**	**70**	**4**	**0**	**1**
BARRAULT, Doug *No playoffs*	Right wing								
BARRETT, Fred	Defense								
1973	Minnesota	6	0	0	0	4	0	0	0
1977	Minnesota	2	0	0	0	2	0	0	0
1980	Minnesota	14	0	0	0	22	0	0	0
1981	Minnesota	14	0	1	1	16	0	0	0
1982	Minnesota	4	0	1	1	16	0	0	0
1983	Minnesota	4	0	0	0	0	0	0	0
Playoff Totals		**44**	**0**	**2**	**2**	**60**	**0**	**0**	**0**
BARRETT, John	Defense								
1984	Detroit	4	0	0	0	4	0	0	0
1985	Detroit	3	0	1	1	11	0	0	0
1986	Washington	9	2	1	3	35	0	0	1
Playoff Totals		**16**	**2**	**2**	**4**	**50**	**0**	**0**	**1**
BARRIE, Doug *No playoffs*	Defense								
BARRIE, Len	Center								
1995	Pittsburgh	4	1	0	1	8	1	0	0
Playoff Totals		**4**	**1**	**0**	**1**	**8**	**1**	**0**	**0**
BARRY, Ed *No playoffs*	Left wing								
BARRY, Marty	Center								
1930	Boston	6	3	3	*6	14	....	....	....
1931	Boston	5	1	1	2	4	....	....	....
1933	Boston	5	2	2	4	6	....	....	....
1935	Boston	4	0	0	0	2	....	....	....
1936◆	Detroit	7	2	4	6	6	....	....	....
1937◆	Detroit	10	*4	*7	*11	2	....	....	....
1939	Detroit	6	3	1	4	0	....	....	....
Playoff Totals		**43**	**15**	**18**	**33**	**34**	....	....	....
BARRY, Ray *No playoffs*	Center								
BARTECKO, Lubos	Left wing								
1999	St. Louis	5	0	0	0	2	0	0	0
Playoff Totals		**5**	**0**	**0**	**0**	**2**	**0**	**0**	**0**
BARTEL, Robin	Defense								
1986	Calgary	6	0	0	0	16	0	0	0
Playoff Totals		**6**	**0**	**0**	**0**	**16**	**0**	**0**	**0**
BARTLETT, Jim	Left wing								
1955	Montreal	2	0	0	0	0	0	0	0
Playoff Totals		**2**	**0**	**0**	**0**	**0**	**0**	**0**	**0**
BARTON, Cliff *No playoffs*	Right wing								
BASHKIROV, Andrei *No playoffs*	Left wing								
BASSEN, Bob	Center								
1986	NY Islanders	3	0	1	1	0	0	0	0
1987	NY Islanders	14	1	2	3	21	0	0	0
1988	NY Islanders	6	0	1	1	23	0	0	0
1989	Chicago	10	1	1	2	34	0	0	0
1990	Chicago	1	0	0	0	2	0	0	0
1991	St. Louis	13	1	3	4	24	0	0	0
1992	St. Louis	6	0	2	2	4	0	0	0
1993	St. Louis	11	0	0	0	10	0	0	0
1995	Quebec	5	2	4	6	0	0	0	0
1997	Dallas	7	3	1	4	4	0	0	0
1998	Dallas	17	1	0	1	12	0	0	0
Playoff Totals		**93**	**9**	**15**	**24**	**134**	**0**	**0**	**0**
BAST, Ryan *No playoffs*	Defense								
BATES, Shawn	Center								
1999	Boston	12	0	0	0	4	0	0	0
Playoff Totals		**12**	**0**	**0**	**0**	**4**	**0**	**0**	**0**
BATHE, Frank	Defense								
1979	Philadelphia	6	1	0	1	12	0	0	0
1980	Philadelphia	1	0	0	0	0	0	0	0
1981	Philadelphia	12	0	3	3	16	0	0	0
1982	Philadelphia	4	0	0	0	2	0	0	0
1983	Philadelphia	3	0	0	0	12	0	0	0
1984	Philadelphia	1	0	0	0	0	0	0	0
Playoff Totals		**27**	**1**	**3**	**4**	**42**	**0**	**0**	**0**

Season	Club	GP	G	A	Pts	PIM	PP	SH	GW
BATHGATE, Andy	Center								
1956	NY Rangers	5	1	2	3	2	....	....	....
1957	NY Rangers	5	2	0	2	27	....	....	....
1958	NY Rangers	6	5	3	8	6	....	....	....
1962	NY Rangers	6	1	2	3	4	....	....	....
1964◆	Toronto	14	5	4	9	25	....	....	....
1965	Toronto	6	1	0	1	6	....	....	....
1966	Detroit	12	*6	3	9	6	....	....	....
Playoff Totals		**54**	**21**	**14**	**35**	**76**	....	....	....
BATHGATE, Frank *No playoffs*	Center								
BATTAGLIA, Bates	Left wing								
1999	Carolina	6	0	3	3	8	0	0	0
Playoff Totals		**6**	**0**	**3**	**3**	**8**	**0**	**0**	**0**
BATTERS, Jeff *No playoffs*	Defense								
BATYRSHIN, Ruslan *No playoffs*	Defense								
BAUER, Bobby	Right wing								
1937	Boston	1	0	0	0	0	....	....	....
1938	Boston	3	0	0	0	2	....	....	....
1939◆	Boston	12	3	2	5	0	....	....	....
1940	Boston	6	1	0	1	2	....	....	....
1941◆	Boston	11	2	2	4	0	....	....	....
1946	Boston	10	4	3	7	2	....	....	....
1947	Boston	5	1	1	2	0	....	....	....
Playoff Totals		**48**	**11**	**8**	**19**	**6**	....	....	....
BAUMGARTNER, Ken	Left wing								
1988	Los Angeles	5	0	1	1	28	0	0	0
1989	Los Angeles	5	0	0	0	8	0	0	0
1990	NY Islanders	4	0	0	0	27	0	0	0
1993	Toronto	7	1	0	1	0	0	0	0
1994	Toronto	10	0	0	0	18	0	0	0
1997	Anaheim	11	0	1	1	11	0	0	0
1998	Boston	6	0	0	0	14	0	0	0
1999	Boston	3	0	0	0	0	0	0	0
Playoff Totals		**51**	**1**	**2**	**3**	**106**	**0**	**0**	**0**
BAUMGARTNER, Mike *No playoffs*	Defense								
BAUMGARTNER, Nolan	Defense								
1996	Washington	1	0	0	0	10	0	0	0
Playoff Totals		**1**	**0**	**0**	**0**	**10**	**0**	**0**	**0**
BAUN, Bob	Defense								
1959	Toronto	12	0	0	0	24	0	0	0
1960	Toronto	10	1	0	1	17	0	0	0
1961	Toronto	3	0	0	0	8	0	0	0
1962◆	Toronto	12	0	3	3	19	0	0	0
1963◆	Toronto	10	0	3	3	6	0	0	0
1964◆	Toronto	14	2	3	5	*42	0	0	1
1965	Toronto	6	0	1	1	14	0	0	0
1966	Toronto	4	0	1	1	8	0	0	0
1967◆	Toronto	10	0	0	0	4	0	0	0
1970	Detroit	4	0	0	0	6	0	0	0
1971	Toronto	6	0	1	1	19	0	0	0
1972	Toronto	5	0	0	0	4	0	0	0
Playoff Totals		**96**	**3**	**12**	**15**	**171**	**0**	**0**	**1**
BAUTIN, Sergei	Defense								
1993	Winnipeg	6	0	0	0	2	0	0	0
Playoff Totals		**6**	**0**	**0**	**0**	**2**	**0**	**0**	**0**
BAWA, Robin	Right wing								
1992	Vancouver	1	0	0	0	0	0	0	0
Playoff Totals		**1**	**0**	**0**	**0**	**0**	**0**	**0**	**0**
BAXTER, Paul	Defense								
1981	Pittsburgh	5	0	1	1	28	0	0	0
1982	Pittsburgh	5	0	0	0	14	0	0	0
1984	Calgary	11	0	2	2	37	0	0	0
1985	Calgary	4	0	1	1	18	0	0	0
1986	Calgary	13	0	1	1	55	0	0	0
1987	Calgary	2	0	0	0	10	0	0	0
Playoff Totals		**40**	**0**	**5**	**5**	**162**	**0**	**0**	**0**
BEADLE, Sandy *No playoffs*	Left wing								
BEATON, Frank *No playoffs*	Left wing								
BEATTIE, Red	Left wing								
1931	Boston	4	0	0	0	0	....	....	....
1933	Boston	5	0	0	0	2	....	....	....
1935	Boston	4	1	0	1	2	....	....	....
1936	Boston	2	0	0	0	2	....	....	....
1937	Boston	3	1	0	1	0	....	....	....
1938	NY Americans	6	2	2	4	2	....	....	....
Playoff Totals		**24**	**4**	**2**	**6**	**8**	....	....	....
BEAUDIN, Norm *No playoffs*	Right wing								
BEAUDOIN, Serge *No playoffs*	Defense								
BEAUDOIN, Yves *No playoffs*	Defense								
BEAUFAIT, Mark *No playoffs*	Center								
BECK, Barry	Defense								
1978	Colorado	2	0	1	1	0	0	0	0
1980	NY Rangers	9	1	4	5	6	1	0	0
1981	NY Rangers	14	5	8	13	32	1	1	0
1982	NY Rangers	10	1	5	6	14	1	0	0
1983	NY Rangers	9	2	4	6	8	0	0	0
1984	NY Rangers	4	1	0	1	6	0	0	0
1985	NY Rangers	3	0	1	1	11	0	0	0
Playoff Totals		**51**	**10**	**23**	**33**	**77**	**3**	**1**	**0**

Season	Club	GP	G	A	Pts	PIM	PP	SH	GW
BECKETT, Bob *No playoffs*	Center								
BEDARD, James *No playoffs*	Defense								
BEDDOES, Clayton *No playoffs*	Center								
BEDNARSKI, John	Defense								
1975	NY Rangers	1	0	0	0	17	0	0	0
Playoff Totals		**1**	**0**	**0**	**0**	**17**	**0**	**0**	**0**
BEERS, Bob	Defense								
1990	Boston	14	1	1	2	18	0	0	0
1991	Boston	6	0	0	0	4	0	0	0
1992	Boston	1	0	0	0	0	0	0	0
Playoff Totals		**21**	**1**	**1**	**2**	**22**	**0**	**0**	**0**
BEERS, Eddy	Left wing								
1983	Calgary	8	1	1	2	27	0	0	1
1984	Calgary	11	2	5	7	12	0	0	0
1985	Calgary	3	1	0	1	0	1	0	0
1986	St. Louis	19	3	4	7	8	2	0	1
Playoff Totals		**41**	**7**	**10**	**17**	**47**	**3**	**0**	**2**
BEGIN, Steve *No playoffs*	Center								
BEHLING, Dick *No playoffs*	Defense								
BEISLER, Frank *No playoffs*	Defense								
BEKAR, Derek *No playoffs*	Left wing								
BELAK, Wade *No playoffs*	Defense								
BELANGER, Alain *No playoffs*	Right wing								
BELANGER, Jesse	Center								
1993◆	Montreal	9	0	1	1	0	0	0	0
1996	Vancouver	3	0	2	2	2	0	0	0
Playoff Totals		**12**	**0**	**3**	**3**	**2**	**0**	**0**	**0**
BELANGER, Ken	Left wing								
1999	Boston	12	1	0	1	16	0	0	0
Playoff Totals		**12**	**1**	**0**	**1**	**16**	**0**	**0**	**0**
BELANGER, Roger *No playoffs*	Center								
BELISLE, Danny *No playoffs*	Right wing								
BELIVEAU, Jean	Center								
1954	Montreal	10	2	*8	10	4	....	....	....
1955	Montreal	12	6	7	13	18	....	....	....
1956◆	Montreal	10	*12	7	*19	22	....	....	....
1957◆	Montreal	10	6	6	12	15	....	....	....
1958◆	Montreal	10	4	8	12	10	....	....	....
1959◆	Montreal	3	1	4	5	4	....	....	....
1960◆	Montreal	8	5	2	7	6	....	....	....
1961	Montreal	6	0	5	5	0	....	....	....
1962	Montreal	6	2	1	3	4	....	....	....
1963	Montreal	5	2	1	3	2	....	....	....
1964	Montreal	5	2	0	2	18	....	....	....
1965◆	Montreal	13	8	8	16	34	....	....	....
1966◆	Montreal	10	5	5	10	6	....	....	....
1967	Montreal	10	6	5	11	*26	....	....	....
1968◆	Montreal	10	7	4	11	6	3	0	1
1969◆	Montreal	14	5	*10	15	8	1	1	0
1971◆	Montreal	20	6	*16	22	28	2	0	0
Playoff Totals		**162**	**79**	**97**	**176**	**211**	....	....	....
BELL, Billy	Center/right wing								
1922	Ottawa	1	0	0	0	0	0	0	0
1923	Mtl. Canadiens	2	0	0	0	0	0	0	0
1924◆	Mtl. Canadiens	5	0	0	0	0	0	0	0
Playoff Totals		**8**	**0**	**0**	**0**	**0**	**0**	**0**	**0**
BELL, Bruce	Defense								
1985	Quebec	16	2	2	4	21	1	0	0
1986	St. Louis	14	0	2	2	13	0	0	0
1987	St. Louis	4	1	1	2	7	0	0	0
Playoff Totals		**34**	**3**	**5**	**8**	**41**	**1**	**0**	**0**
BELL, Harry *No playoffs*	Right wing/defense								
BELL, Joe *No playoffs*	Left wing								
BELLAND, Neil	Defense								
1982	Vancouver	17	1	7	8	16	1	0	0
1984	Vancouver	4	1	2	3	7	0	0	1
Playoff Totals		**21**	**2**	**9**	**11**	**23**	**1**	**0**	**1**
BELLEFEUILLE, Pete *No playoffs*	Right wing								
BELLEMER, Andy *No playoffs*	Defense								
BELLOWS, Brian	Left wing								
1983	Minnesota	9	5	4	9	18	2	0	0
1984	Minnesota	16	2	12	14	6	0	1	0
1985	Minnesota	9	2	4	6	9	0	1	0
1986	Minnesota	5	5	0	5	16	3	0	0
1989	Minnesota	5	2	3	5	8	2	0	0
1990	Minnesota	7	4	3	7	10	3	0	1
1991	Minnesota	23	10	19	29	30	6	0	1
1992	Minnesota	7	4	4	8	14	2	0	1
1993◆	Montreal	18	6	9	15	18	2	0	0
1994	Montreal	6	1	2	3	2	0	0	0
1996	Tampa Bay	6	2	0	2	4	0	0	1
1997	Anaheim	11	2	4	6	2	1	0	0
1998	Washington	21	6	7	13	6	2	0	1
Playoff Totals		**143**	**51**	**71**	**122**	**143**	**23**	**2**	**5**
BEND, Lin *No playoffs*	Center								
BENDA, Jan *No playoffs*	Center								
BENNETT, Adam *No playoffs*	Defense								

Season	Club	GP	G	A	Pts	PIM	PP	SH	GW
BENNETT, Bill	*No playoffs*								Left wing
BENNETT, Curt									Left wing
1971	St. Louis	2	0	0	0	0	0	0	0
1972	St. Louis	10	0	0	0	12	0	0	0
1974	Atlanta	4	0	1	1	34	0	0	0
1976	Atlanta	2	0	0	0	4	0	0	0
1977	Atlanta	3	1	0	1	7	0	0	0
Playoff Totals		**21**	**1**	**1**	**2**	**57**	**0**	**0**	**0**
BENNETT, Frank	*No playoffs*								Left wing/defense
BENNETT, Harvey									Center
1977	Philadelphia	4	0	0	0	2	0	0	0
Playoff Totals		**4**	**0**	**0**	**0**	**2**	**0**	**0**	**0**
BENNETT, Max	*No playoffs*								Right wing
BENNETT, Rick	*No playoffs*								Left wing
BENNING, Brian									Defense
1986	St. Louis	6	1	2	3	13	1	0	0
1987	St. Louis	6	0	4	4	9	0	0	0
1988	St. Louis	10	1	6	7	25	1	0	0
1989	St. Louis	7	1	1	2	11	1	0	0
1990	Los Angeles	7	0	2	2	10	0	0	0
1991	Los Angeles	12	0	5	5	6	0	0	0
Playoff Totals		**48**	**3**	**20**	**23**	**74**	**3**	**0**	**0**
BENNING, Jim									Defense
1983	Toronto	4	1	1	2	2	0	0	0
1989	Vancouver	3	0	0	0	0	0	0	0
Playoff Totals		**7**	**1**	**1**	**2**	**2**	**0**	**0**	**0**
BENOIT, Joe									Right wing
1941	Montreal	3	4	0	4	2	....	....	....
1942	Montreal	3	1	0	1	5	....	....	....
1943	Montreal	5	1	3	4	4	....	....	....
Playoff Totals		**11**	**6**	**3**	**9**	**11**	....	....	....
BENSON, Bill	*No playoffs*								Center
BENSON, Bobby	*No playoffs*								Defense
BENTLEY, Doug									Left wing
1940	Chicago	2	0	0	0	0	....	....	....
1941	Chicago	5	1	1	2	4	....	....	....
1942	Chicago	3	0	1	1	4	....	....	....
1944	Chicago	9	8	4	12	4	....	....	....
1946	Chicago	4	0	2	2	0	....	....	....
Playoff Totals		**23**	**9**	**8**	**17**	**12**	....	....	....
BENTLEY, Max									Center
1941	Chicago	4	1	3	4	2	....	....	....
1942	Chicago	3	2	0	2	0	....	....	....
1946	Chicago	4	1	0	1	4	....	....	....
1948◆	Toronto	9	4	*7	11	0	....	....	....
1949◆	Toronto	9	4	3	7	2	....	....	....
1950	Toronto	7	3	3	6	0	....	....	....
1951◆	Toronto	11	2	*11	*13	4	....	....	....
1952	Toronto	4	1	0	1	2	....	....	....
Playoff Totals		**51**	**18**	**27**	**45**	**14**	....	....	....
BENTLEY, Reggie	*No playoffs*								Left wing
BENYSEK, Ladislav	*No playoffs*								Defense
BERALDO, Paul	*No playoffs*								Right wing
BERANEK, Josef									Left wing/Center
1992	Edmonton	12	2	1	3	0	1	0	1
1995	Vancouver	11	1	1	2	12	0	0	0
1996	Vancouver	3	2	1	3	0	0	0	0
1997	Pittsburgh	5	0	0	0	2	0	0	0
1999	Edmonton	2	0	0	0	4	0	0	0
Playoff Totals		**33**	**5**	**3**	**8**	**18**	**1**	**0**	**1**
BERARD, Bryan									Defense
1999	Toronto	17	1	8	9	8	1	0	0
Playoff Totals		**17**	**1**	**8**	**9**	**8**	**1**	**0**	**0**
BEREHOWSKY, Drake									Defense
1995	Pittsburgh	1	0	0	0	0	0	0	0
1998	Edmonton	12	1	2	3	14	0	0	1
Playoff Totals		**13**	**1**	**2**	**3**	**14**	**0**	**0**	**1**
BERENSON, Red									Center
1962	Montreal	5	2	0	2	0	0	0	0
1963	Montreal	5	0	0	0	0	0	0	0
1964	Montreal	7	0	0	0	4	0	0	0
1965◆	Montreal	9	0	1	1	2	0	0	0
1967	NY Rangers	4	0	1	1	2	0	0	0
1968	St. Louis	18	5	2	7	9	1	1	0
1969	St. Louis	12	7	3	10	20	2	1	0
1970	St. Louis	16	7	5	12	8	3	1	1
1975	St. Louis	2	1	0	1	0	1	0	0
1976	St. Louis	3	1	2	3	0	0	0	0
1977	St. Louis	4	0	0	0	4	0	0	0
Playoff Totals		**85**	**23**	**14**	**37**	**49**	**7**	**3**	**1**
BEREZAN, Perry									Center
1985	Calgary	2	1	0	1	4	1	0	0
1986	Calgary	8	1	1	2	6	0	0	1
1987	Calgary	2	0	2	2	7	0	0	0
1988	Calgary	8	0	2	2	13	0	0	0
1989	Minnesota	5	1	2	3	4	0	0	0
1990	Minnesota	5	1	0	1	0	0	0	0
1991	Minnesota	1	0	0	0	0	0	0	0
Playoff Totals		**31**	**4**	**7**	**11**	**34**	**1**	**0**	**1**

Season	Club	GP	G	A	Pts	PIM	PP	SH	GW
BEREZIN, Sergei									Left wing
1999	Toronto	17	6	6	12	4	2	0	2
Playoff Totals		**17**	**6**	**6**	**12**	**4**	**2**	**0**	**2**
BERG, Aki									Defense
1998	Los Angeles	4	0	3	3	0	0	0	0
Playoff Totals		**4**	**0**	**3**	**3**	**0**	**0**	**0**	**0**
BERG, Bill									Left wing
1993	Toronto	21	1	1	2	18	0	0	0
1994	Toronto	18	1	2	3	10	0	0	0
1995	Toronto	7	0	1	1	4	0	0	0
1996	NY Rangers	10	1	0	1	0	0	0	0
1997	NY Rangers	3	0	0	0	2	0	0	0
1999	Ottawa	2	0	0	0	0	0	0	0
Playoff Totals		**61**	**3**	**4**	**7**	**34**	**0**	**0**	**0**
BERGDINON, Fred	*No playoffs*								Right wing
BERGEN, Todd									Center
1985	Philadelphia	17	4	9	13	8	2	0	1
Playoff Totals		**17**	**4**	**9**	**13**	**8**	**2**	**0**	**1**
BERGER, Mike	*No playoffs*								Defense
BERGERON, Michel	*No playoffs*								Right wing
BERGERON, Yves	*No playoffs*								Right wing
BERGEVIN, Marc									Defense
1985	Chicago	6	0	3	3	2	0	0	0
1986	Chicago	3	0	0	0	0	0	0	0
1987	Chicago	3	1	0	1	2	0	0	0
1992	Hartford	5	0	0	0	2	0	0	0
1996	Detroit	17	1	0	1	14	1	0	0
1997	St. Louis	6	1	0	1	8	0	0	0
1998	St. Louis	10	0	1	1	8	0	0	0
Playoff Totals		**50**	**3**	**4**	**7**	**36**	**1**	**0**	**0**
BERGKVIST, Stefan									Defense
1996	Pittsburgh	4	0	0	0	2	0	0	0
Playoff Totals		**4**	**0**	**0**	**0**	**2**	**0**	**0**	**0**
BERGLAND, Tim									Right wing
1990	Washington	15	1	1	2	10	0	0	0
1991	Washington	11	1	1	2	12	0	0	0
Playoff Totals		**26**	**2**	**2**	**4**	**22**	**0**	**0**	**0**
BERGLOFF, Bob	*No playoffs*								Defense
BERGLUND, Bo									Right wing
1984	Quebec	7	2	0	2	4	0	0	1
1985	Minnesota	2	0	0	0	2	0	0	0
Playoff Totals		**9**	**2**	**0**	**2**	**6**	**0**	**0**	**1**
BERGMAN, Gary									Defense
1965	Detroit	5	0	1	1	4	0	0	0
1966	Detroit	12	0	3	3	14	0	0	0
1970	Detroit	4	0	1	1	2	0	0	0
Playoff Totals		**21**	**0**	**5**	**5**	**20**	**0**	**0**	**0**
BERGMAN, Thommie									Defense
1978	Detroit	7	0	2	2	2	0	0	0
Playoff Totals		**7**	**0**	**2**	**2**	**2**	**0**	**0**	**0**
BERGQVIST, Jonas	*No playoffs*								Right wing
BERLINQUETTE, Louis									Left wing
1918	Mtl. Canadiens	2	0	0	0	0	....	....	....
1919	Mtl. Canadiens	10	1	4	5	9	....	....	....
1923	Mtl. Canadiens	2	0	2	2	0	....	....	....
1926	Pittsburgh	2	0	0	0	0	....	....	....
Playoff Totals		**16**	**1**	**6**	**7**	**9**	....	....	....
BERNIER, Serge									Right wing
1971	Philadelphia	4	1	1	2	0	1	0	0
1981	Quebec	1	0	0	0	0	0	0	0
Playoff Totals		**5**	**1**	**1**	**2**	**0**	**1**	**0**	**0**
BERRY, Bob									Left wing
1974	Los Angeles	5	0	0	0	0	0	0	0
1975	Los Angeles	3	1	2	3	2	0	0	0
1976	Los Angeles	9	1	1	2	0	0	0	1
1977	Los Angeles	9	0	3	3	4	0	0	0
Playoff Totals		**26**	**2**	**6**	**8**	**6**	**0**	**0**	**1**
BERRY, Brad									Defense
1986	Winnipeg	3	0	0	0	0	0	0	0
1987	Winnipeg	7	0	1	1	14	0	0	0
1990	Winnipeg	1	0	0	0	0	0	0	0
1992	Minnesota	2	0	0	0	2	0	0	0
Playoff Totals		**13**	**0**	**1**	**1**	**16**	**0**	**0**	**0**
BERRY, Doug	*No playoffs*								Center
BERRY, Fred	*No playoffs*								Center
BERRY, Ken	*No playoffs*								Left wing
BERTRAND, Eric	*No playoffs*								Left wing
BERTUZZI, Todd	*No playoffs*								Center

Season	Club	GP	G	A	Pts	PIM	PP	SH	GW
BERUBE, Craig									Left wing
1987	Philadelphia	5	0	0	0	17	0	0	0
1989	Philadelphia	16	0	0	0	56	0	0	0
1993	Calgary	6	0	1	1	21	0	0	0
1994	Washington	8	0	0	0	21	0	0	0
1995	Washington	7	0	0	0	29	0	0	0
1996	Washington	2	0	0	0	19	0	0	0
1998	Washington	21	1	0	1	21	0	0	1
1999	Philadelphia	6	1	0	1	4	0	0	0
Playoff Totals		**71**	**2**	**1**	**3**	**188**	**0**	**0**	**1**
BESLER, Phil	*No playoffs*								Right wing
BESSONE, Pete	*No playoffs*								Defense
BETHEL, John	*No playoffs*								Left wing
BETIK, Karel	*No playoffs*								Defense
BETS, Maxim	*No playoffs*								Left wing
BETTIO, Sam	*No playoffs*								Left wing
BEUKEBOOM, Jeff									Defense
1986	Edmonton	1	0	0	0	4	0	0	0
1988◆	Edmonton	7	0	0	0	16	0	0	0
1989	Edmonton	1	0	0	0	2	0	0	0
1990◆	Edmonton	2	0	0	0	0	0	0	0
1991	Edmonton	18	1	3	4	28	0	0	0
1992	NY Rangers	13	2	3	5	47	0	0	0
1994◆	NY Rangers	22	0	6	6	50	0	0	0
1995	NY Rangers	9	0	0	0	10	0	0	0
1996	NY Rangers	11	0	3	3	6	0	0	0
1997	NY Rangers	15	0	1	1	34	0	0	0
Playoff Totals		**99**	**3**	**16**	**19**	**197**	**0**	**0**	**0**
BEVERLEY, Nick									Defense
1973	Boston	4	0	0	0	0	0	0	0
1975	NY Rangers	3	0	1	1	0	0	0	0
Playoff Totals		**7**	**0**	**1**	**1**	**0**	**0**	**0**	**0**
BIALOWAS, Dwight	*No playoffs*								Defense
BIALOWAS, Frank	*No playoffs*								Left wing
BIANCHIN, Wayne									Left wing
1977	Pittsburgh	3	0	1	1	6	0	0	0
Playoff Totals		**3**	**0**	**1**	**1**	**6**	**0**	**0**	**0**
BICANEK, Radim									Defense
1997	Ottawa	7	0	0	0	8	0	0	0
Playoff Totals		**7**	**0**	**0**	**0**	**8**	**0**	**0**	**0**
BIDNER, Todd	*No playoffs*								Left wing
BIGGS, Don	*No playoffs*								Center
BIGNELL, Larry									Defense
1975	Pittsburgh	3	0	0	0	2	0	0	0
Playoff Totals		**3**	**0**	**0**	**0**	**2**	**0**	**0**	**0**
BILODEAU, Gilles	*No playoffs*								Left wing
BIONDA, Jack									Defense
1957	Boston	10	0	1	1	14	0	0	0
1959	Boston	1	0	0	0	0	0	0	0
Playoff Totals		**11**	**0**	**1**	**1**	**14**	**0**	**0**	**0**
BIRON, Mathieu	*No playoffs*								Defense
BISSETT, Tom	*No playoffs*								Center
BJUGSTAD, Scott									Right wing
1986	Minnesota	5	0	1	1	0	0	0	0
1990	Los Angeles	2	0	0	0	2	0	0	0
1991	Los Angeles	2	0	0	0	0	0	0	0
Playoff Totals		**9**	**0**	**1**	**1**	**2**	**0**	**0**	**0**
BLACK, James									Left wing
1996	Chicago	8	1	0	1	2	0	0	0
1997	Chicago	5	1	1	2	2	0	0	0
Playoff Totals		**13**	**2**	**1**	**3**	**4**	**0**	**0**	**0**
BLACK, Stephen									Left wing
1950◆	Detroit	13	0	0	0	13	0	0	0
Playoff Totals		**13**	**0**	**0**	**0**	**13**	**0**	**0**	**0**
BLACKBURN, Bob									Defense
1970	Pittsburgh	6	0	0	0	4	0	0	0
Playoff Totals		**6**	**0**	**0**	**0**	**4**	**0**	**0**	**0**
BLACKBURN, Don									Left wing
1968	Philadelphia	7	3	0	3	8	1	0	1
1969	Philadelphia	4	0	0	0	2	0	0	0
1970	NY Rangers	1	0	0	0	0	0	0	0
Playoff Totals		**12**	**3**	**0**	**3**	**10**	**1**	**0**	**1**
BLADE, Hank	*No playoffs*								Left wing
BLADON, Tom									Defense
1973	Philadelphia	11	0	4	4	2	0	0	0
1974◆	Philadelphia	16	4	6	10	25	3	0	1
1975◆	Philadelphia	13	1	3	4	12	1	0	0
1976	Philadelphia	16	2	6	8	14	1	0	0
1977	Philadelphia	10	1	3	4	4	0	0	0
1978	Philadelphia	12	0	2	2	11	0	0	0
1979	Pittsburgh	7	0	4	4	2	0	0	0
1980	Pittsburgh	1	0	1	1	0	0	0	0
Playoff Totals		**86**	**8**	**29**	**37**	**70**	**5**	**0**	**1**
BLAINE, Garry	*No playoffs*								Right wing

Season	Club	GP	G	A	Pts	PIM	PP	SH	GW
BLAIR, Andy									Center
1929	Toronto	4	*3	0	*3	2	....	....	....
1931	Toronto	2	1	0	1	0	....	....	....
1932◆	Toronto	7	2	2	4	6	....	....	....
1933	Toronto	9	0	2	2	4	....	....	....
1934	Toronto	5	0	2	2	16	....	....	....
1935	Toronto	2	0	0	0	2	....	....	....
1936	Toronto	9	0	0	0	2	....	....	....
Playoff Totals		**38**	**6**	**6**	**12**	**32**	....	....	....
BLAIR, Chuck	*No playoffs*								Right wing
BLAIR, Dusty	*No playoffs*								Center
BLAISDELL, Mike									Right wing
1988	Toronto	6	1	2	3	10	0	0	0
Playoff Totals		**6**	**1**	**2**	**3**	**10**	**0**	**0**	**0**
BLAKE, Bob	*No playoffs*								Left wing
BLAKE, Jason	*No playoffs*								Center
BLAKE, Mickey	*No playoffs*								Left wing/defense
BLAKE, Rob									Defense
1990	Los Angeles	8	1	3	4	4	1	0	0
1991	Los Angeles	12	1	4	5	26	1	0	0
1992	Los Angeles	6	2	1	3	12	0	0	0
1993	Los Angeles	23	4	6	10	46	1	1	0
1998	Los Angeles	4	0	0	0	6	0	0	0
Playoff Totals		**53**	**8**	**14**	**22**	**94**	**3**	**1**	**0**
BLAKE, Toe									Left wing
1935◆	Mtl. Maroons	1	0	0	0	0	....	....	....
1937	Mtl. Canadiens	5	1	0	1	0	....	....	....
1938	Mtl. Canadiens	3	3	1	4	2	....	....	....
1939	Mtl. Canadiens	3	1	1	2	2	....	....	....
1941	Montreal	3	0	3	3	5	....	....	....
1942	Montreal	3	0	3	3	2	....	....	....
1943	Montreal	5	4	3	7	0	....	....	....
1944◆	Montreal	9	7	*11	*18	2	....	....	....
1945	Montreal	6	0	2	2	5	....	....	....
1946◆	Montreal	9	*7	6	13	5	....	....	....
1947	Montreal	11	2	*7	9	0	....	....	....
Playoff Totals		**58**	**25**	**37**	**62**	**23**	....	....	....
BLIGHT, Rick									Right wing
1976	Vancouver	2	0	1	1	0	0	0	0
1979	Vancouver	3	0	4	4	2	0	0	0
Playoff Totals		**5**	**0**	**5**	**5**	**2**	**0**	**0**	**0**
BLINCO, Russ									Center
1934	Mtl. Maroons	4	0	1	1	0	....	....	....
1935◆	Mtl. Maroons	7	2	2	4	2	....	....	....
1936	Mtl. Maroons	3	0	0	0	0	....	....	....
1937	Mtl. Maroons	5	1	0	1	2	....	....	....
Playoff Totals		**19**	**3**	**3**	**6**	**4**	....	....	....
BLOCK, Ken	*No playoffs*								Defense
BLOEMBERG, Jeff									Defense
1990	NY Rangers	7	0	3	3	5	0	0	0
Playoff Totals		**7**	**0**	**3**	**3**	**5**	**0**	**0**	**0**
BLOMQVIST, Timo									Defense
1983	Washington	3	0	0	0	16	0	0	0
1984	Washington	8	0	0	0	8	0	0	0
1985	Washington	2	0	0	0	0	0	0	0
Playoff Totals		**13**	**0**	**0**	**0**	**24**	**0**	**0**	**0**
BLOMSTEN, Arto	*No playoffs*								Defense
BLOOM, Mike	*No playoffs*								Left wing
BLOUIN, Sylvain	*No playoffs*								Left wing
BLUM, John									Defense
1984	Boston	3	0	0	0	4	0	0	0
1985	Boston	5	0	0	0	13	0	0	0
1986	Boston	3	0	0	0	6	0	0	0
1987	Washington	6	0	1	1	4	0	0	0
1988	Boston	3	0	1	1	0	0	0	0
Playoff Totals		**20**	**0**	**2**	**2**	**27**	**0**	**0**	**0**
BODAK, Bob	*No playoffs*								Left wing
BODDY, Gregg									Defense
1975	Vancouver	3	0	0	0	0	0	0	0
Playoff Totals		**3**	**0**	**0**	**0**	**0**	**0**	**0**	**0**
BODGER, Doug									Defense
1989	Buffalo	5	1	1	2	11	1	0	0
1990	Buffalo	6	1	5	6	6	0	0	0
1991	Buffalo	4	0	1	1	0	0	0	0
1992	Buffalo	7	2	1	3	2	2	0	1
1993	Buffalo	8	2	3	5	0	2	0	0
1994	Buffalo	7	0	3	3	6	0	0	0
1995	Buffalo	5	0	4	4	0	0	0	0
1998	New Jersey	5	0	0	0	0	0	0	0
Playoff Totals		**47**	**6**	**18**	**24**	**25**	**5**	**0**	**1**
BODNAR, Gus									Center
1944	Toronto	5	0	0	0	0	....	....	....
1945◆	Toronto	13	3	1	4	4	....	....	....
1947◆	Toronto	1	0	0	0	0	....	....	....
1953	Chicago	7	1	1	2	2	....	....	....
1954	Boston	1	0	0	0	0	....	....	....
1955	Boston	5	0	1	1	4	....	....	....
Playoff Totals		**32**	**4**	**3**	**7**	**10**	....	....	....

Season	Club	GP	G	A	Pts	PIM	PP	SH	GW
BOEHM, Ron	*No playoffs*								Left wing
BOESCH, Garth									Defense
1947◆	Toronto	11	0	2	2	6	....	....	....
1948◆	Toronto	8	2	1	3	2	....	....	....
1949◆	Toronto	9	0	2	2	6	....	....	....
1950	Toronto	6	0	0	0	4	....	....	....
Playoff Totals		**34**	**2**	**5**	**7**	**18**	....	....	....
BOH, Rick	*No playoffs*								Center
BOHONOS, Lonny									Right wing
1999	Toronto	9	3	6	9	2	0	0	0
Playoff Totals		**9**	**3**	**6**	**9**	**2**	**0**	**0**	**0**
BOILEAU, Marc	*No playoffs*								Center
BOILEAU, Patrick	*No playoffs*								Defense
BOILEAU, Rene	*No playoffs*								Center
BOIMISTRUCK, Fred	*No playoffs*								Defense
BOISVERT, Serge									Right wing
1985	Montreal	12	3	5	8	2	1	0	0
1986◆	Montreal	8	0	1	1	0	0	0	0
1988	Montreal	3	0	1	1	2	0	0	0
Playoff Totals		**23**	**3**	**7**	**10**	**4**	**1**	**0**	**0**
BOIVIN, Claude	*No playoffs*								Left wing
BOIVIN, Leo									Defense
1954	Toronto	5	0	0	0	2	0	0	0
1955	Boston	5	0	1	1	4	0	0	0
1957	Boston	10	2	3	5	12	0	0	0
1958	Boston	12	0	3	3	21	0	0	0
1959	Boston	7	1	2	3	4	0	0	0
1966	Detroit	12	0	1	1	16	0	0	0
1970	Minnesota	3	0	0	0	0	0	0	0
Playoff Totals		**54**	**3**	**10**	**13**	**59**	**0**	**0**	**0**
BOLAND, Mike A.	*No playoffs*								Right wing
BOLAND, Mike J.									Defense
1979	Buffalo	3	1	0	1	2	0	0	0
Playoff Totals		**3**	**1**	**0**	**1**	**2**	**0**	**0**	**0**
BOLDIREV, Ivan									Center
1975	Chicago	8	4	2	6	2	1	0	1
1976	Chicago	4	0	1	1	0	0	0	0
1977	Chicago	2	0	1	1	0	0	0	0
1978	Chicago	4	0	2	2	2	0	0	0
1979	Atlanta	2	0	2	2	2	0	0	0
1980	Vancouver	4	0	2	2	0	0	0	0
1981	Vancouver	1	1	1	2	0	0	0	0
1982	Vancouver	17	8	3	11	4	3	0	1
1984	Detroit	4	0	5	5	4	0	0	0
1985	Detroit	2	0	1	1	0	0	0	0
Playoff Totals		**48**	**13**	**20**	**33**	**14**	**4**	**0**	**2**
BOLDUC, Danny									Left wing
1984	Calgary	1	0	0	0	0	0	0	0
Playoff Totals		**1**	**0**	**0**	**0**	**0**	**0**	**0**	**0**
BOLDUC, Michel	*No playoffs*								Defense
BOLL, Buzz									Left wing
1933	Toronto	1	0	0	0	0	....	....	....
1934	Toronto	5	0	0	0	9	....	....	....
1935	Toronto	6	0	0	0	0	....	....	....
1936	Toronto	9	*7	3	*10	2	....	....	....
1937	Toronto	2	0	0	0	0	....	....	....
1938	Toronto	7	0	0	0	2	....	....	....
1940	NY Americans	1	0	0	0	0	....	....	....
Playoff Totals		**31**	**7**	**3**	**10**	**13**	....	....	....
BOLONCHUK, Larry	*No playoffs*								Defense
BOLTON, Hugh									Defense
1952	Toronto	3	0	0	0	4	0	0	0
1954	Toronto	5	0	1	1	4	0	0	0
1955	Toronto	4	0	3	3	6	0	0	0
1956	Toronto	5	0	1	1	0	0	0	0
Playoff Totals		**17**	**0**	**5**	**5**	**14**	**0**	**0**	**0**
BOMBARDIR, Brad									Defense
1999	New Jersey	5	0	0	0	0	0	0	0
Playoff Totals		**5**	**0**	**0**	**0**	**0**	**0**	**0**	**0**
BONAR, Dan									Center
1981	Los Angeles	4	1	1	2	11	0	1	0
1982	Los Angeles	10	2	3	5	11	0	0	0
Playoff Totals		**14**	**3**	**4**	**7**	**22**	**0**	**1**	**0**
BONDRA, Peter									Right wing
1991	Washington	4	0	1	1	2	0	0	0
1992	Washington	7	6	2	8	4	1	0	0
1993	Washington	6	0	6	6	0	0	0	0
1994	Washington	9	2	4	6	4	0	0	1
1995	Washington	7	5	3	8	10	2	0	1
1996	Washington	6	3	2	5	8	2	0	1
1998	Washington	17	7	5	12	12	3	0	2
Playoff Totals		**56**	**23**	**23**	**46**	**40**	**8**	**0**	**5**
BONIN, Brian									Center
1999	Pittsburgh	3	0	0	0	0	0	0	0
Playoff Totals		**3**	**0**	**0**	**0**	**0**	**0**	**0**	**0**

Season	Club	GP	G	A	Pts	PIM	PP	SH	GW
BONIN, Marcel									Right/left wing
1953	Detroit	5	0	1	1	0	0	0	0
1955◆	Detroit	11	0	2	2	4	0	0	0
1958◆	Montreal	9	0	1	1	2	0	0	0
1959◆	Montreal	11	*10	5	15	4	4	0	3
1960◆	Montreal	8	1	4	5	12	0	0	0
1961	Montreal	6	0	1	1	29	0	0	0
Playoff Totals		**50**	**11**	**14**	**25**	**51**	**4**	**0**	**3**
BONK, Radek									Center
1997	Ottawa	7	0	1	1	4	0	0	0
1998	Ottawa	5	0	0	0	2	0	0	0
1999	Ottawa	4	0	0	0	6	0	0	0
Playoff Totals		**16**	**0**	**1**	**1**	**12**	**0**	**0**	**0**
BONNI, Ryan	*No playoffs*								Defense
BONSIGNORE, Jason	*No playoffs*								Center
BONVIE, Dennis	*No playoffs*								Right wing/Defense
BOO, Jim	*No playoffs*								Defense
BOONE, Buddy									Right wing
1957	Boston	10	1	0	1	12	0	0	0
1958	Boston	12	1	1	2	13	0	0	0
Playoff Totals		**22**	**2**	**1**	**3**	**25**	**0**	**0**	**0**
BOOTHMAN, George									Center/defense
1944	Toronto	5	2	1	3	2	....	....	....
Playoff Totals		**5**	**2**	**1**	**3**	**2**	....	....	....
BORDELEAU, Christian									Center
1969◆	Montreal	6	1	0	1	0	0	0	1
1971	St. Louis	5	0	1	1	17	0	0	0
1972	Chicago	8	3	6	9	0	0	0	1
Playoff Totals		**19**	**4**	**7**	**11**	**17**	**0**	**0**	**2**
BORDELEAU, J.P.									Right wing
1970	Chicago	1	0	0	0	0	0	0	0
1973	Chicago	14	1	0	1	4	1	0	0
1974	Chicago	11	0	2	2	2	0	0	0
1975	Chicago	7	2	2	4	2	0	0	0
1976	Chicago	4	0	0	0	0	0	0	0
1977	Chicago	2	0	0	0	2	0	0	0
1978	Chicago	4	0	1	1	0	0	0	0
1979	Chicago	4	0	1	1	2	0	0	0
1980	Chicago	1	0	0	0	0	0	0	0
Playoff Totals		**48**	**3**	**6**	**9**	**12**	**1**	**0**	**0**
BORDELEAU, Paulin									Right wing
1975	Vancouver	5	2	1	3	0	1	0	0
Playoff Totals		**5**	**2**	**1**	**3**	**0**	**1**	**0**	**0**
BORDELEAU, Sebastien									Center
1998	Montreal	5	0	0	0	2	0	0	0
Playoff Totals		**5**	**0**	**0**	**0**	**2**	**0**	**0**	**0**
BOROTSIK, Jack	*No playoffs*								Center
BORSATO, Luciano									Center
1992	Winnipeg	1	0	0	0	0	0	0	0
1993	Winnipeg	6	1	0	1	4	0	1	0
Playoff Totals		**7**	**1**	**0**	**1**	**4**	**0**	**1**	**0**
BORSCHEVSKY, Nikolai									Right wing
1993	Toronto	16	2	7	9	0	0	0	1
1994	Toronto	15	2	2	4	4	1	0	0
Playoff Totals		**31**	**4**	**9**	**13**	**4**	**1**	**0**	**1**
BOSCHMAN, Laurie									Center
1980	Toronto	3	1	1	2	18	1	0	0
1981	Toronto	3	0	0	0	7	0	0	0
1982	Edmonton	3	0	1	1	4	0	0	0
1983	Winnipeg	3	0	1	1	12	0	0	0
1984	Winnipeg	3	0	1	1	5	0	0	0
1985	Winnipeg	8	2	1	3	21	0	1	0
1986	Winnipeg	3	0	1	1	6	0	0	0
1987	Winnipeg	10	2	3	5	32	1	0	0
1988	Winnipeg	5	1	3	4	9	0	0	0
1990	Winnipeg	2	0	0	0	2	0	0	0
1991	New Jersey	7	1	1	2	16	0	0	0
1992	New Jersey	7	1	0	1	8	0	0	1
Playoff Totals		**57**	**8**	**13**	**21**	**140**	**2**	**1**	**1**
BOSSY, Mike									Right wing
1978	NY Islanders	7	2	2	4	2	0	0	1
1979	NY Islanders	10	6	2	8	2	2	0	1
1980◆	NY Islanders	16	10	13	23	8	6	0	1
1981◆	NY Islanders	18	*17	*18	*35	4	9	0	3
1982◆	NY Islanders	19	*17	10	27	0	6	0	3
1983◆	NY Islanders	19	*17	9	26	10	6	0	5
1984	NY Islanders	21	8	10	18	4	2	0	3
1985	NY Islanders	10	5	6	11	4	2	0	0
1986	NY Islanders	3	1	2	3	4	0	0	0
1987	NY Islanders	6	2	3	5	0	2	0	0
Playoff Totals		**129**	**85**	**75**	**160**	**38**	***35**	**0**	**17**
BOSTROM, Helge									Defense
1930	Chicago	2	0	0	0	0	0	0	0
1931	Chicago	9	0	0	0	16	0	0	0
1932	Chicago	2	0	0	0	0	0	0	0
Playoff Totals		**13**	**0**	**0**	**0**	**16**	**0**	**0**	**0**
BOTELL, Mark	*No playoffs*								Defense

Season	Club	GP	G	A	Pts	PIM	PP	SH	GW
BOTHWELL, Tim	Defense								
1980	NY Rangers	9	0	0	0	8	0	0	0
1984	St. Louis	11	0	2	2	14	0	0	0
1985	St. Louis	3	0	0	0	2	0	0	0
1986	Hartford	10	0	0	0	8	0	0	0
1987	St. Louis	6	0	0	0	6	0	0	0
1988	St. Louis	10	0	1	1	18	0	0	0
Playoff Totals		**49**	**0**	**3**	**3**	**56**	**0**	**0**	**0**
BOTTERILL, Jason	*No playoffs* Left wing								
BOTTING, Cam	*No playoffs* Right wing								
BOUCHA, Henry	*No playoffs* Center								
BOUCHARD, Butch	Defense								
1942	Montreal	3	1	1	2	0	....	....	....
1943	Montreal	5	0	1	1	4	....	....	....
1944◆	Montreal	9	1	3	4	4	....	....	....
1945	Montreal	6	3	4	7	4	....	....	....
1946◆	Montreal	9	2	1	3	17	....	....	....
1947	Montreal	11	0	3	3	21	....	....	....
1949	Montreal	7	0	0	0	6	....	....	....
1950	Montreal	5	0	2	2	2	....	....	....
1951	Montreal	11	1	1	2	2	....	....	....
1952	Montreal	11	0	2	2	14	....	....	....
1953◆	Montreal	12	1	1	2	6	....	....	....
1954	Montreal	11	2	1	3	4	....	....	....
1955	Montreal	12	0	1	1	37	....	....	....
1956◆	Montreal	1	0	0	0	0	....	....	....
Playoff Totals		**113**	**11**	**21**	**32**	**121**	**....**	**....**	**....**
BOUCHARD, Dick	*No playoffs* Right wing								
BOUCHARD, Edmond	*No playoffs* Left wing/defense								
BOUCHARD, Joel	*No playoffs* Defense								
BOUCHARD, Pierre	Defense								
1971◆	Montreal	13	0	1	1	10	0	0	0
1972	Montreal	1	0	0	0	0	0	0	0
1973◆	Montreal	17	1	3	4	13	0	0	0
1974	Montreal	6	0	2	2	4	0	0	0
1975	Montreal	10	0	2	2	10	0	0	0
1976◆	Montreal	13	2	0	2	8	1	0	1
1977◆	Montreal	6	0	1	1	6	0	0	0
1978◆	Montreal	10	0	1	1	5	0	0	0
Playoff Totals		**76**	**3**	**10**	**13**	**56**	**1**	**0**	**1**
BOUCHER, Billy	Right wing								
1923	Mtl. Canadiens	2	1	0	1	2	....	....	....
1924◆	Mtl. Canadiens	6	5	1	6	15	....	....	....
1925	Mtl. Canadiens	6	2	1	3	17	....	....	....
1927	Boston	8	0	0	0	2	....	....	....
Playoff Totals		**22**	**8**	**2**	**10**	**36**	**....**	**....**	**....**
BOUCHER, Bobby	Center								
1924	Mtl. Canadiens	5	0	0	0	0	....	....	....
Playoff Totals		**5**	**0**	**0**	**0**	**0**	**....**	**....**	**....**
BOWCHER, Clarence	*No playoffs* Defense								
BOUCHER, Frank	Center								
1922	Ottawa	1	0	0	0	0	....	....	....
1927	NY Rangers	2	0	0	0	4	....	....	....
1928◆	NY Rangers	9	*7	1	*8	2	....	....	....
1929	NY Rangers	6	1	0	1	0	....	....	....
1930	NY Rangers	3	1	1	2	0	....	....	....
1931	NY Rangers	4	0	2	2	0	....	....	....
1932	NY Rangers	7	3	*6	*9	0	....	....	....
1933◆	NY Rangers	8	2	2	4	6	....	....	....
1934	NY Rangers	2	0	0	0	0	....	....	....
1935	NY Rangers	4	0	3	3	0	....	....	....
1937	NY Rangers	9	2	3	5	0	....	....	....
Playoff Totals		**55**	**16**	**18**	**34**	**12**	**....**	**....**	**....**
BOUCHER, Georges	Defense								
1919	Ottawa	5	2	0	2	9	....	....	....
1920◆	Ottawa	5	2	0	2	2	....	....	....
1921◆	Ottawa	7	*5	0	5	19	....	....	....
1922	Ottawa	2	0	0	0	4	....	....	....
1923◆	Ottawa	8	2	1	3	8	....	....	....
1924	Ottawa	2	0	1	1	4	....	....	....
1926	Ottawa	2	0	0	0	10	....	....	....
1927◆	Ottawa	6	0	0	0	43	....	....	....
1928	Ottawa	2	0	0	0	4	....	....	....
1930	Mtl. Maroons	3	0	0	0	2	....	....	....
1932	Chicago	2	0	1	1	0	....	....	....
Playoff Totals		**44**	**11**	**3**	**14**	**105**	**....**	**....**	**....**
BOUCHER, Philippe	Defense								
1994	Buffalo	7	1	1	2	2	1	0	0
Playoff Totals		**7**	**1**	**1**	**2**	**2**	**1**	**0**	**0**
BOUDREAU, Bruce	Center								
1977	Toronto	3	0	0	0	0	0	0	0
1981	Toronto	2	1	0	1	0	0	0	0
1983	Toronto	4	1	0	1	0	0	0	0
Playoff Totals		**9**	**2**	**0**	**2**	**0**	**0**	**0**	**0**
BOUDRIAS, Andre	Left wing								
1968	Minnesota	14	3	6	9	8	0	0	1
1970	St. Louis	14	2	4	6	4	1	0	0
1975	Vancouver	5	1	0	1	0	0	0	0
1976	Vancouver	1	0	0	0	0	0	0	0
Playoff Totals		**34**	**6**	**10**	**16**	**12**	**1**	**0**	**1**

Season	Club	GP	G	A	Pts	PIM	PP	SH	GW
BOUGHNER, Barry	*No playoffs* Left wing								
BOUGHNER, Bob	Defense								
1997	Buffalo	11	0	1	1	9	0	0	0
1998	Buffalo	14	0	4	4	15	0	0	0
Playoff Totals		**25**	**0**	**5**	**5**	**24**	**0**	**0**	**0**
BOUILLON, Francis	*No playoffs* Defense								
BOURBONNAIS, Dan	*No playoffs* Left wing								
BOURBONNAIS, Rick	Right wing								
1977	St. Louis	4	0	1	1	0	0	0	0
Playoff Totals		**4**	**0**	**1**	**1**	**0**	**0**	**0**	**0**
BOURCIER, Conrad	*No playoffs* Center								
BOURCIER, Jean	*No playoffs* Left wing								
BOURGEAULT, Leo	Defense								
1927	NY Rangers	2	0	0	0	4	....	....	....
1928◆	NY Rangers	9	0	0	0	8	....	....	....
1929	NY Rangers	6	0	0	0	2	....	....	....
1930	NY Rangers	3	1	1	2	6	....	....	....
1933	Mtl. Canadiens	2	0	0	0	0	....	....	....
1934	Mtl. Canadiens	2	0	0	0	0	....	....	....
Playoff Totals		**24**	**1**	**1**	**2**	**18**	**....**	**....**	**....**
BOURGEOIS, Charlie	Defense								
1982	Calgary	3	0	0	0	7	0	0	0
1984	Calgary	8	0	1	1	27	0	0	0
1985	Calgary	4	0	0	0	17	0	0	0
1986	St. Louis	19	2	2	4	116	1	0	0
1987	St. Louis	6	0	0	0	27	0	0	0
Playoff Totals		**40**	**2**	**3**	**5**	**194**	**1**	**0**	**0**
BOURNE, Bob	Center								
1975	NY Islanders	9	1	2	3	4	1	0	0
1977	NY Islanders	8	2	0	2	4	0	0	0
1978	NY Islanders	7	2	3	5	2	1	0	0
1979	NY Islanders	10	1	3	4	6	0	0	0
1980◆	NY Islanders	21	10	10	20	10	5	2	1
1981◆	NY Islanders	14	4	6	10	19	1	1	1
1982◆	NY Islanders	19	9	7	16	36	3	1	0
1983◆	NY Islanders	20	8	20	28	14	0	1	2
1984	NY Islanders	8	1	1	2	7	0	0	1
1985	NY Islanders	10	0	2	2	6	0	0	0
1986	NY Islanders	3	0	0	0	0	0	0	0
1987	Los Angeles	5	2	1	3	0	0	0	0
1988	Los Angeles	5	0	1	1	0	0	0	0
Playoff Totals		**139**	**40**	**56**	**96**	**108**	**11**	**5**	**5**
BOURQUE, Phil	Left wing								
1989	Pittsburgh	11	4	1	5	66	0	0	1
1991◆	Pittsburgh	24	6	7	13	16	0	0	0
1992◆	Pittsburgh	21	3	4	7	25	2	0	0
Playoff Totals		**56**	**13**	**12**	**25**	**107**	**2**	**0**	**1**
BOURQUE, Ray	Defense								
1980	Boston	10	2	9	11	27	0	0	0
1981	Boston	3	0	1	1	2	0	0	0
1982	Boston	9	1	5	6	16	0	0	1
1983	Boston	17	8	15	23	10	2	0	1
1984	Boston	3	0	2	2	0	0	0	0
1985	Boston	5	0	3	3	4	0	0	0
1986	Boston	3	0	0	0	0	0	0	0
1987	Boston	4	1	2	3	0	0	0	0
1988	Boston	23	3	18	21	26	0	0	1
1989	Boston	10	0	4	4	6	0	0	0
1990	Boston	17	5	12	17	16	1	0	0
1991	Boston	19	7	18	25	12	3	0	0
1992	Boston	12	3	6	9	12	2	0	0
1993	Boston	4	1	0	1	2	1	0	0
1994	Boston	13	2	8	10	0	1	0	0
1995	Boston	5	0	3	3	0	0	0	0
1996	Boston	5	1	6	7	2	1	0	0
1998	Boston	6	1	4	5	2	1	0	0
1999	Boston	12	1	9	10	14	0	0	0
Playoff Totals		**180**	**36**	**125**	**161**	**151**	**12**	**0**	**3**
BOUTETTE, Pat	Center/right wing								
1976	Toronto	10	1	4	5	16	0	0	0
1977	Toronto	9	0	4	4	17	0	0	0
1978	Toronto	13	3	3	6	40	0	0	0
1979	Toronto	6	2	2	4	22	0	0	0
1980	Hartford	3	1	0	1	6	0	1	0
1982	Pittsburgh	5	3	1	4	8	2	0	0
Playoff Totals		**46**	**10**	**14**	**24**	**109**	**2**	**1**	**0**
BOUTILIER, Paul	Defense								
1983◆	NY Islanders	2	0	0	0	2	0	0	0
1984	NY Islanders	21	1	7	8	10	0	0	1
1985	NY Islanders	10	0	2	2	16	0	0	0
1986	NY Islanders	3	0	0	0	2	0	0	0
1988	Winnipeg	5	0	0	0	15	0	0	0
Playoff Totals		**41**	**1**	**9**	**10**	**45**	**0**	**0**	**1**
BOWEN, Jason	*No playoffs* Defense								
BOWMAN, Kirk	Left wing								
1977	Chicago	2	1	0	1	0	1	0	0
1978	Chicago	3	0	0	0	0	0	0	0
1979	Chicago	2	0	0	0	0	0	0	0
Playoff Totals		**7**	**1**	**0**	**1**	**0**	**1**	**0**	**0**

Season	Club	GP	G	A	Pts	PIM	PP	SH	GW
BOWMAN, Ralph	Defense								
1936◆	Detroit	7	2	1	3	2	....	....	....
1937◆	Detroit	10	0	1	1	4	....	....	....
1939	Detroit	5	0	0	0	0	....	....	....
Playoff Totals		**22**	**2**	**2**	**4**	**6**	**....**	**....**	**....**
BOWNASS, Jack	*No playoffs* Defense								
BOWNESS, Rick	Right wing								
1978	Detroit	4	0	0	0	2	0	0	0
1982	Winnipeg	1	0	0	0	0	....	....	....
Playoff Totals		**5**	**0**	**0**	**0**	**2**	**....**	**....**	**....**
BOYD, Bill	Right wing								
1928◆	NY Rangers	9	0	0	0	4	0	0	0
1929	NY Rangers	1	0	0	0	0	0	0	0
Playoff Totals		**10**	**0**	**0**	**0**	**4**	**0**	**0**	**0**
BOYD, Irwin	Right wing								
1943	Boston	5	0	1	1	4	0	0	0
Playoff Totals		**5**	**0**	**1**	**1**	**4**	**0**	**0**	**0**
BOYD, Randy	Defense								
1982	Pittsburgh	3	0	0	0	11	0	0	0
1985	Chicago	3	0	1	1	7	0	0	0
1986	NY Islanders	3	0	0	0	2	0	0	0
1987	NY Islanders	4	0	1	1	6	0	0	0
Playoff Totals		**13**	**0**	**2**	**2**	**26**	**0**	**0**	**0**
BOYER, Wally	Center								
1966	Toronto	4	0	1	1	0	0	0	0
1967	Chicago	1	0	0	0	0	0	0	0
1970	Pittsburgh	10	1	2	3	0	0	1	0
Playoff Totals		**15**	**1**	**3**	**4**	**0**	**0**	**1**	**0**
BOYER, Zac	Right wing								
1995	Dallas	2	0	0	0	0	0	0	0
Playoff Totals		**2**	**0**	**0**	**0**	**0**	**0**	**0**	**0**
BOYKO, Darren	*No playoffs* Center								
BOYLE, Dan	*No playoffs* Defense								
BOZEK, Steve	Left wing								
1982	Los Angeles	10	4	1	5	6	2	0	1
1984	Calgary	10	3	1	4	15	1	0	0
1985	Calgary	3	1	0	1	4	1	0	0
1986	Calgary	14	2	6	8	32	0	0	0
1987	Calgary	4	1	0	1	2	0	0	0
1988	St. Louis	7	1	1	2	6	0	0	0
1989	Vancouver	7	0	2	2	4	0	0	0
1991	Vancouver	3	0	0	0	0	0	0	0
Playoff Totals		**58**	**12**	**11**	**23**	**69**	**4**	**0**	**1**
BOZON, Philippe	Left wing								
1992	St. Louis	6	1	0	1	27	0	0	0
1993	St. Louis	9	1	0	1	0	0	0	0
1994	St. Louis	4	0	0	0	4	0	0	0
Playoff Totals		**19**	**2**	**0**	**2**	**31**	**0**	**0**	**0**
BRACKENBOROUGH, John	*No playoffs* Left wing/center								
BRACKENBURY, Curt	Right wing								
1981	Edmonton	2	0	0	0	0	0	0	0
Playoff Totals		**2**	**0**	**0**	**0**	**0**	**0**	**0**	**0**
BRADLEY, Bart	*No playoffs* Center								
BRADLEY, Brian	Center								
1986	Calgary	1	0	0	0	0	0	0	0
1989	Vancouver	7	3	4	7	10	1	0	0
1996	Tampa Bay	5	0	3	3	6	0	0	0
Playoff Totals		**13**	**3**	**7**	**10**	**16**	**1**	**0**	**0**
BRADLEY, Lyle	*No playoffs* Center/right wing								
BRADY, Neil	*No playoffs* Center								
BRAGNALO, Rick	*No playoffs* Center								
BRANIGAN, Andy	*No playoffs* Defense								
BRASAR, Per-Olov	Left wing								
1980	Vancouver	4	1	2	3	0	0	0	1
1981	Vancouver	3	0	0	0	0	0	0	0
1982	Vancouver	6	0	0	0	0	0	0	0
Playoff Totals		**13**	**1**	**2**	**3**	**0**	**0**	**0**	**1**
BRASHEAR, Donald	Left wing								
1994	Montreal	2	0	0	0	0	0	0	0
1996	Montreal	6	0	0	0	2	0	0	0
Playoff Totals		**8**	**0**	**0**	**0**	**2**	**0**	**0**	**0**
BRAYSHAW, Russ	*No playoffs* Left wing								
BREAULT, Francois	*No playoffs* Right wing								
BREITENBACH, Ken	Defense								
1976	Buffalo	1	0	0	0	0	0	0	0
1977	Buffalo	4	0	0	0	0	0	0	0
1979	Buffalo	3	0	1	1	4	0	0	0
Playoff Totals		**8**	**0**	**1**	**1**	**4**	**0**	**0**	**0**
BRENNAN, Dan	*No playoffs* Left wing								
BRENNAN, Doug	Defense								
1932	NY Rangers	7	1	0	1	10	....	....	....
1933◆	NY Rangers	8	0	0	0	11	....	....	....
1934	NY Rangers	1	0	0	0	0	....	....	....
Playoff Totals		**16**	**1**	**0**	**1**	**21**	**....**	**....**	**....**
BRENNAN, Rich	*No playoffs* Defense								

Season	Club	GP	G	A	Pts	PIM	PP	SH	GW
BRENNAN, Tom *No playoffs*	Right wing								
BRENNEMAN, John *No playoffs*	Left wing								
BRETTO, Joe *No playoffs*	Defense								
BREWER, Carl	Defense								
1959	Toronto	12	0	6	6	*40	0	0	0
1960	Toronto	10	2	3	5	16	0	0	0
1961	Toronto	5	0	0	0	4	0	0	0
1962♦	Toronto	8	0	2	2	22	0	0	0
1963♦	Toronto	10	0	1	1	12	0	0	0
1964♦	Toronto	12	0	1	1	30	0	0	0
1965	Toronto	6	1	2	3	12	0	0	0
1970	Detroit	4	0	0	0	2	0	0	0
1971	St. Louis	5	0	2	2	8	0	0	0
Playoff Totals		**72**	**3**	**17**	**20**	**146**	**0**	**0**	**0**
BREWER, Eric *No playoffs*	Defense								
BRICKLEY, Andy	Left wing/Center								
1988	New Jersey	4	0	1	1	4	0	0	0
1989	Boston	10	0	2	2	0	0	0	0
1990	Boston	2	0	0	0	0	0	0	0
1993	Winnipeg	1	1	1	2	0	0	0	0
Playoff Totals		**17**	**1**	**4**	**5**	**4**	**0**	**0**	**0**
BRIDEN, Archie *No playoffs*	Left wing								
BRIDGMAN, Mel	Center								
1976	Philadelphia	16	6	8	14	31	0	0	2
1977	Philadelphia	7	1	0	1	8	0	1	0
1978	Philadelphia	12	1	7	8	36	0	0	1
1979	Philadelphia	8	1	2	3	17	0	0	0
1980	Philadelphia	19	2	9	11	70	0	0	0
1981	Philadelphia	12	2	4	6	39	0	0	0
1982	Calgary	3	2	0	2	14	0	0	0
1983	Calgary	9	3	4	7	33	2	0	0
1987	Detroit	16	5	2	7	28	0	1	1
1988	Detroit	16	4	1	5	12	0	0	0
1989	Vancouver	7	1	2	3	10	1	0	0
Playoff Totals		**125**	**28**	**39**	**67**	**298**	**3**	**2**	**4**
BRIERE, Daniel *No playoffs*	Center								
BRIERE, Michel	Center								
1970	Pittsburgh	10	5	3	8	17	1	3	0
Playoff Totals		**10**	**5**	**3**	**8**	**17**	**1**	**3**	**0**
BRIGLEY, Travis *No playoffs*	Left wing								
BRIMANIS, Aris *No playoffs*	Defense								
BRIND'AMOUR, Rod	Center								
1989	St. Louis	5	2	0	2	4	0	0	0
1990	St. Louis	12	5	8	13	6	1	0	0
1991	St. Louis	13	2	5	7	10	1	0	0
1995	Philadelphia	15	6	9	15	8	2	1	1
1996	Philadelphia	12	2	5	7	6	1	0	0
1997	Philadelphia	19	*13	8	21	10	4	2	1
1998	Philadelphia	5	2	2	4	7	0	0	0
1999	Philadelphia	6	1	3	4	0	0	0	0
Playoff Totals		**87**	**33**	**40**	**73**	**51**	**9**	**3**	**2**
BRINDLEY, Doug *No playoffs*	Left wing/center								
BRINK, Milt *No playoffs*	Center								
BRISEBOIS, Patrice	Defense								
1992	Montreal	11	2	4	6	6	1	0	1
1993♦	Montreal	20	0	4	4	18	0	0	0
1994	Montreal	7	0	4	4	6	0	0	0
1996	Montreal	6	1	2	3	6	0	0	0
1997	Montreal	3	1	1	2	24	0	0	1
1998	Montreal	10	1	0	1	0	0	0	0
Playoff Totals		**57**	**5**	**15**	**20**	**60**	**1**	**0**	**2**
BRISSON, Gerry *No playoffs*	Right wing								
BRITZ, Greg *No playoffs*	Right wing								
BROADBENT, Punch	Right wing								
1919	Ottawa	5	2	3	5	*28	....	....	....
1920♦	Ottawa	4	0	0	0	3	....	....	....
1921♦	Ottawa	6	2	2	4	4	....	....	....
1922	Ottawa	2	0	1	1	8	....	....	....
1923♦	Ottawa	8	*6	1	*7	*12	....	....	....
1924	Ottawa	2	0	0	0	4	....	....	....
1926♦	Mtl. Maroons	8	2	0	2	*36	....	....	....
1927	Mtl. Maroons	2	0	0	0	0	....	....	....
1928	Ottawa	2	0	0	0	0	....	....	....
1929	NY Americans	2	0	0	0	2	....	....	....
Playoff Totals		**41**	**12**	**7**	**19**	**97**	....	....	....
BROCHU, Stephane *No playoffs*	Defense								
BRODEN, Connie	Center								
1957♦	Montreal	6	0	1	1	0	0	0	0
1958♦	Montreal	1	0	0	0	0	0	0	0
Playoff Totals		**7**	**0**	**1**	**1**	**0**	**0**	**0**	**0**
BROOKE, Bob	Center								
1984	NY Rangers	5	0	0	0	7	0	0	0
1985	NY Rangers	3	0	0	0	8	0	0	0
1986	NY Rangers	16	6	9	15	28	0	2	2
1989	Minnesota	5	3	0	3	2	0	0	0
1990	New Jersey	5	0	0	0	14	0	0	0
Playoff Totals		**34**	**9**	**9**	**18**	**59**	**0**	**2**	**2**
BROOKS, Gord *No playoffs*	Right wing								

Season	Club	GP	G	A	Pts	PIM	PP	SH	GW
BROPHY, Bernie	Left wing								
1929	Detroit	2	0	0	0	2	0	0	0
Playoff Totals		**2**	**0**	**0**	**0**	**2**	**0**	**0**	**0**
BROSSART, Willie	Left wing								
1974	Toronto	1	0	0	0	0	0	0	0
Playoff Totals		**1**	**0**	**0**	**0**	**0**	**0**	**0**	**0**
BROTEN, Aaron	Left wing/Center								
1988	New Jersey	20	5	11	16	20	3	0	1
1990	Minnesota	7	0	5	5	8	0	0	0
1992	Winnipeg	7	2	2	4	12	0	0	0
Playoff Totals		**34**	**7**	**18**	**25**	**40**	**3**	**0**	**1**
BROTEN, Neal	Center								
1981	Minnesota	19	1	7	8	9	0	0	1
1982	Minnesota	4	0	2	2	0	0	0	0
1983	Minnesota	9	1	6	7	10	1	0	0
1984	Minnesota	16	5	5	10	4	2	0	1
1985	Minnesota	9	2	5	7	10	0	0	0
1986	Minnesota	5	3	2	5	2	1	0	0
1989	Minnesota	5	2	2	4	4	1	1	0
1990	Minnesota	7	2	2	4	18	1	0	0
1991	Minnesota	23	9	13	22	6	2	1	0
1992	Minnesota	7	1	5	6	2	0	0	0
1994	Dallas	9	2	1	3	6	0	0	1
1995♦	New Jersey	20	7	12	19	6	1	0	4
1997	Dallas	2	0	1	1	0	0	0	0
Playoff Totals		**135**	**35**	**63**	**98**	**77**	**9**	**2**	**7**
BROTEN, Paul	Right wing								
1990	NY Rangers	6	1	1	2	2	0	1	0
1991	NY Rangers	5	0	0	0	2	0	0	0
1992	NY Rangers	13	1	2	3	10	0	0	0
1994	Dallas	9	1	1	2	2	0	0	0
1995	Dallas	5	1	2	3	2	0	0	0
Playoff Totals		**38**	**4**	**6**	**10**	**18**	**0**	**1**	**0**
BROUSSEAU, Paul *No playoffs*	Right wing								
BROWN, Adam	Left wing								
1942	Detroit	10	0	2	2	4	....	....	....
1943♦	Detroit	6	1	1	2	2	....	....	....
1944	Detroit	5	0	0	0	8	....	....	....
1946	Detroit	5	1	1	2	0	....	....	....
Playoff Totals		**26**	**2**	**4**	**6**	**14**	....	....	....
BROWN, Arnie	Defense								
1967	NY Rangers	4	0	0	0	6	0	0	0
1968	NY Rangers	6	0	1	1	8	0	0	0
1969	NY Rangers	4	0	1	1	0	0	0	0
1970	NY Rangers	4	0	4	4	9	0	0	0
1974	Atlanta	4	0	0	0	0	0	0	0
Playoff Totals		**22**	**0**	**6**	**6**	**23**	**0**	**0**	**0**
BROWN, Brad *No playoffs*	Defense								
BROWN, Cam *No playoffs*	Left wing								
BROWN, Connie	Center								
1940	Detroit	5	2	1	3	0	....	....	....
1941	Detroit	9	0	2	2	0	....	....	....
Playoff Totals		**14**	**2**	**3**	**5**	**0**	....	....	....
BROWN, Curtis	Center								
1998	Buffalo	13	1	2	3	10	1	0	0
1999	Buffalo	21	7	6	13	10	3	0	3
Playoff Totals		**34**	**8**	**8**	**16**	**20**	**4**	**0**	**3**
BROWN, David	Right wing								
1984	Philadelphia	2	0	0	0	12	0	0	0
1985	Philadelphia	11	0	0	0	59	0	0	0
1986	Philadelphia	5	0	0	0	16	0	0	0
1987	Philadelphia	26	1	2	3	59	0	0	0
1988	Philadelphia	7	1	0	1	27	0	0	0
1989	Edmonton	7	0	0	0	6	0	0	0
1990♦	Edmonton	3	0	0	0	0	0	0	0
1991	Edmonton	16	0	1	1	30	0	0	0
1995	Philadelphia	3	0	0	0	0	0	0	0
Playoff Totals		**80**	**2**	**3**	**5**	**209**	**0**	**0**	**0**
BROWN, Doug	Right wing								
1988	New Jersey	19	5	1	6	6	0	1	1
1990	New Jersey	6	0	1	1	2	0	0	0
1991	New Jersey	7	2	2	4	2	0	1	0
1994	Pittsburgh	6	0	0	0	2	0	0	0
1995	Detroit	18	4	8	12	2	0	1	1
1996	Detroit	13	3	3	6	4	0	1	0
1997♦	Detroit	14	3	3	6	2	0	0	0
1998♦	Detroit	9	4	2	6	0	3	0	1
1999	Detroit	10	2	2	4	4	1	0	1
Playoff Totals		**102**	**23**	**22**	**45**	**24**	**4**	**4**	**4**
BROWN, Fred	Left wing								
1928	Mtl. Maroons	9	0	0	0	0	0	0	0
Playoff Totals		**9**	**0**	**0**	**0**	**0**	**0**	**0**	**0**
BROWN, George	Center								
1937	Mtl. Canadiens	4	0	0	0	0	0	0	0
1938	Mtl. Canadiens	3	0	0	0	2	0	0	0
Playoff Totals		**7**	**0**	**0**	**0**	**2**	**0**	**0**	**0**
BROWN, Gerry	Left wing								
1942	Detroit	12	2	1	3	4	....	....	....
Playoff Totals		**12**	**2**	**1**	**3**	**4**	....	....	....

Season	Club	GP	G	A	Pts	PIM	PP	SH	GW
BROWN, Greg	Defense								
1994	Pittsburgh	6	0	1	1	4	0	0	0
Playoff Totals		**6**	**0**	**1**	**1**	**4**	**0**	**0**	**0**
BROWN, Harold *No playoffs*	Right wing								
BROWN, Jeff	Defense								
1986	Quebec	1	0	0	0	0	0	0	0
1987	Quebec	13	3	3	6	2	2	0	0
1990	St. Louis	12	2	10	12	4	1	0	1
1991	St. Louis	13	3	9	12	6	0	0	0
1992	St. Louis	6	2	1	3	2	0	0	1
1993	St. Louis	11	3	8	11	6	1	0	2
1994	Vancouver	24	6	9	15	37	3	0	0
1995	Vancouver	5	1	3	4	2	0	0	0
1998	Washington	2	0	2	2	0	0	0	0
Playoff Totals		**87**	**20**	**45**	**65**	**59**	**7**	**0**	**4**
BROWN, Jim *No playoffs*	Defense								
BROWN, Keith	Defense								
1980	Chicago	6	0	0	0	4	0	0	0
1981	Chicago	3	0	2	2	2	0	0	0
1982	Chicago	4	0	2	2	5	0	0	0
1983	Chicago	7	0	0	0	11	0	0	0
1984	Chicago	5	0	1	1	10	0	0	0
1985	Chicago	11	2	7	9	31	1	0	0
1986	Chicago	3	0	1	1	9	0	0	0
1987	Chicago	4	0	1	1	6	0	0	0
1988	Chicago	5	0	2	2	10	0	0	0
1989	Chicago	13	1	3	4	25	0	0	0
1990	Chicago	18	0	4	4	43	0	0	0
1991	Chicago	6	1	0	1	8	0	0	0
1992	Chicago	14	0	8	8	18	0	0	0
1993	Chicago	4	0	1	1	2	0	0	0
Playoff Totals		**103**	**4**	**32**	**36**	**184**	**1**	**0**	**0**
BROWN, Kevin *No playoffs*	Right wing								
BROWN, Larry	Defense								
1971	NY Rangers	11	0	1	1	0	0	0	0
1974	Los Angeles	2	0	0	0	0	0	0	0
1975	Los Angeles	3	0	2	2	0	0	0	0
1976	Los Angeles	9	0	0	0	2	0	0	0
1977	Los Angeles	9	0	1	1	6	0	0	0
1978	Los Angeles	1	0	0	0	2	0	0	0
Playoff Totals		**35**	**0**	**4**	**4**	**10**	**0**	**0**	**0**
BROWN, Rob	Right wing								
1989	Pittsburgh	11	5	3	8	22	1	0	3
1991	Hartford	5	1	0	1	7	1	0	1
1992	Chicago	8	2	4	6	4	1	0	0
1998	Pittsburgh	6	1	0	1	4	1	0	0
1999	Pittsburgh	13	2	5	7	8	2	0	0
Playoff Totals		**43**	**11**	**12**	**23**	**45**	**6**	**0**	**4**
BROWN, Sean	Defense								
1999	Edmonton	1	0	0	0	10	0	0	0
Playoff Totals		**1**	**0**	**0**	**0**	**10**	**0**	**0**	**0**
BROWN, Stan	Defense								
1927	NY Rangers	2	0	0	0	0	0	0	0
Playoff Totals		**2**	**0**	**0**	**0**	**0**	**0**	**0**	**0**
BROWN, Wayne	Right wing								
1954	Boston	4	0	0	0	2	0	0	0
Playoff Totals		**4**	**0**	**0**	**0**	**2**	**0**	**0**	**0**
BROWNE, Cecil *No playoffs*	Left wing								
BROWNSCHIDLE, Jack	Defense								
1980	St. Louis	3	0	0	0	0	0	0	0
1981	St. Louis	11	0	3	3	2	0	0	0
1982	St. Louis	8	0	2	2	14	0	0	0
1983	St. Louis	4	0	0	0	2	0	0	0
Playoff Totals		**26**	**0**	**5**	**5**	**18**	**0**	**0**	**0**
BROWNSCHIDLE, Jeff *No playoffs*	Defense								
BRUBAKER, Jeff	Left wing								
1982	Montreal	2	0	0	0	27	0	0	0
Playoff Totals		**2**	**0**	**0**	**0**	**27**	**0**	**0**	**0**
BRUCE, David	Left wing								
1986	Vancouver	1	0	0	0	0	0	0	0
1991	St. Louis	2	0	0	0	2	0	0	0
Playoff Totals		**3**	**0**	**0**	**0**	**2**	**0**	**0**	**0**
BRUCE, Gordie	Left wing								
1941♦	Boston	2	0	0	0	0	....	....	....
1942	Boston	5	2	3	5	4	....	....	....
Playoff Totals		**7**	**2**	**3**	**5**	**4**	....	....	....
BRUCE, Morley	Defense/center								
1920♦	Ottawa	5	0	0	0	0	0	0	0
1921♦	Ottawa	2	0	0	0	2	0	0	0
1922	Ottawa	1	0	0	0	0	0	0	0
Playoff Totals		**8**	**0**	**0**	**0**	**2**	**0**	**0**	**0**
BRUMWELL, Murray	Defense								
1982	Minnesota	2	0	0	0	2	0	0	0
Playoff Totals		**2**	**0**	**0**	**0**	**2**	**0**	**0**	**0**

Season	Club	GP	G	A	Pts	PIM	PP	SH	GW
BRUNET, Benoit	Left wing								
1993◆	Montreal	20	2	8	10	8	1	0	1
1994	Montreal	7	1	4	5	16	0	0	0
1996	Montreal	3	0	2	2	0	0	0	0
1997	Montreal	4	1	3	4	4	0	1	0
1998	Montreal	8	1	0	1	4	0	0	1
Playoff Totals		**42**	**5**	**17**	**22**	**32**	**1**	**1**	**2**
BRUNETEAU, Eddie	Right wing								
1941	Detroit	3	0	0	0	0	....	....	....
1945	Detroit	14	5	2	7	0	....	....	....
1946	Detroit	4	1	0	1	0	....	....	....
1947	Detroit	4	1	4	5	0	....	....	....
1948	Detroit	6	0	0	0	0	....	....	....
Playoff Totals		**31**	**7**	**6**	**13**	**0**	....	....	....
BRUNETEAU, Mud	Right wing								
1936◆	Detroit	7	2	2	4	4	....	....	....
1937◆	Detroit	10	2	0	2	6	....	....	....
1939	Detroit	6	0	0	0	0	....	....	....
1940	Detroit	5	3	2	5	0	....	....	....
1941	Detroit	9	2	1	3	2	....	....	....
1942	Detroit	12	5	1	6	6	....	....	....
1943◆	Detroit	9	5	4	9	0	....	....	....
1944	Detroit	5	1	2	3	2	....	....	....
1945	Detroit	14	3	2	5	2	....	....	....
Playoff Totals		**77**	**23**	**14**	**37**	**22**	....	....	....
BRUNETTE, Andrew	Left wing								
1996	Washington	6	1	3	4	0	0	0	0
Playoff Totals		**6**	**1**	**3**	**4**	**0**	**0**	**0**	**0**
BRYDGE, Bill	Defense								
1929	Detroit	2	0	0	0	4	0	0	0
Playoff Totals		**2**	**0**	**0**	**0**	**4**	**0**	**0**	**0**
BRYDGES, Paul *No playoffs*	Center								
BRYDSON, Glenn	Right wing								
1931	Mtl. Maroons	2	0	0	0	0	0	0	0
1932	Mtl. Maroons	4	0	0	0	4	0	0	0
1933	Mtl. Maroons	2	0	0	0	0	0	0	0
1934	Mtl. Maroons	1	0	0	0	0	0	0	0
1936	Chicago	2	0	0	0	4	0	0	0
Playoff Totals		**11**	**0**	**0**	**0**	**8**	**0**	**0**	**0**
BRYDSON, Gord *No playoffs*	Center/right wing								
BRYLIN, Sergei	Center								
1995◆	New Jersey	12	1	2	3	4	0	0	0
1999	New Jersey	5	3	1	4	4	1	0	1
Playoff Totals		**17**	**4**	**3**	**7**	**8**	**1**	**0**	**1**
BUBLA, Jiri	Defense								
1983	Vancouver	1	0	0	0	5	0	0	0
1984	Vancouver	2	0	0	0	0	0	0	0
1986	Vancouver	3	0	0	0	2	0	0	0
Playoff Totals		**6**	**0**	**0**	**0**	**7**	**0**	**0**	**0**
BUCHANAN, Al *No playoffs*	Left wing								
BUCHANAN, Bucky *No playoffs*	Center/Right wing								
BUCHANAN, Jeff *No playoffs*	Defense								
BUCHANAN, Mike *No playoffs*	Defense								
BUCHANAN, Ron *No playoffs*	Center								
BUCHBERGER, Kelly	Right wing								
1987◆	Edmonton	3	0	1	1	5	0	0	0
1990◆	Edmonton	19	0	5	5	13	0	0	0
1991	Edmonton	12	2	1	3	25	0	0	0
1992	Edmonton	16	1	4	5	32	0	0	0
1997	Edmonton	12	5	2	7	16	0	0	1
1998	Edmonton	12	1	2	3	25	0	0	0
1999	Edmonton	4	0	0	0	0	0	0	0
Playoff Totals		**78**	**9**	**15**	**24**	**116**	**0**	**0**	**1**
BUCYK, John	Left wing								
1956	Detroit	10	1	1	2	8	0	0	0
1957	Detroit	5	0	1	1	0	0	0	0
1958	Boston	12	0	4	4	16	0	0	0
1959	Boston	7	2	4	6	6	0	0	0
1968	Boston	3	0	2	2	0	0	0	0
1969	Boston	10	5	6	11	0	2	1	0
1970◆	Boston	14	11	8	19	2	4	1	0
1971	Boston	7	2	5	7	0	0	0	0
1972◆	Boston	15	9	11	20	6	0	0	0
1973	Boston	5	0	3	3	0	0	0	0
1974	Boston	16	8	10	18	4	3	0	1
1975	Boston	3	1	0	1	0	0	0	0
1976	Boston	12	2	7	9	0	2	0	0
1977	Boston	5	0	0	0	0	0	0	0
Playoff Totals		**124**	**41**	**62**	**103**	**42**	**11**	**2**	**1**
BUCYK, Randy	Center								
1986◆	Montreal	2	0	0	0	0	0	0	0
Playoff Totals		**2**	**0**	**0**	**0**	**0**	**0**	**0**	**0**
BUHR, Doug *No playoffs*	Left wing								
BUKOVICH, Tony	Left wing/center								
1945	Detroit	6	0	1	1	0	0	0	0
Playoff Totals		**6**	**0**	**1**	**1**	**0**	**0**	**0**	**0**
BULIS, Jan *No playoffs*	Center								

Season	Club	GP	G	A	Pts	PIM	PP	SH	GW
BULLARD, Mike	Center								
1981	Pittsburgh	4	3	3	6	0	1	0	1
1982	Pittsburgh	5	1	1	2	4	0	0	0
1987	Calgary	6	4	3	7	2	3	0	1
1988	Calgary	6	0	2	2	6	0	0	0
1989	Philadelphia	19	3	9	12	32	1	0	0
Playoff Totals		**40**	**11**	**18**	**29**	**44**	**5**	**0**	**2**
BULLER, Hy *No playoffs*	Defense								
BULLEY, Ted	Left wing								
1978	Chicago	4	1	1	2	2	0	0	0
1979	Chicago	2	0	0	0	0	0	0	0
1980	Chicago	7	2	3	5	10	0	0	0
1982	Chicago	15	2	1	3	12	0	0	1
1983	Washington	1	0	0	0	0	0	0	0
Playoff Totals		**29**	**5**	**5**	**10**	**24**	**0**	**0**	**1**
BURAKOVSKY, Robert *No playoffs*	Right wing								
BURCH, Billy	Center/left wing								
1929	NY Americans	2	0	0	0	0	0	0	0
Playoff Totals		**2**	**0**	**0**	**0**	**0**	**0**	**0**	**0**
BURCHELL, Fred *No playoffs*	Center								
BURDON, Glen *No playoffs*	Center								
BURE, Pavel	Right wing								
1992	Vancouver	13	6	4	10	14	0	0	0
1993	Vancouver	12	5	7	12	8	0	0	1
1994	Vancouver	24	*16	15	31	40	3	0	2
1995	Vancouver	11	7	6	13	10	2	2	0
Playoff Totals		**60**	**34**	**32**	**66**	**72**	**5**	**2**	**3**
BURE, Valeri	Right wing								
1996	Montreal	6	0	1	1	6	0	0	0
1997	Montreal	5	0	1	1	2	0	0	0
Playoff Totals		**11**	**0**	**2**	**2**	**8**	**0**	**0**	**0**
BUREAU, Marc	Center								
1991	Minnesota	23	3	2	5	20	0	1	0
1992	Minnesota	5	0	0	0	14	0	0	0
1996	Montreal	6	1	1	2	4	0	0	0
1998	Montreal	10	1	2	3	6	0	0	0
1999	Philadelphia	6	0	2	2	2	0	0	0
Playoff Totals		**50**	**5**	**7**	**12**	**46**	**0**	**1**	**0**
BUREGA, Bill *No playoffs*	Defense								
BURKE, Eddie *No playoffs*	Right wing/center								
BURKE, Marty	Defense								
1928	Pittsburgh	2	1	0	1	2	....	....	....
1929	Mtl. Canadiens	3	0	0	0	8	....	....	....
1930◆	Mtl. Canadiens	6	0	1	1	6	....	....	....
1931◆	Mtl. Canadiens	10	1	2	3	10	....	....	....
1932	Mtl. Canadiens	4	0	0	0	12	....	....	....
1934	Mtl. Canadiens	2	0	1	1	2	....	....	....
1935	Chicago	2	0	0	0	2	....	....	....
1936	Chicago	2	0	0	0	2	....	....	....
Playoff Totals		**31**	**2**	**4**	**6**	**44**	....	....	....
BURMEISTER, Roy *No playoffs*	Left wing								
BURNETT, Kelly *No playoffs*	Center								
BURNS, Bobby *No playoffs*	Left wing								
BURNS, Charlie	Center								
1970	Minnesota	6	1	0	1	2	0	0	0
1971	Minnesota	12	3	3	6	2	0	0	1
1972	Minnesota	7	1	1	2	2	0	0	0
1973	Minnesota	6	0	0	0	0	0	0	0
Playoff Totals		**31**	**5**	**4**	**9**	**6**	**0**	**0**	**1**
BURNS, Gary	Left wing/center								
1981	NY Rangers	1	0	0	0	2	0	0	0
1982	NY Rangers	4	0	0	0	0	0	0	0
Playoff Totals		**5**	**0**	**0**	**0**	**2**	**0**	**0**	**0**
BURNS, Norm *No playoffs*	Center								
BURNS, Robin *No playoffs*	Left wing								
BURR, Shawn	Left wing/Center								
1987	Detroit	16	7	2	9	20	0	0	2
1988	Detroit	9	3	1	4	14	0	0	1
1989	Detroit	6	1	2	3	6	0	0	0
1991	Detroit	7	0	4	4	15	0	0	0
1992	Detroit	11	1	5	6	10	0	0	0
1993	Detroit	7	2	1	3	2	0	1	0
1994	Detroit	7	2	0	2	6	0	0	2
1995	Detroit	16	0	2	2	6	0	0	0
1996	Tampa Bay	6	0	2	2	8	0	0	0
1998	San Jose	6	0	0	0	8	0	0	0
Playoff Totals		**91**	**16**	**19**	**35**	**95**	**0**	**1**	**5**
BURRIDGE, Randy	Left wing								
1986	Boston	3	0	4	4	12	0	0	0
1987	Boston	2	1	0	1	2	0	0	0
1988	Boston	23	2	10	12	16	0	0	0
1989	Boston	10	5	2	7	6	1	1	0
1990	Boston	21	4	11	15	14	0	1	0
1991	Boston	19	0	3	3	39	0	0	0
1992	Washington	2	0	1	1	0	0	0	0
1993	Washington	4	1	0	1	0	0	0	0
1994	Washington	11	0	2	2	12	0	0	0
1997	Buffalo	12	5	1	6	2	0	0	0
Playoff Totals		**107**	**18**	**34**	**52**	**103**	**1**	**2**	**0**

Season	Club	GP	G	A	Pts	PIM	PP	SH	GW
BURROWS, Dave	Defense								
1972	Pittsburgh	4	0	0	0	4	0	0	0
1975	Pittsburgh	9	1	1	2	12	0	0	1
1976	Pittsburgh	3	0	0	0	0	0	0	0
1977	Pittsburgh	3	0	2	2	0	0	0	0
1979	Toronto	6	0	1	1	7	0	0	0
1980	Toronto	3	0	1	1	2	0	0	0
1981	Pittsburgh	1	0	0	0	0	0	0	0
Playoff Totals		**29**	**1**	**5**	**6**	**25**	**0**	**0**	**1**
BURRY, Bert *No playoffs*	Defense								
BURT, Adam	Defense								
1990	Hartford	2	0	0	0	0	0	0	0
1992	Hartford	2	0	0	0	0	0	0	0
1999	Philadelphia	6	0	0	0	4	0	0	0
Playoff Totals		**10**	**0**	**0**	**0**	**4**	**0**	**0**	**0**
BURTON, Cummy	Right wing								
1956	Detroit	3	0	0	0	0	0	0	0
Playoff Totals		**3**	**0**	**0**	**0**	**0**	**0**	**0**	**0**
BURTON, Nelson *No playoffs*	Left wing								
BUSH, Eddie	Defense								
1942	Detroit	11	1	6	7	23	....	....	....
Playoff Totals		**11**	**1**	**6**	**7**	**23**	....	....	....
BUSKAS, Rod	Defense								
1989	Pittsburgh	10	0	0	0	23	0	0	0
1991	Los Angeles	2	0	2	2	22	0	0	0
1992	Chicago	6	0	1	1	0	0	0	0
Playoff Totals		**18**	**0**	**3**	**3**	**45**	**0**	**0**	**0**
BUSNIUK, Mike	Defense								
1980	Philadelphia	19	2	4	6	23	0	0	0
1981	Philadelphia	6	0	1	1	11	0	0	0
Playoff Totals		**25**	**2**	**5**	**7**	**34**	**0**	**0**	**0**
BUSNIUK, Ron *No playoffs*	Right wing								
BUSWELL, Walt	Defense								
1933	Detroit	4	0	0	0	4	....	....	....
1934	Detroit	9	0	1	1	2	....	....	....
1937	Mtl. Canadiens	5	0	0	0	2	....	....	....
1938	Mtl. Canadiens	3	0	0	0	0	....	....	....
1939	Mtl. Canadiens	3	2	0	2	2	....	....	....
Playoff Totals		**24**	**2**	**1**	**3**	**10**	....	....	....
BUTCHER, Garth	Defense								
1982	Vancouver	1	0	0	0	0	0	0	0
1983	Vancouver	3	1	0	1	2	0	0	0
1986	Vancouver	3	0	0	0	0	0	0	0
1989	Vancouver	7	1	1	2	22	0	0	1
1991	St. Louis	13	2	1	3	54	0	0	0
1992	St. Louis	5	1	2	3	16	0	0	0
1993	St. Louis	11	1	1	2	20	0	0	1
1995	Toronto	7	0	0	0	8	0	0	0
Playoff Totals		**50**	**6**	**5**	**11**	**122**	**0**	**0**	**2**
BUTENSCHON, Sven *No playoffs*	Defense								
BUTLER, Dick *No playoffs*	Right wing								
BUTLER, Jerry	Right wing								
1974	NY Rangers	12	0	2	2	25	0	0	0
1975	NY Rangers	3	1	0	1	16	0	0	0
1976	St. Louis	3	0	0	0	0	0	0	0
1977	St. Louis	4	0	0	0	14	0	0	0
1978	Toronto	13	1	1	2	18	0	0	0
1979	Toronto	6	0	0	0	4	0	0	0
1980	Vancouver	4	0	0	0	2	0	0	0
1981	Vancouver	3	1	0	1	0	0	0	0
Playoff Totals		**48**	**3**	**3**	**6**	**79**	**0**	**0**	**0**
BUTSAYEV, Viacheslav *No playoffs*	Center								
BUTSAYEV, Yuri *No playoffs*	Center								
BUTTERS, Bill *No playoffs*	Defense								
BUTTREY, Gord *No playoffs*	Left/right wing								
BUYNAK, Gordon *No playoffs*	Defense								
BUZEK, Petr *No playoffs*	Defense								
BYAKIN, Ilja *No playoffs*	Defense								
BYCE, John	Center								
1990	Boston	8	2	0	2	2	0	0	0
Playoff Totals		**8**	**2**	**0**	**2**	**2**	**0**	**0**	**0**
BYERS, Gord *No playoffs*	Defense								
BYERS, Jerry *No playoffs*	Left wing								
BYERS, Lyndon	Right wing								
1987	Boston	1	0	0	0	0	0	0	0
1988	Boston	11	1	2	3	62	0	0	0
1989	Boston	2	0	0	0	0	0	0	0
1990	Boston	17	1	0	1	12	0	0	0
1991	Boston	1	0	0	0	10	0	0	0
1992	Boston	5	0	0	0	12	0	0	0
Playoff Totals		**37**	**2**	**2**	**4**	**96**	**0**	**0**	**0**
BYERS, Mike	Right wing								
1969	Philadelphia	4	0	1	1	0	0	0	0
Playoff Totals		**4**	**0**	**1**	**1**	**0**	**0**	**0**	**0**
BYLSMA, Dan	Right wing								
1998	Los Angeles	2	0	0	0	0	0	0	0
Playoff Totals		**2**	**0**	**0**	**0**	**0**	**0**	**0**	**0**

Season	Club	GP	G	A	Pts	PIM	PP	SH	GW
BYRAM, Shawn *No playoffs*									Left wing
CAFFERY, Jack									Center
1957	Boston	10	1	0	1	4	0	0	0
Playoff Totals		**10**	**1**	**0**	**1**	**4**	**0**	**0**	**0**
CAFFERY, Terry									Center
1971	Minnesota	1	0	0	0	0	0	0	0
Playoff Totals		**1**	**0**	**0**	**0**	**0**	**0**	**0**	**0**
CAHAN, Larry									Defense
1955	Toronto	4	0	0	0	0	0	0	0
1957	NY Rangers	3	0	0	0	2	0	0	0
1958	NY Rangers	5	0	0	0	4	0	0	0
1962	NY Rangers	6	0	0	0	10	0	0	0
1969	Los Angeles	11	1	1	2	22	0	1	0
Playoff Totals		**29**	**1**	**1**	**2**	**38**	**0**	**1**	**0**
CAHILL, Charles *No playoffs*									Right wing
CAIN, Francis *No playoffs*									Defense
CAIN, Herb									Left wing
1934	Mtl. Maroons	4	0	0	0	0	....	....	....
1935◆	Mtl. Maroons	7	1	0	1	2	....	....	....
1936	Mtl. Maroons	3	0	1	1	0	....	....	....
1937	Mtl. Maroons	5	1	1	2	0	....	....	....
1939	Mtl. Canadiens	3	0	0	0	2	....	....	....
1940	Boston	6	1	3	4	2	....	....	....
1941◆	Boston	11	3	2	5	5	....	....	....
1942	Boston	5	1	0	1	0	....	....	....
1943	Boston	7	4	2	6	0	....	....	....
1945	Boston	7	5	2	7	0	....	....	....
1946	Boston	9	0	2	2	2	....	....	....
Playoff Totals		**67**	**16**	**13**	**29**	**13**	....	....	....
CAIRNS, Don *No playoffs*									Left wing
CAIRNS, Eric									Defense
1997	NY Rangers	3	0	0	0	0	0	0	0
Playoff Totals		**3**	**0**	**0**	**0**	**0**	**0**	**0**	**0**
CALDER, Eric *No playoffs*									Defense
CALDER, Kyle *No playoffs*									Center
CALLADINE, Norm *No playoffs*									Center
CALLANDER, Drew *No playoffs*									Center/right wing
CALLANDER, Jock									Right wing
1989	Pittsburgh	10	2	5	7	10	0	0	0
1992◆	Pittsburgh	12	1	3	4	2	0	0	0
Playoff Totals		**22**	**3**	**8**	**11**	**12**	**0**	**0**	**0**
CALLIGHEN, Brett									Center
1980	Edmonton	3	0	2	2	0	0	0	0
1981	Edmonton	9	4	4	8	6	1	0	1
1982	Edmonton	2	0	0	0	2	0	0	0
Playoff Totals		**14**	**4**	**6**	**10**	**8**	**1**	**0**	**1**
CALLIGHEN, Patsy									Defense
1928◆	NY Rangers	9	0	0	0	0	0	0	0
Playoff Totals		**9**	**0**	**0**	**0**	**0**	**0**	**0**	**0**
CALOUN, Jan *No playoffs*									Right wing
CAMAZZOLA, James *No playoffs*									Left wing
CAMAZZOLA, Tony *No playoffs*									Defense
CAMERON, Al									Defense
1978	Detroit	7	0	1	1	2	0	0	0
Playoff Totals		**7**	**0**	**1**	**1**	**2**	**0**	**0**	**0**
CAMERON, Billy									Right wing
1924◆	Mtl. Canadiens	6	0	0	0	0	0	0	0
Playoff Totals		**6**	**0**	**0**	**0**	**0**	**0**	**0**	**0**
CAMERON, Craig									Right wing
1968	St. Louis	14	1	0	1	11	0	0	0
1969	St. Louis	2	0	0	0	0	0	0	0
1971	St. Louis	6	2	0	2	4	0	0	0
1972	Minnesota	5	0	1	1	2	0	0	0
Playoff Totals		**27**	**3**	**1**	**4**	**17**	**0**	**0**	**0**
CAMERON, Dave *No playoffs*									Center
CAMERON, Harry									Defense
1918◆	Toronto	7	6	3	9	12	....	....	....
1919	Ottawa	5	6	0	6	6	....	....	....
1921	Toronto	2	0	0	0	2	....	....	....
1922◆	Toronto	6	0	4	4	19	....	....	....
Playoff Totals		**20**	**12**	**7**	**19**	**39**	....	....	....
CAMERON, Scotty *No playoffs*									Center
CAMPBELL, Brian *No playoffs*									Defense
CAMPBELL, Bryan									Center
1969	Los Angeles	6	2	1	3	0	0	0	1
1970	Chicago	8	1	2	3	0	1	0	0
1971	Chicago	4	0	1	1	0	0	0	0
1972	Chicago	4	0	0	0	2	0	0	0
Playoff Totals		**22**	**3**	**4**	**7**	**2**	**1**	**0**	**1**

Season	Club	GP	G	A	Pts	PIM	PP	SH	GW
CAMPBELL, Colin									Defense
1975	Pittsburgh	9	1	3	4	21	0	1	1
1976	Pittsburgh	3	0	0	0	0	0	0	0
1979	Pittsburgh	7	1	4	5	30	0	0	0
1980	Edmonton	3	0	0	0	11	0	0	0
1981	Vancouver	3	0	1	1	9	0	0	0
1982	Vancouver	16	2	2	4	89	0	0	1
1984	Detroit	4	0	0	0	21	0	0	0
Playoff Totals		**45**	**4**	**10**	**14**	**181**	**0**	**1**	**2**
CAMPBELL, Dave *No playoffs*									Defense
CAMPBELL, Don *No playoffs*									Left wing
CAMPBELL, Earl									Defense
1924	Ottawa	2	0	0	0	0	0	0	0
Playoff Totals		**2**	**0**	**0**	**0**	**0**	**0**	**0**	**0**
CAMPBELL, Jim									Right wing
1997	St. Louis	4	1	0	1	6	1	0	0
1998	St. Louis	10	7	3	10	12	4	0	2
Playoff Totals		**14**	**8**	**3**	**11**	**18**	**5**	**0**	**2**
CAMPBELL, Scott *No playoffs*									Defense
CAMPBELL, Wade									Defense
1984	Winnipeg	3	0	0	0	7	0	0	0
1985	Winnipeg	3	0	0	0	2	0	0	0
1987	Boston	4	0	0	0	11	0	0	0
Playoff Totals		**10**	**0**	**0**	**0**	**20**	**0**	**0**	**0**
CAMPEAU, Tod									Center
1949	Montreal	1	0	0	0	0	0	0	0
Playoff Totals		**1**	**0**	**0**	**0**	**0**	**0**	**0**	**0**
CAMPEDELLI, Dom *No playoffs*									Defense
CAPUANO, Dave									Left wing
1991	Vancouver	6	1	1	2	5	0	0	0
Playoff Totals		**6**	**1**	**1**	**2**	**5**	**0**	**0**	**0**
CAPUANO, Jack *No playoffs*									Defense
CARBOL, Leo *No playoffs*									Defense
CARBONNEAU, Guy									Center
1983	Montreal	3	0	0	0	2	0	0	0
1984	Montreal	15	4	3	7	12	0	0	1
1985	Montreal	12	4	3	7	8	0	1	1
1986◆	Montreal	20	7	5	12	35	0	2	1
1987	Montreal	17	3	8	11	20	0	0	0
1988	Montreal	11	0	4	4	2	0	0	0
1989	Montreal	21	4	5	9	10	0	1	0
1990	Montreal	11	2	3	5	6	0	0	0
1991	Montreal	13	1	5	6	10	0	0	1
1992	Montreal	11	1	1	2	6	0	0	0
1993◆	Montreal	20	3	3	6	10	0	1	2
1994	Montreal	7	1	3	4	4	0	0	0
1995	St. Louis	7	1	2	3	6	0	0	0
1997	Dallas	7	0	1	1	6	0	0	0
1998	Dallas	16	3	1	4	6	0	0	0
1999◆	Dallas	17	2	4	6	6	0	0	1
Playoff Totals		**208**	**36**	**51**	**87**	**149**	**0**	**5**	**7**
CARDIN, Claude *No playoffs*									Left wing
CARDWELL, Steve									Left wing
1972	Pittsburgh	4	0	0	0	2	0	0	0
Playoff Totals		**4**	**0**	**0**	**0**	**2**	**0**	**0**	**0**
CAREY, George *No playoffs*									Right wing
CARKNER, Terry									Defense
1987	NY Rangers	1	0	0	0	0	0	0	0
1989	Philadelphia	19	1	5	6	28	0	1	0
1994	Detroit	7	0	0	0	4	0	0	0
1996	Florida	22	0	4	4	10	0	0	0
1997	Florida	5	0	0	0	6	0	0	0
Playoff Totals		**54**	**1**	**9**	**10**	**48**	**0**	**1**	**0**
CARLETON, Wayne									Left wing
1970◆	Boston	14	2	4	6	14	0	0	0
1971	Boston	4	0	0	0	0	0	0	0
Playoff Totals		**18**	**2**	**4**	**6**	**14**	**0**	**0**	**0**
CARLIN, Brian *No playoffs*									Left wing
CARLSON, Jack									Left wing
1981	Minnesota	15	1	2	3	50	0	0	0
1982	Minnesota	1	0	0	0	15	0	0	0
1983	St. Louis	4	0	0	0	5	0	0	0
1984	St. Louis	5	0	0	0	2	0	0	0
Playoff Totals		**25**	**1**	**2**	**3**	**72**	**0**	**0**	**0**
CARLSON, Kent									Defense
1986	St. Louis	5	0	0	0	11	0	0	0
1988	St. Louis	3	0	0	0	2	0	0	0
Playoff Totals		**8**	**0**	**0**	**0**	**13**	**0**	**0**	**0**
CARLSON, Steve									Center
1980	Los Angeles	4	1	1	2	7	0	0	0
Playoff Totals		**4**	**1**	**1**	**2**	**7**	**0**	**0**	**0**
CARLSSON, Anders									Center
1988	New Jersey	3	1	0	1	2	0	0	1
Playoff Totals		**3**	**1**	**0**	**1**	**2**	**0**	**0**	**1**

Season	Club	GP	G	A	Pts	PIM	PP	SH	GW
CARLYLE, Randy									Defense
1977	Toronto	9	0	1	1	20	0	0	0
1978	Toronto	7	0	1	1	8	0	0	0
1979	Pittsburgh	7	0	0	0	12	0	0	0
1980	Pittsburgh	5	1	0	1	4	0	0	0
1981	Pittsburgh	5	4	5	9	9	0	1	0
1982	Pittsburgh	5	1	3	4	16	0	0	0
1984	Winnipeg	3	0	2	2	4	0	0	0
1985	Winnipeg	8	1	5	6	13	1	0	0
1987	Winnipeg	10	1	5	6	18	0	0	0
1988	Winnipeg	5	0	2	2	10	0	0	0
1992	Winnipeg	5	1	0	1	6	0	0	0
Playoff Totals		**69**	**9**	**24**	**33**	**120**	**1**	**1**	**0**
CARNBACK, Patrik *No playoffs*									Center
CARNEY, Keith									Defense
1992	Buffalo	7	0	3	3	0	0	0	0
1993	Buffalo	8	0	3	3	6	0	0	0
1994	Chicago	6	0	1	1	4	0	0	0
1995	Chicago	4	0	1	1	0	0	0	0
1996	Chicago	10	0	3	3	4	0	0	0
1997	Chicago	6	1	1	2	2	0	0	0
1998	Phoenix	6	0	0	0	4	0	0	0
1999	Phoenix	7	1	2	3	10	0	0	0
Playoff Totals		**54**	**2**	**14**	**16**	**30**	**0**	**0**	**0**
CARON, Alain *No playoffs*									Right wing
CARPENTER, Bob									Center
1983	Washington	4	1	0	1	2	0	0	0
1984	Washington	8	2	1	3	25	1	0	0
1985	Washington	5	1	4	5	8	0	0	0
1986	Washington	9	5	4	9	12	2	0	1
1987	Los Angeles	5	1	2	3	2	0	0	0
1988	Los Angeles	5	1	1	2	0	0	0	0
1989	Boston	8	1	1	2	4	1	0	1
1990	Boston	21	4	6	10	39	2	0	1
1991	Boston	1	0	1	1	2	0	0	0
1992	Boston	8	0	1	1	6	0	0	0
1993	Washington	6	1	4	5	6	0	0	0
1994	New Jersey	20	1	7	8	20	0	0	0
1995◆	New Jersey	17	1	4	5	6	1	0	0
1997	New Jersey	10	1	2	3	2	0	0	0
1998	New Jersey	6	1	0	1	0	0	0	0
1999	New Jersey	7	0	0	0	2	0	0	0
Playoff Totals		**140**	**21**	**38**	**59**	**136**	**7**	**0**	**3**
CARPENTER, Eddie *No playoffs*									Defense
CARR, Al *No playoffs*									Left wing
CARR, Gene									Center
1972	NY Rangers	16	1	3	4	21	0	0	0
1973	NY Rangers	1	0	1	1	0	0	0	0
1974	Los Angeles	5	2	1	3	14	1	0	0
1975	Los Angeles	3	1	2	3	29	0	0	0
1977	Los Angeles	9	1	1	2	2	0	0	0
1979	Atlanta	1	0	0	0	0	0	0	0
Playoff Totals		**35**	**5**	**8**	**13**	**66**	**1**	**0**	**0**
CARR, Lorne									Right wing
1936	NY Americans	5	1	1	2	0	....	....	....
1938	NY Americans	6	3	1	4	2	....	....	....
1939	NY Americans	2	0	0	0	0	....	....	....
1940	NY Americans	3	0	0	0	0	....	....	....
1942◆	Toronto	13	3	2	5	6	....	....	....
1943	Toronto	6	1	2	3	0	....	....	....
1944	Toronto	5	0	1	1	0	....	....	....
1945◆	Toronto	13	2	2	4	5	....	....	....
Playoff Totals		**53**	**10**	**9**	**19**	**13**	....	....	....
CARRIERE, Larry									Defense
1973	Buffalo	6	0	1	1	8	0	0	0
1975	Buffalo	17	0	2	2	32	0	0	0
1976	Atlanta	2	0	0	0	2	0	0	0
1980	Toronto	2	0	0	0	0	0	0	0
Playoff Totals		**27**	**0**	**3**	**3**	**42**	**0**	**0**	**0**
CARRIGAN, Gene									Center
1934	Detroit	4	0	0	0	0	0	0	0
Playoff Totals		**4**	**0**	**0**	**0**	**0**	**0**	**0**	**0**
CARROLL, Billy									Center
1981◆	NY Islanders	18	3	9	12	4	0	1	1
1982◆	NY Islanders	19	2	2	4	8	0	2	0
1983◆	NY Islanders	20	1	1	2	2	0	1	0
1984	NY Islanders	5	0	0	0	0	0	0	0
1985◆	Edmonton	9	0	0	0	4	0	0	0
Playoff Totals		**71**	**6**	**12**	**18**	**18**	**0**	**4**	**1**
CARROLL, George *No playoffs*									Defense
CARROLL, Greg *No playoffs*									Center
CARRUTHERS, Dwight *No playoffs*									Defense
CARSE, Bill									Center
1939	NY Rangers	6	1	1	2	0	....	....	....
1940	Chicago	2	1	0	1	0	....	....	....
1941	Chicago	2	0	0	0	0	....	....	....
1942	Chicago	3	1	1	2	0	....	....	....
Playoff Totals		**13**	**3**	**2**	**5**	**0**	....	....	....

Season	Club	GP	G	A	Pts	PIM	PP	SH	GW
CARSE, Bob									Left wing
1940	Chicago	2	0	0	0	0	0	0	0
1941	Chicago	5	0	0	0	2	0	0	0
1942	Chicago	3	0	2	2	0	0	0	0
Playoff Totals		**10**	**0**	**2**	**2**	**2**	**0**	**0**	**0**
CARSON, Bill									Center
1929◆	Boston	5	2	0	2	8	....	....	....
1930	Boston	6	1	0	1	6	....	....	....
Playoff Totals		**11**	**3**	**0**	**3**	**14**	....	....	....
CARSON, Frank									Right wing
1926◆	Mtl. Maroons	8	0	0	0	0	0	0	0
1927	Mtl. Maroons	2	0	0	0	2	0	0	0
1928	Mtl. Maroons	9	0	0	0	0	0	0	0
1932	Detroit	2	0	0	0	2	0	0	0
1933	Detroit	4	0	1	1	0	0	0	0
1934	Detroit	6	0	1	1	5	0	0	0
Playoff Totals		**31**	**0**	**2**	**2**	**9**	**0**	**0**	**0**
CARSON, Gerry									Defense
1929	NY Rangers	5	0	0	0	0	0	0	0
1930◆	Mtl. Canadiens	6	0	0	0	0	0	0	0
1933	Mtl. Canadiens	2	0	0	0	2	0	0	0
1934	Mtl. Canadiens	2	0	0	0	2	0	0	0
1935	Mtl. Canadiens	2	0	0	0	4	0	0	0
1937	Mtl. Maroons	5	0	0	0	4	0	0	0
Playoff Totals		**22**	**0**	**0**	**0**	**12**	**0**	**0**	**0**
CARSON, Jimmy									Center
1987	Los Angeles	5	1	2	3	6	0	0	0
1988	Los Angeles	5	5	3	8	4	1	0	0
1989	Edmonton	7	2	1	3	6	1	0	1
1991	Detroit	7	2	1	3	4	0	0	1
1992	Detroit	11	2	3	5	0	0	0	0
1993	Los Angeles	18	5	4	9	2	2	0	0
1994	Vancouver	2	0	1	1	0	0	0	0
Playoff Totals		**55**	**17**	**15**	**32**	**22**	**4**	**0**	**2**
CARSON, Lindsay									Center
1983	Philadelphia	1	0	0	0	0	0	0	0
1984	Philadelphia	1	0	0	0	5	0	0	0
1985	Philadelphia	17	0	3	3	24	0	0	0
1986	Philadelphia	1	0	0	0	5	0	0	0
1987	Philadelphia	24	3	5	8	22	0	0	0
1988	Hartford	5	1	2	3	0	0	0	0
Playoff Totals		**49**	**4**	**10**	**14**	**56**	**0**	**0**	**0**
CARTER, Anson									Center
1998	Boston	6	1	1	2	0	0	0	0
1999	Boston	12	4	3	7	0	1	0	1
Playoff Totals		**18**	**5**	**4**	**9**	**0**	**1**	**0**	**1**
CARTER, Billy *No playoffs*									Center
CARTER, John									Left wing
1989	Boston	10	1	2	3	6	0	0	0
1990	Boston	21	6	3	9	45	0	1	0
Playoff Totals		**31**	**7**	**5**	**12**	**51**	**0**	**1**	**0**
CARTER, Ron *No playoffs*									Right wing
CARVETH, Joe									Right wing
1942	Detroit	9	4	0	4	0	....	....	....
1943◆	Detroit	10	*6	2	8	4	....	....	....
1944	Detroit	5	2	1	3	8	....	....	....
1945	Detroit	14	5	*6	*11	2	....	....	....
1946	Detroit	5	0	1	1	0	....	....	....
1947	Boston	5	2	1	3	0	....	....	....
1949	Montreal	7	0	1	1	8	....	....	....
1950◆	Detroit	14	2	4	6	6	....	....	....
Playoff Totals		**69**	**21**	**16**	**37**	**28**	....	....	....
CASHMAN, Wayne									Right wing
1968	Boston	1	0	0	0	0	0	0	0
1969	Boston	6	0	1	1	0	0	0	0
1970◆	Boston	14	5	4	9	50	0	2	0
1971	Boston	7	3	2	5	15	0	0	1
1972◆	Boston	15	4	7	11	42	1	0	0
1973	Boston	5	1	1	2	4	0	0	0
1974	Boston	16	5	9	14	46	1	0	1
1975	Boston	1	0	2	2	0	0	0	0
1976	Boston	11	1	5	6	16	0	0	0
1977	Boston	14	1	8	9	18	0	0	0
1978	Boston	15	4	6	10	13	3	0	2
1979	Boston	10	4	5	9	8	1	0	1
1980	Boston	10	3	3	6	32	1	0	0
1981	Boston	3	0	1	1	0	0	0	0
1982	Boston	9	0	2	2	6	0	0	0
1983	Boston	8	0	1	1	0	0	0	0
Playoff Totals		**145**	**31**	**57**	**88**	**250**	**7**	**2**	**5**
CASSELMAN, Mike *No playoffs*									Center
CASSELS, Andrew									Center
1991	Montreal	8	0	2	2	2	0	0	0
1992	Hartford	7	2	4	6	6	1	0	0
Playoff Totals		**15**	**2**	**6**	**8**	**8**	**1**	**0**	**0**
CASSIDY, Bruce									Defense
1989	Chicago	1	0	0	0	0	0	0	0
Playoff Totals		**1**	**0**	**0**	**0**	**0**	**0**	**0**	**0**
CASSIDY, Tom *No playoffs*									Center
CASSOLATO, Tony *No playoffs*									Right wing

Season	Club	GP	G	A	Pts	PIM	PP	SH	GW
CAUFIELD, Jay									Right wing
1987	NY Rangers	3	0	0	0	12	0	0	0
1989	Pittsburgh	9	0	0	0	28	0	0	0
1992◆	Pittsburgh	5	0	0	0	2	0	0	0
Playoff Totals		**17**	**0**	**0**	**0**	**42**	**0**	**0**	**0**
CAVALLINI, Gino									Left wing
1985	Calgary	3	0	0	0	4	0	0	0
1986	St. Louis	17	4	5	9	10	0	0	2
1987	St. Louis	6	3	1	4	2	1	0	1
1988	St. Louis	10	5	5	10	19	2	0	0
1989	St. Louis	9	0	2	2	17	0	0	0
1990	St. Louis	12	1	3	4	12	0	0	1
1991	St. Louis	13	1	3	4	2	0	0	0
1993	Quebec	4	0	0	0	0	0	0	0
Playoff Totals		**74**	**14**	**19**	**33**	**66**	**3**	**0**	**4**
CAVALLINI, Paul									Defense
1988	St. Louis	10	1	6	7	26	0	1	0
1989	St. Louis	10	2	2	4	14	0	0	0
1990	St. Louis	12	2	3	5	20	0	0	0
1991	St. Louis	13	2	3	5	20	1	0	0
1992	St. Louis	4	0	1	1	6	0	0	0
1993	Washington	6	0	2	2	18	0	0	0
1994	Dallas	9	1	8	9	4	1	0	1
1995	Dallas	5	0	2	2	6	0	0	0
Playoff Totals		**69**	**8**	**27**	**35**	**114**	**2**	**1**	**1**
CERESINO, Ray *No playoffs*									Right wing
CERNIK, Frantisek *No playoffs*									Left/Right wing
CHABOT, John									Center
1984	Montreal	11	1	4	5	0	0	0	1
1988	Detroit	16	4	15	19	2	1	0	0
1989	Detroit	6	1	1	2	0	0	0	1
Playoff Totals		**33**	**6**	**20**	**26**	**2**	**1**	**0**	**2**
CHAD, John									Right wing
1940	Chicago	2	0	0	0	0	0	0	0
1941	Chicago	5	0	0	0	2	0	0	0
1946	Chicago	3	0	1	1	0	0	0	0
Playoff Totals		**10**	**0**	**1**	**1**	**2**	**0**	**0**	**0**
CHALMERS, Bill *No playoffs*									Center
CHALUPA, Milan *No playoffs*									Defense
CHAMBERLAIN, Murph									Left wing
1938	Toronto	5	0	0	0	2	....	....	....
1939	Toronto	10	2	5	7	4	....	....	....
1940	Toronto	3	0	0	0	0	....	....	....
1941	Montreal	3	0	2	2	11	....	....	....
1943	Boston	6	1	1	2	12	....	....	....
1944◆	Montreal	9	5	3	8	12	....	....	....
1945	Montreal	6	1	1	2	10	....	....	....
1946◆	Montreal	9	4	2	6	18	....	....	....
1947	Montreal	11	1	3	4	19	....	....	....
1949	Montreal	4	0	0	0	8	....	....	....
Playoff Totals		**66**	**14**	**17**	**31**	**96**	....	....	....
CHAMBERS, Shawn									Defense
1989	Minnesota	3	0	2	2	0	0	0	0
1990	Minnesota	7	2	1	3	10	1	0	0
1991	Minnesota	23	0	7	7	16	0	0	0
1995◆	New Jersey	20	4	5	9	2	2	0	0
1997	New Jersey	10	1	6	7	6	1	0	0
1998	Dallas	14	0	3	3	20	0	0	0
1999◆	Dallas	17	0	2	2	18	0	0	0
Playoff Totals		**94**	**7**	**26**	**33**	**72**	**4**	**0**	**0**
CHAMPAGNE, Andre *No playoffs*									Left wing
CHAPDELAINE, Rene *No playoffs*									Defense
CHAPMAN, Art									Center
1931	Boston	5	0	1	1	7	....	....	....
1933	Boston	5	0	0	0	2	....	....	....
1936	NY Americans	5	0	3	3	0	....	....	....
1938	NY Americans	6	0	1	1	0	....	....	....
1939	NY Americans	2	0	0	0	0	....	....	....
1940	NY Americans	3	1	0	1	0	....	....	....
Playoff Totals		**26**	**1**	**5**	**6**	**9**	....	....	....
CHAPMAN, Blair									Right wing
1977	Pittsburgh	3	1	1	2	7	0	0	0
1979	Pittsburgh	7	1	0	1	2	0	0	0
1980	St. Louis	3	0	0	0	0	0	0	0
1981	St. Louis	9	2	5	7	6	0	0	0
1982	St. Louis	3	0	0	0	0	0	0	0
Playoff Totals		**25**	**4**	**6**	**10**	**15**	**0**	**0**	**0**
CHAPMAN, Brian *No playoffs*									Defense
CHARA, Zdeno *No playoffs*									Defense
CHARBONNEAU, Jose									Right wing
1988	Montreal	8	0	0	0	4	0	0	0
1994	Vancouver	3	1	0	1	4	0	0	0
Playoff Totals		**11**	**1**	**0**	**1**	**8**	**0**	**0**	**0**
CHARBONNEAU, Stephane *No playoffs*									Right wing
CHARLEBOIS, Bob *No playoffs*									Left wing
CHARLESWORTH, Todd *No playoffs*									Defense
CHARRON, Eric									Defense
1996	Washington	6	0	0	0	8	0	0	0
Playoff Totals		**6**	**0**	**0**	**0**	**8**	**0**	**0**	**0**

Season	Club	GP	G	A	Pts	PIM	PP	SH	GW
CHARRON, Guy *No playoffs*									Center
CHARTIER, Dave *No playoffs*									Center
CHARTRAND, Brad *No playoffs*									Right wing
CHARTRAW, Rick									Defense/right wing
1976◆	Montreal	2	0	0	0	0	0	0	0
1977◆	Montreal	13	2	1	3	17	0	0	0
1978◆	Montreal	10	1	0	1	10	0	0	1
1979◆	Montreal	16	2	1	3	24	0	0	0
1980	Montreal	10	2	2	4	0	0	0	0
1981	Los Angeles	4	0	1	1	4	0	0	0
1982	Los Angeles	10	0	2	2	17	0	0	0
1983	NY Rangers	9	0	2	2	6	0	0	0
1984◆	Edmonton	1	0	0	0	2	0	0	0
Playoff Totals		**75**	**7**	**9**	**16**	**80**	**0**	**0**	**1**
CHASE, Kelly									Right wing
1990	St. Louis	9	1	0	1	46	0	0	0
1991	St. Louis	6	0	0	0	18	0	0	0
1992	St. Louis	1	0	0	0	7	0	0	0
1994	St. Louis	4	0	1	1	6	0	0	0
1998	St. Louis	7	0	0	0	23	0	0	0
Playoff Totals		**27**	**1**	**1**	**2**	**100**	**0**	**0**	**0**
CHASSE, Denis									Right wing
1995	St. Louis	7	1	7	8	23	0	0	0
Playoff Totals		**7**	**1**	**7**	**8**	**23**	**0**	**0**	**0**
CHEBATURKIN, Vladimir *No playoffs*									Defense
CHECK, Lude *No playoffs*									Left wing
CHELIOS, Chris									Defense
1984	Montreal	15	1	9	10	17	1	0	0
1985	Montreal	9	2	8	10	17	2	0	0
1986◆	Montreal	20	2	9	11	49	1	0	0
1987	Montreal	17	4	9	13	38	2	1	0
1988	Montreal	11	3	1	4	29	1	0	0
1989	Montreal	21	4	15	19	28	1	0	2
1990	Montreal	5	0	1	1	8	0	0	0
1991	Chicago	6	1	7	8	46	1	0	0
1992	Chicago	18	6	15	21	37	3	0	1
1993	Chicago	4	0	2	2	14	0	0	0
1994	Chicago	6	1	1	2	8	1	0	0
1995	Chicago	16	4	7	11	12	0	1	3
1996	Chicago	9	0	3	3	8	0	0	0
1997	Chicago	6	0	1	1	8	0	0	0
1999	Detroit	10	0	4	4	14	0	0	0
Playoff Totals		**173**	**28**	**92**	**120**	**333**	**13**	**2**	**6**
CHERNOFF, Mike *No playoffs*									Left wing
CHERNOMAZ, Rich *No playoffs*									Right wing
CHERRY, Dick									Defense
1969	Philadelphia	4	1	0	1	4	0	0	0
Playoff Totals		**4**	**1**	**0**	**1**	**4**	**0**	**0**	**0**
CHERRY, Don									Defense
1955	Boston	1	0	0	0	0	0	0	0
Playoff Totals		**1**	**0**	**0**	**0**	**0**	**0**	**0**	**0**
CHERVYAKOV, Denis *No playoffs*									Defense
CHEVREFILS, Real									Left wing
1952	Boston	7	1	1	2	6	....	....	....
1953	Boston	7	0	1	1	6	....	....	....
1955	Boston	5	2	1	3	4	....	....	....
1957	Boston	10	2	1	3	4	....	....	....
1958	Boston	1	0	0	0	0	....	....	....
Playoff Totals		**30**	**5**	**4**	**9**	**20**	....	....	....
CHIASSON, Steve									Defense
1987	Detroit	2	0	0	0	19	0	0	0
1988	Detroit	9	2	2	4	31	1	0	0
1989	Detroit	5	2	1	3	6	1	0	0
1991	Detroit	5	3	1	4	19	1	0	0
1992	Detroit	11	1	5	6	12	1	0	0
1993	Detroit	7	2	2	4	19	1	0	1
1994	Detroit	7	2	3	5	2	2	0	1
1995	Calgary	7	1	2	3	9	1	0	0
1996	Calgary	4	2	1	3	0	0	0	0
1999	Carolina	6	1	2	3	2	1	0	0
Playoff Totals		**63**	**16**	**19**	**35**	**119**	**9**	**0**	**2**
CHIBIREV, Igor *No playoffs*									Center
CHICOINE, Dan									Right wing
1980	Minnesota	1	0	0	0	0	0	0	0
Playoff Totals		**1**	**0**	**0**	**0**	**0**	**0**	**0**	**0**
CHINNICK, Rick *No playoffs*									Right wing
CHIPPERFIELD, Ron *No playoffs*									Center
CHISHOLM, Art *No playoffs*									Center/Defense
CHISHOLM, Colin *No playoffs*									Defense
CHISHOLM, Lex									Center/right wing
1941	Toronto	3	1	0	1	0	....	....	....
Playoff Totals		**3**	**1**	**0**	**1**	**0**	....	....	....
CHORNEY, Marc									Defense
1981	Pittsburgh	2	0	1	1	2	0	0	0
1982	Pittsburgh	5	0	0	0	0	0	0	0
Playoff Totals		**7**	**0**	**1**	**1**	**2**	**0**	**0**	**0**

Season	Club	GP	G	A	Pts	PIM	PP	SH	GW
CHORSKE, Tom									Left wing
1992	New Jersey	7	0	3	3	4	0	0	0
1993	New Jersey	1	0	0	0	0	0	0	0
1994	New Jersey	20	4	3	7	0	0	0	1
1995◆	New Jersey	17	1	5	6	4	0	0	0
1997	Ottawa	5	0	1	1	2	0	0	0
Playoff Totals		**50**	**5**	**12**	**17**	**10**	**0**	**0**	**1**
CHOUINARD, Gene	*No playoffs*								Defense
CHOUINARD, Guy									Center
1976	Atlanta	2	0	0	0	0	0	0	0
1977	Atlanta	3	2	0	2	0	1	0	0
1978	Atlanta	2	1	0	1	0	0	0	0
1979	Atlanta	2	1	2	3	0	1	0	0
1980	Atlanta	4	1	3	4	4	1	0	0
1981	Calgary	16	3	14	17	4	0	0	0
1982	Calgary	3	0	1	1	0	0	0	0
1983	Calgary	9	1	6	7	4	0	0	0
1984	St. Louis	5	0	2	2	0	0	0	0
Playoff Totals		**46**	**9**	**28**	**37**	**12**	**3**	**0**	**0**
CHRISTIAN, Dave									Right wing
1982	Winnipeg	4	0	1	1	2	0	0	0
1983	Winnipeg	3	0	0	0	0	0	0	0
1984	Washington	8	5	4	9	5	1	0	0
1985	Washington	5	1	1	2	0	0	0	0
1986	Washington	9	4	4	8	0	1	0	0
1987	Washington	7	1	3	4	6	0	0	1
1988	Washington	14	5	6	11	6	1	0	0
1989	Washington	6	1	1	2	0	1	0	0
1990	Boston	21	4	1	5	4	1	0	0
1991	Boston	19	8	4	12	4	0	0	2
1992	St. Louis	4	3	0	3	0	0	0	0
1993	Chicago	1	0	0	0	0	0	0	0
1994	Chicago	1	0	0	0	0	0	0	0
Playoff Totals		**102**	**32**	**25**	**57**	**27**	**5**	**0**	**3**
CHRISTIAN, Jeff	*No playoffs*								Left wing
CHRISTIE, Mike									Defense
1978	Colorado	2	0	0	0	0	0	0	0
Playoff Totals		**2**	**0**	**0**	**0**	**0**	**0**	**0**	**0**
CHRISTIE, Ryan	*No playoffs*								Left wing
CHRISTOFF, Steve									Center
1980	Minnesota	14	8	4	12	7	2	0	0
1981	Minnesota	18	8	8	16	16	5	0	1
1982	Minnesota	2	0	0	0	2	0	0	0
1983	Calgary	1	0	0	0	0	0	0	0
Playoff Totals		**35**	**16**	**12**	**28**	**25**	**7**	**0**	**1**
CHRYSTAL, Bob	*No playoffs*								Defense
CHUBAROV, Artem	*No playoffs*								Center
CHURCH, Brad	*No playoffs*								Left wing
CHURCH, Jack									Defense
1939	Toronto	1	0	0	0	0	....	....	....
1940	Toronto	10	1	1	2	6	....	....	....
1941	Toronto	5	0	0	0	8	....	....	....
1946	Boston	9	0	0	0	4	....	....	....
Playoff Totals		**25**	**1**	**1**	**2**	**18**	....	....	....
CHURLA, Shane									Right wing
1987	Hartford	2	0	0	0	42	0	0	0
1988	Calgary	7	0	1	1	17	0	0	0
1990	Minnesota	7	0	0	0	44	0	0	0
1991	Minnesota	22	2	1	3	90	0	0	1
1994	Dallas	9	1	3	4	35	1	0	0
1995	Dallas	5	0	0	0	20	0	0	0
1996	NY Rangers	11	2	2	4	14	0	0	0
1997	NY Rangers	15	0	0	0	20	0	0	0
Playoff Totals		**78**	**5**	**7**	**12**	**282**	**1**	**0**	**1**
CHYCHRUN, Jeff									Defense
1989	Philadelphia	19	0	2	2	65	0	0	0
Playoff Totals		**19**	**0**	**2**	**2**	**65**	**0**	**0**	**0**
CHYNOWETH, Dean									Defense
1994	NY Islanders	2	0	0	0	2	0	0	0
1996	Boston	4	0	0	0	24	0	0	0
Playoff Totals		**6**	**0**	**0**	**0**	**26**	**0**	**0**	**0**
CHYZOWSKI, Dave									Left wing
1994	NY Islanders	2	0	0	0	0	0	0	0
Playoff Totals		**2**	**0**	**0**	**0**	**0**	**0**	**0**	**0**
CIAVAGLIA, Peter	*No playoffs*								Center

Season	Club	GP	G	A	Pts	PIM	PP	SH	GW
CICCARELLI, Dino									Right wing
1981	Minnesota	19	14	7	21	25	5	0	3
1982	Minnesota	4	3	1	4	2	2	0	1
1983	Minnesota	9	4	6	10	11	1	0	2
1984	Minnesota	16	4	5	9	27	1	0	1
1985	Minnesota	9	3	3	6	8	1	0	0
1986	Minnesota	5	0	1	1	6	0	0	0
1989	Washington	6	3	3	6	12	3	0	0
1990	Washington	8	8	3	11	6	1	0	1
1991	Washington	11	5	4	9	22	3	0	2
1992	Washington	7	5	4	9	14	1	0	0
1993	Detroit	7	4	2	6	16	3	0	0
1994	Detroit	7	5	2	7	14	1	0	0
1995	Detroit	16	9	2	11	22	6	0	2
1996	Detroit	17	6	2	8	26	6	0	1
Playoff Totals		**141**	**73**	**45**	**118**	**211**	**34**	**0**	**13**
CICCONE, Enrico									Defense
1996	Chicago	9	1	0	1	30	0	0	0
1997	Chicago	4	0	0	0	18	0	0	0
Playoff Totals		**13**	**1**	**0**	**1**	**48**	**0**	**0**	**0**
CICHOCKI, Chris	*No playoffs*								Right wing
CIERNIK, Ivan	*No playoffs*								Left wing
CIERNY, Jozef	*No playoffs*								Left wing
CIESLA, Hank									Center
1958	NY Rangers	6	0	2	2	0	0	0	0
Playoff Totals		**6**	**0**	**2**	**2**	**0**	**0**	**0**	**0**
CIGER, Zdeno									Left wing
1991	New Jersey	6	0	2	2	4	0	0	0
1992	New Jersey	7	2	4	6	0	0	0	1
Playoff Totals		**13**	**2**	**6**	**8**	**4**	**0**	**0**	**1**
CIMELLARO, Tony	*No playoffs*								Center
CIMETTA, Robert									Left/Right wing
1989	Boston	1	0	0	0	15	0	0	0
Playoff Totals		**1**	**0**	**0**	**0**	**15**	**0**	**0**	**0**
CIRELLA, Joe									Defense
1988	New Jersey	19	0	7	7	49	0	0	0
1991	NY Rangers	6	0	2	2	26	0	0	0
1992	NY Rangers	13	0	4	4	23	0	0	0
Playoff Totals		**38**	**0**	**13**	**13**	**98**	**0**	**0**	**0**
CIRONE, Jason	*No playoffs*								Center
CLACKSON, Kim									Defense
1980	Pittsburgh	3	0	0	0	37	0	0	0
1981	Quebec	5	0	0	0	33	0	0	0
Playoff Totals		**8**	**0**	**0**	**0**	**70**	**0**	**0**	**0**
CLANCY, King									Defense
1922	Ottawa	2	0	0	0	2	....	....	....
1923◆	Ottawa	8	1	0	1	2	....	....	....
1924	Ottawa	2	0	0	0	4	....	....	....
1926	Ottawa	2	1	0	1	8	....	....	....
1927◆	Ottawa	6	1	1	2	14	....	....	....
1928	Ottawa	2	0	0	0	6	....	....	....
1930	Ottawa	2	0	1	1	2	....	....	....
1931	Toronto	2	1	0	1	0	....	....	....
1932◆	Toronto	7	2	1	3	14	....	....	....
1933	Toronto	9	0	3	3	14	....	....	....
1934	Toronto	3	0	0	0	8	....	....	....
1935	Toronto	7	1	0	1	8	....	....	....
1936	Toronto	9	2	2	4	10	....	....	....
Playoff Totals		**61**	**9**	**8**	**17**	**92**	....	....	....
CLANCY, Terry	*No playoffs*								Right wing
CLAPPER, Dit									Right wing/defense
1928	Boston	2	0	0	0	2	....	....	....
1929◆	Boston	5	1	0	1	0	....	....	....
1930	Boston	6	4	0	4	4	....	....	....
1931	Boston	5	2	4	6	4	....	....	....
1933	Boston	5	1	1	2	2	....	....	....
1935	Boston	3	1	0	1	0	....	....	....
1936	Boston	2	0	1	1	0	....	....	....
1937	Boston	3	2	0	2	5	....	....	....
1938	Boston	3	0	0	0	12	....	....	....
1939◆	Boston	12	0	1	1	6	....	....	....
1940	Boston	5	0	2	2	2	....	....	....
1941◆	Boston	11	0	5	5	4	....	....	....
1943	Boston	9	2	3	5	9	....	....	....
1945	Boston	7	0	0	0	0	....	....	....
1946	Boston	4	0	0	0	0	....	....	....
Playoff Totals		**82**	**13**	**17**	**30**	**50**	....	....	....
CLARK, Brett	*No playoffs*								Defense
CLARK, Chris	*No playoffs*								Right wing
CLARK, Dan	*No playoffs*								Defense
CLARK, Dean	*No playoffs*								Defense
CLARK, Gordie									Right wing
1976	Boston	1	0	0	0	0	0	0	0
Playoff Totals		**1**	**0**	**0**	**0**	**0**	**0**	**0**	**0**
CLARK, Nobby	*No playoffs*								Defense

Season	Club	GP	G	A	Pts	PIM	PP	SH	GW
CLARK, Wendel									Left wing/defense
1986	Toronto	10	5	1	6	47	1	0	1
1987	Toronto	13	6	5	11	38	3	0	1
1990	Toronto	5	1	1	2	19	0	0	0
1993	Toronto	21	10	10	20	51	2	0	1
1994	Toronto	18	9	7	16	24	2	0	1
1995	Quebec	6	1	2	3	6	0	0	0
1996	Toronto	6	2	2	4	2	1	0	0
1999	Detroit	10	2	3	5	10	1	0	0
Playoff Totals		**89**	**36**	**31**	**67**	**197**	**10**	**0**	**4**
CLARKE, Bobby									Center
1971	Philadelphia	4	0	0	0	2	0	0	0
1973	Philadelphia	11	2	6	8	6	2	0	1
1974◆	Philadelphia	17	5	11	16	42	1	0	2
1975◆	Philadelphia	17	4	*12	16	16	2	1	2
1976	Philadelphia	16	2	*14	16	28	1	0	0
1977	Philadelphia	10	5	5	10	8	2	0	0
1978	Philadelphia	12	4	7	11	8	1	0	0
1979	Philadelphia	8	2	4	6	8	1	0	0
1980	Philadelphia	19	8	12	20	16	3	0	2
1981	Philadelphia	12	3	3	6	6	0	1	0
1982	Philadelphia	4	4	2	6	4	1	1	0
1983	Philadelphia	3	1	0	1	2	0	0	0
1984	Philadelphia	3	2	1	3	6	0	0	0
Playoff Totals		**136**	**42**	**77**	**119**	**152**	**14**	**3**	**7**
CLEARY, Daniel	*No playoffs*								Left wing
CLEGHORN, Odie									Right wing/Center
1919	Mtl. Canadiens	10	8	1	9	9	....	....	....
1923	Mtl. Canadiens	2	0	0	0	2	....	....	....
1924◆	Mtl. Canadiens	6	0	1	1	0	....	....	....
1925	Mtl. Canadiens	5	0	1	1	0	....	....	....
1926	Pittsburgh	1	0	0	0	0	....	....	....
Playoff Totals		**24**	**8**	**3**	**11**	**11**	....	....	....
CLEGHORN, Sprague									Defense
1919	Ottawa	5	2	2	4	12	....	....	....
1920◆	Ottawa	5	0	1	1	4	....	....	....
1921	Toronto	1	0	0	0	0	....	....	....
1921◆	Ottawa	5	1	2	3	36	....	....	....
1923	Mtl. Canadiens	1	0	0	0	0	....	....	....
1924◆	Mtl. Canadiens	6	2	1	3	2	....	....	....
1925	Mtl. Canadiens	6	1	2	3	4	....	....	....
1927	Boston	8	1	0	1	8	....	....	....
1928	Boston	2	0	0	0	0	....	....	....
Playoff Totals		**39**	**7**	**8**	**15**	**66**	....	....	....
CLEMENT, Bill									Center
1973	Philadelphia	2	0	0	0	0	0	0	0
1974◆	Philadelphia	4	1	0	1	4	0	0	0
1975◆	Philadelphia	12	1	0	1	8	0	0	0
1976	Atlanta	2	0	1	1	0	0	0	0
1977	Atlanta	3	1	1	2	0	0	1	0
1978	Atlanta	2	0	0	0	2	0	0	0
1979	Atlanta	2	0	0	0	0	0	0	0
1980	Atlanta	4	0	0	0	4	0	0	0
1981	Calgary	16	2	1	3	6	0	0	0
1982	Calgary	3	0	0	0	2	0	0	0
Playoff Totals		**50**	**5**	**3**	**8**	**26**	**0**	**1**	**0**
CLINE, Bruce	*No playoffs*								Right wing
CLIPPINGDALE, Steve									Left wing
1977	Los Angeles	1	0	0	0	0	0	0	0
Playoff Totals		**1**	**0**	**0**	**0**	**0**	**0**	**0**	**0**
CLOUTIER, Real									Right wing
1981	Quebec	3	0	0	0	10	0	0	0
1982	Quebec	16	7	5	12	10	1	0	1
1983	Quebec	4	0	0	0	0	0	0	0
1984	Buffalo	2	0	0	0	0	0	0	0
Playoff Totals		**25**	**7**	**5**	**12**	**20**	**1**	**0**	**1**
CLOUTIER, Rejean	*No playoffs*								Defense
CLOUTIER, Roland	*No playoffs*								Center
CLOUTIER, Sylvain	*No playoffs*								Center
CLUNE, Wally	*No playoffs*								Defense
CLYMER, Ben	*No playoffs*								Defense
COALTER, Gary	*No playoffs*								Right wing
COATES, Steve	*No playoffs*								Right wing
COCHRANE, Glen									Defense
1981	Philadelphia	6	1	1	2	18	0	0	0
1982	Philadelphia	2	0	0	0	2	0	0	0
1983	Philadelphia	3	0	0	0	4	0	0	0
1986	Vancouver	2	0	0	0	5	0	0	0
1988	Chicago	5	0	0	0	2	0	0	0
Playoff Totals		**18**	**1**	**1**	**2**	**31**	**0**	**0**	**0**

Season	Club	GP	G	A	Pts	PIM	PP	SH	GW
COFFEY, Paul									Defense
1981	Edmonton	9	4	3	7	22	1	0	0
1982	Edmonton	5	1	1	2	6	1	0	0
1983	Edmonton	16	7	7	14	14	2	2	0
1984◆	Edmonton	19	8	14	22	21	2	0	1
1985◆	Edmonton	18	12	25	37	44	3	1	4
1986	Edmonton	10	1	9	10	30	1	0	0
1987◆	Edmonton	17	3	8	11	30	1	0	1
1989	Pittsburgh	11	2	13	15	31	2	0	1
1991◆	Pittsburgh	12	2	9	11	6	0	0	0
1992	Los Angeles	6	4	3	7	2	3	0	0
1993	Detroit	7	2	9	11	2	0	0	0
1994	Detroit	7	1	6	7	8	0	0	0
1995	Detroit	18	6	12	18	10	2	1	0
1996	Detroit	17	5	9	14	30	3	2	1
1997	Philadelphia	17	1	8	9	6	0	0	0
1999	Carolina	5	0	1	1	2	0	0	0
Playoff Totals		**194**	**59**	**137**	**196**	**264**	**21**	**6**	**8**
COFLIN, Hugh	*No playoffs*								Defense
COLE, Danton									Center/Right wing
1995◆	New Jersey	1	0	0	0	0	0	0	0
Playoff Totals		**1**	**0**	**0**	**0**	**0**	**0**	**0**	**0**
COLLEY, Tom	*No playoffs*								Center
COLLINGS, Norm	*No playoffs*								Forward
COLLINS, Bill									Right wing
1968	Minnesota	10	2	4	6	4	0	0	1
1970	Minnesota	6	0	1	1	8	0	0	0
1975	St. Louis	2	1	0	1	0	0	0	0
Playoff Totals		**18**	**3**	**5**	**8**	**12**	**0**	**0**	**1**
COLLINS, Gary									Center
1959	Toronto	2	0	0	0	0	0	0	0
Playoff Totals		**2**	**0**	**0**	**0**	**0**	**0**	**0**	**0**
COLLYARD, Bob	*No playoffs*								Center
COLMAN, Michael	*No playoffs*								Defense
COLVILLE, Mac									Right wing/defense
1937	NY Rangers	9	1	2	3	2	....	....	....
1938	NY Rangers	3	0	2	2	0	....	....	....
1939	NY Rangers	7	1	2	3	4	....	....	....
1940◆	NY Rangers	12	3	2	5	6	....	....	....
1941	NY Rangers	3	1	1	2	2	....	....	....
1942	NY Rangers	6	3	1	4	0	....	....	....
Playoff Totals		**40**	**9**	**10**	**19**	**14**	....	....	....
COLVILLE, Neil									Center/defense
1937	NY Rangers	9	3	3	6	0	....	....	....
1938	NY Rangers	3	0	1	1	0	....	....	....
1939	NY Rangers	7	0	2	2	2	....	....	....
1940◆	NY Rangers	12	2	*7	*9	18	....	....	....
1941	NY Rangers	3	1	1	2	0	....	....	....
1942	NY Rangers	6	0	5	5	6	....	....	....
1948	NY Rangers	6	1	0	1	6	....	....	....
Playoff Totals		**46**	**7**	**19**	**26**	**32**	....	....	....
COLWILL, Les	*No playoffs*								Right wing
COMEAU, Rey									Center
1974	Atlanta	4	2	1	3	6	1	0	0
1977	Atlanta	3	0	0	0	2	0	0	0
1978	Atlanta	2	0	0	0	0	0	0	0
Playoff Totals		**9**	**2**	**1**	**3**	**8**	**1**	**0**	**0**
COMRIE, Paul	*No playoffs*								Center
CONACHER, Brian									Left wing
1967◆	Toronto	12	3	2	5	21	0	0	2
Playoff Totals		**12**	**3**	**2**	**5**	**21**	**0**	**0**	**2**
CONACHER, Charlie									Right wing
1931	Toronto	2	0	1	1	0	....	....	....
1932◆	Toronto	7	*6	2	8	6	....	....	....
1933	Toronto	9	1	1	2	10	....	....	....
1934	Toronto	5	3	2	5	0	....	....	....
1935	Toronto	7	1	*4	5	6	....	....	....
1936	Toronto	9	3	2	5	12	....	....	....
1937	Toronto	2	0	0	0	5	....	....	....
1939	Detroit	5	2	5	7	2	....	....	....
1940	NY Americans	3	1	1	2	8	....	....	....
Playoff Totals		**49**	**17**	**18**	**35**	**49**	....	....	....
CONACHER, Jim									Center
1946	Detroit	5	1	1	2	0	....	....	....
1947	Detroit	5	2	1	3	2	....	....	....
1948	Detroit	9	2	0	2	2	....	....	....
Playoff Totals		**19**	**5**	**2**	**7**	**4**	....	....	....
CONACHER, Lionel									Defense
1926	Pittsburgh	2	0	0	0	0	....	....	....
1929	NY Americans	2	0	0	0	10	....	....	....
1931	Mtl. Maroons	2	0	0	0	2	....	....	....
1932	Mtl. Maroons	4	0	0	0	2	....	....	....
1933	Mtl. Maroons	2	0	1	1	0	....	....	....
1934◆	Chicago	8	2	0	2	4	....	....	....
1935◆	Mtl. Maroons	7	0	0	0	14	....	....	....
1936	Mtl. Maroons	3	0	0	0	0	....	....	....
1937	Mtl. Maroons	5	0	1	1	2	....	....	....
Playoff Totals		**35**	**2**	**2**	**4**	**34**	....	....	....

Season	Club	GP	G	A	Pts	PIM	PP	SH	GW
CONACHER, Pat									Left wing
1980	NY Rangers	3	0	1	1	2	0	0	0
1984◆	Edmonton	3	1	0	1	2	0	0	0
1988	New Jersey	17	2	2	4	14	0	1	1
1990	New Jersey	5	1	0	1	10	0	0	0
1991	New Jersey	7	0	2	2	2	0	0	0
1992	New Jersey	7	1	1	2	4	0	1	0
1993	Los Angeles	24	6	4	10	6	0	0	0
Playoff Totals		**66**	**11**	**10**	**21**	**40**	**0**	**2**	**1**
CONACHER, Pete									Left wing
1953	Chicago	2	0	0	0	0	0	0	0
1956	NY Rangers	5	0	0	0	0	0	0	0
Playoff Totals		**7**	**0**	**0**	**0**	**0**	**0**	**0**	**0**
CONACHER, Roy									Left wing
1939◆	Boston	12	6	4	10	12	....	....	....
1940	Boston	6	2	1	3	0	....	....	....
1941◆	Boston	11	1	5	6	0	....	....	....
1942	Boston	5	2	1	3	0	....	....	....
1946	Boston	3	0	0	0	0	....	....	....
1947	Detroit	5	4	4	8	2	....	....	....
Playoff Totals		**42**	**15**	**15**	**30**	**14**	....	....	....
CONN, Hugh	*No playoffs*								Left wing
CONN, Rob	*No playoffs*								Left/Right wing
CONNELLY, Bert									Left wing
1935	NY Rangers	4	1	0	1	0	....	....	....
1938◆	Chicago	10	0	0	0	0	....	....	....
Playoff Totals		**14**	**1**	**0**	**1**	**0**	....	....	....
CONNELLY, Wayne									Center
1968	Minnesota	14	*8	3	11	2	3	0	0
1970	Detroit	4	1	3	4	2	1	0	0
1971	St. Louis	6	2	1	3	0	1	0	1
Playoff Totals		**24**	**11**	**7**	**18**	**4**	**5**	**0**	**1**
CONNOLLY, Tim	*No playoffs*								Center
CONNOR, Cam									Right wing
1979◆	Montreal	8	1	0	1	0	0	0	1
1980	NY Rangers	2	0	0	0	2	0	0	0
1982	NY Rangers	10	4	0	4	4	1	0	1
Playoff Totals		**20**	**5**	**0**	**5**	**6**	**1**	**0**	**2**
CONNOR, Harry									Left wing
1928	Boston	2	0	0	0	0	0	0	0
1929	NY Americans	2	0	0	0	2	0	0	0
1930	Boston	6	0	0	0	0	0	0	0
Playoff Totals		**10**	**0**	**0**	**0**	**2**	**0**	**0**	**0**
CONNORS, Bobby									Left wing/Defense
1929	Detroit	2	0	0	0	10	0	0	0
Playoff Totals		**2**	**0**	**0**	**0**	**10**	**0**	**0**	**0**
CONROY, Al	*No playoffs*								Center
CONROY, Craig									Center
1997	St. Louis	6	0	0	0	8	0	0	0
1998	St. Louis	10	1	2	3	8	0	0	1
1999	St. Louis	13	2	1	3	6	0	0	0
Playoff Totals		**29**	**3**	**3**	**6**	**22**	**0**	**0**	**1**
CONTINI, Joe									Center
1978	Colorado	2	0	0	0	0	0	0	0
Playoff Totals		**2**	**0**	**0**	**0**	**0**	**0**	**0**	**0**
CONVERY, Brandon									Center
1996	Toronto	5	0	0	0	2	0	0	0
Playoff Totals		**5**	**0**	**0**	**0**	**2**	**0**	**0**	**0**
CONVEY, Eddie	*No playoffs*								Left wing/center
COOK, Bill									Right wing
1927	NY Rangers	2	1	0	1	6	....	....	....
1928◆	NY Rangers	9	2	3	5	26	....	....	....
1929	NY Rangers	6	0	0	0	6	....	....	....
1930	NY Rangers	4	0	1	1	11	....	....	....
1931	NY Rangers	4	3	0	3	4	....	....	....
1932	NY Rangers	7	3	3	6	2	....	....	....
1933◆	NY Rangers	8	3	2	5	4	....	....	....
1934	NY Rangers	2	0	0	0	2	....	....	....
1935	NY Rangers	4	1	2	3	7	....	....	....
Playoff Totals		**46**	**13**	**11**	**24**	**68**	....	....	....
COOK, Bob	*No playoffs*								Right wing
COOK, Bud	*No playoffs*								Center
COOK, Bun									Left wing
1927	NY Rangers	2	0	0	0	6	....	....	....
1928◆	NY Rangers	9	2	1	3	10	....	....	....
1929	NY Rangers	6	1	0	1	12	....	....	....
1930	NY Rangers	4	2	0	2	2	....	....	....
1931	NY Rangers	4	0	0	0	2	....	....	....
1932	NY Rangers	7	6	2	8	12	....	....	....
1933◆	NY Rangers	8	2	0	2	4	....	....	....
1934	NY Rangers	2	0	0	0	2	....	....	....
1935	NY Rangers	4	2	0	2	0	....	....	....
Playoff Totals		**46**	**15**	**3**	**18**	**50**	....	....	....
COOK, Lloyd	*No playoffs*								Defense

Season	Club	GP	G	A	Pts	PIM	PP	SH	GW
COOK, Tom									Center
1930	Chicago	2	0	1	1	4	....	....	....
1931	Chicago	9	1	3	4	11	....	....	....
1932	Chicago	2	0	0	0	2	....	....	....
1934◆	Chicago	8	1	0	1	0	....	....	....
1935	Chicago	2	0	0	0	2	....	....	....
1936	Chicago	1	0	0	0	0	....	....	....
Playoff Totals		**24**	**2**	**4**	**6**	**19**	....	....	....
COOKE, Matt	*No playoffs*								Left wing
COOPER, Carson									Right wing
1927	Mtl. Canadiens	3	0	0	0	0	0	0	0
1929	Detroit	2	0	0	0	2	0	0	0
1932	Detroit	2	0	0	0	0	0	0	0
Playoff Totals		**7**	**0**	**0**	**0**	**2**	**0**	**0**	**0**
COOPER, David	*No playoffs*								Defense
COOPER, Ed	*No playoffs*								Left wing
COOPER, Hal	*No playoffs*								Right wing
COOPER, Joe									Defense
1937	NY Rangers	9	1	1	2	12	....	....	....
1938	NY Rangers	3	0	0	0	4	....	....	....
1940	Chicago	2	0	0	0	0	....	....	....
1941	Chicago	5	1	0	1	8	....	....	....
1942	Chicago	3	0	2	2	2	....	....	....
1944	Chicago	9	1	1	2	18	....	....	....
1946	Chicago	4	0	1	1	14	....	....	....
Playoff Totals		**35**	**3**	**5**	**8**	**58**	....	....	....
COPP, Bob	*No playoffs*								Defense
CORBEAU, Bert									Defense
1918	Mtl. Canadiens	2	1	1	2	11	....	....	....
1919	Mtl. Canadiens	10	1	2	3	20	....	....	....
1925	Toronto	2	0	0	0	0	....	....	....
Playoff Totals		**14**	**2**	**3**	**5**	**31**	....	....	....
CORBET, Rene									Left wing
1995	Quebec	2	0	1	1	0	0	0	0
1996◆	Colorado	8	3	2	5	2	1	0	1
1997	Colorado	17	2	2	4	27	0	0	0
1998	Colorado	2	0	0	0	2	0	0	0
Playoff Totals		**29**	**5**	**5**	**10**	**31**	**1**	**0**	**1**
CORBETT, Michael									Right wing/defense
1968	Los Angeles	2	0	1	1	2	0	0	0
Playoff Totals		**2**	**0**	**1**	**1**	**2**	**0**	**0**	**0**
CORCORAN, Norm									Center/right wing
1955	Boston	4	0	0	0	6	0	0	0
Playoff Totals		**4**	**0**	**0**	**0**	**6**	**0**	**0**	**0**
CORKUM, Bob									Center
1990	Buffalo	5	1	0	1	4	0	0	0
1992	Buffalo	4	1	0	1	0	1	0	0
1993	Buffalo	5	0	0	0	2	0	0	0
1996	Philadelphia	12	1	2	3	6	0	0	0
1997	Phoenix	7	2	2	4	4	0	0	1
1998	Phoenix	6	1	0	1	4	0	0	0
1999	Phoenix	7	0	1	1	4	0	0	0
Playoff Totals		**46**	**6**	**5**	**11**	**24**	**1**	**0**	**1**
CORMIER, Roger	*No playoffs*								Right wing
CORNFORTH, Mark	*No playoffs*								Defense
CORRIGAN, Chuck	*No playoffs*								Right wing
CORRIGAN, Mike									Left wing
1974	Los Angeles	3	0	1	1	4	0	0	0
1975	Los Angeles	3	0	0	0	4	0	0	0
1976	Los Angeles	9	2	2	4	12	0	0	0
1977	Pittsburgh	2	0	0	0	0	0	0	0
Playoff Totals		**17**	**2**	**3**	**5**	**20**	**0**	**0**	**0**
CORRIVEAU, Andre	*No playoffs*								Right wing
CORRIVEAU, Yvon									Left wing
1986	Washington	4	0	3	3	2	0	0	0
1988	Washington	13	1	2	3	30	0	0	0
1989	Washington	1	0	0	0	0	0	0	0
1990	Hartford	4	1	0	1	0	0	0	0
1992	Hartford	7	3	2	5	18	2	0	1
Playoff Totals		**29**	**5**	**7**	**12**	**50**	**2**	**0**	**1**
CORSON, Shayne									Left wing
1987	Montreal	17	6	5	11	30	1	1	1
1988	Montreal	3	1	0	1	12	0	0	0
1989	Montreal	21	4	5	9	65	2	0	2
1990	Montreal	11	2	8	10	20	0	0	0
1991	Montreal	13	9	6	15	36	4	1	3
1992	Montreal	10	2	5	7	15	0	0	0
1996	St. Louis	13	8	6	14	22	6	1	1
1997	Montreal	5	1	0	1	4	0	1	0
1998	Montreal	10	3	6	9	26	1	0	1
Playoff Totals		**103**	**36**	**41**	**77**	**230**	**14**	**4**	**8**
CORY, Ross	*No playoffs*								Defense
COSSETTE, Jacques									Right wing
1979	Pittsburgh	3	0	1	1	4	0	0	0
Playoff Totals		**3**	**0**	**1**	**1**	**4**	**0**	**0**	**0**

Season	Club	GP	G	A	Pts	PIM	PP	SH	GW
COSTELLO, Les	Left wing								
1948♦	Toronto	5	2	2	4	2	....	....	....
1950	Toronto	1	0	0	0	0	....	....	....
Playoff Totals		**6**	**2**	**2**	**4**	**2**	....	....	....
COSTELLO, Murray	Center								
1955	Boston	1	0	0	0	2	0	0	0
1956	Detroit	4	0	0	0	0	0	0	0
Playoff Totals		**5**	**0**	**0**	**0**	**2**	**0**	**0**	**0**
COSTELLO, Rich	*No playoffs* Center								
COTCH, Charlie	*No playoffs* Left wing								
COTE, Alain	Defense								
1991	Montreal	11	0	2	2	26	0	0	0
Playoff Totals		**11**	**0**	**2**	**2**	**26**	**0**	**0**	**0**
COTE, Alain	Left wing								
1981	Quebec	4	0	0	0	6	0	0	0
1982	Quebec	16	1	2	3	8	0	0	0
1983	Quebec	4	0	3	3	0	0	0	0
1984	Quebec	9	0	2	2	17	0	0	0
1985	Quebec	18	5	5	10	11	0	0	1
1986	Quebec	3	1	0	1	0	0	0	0
1987	Quebec	13	2	3	5	2	0	0	0
Playoff Totals		**67**	**9**	**15**	**24**	**44**	**0**	**0**	**1**
COTE, Patrick	*No playoffs* Left wing								
COTE, Ray	Center								
1983	Edmonton	14	3	2	5	0	0	0	0
Playoff Totals		**14**	**3**	**2**	**5**	**0**	**0**	**0**	**0**
COTE, Sylvain	Defense								
1987	Hartford	2	0	2	2	2	0	0	0
1988	Hartford	6	1	1	2	4	1	0	0
1989	Hartford	3	0	1	1	4	0	0	0
1990	Hartford	5	0	0	0	2	0	0	0
1991	Hartford	6	0	2	2	2	0	0	0
1992	Washington	7	1	2	3	4	0	0	0
1993	Washington	6	1	1	2	4	0	0	0
1994	Washington	9	1	8	9	6	0	0	0
1995	Washington	7	1	3	4	2	0	0	0
1996	Washington	6	2	0	2	12	1	0	0
1999	Toronto	17	2	1	3	10	0	0	0
Playoff Totals		**74**	**9**	**21**	**30**	**52**	**2**	**0**	**0**
COTTON, Baldy	Left wing								
1926	Pittsburgh	2	1	0	1	0	....	....	....
1928	Pittsburgh	2	1	1	2	2	....	....	....
1929	Toronto	4	0	0	0	2	....	....	....
1931	Toronto	2	0	0	0	2	....	....	....
1932♦	Toronto	7	2	2	4	8	....	....	....
1933	Toronto	9	0	3	3	6	....	....	....
1934	Toronto	5	0	2	2	0	....	....	....
1935	Toronto	7	0	0	0	17	....	....	....
1936	NY Americans	5	0	1	1	9	....	....	....
Playoff Totals		**43**	**4**	**9**	**13**	**46**	....	....	....
COUGHLIN, Jack	*No playoffs* Right wing								
COULIS, Tim	Left wing								
1985	Minnesota	3	1	0	1	2	0	0	1
Playoff Totals		**3**	**1**	**0**	**1**	**2**	**0**	**0**	**1**
COULSON, D'arcy	*No playoffs* Defense								
COULTER, Art	Defense								
1932	Chicago	2	1	0	1	0	....	....	....
1934♦	Chicago	8	1	0	1	10	....	....	....
1935	Chicago	2	0	0	0	5	....	....	....
1937	NY Rangers	9	0	3	3	15	....	....	....
1939	NY Rangers	7	1	1	2	6	....	....	....
1940♦	NY Rangers	12	1	0	1	21	....	....	....
1941	NY Rangers	3	0	0	0	0	....	....	....
1942	NY Rangers	6	0	1	1	4	....	....	....
Playoff Totals		**49**	**4**	**5**	**9**	**61**	....	....	....
COULTER, Neal	*No playoffs* Right wing								
COURNOYER, Yvan	Right wing								
1965♦	Montreal	12	3	1	4	0	3	0	1
1966♦	Montreal	10	2	3	5	2	1	0	1
1967	Montreal	10	2	3	5	6	2	0	1
1968♦	Montreal	13	6	8	14	4	3	0	1
1969♦	Montreal	14	4	7	11	5	0	2	2
1971♦	Montreal	20	10	12	22	6	2	0	1
1972	Montreal	6	2	1	3	2	0	0	0
1973♦	Montreal	17	*15	10	*25	2	3	0	3
1974	Montreal	6	5	2	7	2	0	0	2
1975	Montreal	11	5	6	11	4	2	0	0
1976♦	Montreal	13	3	6	9	4	2	0	1
1978♦	Montreal	15	7	4	11	10	0	0	2
Playoff Totals		**147**	**64**	**63**	**127**	**47**	**18**	**2**	**15**
COURTEAU, Yves	Right wing								
1986	Calgary	1	0	0	0	0	0	0	0
Playoff Totals		**1**	**0**	**0**	**0**	**0**	**0**	**0**	**0**
COURTENAY, Ed	*No playoffs* Right wing								

Season	Club	GP	G	A	Pts	PIM	PP	SH	GW
COURTNALL, Geoff	Left wing								
1985	Boston	5	0	2	2	7	0	0	0
1986	Boston	3	0	0	0	2	0	0	0
1987	Boston	1	0	0	0	0	0	0	0
1988♦	Edmonton	19	0	3	3	23	0	0	0
1989	Washington	6	2	5	7	12	1	0	0
1990	Washington	15	4	9	13	32	1	0	2
1991	Vancouver	6	3	5	8	4	0	0	0
1992	Vancouver	12	6	8	14	20	2	0	1
1993	Vancouver	12	4	10	14	12	1	0	1
1994	Vancouver	24	9	10	19	51	0	1	3
1995	Vancouver	11	4	2	6	34	3	1	1
1996	St. Louis	13	0	3	3	14	0	0	0
1997	St. Louis	6	3	1	4	23	1	0	2
1998	St. Louis	10	2	8	10	18	1	0	0
1999	St. Louis	13	2	4	6	10	2	0	0
Playoff Totals		**156**	**39**	**70**	**109**	**262**	**12**	**2**	**10**
COURTNALL, Russ	Right wing								
1986	Toronto	10	3	6	9	8	1	0	0
1987	Toronto	13	3	4	7	11	1	0	0
1988	Toronto	6	2	1	3	0	0	0	0
1989	Montreal	21	8	5	13	18	1	0	2
1990	Montreal	11	5	1	6	10	0	0	0
1991	Montreal	13	8	3	11	7	2	2	1
1992	Montreal	10	1	1	2	4	0	0	1
1994	Dallas	9	1	8	9	0	0	0	0
1995	Vancouver	11	4	8	12	21	0	2	1
1996	Vancouver	6	1	3	4	2	0	0	0
1997	NY Rangers	15	3	4	7	0	1	0	0
1998	Los Angeles	4	0	0	0	2	0	0	0
Playoff Totals		**129**	**39**	**44**	**83**	**83**	**6**	**4**	**5**
COURVILLE, Larry	*No playoffs* Left wing								
COUTU, Billy	Defense								
1918	Mtl. Canadiens	2	0	0	0	0	....	....	....
1919	Mtl. Canadiens	10	0	2	2	8	....	....	....
1923	Mtl. Canadiens	1	0	0	0	*12	....	....	....
1924♦	Mtl. Canadiens	6	0	0	0	2	....	....	....
1925	Mtl. Canadiens	6	1	0	1	14	....	....	....
1927	Boston	7	1	0	1	4	....	....	....
Playoff Totals		**32**	**2**	**2**	**4**	**40**	....	....	....
COUTURE, Gerry	Right wing								
1945	Detroit	2	0	0	0	0	....	....	....
1946	Detroit	5	0	2	2	0	....	....	....
1947	Detroit	1	0	0	0	0	....	....	....
1949	Detroit	10	2	0	2	2	....	....	....
1950♦	Detroit	14	5	4	9	2	....	....	....
1951	Detroit	6	1	1	2	0	....	....	....
1953	Chicago	7	1	0	1	0	....	....	....
Playoff Totals		**45**	**9**	**7**	**16**	**4**	....	....	....
COUTURE, Rosie	Right wing								
1930	Chicago	2	0	0	0	2	....	....	....
1931	Chicago	9	0	3	3	2	....	....	....
1932	Chicago	2	0	0	0	2	....	....	....
1934♦	Chicago	8	1	2	3	4	....	....	....
1935	Chicago	2	0	0	0	5	....	....	....
Playoff Totals		**23**	**1**	**5**	**6**	**15**	....	....	....
COUTURIER, Sylvain	*No playoffs* Center								
COWICK, Bruce	Left wing								
1974♦	Philadelphia	8	0	0	0	9	0	0	0
Playoff Totals		**8**	**0**	**0**	**0**	**9**	**0**	**0**	**0**
COWIE, Rob	*No playoffs* Defense								
COWLEY, Bill	Center								
1936	Boston	2	2	1	3	2	....	....	....
1937	Boston	3	0	3	3	0	....	....	....
1938	Boston	3	2	0	2	0	....	....	....
1939♦	Boston	12	3	11	14	2	....	....	....
1940	Boston	6	0	1	1	7	....	....	....
1941♦	Boston	2	0	0	0	0	....	....	....
1942	Boston	5	0	3	3	5	....	....	....
1943	Boston	9	1	7	8	4	....	....	....
1945	Boston	7	3	3	6	0	....	....	....
1946	Boston	10	1	3	4	2	....	....	....
1947	Boston	5	0	2	2	0	....	....	....
Playoff Totals		**64**	**12**	**34**	**46**	**22**	....	....	....
COX, Danny	Left wing								
1929	Toronto	4	0	1	1	4	0	0	0
1930	Ottawa	2	0	0	0	0	0	0	0
1932	Detroit	2	0	0	0	2	0	0	0
1934	NY Rangers	2	0	0	0	0	0	0	0
Playoff Totals		**10**	**0**	**1**	**1**	**6**	**0**	**0**	**0**
COXE, Craig	Left wing								
1986	Vancouver	3	0	0	0	2	0	0	0
1988	Calgary	2	1	0	1	16	0	0	0
Playoff Totals		**5**	**1**	**0**	**1**	**18**	**0**	**0**	**0**
CRAIG, Mike	Right wing								
1991	Minnesota	10	1	1	2	20	1	0	1
1992	Minnesota	4	1	0	1	7	0	0	0
1994	Dallas	4	0	0	0	2	0	0	0
1995	Toronto	2	0	1	1	2	0	0	0
1996	Toronto	6	0	0	0	18	0	0	0
Playoff Totals		**26**	**2**	**2**	**4**	**49**	**1**	**0**	**1**

Season	Club	GP	G	A	Pts	PIM	PP	SH	GW
CRAIGHEAD, John	*No playoffs* Right wing								
CRAIGWELL, Dale	*No playoffs* Center								
CRASHLEY, Bart	*No playoffs* Defense								
CRAVEN, Murray	Left wing								
1985	Philadelphia	19	4	6	10	11	1	1	1
1986	Philadelphia	5	0	3	3	4	0	0	0
1987	Philadelphia	12	3	1	4	9	2	0	0
1988	Philadelphia	7	2	5	7	4	0	0	1
1989	Philadelphia	1	0	0	0	0	0	0	0
1992	Hartford	7	3	3	6	6	0	1	0
1993	Vancouver	12	4	6	10	4	1	0	1
1994	Vancouver	22	4	9	13	18	0	0	1
1995	Chicago	16	5	5	10	4	0	0	1
1996	Chicago	9	1	4	5	2	1	0	0
1997	Chicago	2	0	0	0	2	0	0	0
1998	San Jose	6	1	1	2	0	0	0	0
Playoff Totals		**118**	**27**	**43**	**70**	**64**	**5**	**2**	**5**
CRAWFORD, Bob	Right wing								
1983	St. Louis	4	0	0	0	0	0	0	0
1986	NY Rangers	7	0	1	1	8	0	0	0
Playoff Totals		**11**	**0**	**1**	**1**	**8**	**0**	**0**	**0**
CRAWFORD, Bobby	*No playoffs* Right wing								
CRAWFORD, Jack	Defense								
1939♦	Boston	12	1	1	2	9	....	....	....
1940	Boston	6	0	0	0	0	....	....	....
1941♦	Boston	11	0	2	2	7	....	....	....
1942	Boston	5	0	1	1	4	....	....	....
1943	Boston	6	1	1	2	10	....	....	....
1945	Boston	7	0	5	5	0	....	....	....
1946	Boston	10	1	2	3	4	....	....	....
1947	Boston	2	1	0	1	0	....	....	....
1948	Boston	4	0	1	1	2	....	....	....
1949	Boston	3	0	0	0	0	....	....	....
Playoff Totals		**66**	**4**	**13**	**17**	**36**	....	....	....
CRAWFORD, Lou	*No playoffs* Left wing								
CRAWFORD, Marc	Left wing								
1982	Vancouver	14	1	0	1	11	0	0	0
1983	Vancouver	3	0	1	1	25	0	0	0
1986	Vancouver	3	0	1	1	8	0	0	0
Playoff Totals		**20**	**1**	**2**	**3**	**44**	**0**	**0**	**0**
CRAWFORD, Rusty	Left wing								
1918♦	Toronto	2	2	1	3	9	....	....	....
Playoff Totals		**2**	**2**	**1**	**3**	**9**	....	....	....
CREIGHTON, Adam	Center								
1989	Chicago	15	5	6	11	44	3	1	0
1990	Chicago	20	3	6	9	59	0	1	0
1991	Chicago	6	0	1	1	10	0	0	0
1995	St. Louis	7	2	0	2	16	1	0	1
1996	St. Louis	13	1	1	2	8	0	0	0
Playoff Totals		**61**	**11**	**14**	**25**	**137**	**4**	**2**	**1**
CREIGHTON, Dave	Center								
1949	Boston	3	0	0	0	0	....	....	....
1951	Boston	5	0	1	1	0	....	....	....
1952	Boston	7	2	1	3	2	....	....	....
1953	Boston	11	4	5	9	10	....	....	....
1954	Boston	4	0	0	0	0	....	....	....
1956	NY Rangers	5	0	0	0	4	....	....	....
1957	NY Rangers	5	2	2	4	2	....	....	....
1958	NY Rangers	6	3	3	6	2	....	....	....
1959	Toronto	5	0	1	1	0	....	....	....
Playoff Totals		**51**	**11**	**13**	**24**	**20**	....	....	....
CREIGHTON, Jimmy	*No playoffs* Forward								
CRESSMAN, Dave	*No playoffs* Left wing								
CRESSMAN, Glen	*No playoffs* Center								
CRISP, Terry	Center								
1968	St. Louis	18	1	5	6	6	0	0	0
1969	St. Louis	12	3	4	7	20	0	2	0
1970	St. Louis	16	2	3	5	2	1	0	0
1971	St. Louis	6	1	0	1	2	0	0	0
1972	St. Louis	11	1	3	4	2	0	0	0
1973	Philadelphia	11	3	2	5	2	1	0	0
1974♦	Philadelphia	17	2	2	4	4	0	1	1
1975♦	Philadelphia	9	2	4	6	0	0	0	0
1976	Philadelphia	10	0	5	5	2	0	0	0
Playoff Totals		**110**	**15**	**28**	**43**	**40**	**2**	**3**	**1**
CRISTOFOLI, Ed	*No playoffs* Right wing								
CROGHEN, Maurice	*No playoffs* Defense								
CROMBEEN, Mike	Right wing								
1980	St. Louis	2	0	0	0	0	0	0	0
1981	St. Louis	11	3	0	3	8	0	0	2
1982	St. Louis	10	3	1	4	20	0	0	1
1983	St. Louis	4	0	1	1	4	0	0	0
Playoff Totals		**27**	**6**	**2**	**8**	**32**	**0**	**0**	**3**
CRONIN, Shawn	Defense								
1990	Winnipeg	5	0	0	0	7	0	0	0
1992	Winnipeg	4	0	0	0	6	0	0	0
1994	San Jose	14	1	0	1	20	0	0	0
1995	San Jose	9	0	0	0	5	0	0	0
Playoff Totals		**32**	**1**	**0**	**1**	**38**	**0**	**0**	**0**

Season	Club	GP	G	A	Pts	PIM	PP	SH	GW
CROSS, Cory									Defense
1996	Tampa Bay	6	0	0	0	22	0	0	0
Playoff Totals		**6**	**0**	**0**	**0**	**22**	**0**	**0**	**0**
CROSSETT, Stan	*No playoffs*								Defense
CROSSMAN, Doug									Defense
1982	Chicago	11	0	3	3	4	0	0	0
1983	Chicago	13	3	7	10	6	1	0	0
1984	Philadelphia	3	0	0	0	0	0	0	0
1985	Philadelphia	19	4	6	10	38	3	0	0
1986	Philadelphia	5	0	1	1	4	0	0	0
1987	Philadelphia	26	4	14	18	31	2	0	0
1988	Philadelphia	7	1	1	2	8	1	0	0
1989	Los Angeles	2	0	1	1	2	0	0	0
1990	NY Islanders	5	0	1	1	6	0	0	0
1991	Detroit	6	0	5	5	6	0	0	0
Playoff Totals		**97**	**12**	**39**	**51**	**105**	**7**	**0**	**0**
CROTEAU, Gary									Left wing
1969	Los Angeles	11	3	2	5	8	1	0	0
Playoff Totals		**11**	**3**	**2**	**5**	**8**	**1**	**0**	**0**
CROWDER, Bruce									Right wing
1982	Boston	11	5	3	8	9	1	0	0
1983	Boston	17	3	1	4	32	0	0	1
1984	Boston	3	0	0	0	0	0	0	0
Playoff Totals		**31**	**8**	**4**	**12**	**41**	**1**	**0**	**1**
CROWDER, Keith									Right wing
1981	Boston	3	2	0	2	9	0	0	0
1982	Boston	11	2	2	4	14	0	0	0
1983	Boston	17	1	6	7	54	1	0	0
1984	Boston	3	0	0	0	7	0	0	0
1985	Boston	4	3	2	5	19	0	0	1
1986	Boston	3	2	0	2	21	0	0	0
1987	Boston	4	0	1	1	4	0	0	0
1988	Boston	23	3	9	12	44	1	0	0
1989	Boston	10	0	2	2	37	0	0	0
1990	Los Angeles	7	1	0	1	9	0	0	0
Playoff Totals		**85**	**14**	**22**	**36**	**218**	**2**	**0**	**1**
CROWDER, Troy									Right wing
1988	New Jersey	1	0	0	0	12	0	0	0
1990	New Jersey	2	0	0	0	10	0	0	0
1992	Detroit	1	0	0	0	0	0	0	0
Playoff Totals		**4**	**0**	**0**	**0**	**22**	**0**	**0**	**0**
CROWE, Philip									Left wing
1997	Ottawa	3	0	0	0	16	0	0	0
Playoff Totals		**3**	**0**	**0**	**0**	**16**	**0**	**0**	**0**
CROWLEY, Mike	*No playoffs*								Defense
CROWLEY, Ted	*No playoffs*								Defense
CROZIER, Joe	*No playoffs*								Defense
CRUTCHFIELD, Nels									Center
1935	Mtl. Canadiens	2	0	1	1	22	0	0	0
Playoff Totals		**2**	**0**	**1**	**1**	**22**	**0**	**0**	**0**
CULHANE, Jim	*No playoffs*								Defense
CULLEN, Barry									Right wing
1959	Toronto	2	0	0	0	0	0	0	0
1960	Detroit	4	0	0	0	2	0	0	0
Playoff Totals		**6**	**0**	**0**	**0**	**2**	**0**	**0**	**0**
CULLEN, Brian									Center
1955	Toronto	4	1	0	1	0	1	0	0
1956	Toronto	5	1	0	1	2	1	0	0
1959	Toronto	10	1	0	1	0	0	0	0
Playoff Totals		**19**	**3**	**0**	**3**	**2**	**2**	**0**	**0**
CULLEN, John									Center
1989	Pittsburgh	11	3	6	9	28	0	0	0
1991	Hartford	6	2	7	9	10	0	0	0
1992	Hartford	7	2	1	3	12	1	0	1
1993	Toronto	12	2	3	5	0	1	0	0
1994	Toronto	3	0	0	0	0	0	0	0
1995	Pittsburgh	9	0	2	2	8	0	0	0
1996	Tampa Bay	5	3	3	6	0	0	1	0
Playoff Totals		**53**	**12**	**22**	**34**	**58**	**2**	**1**	**1**
CULLEN, Matt									Center
1999	Anaheim	4	0	0	0	0	0	0	0
Playoff Totals		**4**	**0**	**0**	**0**	**0**	**0**	**0**	**0**
CULLEN, Ray									Center
1968	Minnesota	14	2	6	8	2	1	0	0
1970	Minnesota	6	1	4	5	0	0	0	0
Playoff Totals		**20**	**3**	**10**	**13**	**2**	**1**	**0**	**0**
CULLIMORE, Jassen									Defense
1995	Vancouver	11	0	0	0	12	0	0	0
1997	Montreal	2	0	0	0	2	0	0	0
Playoff Totals		**13**	**0**	**0**	**0**	**14**	**0**	**0**	**0**
CUMMINS, Barry	*No playoffs*								Defense
CUMMINS, Jim									Right wing
1995	Chicago	14	1	1	2	4	0	0	1
1996	Chicago	10	0	0	0	2	0	0	0
1997	Chicago	6	0	0	0	24	0	0	0
1998	Phoenix	3	0	0	0	4	0	0	0
1999	Phoenix	3	0	1	1	0	0	0	0
Playoff Totals		**36**	**1**	**2**	**3**	**34**	**0**	**0**	**1**

Season	Club	GP	G	A	Pts	PIM	PP	SH	GW
CUNNEYWORTH, Randy									Left wing
1989	Pittsburgh	11	3	5	8	26	1	0	1
1990	Hartford	4	0	0	0	2	0	0	0
1991	Hartford	1	0	0	0	0	0	0	0
1992	Hartford	7	3	0	3	9	1	1	1
1994	Chicago	6	0	0	0	8	0	0	0
1997	Ottawa	7	1	1	2	10	0	0	0
1998	Ottawa	6	0	1	1	6	0	0	0
1999	Buffalo	3	0	0	0	0	0	0	0
Playoff Totals		**45**	**7**	**7**	**14**	**61**	**2**	**1**	**2**
CUNNINGHAM, Bob	*No playoffs*								Center
CUNNINGHAM, Jim	*No playoffs*								Left wing
CUNNINGHAM, Les									Center
1940	Chicago	1	0	0	0	0	0	0	0
Playoff Totals		**1**	**0**	**0**	**0**	**0**	**0**	**0**	**0**
CUPOLO, Bill									Right wing
1945	Boston	7	1	2	3	0	....	....	....
Playoff Totals		**7**	**1**	**2**	**3**	**0**	....	....	....
CURRAN, Brian									Defense
1984	Boston	3	0	0	0	7	0	0	0
1986	Boston	2	0	0	0	4	0	0	0
1987	NY Islanders	8	0	0	0	51	0	0	0
1988	Toronto	6	0	0	0	41	0	0	0
1990	Toronto	5	0	1	1	19	0	0	0
Playoff Totals		**24**	**0**	**1**	**1**	**122**	**0**	**0**	**0**
CURRIE, Dan	*No playoffs*								Left wing
CURRIE, Glen									Center
1983	Washington	4	0	3	3	4	0	0	0
1984	Washington	8	1	0	1	0	0	0	0
Playoff Totals		**12**	**1**	**3**	**4**	**4**	**0**	**0**	**0**
CURRIE, Hugh	*No playoffs*								Defense
CURRIE, Tony									Right wing
1980	St. Louis	2	0	0	0	0	0	0	0
1981	St. Louis	11	4	12	16	4	1	0	0
1982	Vancouver	3	0	0	0	10	0	0	0
Playoff Totals		**16**	**4**	**12**	**16**	**14**	**1**	**0**	**0**
CURRY, Floyd									Right wing
1949	Montreal	2	0	0	0	2	....	....	....
1950	Montreal	5	1	0	1	2	....	....	....
1951	Montreal	11	0	2	2	2	....	....	....
1952	Montreal	11	4	3	*7	6	....	....	....
1953◆	Montreal	12	2	1	3	2	....	....	....
1954	Montreal	11	4	0	4	4	....	....	....
1955	Montreal	12	8	4	12	4	....	....	....
1956◆	Montreal	10	1	5	6	12	....	....	....
1957◆	Montreal	10	3	2	5	2	....	....	....
1958◆	Montreal	7	0	0	0	2	....	....	....
Playoff Totals		**91**	**23**	**17**	**40**	**38**	....	....	....
CURTALE, Tony	*No playoffs*								Defense
CURTIS, Paul									Defense
1973	St. Louis	5	0	0	0	2	0	0	0
Playoff Totals		**5**	**0**	**0**	**0**	**2**	**0**	**0**	**0**
CUSHENAN, Ian	*No playoffs*								Defense
CUSSON, Jean	*No playoffs*								Left wing
CYR, Denis									Right wing
1983	Chicago	1	0	0	0	0	0	0	0
1985	St. Louis	3	0	0	0	0	0	0	0
Playoff Totals		**4**	**0**	**0**	**0**	**0**	**0**	**0**	**0**
CYR, Paul									Left wing
1983	Buffalo	10	1	3	4	6	1	0	0
1984	Buffalo	3	0	1	1	0	0	0	0
1985	Buffalo	5	2	2	4	15	0	0	0
1991	Hartford	6	1	0	1	10	0	0	0
Playoff Totals		**24**	**4**	**6**	**10**	**31**	**1**	**0**	**0**
CZERKAWSKI, Mariusz									Right wing
1994	Boston	13	3	3	6	4	1	0	0
1995	Boston	5	1	0	1	0	0	0	0
1997	Edmonton	12	2	1	3	10	0	0	0
Playoff Totals		**30**	**6**	**4**	**10**	**14**	**1**	**0**	**0**
DACKELL, Andreas									Right wing
1997	Ottawa	7	1	0	1	0	0	0	0
1998	Ottawa	11	1	1	2	2	1	0	0
1999	Ottawa	4	0	1	1	0	0	0	0
Playoff Totals		**22**	**2**	**2**	**4**	**2**	**1**	**0**	**0**
DAHL, Kevin									Defense
1993	Calgary	6	0	2	2	8	0	0	0
1994	Calgary	6	0	0	0	4	0	0	0
1995	Calgary	3	0	0	0	0	0	0	0
1996	Calgary	1	0	0	0	0	0	0	0
Playoff Totals		**16**	**0**	**2**	**2**	**12**	**0**	**0**	**0**

Season	Club	GP	G	A	Pts	PIM	PP	SH	GW
DAHLEN, Ulf									Right wing
1989	NY Rangers	4	0	0	0	0	0	0	0
1990	Minnesota	7	1	4	5	2	0	0	0
1991	Minnesota	15	2	6	8	4	0	0	0
1992	Minnesota	7	0	3	3	2	0	0	0
1994	San Jose	14	6	2	8	0	3	0	1
1995	San Jose	11	5	4	9	0	3	0	1
1997	Chicago	5	0	1	1	0	0	0	0
Playoff Totals		**63**	**14**	**20**	**34**	**8**	**6**	**0**	**2**
DAHLIN, Kjell									Right wing
1986◆	Montreal	16	2	3	5	4	0	0	0
1987	Montreal	8	2	4	6	0	0	0	0
1988	Montreal	11	2	4	6	2	0	0	0
Playoff Totals		**35**	**6**	**11**	**17**	**6**	**0**	**0**	**0**
DAHLQUIST, Chris									Defense
1989	Pittsburgh	2	0	0	0	0	0	0	0
1991	Minnesota	23	1	6	7	20	0	0	0
1992	Minnesota	7	0	0	0	6	0	0	0
1993	Calgary	6	3	1	4	4	0	0	0
1994	Calgary	1	0	0	0	0	0	0	0
Playoff Totals		**39**	**4**	**7**	**11**	**30**	**0**	**0**	**0**
DAHLSTROM, Cully									Center
1938◆	Chicago	10	3	1	4	2	....	....	....
1940	Chicago	2	0	0	0	0	....	....	....
1941	Chicago	5	3	3	6	2	....	....	....
1942	Chicago	3	0	0	0	0	....	....	....
1944	Chicago	9	0	4	4	0	....	....	....
Playoff Totals		**29**	**6**	**8**	**14**	**4**	....	....	....
DAIGLE, Alain									Right wing
1975	Chicago	2	0	0	0	0	0	0	0
1976	Chicago	4	0	0	0	0	0	0	0
1977	Chicago	1	0	0	0	0	0	0	0
1978	Chicago	4	0	1	1	0	0	0	0
1979	Chicago	4	0	0	0	0	0	0	0
1980	Chicago	2	0	0	0	0	0	0	0
Playoff Totals		**17**	**0**	**1**	**1**	**0**	**0**	**0**	**0**
DAIGLE, Alexandre									Center
1997	Ottawa	7	0	0	0	2	0	0	0
1998	Philadelphia	5	0	2	2	0	0	0	0
Playoff Totals		**12**	**0**	**2**	**2**	**2**	**0**	**0**	**0**
DAIGNEAULT, J.J.									Defense
1986	Vancouver	3	0	2	2	0	0	0	0
1987	Philadelphia	9	1	0	1	0	0	0	1
1990	Montreal	9	0	0	0	2	0	0	0
1991	Montreal	5	0	1	1	0	0	0	0
1992	Montreal	11	0	3	3	4	0	0	0
1993◆	Montreal	20	1	3	4	22	0	0	0
1994	Montreal	7	0	1	1	12	0	0	0
1996	Pittsburgh	17	1	9	10	36	1	0	1
1997	Anaheim	11	2	7	9	16	1	0	1
1999	Phoenix	6	0	0	0	8	0	0	0
Playoff Totals		**98**	**5**	**26**	**31**	**100**	**2**	**0**	**3**
DAILEY, Bob									Defense
1975	Vancouver	5	1	3	4	14	0	0	0
1976	Vancouver	2	1	1	2	0	1	0	0
1977	Philadelphia	10	4	9	13	15	2	0	0
1978	Philadelphia	12	1	5	6	22	0	0	0
1979	Philadelphia	8	1	2	3	14	0	0	0
1980	Philadelphia	19	4	13	17	22	1	1	2
1981	Philadelphia	7	0	1	1	18	0	0	0
Playoff Totals		**63**	**12**	**34**	**46**	**105**	**4**	**1**	**2**
DALEY, Frank									Left wing/Center
1929	Detroit	2	0	0	0	0	0	0	0
Playoff Totals		**2**	**0**	**0**	**0**	**0**	**0**	**0**	**0**
DALEY, Pat	*No playoffs*								Left wing
DALGARNO, Brad									Right wing
1987	NY Islanders	1	0	1	1	0	0	0	0
1988	NY Islanders	4	0	0	0	19	0	0	0
1993	NY Islanders	18	2	2	4	14	0	0	0
1994	NY Islanders	4	0	1	1	4	0	0	0
Playoff Totals		**27**	**2**	**4**	**6**	**37**	**0**	**0**	**0**
DALLMAN, Marty	*No playoffs*								Center
DALLMAN, Rod									Left wing
1990	NY Islanders	1	0	1	1	0	0	0	0
Playoff Totals		**1**	**0**	**1**	**1**	**0**	**0**	**0**	**0**
DAME, Bunny	*No playoffs*								Left wing
DAMORE, Hank	*No playoffs*								Center
DAMPHOUSSE, Vincent									Center
1987	Toronto	12	1	5	6	8	1	0	0
1988	Toronto	6	0	1	1	10	0	0	0
1990	Toronto	5	0	2	2	2	0	0	0
1992	Edmonton	16	6	8	14	8	1	0	0
1993◆	Montreal	20	11	12	23	16	5	0	3
1994	Montreal	7	1	2	3	8	0	0	0
1996	Montreal	6	4	4	8	0	0	1	2
1997	Montreal	5	0	0	0	2	0	0	0
1998	Montreal	10	3	6	9	22	1	0	0
1999	San Jose	6	3	2	5	6	0	2	0
Playoff Totals		**93**	**29**	**42**	**71**	**82**	**8**	**3**	**5**

Season	Club	GP	G	A	Pts	PIM	PP	SH	GW
DANDENAULT, Mathieu	Right wing/defense								
1998◆	Detroit	3	1	0	1	0	1	0	0
1999	Detroit	10	0	1	1	0	0	0	0
Playoff Totals		**13**	**1**	**1**	**2**	**0**	**1**	**0**	**0**
DANEYKO, Ken	Defense								
1988	New Jersey	20	1	6	7	83	0	0	1
1990	New Jersey	6	2	0	2	21	0	0	0
1991	New Jersey	7	0	1	1	10	0	0	0
1992	New Jersey	7	0	3	3	16	0	0	0
1993	New Jersey	5	0	0	0	8	0	0	0
1994	New Jersey	20	0	1	1	45	0	0	0
1995◆	New Jersey	20	1	0	1	22	0	0	0
1997	New Jersey	10	0	0	0	28	0	0	0
1998	New Jersey	6	0	1	1	10	0	0	0
1999	New Jersey	7	0	0	0	8	0	0	0
Playoff Totals		**108**	**4**	**12**	**16**	**251**	**0**	**0**	**1**
DANIELS, Jeff	Left wing								
1993	Pittsburgh	12	3	2	5	0	0	0	1
Playoff Totals		**12**	**3**	**2**	**5**	**0**	**0**	**0**	**1**
DANIELS, Kimbi	*No playoffs* — Center								
DANIELS, Scott	Left wing								
1998	New Jersey	1	0	0	0	0	0	0	0
Playoff Totals		**1**	**0**	**0**	**0**	**0**	**0**	**0**	**0**
DAOUST, Dan	Center								
1986	Toronto	10	2	2	4	19	0	0	0
1987	Toronto	13	5	2	7	42	0	0	2
1988	Toronto	4	0	0	0	2	0	0	0
1990	Toronto	5	0	1	1	20	0	0	0
Playoff Totals		**32**	**7**	**5**	**12**	**83**	**0**	**0**	**2**
DARBY, Craig	*No playoffs* — Center								
DARK, Michael	*No playoffs* — Defense								
DARRAGH, Harold	Left wing								
1926	Pittsburgh	2	1	0	1	0	....	....	....
1928	Pittsburgh	2	0	1	1	0	....	....	....
1931	Boston	5	0	1	1	2	....	....	....
1932◆	Toronto	7	0	1	1	2	....	....	....
Playoff Totals		**16**	**1**	**3**	**4**	**4**	....	....	....
DARRAGH, Jack	Right wing								
1919	Ottawa	7	4	0	4	3	....	....	....
1920◆	Ottawa	5	5	*2	*7	3	....	....	....
1921◆	Ottawa	7	*5	0	5	7	....	....	....
1923◆	Ottawa	2	1	0	1	2	....	....	....
1924	Ottawa	2	0	0	0	2	....	....	....
Playoff Totals		**23**	**15**	**2**	**17**	**17**	....	....	....
DAVID, Richard	Left wing								
1982	Quebec	1	0	0	0	0	0	0	0
Playoff Totals		**1**	**0**	**0**	**0**	**0**	**0**	**0**	**0**
DAVIDSON, Bob	Left wing								
1936	Toronto	9	1	3	4	2	....	....	....
1937	Toronto	2	0	0	0	5	....	....	....
1938	Toronto	7	0	2	2	10	....	....	....
1939	Toronto	10	1	1	2	6	....	....	....
1940	Toronto	10	0	3	3	16	....	....	....
1941	Toronto	7	0	2	2	7	....	....	....
1942◆	Toronto	13	1	2	3	20	....	....	....
1943	Toronto	6	1	2	3	7	....	....	....
1944	Toronto	5	0	0	0	4	....	....	....
1945◆	Toronto	13	1	2	3	2	....	....	....
Playoff Totals		**82**	**5**	**17**	**22**	**79**	....	....	....
DAVIDSON, Gord	*No playoffs* — Defense								
DAVIDSSON, Johan	Center								
1999	Anaheim	1	0	0	0	0	0	0	0
Playoff Totals		**1**	**0**	**0**	**0**	**0**	**0**	**0**	**0**
DAVIE, Bob	*No playoffs* — Defense								
DAVIES, Buck	Center								
1948	NY Rangers	1	0	0	0	0	0	0	0
Playoff Totals		**1**	**0**	**0**	**0**	**0**	**0**	**0**	**0**
DAVIS, Bob	*No playoffs* — Right wing								
DAVIS, Kim	Center								
1980	Pittsburgh	4	0	0	0	0	0	0	0
Playoff Totals		**4**	**0**	**0**	**0**	**0**	**0**	**0**	**0**
DAVIS, Lorne	Right wing								
1953◆	Montreal	7	1	1	2	2	....	....	....
1954	Montreal	11	2	0	2	8	....	....	....
Playoff Totals		**18**	**3**	**1**	**4**	**10**	....	....	....
DAVIS, Mal	Left wing								
1983	Buffalo	6	1	0	1	0	0	0	0
1984	Buffalo	1	0	0	0	0	0	0	0
Playoff Totals		**7**	**1**	**0**	**1**	**0**	**0**	**0**	**0**
DAVISON, Murray	*No playoffs* — Defense								
DAVYDOV, Evgeny	Left wing								
1992	Winnipeg	7	2	2	4	2	1	0	0
1993	Winnipeg	4	0	0	0	0	0	0	0
Playoff Totals		**11**	**2**	**2**	**4**	**2**	**1**	**0**	**0**

Season	Club	GP	G	A	Pts	PIM	PP	SH	GW
DAWE, Jason	Right wing								
1994	Buffalo	6	0	1	1	6	0	0	0
1995	Buffalo	5	2	1	3	6	0	0	0
1997	Buffalo	11	2	1	3	6	0	0	0
Playoff Totals		**22**	**4**	**3**	**7**	**18**	**0**	**0**	**0**
DAWES, Bobby	Defense/Center								
1949◆	Toronto	9	0	0	0	2	0	0	0
1951	Montreal	1	0	0	0	0	0	0	0
Playoff Totals		**10**	**0**	**0**	**0**	**2**	**0**	**0**	**0**
DAY, Hap	Defense								
1925	Toronto	2	0	0	0	0	....	....	....
1929	Toronto	4	1	0	1	4	....	....	....
1931	Toronto	2	0	3	3	7	....	....	....
1932◆	Toronto	7	3	3	6	6	....	....	....
1933	Toronto	9	0	1	1	*21	....	....	....
1934	Toronto	5	0	0	0	6	....	....	....
1935	Toronto	7	0	0	0	4	....	....	....
1936	Toronto	9	0	0	0	8	....	....	....
1937	Toronto	2	0	0	0	0	....	....	....
1938	NY Americans	6	0	0	0	0	....	....	....
Playoff Totals		**53**	**4**	**7**	**11**	**56**	....	....	....
DAY, Joe	*No playoffs* — Center								
DAZE, Eric	Left wing								
1995	Chicago	16	0	1	1	4	0	0	0
1996	Chicago	10	3	5	8	0	0	0	1
1997	Chicago	6	2	1	3	2	0	0	0
Playoff Totals		**32**	**5**	**7**	**12**	**6**	**0**	**0**	**1**
DEA, Billy	Left wing								
1957	Detroit	5	2	0	2	2	1	0	0
1967	Chicago	2	0	0	0	2	0	0	0
1970	Detroit	4	0	1	1	2	0	0	0
Playoff Totals		**11**	**2**	**1**	**3**	**6**	**1**	**0**	**0**
DEACON, Don	Left wing								
1939	Detroit	2	2	1	3	0	....	....	....
Playoff Totals		**2**	**2**	**1**	**3**	**0**	....	....	....
DEADMARSH, Adam	Center								
1995	Quebec	6	0	1	1	0	0	0	0
1996◆	Colorado	22	5	12	17	25	1	0	0
1997	Colorado	17	3	6	9	24	1	0	1
1998	Colorado	7	2	0	2	4	1	0	0
1999	Colorado	19	8	4	12	20	3	0	0
Playoff Totals		**71**	**18**	**23**	**41**	**73**	**6**	**0**	**1**
DEADMARSH, Butch	Left wing								
1974	Atlanta	4	0	0	0	17	0	0	0
Playoff Totals		**4**	**0**	**0**	**0**	**17**	**0**	**0**	**0**
DEAN, Barry	*No playoffs* — Left wing								
DEAN, Kevin	Defense								
1995◆	New Jersey	3	0	2	2	0	0	0	0
1997	New Jersey	1	1	0	1	0	0	0	1
1998	New Jersey	5	1	0	1	2	0	0	0
1999	New Jersey	7	0	0	0	0	0	0	0
Playoff Totals		**16**	**2**	**2**	**4**	**2**	**0**	**0**	**1**
DEBENEDET, Nelson	*No playoffs* — Left wing								
DEBLOIS, Lucien	Center								
1978	NY Rangers	3	0	0	0	2	0	0	0
1979	NY Rangers	9	2	0	2	4	1	0	0
1982	Winnipeg	4	2	1	3	4	0	0	0
1983	Winnipeg	3	0	0	0	5	0	0	0
1984	Winnipeg	3	0	1	1	4	0	0	0
1985	Montreal	8	2	4	6	4	1	0	0
1986◆	Montreal	11	0	0	0	7	0	0	0
1987	NY Rangers	2	0	0	0	2	0	0	0
1989	NY Rangers	4	0	0	0	4	0	0	0
1992	Winnipeg	5	1	0	1	2	0	0	1
Playoff Totals		**52**	**7**	**6**	**13**	**38**	**2**	**0**	**1**
DEBOL, Dave	Center								
1980	Hartford	3	0	0	0	0	0	0	0
Playoff Totals		**3**	**0**	**0**	**0**	**0**	**0**	**0**	**0**
DeBRUSK, Louie	Left wing								
1997	Edmonton	6	0	0	0	4	0	0	0
1999	Phoenix	6	2	0	2	6	0	0	0
Playoff Totals		**12**	**2**	**0**	**2**	**10**	**0**	**0**	**0**
DEFAZIO, Dean	*No playoffs* — Left wing								
DEGRAY, Dale	Defense								
1988	Toronto	5	0	1	1	16	0	0	0
1989	Los Angeles	8	1	2	3	12	1	0	0
Playoff Totals		**13**	**1**	**3**	**4**	**28**	**1**	**0**	**0**
DELISLE, Jonathan	*No playoffs* — Right wing								
DELISLE, Xavier	*No playoffs* — Center								
DELMONTE, Armand	*No playoffs* — Right wing								
DELMORE, Andy	*No playoffs* — Defense								

Season	Club	GP	G	A	Pts	PIM	PP	SH	GW
DELORME, Gilbert	Defense								
1983	Montreal	3	0	0	0	2	0	0	0
1984	St. Louis	11	1	3	4	11	0	0	0
1985	St. Louis	3	0	0	0	0	0	0	0
1986	Quebec	2	0	0	0	5	0	0	0
1987	Detroit	16	0	2	2	14	0	0	0
1988	Detroit	15	0	3	3	22	0	0	0
1989	Detroit	6	0	1	1	2	0	0	0
Playoff Totals		**56**	**1**	**9**	**10**	**56**	**0**	**0**	**0**
DELORME, Ron	Center								
1978	Colorado	2	0	0	0	10	0	0	0
1982	Vancouver	15	0	2	2	31	0	0	0
1983	Vancouver	4	0	0	0	10	0	0	0
1984	Vancouver	4	1	0	1	8	0	0	0
Playoff Totals		**25**	**1**	**2**	**3**	**59**	**0**	**0**	**0**
DELORY, Val	*No playoffs* — Left wing								
DELPARTE, Guy	*No playoffs* — Left wing								
DELVECCHIO, Alex	Center								
1952◆	Detroit	8	0	3	3	4	....	....	....
1953	Detroit	6	2	4	6	2	....	....	....
1954◆	Detroit	12	2	7	9	7	....	....	....
1955◆	Detroit	11	7	8	15	2	....	....	....
1956	Detroit	10	7	3	10	2	....	....	....
1957	Detroit	5	3	2	5	2	....	....	....
1958	Detroit	4	0	1	1	0	....	....	....
1960	Detroit	6	2	6	8	0	....	....	....
1961	Detroit	11	4	5	9	0	....	....	....
1963	Detroit	11	3	6	9	2	....	....	....
1964	Detroit	14	3	8	11	0	....	....	....
1965	Detroit	7	2	3	5	4	....	....	....
1966	Detroit	12	0	*11	11	4	....	....	....
1970	Detroit	4	0	2	2	0	0	0	0
Playoff Totals		**121**	**35**	**69**	**104**	**29**	....	....	....
DEMARCO, Ab Jr.	Defense								
1970	NY Rangers	5	0	0	0	2	0	0	0
1972	NY Rangers	4	0	1	1	0	0	0	0
1973	St. Louis	4	1	1	2	2	1	0	0
1975	Vancouver	2	0	0	0	0	0	0	0
1976	Los Angeles	9	0	0	0	11	0	0	0
1977	Los Angeles	1	0	0	0	2	0	0	0
Playoff Totals		**25**	**1**	**2**	**3**	**17**	**1**	**0**	**0**
DEMARCO, Ab Sr.	Center								
1940	Chicago	2	0	0	0	0	....	....	....
1943	Boston	9	3	0	3	2	....	....	....
Playoff Totals		**11**	**3**	**0**	**3**	**2**	....	....	....
DEMERS, Tony	Right wing								
1941	Montreal	2	0	0	0	0	0	0	0
Playoff Totals		**2**	**0**	**0**	**0**	**0**	**0**	**0**	**0**
DEMITRA, Pavol	Left wing								
1997	St. Louis	6	1	3	4	6	0	0	0
1998	St. Louis	10	3	3	6	2	0	0	0
1999	St. Louis	13	5	4	9	4	3	0	1
Playoff Totals		**29**	**9**	**10**	**19**	**12**	**3**	**0**	**1**
DEMPSEY, Nathan	*No playoffs* — Defense								
DENIS, Jean-Paul	*No playoffs* — Right wing								
DENIS, Lulu	*No playoffs* — Right wing								
DENNENY, Corb	Center								
1918◆	Toronto	7	3	1	4	3	....	....	....
1921	Toronto	2	0	0	0	4	....	....	....
1922◆	Toronto	7	4	*2	6	2	....	....	....
Playoff Totals		**16**	**7**	**3**	**10**	**9**	....	....	....
DENNENY, Cy	Left wing								
1919	Ottawa	7	5	3	8	9	....	....	....
1920◆	Ottawa	5	0	2	2	3	....	....	....
1921◆	Ottawa	7	4	2	*6	15	....	....	....
1922	Ottawa	2	2	0	2	4	....	....	....
1923◆	Ottawa	8	3	1	4	6	....	....	....
1924	Ottawa	2	2	0	2	10	....	....	....
1926	Ottawa	2	0	0	0	4	....	....	....
1927◆	Ottawa	6	*5	0	5	0	....	....	....
1928	Ottawa	2	0	0	0	0	....	....	....
1929◆	Boston	2	0	0	0	0	....	....	....
Playoff Totals		**43**	**21**	**8**	**29**	**51**	....	....	....
DENNIS, Norm	Center								
1970	St. Louis	2	0	0	0	2	0	0	0
1971	St. Louis	3	0	0	0	0	0	0	0
Playoff Totals		**5**	**0**	**0**	**0**	**2**	**0**	**0**	**0**
DENOIRD, Gerry	*No playoffs* — Center								
DEPALMA, Larry	Left wing								
1989	Minnesota	2	0	0	0	6	0	0	0
1994	Pittsburgh	1	0	0	0	0	0	0	0
Playoff Totals		**3**	**0**	**0**	**0**	**6**	**0**	**0**	**0**
DERLAGO, Bill	Center								
1980	Toronto	3	0	0	0	4	0	0	0
1981	Toronto	3	1	0	1	2	1	0	0
1983	Toronto	4	3	0	3	2	2	0	0
1986	Winnipeg	3	1	0	1	0	0	0	0
Playoff Totals		**13**	**5**	**0**	**5**	**8**	**3**	**0**	**0**
DESAULNIERS, Gerard	*No playoffs* — Center								

Season	Club	GP	G	A	Pts	PIM	PP	SH	GW
DESILETS, Joffre	Right wing								
1937	Mtl. Canadiens	5	1	0	1	0	....	....	....
1938	Mtl. Canadiens	2	0	0	0	7	....	....	....
Playoff Totals		**7**	**1**	**0**	**1**	**7**	....	....	....
DESJARDINS, Eric	Defense								
1989	Montreal	14	1	1	2	6	1	0	0
1990	Montreal	6	0	0	0	10	0	0	0
1991	Montreal	13	1	4	5	8	1	0	0
1992	Montreal	11	3	3	6	4	1	0	0
1993◆	Montreal	20	4	10	14	23	1	0	1
1994	Montreal	7	0	2	2	4	0	0	0
1995	Philadelphia	15	4	4	8	10	1	0	2
1996	Philadelphia	12	0	6	6	2	0	0	0
1997	Philadelphia	19	2	8	10	12	0	0	0
1998	Philadelphia	5	0	1	1	0	0	0	0
1999	Philadelphia	6	2	2	4	4	1	0	1
Playoff Totals		**128**	**17**	**41**	**58**	**83**	**6**	**0**	**4**
DESJARDINS, Martin *No playoffs*	Center								
DESJARDINS, Vic	Center								
1931	Chicago	9	0	0	0	0	0	0	0
1932	NY Rangers	7	0	0	0	0	0	0	0
Playoff Totals		**16**	**0**	**0**	**0**	**0**	**0**	**0**	**0**
DESLAURIERS, Jacques *No playoffs*	Defense								
DEULING, Jarrett *No playoffs*	Left wing								
DEVEREAUX, Boyd	Center								
1999	Edmonton	1	0	0	0	0	0	0	0
Playoff Totals		**1**	**0**	**0**	**0**	**0**	**0**	**0**	**0**
DEVINE, Kevin *No playoffs*	Left wing								
de VRIES, Greg	Defense								
1997	Edmonton	12	0	1	1	8	0	0	0
1998	Edmonton	7	0	0	0	21	0	0	0
1999	Colorado	19	0	2	2	22	0	0	0
Playoff Totals		**38**	**0**	**3**	**3**	**51**	**0**	**0**	**0**
DEWAR, Tom *No playoffs*	Defense								
DEWSBURY, Al	Defense								
1947	Detroit	2	0	0	0	4	....	....	....
1948	Detroit	1	0	0	0	0	....	....	....
1950◆	Detroit	4	0	3	3	8	....	....	....
1953	Chicago	7	1	2	3	4	....	....	....
Playoff Totals		**14**	**1**	**5**	**6**	**16**	....	....	....
DEZIEL, Michel	Left wing								
1975	Buffalo	1	0	0	0	0	0	0	0
Playoff Totals		**1**	**0**	**0**	**0**	**0**	**0**	**0**	**0**
DHEERE, Marcel	Left wing								
1943	Montreal	5	0	0	0	6	0	0	0
Playoff Totals		**5**	**0**	**0**	**0**	**6**	**0**	**0**	**0**
DIACHUK, Edward *No playoffs*	Left wing								
DICK, Harry *No playoffs*	Defense								
DICKENS, Ernie	Defense								
1942◆	Toronto	13	0	0	0	4	0	0	0
Playoff Totals		**13**	**0**	**0**	**0**	**4**	**0**	**0**	**0**
DICKENSON, Herb *No playoffs*	Left/right wing								
DIDUCK, Gerald	Defense								
1987	NY Islanders	14	0	1	1	35	0	0	0
1988	NY Islanders	6	1	0	1	42	1	0	0
1990	NY Islanders	5	0	0	0	12	0	0	0
1991	Vancouver	6	1	0	1	11	1	0	0
1992	Vancouver	5	0	0	0	10	0	0	0
1993	Vancouver	12	4	2	6	12	0	0	0
1994	Vancouver	24	1	7	8	22	0	0	0
1995	Chicago	16	1	3	4	22	0	0	0
1997	Phoenix	7	0	0	0	10	0	0	0
1998	Phoenix	6	0	2	2	20	0	0	0
1999	Phoenix	3	0	0	0	2	0	0	0
Playoff Totals		**104**	**8**	**15**	**23**	**198**	**2**	**0**	**0**
DIETRICH, Don *No playoffs*	Defense								
DILL, Bob *No playoffs*	Defense								
DILLABOUGH, Bob	Center								
1963	Detroit	1	0	0	0	0	0	0	0
1964	Detroit	1	0	0	0	0	0	0	0
1965	Detroit	4	0	0	0	0	0	0	0
1969	Oakland	7	3	0	3	0	0	1	0
1970	Oakland	4	0	0	0	0	0	0	0
Playoff Totals		**17**	**3**	**0**	**3**	**0**	**0**	**1**	**0**
DILLON, Cecil	Right wing								
1931	NY Rangers	4	0	1	1	2	....	....	....
1932	NY Rangers	7	2	1	3	4	....	....	....
1933◆	NY Rangers	8	8	2	10	6	....	....	....
1934	NY Rangers	2	0	1	1	2	....	....	....
1935	NY Rangers	4	2	1	3	0	....	....	....
1937	NY Rangers	9	0	3	3	0	....	....	....
1938	NY Rangers	3	1	0	1	0	....	....	....
1939	NY Rangers	1	0	0	0	0	....	....	....
1940	Detroit	5	1	0	1	0	....	....	....
Playoff Totals		**43**	**14**	**9**	**23**	**14**	....	....	....
DILLON, Gary *No playoffs*	Center								

Season	Club	GP	G	A	Pts	PIM	PP	SH	GW
DILLON, Wayne	Center								
1978	NY Rangers	3	0	1	1	0	0	0	0
Playoff Totals		**3**	**0**	**1**	**1**	**0**	**0**	**0**	**0**
DiMAIO, Rob	Center								
1990	NY Islanders	1	1	0	1	4	0	0	0
1995	Philadelphia	15	2	4	6	4	0	1	1
1996	Philadelphia	3	0	0	0	0	0	0	0
1998	Boston	6	1	0	1	8	0	0	0
1999	Boston	12	2	0	2	8	0	0	1
Playoff Totals		**37**	**6**	**4**	**10**	**24**	**0**	**1**	**2**
DINEEN, Bill	Right wing								
1954◆	Detroit	12	0	0	0	2	0	0	0
1955◆	Detroit	11	0	1	1	8	0	0	0
1956	Detroit	10	1	0	1	8	0	0	0
1957	Detroit	4	0	0	0	0	0	0	0
Playoff Totals		**37**	**1**	**1**	**2**	**18**	**0**	**0**	**0**
DINEEN, Gary *No playoffs*	Center								
DINEEN, Gord	Defense								
1984	NY Islanders	9	1	1	2	28	0	0	0
1985	NY Islanders	10	0	0	0	26	0	0	0
1986	NY Islanders	3	0	0	0	2	0	0	0
1987	NY Islanders	7	0	4	4	4	0	0	0
1989	Pittsburgh	11	0	2	2	8	0	0	0
Playoff Totals		**40**	**1**	**7**	**8**	**68**	**0**	**0**	**0**
DINEEN, Kevin	Right wing								
1986	Hartford	10	6	7	13	18	1	0	2
1987	Hartford	6	2	1	3	31	1	0	0
1988	Hartford	6	4	4	8	8	1	0	1
1989	Hartford	4	1	0	1	10	0	0	0
1990	Hartford	6	3	2	5	18	0	0	1
1991	Hartford	6	1	0	1	16	0	0	0
1995	Philadelphia	15	6	4	10	18	1	0	1
1999	Carolina	6	0	0	0	8	0	0	0
Playoff Totals		**59**	**23**	**18**	**41**	**127**	**4**	**0**	**5**
DINEEN, Peter *No playoffs*	Defense								
DINGMAN, Chris *No playoffs*	Left wing								
DINSMORE, Chuck	Center								
1926◆	Mtl. Maroons	8	1	0	1	6	....	....	....
1930	Mtl. Maroons	4	0	0	0	0	....	....	....
Playoff Totals		**12**	**1**	**0**	**1**	**6**	....	....	....
DIONNE, Gilbert	Left wing								
1992	Montreal	11	3	4	7	10	1	0	1
1993◆	Montreal	20	6	6	12	20	1	0	1
1994	Montreal	5	1	2	3	0	1	0	0
1995	Philadelphia	3	0	0	0	4	0	0	0
Playoff Totals		**39**	**10**	**12**	**22**	**34**	**2**	**0**	**2**
DIONNE, Marcel	Center								
1976	Los Angeles	9	6	1	7	0	3	0	0
1977	Los Angeles	9	5	9	14	2	1	0	1
1978	Los Angeles	2	0	0	0	0	0	0	0
1979	Los Angeles	2	0	1	1	0	0	0	0
1980	Los Angeles	4	0	3	3	4	0	0	0
1981	Los Angeles	4	1	3	4	7	1	0	0
1982	Los Angeles	10	7	4	11	0	4	0	0
1985	Los Angeles	3	1	2	3	2	1	0	0
1987	NY Rangers	6	1	1	2	2	1	0	0
Playoff Totals		**49**	**21**	**24**	**45**	**17**	**11**	**0**	**1**
DI PIETRO, Paul	Center								
1993◆	Montreal	17	8	5	13	8	0	0	1
1994	Montreal	7	2	4	6	2	2	0	1
1995	Toronto	7	1	1	2	0	0	0	0
Playoff Totals		**31**	**11**	**10**	**21**	**10**	**2**	**0**	**2**
DIRK, Robert	Defense								
1988	St. Louis	6	0	1	1	2	0	0	0
1990	St. Louis	3	0	0	0	0	0	0	0
1991	Vancouver	6	0	0	0	13	0	0	0
1992	Vancouver	13	0	0	0	20	0	0	0
1993	Vancouver	9	0	0	0	6	0	0	0
1994	Chicago	2	0	0	0	15	0	0	0
Playoff Totals		**39**	**0**	**1**	**1**	**56**	**0**	**0**	**0**
DJOOS, Per *No playoffs*	Defense								
DOAK, Gary	Defense								
1968	Boston	4	0	0	0	4	0	0	0
1970◆	Boston	8	0	0	0	9	0	0	0
1972	NY Rangers	12	0	0	0	46	0	0	0
1973	Boston	2	0	0	0	2	0	0	0
1975	Boston	3	0	0	0	4	0	0	0
1976	Boston	12	1	0	1	22	0	0	0
1977	Boston	14	0	2	2	26	0	0	0
1978	Boston	12	1	0	1	4	0	0	1
1979	Boston	7	0	2	2	4	0	0	0
1980	Boston	4	0	0	0	0	0	0	0
Playoff Totals		**78**	**2**	**4**	**6**	**121**	**0**	**0**	**1**
DOAN, Shane	Right wing								
1996	Winnipeg	6	0	0	0	6	0	0	0
1997	Phoenix	4	0	0	0	2	0	0	0
1998	Phoenix	6	1	0	1	6	0	0	0
1999	Phoenix	7	2	2	4	6	0	0	2
Playoff Totals		**23**	**3**	**2**	**5**	**20**	**0**	**0**	**2**

Season	Club	GP	G	A	Pts	PIM	PP	SH	GW
DOBBIN, Brian	Right wing								
1989	Philadelphia	2	0	0	0	17	0	0	0
Playoff Totals		**2**	**0**	**0**	**0**	**17**	**0**	**0**	**0**
DOBSON, Jim *No playoffs*	Right wing								
DOHERTY, Fred *No playoffs*	Right wing								
DOIG, Jason *No playoffs*	Defense								
DOLLAS, Bobby	Defense								
1986	Winnipeg	3	0	0	0	2	0	0	0
1991	Detroit	7	1	0	1	13	0	0	0
1992	Detroit	2	0	1	1	0	0	0	0
1997	Anaheim	11	0	0	0	4	0	0	0
1998	Edmonton	11	0	0	0	16	0	0	0
1999	Pittsburgh	13	1	0	1	6	0	0	0
Playoff Totals		**47**	**2**	**1**	**3**	**41**	**0**	**0**	**0**
DOME, Robert *No playoffs*	Right wing								
DOMENICHELLI, Hnat *No playoffs*	Center								
DOMI, Tie	Right wing								
1992	NY Rangers	6	1	1	2	32	0	0	0
1993	Winnipeg	6	1	0	1	23	0	0	0
1995	Toronto	7	1	0	1	0	0	0	0
1996	Toronto	6	0	2	2	4	0	0	0
1999	Toronto	14	0	2	2	24	0	0	0
Playoff Totals		**39**	**3**	**5**	**8**	**83**	**0**	**0**	**0**
DONALDSON, Gary *No playoffs*	Right wing								
DONATELLI, Clark	Left wing								
1992	Boston	2	0	0	0	0	0	0	0
Playoff Totals		**2**	**0**	**0**	**0**	**0**	**0**	**0**	**0**
DONATO, Ted	Left wing								
1992	Boston	15	3	4	7	4	0	0	1
1993	Boston	4	0	1	1	0	0	0	0
1994	Boston	13	4	2	6	10	2	0	1
1995	Boston	5	0	0	0	4	0	0	0
1996	Boston	5	1	2	3	2	1	0	0
1998	Boston	5	0	0	0	2	0	0	0
1999	Ottawa	1	0	0	0	0	0	0	0
Playoff Totals		**48**	**8**	**9**	**17**	**22**	**3**	**0**	**2**
DONNELLY, Babe	Defense								
1927	Mtl. Maroons	2	0	0	0	0	0	0	0
Playoff Totals		**2**	**0**	**0**	**0**	**0**	**0**	**0**	**0**
DONNELLY, Dave	Center								
1984	Boston	3	0	0	0	0	0	0	0
1985	Boston	1	0	0	0	0	0	0	0
1987	Chicago	1	0	0	0	0	0	0	0
Playoff Totals		**5**	**0**	**0**	**0**	**0**	**0**	**0**	**0**
DONNELLY, Gord	Defense								
1986	Quebec	1	0	0	0	0	0	0	0
1987	Quebec	13	0	0	0	53	0	0	0
1990	Winnipeg	6	0	1	1	8	0	0	0
1992	Buffalo	6	0	1	1	0	0	0	0
Playoff Totals		**26**	**0**	**2**	**2**	**61**	**0**	**0**	**0**
DONNELLY, Mike	Left wing								
1991	Los Angeles	12	5	4	9	6	0	0	0
1992	Los Angeles	6	1	0	1	4	0	0	0
1993	Los Angeles	24	6	7	13	14	0	0	0
1995	Dallas	5	0	1	1	6	0	0	0
Playoff Totals		**47**	**12**	**12**	**24**	**30**	**0**	**0**	**0**
DONOVAN, Shean	Right wing								
1995	San Jose	7	0	1	1	6	0	0	0
1999	Colorado	5	0	0	0	2	0	0	0
Playoff Totals		**12**	**0**	**1**	**1**	**8**	**0**	**0**	**0**
DORAN, John	Defense								
1936	NY Americans	3	0	0	0	0	0	0	0
Playoff Totals		**3**	**0**	**0**	**0**	**0**	**0**	**0**	**0**
DORAN, Lloyd *No playoffs*	Center								
DORATY, Ken	Forward								
1933	Toronto	9	5	0	5	2	....	....	....
1934	Toronto	5	2	2	4	0	....	....	....
1935	Toronto	1	0	0	0	0	....	....	....
Playoff Totals		**15**	**7**	**2**	**9**	**2**	....	....	....
DORE, Andre	Defense								
1982	NY Rangers	10	1	1	2	16	0	0	0
1983	St. Louis	4	0	1	1	8	0	0	0
1984	Quebec	9	0	0	0	8	0	0	0
Playoff Totals		**23**	**1**	**2**	**3**	**32**	**0**	**0**	**0**
DORE, Daniel *No playoffs*	Right wing								
DOREY, Jim	Defense								
1969	Toronto	4	0	1	1	21	0	0	0
1971	Toronto	6	0	1	1	19	0	0	0
1972	NY Rangers	1	0	0	0	0	0	0	0
Playoff Totals		**11**	**0**	**2**	**2**	**40**	**0**	**0**	**0**
DORION, Dan *No playoffs*	Center								

Season	Club	GP	G	A	Pts	PIM	PP	SH	GW
DORNHOEFER, Gary									Right wing
1968	Philadelphia	3	0	0	0	15	0	0	0
1969	Philadelphia	4	0	1	1	20	0	0	0
1971	Philadelphia	2	0	0	0	4	0	0	0
1973	Philadelphia	11	3	3	6	16	1	0	1
1974◆	Philadelphia	14	5	6	11	43	2	1	1
1975◆	Philadelphia	17	5	5	10	33	0	0	2
1976	Philadelphia	16	3	4	7	43	1	0	0
1977	Philadelphia	9	1	0	1	22	0	0	0
1978	Philadelphia	4	0	0	0	7	0	0	0
Playoff Totals		**80**	**17**	**19**	**36**	**203**	**4**	**1**	**4**
DOROHOY, Eddie *No playoffs*									Center/left wing
DOUGLAS, Jordy									Left wing
1983	Minnesota	5	0	0	0	2	0	0	0
1984	Winnipeg	1	0	0	0	2	0	0	0
Playoff Totals		**6**	**0**	**0**	**0**	**4**	**0**	**0**	**0**
DOUGLAS, Kent									Defense
1963◆	Toronto	10	1	1	2	2	0	0	0
1965	Toronto	5	0	1	1	19	0	0	0
1966	Toronto	4	0	1	1	12	0	0	0
Playoff Totals		**19**	**1**	**3**	**4**	**33**	**0**	**0**	**0**
DOUGLAS, Les									Center
1943◆	Detroit	10	3	2	5	2	....	....	....
Playoff Totals		**10**	**3**	**2**	**5**	**2**	....	....	....
DOURIS, Peter									Right wing
1988	Winnipeg	1	0	0	0	0	0	0	0
1990	Boston	8	0	1	1	8	0	0	0
1991	Boston	7	0	1	1	6	0	0	0
1992	Boston	7	2	3	5	0	0	0	1
1993	Boston	4	1	0	1	0	0	0	0
Playoff Totals		**27**	**3**	**5**	**8**	**14**	**0**	**0**	**1**
DOWD, Jim									Center
1994	New Jersey	19	2	6	8	8	0	0	0
1995◆	New Jersey	11	2	1	3	8	0	0	1
1996	Vancouver	1	0	0	0	0	0	0	0
Playoff Totals		**31**	**4**	**7**	**11**	**16**	**0**	**0**	**1**
DOWNIE, Dave *No playoffs*									Center/right wing
DOYON, Mario *No playoffs*									Defense
DRAKE, Dallas									Right wing
1993	Detroit	7	3	3	6	6	1	0	0
1996	Winnipeg	3	0	0	0	0	0	0	0
1997	Phoenix	7	0	1	1	2	0	0	0
1998	Phoenix	4	0	1	1	2	0	0	0
1999	Phoenix	7	4	3	7	4	2	0	1
Playoff Totals		**28**	**7**	**8**	**15**	**14**	**3**	**0**	**1**
DRAPER, Bruce *No playoffs*									Center
DRAPER, Kris									Center
1992	Winnipeg	2	0	0	0	0	0	0	0
1994	Detroit	7	2	2	4	4	0	1	0
1995	Detroit	18	4	1	5	12	0	1	1
1996	Detroit	18	4	2	6	18	0	1	0
1997◆	Detroit	20	2	4	6	12	0	1	0
1998◆	Detroit	19	1	3	4	12	0	0	1
1999	Detroit	10	0	1	1	6	0	0	0
Playoff Totals		**94**	**13**	**13**	**26**	**64**	**0**	**4**	**2**
DRILLON, Gordie									Right wing
1937	Toronto	2	0	0	0	0	....	....	....
1938	Toronto	7	*7	1	8	2	....	....	....
1939	Toronto	10	*7	6	13	4	....	....	....
1940	Toronto	10	3	1	4	0	....	....	....
1941	Toronto	7	3	2	5	2	....	....	....
1942◆	Toronto	9	2	3	5	2	....	....	....
1943	Montreal	5	4	2	6	0	....	....	....
Playoff Totals		**50**	**26**	**15**	**41**	**10**	....	....	....
DRISCOLL, Peter									Left wing
1980	Edmonton	3	0	0	0	0	0	0	0
Playoff Totals		**3**	**0**	**0**	**0**	**0**	**0**	**0**	**0**
DRIVER, Bruce									Defense
1988	New Jersey	20	3	7	10	14	3	0	0
1990	New Jersey	6	1	5	6	6	0	0	0
1991	New Jersey	7	1	2	3	12	1	0	0
1992	New Jersey	7	0	4	4	2	0	0	0
1993	New Jersey	5	1	3	4	4	0	1	0
1994	New Jersey	20	3	5	8	12	2	0	0
1995◆	New Jersey	17	1	6	7	8	1	0	0
1996	NY Rangers	11	0	7	7	4	0	0	0
1997	NY Rangers	15	0	1	1	2	0	0	0
Playoff Totals		**108**	**10**	**40**	**50**	**64**	**7**	**1**	**0**
DROLET, Rene *No playoffs*									Right wing
DROPPA, Ivan *No playoffs*									Defense
DROUILLARD, Clarence *No playoffs*									Center

Season	Club	GP	G	A	Pts	PIM	PP	SH	GW
DROUIN, Jude									Center
1971	Minnesota	12	5	7	12	10	1	0	0
1972	Minnesota	7	4	4	8	6	1	0	1
1973	Minnesota	6	1	3	4	0	0	0	0
1975	NY Islanders	17	6	*12	18	6	1	0	1
1976	NY Islanders	13	6	9	15	0	1	0	1
1977	NY Islanders	12	5	6	11	6	1	0	0
1978	NY Islanders	5	0	0	0	5	0	0	0
Playoff Totals		**72**	**27**	**41**	**68**	**33**	**5**	**0**	**3**
DROUIN, P.C. *No playoffs*									Left wing
DROUIN, Polly									Left wing
1938	Mtl. Canadiens	1	0	0	0	0	0	0	0
1939	Mtl. Canadiens	3	0	1	1	5	0	0	0
1940	Mtl. Canadiens	1	0	0	0	0	0	0	0
Playoff Totals		**5**	**0**	**1**	**1**	**5**	**0**	**0**	**0**
DRUCE, John									Right wing
1989	Washington	1	0	0	0	0	0	0	0
1990	Washington	15	14	3	17	23	8	1	4
1991	Washington	11	1	1	2	7	1	0	0
1992	Washington	7	1	0	1	2	0	0	1
1993	Winnipeg	2	0	0	0	0	0	0	0
1996	Philadelphia	2	0	2	2	2	0	0	0
1997	Philadelphia	13	1	0	1	2	0	1	0
1998	Philadelphia	2	0	0	0	2	0	0	0
Playoff Totals		**53**	**17**	**6**	**23**	**38**	**9**	**2**	**5**
DRUKEN, Harold *No playoffs*									Center
DRULIA, Stan *No playoffs*									Right wing
DRUMMOND, Jim *No playoffs*									Defense
DRURY, Chris									Center
1999	Colorado	19	6	2	8	4	0	0	4
Playoff Totals		**19**	**6**	**2**	**8**	**4**	**0**	**0**	**4**
DRURY, Herb									Defense/right wing
1926	Pittsburgh	2	1	0	1	0	....	....	....
1928	Pittsburgh	2	0	1	1	0	....	....	....
Playoff Totals		**4**	**1**	**1**	**2**	**0**	....	....	....
DRURY, Ted									Center
1997	Anaheim	10	1	0	1	4	0	0	0
1999	Anaheim	4	0	0	0	0	0	0	0
Playoff Totals		**14**	**1**	**0**	**1**	**4**	**0**	**0**	**0**
DUBE, Christian									Center
1997	NY Rangers	3	0	0	0	0	0	0	0
Playoff Totals		**3**	**0**	**0**	**0**	**0**	**0**	**0**	**0**
DUBE, Gilles									Left wing
1954◆	Detroit	2	0	0	0	0	0	0	0
Playoff Totals		**2**	**0**	**0**	**0**	**0**	**0**	**0**	**0**
DUBE, Norm *No playoffs*									Left wing
DUBERMAN, Justin *No playoffs*									Right wing
DUBINSKY, Steve									Center
1994	Chicago	6	0	0	0	10	0	0	0
1997	Chicago	4	1	0	1	4	0	0	0
Playoff Totals		**10**	**1**	**0**	**1**	**14**	**0**	**0**	**0**
DUCHESNE, Gaetan									Left wing
1983	Washington	4	1	1	2	4	0	0	0
1984	Washington	8	2	1	3	2	0	0	1
1985	Washington	5	0	1	1	7	0	0	0
1986	Washington	9	4	3	7	12	0	1	0
1987	Washington	7	3	0	3	14	0	0	0
1990	Minnesota	7	0	0	0	6	0	0	0
1991	Minnesota	23	2	3	5	34	0	0	0
1992	Minnesota	7	1	0	1	6	0	0	0
1994	San Jose	14	1	4	5	12	0	0	0
Playoff Totals		**84**	**14**	**13**	**27**	**97**	**0**	**1**	**1**
DUCHESNE, Steve									Defense
1987	Los Angeles	5	2	2	4	4	1	0	0
1988	Los Angeles	5	1	3	4	14	1	0	0
1989	Los Angeles	11	4	4	8	12	2	0	0
1990	Los Angeles	10	2	9	11	6	1	0	0
1991	Los Angeles	12	4	8	12	8	1	0	0
1993	Quebec	6	0	5	5	6	0	0	0
1994	St. Louis	4	0	2	2	2	0	0	0
1995	St. Louis	7	0	4	4	2	0	0	0
1997	Ottawa	7	1	4	5	0	1	0	1
1998	St. Louis	10	0	4	4	6	0	0	0
1999	Philadelphia	6	0	2	2	2	0	0	0
Playoff Totals		**83**	**14**	**47**	**61**	**62**	**7**	**0**	**1**
DUDLEY, Rick									Left wing
1975	Buffalo	10	3	1	4	26	1	0	1
1979	Buffalo	3	1	1	2	2	0	0	0
1980	Buffalo	12	3	0	3	41	1	0	1
Playoff Totals		**25**	**7**	**2**	**9**	**69**	**2**	**0**	**2**
DUERDEN, Dave *No playoffs*									Left wing

Season	Club	GP	G	A	Pts	PIM	PP	SH	GW
DUFF, Dick									Left wing
1956	Toronto	5	1	4	5	2	....	....	....
1959	Toronto	12	4	3	7	8	....	....	....
1960	Toronto	10	2	4	6	6	....	....	....
1961	Toronto	5	0	1	1	2	....	....	....
1962◆	Toronto	12	3	10	13	20	....	....	....
1963◆	Toronto	10	4	1	5	2	....	....	....
1965◆	Montreal	13	3	6	9	17	....	....	....
1966◆	Montreal	10	2	5	7	2	....	....	....
1967	Montreal	10	2	3	5	4	....	....	....
1968◆	Montreal	13	3	4	7	4	0	0	1
1969◆	Montreal	14	6	8	14	11	3	1	0
Playoff Totals		**114**	**30**	**49**	**79**	**78**	....	....	....
DUFOUR, Luc									Left wing
1983	Boston	17	1	0	1	30	0	0	1
1985	St. Louis	1	0	0	0	2	0	0	0
Playoff Totals		**18**	**1**	**0**	**1**	**32**	**0**	**0**	**1**
DUFOUR, Marc *No playoffs*									Right wing
DUFRESNE, Donald									Defense
1989	Montreal	6	1	1	2	4	0	0	0
1990	Montreal	10	0	1	1	18	0	0	0
1991	Montreal	10	0	1	1	21	0	0	0
1993◆	Montreal	2	0	0	0	0	0	0	0
1995	St. Louis	3	0	0	0	4	0	0	0
1997	Edmonton	3	0	0	0	0	0	0	0
Playoff Totals		**34**	**1**	**3**	**4**	**47**	**0**	**0**	**0**
DUGGAN, Jack									Left wing
1926	Ottawa	2	0	0	0	0	0	0	0
Playoff Totals		**2**	**0**	**0**	**0**	**0**	**0**	**0**	**0**
DUGGAN, Ken *No playoffs*									Defense
DUGUAY, Ron									Center/Right wing
1978	NY Rangers	3	1	1	2	2	1	0	0
1979	NY Rangers	18	5	4	9	11	0	1	0
1980	NY Rangers	9	5	2	7	11	2	0	0
1981	NY Rangers	14	8	9	17	16	0	1	1
1982	NY Rangers	10	5	1	6	31	1	0	0
1983	NY Rangers	9	2	2	4	28	0	0	0
1984	Detroit	4	2	3	5	2	1	0	0
1985	Detroit	3	1	0	1	7	1	0	0
1987	NY Rangers	6	2	0	2	4	1	0	0
1988	Los Angeles	2	0	0	0	0	0	0	0
1989	Los Angeles	11	0	0	0	6	0	0	0
Playoff Totals		**89**	**31**	**22**	**53**	**118**	**7**	**2**	**1**
DUGUID, Lorne									Left wing
1933	Mtl. Maroons	2	0	0	0	4	0	0	0
Playoff Totals		**2**	**0**	**0**	**0**	**4**	**0**	**0**	**0**
DUKOWSKI, Duke									Defense
1927	Chicago	2	0	0	0	0	0	0	0
1930	Chicago	2	0	0	0	6	0	0	0
1934	NY Rangers	2	0	0	0	0	0	0	0
Playoff Totals		**6**	**0**	**0**	**0**	**6**	**0**	**0**	**0**
DUMART, Woody									Left wing
1937	Boston	3	0	0	0	0	....	....	....
1938	Boston	3	0	0	0	0	....	....	....
1939◆	Boston	12	1	3	4	6	....	....	....
1940	Boston	6	1	0	1	0	....	....	....
1941◆	Boston	11	1	3	4	9	....	....	....
1946	Boston	10	4	3	7	0	....	....	....
1947	Boston	5	1	1	2	8	....	....	....
1948	Boston	5	0	0	0	0	....	....	....
1949	Boston	5	3	0	3	0	....	....	....
1951	Boston	6	1	2	3	0	....	....	....
1952	Boston	7	0	1	1	0	....	....	....
1953	Boston	11	0	2	2	0	....	....	....
1954	Boston	4	0	0	0	0	....	....	....
Playoff Totals		**88**	**12**	**15**	**27**	**23**	....	....	....
DUMONT, Jean-Pierre *No playoffs*									Right wing
DUNBAR, Dale *No playoffs*									Defense
DUNCAN, Art									Defense
1929	Toronto	4	0	0	0	4	0	0	0
1931	Toronto	1	0	0	0	0	0	0	0
Playoff Totals		**5**	**0**	**0**	**0**	**4**	**0**	**0**	**0**
DUNCAN, Iain									Left wing
1987	Winnipeg	7	0	2	2	6	0	0	0
1988	Winnipeg	4	0	1	1	0	0	0	0
Playoff Totals		**11**	**0**	**3**	**3**	**6**	**0**	**0**	**0**
DUNCANSON, Craig *No playoffs*									Left wing
DUNDAS, Rocky *No playoffs*									Right wing
DUNLAP, Frank *No playoffs*									Right/left wing
DUNLOP, Blake									Center
1979	Philadelphia	8	1	1	2	4	0	0	0
1980	St. Louis	3	0	2	2	2	0	0	0
1981	St. Louis	11	0	3	3	4	0	0	0
1982	St. Louis	10	2	2	4	4	0	0	0
1983	St. Louis	4	1	1	2	0	1	0	0
1984	Detroit	4	0	1	1	4	0	0	0
Playoff Totals		**40**	**4**	**10**	**14**	**18**	**1**	**0**	**0**

Season	Club	GP	G	A	Pts	PIM	PP	SH	GW
DUNN, Dave	Defense								
1975	Toronto	7	1	1	2	24	0	0	0
1976	Toronto	3	0	0	0	17	0	0	0
Playoff Totals		**10**	**1**	**1**	**2**	**41**	**0**	**0**	**0**
DUNN, Richie	Defense								
1978	Buffalo	1	0	0	0	2	0	0	0
1980	Buffalo	14	2	8	10	8	2	0	0
1981	Buffalo	8	0	5	5	6	0	0	0
1982	Buffalo	4	0	1	1	0	0	0	0
1983	Calgary	9	1	1	2	8	0	0	0
Playoff Totals		**36**	**3**	**15**	**18**	**24**	**2**	**0**	**0**
DUPERE, Denis	Left wing								
1971	Toronto	6	0	0	0	0	0	0	0
1972	Toronto	5	0	0	0	0	0	0	0
1974	Toronto	3	0	0	0	0	0	0	0
1978	Colorado	2	1	0	1	0	1	0	0
Playoff Totals		**16**	**1**	**0**	**1**	**0**	**1**	**0**	**0**
DUPONT, Andre	Defense								
1972	St. Louis	11	1	0	1	20	0	0	0
1973	Philadelphia	11	1	2	3	29	0	0	0
1974◆	Philadelphia	16	4	3	7	67	0	0	0
1975◆	Philadelphia	17	3	2	5	49	1	0	2
1976	Philadelphia	15	2	2	4	46	2	0	0
1977	Philadelphia	10	1	1	2	35	0	0	0
1978	Philadelphia	12	2	1	3	13	0	0	0
1979	Philadelphia	8	0	0	0	17	0	0	0
1980	Philadelphia	19	0	4	4	50	0	0	0
1981	Quebec	1	0	0	0	0	0	0	0
1982	Quebec	16	0	3	3	18	0	0	0
1983	Quebec	4	0	0	0	8	0	0	0
Playoff Totals		**140**	**14**	**18**	**32**	**352**	**3**	**0**	**2**
DUPONT, Jerome	Defense								
1984	Chicago	4	0	0	0	15	0	0	0
1985	Chicago	15	0	2	2	41	0	0	0
1986	Chicago	1	0	0	0	0	0	0	0
Playoff Totals		**20**	**0**	**2**	**2**	**56**	**0**	**0**	**0**
DUPONT, Norm	Left wing								
1980	Montreal	8	1	1	2	0	0	0	1
1982	Winnipeg	4	2	0	2	0	2	0	0
1983	Winnipeg	1	1	1	2	0	1	0	0
Playoff Totals		**13**	**4**	**2**	**6**	**0**	**3**	**0**	**1**
DUPRE, Yanick *No playoffs*	Left wing								
DURBANO, Steve	Defense								
1973	St. Louis	5	0	2	2	8	0	0	0
Playoff Totals		**5**	**0**	**2**	**2**	**8**	**0**	**0**	**0**
DURIS, Vitezslav	Defense								
1981	Toronto	3	0	1	1	2	0	0	0
Playoff Totals		**3**	**0**	**1**	**1**	**2**	**0**	**0**	**0**
DUSSAULT, Norm	Center								
1949	Montreal	2	0	0	0	0	....	....	....
1950	Montreal	5	3	1	4	0	....	....	....
Playoff Totals		**7**	**3**	**1**	**4**	**0**	....	....	....
DUTTON, Red	Defense								
1927	Mtl. Maroons	2	0	0	0	4	....	....	....
1928	Mtl. Maroons	9	1	0	1	27	....	....	....
1930	Mtl. Maroons	4	0	0	0	2	....	....	....
1936	NY Americans	3	0	0	0	0	....	....	....
Playoff Totals		**18**	**1**	**0**	**1**	**33**	....	....	....
DVORAK, Miroslav	Defense								
1983	Philadelphia	3	0	1	1	0	0	0	0
1984	Philadelphia	2	0	0	0	2	0	0	0
1985	Philadelphia	13	0	1	1	4	0	0	0
Playoff Totals		**18**	**0**	**2**	**2**	**6**	**0**	**0**	**0**
DVORAK, Radek	Right wing								
1996	Florida	16	1	3	4	0	0	0	0
1997	Florida	3	0	0	0	0	0	0	0
Playoff Totals		**19**	**1**	**3**	**4**	**0**	**0**	**0**	**0**
DWYER, Gordie *No playoffs*	Left wing								
DWYER, Mike	Left wing								
1981	Calgary	1	1	0	1	0	0	0	0
Playoff Totals		**1**	**1**	**0**	**1**	**0**	**0**	**0**	**0**
DYCK, Henry *No playoffs*	Center/left wing								
DYE, Babe	Right wing								
1921	Toronto	2	0	0	0	7	....	....	....
1922◆	Toronto	7	*11	1	*12	5	....	....	....
1925	Toronto	2	0	0	0	0	....	....	....
1927	Chicago	2	0	0	0	2	....	....	....
1929	NY Americans	2	0	0	0	0	....	....	....
Playoff Totals		**15**	**11**	**1**	**12**	**14**	....	....	....
DYKHUIS, Karl	Defense								
1995	Philadelphia	15	4	4	8	14	2	0	2
1996	Philadelphia	12	2	2	4	22	1	0	0
1997	Philadelphia	18	0	3	3	2	0	0	0
1999	Philadelphia	5	1	0	1	4	0	0	0
Playoff Totals		**50**	**7**	**9**	**16**	**42**	**3**	**0**	**2**
DYKSTRA, Steve	Defense								
1989	Pittsburgh	1	0	0	0	2	0	0	0
Playoff Totals		**1**	**0**	**0**	**0**	**2**	**0**	**0**	**0**

Season	Club	GP	G	A	Pts	PIM	PP	SH	GW
DYTE, Jack *No playoffs*	Defense								
DZIEDZIC, Joe	Left wing								
1996	Pittsburgh	16	1	2	3	19	0	0	0
1997	Pittsburgh	5	0	1	1	4	0	0	0
Playoff Totals		**21**	**1**	**3**	**4**	**23**	**0**	**0**	**0**
EAGLES, Mike	Center/Left wing								
1986	Quebec	3	0	0	0	2	0	0	0
1987	Quebec	4	1	0	1	10	0	0	0
1992	Winnipeg	7	0	0	0	8	0	0	0
1993	Winnipeg	5	0	1	1	6	0	0	0
1995	Washington	7	0	2	2	4	0	0	0
1996	Washington	6	1	1	2	2	0	0	0
1998	Washington	12	0	2	2	2	0	0	0
Playoff Totals		**44**	**2**	**6**	**8**	**34**	**0**	**0**	**0**
EAKIN, Bruce *No playoffs*	Center								
EAKINS, Dallas	Defense								
1997	NY Rangers	4	0	0	0	4	0	0	0
1999	Toronto	1	0	0	0	0	0	0	0
Playoff Totals		**5**	**0**	**0**	**0**	**4**	**0**	**0**	**0**
EASTWOOD, Mike	Center								
1993	Toronto	10	1	2	3	8	0	0	0
1994	Toronto	18	3	2	5	12	1	0	1
1996	Winnipeg	6	0	1	1	2	0	0	0
1997	NY Rangers	15	1	2	3	22	0	0	0
1998	St. Louis	3	1	0	1	0	0	0	1
1999	St. Louis	13	1	1	2	6	0	0	0
Playoff Totals		**65**	**7**	**8**	**15**	**50**	**1**	**0**	**2**
EATON, Mark *No playoffs*	Defense								
EATOUGH, Jeff *No playoffs*	Right wing								
EAVES, Mike	Center								
1980	Minnesota	15	2	5	7	4	0	0	0
1983	Minnesota	9	0	0	0	0	0	0	0
1984	Calgary	11	4	4	8	2	1	1	1
1986	Calgary	8	1	1	2	8	0	0	0
Playoff Totals		**43**	**7**	**10**	**17**	**14**	**1**	**1**	**1**
EAVES, Murray	Center								
1984	Winnipeg	2	0	0	0	2	0	0	0
1985	Winnipeg	2	0	1	1	0	0	0	0
Playoff Totals		**4**	**0**	**1**	**1**	**2**	**0**	**0**	**0**
ECCLESTONE, Tim	Left wing								
1968	St. Louis	12	1	2	3	2	0	0	0
1969	St. Louis	12	2	2	4	20	0	0	0
1970	St. Louis	16	3	4	7	48	1	0	1
1974	Toronto	4	0	1	1	0	0	0	0
1977	Atlanta	3	0	2	2	6	0	0	0
1978	Atlanta	1	0	0	0	0	0	0	0
Playoff Totals		**48**	**6**	**11**	**17**	**76**	**1**	**0**	**1**
EDBERG, Rolf *No playoffs*	Center								
EDDOLLS, Frank	Defense								
1945	Montreal	3	0	0	0	0	0	0	0
1946◆	Montreal	8	0	1	1	2	0	0	0
1947	Montreal	7	0	0	0	4	0	0	0
1948	NY Rangers	2	0	0	0	0	0	0	0
1950	NY Rangers	11	0	1	1	4	0	0	0
Playoff Totals		**31**	**0**	**2**	**2**	**10**	**0**	**0**	**0**
EDESTRAND, Darryl	Defense								
1972	Pittsburgh	4	0	2	2	0	0	0	0
1974	Boston	16	1	2	3	15	0	0	0
1975	Boston	3	0	1	1	7	0	0	0
1976	Boston	12	1	3	4	23	0	0	0
1977	Boston	3	0	0	0	2	0	0	0
1978	Los Angeles	2	1	1	2	4	0	0	0
1979	Los Angeles	2	0	0	0	6	0	0	0
Playoff Totals		**42**	**3**	**9**	**12**	**57**	**0**	**0**	**0**
EDMUNDSON, Garry	Left wing								
1952	Montreal	2	0	0	0	4	0	0	0
1960	Toronto	9	0	1	1	4	0	0	0
Playoff Totals		**11**	**0**	**1**	**1**	**8**	**0**	**0**	**0**
EDUR, Tom *No playoffs*	Defense								
EGAN, Pat	Defense								
1940	NY Americans	2	0	0	0	4	....	....	....
1945	Boston	7	2	0	2	6	....	....	....
1946	Boston	10	3	0	3	8	....	....	....
1947	Boston	5	0	2	2	6	....	....	....
1948	Boston	5	1	1	2	2	....	....	....
1949	Boston	5	0	0	0	16	....	....	....
1950	NY Rangers	12	3	1	4	6	....	....	....
Playoff Totals		**46**	**9**	**4**	**13**	**48**	....	....	....
EGELAND, Allan *No playoffs*	Center								
EGERS, Jack	Right wing								
1970	NY Rangers	5	3	1	4	10	1	0	0
1971	NY Rangers	3	0	0	0	2	0	0	0
1972	St. Louis	11	1	4	5	14	0	0	0
1973	St. Louis	5	0	1	1	2	0	0	0
1974	NY Rangers	8	1	0	1	4	0	0	0
Playoff Totals		**32**	**5**	**6**	**11**	**32**	**1**	**0**	**0**

Season	Club	GP	G	A	Pts	PIM	PP	SH	GW
EHMAN, Gerry	Right wing								
1959	Toronto	12	6	7	13	8	2	0	2
1960	Toronto	9	0	0	0	0	0	0	0
1964◆	Toronto	9	1	0	1	4	0	0	0
1969	Oakland	7	2	2	4	0	0	0	0
1970	Oakland	4	1	1	2	0	1	0	0
Playoff Totals		**41**	**10**	**10**	**20**	**12**	**3**	**0**	**2**
EISENHUT, Neil *No playoffs*	Center								
EKLUND, Per-Erik	Center								
1986	Philadelphia	5	0	2	2	0	0	0	0
1987	Philadelphia	26	7	20	27	2	2	0	0
1988	Philadelphia	7	0	3	3	0	0	0	0
1989	Philadelphia	19	3	8	11	2	3	0	1
1994	Dallas	9	0	3	3	4	0	0	0
Playoff Totals		**66**	**10**	**36**	**46**	**8**	**5**	**0**	**1**
EKMAN, Nils *No playoffs*	Left wing								
ELDEBRINK, Anders	Defense								
1982	Vancouver	13	0	0	0	10	0	0	0
1983	Quebec	1	0	0	0	0	0	0	0
Playoff Totals		**14**	**0**	**0**	**0**	**10**	**0**	**0**	**0**
ELIAS, Patrik	Left wing								
1997	New Jersey	8	2	3	5	4	1	0	0
1998	New Jersey	4	0	1	1	0	0	0	0
1999	New Jersey	7	0	5	5	6	0	0	0
Playoff Totals		**19**	**2**	**9**	**11**	**10**	**1**	**0**	**0**
ELIK, Bo *No playoffs*	Left wing								
ELIK, Todd	Center								
1990	Los Angeles	10	3	9	12	10	1	0	0
1991	Los Angeles	12	2	7	9	6	0	0	0
1992	Minnesota	5	1	1	2	2	0	0	1
1994	San Jose	14	5	5	10	12	1	0	0
1995	St. Louis	7	4	3	7	2	1	1	0
1996	Boston	4	0	2	2	16	0	0	0
Playoff Totals		**52**	**15**	**27**	**42**	**48**	**3**	**1**	**1**
ELLETT, Dave	Defense								
1985	Winnipeg	8	1	5	6	4	1	0	0
1986	Winnipeg	3	0	1	1	0	0	0	0
1987	Winnipeg	10	0	8	8	2	0	0	0
1988	Winnipeg	5	1	2	3	10	1	0	0
1990	Winnipeg	7	2	0	2	6	2	0	1
1993	Toronto	21	4	8	12	8	2	0	0
1994	Toronto	18	3	15	18	31	3	0	0
1995	Toronto	7	0	2	2	0	0	0	0
1996	Toronto	6	0	0	0	4	0	0	0
1997	New Jersey	10	0	3	3	10	0	0	0
1998	Boston	6	0	1	1	6	0	0	0
1999	Boston	8	0	0	0	4	0	0	0
Playoff Totals		**109**	**11**	**45**	**56**	**85**	**9**	**0**	**1**
ELLIOT, Fred *No playoffs*	Right wing								
ELLIS, Ron	Right wing								
1965	Toronto	6	3	0	3	2	0	0	0
1966	Toronto	4	0	0	0	2	0	0	0
1967◆	Toronto	12	2	1	3	4	0	0	0
1969	Toronto	4	2	1	3	2	1	0	0
1971	Toronto	6	1	1	2	2	1	0	0
1972	Toronto	5	1	1	2	4	1	0	0
1974	Toronto	4	2	1	3	0	0	0	0
1975	Toronto	7	3	0	3	2	1	0	0
1978	Toronto	13	3	2	5	0	0	0	2
1979	Toronto	6	1	1	2	2	0	0	0
1980	Toronto	3	0	0	0	0	0	0	0
Playoff Totals		**70**	**18**	**8**	**26**	**20**	**4**	**0**	**2**
ELOMO, Miika *No playoffs*	Left wing								
ELORANTA, Kari	Defense								
1982	St. Louis	5	0	0	0	0	0	0	0
1983	Calgary	9	1	3	4	17	0	0	0
1984	Calgary	6	0	2	2	2	0	0	0
1987	Calgary	6	0	2	2	0	0	0	0
Playoff Totals		**26**	**1**	**7**	**8**	**19**	**0**	**0**	**0**
ELORANTA, Mikko *No playoffs*	Left wing								
ELYNUIK, Pat	Right wing								
1990	Winnipeg	7	2	4	6	2	0	0	0
1992	Winnipeg	7	2	2	4	4	2	0	0
1993	Washington	6	2	3	5	19	0	0	0
Playoff Totals		**20**	**6**	**9**	**15**	**25**	**2**	**0**	**0**
EMBERG, Eddie	Center								
1945	Montreal	2	1	0	1	0	....	....	....
Playoff Totals		**2**	**1**	**0**	**1**	**0**	....	....	....
EMERSON, Nelson	Right wing								
1992	St. Louis	6	3	3	6	21	2	0	0
1993	St. Louis	11	1	6	7	6	0	0	0
1999	Ottawa	4	1	3	4	0	0	0	0
Playoff Totals		**21**	**5**	**12**	**17**	**27**	**2**	**0**	**0**
EMMA, David *No playoffs*	Center								
EMMONS, Gary *No playoffs*	Center								
EMMONS, John *No playoffs*	Center								

Season	Club	GP	G	A	Pts	PIM	PP	SH	GW
EMMS, Hap									Left wing/defense
1932	Detroit	2	0	0	0	2	0	0	0
1933	Detroit	4	0	0	0	8	0	0	0
1934	Detroit	8	0	0	0	2	0	0	0
Playoff Totals		**14**	**0**	**0**	**0**	**12**	**0**	**0**	**0**
ENDEAN, Craig	*No playoffs*								Left wing
ENGBLOM, Brian									Defense
1977◆	Montreal	2	0	0	0	2	0	0	0
1978◆	Montreal	5	0	0	0	2	0	0	0
1979◆	Montreal	16	0	1	1	11	0	0	0
1980	Montreal	10	2	4	6	6	1	0	1
1981	Montreal	3	1	0	1	4	0	0	0
1982	Montreal	5	0	2	2	14	0	0	0
1983	Washington	4	0	2	2	2	0	0	0
1985	Los Angeles	3	0	0	0	2	0	0	0
Playoff Totals		**48**	**3**	**9**	**12**	**43**	**1**	**0**	**1**
ENGELE, Jerry									Defense
1977	Minnesota	2	0	1	1	0	0	0	0
Playoff Totals		**2**	**0**	**1**	**1**	**0**	**0**	**0**	**0**
ENGLISH, John									Defense
1988	Los Angeles	1	0	0	0	0	0	0	0
Playoff Totals		**1**	**0**	**0**	**0**	**0**	**0**	**0**	**0**
ENNIS, Jim	*No playoffs*								Defense
ERICKSON, Aut									Defense
1964	Chicago	6	0	0	0	0	0	0	0
1967◆	Toronto	1	0	0	0	2	0	0	0
Playoff Totals		**7**	**0**	**0**	**0**	**2**	**0**	**0**	**0**
ERICKSON, Bryan									Right wing
1984	Washington	8	2	3	5	7	1	0	0
1987	Los Angeles	3	1	1	2	0	0	0	0
1993	Winnipeg	3	0	0	0	0	0	0	0
Playoff Totals		**14**	**3**	**4**	**7**	**7**	**1**	**0**	**0**
ERICKSON, Grant	*No playoffs*								Left wing
ERIKSSON, Anders									Defense
1996	Detroit	3	0	0	0	0	0	0	0
1998◆	Detroit	18	0	5	5	16	0	0	0
Playoff Totals		**21**	**0**	**5**	**5**	**16**	**0**	**0**	**0**
ERIKSSON, Peter	*No playoffs*								Left wing
ERIKSSON, Roland									Center
1977	Minnesota	2	1	0	1	0	0	0	0
Playoff Totals		**2**	**1**	**0**	**1**	**0**	**0**	**0**	**0**
ERIKSSON, Thomas									Defense
1981	Philadelphia	7	0	2	2	6	0	0	0
1984	Philadelphia	3	0	1	1	0	0	0	0
1985	Philadelphia	9	0	0	0	6	0	0	0
Playoff Totals		**19**	**0**	**3**	**3**	**12**	**0**	**0**	**0**
ERIXON, Jan									Left wing
1984	NY Rangers	5	2	0	2	4	0	0	1
1985	NY Rangers	2	0	0	0	2	0	0	0
1986	NY Rangers	12	0	1	1	4	0	0	0
1987	NY Rangers	6	1	0	1	0	0	0	0
1989	NY Rangers	4	0	1	1	2	0	0	0
1990	NY Rangers	10	1	0	1	2	0	1	0
1991	NY Rangers	6	1	2	3	0	0	0	0
1992	NY Rangers	13	2	3	5	2	0	1	1
Playoff Totals		**58**	**7**	**7**	**14**	**16**	**0**	**2**	**2**
ERREY, Bob									Left wing
1989	Pittsburgh	11	1	2	3	12	0	0	0
1991◆	Pittsburgh	24	5	2	7	29	0	1	0
1992◆	Pittsburgh	14	3	0	3	10	0	1	0
1993	Buffalo	4	0	1	1	10	0	0	0
1994	San Jose	14	3	2	5	10	1	0	0
1995	Detroit	18	1	5	6	30	1	0	0
1996	Detroit	14	0	4	4	8	0	0	0
Playoff Totals		**99**	**13**	**16**	**29**	**109**	**2**	**2**	**0**
ESAU, Len	*No playoffs*								Defense
ESPOSITO, Phil									Center
1964	Chicago	4	0	0	0	0	0	0	0
1965	Chicago	13	3	3	6	15	0	0	0
1966	Chicago	6	1	1	2	2	1	0	0
1967	Chicago	6	0	0	0	7	0	0	0
1968	Boston	4	0	3	3	0	0	0	0
1969	Boston	10	*8	*10	*18	8	5	2	0
1970◆	Boston	14	*13	*14	*27	16	4	2	0
1971	Boston	7	3	7	10	6	2	0	0
1972◆	Boston	15	9	15	*24	24	2	0	3
1973	Boston	2	0	1	1	2	0	0	0
1974	Boston	16	9	5	14	25	4	0	2
1975	Boston	3	4	1	5	0	1	0	0
1978	NY Rangers	3	0	1	1	5	0	0	0
1979	NY Rangers	18	8	12	20	20	2	0	2
1980	NY Rangers	9	3	3	6	8	1	0	1
Playoff Totals		**130**	**61**	**76**	**137**	**138**	**22**	**4**	**8**
EVANS, Chris									Defense
1972	St. Louis	7	1	0	1	4	0	0	0
1973	St. Louis	5	0	1	1	4	0	0	0
Playoff Totals		**12**	**1**	**1**	**2**	**8**	**0**	**0**	**0**

Season	Club	GP	G	A	Pts	PIM	PP	SH	GW
EVANS, Daryl									Left wing
1982	Los Angeles	10	5	8	13	12	1	0	1
1987	Toronto	1	0	0	0	0	0	0	0
Playoff Totals		**11**	**5**	**8**	**13**	**12**	**1**	**0**	**1**
EVANS, Doug									Left wing
1987	St. Louis	5	0	0	0	10	0	0	0
1988	St. Louis	2	0	0	0	0	0	0	0
1989	St. Louis	7	1	2	3	16	0	0	0
1990	Winnipeg	7	2	2	4	10	0	0	0
1992	Winnipeg	1	0	0	0	2	0	0	0
Playoff Totals		**22**	**3**	**4**	**7**	**38**	**0**	**0**	**0**
EVANS, Jack									Defense
1956	NY Rangers	5	1	0	1	18	....	....	....
1957	NY Rangers	5	0	1	1	4	....	....	....
1958	NY Rangers	6	0	0	0	17	....	....	....
1959	Chicago	6	0	0	0	10	....	....	....
1960	Chicago	4	0	0	0	4	....	....	....
1961◆	Chicago	12	1	1	2	14	....	....	....
1962	Chicago	12	0	0	0	26	....	....	....
1963	Chicago	6	0	0	0	4	....	....	....
Playoff Totals		**56**	**2**	**2**	**4**	**97**	....	....	....
EVANS, John Paul									Center
1983	Philadelphia	1	0	0	0	0	0	0	0
Playoff Totals		**1**	**0**	**0**	**0**	**0**	**0**	**0**	**0**
EVANS, Kevin	*No playoffs*								Left wing
EVANS, Paul									Center/left wing
1977	Toronto	2	0	0	0	0	0	0	0
Playoff Totals		**2**	**0**	**0**	**0**	**0**	**0**	**0**	**0**
EVANS, Shawn	*No playoffs*								Defense
EVANS, Stewart									Defense
1933	Detroit	4	0	0	0	6	0	0	0
1934	Mtl. Maroons	4	0	0	0	4	0	0	0
1935◆	Mtl. Maroons	7	0	0	0	8	0	0	0
1936	Mtl. Maroons	3	0	0	0	0	0	0	0
1937	Mtl. Maroons	5	0	0	0	0	0	0	0
1939	Mtl. Canadiens	3	0	0	0	2	0	0	0
Playoff Totals		**26**	**0**	**0**	**0**	**20**	**0**	**0**	**0**
EVASON, Dean									Center
1986	Hartford	10	1	4	5	10	0	0	0
1987	Hartford	5	3	2	5	35	0	0	0
1988	Hartford	6	1	1	2	2	0	0	0
1989	Hartford	4	1	2	3	10	0	1	0
1990	Hartford	7	2	2	4	22	0	0	0
1991	Hartford	6	0	4	4	29	0	0	0
1994	Dallas	9	0	2	2	12	0	0	0
1995	Dallas	5	1	2	3	12	0	1	0
1996	Calgary	3	0	1	1	0	0	0	0
Playoff Totals		**55**	**9**	**20**	**29**	**132**	**0**	**2**	**0**
EWEN, Todd									Right wing
1987	St. Louis	4	0	0	0	23	0	0	0
1988	St. Louis	6	0	0	0	21	0	0	0
1989	St. Louis	2	0	0	0	21	0	0	0
1990	Montreal	10	0	0	0	4	0	0	0
1992	Montreal	3	0	0	0	18	0	0	0
1993◆	Montreal	1	0	0	0	0	0	0	0
Playoff Totals		**26**	**0**	**0**	**0**	**87**	**0**	**0**	**0**
EZINICKI, Bill									Right wing
1947◆	Toronto	11	0	2	2	30	....	....	....
1948◆	Toronto	9	3	1	4	6	....	....	....
1949◆	Toronto	9	1	4	5	20	....	....	....
1950	Toronto	5	0	0	0	13	....	....	....
1951	Boston	6	1	1	2	18	....	....	....
Playoff Totals		**40**	**5**	**8**	**13**	**87**	....	....	....
FAHEY, Trevor	*No playoffs*								Left wing
FAIRBAIRN, Bill									Right wing
1970	NY Rangers	6	0	1	1	10	0	0	0
1971	NY Rangers	4	0	0	0	0	0	0	0
1972	NY Rangers	16	5	7	12	11	2	0	1
1973	NY Rangers	10	1	8	9	2	0	0	0
1974	NY Rangers	13	3	5	8	6	0	0	0
1975	NY Rangers	3	4	0	4	13	2	1	0
1977	Minnesota	2	0	1	1	0	0	0	0
Playoff Totals		**54**	**13**	**22**	**35**	**42**	**4**	**1**	**1**
FAIRCHILD, Kelly	*No playoffs*								Center
FALKENBERG, Bob	*No playoffs*								Defense
FALLOON, Pat									Right wing
1994	San Jose	14	1	2	3	6	0	0	0
1995	San Jose	11	3	1	4	0	0	0	0
1996	Philadelphia	12	3	2	5	2	2	0	0
1997	Philadelphia	14	3	1	4	2	1	0	0
1998	Ottawa	1	0	0	0	0	0	0	0
1999	Edmonton	4	0	1	1	4	0	0	0
Playoff Totals		**56**	**10**	**7**	**17**	**14**	**3**	**0**	**0**
FARRANT, Walt	*No playoffs*								Right wing
FARRISH, Dave									Defense
1978	NY Rangers	3	0	0	0	0	0	0	0
1979	NY Rangers	7	0	2	2	14	0	0	0
1980	Toronto	3	0	0	0	10	0	0	0
1981	Toronto	1	0	0	0	0	0	0	0
Playoff Totals		**14**	**0**	**2**	**2**	**24**	**0**	**0**	**0**

Season	Club	GP	G	A	Pts	PIM	PP	SH	GW
FASHOWAY, Gordie	*No playoffs*								Left wing
FATA, Rico	*No playoffs*								Center
FAUBERT, Mario									Defense
1977	Pittsburgh	3	1	0	1	2	1	0	0
1980	Pittsburgh	2	0	1	1	0	0	0	0
1981	Pittsburgh	5	1	1	2	4	1	0	0
Playoff Totals		**10**	**2**	**2**	**4**	**6**	**2**	**0**	**0**
FAULKNER, Alex									Center
1963	Detroit	8	5	0	5	2	1	0	3
1964	Detroit	4	0	0	0	0	0	0	0
Playoff Totals		**12**	**5**	**0**	**5**	**2**	**1**	**0**	**3**
FAUSS, Ted	*No playoffs*								Defense
FAUST, Andre	*No playoffs*								Center
FEAMSTER, Dave									Defense
1982	Chicago	15	2	4	6	53	0	0	1
1983	Chicago	13	1	0	1	4	0	0	0
1984	Chicago	5	0	1	1	4	0	0	0
Playoff Totals		**33**	**3**	**5**	**8**	**61**	**0**	**0**	**1**
FEATHERSTONE, Glen									Defense
1989	St. Louis	6	0	0	0	25	0	0	0
1990	St. Louis	12	0	2	2	47	0	0	0
1991	St. Louis	9	0	0	0	31	0	0	0
1994	Boston	1	0	0	0	0	0	0	0
Playoff Totals		**28**	**0**	**2**	**2**	**103**	**0**	**0**	**0**
FEATHERSTONE, Tony									Right wing
1970	Oakland	2	0	0	0	0	0	0	0
Playoff Totals		**2**	**0**	**0**	**0**	**0**	**0**	**0**	**0**
FEDERKO, Bernie									Center
1977	St. Louis	4	1	1	2	2	0	0	0
1980	St. Louis	3	1	0	1	2	0	0	0
1981	St. Louis	11	8	10	18	2	4	0	1
1982	St. Louis	10	3	15	18	10	1	0	1
1983	St. Louis	4	2	3	5	0	1	0	0
1984	St. Louis	11	4	4	8	10	1	0	1
1985	St. Louis	3	0	2	2	4	0	0	0
1986	St. Louis	19	7	14	*21	17	1	0	1
1987	St. Louis	6	3	3	6	18	1	0	0
1988	St. Louis	10	2	6	8	18	2	0	0
1989	St. Louis	10	4	8	12	0	2	0	0
Playoff Totals		**91**	**35**	**66**	**101**	**83**	**13**	**0**	**4**
FEDOROV, Sergei									Center
1991	Detroit	7	1	5	6	4	0	0	1
1992	Detroit	11	5	5	10	8	1	2	1
1993	Detroit	7	3	6	9	23	1	1	0
1994	Detroit	7	1	7	8	6	0	0	0
1995	Detroit	17	7	*17	*24	6	3	0	0
1996	Detroit	19	2	*18	20	10	0	0	2
1997◆	Detroit	20	8	12	20	12	3	0	4
1998◆	Detroit	22	*10	10	20	12	2	1	1
1999	Detroit	10	1	8	9	8	0	0	0
Playoff Totals		**120**	**38**	**88**	**126**	**89**	**10**	**4**	**9**
FEDOTOV, Anatoli	*No playoffs*								Defense
FEDYK, Brent									Left wing
1991	Detroit	6	1	0	1	2	0	0	1
1992	Detroit	1	0	0	0	2	0	0	0
1995	Philadelphia	9	2	2	4	8	0	0	0
Playoff Totals		**16**	**3**	**2**	**5**	**12**	**0**	**0**	**1**
FELIX, Chris									Defense
1988	Washington	1	0	0	0	0	0	0	0
1989	Washington	1	0	1	1	0	0	0	0
Playoff Totals		**2**	**0**	**1**	**1**	**0**	**0**	**0**	**0**
FELSNER, Brian	*No playoffs*								Left wing
FELSNER, Denny									Left wing
1992	St. Louis	1	0	0	0	0	0	0	0
1993	St. Louis	9	2	3	5	2	1	0	0
Playoff Totals		**10**	**2**	**3**	**5**	**2**	**1**	**0**	**0**
FELTRIN, Tony	*No playoffs*								Defense
FENTON, Paul									Left wing
1988	Los Angeles	5	2	1	3	2	1	0	0
1990	Winnipeg	7	2	0	2	23	2	0	0
1991	Calgary	5	0	0	0	2	0	0	0
Playoff Totals		**17**	**4**	**1**	**5**	**27**	**3**	**0**	**0**
FENYVES, David									Defense
1983	Buffalo	4	0	0	0	0	0	0	0
1984	Buffalo	2	0	0	0	7	0	0	0
1985	Buffalo	5	0	0	0	2	0	0	0
Playoff Totals		**11**	**0**	**0**	**0**	**9**	**0**	**0**	**0**
FERENCE, Andrew	*No playoffs*								Defense

Season	Club	GP	G	A	Pts	PIM	PP	SH	GW
FERGUS, Tom	Center								
1982	Boston	6	3	0	3	0	2	0	0
1983	Boston	15	2	2	4	15	0	0	0
1984	Boston	3	2	0	2	9	1	0	0
1985	Boston	5	0	0	0	4	0	0	0
1986	Toronto	10	5	7	12	6	3	0	1
1987	Toronto	2	0	1	1	2	0	0	0
1988	Toronto	6	2	3	5	2	0	1	0
1990	Toronto	5	2	1	3	4	0	0	0
1992	Vancouver	13	5	3	8	6	0	0	1
Playoff Totals		**65**	**21**	**17**	**38**	**48**	**6**	**1**	**2**
FERGUSON, Craig *No playoffs*	Center								
FERGUSON, George	Center								
1974	Toronto	3	0	1	1	2	0	0	0
1975	Toronto	7	1	0	1	7	0	0	0
1976	Toronto	10	2	4	6	2	0	0	1
1977	Toronto	9	0	3	3	7	0	0	0
1978	Toronto	13	5	1	6	7	0	0	0
1979	Pittsburgh	7	2	1	3	0	0	0	1
1980	Pittsburgh	5	0	3	3	4	0	0	0
1981	Pittsburgh	5	2	6	8	9	0	0	0
1982	Pittsburgh	5	0	1	1	0	0	0	0
1983	Minnesota	9	0	3	3	4	0	0	0
1984	Minnesota	13	2	0	2	2	0	0	1
Playoff Totals		**86**	**14**	**23**	**37**	**44**	**0**	**0**	**3**
FERGUSON, John	Left wing								
1964	Montreal	7	0	1	1	25	0	0	0
1965◆	Montreal	13	3	1	4	28	0	0	0
1966◆	Montreal	10	2	0	2	*44	0	0	0
1967	Montreal	10	4	2	6	22	1	0	2
1968◆	Montreal	13	3	5	8	25	0	0	1
1969◆	Montreal	14	4	3	7	*80	2	2	0
1971◆	Montreal	18	4	6	10	36	1	0	1
Playoff Totals		**85**	**20**	**18**	**38**	**260**	**4**	**2**	**4**
FERGUSON, Lorne	Left wing								
1951	Boston	6	1	0	1	2	....	....	....
1955	Boston	4	1	0	1	2	....	....	....
1956	Detroit	10	1	2	3	12	....	....	....
1957	Detroit	5	1	0	1	6	....	....	....
1959	Chicago	6	2	1	3	2	....	....	....
Playoff Totals		**31**	**6**	**3**	**9**	**24**	....	....	....
FERGUSON, Norm	Right wing								
1969	Oakland	7	1	4	5	7	0	0	0
1970	Oakland	3	0	0	0	0	0	0	0
Playoff Totals		**10**	**1**	**4**	**5**	**7**	**0**	**0**	**0**
FERGUSON, Scott *No playoffs*	Defense								
FERNER, Mark *No playoffs*	Defense								
FERRARO, Chris *No playoffs*	Center/Right wing								
FERRARO, Peter	Center								
1997	NY Rangers	2	0	0	0	0	0	0	0
Playoff Totals		**2**	**0**	**0**	**0**	**0**	**0**	**0**	**0**
FERRARO, Ray	Center								
1986	Hartford	10	3	6	9	4	3	0	0
1987	Hartford	6	1	1	2	8	0	0	0
1988	Hartford	6	1	1	2	6	1	0	0
1989	Hartford	4	2	0	2	4	0	0	0
1990	Hartford	7	0	3	3	2	0	0	0
1993	NY Islanders	18	13	7	20	18	0	0	0
1994	NY Islanders	4	1	0	1	6	0	0	0
1998	Los Angeles	3	0	1	1	2	0	0	0
Playoff Totals		**58**	**21**	**19**	**40**	**50**	**4**	**0**	**0**
FETISOV, Viacheslav *No playoffs*	Defense								
FETISOV, Viacheslav	Defense								
1990	New Jersey	6	0	2	2	10	0	0	0
1991	New Jersey	7	0	0	0	17	0	0	0
1992	New Jersey	6	0	3	3	8	0	0	0
1993	New Jersey	5	0	2	2	4	0	0	0
1994	New Jersey	14	1	0	1	8	0	0	0
1995	Detroit	18	0	8	8	14	0	0	0
1996	Detroit	19	1	4	5	34	0	0	1
1997◆	Detroit	20	0	4	4	42	0	0	0
1998◆	Detroit	21	0	3	3	10	0	0	0
Playoff Totals		**116**	**2**	**26**	**28**	**147**	**0**	**0**	**1**
FIDLER, Mike *No playoffs*	Left wing								
FIELD, Wilf	Defense								
1939	NY Americans	2	0	0	0	2	0	0	0
Playoff Totals		**2**	**0**	**0**	**0**	**2**	**0**	**0**	**0**
FIELDER, Guyle	Center								
1953	Detroit	4	0	0	0	0	0	0	0
1954	Boston	2	0	0	0	2	0	0	0
Playoff Totals		**6**	**0**	**0**	**0**	**2**	**0**	**0**	**0**
FILIMONOV, Dmitri *No playoffs*	Defense								
FILLION, Bob	Left wing								
1944◆	Montreal	3	0	0	0	0	....	....	....
1945	Montreal	1	3	0	3	0	....	....	....
1946◆	Montreal	9	4	3	7	6	....	....	....
1947	Montreal	8	0	0	0	0	....	....	....
1949	Montreal	7	0	1	1	4	....	....	....
1950	Montreal	5	0	0	0	0	....	....	....
Playoff Totals		**33**	**7**	**4**	**11**	**10**	....	....	....
FILLION, Marcel *No playoffs*	Left wing								
FILMORE, Tommy *No playoffs*	Right wing								
FINKBEINER, Lloyd *No playoffs*	Left wing/defense								
FINLEY, Jeff	Defense								
1988	NY Islanders	1	0	0	0	2	0	0	0
1990	NY Islanders	5	0	2	2	2	0	0	0
1996	Winnipeg	6	0	0	0	4	0	0	0
1997	Phoenix	1	0	0	0	2	0	0	0
1999	St. Louis	13	1	2	3	8	0	0	1
Playoff Totals		**26**	**1**	**4**	**5**	**18**	**0**	**0**	**1**
FINN, Steven	Defense								
1987	Quebec	13	0	2	2	29	0	0	0
1993	Quebec	6	0	1	1	8	0	0	0
1995	Quebec	4	0	1	1	2	0	0	0
Playoff Totals		**23**	**0**	**4**	**4**	**39**	**0**	**0**	**0**
FINNEY, Sid	Center								
1953	Chicago	7	0	2	2	0	0	0	0
Playoff Totals		**7**	**0**	**2**	**2**	**0**	**0**	**0**	**0**
FINNIGAN, Ed *No playoffs*	Left wing								
FINNIGAN, Frank	Right wing								
1924	Ottawa	2	0	0	0	2	....	....	....
1926	Ottawa	2	0	0	0	0	....	....	....
1927◆	Ottawa	6	3	0	3	0	....	....	....
1928	Ottawa	2	0	1	1	6	....	....	....
1930	Ottawa	1	0	0	0	4	....	....	....
1932◆	Toronto	7	2	3	5	8	....	....	....
1935	Toronto	7	1	2	3	2	....	....	....
1936	Toronto	9	0	3	3	0	....	....	....
1937	Toronto	2	0	0	0	0	....	....	....
Playoff Totals		**38**	**6**	**9**	**15**	**22**	....	....	....
FIORENTINO, Peter *No playoffs*	Defense								
FISCHER, Jiri *No playoffs*	Defense								
FISCHER, Ron *No playoffs*	Defense								
FISHER, Alvin *No playoffs*	Right wing								
FISHER, Craig *No playoffs*	Center								
FISHER, Dunc	Right wing								
1948	NY Rangers	1	0	1	1	0	....	....	....
1950	NY Rangers	12	3	3	6	14	....	....	....
1951	Boston	6	1	0	1	0	....	....	....
1952	Boston	2	0	0	0	0	....	....	....
Playoff Totals		**21**	**4**	**4**	**8**	**14**	....	....	....
FISHER, Joe	Right wing								
1940	Detroit	5	1	1	2	0	....	....	....
1941	Detroit	5	1	0	1	6	....	....	....
1942	Detroit	1	0	0	0	0	....	....	....
1943◆	Detroit	1	0	0	0	0	....	....	....
Playoff Totals		**12**	**2**	**1**	**3**	**6**	....	....	....
FISHER, Mike *No playoffs*	Center								
FITCHNER, Bob	Center								
1981	Quebec	3	0	0	0	10	0	0	0
Playoff Totals		**3**	**0**	**0**	**0**	**10**	**0**	**0**	**0**
FITZGERALD, Rusty	Center								
1995	Pittsburgh	5	0	0	0	4	0	0	0
Playoff Totals		**5**	**0**	**0**	**0**	**4**	**0**	**0**	**0**
FITZGERALD, Tom	Right wing/Center								
1990	NY Islanders	4	1	0	1	4	0	0	0
1993	NY Islanders	18	2	5	7	18	0	0	0
1996	Florida	22	4	4	8	34	0	0	2
1997	Florida	5	0	1	1	0	0	0	0
1998	Colorado	7	0	1	1	20	0	0	0
Playoff Totals		**56**	**7**	**11**	**18**	**76**	**0**	**0**	**2**
FITZPATRICK, Rory	Defense								
1996	Montreal	6	1	1	2	0	0	0	0
Playoff Totals		**6**	**1**	**1**	**2**	**0**	**0**	**0**	**0**
FITZPATRICK, Ross *No playoffs*	Center								
FITZPATRICK, Sandy	Center								
1968	Minnesota	12	0	0	0	0	0	0	0
Playoff Totals		**12**	**0**	**0**	**0**	**0**	**0**	**0**	**0**
FLAMAN, Fern	Defense								
1947	Boston	5	0	0	0	8	....	....	....
1948	Boston	5	0	0	0	12	....	....	....
1949	Boston	5	0	1	1	8	....	....	....
1951◆	Toronto	9	1	0	1	8	....	....	....
1952	Toronto	4	0	2	2	18	....	....	....
1954	Toronto	2	0	0	0	0	....	....	....
1955	Boston	4	1	0	1	2	....	....	....
1957	Boston	10	0	3	3	19	....	....	....
1958	Boston	12	2	2	4	10	....	....	....
1959	Boston	7	0	0	0	8	....	....	....
Playoff Totals		**63**	**4**	**8**	**12**	**93**	....	....	....
FLATLEY, Pat	Right wing								
1984	NY Islanders	21	9	6	15	14	1	0	1
1985	NY Islanders	4	1	0	1	6	0	0	0
1986	NY Islanders	3	0	0	0	21	0	0	0
1987	NY Islanders	11	3	2	5	6	0	0	0
1990	NY Islanders	5	3	0	3	2	2	0	0
1993	NY Islanders	15	2	7	9	12	0	0	0
1997	NY Rangers	11	0	0	0	14	0	0	0
Playoff Totals		**70**	**18**	**15**	**33**	**75**	**3**	**0**	**1**
FLEMING, Gerry *No playoffs*	Left wing								
FLEMING, Reggie	Defense/left wing								
1961◆	Chicago	12	1	0	1	12	0	1	0
1962	Chicago	12	2	2	4	27	0	0	1
1963	Chicago	6	0	0	0	27	0	0	0
1964	Chicago	7	0	0	0	18	0	0	0
1967	NY Rangers	4	0	2	2	11	0	0	0
1968	NY Rangers	6	0	2	2	4	0	0	0
1969	NY Rangers	3	0	0	0	7	0	0	0
Playoff Totals		**50**	**3**	**6**	**9**	**106**	**0**	**1**	**1**
FLESCH, John *No playoffs*	Left wing								
FLETCHER, Steven	Left wing/Defense								
1988	Montreal	1	0	0	0	5	0	0	0
Playoff Totals		**1**	**0**	**0**	**0**	**5**	**0**	**0**	**0**
FLETT, Bill	Right wing								
1968	Los Angeles	7	1	2	3	8	0	0	0
1969	Los Angeles	10	3	4	7	11	1	1	0
1973	Philadelphia	11	3	4	7	0	0	1	1
1974◆	Philadelphia	17	0	6	6	21	0	0	0
1975	Toronto	5	0	0	0	2	0	0	0
1976	Atlanta	2	0	0	0	0	0	0	0
Playoff Totals		**52**	**7**	**16**	**23**	**42**	**1**	**2**	**1**
FLEURY, Theoren	Right wing								
1989◆	Calgary	22	5	6	11	24	3	0	3
1990	Calgary	6	2	3	5	10	0	0	0
1991	Calgary	7	2	5	7	14	0	0	1
1993	Calgary	6	5	7	12	27	3	1	0
1994	Calgary	7	6	4	10	5	1	0	2
1995	Calgary	7	7	7	14	2	2	1	0
1996	Calgary	4	2	1	3	14	0	0	0
1999	Colorado	18	5	12	17	20	2	0	0
Playoff Totals		**77**	**34**	**45**	**79**	**116**	**11**	**2**	**6**
FLICHEL, Todd *No playoffs*	Defense								
FLOCKHART, Rob	Left wing								
1980	Minnesota	1	1	0	1	2	0	0	0
Playoff Totals		**1**	**1**	**0**	**1**	**2**	**0**	**0**	**0**
FLOCKHART, Ron	Center								
1981	Philadelphia	3	1	0	1	2	0	0	0
1982	Philadelphia	4	0	1	1	2	0	0	0
1983	Philadelphia	2	1	1	2	2	1	0	0
1985	Montreal	2	1	1	2	2	0	0	1
1986	St. Louis	8	1	3	4	6	0	0	0
Playoff Totals		**19**	**4**	**6**	**10**	**14**	**1**	**0**	**1**
FLOYD, Larry *No playoffs*	Center								
FOGARTY, Bryan *No playoffs*	Defense								
FOGOLIN Jr., Lee	Defense								
1975	Buffalo	8	0	0	0	6	0	0	0
1976	Buffalo	9	0	4	4	23	0	0	0
1977	Buffalo	4	0	0	0	2	0	0	0
1978	Buffalo	6	0	2	2	23	0	0	0
1979	Buffalo	3	0	0	0	4	0	0	0
1980	Edmonton	3	0	0	0	4	0	0	0
1981	Edmonton	9	0	0	0	12	0	0	0
1982	Edmonton	5	1	1	2	14	0	1	0
1983	Edmonton	16	0	5	5	36	0	0	0
1984◆	Edmonton	19	1	4	5	23	0	0	0
1985◆	Edmonton	18	3	1	4	16	0	0	1
1986	Edmonton	8	0	2	2	10	0	0	0
Playoff Totals		**108**	**5**	**19**	**24**	**173**	**0**	**1**	**1**
FOGOLIN Sr., Lee	Defense								
1948	Detroit	2	0	1	1	6	0	0	0
1949	Detroit	9	0	0	0	4	0	0	0
1950◆	Detroit	10	0	0	0	16	0	0	0
1953	Chicago	7	0	1	1	4	0	0	0
Playoff Totals		**28**	**0**	**2**	**2**	**30**	**0**	**0**	**0**
FOLCO, Peter *No playoffs*	Defense								
FOLEY, Gerry	Right wing								
1957	NY Rangers	3	0	0	0	0	0	0	0
1958	NY Rangers	6	0	1	1	2	0	0	0
Playoff Totals		**9**	**0**	**1**	**1**	**2**	**0**	**0**	**0**
FOLEY, Rick	Defense								
1971	Chicago	4	0	1	1	4	0	0	0
Playoff Totals		**4**	**0**	**1**	**1**	**4**	**0**	**0**	**0**

FOLIGNO, Mike Right wing

Season	Club	GP	G	A	Pts	PIM	PP	SH	GW
1982	Buffalo	4	2	0	2	9	2	0	0
1983	Buffalo	10	2	3	5	39	0	0	0
1984	Buffalo	3	2	1	3	19	0	0	0
1985	Buffalo	5	1	3	4	12	0	0	0
1988	Buffalo	6	3	2	5	31	0	0	0
1989	Buffalo	5	3	1	4	21	1	1	1
1990	Buffalo	6	0	1	1	12	0	0	0
1993	Toronto	18	2	6	8	42	1	0	2
Playoff Totals		**57**	**15**	**17**	**32**	**185**	**4**	**1**	**3**

FOLK, Bill *No playoffs* Defense

FONTAINE, Len *No playoffs* Right wing

FONTAS, Jon *No playoffs* Center

FONTEYNE, Val Left wing

Season	Club	GP	G	A	Pts	PIM	PP	SH	GW
1960	Detroit	6	0	4	4	0	0	0	0
1961	Detroit	11	2	3	5	0	0	0	0
1963	Detroit	11	0	0	0	2	0	0	0
1965	Detroit	5	0	1	1	0	0	0	0
1966	Detroit	12	1	0	1	4	0	1	0
1970	Pittsburgh	10	0	2	2	0	0	0	0
1972	Pittsburgh	4	0	0	0	2	0	0	0
Playoff Totals		**59**	**3**	**10**	**13**	**8**	**0**	**1**	**0**

FONTINATO, Lou Defense

Season	Club	GP	G	A	Pts	PIM	PP	SH	GW
1956	NY Rangers	4	0	0	0	6	0	0	0
1957	NY Rangers	5	0	0	0	7	0	0	0
1958	NY Rangers	6	0	1	1	6	0	0	0
1962	Montreal	6	0	1	1	23	0	0	0
Playoff Totals		**21**	**0**	**2**	**2**	**42**	**0**	**0**	**0**

FOOTE, Adam Defense

Season	Club	GP	G	A	Pts	PIM	PP	SH	GW
1993	Quebec	6	0	1	1	2	0	0	0
1995	Quebec	6	0	1	1	14	0	0	0
1996♦	Colorado	22	1	3	4	36	0	0	0
1997	Colorado	17	0	4	4	62	0	0	0
1998	Colorado	7	0	0	0	23	0	0	0
1999	Colorado	19	2	3	5	24	1	0	0
Playoff Totals		**77**	**3**	**12**	**15**	**161**	**1**	**0**	**0**

FORBES, Colin Left wing

Season	Club	GP	G	A	Pts	PIM	PP	SH	GW
1997	Philadelphia	3	0	0	0	0	0	0	0
1998	Philadelphia	5	0	0	0	2	0	0	0
Playoff Totals		**8**	**0**	**0**	**0**	**2**	**0**	**0**	**0**

FORBES, Dave Left wing

Season	Club	GP	G	A	Pts	PIM	PP	SH	GW
1974	Boston	16	0	2	2	6	0	0	0
1975	Boston	3	0	0	0	0	0	0	0
1976	Boston	12	1	1	2	5	0	1	0
1977	Boston	14	0	1	1	2	0	0	0
Playoff Totals		**45**	**1**	**4**	**5**	**13**	**0**	**1**	**0**

FORBES, Mike *No playoffs* Defense

FOREY, Connie *No playoffs* Left wing

FORSBERG, Peter Center

Season	Club	GP	G	A	Pts	PIM	PP	SH	GW
1995	Quebec	6	2	4	6	4	1	0	0
1996♦	Colorado	22	10	11	21	18	3	0	1
1997	Colorado	14	5	12	17	10	3	0	0
1998	Colorado	7	6	5	11	12	2	0	0
1999	Colorado	19	8	16	*24	31	1	1	0
Playoff Totals		**68**	**31**	**48**	**79**	**75**	**10**	**1**	**1**

FORSEY, Jack Right wing

Season	Club	GP	G	A	Pts	PIM	PP	SH	GW
1943	Toronto	3	0	1	1	0	0	0	0
Playoff Totals		**3**	**0**	**1**	**1**	**0**	**0**	**0**	**0**

FORSLUND, Gus *No playoffs* Right wing

FORSLUND, Tomas *No playoffs* Right wing

FORSYTH, Alex *No playoffs* Center

FORTIER, Dave Defense

Season	Club	GP	G	A	Pts	PIM	PP	SH	GW
1975	NY Islanders	14	0	2	2	33	0	0	0
1976	NY Islanders	6	0	0	0	0	0	0	0
Playoff Totals		**20**	**0**	**2**	**2**	**33**	**0**	**0**	**0**

FORTIER, Marc *No playoffs* Center

FORTIN, Ray Defense

Season	Club	GP	G	A	Pts	PIM	PP	SH	GW
1968	St. Louis	3	0	0	0	2	0	0	0
1970	St. Louis	3	0	0	0	6	0	0	0
Playoff Totals		**6**	**0**	**0**	**0**	**8**	**0**	**0**	**0**

FOSTER, Corey Defense

Season	Club	GP	G	A	Pts	PIM	PP	SH	GW
1996	Pittsburgh	3	0	0	0	4	0	0	0
Playoff Totals		**3**	**0**	**0**	**0**	**4**	**0**	**0**	**0**

FOSTER, Dwight Right wing

Season	Club	GP	G	A	Pts	PIM	PP	SH	GW
1979	Boston	11	1	3	4	0	0	0	0
1980	Boston	9	3	5	8	2	0	1	1
1981	Boston	3	1	1	2	0	0	0	0
1984	Detroit	3	0	1	1	0	0	0	0
1985	Detroit	3	0	0	0	0	0	0	0
1986	Boston	3	0	2	2	2	0	0	0
1987	Boston	3	0	0	0	0	0	0	0
Playoff Totals		**35**	**5**	**12**	**17**	**4**	**0**	**1**	**1**

FOSTER, Herb *No playoffs* Left wing

FOSTER, Yip *No playoffs* Defense

FOTIU, Nick Left wing

Season	Club	GP	G	A	Pts	PIM	PP	SH	GW
1978	NY Rangers	3	0	0	0	5	0	0	0
1979	NY Rangers	4	0	0	0	6	0	0	0
1980	Hartford	3	0	0	0	6	0	0	0
1981	NY Rangers	2	0	0	0	4	0	0	0
1982	NY Rangers	10	0	2	2	6	0	0	0
1983	NY Rangers	5	0	1	1	6	0	0	0
1986	Calgary	11	0	1	1	34	0	0	0
Playoff Totals		**38**	**0**	**4**	**4**	**67**	**0**	**0**	**0**

FOWLER, Jimmy Defense

Season	Club	GP	G	A	Pts	PIM	PP	SH	GW
1937	Toronto	2	0	0	0	0	0	0	0
1938	Toronto	7	0	2	2	0	0	0	0
1939	Toronto	9	0	1	1	2	0	0	0
Playoff Totals		**18**	**0**	**3**	**3**	**2**	**0**	**0**	**0**

FOWLER, Tom *No playoffs* Center

FOX, Greg Defense

Season	Club	GP	G	A	Pts	PIM	PP	SH	GW
1978	Atlanta	2	0	1	1	8	0	0	0
1979	Chicago	4	0	1	1	0	0	0	0
1980	Chicago	7	0	0	0	8	0	0	0
1981	Chicago	3	0	1	1	2	0	0	0
1982	Chicago	15	1	3	4	27	0	0	1
1983	Chicago	13	0	3	3	22	0	0	0
Playoff Totals		**44**	**1**	**9**	**10**	**67**	**0**	**0**	**1**

FOX, Jim Right wing

Season	Club	GP	G	A	Pts	PIM	PP	SH	GW
1981	Los Angeles	4	0	1	1	0	0	0	0
1982	Los Angeles	9	1	4	5	0	0	0	0
1985	Los Angeles	3	0	1	1	0	0	0	0
1987	Los Angeles	5	3	2	5	0	1	0	0
1988	Los Angeles	1	0	0	0	0	0	0	0
Playoff Totals		**22**	**4**	**8**	**12**	**0**	**1**	**0**	**0**

FOYSTON, Frank *No playoffs* Center/Right wing

FRAMPTON, Bob Left wing

Season	Club	GP	G	A	Pts	PIM	PP	SH	GW
1950	Montreal	3	0	0	0	0	0	0	0
Playoff Totals		**3**	**0**	**0**	**0**	**0**	**0**	**0**	**0**

FRANCESCHETTI, Lou Right wing

Season	Club	GP	G	A	Pts	PIM	PP	SH	GW
1984	Washington	3	0	0	0	8	0	0	0
1985	Washington	5	1	1	2	15	0	0	0
1986	Washington	8	0	0	0	15	0	0	0
1987	Washington	7	0	0	0	23	0	0	0
1988	Washington	4	0	0	0	14	0	0	0
1989	Washington	6	1	0	1	8	0	0	1
1990	Toronto	5	0	1	1	26	0	0	0
1991	Buffalo	6	1	0	1	2	0	0	0
Playoff Totals		**44**	**3**	**2**	**5**	**111**	**0**	**0**	**1**

FRANCIS, Bobby *No playoffs* Center

FRANCIS, Ron Center

Season	Club	GP	G	A	Pts	PIM	PP	SH	GW
1986	Hartford	10	1	2	3	4	0	0	0
1987	Hartford	6	2	2	4	6	1	0	0
1988	Hartford	6	2	5	7	2	1	0	0
1989	Hartford	4	0	2	2	0	0	0	0
1990	Hartford	7	3	3	6	8	1	0	0
1991♦	Pittsburgh	24	7	10	17	24	0	0	4
1992♦	Pittsburgh	21	8	*19	27	6	2	0	2
1993	Pittsburgh	12	6	11	17	19	1	0	1
1994	Pittsburgh	6	0	2	2	6	0	0	0
1995	Pittsburgh	12	6	13	19	4	2	0	0
1996	Pittsburgh	11	3	6	9	4	2	0	1
1997	Pittsburgh	5	1	2	3	2	1	0	0
1998	Pittsburgh	6	1	5	6	2	0	0	0
1999	Carolina	3	0	1	1	0	0	0	0
Playoff Totals		**133**	**40**	**83**	**123**	**87**	**11**	**0**	**8**

FRASER, Archie *No playoffs* Center

FRASER, Charles *No playoffs* Defense

FRASER, Curt Left wing

Season	Club	GP	G	A	Pts	PIM	PP	SH	GW
1979	Vancouver	3	0	2	2	6	0	0	0
1980	Vancouver	4	0	0	0	2	0	0	0
1981	Vancouver	3	1	0	1	2	0	0	0
1982	Vancouver	17	3	7	10	98	0	0	0
1983	Chicago	13	4	4	8	18	1	0	1
1984	Chicago	5	0	0	0	14	0	0	0
1985	Chicago	15	6	3	9	36	0	0	1
1986	Chicago	3	0	1	1	12	0	0	0
1987	Chicago	2	1	1	2	10	0	0	0
Playoff Totals		**65**	**15**	**18**	**33**	**198**	**1**	**0**	**2**

FRASER, Gord Defense

Season	Club	GP	G	A	Pts	PIM	PP	SH	GW
1927	Chicago	2	1	0	1	6	....	....	....
Playoff Totals		**2**	**1**	**0**	**1**	**6**	....	....	....

FRASER, Harvey *No playoffs* Center

FRASER, Iain Center

Season	Club	GP	G	A	Pts	PIM	PP	SH	GW
1996	Winnipeg	4	0	0	0	0	0	0	0
Playoff Totals		**4**	**0**	**0**	**0**	**0**	**0**	**0**	**0**

FRASER, Scott Center

Season	Club	GP	G	A	Pts	PIM	PP	SH	GW
1998	Edmonton	11	1	1	2	0	0	0	0
Playoff Totals		**11**	**1**	**1**	**2**	**0**	**0**	**0**	**0**

FRAWLEY, Dan Right wing

Season	Club	GP	G	A	Pts	PIM	PP	SH	GW
1985	Chicago	1	0	0	0	0	0	0	0
Playoff Totals		**1**	**0**	**0**	**0**	**0**	**0**	**0**	**0**

FREADRICH, Kyle *No playoffs* Left wing

FREDRICKSON, Frank Center

Season	Club	GP	G	A	Pts	PIM	PP	SH	GW
1927	Boston	8	2	2	4	20	....	....	....
1928	Boston	2	0	1	1	4	....	....	....
Playoff Totals		**10**	**2**	**3**	**5**	**24**	....	....	....

FREER, Mark *No playoffs* Center

FREW, Irv Defense

Season	Club	GP	G	A	Pts	PIM	PP	SH	GW
1934	Mtl. Maroons	4	0	0	0	6	0	0	0
Playoff Totals		**4**	**0**	**0**	**0**	**6**	**0**	**0**	**0**

FRIDAY, Tim *No playoffs* Defense

FRIDGEN, Dan *No playoffs* Left wing

FRIEDMAN, Doug *No playoffs* Left wing

FRIESEN, Jeff Center

Season	Club	GP	G	A	Pts	PIM	PP	SH	GW
1995	San Jose	11	1	5	6	4	0	0	0
1998	San Jose	6	0	1	1	2	0	0	0
1999	San Jose	6	2	2	4	14	1	0	0
Playoff Totals		**23**	**3**	**8**	**11**	**20**	**1**	**0**	**0**

FRIEST, Ron Left wing

Season	Club	GP	G	A	Pts	PIM	PP	SH	GW
1982	Minnesota	2	0	0	0	5	0	0	0
1983	Minnesota	4	1	0	1	2	0	0	0
Playoff Totals		**6**	**1**	**0**	**1**	**7**	**0**	**0**	**0**

FRIG, Len Defense

Season	Club	GP	G	A	Pts	PIM	PP	SH	GW
1973	Chicago	4	1	1	2	0	1	0	0
1974	Chicago	7	1	0	1	0	1	0	0
1980	St. Louis	3	0	0	0	0	0	0	0
Playoff Totals		**14**	**2**	**1**	**3**	**0**	**2**	**0**	**0**

FROST, Harry Right wing

Season	Club	GP	G	A	Pts	PIM	PP	SH	GW
1939♦	Boston	1	0	0	0	0	0	0	0
Playoff Totals		**1**	**0**	**0**	**0**	**0**	**0**	**0**	**0**

FRYCER, Miroslav Right wing

Season	Club	GP	G	A	Pts	PIM	PP	SH	GW
1983	Toronto	4	2	5	7	0	0	0	0
1986	Toronto	10	1	3	4	10	0	0	0
1988	Toronto	3	0	0	0	6	0	0	0
Playoff Totals		**17**	**3**	**8**	**11**	**16**	**0**	**0**	**0**

FRYDAY, Bob *No playoffs* Right wing

FTOREK, Robbie Center/left wing

Season	Club	GP	G	A	Pts	PIM	PP	SH	GW
1981	Quebec	5	1	2	3	17	1	0	0
1982	NY Rangers	10	7	4	11	11	4	0	1
1983	NY Rangers	4	1	0	1	0	0	0	0
Playoff Totals		**19**	**9**	**6**	**15**	**28**	**5**	**0**	**1**

FULLAN, Larry *No playoffs* Left wing

FUSCO, Mark *No playoffs* Defense

GADSBY, Bill Defense

Season	Club	GP	G	A	Pts	PIM	PP	SH	GW
1953	Chicago	7	0	1	1	4	....	....	....
1956	NY Rangers	5	1	3	4	4	....	....	....
1957	NY Rangers	5	1	2	3	2	....	....	....
1958	NY Rangers	6	0	3	3	4	....	....	....
1963	Detroit	11	1	4	5	*36	....	....	....
1964	Detroit	14	0	4	4	22	....	....	....
1965	Detroit	7	0	3	3	8	....	....	....
1966	Detroit	12	1	3	4	12	....	....	....
Playoff Totals		**67**	**4**	**23**	**27**	**92**	....	....	....

GAETZ, Link *No playoffs* Defense

GAGE, Jody *No playoffs* Right wing

GAGNE, Art Right wing

Season	Club	GP	G	A	Pts	PIM	PP	SH	GW
1927	Mtl. Canadiens	4	0	0	0	0	....	....	....
1928	Mtl. Canadiens	2	1	1	2	4	....	....	....
1929	Mtl. Canadiens	3	0	0	0	12	....	....	....
1930	Ottawa	2	1	0	1	4	....	....	....
Playoff Totals		**11**	**2**	**1**	**3**	**20**	....	....	....

GAGNE, Paul *No playoffs* Left wing

GAGNE, Pierre *No playoffs* Left wing

GAGNE, Simon *No playoffs* Center

GAGNER, Dave Center

Season	Club	GP	G	A	Pts	PIM	PP	SH	GW
1990	Minnesota	7	2	3	5	16	1	0	0
1991	Minnesota	23	12	15	27	28	6	1	1
1992	Minnesota	7	2	4	6	8	2	0	0
1994	Dallas	9	5	1	6	2	3	0	0
1995	Dallas	5	1	1	2	4	1	0	0
1996	Toronto	6	0	2	2	6	0	0	0
Playoff Totals		**57**	**22**	**26**	**48**	**64**	**13**	**1**	**1**

GAGNON, Germaine Left wing

Season	Club	GP	G	A	Pts	PIM	PP	SH	GW
1974	Chicago	11	2	2	4	2	1	0	1
1975	Chicago	8	0	1	1	0	0	0	0
Playoff Totals		**19**	**2**	**3**	**5**	**2**	**1**	**0**	**1**

GAGNON, Johnny Right wing

Season	Club	GP	G	A	Pts	PIM	PP	SH	GW
1931♦	Mtl. Canadiens	10	*6	2	8	8	....	....	....
1932	Mtl. Canadiens	4	1	1	2	4	....	....	....
1933	Mtl. Canadiens	2	0	2	2	0	....	....	....
1934	Mtl. Canadiens	2	1	0	1	2	....	....	....
1935	Mtl. Canadiens	2	0	1	1	2	....	....	....
1937	Mtl. Canadiens	5	2	1	3	9	....	....	....
1938	Mtl. Canadiens	3	1	3	4	2	....	....	....
1939	Mtl. Canadiens	3	0	2	2	10	....	....	....
1940	NY Americans	1	1	0	1	0	....	....	....
Playoff Totals		**32**	**12**	**12**	**24**	**37**	....	....	....

GAGNON, Sean *No playoffs* Defense

Season	Club	GP	G	A	Pts	PIM	PP	SH	GW
GAINEY, Bob									Left wing
1974	Montreal	6	0	0	0	6	0	0	0
1975	Montreal	11	2	4	6	4	0	0	1
1976◆	Montreal	13	1	3	4	20	0	0	0
1977◆	Montreal	14	4	1	5	25	0	1	1
1978◆	Montreal	15	2	7	9	14	0	1	0
1979◆	Montreal	16	6	10	16	10	0	0	1
1980	Montreal	10	1	1	2	4	0	0	1
1981	Montreal	3	0	0	0	2	0	0	0
1982	Montreal	5	0	1	1	8	0	0	0
1983	Montreal	3	0	0	0	4	0	0	0
1984	Montreal	15	1	5	6	9	0	0	0
1985	Montreal	12	1	3	4	13	0	0	0
1986◆	Montreal	20	5	5	10	12	0	1	3
1987	Montreal	17	1	3	4	6	0	0	0
1988	Montreal	6	0	1	1	6	0	0	0
1989	Montreal	16	1	4	5	8	0	0	0
Playoff Totals		**182**	**25**	**48**	**73**	**151**	**0**	**3**	**7**
GAINOR, Norm									Center
1928	Boston	2	0	0	0	6	....	....	....
1929◆	Boston	5	2	0	2	4	....	....	....
1930	Boston	3	0	0	0	0	....	....	....
1931	Boston	5	0	1	1	2	....	....	....
1932	NY Rangers	7	0	0	0	2	....	....	....
Playoff Totals		**22**	**2**	**1**	**3**	**14**	....	....	....
GALANOV, Maxim									Defense
1999	Pittsburgh	1	0	0	0	0	0	0	0
Playoff Totals		**1**	**0**	**0**	**0**	**0**	**0**	**0**	**0**
GALARNEAU, Michel *No playoffs*									Center
GALBRAITH, Percy									Left wing/defense
1927	Boston	8	3	*3	*6	2	....	....	....
1928	Boston	2	0	1	1	6	....	....	....
1929◆	Boston	5	0	0	0	2	....	....	....
1930	Boston	6	1	3	4	8	....	....	....
1931	Boston	5	0	0	0	6	....	....	....
1933	Boston	5	0	0	0	0	....	....	....
Playoff Totals		**31**	**4**	**7**	**11**	**24**	....	....	....
GALLAGHER, John									Defense
1931	Mtl. Maroons	2	0	0	0	0	....	....	....
1933	Detroit	4	1	1	2	4	....	....	....
1937◆	Detroit	10	1	0	1	17	....	....	....
1938	NY Americans	6	0	2	2	6	....	....	....
1939	NY Americans	2	0	0	0	0	....	....	....
Playoff Totals		**24**	**2**	**3**	**5**	**27**	....	....	....
GALLANT, Gerard									Left wing
1985	Detroit	3	0	0	0	11	0	0	0
1987	Detroit	16	8	6	14	43	2	0	0
1988	Detroit	16	6	9	15	55	1	0	1
1989	Detroit	6	1	2	3	40	0	0	0
1992	Detroit	11	2	2	4	25	0	0	1
1993	Detroit	6	1	2	3	4	0	0	0
Playoff Totals		**58**	**18**	**21**	**39**	**178**	**3**	**0**	**2**
GALLEY, Garry									Defense
1985	Los Angeles	3	1	0	1	2	0	0	0
1987	Washington	2	0	0	0	0	0	0	0
1988	Washington	13	2	4	6	13	0	0	0
1989	Boston	9	0	1	1	33	0	0	0
1990	Boston	21	3	3	6	34	1	0	2
1991	Boston	16	1	5	6	17	0	0	0
1995	Buffalo	5	0	3	3	4	0	0	0
1997	Buffalo	12	0	6	6	14	0	0	0
1998	Los Angeles	4	0	1	1	2	0	0	0
Playoff Totals		**85**	**7**	**23**	**30**	**119**	**1**	**0**	**2**
GALLIMORE, Jamie *No playoffs*									Right wing
GALLINGER, Don									Center
1943	Boston	9	3	1	4	10	....	....	....
1946	Boston	10	2	4	6	2	....	....	....
1947	Boston	4	0	0	0	7	....	....	....
Playoff Totals		**23**	**5**	**5**	**10**	**19**	....	....	....
GAMBLE, Dick									Left wing
1952	Montreal	7	0	2	2	0	....	....	....
1953◆	Montreal	5	1	0	1	2	....	....	....
1955	Montreal	2	0	0	0	2	....	....	....
Playoff Totals		**14**	**1**	**2**	**3**	**4**	....	....	....
GAMBUCCI, Gary *No playoffs*									Center
GANCHAR, Perry									Right wing
1984	St. Louis	7	3	1	4	0	2	0	0
Playoff Totals		**7**	**3**	**1**	**4**	**0**	**2**	**0**	**0**
GANS, Dave *No playoffs*									Center
GARDINER, Bruce									Center
1997	Ottawa	7	0	1	1	2	0	0	0
1998	Ottawa	11	1	3	4	2	0	0	1
1999	Ottawa	3	0	0	0	4	0	0	0
Playoff Totals		**21**	**1**	**4**	**5**	**8**	**0**	**0**	**1**
GARDINER, Herb									Defense
1927	Mtl. Canadiens	4	0	0	0	10	0	0	0
1928	Mtl. Canadiens	2	0	1	1	4	0	0	0
1929	Mtl. Canadiens	3	0	0	0	2	0	0	0
Playoff Totals		**9**	**0**	**1**	**1**	**16**	**0**	**0**	**0**

Season	Club	GP	G	A	Pts	PIM	PP	SH	GW
GARDNER, Bill									Center
1982	Chicago	15	1	4	5	6	0	0	0
1983	Chicago	13	1	0	1	9	1	0	0
1984	Chicago	5	0	1	1	0	0	0	0
1985	Chicago	12	1	3	4	2	0	0	0
Playoff Totals		**45**	**3**	**8**	**11**	**17**	**1**	**0**	**0**
GARDNER, Cal									Center
1948	NY Rangers	5	0	0	0	0	....	....	....
1949◆	Toronto	9	2	5	7	0	....	....	....
1950	Toronto	7	1	0	1	4	....	....	....
1951◆	Toronto	11	1	1	2	4	....	....	....
1952	Toronto	3	0	0	0	2	....	....	....
1953	Chicago	7	0	2	2	4	....	....	....
1954	Boston	4	1	1	2	0	....	....	....
1955	Boston	5	0	0	0	4	....	....	....
1957	Boston	10	2	1	3	2	....	....	....
Playoff Totals		**61**	**7**	**10**	**17**	**20**	....	....	....
GARDNER, Dave *No playoffs*									Center
GARDNER, Paul									Center
1979	Toronto	6	0	1	1	4	0	0	0
1981	Pittsburgh	5	1	0	1	8	1	0	0
1982	Pittsburgh	5	1	5	6	2	1	0	0
Playoff Totals		**16**	**2**	**6**	**8**	**14**	**2**	**0**	**0**
GARE, Danny									Right wing
1975	Buffalo	17	7	6	13	19	0	0	1
1976	Buffalo	9	5	2	7	21	0	0	2
1977	Buffalo	4	0	0	0	18	0	0	0
1978	Buffalo	8	4	6	10	37	2	0	0
1979	Buffalo	3	0	0	0	9	0	0	0
1980	Buffalo	14	4	7	11	35	4	0	1
1981	Buffalo	3	3	0	3	8	2	0	1
1984	Detroit	4	2	0	2	38	0	0	0
1985	Detroit	2	0	0	0	10	0	0	0
Playoff Totals		**64**	**25**	**21**	**46**	**195**	**8**	**0**	**5**
GARIEPY, Ray *No playoffs*									Defense
GARLAND, Scott									Center
1976	Toronto	7	1	2	3	35	1	0	0
Playoff Totals		**7**	**1**	**2**	**3**	**35**	**1**	**0**	**0**
GARNER, Rob *No playoffs*									Center
GARPENLOV, Johan									Left wing
1991	Detroit	6	0	1	1	4	0	0	0
1994	San Jose	14	4	6	10	6	0	0	2
1996	Florida	20	4	2	6	8	0	0	0
1997	Florida	4	2	0	2	4	2	0	1
Playoff Totals		**44**	**10**	**9**	**19**	**22**	**2**	**0**	**3**
GARRETT, Red *No playoffs*									Defense
GARTNER, Mike									Right wing
1983	Washington	4	0	0	0	4	0	0	0
1984	Washington	8	3	7	10	16	2	0	0
1985	Washington	5	4	3	7	9	1	0	1
1986	Washington	9	2	10	12	4	0	0	0
1987	Washington	7	4	3	7	14	0	0	0
1988	Washington	14	3	4	7	14	1	0	0
1989	Minnesota	5	0	0	0	6	0	0	0
1990	NY Rangers	10	5	3	8	12	4	0	1
1991	NY Rangers	6	1	1	2	0	1	0	0
1992	NY Rangers	13	8	8	16	4	3	0	1
1994	Toronto	18	5	6	11	14	1	0	3
1995	Toronto	5	2	2	4	2	0	0	0
1996	Toronto	6	4	1	5	4	2	0	1
1997	Phoenix	7	1	2	3	4	0	0	0
1998	Phoenix	5	1	0	1	18	1	0	0
Playoff Totals		**122**	**43**	**50**	**93**	**125**	**16**	**0**	**7**
GASSOFF, Bob									Defense
1975	St. Louis	2	0	0	0	0	0	0	0
1976	St. Louis	3	0	0	0	6	0	0	0
1977	St. Louis	4	0	1	1	10	0	0	0
Playoff Totals		**9**	**0**	**1**	**1**	**16**	**0**	**0**	**0**
GASSOFF, Brad									Left wing
1979	Vancouver	3	0	0	0	0	0	0	0
Playoff Totals		**3**	**0**	**0**	**0**	**0**	**0**	**0**	**0**
GATZOS, Steve									Right wing
1982	Pittsburgh	1	0	0	0	0	0	0	0
Playoff Totals		**1**	**0**	**0**	**0**	**0**	**0**	**0**	**0**
GAUDREAU, Rob									Right wing
1994	San Jose	14	2	0	2	0	1	1	0
Playoff Totals		**14**	**2**	**0**	**2**	**0**	**1**	**1**	**0**
GAUDREAULT, Armand									Left wing
1945	Boston	7	0	2	2	8	0	0	0
Playoff Totals		**7**	**0**	**2**	**2**	**8**	**0**	**0**	**0**
GAUDREAULT, Leo *No playoffs*									Left wing/center
GAUL, Michael *No playoffs*									Defense
GAULIN, Jean-Marc									Right wing
1985	Quebec	1	0	0	0	0	0	0	0
Playoff Totals		**1**	**0**	**0**	**0**	**0**	**0**	**0**	**0**
GAUME, Dallas *No playoffs*									Center

Season	Club	GP	G	A	Pts	PIM	PP	SH	GW
GAUTHIER, Art									Center
1927	Mtl. Canadiens	1	0	0	0	0	0	0	0
Playoff Totals		**1**	**0**	**0**	**0**	**0**	**0**	**0**	**0**
GAUTHIER, Daniel *No playoffs*									Left wing
GAUTHIER, Denis *No playoffs*									Defense
GAUTHIER, Fern									Right wing
1945	Montreal	4	0	0	0	0	....	....	....
1946	Detroit	5	3	0	3	2	....	....	....
1947	Detroit	3	1	0	1	0	....	....	....
1948	Detroit	10	1	1	2	5	....	....	....
Playoff Totals		**22**	**5**	**1**	**6**	**7**	....	....	....
GAUTHIER, Jean									Defense
1963	Montreal	5	0	0	0	12	0	0	0
1965◆	Montreal	2	0	0	0	4	0	0	0
1968	Philadelphia	7	1	3	4	6	1	0	0
Playoff Totals		**14**	**1**	**3**	**4**	**22**	**1**	**0**	**0**
GAUTHIER, Luc *No playoffs*									Defense
GAUVREAU, Jocelyn *No playoffs*									Defense
GAVEY, Aaron									Center
1996	Tampa Bay	6	0	0	0	4	0	0	0
Playoff Totals		**6**	**0**	**0**	**0**	**4**	**0**	**0**	**0**
GAVIN, Stew									Left wing
1983	Toronto	4	0	0	0	0	0	0	0
1986	Hartford	10	4	1	5	13	0	0	0
1987	Hartford	6	2	4	6	10	0	0	0
1988	Hartford	6	2	2	4	4	0	0	0
1989	Minnesota	5	3	1	4	10	0	0	0
1990	Minnesota	7	0	2	2	12	0	0	0
1991	Minnesota	21	3	10	13	20	0	1	1
1992	Minnesota	7	0	0	0	6	0	0	0
Playoff Totals		**66**	**14**	**20**	**34**	**75**	**0**	**1**	**1**
GEALE, Bob *No playoffs*									Center
GEE, George									Center
1946	Chicago	4	1	1	2	4	....	....	....
1949	Detroit	10	1	3	4	22	....	....	....
1950◆	Detroit	14	3	*6	9	0	....	....	....
1951	Detroit	6	0	1	1	0	....	....	....
1953	Chicago	7	1	2	3	6	....	....	....
Playoff Totals		**41**	**6**	**13**	**19**	**32**	....	....	....
GELDART, Gary *No playoffs*									Defense
GELINAS, Martin									Left wing
1990◆	Edmonton	20	2	3	5	6	0	0	0
1991	Edmonton	18	3	6	9	25	0	0	1
1992	Edmonton	15	1	3	4	10	0	0	0
1994	Vancouver	24	5	4	9	14	2	0	1
1995	Vancouver	3	0	1	1	0	0	0	0
1996	Vancouver	6	1	1	2	12	1	0	0
1999	Carolina	6	0	3	3	2	0	0	0
Playoff Totals		**92**	**12**	**21**	**33**	**69**	**3**	**0**	**2**
GENDRON, Jean-Guy									Left wing
1956	NY Rangers	5	2	1	3	2	1	0	0
1957	NY Rangers	5	0	1	1	6	0	0	0
1958	NY Rangers	6	1	0	1	11	0	0	1
1959	Boston	7	1	0	1	18	0	0	1
1961	Montreal	5	0	0	0	2	0	0	0
1962	NY Rangers	6	3	1	4	2	0	0	0
1969	Philadelphia	4	0	0	0	6	0	0	0
1971	Philadelphia	4	0	1	1	0	0	0	0
Playoff Totals		**42**	**7**	**4**	**11**	**47**	**1**	**0**	**2**
GENDRON, Martin *No playoffs*									Right wing
GEOFFRION, Bernie									Right wing
1951	Montreal	11	1	1	2	6	....	....	....
1952	Montreal	11	3	1	4	6	....	....	....
1953◆	Montreal	12	*6	4	10	12	....	....	....
1954	Montreal	11	6	5	11	18	....	....	....
1955	Montreal	12	8	5	13	8	....	....	....
1956◆	Montreal	10	5	9	14	6	....	....	....
1957◆	Montreal	10	*11	7	*18	2	....	....	....
1958◆	Montreal	10	6	5	11	2	....	....	....
1959◆	Montreal	11	5	8	13	10	....	....	....
1960◆	Montreal	8	2	*10	*12	4	....	....	....
1961	Montreal	4	2	1	3	0	....	....	....
1962	Montreal	5	0	1	1	6	....	....	....
1963	Montreal	5	0	1	1	4	....	....	....
1964	Montreal	7	1	1	2	4	....	....	....
1967	NY Rangers	4	2	0	2	0	....	....	....
1968	NY Rangers	1	0	1	1	0	0	0	0
Playoff Totals		**132**	**58**	**60**	**118**	**88**	....	....	....
GEOFFRION, Danny									Right wing
1980	Montreal	2	0	0	0	7	0	0	0
Playoff Totals		**2**	**0**	**0**	**0**	**7**	**0**	**0**	**0**
GERAN, Gerry *No playoffs*									Center
GERARD, Eddie									Left wing/defense
1919	Ottawa	5	3	0	3	3	....	....	....
1920◆	Ottawa	5	2	1	3	3	....	....	....
1921◆	Ottawa	7	1	0	1	*53	....	....	....
1922	Ottawa	2	0	0	0	8	....	....	....
1922◆	Toronto	1	0	0	0	0	....	....	....
1923◆	Ottawa	7	1	0	1	4	....	....	....
Playoff Totals		**27**	**7**	**1**	**8**	**71**	....	....	....

GERMAIN, Eric — Defense

Season	Club	GP	G	A	Pts	PIM	PP	SH	GW
1988	Los Angeles	1	0	0	0	4	0	0	0
Playoff Totals		**1**	**0**	**0**	**0**	**4**	**0**	**0**	**0**

GERNANDER, Ken — Center

Season	Club	GP	G	A	Pts	PIM	PP	SH	GW
1996	NY Rangers	6	0	0	0	0	0	0	0
1997	NY Rangers	9	0	0	0	0	0	0	0
Playoff Totals		**15**	**0**	**0**	**0**	**0**	**0**	**0**	**0**

GETLIFFE, Ray — Center/left wing

Season	Club	GP	G	A	Pts	PIM	PP	SH	GW
1936	Boston	2	0	0	0	0	....	....	....
1937	Boston	3	2	1	3	2	....	....	....
1938	Boston	3	0	1	1	2	....	....	....
1939◆	Boston	11	1	1	2	2	....	....	....
1941	Montreal	3	1	1	2	0	....	....	....
1942	Montreal	3	0	0	0	0	....	....	....
1943	Montreal	5	0	1	1	8	....	....	....
1944◆	Montreal	9	5	4	9	16	....	....	....
1945	Montreal	6	0	1	1	0	....	....	....
Playoff Totals		**45**	**9**	**10**	**19**	**30**	....	....	....

GIALLONARDO, Mario *No playoffs* — Defense

GIBBS, Barry — Defense

Season	Club	GP	G	A	Pts	PIM	PP	SH	GW
1970	Minnesota	6	1	0	1	7	1	0	0
1971	Minnesota	12	0	1	1	47	0	0	0
1972	Minnesota	7	1	1	2	9	0	0	0
1973	Minnesota	5	1	0	1	0	1	0	0
1976	Atlanta	2	1	0	1	2	0	0	0
1977	Atlanta	3	0	0	0	2	0	0	0
1980	Los Angeles	1	0	0	0	0	0	0	0
Playoff Totals		**36**	**4**	**2**	**6**	**67**	**2**	**0**	**0**

GIBSON, Don *No playoffs* — Defense

GIBSON, Doug — Center

Season	Club	GP	G	A	Pts	PIM	PP	SH	GW
1974	Boston	1	0	0	0	0	0	0	0
Playoff Totals		**1**	**0**	**0**	**0**	**0**	**0**	**0**	**0**

GIBSON, John *No playoffs* — Defense

GIESEBRECHT, Gus — Center

Season	Club	GP	G	A	Pts	PIM	PP	SH	GW
1939	Detroit	6	0	2	2	0	....	....	....
1941	Detroit	9	2	1	3	0	....	....	....
1942	Detroit	2	0	0	0	0	....	....	....
Playoff Totals		**17**	**2**	**3**	**5**	**0**	....	....	....

GIFFIN, Lee *No playoffs* — Right wing

GILBERT, Ed *No playoffs* — Center

GILBERT, Greg — Left wing

Season	Club	GP	G	A	Pts	PIM	PP	SH	GW
1982◆	NY Islanders	4	1	1	2	2	0	0	0
1983◆	NY Islanders	10	1	0	1	14	0	0	0
1984	NY Islanders	21	5	7	12	39	2	0	1
1986	NY Islanders	2	0	0	0	9	0	0	0
1987	NY Islanders	10	2	2	4	6	0	0	1
1988	NY Islanders	4	0	0	0	6	0	0	0
1989	Chicago	15	1	5	6	20	0	0	0
1990	Chicago	19	5	8	13	34	0	0	0
1991	Chicago	5	0	1	1	2	0	0	0
1992	Chicago	10	1	3	4	16	0	0	1
1993	Chicago	3	0	0	0	0	0	0	0
1994◆	NY Rangers	23	1	3	4	8	0	0	0
1995	St. Louis	7	0	3	3	6	0	0	0
Playoff Totals		**133**	**17**	**33**	**50**	**162**	**2**	**0**	**3**

GILBERT, Jeannot *No playoffs* — Center

GILBERT, Rod — Right wing

Season	Club	GP	G	A	Pts	PIM	PP	SH	GW
1962	NY Rangers	4	2	3	5	4	0	0	0
1967	NY Rangers	4	2	2	4	6	1	0	0
1968	NY Rangers	6	5	0	5	4	0	0	0
1969	NY Rangers	4	1	0	1	2	0	0	0
1970	NY Rangers	6	4	5	9	0	3	0	0
1971	NY Rangers	13	4	6	10	8	1	0	1
1972	NY Rangers	16	7	8	15	11	4	0	2
1973	NY Rangers	10	5	1	6	2	0	0	1
1974	NY Rangers	13	3	5	8	4	1	0	1
1975	NY Rangers	3	1	3	4	2	0	0	0
Playoff Totals		**79**	**34**	**33**	**67**	**43**	**10**	**0**	**5**

GILBERTSON, Stan — Left wing

Season	Club	GP	G	A	Pts	PIM	PP	SH	GW
1976	Pittsburgh	3	1	1	2	2	0	0	0
Playoff Totals		**3**	**1**	**1**	**2**	**2**	**0**	**0**	**0**

GILCHRIST, Brent — Left wing

Season	Club	GP	G	A	Pts	PIM	PP	SH	GW
1989	Montreal	9	1	1	2	10	0	0	0
1990	Montreal	8	2	0	2	2	0	0	0
1991	Montreal	13	5	3	8	6	0	0	1
1992	Montreal	11	2	4	6	6	1	0	0
1994	Dallas	9	3	1	4	2	1	0	0
1995	Dallas	5	0	1	1	2	0	0	0
1997	Dallas	6	2	2	4	2	0	0	0
1998◆	Detroit	15	2	1	3	12	0	0	0
1999	Detroit	3	0	0	0	0	0	0	0
Playoff Totals		**79**	**17**	**13**	**30**	**42**	**2**	**0**	**1**

GILES, Curt — Defense

Season	Club	GP	G	A	Pts	PIM	PP	SH	GW
1980	Minnesota	12	2	4	6	10	2	0	0
1981	Minnesota	19	1	4	5	14	0	0	0
1982	Minnesota	4	0	0	0	2	0	0	0
1983	Minnesota	5	0	2	2	6	0	0	0
1984	Minnesota	16	1	3	4	25	1	0	0
1985	Minnesota	9	0	0	0	17	0	0	0
1986	Minnesota	5	0	1	1	10	0	0	0
1987	NY Rangers	5	0	0	0	6	0	0	0
1989	Minnesota	5	0	0	0	4	0	0	0
1990	Minnesota	7	0	1	1	6	0	0	0
1991	Minnesota	10	1	0	1	16	0	0	0
1992	St. Louis	3	1	1	2	0	1	0	0
1993	St. Louis	3	0	0	0	2	0	0	0
Playoff Totals		**103**	**6**	**16**	**22**	**118**	**4**	**0**	**0**

GILHEN, Randy — Center

Season	Club	GP	G	A	Pts	PIM	PP	SH	GW
1988	Winnipeg	4	1	0	1	10	0	1	1
1991◆	Pittsburgh	16	1	0	1	14	0	0	0
1992	NY Rangers	13	1	2	3	2	0	0	0
Playoff Totals		**33**	**3**	**2**	**5**	**26**	**0**	**1**	**1**

GILL, Hal — Defense

Season	Club	GP	G	A	Pts	PIM	PP	SH	GW
1998	Boston	6	0	0	0	4	0	0	0
1999	Boston	12	0	0	0	14	0	0	0
Playoff Totals		**18**	**0**	**0**	**0**	**18**	**0**	**0**	**0**

GILL, Todd — Defense

Season	Club	GP	G	A	Pts	PIM	PP	SH	GW
1986	Toronto	1	0	0	0	0	0	0	0
1987	Toronto	13	2	2	4	42	0	0	0
1988	Toronto	6	1	3	4	20	1	0	0
1990	Toronto	5	0	3	3	16	0	0	0
1993	Toronto	21	1	10	11	26	0	0	0
1994	Toronto	18	1	5	6	37	0	0	1
1995	Toronto	7	0	3	3	6	0	0	0
1996	Toronto	6	0	0	0	24	0	0	0
1998	St. Louis	10	2	2	4	10	1	1	0
1999	Detroit	2	0	1	1	0	0	0	0
Playoff Totals		**89**	**7**	**29**	**36**	**181**	**2**	**1**	**1**

GILLEN, Don *No playoffs* — Right wing

GILLIE, Farrand *No playoffs* — Left wing/defense

GILLIES, Clark — Left wing

Season	Club	GP	G	A	Pts	PIM	PP	SH	GW
1975	NY Islanders	17	4	2	6	36	0	0	2
1976	NY Islanders	13	2	4	6	16	0	0	1
1977	NY Islanders	12	4	4	8	15	0	0	4
1978	NY Islanders	7	2	0	2	15	1	0	0
1979	NY Islanders	10	1	2	3	11	0	0	0
1980◆	NY Islanders	21	6	10	16	63	1	0	2
1981◆	NY Islanders	18	6	9	15	28	3	0	0
1982◆	NY Islanders	19	8	6	14	34	4	0	3
1983◆	NY Islanders	8	0	2	2	10	0	0	0
1984	NY Islanders	21	12	7	19	19	3	0	0
1985	NY Islanders	10	1	0	1	9	0	0	0
1986	NY Islanders	3	1	0	1	6	0	0	0
1988	Buffalo	5	0	1	1	25	0	0	0
Playoff Totals		**164**	**47**	**47**	**94**	**287**	**12**	**0**	**12**

GILLIS, Jere — Left wing

Season	Club	GP	G	A	Pts	PIM	PP	SH	GW
1979	Vancouver	1	0	1	1	0	0	0	0
1981	NY Rangers	14	2	5	7	9	0	0	0
1984	Vancouver	4	2	1	3	0	0	0	0
Playoff Totals		**19**	**4**	**7**	**11**	**9**	**0**	**0**	**0**

GILLIS, Mike — Left wing

Season	Club	GP	G	A	Pts	PIM	PP	SH	GW
1981	Boston	1	0	0	0	0	0	0	0
1982	Boston	11	1	2	3	6	0	0	0
1983	Boston	12	1	3	4	2	0	0	0
1984	Boston	3	0	0	0	2	0	0	0
Playoff Totals		**27**	**2**	**5**	**7**	**10**	**0**	**0**	**0**

GILLIS, Paul — Center

Season	Club	GP	G	A	Pts	PIM	PP	SH	GW
1984	Quebec	1	0	0	0	2	0	0	0
1985	Quebec	18	1	7	8	73	0	0	0
1986	Quebec	3	0	2	2	14	0	0	0
1987	Quebec	13	2	4	6	65	0	0	0
1991	Chicago	2	0	0	0	2	0	0	0
1992	Hartford	5	0	1	1	0	0	0	0
Playoff Totals		**42**	**3**	**14**	**17**	**156**	**0**	**0**	**0**

GILMOUR, Doug — Center

Season	Club	GP	G	A	Pts	PIM	PP	SH	GW
1984	St. Louis	11	2	9	11	10	1	0	1
1985	St. Louis	3	1	1	2	2	0	0	0
1986	St. Louis	19	9	12	*21	25	1	2	2
1987	St. Louis	6	2	2	4	16	1	0	1
1988	St. Louis	10	3	14	17	18	1	0	0
1989◆	Calgary	22	11	11	22	20	3	0	3
1990	Calgary	6	3	1	4	8	0	0	1
1991	Calgary	7	1	1	2	0	0	0	1
1993	Toronto	21	10	*25	35	30	4	0	1
1994	Toronto	18	6	22	28	42	5	0	1
1995	Toronto	7	0	6	6	6	0	0	0
1996	Toronto	6	1	7	8	12	1	0	0
1997	New Jersey	10	0	4	4	14	0	0	0
1998	New Jersey	6	5	2	7	4	1	0	1
Playoff Totals		**152**	**54**	**117**	**171**	**207**	**18**	**2**	**12**

GINGRAS, Gaston — Defense

Season	Club	GP	G	A	Pts	PIM	PP	SH	GW
1980	Montreal	10	1	6	7	8	0	0	0
1981	Montreal	1	1	0	1	0	1	0	0
1982	Montreal	5	0	1	1	0	0	0	0
1983	Toronto	3	1	2	3	2	0	0	0
1986◆	Montreal	11	2	3	5	4	1	0	0
1987	Montreal	5	0	2	2	0	0	0	0
1988	St. Louis	10	1	3	4	4	0	0	0
1989	St. Louis	7	0	1	1	2	0	0	0
Playoff Totals		**52**	**6**	**18**	**24**	**20**	**2**	**0**	**0**

GIRARD, Bob *No playoffs* — Left wing

GIRARD, Jonathan *No playoffs* — Defense

GIRARD, Kenny *No playoffs* — Right wing

GIROUX, Art — Right wing

Season	Club	GP	G	A	Pts	PIM	PP	SH	GW
1933	Mtl. Canadiens	2	0	0	0	0	0	0	0
Playoff Totals		**2**	**0**	**0**	**0**	**0**	**0**	**0**	**0**

GIROUX, Larry — Defense

Season	Club	GP	G	A	Pts	PIM	PP	SH	GW
1978	Detroit	2	0	0	0	2	0	0	0
1980	Hartford	3	0	0	0	2	0	0	0
Playoff Totals		**5**	**0**	**0**	**0**	**4**	**0**	**0**	**0**

GIROUX, Pierre *No playoffs* — Center

GIROUX, Ray *No playoffs* — Defense

GLADNEY, Bob *No playoffs* — Defense

GLADU, Jean-Paul — Left wing

Season	Club	GP	G	A	Pts	PIM	PP	SH	GW
1945	Boston	7	2	2	4	0	....	....	....
Playoff Totals		**7**	**2**	**2**	**4**	**0**	....	....	....

GLENNIE, Brian — Defense

Season	Club	GP	G	A	Pts	PIM	PP	SH	GW
1971	Toronto	3	0	0	0	0	0	0	0
1972	Toronto	5	0	0	0	25	0	0	0
1974	Toronto	3	0	0	0	10	0	0	0
1976	Toronto	6	0	1	1	15	0	0	0
1977	Toronto	2	0	0	0	0	0	0	0
1978	Toronto	13	0	0	0	16	0	0	0
Playoff Totals		**32**	**0**	**1**	**1**	**66**	**0**	**0**	**0**

GLENNON, Matt *No playoffs* — Left wing

GLOECKNER, Lorry *No playoffs* — Defense

GLOOR, Dan *No playoffs* — Center

GLOVER, Fred — Center

Season	Club	GP	G	A	Pts	PIM	PP	SH	GW
1949	Detroit	2	0	0	0	0	0	0	0
1951	Detroit	6	0	0	0	0	0	0	0
Playoff Totals		**8**	**0**	**0**	**0**	**0**	**0**	**0**	**0**

GLOVER, Howie — Right wing

Season	Club	GP	G	A	Pts	PIM	PP	SH	GW
1961	Detroit	11	1	2	3	2	1	0	0
Playoff Totals		**11**	**1**	**2**	**3**	**2**	**1**	**0**	**0**

GLYNN, Brian — Defense

Season	Club	GP	G	A	Pts	PIM	PP	SH	GW
1988	Calgary	1	0	0	0	0	0	0	0
1991	Minnesota	23	2	6	8	18	2	0	0
1992	Edmonton	16	4	1	5	12	1	0	1
1994	Vancouver	17	0	3	3	10	0	0	0
Playoff Totals		**57**	**6**	**10**	**16**	**40**	**3**	**0**	**1**

GODDEN, Ernie *No playoffs* — Center

GODFREY, Warren — Defense

Season	Club	GP	G	A	Pts	PIM	PP	SH	GW
1953	Boston	11	0	1	1	2	0	0	0
1954	Boston	4	0	0	0	4	0	0	0
1955	Boston	3	0	0	0	0	0	0	0
1957	Detroit	5	0	0	0	6	0	0	0
1958	Detroit	4	0	0	0	0	0	0	0
1960	Detroit	6	1	0	1	10	0	0	0
1961	Detroit	11	0	2	2	18	0	0	0
1965	Detroit	4	0	1	1	2	0	0	0
1966	Detroit	4	0	0	0	0	0	0	0
Playoff Totals		**52**	**1**	**4**	**5**	**42**	**0**	**0**	**0**

GODIN, Eddy *No playoffs* — Right wing

GODIN, Sammy *No playoffs* — Right wing

GODYNYUK, Alexander *No playoffs* — Defense

GOEGAN, Pete — Defense

Season	Club	GP	G	A	Pts	PIM	PP	SH	GW
1958	Detroit	4	0	0	0	18	0	0	0
1960	Detroit	6	1	0	1	13	0	0	0
1961	Detroit	11	0	1	1	18	0	0	0
1963	Detroit	11	0	2	2	12	0	0	0
1966	Detroit	1	0	0	0	0	0	0	0
Playoff Totals		**33**	**1**	**3**	**4**	**61**	**0**	**0**	**0**

GOERTZ, Dave *No playoffs* — Defense

GOLDHAM, Bob — Defense

Season	Club	GP	G	A	Pts	PIM	PP	SH	GW
1942◆	Toronto	13	2	2	4	31	....	....	....
1951	Detroit	6	0	1	1	2	....	....	....
1952◆	Detroit	8	0	1	1	8	....	....	....
1953	Detroit	6	1	1	2	2	....	....	....
1954◆	Detroit	12	0	2	2	2	....	....	....
1955◆	Detroit	11	0	4	4	4	....	....	....
1956	Detroit	10	0	3	3	4	....	....	....
Playoff Totals		**66**	**3**	**14**	**17**	**53**	....	....	....

GOLDMANN, Erich *No playoffs* — Defense

Season	Club	GP	G	A	Pts	PIM	PP	SH	GW
GOLDSWORTHY, Bill									Right wing
1968	Minnesota	14	*8	7	*15	12	1	0	1
1970	Minnesota	6	4	3	7	6	3	2	0
1971	Minnesota	7	2	4	6	6	0	0	0
1972	Minnesota	7	2	3	5	6	0	0	1
1973	Minnesota	6	2	2	4	0	1	0	0
Playoff Totals		**40**	**18**	**19**	**37**	**30**	**5**	**2**	**2**
GOLDSWORTHY, Leroy									Right wing
1929	NY Rangers	1	0	0	0	0	....	....	....
1930	NY Rangers	4	0	0	0	2	....	....	....
1933	Detroit	2	0	0	0	0	....	....	....
1934◆	Chicago	7	0	0	0	0	....	....	....
1935	Mtl. Canadiens	2	1	0	1	0	....	....	....
1937	Boston	3	0	0	0	0	....	....	....
1938	Boston	3	0	0	0	2	....	....	....
1939	NY Americans	2	0	0	0	0	....	....	....
Playoff Totals		**24**	**1**	**0**	**1**	**4**	....	....	....
GOLDUP, Glenn									Right wing
1977	Los Angeles	8	2	2	4	2	0	0	0
1978	Los Angeles	2	1	0	1	11	0	0	0
1979	Los Angeles	2	0	1	1	9	0	0	0
1980	Los Angeles	4	1	0	1	0	0	0	0
Playoff Totals		**16**	**4**	**3**	**7**	**22**	**0**	**0**	**0**
GOLDUP, Hank									Left wing
1940	Toronto	10	*5	1	6	4	....	....	....
1941	Toronto	7	0	0	0	0	....	....	....
1942◆	Toronto	9	0	0	0	2	....	....	....
Playoff Totals		**26**	**5**	**1**	**6**	**6**	....	....	....
GOLUBOVSKY, Yan	*No playoffs*								Defense
GOMEZ, Scott	*No playoffs*								Center
GONCHAR, Sergei									Defense
1995	Washington	7	2	2	4	2	0	0	1
1996	Washington	6	2	4	6	4	1	0	0
1998	Washington	21	7	4	11	30	3	1	2
Playoff Totals		**34**	**11**	**10**	**21**	**36**	**4**	**1**	**3**
GONEAU, Daniel	*No playoffs*								Left wing
GOODEN, Bill	*No playoffs*								Left wing
GOODENOUGH, Larry									Defense
1975◆	Philadelphia	5	0	4	4	2	0	0	0
1976	Philadelphia	16	3	11	14	6	1	0	0
1979	Vancouver	1	0	0	0	2	0	0	0
Playoff Totals		**22**	**3**	**15**	**18**	**10**	**1**	**0**	**0**
GOODFELLOW, Ebbie									Center/Defense
1932	Detroit	2	0	0	0	0	....	....	....
1933	Detroit	4	1	0	1	11	....	....	....
1934	Detroit	9	4	3	7	12	....	....	....
1936◆	Detroit	7	1	0	1	4	....	....	....
1937◆	Detroit	9	2	2	4	12	....	....	....
1939	Detroit	6	0	0	0	8	....	....	....
1940	Detroit	5	0	2	2	9	....	....	....
1941	Detroit	3	0	1	1	9	....	....	....
Playoff Totals		**45**	**8**	**8**	**16**	**65**	....	....	....
GORDIOUK, Viktor	*No playoffs*								Left wing
GORDON, Fred									Right wing
1928	Boston	2	0	0	0	0	0	0	0
Playoff Totals		**2**	**0**	**0**	**0**	**0**	**0**	**0**	**0**
GORDON, Jackie									Center
1950	NY Rangers	9	1	1	2	7	....	....	....
Playoff Totals		**9**	**1**	**1**	**2**	**7**	....	....	....
GORDON, Robb	*No playoffs*								Center
GORENCE, Tom									Right wing
1979	Philadelphia	7	3	1	4	0	1	0	0
1980	Philadelphia	15	3	3	6	18	1	0	0
1981	Philadelphia	12	3	2	5	29	0	0	0
1982	Philadelphia	3	0	0	0	0	0	0	0
Playoff Totals		**37**	**9**	**6**	**15**	**47**	**2**	**0**	**0**
GORING, Butch									Center
1974	Los Angeles	5	0	1	1	0	0	0	0
1975	Los Angeles	3	0	0	0	0	0	0	0
1976	Los Angeles	9	2	3	5	4	1	0	2
1977	Los Angeles	9	7	5	12	0	3	0	2
1978	Los Angeles	2	0	0	0	2	0	0	0
1979	Los Angeles	2	0	0	0	0	0	0	0
1980◆	NY Islanders	21	7	12	19	2	1	0	0
1981◆	NY Islanders	18	10	10	20	6	4	2	2
1982◆	NY Islanders	19	6	5	11	12	1	0	2
1983◆	NY Islanders	20	4	8	12	4	0	0	1
1984	NY Islanders	21	1	5	6	2	1	0	0
1985	Boston	5	1	1	2	0	0	0	0
Playoff Totals		**134**	**38**	**50**	**88**	**32**	**11**	**2**	**9**
GORMAN, Dave	*No playoffs*								Right wing
GORMAN, Ed									Defense
1926	Ottawa	2	0	0	0	2	0	0	0
1927◆	Ottawa	6	0	0	0	0	0	0	0
Playoff Totals		**8**	**0**	**0**	**0**	**2**	**0**	**0**	**0**
GOSSELIN, Benoit	*No playoffs*								Left wing
GOSSELIN, Guy	*No playoffs*								Defense

Season	Club	GP	G	A	Pts	PIM	PP	SH	GW
GOTAAS, Steve									Center
1989	Minnesota	3	0	1	1	5	0	0	0
Playoff Totals		**3**	**0**	**1**	**1**	**5**	**0**	**0**	**0**
GOTTSELIG, Johnny									Left wing
1930	Chicago	2	0	0	0	4	....	....	....
1931	Chicago	9	3	3	6	2	....	....	....
1932	Chicago	2	0	0	0	2	....	....	....
1934◆	Chicago	8	4	3	7	4	....	....	....
1935	Chicago	2	0	0	0	0	....	....	....
1936	Chicago	2	0	2	2	0	....	....	....
1938◆	Chicago	10	5	3	*8	4	....	....	....
1940	Chicago	2	0	1	1	0	....	....	....
1944	Chicago	6	1	1	2	2	....	....	....
Playoff Totals		**43**	**13**	**13**	**26**	**18**	....	....	....
GOULD, Bobby									Right wing
1981	Calgary	11	3	1	4	4	0	0	0
1983	Washington	4	5	0	5	4	1	0	1
1984	Washington	5	0	2	2	4	0	0	0
1985	Washington	5	0	1	1	2	0	0	0
1986	Washington	9	4	3	7	11	0	0	0
1987	Washington	7	0	3	3	8	0	0	0
1988	Washington	14	3	1	4	21	0	2	0
1989	Washington	6	0	2	2	0	0	0	0
1990	Boston	17	0	0	0	4	0	0	0
Playoff Totals		**78**	**15**	**13**	**28**	**58**	**1**	**2**	**1**
GOULD, John									Right wing
1975	Vancouver	5	2	2	4	0	1	0	0
1976	Vancouver	2	1	0	1	0	0	1	0
1977	Atlanta	3	0	0	0	2	0	0	0
1978	Atlanta	2	0	0	0	2	0	0	0
1979	Atlanta	2	0	0	0	0	0	0	0
Playoff Totals		**14**	**3**	**2**	**5**	**4**	**1**	**1**	**0**
GOULD, Larry	*No playoffs*								Left wing
GOULET, Michel									Left wing
1981	Quebec	4	3	4	7	7	0	0	1
1982	Quebec	16	8	5	13	6	2	2	0
1983	Quebec	4	0	0	0	6	0	0	0
1984	Quebec	9	2	4	6	17	0	0	0
1985	Quebec	17	11	10	21	17	7	0	0
1986	Quebec	3	1	2	3	10	1	0	0
1987	Quebec	13	9	5	14	35	4	0	2
1990	Chicago	14	2	4	6	6	0	0	0
1992	Chicago	9	3	4	7	6	0	0	1
1993	Chicago	3	0	1	1	0	0	0	0
Playoff Totals		**92**	**39**	**39**	**78**	**110**	**14**	**2**	**4**
GOUPILLE, Red									Defense
1938	Mtl. Canadiens	3	2	0	2	4	....	....	....
1941	Montreal	2	0	0	0	0	....	....	....
1942	Montreal	3	0	0	0	2	....	....	....
Playoff Totals		**8**	**2**	**0**	**2**	**6**	....	....	....
GOVEDARIS, Chris									Left wing
1990	Hartford	2	0	0	0	2	0	0	0
1994	Toronto	2	0	0	0	0	0	0	0
Playoff Totals		**4**	**0**	**0**	**0**	**2**	**0**	**0**	**0**
GOYER, Gerry									Center
1968	Chicago	3	0	0	0	2	0	0	0
Playoff Totals		**3**	**0**	**0**	**0**	**2**	**0**	**0**	**0**
GOYETTE, Phil									Center
1957◆	Montreal	10	2	1	3	4	....	....	....
1958◆	Montreal	10	4	1	5	4	....	....	....
1959◆	Montreal	10	0	4	4	0	....	....	....
1960◆	Montreal	8	2	1	3	4	....	....	....
1961	Montreal	6	3	3	6	0	....	....	....
1962	Montreal	6	1	4	5	2	....	....	....
1963	Montreal	2	0	0	0	0	....	....	....
1967	NY Rangers	4	1	0	1	0	....	....	....
1968	NY Rangers	6	0	1	1	4	0	0	0
1969	NY Rangers	3	0	0	0	0	0	0	0
1970	St. Louis	16	3	11	14	6	1	2	0
1972	NY Rangers	13	1	3	4	2	1	0	0
Playoff Totals		**94**	**17**	**29**	**46**	**26**	....	....	....
GRABOSKI, Tony									Left wing/Defense
1941	Montreal	3	0	0	0	6	0	0	0
Playoff Totals		**3**	**0**	**0**	**0**	**6**	**0**	**0**	**0**
GRACIE, Bob									Center/left wing
1931	Toronto	2	0	0	0	0	....	....	....
1932◆	Toronto	7	3	1	4	0	....	....	....
1933	Toronto	9	0	1	1	0	....	....	....
1935◆	Mtl. Maroons	7	0	2	2	2	....	....	....
1936	Mtl. Maroons	3	0	1	1	0	....	....	....
1937	Mtl. Maroons	5	1	2	3	2	....	....	....
Playoff Totals		**33**	**4**	**7**	**11**	**4**	....	....	....

Season	Club	GP	G	A	Pts	PIM	PP	SH	GW
GRADIN, Thomas									Center
1979	Vancouver	3	4	1	5	4	0	0	0
1980	Vancouver	4	0	2	2	0	0	0	0
1981	Vancouver	3	1	3	4	0	0	0	0
1982	Vancouver	17	9	10	19	10	4	0	0
1983	Vancouver	4	1	3	4	2	0	0	0
1984	Vancouver	4	0	1	1	2	0	0	0
1986	Vancouver	3	2	1	3	2	0	0	0
1987	Boston	4	0	4	4	0	0	0	0
Playoff Totals		**42**	**17**	**25**	**42**	**20**	**4**	**0**	**0**
GRAHAM, Dirk									Left/Right wing
1984	Minnesota	1	0	0	0	2	0	0	0
1985	Minnesota	9	0	4	4	7	0	0	0
1986	Minnesota	5	3	1	4	2	0	1	2
1988	Chicago	4	1	2	3	4	0	0	0
1989	Chicago	16	2	4	6	38	1	0	0
1990	Chicago	5	1	5	6	2	0	1	0
1991	Chicago	6	1	2	3	17	0	0	0
1992	Chicago	18	7	5	12	8	0	0	1
1993	Chicago	4	0	0	0	0	0	0	0
1994	Chicago	6	0	1	1	4	0	0	0
1995	Chicago	16	2	3	5	8	0	0	1
Playoff Totals		**90**	**17**	**27**	**44**	**92**	**1**	**2**	**4**
GRAHAM, Leth									Left wing
1921◆	Ottawa	1	0	0	0	0	0	0	0
Playoff Totals		**1**	**0**	**0**	**0**	**0**	**0**	**0**	**0**
GRAHAM, Pat									Left wing
1982	Pittsburgh	4	0	0	0	2	0	0	0
Playoff Totals		**4**	**0**	**0**	**0**	**2**	**0**	**0**	**0**
GRAHAM, Rod	*No playoffs*								Left wing
GRAHAM, Ted									Defense
1930	Chicago	2	0	0	0	8	....	....	....
1931	Chicago	9	0	0	0	12	....	....	....
1932	Chicago	2	0	0	0	2	....	....	....
1934	Detroit	9	3	1	4	8	....	....	....
1936	Boston	2	0	0	0	0	....	....	....
Playoff Totals		**24**	**3**	**1**	**4**	**30**	....	....	....
GRANATO, Tony									Right wing
1989	NY Rangers	4	1	1	2	21	0	0	0
1990	Los Angeles	10	5	4	9	12	2	1	2
1991	Los Angeles	12	1	4	5	28	0	0	0
1992	Los Angeles	6	1	5	6	10	0	0	0
1993	Los Angeles	24	6	11	17	50	1	0	1
1998	San Jose	1	0	0	0	0	0	0	0
1999	San Jose	6	1	1	2	2	0	0	0
Playoff Totals		**63**	**15**	**26**	**41**	**123**	**3**	**1**	**3**
GRAND PIERRE, Jean-Luc	*No playoffs*								Defense
GRANT, Danny									Right wing
1968◆	Montreal	10	0	3	3	5	0	0	0
1970	Minnesota	6	0	2	2	4	0	0	0
1971	Minnesota	12	5	5	10	8	3	0	1
1972	Minnesota	7	2	1	3	0	0	0	0
1973	Minnesota	6	3	1	4	0	0	0	0
1978	Los Angeles	2	0	2	2	2	0	0	0
Playoff Totals		**43**	**10**	**14**	**24**	**19**	**3**	**0**	**1**
GRATTON, Benoit	*No playoffs*								Left wing
GRATTON, Chris									Center
1996	Tampa Bay	6	0	2	2	27	0	0	0
1998	Philadelphia	5	2	0	2	10	0	0	0
Playoff Totals		**11**	**2**	**2**	**4**	**37**	**0**	**0**	**0**
GRATTON, Dan	*No playoffs*								Center
GRATTON, Norm									Left wing
1973	Buffalo	6	0	1	1	2	0	0	0
Playoff Totals		**6**	**0**	**1**	**1**	**2**	**0**	**0**	**0**
GRAVELLE, Leo									Right wing
1947	Montreal	6	2	0	2	2	....	....	....
1949	Montreal	7	2	1	3	0	....	....	....
1950	Montreal	4	0	0	0	0	....	....	....
Playoff Totals		**17**	**4**	**1**	**5**	**2**	....	....	....
GRAVES, Adam									Center
1989	Detroit	5	0	0	0	4	0	0	0
1990◆	Edmonton	22	5	6	11	17	0	0	1
1991	Edmonton	18	2	4	6	22	0	0	0
1992	NY Rangers	10	5	3	8	22	1	0	1
1994◆	NY Rangers	23	10	7	17	24	3	0	0
1995	NY Rangers	10	4	4	8	8	2	0	0
1996	NY Rangers	10	7	1	8	4	6	0	2
1997	NY Rangers	15	2	1	3	12	1	0	2
Playoff Totals		**113**	**35**	**26**	**61**	**113**	**13**	**0**	**6**
GRAVES, Hilliard									Right wing
1976	Atlanta	2	0	0	0	0	0	0	0
Playoff Totals		**2**	**0**	**0**	**0**	**0**	**0**	**0**	**0**
GRAVES, Steve	*No playoffs*								Left wing
GRAY, Alex									Right wing
1928◆	NY Rangers	9	1	0	1	0	....	....	....
1929	Toronto	4	0	0	0	0	....	....	....
Playoff Totals		**13**	**1**	**0**	**1**	**0**	....	....	....

Season	Club	GP	G	A	Pts	PIM	PP	SH	GW
GRAY, Terry									Right wing
1968	Los Angeles	7	0	2	2	10	0	0	0
1969	St. Louis	11	3	2	5	8	1	0	0
1970	St. Louis	16	2	1	3	4	1	1	0
1971	St. Louis	1	0	0	0	0	0	0	0
Playoff Totals		**35**	**5**	**5**	**10**	**22**	**2**	**1**	**0**
GREEN, Josh	*No playoffs*								Left wing
GREEN, Red									Left wing
1929♦	Boston	1	0	0	0	0	0	0	0
Playoff Totals		**1**	**0**	**0**	**0**	**0**	**0**	**0**	**0**
GREEN, Rick									Defense
1983	Montreal	3	0	0	0	2	0	0	0
1984	Montreal	15	1	2	3	33	0	0	0
1985	Montreal	12	0	3	3	14	0	0	0
1986♦	Montreal	18	1	4	5	8	0	0	0
1987	Montreal	17	0	4	4	8	0	0	0
1988	Montreal	11	0	2	2	2	0	0	0
1989	Montreal	21	1	1	2	6	0	0	0
1991	Detroit	3	0	0	0	0	0	0	0
Playoff Totals		**100**	**3**	**16**	**19**	**73**	**0**	**0**	**0**
GREEN, Shorty	*No playoffs*								Right wing
GREEN, Ted									Defense
1968	Boston	4	1	1	2	11	1	0	0
1969	Boston	10	2	7	9	18	0	0	0
1971	Boston	7	1	0	1	25	0	0	0
1972♦	Boston	10	0	0	0	0	0	0	0
Playoff Totals		**31**	**4**	**8**	**12**	**54**	**1**	**0**	**0**
GREEN, Travis									Center
1993	NY Islanders	12	3	1	4	6	0	0	0
1994	NY Islanders	4	0	0	0	2	0	0	0
1999	Anaheim	4	0	1	1	4	0	0	0
Playoff Totals		**20**	**3**	**2**	**5**	**12**	**0**	**0**	**0**
GREENLAW, Jeff									Left wing
1988	Washington	1	0	0	0	19	0	0	0
1991	Washington	1	0	0	0	2	0	0	0
Playoff Totals		**2**	**0**	**0**	**0**	**21**	**0**	**0**	**0**
GREGG, Randy									Defense
1982	Edmonton	4	0	0	0	0	0	0	0
1983	Edmonton	16	2	4	6	13	0	1	1
1984♦	Edmonton	19	3	7	10	21	0	0	1
1985♦	Edmonton	17	0	6	6	12	0	0	0
1986	Edmonton	10	1	0	1	12	0	0	0
1987♦	Edmonton	18	3	6	9	17	1	0	1
1988♦	Edmonton	19	1	8	9	24	0	0	1
1989	Edmonton	7	1	0	1	4	0	0	0
1990♦	Edmonton	20	2	6	8	16	1	0	0
1992	Vancouver	7	0	1	1	8	0	0	0
Playoff Totals		**137**	**13**	**38**	**51**	**127**	**2**	**1**	**4**
GREIG, Bruce	*No playoffs*								Left wing
GREIG, Mark									Right wing
1999	Philadelphia	2	0	1	1	0	0	0	0
Playoff Totals		**2**	**0**	**1**	**1**	**0**	**0**	**0**	**0**
GRENIER, Lucien									Right wing
1969♦	Montreal	2	0	0	0	0	0	0	0
Playoff Totals		**2**	**0**	**0**	**0**	**0**	**0**	**0**	**0**
GRENIER, Richard	*No playoffs*								Center
GRESCHNER, Ron									Defense
1975	NY Rangers	3	0	1	1	2	0	0	0
1978	NY Rangers	3	0	0	0	2	0	0	0
1979	NY Rangers	18	7	5	12	16	4	1	3
1980	NY Rangers	9	0	6	6	10	0	0	0
1981	NY Rangers	14	4	8	12	17	1	0	0
1983	NY Rangers	8	2	2	4	12	2	0	0
1984	NY Rangers	2	1	0	1	2	0	0	0
1985	NY Rangers	2	0	3	3	12	0	0	0
1986	NY Rangers	5	3	1	4	11	0	0	0
1987	NY Rangers	6	0	5	5	0	0	0	0
1989	NY Rangers	4	0	1	1	6	0	0	0
1990	NY Rangers	10	0	0	0	16	0	0	0
Playoff Totals		**84**	**17**	**32**	**49**	**106**	**7**	**1**	**3**
GRETZKY, Brent	*No playoffs*								Center
GRETZKY, Wayne									Center
1980	Edmonton	3	2	1	3	0	0	0	0
1981	Edmonton	9	7	14	21	4	2	1	1
1982	Edmonton	5	5	7	12	8	1	1	1
1983	Edmonton	16	12	*26	*38	4	2	3	3
1984♦	Edmonton	19	13	*22	*35	12	2	0	3
1985♦	Edmonton	18	17	*30	*47	4	4	2	3
1986	Edmonton	10	8	11	19	2	4	1	2
1987♦	Edmonton	21	5	*29	*34	6	2	0	0
1988♦	Edmonton	19	12	*31	*43	16	5	1	3
1989	Los Angeles	11	5	17	22	0	1	1	0
1990	Los Angeles	7	3	7	10	0	1	0	0
1991	Los Angeles	12	4	11	15	2	1	0	2
1992	Los Angeles	6	2	5	7	2	1	0	2
1993	Los Angeles	24	*15	*25	*40	4	4	1	3
1996	St. Louis	13	2	14	16	0	1	0	1
1997	NY Rangers	15	10	10	20	2	3	0	2
Playoff Totals		**208**	***122**	***260**	***382**	**66**	**34**	**11**	***24**

Season	Club	GP	G	A	Pts	PIM	PP	SH	GW
GRIER, Michael									Right wing
1997	Edmonton	12	3	1	4	4	1	0	1
1998	Edmonton	12	2	2	4	13	0	0	1
1999	Edmonton	4	1	1	2	6	0	0	0
Playoff Totals		**28**	**6**	**4**	**10**	**23**	**1**	**0**	**2**
GRIEVE, Brent	*No playoffs*								Left wing
GRIGOR, George									Center
1944	Chicago	1	0	0	0	0	0	0	0
Playoff Totals		**1**	**0**	**0**	**0**	**0**	**0**	**0**	**0**
GRIMSON, Stu									Left wing
1991	Chicago	5	0	0	0	46	0	0	0
1992	Chicago	14	0	1	1	10	0	0	0
1993	Chicago	2	0	0	0	4	0	0	0
1995	Detroit	11	1	0	1	26	0	0	0
1996	Detroit	2	0	0	0	0	0	0	0
1999	Anaheim	3	0	0	0	30	0	0	0
Playoff Totals		**37**	**1**	**1**	**2**	**116**	**0**	**0**	**0**
GRISDALE, John									Defense
1975	Vancouver	5	0	1	1	13	0	0	0
1976	Vancouver	2	0	0	0	0	0	0	0
1979	Vancouver	3	0	0	0	2	0	0	0
Playoff Totals		**10**	**0**	**1**	**1**	**15**	**0**	**0**	**0**
GROLEAU, Francois	*No playoffs*								Defense
GRONMAN, Tuomas									Defense
1998	Pittsburgh	1	0	0	0	0	0	0	0
Playoff Totals		**1**	**0**	**0**	**0**	**0**	**0**	**0**	**0**
GRONSDAHL, Lloyd	*No playoffs*								Right wing
GRONSTRAND, Jari									Defense
1990	NY Islanders	3	0	0	0	4	0	0	0
Playoff Totals		**3**	**0**	**0**	**0**	**4**	**0**	**0**	**0**
GROSEK, Michal									Left wing
1997	Buffalo	12	3	3	6	8	0	0	0
1998	Buffalo	15	6	4	10	28	2	0	3
1999	Buffalo	13	0	4	4	28	0	0	0
Playoff Totals		**40**	**9**	**11**	**20**	**64**	**2**	**0**	**3**
GROSS, Lloyd									Left wing
1934	Detroit	1	0	0	0	0	0	0	0
Playoff Totals		**1**	**0**	**0**	**0**	**0**	**0**	**0**	**0**
GROSSO, Don									Left wing/center
1939	Detroit	3	1	2	3	7	....	....	....
1940	Detroit	5	0	0	0	0	....	....	....
1941	Detroit	9	1	4	5	0	....	....	....
1942	Detroit	12	*8	6	*14	29	....	....	....
1943♦	Detroit	10	4	2	6	10	....	....	....
1944	Detroit	5	1	0	1	0	....	....	....
1946	Chicago	4	0	0	0	17	....	....	....
Playoff Totals		**48**	**15**	**14**	**29**	**63**	....	....	....
GROSVENOR, Len									Center/right wing
1928	Ottawa	2	0	0	0	2	0	0	0
1933	Mtl. Canadiens	2	0	0	0	0	0	0	0
Playoff Totals		**4**	**0**	**0**	**0**	**2**	**0**	**0**	**0**
GROULX, Wayne	*No playoffs*								Center
GRUDEN, John									Defense
1996	Boston	3	0	1	1	0	0	0	0
Playoff Totals		**3**	**0**	**1**	**1**	**0**	**0**	**0**	**0**
GRUEN, Danny	*No playoffs*								Left wing
GRUHL, Scott	*No playoffs*								Left wing
GRYP, Bob	*No playoffs*								Left wing
GUAY, Francois	*No playoffs*								Center
GUAY, Paul									Right wing
1984	Philadelphia	3	0	0	0	4	0	0	0
1987	Los Angeles	2	0	0	0	0	0	0	0
1988	Los Angeles	4	0	1	1	8	0	0	0
Playoff Totals		**9**	**0**	**1**	**1**	**12**	**0**	**0**	**0**
GUERARD, Daniel	*No playoffs*								Right wing
GUERARD, Stephane	*No playoffs*								Defense
GUERIN, Bill									Right wing
1992	New Jersey	6	3	0	3	4	0	0	0
1993	New Jersey	5	1	1	2	4	0	0	0
1994	New Jersey	17	2	1	3	35	0	0	1
1995♦	New Jersey	20	3	8	11	30	1	0	0
1997	New Jersey	8	2	1	3	18	1	0	1
1998	Edmonton	12	7	1	8	17	4	0	0
1999	Edmonton	3	0	2	2	2	0	0	0
Playoff Totals		**71**	**18**	**14**	**32**	**110**	**6**	**0**	**2**
GUEVREMONT, Jocelyn									Defense
1975	Buffalo	17	0	6	6	14	0	0	0
1976	Buffalo	9	0	5	5	2	0	0	0
1977	Buffalo	6	3	4	7	0	1	0	0
1978	Buffalo	8	1	2	3	2	0	0	0
Playoff Totals		**40**	**4**	**17**	**21**	**18**	**1**	**0**	**0**
GUIDOLIN, Aldo	*No playoffs*								Right wing/Defense

Season	Club	GP	G	A	Pts	PIM	PP	SH	GW
GUIDOLIN, Bep									Left wing
1943	Boston	9	0	4	4	12	....	....	....
1946	Boston	10	5	2	7	13	....	....	....
1947	Boston	3	0	1	1	6	....	....	....
1948	Detroit	2	0	0	0	4	....	....	....
Playoff Totals		**24**	**5**	**7**	**12**	**35**	....	....	....
GUINDON, Bobby	*No playoffs*								Left wing
GUOLLA, Stephen	*No playoffs*								Left wing
GUREN, Miloslav	*No playoffs*								Defense
GUSAROV, Alexei									Defense
1993	Quebec	5	0	1	1	0	0	0	0
1996♦	Colorado	21	0	9	9	12	0	0	0
1997	Colorado	17	0	3	3	14	0	0	0
1998	Colorado	7	0	1	1	6	0	0	0
1999	Colorado	5	0	0	0	2	0	0	0
Playoff Totals		**55**	**0**	**14**	**14**	**34**	**0**	**0**	**0**
GUSEV, Sergey	*No playoffs*								Defense
GUSMANOV, Ravil	*No playoffs*								Left wing
GUSTAFSSON, Bengt-Ake									Right wing
1983	Washington	4	0	1	1	4	0	0	0
1984	Washington	5	2	3	5	0	2	0	0
1985	Washington	5	1	3	4	0	1	0	0
1988	Washington	14	4	9	13	6	2	0	1
1989	Washington	4	2	3	5	6	1	0	0
Playoff Totals		**32**	**9**	**19**	**28**	**16**	**6**	**0**	**1**
GUSTAFSSON, Per									Defense
1998	Ottawa	1	0	0	0	0	0	0	0
Playoff Totals		**1**	**0**	**0**	**0**	**0**	**0**	**0**	**0**
GUSTAVSSON, Peter	*No playoffs*								Left wing
GUY, Kevan									Defense
1987	Calgary	4	0	1	1	23	0	0	0
1989	Vancouver	1	0	0	0	0	0	0	0
Playoff Totals		**5**	**0**	**1**	**1**	**23**	**0**	**0**	**0**
HAANPAA, Ari									Right wing
1987	NY Islanders	6	0	0	0	10	0	0	0
Playoff Totals		**6**	**0**	**0**	**0**	**10**	**0**	**0**	**0**
HAAS, David	*No playoffs*								Left wing
HABSCHEID, Marc									Right wing/Center
1986	Minnesota	2	0	0	0	0	0	0	0
1989	Minnesota	5	1	3	4	13	0	0	0
1991	Detroit	5	0	0	0	0	0	0	0
Playoff Totals		**12**	**1**	**3**	**4**	**13**	**0**	**0**	**0**
HACHBORN, Len									Center
1984	Philadelphia	3	0	0	0	7	0	0	0
1985	Philadelphia	4	0	3	3	0	0	0	0
Playoff Totals		**7**	**0**	**3**	**3**	**7**	**0**	**0**	**0**
HADDON, Lloyd									Defense
1960	Detroit	1	0	0	0	0	0	0	0
Playoff Totals		**1**	**0**	**0**	**0**	**0**	**0**	**0**	**0**
HADFIELD, Vic									Left wing
1962	NY Rangers	4	0	0	0	2	0	0	0
1967	NY Rangers	4	1	0	1	17	0	0	0
1968	NY Rangers	6	1	2	3	6	1	0	0
1969	NY Rangers	4	2	1	3	2	0	0	0
1971	NY Rangers	12	8	5	13	46	1	0	1
1972	NY Rangers	16	7	9	16	22	2	0	1
1973	NY Rangers	9	2	2	4	11	0	0	1
1974	NY Rangers	6	1	0	1	0	0	0	0
1975	Pittsburgh	9	4	2	6	0	0	1	0
1976	Pittsburgh	3	1	0	1	11	0	0	0
Playoff Totals		**73**	**27**	**21**	**48**	**117**	**4**	**1**	**3**
HAGGARTY, Jim									Left wing
1942	Montreal	3	2	1	3	0	....	....	....
Playoff Totals		**3**	**2**	**1**	**3**	**0**	....	....	....
HAGGERTY, Sean	*No playoffs*								Left wing
HAGGLUND, Roger	*No playoffs*								Defense
HAGMAN, Matti									Center
1977	Boston	8	0	1	1	0	0	0	0
1981	Edmonton	9	4	1	5	6	0	0	2
1982	Edmonton	3	1	0	1	0	0	0	0
Playoff Totals		**20**	**5**	**2**	**7**	**6**	**0**	**0**	**2**
HAIDY, Gord									Right wing
1950♦	Detroit	1	0	0	0	0	0	0	0
Playoff Totals		**1**	**0**	**0**	**0**	**0**	**0**	**0**	**0**
HAJDU, Richard	*No playoffs*								Left wing
HAJT, Bill									Defense
1975	Buffalo	17	1	4	5	18	0	0	0
1976	Buffalo	9	0	1	1	15	0	0	0
1977	Buffalo	6	0	1	1	4	0	0	0
1978	Buffalo	8	0	0	0	2	0	0	0
1980	Buffalo	14	0	5	5	4	0	0	0
1981	Buffalo	8	0	2	2	17	0	0	0
1982	Buffalo	2	0	0	0	0	0	0	0
1983	Buffalo	10	0	0	0	4	0	0	0
1984	Buffalo	3	0	0	0	0	0	0	0
1985	Buffalo	3	1	3	4	6	0	0	0
Playoff Totals		**80**	**2**	**16**	**18**	**70**	**0**	**0**	**0**

HAKANSSON, Anders — Left wing

Season	Club	GP	G	A	Pts	PIM	PP	SH	GW
1982	Minnesota	3	0	0	0	2	0	0	0
1985	Los Angeles	3	0	0	0	0	0	0	0
Playoff Totals		**6**	**0**	**0**	**0**	**2**	**0**	**0**	**0**

HALDERSON, Harold *No playoffs* — Defense

HALE, Larry — Defense

Season	Club	GP	G	A	Pts	PIM	PP	SH	GW
1969	Philadelphia	4	0	0	0	10	0	0	0
1971	Philadelphia	4	0	0	0	2	0	0	0
Playoff Totals		**8**	**0**	**0**	**0**	**12**	**0**	**0**	**0**

HALEY, Len — Right wing

Season	Club	GP	G	A	Pts	PIM	PP	SH	GW
1960	Detroit	6	1	3	4	6	0	0	1
Playoff Totals		**6**	**1**	**3**	**4**	**6**	**0**	**0**	**1**

HALKIDIS, Bob — Defense

Season	Club	GP	G	A	Pts	PIM	PP	SH	GW
1985	Buffalo	4	0	0	0	19	0	0	0
1988	Buffalo	4	0	0	0	22	0	0	0
1990	Los Angeles	8	0	1	1	8	0	0	0
1991	Los Angeles	3	0	0	0	0	0	0	0
1994	Detroit	1	0	0	0	2	0	0	0
Playoff Totals		**20**	**0**	**1**	**1**	**51**	**0**	**0**	**0**

HALKO, Steven — Defense

Season	Club	GP	G	A	Pts	PIM	PP	SH	GW
1999	Carolina	4	0	0	0	2	0	0	0
Playoff Totals		**4**	**0**	**0**	**0**	**2**	**0**	**0**	**0**

HALL, Bob *No playoffs* — Forward

HALL, Del *No playoffs* — Center

HALL, Joe — Defense

Season	Club	GP	G	A	Pts	PIM	PP	SH	GW
1918	Mtl. Canadiens	2	0	1	1	13	0	0	0
1919	Mtl. Canadiens	10	0	0	0	26	0	0	0
Playoff Totals		**12**	**0**	**1**	**1**	**39**	**0**	**0**	**0**

HALL, Murray — Right wing

Season	Club	GP	G	A	Pts	PIM	PP	SH	GW
1963	Chicago	4	0	0	0	0	0	0	0
1965	Detroit	1	0	0	0	0	0	0	0
1966	Detroit	1	0	0	0	0	0	0	0
Playoff Totals		**6**	**0**	**0**	**0**	**0**	**0**	**0**	**0**

HALL, Taylor *No playoffs* — Left wing

HALL, Wayne *No playoffs* — Left wing

HALLER, Kevin — Defense

Season	Club	GP	G	A	Pts	PIM	PP	SH	GW
1991	Buffalo	6	1	4	5	10	0	0	0
1992	Montreal	9	0	0	0	6	0	0	0
1993♦	Montreal	17	1	6	7	16	1	0	0
1994	Montreal	7	1	1	2	19	0	0	0
1995	Philadelphia	15	4	4	8	10	0	1	1
1996	Philadelphia	6	0	1	1	8	0	0	0
1999	Anaheim	4	0	0	0	2	0	0	0
Playoff Totals		**64**	**7**	**16**	**23**	**71**	**1**	**1**	**1**

HALLIDAY, Milt — Left wing

Season	Club	GP	G	A	Pts	PIM	PP	SH	GW
1927♦	Ottawa	6	0	0	0	0	0	0	0
Playoff Totals		**6**	**0**	**0**	**0**	**0**	**0**	**0**	**0**

HALLIN, Mats — Left wing

Season	Club	GP	G	A	Pts	PIM	PP	SH	GW
1983♦	NY Islanders	7	1	0	1	6	0	0	1
1984	NY Islanders	6	0	0	0	7	0	0	0
1985	NY Islanders	1	0	0	0	0	0	0	0
1986	Minnesota	1	0	0	0	0	0	0	0
Playoff Totals		**15**	**1**	**0**	**1**	**13**	**0**	**0**	**1**

HALPERN, Jeff *No playoffs* — Center

HALVERSON, Trevor *No playoffs* — Left wing

HALWARD, Doug — Defense

Season	Club	GP	G	A	Pts	PIM	PP	SH	GW
1976	Boston	1	0	0	0	0	0	0	0
1977	Boston	6	0	0	0	4	0	0	0
1979	Los Angeles	1	0	0	0	12	0	0	0
1980	Los Angeles	1	0	0	0	2	0	0	0
1981	Vancouver	2	0	1	1	6	0	0	0
1982	Vancouver	15	2	4	6	44	0	0	1
1983	Vancouver	4	1	0	1	21	0	0	0
1984	Vancouver	4	3	1	4	2	2	0	0
1986	Vancouver	3	0	0	0	4	0	0	0
1988	Detroit	8	1	4	5	18	0	0	0
1989	Edmonton	2	0	0	0	0	0	0	0
Playoff Totals		**47**	**7**	**10**	**17**	**113**	**2**	**0**	**1**

HAMEL, Denis *No playoffs* — Left wing

HAMEL, Gilles — Left wing

Season	Club	GP	G	A	Pts	PIM	PP	SH	GW
1981	Buffalo	5	0	1	1	4	0	0	0
1983	Buffalo	9	2	2	4	2	1	0	0
1984	Buffalo	3	0	2	2	2	0	0	0
1985	Buffalo	1	0	0	0	0	0	0	0
1987	Winnipeg	8	2	0	2	2	0	0	2
1988	Winnipeg	1	0	0	0	0	0	0	0
Playoff Totals		**27**	**4**	**5**	**9**	**10**	**1**	**0**	**2**

HAMEL, Herb *No playoffs* — Right wing

HAMEL, Jean — Defense

Season	Club	GP	G	A	Pts	PIM	PP	SH	GW
1973	St. Louis	2	0	0	0	0	0	0	0
1978	Detroit	7	0	0	0	10	0	0	0
1982	Quebec	5	0	0	0	16	0	0	0
1983	Quebec	4	0	0	0	2	0	0	0
1984	Montreal	15	0	2	2	16	0	0	0
Playoff Totals		**33**	**0**	**2**	**2**	**44**	**0**	**0**	**0**

HAMILL, Red — Left wing

Season	Club	GP	G	A	Pts	PIM	PP	SH	GW
1939♦	Boston	12	0	0	0	8	....	....	....
1940	Boston	5	0	1	1	5	....	....	....
1942	Chicago	3	0	1	1	0	....	....	....
1946	Chicago	4	1	0	1	7	....	....	....
Playoff Totals		**24**	**1**	**2**	**3**	**20**	....	....	....

HAMILTON, Al — Defense

Season	Club	GP	G	A	Pts	PIM	PP	SH	GW
1969	NY Rangers	1	0	0	0	0	0	0	0
1970	NY Rangers	5	0	0	0	2	0	0	0
1980	Edmonton	1	0	0	0	0	0	0	0
Playoff Totals		**7**	**0**	**0**	**0**	**2**	**0**	**0**	**0**

HAMILTON, Chuck *No playoffs* — Left wing

HAMILTON, Jack — Center

Season	Club	GP	G	A	Pts	PIM	PP	SH	GW
1943	Toronto	6	1	1	2	0	....	....	....
1944	Toronto	5	1	0	1	0	....	....	....
Playoff Totals		**11**	**2**	**1**	**3**	**0**	....	....	....

HAMILTON, Jim — Right wing

Season	Club	GP	G	A	Pts	PIM	PP	SH	GW
1979	Pittsburgh	5	3	0	3	0	1	0	0
1981	Pittsburgh	1	0	0	0	0	0	0	0
Playoff Totals		**6**	**3**	**0**	**3**	**0**	**1**	**0**	**0**

HAMILTON, Reg — Defense

Season	Club	GP	G	A	Pts	PIM	PP	SH	GW
1937	Toronto	2	0	1	1	2	....	....	....
1938	Toronto	7	0	1	1	2	....	....	....
1939	Toronto	10	0	2	2	4	....	....	....
1940	Toronto	10	0	0	0	0	....	....	....
1941	Toronto	7	1	2	3	13	....	....	....
1943	Toronto	6	1	1	2	9	....	....	....
1944	Toronto	5	1	0	1	8	....	....	....
1945♦	Toronto	13	0	0	0	6	....	....	....
1946	Chicago	4	0	1	1	2	....	....	....
Playoff Totals		**64**	**3**	**8**	**11**	**46**	....	....	....

HAMMARSTROM, Inge — Left wing

Season	Club	GP	G	A	Pts	PIM	PP	SH	GW
1974	Toronto	4	1	0	1	0	0	0	0
1975	Toronto	7	1	3	4	4	0	0	1
1977	Toronto	2	0	0	0	0	0	0	0
Playoff Totals		**13**	**2**	**3**	**5**	**4**	**0**	**0**	**1**

HAMMOND, Ken — Defense

Season	Club	GP	G	A	Pts	PIM	PP	SH	GW
1985	Los Angeles	3	0	0	0	4	0	0	0
1988	Los Angeles	2	0	0	0	4	0	0	0
1991	Boston	8	0	0	0	10	0	0	0
1992	Vancouver	2	0	0	0	6	0	0	0
Playoff Totals		**15**	**0**	**0**	**0**	**24**	**0**	**0**	**0**

HAMPSON, Gord *No playoffs* — Left wing

HAMPSON, Ted — Center

Season	Club	GP	G	A	Pts	PIM	PP	SH	GW
1962	NY Rangers	6	0	1	1	0	0	0	0
1969	Oakland	7	3	4	7	2	2	0	0
1970	Oakland	4	1	1	2	0	0	0	0
1971	Minnesota	11	3	3	6	0	1	0	0
1972	Minnesota	7	0	1	1	0	0	0	0
Playoff Totals		**35**	**7**	**10**	**17**	**2**	**3**	**0**	**0**

HAMPTON, Rick — Left wing/defense

Season	Club	GP	G	A	Pts	PIM	PP	SH	GW
1979	Los Angeles	2	0	0	0	0	0	0	0
Playoff Totals		**2**	**0**	**0**	**0**	**0**	**0**	**0**	**0**

HAMR, Radek *No playoffs* — Defense

HAMRLIK, Roman — Defense

Season	Club	GP	G	A	Pts	PIM	PP	SH	GW
1996	Tampa Bay	5	0	1	1	4	0	0	0
1998	Edmonton	12	0	6	6	12	0	0	0
1999	Edmonton	3	0	0	0	2	0	0	0
Playoff Totals		**20**	**0**	**7**	**7**	**18**	**0**	**0**	**0**

HAMWAY, Mark — Right wing

Season	Club	GP	G	A	Pts	PIM	PP	SH	GW
1986	NY Islanders	1	0	0	0	0	0	0	0
Playoff Totals		**1**	**0**	**0**	**0**	**0**	**0**	**0**	**0**

HANDY, Ron *No playoffs* — Left wing

HANDZUS, Michal — Center

Season	Club	GP	G	A	Pts	PIM	PP	SH	GW
1999	St. Louis	11	0	2	2	8	0	0	0
Playoff Totals		**11**	**0**	**2**	**2**	**8**	**0**	**0**	**0**

HANGSLEBEN, Al *No playoffs* — Defense

HANKINSON, Ben — Right wing

Season	Club	GP	G	A	Pts	PIM	PP	SH	GW
1994	New Jersey	2	1	0	1	4	0	0	0
Playoff Totals		**2**	**1**	**0**	**1**	**4**	**0**	**0**	**0**

HANNA, John *No playoffs* — Defense

HANNAN, Dave — Center

Season	Club	GP	G	A	Pts	PIM	PP	SH	GW
1988♦	Edmonton	12	1	1	2	8	0	0	1
1989	Pittsburgh	8	0	1	1	4	0	0	0
1990	Toronto	3	1	0	1	4	0	0	1
1992	Buffalo	7	2	0	2	2	2	0	0
1993	Buffalo	8	1	1	2	18	0	0	0
1994	Buffalo	7	1	0	1	6	0	0	1
1995	Buffalo	5	0	2	2	2	0	0	0
1996♦	Colorado	13	0	2	2	2	0	0	0
Playoff Totals		**63**	**6**	**7**	**13**	**46**	**2**	**0**	**3**

HANNAN, Scott *No playoffs* — Defense

HANNIGAN, Gord — Center

Season	Club	GP	G	A	Pts	PIM	PP	SH	GW
1954	Toronto	5	2	0	2	4	1	0	1
1956	Toronto	4	0	0	0	4	0	0	0
Playoff Totals		**9**	**2**	**0**	**2**	**8**	**1**	**0**	**1**

HANNIGAN, Pat — Left wing

Season	Club	GP	G	A	Pts	PIM	PP	SH	GW
1962	NY Rangers	4	0	0	0	2	0	0	0
1968	Philadelphia	7	1	2	3	9	0	0	0
Playoff Totals		**11**	**1**	**2**	**3**	**11**	**0**	**0**	**0**

HANNIGAN, Ray *No playoffs* — Right wing

HANSEN, Richie *No playoffs* — Center

HANSEN, Tavis — Center

Season	Club	GP	G	A	Pts	PIM	PP	SH	GW
1999	Phoenix	2	0	0	0	0	0	0	0
Playoff Totals		**2**	**0**	**0**	**0**	**0**	**0**	**0**	**0**

HANSON, Dave *No playoffs* — Defense

HANSON, Emil *No playoffs* — Right wing/defense

HANSON, Keith *No playoffs* — Defense

HANSON, Oscar *No playoffs* — Center

HARBARUK, Nick — Right wing

Season	Club	GP	G	A	Pts	PIM	PP	SH	GW
1970	Pittsburgh	10	3	0	3	20	0	1	0
1972	Pittsburgh	4	0	1	1	0	0	0	0
Playoff Totals		**14**	**3**	**1**	**4**	**20**	**0**	**1**	**0**

HARDING, Jeff *No playoffs* — Right wing

HARDY, Joe — Center

Season	Club	GP	G	A	Pts	PIM	PP	SH	GW
1970	Oakland	4	0	0	0	0	0	0	0
Playoff Totals		**4**	**0**	**0**	**0**	**0**	**0**	**0**	**0**

HARDY, Mark — Defense

Season	Club	GP	G	A	Pts	PIM	PP	SH	GW
1980	Los Angeles	4	1	1	2	9	0	0	0
1981	Los Angeles	4	1	2	3	4	1	0	0
1982	Los Angeles	10	1	2	3	9	0	0	0
1985	Los Angeles	3	0	1	1	2	0	0	0
1987	Los Angeles	5	1	2	3	10	0	0	0
1989	NY Rangers	4	0	1	1	31	0	0	0
1990	NY Rangers	3	0	1	1	2	0	0	0
1991	NY Rangers	6	0	1	1	30	0	0	0
1992	NY Rangers	13	0	3	3	31	0	0	0
1993	Los Angeles	15	1	2	3	30	0	0	0
Playoff Totals		**67**	**5**	**16**	**21**	**158**	**1**	**0**	**0**

HARGREAVES, Jim *No playoffs* — Defense

HARKINS, Brett *No playoffs* — Left wing

HARKINS, Todd *No playoffs* — Center

HARLOCK, David *No playoffs* — Defense

HARLOW, Scott *No playoffs* — Left wing

HARMON, Glen — Defense

Season	Club	GP	G	A	Pts	PIM	PP	SH	GW
1943	Montreal	5	0	1	1	2	....	....	....
1944♦	Montreal	9	1	2	3	4	....	....	....
1945	Montreal	6	1	0	1	2	....	....	....
1946♦	Montreal	9	1	4	5	0	....	....	....
1947	Montreal	11	1	1	2	4	....	....	....
1949	Montreal	7	1	1	2	4	....	....	....
1950	Montreal	5	0	1	1	21	....	....	....
1951	Montreal	1	0	0	0	0	....	....	....
Playoff Totals		**53**	**5**	**10**	**15**	**37**	....	....	....

HARMS, John — Right wing

Season	Club	GP	G	A	Pts	PIM	PP	SH	GW
1944	Chicago	4	3	0	3	2	....	....	....
Playoff Totals		**4**	**3**	**0**	**3**	**2**	....	....	....

HARNOTT, Walter *No playoffs* — Left wing

HARPER, Terry — Defense

Season	Club	GP	G	A	Pts	PIM	PP	SH	GW
1963	Montreal	5	1	0	1	8	0	0	0
1964	Montreal	7	0	0	0	6	0	0	0
1965♦	Montreal	13	0	0	0	19	0	0	0
1966♦	Montreal	10	2	3	5	18	0	0	1
1967	Montreal	10	0	1	1	15	0	0	0
1968♦	Montreal	13	0	1	1	8	0	0	0
1969♦	Montreal	11	0	0	0	8	0	0	0
1971♦	Montreal	20	0	6	6	28	0	0	0
1972	Montreal	5	1	1	2	6	0	0	0
1974	Los Angeles	5	0	0	0	16	0	0	0
1975	Los Angeles	3	0	0	0	2	0	0	0
1978	Detroit	7	0	1	1	4	0	0	0
1980	St. Louis	3	0	0	0	2	0	0	0
Playoff Totals		**112**	**4**	**13**	**17**	**140**	**0**	**0**	**1**

HARRER, Tim *No playoffs* — Right wing

HARRINGTON, Hago — Left wing

Season	Club	GP	G	A	Pts	PIM	PP	SH	GW
1928	Boston	2	0	0	0	0	....	....	....
1933	Mtl. Canadiens	2	1	0	1	2	....	....	....
Playoff Totals		**4**	**1**	**0**	**1**	**2**	....	....	....

HARRIS, Billy — Right wing

Season	Club	GP	G	A	Pts	PIM	PP	SH	GW
1975	NY Islanders	17	3	7	10	12	2	0	1
1976	NY Islanders	13	5	2	7	10	1	0	0
1977	NY Islanders	12	7	7	14	8	2	0	1
1978	NY Islanders	7	0	0	0	4	0	0	0
1979	NY Islanders	10	2	1	3	10	1	0	1
1980	Los Angeles	4	0	0	0	2	0	0	0
1981	Los Angeles	4	2	1	3	0	0	0	0
1983	Toronto	4	0	1	1	2	0	0	0
Playoff Totals		**71**	**19**	**19**	**38**	**48**	**6**	**0**	**3**

HARRIS, Billy Center

Season	Club	GP	G	A	Pts	PIM	PP	SH	GW
1956	Toronto	5	1	0	1	4	....	....	....
1959	Toronto	12	3	4	7	16	....	....	....
1960	Toronto	9	0	3	3	4	....	....	....
1961	Toronto	5	1	0	1	0	....	....	....
1962◆	Toronto	12	2	1	3	2	....	....	....
1963◆	Toronto	10	0	1	1	0	....	....	....
1964◆	Toronto	9	1	1	2	4	....	....	....
Playoff Totals		**62**	**8**	**10**	**18**	**30**	....	....	....

HARRIS, Duke *No playoffs* Right wing

HARRIS, Henry *No playoffs* Right wing

HARRIS, Hugh Center

Season	Club	GP	G	A	Pts	PIM	PP	SH	GW
1973	Buffalo	3	0	0	0	0	0	0	0
Playoff Totals		**3**	**0**	**0**	**0**	**0**	**0**	**0**	**0**

HARRIS, Ron Defense

Season	Club	GP	G	A	Pts	PIM	PP	SH	GW
1970	Detroit	4	0	0	0	8	0	0	0
1973	NY Rangers	10	0	3	3	2	0	0	0
1974	NY Rangers	11	3	0	3	14	0	0	2
1975	NY Rangers	3	1	0	1	9	0	0	1
Playoff Totals		**28**	**4**	**3**	**7**	**33**	**0**	**0**	**3**

HARRIS, Smokey *No playoffs* Left wing

HARRIS, Ted Defense

Season	Club	GP	G	A	Pts	PIM	PP	SH	GW
1965◆	Montreal	13	0	5	5	45	0	0	0
1966◆	Montreal	10	0	0	0	38	0	0	0
1967	Montreal	10	0	1	1	19	0	0	0
1968◆	Montreal	13	0	4	4	22	0	0	0
1969◆	Montreal	14	1	2	3	34	0	0	0
1971	Minnesota	12	0	4	4	36	0	0	0
1972	Minnesota	7	0	1	1	17	0	0	0
1973	Minnesota	5	0	1	1	15	0	0	0
1975◆	Philadelphia	16	0	4	4	4	0	0	0
Playoff Totals		**100**	**1**	**22**	**23**	**230**	**0**	**0**	**0**

HARRISON, Ed Center/left wing

Season	Club	GP	G	A	Pts	PIM	PP	SH	GW
1948	Boston	5	1	0	1	2	....	....	....
1949	Boston	4	0	0	0	0	....	....	....
Playoff Totals		**9**	**1**	**0**	**1**	**2**	....	....	....

HARRISON, Jim Center

Season	Club	GP	G	A	Pts	PIM	PP	SH	GW
1971	Toronto	6	0	1	1	33	0	0	0
1972	Toronto	5	1	0	1	10	0	0	1
1977	Chicago	2	0	0	0	0	0	0	0
Playoff Totals		**13**	**1**	**1**	**2**	**43**	**0**	**0**	**1**

HART, Gerry Defense

Season	Club	GP	G	A	Pts	PIM	PP	SH	GW
1975	NY Islanders	17	2	2	4	42	0	0	1
1976	NY Islanders	13	1	3	4	24	0	0	0
1977	NY Islanders	12	0	2	2	23	0	0	0
1978	NY Islanders	7	0	0	0	16	0	0	0
1979	NY Islanders	9	0	2	2	10	0	0	0
1981	St. Louis	10	0	0	0	27	0	0	0
1982	St. Louis	10	0	3	3	33	0	0	0
Playoff Totals		**78**	**3**	**12**	**15**	**175**	**0**	**0**	**1**

HART, Gizzy Left wing

Season	Club	GP	G	A	Pts	PIM	PP	SH	GW
1927	Mtl. Canadiens	4	0	0	0	0	0	0	0
1928	Mtl. Canadiens	2	0	0	0	0	0	0	0
1933	Mtl. Canadiens	2	0	1	1	0	0	0	0
Playoff Totals		**8**	**0**	**1**	**1**	**0**	**0**	**0**	**0**

HARTMAN, Mike Left wing

Season	Club	GP	G	A	Pts	PIM	PP	SH	GW
1988	Buffalo	6	0	0	0	35	0	0	0
1989	Buffalo	5	0	0	0	34	0	0	0
1990	Buffalo	6	0	0	0	18	0	0	0
1991	Buffalo	2	0	0	0	17	0	0	0
1992	Winnipeg	2	0	0	0	2	0	0	0
Playoff Totals		**21**	**0**	**0**	**0**	**106**	**0**	**0**	**0**

HARTSBURG, Craig Defense

Season	Club	GP	G	A	Pts	PIM	PP	SH	GW
1980	Minnesota	15	3	1	4	17	2	0	0
1981	Minnesota	19	3	12	15	16	3	0	0
1982	Minnesota	4	1	2	3	14	0	0	0
1983	Minnesota	9	3	8	11	7	2	0	0
1985	Minnesota	9	5	3	8	14	3	0	0
1986	Minnesota	5	0	1	1	2	0	0	0
Playoff Totals		**61**	**15**	**27**	**42**	**70**	**10**	**0**	**0**

HARVEY, Buster Right wing

Season	Club	GP	G	A	Pts	PIM	PP	SH	GW
1971	Minnesota	7	0	0	0	4	0	0	0
1972	Minnesota	1	0	0	0	0	0	0	0
1973	Minnesota	6	0	2	2	4	0	0	0
Playoff Totals		**14**	**0**	**2**	**2**	**8**	**0**	**0**	**0**

HARVEY, Doug Defense

Season	Club	GP	G	A	Pts	PIM	PP	SH	GW
1949	Montreal	7	0	1	1	10	....	....	....
1950	Montreal	5	0	2	2	10	....	....	....
1951	Montreal	11	0	5	5	12	....	....	....
1952	Montreal	11	0	3	3	8	....	....	....
1953◆	Montreal	12	0	5	5	8	....	....	....
1954	Montreal	10	0	2	2	12	....	....	....
1955	Montreal	12	0	8	8	6	....	....	....
1956◆	Montreal	10	2	5	7	10	....	....	....
1957◆	Montreal	10	0	7	7	10	....	....	....
1958◆	Montreal	10	2	9	11	16	....	....	....
1959◆	Montreal	11	1	11	12	22	....	....	....
1960◆	Montreal	8	3	0	3	6	....	....	....
1961	Montreal	6	0	1	1	8	....	....	....
1962	NY Rangers	6	0	1	1	2	....	....	....
1968	St. Louis	8	0	4	4	12	....	....	....
Playoff Totals		**137**	**8**	**64**	**72**	**152**	....	....	....

HARVEY, Hugh *No playoffs* Center/left wing

HARVEY, Todd Center

Season	Club	GP	G	A	Pts	PIM	PP	SH	GW
1995	Dallas	5	0	0	0	8	0	0	0
1997	Dallas	7	0	1	1	10	0	0	0
Playoff Totals		**12**	**0**	**1**	**1**	**18**	**0**	**0**	**0**

HASSARD, Bob *No playoffs* Center

HATCHER, Derian Defense

Season	Club	GP	G	A	Pts	PIM	PP	SH	GW
1992	Minnesota	5	0	2	2	8	0	0	0
1994	Dallas	9	0	2	2	14	0	0	0
1997	Dallas	7	0	2	2	20	0	0	0
1998	Dallas	17	3	3	6	39	2	0	0
1999◆	Dallas	18	1	6	7	24	0	0	0
Playoff Totals		**56**	**4**	**15**	**19**	**105**	**2**	**0**	**0**

HATCHER, Kevin Defense

Season	Club	GP	G	A	Pts	PIM	PP	SH	GW
1985	Washington	1	0	0	0	0	0	0	0
1986	Washington	9	1	1	2	19	0	0	0
1987	Washington	7	1	0	1	20	0	0	0
1988	Washington	14	5	7	12	55	1	0	1
1989	Washington	6	1	4	5	20	1	0	0
1990	Washington	11	0	8	8	32	0	0	0
1991	Washington	11	3	3	6	8	2	0	0
1992	Washington	7	2	4	6	19	0	1	0
1993	Washington	6	0	1	1	14	0	0	0
1994	Washington	11	3	4	7	37	0	1	0
1995	Dallas	5	2	1	3	2	1	0	1
1997	Pittsburgh	5	1	1	2	4	1	0	0
1998	Pittsburgh	6	1	0	1	12	1	0	0
1999	Pittsburgh	13	2	3	5	4	1	0	0
Playoff Totals		**112**	**22**	**37**	**59**	**246**	**8**	**2**	**2**

HATOUM, Ed *No playoffs* Right wing

HAUER, Brett *No playoffs* Defense

HAVELID, Niclas *No playoffs* Defense

HAWERCHUK, Dale Center

Season	Club	GP	G	A	Pts	PIM	PP	SH	GW
1982	Winnipeg	4	1	7	8	5	0	0	0
1983	Winnipeg	3	1	4	5	8	1	0	0
1984	Winnipeg	3	1	1	2	0	1	0	0
1985	Winnipeg	3	2	1	3	4	1	0	0
1986	Winnipeg	3	0	3	3	0	0	0	0
1987	Winnipeg	10	5	8	13	4	3	0	0
1988	Winnipeg	5	3	4	7	16	2	0	0
1990	Winnipeg	7	3	5	8	2	0	0	1
1991	Buffalo	6	2	4	6	10	1	0	0
1992	Buffalo	7	2	5	7	0	0	0	0
1993	Buffalo	8	5	9	14	2	3	0	0
1994	Buffalo	7	0	7	7	4	0	0	0
1995	Buffalo	2	0	0	0	0	0	0	0
1996	Philadelphia	12	3	6	9	12	1	0	0
1997	Philadelphia	17	2	5	7	0	1	0	1
Playoff Totals		**97**	**30**	**69**	**99**	**67**	**14**	**0**	**2**

HAWGOOD, Greg Defense

Season	Club	GP	G	A	Pts	PIM	PP	SH	GW
1988	Boston	3	1	0	1	0	0	0	0
1989	Boston	10	0	2	2	2	0	0	0
1990	Boston	15	1	3	4	12	1	0	0
1992	Edmonton	13	0	3	3	23	0	0	0
1994	Pittsburgh	1	0	0	0	0	0	0	0
Playoff Totals		**42**	**2**	**8**	**10**	**37**	**1**	**0**	**0**

HAWKINS, Todd *No playoffs* Left/Right wing

HAWORTH, Alan Center

Season	Club	GP	G	A	Pts	PIM	PP	SH	GW
1981	Buffalo	7	4	4	8	2	3	0	1
1982	Buffalo	3	0	1	1	2	0	0	0
1983	Washington	4	0	0	0	2	0	0	0
1984	Washington	8	3	2	5	4	1	0	0
1985	Washington	5	1	0	1	0	0	0	1
1986	Washington	9	4	6	10	11	1	0	0
1987	Washington	6	0	3	3	7	0	0	0
Playoff Totals		**42**	**12**	**16**	**28**	**28**	**5**	**0**	**2**

HAWORTH, Gord *No playoffs* Center

HAWRYLIW, Neil *No playoffs* Right wing

HAY, Bill Center

Season	Club	GP	G	A	Pts	PIM	PP	SH	GW
1960	Chicago	4	1	2	3	2	....	....	....
1961◆	Chicago	12	2	5	7	20	....	....	....
1962	Chicago	12	3	7	10	18	....	....	....
1963	Chicago	6	3	2	5	6	....	....	....
1964	Chicago	7	3	1	4	4	....	....	....
1965	Chicago	14	3	1	4	4	....	....	....
1966	Chicago	6	0	2	2	4	....	....	....
1967	Chicago	6	0	1	1	4	....	....	....
Playoff Totals		**67**	**15**	**21**	**36**	**62**	....	....	....

HAY, Dwayne *No playoffs* Left wing

HAY, George Left wing

Season	Club	GP	G	A	Pts	PIM	PP	SH	GW
1927	Chicago	2	1	2	3	2	....	....	....
1929	Detroit	2	1	0	1	0	....	....	....
1933	Detroit	4	0	1	1	0	....	....	....
Playoff Totals		**8**	**2**	**3**	**5**	**2**	....	....	....

HAY, Jim Defense

Season	Club	GP	G	A	Pts	PIM	PP	SH	GW
1953	Detroit	4	0	0	0	2	0	0	0
1955◆	Detroit	5	1	0	1	0	0	0	0
Playoff Totals		**9**	**1**	**0**	**1**	**2**	**0**	**0**	**0**

HAYEK, Peter *No playoffs* Defense

HAYES, Chris Left wing

Season	Club	GP	G	A	Pts	PIM	PP	SH	GW
1972◆	Boston	1	0	0	0	0	0	0	0
Playoff Totals		**1**	**0**	**0**	**0**	**0**	**0**	**0**	**0**

HAYNES, Paul Center

Season	Club	GP	G	A	Pts	PIM	PP	SH	GW
1932	Mtl. Maroons	4	0	0	0	0	....	....	....
1933	Mtl. Maroons	2	0	0	0	2	....	....	....
1934	Mtl. Maroons	4	0	1	1	2	....	....	....
1935	Boston	3	0	0	0	0	....	....	....
1937	Mtl. Canadiens	5	2	3	5	0	....	....	....
1938	Mtl. Canadiens	3	0	4	4	5	....	....	....
1939	Mtl. Canadiens	3	0	0	0	4	....	....	....
Playoff Totals		**24**	**2**	**8**	**10**	**13**	....	....	....

HAYWARD, Rick *No playoffs* Defense

HAZLETT, Steve *No playoffs* Left wing

HEAD, Galen *No playoffs* Right wing

HEADLEY, Fern Defense

Season	Club	GP	G	A	Pts	PIM	PP	SH	GW
1925	Mtl. Canadiens	5	0	0	0	0	0	0	0
Playoff Totals		**5**	**0**	**0**	**0**	**0**	**0**	**0**	**0**

HEALEY, Dick *No playoffs* Defense

HEALEY, Paul *No playoffs* Right wing

HEAPHY, Shawn *No playoffs* Center

HEASLIP, Mark Right wing

Season	Club	GP	G	A	Pts	PIM	PP	SH	GW
1978	NY Rangers	3	0	0	0	0	0	0	0
1979	Los Angeles	2	0	0	0	2	0	0	0
Playoff Totals		**5**	**0**	**0**	**0**	**2**	**0**	**0**	**0**

HEATH, Randy *No playoffs* Left wing

HEBENTON, Andy Right wing

Season	Club	GP	G	A	Pts	PIM	PP	SH	GW
1956	NY Rangers	5	1	0	1	2	....	....	....
1957	NY Rangers	6	2	0	2	2	....	....	....
1958	NY Rangers	6	2	3	5	4	....	....	....
1962	NY Rangers	6	1	2	3	0	....	....	....
Playoff Totals		**22**	**6**	**5**	**11**	**8**	....	....	....

HECHT, Jochen Center

Season	Club	GP	G	A	Pts	PIM	PP	SH	GW
1999	St. Louis	5	2	0	2	0	0	0	0
Playoff Totals		**5**	**2**	**0**	**2**	**0**	**0**	**0**	**0**

HEDBERG, Anders Right wing

Season	Club	GP	G	A	Pts	PIM	PP	SH	GW
1979	NY Rangers	18	4	5	9	12	0	1	1
1980	NY Rangers	9	3	2	5	7	0	0	1
1981	NY Rangers	14	8	8	16	6	3	0	0
1983	NY Rangers	9	4	8	12	4	1	0	0
1984	NY Rangers	5	1	0	1	0	0	0	0
1985	NY Rangers	3	2	1	3	2	0	0	0
Playoff Totals		**58**	**22**	**24**	**46**	**31**	**4**	**1**	**2**

HEDICAN, Bret Defense

Season	Club	GP	G	A	Pts	PIM	PP	SH	GW
1992	St. Louis	5	0	0	0	0	0	0	0
1993	St. Louis	10	0	0	0	14	0	0	0
1994	Vancouver	24	1	6	7	16	0	0	0
1995	Vancouver	11	0	2	2	6	0	0	0
1996	Vancouver	6	0	1	1	10	0	0	0
Playoff Totals		**56**	**1**	**9**	**10**	**46**	**0**	**0**	**0**

HEFFERNAN, Frank *No playoffs* Defense

HEFFERNAN, Gerry Right wing

Season	Club	GP	G	A	Pts	PIM	PP	SH	GW
1942	Montreal	2	2	1	3	0	....	....	....
1943	Montreal	2	0	0	0	0	....	....	....
1944◆	Montreal	7	1	2	3	8	....	....	....
Playoff Totals		**11**	**3**	**3**	**6**	**8**	....	....	....

HEIDT, Michael *No playoffs* Defense

HEINDL, Bill *No playoffs* Left wing

HEINRICH, Lionel *No playoffs* Left wing

HEINS, Shawn *No playoffs* Defense

Season	Club	GP	G	A	Pts	PIM	PP	SH	GW
HEINZE, Steve									Right wing
1992	Boston	7	0	3	3	17	0	0	0
1993	Boston	4	1	1	2	2	0	0	0
1994	Boston	13	2	3	5	7	0	0	0
1995	Boston	5	0	0	0	0	0	0	0
1996	Boston	5	1	1	2	4	0	1	0
1998	Boston	6	0	0	0	6	0	0	0
1999	Boston	12	4	3	7	0	2	0	0
Playoff Totals		**52**	**8**	**11**	**19**	**36**	**2**	**1**	**0**
HEISKALA, Earl	*No playoffs*								Left wing
HEJDUK, Milan									Right wing
1999	Colorado	16	6	6	12	4	1	0	3
Playoff Totals		**16**	**6**	**6**	**12**	**4**	**1**	**0**	**3**
HELANDER, Peter	*No playoffs*								Defense
HELENIUS, Sami	*No playoffs*								Defense
HELLER, Ott									Defense
1932	NY Rangers	7	3	1	4	8	....	....	....
1933◆	NY Rangers	8	3	0	3	10	....	....	....
1934	NY Rangers	2	0	0	0	0	....	....	....
1935	NY Rangers	4	0	1	1	4	....	....	....
1937	NY Rangers	9	0	0	0	11	....	....	....
1938	NY Rangers	3	0	1	1	2	....	....	....
1939	NY Rangers	7	0	1	1	10	....	....	....
1940◆	NY Rangers	12	0	3	3	12	....	....	....
1941	NY Rangers	3	0	1	1	4	....	....	....
1942	NY Rangers	6	0	0	0	0	....	....	....
Playoff Totals		**61**	**6**	**8**	**14**	**61**	....	....	....
HELMAN, Harry									Right wing
1923◆	Ottawa	4	0	0	0	0	0	0	0
Playoff Totals		**4**	**0**	**0**	**0**	**0**	**0**	**0**	**0**
HELMER, Bryan	*No playoffs*								Defense
HELMINEN, Raimo									Center
1986	NY Rangers	2	0	0	0	0	0	0	0
Playoff Totals		**2**	**0**	**0**	**0**	**0**	**0**	**0**	**0**
HEMMERLING, Tony	*No playoffs*								Left wing
HENDERSON, Archie	*No playoffs*								Right wing
HENDERSON, Jay	*No playoffs*								Left wing
HENDERSON, Matt	*No playoffs*								Right wing
HENDERSON, Murray									Defense
1945	Boston	7	0	1	1	2	....	....	....
1946	Boston	10	1	1	2	4	....	....	....
1947	Boston	4	0	0	0	4	....	....	....
1948	Boston	3	1	0	1	5	....	....	....
1949	Boston	5	0	1	1	2	....	....	....
1951	Boston	5	0	0	0	2	....	....	....
1952	Boston	7	0	0	0	4	....	....	....
Playoff Totals		**41**	**2**	**3**	**5**	**23**	....	....	....
HENDERSON, Paul									Right wing
1964	Detroit	14	2	3	5	6	0	0	0
1965	Detroit	7	0	2	2	0	0	0	0
1966	Detroit	12	3	3	6	10	1	0	2
1969	Toronto	4	0	1	1	0	0	0	0
1971	Toronto	6	5	1	6	4	1	0	2
1972	Toronto	5	1	2	3	6	0	0	0
1974	Toronto	4	0	2	2	2	0	0	0
1980	Atlanta	4	0	0	0	0	0	0	0
Playoff Totals		**56**	**11**	**14**	**25**	**28**	**2**	**0**	**4**
HENDRICKSON, Darby									Center
1994	Toronto	2	0	0	0	0	0	0	0
Playoff Totals		**2**	**0**	**0**	**0**	**0**	**0**	**0**	**0**
HENDRICKSON, John	*No playoffs*								Defense
HENNING, Lorne									Center
1975	NY Islanders	17	0	2	2	0	0	0	0
1976	NY Islanders	13	2	0	2	2	1	1	0
1977	NY Islanders	12	0	1	1	0	0	0	0
1978	NY Islanders	7	0	0	0	4	0	0	0
1979	NY Islanders	10	2	0	2	0	0	1	0
1980◆	NY Islanders	21	3	4	7	2	0	3	1
1981◆	NY Islanders	1	0	0	0	0	0	0	0
Playoff Totals		**81**	**7**	**7**	**14**	**8**	**1**	**5**	**1**
HENRY, Camille									Center
1957	NY Rangers	5	2	3	5	0	1	0	0
1958	NY Rangers	6	1	4	5	5	1	0	0
1962	NY Rangers	5	0	0	0	0	0	0	0
1965	Chicago	14	1	0	1	2	1	0	0
1968	NY Rangers	6	0	0	0	0	0	0	0
1969	St. Louis	11	2	5	7	0	1	0	0
Playoff Totals		**47**	**6**	**12**	**18**	**7**	**4**	**0**	**0**
HENRY, Dale									Left wing
1987	NY Islanders	8	0	0	0	2	0	0	0
1988	NY Islanders	6	1	0	1	17	0	1	0
Playoff Totals		**14**	**1**	**0**	**1**	**19**	**0**	**1**	**0**
HEPPLE, Alan	*No playoffs*								Defense
HERBERS, Ian	*No playoffs*								Defense
HERBERTS, Jimmy									Center/right wing
1927	Boston	8	3	0	3	8	....	....	....
1929	Detroit	1	0	0	0	2	....	....	....
Playoff Totals		**9**	**3**	**0**	**3**	**10**	....	....	....
HERCHENRATTER, Art	*No playoffs*								Left wing
HERGERTS, Fred	*No playoffs*								Center
HERGESHEIMER, Philip									Right wing
1940	Chicago	1	0	0	0	0	0	0	0
1941	Chicago	5	0	0	0	2	0	0	0
Playoff Totals		**6**	**0**	**0**	**0**	**2**	**0**	**0**	**0**
HERGESHEIMER, Wally									Right wing
1956	NY Rangers	5	1	0	1	0	0	0	0
Playoff Totals		**5**	**1**	**0**	**1**	**0**	**0**	**0**	**0**
HERON, Red									Center
1939	Toronto	2	0	0	0	4	....	....	....
1940	Toronto	9	2	0	2	2	....	....	....
1941	Toronto	7	0	2	2	0	....	....	....
1942	Montreal	3	0	0	0	0	....	....	....
Playoff Totals		**21**	**2**	**2**	**4**	**6**	....	....	....
HEROUX, Yves	*No playoffs*								Right wing
HERPERGER, Chris	*No playoffs*								Left wing
HERR, Matt	*No playoffs*								Center
HERTER, Jason	*No playoffs*								Defense
HERVEY, Matt									Defense
1992	Boston	5	0	0	0	6	0	0	0
Playoff Totals		**5**	**0**	**0**	**0**	**6**	**0**	**0**	**0**
HESS, Bob									Defense
1975	St. Louis	1	0	0	0	2	0	0	0
1976	St. Louis	1	0	1	1	0	0	0	0
1977	St. Louis	1	0	0	0	0	0	0	0
1981	Buffalo	1	1	0	1	0	0	0	0
Playoff Totals		**4**	**1**	**1**	**2**	**2**	**0**	**0**	**0**
HEWARD, Jamie	*No playoffs*								Defense
HEXIMER, Orville									Left wing/center
1933	Boston	5	0	0	0	2	0	0	0
Playoff Totals		**5**	**0**	**0**	**0**	**2**	**0**	**0**	**0**
HEXTALL, Bryan Jr.									Center
1970	Pittsburgh	10	0	1	1	34	0	0	0
1972	Pittsburgh	4	0	2	2	9	0	0	0
1974	Atlanta	4	0	1	1	16	0	0	0
Playoff Totals		**18**	**0**	**4**	**4**	**59**	**0**	**0**	**0**
HEXTALL, Bryan Sr.									Right wing
1938	NY Rangers	3	2	0	2	0	....	....	....
1939	NY Rangers	7	0	1	1	4	....	....	....
1940◆	NY Rangers	12	4	3	7	11	....	....	....
1941	NY Rangers	3	0	1	1	0	....	....	....
1942	NY Rangers	6	1	1	2	4	....	....	....
1948	NY Rangers	6	1	3	4	0	....	....	....
Playoff Totals		**37**	**8**	**9**	**17**	**19**	....	....	....
HEXTALL, Dennis									Left wing
1968	NY Rangers	2	0	0	0	0	0	0	0
1972	Minnesota	7	0	2	2	19	0	0	0
1973	Minnesota	6	2	0	2	16	0	0	2
1978	Detroit	7	1	1	2	10	0	1	1
Playoff Totals		**22**	**3**	**3**	**6**	**45**	**0**	**1**	**3**
HEYLIGER, Vic	*No playoffs*								Center
HICKE, Bill									Right wing
1959◆	Montreal	1	0	0	0	0	0	0	0
1960◆	Montreal	7	1	2	3	0	0	0	1
1961	Montreal	5	2	0	2	19	0	0	1
1962	Montreal	6	0	2	2	14	0	0	0
1963	Montreal	5	0	0	0	0	0	0	0
1964	Montreal	7	0	2	2	2	0	0	0
1969	Oakland	7	0	3	3	4	0	0	0
1970	Oakland	4	0	1	1	2	0	0	0
Playoff Totals		**42**	**3**	**10**	**13**	**41**	**0**	**0**	**2**
HICKE, Ernie									Left wing
1977	Minnesota	2	1	0	1	0	0	0	0
Playoff Totals		**2**	**1**	**0**	**1**	**0**	**0**	**0**	**0**
HICKEY, Greg	*No playoffs*								Left wing
HICKEY, Pat									Left wing
1978	NY Rangers	3	2	0	2	0	1	0	0
1979	NY Rangers	18	1	7	8	6	0	0	0
1980	Toronto	3	0	0	0	2	0	0	0
1981	Toronto	2	0	0	0	0	0	0	0
1982	Quebec	15	1	3	4	21	1	0	0
1984	St. Louis	11	1	1	2	6	0	1	0
1985	St. Louis	3	0	0	0	2	0	0	0
Playoff Totals		**55**	**5**	**11**	**16**	**37**	**2**	**1**	**0**
HICKS, Alex									Left wing
1997	Pittsburgh	5	0	1	1	2	0	0	0
1998	Pittsburgh	6	0	0	0	2	0	0	0
Playoff Totals		**11**	**0**	**1**	**1**	**4**	**0**	**0**	**0**
HICKS, Doug									Defense
1977	Minnesota	2	0	0	0	7	0	0	0
1978	Chicago	4	1	0	1	2	1	0	0
1980	Edmonton	3	0	0	0	2	0	0	0
1981	Edmonton	9	1	1	2	4	0	0	0
Playoff Totals		**18**	**2**	**1**	**3**	**15**	**1**	**0**	**0**
HICKS, Glenn	*No playoffs*								Left wing
HICKS, Harold	*No playoffs*								Defense
HICKS, Wayne									Right wing
1960	Chicago	1	0	1	1	0	0	0	0
1961◆	Chicago	1	0	0	0	2	0	0	0
Playoff Totals		**2**	**0**	**1**	**1**	**2**	**0**	**0**	**0**
HIDI, Andre									Left wing
1984	Washington	2	0	0	0	0	0	0	0
Playoff Totals		**2**	**0**	**0**	**0**	**0**	**0**	**0**	**0**
HIEMER, Uli	*No playoffs*								Defense
HIGGINS, Matt	*No playoffs*								Center
HIGGINS, Paul									Right wing
1983	Toronto	1	0	0	0	0	0	0	0
Playoff Totals		**1**	**0**	**0**	**0**	**0**	**0**	**0**	**0**
HIGGINS, Tim									Right wing
1979	Chicago	4	0	0	0	0	0	0	0
1980	Chicago	7	0	3	3	10	0	0	0
1981	Chicago	3	0	0	0	0	0	0	0
1982	Chicago	12	3	1	4	15	0	0	0
1983	Chicago	13	1	3	4	10	0	0	0
1987	Detroit	12	0	1	1	16	0	0	0
1988	Detroit	13	1	0	1	26	0	0	1
1989	Detroit	1	0	0	0	0	0	0	0
Playoff Totals		**65**	**5**	**8**	**13**	**77**	**0**	**0**	**1**
HILDEBRAND, Ike	*No playoffs*								Right wing
HILL, Al									Center
1979	Philadelphia	7	1	0	1	2	0	0	0
1980	Philadelphia	19	3	5	8	19	1	0	0
1981	Philadelphia	12	2	4	6	18	0	0	1
1982	Philadelphia	3	0	0	0	0	0	0	0
1987	Philadelphia	9	2	1	3	0	0	0	0
1988	Philadelphia	1	0	1	1	4	0	0	0
Playoff Totals		**51**	**8**	**11**	**19**	**43**	**1**	**0**	**1**
HILL, Brian	*No playoffs*								Right wing
HILL, Mel									Right wing
1938	Boston	1	0	0	0	0	....	....	....
1939◆	Boston	12	6	3	9	12	....	....	....
1940	Boston	3	0	0	0	0	....	....	....
1941◆	Boston	8	1	1	2	0	....	....	....
1943	Toronto	6	3	0	3	0	....	....	....
1945◆	Toronto	13	2	3	5	6	....	....	....
Playoff Totals		**43**	**12**	**7**	**19**	**18**	....	....	....
HILL, Sean									Defense
1991	Montreal	1	0	0	0	0	0	0	0
1992	Montreal	4	1	0	1	2	0	0	0
1993◆	Montreal	3	0	0	0	4	0	0	0
Playoff Totals		**8**	**1**	**0**	**1**	**6**	**0**	**0**	**0**
HILLER, Dutch									Left wing
1938	NY Rangers	1	0	0	0	0	....	....	....
1939	NY Rangers	7	1	0	1	9	....	....	....
1940◆	NY Rangers	12	2	4	6	2	....	....	....
1941	NY Rangers	3	0	0	0	0	....	....	....
1942	Boston	5	0	1	1	0	....	....	....
1943	Montreal	5	1	0	1	4	....	....	....
1945	Montreal	6	1	1	2	4	....	....	....
1946◆	Montreal	9	4	2	6	2	....	....	....
Playoff Totals		**48**	**9**	**8**	**17**	**21**	....	....	....
HILLER, Jim									Right wing
1993	Detroit	2	0	0	0	4	0	0	0
Playoff Totals		**2**	**0**	**0**	**0**	**4**	**0**	**0**	**0**
HILLIER, Randy									Defense
1982	Boston	8	0	1	1	16	0	0	0
1983	Boston	3	0	0	0	4	0	0	0
1989	Pittsburgh	9	0	1	1	49	0	0	0
1991◆	Pittsburgh	8	0	0	0	24	0	0	0
Playoff Totals		**28**	**0**	**2**	**2**	**93**	**0**	**0**	**0**
HILLMAN, Floyd	*No playoffs*								Defense
HILLMAN, Larry									Defense
1955◆	Detroit	3	0	0	0	0	0	0	0
1956	Detroit	10	0	1	1	6	0	0	0
1958	Boston	11	0	2	2	6	0	0	0
1959	Boston	7	0	1	1	0	0	0	0
1961	Toronto	5	0	0	0	0	0	0	0
1964◆	Toronto	11	0	0	0	2	0	0	0
1966	Toronto	4	1	1	2	6	0	0	0
1967◆	Toronto	12	1	2	3	0	0	0	0
1969◆	Montreal	1	0	0	0	0	0	0	0
1971	Philadelphia	4	0	2	2	2	0	0	0
1973	Buffalo	6	0	0	0	8	0	0	0
Playoff Totals		**74**	**2**	**9**	**11**	**30**	**0**	**0**	**0**
HILLMAN, Wayne									Defense
1961◆	Chicago	1	0	0	0	0	0	0	0
1963	Chicago	6	0	2	2	2	0	0	0
1964	Chicago	7	0	1	1	15	0	0	0
1967	NY Rangers	4	0	0	0	2	0	0	0
1968	NY Rangers	2	0	0	0	0	0	0	0
1973	Philadelphia	8	0	0	0	0	0	0	0
Playoff Totals		**28**	**0**	**3**	**3**	**19**	**0**	**0**	**0**
HILWORTH, John	*No playoffs*								Defense

Season	Club	GP	G	A	Pts	PIM	PP	SH	GW
HIMES, Normie	Center								
1929	NY Americans	2	0	0	0	0	0	0	0
Playoff Totals		**2**	**0**	**0**	**0**	**0**	**0**	**0**	**0**
HINDMARCH, Dave	Right wing								
1981	Calgary	6	0	0	0	2	0	0	0
1983	Calgary	4	0	0	0	4	0	0	0
Playoff Totals		**10**	**0**	**0**	**0**	**6**	**0**	**0**	**0**
HINOTE, Dan *No playoffs*	Right wing								
HINSE, Andre *No playoffs*	Left wing								
HINTON, Dan *No playoffs*	Left wing								
HIRSCH, Tom	Defense								
1984	Minnesota	12	0	0	0	6	0	0	0
Playoff Totals		**12**	**0**	**0**	**0**	**6**	**0**	**0**	**0**
HIRSCHFELD, Bert	Left wing								
1950	Montreal	5	1	0	1	0	....	....	....
Playoff Totals		**5**	**1**	**0**	**1**	**0**	....	....	....
HISLOP, Jamie	Right wing								
1981	Calgary	16	3	0	3	5	1	0	1
1982	Calgary	3	0	0	0	0	0	0	0
1983	Calgary	9	0	2	2	6	0	0	0
Playoff Totals		**28**	**3**	**2**	**5**	**11**	**1**	**0**	**1**
HITCHMAN, Lionel	Defense								
1923♦	Ottawa	7	1	0	1	4	....	....	....
1924	Ottawa	2	0	0	0	4	....	....	....
1927	Boston	8	1	0	1	31	....	....	....
1928	Boston	2	0	0	0	2	....	....	....
1929♦	Boston	5	0	1	1	22	....	....	....
1930	Boston	6	1	0	1	14	....	....	....
1931	Boston	5	0	0	0	0	....	....	....
1933	Boston	5	1	0	1	0	....	....	....
Playoff Totals		**40**	**4**	**1**	**5**	**77**	....	....	....
HLAVAC, Jan *No playoffs*	Left wing								
HLINKA, Ivan	Center								
1982	Vancouver	12	2	6	8	4	2	0	0
1983	Vancouver	4	1	4	5	4	0	0	0
Playoff Totals		**16**	**3**	**10**	**13**	**8**	**2**	**0**	**0**
HLUSHKO, Todd	Center								
1995	Calgary	1	0	0	0	2	0	0	0
1999	Pittsburgh	2	0	0	0	0	0	0	0
Playoff Totals		**3**	**0**	**0**	**0**	**2**	**0**	**0**	**0**
HOCKING, Justin *No playoffs*	Defense								
HODGE, Ken	Right wing								
1966	Chicago	5	0	0	0	8	0	0	0
1967	Chicago	6	0	0	0	4	0	0	0
1968	Boston	4	3	0	3	2	0	0	0
1969	Boston	10	5	7	12	4	2	0	0
1970♦	Boston	14	3	10	13	7	0	1	0
1971	Boston	7	2	5	7	6	0	0	0
1972♦	Boston	15	9	8	17	*62	2	1	3
1973	Boston	5	1	0	1	7	1	0	0
1974	Boston	16	6	10	16	16	1	0	1
1975	Boston	3	1	1	2	0	1	0	0
1976	Boston	12	4	6	10	4	4	0	1
Playoff Totals		**97**	**34**	**47**	**81**	**120**	**11**	**2**	**5**
HODGE, Ken	Center/Right wing								
1991	Boston	15	4	6	10	6	1	0	1
Playoff Totals		**15**	**4**	**6**	**10**	**6**	**1**	**0**	**1**
HODGSON, Dan *No playoffs*	Center								
HODGSON, Rick	Defense								
1980	Hartford	1	0	0	0	0	0	0	0
Playoff Totals		**1**	**0**	**0**	**0**	**0**	**0**	**0**	**0**
HODGSON, Ted *No playoffs*	Right wing								
HOEKSTRA, Cecil *No playoffs*	Center								
HOEKSTRA, Ed	Center								
1968	Philadelphia	7	0	1	1	0	0	0	0
Playoff Totals		**7**	**0**	**1**	**1**	**0**	**0**	**0**	**0**
HOENE, Phil *No playoffs*	Left wing								
HOFFINGER, Val *No playoffs*	Defense								
HOFFMAN, Mike *No playoffs*	Left wing								
HOFFMEYER, Bob	Defense								
1982	Philadelphia	2	0	1	1	25	0	0	0
1983	Philadelphia	1	0	0	0	0	0	0	0
Playoff Totals		**3**	**0**	**1**	**1**	**25**	**0**	**0**	**0**
HOFFORD, Jim *No playoffs*	Defense								
HOGABOAM, Bill	Center								
1977	Minnesota	2	0	0	0	0	0	0	0
Playoff Totals		**2**	**0**	**0**	**0**	**0**	**0**	**0**	**0**
HOGANSON, Dale	Defense								
1981	Quebec	5	0	3	3	10	0	0	0
1982	Quebec	6	0	0	0	2	0	0	0
Playoff Totals		**11**	**0**	**3**	**3**	**12**	**0**	**0**	**0**
HOGLUND, Jonas	Right wing								
1998	Montreal	10	2	0	2	0	0	0	0
Playoff Totals		**10**	**2**	**0**	**2**	**0**	**0**	**0**	**0**
HOGUE, Benoit	Center								
1989	Buffalo	5	0	0	0	17	0	0	0
1990	Buffalo	3	0	0	0	10	0	0	0
1991	Buffalo	5	3	1	4	10	0	0	0
1993	NY Islanders	18	6	6	12	31	0	0	0
1994	NY Islanders	4	0	1	1	4	0	0	0
1995	Toronto	7	0	0	0	6	0	0	0
1997	Dallas	7	2	2	4	6	1	0	0
1998	Dallas	17	4	2	6	16	1	0	2
1999♦	Dallas	14	0	2	2	16	0	0	0
Playoff Totals		**80**	**15**	**14**	**29**	**116**	**2**	**0**	**2**
HOLAN, Milos *No playoffs*	Defense								
HOLBROOK, Terry	Right wing								
1973	Minnesota	6	0	0	0	0	0	0	0
Playoff Totals		**6**	**0**	**0**	**0**	**0**	**0**	**0**	**0**
HOLDEN, Josh *No playoffs*	Center								
HOLIK, Bobby	Left wing								
1991	Hartford	6	0	0	0	7	0	0	0
1992	Hartford	7	0	1	1	6	0	0	0
1993	New Jersey	5	1	1	2	6	0	0	0
1994	New Jersey	20	0	3	3	6	0	0	0
1995♦	New Jersey	20	4	4	8	22	2	0	1
1997	New Jersey	10	2	3	5	4	1	0	0
1998	New Jersey	5	0	0	0	8	0	0	0
1999	New Jersey	7	0	7	7	6	0	0	0
Playoff Totals		**80**	**7**	**19**	**26**	**65**	**3**	**0**	**1**
HOLLAND, Jason *No playoffs*	Defense								
HOLLAND, Jerry *No playoffs*	Left wing								
HOLLETT, Flash	Defense								
1935	Toronto	7	0	0	0	6	....	....	....
1937	Boston	3	0	0	0	2	....	....	....
1938	Boston	3	0	1	1	0	....	....	....
1939♦	Boston	12	1	3	4	2	....	....	....
1940	Boston	5	1	2	3	2	....	....	....
1941♦	Boston	11	3	4	7	8	....	....	....
1942	Boston	5	0	1	1	2	....	....	....
1943	Boston	9	0	9	9	4	....	....	....
1944	Detroit	5	0	0	0	6	....	....	....
1945	Detroit	14	3	4	7	6	....	....	....
1946	Detroit	5	0	2	2	0	....	....	....
Playoff Totals		**79**	**8**	**26**	**34**	**38**	....	....	....
HOLLINGER, Terry *No playoffs*	Defense								
HOLLINGWORTH, Gord	Defense								
1956	Detroit	3	0	0	0	2	0	0	0
Playoff Totals		**3**	**0**	**0**	**0**	**2**	**0**	**0**	**0**
HOLLOWAY, Bruce *No playoffs*	Defense								
HOLMES, Bill *No playoffs*	Center								
HOLMES, Chuck *No playoffs*	Right wing								
HOLMES, Lou	Center/left wing								
1932	Chicago	2	0	0	0	2	0	0	0
Playoff Totals		**2**	**0**	**0**	**0**	**2**	**0**	**0**	**0**
HOLMES, Warren *No playoffs*	Center								
HOLMGREN, Paul	Right wing								
1977	Philadelphia	10	1	1	2	25	0	0	0
1978	Philadelphia	12	1	4	5	26	0	0	0
1979	Philadelphia	8	1	5	6	22	0	0	0
1980	Philadelphia	18	10	10	20	47	3	0	1
1981	Philadelphia	12	5	9	14	49	2	0	1
1982	Philadelphia	4	1	2	3	6	0	0	0
1983	Philadelphia	3	0	0	0	6	0	0	0
1984	Minnesota	12	0	1	1	6	0	0	0
1985	Minnesota	3	0	0	0	8	0	0	0
Playoff Totals		**82**	**19**	**32**	**51**	**195**	**5**	**0**	**2**
HOLMSTROM, Tomas	Left wing								
1997♦	Detroit	1	0	0	0	0	0	0	0
1998♦	Detroit	22	7	12	19	16	2	0	0
1999	Detroit	10	4	3	7	4	2	0	1
Playoff Totals		**33**	**11**	**15**	**26**	**20**	**4**	**0**	**1**
HOLOTA, John *No playoffs*	Center								
HOLST, Greg *No playoffs*	Center								
HOLT, Gary *No playoffs*	Left wing								
HOLT, Randy	Defense								
1977	Chicago	2	0	0	0	7	0	0	0
1979	Los Angeles	2	0	0	0	4	0	0	0
1981	Calgary	13	2	2	4	52	0	0	1
1983	Washington	4	0	1	1	20	0	0	0
Playoff Totals		**21**	**2**	**3**	**5**	**83**	**0**	**0**	**1**
HOLWAY, Albert	Defense								
1925	Toronto	2	0	0	0	0	0	0	0
1926♦	Mtl. Maroons	6	0	0	0	2	0	0	0
Playoff Totals		**8**	**0**	**0**	**0**	**2**	**0**	**0**	**0**
HOLZINGER, Brian	Center								
1995	Buffalo	4	2	1	3	2	1	0	0
1997	Buffalo	12	2	5	7	8	0	0	0
1998	Buffalo	15	4	7	11	18	1	1	0
1999	Buffalo	21	3	5	8	33	1	0	0
Playoff Totals		**52**	**11**	**18**	**29**	**61**	**3**	**1**	**0**
HOMENUKE, Ron *No playoffs*	Right wing								
HOOVER, Ron	Center								
1991	Boston	8	0	0	0	18	0	0	0
Playoff Totals		**8**	**0**	**0**	**0**	**18**	**0**	**0**	**0**
HOPKINS, Dean	Right wing								
1980	Los Angeles	4	0	1	1	5	0	0	0
1981	Los Angeles	4	1	0	1	9	0	0	1
1982	Los Angeles	10	0	4	4	15	0	0	0
Playoff Totals		**18**	**1**	**5**	**6**	**29**	**0**	**0**	**1**
HOPKINS, Larry	Left wing								
1982	Winnipeg	4	0	0	0	2	0	0	0
1983	Winnipeg	2	0	0	0	0	0	0	0
Playoff Totals		**6**	**0**	**0**	**0**	**2**	**0**	**0**	**0**
HORACEK, Tony	Left wing								
1992	Chicago	2	1	0	1	2	0	0	0
Playoff Totals		**2**	**1**	**0**	**1**	**2**	**0**	**0**	**0**
HORAVA, Miloslav	Defense								
1990	NY Rangers	2	0	1	1	0	0	0	0
Playoff Totals		**2**	**0**	**1**	**1**	**0**	**0**	**0**	**0**
HORBUL, Doug *No playoffs*	Left wing								
HORDY, Mike *No playoffs*	Defense								
HORECK, Pete	Left wing								
1946	Chicago	4	0	0	0	2	....	....	....
1947	Detroit	5	2	0	2	6	....	....	....
1948	Detroit	10	3	*7	10	12	....	....	....
1949	Detroit	11	1	1	2	10	....	....	....
1951	Boston	4	0	0	0	13	....	....	....
Playoff Totals		**34**	**6**	**8**	**14**	**43**	....	....	....
HORNE, George	Right wing								
1929	Toronto	4	0	0	0	4	0	0	0
Playoff Totals		**4**	**0**	**0**	**0**	**4**	**0**	**0**	**0**
HORNER, Red	Defense								
1929	Toronto	4	1	0	1	2	....	....	....
1931	Toronto	2	0	0	0	4	....	....	....
1932♦	Toronto	7	2	2	4	20	....	....	....
1933	Toronto	9	1	0	1	10	....	....	....
1934	Toronto	5	1	0	1	6	....	....	....
1935	Toronto	7	0	1	1	4	....	....	....
1936	Toronto	9	1	2	3	*22	....	....	....
1937	Toronto	2	0	0	0	7	....	....	....
1938	Toronto	7	0	1	1	14	....	....	....
1939	Toronto	10	1	2	3	*26	....	....	....
1940	Toronto	9	0	2	2	55	....	....	....
Playoff Totals		**71**	**7**	**10**	**17**	**170**	....	....	....
HORNUNG, Larry	Defense								
1972	St. Louis	11	0	2	2	2	0	0	0
Playoff Totals		**11**	**0**	**2**	**2**	**2**	**0**	**0**	**0**
HORTON, Tim	Defense								
1950	Toronto	1	0	0	0	2	....	....	....
1954	Toronto	5	1	1	2	4	....	....	....
1956	Toronto	2	0	0	0	4	....	....	....
1959	Toronto	12	0	3	3	16	....	....	....
1960	Toronto	10	0	1	1	6	....	....	....
1961	Toronto	5	0	0	0	0	....	....	....
1962♦	Toronto	12	3	13	16	16	....	....	....
1963♦	Toronto	10	1	3	4	10	....	....	....
1964♦	Toronto	14	0	4	4	20	....	....	....
1965	Toronto	6	0	2	2	13	....	....	....
1966	Toronto	4	1	0	1	12	....	....	....
1967♦	Toronto	12	3	5	8	25	....	....	....
1969	Toronto	4	0	0	0	7	0	0	0
1970	NY Rangers	6	1	1	2	28	0	0	0
1971	NY Rangers	13	1	4	5	14	0	0	0
1972	Pittsburgh	4	0	1	1	2	0	0	0
1973	Buffalo	6	0	1	1	4	0	0	0
Playoff Totals		**126**	**11**	**39**	**50**	**183**	....	....	....
HORVATH, Bronco	Center								
1956	NY Rangers	5	1	2	3	4	....	....	....
1958	Boston	12	5	3	8	8	....	....	....
1959	Boston	7	2	3	5	0	....	....	....
1962	Chicago	12	4	1	5	6	....	....	....
Playoff Totals		**36**	**12**	**9**	**21**	**18**	....	....	....
HOSPODAR, Ed	Defense								
1980	NY Rangers	7	1	0	1	42	0	0	1
1981	NY Rangers	12	2	0	2	*93	0	0	0
1985	Philadelphia	18	1	1	2	69	0	0	0
1986	Minnesota	2	0	0	0	2	0	0	0
1987	Philadelphia	5	0	0	0	2	0	0	0
Playoff Totals		**44**	**4**	**1**	**5**	**208**	**0**	**0**	**1**
HOSSA, Marian	Left wing								
1999	Ottawa	4	0	2	2	4	0	0	0
Playoff Totals		**4**	**0**	**2**	**2**	**4**	**0**	**0**	**0**
HOSTAK, Martin *No playoffs*	Center								
HOTHAM, Greg	Defense								
1982	Pittsburgh	5	0	3	3	6	0	0	0
Playoff Totals		**5**	**0**	**3**	**3**	**6**	**0**	**0**	**0**
HOUCK, Paul *No playoffs*	Right wing								

Season	Club	GP	G	A	Pts	PIM	PP	SH	GW
HOUDA, Doug	Defense								
1989	Detroit	6	0	1	1	0	0	0	0
1991	Hartford	6	0	0	0	8	0	0	0
1992	Hartford	6	0	2	2	13	0	0	0
Playoff Totals		**18**	**0**	**3**	**3**	**21**	**0**	**0**	**0**
HOUDE, Claude	*No playoffs* Defense								
HOUDE, Eric	*No playoffs* Center								
HOUGH, Mike	Left wing								
1987	Quebec	9	0	3	3	26	0	0	0
1993	Quebec	6	0	1	1	2	0	0	0
1996	Florida	22	4	1	5	8	0	0	2
1997	Florida	5	1	0	1	2	0	0	0
Playoff Totals		**42**	**5**	**5**	**10**	**38**	**0**	**0**	**2**
HOULDER, Bill	Defense								
1993	Buffalo	8	0	2	2	4	0	0	0
1995	St. Louis	4	1	1	2	0	0	0	0
1996	Tampa Bay	6	0	1	1	4	0	0	0
1998	San Jose	6	1	2	3	2	0	0	0
1999	San Jose	6	3	0	3	4	3	0	0
Playoff Totals		**30**	**5**	**6**	**11**	**14**	**3**	**0**	**0**
HOULE, Rejean	Left/right wing								
1971◆	Montreal	20	2	5	7	20	0	0	1
1972	Montreal	6	0	0	0	2	0	0	0
1973◆	Montreal	17	3	6	9	0	0	0	0
1977◆	Montreal	6	0	1	1	4	0	0	0
1978◆	Montreal	15	3	8	11	14	0	0	0
1979◆	Montreal	7	1	5	6	2	0	0	0
1980	Montreal	10	4	5	9	12	1	0	0
1981	Montreal	3	1	0	1	6	0	0	0
1982	Montreal	5	0	4	4	6	0	0	0
1983	Montreal	1	0	0	0	0	0	0	0
Playoff Totals		**90**	**14**	**34**	**48**	**66**	**1**	**0**	**1**
HOUSLEY, Phil	Defense								
1983	Buffalo	10	3	4	7	2	1	0	0
1984	Buffalo	3	0	0	0	6	0	0	0
1985	Buffalo	5	3	2	5	2	0	0	0
1988	Buffalo	6	2	4	6	6	1	0	0
1989	Buffalo	5	1	3	4	2	0	0	0
1990	Buffalo	6	1	4	5	4	1	0	0
1992	Winnipeg	7	1	4	5	0	1	0	1
1993	Winnipeg	6	0	7	7	2	0	0	0
1994	St. Louis	4	2	1	3	4	2	0	0
1995	Calgary	7	0	9	9	0	0	0	0
1998	Washington	18	0	4	4	4	0	0	0
Playoff Totals		**77**	**13**	**42**	**55**	**32**	**6**	**0**	**1**
HOUSTON, Ken	Right wing								
1976	Atlanta	2	0	0	0	0	0	0	0
1977	Atlanta	3	0	0	0	4	0	0	0
1978	Atlanta	2	0	0	0	0	0	0	0
1979	Atlanta	1	0	0	0	16	0	0	0
1980	Atlanta	4	1	1	2	10	0	0	0
1981	Calgary	16	7	8	15	28	5	0	1
1982	Calgary	3	1	0	1	4	0	0	0
1983	Washington	4	1	0	1	4	0	0	0
Playoff Totals		**35**	**10**	**9**	**19**	**66**	**5**	**0**	**1**
HOWARD, Jack	*No playoffs* Defense								
HOWATT, Garry	Left wing								
1975	NY Islanders	17	3	3	6	59	0	0	1
1976	NY Islanders	13	5	5	10	23	0	0	1
1977	NY Islanders	12	1	1	2	28	0	0	0
1978	NY Islanders	7	0	1	1	62	0	0	0
1979	NY Islanders	9	0	1	1	18	0	0	0
1980◆	NY Islanders	21	3	1	4	84	0	0	1
1981◆	NY Islanders	8	0	2	2	15	0	0	0
Playoff Totals		**87**	**12**	**14**	**26**	**289**	**0**	**0**	**3**
HOWE, Gordie	Right wing								
1947	Detroit	5	0	0	0	18	....	....	....
1948	Detroit	10	1	1	2	11	....	....	....
1949	Detroit	11	*8	3	*11	19	....	....	....
1950◆	Detroit	1	0	0	0	7	....	....	....
1951	Detroit	6	4	3	7	4	....	....	....
1952◆	Detroit	8	2	*5	*7	2	....	....	....
1953	Detroit	6	2	5	7	2	....	....	....
1954◆	Detroit	12	4	5	9	*31	....	....	....
1955◆	Detroit	11	*9	*11	20	24	....	....	....
1956	Detroit	10	3	9	12	8	....	....	....
1957	Detroit	5	2	5	7	6	....	....	....
1958	Detroit	4	1	1	2	0	....	....	....
1960	Detroit	6	1	5	6	4	....	....	....
1961	Detroit	11	4	11	*15	10	....	....	....
1963	Detroit	11	7	9	*16	22	....	....	....
1964	Detroit	14	*9	10	*19	16	....	....	....
1965	Detroit	7	4	2	6	20	....	....	....
1966	Detroit	12	4	6	10	12	....	....	....
1970	Detroit	4	2	0	2	2	1	0	0
1980	Hartford	3	1	1	2	2	0	0	0
Playoff Totals		**157**	**68**	**92**	**160**	**220**	....	....	....

Season	Club	GP	G	A	Pts	PIM	PP	SH	GW
HOWE, Mark	Defense								
1980	Hartford	3	1	2	3	2	0	0	0
1983	Philadelphia	3	0	2	2	4	0	0	0
1984	Philadelphia	3	0	0	0	2	0	0	0
1985	Philadelphia	19	3	8	11	6	1	0	1
1986	Philadelphia	5	0	4	4	0	0	0	0
1987	Philadelphia	26	2	10	12	4	0	0	0
1988	Philadelphia	7	3	6	9	4	0	0	0
1989	Philadelphia	19	0	15	15	10	0	0	0
1993	Detroit	7	1	3	4	2	0	0	0
1994	Detroit	6	0	1	1	0	0	0	0
1995	Detroit	3	0	0	0	0	0	0	0
Playoff Totals		**101**	**10**	**51**	**61**	**34**	**1**	**0**	**1**
HOWE, Marty	Defense								
1980	Hartford	3	1	1	2	0	0	0	0
1983	Boston	12	0	1	1	9	0	0	0
Playoff Totals		**15**	**1**	**2**	**3**	**9**	**0**	**0**	**0**
HOWE, Syd	Center/Left wing								
1930	Ottawa	2	0	0	0	0	....	....	....
1936◆	Detroit	7	3	3	6	2	....	....	....
1937◆	Detroit	10	2	5	7	0	....	....	....
1939	Detroit	6	3	1	4	4	....	....	....
1940	Detroit	5	2	2	4	2	....	....	....
1941	Detroit	9	1	*7	8	0	....	....	....
1942	Detroit	12	3	5	8	0	....	....	....
1943◆	Detroit	7	1	2	3	0	....	....	....
1944	Detroit	5	2	2	4	0	....	....	....
1945	Detroit	7	0	0	0	2	....	....	....
Playoff Totals		**70**	**17**	**27**	**44**	**10**	....	....	....
HOWE, Vic	*No playoffs* Right wing								
HOWELL, Harry	Defense								
1956	NY Rangers	5	0	1	1	4	....	....	....
1957	NY Rangers	5	1	0	1	6	....	....	....
1958	NY Rangers	6	1	0	1	8	....	....	....
1962	NY Rangers	6	0	1	1	8	....	....	....
1967	NY Rangers	4	0	0	0	4	....	....	....
1968	NY Rangers	6	1	0	1	0	1	0	1
1969	NY Rangers	2	0	0	0	0	0	0	0
1970	Oakland	4	0	1	1	2	0	0	0
Playoff Totals		**38**	**3**	**3**	**6**	**32**	....	....	....
HOWELL, Ron	*No playoffs* Defense/left wing								
HOWSE, Don	Left wing								
1980	Los Angeles	2	0	0	0	0	0	0	0
Playoff Totals		**2**	**0**	**0**	**0**	**0**	**0**	**0**	**0**
HOWSON, Scott	*No playoffs* Center								
HOYDA, Dave	Left wing								
1978	Philadelphia	9	0	0	0	17	0	0	0
1979	Philadelphia	3	0	0	0	0	0	0	0
Playoff Totals		**12**	**0**	**0**	**0**	**17**	**0**	**0**	**0**
HRDINA, Jan	Center								
1999	Pittsburgh	13	4	1	5	12	1	0	1
Playoff Totals		**13**	**4**	**1**	**5**	**12**	**1**	**0**	**1**
HRDINA, Jiri	Center								
1988	Calgary	1	0	0	0	0	0	0	0
1989◆	Calgary	4	0	0	0	0	0	0	0
1990	Calgary	6	0	1	1	2	0	0	0
1991◆	Pittsburgh	14	2	2	4	6	0	0	1
1992◆	Pittsburgh	21	0	2	2	16	0	0	0
Playoff Totals		**46**	**2**	**5**	**7**	**24**	**0**	**0**	**1**
HRECHKOSY, Dave	Left wing								
1976	St. Louis	3	1	0	1	2	0	0	0
Playoff Totals		**3**	**1**	**0**	**1**	**2**	**0**	**0**	**0**
HRKAC, Tony	Center								
1987	St. Louis	3	0	0	0	0	0	0	0
1988	St. Louis	10	6	1	7	4	3	1	1
1989	St. Louis	4	1	1	2	0	0	0	1
1992	Chicago	3	0	0	0	2	0	0	0
1994	St. Louis	4	0	0	0	0	0	0	0
1998	Edmonton	12	0	3	3	2	0	0	0
1999◆	Dallas	5	0	2	2	4	0	0	0
Playoff Totals		**41**	**7**	**7**	**14**	**12**	**3**	**1**	**2**
HRYCUIK, Jim	*No playoffs* Center								
HRYMNAK, Steve	Defense								
1953	Detroit	2	0	0	0	0	0	0	0
Playoff Totals		**2**	**0**	**0**	**0**	**0**	**0**	**0**	**0**
HRYNEWICH, Tim	*No playoffs* Left wing								
HUARD, Bill	Left wing								
1995	Quebec	1	0	0	0	0	0	0	0
1998	Edmonton	4	0	0	0	2	0	0	0
Playoff Totals		**5**	**0**	**0**	**0**	**2**	**0**	**0**	**0**
HUARD, Rolly	*No playoffs* Center								
HUBER, Willie	Defense								
1984	NY Rangers	4	1	1	2	9	0	0	0
1985	NY Rangers	2	1	0	1	2	1	0	0
1986	NY Rangers	16	3	2	5	16	2	0	0
1987	NY Rangers	6	0	2	2	6	0	0	0
1988	Philadelphia	5	0	0	0	2	0	0	0
Playoff Totals		**33**	**5**	**5**	**10**	**35**	**3**	**0**	**0**
HUBICK, Greg	*No playoffs* Defense								

Season	Club	GP	G	A	Pts	PIM	PP	SH	GW
HUCK, Fran	Center								
1971	St. Louis	6	1	2	3	2	0	0	0
1973	St. Louis	5	2	2	4	0	1	0	0
Playoff Totals		**11**	**3**	**4**	**7**	**2**	**1**	**0**	**0**
HUCUL, Fred	Defense								
1953	Chicago	6	1	0	1	10	....	....	....
Playoff Totals		**6**	**1**	**0**	**1**	**10**	....	....	....
HUDDY, Charlie	Defense								
1982	Edmonton	5	1	2	3	14	0	1	0
1983	Edmonton	15	1	6	7	10	0	0	0
1984◆	Edmonton	12	1	9	10	8	0	0	0
1985◆	Edmonton	18	3	17	20	17	1	0	0
1986	Edmonton	7	0	2	2	0	0	0	0
1987◆	Edmonton	21	1	7	8	21	0	0	0
1988◆	Edmonton	13	4	5	9	10	2	0	0
1989	Edmonton	7	2	0	2	4	1	0	0
1990◆	Edmonton	22	0	6	6	11	0	0	0
1991	Edmonton	18	3	7	10	10	1	0	0
1992	Los Angeles	6	1	1	2	10	0	0	1
1993	Los Angeles	23	1	4	5	12	0	0	0
1995	Buffalo	3	0	0	0	0	0	0	0
1996	St. Louis	13	1	0	1	8	0	0	0
Playoff Totals		**183**	**19**	**66**	**85**	**135**	**5**	**1**	**1**
HUDSON, Dave	Center								
1978	Colorado	2	1	1	2	0	0	0	0
Playoff Totals		**2**	**1**	**1**	**2**	**0**	**0**	**0**	**0**
HUDSON, Lex	Defense								
1979	Pittsburgh	2	0	0	0	0	0	0	0
Playoff Totals		**2**	**0**	**0**	**0**	**0**	**0**	**0**	**0**
HUDSON, Mike	Center/Left wing								
1989	Chicago	10	1	2	3	18	1	0	0
1990	Chicago	4	0	0	0	2	0	0	0
1991	Chicago	6	0	2	2	8	0	0	0
1992	Chicago	16	3	5	8	26	0	0	0
1995	Pittsburgh	11	0	0	0	6	0	0	0
1996	St. Louis	2	0	1	1	4	0	0	0
Playoff Totals		**49**	**4**	**10**	**14**	**64**	**1**	**0**	**0**
HUDSON, Ron	*No playoffs* Center								
HUFFMAN, Kerry	Defense								
1988	Philadelphia	2	0	0	0	0	0	0	0
1993	Quebec	3	0	0	0	0	0	0	0
1996	Philadelphia	6	0	0	0	2	0	0	0
Playoff Totals		**11**	**0**	**0**	**0**	**2**	**0**	**0**	**0**
HUGGINS, Al	*No playoffs* Left wing								
HUGHES, Al	*No playoffs* Center/left wing								
HUGHES, Brent	Defense								
1968	Los Angeles	7	0	0	0	10	0	0	0
1969	Los Angeles	11	1	3	4	37	0	0	0
1971	Philadelphia	4	0	0	0	6	0	0	0
Playoff Totals		**22**	**1**	**3**	**4**	**53**	**0**	**0**	**0**
HUGHES, Brent	Left wing								
1992	Boston	10	2	0	2	20	0	0	0
1993	Boston	1	0	0	0	2	0	0	0
1994	Boston	13	2	1	3	27	0	0	1
1995	Boston	5	0	0	0	4	0	0	0
Playoff Totals		**29**	**4**	**1**	**5**	**53**	**0**	**0**	**1**
HUGHES, Frank	*No playoffs* Left wing								
HUGHES, Howie	Right wing								
1968	Los Angeles	7	2	0	2	0	1	0	0
1969	Los Angeles	7	0	0	0	2	0	0	0
Playoff Totals		**14**	**2**	**0**	**2**	**2**	**1**	**0**	**0**
HUGHES, Jack	*No playoffs* Defense								
HUGHES, James	*No playoffs* Defense								
HUGHES, John	Defense								
1980	Vancouver	4	0	0	0	10	0	0	0
1981	NY Rangers	3	0	1	1	6	0	0	0
Playoff Totals		**7**	**0**	**1**	**1**	**16**	**0**	**0**	**0**
HUGHES, Pat	Right wing								
1979◆	Montreal	8	1	2	3	4	0	0	0
1980	Pittsburgh	5	0	0	0	21	0	0	0
1981	Edmonton	5	0	5	5	16	0	0	0
1982	Edmonton	5	2	1	3	6	0	0	0
1983	Edmonton	16	2	5	7	14	0	0	1
1984◆	Edmonton	19	2	11	13	12	0	0	0
1985◆	Edmonton	10	1	1	2	4	0	0	0
1987	Hartford	3	0	0	0	0	0	0	0
Playoff Totals		**71**	**8**	**25**	**33**	**77**	**0**	**0**	**1**
HUGHES, Ryan	*No playoffs* Center								
HULBIG, Joe	Left wing								
1997	Edmonton	6	0	1	1	2	0	0	0
Playoff Totals		**6**	**0**	**1**	**1**	**2**	**0**	**0**	**0**

Season	Club	GP	G	A	Pts	PIM	PP	SH	GW
HULL, Bobby									Left wing
1959	Chicago	6	1	1	2	2	....	....	....
1960	Chicago	3	1	0	1	2	....	....	....
1961♦	Chicago	12	4	10	14	4	....	....	....
1962	Chicago	12	*8	6	14	12	....	....	....
1963	Chicago	5	*8	2	10	4	....	....	....
1964	Chicago	7	2	5	7	2	....	....	....
1965	Chicago	14	*10	7	*17	27	....	....	....
1966	Chicago	6	2	2	4	10	....	....	....
1967	Chicago	6	4	2	6	0	....	....	....
1968	Chicago	11	4	6	10	15	1	1	1
1970	Chicago	8	3	8	11	2	0	0	0
1971	Chicago	18	11	14	25	16	6	0	4
1972	Chicago	8	4	4	8	6	0	1	0
1980	Hartford	3	0	0	0	0	0	0	0
Playoff Totals		**119**	**62**	**67**	**129**	**102**	....	....	....
HULL, Brett									Right wing
1986	Calgary	2	0	0	0	0	0	0	0
1987	Calgary	4	2	1	3	0	0	0	0
1988	St. Louis	10	7	2	9	4	4	0	3
1989	St. Louis	10	5	5	10	6	1	0	2
1990	St. Louis	12	13	8	21	17	7	0	3
1991	St. Louis	13	11	8	19	4	3	0	2
1992	St. Louis	6	4	4	8	4	1	1	1
1993	St. Louis	11	8	5	13	2	5	0	2
1994	St. Louis	4	2	1	3	0	1	0	0
1995	St. Louis	7	6	2	8	0	2	0	0
1996	St. Louis	13	6	5	11	10	2	1	1
1997	St. Louis	6	2	7	9	2	0	0	0
1998	St. Louis	10	3	3	6	2	1	0	1
1999♦	Dallas	22	8	7	15	4	3	0	2
Playoff Totals		**130**	**77**	**58**	**135**	**55**	**30**	**2**	**17**
HULL, Dennis									Left wing
1965	Chicago	6	0	0	0	0	0	0	0
1966	Chicago	3	0	0	0	0	0	0	0
1967	Chicago	6	0	1	1	12	0	0	0
1968	Chicago	11	1	3	4	6	0	0	1
1970	Chicago	8	5	2	7	0	0	1	0
1971	Chicago	18	7	6	13	2	2	0	1
1972	Chicago	8	4	2	6	4	1	0	0
1973	Chicago	16	9	*15	24	4	4	0	1
1974	Chicago	10	6	3	9	0	1	0	1
1975	Chicago	5	0	2	2	0	0	0	0
1976	Chicago	4	0	0	0	0	0	0	0
1977	Chicago	2	1	0	1	0	1	0	0
1978	Detroit	7	0	0	0	2	0	0	0
Playoff Totals		**104**	**33**	**34**	**67**	**30**	**9**	**1**	**4**
HULL, Jody									Right wing
1989	Hartford	1	0	0	0	2	0	0	0
1990	Hartford	5	0	1	1	2	0	0	0
1996	Florida	14	3	2	5	0	0	0	0
1997	Florida	5	0	0	0	0	0	0	0
1999	Philadelphia	6	0	0	0	4	0	0	0
Playoff Totals		**31**	**3**	**3**	**6**	**8**	**0**	**0**	**0**
HULSE, Cale									Defense
1996	Calgary	1	0	0	0	0	0	0	0
Playoff Totals		**1**	**0**	**0**	**0**	**0**	**0**	**0**	**0**
HUNT, Fred *No playoffs*									Right wing
HUNTER, Dale									Center
1981	Quebec	5	4	2	6	34	0	0	1
1982	Quebec	16	3	7	10	52	1	0	2
1983	Quebec	4	2	1	3	24	0	1	0
1984	Quebec	9	2	3	5	41	0	0	0
1985	Quebec	17	4	6	10	*97	0	1	2
1986	Quebec	3	0	0	0	15	0	0	0
1987	Quebec	13	1	7	8	56	1	0	0
1988	Washington	14	7	5	12	98	4	0	1
1989	Washington	6	0	4	4	29	0	0	0
1990	Washington	15	4	8	12	61	1	0	0
1991	Washington	11	1	9	10	41	0	0	0
1992	Washington	7	1	4	5	16	0	0	0
1993	Washington	6	7	1	8	35	4	0	1
1994	Washington	7	0	3	3	14	0	0	0
1995	Washington	7	4	4	8	24	2	0	0
1996	Washington	6	1	5	6	24	0	0	0
1998	Washington	21	0	4	4	30	0	0	0
1999	Colorado	19	1	3	4	38	0	0	0
Playoff Totals		**186**	**42**	**76**	**118**	***729**	**13**	**2**	**7**
HUNTER, Dave									Left wing
1980	Edmonton	3	0	0	0	7	0	0	0
1981	Edmonton	9	0	0	0	28	0	0	0
1982	Edmonton	5	0	1	1	26	0	0	0
1983	Edmonton	16	4	7	11	60	0	0	0
1984♦	Edmonton	17	5	5	10	14	1	1	0
1985♦	Edmonton	18	2	5	7	33	0	0	0
1986	Edmonton	10	2	3	5	23	0	0	0
1987♦	Edmonton	21	3	3	6	20	0	0	0
1989	Edmonton	6	0	0	0	0	0	0	0
Playoff Totals		**105**	**16**	**24**	**40**	**211**	**1**	**1**	**0**
HUNTER, Mark									Right wing
1982	Montreal	5	0	0	0	20	0	0	0
1984	Montreal	14	2	1	3	69	0	0	0
1985	Montreal	11	0	3	3	13	0	0	0
1986	St. Louis	19	7	7	14	48	2	0	1
1987	St. Louis	5	0	3	3	10	0	0	0
1988	St. Louis	5	2	3	5	24	1	0	0
1989♦	Calgary	10	2	2	4	23	0	0	0
1991	Hartford	6	5	1	6	17	3	0	0
1992	Hartford	4	0	0	0	6	0	0	0
Playoff Totals		**79**	**18**	**20**	**38**	**230**	**6**	**0**	**1**
HUNTER, Tim									Right wing
1983	Calgary	9	1	0	1	*70	1	0	0
1984	Calgary	7	0	0	0	21	0	0	0
1985	Calgary	4	0	0	0	24	0	0	0
1986	Calgary	19	0	3	3	108	0	0	0
1987	Calgary	6	0	0	0	51	0	0	0
1988	Calgary	9	4	0	4	32	0	0	2
1989♦	Calgary	19	0	4	4	32	0	0	0
1990	Calgary	6	0	0	0	4	0	0	0
1991	Calgary	7	0	0	0	10	0	0	0
1993	Vancouver	11	0	0	0	26	0	0	0
1994	Vancouver	24	0	0	0	26	0	0	0
1995	Vancouver	11	0	0	0	22	0	0	0
Playoff Totals		**132**	**5**	**7**	**12**	**426**	**1**	**0**	**2**
HURAS, Larry *No playoffs*									Defense
HURLBURT, Bob *No playoffs*									Left wing
HURLBUT, Mike *No playoffs*									Defense
HURLEY, Paul *No playoffs*									Defense
HURST, Ron									Right wing
1956	Toronto	3	0	2	2	4	0	0	0
Playoff Totals		**3**	**0**	**2**	**2**	**4**	**0**	**0**	**0**
HUSCROFT, Jamie									Defense
1990	New Jersey	5	0	0	0	16	0	0	0
1991	New Jersey	3	0	0	0	6	0	0	0
1994	Boston	4	0	0	0	9	0	0	0
1995	Boston	5	0	0	0	11	0	0	0
1996	Calgary	4	0	1	1	4	0	0	0
Playoff Totals		**21**	**0**	**1**	**1**	**46**	**0**	**0**	**0**
HUSKA, Ryan *No playoffs*									Left wing
HUSTON, Ron *No playoffs*									Center
HUTCHINSON, Ron *No playoffs*									Center
HUTCHISON, Dave									Defense
1975	Los Angeles	2	0	0	0	22	0	0	0
1976	Los Angeles	9	0	3	3	29	0	0	0
1977	Los Angeles	9	1	4	5	17	0	0	0
1979	Toronto	6	0	3	3	23	0	0	0
1980	Chicago	6	0	0	0	12	0	0	0
1981	Chicago	2	0	0	0	2	0	0	0
1982	Chicago	14	1	2	3	44	0	0	0
Playoff Totals		**48**	**2**	**12**	**14**	**149**	**0**	**0**	**0**
HUTTON, Bill									Defense/Right wing
1930	Ottawa	2	0	0	0	0	0	0	0
Playoff Totals		**2**	**0**	**0**	**0**	**0**	**0**	**0**	**0**
HYLAND, Harry *No playoffs*									Right wing
HYNES, Dave *No playoffs*									Left wing
HYNES, Gord									Defense
1992	Boston	12	1	2	3	6	0	0	0
Playoff Totals		**12**	**1**	**2**	**3**	**6**	**0**	**0**	**0**
IAFRATE, Al									Defense
1986	Toronto	10	0	3	3	4	0	0	0
1987	Toronto	13	1	3	4	11	1	0	0
1988	Toronto	6	3	4	7	6	2	0	0
1991	Washington	10	1	3	4	22	0	0	1
1992	Washington	7	4	2	6	14	1	0	0
1993	Washington	6	6	0	6	4	3	0	1
1994	Boston	13	3	1	4	6	1	0	1
1998	San Jose	6	1	0	1	10	1	0	0
Playoff Totals		**71**	**19**	**16**	**35**	**77**	**9**	**0**	**3**
IGINLA, Jarome									Right wing
1996	Calgary	2	1	1	2	0	0	0	0
Playoff Totals		**2**	**1**	**1**	**2**	**0**	**0**	**0**	**0**
IGNATJEV, Victor									Defense
1999	Pittsburgh	1	0	0	0	2	0	0	0
Playoff Totals		**1**	**0**	**0**	**0**	**2**	**0**	**0**	**0**
IHNACAK, Miroslav									Left wing
1987	Toronto	1	0	0	0	0	0	0	0
Playoff Totals		**1**	**0**	**0**	**0**	**0**	**0**	**0**	**0**
IHNACAK, Peter									Center
1986	Toronto	10	2	3	5	12	0	0	1
1987	Toronto	13	2	4	6	9	0	0	0
1988	Toronto	5	0	3	3	4	0	0	0
Playoff Totals		**28**	**4**	**10**	**14**	**25**	**0**	**0**	**1**
IMLACH, Brent *No playoffs*									Forward
INGARFIELD, Earl									Center
1962	NY Rangers	6	3	2	5	2	1	0	0
1967	NY Rangers	4	1	0	1	2	0	0	0
1969	Oakland	7	4	6	10	2	0	1	1
1970	Oakland	4	1	0	1	4	1	0	0
Playoff Totals		**21**	**9**	**8**	**17**	**10**	**2**	**1**	**1**
INGARFIELD, Earl Jr.									Center
1980	Atlanta	2	0	1	1	0	0	0	0
Playoff Totals		**2**	**0**	**1**	**1**	**0**	**0**	**0**	**0**
INGLIS, Billy									Center
1969	Los Angeles	11	1	2	3	4	0	0	0
Playoff Totals		**11**	**1**	**2**	**3**	**4**	**0**	**0**	**0**
INGOLDSBY, Johnny *No playoffs*									Right wing/defense
INGRAM, Frank									Right wing
1930	Chicago	2	0	0	0	0	0	0	0
1931	Chicago	9	0	1	1	2	0	0	0
Playoff Totals		**11**	**0**	**1**	**1**	**2**	**0**	**0**	**0**
INGRAM, John J. *No playoffs*									Center
INGRAM, Ron									Defense
1963	Chicago	2	0	0	0	0	0	0	0
Playoff Totals		**2**	**0**	**0**	**0**	**0**	**0**	**0**	**0**
INTRANUOVO, Ralph *No playoffs*									Center
IRVIN, Dick									Center
1927	Chicago	2	2	0	2	4	....	....	....
Playoff Totals		**2**	**2**	**0**	**2**	**4**	....	....	....
IRVINE, Ted									Left wing
1968	Los Angeles	6	1	3	4	2	0	0	0
1969	Los Angeles	11	5	1	6	7	1	1	0
1970	NY Rangers	6	1	2	3	8	0	1	0
1971	NY Rangers	12	1	2	3	28	0	0	0
1972	NY Rangers	16	4	5	9	19	0	0	0
1973	NY Rangers	10	1	3	4	20	1	0	0
1974	NY Rangers	13	3	5	8	16	0	0	0
1975	NY Rangers	3	0	1	1	11	0	0	0
1976	St. Louis	3	0	2	2	2	0	0	0
1977	St. Louis	3	0	0	0	2	0	0	0
Playoff Totals		**83**	**16**	**24**	**40**	**115**	**2**	**2**	**0**
IRWIN, Ivan									Defense
1956	NY Rangers	5	0	0	0	8	0	0	0
Playoff Totals		**5**	**0**	**0**	**0**	**8**	**0**	**0**	**0**
ISAKSSON, Ulf *No playoffs*									Left wing
ISBISTER, Brad									Right wing
1998	Phoenix	5	0	0	0	2	0	0	0
Playoff Totals		**5**	**0**	**0**	**0**	**2**	**0**	**0**	**0**
ISSEL, Kim *No playoffs*									Right wing
JACKMAN, Richard *No playoffs*									Defense
JACKSON, Art									Center
1935	Toronto	1	0	0	0	2	....	....	....
1936	Toronto	8	0	3	3	2	....	....	....
1938	Boston	3	0	0	0	0	....	....	....
1939	NY Americans	2	0	0	0	2	....	....	....
1940	Boston	5	1	2	3	0	....	....	....
1941♦	Boston	11	1	3	4	16	....	....	....
1942	Boston	5	0	1	1	0	....	....	....
1943	Boston	9	6	3	9	7	....	....	....
1945♦	Toronto	8	0	0	0	0	....	....	....
Playoff Totals		**52**	**8**	**12**	**20**	**29**	....	....	....
JACKSON, Busher									Left wing
1931	Toronto	2	0	0	0	0	....	....	....
1932♦	Toronto	7	5	2	7	13	....	....	....
1933	Toronto	9	3	1	4	2	....	....	....
1934	Toronto	5	1	0	1	8	....	....	....
1935	Toronto	7	3	2	*5	2	....	....	....
1936	Toronto	9	3	2	5	4	....	....	....
1937	Toronto	2	1	0	1	2	....	....	....
1938	Toronto	6	1	0	1	8	....	....	....
1939	Toronto	7	0	1	1	2	....	....	....
1940	NY Americans	3	0	1	1	2	....	....	....
1942	Boston	5	0	1	1	0	....	....	....
1943	Boston	9	1	2	3	10	....	....	....
Playoff Totals		**71**	**18**	**12**	**30**	**53**	....	....	....
JACKSON, Dane									Right wing
1995	Vancouver	6	0	0	0	10	0	0	0
Playoff Totals		**6**	**0**	**0**	**0**	**10**	**0**	**0**	**0**
JACKSON, Don									Defense
1980	Minnesota	1	0	0	0	0	0	0	0
1983	Edmonton	16	3	3	6	30	0	0	0
1984♦	Edmonton	19	1	2	3	32	0	0	0
1985♦	Edmonton	9	0	0	0	64	0	0	0
1986	Edmonton	8	0	0	0	21	0	0	0
Playoff Totals		**53**	**4**	**5**	**9**	**147**	**0**	**0**	**0**
JACKSON, Harold									Defense
1938♦	Chicago	1	0	0	0	2	....	....	....
1943♦	Detroit	6	0	1	1	4	....	....	....
1944	Detroit	5	0	0	0	11	....	....	....
1945	Detroit	14	1	1	2	10	....	....	....
1946	Detroit	5	0	0	0	6	....	....	....
Playoff Totals		**31**	**1**	**2**	**3**	**33**	....	....	....

Season	Club	GP	G	A	Pts	PIM	PP	SH	GW
JACKSON, Jack	*No playoffs*								Defense
JACKSON, Jeff									Left wing
1987	NY Rangers	6	1	1	2	16	0	0	0
Playoff Totals		**6**	**1**	**1**	**2**	**16**	**0**	**0**	**0**
JACKSON, Jim									Left wing
1983	Calgary	8	2	1	3	2	0	0	0
1984	Calgary	6	1	1	2	4	0	1	0
Playoff Totals		**14**	**3**	**2**	**5**	**6**	**0**	**1**	**0**
JACKSON, Lloyd	*No playoffs*								Center
JACKSON, Stan	*No playoffs*								Left wing
JACKSON, Walter	*No playoffs*								Left wing
JACOBS, Paul	*No playoffs*								Defense
JACOBS, Tim	*No playoffs*								Defense
JAGR, Jaromir									Right wing
1991♦	Pittsburgh	24	3	10	13	6	1	0	1
1992♦	Pittsburgh	21	11	13	24	6	2	0	4
1993	Pittsburgh	12	5	4	9	23	1	0	1
1994	Pittsburgh	6	2	4	6	16	0	0	1
1995	Pittsburgh	12	10	5	15	6	2	1	1
1996	Pittsburgh	18	11	12	23	18	5	1	1
1997	Pittsburgh	5	4	4	8	4	2	0	0
1998	Pittsburgh	6	4	5	9	2	1	0	0
1999	Pittsburgh	9	5	7	12	16	1	0	1
Playoff Totals		**113**	**55**	**64**	**119**	**97**	**15**	**2**	**10**
JAKOPIN, John	*No playoffs*								Defense
JALO, Risto	*No playoffs*								Center
JALONEN, Kari									Center
1983	Calgary	5	1	0	1	0	0	0	0
Playoff Totals		**5**	**1**	**0**	**1**	**0**	**0**	**0**	**0**
JAMES, Gerry									Right wing
1956	Toronto	5	1	0	1	8	0	1	0
1960	Toronto	10	0	0	0	0	0	0	0
Playoff Totals		**15**	**1**	**0**	**1**	**8**	**0**	**1**	**0**
JAMES, Val	*No playoffs*								Left wing
JAMIESON, Jim	*No playoffs*								Defense
JANKOWSKI, Lou									Center/right wing
1953	Detroit	1	0	0	0	0	0	0	0
Playoff Totals		**1**	**0**	**0**	**0**	**0**	**0**	**0**	**0**
JANNEY, Craig									Center
1988	Boston	23	6	10	16	11	4	0	1
1989	Boston	10	4	9	13	21	0	0	0
1990	Boston	18	3	19	22	2	1	0	2
1991	Boston	18	4	18	22	11	4	0	0
1992	St. Louis	6	0	6	6	0	0	0	0
1993	St. Louis	11	2	9	11	0	1	0	2
1994	St. Louis	4	1	3	4	0	0	0	0
1995	San Jose	11	3	4	7	4	0	0	1
1996	Winnipeg	6	1	2	3	0	0	0	0
1997	Phoenix	7	0	3	3	4	0	0	0
1998	Phoenix	6	0	3	3	0	0	0	0
Playoff Totals		**120**	**24**	**86**	**110**	**53**	**10**	**0**	**6**
JANSSENS, Mark									Center
1990	NY Rangers	9	2	1	3	10	0	0	1
1991	NY Rangers	6	3	0	3	6	0	0	0
1997	Anaheim	11	0	0	0	15	0	0	0
1998	Phoenix	1	0	0	0	2	0	0	0
Playoff Totals		**27**	**5**	**1**	**6**	**33**	**0**	**0**	**1**
JANTUNEN, Marko	*No playoffs*								Center
JARRETT, Doug									Defense
1965	Chicago	11	1	0	1	10	0	0	0
1966	Chicago	5	0	1	1	9	0	0	0
1967	Chicago	6	0	3	3	8	0	0	0
1968	Chicago	11	4	0	4	9	0	0	0
1970	Chicago	8	1	0	1	4	0	0	0
1971	Chicago	18	1	6	7	14	0	0	0
1972	Chicago	8	0	2	2	16	0	0	0
1973	Chicago	15	0	3	3	2	0	0	0
1974	Chicago	10	0	1	1	6	0	0	0
1975	Chicago	7	0	0	0	4	0	0	0
Playoff Totals		**99**	**7**	**16**	**23**	**82**	**0**	**0**	**0**
JARRETT, Gary									Left wing
1969	Oakland	7	2	1	3	4	0	1	0
1970	Oakland	4	1	0	1	5	1	0	0
Playoff Totals		**11**	**3**	**1**	**4**	**9**	**1**	**1**	**0**
JARRY, Pierre									Left wing
1972	Toronto	5	0	1	1	0	0	0	0
Playoff Totals		**5**	**0**	**1**	**1**	**0**	**0**	**0**	**0**
JARVENPAA, Hannu	*No playoffs*								Right wing
JARVI, Iiro	*No playoffs*								Right wing

Season	Club	GP	G	A	Pts	PIM	PP	SH	GW
JARVIS, Doug									Center
1976♦	Montreal	13	2	1	3	2	0	0	0
1977♦	Montreal	14	0	7	7	2	0	0	0
1978♦	Montreal	15	3	5	8	12	1	0	1
1979♦	Montreal	12	1	3	4	4	0	0	0
1980	Montreal	10	4	4	8	2	0	1	0
1981	Montreal	3	0	0	0	0	0	0	0
1982	Montreal	5	1	0	1	4	0	1	0
1983	Washington	4	0	1	1	0	0	0	0
1984	Washington	8	2	3	5	6	0	0	0
1985	Washington	5	1	0	1	2	0	0	0
1986	Hartford	10	0	3	3	4	0	0	0
1987	Hartford	6	0	0	0	4	0	0	0
Playoff Totals		**105**	**14**	**27**	**41**	**42**	**1**	**2**	**1**
JARVIS, Jim	*No playoffs*								Left wing
JARVIS, Wes									Center
1987	Toronto	2	0	0	0	2	0	0	0
Playoff Totals		**2**	**0**	**0**	**0**	**2**	**0**	**0**	**0**
JAVANAINEN, Arto	*No playoffs*								Right wing
JAY, Bob	*No playoffs*								Defense
JEFFREY, Larry									Left wing
1963	Detroit	9	3	3	6	8	1	0	0
1964	Detroit	14	1	6	7	28	0	0	1
1965	Detroit	2	0	0	0	0	0	0	0
1967♦	Toronto	6	0	1	1	4	0	0	0
1968	NY Rangers	3	0	0	0	0	0	0	0
1969	NY Rangers	4	0	0	0	2	0	0	0
Playoff Totals		**38**	**4**	**10**	**14**	**42**	**1**	**0**	**1**
JELINEK, Tomas	*No playoffs*								Right wing
JENKINS, Dean	*No playoffs*								Right wing
JENKINS, Roger									Right wing/defense
1931	Chicago	3	0	0	0	0	....	....	....
1934♦	Chicago	8	0	0	0	0	....	....	....
1935	Mtl. Canadiens	2	1	0	1	2	....	....	....
1936	Boston	2	0	1	1	2	....	....	....
1938♦	Chicago	10	0	*6	6	8	....	....	....
Playoff Totals		**25**	**1**	**7**	**8**	**12**	....	....	....
JENNINGS, Bill									Right wing
1941	Detroit	9	2	2	4	0	....	....	....
1944	Detroit	4	0	0	0	0	....	....	....
1945	Boston	7	2	2	4	6	....	....	....
Playoff Totals		**20**	**4**	**4**	**8**	**6**	....	....	....
JENNINGS, Grant									Defense
1988	Washington	1	0	0	0	0	0	0	0
1989	Hartford	4	1	0	1	17	1	0	0
1990	Hartford	7	0	0	0	13	0	0	0
1991♦	Pittsburgh	13	1	1	2	16	0	0	0
1992♦	Pittsburgh	10	0	0	0	12	0	0	0
1993	Pittsburgh	12	0	0	0	8	0	0	0
1994	Pittsburgh	3	0	0	0	2	0	0	0
1995	Toronto	4	0	0	0	0	0	0	0
Playoff Totals		**54**	**2**	**1**	**3**	**68**	**1**	**0**	**0**
JENSEN, Chris	*No playoffs*								Right wing
JENSEN, David	*No playoffs*								Defense
JENSEN, David A.									Center
1986	Washington	4	0	0	0	0	0	0	0
1987	Washington	7	0	0	0	2	0	0	0
Playoff Totals		**11**	**0**	**0**	**0**	**2**	**0**	**0**	**0**
JENSEN, Steve									Left wing
1977	Minnesota	2	0	1	1	0	0	0	0
1979	Los Angeles	2	0	0	0	0	0	0	0
1980	Los Angeles	4	0	0	0	2	0	0	0
1981	Los Angeles	4	0	2	2	7	0	0	0
Playoff Totals		**12**	**0**	**3**	**3**	**9**	**0**	**0**	**0**
JEREMIAH, Ed	*No playoffs*								Right wing/defense
JERRARD, Paul	*No playoffs*								Defense
JERWA, Frank	*No playoffs*								Left wing/defense
JERWA, Joe									Defense
1931	NY Rangers	4	0	0	0	4	....	....	....
1936	NY Americans	5	2	3	5	2	....	....	....
1938	NY Americans	6	0	0	0	8	....	....	....
1939	NY Americans	2	0	0	0	2	....	....	....
Playoff Totals		**17**	**2**	**3**	**5**	**16**	....	....	....
JIRIK, Jaroslav	*No playoffs*								left wing
JOANETTE, Rosario	*No playoffs*								Center
JODZIO, Rick	*No playoffs*								Left wing
JOHANNESEN, Glenn	*No playoffs*								Left wing
JOHANNSON, John	*No playoffs*								Center
JOHNSON, Bill	*No playoffs*								Center/right wing
JOHANSEN, Trevor									Defense
1978	Toronto	13	0	3	3	21	0	0	0
Playoff Totals		**13**	**0**	**3**	**3**	**21**	**0**	**0**	**0**
JOHANSSON, Andreas									Center
1998	Pittsburgh	1	0	0	0	0	0	0	0
1999	Ottawa	2	0	0	0	0	0	0	0
Playoff Totals		**3**	**0**	**0**	**0**	**0**	**0**	**0**	**0**
JOHANSSON, Bjorn	*No playoffs*								Defense

Season	Club	GP	G	A	Pts	PIM	PP	SH	GW
JOHANSSON, Calle									Defense
1988	Buffalo	6	0	1	1	0	0	0	0
1989	Washington	6	1	2	3	0	1	0	0
1990	Washington	15	1	6	7	4	0	0	0
1991	Washington	10	2	7	9	8	1	0	0
1992	Washington	7	0	5	5	4	0	0	0
1993	Washington	6	0	5	5	4	0	0	0
1994	Washington	6	1	3	4	4	0	0	1
1995	Washington	7	3	1	4	0	1	0	0
1998	Washington	21	2	8	10	16	0	0	0
Playoff Totals		**84**	**10**	**38**	**48**	**40**	**3**	**0**	**1**
JOHANSSON, Roger									Defense
1993	Calgary	5	0	1	1	2	0	0	0
Playoff Totals		**5**	**0**	**1**	**1**	**2**	**0**	**0**	**0**
JOHNS, Don	*No playoffs*								Defense
JOHNSON, Al									Right wing/center
1961	Detroit	11	2	2	4	6	0	0	1
Playoff Totals		**11**	**2**	**2**	**4**	**6**	**0**	**0**	**1**
JOHNSON, Brian	*No playoffs*								Right wing
JOHNSON, Craig									Left wing
1995	St. Louis	1	0	0	0	2	0	0	0
1998	Los Angeles	4	1	0	1	4	0	0	0
Playoff Totals		**5**	**1**	**0**	**1**	**6**	**0**	**0**	**0**
JOHNSON, Danny	*No playoffs*								Center
JOHNSON, Earl	*No playoffs*								Left wing
JOHNSON, Greg									Center
1994	Detroit	7	2	2	4	2	1	0	0
1995	Detroit	1	0	0	0	0	0	0	0
1996	Detroit	13	3	1	4	8	0	0	0
1997	Pittsburgh	5	1	0	1	2	0	0	0
Playoff Totals		**26**	**6**	**3**	**9**	**12**	**1**	**0**	**0**
JOHNSON, Ivan									Defense
1927	NY Rangers	2	0	0	0	8	....	....	....
1928♦	NY Rangers	9	1	1	2	*46	....	....	....
1929	NY Rangers	6	0	0	0	26	....	....	....
1930	NY Rangers	4	0	0	0	14	....	....	....
1931	NY Rangers	4	1	0	1	17	....	....	....
1932	NY Rangers	7	2	0	2	*24	....	....	....
1933♦	NY Rangers	8	1	0	1	14	....	....	....
1934	NY Rangers	2	0	0	0	4	....	....	....
1935	NY Rangers	4	0	0	0	2	....	....	....
1937	NY Rangers	9	0	1	1	4	....	....	....
1938	NY Americans	6	0	0	0	2	....	....	....
Playoff Totals		**61**	**5**	**2**	**7**	**161**	....	....	....
JOHNSON, Jim									Center
1969	Philadelphia	3	0	0	0	2	0	0	0
1971	Philadelphia	4	0	2	2	0	0	0	0
Playoff Totals		**7**	**0**	**2**	**2**	**2**	**0**	**0**	**0**
JOHNSON, Jim									Defense
1989	Pittsburgh	11	0	5	5	44	0	0	0
1991	Minnesota	14	0	1	1	52	0	0	0
1992	Minnesota	7	1	3	4	18	0	0	0
1995	Washington	7	0	2	2	8	0	0	0
1996	Washington	6	0	0	0	6	0	0	0
1997	Phoenix	6	0	0	0	4	0	0	0
Playoff Totals		**51**	**1**	**11**	**12**	**132**	**0**	**0**	**0**
JOHNSON, Mark									Center
1980	Pittsburgh	5	2	2	4	0	1	0	1
1981	Pittsburgh	5	2	1	3	6	1	0	0
1982	Minnesota	4	2	0	2	0	1	0	0
1985	St. Louis	3	0	1	1	0	0	0	0
1988	New Jersey	18	10	8	18	4	5	0	1
1990	New Jersey	2	0	0	0	0	0	0	0
Playoff Totals		**37**	**16**	**12**	**28**	**10**	**8**	**0**	**2**
JOHNSON, Matt									Left wing
1998	Los Angeles	4	0	0	0	6	0	0	0
Playoff Totals		**4**	**0**	**0**	**0**	**6**	**0**	**0**	**0**
JOHNSON, Mike									Right wing
1999	Toronto	17	3	2	5	4	0	0	1
Playoff Totals		**17**	**3**	**2**	**5**	**4**	**0**	**0**	**1**
JOHNSON, Norm									Center
1958	Boston	12	4	0	4	6	....	....	....
1960	Chicago	2	0	0	0	0	....	....	....
Playoff Totals		**14**	**4**	**0**	**4**	**6**	....	....	....
JOHNSON, Ryan	*No playoffs*								Center
JOHNSON, Terry									Defense
1981	Quebec	2	0	0	0	0	0	0	0
1984	St. Louis	11	0	1	1	25	0	0	0
1985	St. Louis	3	0	0	0	19	0	0	0
1986	Calgary	17	0	3	3	64	0	0	0
1987	Toronto	2	0	0	0	0	0	0	0
1988	Toronto	3	0	0	0	10	0	0	0
Playoff Totals		**38**	**0**	**4**	**4**	**118**	**0**	**0**	**0**

Season	Club	GP	G	A	Pts	PIM	PP	SH	GW
JOHNSON, Tom	Defense								
1950	Montreal	1	0	0	0	0	....	....	....
1951	Montreal	11	0	0	0	6	....	....	....
1952	Montreal	11	1	0	1	2	....	....	....
1953♦	Montreal	12	2	3	5	8	....	....	....
1954	Montreal	11	1	2	3	30	....	....	....
1955	Montreal	12	2	0	2	22	....	....	....
1956♦	Montreal	10	0	2	2	8	....	....	....
1957♦	Montreal	10	0	2	2	13	....	....	....
1958♦	Montreal	2	0	0	0	0	....	....	....
1959♦	Montreal	11	2	3	5	8	....	....	....
1960♦	Montreal	8	0	1	1	4	....	....	....
1961	Montreal	6	0	1	1	8	....	....	....
1962	Montreal	6	0	1	1	0	....	....	....
Playoff Totals		**111**	**8**	**15**	**23**	**109**	....	....	....
JOHNSON, Virgil	Defense								
1938♦	Chicago	10	0	0	0	0	0	0	0
1944	Chicago	9	0	3	3	4	0	0	0
Playoff Totals		**19**	**0**	**3**	**3**	**4**	**0**	**0**	**0**
JOHNSSON, Kim *No playoffs*	Defense								
JOHNSTON, Bernie	Center								
1980	Hartford	3	0	1	1	0	0	0	0
Playoff Totals		**3**	**0**	**1**	**1**	**0**	**0**	**0**	**0**
JOHNSTON, George *No playoffs*	Right wing								
JOHNSTON, Greg	Right wing								
1987	Boston	4	0	0	0	0	0	0	0
1988	Boston	3	0	1	1	2	0	0	0
1989	Boston	10	1	0	1	6	0	1	0
1990	Boston	5	1	0	1	4	0	0	1
Playoff Totals		**22**	**2**	**1**	**3**	**12**	**0**	**1**	**1**
JOHNSTON, Jay *No playoffs*	Defense								
JOHNSTON, Joey *No playoffs*	Left wing								
JOHNSTON, Larry *No playoffs*	Defense								
JOHNSTON, Marshall	Defense								
1970	Minnesota	6	0	0	0	2	0	0	0
Playoff Totals		**6**	**0**	**0**	**0**	**2**	**0**	**0**	**0**
JOHNSTON, Randy *No playoffs*	Defense								
JOHNSTONE, Eddie	Right wing								
1979	NY Rangers	17	5	0	5	10	0	1	1
1980	NY Rangers	9	0	1	1	25	0	0	0
1981	NY Rangers	8	2	2	4	4	0	0	1
1982	NY Rangers	10	2	6	8	25	1	0	0
1983	NY Rangers	9	4	1	5	19	1	1	0
1984	Detroit	2	0	0	0	0	0	0	0
Playoff Totals		**55**	**13**	**10**	**23**	**83**	**2**	**2**	**2**
JOHNSTONE, Ross	Defense								
1944	Toronto	3	0	0	0	0	0	0	0
Playoff Totals		**3**	**0**	**0**	**0**	**0**	**0**	**0**	**0**
JOKINEN, Olli *No playoffs*	Center								
JOLIAT, Aurel	Left wing								
1923	Mtl. Canadiens	2	1	1	2	8	....	....	....
1924♦	Mtl. Canadiens	6	4	*4	8	10	....	....	....
1925	Mtl. Canadiens	5	2	2	4	*21	....	....	....
1927	Mtl. Canadiens	4	1	0	1	10	....	....	....
1928	Mtl. Canadiens	2	0	0	0	4	....	....	....
1929	Mtl. Canadiens	3	1	1	2	10	....	....	....
1930♦	Mtl. Canadiens	6	0	2	2	6	....	....	....
1931♦	Mtl. Canadiens	10	0	*4	4	12	....	....	....
1932	Mtl. Canadiens	4	2	0	2	4	....	....	....
1933	Mtl. Canadiens	2	2	1	3	2	....	....	....
1934	Mtl. Canadiens	3	0	1	1	0	....	....	....
1935	Mtl. Canadiens	2	1	0	1	0	....	....	....
1937	Mtl. Canadiens	5	0	3	3	2	....	....	....
Playoff Totals		**54**	**14**	**19**	**33**	**89**	....	....	....
JOLIAT, Rene *No playoffs*	Right wing/defense								
JOLY, Greg	Defense								
1978	Detroit	5	0	0	0	8	0	0	0
Playoff Totals		**5**	**0**	**0**	**0**	**8**	**0**	**0**	**0**
JOLY, Yvan	Right wing								
1980	Montreal	1	0	0	0	0	0	0	0
Playoff Totals		**1**	**0**	**0**	**0**	**0**	**0**	**0**	**0**
JOMPHE, Jean-Francois *No playoffs*	Center								
JONATHAN, Stan	Left wing								
1977	Boston	14	4	2	6	24	0	0	1
1978	Boston	15	0	1	1	36	0	0	0
1979	Boston	11	4	1	5	12	0	0	0
1980	Boston	9	0	0	0	29	0	0	0
1981	Boston	3	0	0	0	30	0	0	0
1982	Boston	11	0	0	0	6	0	0	0
Playoff Totals		**63**	**8**	**4**	**12**	**137**	**0**	**0**	**1**
JONES, Bob *No playoffs*	Left wing								
JONES, Brad	Left wing								
1988	Winnipeg	1	0	0	0	0	0	0	0
1991	Los Angeles	8	1	1	2	2	0	0	1
Playoff Totals		**9**	**1**	**1**	**2**	**2**	**0**	**0**	**1**
JONES, Buck	Defense								
1939	Detroit	6	0	1	1	10	0	0	0
1943	Toronto	6	0	0	0	8	0	0	0
Playoff Totals		**12**	**0**	**1**	**1**	**18**	**0**	**0**	**0**
JONES, Jim *No playoffs*	Defense								
JONES, Jimmy	Right wing								
1978	Toronto	13	1	5	6	7	0	0	0
1979	Toronto	6	0	0	0	4	0	0	0
Playoff Totals		**19**	**1**	**5**	**6**	**11**	**0**	**0**	**0**
JONES, Keith	Right wing								
1993	Washington	6	0	0	0	10	0	0	0
1994	Washington	11	0	1	1	36	0	0	0
1995	Washington	7	4	4	8	22	1	0	0
1996	Washington	2	0	0	0	7	0	0	0
1997	Colorado	6	3	3	6	4	1	0	0
1998	Colorado	7	0	0	0	13	0	0	0
1999	Philadelphia	6	2	1	3	14	0	0	0
Playoff Totals		**45**	**9**	**9**	**18**	**106**	**2**	**0**	**0**
JONES, Ron *No playoffs*	Defense								
JONES, Ty *No playoffs*	Right wing								
JONSSON, Hans *No playoffs*	Defense								
JONSSON, Jorgen *No playoffs*	Left wing								
JONSSON, Kenny	Defense								
1995	Toronto	4	0	0	0	0	0	0	0
Playoff Totals		**4**	**0**	**0**	**0**	**0**	**0**	**0**	**0**
JONSSON, Tomas	Defense								
1982♦	NY Islanders	10	0	2	2	21	0	0	0
1983♦	NY Islanders	20	2	10	12	18	0	0	0
1984	NY Islanders	21	3	5	8	22	2	0	0
1985	NY Islanders	7	1	2	3	10	1	0	0
1986	NY Islanders	3	0	1	1	4	0	0	0
1987	NY Islanders	10	1	4	5	6	1	0	0
1988	NY Islanders	5	2	2	4	10	1	0	0
1989	Edmonton	4	2	0	2	6	2	0	0
Playoff Totals		**80**	**11**	**26**	**37**	**97**	**7**	**0**	**0**
JOSEPH, Anthony *No playoffs*	Right wing								
JOSEPH, Chris	Defense								
1992	Edmonton	5	1	3	4	2	0	0	0
1995	Pittsburgh	10	1	1	2	12	0	0	0
1996	Pittsburgh	15	1	0	1	8	0	0	0
1998	Philadelphia	1	0	0	0	2	0	0	0
Playoff Totals		**31**	**3**	**4**	**7**	**24**	**0**	**0**	**0**
JOVANOVSKI, Ed	Defense								
1996	Florida	22	1	8	9	52	0	0	0
1997	Florida	5	0	0	0	4	0	0	0
Playoff Totals		**27**	**1**	**8**	**9**	**56**	**0**	**0**	**0**
JOYAL, Eddie	Center								
1963	Detroit	11	1	0	1	2	1	0	0
1964	Detroit	14	2	3	5	10	0	0	1
1965	Detroit	7	1	1	2	4	1	0	0
1968	Los Angeles	7	4	1	5	2	3	0	1
1969	Los Angeles	11	3	3	6	0	1	0	0
Playoff Totals		**50**	**11**	**8**	**19**	**18**	**6**	**0**	**2**
JOYCE, Bob	Left wing								
1988	Boston	23	8	6	14	18	3	0	1
1989	Boston	9	5	2	7	2	0	0	0
1990	Washington	14	2	1	3	9	0	0	0
Playoff Totals		**46**	**15**	**9**	**24**	**29**	**3**	**0**	**1**
JOYCE, Duane *No playoffs*	Defense								
JUCKES, Bing *No playoffs*	Left wing								
JUHLIN, Patrik	Left wing								
1995	Philadelphia	13	1	0	1	2	0	0	0
Playoff Totals		**13**	**1**	**0**	**1**	**2**	**0**	**0**	**0**
JULIEN, Claude *No playoffs*	Defense								
JUNEAU, Joe	Center								
1992	Boston	15	4	8	12	21	2	0	0
1993	Boston	4	2	4	6	6	2	0	0
1994	Washington	11	4	5	9	6	2	0	1
1995	Washington	7	2	6	8	2	0	0	0
1996	Washington	5	0	7	7	6	0	0	0
1998	Washington	21	7	10	17	8	1	1	4
1999	Buffalo	20	3	8	11	10	0	1	0
Playoff Totals		**83**	**22**	**48**	**70**	**59**	**7**	**2**	**5**
JUNKER, Steve	Left wing								
1993	NY Islanders	3	0	1	1	0	0	0	0
Playoff Totals		**3**	**0**	**1**	**1**	**0**	**0**	**0**	**0**
JUTILA, Timo *No playoffs*	Defense								
JUZDA, Bill	Defense								
1942	NY Rangers	6	0	1	1	4	0	0	0
1948	NY Rangers	6	0	0	0	9	0	0	0
1949♦	Toronto	9	0	2	2	8	0	0	0
1950	Toronto	7	0	0	0	16	0	0	0
1951♦	Toronto	11	0	0	0	7	0	0	0
1952	Toronto	3	0	0	0	2	0	0	0
Playoff Totals		**42**	**0**	**3**	**3**	**46**	**0**	**0**	**0**
KABEL, Bob *No playoffs*	Center								
KABERLE, Frantisek *No playoffs*	Defense								
KABERLE, Tomas	Defense								
1999	Toronto	14	0	3	3	2	0	0	0
Playoff Totals		**14**	**0**	**3**	**3**	**2**	**0**	**0**	**0**
KACHOWSKI, Mark *No playoffs*	Left wing								
KACHUR, Ed *No playoffs*	Right wing								
KAESE, Trent *No playoffs*	Right wing								
KAISER, Vern	Left wing								
1951	Montreal	2	0	0	0	0	0	0	0
Playoff Totals		**2**	**0**	**0**	**0**	**0**	**0**	**0**	**0**
KALBFLEISH, Walter	Defense								
1936	NY Americans	5	0	0	0	2	0	0	0
Playoff Totals		**5**	**0**	**0**	**0**	**2**	**0**	**0**	**0**
KALETA, Alex	Left wing								
1942	Chicago	3	1	2	3	0	....	....	....
1946	Chicago	4	0	1	1	2	....	....	....
1950	NY Rangers	10	0	3	3	0	....	....	....
Playoff Totals		**17**	**1**	**6**	**7**	**2**	....	....	....
KALININ, Dimitri *No playoffs*	Defense								
KALLUR, Anders	Right wing								
1981♦	NY Islanders	12	4	3	7	10	0	2	0
1982♦	NY Islanders	19	1	6	7	8	0	1	0
1983♦	NY Islanders	20	3	12	15	12	1	1	0
1984	NY Islanders	17	2	2	4	2	0	1	1
1985	NY Islanders	10	2	0	2	0	0	0	0
Playoff Totals		**78**	**12**	**23**	**35**	**32**	**1**	**5**	**1**
KAMENSKY, Valeri	Left wing								
1993	Quebec	6	0	1	1	6	0	0	0
1995	Quebec	2	1	0	1	0	0	0	0
1996♦	Colorado	22	10	12	22	28	3	0	2
1997	Colorado	17	8	14	22	16	5	0	2
1998	Colorado	7	2	3	5	18	1	0	0
1999	Colorado	10	4	5	9	4	1	0	1
Playoff Totals		**64**	**25**	**35**	**60**	**72**	**10**	**0**	**5**
KAMINSKI, Kevin	Center								
1995	Washington	5	0	0	0	36	0	0	0
1996	Washington	3	0	0	0	16	0	0	0
Playoff Totals		**8**	**0**	**0**	**0**	**52**	**0**	**0**	**0**
KAMINSKY, Max	Center								
1935	Boston	4	0	0	0	0	0	0	0
Playoff Totals		**4**	**0**	**0**	**0**	**0**	**0**	**0**	**0**
KAMINSKY, Yan	Right wing								
1994	NY Islanders	2	0	0	0	4	0	0	0
Playoff Totals		**2**	**0**	**0**	**0**	**4**	**0**	**0**	**0**
KAMPMAN, Rudolph	Defense								
1938	Toronto	7	0	1	1	6	....	....	....
1939	Toronto	10	1	1	2	20	....	....	....
1940	Toronto	10	0	0	0	0	....	....	....
1941	Toronto	7	0	0	0	0	....	....	....
1942♦	Toronto	13	0	2	2	12	....	....	....
Playoff Totals		**47**	**1**	**4**	**5**	**38**	....	....	....
KANE, Francis *No playoffs*	Defense								
KANNEGIESSER, Gord *No playoffs*	Defense								
KANNEGIESSER, Sheldon	Defense								
1973	NY Rangers	1	0	0	0	2	0	0	0
1974	Los Angeles	5	0	1	1	0	0	0	0
1975	Los Angeles	3	0	1	1	4	0	0	0
1976	Los Angeles	9	0	0	0	4	0	0	0
Playoff Totals		**18**	**0**	**2**	**2**	**10**	**0**	**0**	**0**
KAPANEN, Sami	Left wing								
1999	Carolina	5	1	1	2	0	0	0	0
Playoff Totals		**5**	**1**	**1**	**2**	**0**	**0**	**0**	**0**
KARABIN, Ladislav *No playoffs*	Left wing								
KARALAHTI, Jere *No playoffs*	Defense								
KARAMNOV, Vitali	Left wing								
1995	St. Louis	2	0	0	0	2	0	0	0
Playoff Totals		**2**	**0**	**0**	**0**	**2**	**0**	**0**	**0**
KARIYA, Paul	Left wing								
1997	Anaheim	11	7	6	13	4	4	0	1
1999	Anaheim	3	1	3	4	0	0	0	0
Playoff Totals		**14**	**8**	**9**	**17**	**4**	**4**	**0**	**1**
KARIYA, Steve *No playoffs*	Left wing								
KARJALAINEN, Kyosti	Right wing								
1992	Los Angeles	3	0	1	1	2	0	0	0
Playoff Totals		**3**	**0**	**1**	**1**	**2**	**0**	**0**	**0**
KARLANDER, Al	Center								
1970	Detroit	4	0	1	1	0	0	0	0
Playoff Totals		**4**	**0**	**1**	**1**	**0**	**0**	**0**	**0**
KARLSSON, Andreas *No playoffs*	Center								
KARPA, Dave	Defense								
1993	Quebec	3	0	0	0	0	0	0	0
1997	Anaheim	8	1	1	2	20	0	0	1
1999	Carolina	2	0	0	0	2	0	0	0
Playoff Totals		**13**	**1**	**1**	**2**	**22**	**0**	**0**	**1**
KARPOV, Valeri *No playoffs*	Right wing								

Season	Club	GP	G	A	Pts	PIM	PP	SH	GW
KARPOVTSEV, Alexander	Defense								
1994◆	NY Rangers	17	0	4	4	12	0	0	0
1995	NY Rangers	8	1	0	1	0	0	0	0
1996	NY Rangers	6	0	1	1	4	0	0	0
1997	NY Rangers	13	1	3	4	20	1	0	0
1999	Toronto	14	1	3	4	12	1	0	0
Playoff Totals		**58**	**3**	**11**	**14**	**48**	**2**	**0**	**0**
KASATONOV, Alexei	Defense								
1990	New Jersey	6	0	3	3	14	0	0	0
1991	New Jersey	7	1	3	4	10	0	0	0
1992	New Jersey	7	1	1	2	12	0	0	0
1993	New Jersey	4	0	0	0	0	0	0	0
1994	St. Louis	4	2	0	2	2	0	0	0
1995	Boston	5	0	0	0	2	0	0	0
Playoff Totals		**33**	**4**	**7**	**11**	**40**	**0**	**0**	**0**
KASPARAITIS, Darius	Defense								
1993	NY Islanders	18	0	5	5	31	0	0	0
1994	NY Islanders	4	0	0	0	8	0	0	0
1997	Pittsburgh	5	0	0	0	6	0	0	0
1998	Pittsburgh	5	0	0	0	8	0	0	0
Playoff Totals		**32**	**0**	**5**	**5**	**53**	**0**	**0**	**0**
KASPER, Steve	Center								
1981	Boston	3	0	1	1	0	0	0	0
1982	Boston	11	3	6	9	22	1	0	0
1983	Boston	12	2	1	3	10	0	1	0
1984	Boston	3	0	0	0	7	0	0	0
1985	Boston	5	1	0	1	9	0	0	0
1986	Boston	3	1	0	1	4	0	1	0
1987	Boston	3	0	2	2	0	0	0	0
1988	Boston	23	7	6	13	10	0	1	0
1989	Los Angeles	11	1	5	6	10	0	0	0
1990	Los Angeles	10	1	1	2	2	0	0	0
1991	Los Angeles	10	4	6	10	8	0	1	0
Playoff Totals		**94**	**20**	**28**	**48**	**82**	**1**	**4**	**0**
KASTELIC, Ed	Right/Left wing								
1987	Washington	5	1	0	1	13	1	0	0
1988	Washington	1	0	0	0	19	0	0	0
1990	Hartford	2	0	0	0	0	0	0	0
Playoff Totals		**8**	**1**	**0**	**1**	**32**	**1**	**0**	**0**
KASZYCKI, Mike	Center								
1978	NY Islanders	7	1	3	4	4	0	0	0
1979	NY Islanders	10	1	3	4	4	0	0	0
1980	Toronto	2	0	0	0	2	0	0	0
Playoff Totals		**19**	**2**	**6**	**8**	**10**	**0**	**0**	**0**
KEA, Ed	Defense								
1976	Atlanta	2	0	0	0	7	0	0	0
1977	Atlanta	3	0	1	1	2	0	0	0
1978	Atlanta	1	0	0	0	0	0	0	0
1979	Atlanta	2	0	0	0	0	0	0	0
1980	St. Louis	3	0	0	0	2	0	0	0
1981	St. Louis	11	1	2	3	12	0	0	0
1982	St. Louis	10	1	1	2	16	0	0	0
Playoff Totals		**32**	**2**	**4**	**6**	**39**	**0**	**0**	**0**
KEANE, Mike	Right wing								
1989	Montreal	21	4	3	7	17	2	0	0
1990	Montreal	11	0	1	1	8	0	0	0
1991	Montreal	12	3	2	5	6	0	0	0
1992	Montreal	8	1	1	2	16	0	0	0
1993◆	Montreal	19	2	13	15	6	0	0	0
1994	Montreal	6	3	1	4	4	0	0	0
1996◆	Colorado	22	3	2	5	16	0	0	1
1997	Colorado	17	3	1	4	24	0	0	1
1998	Dallas	17	4	4	8	0	0	1	1
1999◆	Dallas	23	5	2	7	6	0	1	1
Playoff Totals		**156**	**28**	**30**	**58**	**103**	**2**	**2**	**4**
KEARNS, Dennis	Defense								
1975	Vancouver	4	0	0	0	4	0	0	0
1976	Vancouver	2	0	1	1	0	0	0	0
1979	Vancouver	3	1	1	2	2	1	0	0
1980	Vancouver	2	0	0	0	2	0	0	0
Playoff Totals		**11**	**1**	**2**	**3**	**8**	**1**	**0**	**0**
KEATING, Jack *No playoffs*	Left wing								
KEATING, Jack *No playoffs*	Left wing								
KEATING, Mike *No playoffs*	Left wing								
KEATS, Duke *No playoffs*	Center								
KECZMER, Dan	Defense								
1994	Calgary	3	0	0	0	4	0	0	0
1995	Calgary	7	0	1	1	2	0	0	0
1998	Dallas	2	0	0	0	2	0	0	0
Playoff Totals		**12**	**0**	**1**	**1**	**8**	**0**	**0**	**0**
KEELING, Butch	Left wing								
1929	NY Rangers	6	*3	0	*3	2	....	....	....
1930	NY Rangers	4	0	3	3	8	....	....	....
1931	NY Rangers	4	1	1	2	0	....	....	....
1932	NY Rangers	7	2	1	3	12	....	....	....
1933◆	NY Rangers	8	0	2	2	8	....	....	....
1934	NY Rangers	2	0	0	0	0	....	....	....
1935	NY Rangers	4	2	1	3	0	....	....	....
1937	NY Rangers	9	3	2	5	2	....	....	....
1938	NY Rangers	3	0	1	1	2	....	....	....
Playoff Totals		**47**	**11**	**11**	**22**	**34**	....	....	....

Season	Club	GP	G	A	Pts	PIM	PP	SH	GW
KEENAN, Larry	Left wing								
1968	St. Louis	18	4	5	9	4	1	0	2
1969	St. Louis	12	4	5	9	8	1	2	0
1970	St. Louis	16	7	6	13	0	4	2	0
Playoff Totals		**46**	**15**	**16**	**31**	**12**	**6**	**4**	**2**
KEHOE, Rick	Right wing								
1972	Toronto	2	0	0	0	2	0	0	0
1975	Pittsburgh	9	0	2	2	0	0	0	0
1976	Pittsburgh	3	0	0	0	0	0	0	0
1977	Pittsburgh	3	0	2	2	0	0	0	0
1979	Pittsburgh	7	0	2	2	0	0	0	0
1980	Pittsburgh	5	2	5	7	0	2	0	0
1981	Pittsburgh	5	0	3	3	0	0	0	0
1982	Pittsburgh	5	2	3	5	2	0	0	2
Playoff Totals		**39**	**4**	**17**	**21**	**4**	**2**	**0**	**2**
KEKALAINEN, Jarmo *No playoffs*	Left wing								
KELLER, Ralph *No playoffs*	Defense								
KELLGREN, Christer *No playoffs*	Right wing								
KELLY, Bob	Left wing								
1975	Pittsburgh	9	5	3	8	17	1	0	0
1976	Pittsburgh	3	0	0	0	2	0	0	0
1977	Pittsburgh	3	1	0	1	4	0	0	0
1978	Chicago	4	0	0	0	8	0	0	0
1979	Chicago	4	0	0	0	9	0	0	0
Playoff Totals		**23**	**6**	**3**	**9**	**40**	**1**	**0**	**0**
KELLY, Bob	Left wing								
1971	Philadelphia	4	1	0	1	2	0	0	0
1973	Philadelphia	11	0	1	1	8	0	0	0
1974◆	Philadelphia	5	0	0	0	11	0	0	0
1975◆	Philadelphia	16	3	3	6	15	0	0	1
1976	Philadelphia	16	0	2	2	44	0	0	0
1977	Philadelphia	10	0	1	1	18	0	0	0
1978	Philadelphia	12	3	5	8	26	0	0	0
1979	Philadelphia	8	1	1	2	10	1	0	0
1980	Philadelphia	19	1	1	2	38	0	0	0
Playoff Totals		**101**	**9**	**14**	**23**	**172**	**1**	**0**	**1**
KELLY, Dave *No playoffs*	Right wing								
KELLY, John Paul	Left wing								
1980	Los Angeles	3	0	0	0	2	0	0	0
1981	Los Angeles	4	0	1	1	25	0	0	0
1982	Los Angeles	10	1	0	1	14	1	0	0
1985	Los Angeles	1	0	0	0	0	0	0	0
Playoff Totals		**18**	**1**	**1**	**2**	**41**	**1**	**0**	**0**
KELLY, Pete	Right wing								
1936◆	Detroit	7	1	1	2	2	....	....	....
1937◆	Detroit	8	2	0	2	0	....	....	....
1939	Detroit	4	0	0	0	0	....	....	....
Playoff Totals		**19**	**3**	**1**	**4**	**2**	....	....	....
KELLY, Red	Defense/center								
1948	Detroit	10	3	2	5	2	....	....	....
1949	Detroit	11	1	1	2	10	....	....	....
1950◆	Detroit	14	1	3	4	2	....	....	....
1951	Detroit	6	0	1	1	0	....	....	....
1952◆	Detroit	5	1	0	1	0	....	....	....
1953	Detroit	6	0	4	4	0	....	....	....
1954◆	Detroit	12	5	1	6	0	....	....	....
1955◆	Detroit	11	2	4	6	17	....	....	....
1956	Detroit	10	2	4	6	2	....	....	....
1957	Detroit	5	1	0	1	0	....	....	....
1958	Detroit	4	0	1	1	2	....	....	....
1960	Toronto	10	3	8	11	2	....	....	....
1961	Toronto	2	1	0	1	0	....	....	....
1962◆	Toronto	12	4	6	10	0	....	....	....
1963◆	Toronto	10	2	6	8	6	....	....	....
1964◆	Toronto	14	4	9	13	4	....	....	....
1965	Toronto	6	3	2	5	2	....	....	....
1966	Toronto	4	0	2	2	0	....	....	....
1967◆	Toronto	12	0	5	5	2	....	....	....
Playoff Totals		**164**	**33**	**59**	**92**	**51**	....	....	....
KELLY, Regis	Right wing								
1935	Toronto	7	2	0	2	4	....	....	....
1936	Toronto	9	2	3	5	4	....	....	....
1938	Toronto	7	2	2	4	2	....	....	....
1939	Toronto	9	1	0	1	0	....	....	....
1940	Toronto	6	0	1	1	0	....	....	....
Playoff Totals		**38**	**7**	**6**	**13**	**10**	....	....	....
KELLY, Steve	Center								
1997	Edmonton	6	0	0	0	2	0	0	0
Playoff Totals		**6**	**0**	**0**	**0**	**2**	**0**	**0**	**0**
KEMP, Kevin *No playoffs*	Defense								
KEMP, Stan *No playoffs*	Defense								
KENADY, Chris *No playoffs*	Right wing								
KENDALL, Bill	Right wing								
1934◆	Chicago	2	0	0	0	0	0	0	0
1935	Chicago	2	0	0	0	0	0	0	0
1936	Chicago	2	0	0	0	0	0	0	0
Playoff Totals		**6**	**0**	**0**	**0**	**0**	**0**	**0**	**0**

Season	Club	GP	G	A	Pts	PIM	PP	SH	GW
KENNEDY, Dean	Defense								
1987	Los Angeles	5	0	2	2	10	0	0	0
1988	Los Angeles	4	0	1	1	10	0	0	0
1989	Los Angeles	11	0	2	2	8	0	0	0
1990	Buffalo	6	1	1	2	12	0	0	0
1991	Buffalo	2	0	1	1	17	0	0	0
1992	Winnipeg	2	0	0	0	0	0	0	0
1993	Winnipeg	6	0	0	0	2	0	0	0
Playoff Totals		**36**	**1**	**7**	**8**	**59**	**0**	**0**	**0**
KENNEDY, Forbes	Center								
1958	Detroit	4	1	0	1	12	0	0	1
1968	Philadelphia	7	1	4	5	14	0	1	0
1969	Toronto	1	0	0	0	38	0	0	0
Playoff Totals		**12**	**2**	**4**	**6**	**64**	**0**	**1**	**1**
KENNEDY, Mike	Center								
1995	Dallas	5	0	0	0	9	0	0	0
Playoff Totals		**5**	**0**	**0**	**0**	**9**	**0**	**0**	**0**
KENNEDY, Sheldon	Right wing								
1993	Detroit	7	1	1	2	2	0	0	0
1994	Detroit	7	1	2	3	0	0	0	0
1995	Calgary	7	3	1	4	16	0	1	0
1996	Calgary	3	1	0	1	2	0	0	0
Playoff Totals		**24**	**6**	**4**	**10**	**20**	**0**	**1**	**0**
KENNEDY, Ted	Center								
1944	Toronto	5	1	1	2	4	....	....	....
1945◆	Toronto	13	*7	2	9	2	....	....	....
1947◆	Toronto	11	4	5	9	4	....	....	....
1948◆	Toronto	9	*8	6	*14	0	....	....	....
1949◆	Toronto	9	2	*6	8	2	....	....	....
1950	Toronto	7	1	2	3	8	....	....	....
1951◆	Toronto	11	4	5	9	6	....	....	....
1952	Toronto	4	0	0	0	4	....	....	....
1954	Toronto	5	1	1	2	2	....	....	....
1955	Toronto	4	1	3	4	0	....	....	....
Playoff Totals		**78**	**29**	**31**	**60**	**32**	....	....	....
KENNY, Ernest *No playoffs*	Defense								
KEON, Dave	Center								
1961	Toronto	5	1	1	2	0	....	....	....
1962◆	Toronto	12	5	3	8	0	....	....	....
1963◆	Toronto	10	7	5	12	0	....	....	....
1964◆	Toronto	14	7	2	9	2	....	....	....
1965	Toronto	6	2	2	4	2	....	....	....
1966	Toronto	4	0	2	2	0	....	....	....
1967◆	Toronto	12	3	5	8	0	....	....	....
1969	Toronto	4	1	3	4	2	0	0	1
1971	Toronto	6	3	2	5	0	0	0	0
1972	Toronto	5	2	3	5	0	0	0	0
1974	Toronto	4	1	2	3	0	0	0	0
1975	Toronto	7	0	5	5	0	0	0	0
1980	Hartford	3	0	1	1	0	0	0	0
Playoff Totals		**92**	**32**	**36**	**68**	**6**	....	....	....
KERCH, Alexander *No playoffs*	Left wing								
KERR, Alan	Right wing								
1985	NY Islanders	4	1	0	1	4	1	0	0
1986	NY Islanders	1	0	0	0	0	0	0	0
1987	NY Islanders	14	1	4	5	25	0	0	0
1988	NY Islanders	6	1	0	1	14	0	0	0
1990	NY Islanders	4	0	0	0	10	0	0	0
1992	Detroit	9	2	0	2	17	0	0	0
Playoff Totals		**38**	**5**	**4**	**9**	**70**	**1**	**0**	**0**
KERR, Reg	Left wing								
1979	Chicago	4	1	0	1	5	0	0	0
1981	Chicago	3	0	0	0	2	0	0	0
Playoff Totals		**7**	**1**	**0**	**1**	**7**	**0**	**0**	**0**
KERR, Tim	Center/Right wing								
1981	Philadelphia	10	1	3	4	2	1	0	0
1982	Philadelphia	4	0	2	2	2	0	0	0
1983	Philadelphia	2	2	0	2	0	0	0	0
1984	Philadelphia	3	0	0	0	0	0	0	0
1985	Philadelphia	12	10	4	14	13	4	0	1
1986	Philadelphia	5	3	3	6	8	1	0	0
1987	Philadelphia	12	8	5	13	2	5	0	3
1988	Philadelphia	6	1	3	4	4	1	0	0
1989	Philadelphia	19	14	11	25	27	8	0	2
1992	NY Rangers	8	1	0	1	0	1	0	0
Playoff Totals		**81**	**40**	**31**	**71**	**58**	**21**	**0**	**6**
KESA, Dan	Right wing								
1999	Pittsburgh	13	1	0	1	0	1	0	1
Playoff Totals		**13**	**1**	**0**	**1**	**0**	**1**	**0**	**1**
KESSELL, Rick *No playoffs*	Center								
KETOLA, Veli-Pekka *No playoffs*	Center								
KETTER, Kerry *No playoffs*	Defense								
KHARIN, Sergei *No playoffs*	Right wing								
KHMYLEV, Yuri	Left wing								
1993	Buffalo	8	4	3	7	4	1	0	1
1994	Buffalo	7	3	1	4	8	0	0	0
1995	Buffalo	5	0	1	1	8	0	0	0
1996	St. Louis	6	1	1	2	4	0	0	1
Playoff Totals		**26**	**8**	**6**	**14**	**24**	**1**	**0**	**2**

Season	Club	GP	G	A	Pts	PIM	PP	SH	GW
KHRISTICH, Dmitri	Left wing/Center								
1991	Washington	11	1	3	4	6	0	0	0
1992	Washington	7	3	2	5	15	3	0	1
1993	Washington	6	2	5	7	2	1	0	0
1994	Washington	11	2	3	5	10	0	0	0
1995	Washington	7	1	4	5	0	0	0	0
1998	Boston	6	2	2	4	2	2	0	0
1999	Boston	12	3	4	7	6	0	0	1
Playoff Totals		**60**	**14**	**23**	**37**	**41**	**6**	**0**	**2**
KIDD, Ian *No playoffs*	Defense								
KIESSLING, Udo *No playoffs*	Defense								
KILGER, Chad	Center								
1996	Winnipeg	4	1	0	1	0	0	0	1
1999	Edmonton	4	0	0	0	4	0	0	0
Playoff Totals		**8**	**1**	**0**	**1**	**4**	**0**	**0**	**1**
KILREA, Brian *No playoffs*	Center								
KILREA, Hec	Left wing								
1926	Ottawa	2	0	0	0	0	....	....	....
1927♦	Ottawa	6	1	1	2	4	....	....	....
1928	Ottawa	2	1	0	1	0	....	....	....
1930	Ottawa	2	0	0	0	4	....	....	....
1932	Detroit	2	0	0	0	0	....	....	....
1934	Toronto	5	2	0	2	2	....	....	....
1935	Toronto	6	0	0	0	4	....	....	....
1936♦	Detroit	7	0	3	3	2	....	....	....
1937♦	Detroit	10	3	1	4	2	....	....	....
1939	Detroit	6	1	2	3	0	....	....	....
Playoff Totals		**48**	**8**	**7**	**15**	**18**	....	....	....
KILREA, Ken	Left wing								
1939	Detroit	3	1	1	2	4	....	....	....
1940	Detroit	5	1	1	2	0	....	....	....
1941	Detroit	5	0	0	0	0	....	....	....
1944	Detroit	2	0	0	0	0	....	....	....
Playoff Totals		**15**	**2**	**2**	**4**	**4**	....	....	....
KILREA, Wally	Right wing/center								
1930	Ottawa	2	0	0	0	0	....	....	....
1933	Mtl. Maroons	2	0	0	0	0	....	....	....
1934	Mtl. Maroons	4	0	0	0	0	....	....	....
1936♦	Detroit	7	2	2	4	2	....	....	....
1937♦	Detroit	10	0	2	2	4	....	....	....
Playoff Totals		**25**	**2**	**4**	**6**	**6**	....	....	....
KIMBLE, Darin	Right wing								
1991	St. Louis	13	0	0	0	38	0	0	0
1992	St. Louis	5	0	0	0	7	0	0	0
1993	Boston	4	0	0	0	2	0	0	0
1994	Chicago	1	0	0	0	5	0	0	0
Playoff Totals		**23**	**0**	**0**	**0**	**52**	**0**	**0**	**0**
KINDRACHUK, Orest	Center								
1974♦	Philadelphia	17	5	4	9	17	0	0	0
1975♦	Philadelphia	14	0	2	2	12	0	0	0
1976	Philadelphia	16	4	7	11	4	1	0	2
1977	Philadelphia	10	2	1	3	0	1	0	0
1978	Philadelphia	12	5	5	10	13	2	0	1
1979	Pittsburgh	7	4	1	5	7	0	0	1
Playoff Totals		**76**	**20**	**20**	**40**	**53**	**4**	**0**	**4**
KING, Derek	Left wing								
1988	NY Islanders	5	0	2	2	2	0	0	0
1990	NY Islanders	4	0	0	0	4	0	0	0
1993	NY Islanders	18	3	11	14	14	0	0	0
1994	NY Islanders	4	0	1	1	0	0	0	0
1999	Toronto	16	1	3	4	4	0	0	0
Playoff Totals		**47**	**4**	**17**	**21**	**24**	**0**	**0**	**0**
KING, Frank *No playoffs*	Center								
KING, Kris	Left wing								
1989	Detroit	2	0	0	0	2	0	0	0
1990	NY Rangers	10	0	1	1	38	0	0	0
1991	NY Rangers	6	2	0	2	36	0	0	1
1992	NY Rangers	13	4	1	5	14	0	0	3
1993	Winnipeg	6	1	1	2	4	0	0	0
1996	Winnipeg	5	0	1	1	4	0	0	0
1997	Phoenix	7	0	0	0	17	0	0	0
1999	Toronto	17	1	1	2	25	0	0	0
Playoff Totals		**66**	**8**	**5**	**13**	**140**	**0**	**0**	**4**
KING, Steven *No playoffs*	Right wing								
KING, Wayne *No playoffs*	Center								
KINSELLA, Brian *No playoffs*	Center								
KINSELLA, Ray *No playoffs*	Left wing								
KIPRUSOFF, Marko *No playoffs*	Defense								
KIRK, Bobby *No playoffs*	Right wing								
KIRKPATRICK, Bob *No playoffs*	Center								
KIRTON, Mark	Center								
1983	Vancouver	4	1	2	3	7	0	0	0
Playoff Totals		**4**	**1**	**2**	**3**	**7**	**0**	**0**	**0**

Season	Club	GP	G	A	Pts	PIM	PP	SH	GW
KISIO, Kelly	Center								
1984	Detroit	4	1	0	1	4	0	0	0
1985	Detroit	3	0	2	2	2	0	0	0
1987	NY Rangers	4	0	1	1	2	0	0	0
1989	NY Rangers	4	0	0	0	9	0	0	0
1990	NY Rangers	10	2	8	10	8	0	1	0
1994	Calgary	7	0	2	2	8	0	0	0
1995	Calgary	7	3	2	5	19	1	0	0
Playoff Totals		**39**	**6**	**15**	**21**	**52**	**1**	**1**	**0**
KITCHEN, Bill	Defense								
1982	Montreal	3	0	1	1	0	0	0	0
Playoff Totals		**3**	**0**	**1**	**1**	**0**	**0**	**0**	**0**
KITCHEN, Hobie *No playoffs*	Defense								
KITCHEN, Mike	Defense								
1978	Colorado	2	0	0	0	2	0	0	0
Playoff Totals		**2**	**0**	**0**	**0**	**2**	**0**	**0**	**0**
KJELLBERG, Patrik *No playoffs*	Left wing								
KLASSEN, Ralph	Center								
1978	Colorado	2	0	0	0	0	0	0	0
1980	St. Louis	3	0	0	0	0	0	0	0
1981	St. Louis	11	2	0	2	2	0	0	0
1982	St. Louis	10	2	2	4	10	0	0	0
Playoff Totals		**26**	**4**	**2**	**6**	**12**	**0**	**0**	**0**
KLATT, Trent	Right wing								
1992	Minnesota	6	0	0	0	2	0	0	0
1994	Dallas	9	2	1	3	4	1	0	0
1995	Dallas	5	1	0	1	0	1	0	0
1996	Philadelphia	12	4	1	5	0	0	0	0
1997	Philadelphia	19	4	3	7	12	0	0	2
1998	Philadelphia	5	0	0	0	0	0	0	0
Playoff Totals		**56**	**11**	**5**	**16**	**18**	**2**	**0**	**2**
KLEE, Ken	Right wing								
1995	Washington	7	0	0	0	4	0	0	0
1996	Washington	1	0	0	0	0	0	0	0
1998	Washington	9	1	0	1	10	0	0	0
Playoff Totals		**17**	**1**	**0**	**1**	**14**	**0**	**0**	**0**
KLEIN, Lloyd	Left wing								
1936	NY Americans	5	0	0	0	2	0	0	0
Playoff Totals		**5**	**0**	**0**	**0**	**2**	**0**	**0**	**0**
KLEINENDORST, Scot	Defense								
1983	NY Rangers	6	0	2	2	2	0	0	0
1986	Hartford	10	0	1	1	18	0	0	0
1987	Hartford	4	1	3	4	20	0	0	0
1988	Hartford	3	1	1	2	0	0	0	0
1990	Washington	3	0	0	0	0	0	0	0
Playoff Totals		**26**	**2**	**7**	**9**	**40**	**0**	**0**	**0**
KLEMM, Jon	Defense								
1996♦	Colorado	15	2	1	3	0	1	0	0
1997	Colorado	17	1	1	2	6	0	0	0
1998	Colorado	4	0	0	0	0	0	0	0
1999	Colorado	19	0	1	1	10	0	0	0
Playoff Totals		**55**	**3**	**3**	**6**	**16**	**1**	**0**	**0**
KLIMA, Petr	Right/Left wing								
1987	Detroit	13	1	2	3	4	0	0	0
1988	Detroit	12	10	8	18	10	2	1	4
1989	Detroit	6	2	4	6	19	1	0	0
1990♦	Edmonton	21	5	0	5	8	1	0	1
1991	Edmonton	18	7	6	13	16	1	0	3
1992	Edmonton	15	1	4	5	8	0	0	0
1996	Tampa Bay	4	2	0	2	14	2	0	0
1997	Edmonton	6	0	0	0	4	0	0	0
Playoff Totals		**95**	**28**	**24**	**52**	**83**	**7**	**1**	**8**
KLIMOVICH, Sergei *No playoffs*	Center								
KLINGBEIL, Ike *No playoffs*	Defense								
KLUKAY, Joe	Left wing								
1943	Toronto	1	0	0	0	0	....	....	....
1947♦	Toronto	11	1	0	1	0	....	....	....
1948♦	Toronto	9	1	1	2	2	....	....	....
1949♦	Toronto	9	2	3	5	4	....	....	....
1950	Toronto	7	3	0	3	4	....	....	....
1951♦	Toronto	11	4	3	7	0	....	....	....
1952	Toronto	4	1	1	2	0	....	....	....
1953	Boston	11	1	2	3	9	....	....	....
1954	Boston	4	0	0	0	0	....	....	....
1955	Toronto	4	0	0	0	4	....	....	....
Playoff Totals		**71**	**13**	**10**	**23**	**23**	....	....	....
KLUZAK, Gord	Defense								
1983	Boston	17	1	4	5	54	0	0	0
1984	Boston	3	0	0	0	0	0	0	0
1986	Boston	3	1	1	2	16	1	0	0
1988	Boston	23	4	8	12	59	0	1	1
Playoff Totals		**46**	**6**	**13**	**19**	**129**	**1**	**1**	**1**
KNIBBS, Bill *No playoffs*	Center								
KNIPSCHEER, Fred	Center								
1994	Boston	12	2	1	3	6	0	0	1
1995	Boston	4	0	0	0	0	0	0	0
Playoff Totals		**16**	**2**	**1**	**3**	**6**	**0**	**0**	**1**
KNOTT, Nick *No playoffs*	Defense								
KNOX, Paul *No playoffs*	Right wing								

Season	Club	GP	G	A	Pts	PIM	PP	SH	GW
KNUBLE, Mike	Right wing								
1998♦	Detroit	3	0	1	1	0	0	0	0
Playoff Totals		**3**	**0**	**1**	**1**	**0**	**0**	**0**	**0**
KNUTSEN, Espen *No playoffs*	Center								
KOCUR, Joe	Right wing								
1985	Detroit	3	1	0	1	5	0	0	0
1987	Detroit	16	2	3	5	71	1	0	2
1988	Detroit	10	0	1	1	13	0	0	0
1989	Detroit	3	0	1	1	6	0	0	0
1991	NY Rangers	6	0	2	2	21	0	0	0
1992	NY Rangers	12	1	1	2	38	0	0	0
1994♦	NY Rangers	20	1	1	2	17	0	0	0
1995	NY Rangers	10	0	0	0	8	0	0	0
1996	Vancouver	1	0	0	0	0	0	0	0
1997♦	Detroit	19	1	3	4	22	0	0	0
1998♦	Detroit	18	4	0	4	30	0	0	0
Playoff Totals		**118**	**10**	**12**	**22**	**231**	**1**	**0**	**2**
KOHN, Ladislav	Right wing								
1999	Toronto	2	0	0	0	5	0	0	0
Playoff Totals		**2**	**0**	**0**	**0**	**5**	**0**	**0**	**0**
KOIVU, Saku	Center								
1996	Montreal	6	3	1	4	8	0	0	0
1997	Montreal	5	1	3	4	10	0	0	0
1998	Montreal	6	2	3	5	2	1	0	0
Playoff Totals		**17**	**6**	**7**	**13**	**20**	**1**	**0**	**0**
KOLESAR, Mark	Left wing								
1996	Toronto	3	1	0	1	2	0	1	0
Playoff Totals		**3**	**1**	**0**	**1**	**2**	**0**	**1**	**0**
KOLSTAD, Dean *No playoffs*	Defense								
KOMADOSKI, Neil	Defense								
1974	Los Angeles	2	0	0	0	12	0	0	0
1975	Los Angeles	3	0	0	0	2	0	0	0
1976	Los Angeles	9	0	0	0	18	0	0	0
1977	Los Angeles	9	0	2	2	15	0	0	0
Playoff Totals		**23**	**0**	**2**	**2**	**47**	**0**	**0**	**0**
KOMARNISKI, Zenith *No playoffs*	Defense								
KONIK, George *No playoffs*	Defense/left wing								
KONOWALCHUK, Steve	Center								
1993	Washington	2	0	1	1	0	0	0	0
1994	Washington	11	0	1	1	10	0	0	0
1995	Washington	7	2	5	7	12	0	1	0
1996	Washington	2	0	2	2	0	0	0	0
Playoff Totals		**22**	**2**	**9**	**11**	**22**	**0**	**1**	**0**
KONROYD, Steve	Defense								
1982	Calgary	3	0	0	0	12	0	0	0
1983	Calgary	9	2	1	3	18	0	0	0
1984	Calgary	8	1	2	3	8	0	0	0
1985	Calgary	4	1	4	5	2	0	1	0
1986	NY Islanders	3	0	0	0	6	0	0	0
1987	NY Islanders	14	1	4	5	10	0	0	0
1988	NY Islanders	6	1	0	1	4	0	1	0
1989	Chicago	16	2	0	2	10	0	0	0
1990	Chicago	20	1	3	4	19	0	0	0
1991	Chicago	6	1	0	1	8	0	0	0
1992	Hartford	7	0	1	1	2	0	0	0
1993	Detroit	1	0	0	0	0	0	0	0
Playoff Totals		**97**	**10**	**15**	**25**	**99**	**0**	**3**	**0**
KONSTANTINOV, Vladimir	Defense								
1992	Detroit	11	0	1	1	16	0	0	0
1993	Detroit	7	0	1	1	8	0	0	0
1994	Detroit	7	0	2	2	4	0	0	0
1995	Detroit	18	1	1	2	22	0	0	1
1996	Detroit	19	4	5	9	28	0	1	0
1997♦	Detroit	20	0	4	4	29	0	0	0
Playoff Totals		**82**	**5**	**14**	**19**	**107**	**0**	**1**	**1**
KONTOS, Chris	Left wing/Center								
1988	Los Angeles	4	1	0	1	4	0	0	0
1989	Los Angeles	11	9	0	9	8	6	0	1
1990	Los Angeles	5	1	0	1	0	0	1	0
Playoff Totals		**20**	**11**	**0**	**11**	**12**	**6**	**1**	**1**
KOPAK, Russ *No playoffs*	Center								
KORAB, Jerry	Defense								
1971	Chicago	7	1	0	1	20	0	0	0
1972	Chicago	8	0	1	1	20	0	0	0
1973	Chicago	15	0	0	0	22	0	0	0
1975	Buffalo	16	3	2	5	32	1	0	0
1976	Buffalo	9	1	3	4	12	0	0	0
1977	Buffalo	6	2	4	6	8	1	0	1
1978	Buffalo	8	0	5	5	6	0	0	0
1979	Buffalo	3	1	0	1	4	0	0	0
1980	Los Angeles	3	0	1	1	11	0	0	0
1981	Los Angeles	4	0	0	0	33	0	0	0
1982	Los Angeles	10	0	2	2	26	0	0	0
1984	Buffalo	3	0	0	0	5	0	0	0
1985	Buffalo	1	0	0	0	2	0	0	0
Playoff Totals		**93**	**8**	**18**	**26**	**201**	**2**	**0**	**1**
KORDIC, Dan	Left wing								
1997	Philadelphia	12	1	0	1	22	0	0	0
Playoff Totals		**12**	**1**	**0**	**1**	**22**	**0**	**0**	**0**

Season	Club	GP	G	A	Pts	PIM	PP	SH	GW
KORDIC, John									Right wing
1986◆	Montreal	18	0	0	0	53	0	0	0
1987	Montreal	11	2	0	2	19	0	0	1
1988	Montreal	7	2	2	4	26	0	0	0
1990	Toronto	5	0	1	1	33	0	0	0
Playoff Totals		**41**	**4**	**3**	**7**	**131**	**0**	**0**	**1**
KORN, Jim									Defense
1983	Toronto	3	0	0	0	26	0	0	0
1988	New Jersey	9	0	2	2	71	0	0	0
1990	Calgary	4	1	0	1	12	0	0	0
Playoff Totals		**16**	**1**	**2**	**3**	**109**	**0**	**0**	**0**
KORNEY, Mike	*No playoffs*								Right wing
KOROLEV, Evgeny	*No playoffs*								Defense
KOROLEV, Igor									Center/left wing
1993	St. Louis	3	0	0	0	0	0	0	0
1994	St. Louis	2	0	0	0	0	0	0	0
1996	Winnipeg	6	0	3	3	0	0	0	0
1997	Phoenix	1	0	0	0	0	0	0	0
1999	Toronto	1	0	0	0	0	0	0	0
Playoff Totals		**13**	**0**	**3**	**3**	**0**	**0**	**0**	**0**
KOROLL, Cliff									Right wing
1970	Chicago	8	1	4	5	9	0	0	0
1971	Chicago	18	7	9	16	18	3	0	1
1972	Chicago	8	0	0	0	11	0	0	0
1973	Chicago	16	4	6	10	6	0	0	0
1974	Chicago	11	2	5	7	13	1	0	0
1975	Chicago	8	3	5	8	8	2	0	0
1976	Chicago	4	1	0	1	0	1	0	0
1977	Chicago	2	0	0	0	0	0	0	0
1978	Chicago	4	1	0	1	0	0	0	0
1979	Chicago	4	0	0	0	0	0	0	0
1980	Chicago	2	0	0	0	2	0	0	0
Playoff Totals		**85**	**19**	**29**	**48**	**67**	**7**	**0**	**1**
KOROLYUK, Alexander									Right wing
1999	San Jose	6	1	3	4	2	0	0	1
Playoff Totals		**6**	**1**	**3**	**4**	**2**	**0**	**0**	**1**
KORTKO, Roger									Center
1985	NY Islanders	10	0	3	3	17	0	0	0
Playoff Totals		**10**	**0**	**3**	**3**	**17**	**0**	**0**	**0**
KOSTYNSKI, Doug	*No playoffs*								Center
KOTANEN, Dick	*No playoffs*								Defense
KOTSOPOULOS, Chris									Defense
1981	NY Rangers	14	0	3	3	63	0	0	0
1986	Toronto	10	1	0	1	14	0	0	0
1987	Toronto	7	0	0	0	14	0	0	0
Playoff Totals		**31**	**1**	**3**	**4**	**91**	**0**	**0**	**0**
KOVALENKO, Andrei									Right wing
1993	Quebec	4	1	0	1	2	0	0	0
1995	Quebec	6	0	1	1	2	0	0	0
1996	Montreal	6	0	0	0	6	0	0	0
1997	Edmonton	12	4	3	7	6	3	0	0
1998	Edmonton	1	0	0	0	2	0	0	0
1999	Carolina	4	0	2	2	2	0	0	0
Playoff Totals		**33**	**5**	**6**	**11**	**20**	**3**	**0**	**0**
KOVALEV, Alexei									Right wing
1994◆	NY Rangers	23	9	12	21	18	5	0	2
1995	NY Rangers	10	4	7	11	10	0	0	0
1996	NY Rangers	11	3	4	7	14	0	0	1
1999	Pittsburgh	10	5	7	12	14	0	0	1
Playoff Totals		**54**	**21**	**30**	**51**	**56**	**5**	**0**	**4**
KOWAL, Joe									Left wing
1978	Buffalo	2	0	0	0	0	0	0	0
Playoff Totals		**2**	**0**	**0**	**0**	**0**	**0**	**0**	**0**
KOZAK, Don									Right wing
1974	Los Angeles	5	0	0	0	33	0	0	0
1975	Los Angeles	3	1	1	2	7	0	0	0
1976	Los Angeles	9	1	0	1	12	0	0	1
1977	Los Angeles	9	4	1	5	17	1	0	0
1979	Vancouver	3	1	0	1	0	0	0	0
Playoff Totals		**29**	**7**	**2**	**9**	**69**	**1**	**0**	**1**
KOZAK, Les	*No playoffs*								Left wing
KOZLOV, Viktor	*No playoffs*								Center
KOZLOV, Vyacheslav									Center
1993	Detroit	4	0	2	2	2	0	0	0
1994	Detroit	7	2	5	7	12	0	0	0
1995	Detroit	18	9	7	16	10	1	0	4
1996	Detroit	19	5	7	12	10	2	0	1
1997◆	Detroit	20	8	5	13	14	4	0	2
1998◆	Detroit	22	6	8	14	10	1	0	4
1999	Detroit	10	6	1	7	4	3	0	0
Playoff Totals		**100**	**36**	**35**	**71**	**62**	**11**	**0**	**11**
KRAFTCHECK, Stephen									Defense
1951	Boston	6	0	0	0	7	0	0	0
Playoff Totals		**6**	**0**	**0**	**0**	**7**	**0**	**0**	**0**
KRAKE, Skip									Center
1968	Boston	4	0	0	0	2	0	0	0
1969	Los Angeles	6	1	0	1	15	0	0	0
Playoff Totals		**10**	**1**	**0**	**1**	**17**	**0**	**0**	**0**

Season	Club	GP	G	A	Pts	PIM	PP	SH	GW
KRAVCHUK, Igor									Defense
1992	Chicago	18	2	6	8	8	1	0	0
1996	St. Louis	10	1	5	6	4	0	0	1
1997	St. Louis	2	0	0	0	2	0	0	0
1998	Ottawa	11	2	3	5	4	0	0	0
1999	Ottawa	4	0	0	0	0	0	0	0
Playoff Totals		**45**	**5**	**14**	**19**	**18**	**1**	**0**	**1**
KRAVETS, Mikhail	*No playoffs*								Right wing
KRENTZ, Dale									Left wing
1988	Detroit	2	0	0	0	0	0	0	0
Playoff Totals		**2**	**0**	**0**	**0**	**0**	**0**	**0**	**0**
KRIVOKRASOV, Sergei									Right wing
1995	Chicago	10	0	0	0	8	0	0	0
1996	Chicago	5	1	0	1	2	0	0	1
1997	Chicago	6	1	0	1	4	0	0	0
Playoff Totals		**21**	**2**	**0**	**2**	**14**	**0**	**0**	**1**
KROG, Jason	*No playoffs*								Center
KROL, Joe	*No playoffs*								Left wing
KROMM, Rich									Left wing
1984	Calgary	11	1	1	2	9	0	0	0
1985	Calgary	3	0	1	1	4	0	0	0
1986	NY Islanders	3	0	1	1	0	0	0	0
1987	NY Islanders	14	1	3	4	4	0	0	0
1988	NY Islanders	5	0	0	0	5	0	0	0
Playoff Totals		**36**	**2**	**6**	**8**	**22**	**0**	**0**	**0**
KRON, Robert									Left wing
1992	Vancouver	11	1	2	3	2	0	1	0
1999	Carolina	5	2	0	2	0	0	0	1
Playoff Totals		**16**	**3**	**2**	**5**	**2**	**0**	**1**	**1**
KROOK, Kevin	*No playoffs*								Defense
KROUPA, Vlastimil									Defense
1994	San Jose	14	1	2	3	21	0	0	1
1995	San Jose	6	0	0	0	4	0	0	0
Playoff Totals		**20**	**1**	**2**	**3**	**25**	**0**	**0**	**1**
KRULICKI, Jim	*No playoffs*								Left wing
KRUPP, Uwe									Defense
1988	Buffalo	6	0	0	0	15	0	0	0
1989	Buffalo	5	0	1	1	4	0	0	0
1990	Buffalo	6	0	0	0	4	0	0	0
1991	Buffalo	6	1	1	2	6	1	0	0
1993	NY Islanders	18	1	5	6	12	0	0	0
1994	NY Islanders	4	0	1	1	4	0	0	0
1995	Quebec	5	0	2	2	2	0	0	0
1996◆	Colorado	22	4	12	16	33	1	0	2
1998	Colorado	7	0	1	1	4	0	0	0
Playoff Totals		**79**	**6**	**23**	**29**	**84**	**2**	**0**	**2**
KRUPPKE, Gord	*No playoffs*								Defense
KRUSE, Paul									Left wing
1994	Calgary	7	0	0	0	14	0	0	0
1995	Calgary	7	4	2	6	10	0	1	0
1996	Calgary	3	0	0	0	4	0	0	0
1998	Buffalo	1	1	0	1	4	0	0	0
1999	Buffalo	10	0	0	0	4	0	0	0
Playoff Totals		**28**	**5**	**2**	**7**	**36**	**0**	**1**	**0**
KRUSHELNYSKI, Mike									Left wing/Center
1982	Boston	1	0	0	0	2	0	0	0
1983	Boston	17	8	6	14	12	2	0	0
1984	Boston	2	0	0	0	0	0	0	0
1985◆	Edmonton	18	5	8	13	22	2	0	2
1986	Edmonton	10	4	5	9	16	1	0	2
1987◆	Edmonton	21	3	4	7	18	0	0	1
1988◆	Edmonton	19	4	6	10	12	0	0	0
1989	Los Angeles	11	1	4	5	4	1	0	0
1990	Los Angeles	10	1	3	4	12	0	0	1
1993	Toronto	16	3	7	10	8	1	0	0
1994	Toronto	6	0	0	0	0	0	0	0
1995	Detroit	8	0	0	0	0	0	0	0
Playoff Totals		**139**	**29**	**43**	**72**	**106**	**7**	**0**	**6**
KRUTOV, Vladimir	*No playoffs*								Left wing
KRYGIER, Todd									Left wing
1990	Hartford	7	2	1	3	4	0	0	0
1991	Hartford	6	0	2	2	0	0	0	0
1992	Washington	5	2	1	3	4	0	0	0
1993	Washington	6	1	1	2	4	0	1	0
1994	Washington	5	2	0	2	10	0	0	0
1996	Washington	6	2	0	2	12	0	0	1
1998	Washington	13	1	2	3	6	0	0	1
Playoff Totals		**48**	**10**	**7**	**17**	**40**	**0**	**1**	**2**
KRYSKOW, Dave									Left wing
1973	Chicago	3	2	0	2	0	0	0	0
1974	Chicago	7	0	0	0	2	0	0	0
1976	Atlanta	2	0	0	0	2	0	0	0
Playoff Totals		**12**	**2**	**0**	**2**	**4**	**0**	**0**	**0**
KRYZNOWSKI, Ed									Defense
1949	Boston	5	0	1	1	2	0	0	0
1951	Boston	6	0	0	0	2	0	0	0
1952	Boston	7	0	0	0	0	0	0	0
Playoff Totals		**18**	**0**	**1**	**1**	**4**	**0**	**0**	**0**
KUBA, Filip	*No playoffs*								Defense

Season	Club	GP	G	A	Pts	PIM	PP	SH	GW
KUBINA, Pavel	*No playoffs*								Defense
KUCERA, Frantisek									Defense
1992	Chicago	6	0	0	0	0	0	0	0
1996	Vancouver	6	0	1	1	0	0	0	0
Playoff Totals		**12**	**0**	**1**	**1**	**0**	**0**	**0**	**0**
KUDASHOV, Alexei	*No playoffs*								Center
KUDELSKI, Bob									Right wing
1990	Los Angeles	8	1	2	3	2	0	0	0
1991	Los Angeles	8	3	2	5	2	0	0	0
1992	Los Angeles	6	0	0	0	0	0	0	0
Playoff Totals		**22**	**4**	**4**	**8**	**4**	**0**	**0**	**0**
KUHN, Gord	*No playoffs*								Right wing
KUKULOWICZ, Aggie	*No playoffs*								Center
KULAK, Stu									Right wing
1987	NY Rangers	3	0	0	0	2	0	0	0
Playoff Totals		**3**	**0**	**0**	**0**	**2**	**0**	**0**	**0**
KULLMAN, Arnie	*No playoffs*								Center
KULLMAN, Eddie									Right wing
1948	NY Rangers	6	1	0	1	2	....	....	....
Playoff Totals		**6**	**1**	**0**	**1**	**2**	....	....	....
KUMPEL, Mark									Right wing
1985	Quebec	18	3	4	7	4	0	0	1
1986	Quebec	2	1	0	1	0	0	0	0
1987	Detroit	8	0	0	0	4	0	0	0
1988	Winnipeg	4	0	0	0	4	0	0	0
1990	Winnipeg	7	2	0	2	2	0	0	0
Playoff Totals		**39**	**6**	**4**	**10**	**14**	**0**	**0**	**1**
KUNTZ, Alan									Left wing
1942	NY Rangers	6	1	0	1	2	....	....	....
Playoff Totals		**6**	**1**	**0**	**1**	**2**	....	....	....
KUNTZ, Murray	*No playoffs*								Left wing
KURRI, Jari									Right wing
1981	Edmonton	9	5	7	12	4	0	0	0
1982	Edmonton	5	2	5	7	10	0	0	0
1983	Edmonton	16	8	15	23	8	2	2	0
1984◆	Edmonton	19	*14	14	28	13	4	0	0
1985◆	Edmonton	18	*19	12	31	6	1	2	2
1986	Edmonton	10	2	10	12	4	0	1	0
1987◆	Edmonton	21	*15	10	25	20	4	1	5
1988◆	Edmonton	19	*14	17	31	12	5	0	3
1989	Edmonton	7	3	5	8	6	0	1	0
1990◆	Edmonton	22	10	15	25	18	6	0	3
1992	Los Angeles	4	1	2	3	4	1	0	0
1993	Los Angeles	24	9	8	17	12	2	2	0
1996	NY Rangers	11	3	5	8	2	0	1	1
1997	Anaheim	11	1	2	3	4	0	0	0
1998	Colorado	4	0	0	0	0	0	0	0
Playoff Totals		**200**	**106**	**127**	**233**	**123**	**25**	**10**	**14**
KURTENBACH, Orland									Center
1966	Toronto	4	0	0	0	20	0	0	0
1967	NY Rangers	3	0	2	2	0	0	0	0
1968	NY Rangers	6	1	0	1	26	0	0	0
1970	NY Rangers	6	1	2	3	24	0	0	0
Playoff Totals		**19**	**2**	**4**	**6**	**70**	**0**	**0**	**0**
KURVERS, Tom									Defense
1985	Montreal	12	0	6	6	6	0	0	0
1988	New Jersey	19	6	9	15	38	3	0	1
1990	Toronto	5	0	3	3	4	0	0	0
1991	Vancouver	6	2	2	4	12	1	0	0
1993	NY Islanders	12	0	2	2	6	0	0	0
1994	NY Islanders	3	0	0	0	2	0	0	0
Playoff Totals		**57**	**8**	**22**	**30**	**68**	**4**	**0**	**1**
KURYLUK, Merv									Left wing
1962	Chicago	2	0	0	0	0	0	0	0
Playoff Totals		**2**	**0**	**0**	**0**	**0**	**0**	**0**	**0**
KUSHNER, Dale	*No playoffs*								Right wing
KUZYK, Ken	*No playoffs*								Right wing
KVARTALNOV, Dmitri									Left wing
1993	Boston	4	0	0	0	0	0	0	0
Playoff Totals		**4**	**0**	**0**	**0**	**0**	**0**	**0**	**0**
KVASHA, Oleg	*No playoffs*								Left wing
KWONG, Larry	*No playoffs*								Right wing
KYLE, Bill	*No playoffs*								Center
KYLE, Gus									Defense
1950	NY Rangers	12	1	2	3	30	....	....	....
1952	Boston	2	0	0	0	4	....	....	....
Playoff Totals		**14**	**1**	**2**	**3**	**34**	....	....	....
KYLLONEN, Markku	*No playoffs*								Left wing
KYPREOS, Nick									Left wing
1990	Washington	7	1	0	1	15	0	0	0
1991	Washington	9	0	1	1	38	0	0	0
1994◆	NY Rangers	3	0	0	0	2	0	0	0
1995	NY Rangers	10	0	2	2	6	0	0	0
1996	Toronto	5	0	0	0	4	0	0	0
Playoff Totals		**34**	**1**	**3**	**4**	**65**	**0**	**0**	**0**

Season	Club	GP	G	A	Pts	PIM	PP	SH	GW
KYTE, Jim									Defense
1984	Winnipeg	3	0	0	0	11	0	0	0
1985	Winnipeg	8	0	0	0	14	0	0	0
1986	Winnipeg	3	0	0	0	12	0	0	0
1987	Winnipeg	10	0	4	4	36	0	0	0
1991	Calgary	7	0	0	0	7	0	0	0
1995	San Jose	11	0	2	2	14	0	0	0
Playoff Totals		**42**	**0**	**6**	**6**	**94**	**0**	**0**	**0**
LAAKSONEN, Antti	*No playoffs*								Left wing
LABADIE, Mike	*No playoffs*								Right wing
LABATTE, Neil	*No playoffs*								Center/defense
L'ABBE, Moe	*No playoffs*								Right wing
LABELLE, Marc	*No playoffs*								Left wing
LABINE, Leo									Right wing
1952	Boston	5	0	1	1	4	....	....	....
1953	Boston	7	2	1	3	*19	....	....	....
1954	Boston	4	0	1	1	8	....	....	....
1955	Boston	5	2	1	3	11	....	....	....
1957	Boston	10	2	3	5	*14	....	....	....
1958	Boston	11	0	2	2	10	....	....	....
1959	Boston	7	2	1	3	12	....	....	....
1961	Detroit	11	3	2	5	4	....	....	....
Playoff Totals		**60**	**11**	**12**	**23**	**82**	....	....	....
LABOSSIERRE, Gord									Center
1968	Los Angeles	7	2	3	5	24	0	0	0
1971	Minnesota	3	0	0	0	4	0	0	0
Playoff Totals		**10**	**2**	**3**	**5**	**28**	**0**	**0**	**0**
LABOVITCH, Max	*No playoffs*								Right wing
LABRAATEN, Daniel									Left wing
1981	Calgary	5	1	0	1	4	1	0	1
1982	Calgary	3	0	0	0	0	0	0	0
Playoff Totals		**8**	**1**	**0**	**1**	**4**	**1**	**0**	**1**
LABRE, Yvon	*No playoffs*								Defense
LABRIE, Guy	*No playoffs*								Defense
LACH, Elmer									Center
1941	Montreal	3	1	0	1	0	....	....	....
1943	Montreal	5	2	4	6	6	....	....	....
1944◆	Montreal	9	2	*11	13	4	....	....	....
1945	Montreal	6	4	4	8	2	....	....	....
1946◆	Montreal	9	5	*12	*17	4	....	....	....
1949	Montreal	1	0	0	0	4	....	....	....
1950	Montreal	5	1	2	3	4	....	....	....
1951	Montreal	11	2	2	4	2	....	....	....
1952	Montreal	11	1	2	3	4	....	....	....
1953◆	Montreal	12	1	6	7	6	....	....	....
1954	Montreal	4	0	2	2	0	....	....	....
Playoff Totals		**76**	**19**	**45**	**64**	**36**	....	....	....
LACHANCE, Michel	*No playoffs*								Defense
LACHANCE, Scott									Defense
1994	NY Islanders	3	0	0	0	0	0	0	0
Playoff Totals		**3**	**0**	**0**	**0**	**0**	**0**	**0**	**0**
LACOMBE, Francois									Defense
1969	Oakland	3	1	0	1	0	0	0	0
Playoff Totals		**3**	**1**	**0**	**1**	**0**	**0**	**0**	**0**
LACOMBE, Normand									Right wing
1988◆	Edmonton	19	3	0	3	28	0	0	1
1989	Edmonton	7	2	1	3	21	0	0	0
Playoff Totals		**26**	**5**	**1**	**6**	**49**	**0**	**0**	**1**
LaCOUTURE, Dan	*No playoffs*								Left wing
LACROIX, Andre									Center
1968	Philadelphia	7	2	3	5	0	1	0	0
1969	Philadelphia	4	0	0	0	0	0	0	0
1971	Philadelphia	4	0	2	2	0	0	0	0
1972	Chicago	1	0	0	0	0	0	0	0
Playoff Totals		**16**	**2**	**5**	**7**	**0**	**1**	**0**	**0**
LACROIX, Daniel									Left wing
1997	Philadelphia	12	0	1	1	22	0	0	0
1998	Philadelphia	4	0	0	0	4	0	0	0
Playoff Totals		**16**	**0**	**1**	**1**	**26**	**0**	**0**	**0**
LACROIX, Eric									Left wing
1994	Toronto	2	0	0	0	0	0	0	0
1997	Colorado	17	1	4	5	19	0	0	0
1998	Colorado	7	0	0	0	6	0	0	0
Playoff Totals		**26**	**1**	**4**	**5**	**25**	**0**	**0**	**0**
LACROIX, Pierre									Defense
1981	Quebec	5	0	2	2	10	0	0	0
1982	Quebec	3	0	0	0	0	0	0	0
Playoff Totals		**8**	**0**	**2**	**2**	**10**	**0**	**0**	**0**
LADOUCEUR, Randy									Defense
1984	Detroit	4	1	0	1	6	0	1	0
1985	Detroit	3	1	0	1	0	0	0	0
1987	Hartford	6	0	2	2	12	0	0	0
1988	Hartford	6	1	1	2	4	0	0	0
1989	Hartford	1	0	0	0	10	0	0	0
1990	Hartford	7	1	0	1	10	0	0	1
1991	Hartford	6	1	4	5	6	0	0	0
1992	Hartford	7	0	1	1	11	0	0	0
Playoff Totals		**40**	**5**	**8**	**13**	**59**	**0**	**1**	**1**

Season	Club	GP	G	A	Pts	PIM	PP	SH	GW
LaFAYETTE, Nathan									Center
1994	Vancouver	20	2	7	9	4	0	0	0
1995	NY Rangers	8	0	0	0	2	0	0	0
1998	Los Angeles	4	0	0	0	2	0	0	0
Playoff Totals		**32**	**2**	**7**	**9**	**8**	**0**	**0**	**0**
LAFLAMME, Christian									Defense
1999	Edmonton	4	0	1	1	2	0	0	0
Playoff Totals		**4**	**0**	**1**	**1**	**2**	**0**	**0**	**0**
LAFLEUR, Guy									Right wing
1972	Montreal	6	1	4	5	2	0	0	0
1973◆	Montreal	17	3	5	8	9	2	0	1
1974	Montreal	6	0	1	1	4	0	0	0
1975	Montreal	11	12	7	19	15	4	0	4
1976◆	Montreal	13	7	10	17	2	0	0	3
1977◆	Montreal	14	9	*17	*26	6	1	0	2
1978◆	Montreal	15	*10	11	*21	16	3	0	2
1979◆	Montreal	16	10	*13	*23	0	2	0	2
1980	Montreal	3	3	1	4	0	0	0	0
1981	Montreal	3	0	1	1	2	0	0	0
1982	Montreal	5	2	1	3	4	2	0	0
1983	Montreal	3	0	2	2	2	0	0	0
1984	Montreal	12	0	3	3	5	0	0	0
1989	NY Rangers	4	1	0	1	0	1	0	0
Playoff Totals		**128**	**58**	**76**	**134**	**67**	**15**	**0**	**14**
LAFLEUR, Roland	*No playoffs*								Left wing
LaFONTAINE, Pat									Center
1984	NY Islanders	16	3	6	9	8	0	0	0
1985	NY Islanders	9	1	2	3	4	0	0	0
1986	NY Islanders	3	1	0	1	0	1	0	0
1987	NY Islanders	14	5	7	12	10	1	0	2
1988	NY Islanders	6	4	5	9	8	1	0	1
1990	NY Islanders	2	0	1	1	0	0	0	0
1992	Buffalo	7	8	3	11	4	5	1	1
1993	Buffalo	7	2	10	12	0	1	0	0
1995	Buffalo	5	2	2	4	2	1	0	0
Playoff Totals		**69**	**26**	**36**	**62**	**36**	**10**	**1**	**4**
LAFORCE, Ernie	*No playoffs*								Defense
LAFOREST, Bob	*No playoffs*								Right wing
LAFORGE, Claude									Left wing
1968	Philadelphia	5	1	2	3	15	0	0	0
Playoff Totals		**5**	**1**	**2**	**3**	**15**	**0**	**0**	**0**
LAFORGE, Marc	*No playoffs*								Left wing
LAFRAMBOISE, Pete									Left wing/center
1975	Pittsburgh	9	1	0	1	0	0	0	0
Playoff Totals		**9**	**1**	**0**	**1**	**0**	**0**	**0**	**0**
LAFRANCE, Adie									Left wing
1934	Mtl. Canadiens	2	0	0	0	0	0	0	0
Playoff Totals		**2**	**0**	**0**	**0**	**0**	**0**	**0**	**0**
LAFRANCE, Leo	*No playoffs*								Left wing
LAFRENIERE, Jason									Center
1987	Quebec	12	1	5	6	2	1	0	0
1989	NY Rangers	3	0	0	0	17	0	0	0
Playoff Totals		**15**	**1**	**5**	**6**	**19**	**1**	**0**	**0**
LAFRENIERE, Roger	*No playoffs*								Left wing
LAGACE, Jean-Guy	*No playoffs*								Defense
LAIDLAW, Tom									Defense
1981	NY Rangers	14	1	4	5	18	0	0	1
1982	NY Rangers	10	0	3	3	14	0	0	0
1983	NY Rangers	9	1	1	2	10	0	0	0
1984	NY Rangers	5	0	0	0	8	0	0	0
1985	NY Rangers	3	0	2	2	4	0	0	0
1986	NY Rangers	7	0	2	2	12	0	0	0
1987	Los Angeles	5	0	0	0	2	0	0	0
1988	Los Angeles	5	0	2	2	4	0	0	0
1989	Los Angeles	11	2	3	5	6	0	0	0
Playoff Totals		**69**	**4**	**17**	**21**	**78**	**0**	**0**	**1**
LAIRD, Robbie	*No playoffs*								Left wing
LAJEUNESSE, Serge	*No playoffs*								Defense/right wing
LAKOVIC, Sasha	*No playoffs*								Right wing
LALANDE, Hec	*No playoffs*								Center
LALONDE, Bobby									Center
1975	Vancouver	5	0	0	0	0	0	0	0
1976	Vancouver	1	0	0	0	2	0	0	0
1978	Atlanta	1	1	0	1	0	0	0	0
1979	Atlanta	2	1	0	1	0	1	0	0
1980	Boston	4	0	1	1	2	0	0	0
1981	Boston	3	2	1	3	2	0	2	0
Playoff Totals		**16**	**4**	**2**	**6**	**6**	**1**	**2**	**0**
LALONDE, Newsy									Center
1918	Mtl. Canadiens	2	4	2	6	17	....	....	....
1919	Mtl. Canadiens	10	*17	1	*18	18	....	....	....
Playoff Totals		**12**	**21**	**3**	**24**	**35**	....	....	....
LALONDE, Ron	*No playoffs*								Center

Season	Club	GP	G	A	Pts	PIM	PP	SH	GW
LALOR, Mike									Defense
1986◆	Montreal	17	1	2	3	29	0	0	1
1987	Montreal	13	2	1	3	29	0	0	0
1988	Montreal	11	0	0	0	11	0	0	0
1989	St. Louis	10	1	1	2	14	1	0	0
1990	St. Louis	12	0	2	2	31	0	0	0
1991	Washington	10	1	2	3	22	0	0	0
1992	Winnipeg	7	0	0	0	19	0	0	0
1993	Winnipeg	4	0	2	2	4	0	0	0
1994	Dallas	5	0	0	0	6	0	0	0
1995	Dallas	3	0	0	0	2	0	0	0
Playoff Totals		**92**	**5**	**10**	**15**	**167**	**1**	**0**	**1**
LAMB, Joe									Right wing
1928	Mtl. Maroons	8	1	0	1	32	....	....	....
1930	Ottawa	2	0	0	0	11	....	....	....
1933	Boston	5	0	1	1	6	....	....	....
1936	Mtl. Maroons	3	0	0	0	2	....	....	....
Playoff Totals		**18**	**1**	**1**	**2**	**51**	....	....	....
LAMB, Mark									Center
1987	Detroit	11	0	0	0	11	0	0	0
1989	Edmonton	6	0	2	2	8	0	0	0
1990◆	Edmonton	22	6	11	17	2	1	0	2
1991	Edmonton	15	0	5	5	20	0	0	0
1992	Edmonton	16	1	1	2	10	0	0	0
Playoff Totals		**70**	**7**	**19**	**26**	**51**	**1**	**0**	**2**
LAMBERT, Dan	*No playoffs*								Defense
LAMBERT, Denny									Left wing
1997	Ottawa	6	0	1	1	9	0	0	0
1998	Ottawa	11	0	0	0	19	0	0	0
Playoff Totals		**17**	**0**	**1**	**1**	**28**	**0**	**0**	**0**
LAMBERT, Lane									Right wing
1984	Detroit	4	0	0	0	10	0	0	0
1987	Quebec	13	2	4	6	30	0	0	0
Playoff Totals		**17**	**2**	**4**	**6**	**40**	**0**	**0**	**0**
LAMBERT, Yvon									Left wing
1974	Montreal	5	0	0	0	7	0	0	0
1975	Montreal	11	4	2	6	0	2	0	0
1976◆	Montreal	12	2	3	5	18	0	0	1
1977◆	Montreal	14	3	3	6	12	1	0	0
1978◆	Montreal	15	2	4	6	6	1	0	1
1979◆	Montreal	16	5	6	11	16	2	0	1
1980	Montreal	10	8	4	12	4	1	0	1
1981	Montreal	3	0	0	0	2	0	0	0
1982	Buffalo	4	3	0	3	2	1	0	0
Playoff Totals		**90**	**27**	**22**	**49**	**67**	**8**	**0**	**4**
LAMBY, Dick	*No playoffs*								Defense
LAMIRANDE, Jean-Paul									Left wing/defense
1948	NY Rangers	6	0	0	0	4	0	0	0
1950	NY Rangers	2	0	0	0	0	0	0	0
Playoff Totals		**8**	**0**	**0**	**0**	**4**	**0**	**0**	**0**
LAMMENS, Hank	*No playoffs*								Defense
LAMOUREUX, Leo									Center/Defense
1944◆	Montreal	9	0	3	3	8	....	....	....
1945	Montreal	6	1	1	2	2	....	....	....
1946◆	Montreal	9	0	2	2	2	....	....	....
1947	Montreal	4	0	0	0	4	....	....	....
Playoff Totals		**28**	**1**	**6**	**7**	**16**	....	....	....
LAMOUREUX, Mitch	*No playoffs*								Center
LAMPMAN, Mike	*No playoffs*								Left wing
LANCIEN, Jack									Defense
1948	NY Rangers	2	0	0	0	2	0	0	0
1950	NY Rangers	4	0	1	1	0	0	0	0
Playoff Totals		**6**	**0**	**1**	**1**	**2**	**0**	**0**	**0**
LANDON, Larry	*No playoffs*								Right wing
LANDRY, Eric	*No playoffs*								Center
LANE, Gord									Defense
1980◆	NY Islanders	21	1	3	4	*85	0	0	0
1981◆	NY Islanders	12	1	5	6	32	0	0	0
1982◆	NY Islanders	19	0	4	4	61	0	0	0
1983◆	NY Islanders	18	1	2	3	32	0	0	1
1984	NY Islanders	4	0	0	0	2	0	0	0
1985	NY Islanders	1	0	0	0	2	0	0	0
Playoff Totals		**75**	**3**	**14**	**17**	**214**	**0**	**0**	**1**
LANE, Myles									Defense
1929◆	Boston	5	0	0	0	0	0	0	0
1930	Boston	6	0	0	0	0	0	0	0
Playoff Totals		**11**	**0**	**0**	**0**	**0**	**0**	**0**	**0**
LANG, Robert									Center
1998	Pittsburgh	6	0	3	3	2	0	0	0
1999	Pittsburgh	12	0	2	2	0	0	0	0
Playoff Totals		**18**	**0**	**5**	**5**	**2**	**0**	**0**	**0**
LANGDON, Darren									Left wing
1996	NY Rangers	2	0	0	0	0	0	0	0
1997	NY Rangers	10	0	0	0	2	0	0	0
Playoff Totals		**12**	**0**	**0**	**0**	**2**	**0**	**0**	**0**
LANGDON, Steve									Left wing
1976	Boston	4	0	0	0	0	0	0	0
Playoff Totals		**4**	**0**	**0**	**0**	**0**	**0**	**0**	**0**

Season	Club	GP	G	A	Pts	PIM	PP	SH	GW
LANGELLE, Pete									Center
1939	Toronto	11	1	2	3	2	....	....	....
1940	Toronto	10	0	3	3	0	....	....	....
1941	Toronto	7	1	1	2	0	....	....	....
1942◆	Toronto	13	3	3	6	2	....	....	....
Playoff Totals		**41**	**5**	**9**	**14**	**4**	....	....	....
LANGENBRUNNER, Jamie									Center
1997	Dallas	5	1	1	2	14	0	0	1
1998	Dallas	16	1	4	5	14	0	0	1
1999◆	Dallas	23	10	7	17	16	4	0	3
Playoff Totals		**44**	**12**	**12**	**24**	**44**	**4**	**0**	**5**
LANGEVIN, Chris	*No playoffs*								Left wing
LANGEVIN, Dave									Defense
1980◆	NY Islanders	21	0	3	3	32	0	0	0
1981◆	NY Islanders	18	0	3	3	25	0	0	0
1982◆	NY Islanders	19	2	4	6	16	0	0	1
1983◆	NY Islanders	8	0	2	2	2	0	0	0
1984	NY Islanders	12	0	4	4	18	0	0	0
1985	NY Islanders	4	0	0	0	4	0	0	0
1986	Minnesota	5	0	1	1	9	0	0	0
Playoff Totals		**87**	**2**	**17**	**19**	**106**	**0**	**0**	**1**
LANGKOW, Daymond									Center
1999	Philadelphia	6	0	2	2	2	0	0	0
Playoff Totals		**6**	**0**	**2**	**2**	**2**	**0**	**0**	**0**
LANGLAIS, Alain	*No playoffs*								Left wing
LANGLOIS, Albert									Defense
1958◆	Montreal	7	0	1	1	4	0	0	0
1959◆	Montreal	7	0	0	0	4	0	0	0
1960◆	Montreal	8	0	3	3	18	0	0	0
1961	Montreal	5	0	0	0	6	0	0	0
1962	NY Rangers	6	0	1	1	2	0	0	0
1964	Detroit	14	0	0	0	12	0	0	0
1965	Detroit	6	1	0	1	4	0	0	0
Playoff Totals		**53**	**1**	**5**	**6**	**50**	**0**	**0**	**0**
LANGLOIS, Charlie									Right wing/defense
1928	Mtl. Canadiens	2	0	0	0	0	0	0	0
Playoff Totals		**2**	**0**	**0**	**0**	**0**	**0**	**0**	**0**
LANGWAY, Rod									Defense
1979◆	Montreal	8	0	0	0	16	0	0	0
1980	Montreal	10	3	3	6	2	1	0	0
1981	Montreal	3	0	0	0	6	0	0	0
1982	Montreal	5	0	3	3	18	0	0	0
1983	Washington	4	0	0	0	0	0	0	0
1984	Washington	8	0	5	5	7	0	0	0
1985	Washington	5	0	1	1	6	0	0	0
1986	Washington	9	1	2	3	6	1	0	0
1987	Washington	7	0	1	1	2	0	0	0
1988	Washington	6	0	0	0	8	0	0	0
1989	Washington	6	0	0	0	6	0	0	0
1990	Washington	15	1	4	5	12	0	0	1
1991	Washington	11	0	2	2	6	0	0	0
1992	Washington	7	0	1	1	2	0	0	0
Playoff Totals		**104**	**5**	**22**	**27**	**97**	**2**	**0**	**1**
LANK, Jeff	*No playoffs*								Defense
LANTHIER, Jean-Marc	*No playoffs*								Right wing
LANYON, Ted	*No playoffs*								Defense
LANZ, Rick									Defense
1981	Vancouver	3	0	0	0	4	0	0	0
1983	Vancouver	4	2	1	3	0	1	0	0
1984	Vancouver	4	0	4	4	2	0	0	0
1986	Vancouver	3	0	0	0	0	0	0	0
1987	Toronto	13	1	3	4	27	0	0	1
1988	Toronto	1	0	0	0	2	0	0	0
Playoff Totals		**28**	**3**	**8**	**11**	**35**	**1**	**0**	**1**
LAPERRIERE, Daniel	*No playoffs*								Defense
LAPERRIERE, Ian									Center
1995	St. Louis	7	0	4	4	21	0	0	0
1998	Los Angeles	4	1	0	1	6	0	0	0
Playoff Totals		**11**	**1**	**4**	**5**	**27**	**0**	**0**	**0**
LAPERRIERE, Jacques									Defense
1963	Montreal	5	0	1	1	4	0	0	0
1964	Montreal	7	1	1	2	8	0	1	0
1965◆	Montreal	6	1	1	2	16	1	0	0
1967	Montreal	9	0	1	1	9	0	0	0
1968◆	Montreal	13	1	3	4	20	0	0	0
1969◆	Montreal	14	1	3	4	28	1	0	0
1971◆	Montreal	20	4	9	13	12	1	0	1
1972	Montreal	4	0	0	0	2	0	0	0
1973◆	Montreal	10	1	3	4	2	0	0	0
Playoff Totals		**88**	**9**	**22**	**31**	**101**	**3**	**1**	**1**
LAPLANTE, Darryl	*No playoffs*								Center
LAPOINTE, Claude									Center
1993	Quebec	6	2	4	6	8	0	0	0
1995	Quebec	5	0	0	0	8	0	0	0
1996	Calgary	2	0	0	0	0	0	0	0
Playoff Totals		**13**	**2**	**4**	**6**	**16**	**0**	**0**	**0**

Season	Club	GP	G	A	Pts	PIM	PP	SH	GW
LAPOINTE, Guy									Defense
1971◆	Montreal	20	4	5	9	34	1	0	2
1972	Montreal	6	0	1	1	0	0	0	0
1973◆	Montreal	17	6	7	13	20	2	0	1
1974	Montreal	6	0	2	2	4	0	0	0
1975	Montreal	11	6	4	10	4	3	1	0
1976◆	Montreal	13	3	3	6	12	1	0	1
1977◆	Montreal	12	3	9	12	4	1	0	0
1978◆	Montreal	14	1	6	7	16	1	0	0
1979◆	Montreal	10	2	6	8	10	1	0	0
1980	Montreal	2	0	0	0	0	0	0	0
1981	Montreal	1	0	0	0	17	0	0	0
1982	St. Louis	7	1	0	1	8	1	0	1
1983	St. Louis	4	0	1	1	9	0	0	0
Playoff Totals		**123**	**26**	**44**	**70**	**138**	**11**	**1**	**5**
LAPOINTE, Martin									Right wing
1992	Detroit	3	0	1	1	4	0	0	0
1994	Detroit	4	0	0	0	6	0	0	0
1995	Detroit	2	0	1	1	8	0	0	0
1996	Detroit	11	1	2	3	12	0	0	0
1997◆	Detroit	20	4	8	12	60	1	0	1
1998◆	Detroit	21	9	6	15	20	2	1	1
1999	Detroit	10	0	2	2	20	0	0	0
Playoff Totals		**71**	**14**	**20**	**34**	**130**	**3**	**1**	**2**
LAPOINTE, Rick									Defense
1977	Philadelphia	10	0	0	0	7	0	0	0
1978	Philadelphia	12	0	3	3	19	0	0	0
1979	Philadelphia	7	0	1	1	14	0	0	0
1980	St. Louis	3	0	1	1	6	0	0	0
1981	St. Louis	8	2	2	4	12	0	0	0
1982	St. Louis	3	0	0	0	6	0	0	0
1984	Quebec	3	0	0	0	0	0	0	0
Playoff Totals		**46**	**2**	**7**	**9**	**64**	**0**	**0**	**0**
LAPPIN, Peter	*No playoffs*								Right wing
LAPRADE, Edgar									Center
1948	NY Rangers	6	1	4	5	0	....	....	....
1950	NY Rangers	12	3	5	8	4	....	....	....
Playoff Totals		**18**	**4**	**9**	**13**	**4**	....	....	....
LAPRAIRIE, Benjamin	*No playoffs*								Defense
LARAQUE, Georges									Right wing
1999	Edmonton	4	0	0	0	2	0	0	0
Playoff Totals		**4**	**0**	**0**	**0**	**2**	**0**	**0**	**0**
LARIONOV, Igor									Center
1991	Vancouver	6	1	0	1	6	0	0	0
1992	Vancouver	13	3	7	10	4	1	0	0
1994	San Jose	14	5	13	18	10	0	0	0
1995	San Jose	11	1	8	9	2	0	0	0
1996	Detroit	19	6	7	13	6	3	0	2
1997◆	Detroit	20	4	8	12	8	3	0	1
1998◆	Detroit	22	3	10	13	12	0	0	0
1999	Detroit	7	0	2	2	0	0	0	0
Playoff Totals		**112**	**23**	**55**	**78**	**48**	**7**	**0**	**3**
LARIVIERE, Garry									Defense
1981	Edmonton	9	0	3	3	8	0	0	0
1982	Edmonton	4	0	1	1	0	0	0	0
1983	Edmonton	1	0	1	1	0	0	0	0
Playoff Totals		**14**	**0**	**5**	**5**	**8**	**0**	**0**	**0**
LARMER, Jeff									Left wing
1984	Chicago	5	1	0	1	2	1	0	0
Playoff Totals		**5**	**1**	**0**	**1**	**2**	**1**	**0**	**0**
LARMER, Steve									Right wing
1983	Chicago	11	5	7	12	8	2	0	1
1984	Chicago	5	2	2	4	7	1	0	0
1985	Chicago	15	9	13	22	14	5	0	1
1986	Chicago	3	0	3	3	4	0	0	0
1987	Chicago	4	0	0	0	2	0	0	0
1988	Chicago	5	1	6	7	0	1	0	0
1989	Chicago	16	8	9	17	22	3	0	2
1990	Chicago	20	7	15	22	2	2	2	2
1991	Chicago	6	5	1	6	4	1	0	0
1992	Chicago	18	8	7	15	6	3	0	0
1993	Chicago	4	0	3	3	0	0	0	0
1994◆	NY Rangers	23	9	7	16	14	3	0	0
1995	NY Rangers	10	2	2	4	6	0	1	1
Playoff Totals		**140**	**56**	**75**	**131**	**89**	**21**	**3**	**7**
LAROCHELLE, Wildor									Right wing
1927	Mtl. Canadiens	4	0	0	0	0	....	....	....
1928	Mtl. Canadiens	2	0	0	0	0	....	....	....
1930◆	Mtl. Canadiens	6	1	0	1	12	....	....	....
1931◆	Mtl. Canadiens	10	1	2	3	8	....	....	....
1932	Mtl. Canadiens	4	2	1	3	4	....	....	....
1933	Mtl. Canadiens	2	1	0	1	0	....	....	....
1934	Mtl. Canadiens	2	1	1	2	0	....	....	....
1935	Mtl. Canadiens	2	0	0	0	0	....	....	....
1936	Chicago	2	0	0	0	0	....	....	....
Playoff Totals		**34**	**6**	**4**	**10**	**24**	....	....	....
LAROCQUE, Denis	*No playoffs*								Defense
LAROCQUE, Mario	*No playoffs*								Defense
LAROSE, Charles	*No playoffs*								Left wing

Season	Club	GP	G	A	Pts	PIM	PP	SH	GW
LAROSE, Claude									Right wing
1964	Montreal	2	1	0	1	0	0	0	0
1965◆	Montreal	13	0	1	1	14	0	0	0
1966◆	Montreal	6	0	1	1	31	0	0	0
1967	Montreal	10	1	5	6	15	0	0	0
1968◆	Montreal	12	3	2	5	8	0	0	0
1970	Minnesota	6	1	1	2	25	0	0	0
1971◆	Montreal	11	1	0	1	10	0	0	0
1972	Montreal	6	2	1	3	23	0	0	0
1973◆	Montreal	17	3	4	7	6	0	0	0
1974	Montreal	5	0	2	2	11	0	0	0
1975	St. Louis	2	1	1	2	0	0	0	0
1976	St. Louis	3	0	0	0	0	0	0	0
1977	St. Louis	4	1	0	1	0	0	0	0
Playoff Totals		**97**	**14**	**18**	**32**	**143**	**0**	**0**	**0**
LAROSE, Claude									Left wing
1982	NY Rangers	2	0	0	0	0	0	0	0
Playoff Totals		**2**	**0**	**0**	**0**	**0**	**0**	**0**	**0**
LAROSE, Guy									Center
1995	Boston	4	0	0	0	0	0	0	0
Playoff Totals		**4**	**0**	**0**	**0**	**0**	**0**	**0**	**0**
LAROUCHE, Pierre									Center
1975	Pittsburgh	9	2	5	7	2	0	0	1
1976	Pittsburgh	3	0	1	1	0	0	0	0
1977	Pittsburgh	3	0	3	3	0	0	0	0
1978◆	Montreal	5	2	1	3	4	1	0	1
1979◆	Montreal	6	1	3	4	0	0	0	1
1980	Montreal	9	1	7	8	2	0	0	0
1981	Montreal	2	0	2	2	0	0	0	0
1984	NY Rangers	5	3	1	4	2	2	0	0
1986	NY Rangers	16	8	9	17	2	4	0	1
1987	NY Rangers	6	3	2	5	4	0	0	1
Playoff Totals		**64**	**20**	**34**	**54**	**16**	**7**	**0**	**5**
LAROUCHE, Steve	*No playoffs*								Center
LARSEN, Brad	*No playoffs*								Left wing
LARSON, Norman	*No playoffs*								Right wing
LARSON, Reed									Defense
1978	Detroit	7	0	2	2	4	0	0	0
1984	Detroit	4	2	0	2	21	2	0	0
1985	Detroit	3	1	2	3	20	0	0	0
1986	Boston	3	1	0	1	6	1	0	0
1987	Boston	4	0	2	2	2	0	0	0
1988	Boston	8	0	1	1	6	0	0	0
1989	Minnesota	3	0	0	0	4	0	0	0
Playoff Totals		**32**	**4**	**7**	**11**	**63**	**3**	**0**	**0**
LARTER, Tyler	*No playoffs*								Center
LATAL, Jiri	*No playoffs*								Defense
LATOS, James	*No playoffs*								Right wing
LATREILLE, Phil	*No playoffs*								Center/right wing
LATTA, David	*No playoffs*								Left wing
LAUDER, Martin	*No playoffs*								Defense/center
LAUEN, Mike	*No playoffs*								Right wing
LAUER, Brad									Left wing
1987	NY Islanders	6	2	0	2	4	0	0	0
1988	NY Islanders	5	3	1	4	4	0	0	0
1990	NY Islanders	4	0	2	2	10	0	0	0
1992	Chicago	7	1	1	2	2	0	0	0
1996	Pittsburgh	12	1	1	2	4	0	0	0
Playoff Totals		**34**	**7**	**5**	**12**	**24**	**0**	**0**	**0**
LAUGHLIN, Craig									Right wing
1982	Montreal	3	0	1	1	0	0	0	0
1983	Washington	4	1	0	1	0	0	0	0
1984	Washington	8	4	2	6	6	1	0	3
1985	Washington	5	0	0	0	2	0	0	0
1986	Washington	9	1	2	3	10	0	0	1
1987	Washington	1	0	0	0	0	0	0	0
1988	Los Angeles	3	0	1	1	2	0	0	0
Playoff Totals		**33**	**6**	**6**	**12**	**20**	**1**	**0**	**4**
LAUGHTON, Mike									Center
1969	Oakland	7	2	3	5	0	0	0	0
1970	Oakland	4	0	1	1	0	0	0	0
Playoff Totals		**11**	**2**	**4**	**6**	**0**	**0**	**0**	**0**
LAUKKANEN, Janne									Defense
1995	Quebec	6	1	0	1	2	0	0	0
1997	Ottawa	7	0	1	1	6	0	0	0
1998	Ottawa	11	2	2	4	8	1	0	1
1999	Ottawa	4	0	0	0	4	0	0	0
Playoff Totals		**28**	**3**	**3**	**6**	**20**	**1**	**0**	**1**
LAURENCE, Don	*No playoffs*								Center
LAUS, Paul									Defense
1996	Florida	21	2	6	8	*62	0	0	0
1997	Florida	5	0	1	1	4	0	0	0
Playoff Totals		**26**	**2**	**7**	**9**	**66**	**0**	**0**	**0**
LAVALLEE, Kevin									Left wing
1981	Calgary	8	2	3	5	4	1	0	1
1982	Calgary	3	0	0	0	7	0	0	0
1983	Calgary	8	1	3	4	4	0	0	0
1986	St. Louis	13	2	2	4	6	0	0	0
Playoff Totals		**32**	**5**	**8**	**13**	**21**	**1**	**0**	**1**

Season	Club	GP	G	A	Pts	PIM	PP	SH	GW
LAVARRE, Mark	Right wing								
1988	Chicago	1	0	0	0	2	0	0	0
Playoff Totals		**1**	**0**	**0**	**0**	**2**	**0**	**0**	**0**
LAVENDER, Brian	Left wing								
1972	St. Louis	3	0	0	0	2	0	0	0
Playoff Totals		**3**	**0**	**0**	**0**	**2**	**0**	**0**	**0**
LAVIGNE, Eric *No playoffs*	Defense								
LAVIOLETTE, Jack	Defense/right wing								
1918	Mtl. Canadiens	2	0	0	0	0	0	0	0
Playoff Totals		**2**	**0**	**0**	**0**	**0**	**0**	**0**	**0**
LAVIOLETTE, Peter *No playoffs*	Defense								
LAVOIE, Dominic *No playoffs*	Defense								
LAWLESS, Paul	Left wing								
1986	Hartford	1	0	0	0	0	0	0	0
1987	Hartford	2	0	2	2	2	0	0	0
Playoff Totals		**3**	**0**	**2**	**2**	**2**	**0**	**0**	**0**
LAWRENCE, Mark *No playoffs*	Right wing								
LAWSON, Danny	Right wing								
1970	Minnesota	6	0	1	1	2	0	0	0
1971	Minnesota	10	0	0	0	0	0	0	0
Playoff Totals		**16**	**0**	**1**	**1**	**2**	**0**	**0**	**0**
LAWTON, Brian	Left wing								
1984	Minnesota	5	0	0	0	10	0	0	0
1986	Minnesota	3	0	1	1	2	0	0	0
1989	Hartford	3	1	0	1	0	0	0	0
Playoff Totals		**11**	**1**	**1**	**2**	**12**	**0**	**0**	**0**
LAXDAL, Derek	Right wing								
1990	NY Islanders	1	0	2	2	2	0	0	0
Playoff Totals		**1**	**0**	**2**	**2**	**2**	**0**	**0**	**0**
LAYCOE, Hal	Defense								
1949	Montreal	7	0	1	1	13	....	....	....
1950	Montreal	2	0	0	0	0	....	....	....
1951	Boston	6	0	1	1	5	....	....	....
1952	Boston	7	1	1	2	11	....	....	....
1953	Boston	11	0	2	2	10	....	....	....
1954	Boston	2	0	0	0	0	....	....	....
1955	Boston	5	1	0	1	0	....	....	....
Playoff Totals		**40**	**2**	**5**	**7**	**39**	....	....	....
LAZARO, Jeff	Left wing								
1991	Boston	19	3	2	5	30	0	0	0
1992	Boston	9	0	1	1	2	0	0	0
Playoff Totals		**28**	**3**	**3**	**6**	**32**	**0**	**0**	**0**
LEACH, Jamie *No playoffs*	Right wing								
LEACH, Larry	Center								
1959	Boston	7	1	1	2	8	0	1	0
Playoff Totals		**7**	**1**	**1**	**2**	**8**	**0**	**1**	**0**
LEACH, Reggie	Right wing								
1971	Boston	3	0	0	0	0	0	0	0
1975♦	Philadelphia	17	8	2	10	6	2	0	2
1976	Philadelphia	16	*19	5	*24	8	2	0	2
1977	Philadelphia	10	4	5	9	0	0	0	2
1978	Philadelphia	12	2	2	4	0	1	0	0
1979	Philadelphia	8	5	1	6	0	3	0	2
1980	Philadelphia	19	9	7	16	6	2	1	0
1981	Philadelphia	9	0	0	0	2	0	0	0
Playoff Totals		**94**	**47**	**22**	**69**	**22**	**10**	**1**	**8**
LEACH, Stephen	Right wing								
1986	Washington	6	0	1	1	0	0	0	0
1988	Washington	9	2	1	3	0	0	0	1
1989	Washington	6	1	0	1	12	1	0	0
1990	Washington	14	2	2	4	8	0	0	0
1991	Washington	9	1	2	3	8	0	0	0
1992	Boston	15	4	0	4	10	0	0	1
1993	Boston	4	1	1	2	2	0	0	0
1994	Boston	5	0	1	1	2	0	0	0
1996	St. Louis	11	3	2	5	10	1	0	1
1997	St. Louis	6	0	0	0	33	0	0	0
1999	Phoenix	7	1	1	2	2	0	0	0
Playoff Totals		**92**	**15**	**11**	**26**	**87**	**2**	**0**	**3**
LEAVINS, Jim *No playoffs*	Defense								
LEBEAU, Patrick *No playoffs*	Left wing								
LEBEAU, Stephan	Center								
1990	Montreal	2	3	0	3	0	0	0	1
1991	Montreal	7	2	1	3	2	0	0	0
1992	Montreal	8	1	3	4	4	1	0	0
1993♦	Montreal	13	3	3	6	6	1	0	1
Playoff Totals		**30**	**9**	**7**	**16**	**12**	**2**	**0**	**2**
LEBLANC, Fern *No playoffs*	Center								
LEBLANC, J.P.	Center								
1978	Detroit	2	0	0	0	0	0	0	0
Playoff Totals		**2**	**0**	**0**	**0**	**0**	**0**	**0**	**0**
LeBLANC, John	Right wing								
1989	Edmonton	1	0	0	0	0	0	0	0
Playoff Totals		**1**	**0**	**0**	**0**	**0**	**0**	**0**	**0**
LeBOUTILLIER, Peter *No playoffs*	Right wing								
LEBRUN, Al *No playoffs*	Defense								

Season	Club	GP	G	A	Pts	PIM	PP	SH	GW
LECAINE, Bill *No playoffs*	Left wing								
LECAVALIER, Vincent *No playoffs*	Center								
LECLAIR, Jackie	Center								
1955	Montreal	12	5	0	5	2	1	0	0
1956♦	Montreal	8	1	1	2	4	0	0	0
Playoff Totals		**20**	**6**	**1**	**7**	**6**	**1**	**0**	**0**
LeCLAIR, John	Left wing								
1991	Montreal	3	0	0	0	0	0	0	0
1992	Montreal	8	1	1	2	4	0	0	0
1993♦	Montreal	20	4	6	10	14	0	0	3
1994	Montreal	7	2	1	3	8	1	0	0
1995	Philadelphia	15	5	7	12	4	1	0	1
1996	Philadelphia	11	6	5	11	6	4	0	1
1997	Philadelphia	19	9	12	21	10	4	0	3
1998	Philadelphia	5	1	1	2	8	1	0	1
1999	Philadelphia	6	3	0	3	12	2	0	0
Playoff Totals		**94**	**31**	**33**	**64**	**66**	**13**	**0**	**9**
LECLERC, Mike	Left wing								
1997	Anaheim	1	0	0	0	0	0	0	0
1999	Anaheim	1	0	0	0	0	0	0	0
Playoff Totals		**2**	**0**	**0**	**0**	**0**	**0**	**0**	**0**
LECLERC, Rene *No playoffs*	Right wing								
LECUYER, Doug	Left wing								
1980	Chicago	7	4	0	4	15	0	0	1
Playoff Totals		**7**	**4**	**0**	**4**	**15**	**0**	**0**	**1**
LEDINGHAM, Walt *No playoffs*	Left wing								
LEDUC, Albert	Defense								
1927	Mtl. Canadiens	4	0	0	0	2	....	....	....
1928	Mtl. Canadiens	2	1	0	1	5	....	....	....
1929	Mtl. Canadiens	3	1	0	1	4	....	....	....
1930♦	Mtl. Canadiens	6	1	3	4	8	....	....	....
1931♦	Mtl. Canadiens	7	0	2	2	9	....	....	....
1932	Mtl. Canadiens	4	1	1	2	2	....	....	....
1933	Mtl. Canadiens	2	1	0	1	2	....	....	....
Playoff Totals		**28**	**5**	**6**	**11**	**32**	....	....	....
LEDUC, Rich	Center								
1974	Boston	5	0	0	0	9	0	0	0
Playoff Totals		**5**	**0**	**0**	**0**	**9**	**0**	**0**	**0**
LEDYARD, Grant	Defense								
1985	NY Rangers	3	0	2	2	4	0	0	0
1987	Los Angeles	5	0	0	0	10	0	0	0
1988	Washington	14	1	0	1	30	0	0	0
1989	Buffalo	5	1	2	3	2	0	0	0
1991	Buffalo	6	3	3	6	10	0	0	0
1993	Buffalo	8	0	0	0	8	0	0	0
1994	Dallas	9	1	2	3	6	0	0	1
1995	Dallas	3	0	0	0	2	0	0	0
1997	Dallas	7	0	2	2	0	0	0	0
1998	Boston	6	0	0	0	2	0	0	0
1999	Boston	2	0	0	0	2	0	0	0
Playoff Totals		**68**	**6**	**11**	**17**	**76**	**0**	**0**	**1**
LEE, Bobby *No playoffs*	Center								
LEE, Edward *No playoffs*	Right wing								
LEE, Peter	Right wing								
1979	Pittsburgh	7	0	3	3	0	0	0	0
1980	Pittsburgh	4	0	1	1	0	0	0	0
1981	Pittsburgh	5	0	4	4	4	0	0	0
1982	Pittsburgh	3	0	0	0	0	0	0	0
Playoff Totals		**19**	**0**	**8**	**8**	**4**	**0**	**0**	**0**
LEEMAN, Gary	Right wing								
1983	Toronto	2	0	0	0	0	0	0	0
1986	Toronto	10	2	10	12	2	0	0	0
1987	Toronto	5	0	1	1	14	0	0	0
1988	Toronto	2	2	0	2	2	2	0	0
1990	Toronto	5	3	3	6	16	2	0	0
1993♦	Montreal	11	1	2	3	2	0	0	0
1994	Montreal	1	0	0	0	0	0	0	0
Playoff Totals		**36**	**8**	**16**	**24**	**36**	**4**	**0**	**0**
LEETCH, Brian	Defense								
1989	NY Rangers	4	3	2	5	2	2	0	0
1991	NY Rangers	6	1	3	4	0	0	0	0
1992	NY Rangers	13	4	11	15	4	1	1	0
1994♦	NY Rangers	23	11	*23	*34	6	4	0	4
1995	NY Rangers	10	6	8	14	8	3	0	1
1996	NY Rangers	11	1	6	7	4	1	0	0
1997	NY Rangers	15	2	8	10	6	1	0	1
Playoff Totals		**82**	**28**	**61**	**89**	**30**	**12**	**1**	**6**
LEFEBVRE, Patrice *No playoffs*	Right wing								
LEFEBVRE, Sylvain	Defense								
1990	Montreal	6	0	0	0	2	0	0	0
1991	Montreal	11	1	0	1	6	0	0	0
1992	Montreal	2	0	0	0	2	0	0	0
1993	Toronto	21	3	3	6	20	0	0	0
1994	Toronto	18	0	3	3	16	0	0	0
1995	Quebec	6	0	2	2	2	0	0	0
1996♦	Colorado	22	0	5	5	12	0	0	0
1997	Colorado	17	0	0	0	25	0	0	0
1998	Colorado	7	0	0	0	4	0	0	0
1999	Colorado	19	0	1	1	12	0	0	0
Playoff Totals		**129**	**4**	**14**	**18**	**101**	**0**	**0**	**0**

Season	Club	GP	G	A	Pts	PIM	PP	SH	GW
LEFLEY, Bryan	Defense/left wing								
1978	Colorado	2	0	0	0	0	0	0	0
Playoff Totals		**2**	**0**	**0**	**0**	**0**	**0**	**0**	**0**
LEFLEY, Chuck	Left wing								
1971♦	Montreal	1	0	0	0	0	0	0	0
1973♦	Montreal	17	3	5	8	6	0	0	0
1974	Montreal	6	0	1	1	0	0	0	0
1975	St. Louis	2	0	0	0	2	0	0	0
1976	St. Louis	2	2	1	3	0	0	1	0
1977	St. Louis	1	0	1	1	2	0	0	0
Playoff Totals		**29**	**5**	**8**	**13**	**10**	**0**	**1**	**0**
LEGER, Roger	Defense								
1947	Montreal	11	0	6	6	10	0	0	0
1949	Montreal	5	0	1	1	2	0	0	0
1950	Montreal	4	0	0	0	2	0	0	0
Playoff Totals		**20**	**0**	**7**	**7**	**14**	**0**	**0**	**0**
LEGGE, Barry *No playoffs*	Defense								
LEGGE, Randy *No playoffs*	Defense								
LEGWAND, David *No playoffs*	Center								
LEHMANN, Tommy *No playoffs*	Center								
LEHTINEN, Jere	Right wing								
1997	Dallas	7	2	2	4	0	0	0	0
1998	Dallas	12	3	5	8	2	1	0	0
1999♦	Dallas	23	10	3	13	2	1	1	0
Playoff Totals		**42**	**15**	**10**	**25**	**4**	**2**	**1**	**0**
LEHTO, Petteri *No playoffs*	Defense								
LEHTONEN, Antero *No playoffs*	Left wing								
LEHVONEN, Henri *No playoffs*	Defense								
LEIER, Edward *No playoffs*	Center								
LEINONEN, Mikko	Center								
1982	NY Rangers	7	1	6	7	20	0	0	0
1983	NY Rangers	7	1	3	4	4	1	0	0
1984	NY Rangers	5	0	2	2	4	0	0	0
1985	Washington	1	0	0	0	0	0	0	0
Playoff Totals		**20**	**2**	**11**	**13**	**28**	**1**	**0**	**0**
LEITER, Bobby	Center								
1972	Pittsburgh	4	3	0	3	0	1	0	0
1974	Atlanta	4	0	0	0	2	0	0	0
Playoff Totals		**8**	**3**	**0**	**3**	**2**	**1**	**0**	**0**
LEITER, Ken	Defense								
1987	NY Islanders	11	0	5	5	6	0	0	0
1988	NY Islanders	4	0	1	1	2	0	0	0
Playoff Totals		**15**	**0**	**6**	**6**	**8**	**0**	**0**	**0**
LEMAIRE, Jacques	Center								
1968♦	Montreal	13	7	6	13	6	2	0	2
1969♦	Montreal	14	4	2	6	6	1	0	0
1971♦	Montreal	20	9	10	19	17	4	0	1
1972	Montreal	6	2	1	3	2	0	0	0
1973♦	Montreal	17	7	13	20	2	3	0	1
1974	Montreal	6	0	4	4	2	0	0	0
1975	Montreal	11	5	7	12	4	1	0	0
1976♦	Montreal	13	3	3	6	2	1	1	1
1977♦	Montreal	14	7	12	19	6	1	0	3
1978♦	Montreal	15	6	8	14	10	0	0	1
1979♦	Montreal	16	*11	12	*23	6	6	0	2
Playoff Totals		**145**	**61**	**78**	**139**	**63**	**19**	**1**	**11**
LEMAY, Moe	Left wing								
1984	Vancouver	4	0	0	0	12	0	0	0
1987♦	Edmonton	9	2	1	3	11	0	0	1
1988	Boston	15	4	2	6	32	0	0	0
Playoff Totals		**28**	**6**	**3**	**9**	**55**	**0**	**0**	**1**
LEMELIN, Roger *No playoffs*	Defense								
LEMIEUX, Alain	Center								
1983	St. Louis	4	0	1	1	0	0	0	0
1985	Quebec	14	3	3	6	0	2	0	0
1986	Quebec	1	1	2	3	0	1	0	0
Playoff Totals		**19**	**4**	**6**	**10**	**0**	**3**	**0**	**0**
LEMIEUX, Bob *No playoffs*	Defense								
LEMIEUX, Claude	Right wing								
1986♦	Montreal	20	10	6	16	68	4	0	4
1987	Montreal	17	4	9	13	41	2	0	0
1988	Montreal	11	3	2	5	20	0	0	2
1989	Montreal	18	4	3	7	58	0	0	0
1990	Montreal	11	1	3	4	38	0	0	1
1991	New Jersey	7	4	0	4	34	2	0	1
1992	New Jersey	7	4	3	7	26	1	0	0
1993	New Jersey	5	2	0	2	19	1	0	0
1994	New Jersey	20	7	11	18	44	0	0	2
1995♦	New Jersey	20	*13	3	16	20	0	0	3
1996♦	Colorado	19	5	7	12	55	3	0	0
1997	Colorado	17	*13	10	23	32	4	0	4
1998	Colorado	7	3	3	6	8	1	0	1
1999	Colorado	19	3	11	14	26	1	0	0
Playoff Totals		**198**	**76**	**71**	**147**	**489**	**19**	**0**	**18**
LEMIEUX, Jacques	Defense								
1969	Los Angeles	1	0	0	0	0	0	0	0
Playoff Totals		**1**	**0**	**0**	**0**	**0**	**0**	**0**	**0**

Season	Club	GP	G	A	Pts	PIM	PP	SH	GW
LEMIEUX, Jean									Defense
1974	Atlanta	3	1	1	2	0	1	0	0
Playoff Totals		**3**	**1**	**1**	**2**	**0**	**1**	**0**	**0**
LEMIEUX, Jocelyn									Right wing
1987	St. Louis	5	0	1	1	6	0	0	0
1988	St. Louis	5	0	0	0	15	0	0	0
1990	Chicago	18	1	8	9	28	0	0	0
1991	Chicago	4	0	0	0	0	0	0	0
1992	Chicago	18	3	1	4	33	0	0	2
1993	Chicago	4	1	0	1	2	0	0	0
1996	Calgary	4	0	0	0	0	0	0	0
1997	Phoenix	2	0	0	0	4	0	0	0
Playoff Totals		**60**	**5**	**10**	**15**	**88**	**0**	**0**	**2**
LEMIEUX, Mario									Center
1989	Pittsburgh	11	12	7	19	16	7	1	0
1991◆	Pittsburgh	23	16	*28	*44	16	6	2	0
1992◆	Pittsburgh	15	*16	18	*34	2	8	2	5
1993	Pittsburgh	11	8	10	18	10	3	1	1
1994	Pittsburgh	6	4	3	7	2	1	0	0
1996	Pittsburgh	18	11	16	27	33	3	1	2
1997	Pittsburgh	5	3	3	6	4	0	0	0
Playoff Totals		**89**	**70**	**85**	**155**	**83**	**28**	**7**	**8**
LEMIEUX, Real									Left wing
1968	Los Angeles	7	1	1	2	0	0	0	0
1969	Los Angeles	11	1	3	4	10	1	0	0
Playoff Totals		**18**	**2**	**4**	**6**	**10**	**1**	**0**	**0**
LEMIEUX, Richard									Center
1976	Atlanta	2	0	0	0	0	0	0	0
Playoff Totals		**2**	**0**	**0**	**0**	**0**	**0**	**0**	**0**
LENARDON, Tim *No playoffs*									Center
LEPINE, Hec *No playoffs*									Center
LEPINE, Pit									Center
1927	Mtl. Canadiens	4	0	0	0	4	....	....	....
1928	Mtl. Canadiens	1	0	0	0	0	....	....	....
1929	Mtl. Canadiens	3	0	0	0	2	....	....	....
1930◆	Mtl. Canadiens	6	2	2	4	6	....	....	....
1931◆	Mtl. Canadiens	10	4	2	6	6	....	....	....
1932	Mtl. Canadiens	3	1	0	1	4	....	....	....
1933	Mtl. Canadiens	2	0	0	0	2	....	....	....
1934	Mtl. Canadiens	2	0	0	0	0	....	....	....
1935	Mtl. Canadiens	2	0	0	0	2	....	....	....
1937	Mtl. Canadiens	5	0	1	1	0	....	....	....
1938	Mtl. Canadiens	3	0	0	0	0	....	....	....
Playoff Totals		**41**	**7**	**5**	**12**	**26**	....	....	....
LEROUX, Francois									Defense
1995	Pittsburgh	12	0	2	2	14	0	0	0
1996	Pittsburgh	18	1	1	2	20	0	0	1
1997	Pittsburgh	3	0	0	0	0	0	0	0
Playoff Totals		**33**	**1**	**3**	**4**	**34**	**0**	**0**	**1**
LEROUX, Gaston *No playoffs*									Defense
LEROUX, Jean-Yves *No playoffs*									Left wing
LESCHYSHYN, Curtis									Defense
1993	Quebec	6	1	1	2	6	1	0	0
1995	Quebec	3	0	1	1	4	0	0	0
1996◆	Colorado	17	1	2	3	8	0	0	0
1999	Carolina	6	0	0	0	6	0	0	0
Playoff Totals		**32**	**2**	**4**	**6**	**24**	**1**	**0**	**0**
LESIEUR, Art									Defense
1931◆	Mtl. Canadiens	10	0	0	0	4	0	0	0
1932	Mtl. Canadiens	4	0	0	0	0	0	0	0
Playoff Totals		**14**	**0**	**0**	**0**	**4**	**0**	**0**	**0**
LESSARD, Rick *No playoffs*									Defense
LESUK, Bill									Left wing
1969	Boston	1	0	0	0	0	0	0	0
1970◆	Boston	2	0	0	0	0	0	0	0
1971	Philadelphia	4	1	0	1	8	1	0	0
1974	Los Angeles	2	0	0	0	4	0	0	0
Playoff Totals		**9**	**1**	**0**	**1**	**12**	**1**	**0**	**0**
LESWICK, Jack *No playoffs*									Center
LESWICK, Pete *No playoffs*									Center/right wing
LESWICK, Tony									Right/left wing
1948	NY Rangers	6	3	2	5	8	....	....	....
1950	NY Rangers	12	2	4	6	12	....	....	....
1952◆	Detroit	8	3	1	4	22	....	....	....
1953	Detroit	6	1	0	1	11	....	....	....
1954◆	Detroit	12	3	1	4	18	....	....	....
1955◆	Detroit	11	1	2	3	20	....	....	....
1958	Detroit	4	0	0	0	0	....	....	....
Playoff Totals		**59**	**13**	**10**	**23**	**91**	....	....	....
LETANG, Alan *No playoffs*									Defense
LETOWSKI, Trevor *No playoffs*									Center
LEVANDOSKI, Joseph *No playoffs*									Right wing
LEVEILLE, Normand *No playoffs*									Left wing
LEVEQUE, Guy *No playoffs*									Center

Season	Club	GP	G	A	Pts	PIM	PP	SH	GW
LEVER, Don									Left wing
1975	Vancouver	5	0	1	1	4	0	0	0
1976	Vancouver	2	0	0	0	0	0	0	0
1979	Vancouver	3	2	1	3	2	1	0	1
1980	Atlanta	4	1	1	2	0	1	0	0
1981	Calgary	16	4	7	11	20	0	0	0
Playoff Totals		**30**	**7**	**10**	**17**	**26**	**2**	**0**	**1**
LEVIE, Craig									Defense
1984	Minnesota	15	2	3	5	32	0	0	0
1985	St. Louis	1	0	0	0	0	0	0	0
Playoff Totals		**16**	**2**	**3**	**5**	**32**	**0**	**0**	**0**
LEVINS, Scott *No playoffs*									Center/Right wing
LEVINSKY, Alex									Defense
1931	Toronto	2	0	0	0	0	....	....	....
1932◆	Toronto	7	0	0	0	6	....	....	....
1933	Toronto	9	1	0	1	14	....	....	....
1934	Toronto	5	0	0	0	6	....	....	....
1935	Chicago	2	0	0	0	0	....	....	....
1936	Chicago	2	0	1	1	0	....	....	....
1938◆	Chicago	10	1	0	1	0	....	....	....
Playoff Totals		**37**	**2**	**1**	**3**	**26**	....	....	....
LEVO, Tapio *No playoffs*									Defense
LEWICKI, Danny									Left wing
1951◆	Toronto	9	0	0	0	0	0	0	0
1956	NY Rangers	5	0	3	3	0	0	0	0
1957	NY Rangers	5	0	1	1	2	0	0	0
1958	NY Rangers	6	0	0	0	6	0	0	0
1959	Chicago	3	0	0	0	0	0	0	0
Playoff Totals		**28**	**0**	**4**	**4**	**8**	**0**	**0**	**0**
LEWIS, Dale *No playoffs*									Left wing
LEWIS, Dave									Defense
1975	NY Islanders	17	0	1	1	28	0	0	0
1976	NY Islanders	13	0	1	1	44	0	0	0
1977	NY Islanders	12	1	6	7	4	0	0	0
1978	NY Islanders	7	0	1	1	11	0	0	0
1979	NY Islanders	10	0	0	0	4	0	0	0
1980	Los Angeles	4	0	1	1	2	0	0	0
1981	Los Angeles	4	0	2	2	4	0	0	0
1982	Los Angeles	10	0	4	4	36	0	0	0
1987	Detroit	14	0	4	4	10	0	0	0
Playoff Totals		**91**	**1**	**20**	**21**	**143**	**0**	**0**	**0**
LEWIS, Doug *No playoffs*									Left wing
LEWIS, Herbie									Left wing
1932	Detroit	2	0	0	0	0	....	....	....
1933	Detroit	4	1	0	1	0	....	....	....
1934	Detroit	9	*5	2	7	2	....	....	....
1936◆	Detroit	7	2	3	5	0	....	....	....
1937◆	Detroit	10	*4	3	7	4	....	....	....
1939	Detroit	6	1	2	3	0	....	....	....
Playoff Totals		**38**	**13**	**10**	**23**	**6**	....	....	....
LEY, Rick									Defense
1969	Toronto	3	0	0	0	9	0	0	0
1971	Toronto	6	0	2	2	4	0	0	0
1972	Toronto	5	0	0	0	7	0	0	0
Playoff Totals		**14**	**0**	**2**	**2**	**20**	**0**	**0**	**0**
LIBA, Igor									Left wing
1989	Los Angeles	2	0	0	0	2	0	0	0
Playoff Totals		**2**	**0**	**0**	**0**	**2**	**0**	**0**	**0**
LIBBY, Jeff *No playoffs*									Defense
LIBETT, Nick									Left wing
1970	Detroit	4	2	0	2	2	1	0	0
1978	Detroit	7	3	1	4	0	1	0	0
1980	Pittsburgh	5	1	1	2	0	1	0	0
Playoff Totals		**16**	**6**	**2**	**8**	**2**	**3**	**0**	**0**
LICARI, Tony *No playoffs*									Right wing
LIDDINGTON, Bob *No playoffs*									Left wing
LIDSTER, Doug									Defense
1984	Vancouver	2	0	1	1	0	0	0	0
1986	Vancouver	3	0	1	1	2	0	0	0
1989	Vancouver	7	1	1	2	9	0	0	0
1991	Vancouver	6	0	2	2	6	0	0	0
1992	Vancouver	11	1	2	3	11	0	0	0
1993	Vancouver	12	0	3	3	8	0	0	0
1994◆	NY Rangers	9	2	0	2	10	0	0	0
1995	St. Louis	4	0	0	0	2	0	0	0
1996	NY Rangers	7	1	0	1	6	1	0	0
1997	NY Rangers	15	1	5	6	8	0	0	0
1999◆	Dallas	4	0	0	0	2	0	0	0
Playoff Totals		**80**	**6**	**15**	**21**	**64**	**1**	**0**	**0**
LIDSTROM, Nicklas									Defense
1992	Detroit	11	1	2	3	0	1	0	0
1993	Detroit	7	1	0	1	0	1	0	0
1994	Detroit	7	3	2	5	0	1	1	0
1995	Detroit	18	4	12	16	8	3	0	2
1996	Detroit	19	5	9	14	10	1	0	0
1997◆	Detroit	20	2	6	8	2	0	0	0
1998◆	Detroit	22	6	13	19	8	2	0	2
1999	Detroit	10	2	9	11	4	2	0	0
Playoff Totals		**114**	**24**	**53**	**77**	**32**	**11**	**1**	**4**
LILLEY, John *No playoffs*									Right wing

Season	Club	GP	G	A	Pts	PIM	PP	SH	GW
LIND, Juha									Center
1998	Dallas	15	2	2	4	8	0	0	1
Playoff Totals		**15**	**2**	**2**	**4**	**8**	**0**	**0**	**1**
LINDBERG, Chris									Left wing
1993	Calgary	2	0	1	1	2	0	0	0
Playoff Totals		**2**	**0**	**1**	**1**	**2**	**0**	**0**	**0**
LINDBOM, Johan *No playoffs*									Left wing
LINDEN, Jamie *No playoffs*									Right wing
LINDEN, Trevor									Center/Right wing
1989	Vancouver	7	3	4	7	8	2	1	0
1991	Vancouver	6	0	7	7	2	0	0	0
1992	Vancouver	13	4	8	12	6	2	0	1
1993	Vancouver	12	5	8	13	16	2	0	1
1994	Vancouver	24	12	13	25	18	5	1	1
1995	Vancouver	11	2	6	8	12	1	0	0
1996	Vancouver	6	4	4	8	6	2	0	0
Playoff Totals		**79**	**30**	**50**	**80**	**68**	**14**	**2**	**3**
LINDGREN, Lars									Defense
1979	Vancouver	3	0	0	0	6	0	0	0
1980	Vancouver	2	0	1	1	0	0	0	0
1982	Vancouver	16	2	4	6	6	0	0	0
1983	Vancouver	4	1	1	2	2	0	0	0
1984	Minnesota	15	2	0	2	6	0	0	0
Playoff Totals		**40**	**5**	**6**	**11**	**20**	**0**	**0**	**0**
LINDGREN, Mats									Center
1997	Edmonton	12	0	4	4	0	0	0	0
1998	Edmonton	12	1	1	2	10	0	0	0
Playoff Totals		**24**	**1**	**5**	**6**	**10**	**0**	**0**	**0**
LINDHOLM, Mikael *No playoffs*									Center
LINDQUIST, Fredrik *No playoffs*									Center
LINDROS, Brett *No playoffs*									Right wing
LINDROS, Eric									Center
1995	Philadelphia	12	4	11	15	18	0	0	1
1996	Philadelphia	12	6	6	12	43	3	0	2
1997	Philadelphia	19	12	14	*26	40	4	0	1
1998	Philadelphia	5	1	2	3	17	0	0	0
Playoff Totals		**48**	**23**	**33**	**56**	**118**	**7**	**0**	**4**
LINDSAY, Bill									Left wing
1996	Florida	22	5	5	10	18	0	1	1
1997	Florida	3	0	1	1	8	0	0	0
Playoff Totals		**25**	**5**	**6**	**11**	**26**	**0**	**1**	**1**
LINDSAY, Ted									Left wing
1945	Detroit	14	2	0	2	6	....	....	....
1946	Detroit	5	0	1	1	0	....	....	....
1947	Detroit	5	2	2	4	10	....	....	....
1948	Detroit	10	3	1	4	6	....	....	....
1949	Detroit	11	2	*6	8	31	....	....	....
1950◆	Detroit	13	4	4	8	16	....	....	....
1951	Detroit	6	0	1	1	8	....	....	....
1952◆	Detroit	8	*5	2	*7	8	....	....	....
1953	Detroit	6	4	4	8	6	....	....	....
1954◆	Detroit	12	4	4	8	14	....	....	....
1955◆	Detroit	11	7	12	19	12	....	....	....
1956	Detroit	10	6	3	9	22	....	....	....
1957	Detroit	5	2	4	6	8	....	....	....
1959	Chicago	6	2	4	6	13	....	....	....
1960	Chicago	4	1	1	2	0	....	....	....
1965	Detroit	7	3	0	3	34	....	....	....
Playoff Totals		**133**	**47**	**49**	**96**	**194**	....	....	....
LINDSTROM, Willy									Right wing
1982	Winnipeg	4	2	1	3	2	0	0	0
1983	Edmonton	16	2	11	13	4	1	0	0
1984◆	Edmonton	19	5	5	10	10	3	0	0
1985◆	Edmonton	18	5	1	6	8	0	0	1
Playoff Totals		**57**	**14**	**18**	**32**	**24**	**4**	**0**	**1**
LING, David *No playoffs*									Right wing
LINSEMAN, Ken									Center
1979	Philadelphia	8	2	6	8	22	0	0	1
1980	Philadelphia	17	4	*18	22	40	0	0	1
1981	Philadelphia	12	4	16	20	67	0	0	3
1982	Philadelphia	4	1	2	3	6	1	0	0
1983	Edmonton	16	6	8	14	22	1	0	1
1984◆	Edmonton	19	10	4	14	65	3	1	4
1985	Boston	5	4	6	10	8	0	0	1
1986	Boston	3	0	1	1	17	0	0	0
1987	Boston	4	1	1	2	22	0	0	0
1988	Boston	23	11	14	25	56	4	1	0
1991	Edmonton	2	0	1	1	0	0	0	0
Playoff Totals		**113**	**43**	**77**	**120**	**325**	**9**	**2**	**11**
LINTNER, Richard *No playoffs*									Defense
LIPUMA, Chris *No playoffs*									Defense
LISCOMBE, Carl									Left wing
1939	Detroit	6	0	0	0	2	....	....	....
1941	Detroit	8	4	3	7	12	....	....	....
1942	Detroit	12	6	6	12	2	....	....	....
1943◆	Detroit	10	*6	8	*14	2	....	....	....
1944	Detroit	5	1	0	1	2	....	....	....
1945	Detroit	14	4	2	6	0	....	....	....
1946	Detroit	4	1	0	1	0	....	....	....
Playoff Totals		**59**	**22**	**19**	**41**	**20**	....	....	....

Season	Club	GP	G	A	Pts	PIM	PP	SH	GW
LITZENBERGER, Ed									Center/right wing
1959	Chicago	6	3	5	8	8	....	....	....
1960	Chicago	4	0	1	1	4	....	....	....
1961♦	Chicago	10	1	3	4	2	....	....	....
1962♦	Toronto	10	0	2	2	4	....	....	....
1963♦	Toronto	9	1	2	3	6	....	....	....
1964♦	Toronto	1	0	0	0	10	....	....	....
Playoff Totals		**40**	**5**	**13**	**18**	**34**	....	....	....
LOACH, Lonnie									Left wing
1993	Los Angeles	1	0	0	0	0	0	0	0
Playoff Totals		**1**	**0**	**0**	**0**	**0**	**0**	**0**	**0**
LOCAS, Jacques	*No playoffs*								Right wing
LOCHEAD, Bill									Left wing
1978	Detroit	7	3	0	3	6	0	0	1
Playoff Totals		**7**	**3**	**0**	**3**	**6**	**0**	**0**	**1**
LOCKING, Norm	*No playoffs*								Left wing/center
LOEWEN, Darcy	*No playoffs*								Left wing
LOFTHOUSE, Mark	*No playoffs*								Right wing/center
LOGAN, Dave									Defense
1978	Chicago	4	0	0	0	8	0	0	0
1979	Chicago	4	0	0	0	2	0	0	0
1980	Vancouver	4	0	0	0	0	0	0	0
Playoff Totals		**12**	**0**	**0**	**0**	**10**	**0**	**0**	**0**
LOGAN, Robert	*No playoffs*								Right wing
LOISELLE, Claude									Center
1985	Detroit	3	0	2	2	0	0	0	0
1988	New Jersey	20	4	6	10	50	0	2	0
1993	NY Islanders	18	0	3	3	10	0	0	0
Playoff Totals		**41**	**4**	**11**	**15**	**60**	**0**	**2**	**0**
LOMAKIN, Andrei	*No playoffs*								Right wing
LONEY, Brian	*No playoffs*								Right wing
LONEY, Troy									Left wing
1989	Pittsburgh	11	1	3	4	24	0	0	0
1991♦	Pittsburgh	24	2	2	4	41	0	0	0
1992♦	Pittsburgh	21	4	5	9	32	0	0	0
1993	Pittsburgh	10	1	4	5	0	0	0	0
1995	NY Rangers	1	0	0	0	0	0	0	0
Playoff Totals		**67**	**8**	**14**	**22**	**97**	**0**	**0**	**0**
LONG, Barry									Defense
1974	Los Angeles	5	0	1	1	18	0	0	0
Playoff Totals		**5**	**0**	**1**	**1**	**18**	**0**	**0**	**0**
LONG, Stanley									Defense
1952	Montreal	3	0	0	0	0	0	0	0
Playoff Totals		**3**	**0**	**0**	**0**	**0**	**0**	**0**	**0**
LONSBERRY, Ross									Left wing
1973	Philadelphia	11	4	3	7	9	0	0	1
1974♦	Philadelphia	17	4	9	13	18	1	1	1
1975♦	Philadelphia	17	4	3	7	10	1	0	1
1976	Philadelphia	16	4	3	7	2	1	0	1
1977	Philadelphia	10	1	2	3	29	0	0	0
1978	Philadelphia	12	2	2	4	6	1	0	1
1979	Pittsburgh	7	0	2	2	9	0	0	0
1980	Pittsburgh	5	2	1	3	2	0	0	1
1981	Pittsburgh	5	0	0	0	2	0	0	0
Playoff Totals		**100**	**21**	**25**	**46**	**87**	**4**	**1**	**6**
LOOB, Hakan									Right wing
1984	Calgary	11	2	3	5	2	1	0	2
1985	Calgary	4	3	3	6	0	0	1	0
1986	Calgary	22	4	10	14	6	1	2	0
1987	Calgary	5	1	2	3	0	0	1	0
1988	Calgary	9	8	1	9	4	2	2	0
1989♦	Calgary	22	8	9	17	4	2	2	1
Playoff Totals		**73**	**26**	**28**	**54**	**16**	**6**	**8**	**3**
LOOB, Peter	*No playoffs*								Defense
LORENTZ, Jim									Center/right wing
1970♦	Boston	11	1	0	1	4	0	0	0
1971	St. Louis	6	0	1	1	4	0	0	0
1973	Buffalo	6	0	3	3	2	0	0	0
1975	Buffalo	16	6	4	10	6	0	0	2
1976	Buffalo	9	1	2	3	6	0	0	0
1977	Buffalo	6	4	0	4	8	0	0	0
Playoff Totals		**54**	**12**	**10**	**22**	**30**	**0**	**0**	**2**
LORIMER, Bob									Defense
1979	NY Islanders	10	1	3	4	15	0	0	0
1980♦	NY Islanders	21	1	3	4	41	0	0	1
1981♦	NY Islanders	18	1	4	5	27	0	0	0
Playoff Totals		**49**	**3**	**10**	**13**	**83**	**0**	**0**	**1**
LORRAIN, Rod									Right wing
1937	Mtl. Canadiens	5	0	0	0	0	0	0	0
1938	Mtl. Canadiens	3	0	0	0	0	0	0	0
1939	Mtl. Canadiens	3	0	3	3	0	0	0	0
Playoff Totals		**11**	**0**	**3**	**3**	**0**	**0**	**0**	**0**
LOUGHLIN, Clem	*No playoffs*								Defense
LOUGHLIN, Wilf	*No playoffs*								Defense/left wing
LOVSIN, Ken	*No playoffs*								Defense
LOWDERMILK, Dwayne	*No playoffs*								Defense
LOWE, Darren	*No playoffs*								Right wing
LOWE, Kevin									Defense
1980	Edmonton	3	0	1	1	0	0	0	0
1981	Edmonton	9	0	2	2	11	0	0	0
1982	Edmonton	5	0	3	3	0	0	0	0
1983	Edmonton	16	1	8	9	10	0	0	0
1984♦	Edmonton	19	3	7	10	16	0	0	0
1985♦	Edmonton	16	0	5	5	8	0	0	0
1986	Edmonton	10	1	3	4	15	0	0	0
1987♦	Edmonton	21	2	4	6	22	0	2	1
1988♦	Edmonton	19	0	2	2	26	0	0	0
1989	Edmonton	7	1	2	3	4	0	0	0
1990♦	Edmonton	20	0	2	2	10	0	0	0
1991	Edmonton	14	1	1	2	14	0	0	0
1992	Edmonton	11	0	3	3	16	0	0	0
1994♦	NY Rangers	22	1	0	1	20	0	0	0
1995	NY Rangers	10	0	1	1	12	0	0	0
1996	NY Rangers	10	0	4	4	4	0	0	0
1997	Edmonton	1	0	0	0	0	0	0	0
1998	Edmonton	1	0	0	0	4	0	0	0
Playoff Totals		**214**	**10**	**48**	**58**	**192**	**0**	**2**	**1**
LOWE, Norm	*No playoffs*								Center
LOWE, Ross									Defense/left wing
1951	Montreal	2	0	0	0	0	0	0	0
Playoff Totals		**2**	**0**	**0**	**0**	**0**	**0**	**0**	**0**
LOWREY, Ed	*No playoffs*								Center
LOWERY, Fred									Right wing
1926	Pittsburgh	2	0	0	0	6	0	0	0
Playoff Totals		**2**	**0**	**0**	**0**	**6**	**0**	**0**	**0**
LOWREY, Gerry									Left wing
1932	Chicago	2	1	0	1	2	....	....	....
Playoff Totals		**2**	**1**	**0**	**1**	**2**	....	....	....
LOWRY, Dave									Left wing
1986	Vancouver	3	0	0	0	0	0	0	0
1989	St. Louis	10	0	5	5	4	0	0	0
1990	St. Louis	12	2	1	3	39	0	0	0
1991	St. Louis	13	1	4	5	35	0	0	0
1992	St. Louis	6	0	1	1	20	0	0	0
1993	St. Louis	11	2	0	2	14	0	1	0
1996	Florida	22	10	7	17	39	4	0	2
1997	Florida	5	0	0	0	0	0	0	0
1998	San Jose	6	0	0	0	18	0	0	0
1999	San Jose	1	0	0	0	0	0	0	0
Playoff Totals		**89**	**15**	**18**	**33**	**169**	**4**	**1**	**2**
LUCAS, Danny	*No playoffs*								Right wing
LUCAS, Dave	*No playoffs*								Defense
LUCE, Don									Center
1970	NY Rangers	5	0	1	1	4	0	0	0
1973	Buffalo	6	1	1	2	2	0	0	0
1975	Buffalo	16	5	8	13	19	0	1	0
1976	Buffalo	9	4	3	7	6	0	0	1
1977	Buffalo	6	3	1	4	2	2	0	0
1978	Buffalo	8	0	2	2	6	0	0	0
1979	Buffalo	3	1	1	2	0	0	0	0
1980	Buffalo	14	3	3	6	11	0	1	1
1981	Los Angeles	4	0	2	2	2	0	0	0
Playoff Totals		**71**	**17**	**22**	**39**	**52**	**2**	**2**	**2**
LUDVIG, Jan	*No playoffs*								Right wing
LUDWIG, Craig									Defense
1983	Montreal	3	0	0	0	2	0	0	0
1984	Montreal	15	0	3	3	23	0	0	0
1985	Montreal	12	0	2	2	6	0	0	0
1986♦	Montreal	20	0	1	1	48	0	0	0
1987	Montreal	17	2	3	5	30	0	0	1
1988	Montreal	11	1	1	2	6	0	0	0
1989	Montreal	21	0	2	2	24	0	0	0
1990	Montreal	11	0	1	1	16	0	0	0
1992	Minnesota	7	0	1	1	19	0	0	0
1994	Dallas	9	0	3	3	8	0	0	0
1995	Dallas	4	0	1	1	2	0	0	0
1997	Dallas	7	0	2	2	18	0	0	0
1998	Dallas	17	0	1	1	22	0	0	0
1999♦	Dallas	23	1	4	5	20	0	0	0
Playoff Totals		**177**	**4**	**25**	**29**	**244**	**0**	**0**	**1**
LUDZIK, Steve									Center
1983	Chicago	13	3	5	8	20	0	0	0
1984	Chicago	4	0	1	1	9	0	0	0
1985	Chicago	15	1	1	2	16	0	0	0
1986	Chicago	3	0	0	0	12	0	0	0
1987	Chicago	4	0	0	0	0	0	0	0
1988	Chicago	5	0	1	1	13	0	0	0
Playoff Totals		**44**	**4**	**8**	**12**	**70**	**0**	**0**	**0**
LUHNING, Warren	*No playoffs*								Right wing
LUKOWICH, Bernie									Right wing
1975	St. Louis	2	0	0	0	0	0	0	0
Playoff Totals		**2**	**0**	**0**	**0**	**0**	**0**	**0**	**0**
LUKOWICH, Brad									Defense
1999♦	Dallas	8	0	1	1	4	0	0	0
Playoff Totals		**8**	**0**	**1**	**1**	**4**	**0**	**0**	**0**
LUKOWICH, Morris									Left wing
1982	Winnipeg	4	0	2	2	16	0	0	0
1984	Winnipeg	3	0	0	0	0	0	0	0
1985	Boston	1	0	0	0	0	0	0	0
1987	Los Angeles	3	0	0	0	8	0	0	0
Playoff Totals		**11**	**0**	**2**	**2**	**24**	**0**	**0**	**0**
LUKSA, Charlie	*No playoffs*								Defense
LUMLEY, Dave									Right wing
1980	Edmonton	3	1	0	1	12	1	0	0
1981	Edmonton	7	1	0	1	4	0	0	0
1982	Edmonton	5	2	1	3	21	0	0	0
1983	Edmonton	16	0	0	0	19	0	0	0
1984♦	Edmonton	19	2	5	7	44	0	0	0
1985♦	Edmonton	8	0	0	0	29	0	0	0
1986	Edmonton	3	0	2	2	2	0	0	0
Playoff Totals		**61**	**6**	**8**	**14**	**131**	**1**	**0**	**0**
LUMME, Jyrki									Defense
1991	Vancouver	6	2	3	5	0	1	1	0
1992	Vancouver	13	2	3	5	4	1	0	1
1993	Vancouver	12	0	5	5	6	0	0	0
1994	Vancouver	24	2	11	13	16	2	0	1
1995	Vancouver	11	2	6	8	8	1	0	0
1996	Vancouver	6	1	3	4	2	1	0	0
1999	Phoenix	7	0	1	1	6	0	0	0
Playoff Totals		**79**	**9**	**32**	**41**	**42**	**6**	**1**	**2**
LUND, Pentti									Right wing
1947	Boston	1	0	0	0	0	....	....	....
1948	Boston	2	0	0	0	0	....	....	....
1950	NY Rangers	12	6	5	11	0	....	....	....
1952	Boston	2	1	0	1	0	....	....	....
1953	Boston	2	0	0	0	0	....	....	....
Playoff Totals		**19**	**7**	**5**	**12**	**0**	....	....	....
LUNDBERG, Brian	*No playoffs*								Defense
LUNDE, Len									Center
1960	Detroit	6	1	2	3	0	1	0	0
1961	Detroit	10	2	0	2	0	2	0	0
1963	Chicago	4	0	0	0	2	0	0	0
Playoff Totals		**20**	**3**	**2**	**5**	**2**	**3**	**0**	**0**
LUNDHOLM, Bengt									Left wing
1982	Winnipeg	4	1	1	2	2	0	0	0
1983	Winnipeg	3	0	1	1	2	0	0	0
1985	Winnipeg	5	2	2	4	8	0	2	0
1986	Winnipeg	2	0	0	0	2	0	0	0
Playoff Totals		**14**	**3**	**4**	**7**	**14**	**0**	**2**	**0**
LUNDRIGAN, Joe	*No playoffs*								Defense
LUNDSTROM, Tord	*No playoffs*								Left wing
LUNDY, Pat									Center
1946	Detroit	2	1	0	1	0	....	....	....
1947	Detroit	5	0	1	1	2	....	....	....
1948	Detroit	5	1	1	2	0	....	....	....
1949	Detroit	4	0	0	0	0	....	....	....
Playoff Totals		**16**	**2**	**2**	**4**	**2**	....	....	....
LUONGO, Chris	*No playoffs*								Defense
LUPIEN, Gilles									Defense
1978♦	Montreal	8	0	0	0	17	0	0	0
1979♦	Montreal	13	0	0	0	2	0	0	0
1980	Montreal	4	0	0	0	2	0	0	0
Playoff Totals		**25**	**0**	**0**	**0**	**21**	**0**	**0**	**0**
LUPUL, Gary									Center/left wing
1980	Vancouver	4	1	0	1	0	1	0	0
1982	Vancouver	10	2	3	5	4	0	0	1
1983	Vancouver	4	1	3	4	0	0	0	0
1984	Vancouver	4	0	1	1	7	0	0	0
1986	Vancouver	3	0	0	0	0	0	0	0
Playoff Totals		**25**	**4**	**7**	**11**	**11**	**1**	**0**	**1**
LYASHENKO, Roman	*No playoffs*								Center
LYLE, George	*No playoffs*								Left wing
LYNCH, Jack	*No playoffs*								Defense
LYNN, Vic									Left wing/defense
1947♦	Toronto	11	4	1	5	16	....	....	....
1948♦	Toronto	9	2	5	7	*20	....	....	....
1949♦	Toronto	8	0	1	1	2	....	....	....
1950	Toronto	7	0	2	2	2	....	....	....
1951	Boston	5	0	0	0	2	....	....	....
1953	Chicago	7	1	1	2	4	....	....	....
Playoff Totals		**47**	**7**	**10**	**17**	**46**	....	....	....
LYON, Steve	*No playoffs*								Defense/right wing
LYONS, Ron									Left wing
1931	Boston	5	0	0	0	0	0	0	0
Playoff Totals		**5**	**0**	**0**	**0**	**0**	**0**	**0**	**0**

LYSIAK, Tom Center

Season	Club	GP	G	A	Pts	PIM	PP	SH	GW
1974	Atlanta	4	0	2	2	0	0	0	0
1976	Atlanta	2	0	0	0	2	0	0	0
1977	Atlanta	3	1	3	4	8	1	0	0
1978	Atlanta	2	1	0	1	2	0	0	0
1979	Chicago	4	0	0	0	2	0	0	0
1980	Chicago	7	4	4	8	0	4	0	0
1981	Chicago	3	0	3	3	0	0	0	0
1982	Chicago	15	6	9	15	13	3	0	0
1983	Chicago	13	6	7	13	8	2	0	2
1984	Chicago	5	1	1	2	2	0	0	0
1985	Chicago	15	4	8	12	10	0	0	0
1986	Chicago	3	2	1	3	2	0	0	0
Playoff Totals		**76**	**25**	**38**	**63**	**49**	**10**	**0**	**2**

MacADAM, Al Right wing

Season	Club	GP	G	A	Pts	PIM	PP	SH	GW
1974♦	Philadelphia	1	0	0	0	0	0	0	0
1980	Minnesota	15	7	9	16	4	1	0	2
1981	Minnesota	19	9	10	19	4	1	1	1
1982	Minnesota	4	1	0	1	4	0	0	0
1983	Minnesota	9	2	1	3	2	0	0	0
1984	Minnesota	16	1	4	5	7	0	0	0
Playoff Totals		**64**	**20**	**24**	**44**	**21**	**2**	**1**	**3**

MacDERMID, Paul Right wing

Season	Club	GP	G	A	Pts	PIM	PP	SH	GW
1986	Hartford	10	2	1	3	20	0	0	1
1987	Hartford	6	2	1	3	34	0	0	1
1988	Hartford	6	0	5	5	14	0	0	0
1989	Hartford	4	1	1	2	16	0	0	0
1990	Winnipeg	7	0	2	2	8	0	0	0
1992	Washington	7	0	1	1	22	0	0	0
1995	Quebec	3	0	0	0	2	0	0	0
Playoff Totals		**43**	**5**	**11**	**16**	**116**	**0**	**0**	**2**

MacDONALD, Blair Right wing

Season	Club	GP	G	A	Pts	PIM	PP	SH	GW
1980	Edmonton	3	0	3	3	0	0	0	0
1981	Vancouver	3	0	1	1	2	0	0	0
1982	Vancouver	3	0	0	0	0	0	0	0
1983	Vancouver	2	0	2	2	0	0	0	0
Playoff Totals		**11**	**0**	**6**	**6**	**2**	**0**	**0**	**0**

MacDONALD, Brett *No playoffs* Defense

MacDONALD, Craig Center

Season	Club	GP	G	A	Pts	PIM	PP	SH	GW
1999	Carolina	1	0	0	0	0	0	0	0
Playoff Totals		**1**	**0**	**0**	**0**	**0**	**0**	**0**	**0**

MacDONALD, Doug *No playoffs* Left wing

MacDONALD, Kevin *No playoffs* Defense

MacDONALD, Kilby Left wing

Season	Club	GP	G	A	Pts	PIM	PP	SH	GW
1940♦	NY Rangers	12	0	2	2	4	....	....	....
1941	NY Rangers	3	1	0	1	0	....	....	....
Playoff Totals		**15**	**1**	**2**	**3**	**4**	....	....	....

MacDONALD, Lowell Left wing

Season	Club	GP	G	A	Pts	PIM	PP	SH	GW
1963	Detroit	1	0	0	0	2	0	0	0
1968	Los Angeles	7	3	4	7	2	1	0	1
1969	Los Angeles	7	2	3	5	0	0	1	0
1975	Pittsburgh	9	4	2	6	4	1	0	1
1976	Pittsburgh	3	1	0	1	0	1	0	1
1977	Pittsburgh	3	1	2	3	4	0	0	0
Playoff Totals		**30**	**11**	**11**	**22**	**12**	**3**	**1**	**3**

MacDONALD, Parker Center

Season	Club	GP	G	A	Pts	PIM	PP	SH	GW
1955	Toronto	4	0	0	0	4	....	....	....
1957	NY Rangers	1	1	1	2	0	....	....	....
1958	NY Rangers	6	1	2	3	2	....	....	....
1961	Detroit	9	1	0	1	0	....	....	....
1963	Detroit	11	3	2	5	2	....	....	....
1964	Detroit	14	3	3	6	2	....	....	....
1965	Detroit	7	1	1	2	6	....	....	....
1966	Detroit	9	0	0	0	2	....	....	....
1968	Minnesota	14	4	5	9	2	0	0	2
Playoff Totals		**75**	**14**	**14**	**28**	**20**	....	....	....

MacDOUGALL, Kim *No playoffs* Defense

MacEACHERN, Shane *No playoffs* Center

MACEY, Hub Left wing

Season	Club	GP	G	A	Pts	PIM	PP	SH	GW
1942	NY Rangers	1	0	0	0	0	0	0	0
1947	Montreal	7	0	0	0	0	0	0	0
Playoff Totals		**8**	**0**	**0**	**0**	**0**	**0**	**0**	**0**

MacGREGOR, Bruce Center

Season	Club	GP	G	A	Pts	PIM	PP	SH	GW
1961	Detroit	8	1	2	3	6	....	....	....
1963	Detroit	10	1	4	5	10	....	....	....
1964	Detroit	14	5	2	7	12	....	....	....
1965	Detroit	7	0	2	2	2	....	....	....
1966	Detroit	12	1	4	5	2	....	....	....
1970	Detroit	4	1	0	1	2	0	0	0
1971	NY Rangers	13	0	4	4	2	0	0	0
1972	NY Rangers	16	2	6	8	4	0	1	0
1973	NY Rangers	10	2	2	4	2	0	0	0
1974	NY Rangers	13	6	2	8	2	0	0	2
Playoff Totals		**107**	**19**	**28**	**47**	**44**	....	....	....

MacGREGOR, Randy *No playoffs* Right wing

MacGUIGAN, Garth *No playoffs* Center

MacINNIS, Al Defense

Season	Club	GP	G	A	Pts	PIM	PP	SH	GW
1984	Calgary	11	2	12	14	13	2	0	1
1985	Calgary	4	1	2	3	8	1	0	0
1986	Calgary	21	4	*15	19	30	2	0	0
1987	Calgary	4	1	0	1	0	1	0	0
1988	Calgary	7	3	6	9	18	2	0	0
1989♦	Calgary	22	7	*24	*31	46	5	0	4
1990	Calgary	6	2	3	5	8	1	0	0
1991	Calgary	7	2	3	5	8	2	0	0
1993	Calgary	6	1	6	7	10	1	0	0
1994	Calgary	7	2	6	8	12	1	0	0
1995	St. Louis	7	1	5	6	10	0	0	0
1996	St. Louis	13	3	4	7	20	1	0	0
1997	St. Louis	6	1	2	3	4	1	0	0
1998	St. Louis	8	2	6	8	12	1	0	0
1999	St. Louis	13	4	8	12	20	2	0	0
Playoff Totals		**142**	**36**	**102**	**138**	**219**	**23**	**0**	**5**

MacINTOSH, Ian *No playoffs* Right wing

MacIVER, Don *No playoffs* Defense

MACIVER, Norm Defense

Season	Club	GP	G	A	Pts	PIM	PP	SH	GW
1989	Hartford	1	0	0	0	2	0	0	0
1991	Edmonton	18	0	4	4	8	0	0	0
1992	Edmonton	13	1	2	3	10	0	0	0
1995	Pittsburgh	12	1	4	5	8	0	0	1
1996	Winnipeg	6	1	0	1	2	0	0	0
1998	Phoenix	6	0	1	1	2	0	0	0
Playoff Totals		**56**	**3**	**11**	**14**	**32**	**0**	**0**	**1**

MacKASEY, Blair *No playoffs* Defense

MacKAY, Calum Left wing

Season	Club	GP	G	A	Pts	PIM	PP	SH	GW
1950	Montreal	5	0	1	1	2	....	....	....
1951	Montreal	11	1	0	1	0	....	....	....
1953♦	Montreal	7	1	3	4	10	....	....	....
1954	Montreal	3	0	1	1	0	....	....	....
1955	Montreal	12	3	8	11	8	....	....	....
Playoff Totals		**38**	**5**	**13**	**18**	**20**	....	....	....

MacKAY, Dave Defense

Season	Club	GP	G	A	Pts	PIM	PP	SH	GW
1941	Chicago	5	0	1	1	2	0	0	0
Playoff Totals		**5**	**0**	**1**	**1**	**2**	**0**	**0**	**0**

MacKAY, Mickey Center

Season	Club	GP	G	A	Pts	PIM	PP	SH	GW
1927	Chicago	2	0	0	0	0	0	0	0
1929♦	Boston	3	0	0	0	2	0	0	0
1930	Boston	6	0	0	0	4	0	0	0
Playoff Totals		**11**	**0**	**0**	**0**	**6**	**0**	**0**	**0**

MacKAY, Murdo Right wing/center

Season	Club	GP	G	A	Pts	PIM	PP	SH	GW
1947	Montreal	9	0	1	1	0	....	....	....
1949	Montreal	6	1	1	2	0	....	....	....
Playoff Totals		**15**	**1**	**2**	**3**	**0**	....	....	....

MacKELL, Jack Right wing/defense

Season	Club	GP	G	A	Pts	PIM	PP	SH	GW
1920♦	Ottawa	5	0	0	0	0	0	0	0
1921♦	Ottawa	2	0	0	0	0	0	0	0
Playoff Totals		**7**	**0**	**0**	**0**	**0**	**0**	**0**	**0**

MacKENZIE, Barry *No playoffs* Defense

MacKENZIE, Bill Defense

Season	Club	GP	G	A	Pts	PIM	PP	SH	GW
1934	Mtl. Maroons	4	0	0	0	0	....	....	....
1935	NY Rangers	3	0	0	0	0	....	....	....
1937	Mtl. Canadiens	5	1	0	1	0	....	....	....
1938♦	Chicago	9	0	1	1	11	....	....	....
Playoff Totals		**21**	**1**	**1**	**2**	**11**	....	....	....

MACKEY, David Left wing

Season	Club	GP	G	A	Pts	PIM	PP	SH	GW
1992	St. Louis	1	0	0	0	0	0	0	0
1994	St. Louis	2	0	0	0	2	0	0	0
Playoff Totals		**3**	**0**	**0**	**0**	**2**	**0**	**0**	**0**

MACKEY, Reg Defense

Season	Club	GP	G	A	Pts	PIM	PP	SH	GW
1927	NY Rangers	1	0	0	0	0	0	0	0
Playoff Totals		**1**	**0**	**0**	**0**	**0**	**0**	**0**	**0**

MACKIE, Howie Right wing/defense

Season	Club	GP	G	A	Pts	PIM	PP	SH	GW
1937♦	Detroit	8	0	0	0	0	0	0	0
Playoff Totals		**8**	**0**	**0**	**0**	**0**	**0**	**0**	**0**

MacKINNON, Paul *No playoffs* Defense

MacLEAN, Donald *No playoffs* Center

MacLEAN, John Right wing

Season	Club	GP	G	A	Pts	PIM	PP	SH	GW
1988	New Jersey	20	7	11	18	60	2	0	2
1990	New Jersey	6	4	1	5	12	2	1	0
1991	New Jersey	7	5	3	8	20	1	0	0
1993	New Jersey	5	0	1	1	10	0	0	0
1994	New Jersey	20	6	10	16	22	2	0	1
1995♦	New Jersey	20	5	13	18	14	2	0	0
1997	New Jersey	10	4	5	9	4	2	1	1
1998	San Jose	6	2	3	5	4	1	0	0
Playoff Totals		**94**	**33**	**47**	**80**	**146**	**12**	**2**	**4**

MacLEAN, Paul Right wing

Season	Club	GP	G	A	Pts	PIM	PP	SH	GW
1981	St. Louis	1	0	0	0	0	0	0	0
1982	Winnipeg	4	3	2	5	26	2	0	1
1983	Winnipeg	3	1	2	3	6	1	0	0
1984	Winnipeg	3	1	0	1	0	0	0	0
1985	Winnipeg	8	3	4	7	4	2	0	0
1986	Winnipeg	2	1	0	1	7	0	0	0
1987	Winnipeg	10	5	2	7	16	2	0	0
1988	Winnipeg	5	2	0	2	23	2	0	0
1989	Detroit	5	1	1	2	8	0	0	0
1990	St. Louis	12	4	3	7	20	3	0	0
Playoff Totals		**53**	**21**	**14**	**35**	**110**	**12**	**0**	**1**

MacLEISH, Rick Center

Season	Club	GP	G	A	Pts	PIM	PP	SH	GW
1971	Philadelphia	4	1	0	1	0	0	0	0
1973	Philadelphia	10	3	4	7	2	2	0	1
1974♦	Philadelphia	17	*13	9	*22	20	5	0	4
1975♦	Philadelphia	17	11	9	*20	8	4	0	1
1977	Philadelphia	10	4	9	13	2	2	0	1
1978	Philadelphia	12	7	9	16	4	3	0	3
1979	Philadelphia	7	0	1	1	0	0	0	0
1980	Philadelphia	19	9	6	15	2	1	0	1
1981	Philadelphia	12	5	5	10	0	4	0	0
1982	Pittsburgh	5	1	1	2	0	0	0	0
1984	Detroit	1	0	0	0	0	0	0	0
Playoff Totals		**114**	**54**	**53**	**107**	**38**	**21**	**0**	**11**

MacLELLAN, Brian Left wing

Season	Club	GP	G	A	Pts	PIM	PP	SH	GW
1985	Los Angeles	3	0	1	1	0	0	0	0
1986	NY Rangers	16	2	4	6	15	0	0	1
1989♦	Calgary	21	3	2	5	19	0	0	1
1990	Calgary	6	0	2	2	8	0	0	0
1991	Calgary	1	0	0	0	0	0	0	0
Playoff Totals		**47**	**5**	**9**	**14**	**42**	**0**	**0**	**2**

MacLEOD, Pat *No playoffs* Defense

MacMILLAN, Billy Right wing

Season	Club	GP	G	A	Pts	PIM	PP	SH	GW
1971	Toronto	6	0	3	3	2	0	0	0
1972	Toronto	5	0	0	0	0	0	0	0
1975	NY Islanders	17	0	1	1	23	0	0	0
1976	NY Islanders	13	4	2	6	8	0	0	2
1977	NY Islanders	12	2	0	2	7	0	0	2
Playoff Totals		**53**	**6**	**6**	**12**	**40**	**0**	**0**	**4**

MacMILLAN, Bob Right wing

Season	Club	GP	G	A	Pts	PIM	PP	SH	GW
1976	St. Louis	3	0	1	1	0	0	0	0
1977	St. Louis	4	0	1	1	0	0	0	0
1978	Atlanta	2	0	2	2	0	0	0	0
1979	Atlanta	2	0	1	1	0	0	0	0
1980	Atlanta	4	0	0	0	9	0	0	0
1981	Calgary	16	8	6	14	7	2	0	1
Playoff Totals		**31**	**8**	**11**	**19**	**16**	**2**	**0**	**1**

MacMILLAN, John Right wing

Season	Club	GP	G	A	Pts	PIM	PP	SH	GW
1961	Toronto	4	0	0	0	0	0	0	0
1962♦	Toronto	3	0	0	0	0	0	0	0
1963♦	Toronto	1	0	0	0	0	0	0	0
1964	Detroit	4	0	1	1	2	0	0	0
Playoff Totals		**12**	**0**	**1**	**1**	**2**	**0**	**0**	**0**

MacNEIL, Al Defense

Season	Club	GP	G	A	Pts	PIM	PP	SH	GW
1962	Montreal	5	0	0	0	2	0	0	0
1963	Chicago	4	0	1	1	4	0	0	0
1964	Chicago	7	0	2	2	25	0	0	0
1965	Chicago	14	0	1	1	34	0	0	0
1966	Chicago	3	0	0	0	0	0	0	0
1967	NY Rangers	4	0	0	0	2	0	0	0
Playoff Totals		**37**	**0**	**4**	**4**	**67**	**0**	**0**	**0**

MacNEIL, Bernie *No playoffs* Left wing

MACOUN, Jamie Defense

Season	Club	GP	G	A	Pts	PIM	PP	SH	GW
1983	Calgary	9	0	2	2	8	0	0	0
1984	Calgary	11	1	0	1	0	1	0	0
1985	Calgary	4	1	0	1	4	0	0	0
1986	Calgary	22	1	6	7	23	0	0	0
1987	Calgary	3	0	1	1	8	0	0	0
1989♦	Calgary	22	3	6	9	30	0	0	1
1990	Calgary	6	0	3	3	10	0	0	0
1991	Calgary	7	0	1	1	4	0	0	0
1993	Toronto	21	0	6	6	36	0	0	0
1994	Toronto	18	1	1	2	12	0	0	0
1995	Toronto	7	1	2	3	8	0	0	0
1996	Toronto	6	0	2	2	8	0	0	0
1998♦	Detroit	22	2	2	4	18	0	0	2
1999	Detroit	1	0	0	0	0	0	0	0
Playoff Totals		**159**	**10**	**32**	**42**	**169**	**1**	**0**	**3**

MacPHERSON, Bud Defense

Season	Club	GP	G	A	Pts	PIM	PP	SH	GW
1951	Montreal	11	0	2	2	8	0	0	0
1952	Montreal	11	0	0	0	0	0	0	0
1953♦	Montreal	4	0	1	1	9	0	0	0
1954	Montreal	3	0	0	0	4	0	0	0
Playoff Totals		**29**	**0**	**3**	**3**	**21**	**0**	**0**	**0**

MacSWEYN, Ralph Defense

Season	Club	GP	G	A	Pts	PIM	PP	SH	GW
1969	Philadelphia	4	0	0	0	4	0	0	0
1971	Philadelphia	4	0	0	0	2	0	0	0
Playoff Totals		**8**	**0**	**0**	**0**	**6**	**0**	**0**	**0**

Season	Club	GP	G	A	Pts	PIM	PP	SH	GW
MacTAVISH, Craig									Center
1980	Boston	10	2	3	5	7	0	0	0
1983	Boston	17	3	1	4	18	0	0	0
1984	Boston	1	0	0	0	0	0	0	0
1986	Edmonton	10	4	4	8	11	1	0	0
1987♦	Edmonton	21	1	9	10	16	0	0	0
1988♦	Edmonton	19	0	1	1	31	0	0	0
1989	Edmonton	7	0	1	1	8	0	0	0
1990♦	Edmonton	22	2	6	8	29	0	0	0
1991	Edmonton	18	3	3	6	20	0	0	1
1992	Edmonton	16	3	0	3	28	0	1	1
1994♦	NY Rangers	23	1	4	5	22	0	0	0
1995	Philadelphia	15	1	4	5	20	0	0	0
1996	St. Louis	13	0	2	2	6	0	0	0
1997	St. Louis	1	0	0	0	2	0	0	0
Playoff Totals		**193**	**20**	**38**	**58**	**218**	**1**	**1**	**2**
MacWilliam, Mike	*No playoffs*								Left wing
MADDEN, John	*No playoffs*								Left wing
MADIGAN, Connie									Defense
1973	St. Louis	5	0	0	0	4	0	0	0
Playoff Totals		**5**	**0**	**0**	**0**	**4**	**0**	**0**	**0**
MADILL, Jeff									Right wing
1991	New Jersey	7	0	2	2	8	0	0	0
Playoff Totals		**7**	**0**	**2**	**2**	**8**	**0**	**0**	**0**
MAGEE, Dean	*No playoffs*								Left wing
MAGGS, Daryl									Defense
1972	Chicago	4	0	0	0	0	0	0	0
Playoff Totals		**4**	**0**	**0**	**0**	**0**	**0**	**0**	**0**
MAGNAN, Marc	*No playoffs*								Left wing
MAGNUSON, Keith									Defense
1970	Chicago	8	1	2	3	17	0	0	0
1971	Chicago	18	0	2	2	*63	0	0	0
1972	Chicago	8	0	1	1	29	0	0	0
1973	Chicago	7	0	2	2	4	0	0	0
1974	Chicago	11	1	0	1	17	0	0	0
1975	Chicago	8	1	2	3	15	0	0	0
1976	Chicago	4	0	0	0	12	0	0	0
1978	Chicago	4	0	0	0	7	0	0	0
Playoff Totals		**68**	**3**	**9**	**12**	**164**	**0**	**0**	**0**
MAGUIRE, Kevin									Right wing
1987	Toronto	1	0	0	0	0	0	0	0
1988	Buffalo	5	0	0	0	50	0	0	0
1989	Buffalo	5	0	0	0	36	0	0	0
Playoff Totals		**11**	**0**	**0**	**0**	**86**	**0**	**0**	**0**
MAHAFFY, John									Center
1945	Montreal	1	0	1	1	0	0	0	0
Playoff Totals		**1**	**0**	**1**	**1**	**0**	**0**	**0**	**0**
MAHOVLICH, Frank									Left wing
1959	Toronto	12	6	5	11	18	....	....	....
1960	Toronto	10	3	1	4	27	....	....	....
1961	Toronto	5	1	1	2	6	....	....	....
1962♦	Toronto	12	6	6	12	*29	....	....	....
1963♦	Toronto	9	0	2	2	8	....	....	....
1964♦	Toronto	14	4	*11	15	20	....	....	....
1965	Toronto	6	0	3	3	9	....	....	....
1966	Toronto	4	1	0	1	10	....	....	....
1967♦	Toronto	12	3	7	10	8	....	....	....
1970	Detroit	4	0	0	0	2	0	0	0
1971♦	Montreal	20	*14	13	*27	18	1	0	0
1972	Montreal	6	3	2	5	2	0	0	1
1973♦	Montreal	17	9	14	23	6	1	0	0
1974	Montreal	6	1	2	3	0	0	0	0
Playoff Totals		**137**	**51**	**67**	**118**	**163**	....	....	....
MAHOVLICH, Pete									Center
1971♦	Montreal	20	10	6	16	43	1	1	1
1972	Montreal	6	0	2	2	12	0	0	0
1973♦	Montreal	17	4	9	13	22	2	1	0
1974	Montreal	6	2	1	3	4	1	0	0
1975	Montreal	11	6	10	16	10	1	0	1
1976♦	Montreal	13	4	8	12	24	2	0	1
1977♦	Montreal	13	4	5	9	19	2	0	1
1979	Pittsburgh	2	0	1	1	0	0	0	0
Playoff Totals		**88**	**30**	**42**	**72**	**134**	**9**	**2**	**4**
MAILHOT, Jacques	*No playoffs*								Left wing
MAILLEY, Frank	*No playoffs*								Defense
MAIR, Adam									Center
1999	Toronto	5	1	0	1	14	0	0	0
Playoff Totals		**5**	**1**	**0**	**1**	**14**	**0**	**0**	**0**
MAIR, Jim									Defense
1971	Philadelphia	3	1	2	3	4	1	0	0
Playoff Totals		**3**	**1**	**2**	**3**	**4**	**1**	**0**	**0**
MAJEAU, Fern									Center/left wing
1944♦	Montreal	1	0	0	0	0	0	0	0
Playoff Totals		**1**	**0**	**0**	**0**	**0**	**0**	**0**	**0**
MAJOR, Bruce	*No playoffs*								Center
MAJOR, Mark	*No playoffs*								Left wing

Season	Club	GP	G	A	Pts	PIM	PP	SH	GW
MAKAROV, Sergei									Right wing
1990	Calgary	6	0	6	6	0	0	0	0
1991	Calgary	3	1	0	1	0	0	0	0
1994	San Jose	14	8	2	10	4	3	0	2
1995	San Jose	11	3	3	6	4	0	0	0
Playoff Totals		**34**	**12**	**11**	**23**	**8**	**3**	**0**	**2**
MAKELA, Mikko									Left wing
1987	NY Islanders	11	2	4	6	8	1	0	1
1988	NY Islanders	6	1	4	5	6	1	0	0
1990	Los Angeles	1	0	0	0	0	0	0	0
Playoff Totals		**18**	**3**	**8**	**11**	**14**	**2**	**0**	**1**
MAKI, Chico									Right wing
1961♦	Chicago	1	0	0	0	0	0	0	0
1963	Chicago	6	0	1	1	2	0	0	0
1964	Chicago	7	0	0	0	15	0	0	0
1965	Chicago	14	3	9	12	8	1	0	0
1966	Chicago	3	1	1	2	0	1	0	0
1967	Chicago	6	0	0	0	0	0	0	0
1968	Chicago	11	2	5	7	4	0	0	1
1970	Chicago	8	2	2	4	2	1	1	0
1971	Chicago	18	6	5	11	6	1	0	0
1972	Chicago	8	1	4	5	4	0	0	1
1973	Chicago	16	2	8	10	0	0	0	0
1974	Chicago	11	0	1	1	2	0	0	0
1976	Chicago	4	0	0	0	0	0	0	0
Playoff Totals		**113**	**17**	**36**	**53**	**43**	**4**	**1**	**2**
MAKI, Wayne									Left wing
1968	Chicago	2	1	0	1	2	0	0	0
Playoff Totals		**2**	**1**	**0**	**1**	**2**	**0**	**0**	**0**
MAKKONEN, Kari	*No playoffs*								Right wing
MALAKHOV, Vladimir									Defense
1993	NY Islanders	17	3	6	9	12	0	0	0
1994	NY Islanders	4	0	0	0	6	0	0	0
1997	Montreal	5	0	0	0	6	0	0	0
1998	Montreal	9	3	4	7	10	2	0	0
Playoff Totals		**35**	**6**	**10**	**16**	**34**	**2**	**0**	**0**
MALEY, David									Left wing
1986♦	Montreal	7	1	3	4	2	0	0	0
1988	New Jersey	20	3	1	4	80	0	0	0
1990	New Jersey	6	0	0	0	25	0	0	0
1992	Edmonton	10	1	1	2	4	0	0	0
1994	NY Islanders	3	0	0	0	0	0	0	0
Playoff Totals		**46**	**5**	**5**	**10**	**111**	**0**	**0**	**0**
MALGUNAS, Stewart	*No playoffs*								Defense
MALHOTRA, Manny	*No playoffs*								Center
MALIK, Marek									Defense
1999	Carolina	4	0	0	0	4	0	0	0
Playoff Totals		**4**	**0**	**0**	**0**	**4**	**0**	**0**	**0**
MALINOWSKI, Merlin	*No playoffs*								Center
MALKOC, Dean	*No playoffs*								Defense
MALLETTE, Troy									Left wing
1990	NY Rangers	10	2	2	4	81	0	0	0
1991	NY Rangers	5	0	0	0	18	0	0	0
Playoff Totals		**15**	**2**	**2**	**4**	**99**	**0**	**0**	**0**
MALONE, Cliff	*No playoffs*								Right wing
MALONE, Greg									Center
1977	Pittsburgh	3	1	1	2	2	0	0	1
1979	Pittsburgh	7	0	1	1	10	0	0	0
1981	Pittsburgh	5	2	3	5	16	0	0	0
1982	Pittsburgh	3	0	0	0	4	0	0	0
1986	Quebec	1	0	0	0	0	0	0	0
1987	Quebec	1	0	0	0	0	0	0	0
Playoff Totals		**20**	**3**	**5**	**8**	**32**	**0**	**0**	**1**
MALONE, Joe									Center/left wing
1918	Mtl. Canadiens	2	0	0	0	0	....	....	....
1919	Mtl. Canadiens	5	5	2	7	3	....	....	....
1923	Mtl. Canadiens	2	0	0	0	0	....	....	....
Playoff Totals		**9**	**5**	**2**	**7**	**3**	....	....	....
MALONEY, Dan									Left wing
1971	Chicago	10	0	1	1	8	0	0	0
1974	Los Angeles	5	0	0	0	2	0	0	0
1975	Los Angeles	3	0	0	0	2	0	0	0
1978	Toronto	13	1	3	4	17	1	0	0
1979	Toronto	6	3	3	6	2	1	0	1
1981	Toronto	3	0	0	0	4	0	0	0
Playoff Totals		**40**	**4**	**7**	**11**	**35**	**2**	**0**	**1**
MALONEY, Dave									Defense
1978	NY Rangers	3	0	0	0	11	0	0	0
1979	NY Rangers	17	3	4	7	45	0	1	0
1980	NY Rangers	8	2	1	3	8	0	1	0
1981	NY Rangers	2	0	2	2	9	0	0	0
1982	NY Rangers	10	1	4	5	6	1	0	1
1983	NY Rangers	7	1	6	7	10	0	0	0
1984	NY Rangers	1	0	0	0	2	0	0	0
1985	Buffalo	1	0	0	0	0	0	0	0
Playoff Totals		**49**	**7**	**17**	**24**	**91**	**1**	**2**	**1**

Season	Club	GP	G	A	Pts	PIM	PP	SH	GW
MALONEY, Don									Left wing
1979	NY Rangers	18	7	*13	20	19	0	0	1
1980	NY Rangers	9	0	4	4	10	0	0	0
1981	NY Rangers	13	1	6	7	13	1	0	0
1982	NY Rangers	10	5	5	10	10	2	0	0
1983	NY Rangers	5	0	1	1	0	0	0	0
1984	NY Rangers	5	1	4	5	0	0	0	0
1985	NY Rangers	3	4	0	4	2	2	0	0
1986	NY Rangers	16	2	1	3	31	0	0	0
1987	NY Rangers	6	2	1	3	6	0	0	0
1989	Hartford	4	0	0	0	8	0	0	0
1990	NY Islanders	5	0	0	0	2	0	0	0
Playoff Totals		**94**	**22**	**35**	**57**	**101**	**5**	**0**	**1**
MALONEY, Phil									Center
1959	Chicago	6	0	0	0	0	0	0	0
Playoff Totals		**6**	**0**	**0**	**0**	**0**	**0**	**0**	**0**
MALTAIS, Steve									Left wing
1990	Washington	1	0	0	0	0	0	0	0
Playoff Totals		**1**	**0**	**0**	**0**	**0**	**0**	**0**	**0**
MALTBY, Kirk									Right wing
1996	Detroit	8	0	1	1	4	0	0	0
1997♦	Detroit	20	5	2	7	24	0	1	1
1998♦	Detroit	22	3	1	4	30	0	1	0
1999	Detroit	10	1	0	1	8	0	0	1
Playoff Totals		**60**	**9**	**4**	**13**	**66**	**0**	**2**	**2**
MALUTA, Ray									Defense
1976	Boston	2	0	0	0	0	0	0	0
Playoff Totals		**2**	**0**	**0**	**0**	**0**	**0**	**0**	**0**
MANASTERSKY, Tom	*No playoffs*								Defense
MANCUSO, Gus	*No playoffs*								Right wing
MANDERVILLE, Kent									Left wing
1993	Toronto	18	1	0	1	8	0	0	0
1994	Toronto	12	1	0	1	4	0	1	0
1995	Toronto	7	0	0	0	6	0	0	0
1999	Carolina	6	0	0	0	2	0	0	0
Playoff Totals		**43**	**2**	**0**	**2**	**20**	**0**	**1**	**0**
MANDICH, Dan									Defense
1983	Minnesota	7	0	0	0	2	0	0	0
Playoff Totals		**7**	**0**	**0**	**0**	**2**	**0**	**0**	**0**
MANELUK, Mike	*No playoffs*								Left wing
MANERY, Kris	*No playoffs*								Center/right wing
MANERY, Randy									Defense
1974	Atlanta	4	0	2	2	4	0	0	0
1976	Atlanta	2	0	0	0	0	0	0	0
1977	Atlanta	3	0	0	0	0	0	0	0
1978	Los Angeles	2	0	0	0	2	0	0	0
1979	Los Angeles	2	0	0	0	6	0	0	0
Playoff Totals		**13**	**0**	**2**	**2**	**12**	**0**	**0**	**0**
MANN, Cameron									Right wing
1999	Boston	1	0	0	0	0	0	0	0
Playoff Totals		**1**	**0**	**0**	**0**	**0**	**0**	**0**	**0**
MANN, Jack	*No playoffs*								Center
MANN, Jimmy									Right wing
1982	Winnipeg	3	0	0	0	7	0	0	0
1983	Winnipeg	1	0	0	0	0	0	0	0
1984	Quebec	3	0	0	0	22	0	0	0
1985	Quebec	13	0	0	0	41	0	0	0
1986	Quebec	2	0	0	0	19	0	0	0
Playoff Totals		**22**	**0**	**0**	**0**	**89**	**0**	**0**	**0**
MANN, Ken	*No playoffs*								Right wing
MANN, Norm									Right wing/center
1936	Toronto	1	0	0	0	0	0	0	0
1941	Toronto	1	0	0	0	0	0	0	0
Playoff Totals		**2**	**0**	**0**	**0**	**0**	**0**	**0**	**0**
MANNERS, Rennison	*No playoffs*								Center
MANNO, Bob									Defense
1979	Vancouver	3	0	1	1	4	0	0	0
1980	Vancouver	4	1	0	1	6	0	0	0
1981	Vancouver	3	0	0	0	2	0	0	0
1984	Detroit	4	0	3	3	0	0	0	0
1985	Detroit	3	1	0	1	0	0	0	0
Playoff Totals		**17**	**2**	**4**	**6**	**12**	**0**	**0**	**0**
MANSON, Dave									Defense
1987	Chicago	3	0	0	0	10	0	0	0
1988	Chicago	5	0	0	0	27	0	0	0
1989	Chicago	16	0	8	8	84	0	0	0
1990	Chicago	20	2	4	6	46	1	0	0
1991	Chicago	6	0	1	1	36	0	0	0
1992	Edmonton	16	3	9	12	44	1	0	0
1996	Winnipeg	6	2	1	3	30	0	0	1
1997	Montreal	5	0	0	0	17	0	0	0
1998	Montreal	10	0	1	1	14	0	0	0
Playoff Totals		**87**	**7**	**24**	**31**	**308**	**2**	**0**	**1**
MANSON, Ray	*No playoffs*								Left wing

Season	Club	GP	G	A	Pts	PIM	PP	SH	GW
MANTHA, Georges	Defense/left wing								
1929	Mtl. Canadiens	3	0	0	0	0	....	....	....
1930♦	Mtl. Canadiens	6	0	0	0	8	....	....	....
1931♦	Mtl. Canadiens	10	5	1	6	4	....	....	....
1932	Mtl. Canadiens	4	0	1	1	8	....	....	....
1935	Mtl. Canadiens	2	0	0	0	4	....	....	....
1937	Mtl. Canadiens	5	0	0	0	0	....	....	....
1938	Mtl. Canadiens	3	1	0	1	0	....	....	....
1939	Mtl. Canadiens	3	0	0	0	0	....	....	....
Playoff Totals		**36**	**6**	**2**	**8**	**24**	....	....	....
MANTHA, Moe	Defense								
1982	Winnipeg	4	1	3	4	16	0	0	0
1983	Winnipeg	2	2	2	4	0	2	0	0
1984	Winnipeg	3	1	0	1	0	0	1	0
1989	Philadelphia	1	0	0	0	0	0	0	0
1990	Winnipeg	7	1	5	6	2	0	0	0
Playoff Totals		**17**	**5**	**10**	**15**	**18**	**2**	**1**	**0**
MANTHA, Sylvio	Defense								
1924♦	Mtl. Canadiens	6	0	0	0	0	....	....	....
1925	Mtl. Canadiens	6	0	0	0	2	....	....	....
1927	Mtl. Canadiens	4	1	0	1	0	....	....	....
1928	Mtl. Canadiens	2	0	0	0	6	....	....	....
1929	Mtl. Canadiens	3	0	0	0	0	....	....	....
1930♦	Mtl. Canadiens	6	2	1	3	18	....	....	....
1931♦	Mtl. Canadiens	10	2	1	3	*26	....	....	....
1932	Mtl. Canadiens	4	0	1	1	8	....	....	....
1933	Mtl. Canadiens	2	0	1	1	2	....	....	....
1934	Mtl. Canadiens	2	0	0	0	2	....	....	....
1935	Mtl. Canadiens	2	0	0	0	2	....	....	....
Playoff Totals		**47**	**5**	**4**	**9**	**66**	....	....	....
MARA, Paul *No playoffs*	Defense								
MARACLE, Bud	Left wing								
1931	NY Rangers	4	0	0	0	0	0	0	0
Playoff Totals		**4**	**0**	**0**	**0**	**0**	**0**	**0**	**0**
MARCETTA, Milan	Center								
1967♦	Toronto	3	0	0	0	0	0	0	0
1968	Minnesota	14	7	7	14	4	1	0	1
Playoff Totals		**17**	**7**	**7**	**14**	**4**	**1**	**0**	**1**
MARCH, Mush	Right wing								
1931	Chicago	9	3	1	4	11	....	....	....
1932	Chicago	2	0	0	0	2	....	....	....
1934♦	Chicago	8	2	2	4	6	....	....	....
1935	Chicago	2	0	0	0	0	....	....	....
1936	Chicago	2	2	3	5	0	....	....	....
1938♦	Chicago	9	2	4	6	12	....	....	....
1940	Chicago	2	1	0	1	2	....	....	....
1941	Chicago	4	2	3	5	0	....	....	....
1942	Chicago	3	0	2	2	4	....	....	....
1944	Chicago	4	0	0	0	4	....	....	....
Playoff Totals		**45**	**12**	**15**	**27**	**41**	....	....	....
MARCHANT, Todd	Center								
1997	Edmonton	12	4	2	6	12	0	3	1
1998	Edmonton	12	1	1	2	10	0	0	0
1999	Edmonton	4	1	1	2	12	0	0	0
Playoff Totals		**28**	**6**	**4**	**10**	**34**	**0**	**3**	**1**
MARCHINKO, Brian *No playoffs*	Center								
MARCHMENT, Bryan	Defense								
1992	Chicago	16	1	0	1	36	0	0	0
1993	Chicago	4	0	0	0	12	0	0	0
1997	Edmonton	3	0	0	0	4	0	0	0
1998	San Jose	6	0	0	0	10	0	0	0
1999	San Jose	6	0	0	0	4	0	0	0
Playoff Totals		**35**	**1**	**0**	**1**	**66**	**0**	**0**	**0**
MARCINYSHYN, Dave *No playoffs*	Defense								
MARCON, Lou *No playoffs*	Defense								
MARCOTTE, Don	Left wing								
1970♦	Boston	14	2	0	2	11	0	0	1
1971	Boston	4	0	0	0	0	0	0	0
1972♦	Boston	14	3	0	3	6	0	1	1
1973	Boston	5	1	1	2	0	0	0	0
1974	Boston	16	4	2	6	8	0	0	1
1975	Boston	3	1	0	1	0	0	0	0
1976	Boston	12	4	2	6	8	1	0	0
1977	Boston	14	5	6	11	10	0	1	0
1978	Boston	15	5	4	9	8	1	0	1
1979	Boston	11	5	3	8	10	0	0	0
1980	Boston	10	2	3	5	4	0	0	1
1981	Boston	3	2	2	4	6	0	0	0
1982	Boston	11	0	4	4	10	0	0	0
Playoff Totals		**132**	**34**	**27**	**61**	**81**	**2**	**2**	**5**
MARHA, Josef *No playoffs*	Center								
MARINI, Hector	Right wing								
1979	NY Islanders	1	0	0	0	0	0	0	0
1981♦	NY Islanders	9	3	6	9	14	0	0	0
Playoff Totals		**10**	**3**	**6**	**9**	**14**	**0**	**0**	**0**
MARINUCCI, Chris *No playoffs*	Center								
MARIO, Frank *No playoffs*	Center								

Season	Club	GP	G	A	Pts	PIM	PP	SH	GW
MARIUCCI, John	Defense								
1941	Chicago	5	0	2	2	16	0	0	0
1942	Chicago	3	0	0	0	0	0	0	0
1946	Chicago	4	0	1	1	10	0	0	0
Playoff Totals		**12**	**0**	**3**	**3**	**26**	**0**	**0**	**0**
MARK, Gordon *No playoffs*	Defense								
MARKELL, John *No playoffs*	Left wing								
MARKER, Gus	Right wing								
1934	Detroit	4	0	0	0	2	....	....	....
1935♦	Mtl. Maroons	7	1	1	2	4	....	....	....
1936	Mtl. Maroons	3	1	0	1	2	....	....	....
1937	Mtl. Maroons	5	0	1	1	0	....	....	....
1939	Toronto	10	2	2	4	0	....	....	....
1940	Toronto	10	1	3	4	23	....	....	....
1941	Toronto	7	0	0	0	5	....	....	....
Playoff Totals		**46**	**5**	**7**	**12**	**36**	....	....	....
MARKHAM, Ray	Center								
1980	NY Rangers	7	1	0	1	24	0	0	0
Playoff Totals		**7**	**1**	**0**	**1**	**24**	**0**	**0**	**0**
MARKLE, Jack *No playoffs*	Right wing								
MARKOV, Danny	Defense								
1999	Toronto	17	0	6	6	18	0	0	0
Playoff Totals		**17**	**0**	**6**	**6**	**18**	**0**	**0**	**0**
MARKS, Jack *No playoffs*	Left wing/defense								
MARKS, John	Left wing								
1973	Chicago	16	1	2	3	2	1	0	1
1974	Chicago	11	2	0	2	8	0	0	1
1975	Chicago	8	2	6	8	34	0	0	1
1976	Chicago	4	0	0	0	10	0	0	0
1977	Chicago	2	0	0	0	4	0	0	0
1978	Chicago	4	0	1	1	0	0	0	0
1979	Chicago	4	0	0	0	2	0	0	0
1980	Chicago	4	0	0	0	0	0	0	0
1981	Chicago	3	0	0	0	0	0	0	0
1982	Chicago	1	0	0	0	0	0	0	0
Playoff Totals		**57**	**5**	**9**	**14**	**60**	**1**	**0**	**3**
MARKWART, Nevin	Left wing								
1985	Boston	1	0	0	0	0	0	0	0
1987	Boston	4	0	0	0	9	0	0	0
1988	Boston	2	0	0	0	2	0	0	0
1991	Boston	12	1	0	1	22	0	0	0
Playoff Totals		**19**	**1**	**0**	**1**	**33**	**0**	**0**	**0**
MARLEAU, Patrick	Center								
1998	San Jose	5	0	1	1	0	0	0	0
1999	San Jose	6	2	1	3	4	2	0	0
Playoff Totals		**11**	**2**	**2**	**4**	**4**	**2**	**0**	**0**
MAROIS, Daniel	Right wing								
1988	Toronto	3	1	0	1	0	0	0	0
1990	Toronto	5	2	2	4	12	2	0	0
1994	Boston	11	0	1	1	16	0	0	0
Playoff Totals		**19**	**3**	**3**	**6**	**28**	**2**	**0**	**0**
MAROIS, Mario	Defense								
1978	NY Rangers	1	0	0	0	5	0	0	0
1979	NY Rangers	18	0	6	6	29	0	0	0
1980	NY Rangers	9	0	2	2	8	0	0	0
1981	Quebec	5	0	1	1	6	0	0	0
1982	Quebec	13	1	2	3	44	0	0	0
1984	Quebec	9	1	4	5	6	0	0	0
1985	Quebec	18	0	8	8	12	0	0	0
1986	Winnipeg	3	1	4	5	6	1	0	0
1987	Winnipeg	10	1	3	4	23	0	0	1
1988	Winnipeg	5	0	4	4	6	0	0	0
1991	St. Louis	9	0	0	0	37	0	0	0
Playoff Totals		**100**	**4**	**34**	**38**	**182**	**1**	**0**	**1**
MAROTTE, Gilles	Defense								
1968	Chicago	11	3	1	4	14	0	0	1
1974	NY Rangers	12	0	1	1	6	0	0	0
1975	NY Rangers	3	0	1	1	4	0	0	0
1977	St. Louis	3	0	0	0	2	0	0	0
Playoff Totals		**29**	**3**	**3**	**6**	**26**	**0**	**0**	**1**
MARQUESS, Mark	Right wing								
1947	Boston	4	0	0	0	0	0	0	0
Playoff Totals		**4**	**0**	**0**	**0**	**0**	**0**	**0**	**0**
MARSH, Brad	Defense								
1979	Atlanta	2	0	0	0	17	0	0	0
1980	Atlanta	4	0	1	1	2	0	0	0
1981	Calgary	16	0	5	5	8	0	0	0
1982	Philadelphia	4	0	0	0	2	0	0	0
1983	Philadelphia	2	0	1	1	0	0	0	0
1984	Philadelphia	3	1	1	2	2	0	0	0
1985	Philadelphia	19	0	6	6	65	0	0	0
1986	Philadelphia	5	0	0	0	2	0	0	0
1987	Philadelphia	26	3	4	7	16	0	1	0
1988	Philadelphia	7	1	0	1	8	0	0	0
1990	Toronto	5	1	0	1	2	0	0	0
1991	Detroit	1	0	0	0	0	0	0	0
1992	Detroit	3	0	0	0	0	0	0	0
Playoff Totals		**97**	**6**	**18**	**24**	**124**	**0**	**1**	**0**
MARSH, Gary *No playoffs*	Left wing								

Season	Club	GP	G	A	Pts	PIM	PP	SH	GW
MARSH, Peter	Right wing								
1981	Chicago	2	1	1	2	2	0	0	0
1982	Chicago	12	0	2	2	31	0	0	0
1983	Chicago	12	0	2	2	0	0	0	0
Playoff Totals		**26**	**1**	**5**	**6**	**33**	**0**	**0**	**0**
MARSHALL, Bert	Defense								
1966	Detroit	12	1	3	4	16	0	0	0
1969	Oakland	7	0	7	7	20	0	0	0
1970	Oakland	4	0	1	1	12	0	0	0
1973	NY Rangers	6	0	1	1	8	0	0	0
1975	NY Islanders	17	2	5	7	16	0	0	0
1976	NY Islanders	13	1	3	4	12	0	0	1
1977	NY Islanders	6	0	0	0	6	0	0	0
1978	NY Islanders	7	0	2	2	9	0	0	0
Playoff Totals		**72**	**4**	**22**	**26**	**99**	**0**	**0**	**1**
MARSHALL, Don	Left wing								
1955	Montreal	12	1	1	2	2	0	0	1
1956♦	Montreal	10	1	0	1	0	0	1	0
1957♦	Montreal	10	1	3	4	2	0	0	0
1958♦	Montreal	10	0	2	2	4	0	0	0
1959♦	Montreal	11	0	2	2	2	0	0	0
1960♦	Montreal	8	2	2	4	0	0	0	0
1961	Montreal	6	0	2	2	0	0	0	0
1962	Montreal	6	0	1	1	2	0	0	0
1963	Montreal	5	0	0	0	0	0	0	0
1967	NY Rangers	4	0	1	1	2	0	0	0
1968	NY Rangers	6	2	1	3	0	0	0	1
1969	NY Rangers	4	1	0	1	0	0	0	0
1970	NY Rangers	1	0	0	0	0	0	0	0
1972	Toronto	1	0	0	0	0	0	0	0
Playoff Totals		**94**	**8**	**15**	**23**	**14**	**0**	**1**	**2**
MARSHALL, Grant	Right wing								
1997	Dallas	5	0	2	2	8	0	0	0
1998	Dallas	17	0	2	2	*47	0	0	0
1999♦	Dallas	14	0	3	3	20	0	0	0
Playoff Totals		**36**	**0**	**7**	**7**	**75**	**0**	**0**	**0**
MARSHALL, Jason	Defense								
1997	Anaheim	7	0	1	1	4	0	0	0
1999	Anaheim	4	1	0	1	10	1	0	0
Playoff Totals		**11**	**1**	**1**	**2**	**14**	**1**	**0**	**0**
MARSHALL, Paul	Left wing								
1980	Pittsburgh	1	0	0	0	0	0	0	0
Playoff Totals		**1**	**0**	**0**	**0**	**0**	**0**	**0**	**0**
MARSHALL, Willie *No playoffs*	Center								
MARSON, Mike *No playoffs*	Left wing								
MARTIN, Clare	Defense								
1942	Boston	5	0	0	0	0	0	0	0
1947	Boston	5	0	1	1	0	0	0	0
1948	Boston	5	0	0	0	6	0	0	0
1950♦	Detroit	10	0	1	1	0	0	0	0
1951	Detroit	2	0	0	0	0	0	0	0
Playoff Totals		**27**	**0**	**2**	**2**	**6**	**0**	**0**	**0**
MARTIN, Craig *No playoffs*	Right wing								
MARTIN, Frank	Defense								
1953	Boston	6	0	1	1	2	0	0	0
1954	Boston	4	0	1	1	0	0	0	0
Playoff Totals		**10**	**0**	**2**	**2**	**2**	**0**	**0**	**0**
MARTIN, Grant	Left wing								
1987	Washington	1	1	0	1	2	0	0	0
Playoff Totals		**1**	**1**	**0**	**1**	**2**	**0**	**0**	**0**
MARTIN, Jack *No playoffs*	Center								
MARTIN, Matt *No playoffs*	Defense								
MARTIN, Pit	Center								
1964	Detroit	14	1	4	5	14	1	0	0
1965	Detroit	3	0	1	1	2	0	0	0
1968	Chicago	11	3	6	9	2	0	0	0
1970	Chicago	8	3	3	6	4	2	1	0
1971	Chicago	17	2	7	9	12	0	0	1
1972	Chicago	8	4	2	6	4	0	0	1
1973	Chicago	15	10	6	16	6	4	0	1
1974	Chicago	7	2	0	2	4	1	0	0
1975	Chicago	8	1	1	2	2	0	0	0
1976	Chicago	4	1	0	1	4	0	0	0
1977	Chicago	2	0	0	0	0	0	0	0
1979	Vancouver	3	0	1	1	2	0	0	0
Playoff Totals		**100**	**27**	**31**	**58**	**56**	**8**	**1**	**3**
MARTIN, Rick	Left wing								
1973	Buffalo	6	3	2	5	12	2	0	0
1975	Buffalo	17	7	8	15	20	5	0	1
1976	Buffalo	9	4	7	11	12	2	0	1
1977	Buffalo	6	2	1	3	9	1	0	1
1978	Buffalo	7	2	4	6	13	1	0	1
1979	Buffalo	3	0	3	3	0	0	0	0
1980	Buffalo	14	6	4	10	8	1	0	0
1981	Los Angeles	1	0	0	0	0	0	0	0
Playoff Totals		**63**	**24**	**29**	**53**	**74**	**12**	**0**	**4**
MARTIN, Ron *No playoffs*	Right wing								

Season	Club	GP	G	A	Pts	PIM	PP	SH	GW
MARTIN, Terry — Left wing									
1977	Buffalo	3	0	2	2	5	0	0	0
1978	Buffalo	8	2	0	2	5	0	0	0
1980	Toronto	3	2	0	2	7	0	0	0
1981	Toronto	3	0	0	0	0	0	0	0
1983	Toronto	4	0	0	0	9	0	0	0
Playoff Totals		**21**	**4**	**2**	**6**	**26**	**0**	**0**	**0**
MARTIN, Tom — Left wing									
1985	Winnipeg	3	0	0	0	2	0	0	0
1989	Hartford	1	0	0	0	4	0	0	0
Playoff Totals		**4**	**0**	**0**	**0**	**6**	**0**	**0**	**0**
MARTIN, Tom *No playoffs* — Right wing									
MARTINEAU, Don *No playoffs* — Right wing									
MARTINI, Darcy *No playoffs* — Defense									
MARTINS, Steve *No playoffs* — Center									
MARTINSON, Steve — Left wing									
1989	Montreal	1	0	0	0	10	0	0	0
Playoff Totals		**1**	**0**	**0**	**0**	**10**	**0**	**0**	**0**
MARUK, Dennis — Center									
1983	Washington	4	1	1	2	2	0	0	0
1984	Minnesota	16	5	5	10	8	1	1	0
1985	Minnesota	9	4	7	11	12	3	0	1
1986	Minnesota	5	4	9	13	4	1	0	0
Playoff Totals		**34**	**14**	**22**	**36**	**26**	**5**	**1**	**1**
MASNICK, Paul — Center									
1951	Montreal	11	2	1	3	4	....	....	....
1952	Montreal	6	1	0	1	12	....	....	....
1953♦	Montreal	6	1	0	1	7	....	....	....
1954	Montreal	10	0	4	4	4	....	....	....
Playoff Totals		**33**	**4**	**5**	**9**	**27**	....	....	....
MASON, Charley — Right wing									
1935	NY Rangers	4	0	1	1	0	0	0	0
Playoff Totals		**4**	**0**	**1**	**1**	**0**	**0**	**0**	**0**
MASSECAR, George *No playoffs* — Left wing									
MASTERS, Jamie — Defense									
1976	St. Louis	1	0	0	0	0	0	0	0
1977	St. Louis	1	0	0	0	0	0	0	0
Playoff Totals		**2**	**0**	**0**	**0**	**0**	**0**	**0**	**0**
MASTERTON, Bill *No playoffs* — Center									
MATHERS, Frank *No playoffs* — Defense									
MATHIASEN, Dwight *No playoffs* — Right wing									
MATHIESON, Jim *No playoffs* — Defense									
MATHIEU, Marquis *No playoffs* — Center									
MATTE, Christian *No playoffs* — Right wing									
MATTE, Joe *No playoffs* — Defense									
MATTE, Roland *No playoffs* — Defense									
MATTEAU, Stephane — Left wing									
1991	Calgary	5	0	1	1	0	0	0	0
1992	Chicago	18	4	6	10	24	1	1	0
1993	Chicago	3	0	1	1	2	0	0	0
1994♦	NY Rangers	23	6	3	9	20	1	0	2
1995	NY Rangers	9	0	1	1	10	0	0	0
1996	St. Louis	11	0	2	2	8	0	0	0
1997	St. Louis	5	0	0	0	0	0	0	0
1998	San Jose	4	0	1	1	0	0	0	0
1999	San Jose	5	0	0	0	6	0	0	0
Playoff Totals		**83**	**10**	**15**	**25**	**70**	**2**	**1**	**2**
MATTIUSSI, Dick — Left wing									
1969	Oakland	7	0	1	1	6	0	0	0
1970	Oakland	1	0	0	0	0	0	0	0
Playoff Totals		**8**	**0**	**1**	**1**	**6**	**0**	**0**	**0**
MATVICHUK, Richard — Defense									
1994	Dallas	7	1	1	2	12	1	0	0
1995	Dallas	5	0	2	2	4	0	0	0
1997	Dallas	7	0	1	1	20	0	0	0
1998	Dallas	16	1	1	2	14	0	0	0
1999♦	Dallas	22	1	5	6	20	0	0	0
Playoff Totals		**57**	**3**	**10**	**13**	**70**	**1**	**0**	**0**
MATZ, Johnny — Center									
1925	Mtl. Canadiens	5	0	0	0	2	0	0	0
Playoff Totals		**5**	**0**	**0**	**0**	**2**	**0**	**0**	**0**
MAXNER, Wayne *No playoffs* — Left wing									
MAXWELL, Brad — Defense									
1980	Minnesota	11	0	8	8	20	0	0	0
1981	Minnesota	18	3	11	14	35	1	0	0
1982	Minnesota	4	0	3	3	13	0	0	0
1983	Minnesota	9	5	6	11	23	2	0	0
1984	Minnesota	16	2	11	13	40	1	0	0
1985	Quebec	18	2	9	11	35	1	0	0
1986	Toronto	3	0	1	1	12	0	0	0
Playoff Totals		**79**	**12**	**49**	**61**	**178**	**5**	**0**	**0**
MAXWELL, Bryan — Defense									
1980	St. Louis	1	0	0	0	9	0	0	0
1981	St. Louis	11	0	1	1	54	0	0	0
1983	Winnipeg	3	1	0	1	23	1	0	0
Playoff Totals		**15**	**1**	**1**	**2**	**86**	**1**	**0**	**0**

Season	Club	GP	G	A	Pts	PIM	PP	SH	GW
MAXWELL, Kevin — Center									
1981	Minnesota	16	3	4	7	24	0	1	0
Playoff Totals		**16**	**3**	**4**	**7**	**24**	**0**	**1**	**0**
MAXWELL, Wally *No playoffs* — Center									
MAY, Alan — Right wing									
1990	Washington	15	0	0	0	37	0	0	0
1991	Washington	11	1	1	2	37	0	0	1
1992	Washington	7	0	0	0	0	0	0	0
1993	Washington	6	0	1	1	6	0	0	0
1994	Dallas	1	0	0	0	0	0	0	0
Playoff Totals		**40**	**1**	**2**	**3**	**80**	**0**	**0**	**1**
MAY, Brad — Left wing									
1992	Buffalo	7	1	4	5	2	0	0	1
1993	Buffalo	8	1	1	2	14	0	0	1
1994	Buffalo	7	0	2	2	9	0	0	0
1995	Buffalo	4	0	0	0	2	0	0	0
1997	Buffalo	10	1	1	2	32	0	0	0
Playoff Totals		**36**	**3**	**8**	**11**	**59**	**0**	**0**	**2**
MAYER, Derek *No playoffs* — Defense									
MAYER, Jim *No playoffs* — Right wing									
MAYER, Pat *No playoffs* — Defense									
MAYER, Shep *No playoffs* — Right wing									
MAYERS, Jamal — Center									
1999	St. Louis	11	0	1	1	8	0	0	0
Playoff Totals		**11**	**0**	**1**	**1**	**8**	**0**	**0**	**0**
MAZUR, Eddie — Defense/left wing									
1951	Montreal	2	0	0	0	0	....	....	....
1952	Montreal	5	2	0	2	4	....	....	....
1953♦	Montreal	7	2	2	4	11	....	....	....
1954	Montreal	11	0	3	3	7	....	....	....
Playoff Totals		**25**	**4**	**5**	**9**	**22**	....	....	....
MAZUR, Jay — Center/Right wing									
1991	Vancouver	6	0	1	1	8	0	0	0
Playoff Totals		**6**	**0**	**1**	**1**	**8**	**0**	**0**	**0**
McADAM, Gary — Left wing									
1976	Buffalo	1	0	0	0	0	0	0	0
1977	Buffalo	6	1	0	1	0	0	0	0
1978	Buffalo	8	2	2	4	7	0	0	0
1979	Pittsburgh	7	2	1	3	0	0	0	0
1980	Pittsburgh	5	1	2	3	9	0	0	0
1982	Calgary	3	0	0	0	0	0	0	0
Playoff Totals		**30**	**6**	**5**	**11**	**16**	**0**	**0**	**0**
McADAM, Sam *No playoffs* — Center/left wing									
McALLISTER, Chris — Defense									
1999	Toronto	6	0	1	1	4	0	0	0
Playoff Totals		**6**	**0**	**1**	**1**	**4**	**0**	**0**	**0**
McALPINE, Chris — Defense									
1997	St. Louis	4	0	1	1	0	0	0	0
1998	St. Louis	10	0	0	0	16	0	0	0
1999	St. Louis	13	0	0	0	2	0	0	0
Playoff Totals		**27**	**0**	**1**	**1**	**18**	**0**	**0**	**0**
McAMMOND, Dean — Center									
1992	Chicago	3	0	0	0	2	0	0	0
1998	Edmonton	12	1	4	5	12	0	0	0
Playoff Totals		**15**	**1**	**4**	**5**	**14**	**0**	**0**	**0**
McANDREW, Hazen *No playoffs* — Defense									
McANEELEY, Ted *No playoffs* — Defense									
McATEE, Jud — Left wing									
1945	Detroit	14	2	1	3	0	....	....	....
Playoff Totals		**14**	**2**	**1**	**3**	**0**	....	....	....
McATEE, Norm *No playoffs* — Center									
McAVOY, George — Defense									
1955	Montreal	4	0	0	0	0	0	0	0
Playoff Totals		**4**	**0**	**0**	**0**	**0**	**0**	**0**	**0**
McBAIN, Andrew — Right wing									
1984	Winnipeg	3	2	0	2	0	0	0	0
1985	Winnipeg	7	1	0	1	0	0	0	0
1987	Winnipeg	9	0	2	2	10	0	0	0
1988	Winnipeg	5	2	5	7	29	0	1	0
Playoff Totals		**24**	**5**	**7**	**12**	**39**	**0**	**1**	**0**
McBAIN, Jason *No playoffs* — Defense									
McBAIN, Mike *No playoffs* — Defense									
McBEAN, Wayne — Defense									
1990	NY Islanders	2	1	1	2	0	0	0	0
Playoff Totals		**2**	**1**	**1**	**2**	**0**	**0**	**0**	**0**
McBRIDE, Cliff *No playoffs* — Right wing/defense									
McBURNEY, Jim *No playoffs* — Left wing									
McCABE, Bryan *No playoffs* — Defense									
McCABE, Stan *No playoffs* — Left wing									
McCAFFREY, Bert — Right wing/defense									
1925	Toronto	2	1	0	1	4	....	....	....
1930♦	Mtl. Canadiens	6	1	1	2	6	....	....	....
Playoff Totals		**8**	**2**	**1**	**3**	**10**	....	....	....
McCAHILL, John *No playoffs* — Defense									

Season	Club	GP	G	A	Pts	PIM	PP	SH	GW
McCAIG, Doug — Defense									
1942	Detroit	2	0	0	0	6	0	0	0
1947	Detroit	5	0	1	1	4	0	0	0
Playoff Totals		**7**	**0**	**1**	**1**	**10**	**0**	**0**	**0**
McCALLUM, Dunc — Defense									
1970	Pittsburgh	10	1	2	3	12	0	0	0
Playoff Totals		**10**	**1**	**2**	**3**	**12**	**0**	**0**	**0**
McCALMON, Eddie *No playoffs* — Right wing									
McCANN, Rick *No playoffs* — Center									
McCARTHY, Dan *No playoffs* — Center									
McCARTHY, Kevin — Defense									
1978	Philadelphia	10	0	1	1	8	0	0	0
1980	Vancouver	4	1	0	1	0	0	0	0
1981	Vancouver	3	0	1	1	0	0	0	0
1983	Vancouver	4	1	1	2	12	0	0	0
Playoff Totals		**21**	**2**	**3**	**5**	**20**	**0**	**0**	**0**
McCARTHY, Sandy — Right wing									
1994	Calgary	7	0	0	0	34	0	0	0
1995	Calgary	6	0	1	1	17	0	0	0
1996	Calgary	4	0	0	0	10	0	0	0
1999	Philadelphia	6	0	1	1	0	0	0	0
Playoff Totals		**23**	**0**	**2**	**2**	**61**	**0**	**0**	**0**
McCARTHY, Steve *No playoffs* — Defense									
McCARTHY, Thomas *No playoffs* — Right wing									
McCARTHY, Tom *No playoffs* — Left wing									
McCARTHY, Tom — Left wing									
1980	Minnesota	15	5	6	11	20	3	0	0
1981	Minnesota	8	0	3	3	6	0	0	0
1982	Minnesota	4	0	2	2	4	0	0	0
1983	Minnesota	9	2	4	6	9	0	0	0
1984	Minnesota	8	1	4	5	6	1	0	1
1985	Minnesota	7	0	2	2	0	0	0	0
1987	Boston	4	1	1	2	4	1	0	0
1988	Boston	13	3	4	7	18	0	0	0
Playoff Totals		**68**	**12**	**26**	**38**	**67**	**5**	**0**	**1**
McCARTNEY, Walt *No playoffs* — Left wing									
McCARTY, Darren — Right wing									
1994	Detroit	7	2	2	4	8	0	0	0
1995	Detroit	18	3	2	5	14	0	0	0
1996	Detroit	19	3	2	5	20	0	0	1
1997♦	Detroit	20	3	4	7	34	0	0	2
1998♦	Detroit	22	3	8	11	34	0	0	1
1999	Detroit	10	1	1	2	23	0	0	0
Playoff Totals		**96**	**15**	**19**	**34**	**133**	**0**	**0**	**4**
McCASKILL, Ted *No playoffs* — Center									
McCAULEY, Alyn *No playoffs* — Center									
McCLANAHAN, Rob — Center									
1980	Buffalo	10	0	1	1	4	0	0	0
1981	Buffalo	5	0	1	1	13	0	0	0
1982	NY Rangers	10	2	5	7	2	0	0	0
1983	NY Rangers	9	2	5	7	12	0	0	1
Playoff Totals		**34**	**4**	**12**	**16**	**31**	**0**	**0**	**1**
McCLEARY, Trent *No playoffs* — Right wing									
McCLELLAND, Kevin — Right wing									
1982	Pittsburgh	5	1	1	2	5	0	0	0
1984♦	Edmonton	18	4	6	10	42	0	0	1
1985♦	Edmonton	18	1	3	4	75	0	0	0
1986	Edmonton	10	1	0	1	32	0	0	0
1987♦	Edmonton	21	2	3	5	43	0	0	0
1988♦	Edmonton	19	2	3	5	68	0	0	0
1989	Edmonton	7	0	2	2	16	0	0	0
Playoff Totals		**98**	**11**	**18**	**29**	**281**	**0**	**0**	**1**
McCORD, Bob — Defense									
1968	Minnesota	14	2	5	7	10	0	0	0
Playoff Totals		**14**	**2**	**5**	**7**	**10**	**0**	**0**	**0**
McCORD, Dennis *No playoffs* — Defense									
McCORMACK, John — Center									
1950	Toronto	6	1	0	1	0	....	....	....
1953♦	Montreal	9	0	0	0	0	....	....	....
1954	Montreal	7	0	1	1	0	....	....	....
Playoff Totals		**22**	**1**	**1**	**2**	**0**	....	....	....
McCOSH, Shawn *No playoffs* — Center									
McCOURT, Dale — Center									
1978	Detroit	7	4	2	6	2	2	0	0
1982	Buffalo	4	2	3	5	0	1	0	0
1983	Buffalo	10	3	2	5	4	2	0	1
Playoff Totals		**21**	**9**	**7**	**16**	**6**	**5**	**0**	**1**
McCREARY, Bill Jr. *No playoffs* — Right wing									
McCREARY, Bill Sr. — Left wing									
1968	St. Louis	15	3	2	5	0	0	2	2
1969	St. Louis	12	1	5	6	14	1	1	0
1970	St. Louis	15	1	7	8	0	0	0	0
1971	St. Louis	6	1	2	3	0	0	0	0
Playoff Totals		**48**	**6**	**16**	**22**	**14**	**1**	**3**	**2**

Season	Club	GP	G	A	Pts	PIM	PP	SH	GW
McCREARY, Keith	Right wing								
1962	Montreal	1	0	0	0	0	0	0	0
1970	Pittsburgh	10	0	4	4	4	0	0	0
1972	Pittsburgh	1	0	0	0	2	0	0	0
1974	Atlanta	4	0	0	0	0	0	0	0
Playoff Totals		**16**	**0**	**4**	**4**	**6**	**0**	**0**	**0**
McCREEDY, Johnny	Right wing								
1942◆	Toronto	13	4	3	7	6	....	....	....
1945◆	Toronto	8	0	0	0	10	....	....	....
Playoff Totals		**21**	**4**	**3**	**7**	**16**	....	....	....
McCRIMMON, Brad	Defense								
1980	Boston	10	1	1	2	28	0	0	0
1981	Boston	3	0	1	1	2	0	0	0
1982	Boston	2	0	0	0	2	0	0	0
1983	Philadelphia	3	0	0	0	4	0	0	0
1984	Philadelphia	1	0	0	0	4	0	0	0
1985	Philadelphia	11	2	1	3	15	0	0	0
1986	Philadelphia	5	2	0	2	2	0	0	1
1987	Philadelphia	26	3	5	8	30	1	0	1
1988	Calgary	9	2	3	5	22	2	0	0
1989◆	Calgary	22	0	3	3	30	0	0	0
1990	Calgary	6	0	2	2	8	0	0	0
1991	Detroit	7	1	1	2	21	0	0	0
1992	Detroit	11	0	1	1	8	0	0	0
Playoff Totals		**116**	**11**	**18**	**29**	**176**	**3**	**0**	**2**
McCRIMMON, Jim *No playoffs*	Defense								
McCULLEY, Bob *No playoffs*	Right wing/defense								
McCURRY, Duke	Left wing								
1926	Pittsburgh	2	0	2	2	4	0	0	0
1928	Pittsburgh	2	0	0	0	0	0	0	0
Playoff Totals		**4**	**0**	**2**	**2**	**4**	**0**	**0**	**0**
McCUTCHEON, Brian *No playoffs*	Left wing								
McCUTCHEON, Darwin *No playoffs*	Defense								
McDILL, Jeff *No playoffs*	Right wing								
McDONAGH, Bill *No playoffs*	Left wing								
McDONALD, Ab	Left wing								
1958◆	Montreal	2	0	0	0	2	....	....	....
1959◆	Montreal	11	1	1	2	6	....	....	....
1961◆	Chicago	8	2	2	4	0	....	....	....
1962	Chicago	12	6	6	12	0	....	....	....
1963	Chicago	6	2	3	5	9	....	....	....
1964	Chicago	7	2	2	4	0	....	....	....
1966	Detroit	10	1	4	5	2	....	....	....
1969	St. Louis	12	2	1	3	10	0	0	0
1970	St. Louis	16	5	10	15	13	3	0	0
Playoff Totals		**84**	**21**	**29**	**50**	**42**	....	....	....
McDONALD, Brian	Center								
1968	Chicago	8	0	0	0	2	0	0	0
Playoff Totals		**8**	**0**	**0**	**0**	**2**	**0**	**0**	**0**
McDONALD, Bucko	Defense								
1936◆	Detroit	7	3	0	3	10	....	....	....
1937◆	Detroit	10	0	0	0	2	....	....	....
1939	Toronto	10	0	0	0	4	....	....	....
1940	Toronto	1	0	0	0	0	....	....	....
1941	Toronto	7	2	0	2	2	....	....	....
1942◆	Toronto	9	0	1	1	2	....	....	....
1943	Toronto	6	1	0	1	4	....	....	....
Playoff Totals		**50**	**6**	**1**	**7**	**24**	....	....	....
McDONALD, Butch	Left wing/center								
1940	Detroit	5	0	2	2	10	0	0	0
Playoff Totals		**5**	**0**	**2**	**2**	**10**	**0**	**0**	**0**
McDONALD, Gerry *No playoffs*	Defense								
McDONALD, Jack *No playoffs*	Right wing								
McDONALD, Jack	Left wing								
1918	Mtl. Canadiens	2	1	0	1	0	....	....	....
1919	Mtl. Canadiens	10	1	4	5	6	....	....	....
Playoff Totals		**12**	**2**	**4**	**6**	**6**	....	....	....
McDONALD, Lanny	Right wing								
1975	Toronto	7	0	0	0	2	0	0	0
1976	Toronto	10	4	4	8	4	2	0	1
1977	Toronto	9	10	7	17	6	3	0	1
1978	Toronto	13	3	4	7	10	1	0	2
1979	Toronto	6	3	2	5	0	0	0	0
1982	Calgary	3	0	1	1	6	0	0	0
1983	Calgary	7	3	4	7	19	1	0	0
1984	Calgary	11	6	7	13	6	3	0	1
1985	Calgary	1	0	0	0	0	0	0	0
1986	Calgary	22	11	7	18	30	4	0	2
1987	Calgary	5	0	0	0	2	0	0	0
1988	Calgary	9	3	1	4	6	0	0	0
1989◆	Calgary	14	1	3	4	29	0	0	0
Playoff Totals		**117**	**44**	**40**	**84**	**120**	**14**	**0**	**7**
McDONALD, Robert *No playoffs*	Right wing								
McDONALD, Terry *No playoffs*	Defense								
McDONNELL, Joe *No playoffs*	Defense								
McDONNELL, Moylan *No playoffs*	Defense								

Season	Club	GP	G	A	Pts	PIM	PP	SH	GW
McDONOUGH, Al	Right wing								
1972	Pittsburgh	4	0	1	1	0	0	0	0
1974	Atlanta	4	0	0	0	2	0	0	0
Playoff Totals		**8**	**0**	**1**	**1**	**2**	**0**	**0**	**0**
McDONOUGH, Hubie	Center								
1990	NY Islanders	5	1	0	1	4	0	0	0
Playoff Totals		**5**	**1**	**0**	**1**	**4**	**0**	**0**	**0**
McDOUGAL, Mike *No playoffs*	Right wing								
McDOUGALL, Bill	Center								
1991	Detroit	1	0	0	0	0	0	0	0
Playoff Totals		**1**	**0**	**0**	**0**	**0**	**0**	**0**	**0**
McEACHERN, Shawn	Left wing								
1992◆	Pittsburgh	19	2	7	9	4	0	0	0
1993	Pittsburgh	12	3	2	5	10	0	0	1
1994	Pittsburgh	6	1	0	1	2	0	0	0
1995	Pittsburgh	11	0	2	2	8	0	0	0
1996	Boston	5	2	1	3	8	0	0	0
1997	Ottawa	7	2	0	2	8	1	0	0
1998	Ottawa	11	0	4	4	8	0	0	0
1999	Ottawa	4	2	0	2	6	1	0	0
Playoff Totals		**75**	**12**	**16**	**28**	**54**	**2**	**0**	**1**
McELMURY, Jim *No playoffs*	Defense								
McEWEN, Mike	Defense								
1979	NY Rangers	18	2	11	13	8	2	0	1
1981◆	NY Islanders	17	6	8	14	6	4	0	0
1982◆	NY Islanders	15	3	7	10	18	2	0	0
1983◆	NY Islanders	12	0	2	2	4	0	0	0
1985	Washington	5	0	1	1	4	0	0	0
1986	Hartford	8	0	4	4	6	0	0	0
1987	Hartford	1	1	1	2	0	1	0	0
1988	Hartford	2	0	2	2	2	0	0	0
Playoff Totals		**78**	**12**	**36**	**48**	**48**	**9**	**0**	**1**
McFADDEN, Jim	Center								
1947	Detroit	4	0	2	2	0	....	....	....
1948	Detroit	10	5	3	8	10	....	....	....
1949	Detroit	8	0	1	1	6	....	....	....
1950◆	Detroit	14	2	3	5	8	....	....	....
1951	Detroit	6	0	0	0	2	....	....	....
1953	Chicago	7	3	0	3	4	....	....	....
Playoff Totals		**49**	**10**	**9**	**19**	**30**	....	....	....
McFADYEN, Don	Center/left wing								
1934◆	Chicago	8	2	2	4	5	....	....	....
1935	Chicago	2	0	0	0	0	....	....	....
1936	Chicago	1	0	0	0	0	....	....	....
Playoff Totals		**11**	**2**	**2**	**4**	**5**	....	....	....
McFALL, Dan *No playoffs*	Defense								
McFARLANE, Gord *No playoffs*	Right wing/defense								
McGEOUGH, Jim *No playoffs*	Center								
McGIBBON, Irv *No playoffs*	Right wing								
McGILL, Bob	Defense								
1986	Toronto	9	0	0	0	35	0	0	0
1987	Toronto	3	0	0	0	0	0	0	0
1988	Chicago	3	0	0	0	2	0	0	0
1989	Chicago	16	0	0	0	33	0	0	0
1990	Chicago	5	0	0	0	2	0	0	0
1991	Chicago	5	0	0	0	2	0	0	0
1992	Detroit	8	0	0	0	14	0	0	0
Playoff Totals		**49**	**0**	**0**	**0**	**88**	**0**	**0**	**0**
McGILL, Jack	Left wing								
1935	Mtl. Canadiens	2	2	0	2	0	....	....	....
1937	Mtl. Canadiens	1	0	0	0	0	....	....	....
Playoff Totals		**3**	**2**	**0**	**2**	**0**	....	....	....
McGILL, Jack	Center								
1942	Boston	5	4	1	5	6	....	....	....
1945	Boston	7	3	3	6	0	....	....	....
1946	Boston	10	0	0	0	0	....	....	....
1947	Boston	5	0	0	0	11	....	....	....
Playoff Totals		**27**	**7**	**4**	**11**	**17**	....	....	....
McGILL, Ryan *No playoffs*	Defense								
McGILLIS, Daniel	Defense								
1997	Edmonton	12	0	5	5	24	0	0	0
1998	Philadelphia	5	1	2	3	10	1	0	0
1999	Philadelphia	6	0	1	1	12	0	0	0
Playoff Totals		**23**	**1**	**8**	**9**	**46**	**1**	**0**	**0**
McGREGOR, Sandy *No playoffs*	Right wing								
McGUIRE, Mickey *No playoffs*	Left wing								
McHUGH, Mike *No playoffs*	Left wing								
McILHARGEY, Jack	Defense								
1976	Philadelphia	15	0	3	3	41	0	0	0
1979	Vancouver	3	0	0	0	2	0	0	0
1980	Philadelphia	9	0	0	0	25	0	0	0
Playoff Totals		**27**	**0**	**3**	**3**	**68**	**0**	**0**	**0**
McINENLY, Bert	Left wing/defense								
1935	Boston	4	0	0	0	2	0	0	0
Playoff Totals		**4**	**0**	**0**	**0**	**2**	**0**	**0**	**0**

Season	Club	GP	G	A	Pts	PIM	PP	SH	GW
McINNIS, Marty	Left wing								
1993	NY Islanders	3	0	1	1	0	0	0	0
1994	NY Islanders	4	0	0	0	0	0	0	0
1999	Anaheim	4	2	0	2	2	2	0	0
Playoff Totals		**11**	**2**	**1**	**3**	**2**	**2**	**0**	**0**
McINTOSH, Bruce *No playoffs*	Defense								
McINTOSH, Paul	Defense								
1975	Buffalo	1	0	0	0	0	0	0	0
1976	Buffalo	1	0	0	0	7	0	0	0
Playoff Totals		**2**	**0**	**0**	**0**	**7**	**0**	**0**	**0**
McINTYRE, Jack	Defense								
1951	Boston	2	0	0	0	0	....	....	....
1952	Boston	7	1	2	3	2	....	....	....
1953	Boston	10	4	2	6	2	....	....	....
1958	Detroit	4	1	1	2	0	....	....	....
1960	Detroit	6	1	1	2	0	....	....	....
Playoff Totals		**29**	**7**	**6**	**13**	**4**	....	....	....
McINTYRE, John	Center								
1990	Toronto	2	0	0	0	2	0	0	0
1991	Los Angeles	12	0	1	1	24	0	0	0
1992	Los Angeles	6	0	4	4	12	0	0	0
1994	Vancouver	24	0	1	1	16	0	0	0
Playoff Totals		**44**	**0**	**6**	**6**	**54**	**0**	**0**	**0**
McINTYRE, Larry *No playoffs*	Defense								
McKAY, Doug	Left wing								
1950◆	Detroit	1	0	0	0	0	0	0	0
Playoff Totals		**1**	**0**	**0**	**0**	**0**	**0**	**0**	**0**
McKAY, Randy	Right wing								
1989	Detroit	2	0	0	0	2	0	0	0
1991	Detroit	5	0	1	1	41	0	0	0
1992	New Jersey	7	1	3	4	10	1	0	0
1993	New Jersey	5	0	0	0	16	0	0	0
1994	New Jersey	20	1	2	3	24	0	0	0
1995◆	New Jersey	19	8	4	12	11	2	0	2
1997	New Jersey	10	1	1	2	0	0	0	0
1998	New Jersey	6	0	1	1	0	0	0	0
1999	New Jersey	7	3	2	5	2	0	0	1
Playoff Totals		**81**	**14**	**14**	**28**	**106**	**3**	**0**	**3**
McKAY, Ray *No playoffs*	Defense								
McKAY, Scott *No playoffs*	Center								
McKECHNIE, Walt	Center								
1968	Minnesota	9	3	2	5	0	0	0	0
1979	Toronto	6	4	3	7	7	0	1	1
Playoff Totals		**15**	**7**	**5**	**12**	**7**	**0**	**1**	**1**
McKEE, Jay	Defense								
1997	Buffalo	3	0	0	0	0	0	0	0
1998	Buffalo	1	0	0	0	0	0	0	0
1999	Buffalo	21	0	3	3	24	0	0	0
Playoff Totals		**25**	**0**	**3**	**3**	**24**	**0**	**0**	**0**
McKEE, Mike *No playoffs*	Left wing								
McKEGNEY, Ian *No playoffs*	Defense								
McKEGNEY, Tony	Left wing								
1979	Buffalo	2	0	1	1	0	0	0	0
1980	Buffalo	14	3	4	7	2	0	0	0
1981	Buffalo	8	5	3	8	2	1	0	0
1982	Buffalo	4	0	0	0	2	0	0	0
1983	Buffalo	10	3	1	4	4	1	0	2
1984	Quebec	7	0	0	0	0	0	0	0
1985	Minnesota	9	8	6	14	0	2	0	1
1986	Minnesota	5	2	1	3	22	0	0	0
1987	NY Rangers	6	0	0	0	12	0	0	0
1988	St. Louis	9	3	6	9	8	1	0	1
1989	St. Louis	3	0	1	1	0	0	0	0
1991	Chicago	2	0	0	0	4	0	0	0
Playoff Totals		**79**	**24**	**23**	**47**	**56**	**5**	**0**	**4**
McKELL, Fleming	Center								
1949◆	Toronto	9	2	4	6	4	....	....	....
1950	Toronto	7	1	1	2	11	....	....	....
1951◆	Toronto	11	2	3	5	9	....	....	....
1952	Boston	5	2	1	3	12	....	....	....
1953	Boston	11	2	*7	9	7	....	....	....
1954	Boston	4	1	1	2	8	....	....	....
1955	Boston	4	0	1	1	0	....	....	....
1957	Boston	10	5	3	8	4	....	....	....
1958	Boston	12	5	14	19	12	....	....	....
1959	Boston	7	2	6	8	8	....	....	....
Playoff Totals		**80**	**22**	**41**	**63**	**75**	....	....	....
McKENDRY, Alex	Left/right wing								
1980◆	NY Islanders	6	2	2	4	0	0	0	0
Playoff Totals		**6**	**2**	**2**	**4**	**0**	**0**	**0**	**0**
McKENNA, Sean	Right wing								
1984	Buffalo	3	1	0	1	2	0	0	0
1985	Buffalo	5	0	1	1	0	0	0	0
1987	Los Angeles	5	0	1	1	0	0	0	0
1988	Toronto	2	0	0	0	0	0	0	0
Playoff Totals		**15**	**1**	**2**	**3**	**2**	**0**	**0**	**0**
McKENNA, Steve	Left wing								
1998	Los Angeles	3	0	1	1	8	0	0	0
Playoff Totals		**3**	**0**	**1**	**1**	**8**	**0**	**0**	**0**

Season	Club	GP	G	A	Pts	PIM	PP	SH	GW
McKENNEY, Don	Center								
1955	Boston	5	1	2	3	4	....	....	....
1957	Boston	10	1	5	6	4	....	....	....
1958	Boston	12	9	8	17	0	....	....	....
1959	Boston	7	2	5	7	0	....	....	....
1964◆	Toronto	12	4	8	12	0	....	....	....
1965	Toronto	6	0	0	0	0	....	....	....
1968	St. Louis	6	1	1	2	2	0	0	0
Playoff Totals		**58**	**18**	**29**	**47**	**10**	....	....	....
McKENNY, Jim	Defense								
1971	Toronto	6	2	1	3	2	1	0	0
1972	Toronto	5	3	0	3	2	2	1	0
1974	Toronto	4	0	2	2	0	0	0	0
1975	Toronto	7	0	1	1	2	0	0	0
1976	Toronto	6	2	3	5	2	1	0	1
1977	Toronto	9	0	2	2	2	0	0	0
Playoff Totals		**37**	**7**	**9**	**16**	**10**	**4**	**1**	**1**
McKENZIE, Brian *No playoffs*	Left wing								
McKENZIE, Jim	Left wing								
1991	Hartford	6	0	0	0	8	0	0	0
1994	Pittsburgh	3	0	0	0	0	0	0	0
1995	Pittsburgh	5	0	0	0	4	0	0	0
1996	Winnipeg	1	0	0	0	2	0	0	0
1997	Phoenix	7	0	0	0	2	0	0	0
1998	Phoenix	1	0	0	0	0	0	0	0
1999	Anaheim	4	0	0	0	4	0	0	0
Playoff Totals		**27**	**0**	**0**	**0**	**20**	**0**	**0**	**0**
McKENZIE, John	Right wing								
1959	Chicago	2	0	0	0	2	0	0	0
1960	Detroit	2	0	0	0	0	0	0	0
1964	Chicago	4	0	1	1	6	0	0	0
1965	Chicago	11	0	1	1	6	0	0	0
1968	Boston	4	1	1	2	8	0	0	0
1969	Boston	10	2	2	4	17	1	0	0
1970◆	Boston	14	5	12	17	35	0	3	0
1971	Boston	7	2	3	5	22	1	0	1
1972◆	Boston	15	5	12	17	37	3	0	0
Playoff Totals		**69**	**15**	**32**	**47**	**133**	**5**	**3**	**1**
McKIM, Andrew *No playoffs*	Center								
McKINNON, Alex *No playoffs*	Right wing								
McKINNON, John	Defense								
1928	Pittsburgh	2	0	0	0	4	0	0	0
Playoff Totals		**2**	**0**	**0**	**0**	**4**	**0**	**0**	**0**
McLAREN, Kyle	Defense								
1996	Boston	5	0	0	0	14	0	0	0
1998	Boston	6	1	0	1	4	1	0	0
1999	Boston	12	0	3	3	10	0	0	0
Playoff Totals		**23**	**1**	**3**	**4**	**28**	**1**	**0**	**0**
McLEAN, Don *No playoffs*	Defense								
McLEAN, Fred *No playoffs*	Defense								
McLEAN, Jack	Center/right wing								
1943	Toronto	6	2	2	4	2	....	....	....
1944	Toronto	3	0	0	0	6	....	....	....
1945◆	Toronto	4	0	0	0	0	....	....	....
Playoff Totals		**13**	**2**	**2**	**4**	**8**	....	....	....
McLEAN, Jeff *No playoffs*	Center								
McLELLAN, John *No playoffs*	Center								
McLELLAN, Scott *No playoffs*	Right wing								
McLELLAN, Todd *No playoffs*	Center								
McLENAHAN, Rollie	Defense								
1946	Detroit	2	0	0	0	0	0	0	0
Playoff Totals		**2**	**0**	**0**	**0**	**0**	**0**	**0**	**0**
McCLEOD, Al *No playoffs*	Defense								
McLEOD, Jackie	Right wing								
1950	NY Rangers	7	0	0	0	0	0	0	0
Playoff Totals		**7**	**0**	**0**	**0**	**0**	**0**	**0**	**0**
McLLWAIN, Dave	Center/Right wing								
1989	Pittsburgh	3	0	1	1	0	0	0	0
1990	Winnipeg	7	0	1	1	2	0	0	0
1993	Toronto	4	0	0	0	0	0	0	0
1996	Pittsburgh	6	0	0	0	0	0	0	0
Playoff Totals		**20**	**0**	**2**	**2**	**2**	**0**	**0**	**0**
McMAHON Jr., Mike	Defense								
1968	Minnesota	14	3	7	10	4	0	2	0
Playoff Totals		**14**	**3**	**7**	**10**	**4**	**0**	**2**	**0**
McMAHON Sr., Mike	Defense								
1943	Montreal	5	0	0	0	14	....	....	....
1944◆	Montreal	8	1	2	3	16	....	....	....
Playoff Totals		**13**	**1**	**2**	**3**	**30**	....	....	....
McMANAMA, Bob	Center								
1975	Pittsburgh	8	0	1	1	6	0	0	0
Playoff Totals		**8**	**0**	**1**	**1**	**6**	**0**	**0**	**0**
McMANUS, Sammy	Left wing								
1935◆	Mtl. Maroons	1	0	0	0	0	0	0	0
Playoff Totals		**1**	**0**	**0**	**0**	**0**	**0**	**0**	**0**
McMURCHY, Tom *No playoffs*	Right wing								

Season	Club	GP	G	A	Pts	PIM	PP	SH	GW
McNAB, Max	Center								
1948	Detroit	3	0	0	0	2	....	....	....
1949	Detroit	10	1	0	1	2	....	....	....
1950◆	Detroit	10	0	0	0	0	....	....	....
1951	Detroit	2	0	0	0	0	....	....	....
Playoff Totals		**25**	**1**	**0**	**1**	**4**	....	....	....
McNAB, Peter	Center								
1975	Buffalo	17	2	6	8	4	0	0	0
1976	Buffalo	8	0	0	0	0	0	0	0
1977	Boston	14	5	3	8	2	2	0	0
1978	Boston	15	8	11	19	2	0	0	2
1979	Boston	11	5	3	8	0	0	0	0
1980	Boston	10	8	6	14	2	3	0	1
1981	Boston	3	3	0	3	0	1	0	0
1982	Boston	11	6	8	14	6	2	0	1
1983	Boston	15	3	5	8	4	0	0	0
1984	Vancouver	3	0	0	0	0	0	0	0
Playoff Totals		**107**	**40**	**42**	**82**	**20**	**8**	**0**	**4**
McNABNEY, Sid	Center								
1951	Montreal	5	0	1	1	2	0	0	0
Playoff Totals		**5**	**0**	**1**	**1**	**2**	**0**	**0**	**0**
McNAMARA, Howard *No playoffs*	Defense								
McNAUGHTON, George *No playoffs*	Right wing/center								
McNEILL, Billy	Right wing								
1958	Detroit	4	1	1	2	4	0	0	0
Playoff Totals		**4**	**1**	**1**	**2**	**4**	**0**	**0**	**0**
McNEILL, Mike *No playoffs*	Right wing								
McNEILL, Stu *No playoffs*	Center								
McPHEE, George	Left wing								
1983	NY Rangers	9	3	3	6	2	1	0	0
1985	NY Rangers	3	1	0	1	7	0	0	0
1986	NY Rangers	11	0	0	0	32	0	0	0
1987	NY Rangers	6	1	0	1	28	1	0	0
Playoff Totals		**29**	**5**	**3**	**8**	**69**	**2**	**0**	**0**
McPHEE, Mike	Left wing								
1984	Montreal	15	1	0	1	31	0	0	0
1985	Montreal	12	4	1	5	32	0	0	0
1986◆	Montreal	20	3	4	7	45	0	1	1
1987	Montreal	17	7	2	9	13	1	0	2
1988	Montreal	11	4	3	7	8	0	1	0
1989	Montreal	20	4	7	11	30	0	0	1
1990	Montreal	9	1	1	2	16	0	0	0
1991	Montreal	13	1	7	8	12	1	0	0
1992	Montreal	8	1	1	2	4	0	0	0
1994	Dallas	9	2	1	3	2	0	0	0
Playoff Totals		**134**	**28**	**27**	**55**	**193**	**2**	**2**	**4**
McRAE, Basil	Left wing								
1982	Quebec	9	1	0	1	34	0	0	0
1987	Quebec	13	3	1	4	*99	0	0	1
1989	Minnesota	5	0	0	0	58	0	0	0
1990	Minnesota	7	1	0	1	24	0	0	0
1991	Minnesota	22	1	1	2	*94	0	0	0
1993	St. Louis	11	0	1	1	24	0	0	0
1994	St. Louis	2	0	0	0	12	0	0	0
1995	St. Louis	7	2	1	3	4	0	0	0
1996	St. Louis	2	0	0	0	0	0	0	0
Playoff Totals		**78**	**8**	**4**	**12**	**349**	**0**	**0**	**1**
McRAE, Chris *No playoffs*	Left wing								
McRAE, Ken	Center								
1994	Toronto	6	0	0	0	4	0	0	0
Playoff Totals		**6**	**0**	**0**	**0**	**4**	**0**	**0**	**0**
McREAVY, Pat	Center								
1941◆	Boston	11	2	2	4	5	....	....	....
1942	Detroit	11	1	1	2	4	....	....	....
Playoff Totals		**22**	**3**	**3**	**6**	**9**	....	....	....
McREYNOLDS, Brian *No playoffs*	Center								
McSHEFFREY, Bryan *No playoffs*	Right wing								
McSORLEY, Marty	Defense								
1986	Edmonton	8	0	2	2	50	0	0	0
1987◆	Edmonton	21	4	3	7	65	0	0	1
1988◆	Edmonton	16	0	3	3	67	0	0	0
1989	Los Angeles	11	0	2	2	33	0	0	0
1990	Los Angeles	10	1	3	4	18	1	0	0
1991	Los Angeles	12	0	0	0	58	0	0	0
1992	Los Angeles	6	1	0	1	21	0	0	0
1993	Los Angeles	24	4	6	10	*60	2	0	1
1996	NY Rangers	4	0	0	0	0	0	0	0
1999	Edmonton	3	0	0	0	2	0	0	0
Playoff Totals		**115**	**10**	**19**	**29**	**374**	**3**	**0**	**2**
McSWEEN, Don *No playoffs*	Defense								
McTAGGART, Jim *No playoffs*	Defense								
McTAVISH, Dale *No playoffs*	Center								
McTAVISH, Gordon *No playoffs*	Center								
McVEIGH, Charley	Center/left wing								
1927	Chicago	2	0	0	0	0	0	0	0
1929	NY Americans	2	0	0	0	2	0	0	0
Playoff Totals		**4**	**0**	**0**	**0**	**2**	**0**	**0**	**0**

Season	Club	GP	G	A	Pts	PIM	PP	SH	GW
McVICAR, Jack	Defense								
1931	Mtl. Maroons	2	0	0	0	2	0	0	0
1932	Mtl. Maroons	4	0	0	0	0	0	0	0
Playoff Totals		**6**	**0**	**0**	**0**	**2**	**0**	**0**	**0**
MEAGHER, Rick	Center								
1986	St. Louis	19	4	4	8	12	0	1	0
1987	St. Louis	6	0	0	0	11	0	0	0
1988	St. Louis	10	0	0	0	8	0	0	0
1989	St. Louis	10	3	2	5	6	0	0	1
1990	St. Louis	8	1	0	1	2	0	0	0
1991	St. Louis	9	0	1	1	2	0	0	0
Playoff Totals		**62**	**8**	**7**	**15**	**41**	**0**	**1**	**1**
MEEHAN, Gerry	Center								
1969	Philadelphia	4	0	0	0	0	0	0	0
1973	Buffalo	6	0	1	1	0	0	0	0
Playoff Totals		**10**	**0**	**1**	**1**	**0**	**0**	**0**	**0**
MEEKE, Brent *No playoffs*	Defense								
MEEKER, Howie	Right wing								
1947◆	Toronto	11	3	3	6	6	....	....	....
1948◆	Toronto	9	2	4	6	15	....	....	....
1950	Toronto	7	0	1	1	4	....	....	....
1951◆	Toronto	11	1	1	2	14	....	....	....
1952	Toronto	4	0	0	0	11	....	....	....
Playoff Totals		**42**	**6**	**9**	**15**	**50**	....	....	....
MEEKER, Mike *No playoffs*	Right wing								
MEEKING, Harry	Left wing								
1918◆	Toronto	7	4	2	6	21	....	....	....
1927	Boston	7	0	0	0	0	....	....	....
Playoff Totals		**14**	**4**	**2**	**6**	**21**	....	....	....
MEGER, Paul	Left wing								
1950	Montreal	2	0	0	0	2	....	....	....
1951	Montreal	11	1	3	4	4	....	....	....
1952	Montreal	11	0	3	3	2	....	....	....
1953◆	Montreal	5	1	2	3	4	....	....	....
1954	Montreal	6	1	0	1	4	....	....	....
Playoff Totals		**35**	**3**	**8**	**11**	**16**	....	....	....
MEIGHAN, Ron *No playoffs*	Defense								
MEISSNER, Barrie *No playoffs*	Left wing								
MEISSNER, Dick *No playoffs*	Right wing								
MELAMETSA, Anssi *No playoffs*	Left wing								
MELANSON, Dean *No playoffs*	Defense								
MELIN, Roger *No playoffs*	Left wing								
MELLANBY, Scott	Right wing								
1987	Philadelphia	24	5	5	10	46	0	0	1
1988	Philadelphia	7	0	1	1	16	0	0	0
1989	Philadelphia	19	4	5	9	28	0	0	0
1992	Edmonton	16	2	1	3	29	1	0	1
1996	Florida	22	3	6	9	44	2	0	0
1997	Florida	5	0	2	2	4	0	0	0
Playoff Totals		**93**	**14**	**20**	**34**	**167**	**3**	**0**	**2**
MELLOR, Tom *No playoffs*	Defense								
MELNYK, Gerry	Center								
1956	Detroit	6	0	0	0	0	0	0	0
1960	Detroit	6	3	0	3	0	0	0	1
1961	Detroit	11	1	0	1	2	0	0	1
1962	Chicago	7	0	0	0	2	0	0	0
1965	Chicago	6	0	0	0	0	0	0	0
1968	St. Louis	17	2	6	8	2	1	1	0
Playoff Totals		**53**	**6**	**6**	**12**	**6**	**1**	**1**	**2**
MELNYK, Larry	Defense								
1982	Boston	11	0	3	3	40	0	0	0
1983	Boston	11	0	0	0	9	0	0	0
1984◆	Edmonton	6	0	1	1	0	0	0	0
1985◆	Edmonton	12	1	3	4	26	0	0	0
1986	NY Rangers	16	1	2	3	46	0	0	0
1987	NY Rangers	6	0	0	0	4	0	0	0
1989	Vancouver	4	0	0	0	2	0	0	0
Playoff Totals		**66**	**2**	**9**	**11**	**127**	**0**	**0**	**0**
MELROSE, Barry	Defense								
1981	Toronto	3	0	1	1	15	0	0	0
1983	Toronto	4	0	1	1	23	0	0	0
Playoff Totals		**7**	**0**	**2**	**2**	**38**	**0**	**0**	**0**
MENARD, Hillary *No playoffs*	Left wing								
MENARD, Howie	Center								
1968	Los Angeles	7	0	5	5	24	0	0	0
1969	Los Angeles	11	3	2	5	12	1	0	0
1970	Oakland	1	0	0	0	0	0	0	0
Playoff Totals		**19**	**3**	**7**	**10**	**36**	**1**	**0**	**0**
MERCREDI, Vic *No playoffs*	Center								
MEREDITH, Greg	Right wing								
1983	Calgary	5	3	1	4	4	0	1	2
Playoff Totals		**5**	**3**	**1**	**4**	**4**	**0**	**1**	**2**
MERKOSKY, Glenn *No playoffs*	Center								
MERONEK, Bill	Center								
1943	Montreal	1	0	0	0	0	0	0	0
Playoff Totals		**1**	**0**	**0**	**0**	**0**	**0**	**0**	**0**

MERRICK, Wayne Center

Season	Club	GP	G	A	Pts	PIM	PP	SH	GW
1973	St. Louis	5	0	1	1	2	0	0	0
1975	St. Louis	2	1	1	2	0	1	0	0
1978	NY Islanders	7	1	0	1	0	0	0	0
1979	NY Islanders	10	2	3	5	2	0	0	0
1980◆	NY Islanders	21	2	4	6	2	0	0	1
1981◆	NY Islanders	18	6	12	18	8	0	0	1
1982◆	NY Islanders	19	6	6	12	6	0	0	1
1983◆	NY Islanders	19	1	3	4	10	0	0	0
1984	NY Islanders	1	0	0	0	0	0	0	0
Playoff Totals		**102**	**19**	**30**	**49**	**30**	**1**	**0**	**3**

MERRILL, Horace *No playoffs* Defense

MERTZIG, Jan *No playoffs* Defense

MESSIER, Eric Defense

Season	Club	GP	G	A	Pts	PIM	PP	SH	GW
1997	Colorado	6	0	0	0	4	0	0	0
1999	Colorado	3	0	0	0	0	0	0	0
Playoff Totals		**9**	**0**	**0**	**0**	**4**	**0**	**0**	**0**

MESSIER, Joby *No playoffs* Defense

MESSIER, Mark Center

Season	Club	GP	G	A	Pts	PIM	PP	SH	GW
1980	Edmonton	3	1	2	3	2	0	1	0
1981	Edmonton	9	2	5	7	13	0	0	0
1982	Edmonton	5	1	2	3	8	0	0	0
1983	Edmonton	15	15	6	21	14	4	2	0
1984◆	Edmonton	19	8	18	26	19	1	1	2
1985◆	Edmonton	18	12	13	25	12	1	1	1
1986	Edmonton	10	4	6	10	18	0	2	0
1987◆	Edmonton	21	12	16	28	16	1	2	1
1988◆	Edmonton	19	11	23	34	29	7	1	0
1989	Edmonton	7	1	11	12	8	0	0	0
1990◆	Edmonton	22	9	*22	*31	20	1	1	1
1991	Edmonton	18	4	11	15	16	1	0	0
1992	NY Rangers	11	7	7	14	6	2	2	0
1994◆	NY Rangers	23	12	18	30	33	2	1	4
1995	NY Rangers	10	3	10	13	8	2	0	1
1996	NY Rangers	11	4	7	11	16	2	0	1
1997	NY Rangers	15	3	9	12	6	0	0	1
Playoff Totals		***236**	**109**	**186**	**295**	**244**	**24**	***14**	**12**

MESSIER, Mitch *No playoffs* Center

MESSIER, Paul *No playoffs* Center

METCALFE, Scott *No playoffs* Left wing

METROPOLIT, Glen *No playoffs* Right wing

METZ, Don Right wing

Season	Club	GP	G	A	Pts	PIM	PP	SH	GW
1939	Toronto	2	0	0	0	0	....	....	....
1940	Toronto	2	0	0	0	0	....	....	....
1941	Toronto	7	1	1	2	2	....	....	....
1942◆	Toronto	4	4	3	7	0	....	....	....
1945◆	Toronto	11	0	1	1	4	....	....	....
1947◆	Toronto	11	2	3	5	4	....	....	....
1948◆	Toronto	2	0	0	0	2	....	....	....
1949◆	Toronto	3	0	0	0	0	....	....	....
Playoff Totals		**42**	**7**	**8**	**15**	**12**	....	....	....

METZ, Nick Left wing

Season	Club	GP	G	A	Pts	PIM	PP	SH	GW
1935	Toronto	6	1	1	2	0	....	....	....
1937	Toronto	2	0	0	0	0	....	....	....
1938	Toronto	7	0	2	2	0	....	....	....
1939	Toronto	10	3	3	6	6	....	....	....
1940	Toronto	9	1	3	4	9	....	....	....
1941	Toronto	7	3	4	7	0	....	....	....
1942◆	Toronto	13	4	4	8	12	....	....	....
1945◆	Toronto	7	1	1	2	2	....	....	....
1947◆	Toronto	6	4	2	6	0	....	....	....
1948◆	Toronto	9	2	0	2	2	....	....	....
Playoff Totals		**76**	**19**	**20**	**39**	**31**	....	....	....

MICHALUK, Art *No playoffs* Defense

MICHALUK, John *No playoffs* Right wing

MICHAYLUK, Dave Left wing

Season	Club	GP	G	A	Pts	PIM	PP	SH	GW
1992◆	Pittsburgh	7	1	1	2	0	0	0	0
Playoff Totals		**7**	**1**	**1**	**2**	**0**	**0**	**0**	**0**

MICHELETTI, Joe Defense

Season	Club	GP	G	A	Pts	PIM	PP	SH	GW
1981	St. Louis	11	1	11	12	10	1	0	0
Playoff Totals		**11**	**1**	**11**	**12**	**10**	**1**	**0**	**0**

MICHELETTI, Pat *No playoffs* Center

MICKEY, Larry Right wing

Season	Club	GP	G	A	Pts	PIM	PP	SH	GW
1969	Toronto	3	0	0	0	5	0	0	0
1973	Buffalo	6	1	0	1	5	0	0	0
Playoff Totals		**9**	**1**	**0**	**1**	**10**	**0**	**0**	**0**

MICKOSKI, Nick Left wing

Season	Club	GP	G	A	Pts	PIM	PP	SH	GW
1948	NY Rangers	2	0	1	1	0	....	....	....
1950	NY Rangers	12	1	5	6	2	....	....	....
1958	Detroit	4	0	0	0	4	....	....	....
Playoff Totals		**18**	**1**	**6**	**7**	**6**	....	....	....

MIDDENDORF, Max *No playoffs* Right wing

MIDDLETON, Rick Right wing

Season	Club	GP	G	A	Pts	PIM	PP	SH	GW
1975	NY Rangers	3	0	0	0	2	0	0	0
1977	Boston	13	5	4	9	0	0	0	1
1978	Boston	15	5	2	7	0	0	0	2
1979	Boston	11	4	8	12	0	2	0	1
1980	Boston	10	4	2	6	5	0	0	0
1981	Boston	3	0	1	1	2	0	0	0
1982	Boston	11	6	9	15	0	2	0	0
1983	Boston	17	11	22	33	6	4	1	1
1984	Boston	3	0	0	0	0	0	0	0
1985	Boston	5	3	0	3	0	0	0	0
1987	Boston	4	2	2	4	0	1	1	0
1988	Boston	19	5	5	10	4	0	1	3
Playoff Totals		**114**	**45**	**55**	**100**	**19**	**9**	**3**	**8**

MIEHM, Kevin Center

Season	Club	GP	G	A	Pts	PIM	PP	SH	GW
1993	St. Louis	2	0	1	1	0	0	0	0
Playoff Totals		**2**	**0**	**1**	**1**	**0**	**0**	**0**	**0**

MIGAY, Rudy Center

Season	Club	GP	G	A	Pts	PIM	PP	SH	GW
1954	Toronto	5	1	0	1	4	....	....	....
1955	Toronto	3	0	0	0	10	....	....	....
1956	Toronto	5	0	0	0	6	....	....	....
1959	Toronto	2	0	0	0	0	....	....	....
Playoff Totals		**15**	**1**	**0**	**1**	**20**	....	....	....

MIKITA, Stan Right wing

Season	Club	GP	G	A	Pts	PIM	PP	SH	GW
1960	Chicago	3	0	1	1	2	....	....	....
1961◆	Chicago	12	*6	5	11	21	....	....	....
1962	Chicago	12	6	*15	*21	19	....	....	....
1963	Chicago	6	3	2	5	2	....	....	....
1964	Chicago	7	3	6	9	8	....	....	....
1965	Chicago	14	3	7	10	*53	....	....	....
1966	Chicago	6	1	2	3	2	....	....	....
1967	Chicago	6	2	2	4	2	....	....	....
1968	Chicago	11	5	7	12	6	2	1	0
1970	Chicago	8	4	6	10	2	3	1	0
1971	Chicago	18	5	13	18	16	1	0	1
1972	Chicago	8	3	1	4	4	0	0	0
1973	Chicago	15	7	13	20	8	1	0	2
1974	Chicago	11	5	6	11	8	1	0	1
1975	Chicago	8	3	4	7	12	1	0	1
1976	Chicago	4	0	0	0	4	0	0	0
1977	Chicago	2	0	1	1	0	0	0	0
1978	Chicago	4	3	0	3	0	2	0	0
Playoff Totals		**155**	**59**	**91**	**150**	**169**	....	....	....

MIKKELSON, Bill *No playoffs* Defense

MIKOL, Jim *No playoffs* Left wing/defense

MIKULCHIK, Oleg *No playoffs* Defense

MILBURY, Mike Defense

Season	Club	GP	G	A	Pts	PIM	PP	SH	GW
1976	Boston	11	0	0	0	29	0	0	0
1977	Boston	13	2	2	4	*47	0	0	1
1978	Boston	15	1	8	9	27	0	0	0
1979	Boston	11	1	7	8	7	0	0	1
1980	Boston	10	0	2	2	50	0	0	0
1981	Boston	2	0	1	1	10	0	0	0
1982	Boston	11	0	4	4	6	0	0	0
1984	Boston	3	0	0	0	12	0	0	0
1985	Boston	5	0	0	0	10	0	0	0
1986	Boston	1	0	0	0	17	0	0	0
1987	Boston	4	0	0	0	4	0	0	0
Playoff Totals		**86**	**4**	**24**	**28**	**219**	**0**	**0**	**2**

MILKS, Hib Left wing/Center

Season	Club	GP	G	A	Pts	PIM	PP	SH	GW
1926	Pittsburgh	2	0	0	0	0	0	0	0
1928	Pittsburgh	2	0	0	0	2	0	0	0
1932	NY Rangers	7	0	0	0	0	0	0	0
Playoff Totals		**11**	**0**	**0**	**0**	**2**	**0**	**0**	**0**

MILLAR, Craig *No playoffs* Defense

MILLAR, Hugh Defense

Season	Club	GP	G	A	Pts	PIM	PP	SH	GW
1947	Detroit	1	0	0	0	0	0	0	0
Playoff Totals		**1**	**0**	**0**	**0**	**0**	**0**	**0**	**0**

MILLAR, Mike *No playoffs* Right wing

MILLEN, Corey Center

Season	Club	GP	G	A	Pts	PIM	PP	SH	GW
1991	NY Rangers	6	1	2	3	0	1	0	0
1992	Los Angeles	6	0	1	1	6	0	0	0
1993	Los Angeles	23	2	4	6	12	0	0	0
1994	New Jersey	7	1	0	1	2	0	0	1
1995	Dallas	5	1	0	1	2	0	0	0
Playoff Totals		**47**	**5**	**7**	**12**	**22**	**1**	**0**	**1**

MILLER, Aaron Defense

Season	Club	GP	G	A	Pts	PIM	PP	SH	GW
1997	Colorado	17	1	2	3	10	0	0	0
1998	Colorado	7	0	0	0	8	0	0	0
1999	Colorado	19	1	5	6	10	0	0	0
Playoff Totals		**43**	**2**	**7**	**9**	**28**	**0**	**0**	**0**

MILLER, Bill Center/defense

Season	Club	GP	G	A	Pts	PIM	PP	SH	GW
1935◆	Mtl. Maroons	7	0	0	0	0	0	0	0
1937	Mtl. Canadiens	5	0	0	0	0	0	0	0
Playoff Totals		**12**	**0**	**0**	**0**	**0**	**0**	**0**	**0**

MILLER, Bob Center

Season	Club	GP	G	A	Pts	PIM	PP	SH	GW
1978	Boston	13	0	3	3	15	0	0	0
1979	Boston	11	1	1	2	8	0	0	0
1980	Boston	10	3	2	5	4	0	1	0
1985	Los Angeles	2	0	1	1	0	0	0	0
Playoff Totals		**36**	**4**	**7**	**11**	**27**	**0**	**1**	**0**

MILLER, Brad *No playoffs* Defense

MILLER, Earl Left wing

Season	Club	GP	G	A	Pts	PIM	PP	SH	GW
1930	Chicago	2	1	0	1	6	....	....	....
1931	Chicago	1	0	0	0	0	....	....	....
1932◆	Toronto	7	0	0	0	0	....	....	....
Playoff Totals		**10**	**1**	**0**	**1**	**6**	....	....	....

MILLER, Jack *No playoffs* Center

MILLER, Jason *No playoffs* Left wing

MILLER, Jay Left wing

Season	Club	GP	G	A	Pts	PIM	PP	SH	GW
1986	Boston	2	0	0	0	17	0	0	0
1988	Boston	12	0	0	0	*124	0	0	0
1989	Los Angeles	11	0	1	1	63	0	0	0
1990	Los Angeles	10	1	1	2	10	0	0	0
1991	Los Angeles	8	0	0	0	17	0	0	0
1992	Los Angeles	5	1	1	2	12	0	0	0
Playoff Totals		**48**	**2**	**3**	**5**	**243**	**0**	**0**	**0**

MILLER, Kelly Left wing

Season	Club	GP	G	A	Pts	PIM	PP	SH	GW
1985	NY Rangers	3	0	0	0	2	0	0	0
1986	NY Rangers	16	3	4	7	4	0	1	0
1987	Washington	7	2	2	4	0	0	0	0
1988	Washington	14	4	4	8	10	0	1	1
1989	Washington	6	1	0	1	2	0	0	1
1990	Washington	15	3	5	8	23	0	1	0
1991	Washington	11	4	2	6	6	0	1	0
1992	Washington	7	1	2	3	4	0	0	0
1993	Washington	6	0	3	3	2	0	0	0
1994	Washington	11	2	7	9	0	1	1	0
1995	Washington	7	0	3	3	4	0	0	0
1996	Washington	6	0	1	1	4	0	0	0
1998	Washington	10	0	1	1	4	0	0	0
Playoff Totals		**119**	**20**	**34**	**54**	**65**	**1**	**5**	**2**

MILLER, Kevin Center

Season	Club	GP	G	A	Pts	PIM	PP	SH	GW
1990	NY Rangers	1	0	0	0	0	0	0	0
1991	Detroit	7	3	2	5	20	0	1	0
1992	Detroit	9	0	2	2	4	0	0	0
1993	St. Louis	10	0	3	3	11	0	0	0
1994	St. Louis	3	1	0	1	4	0	1	0
1995	San Jose	6	0	0	0	2	0	0	0
1996	Pittsburgh	18	3	2	5	8	0	0	0
1997	Chicago	6	0	1	1	0	0	0	0
Playoff Totals		**60**	**7**	**10**	**17**	**49**	**0**	**2**	**0**

MILLER, Kip Center

Season	Club	GP	G	A	Pts	PIM	PP	SH	GW
1999	Pittsburgh	13	2	7	9	19	1	0	0
Playoff Totals		**13**	**2**	**7**	**9**	**19**	**1**	**0**	**0**

MILLER, Paul *No playoffs* Center

MILLER, Perry *No playoffs* Defense

MILLER, Tom *No playoffs* Center

MILLER, Warren Right wing

Season	Club	GP	G	A	Pts	PIM	PP	SH	GW
1980	NY Rangers	6	1	0	1	0	0	0	0
Playoff Totals		**6**	**1**	**0**	**1**	**0**	**0**	**0**	**0**

MILLS, Craig Right wing

Season	Club	GP	G	A	Pts	PIM	PP	SH	GW
1996	Winnipeg	1	0	0	0	0	0	0	0
Playoff Totals		**1**	**0**	**0**	**0**	**0**	**0**	**0**	**0**

MINER, John *No playoffs* Defense

MINOR, Gerry Center

Season	Club	GP	G	A	Pts	PIM	PP	SH	GW
1981	Vancouver	3	0	0	0	8	0	0	0
1982	Vancouver	9	1	3	4	17	0	0	0
Playoff Totals		**12**	**1**	**3**	**4**	**25**	**0**	**0**	**0**

MIRONOV, Boris Defense

Season	Club	GP	G	A	Pts	PIM	PP	SH	GW
1997	Edmonton	12	2	8	10	16	2	0	0
1998	Edmonton	12	3	3	6	27	1	0	1
Playoff Totals		**24**	**5**	**11**	**16**	**43**	**3**	**0**	**1**

MIRONOV, Dmitri Defense

Season	Club	GP	G	A	Pts	PIM	PP	SH	GW
1993	Toronto	14	1	2	3	2	1	0	0
1994	Toronto	18	6	9	15	6	6	0	0
1995	Toronto	6	2	1	3	2	1	0	0
1996	Pittsburgh	15	0	1	1	10	0	0	0
1997	Anaheim	11	1	10	11	10	1	0	0
1998◆	Detroit	7	0	3	3	14	0	0	0
Playoff Totals		**71**	**10**	**26**	**36**	**44**	**9**	**0**	**0**

MISZUK, John Defense

Season	Club	GP	G	A	Pts	PIM	PP	SH	GW
1964	Detroit	3	0	0	0	2	0	0	0
1966	Chicago	3	0	0	0	4	0	0	0
1967	Chicago	2	0	0	0	2	0	0	0
1968	Philadelphia	7	0	3	3	11	0	0	0
1969	Philadelphia	4	0	0	0	0	0	0	0
Playoff Totals		**19**	**0**	**3**	**3**	**19**	**0**	**0**	**0**

MITCHELL, Bill *No playoffs* Defense

MITCHELL, Herb *No playoffs* Left wing

MITCHELL, Jeff *No playoffs* Center/Right wing

MITCHELL, Red *No playoffs* Defense

MITCHELL, Roy *No playoffs* Defense

Season	Club	GP	G	A	Pts	PIM	PP	SH	GW
MODANO, Mike	Center								
1989	Minnesota	2	0	0	0	0	0	0	0
1990	Minnesota	7	1	1	2	12	0	0	0
1991	Minnesota	23	8	12	20	16	3	0	1
1992	Minnesota	7	3	2	5	4	1	0	0
1994	Dallas	9	7	3	10	16	2	0	2
1997	Dallas	7	4	1	5	0	1	1	2
1998	Dallas	17	4	10	14	12	1	0	1
1999◆	Dallas	23	5	*18	23	16	1	1	1
Playoff Totals		**95**	**32**	**47**	**79**	**76**	**9**	**2**	**7**
MODIN, Fredrik	Left wing								
1999	Toronto	8	0	0	0	6	0	0	0
Playoff Totals		**8**	**0**	**0**	**0**	**6**	**0**	**0**	**0**
MODRY, Jaroslav *No playoffs*	Defense								
MOE, Bill	Defense								
1948	NY Rangers	1	0	0	0	0	0	0	0
Playoff Totals		**1**	**0**	**0**	**0**	**0**	**0**	**0**	**0**
MOFFAT, Lyle *No playoffs*	Left wing								
MOFFAT, Ron	Left wing								
1933	Detroit	4	0	0	0	0	0	0	0
1934	Detroit	3	0	0	0	0	0	0	0
Playoff Totals		**7**	**0**	**0**	**0**	**0**	**0**	**0**	**0**
MOGER, Sandy	Center								
1996	Boston	5	2	2	4	12	1	0	0
Playoff Totals		**5**	**2**	**2**	**4**	**12**	**1**	**0**	**0**
MOGILNY, Alexander	Right wing								
1990	Buffalo	4	0	1	1	2	0	0	0
1991	Buffalo	6	0	6	6	2	0	0	0
1992	Buffalo	2	0	2	2	0	0	0	0
1993	Buffalo	7	7	3	10	6	2	0	0
1994	Buffalo	7	4	2	6	6	1	0	0
1995	Buffalo	5	3	2	5	2	0	0	0
1996	Vancouver	6	1	8	9	8	0	0	0
Playoff Totals		**37**	**15**	**24**	**39**	**26**	**3**	**0**	**0**
MOHER, Mike *No playoffs*	Right wing								
MOHNS, Doug	Left wing/defense								
1954	Boston	4	1	0	1	4	....	....	....
1955	Boston	5	0	0	0	4	....	....	....
1957	Boston	10	2	3	5	2	....	....	....
1958	Boston	12	3	10	13	18	....	....	....
1959	Boston	4	0	2	2	12	....	....	....
1965	Chicago	14	3	4	7	21	....	....	....
1966	Chicago	5	1	0	1	4	....	....	....
1967	Chicago	5	0	5	5	8	....	....	....
1968	Chicago	11	1	5	6	12	0	0	0
1970	Chicago	8	0	2	2	15	0	0	0
1971	Minnesota	6	2	2	4	10	1	0	0
1972	Minnesota	4	1	2	3	10	1	0	0
1973	Minnesota	6	0	1	1	2	0	0	0
Playoff Totals		**94**	**14**	**36**	**50**	**122**	....	....	....
MOHNS, Lloyd *No playoffs*	Defense								
MOKOSAK, Carl	Left wing								
1989	Boston	1	0	0	0	0	0	0	0
Playoff Totals		**1**	**0**	**0**	**0**	**0**	**0**	**0**	**0**
MOKOSAK, John *No playoffs*	Defense								
MOLIN, Lars	Left wing								
1982	Vancouver	17	2	9	11	7	0	0	2
1984	Vancouver	2	0	0	0	0	0	0	0
Playoff Totals		**19**	**2**	**9**	**11**	**7**	**0**	**0**	**2**
MOLLER, Mike	Right wing								
1981	Buffalo	3	0	1	1	0	0	0	0
Playoff Totals		**3**	**0**	**1**	**1**	**0**	**0**	**0**	**0**
MOLLER, Randy	Defense								
1982	Quebec	1	0	0	0	0	0	0	0
1983	Quebec	4	1	0	1	4	1	0	1
1984	Quebec	9	1	0	1	45	0	0	0
1985	Quebec	18	2	2	4	40	1	0	0
1986	Quebec	3	0	0	0	26	0	0	0
1987	Quebec	13	1	4	5	23	0	0	0
1990	NY Rangers	10	1	6	7	32	0	0	0
1991	NY Rangers	6	0	2	2	11	0	0	0
1992	Buffalo	7	0	0	0	8	0	0	0
1994	Buffalo	7	0	2	2	8	0	0	0
Playoff Totals		**78**	**6**	**16**	**22**	**197**	**2**	**0**	**1**
MOLLOY, Mitch *No playoffs*	Left wing								
MOLYNEAUX, Larry	Defense								
1938	NY Rangers	3	0	0	0	8	0	0	0
1939	NY Rangers	7	0	0	0	0	0	0	0
Playoff Totals		**10**	**0**	**0**	**0**	**8**	**0**	**0**	**0**

Season	Club	GP	G	A	Pts	PIM	PP	SH	GW
MOMESSO, Sergio	Left wing								
1987	Montreal	11	1	3	4	31	0	0	0
1988	Montreal	6	0	2	2	16	0	0	0
1989	St. Louis	10	2	5	7	24	0	0	0
1990	St. Louis	12	3	2	5	63	0	0	1
1991	Vancouver	6	0	3	3	25	0	0	0
1992	Vancouver	13	0	5	5	30	0	0	0
1993	Vancouver	12	3	0	3	30	0	0	1
1994	Vancouver	24	3	4	7	56	0	0	1
1995	Vancouver	11	3	1	4	16	1	0	0
1996	NY Rangers	11	3	1	4	14	0	0	0
1997	St. Louis	3	0	0	0	6	0	0	0
Playoff Totals		**119**	**18**	**26**	**44**	**311**	**1**	**0**	**3**
MONAHAN, Garry	Left wing								
1971	Toronto	6	2	0	2	2	0	0	0
1972	Toronto	5	0	0	0	0	0	0	0
1974	Toronto	4	0	1	1	7	0	0	0
1975	Vancouver	5	1	0	1	2	0	0	1
1976	Vancouver	2	0	0	0	2	0	0	0
Playoff Totals		**22**	**3**	**1**	**4**	**13**	**0**	**0**	**1**
MONAHAN, Hartland	Right wing								
1978	Los Angeles	2	0	0	0	0	0	0	0
1980	St. Louis	3	0	0	0	0	0	0	0
1981	St. Louis	1	0	0	0	4	0	0	0
Playoff Totals		**6**	**0**	**0**	**0**	**4**	**0**	**0**	**0**
MONDOU, Armand	Left wing								
1929	Mtl. Canadiens	3	0	0	0	2	....	....	....
1930◆	Mtl. Canadiens	6	1	1	2	6	....	....	....
1931◆	Mtl. Canadiens	8	0	0	0	0	....	....	....
1932	Mtl. Canadiens	4	1	2	3	2	....	....	....
1934	Mtl. Canadiens	1	0	1	1	0	....	....	....
1935	Mtl. Canadiens	2	0	1	1	0	....	....	....
1937	Mtl. Canadiens	5	0	0	0	0	....	....	....
1939	Mtl. Canadiens	3	1	0	1	2	....	....	....
Playoff Totals		**32**	**3**	**5**	**8**	**12**	....	....	....
MONDOU, Pierre	Center								
1977◆	Montreal	4	0	0	0	0	0	0	0
1978◆	Montreal	15	3	7	10	4	2	0	1
1979◆	Montreal	16	3	6	9	4	1	0	0
1980	Montreal	4	1	4	5	4	0	0	0
1981	Montreal	3	0	1	1	0	0	0	0
1982	Montreal	5	2	5	7	8	1	1	0
1983	Montreal	3	0	1	1	2	0	0	0
1984	Montreal	14	6	3	9	2	1	0	1
1985	Montreal	5	2	1	3	2	0	0	0
Playoff Totals		**69**	**17**	**28**	**45**	**26**	**5**	**1**	**2**
MONGEAU, Michel	Center								
1990	St. Louis	2	0	1	1	0	0	0	0
Playoff Totals		**2**	**0**	**1**	**1**	**0**	**0**	**0**	**0**
MONGRAIN, Bob	Center								
1980	Buffalo	9	1	2	3	2	0	0	0
1982	Buffalo	1	0	0	0	0	0	0	0
1984	Buffalo	1	0	0	0	0	0	0	0
Playoff Totals		**11**	**1**	**2**	**3**	**2**	**0**	**0**	**0**
MONTEITH, Hank	Left wing								
1970	Detroit	4	0	0	0	0	0	0	0
Playoff Totals		**4**	**0**	**0**	**0**	**0**	**0**	**0**	**0**
MONTGOMERY, Jim	Center								
1995	Philadelphia	7	1	0	1	2	0	0	0
1996	Philadelphia	1	0	0	0	0	0	0	0
Playoff Totals		**8**	**1**	**0**	**1**	**2**	**0**	**0**	**0**
MOORE, Barrie *No playoffs*	Left wing								
MOORE, Dickie	Left wing								
1952	Montreal	11	1	1	2	12	....	....	....
1953◆	Montreal	12	3	2	5	13	....	....	....
1954	Montreal	11	5	*8	*13	8	....	....	....
1955	Montreal	12	1	5	6	22	....	....	....
1956◆	Montreal	10	3	6	9	12	....	....	....
1957◆	Montreal	10	3	7	10	4	....	....	....
1958◆	Montreal	10	4	7	11	4	....	....	....
1959◆	Montreal	11	5	*12	*17	8	....	....	....
1960◆	Montreal	8	*6	4	10	4	....	....	....
1961	Montreal	6	3	1	4	4	....	....	....
1962	Montreal	6	4	2	6	8	....	....	....
1963	Montreal	5	0	1	1	2	....	....	....
1965	Toronto	5	1	1	2	6	....	....	....
1968	St. Louis	18	7	7	14	15	2	0	1
Playoff Totals		**135**	**46**	**64**	**110**	**122**	....	....	....
MORAN, Amby *No playoffs*	Defense								
MORAN, Ian	Right wing								
1995	Pittsburgh	8	0	0	0	0	0	0	0
1997	Pittsburgh	5	1	2	3	4	0	0	0
1998	Pittsburgh	6	0	0	0	2	0	0	0
1999	Pittsburgh	13	0	2	2	8	0	0	0
Playoff Totals		**32**	**1**	**4**	**5**	**14**	**0**	**0**	**0**
MORAVEC, David *No playoffs*	Right wing								

Season	Club	GP	G	A	Pts	PIM	PP	SH	GW
MORE, Jayson	Defense								
1994	San Jose	13	0	2	2	32	0	0	0
1995	San Jose	11	0	4	4	6	0	0	0
1997	Phoenix	7	0	0	0	7	0	0	0
Playoff Totals		**31**	**0**	**6**	**6**	**45**	**0**	**0**	**0**
MOREAU, Ethan	Left wing								
1997	Chicago	6	1	0	1	9	0	0	0
1999	Edmonton	4	0	3	3	6	0	0	0
Playoff Totals		**10**	**1**	**3**	**4**	**15**	**0**	**0**	**0**
MORENZ, Howie	Center								
1924◆	Mtl. Canadiens	6	*7	3	*10	10	....	....	....
1925	Mtl. Canadiens	6	7	1	8	10	....	....	....
1927	Mtl. Canadiens	4	1	0	1	4	....	....	....
1928	Mtl. Canadiens	2	0	0	0	12	....	....	....
1929	Mtl. Canadiens	3	0	0	0	6	....	....	....
1930◆	Mtl. Canadiens	6	3	0	3	10	....	....	....
1931◆	Mtl. Canadiens	10	1	*4	5	10	....	....	....
1932	Mtl. Canadiens	4	1	0	1	4	....	....	....
1933	Mtl. Canadiens	2	0	3	3	2	....	....	....
1934	Mtl. Canadiens	2	1	1	2	0	....	....	....
1935	Chicago	2	0	0	0	0	....	....	....
Playoff Totals		**47**	**21**	**12**	**33**	**68**	....	....	....
MORETTO, Angelo *No playoffs*	Center								
MORGAN, Jason *No playoffs*	Center								
MORIN, Pete	Left wing								
1942	Montreal	1	0	0	0	0	0	0	0
Playoff Totals		**1**	**0**	**0**	**0**	**0**	**0**	**0**	**0**
MORIN, Stephane *No playoffs*	Center								
MORISSETTE, Dave *No playoffs*	Left wing								
MORO, Marc *No playoffs*	Defense								
MOROZOV, Aleksey	Right wing								
1998	Pittsburgh	6	0	1	1	2	0	0	0
1999	Pittsburgh	10	1	1	2	0	0	0	0
Playoff Totals		**16**	**1**	**2**	**3**	**2**	**0**	**0**	**0**
MORRIS, Bernie *No playoffs*	Center/right wing								
MORRIS, Derek *No playoffs*	Defense								
MORRIS, Jon	Center								
1990	New Jersey	6	1	3	4	23	1	0	0
1991	New Jersey	5	0	4	4	2	0	0	0
Playoff Totals		**11**	**1**	**7**	**8**	**25**	**1**	**0**	**0**
MORRIS, Moe	Defense								
1944	Toronto	5	1	2	3	2	....	....	....
1945◆	Toronto	13	3	0	3	*14	....	....	....
Playoff Totals		**18**	**4**	**2**	**6**	**16**	....	....	....
MORRISON, Brendan	Center								
1998	New Jersey	3	0	1	1	0	0	0	0
1999	New Jersey	7	0	2	2	0	0	0	0
Playoff Totals		**10**	**0**	**3**	**3**	**0**	**0**	**0**	**0**
MORRISON, Dave *No playoffs*	Right wing								
MORRISON, Don	Center								
1948	Detroit	3	0	1	1	0	0	0	0
Playoff Totals		**3**	**0**	**1**	**1**	**0**	**0**	**0**	**0**
MORRISON, Doug *No playoffs*	Right wing								
MORRISON, Gary	Right wing								
1980	Philadelphia	5	0	1	1	2	0	0	0
Playoff Totals		**5**	**0**	**1**	**1**	**2**	**0**	**0**	**0**
MORRISON, George	Left wing								
1971	St. Louis	3	0	0	0	0	0	0	0
Playoff Totals		**3**	**0**	**0**	**0**	**0**	**0**	**0**	**0**
MORRISON, Jim	Defense								
1952	Toronto	2	0	0	0	0	0	0	0
1954	Toronto	5	0	0	0	4	0	0	0
1955	Toronto	4	0	1	1	4	0	0	0
1956	Toronto	5	0	0	0	4	0	0	0
1959	Boston	6	0	6	6	16	0	0	0
1960	Detroit	6	0	2	2	0	0	0	0
1970	Pittsburgh	8	0	3	3	10	0	0	0
Playoff Totals		**36**	**0**	**12**	**12**	**38**	**0**	**0**	**0**
MORRISON, John *No playoffs*	Left wing								
MORRISON, Kevin *No playoffs*	Defense								
MORRISON, Lew	Right wing								
1971	Philadelphia	4	0	0	0	2	0	0	0
1975	Pittsburgh	9	0	0	0	0	0	0	0
1976	Pittsburgh	3	0	0	0	0	0	0	0
1977	Pittsburgh	1	0	0	0	0	0	0	0
Playoff Totals		**17**	**0**	**0**	**0**	**2**	**0**	**0**	**0**
MORRISON, Mark *No playoffs*	Center								
MORRISON, Rod	Right wing								
1948	Detroit	3	0	0	0	0	0	0	0
Playoff Totals		**3**	**0**	**0**	**0**	**0**	**0**	**0**	**0**
MORROW, Brenden *No playoffs*	Left wing								

Season	Club	GP	G	A	Pts	PIM	PP	SH	GW
MORROW, Ken									Defense
1980◆	NY Islanders	20	1	2	3	12	0	0	1
1981◆	NY Islanders	18	3	4	7	8	0	0	1
1982◆	NY Islanders	19	0	4	4	8	0	0	0
1983◆	NY Islanders	19	5	7	12	18	0	0	0
1984	NY Islanders	20	1	2	3	20	0	0	1
1985	NY Islanders	10	0	0	0	17	0	0	0
1986	NY Islanders	2	0	0	0	4	0	0	0
1987	NY Islanders	13	1	3	4	2	0	0	0
1988	NY Islanders	6	0	0	0	8	0	0	0
Playoff Totals		**127**	**11**	**22**	**33**	**97**	**0**	**0**	**3**
MORROW, Scott	*No playoffs*								Left wing
MORTON, Dean	*No playoffs*								Defense
MORTSON, Gus									Defense
1947◆	Toronto	11	1	3	4	22	....	....	....
1948◆	Toronto	5	1	2	3	2	....	....	....
1949◆	Toronto	9	2	1	3	8	....	....	....
1950	Toronto	7	0	0	0	18	....	....	....
1951◆	Toronto	11	0	1	1	4	....	....	....
1952	Toronto	4	0	0	0	8	....	....	....
1953	Chicago	7	1	1	2	6	....	....	....
Playoff Totals		**54**	**5**	**8**	**13**	**68**	....	....	....
MOSDELL, Kenny									Center
1946◆	Montreal	9	4	1	5	6	....	....	....
1947	Montreal	4	2	0	2	4	....	....	....
1949	Montreal	7	1	1	2	4	....	....	....
1950	Montreal	5	0	0	0	12	....	....	....
1951	Montreal	11	1	1	2	4	....	....	....
1952	Montreal	2	1	0	1	0	....	....	....
1953◆	Montreal	7	3	2	5	4	....	....	....
1954	Montreal	11	1	0	1	4	....	....	....
1955	Montreal	12	2	7	9	8	....	....	....
1956◆	Montreal	9	1	1	2	2	....	....	....
1959◆	Montreal	3	0	0	0	0	....	....	....
Playoff Totals		**80**	**16**	**13**	**29**	**48**	....	....	....
MOSIENKO, Bill									Right wing
1942	Chicago	3	2	0	2	0	....	....	....
1944	Chicago	8	2	2	4	6	....	....	....
1946	Chicago	4	2	0	2	2	....	....	....
1953	Chicago	7	4	2	6	7	....	....	....
Playoff Totals		**22**	**10**	**4**	**14**	**15**	....	....	....
MOTT, Morris	*No playoffs*								Right wing
MOTTER, Alex									Center
1935	Boston	4	0	0	0	0	....	....	....
1936	Boston	2	0	0	0	0	....	....	....
1939	Detroit	4	0	1	1	0	....	....	....
1940	Detroit	5	1	1	2	15	....	....	....
1941	Detroit	9	1	3	4	4	....	....	....
1942	Detroit	12	1	3	4	20	....	....	....
1943◆	Detroit	5	0	1	1	2	....	....	....
Playoff Totals		**41**	**3**	**9**	**12**	**41**	....	....	....
MOWERS, Mark	*No playoffs*								Right wing
MOXEY, Jim	*No playoffs*								Right wing
MUCKALT, Bill	*No playoffs*								Right wing
MUIR, Bryan									Defense
1997	Edmonton	5	0	0	0	4	0	0	0
Playoff Totals		**5**	**0**	**0**	**0**	**4**	**0**	**0**	**0**
MULHERN, Richard									Defense
1977	Atlanta	3	0	2	2	5	0	0	0
1978	Atlanta	2	0	1	1	0	0	0	0
1979	Los Angeles	1	0	0	0	0	0	0	0
1980	Toronto	1	0	0	0	0	0	0	0
Playoff Totals		**7**	**0**	**3**	**3**	**5**	**0**	**0**	**0**
MULHERN, Ryan	*No playoffs*								Center
MULLEN, Brian									Right wing
1983	Winnipeg	3	1	0	1	0	0	0	0
1984	Winnipeg	3	0	3	3	6	0	0	0
1985	Winnipeg	8	1	2	3	4	0	0	1
1986	Winnipeg	3	1	2	3	6	1	0	0
1987	Winnipeg	9	4	2	6	0	2	0	0
1989	NY Rangers	3	0	1	1	4	0	0	0
1990	NY Rangers	10	2	2	4	8	2	0	0
1991	NY Rangers	5	0	2	2	0	0	0	0
1993	NY Islanders	18	3	4	7	2	0	0	0
Playoff Totals		**62**	**12**	**18**	**30**	**30**	**5**	**0**	**1**

Season	Club	GP	G	A	Pts	PIM	PP	SH	GW
MULLEN, Joe									Right wing
1980	St. Louis	1	0	0	0	0	0	0	0
1982	St. Louis	10	7	11	18	4	1	0	0
1984	St. Louis	6	2	0	2	0	0	0	0
1985	St. Louis	3	0	0	0	0	0	0	0
1986	Calgary	21	*12	7	19	4	4	0	2
1987	Calgary	6	2	1	3	0	1	0	1
1988	Calgary	7	2	4	6	10	0	0	0
1989◆	Calgary	21	*16	8	24	4	6	0	1
1990	Calgary	6	3	0	3	0	0	1	0
1991◆	Pittsburgh	22	8	9	17	4	1	0	1
1992◆	Pittsburgh	9	3	1	4	4	1	0	0
1993	Pittsburgh	12	4	2	6	6	0	1	1
1994	Pittsburgh	6	1	0	1	2	0	0	0
1995	Pittsburgh	12	0	3	3	4	0	0	0
1997	Pittsburgh	1	0	0	0	0	0	0	0
Playoff Totals		**143**	**60**	**46**	**106**	**42**	**14**	**2**	**6**
MULLER, Kirk									Left wing
1988	New Jersey	20	4	8	12	37	0	0	0
1990	New Jersey	6	1	3	4	11	0	0	0
1991	New Jersey	7	0	2	2	10	0	0	0
1992	Montreal	11	4	3	7	31	2	1	1
1993◆	Montreal	20	10	7	17	18	3	0	3
1994	Montreal	7	6	2	8	4	3	0	2
1996	Toronto	6	3	2	5	0	2	0	0
1997	Florida	5	1	2	3	4	1	0	0
Playoff Totals		**82**	**29**	**29**	**58**	**115**	**11**	**1**	**6**
MULOIN, Wayne									Defense
1970	Oakland	4	0	0	0	0	0	0	0
1971	Minnesota	7	0	0	0	2	0	0	0
Playoff Totals		**11**	**0**	**0**	**0**	**2**	**0**	**0**	**0**
MULVENNA, Glenn	*No playoffs*								Center
MULVEY, Grant									Right wing
1975	Chicago	6	2	0	2	6	0	0	0
1976	Chicago	4	0	0	0	2	0	0	0
1977	Chicago	2	1	0	1	2	1	0	0
1978	Chicago	4	2	2	4	0	1	0	0
1979	Chicago	1	0	0	0	2	0	0	0
1980	Chicago	7	1	1	2	8	0	0	0
1981	Chicago	3	0	0	0	0	0	0	0
1982	Chicago	15	4	2	6	50	1	0	0
Playoff Totals		**42**	**10**	**5**	**15**	**70**	**3**	**0**	**0**
MULVEY, Paul	*No playoffs*								Left wing
MUMMERY, Harry									Defense
1918◆	Toronto	7	1	*7	8	38	....	....	....
Playoff Totals		**7**	**1**	**7**	**8**	**38**	....	....	....
MUNI, Craig									Defense
1987◆	Edmonton	14	0	2	2	17	0	0	0
1988◆	Edmonton	19	0	4	4	31	0	0	0
1989	Edmonton	7	0	3	3	8	0	0	0
1990◆	Edmonton	22	0	3	3	16	0	0	0
1991	Edmonton	18	0	3	3	20	0	0	0
1992	Edmonton	3	0	0	0	2	0	0	0
1993	Chicago	4	0	0	0	2	0	0	0
1994	Buffalo	7	0	0	0	4	0	0	0
1995	Buffalo	5	0	1	1	2	0	0	0
1996	Winnipeg	6	0	1	1	2	0	0	0
1997	Pittsburgh	3	0	0	0	0	0	0	0
1998	Dallas	5	0	0	0	4	0	0	0
Playoff Totals		**113**	**0**	**17**	**17**	**108**	**0**	**0**	**0**
MUNRO, Dunc									Defense
1926◆	Mtl. Maroons	6	1	0	1	6	....	....	....
1927	Mtl. Maroons	2	0	0	0	4	....	....	....
1928	Mtl. Maroons	9	0	2	2	8	....	....	....
1930	Mtl. Maroons	4	2	0	2	4	....	....	....
1932	Mtl. Canadiens	4	0	0	0	2	....	....	....
Playoff Totals		**25**	**3**	**2**	**5**	**24**	....	....	....
MUNRO, Gerry	*No playoffs*								Defense
MURDOCH, Bob									Defense
1971◆	Montreal	2	0	0	0	0	0	0	0
1972	Montreal	1	0	0	0	0	0	0	0
1973◆	Montreal	13	0	3	3	10	0	0	0
1974	Los Angeles	5	0	0	0	2	0	0	0
1975	Los Angeles	3	0	1	1	4	0	0	0
1976	Los Angeles	9	0	5	5	15	0	0	0
1977	Los Angeles	9	2	3	5	14	1	0	1
1978	Los Angeles	2	0	1	1	5	0	0	0
1979	Atlanta	2	0	0	0	4	0	0	0
1980	Atlanta	4	1	1	2	2	0	0	0
1981	Calgary	16	1	4	5	36	0	0	0
1982	Calgary	3	0	0	0	0	0	0	0
Playoff Totals		**69**	**4**	**18**	**22**	**92**	**1**	**0**	**1**
MURDOCH, Bob	*No playoffs*								Right wing
MURDOCH, Don									Right wing
1978	NY Rangers	3	1	3	4	4	0	0	1
1979	NY Rangers	18	7	5	12	12	3	0	1
1980	Edmonton	3	2	0	2	0	0	0	0
Playoff Totals		**24**	**10**	**8**	**18**	**16**	**3**	**0**	**2**

Season	Club	GP	G	A	Pts	PIM	PP	SH	GW
MURDOCH, Murray									Left wing
1927	NY Rangers	2	0	0	0	0	....	....	....
1928◆	NY Rangers	9	2	1	3	12	....	....	....
1929	NY Rangers	6	0	0	0	2	....	....	....
1930	NY Rangers	4	3	0	3	6	....	....	....
1931	NY Rangers	4	0	2	2	0	....	....	....
1932	NY Rangers	7	0	2	2	2	....	....	....
1933◆	NY Rangers	8	3	*4	7	2	....	....	....
1934	NY Rangers	2	0	0	0	0	....	....	....
1935	NY Rangers	4	0	2	2	4	....	....	....
1937	NY Rangers	9	1	1	2	0	....	....	....
Playoff Totals		**55**	**9**	**12**	**21**	**28**	....	....	....
MURPHY, Brian	*No playoffs*								Center/left wing
MURPHY, Gord									Defense
1989	Philadelphia	19	2	7	9	13	1	0	1
1992	Boston	15	1	0	1	12	0	0	0
1996	Florida	14	0	4	4	6	0	0	0
1997	Florida	5	0	5	5	4	0	0	0
Playoff Totals		**53**	**3**	**16**	**19**	**35**	**1**	**0**	**1**
MURPHY, Joe									Right wing
1988	Detroit	8	0	1	1	6	0	0	0
1990◆	Edmonton	22	6	8	14	16	0	0	2
1991	Edmonton	15	2	5	7	14	1	0	1
1992	Edmonton	16	8	16	24	12	4	0	2
1993	Chicago	4	0	0	0	8	0	0	0
1994	Chicago	6	1	3	4	25	0	0	0
1995	Chicago	16	9	3	12	29	3	0	3
1996	Chicago	10	6	2	8	33	0	0	2
1997	St. Louis	6	1	1	2	10	1	0	0
1998	San Jose	6	1	1	2	20	1	0	0
1999	San Jose	6	0	3	3	4	0	0	0
Playoff Totals		**115**	**34**	**43**	**77**	**177**	**10**	**0**	**10**
MURPHY, Larry									Defense
1981	Los Angeles	4	3	0	3	2	1	0	0
1982	Los Angeles	10	2	8	10	12	1	0	0
1984	Washington	8	0	3	3	6	0	0	0
1985	Washington	5	2	3	5	0	2	0	0
1986	Washington	9	1	5	6	6	1	0	0
1987	Washington	7	2	2	4	6	0	0	1
1988	Washington	13	4	4	8	33	2	0	1
1989	Minnesota	5	0	2	2	8	0	0	0
1990	Minnesota	7	1	2	3	31	0	0	1
1991◆	Pittsburgh	23	5	18	23	44	4	0	0
1992◆	Pittsburgh	21	6	10	16	19	3	0	1
1993	Pittsburgh	12	2	11	13	10	2	0	1
1994	Pittsburgh	6	0	5	5	0	0	0	0
1995	Pittsburgh	12	2	13	15	0	1	0	0
1996	Toronto	6	0	2	2	4	0	0	0
1997◆	Detroit	20	2	9	11	8	1	0	1
1998◆	Detroit	22	3	12	15	2	1	2	1
1999	Detroit	10	0	2	2	8	0	0	0
Playoff Totals		**200**	**35**	**111**	**146**	**199**	**19**	**2**	**7**
MURPHY, Mike									Right wing
1972	St. Louis	11	2	3	5	6	1	0	0
1973	NY Rangers	10	0	0	0	0	0	0	0
1974	Los Angeles	5	0	4	4	0	0	0	0
1975	Los Angeles	3	3	0	3	4	2	0	1
1976	Los Angeles	9	1	4	5	6	1	0	0
1977	Los Angeles	9	4	9	13	4	1	0	0
1978	Los Angeles	2	0	0	0	0	0	0	0
1979	Los Angeles	2	0	1	1	0	0	0	0
1980	Los Angeles	4	1	0	1	2	0	1	0
1981	Los Angeles	1	0	1	1	0	0	0	0
1982	Los Angeles	10	2	1	3	32	0	0	0
Playoff Totals		**66**	**13**	**23**	**36**	**54**	**5**	**1**	**1**
MURPHY, Rob									Center
1991	Vancouver	4	0	0	0	2	0	0	0
Playoff Totals		**4**	**0**	**0**	**0**	**2**	**0**	**0**	**0**
MURPHY, Ron									Left wing
1956	NY Rangers	5	0	1	1	2	0	0	0
1957	NY Rangers	5	0	0	0	0	0	0	0
1960	Chicago	4	1	0	1	0	0	0	1
1961◆	Chicago	12	2	1	3	0	0	0	1
1963	Chicago	1	0	0	0	0	0	0	0
1964	Chicago	7	0	1	1	8	0	0	0
1965	Detroit	5	0	1	1	4	0	0	0
1968	Boston	4	0	0	0	0	0	0	0
1969	Boston	10	4	4	8	12	0	0	0
Playoff Totals		**53**	**7**	**8**	**15**	**26**	**0**	**0**	**2**
MURRAY, Allan									Defense
1936	NY Americans	5	0	0	0	2	0	0	0
1938	NY Americans	6	0	0	0	6	0	0	0
1940	NY Americans	3	0	0	0	2	0	0	0
Playoff Totals		**14**	**0**	**0**	**0**	**10**	**0**	**0**	**0**
MURRAY, Bob									Defense
1974	Atlanta	4	1	0	1	2	0	0	0
1975	Vancouver	5	0	1	1	13	0	0	0
1976	Vancouver	1	0	0	0	0	0	0	0
Playoff Totals		**10**	**1**	**1**	**2**	**15**	**0**	**0**	**0**

Season	Club	GP	G	A	Pts	PIM	PP	SH	GW
MURRAY, Bob									Defense
1977	Chicago	2	0	1	1	2	0	0	0
1978	Chicago	4	1	4	5	2	0	0	0
1979	Chicago	4	1	0	1	6	0	0	0
1980	Chicago	7	2	4	6	6	0	0	0
1981	Chicago	3	0	0	0	2	0	0	0
1982	Chicago	15	1	6	7	16	0	0	0
1983	Chicago	13	2	3	5	10	1	0	0
1984	Chicago	5	3	1	4	6	1	0	0
1985	Chicago	15	3	6	9	20	1	0	0
1986	Chicago	3	0	2	2	0	0	0	0
1987	Chicago	4	1	0	1	4	0	0	0
1988	Chicago	5	1	3	4	2	1	0	0
1989	Chicago	16	2	3	5	22	1	0	0
1990	Chicago	16	2	4	6	8	0	0	0
Playoff Totals		**112**	**19**	**37**	**56**	**106**	**5**	**0**	**0**
MURRAY, Chris									Right wing
1996	Montreal	4	0	0	0	4	0	0	0
1998	Ottawa	11	1	0	1	8	0	0	0
Playoff Totals		**15**	**1**	**0**	**1**	**12**	**0**	**0**	**0**
MURRAY, Glen									Right wing
1992	Boston	15	4	2	6	10	1	0	0
1994	Boston	13	4	5	9	14	1	0	0
1995	Boston	2	0	0	0	2	0	0	0
1996	Pittsburgh	18	2	6	8	10	0	0	1
1998	Los Angeles	4	2	0	2	6	0	0	0
Playoff Totals		**52**	**12**	**13**	**25**	**42**	**1**	**0**	**1**
MURRAY, Jim	*No playoffs*								Defense
MURRAY, Ken	*No playoffs*								Defense
MURRAY, Leo	*No playoffs*								Center/left wing
MURRAY, Marty	*No playoffs*								Center
MURRAY, Mike	*No playoffs*								Center
MURRAY, Pat	*No playoffs*								Left wing
MURRAY, Randy	*No playoffs*								Defense
MURRAY, Rem									Center/Left wing
1997	Edmonton	12	1	2	3	4	0	0	0
1998	Edmonton	11	1	4	5	2	0	0	0
1999	Edmonton	4	1	1	2	2	0	0	0
Playoff Totals		**27**	**3**	**7**	**10**	**8**	**0**	**0**	**0**
MURRAY, Rob									Center
1990	Washington	9	0	0	0	18	0	0	0
Playoff Totals		**9**	**0**	**0**	**0**	**18**	**0**	**0**	**0**
MURRAY, Terry									Defense
1976	Philadelphia	6	0	1	1	0	0	0	0
1981	Philadelphia	12	2	1	3	10	0	0	0
Playoff Totals		**18**	**2**	**2**	**4**	**10**	**0**	**0**	**0**
MURRAY, Troy									Center
1982	Chicago	7	1	0	1	5	0	0	0
1983	Chicago	2	0	0	0	0	0	0	0
1984	Chicago	5	1	0	1	7	0	0	1
1985	Chicago	15	5	14	19	24	1	0	0
1986	Chicago	2	0	0	0	2	0	0	0
1987	Chicago	4	0	0	0	5	0	0	0
1988	Chicago	5	1	0	1	8	1	0	0
1989	Chicago	16	3	6	9	25	1	0	0
1990	Chicago	20	4	4	8	22	1	0	0
1991	Chicago	6	0	1	1	12	0	0	0
1992	Winnipeg	7	0	0	0	2	0	0	0
1993	Chicago	4	0	0	0	2	0	0	0
1995	Pittsburgh	12	2	1	3	12	0	0	0
1996◆	Colorado	8	0	0	0	19	0	0	0
Playoff Totals		**113**	**17**	**26**	**43**	**145**	**4**	**0**	**1**
MURZYN, Dana									Defense
1986	Hartford	4	0	0	0	10	0	0	0
1987	Hartford	6	2	1	3	29	1	0	1
1988	Calgary	5	2	0	2	13	0	0	0
1989◆	Calgary	21	0	3	3	20	0	0	0
1990	Calgary	6	2	2	4	2	0	0	0
1991	Vancouver	6	0	1	1	8	0	0	0
1992	Vancouver	1	0	0	0	15	0	0	0
1993	Vancouver	12	3	2	5	18	0	0	0
1994	Vancouver	7	0	0	0	4	0	0	0
1995	Vancouver	8	0	1	1	22	0	0	0
1996	Vancouver	6	0	0	0	25	0	0	0
Playoff Totals		**82**	**9**	**10**	**19**	**166**	**1**	**0**	**1**
MUSIL, Frank									Defense
1989	Minnesota	5	1	1	2	4	0	0	0
1990	Minnesota	4	0	0	0	14	0	0	0
1991	Calgary	7	0	0	0	10	0	0	0
1993	Calgary	6	1	1	2	7	0	0	0
1994	Calgary	7	0	1	1	4	0	0	0
1995	Calgary	5	0	1	1	0	0	0	0
1998	Edmonton	7	0	0	0	6	0	0	0
1999	Edmonton	1	0	0	0	2	0	0	0
Playoff Totals		**42**	**2**	**4**	**6**	**47**	**0**	**0**	**0**
MYERS, Hap	*No playoffs*								Defense
MYHRES, Brantt	*No playoffs*								Right wing
MYLES, Vic	*No playoffs*								Defense
MYRVOLD, Anders	*No playoffs*								Defense
NABOKOV, Dmitri	*No playoffs*								Center

Season	Club	GP	G	A	Pts	PIM	PP	SH	GW
NACHBAUR, Don									Center
1983	Edmonton	2	0	0	0	7	0	0	0
1987	Philadelphia	7	1	1	2	15	0	0	1
1988	Philadelphia	2	0	0	0	2	0	0	0
Playoff Totals		**11**	**1**	**1**	**2**	**24**	**0**	**0**	**1**
NAGY, Ladislav	*No playoffs*								Center
NAHRGANG, Jim	*No playoffs*								Defense
NAMESTNIKOV, John									Defense
1995	Vancouver	1	0	0	0	2	0	0	0
1996	Vancouver	1	0	0	0	0	0	0	0
Playoff Totals		**2**	**0**	**0**	**0**	**2**	**0**	**0**	**0**
NANNE, Lou									Defense/right wing
1970	Minnesota	5	0	2	2	2	0	0	0
1971	Minnesota	12	3	6	9	4	0	0	2
1972	Minnesota	7	0	0	0	0	0	0	0
1973	Minnesota	6	1	2	3	0	0	0	0
1977	Minnesota	2	0	0	0	2	0	0	0
Playoff Totals		**32**	**4**	**10**	**14**	**8**	**0**	**0**	**2**
NANTAIS, Rich	*No playoffs*								Left wing
NAPIER, Mark									Right wing
1979◆	Montreal	12	3	2	5	2	0	0	0
1980	Montreal	10	2	6	8	0	1	0	0
1981	Montreal	3	0	0	0	2	0	0	0
1982	Montreal	5	3	2	5	0	1	1	1
1983	Montreal	3	0	0	0	0	0	0	0
1984	Minnesota	12	3	2	5	0	3	0	0
1985◆	Edmonton	18	5	5	10	7	1	0	0
1986	Edmonton	10	1	4	5	0	0	0	0
1988	Buffalo	6	0	3	3	0	0	0	0
1989	Buffalo	3	1	0	1	0	0	0	0
Playoff Totals		**82**	**18**	**24**	**42**	**11**	**6**	**1**	**1**
NASH, Tyson									Left wing
1999	St. Louis	1	0	0	0	2	0	0	0
Playoff Totals		**1**	**0**	**0**	**0**	**2**	**0**	**0**	**0**
NASLUND, Markus									Right wing
1996	Vancouver	6	1	2	3	8	1	0	0
Playoff Totals		**6**	**1**	**2**	**3**	**8**	**1**	**0**	**0**
NASLUND, Mats									Left wing
1983	Montreal	3	1	0	1	0	1	0	0
1984	Montreal	15	6	8	14	4	3	1	3
1985	Montreal	12	7	4	11	6	3	0	2
1986◆	Montreal	20	8	11	19	4	4	0	0
1987	Montreal	17	7	15	22	11	4	0	3
1988	Montreal	6	0	7	7	2	0	0	0
1989	Montreal	21	4	11	15	6	1	0	0
1990	Montreal	3	1	1	2	0	0	0	1
1995	Boston	5	1	0	1	0	0	0	0
Playoff Totals		**102**	**35**	**57**	**92**	**33**	**16**	**1**	**9**
NASREDDINE, Alain	*No playoffs*								Defense
NATTRASS, Ralph	*No playoffs*								Defense
NATTRESS, Ric									Defense
1983	Montreal	3	0	0	0	10	0	0	0
1985	Montreal	2	0	0	0	2	0	0	0
1986	St. Louis	18	1	4	5	24	0	0	0
1987	St. Louis	6	0	0	0	2	0	0	0
1988	Calgary	6	1	3	4	0	0	0	0
1989◆	Calgary	19	0	3	3	20	0	0	0
1990	Calgary	6	2	0	2	0	0	0	0
1991	Calgary	7	1	0	1	2	0	0	1
Playoff Totals		**67**	**5**	**10**	**15**	**60**	**0**	**0**	**1**
NATYSHAK, Mike	*No playoffs*								Right wing
NAZAROV, Andrei									Left wing
1995	San Jose	6	0	0	0	9	0	0	0
Playoff Totals		**6**	**0**	**0**	**0**	**9**	**0**	**0**	**0**
NDUR, Rumun	*No playoffs*								Defense
NEATON, Pat	*No playoffs*								Defense
NECHAEV, Viktor	*No playoffs*								Center
NECKAR, Stanislav									Defense
1998	Ottawa	9	0	0	0	2	0	0	0
1999	Phoenix	6	0	1	1	4	0	0	0
Playoff Totals		**15**	**0**	**1**	**1**	**6**	**0**	**0**	**0**
NEDOMANSKY, Vaclav									Right wing
1978	Detroit	7	3	5	8	0	1	0	0
Playoff Totals		**7**	**3**	**5**	**8**	**0**	**1**	**0**	**0**
NEDVED, Petr									Center
1991	Vancouver	6	0	1	1	0	0	0	0
1992	Vancouver	10	1	4	5	16	0	0	0
1993	Vancouver	12	2	3	5	2	0	0	0
1994	St. Louis	4	0	1	1	4	0	0	0
1995	NY Rangers	10	3	2	5	6	2	0	0
1996	Pittsburgh	18	10	10	20	16	4	0	2
1997	Pittsburgh	5	1	2	3	12	0	1	0
Playoff Totals		**65**	**17**	**23**	**40**	**56**	**6**	**1**	**2**
NEDVED, Zdenek	*No playoffs*								Right wing
NEEDHAM, Mike									Right wing
1992◆	Pittsburgh	5	1	0	1	2	0	0	0
1993	Pittsburgh	9	1	0	1	2	0	0	0
Playoff Totals		**14**	**2**	**0**	**2**	**4**	**0**	**0**	**0**

Season	Club	GP	G	A	Pts	PIM	PP	SH	GW
NEELY, Bob									Left wing
1974	Toronto	4	1	3	4	0	0	0	0
1975	Toronto	3	0	0	0	2	0	0	0
1976	Toronto	10	3	1	4	7	2	0	0
1977	Toronto	9	1	3	4	6	1	0	0
Playoff Totals		**26**	**5**	**7**	**12**	**15**	**3**	**0**	**0**
NEELY, Cam									Right wing
1984	Vancouver	4	2	0	2	2	1	0	0
1986	Vancouver	3	0	0	0	6	0	0	0
1987	Boston	4	5	1	6	8	3	0	0
1988	Boston	23	9	8	17	51	2	0	2
1989	Boston	10	7	2	9	8	4	0	2
1990	Boston	21	12	16	28	51	4	1	2
1991	Boston	19	16	4	20	36	9	0	4
1993	Boston	4	4	1	5	4	1	0	0
1995	Boston	5	2	0	2	2	1	0	1
Playoff Totals		**93**	**57**	**32**	**89**	**168**	**25**	**1**	**11**
NEILSON, Jim									Defense
1967	NY Rangers	4	1	0	1	0	1	0	0
1968	NY Rangers	6	0	2	2	4	0	0	0
1969	NY Rangers	4	0	3	3	5	0	0	0
1970	NY Rangers	6	0	1	1	8	0	0	0
1971	NY Rangers	13	0	3	3	30	0	0	0
1972	NY Rangers	10	0	3	3	8	0	0	0
1973	NY Rangers	10	0	4	4	2	0	0	0
1974	NY Rangers	12	0	1	1	4	0	0	0
Playoff Totals		**65**	**1**	**17**	**18**	**61**	**1**	**0**	**0**
NELSON, Gordie	*No playoffs*								Defense
NELSON, Jeff									Center
1996	Washington	3	0	0	0	4	0	0	0
Playoff Totals		**3**	**0**	**0**	**0**	**4**	**0**	**0**	**0**
NELSON, Todd									Defense
1994	Washington	4	0	0	0	0	0	0	0
Playoff Totals		**4**	**0**	**0**	**0**	**0**	**0**	**0**	**0**
NEMCHINOV, Sergei									Center
1992	NY Rangers	13	1	4	5	8	0	0	0
1994◆	NY Rangers	23	2	5	7	6	0	0	0
1995	NY Rangers	10	4	5	9	2	0	0	1
1996	NY Rangers	6	0	1	1	2	0	0	0
1999	New Jersey	4	0	0	0	0	0	0	0
Playoff Totals		**56**	**7**	**15**	**22**	**18**	**0**	**0**	**1**
NEMECEK, Jan	*No playoffs*								Defense
NEMETH, Steve	*No playoffs*								Center
NEMIROVSKY, David									Right wing
1997	Florida	3	1	0	1	0	0	0	0
Playoff Totals		**3**	**1**	**0**	**1**	**0**	**0**	**0**	**0**
NESTERENKO, Eric									Right wing
1954	Toronto	5	0	1	1	9	....	....	....
1955	Toronto	4	0	1	1	6	....	....	....
1959	Chicago	6	2	2	4	8	....	....	....
1960	Chicago	4	0	0	0	2	....	....	....
1961◆	Chicago	11	2	3	5	6	....	....	....
1962	Chicago	12	0	5	5	22	....	....	....
1963	Chicago	6	2	3	5	8	....	....	....
1964	Chicago	7	2	1	3	8	....	....	....
1965	Chicago	14	2	2	4	16	....	....	....
1966	Chicago	6	1	0	1	4	....	....	....
1967	Chicago	6	1	2	3	2	....	....	....
1968	Chicago	10	0	1	1	2	0	0	0
1970	Chicago	7	1	2	3	4	0	0	0
1971	Chicago	18	0	1	1	19	0	0	0
1972	Chicago	8	0	0	0	11	0	0	0
Playoff Totals		**124**	**13**	**24**	**37**	**127**	....	....	....
NETHERY, Lance									Center
1981	NY Rangers	14	5	3	8	9	0	0	1
Playoff Totals		**14**	**5**	**3**	**8**	**9**	**0**	**0**	**1**
NEUFELD, Ray									Right wing
1980	Hartford	2	1	0	1	0	0	0	0
1986	Winnipeg	3	2	0	2	10	1	0	0
1987	Winnipeg	8	1	1	2	30	0	0	0
1988	Winnipeg	5	2	2	4	6	1	0	0
1989	Boston	10	2	3	5	9	0	0	1
Playoff Totals		**28**	**8**	**6**	**14**	**55**	**2**	**0**	**1**
NEVILLE, Mike									Center
1925	Toronto	2	0	0	0	0	0	0	0
Playoff Totals		**2**	**0**	**0**	**0**	**0**	**0**	**0**	**0**
NEVIN, Bob									Right wing
1961	Toronto	5	1	0	1	2	1	0	0
1962◆	Toronto	12	2	4	6	6	0	0	0
1963◆	Toronto	10	3	0	3	2	0	1	2
1967	NY Rangers	4	0	3	3	2	0	0	0
1968	NY Rangers	6	0	3	3	4	0	0	0
1969	NY Rangers	4	0	2	2	0	0	0	0
1970	NY Rangers	6	1	1	2	2	1	0	0
1971	NY Rangers	13	5	3	8	0	1	0	1
1972	Minnesota	7	1	1	2	0	0	0	0
1974	Los Angeles	5	1	0	1	2	0	0	0
1975	Los Angeles	3	0	0	0	0	0	0	0
1976	Los Angeles	9	2	1	3	4	0	0	1
Playoff Totals		**84**	**16**	**18**	**34**	**24**	**3**	**1**	**4**

Season	Club	GP	G	A	Pts	PIM	PP	SH	GW
NEWBERRY, John	Center								
1983	Montreal	2	0	0	0	0	0	0	0
Playoff Totals		**2**	**0**	**0**	**0**	**0**	**0**	**0**	**0**
NEWELL, Rick *No playoffs*	Defense								
NEWMAN, Dan	Left wing								
1978	NY Rangers	3	0	0	0	4	0	0	0
Playoff Totals		**3**	**0**	**0**	**0**	**4**	**0**	**0**	**0**
NEWMAN, John *No playoffs*	Center/left wing								
NICHOL, Scott *No playoffs*	Center								
NICHOLLS, Bernie	Center								
1982	Los Angeles	10	4	0	4	23	0	0	1
1985	Los Angeles	3	1	1	2	9	0	0	0
1987	Los Angeles	5	2	5	7	6	1	0	0
1988	Los Angeles	5	2	6	8	11	1	0	0
1989	Los Angeles	11	7	9	16	12	3	0	1
1990	NY Rangers	10	7	5	12	16	3	0	0
1991	NY Rangers	5	4	3	7	8	0	0	1
1992	Edmonton	16	8	11	19	25	4	0	1
1993	New Jersey	5	0	0	0	6	0	0	0
1994	New Jersey	16	4	9	13	28	2	1	0
1995	Chicago	16	1	11	12	8	1	0	0
1996	Chicago	10	2	7	9	4	1	0	0
1998	San Jose	6	0	5	5	8	0	0	0
Playoff Totals		**118**	**42**	**72**	**114**	**164**	**16**	**1**	**4**
NICHOLSON, Al *No playoffs*	Left wing								
NICHOLSON, Ed *No playoffs*	Defense								
NICHOLSON, Hickey *No playoffs*	Left wing								
NICHOLSON, Neil	Defense								
1970	Oakland	2	0	0	0	0	0	0	0
Playoff Totals		**2**	**0**	**0**	**0**	**0**	**0**	**0**	**0**
NICHOLSON, Paul *No playoffs*	Left wing								
NICKULAS, Eric	Center								
1999	Boston	1	0	0	0	2	0	0	0
Playoff Totals		**1**	**0**	**0**	**0**	**2**	**0**	**0**	**0**
NICOLSON, Graeme *No playoffs*	Defense								
NIECKAR, Barry *No playoffs*	Left wing								
NIEDERMAYER, Rob	Center								
1996	Florida	22	5	3	8	12	2	0	2
1997	Florida	5	2	1	3	6	1	0	0
Playoff Totals		**27**	**7**	**4**	**11**	**18**	**3**	**0**	**2**
NIEDERMAYER, Scott	Defense								
1993	New Jersey	5	0	3	3	2	0	0	0
1994	New Jersey	20	2	2	4	8	1	0	0
1995♦	New Jersey	20	4	7	11	10	2	0	1
1997	New Jersey	10	2	4	6	6	2	0	1
1998	New Jersey	6	0	2	2	4	0	0	0
1999	New Jersey	7	1	3	4	18	1	0	0
Playoff Totals		**68**	**9**	**21**	**30**	**48**	**6**	**0**	**2**
NIEKAMP, Jim *No playoffs*	Defense								
NIELSEN, Jeff	Right wing								
1999	Anaheim	4	0	0	0	2	0	0	0
Playoff Totals		**4**	**0**	**0**	**0**	**2**	**0**	**0**	**0**
NIELSEN, Kirk *No playoffs*	Right wing								
NIEMINEN, Ville *No playoffs*	Left wing								
NIENHUIS, Kraig	Left wing								
1986	Boston	2	0	0	0	14	0	0	0
Playoff Totals		**2**	**0**	**0**	**0**	**14**	**0**	**0**	**0**
NIEUWENDYK, Joe	Center								
1987	Calgary	6	2	2	4	0	0	0	0
1988	Calgary	8	3	4	7	2	1	0	0
1989♦	Calgary	22	10	4	14	10	6	0	1
1990	Calgary	6	4	6	10	4	1	0	0
1991	Calgary	7	4	1	5	10	2	0	0
1993	Calgary	6	3	6	9	10	1	0	0
1994	Calgary	6	2	2	4	0	1	0	0
1995	Calgary	5	4	3	7	0	2	0	1
1997	Dallas	7	2	2	4	6	0	0	0
1998	Dallas	1	1	0	1	0	0	0	0
1999♦	Dallas	23	*11	10	21	19	3	0	6
Playoff Totals		**97**	**46**	**40**	**86**	**61**	**17**	**0**	**8**
NIGHBOR, Frank	Center								
1919	Ottawa	2	0	2	2	3	....	....	....
1920♦	Ottawa	5	*6	1	*7	2	....	....	....
1921♦	Ottawa	7	1	*4	5	2	....	....	....
1922	Ottawa	2	2	1	3	4	....	....	....
1923♦	Ottawa	8	1	*2	3	10	....	....	....
1924	Ottawa	2	0	1	1	0	....	....	....
1926	Ottawa	2	0	0	0	2	....	....	....
1927♦	Ottawa	6	1	1	2	0	....	....	....
1928	Ottawa	2	0	0	0	2	....	....	....
Playoff Totals		**36**	**11**	**12**	**23**	**25**	....	....	....
NIGRO, Frank	Center								
1983	Toronto	3	0	0	0	2	0	0	0
Playoff Totals		**3**	**0**	**0**	**0**	**2**	**0**	**0**	**0**

Season	Club	GP	G	A	Pts	PIM	PP	SH	GW
NIINIMAA, Janne	Defense								
1997	Philadelphia	19	1	12	13	16	1	0	1
1998	Edmonton	11	1	1	2	12	0	0	1
1999	Edmonton	4	0	0	0	2	0	0	0
Playoff Totals		**34**	**2**	**13**	**15**	**30**	**1**	**0**	**2**
NIKOLISHIN, Andrei	Left wing								
1998	Washington	21	1	13	14	12	1	0	0
Playoff Totals		**21**	**1**	**13**	**14**	**12**	**1**	**0**	**0**
NIKULIN, Igor	Right wing								
1997	Anaheim	1	0	0	0	0	0	0	0
Playoff Totals		**1**	**0**	**0**	**0**	**0**	**0**	**0**	**0**
NILAN, Chris	Right wing								
1980	Montreal	5	0	0	0	2	0	0	0
1981	Montreal	2	0	0	0	0	0	0	0
1982	Montreal	5	1	1	2	22	0	0	0
1983	Montreal	3	0	0	0	5	0	0	0
1984	Montreal	15	1	0	1	*81	0	0	0
1985	Montreal	12	2	1	3	81	1	0	1
1986♦	Montreal	18	1	2	3	*141	1	0	0
1987	Montreal	17	3	0	3	75	0	0	0
1989	NY Rangers	4	0	1	1	38	0	0	0
1990	NY Rangers	4	0	1	1	19	0	0	0
1991	Boston	19	0	2	2	62	0	0	0
1992	Montreal	7	0	1	1	15	0	0	0
Playoff Totals		**111**	**8**	**9**	**17**	**541**	**2**	**0**	**1**
NILL, Jim	Right wing								
1982	Vancouver	16	4	3	7	67	1	0	1
1983	Vancouver	4	0	0	0	6	0	0	0
1984	Boston	3	0	0	0	4	0	0	0
1985	Winnipeg	8	0	1	1	28	0	0	0
1986	Winnipeg	3	0	0	0	4	0	0	0
1987	Winnipeg	3	0	0	0	7	0	0	0
1988	Detroit	16	6	1	7	62	0	1	0
1989	Detroit	6	0	0	0	25	0	0	0
Playoff Totals		**59**	**10**	**5**	**15**	**203**	**1**	**1**	**1**
NILSON, Marcus *No playoffs*	Right wing								
NILSSON, Kent	Center								
1980	Atlanta	4	0	0	0	2	0	0	0
1981	Calgary	14	3	9	12	2	0	0	0
1982	Calgary	3	0	3	3	2	0	0	0
1983	Calgary	9	1	11	12	2	1	0	0
1985	Calgary	3	0	1	1	0	0	0	0
1986	Minnesota	5	1	4	5	0	0	0	0
1987♦	Edmonton	21	6	13	19	6	2	0	0
Playoff Totals		**59**	**11**	**41**	**52**	**14**	**3**	**0**	**0**
NILSSON, Ulf	Center								
1979	NY Rangers	2	0	0	0	2	0	0	0
1980	NY Rangers	9	0	6	6	2	0	0	0
1981	NY Rangers	14	8	8	16	23	3	0	1
Playoff Totals		**25**	**8**	**14**	**22**	**27**	**3**	**0**	**1**
NISTICO, Lou *No playoffs*	Center								
NOBLE, Reg	Center/defense								
1918♦	Toronto	7	3	2	5	21	....	....	....
1921	Toronto	2	0	0	0	0	....	....	....
1922♦	Toronto	7	0	1	1	21	....	....	....
1926♦	Mtl. Maroons	8	1	1	2	12	....	....	....
1927	Mtl. Maroons	2	0	0	0	2	....	....	....
1929	Detroit	2	0	0	0	2	....	....	....
1932	Detroit	2	0	0	0	0	....	....	....
1933	Mtl. Maroons	2	0	0	0	2	....	....	....
Playoff Totals		**32**	**4**	**4**	**8**	**60**	....	....	....
NOEL, Claude *No playoffs*	Center								
NOLAN, Owen	Right wing								
1993	Quebec	5	1	0	1	2	0	0	0
1995	Quebec	6	2	3	5	6	0	0	0
1998	San Jose	6	2	2	4	26	2	0	1
1999	San Jose	6	1	1	2	6	0	0	0
Playoff Totals		**23**	**6**	**6**	**12**	**40**	**2**	**0**	**1**
NOLAN, Paddy *No playoffs*	Left wing/defense								
NOLAN, Ted *No playoffs*	Center								
NOLET, Simon	Right wing								
1968	Philadelphia	1	0	0	0	0	0	0	0
1971	Philadelphia	4	2	1	3	0	1	0	0
1973	Philadelphia	11	3	1	4	4	0	0	0
1974♦	Philadelphia	15	1	1	2	4	0	0	0
1976	Pittsburgh	3	0	0	0	0	0	0	0
Playoff Totals		**34**	**6**	**3**	**9**	**8**	**1**	**0**	**0**
NOONAN, Brian	Right wing								
1988	Chicago	3	0	0	0	4	0	0	0
1989	Chicago	1	0	0	0	0	0	0	0
1992	Chicago	18	6	9	15	30	3	0	1
1993	Chicago	4	3	0	3	4	1	0	0
1994♦	NY Rangers	22	4	7	11	17	2	0	1
1995	NY Rangers	5	0	0	0	8	0	0	0
1996	St. Louis	13	4	1	5	10	0	0	0
1999	Phoenix	5	0	2	2	4	0	0	0
Playoff Totals		**71**	**17**	**19**	**36**	**77**	**6**	**0**	**2**
NORDMARK, Robert	Defense								
1989	Vancouver	7	3	2	5	8	2	0	0
Playoff Totals		**7**	**3**	**2**	**5**	**8**	**2**	**0**	**0**

Season	Club	GP	G	A	Pts	PIM	PP	SH	GW
NORDSTROM, Peter *No playoffs*	Center								
NORIS, Joe *No playoffs*	Center/defense								
NORRIS, Dwayne *No playoffs*	Right wing								
NORRISH, Rod *No playoffs*	Left wing								
NORSTROM, Mattias	Defense								
1995	NY Rangers	3	0	0	0	0	0	0	0
1998	Los Angeles	4	0	0	0	2	0	0	0
Playoff Totals		**7**	**0**	**0**	**0**	**2**	**0**	**0**	**0**
NORTHCOTT, Baldy	Defense/left wing								
1930	Mtl. Maroons	4	0	0	0	4	....	....	....
1931	Mtl. Maroons	2	0	1	1	0	....	....	....
1932	Mtl. Maroons	4	1	2	3	4	....	....	....
1933	Mtl. Maroons	2	0	0	0	4	....	....	....
1934	Mtl. Maroons	4	2	0	2	0	....	....	....
1935♦	Mtl. Maroons	7	*4	1	*5	0	....	....	....
1936	Mtl. Maroons	3	0	0	0	0	....	....	....
1937	Mtl. Maroons	5	1	1	2	2	....	....	....
Playoff Totals		**31**	**8**	**5**	**13**	**14**	....	....	....
NORTON, Jeff	Defense								
1988	NY Islanders	3	0	2	2	13	0	0	0
1990	NY Islanders	4	1	3	4	17	0	0	0
1993	NY Islanders	10	1	1	2	4	0	0	0
1994	San Jose	14	1	5	6	20	0	0	0
1995	St. Louis	7	1	1	2	11	0	0	0
1999	San Jose	6	0	7	7	10	0	0	0
Playoff Totals		**44**	**4**	**19**	**23**	**75**	**0**	**0**	**0**
NORWICH, Craig *No playoffs*	Defense								
NORWOOD, Lee	Defense								
1981	Quebec	3	0	0	0	2	0	0	0
1986	St. Louis	19	2	7	9	64	0	0	0
1987	Detroit	16	1	6	7	31	0	0	1
1988	Detroit	16	2	6	8	40	2	0	0
1989	Detroit	6	1	2	3	16	1	0	0
1991	New Jersey	4	0	0	0	18	0	0	0
1992	St. Louis	1	0	1	1	0	0	0	0
Playoff Totals		**65**	**6**	**22**	**28**	**171**	**3**	**0**	**1**
NOVOSELTSEV, Ivan *No playoffs*	Left wing								
NOVY, Milan	Center								
1983	Washington	2	0	0	0	0	0	0	0
Playoff Totals		**2**	**0**	**0**	**0**	**0**	**0**	**0**	**0**
NOWAK, Hank	Left wing								
1975	Boston	3	1	0	1	0	0	0	0
1976	Boston	10	0	0	0	8	0	0	0
Playoff Totals		**13**	**1**	**0**	**1**	**8**	**0**	**0**	**0**
NUMMINEN, Teppo	Defense								
1990	Winnipeg	7	1	2	3	10	0	0	0
1992	Winnipeg	7	0	0	0	0	0	0	0
1993	Winnipeg	6	1	1	2	2	1	0	0
1996	Winnipeg	6	0	0	0	2	0	0	0
1997	Phoenix	7	3	3	6	0	1	0	1
1998	Phoenix	1	0	0	0	0	0	0	0
1999	Phoenix	7	2	1	3	4	2	0	0
Playoff Totals		**41**	**7**	**7**	**14**	**18**	**4**	**0**	**1**
NURMINEN, Kai *No playoffs*	Left wing								
NYKOLUK, Mike *No playoffs*	Right wing								
NYLANDER, Michael	Center								
1994	Calgary	3	0	0	0	0	0	0	0
1995	Calgary	6	0	6	6	2	0	0	0
1996	Calgary	4	0	0	0	0	0	0	0
Playoff Totals		**13**	**0**	**6**	**6**	**2**	**0**	**0**	**0**
NYLUND, Gary	Defense								
1986	Toronto	10	0	2	2	25	0	0	0
1987	Chicago	4	0	2	2	11	0	0	0
1988	Chicago	5	0	0	0	10	0	0	0
1990	NY Islanders	5	0	2	2	17	0	0	0
Playoff Totals		**24**	**0**	**6**	**6**	**63**	**0**	**0**	**0**
NYROP, Bill	Defense								
1976♦	Montreal	13	0	3	3	12	0	0	0
1977♦	Montreal	8	1	0	1	4	0	0	0
1978♦	Montreal	12	0	4	4	6	0	0	0
1982	Minnesota	2	0	0	0	0	0	0	0
Playoff Totals		**35**	**1**	**7**	**8**	**22**	**0**	**0**	**0**
NYSTROM, Bob	Right wing								
1975	NY Islanders	17	1	3	4	27	0	0	0
1976	NY Islanders	13	3	6	9	30	1	0	0
1977	NY Islanders	12	0	2	2	7	0	0	0
1978	NY Islanders	7	3	1	4	14	1	0	2
1979	NY Islanders	10	3	2	5	4	0	0	1
1980♦	NY Islanders	20	9	9	18	50	0	0	3
1981♦	NY Islanders	18	6	6	12	20	0	0	1
1982♦	NY Islanders	15	5	5	10	32	0	0	0
1983♦	NY Islanders	20	7	6	13	15	0	0	0
1984	NY Islanders	15	0	2	2	8	0	0	0
1985	NY Islanders	10	2	2	4	29	0	0	0
Playoff Totals		**157**	**39**	**44**	**83**	**236**	**2**	**0**	**7**

Season	Club	GP	G	A	Pts	PIM	PP	SH	GW
OATES, Adam									Center
1987	Detroit	16	4	7	11	6	0	0	1
1988	Detroit	16	8	12	20	6	4	0	1
1989	Detroit	6	0	8	8	2	0	0	0
1990	St. Louis	12	2	12	14	4	1	0	0
1991	St. Louis	13	7	13	20	10	2	0	1
1992	Boston	15	5	14	19	4	3	0	2
1993	Boston	4	0	9	9	4	0	0	0
1994	Boston	13	3	9	12	8	2	0	0
1995	Boston	5	1	0	1	2	1	0	0
1996	Boston	5	2	5	7	2	0	1	0
1998	Washington	21	6	11	17	8	1	1	1
Playoff Totals		**126**	**38**	**100**	**138**	**56**	**14**	**2**	**6**
OATMAN, Russell									Left wing
1927	Mtl. Maroons	2	0	0	0	0	....	....	....
1928	Mtl. Maroons	9	1	0	1	18	....	....	....
1929	NY Rangers	4	0	0	0	0	....	....	....
Playoff Totals		**15**	**1**	**0**	**1**	**18**	....	....	....
O'BRIEN, Dennis									Defense
1971	Minnesota	9	0	0	0	20	0	0	0
1972	Minnesota	3	0	1	1	11	0	0	0
1973	Minnesota	6	1	0	1	38	0	0	0
1977	Minnesota	2	0	0	0	4	0	0	0
1978	Boston	14	0	1	1	28	0	0	0
Playoff Totals		**34**	**1**	**2**	**3**	**101**	**0**	**0**	**0**
O'BRIEN, Ellard *No playoffs*									Defense
O'CALLAHAN, Jack									Defense
1983	Chicago	5	0	2	2	2	0	0	0
1984	Chicago	2	0	0	0	2	0	0	0
1985	Chicago	15	3	5	8	25	0	0	0
1986	Chicago	3	0	1	1	4	0	0	0
1987	Chicago	2	0	0	0	2	0	0	0
1988	New Jersey	5	1	3	4	6	0	0	0
Playoff Totals		**32**	**4**	**11**	**15**	**41**	**0**	**0**	**0**
O'CONNELL, Mike									Defense
1979	Chicago	4	0	0	0	4	0	0	0
1980	Chicago	7	0	1	1	0	0	0	0
1981	Boston	3	1	3	4	2	0	1	0
1982	Boston	11	2	2	4	20	0	0	0
1983	Boston	17	3	5	8	12	2	0	1
1984	Boston	3	0	0	0	0	0	0	0
1985	Boston	5	1	5	6	0	1	0	0
1987	Detroit	16	1	4	5	14	0	0	0
1988	Detroit	10	0	4	4	8	0	0	0
1989	Detroit	6	0	0	0	4	0	0	0
Playoff Totals		**82**	**8**	**24**	**32**	**64**	**3**	**1**	**1**
O'CONNOR, Buddy									Center
1942	Montreal	3	0	1	1	0	....	....	....
1943	Montreal	5	4	5	9	0	....	....	....
1944♦	Montreal	8	1	2	3	2	....	....	....
1945	Montreal	2	0	0	0	0	....	....	....
1946♦	Montreal	9	2	3	5	0	....	....	....
1947	Montreal	8	3	4	7	0	....	....	....
1948	NY Rangers	6	1	4	5	0	....	....	....
1950	NY Rangers	12	4	2	6	4	....	....	....
Playoff Totals		**53**	**15**	**21**	**36**	**6**	....	....	....
O'CONNOR, Myles *No playoffs*									Defense
ODDLEIFSON, Chris									Center
1975	Vancouver	5	0	3	3	2	0	0	0
1976	Vancouver	2	1	2	3	0	0	0	0
1979	Vancouver	3	0	1	1	2	0	0	0
1980	Vancouver	4	0	0	0	4	0	0	0
Playoff Totals		**14**	**1**	**6**	**7**	**8**	**0**	**0**	**0**
ODELEIN, Lyle									Defense
1991	Montreal	12	0	0	0	54	0	0	0
1992	Montreal	7	0	0	0	11	0	0	0
1993♦	Montreal	20	1	5	6	30	0	0	0
1994	Montreal	7	0	0	0	17	0	0	0
1996	Montreal	6	1	1	2	6	0	1	0
1997	New Jersey	10	2	2	4	19	1	0	0
1998	New Jersey	6	1	1	2	21	1	0	1
1999	New Jersey	7	0	3	3	10	0	0	0
Playoff Totals		**75**	**5**	**12**	**17**	**168**	**2**	**1**	**1**
ODELEIN, Selmar *No playoffs*									Defense
ODGERS, Jeff									Right wing
1994	San Jose	11	0	0	0	11	0	0	0
1995	San Jose	11	1	1	2	23	0	0	0
1998	Colorado	6	0	0	0	25	0	0	0
1999	Colorado	15	1	0	1	14	0	0	1
Playoff Totals		**43**	**2**	**1**	**3**	**73**	**0**	**0**	**1**
ODJICK, Gino									Left wing
1991	Vancouver	6	0	0	0	18	0	0	0
1992	Vancouver	4	0	0	0	6	0	0	0
1993	Vancouver	1	0	0	0	0	0	0	0
1994	Vancouver	10	0	0	0	18	0	0	0
1995	Vancouver	5	0	0	0	47	0	0	0
1996	Vancouver	6	3	1	4	6	0	0	2
Playoff Totals		**32**	**3**	**1**	**4**	**95**	**0**	**0**	**2**
O'DONNELL, Fred									Right wing
1973	Boston	5	0	1	1	5	0	0	0
Playoff Totals		**5**	**0**	**1**	**1**	**5**	**0**	**0**	**0**
O'DONNELL, Sean									Defense
1998	Los Angeles	4	1	0	1	36	0	0	0
Playoff Totals		**4**	**1**	**0**	**1**	**36**	**0**	**0**	**0**
O'DONOGHUE, Don									Right wing
1970	Oakland	3	0	0	0	0	0	0	0
Playoff Totals		**3**	**0**	**0**	**0**	**0**	**0**	**0**	**0**
ODROWSKI, Gerry									Defense
1961	Detroit	10	0	0	0	4	0	0	0
1963	Detroit	2	0	0	0	2	0	0	0
1969	Oakland	7	0	1	1	2	0	0	0
1972	St. Louis	11	0	0	0	8	0	0	0
Playoff Totals		**30**	**0**	**1**	**1**	**16**	**0**	**0**	**0**
O'DWYER, Bill									Center
1988	Boston	9	0	0	0	0	0	0	0
1990	Boston	1	0	0	0	2	0	0	0
Playoff Totals		**10**	**0**	**0**	**0**	**2**	**0**	**0**	**0**
O'FLAHERTY, Gerry									Left wing
1975	Vancouver	5	2	2	4	6	0	0	0
1976	Vancouver	2	0	0	0	0	0	0	0
Playoff Totals		**7**	**2**	**2**	**4**	**6**	**0**	**0**	**0**
O'FLAHERTY, Peanuts *No playoffs*									Right wing
OGILVIE, Brian *No playoffs*									Center
O'GRADY, George *No playoffs*									Defense
OGRODNICK, John									Left wing
1984	Detroit	4	0	0	0	0	0	0	0
1985	Detroit	3	1	1	2	0	0	0	0
1987	Quebec	13	9	4	13	6	3	0	2
1989	NY Rangers	3	2	0	2	0	1	0	0
1990	NY Rangers	10	6	3	9	0	3	0	1
1991	NY Rangers	4	0	0	0	0	0	0	0
1992	NY Rangers	3	0	0	0	0	0	0	0
1993	Detroit	1	0	0	0	0	0	0	0
Playoff Totals		**41**	**18**	**8**	**26**	**6**	**7**	**0**	**3**
OHLUND, Mattias *No playoffs*									Defense
OJANEN, Janne									Center
1992	New Jersey	3	0	2	2	0	0	0	0
Playoff Totals		**3**	**0**	**2**	**2**	**0**	**0**	**0**	**0**
OKERLUND, Todd *No playoffs*									Right wing
OKSIUTA, Roman									Right wing
1995	Vancouver	10	2	3	5	0	1	0	0
Playoff Totals		**10**	**2**	**3**	**5**	**0**	**1**	**0**	**0**
OLAUSSON, Fredrik									Defense
1987	Winnipeg	10	2	3	5	4	1	0	0
1988	Winnipeg	5	1	1	2	0	0	0	0
1990	Winnipeg	7	0	2	2	2	0	0	0
1992	Winnipeg	7	1	5	6	4	1	0	0
1993	Winnipeg	6	0	2	2	2	0	0	0
1997	Pittsburgh	4	0	1	1	0	0	0	0
1998	Pittsburgh	6	0	3	3	2	0	0	0
1999	Anaheim	4	0	2	2	4	0	0	0
Playoff Totals		**49**	**4**	**19**	**23**	**18**	**2**	**0**	**0**
OLCZYK, Ed									Center
1985	Chicago	15	6	5	11	11	1	1	0
1986	Chicago	3	0	0	0	0	0	0	0
1987	Chicago	4	1	1	2	4	0	0	0
1988	Toronto	6	5	4	9	2	1	1	1
1990	Toronto	5	1	2	3	14	0	0	0
1992	Winnipeg	6	2	1	3	4	0	0	1
1994♦	NY Rangers	1	0	0	0	0	0	0	0
1996	Winnipeg	6	1	2	3	6	0	0	0
1997	Pittsburgh	5	1	0	1	12	0	1	1
1998	Pittsburgh	6	2	0	2	4	1	1	1
Playoff Totals		**57**	**19**	**15**	**34**	**57**	**3**	**4**	**4**
OLIVER, David									Right wing
1997	NY Rangers	3	0	0	0	0	0	0	0
Playoff Totals		**3**	**0**	**0**	**0**	**0**	**0**	**0**	**0**
OLIVER, Harry									Right wing
1927	Boston	8	4	2	*6	4	....	....	....
1928	Boston	2	2	0	2	4	....	....	....
1929♦	Boston	5	1	1	2	8	....	....	....
1930	Boston	6	2	1	3	6	....	....	....
1931	Boston	4	0	0	0	2	....	....	....
1933	Boston	5	0	0	0	0	....	....	....
1936	NY Americans	5	1	2	3	0	....	....	....
Playoff Totals		**35**	**10**	**6**	**16**	**24**	....	....	....
OLIVER, Murray									Center
1960	Detroit	6	1	0	1	4	0	0	0
1969	Toronto	4	1	2	3	0	0	0	0
1971	Minnesota	12	7	4	11	0	2	0	0
1972	Minnesota	7	0	6	6	4	0	0	0
1973	Minnesota	6	0	4	4	2	0	0	0
Playoff Totals		**35**	**9**	**16**	**25**	**10**	**2**	**0**	**0**
OLIWA, Krzysztof									Left wing
1998	New Jersey	6	0	0	0	23	0	0	0
1999	New Jersey	1	0	0	0	2	0	0	0
Playoff Totals		**7**	**0**	**0**	**0**	**25**	**0**	**0**	**0**
OLMSTEAD, Bert									Left wing
1951	Montreal	11	2	4	6	9	....	....	....
1952	Montreal	11	0	1	1	4	....	....	....
1953♦	Montreal	12	2	2	4	4	....	....	....
1954	Montreal	11	0	1	1	19	....	....	....
1955	Montreal	12	0	4	4	21	....	....	....
1956♦	Montreal	10	4	*10	14	8	....	....	....
1957♦	Montreal	10	0	*9	9	13	....	....	....
1958♦	Montreal	9	0	3	3	0	....	....	....
1959	Toronto	12	4	2	6	13	....	....	....
1960	Toronto	10	3	4	7	0	....	....	....
1961	Toronto	3	1	2	3	10	....	....	....
1962♦	Toronto	4	0	1	1	0	....	....	....
Playoff Totals		**115**	**16**	**43**	**59**	**101**	....	....	....
OLSEN, Darryl *No playoffs*									Defense
OLSON, Dennis *No playoffs*									Center
OLSSON, Christer									Defense
1996	St. Louis	3	0	0	0	0	0	0	0
Playoff Totals		**3**	**0**	**0**	**0**	**0**	**0**	**0**	**0**
O'NEIL, Paul *No playoffs*									Center/right wing
O'NEILL, Jeff									Center
1999	Carolina	6	0	1	1	0	0	0	0
Playoff Totals		**6**	**0**	**1**	**1**	**0**	**0**	**0**	**0**
O'NEILL, Jim									Center/right wing
1935	Boston	4	0	0	0	9	....	....	....
1936	Boston	2	1	1	2	4	....	....	....
1941	Montreal	3	0	0	0	0	....	....	....
Playoff Totals		**9**	**1**	**1**	**2**	**13**	....	....	....
O'NEILL, Tom									Right wing
1944	Toronto	4	0	0	0	6	0	0	0
Playoff Totals		**4**	**0**	**0**	**0**	**6**	**0**	**0**	**0**
ORBAN, Bill									Center/left wing
1968	Chicago	3	0	0	0	0	0	0	0
Playoff Totals		**3**	**0**	**0**	**0**	**0**	**0**	**0**	**0**
O'REE, Willie *No playoffs*									Left/right wing
O'REGAN, Tom *No playoffs*									Center/defense
O'REILLY, Terry									Right wing
1973	Boston	5	0	0	0	2	0	0	0
1974	Boston	16	2	5	7	38	0	0	0
1975	Boston	3	0	0	0	17	0	0	0
1976	Boston	12	3	1	4	25	0	0	0
1977	Boston	14	5	6	11	28	0	0	1
1978	Boston	15	5	10	15	40	1	0	1
1979	Boston	11	0	6	6	25	0	0	0
1980	Boston	10	3	6	9	69	2	0	1
1981	Boston	3	1	2	3	12	0	0	0
1982	Boston	11	5	4	9	56	0	0	1
1984	Boston	3	0	0	0	14	0	0	0
1985	Boston	5	1	2	3	9	0	0	0
Playoff Totals		**108**	**25**	**42**	**67**	**335**	**3**	**0**	**4**
ORLANDO, Gates									Center
1985	Buffalo	5	0	4	4	14	0	0	0
Playoff Totals		**5**	**0**	**4**	**4**	**14**	**0**	**0**	**0**
ORLANDO, Jimmy									Defense
1940	Detroit	5	0	0	0	15	0	0	0
1941	Detroit	9	0	2	2	31	0	0	0
1942	Detroit	12	0	4	4	45	0	0	0
1943♦	Detroit	10	0	3	3	14	0	0	0
Playoff Totals		**36**	**0**	**9**	**9**	**105**	**0**	**0**	**0**
ORLESKI, Dave *No playoffs*									Left wing
ORR, Bobby									Defense
1968	Boston	4	0	2	2	2	0	0	0
1969	Boston	10	1	7	8	10	0	0	0
1970♦	Boston	14	9	11	20	14	3	2	1
1971	Boston	7	5	7	12	25	1	1	1
1972♦	Boston	15	5	*19	*24	19	4	0	1
1973	Boston	5	1	1	2	7	0	0	0
1974	Boston	16	4	*14	18	28	1	0	2
1975	Boston	3	1	5	6	2	0	1	0
Playoff Totals		**74**	**26**	**66**	**92**	**107**	**9**	**4**	**5**
ORSZAGH, Vladimir *No playoffs*									Right wing
OSBORNE, Keith *No playoffs*									Right wing
OSBORNE, Mark									Left wing
1984	NY Rangers	5	0	1	1	7	0	0	0
1985	NY Rangers	3	0	0	0	4	0	0	0
1986	NY Rangers	15	2	3	5	26	0	1	1
1987	Toronto	9	1	3	4	6	0	0	0
1988	Toronto	6	1	3	4	16	0	0	1
1990	Toronto	5	2	3	5	12	0	1	0
1993	Toronto	19	1	1	2	16	0	0	0
1994	Toronto	18	4	2	6	52	0	2	1
1995	NY Rangers	7	1	0	1	2	0	0	0
Playoff Totals		**87**	**12**	**16**	**28**	**141**	**0**	**4**	**3**
OSBURN, Randy *No playoffs*									Left wing

Season	Club	GP	G	A	Pts	PIM	PP	SH	GW
O'SHEA, Danny									Center
1970	Minnesota	6	1	0	1	8	0	0	0
1971	Chicago	18	2	5	7	15	0	0	0
1972	St. Louis	10	0	2	2	36	0	0	0
1973	St. Louis	5	0	0	0	2	0	0	0
Playoff Totals		**39**	**3**	**7**	**10**	**61**	**0**	**0**	**0**
O'SHEA, Kevin									Right wing
1972	St. Louis	11	2	1	3	10	0	0	1
1973	St. Louis	1	0	0	0	0	0	0	0
Playoff Totals		**12**	**2**	**1**	**3**	**10**	**0**	**0**	**1**
OSIECKI, Mark	*No playoffs*								Defense
O'SULLIVAN, Chris	*No playoffs*								Defense
OTEVREL, Jaroslav	*No playoffs*								Left wing
OTTO, Joel									Center
1985	Calgary	3	2	1	3	10	1	0	1
1986	Calgary	22	5	10	15	80	3	0	1
1987	Calgary	2	0	2	2	6	0	0	0
1988	Calgary	9	3	2	5	26	1	0	1
1989♦	Calgary	22	6	13	19	46	2	1	1
1990	Calgary	6	2	2	4	2	0	0	0
1991	Calgary	7	1	2	3	8	0	0	0
1993	Calgary	6	4	2	6	4	0	1	1
1994	Calgary	3	0	1	1	4	0	0	0
1995	Calgary	7	0	3	3	2	0	0	0
1996	Philadelphia	12	3	4	7	11	1	0	1
1997	Philadelphia	18	1	5	6	8	0	0	0
1998	Philadelphia	5	0	0	0	0	0	0	0
Playoff Totals		**122**	**27**	**47**	**74**	**207**	**8**	**2**	**6**
OUELLETTE, Eddie									Center
1936	Chicago	1	0	0	0	0	0	0	0
Playoff Totals		**1**	**0**	**0**	**0**	**0**	**0**	**0**	**0**
OUELLETTE, Gerry	*No playoffs*								Right wing
OWCHAR, Dennis									Defense
1975	Pittsburgh	6	0	1	1	4	0	0	0
1976	Pittsburgh	2	0	0	0	2	0	0	0
1978	Colorado	2	1	0	1	2	0	0	0
Playoff Totals		**10**	**1**	**1**	**2**	**8**	**0**	**0**	**0**
OWEN, George									Defense
1929♦	Boston	5	0	0	0	0	....	....	....
1930	Boston	6	0	2	2	6	....	....	....
1931	Boston	5	2	3	5	13	....	....	....
1933	Boston	5	0	0	0	6	....	....	....
Playoff Totals		**21**	**2**	**5**	**7**	**25**	....	....	....
OZOLINSH, Sandis									Defense
1994	San Jose	14	0	10	10	8	0	0	0
1995	San Jose	11	3	2	5	6	1	0	0
1996♦	Colorado	22	5	14	19	16	2	0	1
1997	Colorado	17	4	13	17	24	2	0	1
1998	Colorado	7	0	7	7	14	0	0	0
1999	Colorado	19	4	8	12	22	3	0	1
Playoff Totals		**90**	**16**	**54**	**70**	**90**	**8**	**0**	**3**
PACHAL, Clayton	*No playoffs*								Center/left wing
PADDOCK, John									Right wing
1980	Philadelphia	3	2	0	2	0	0	0	0
1981	Quebec	2	0	0	0	0	0	0	0
Playoff Totals		**5**	**2**	**0**	**2**	**0**	**0**	**0**	**0**
PAEK, Jim									Defense
1991♦	Pittsburgh	8	1	0	1	2	0	0	0
1992♦	Pittsburgh	19	0	4	4	6	0	0	0
Playoff Totals		**27**	**1**	**4**	**5**	**8**	**0**	**0**	**0**
PAIEMENT, Rosaire									Center
1968	Philadelphia	3	3	0	3	0	2	0	1
Playoff Totals		**3**	**3**	**0**	**3**	**0**	**2**	**0**	**1**
PAIEMENT, Wilf									Right wing
1978	Colorado	2	0	0	0	7	0	0	0
1980	Toronto	3	0	2	2	17	0	0	0
1981	Toronto	3	0	0	0	2	0	0	0
1982	Quebec	14	6	6	12	28	1	0	1
1983	Quebec	4	0	1	1	4	0	0	0
1984	Quebec	9	3	1	4	24	0	0	0
1985	Quebec	18	4	2	6	58	0	0	0
1986	NY Rangers	16	5	5	10	45	4	0	0
Playoff Totals		**69**	**18**	**17**	**35**	**185**	**5**	**0**	**1**
PALANGIO, Pete									Left wing
1927	Mtl. Canadiens	4	0	0	0	0	0	0	0
1938♦	Chicago	3	0	0	0	0	0	0	0
Playoff Totals		**7**	**0**	**0**	**0**	**0**	**0**	**0**	**0**
PALAZZARI, Aldo	*No playoffs*								Right wing
PALAZZARI, Doug									Center
1975	St. Louis	2	0	0	0	0	0	0	0
Playoff Totals		**2**	**0**	**0**	**0**	**0**	**0**	**0**	**0**
PALFFY, Zigmund	*No playoffs*								Right wing
PALMER, Brad									Left wing
1981	Minnesota	19	8	5	13	4	1	2	1
1982	Minnesota	3	0	0	0	12	0	0	0
1983	Boston	7	1	0	1	0	0	1	1
Playoff Totals		**29**	**9**	**5**	**14**	**16**	**1**	**3**	**2**
PALMER, Rob	*No playoffs*								Center

Season	Club	GP	G	A	Pts	PIM	PP	SH	GW
PALMER, Robert									Defense
1978	Los Angeles	2	0	0	0	0	0	0	0
1979	Los Angeles	2	0	0	0	2	0	0	0
1980	Los Angeles	4	1	2	3	4	0	0	0
Playoff Totals		**8**	**1**	**2**	**3**	**6**	**0**	**0**	**0**
PANAGABKO, Ed	*No playoffs*								Center
PANDOLFO, Jay									Left wing
1997	New Jersey	6	0	1	1	0	0	0	0
1998	New Jersey	3	0	2	2	0	0	0	0
1999	New Jersey	7	1	0	1	0	0	0	0
Playoff Totals		**16**	**1**	**3**	**4**	**0**	**0**	**0**	**0**
PANKEWICZ, Greg	*No playoffs*								Right wing
PANTELEEV, Grigori	*No playoffs*								Left wing
PAPIKE, Joe									Right wing
1941	Chicago	5	0	2	2	0	0	0	0
Playoff Totals		**5**	**0**	**2**	**2**	**0**	**0**	**0**	**0**
PAPPIN, Jim									Right wing
1964♦	Toronto	11	0	0	0	0	0	0	0
1967♦	Toronto	12	*7	8	*15	12	3	0	1
1970	Chicago	8	3	2	5	6	1	0	0
1971	Chicago	18	10	4	14	24	2	0	1
1972	Chicago	8	2	5	7	4	0	1	1
1973	Chicago	16	8	7	15	24	1	0	1
1974	Chicago	11	3	6	9	29	0	0	2
1975	Chicago	8	0	2	2	2	0	0	0
Playoff Totals		**92**	**33**	**34**	**67**	**101**	**7**	**1**	**6**
PARADISE, Bob									Defense
1972	Minnesota	4	0	0	0	2	0	0	0
1975	Pittsburgh	6	0	1	1	17	0	0	0
1979	Pittsburgh	2	0	0	0	0	0	0	0
Playoff Totals		**12**	**0**	**1**	**1**	**19**	**0**	**0**	**0**
PARGETER, George	*No playoffs*								Left wing
PARISE, Jean-Paul									Left wing
1968	Minnesota	14	2	5	7	10	0	1	0
1970	Minnesota	6	3	2	5	2	2	0	0
1971	Minnesota	12	3	3	6	22	2	0	1
1972	Minnesota	7	3	3	6	6	2	0	0
1973	Minnesota	6	0	0	0	9	0	0	0
1975	NY Islanders	17	8	8	16	22	4	0	1
1976	NY Islanders	13	4	6	10	10	1	0	0
1977	NY Islanders	11	4	4	8	6	1	0	0
Playoff Totals		**86**	**27**	**31**	**58**	**87**	**12**	**1**	**2**
PARIZEAU, Michel	*No playoffs*								Center
PARK, Brad									Defense
1969	NY Rangers	4	0	2	2	7	0	0	0
1970	NY Rangers	5	1	2	3	11	1	0	0
1971	NY Rangers	13	0	4	4	42	0	0	0
1972	NY Rangers	16	4	7	11	21	2	0	1
1973	NY Rangers	10	2	5	7	8	1	0	1
1974	NY Rangers	13	4	8	12	38	1	0	1
1975	NY Rangers	3	1	4	5	2	0	0	0
1976	Boston	11	3	8	11	14	1	1	0
1977	Boston	14	2	10	12	4	0	0	0
1978	Boston	15	9	11	20	14	4	0	0
1979	Boston	11	1	4	5	8	0	0	1
1980	Boston	10	3	6	9	4	0	0	0
1981	Boston	3	1	3	4	11	1	0	0
1982	Boston	11	1	4	5	4	0	0	1
1983	Boston	16	3	9	12	18	1	0	1
1984	Detroit	3	0	3	3	0	0	0	0
1985	Detroit	3	0	0	0	11	0	0	0
Playoff Totals		**161**	**35**	**90**	**125**	**217**	**12**	**1**	**6**
PARK, Richard									Center
1995	Pittsburgh	3	0	0	0	2	0	0	0
1996	Pittsburgh	1	0	0	0	0	0	0	0
1997	Anaheim	11	0	1	1	2	0	0	0
Playoff Totals		**15**	**0**	**1**	**1**	**4**	**0**	**0**	**0**
PARKER, Jeff									Right wing
1989	Buffalo	5	0	0	0	26	0	0	0
Playoff Totals		**5**	**0**	**0**	**0**	**26**	**0**	**0**	**0**
PARKER, Scott	*No playoffs*								Right wing
PARKES, Ernie	*No playoffs*								Right wing
PARKS, Greg									Center
1993	NY Islanders	2	0	0	0	0	0	0	0
Playoff Totals		**2**	**0**	**0**	**0**	**0**	**0**	**0**	**0**
PARRISH, Mark	*No playoffs*								Left wing
PARSONS, George									Left wing
1938	Toronto	7	3	2	5	11	....	....	....
Playoff Totals		**7**	**3**	**2**	**5**	**11**	....	....	....
PASEK, Dusan									Center
1989	Minnesota	2	1	0	1	0	0	0	0
Playoff Totals		**2**	**1**	**0**	**1**	**0**	**0**	**0**	**0**
PASIN, Dave									Right wing
1986	Boston	3	0	1	1	0	0	0	0
Playoff Totals		**3**	**0**	**1**	**1**	**0**	**0**	**0**	**0**

Season	Club	GP	G	A	Pts	PIM	PP	SH	GW
PASLAWSKI, Greg									Right wing
1984	St. Louis	9	1	0	1	2	0	0	0
1985	St. Louis	3	0	0	0	2	0	0	0
1986	St. Louis	17	10	7	17	13	2	0	0
1987	St. Louis	6	1	1	2	4	0	0	0
1988	St. Louis	3	1	1	2	2	1	0	0
1989	St. Louis	9	2	1	3	2	1	0	0
1990	Winnipeg	7	1	3	4	0	0	0	0
1993	Calgary	6	3	0	3	0	0	0	1
Playoff Totals		**60**	**19**	**13**	**32**	**25**	**4**	**0**	**1**
PATERA, Pavel	*No playoffs*								Center
PATERSON, Joe									Left wing
1984	Detroit	3	0	0	0	7	0	0	0
1985	Philadelphia	17	3	4	7	70	1	0	0
1987	Los Angeles	2	0	0	0	0	0	0	0
Playoff Totals		**22**	**3**	**4**	**7**	**77**	**1**	**0**	**0**
PATERSON, Mark	*No playoffs*								Defense
PATERSON, Rick									Center
1979	Chicago	1	0	1	1	0	0	0	0
1980	Chicago	7	0	0	0	5	0	0	0
1981	Chicago	2	1	0	1	0	0	1	0
1982	Chicago	15	3	2	5	21	0	0	0
1983	Chicago	13	1	1	2	4	0	1	1
1984	Chicago	5	1	1	2	6	0	1	0
1985	Chicago	15	1	5	6	15	0	0	0
1986	Chicago	3	0	0	0	0	0	0	0
Playoff Totals		**61**	**7**	**10**	**17**	**51**	**0**	**3**	**1**
PATEY, Doug	*No playoffs*								Right wing
PATEY, Larry									Center
1976	St. Louis	3	1	1	2	2	1	0	1
1977	St. Louis	4	1	0	1	0	0	0	0
1980	St. Louis	3	1	0	1	2	0	0	0
1981	St. Louis	11	2	4	6	30	0	0	0
1982	St. Louis	10	2	4	6	13	0	1	0
1983	St. Louis	4	1	0	1	4	0	0	0
1984	NY Rangers	4	0	1	1	6	0	0	0
1985	NY Rangers	1	0	0	0	0	0	0	0
Playoff Totals		**40**	**8**	**10**	**18**	**57**	**1**	**1**	**1**
PATRICK, Craig									Right wing
1975	St. Louis	2	0	1	1	0	0	0	0
Playoff Totals		**2**	**0**	**1**	**1**	**0**	**0**	**0**	**0**
PATRICK, Glenn	*No playoffs*								Defense
PATRICK, James									Defense
1984	NY Rangers	5	0	3	3	2	0	0	0
1985	NY Rangers	3	0	0	0	4	0	0	0
1986	NY Rangers	16	1	5	6	34	0	0	0
1987	NY Rangers	6	1	2	3	2	2	0	1
1989	NY Rangers	4	0	1	1	2	0	0	0
1990	NY Rangers	10	3	8	11	0	2	0	1
1991	NY Rangers	6	0	0	0	6	0	0	0
1992	NY Rangers	13	0	7	7	12	0	0	0
1994	Calgary	7	0	1	1	6	0	0	0
1995	Calgary	5	0	1	1	0	0	0	0
1996	Calgary	4	0	0	0	2	0	0	0
1999	Buffalo	20	0	1	1	12	0	0	0
Playoff Totals		**99**	**5**	**29**	**34**	**82**	**4**	**0**	**2**
PATRICK, Lester	*No playoffs*								Defense
PATRICK, Lynn									Center/left wing
1935	NY Rangers	4	2	2	4	0	....	....	....
1937	NY Rangers	9	3	0	3	2	....	....	....
1938	NY Rangers	3	0	1	1	2	....	....	....
1939	NY Rangers	7	1	1	2	0	....	....	....
1940♦	NY Rangers	12	2	2	4	4	....	....	....
1941	NY Rangers	3	1	0	1	14	....	....	....
1942	NY Rangers	6	1	0	1	0	....	....	....
Playoff Totals		**44**	**10**	**6**	**16**	**22**	....	....	....
PATRICK, Muzz									Defense
1938	NY Rangers	3	0	0	0	2	....	....	....
1939	NY Rangers	7	1	0	1	17	....	....	....
1940♦	NY Rangers	12	3	0	3	13	....	....	....
1941	NY Rangers	3	0	0	0	2	....	....	....
Playoff Totals		**25**	**4**	**0**	**4**	**34**	....	....	....
PATRICK, Steve									Right wing
1981	Buffalo	5	0	1	1	6	0	0	0
1983	Buffalo	2	0	0	0	0	0	0	0
1984	Buffalo	1	0	0	0	0	0	0	0
1985	NY Rangers	1	0	0	0	0	0	0	0
1986	Quebec	3	0	0	0	6	0	0	0
Playoff Totals		**12**	**0**	**1**	**1**	**12**	**0**	**0**	**0**
PATTERSON, Colin									Right/Left wing
1984	Calgary	11	1	1	2	6	0	0	0
1985	Calgary	4	0	0	0	5	0	0	0
1986	Calgary	19	6	3	9	10	1	1	1
1987	Calgary	6	0	2	2	2	0	0	0
1988	Calgary	9	1	0	1	8	0	1	0
1989♦	Calgary	22	3	10	13	24	0	0	0
1991	Calgary	1	0	0	0	0	0	0	0
1992	Buffalo	5	1	0	1	0	0	0	0
1993	Buffalo	8	0	1	1	2	0	0	0
Playoff Totals		**85**	**12**	**17**	**29**	**57**	**1**	**2**	**1**
PATTERSON, Dennis	*No playoffs*								Defense

Season	Club	GP	G	A	Pts	PIM	PP	SH	GW
PATTERSON, Ed *No playoffs*	Right wing								
PATTERSON, George	Left/right wing								
1929	Mtl. Canadiens	3	0	0	0	2	0	0	0
Playoff Totals		**3**	**0**	**0**	**0**	**2**	**0**	**0**	**0**
PAUL, Butch *No playoffs*	Center								
PAULHUS, Rollie *No playoffs*	Defense								
PAVELICH, Mark	Center								
1982	NY Rangers	6	1	5	6	0	0	0	0
1983	NY Rangers	9	4	5	9	12	2	0	2
1984	NY Rangers	5	2	4	6	0	0	1	0
1985	NY Rangers	3	0	3	3	2	0	0	0
Playoff Totals		**23**	**7**	**17**	**24**	**14**	**2**	**1**	**2**
PAVELICH, Marty	Left wing								
1948	Detroit	10	2	2	4	6	....	....	....
1949	Detroit	9	0	1	1	8	....	....	....
1950◆	Detroit	14	4	2	6	13	....	....	....
1951	Detroit	6	0	1	1	2	....	....	....
1952◆	Detroit	8	2	2	4	2	....	....	....
1953	Detroit	6	2	1	3	7	....	....	....
1954◆	Detroit	12	2	2	4	4	....	....	....
1955◆	Detroit	11	1	3	4	12	....	....	....
1956	Detroit	10	0	1	1	14	....	....	....
1957	Detroit	5	0	0	0	6	....	....	....
Playoff Totals		**91**	**13**	**15**	**28**	**74**	....	....	....
PAVESE, Jim	Defense								
1982	St. Louis	3	0	3	3	2	0	0	0
1983	St. Louis	4	0	0	0	6	0	0	0
1985	St. Louis	1	0	0	0	5	0	0	0
1986	St. Louis	19	0	2	2	51	0	0	0
1987	St. Louis	2	0	0	0	2	0	0	0
1988	Detroit	4	0	1	1	15	0	0	0
1989	Hartford	1	0	0	0	0	0	0	0
Playoff Totals		**34**	**0**	**6**	**6**	**81**	**0**	**0**	**0**
PAYER, Evariste *No playoffs*	Center/left wing								
PAYNE, Davis *No playoffs*	Left wing								
PAYNE, Steve	Left wing								
1980	Minnesota	15	7	7	14	9	3	0	3
1981	Minnesota	19	17	12	29	6	6	0	4
1982	Minnesota	4	4	2	6	2	2	0	0
1983	Minnesota	9	3	6	9	19	1	0	0
1984	Minnesota	15	3	6	9	18	1	0	2
1985	Minnesota	9	1	2	3	6	0	0	0
Playoff Totals		**71**	**35**	**35**	**70**	**60**	**13**	**0**	**9**
PAYNTER, Kent	Defense								
1990	Washington	3	0	0	0	10	0	0	0
1991	Washington	1	0	0	0	0	0	0	0
Playoff Totals		**4**	**0**	**0**	**0**	**10**	**0**	**0**	**0**
PEAKE, Pat	Center								
1994	Washington	8	0	1	1	8	0	0	0
1996	Washington	5	2	1	3	12	2	0	0
Playoff Totals		**13**	**2**	**2**	**4**	**20**	**2**	**0**	**0**
PEARSON, Mel *No playoffs*	Left wing								
PEARSON, Rob	Right wing								
1993	Toronto	14	2	2	4	31	0	0	0
1994	Toronto	14	1	0	1	32	0	0	0
1995	Washington	3	1	0	1	17	0	0	1
1996	St. Louis	2	0	0	0	14	0	0	0
Playoff Totals		**33**	**4**	**2**	**6**	**94**	**0**	**0**	**1**
PEARSON, Scott	Left wing								
1990	Toronto	2	2	0	2	10	0	0	0
1993	Quebec	3	0	0	0	0	0	0	0
1995	Buffalo	5	0	0	0	4	0	0	0
Playoff Totals		**10**	**2**	**0**	**2**	**14**	**0**	**0**	**0**
PECA, Michael	Center								
1995	Vancouver	5	0	1	1	8	0	0	0
1997	Buffalo	10	0	2	2	8	0	0	0
1998	Buffalo	13	3	2	5	8	0	0	1
1999	Buffalo	21	5	8	13	18	2	1	0
Playoff Totals		**49**	**8**	**13**	**21**	**42**	**2**	**1**	**1**
PEDERSEN, Allen	Defense								
1987	Boston	4	0	0	0	4	0	0	0
1988	Boston	21	0	0	0	34	0	0	0
1989	Boston	10	0	0	0	2	0	0	0
1990	Boston	21	0	0	0	41	0	0	0
1991	Boston	8	0	0	0	10	0	0	0
Playoff Totals		**64**	**0**	**0**	**0**	**91**	**0**	**0**	**0**
PEDERSON, Barry	Center								
1982	Boston	11	7	11	18	2	1	0	2
1983	Boston	17	14	18	32	21	1	1	2
1984	Boston	3	0	1	1	2	0	0	0
1986	Boston	3	1	0	1	0	0	0	0
Playoff Totals		**34**	**22**	**30**	**52**	**25**	**2**	**1**	**4**
PEDERSON, Denis	Center								
1997	New Jersey	9	0	0	0	2	0	0	0
1998	New Jersey	6	1	1	2	2	0	1	0
1999	New Jersey	3	0	1	1	0	0	0	0
Playoff Totals		**18**	**1**	**2**	**3**	**4**	**0**	**1**	**0**
PEDERSON, Mark	Left wing								
1990	Montreal	2	0	0	0	0	0	0	0
Playoff Totals		**2**	**0**	**0**	**0**	**0**	**0**	**0**	**0**
PEDERSON, Tom	Defense								
1994	San Jose	14	1	6	7	2	0	1	0
1995	San Jose	10	0	5	5	8	0	0	0
Playoff Totals		**24**	**1**	**11**	**12**	**10**	**0**	**1**	**0**
PEER, Bert *No playoffs*	Right wing								
PEIRSON, Johnny	Right wing								
1948	Boston	5	2	3	5	0	....	....	....
1949	Boston	5	3	1	4	4	....	....	....
1951	Boston	2	1	1	2	2	....	....	....
1952	Boston	7	0	2	2	4	....	....	....
1953	Boston	11	3	6	9	2	....	....	....
1954	Boston	4	0	0	0	2	....	....	....
1957	Boston	10	0	3	3	12	....	....	....
1958	Boston	5	0	1	1	0	....	....	....
Playoff Totals		**49**	**9**	**17**	**26**	**26**	....	....	....
PELENSKY, Perry *No playoffs*	Right wing								
PELLERIN, Scott	Left wing								
1997	St. Louis	6	0	0	0	6	0	0	0
1998	St. Louis	10	0	2	2	10	0	0	0
1999	St. Louis	8	1	0	1	4	0	0	0
Playoff Totals		**24**	**1**	**2**	**3**	**20**	**0**	**0**	**0**
PELLETIER, Roger *No playoffs*	Defense								
PELOFFY, Andre *No playoffs*	Center								
PELTONEN, Ville *No playoffs*	Left wing								
PELUSO, Mike	Left wing								
1991	Chicago	3	0	0	0	2	0	0	0
1992	Chicago	17	1	2	3	8	0	0	1
1994	New Jersey	17	1	0	1	*64	0	0	1
1995◆	New Jersey	20	1	2	3	8	0	0	0
1997	St. Louis	5	0	0	0	25	0	0	0
Playoff Totals		**62**	**3**	**4**	**7**	**107**	**0**	**0**	**2**
PELYK, Mike	Defense								
1969	Toronto	4	0	0	0	8	0	0	0
1971	Toronto	6	0	0	0	10	0	0	0
1972	Toronto	5	0	0	0	8	0	0	0
1974	Toronto	4	0	0	0	4	0	0	0
1977	Toronto	9	0	2	2	4	0	0	0
1978	Toronto	12	0	1	1	7	0	0	0
Playoff Totals		**40**	**0**	**3**	**3**	**41**	**0**	**0**	**0**
PENNEY, Chad *No playoffs*	Left wing								
PENNINGTON, Cliff *No playoffs*	Center								
PEPLINSKI, Jim	Right wing								
1981	Calgary	16	2	3	5	41	0	0	0
1982	Calgary	3	1	0	1	13	1	0	0
1983	Calgary	8	1	1	2	45	0	0	0
1984	Calgary	11	3	4	7	21	0	0	0
1985	Calgary	4	1	3	4	11	0	0	0
1986	Calgary	22	5	9	14	107	0	0	0
1987	Calgary	6	1	0	1	24	0	0	0
1988	Calgary	9	0	5	5	45	0	0	0
1989◆	Calgary	20	1	6	7	75	0	0	0
Playoff Totals		**99**	**15**	**31**	**46**	**382**	**1**	**0**	**0**
PERLINI, Fred *No playoffs*	Center								
PERREAULT, Fern *No playoffs*	Left wing								
PERREAULT, Gilbert	Center								
1973	Buffalo	6	3	7	10	2	1	0	1
1975	Buffalo	17	6	9	15	10	4	0	1
1976	Buffalo	9	4	4	8	4	0	0	0
1977	Buffalo	6	1	8	9	4	0	0	0
1978	Buffalo	8	3	2	5	0	0	0	1
1979	Buffalo	3	1	0	1	2	1	0	0
1980	Buffalo	14	10	11	21	8	3	0	2
1981	Buffalo	8	2	10	12	2	0	0	0
1982	Buffalo	4	0	7	7	0	0	0	0
1983	Buffalo	10	0	7	7	8	0	0	0
1985	Buffalo	5	3	5	8	4	1	0	0
Playoff Totals		**90**	**33**	**70**	**103**	**44**	**10**	**0**	**5**
PERREAULT, Yanic	Center								
1998	Los Angeles	4	1	2	3	6	1	0	0
1999	Toronto	17	3	6	9	6	0	0	2
Playoff Totals		**21**	**4**	**8**	**12**	**12**	**1**	**0**	**2**
PERRY, Brian	Center								
1969	Oakland	6	1	1	2	4	0	0	0
1970	Oakland	2	0	0	0	0	0	0	0
Playoff Totals		**8**	**1**	**1**	**2**	**4**	**0**	**0**	**0**
PERSSON, Ricard	Defense								
1997	St. Louis	6	0	0	0	27	0	0	0
1999	St. Louis	13	0	3	3	17	0	0	0
Playoff Totals		**19**	**0**	**3**	**3**	**44**	**0**	**0**	**0**
PERSSON, Stefan	Defense								
1978	NY Islanders	7	0	2	2	6	0	0	0
1979	NY Islanders	10	0	4	4	8	0	0	0
1980◆	NY Islanders	21	5	10	15	16	4	0	0
1981◆	NY Islanders	7	0	5	5	6	0	0	0
1982◆	NY Islanders	13	1	14	15	9	1	0	0
1983◆	NY Islanders	18	1	5	6	18	1	0	0
1984	NY Islanders	16	0	6	6	2	0	0	0
1985	NY Islanders	10	0	4	4	4	0	0	0
Playoff Totals		**102**	**7**	**50**	**57**	**69**	**6**	**0**	**0**
PESUT, George *No playoffs*	Defense								
PETERS, Frank	Defense								
1931	NY Rangers	4	0	0	0	2	0	0	0
Playoff Totals		**4**	**0**	**0**	**0**	**2**	**0**	**0**	**0**
PETERS, Garry	Center								
1969	Philadelphia	4	1	1	2	16	0	0	1
1971	Philadelphia	4	1	1	2	15	0	0	0
1972◆	Boston	1	0	0	0	0	0	0	0
Playoff Totals		**9**	**2**	**2**	**4**	**31**	**0**	**0**	**1**
PETERS, Steve *No playoffs*	Center								
PETERS Jr., Jimmy	Center								
1969	Los Angeles	11	0	2	2	2	0	0	0
Playoff Totals		**11**	**0**	**2**	**2**	**2**	**0**	**0**	**0**
PETERS Sr., Jimmy	Right wing								
1946◆	Montreal	9	3	1	4	6	....	....	....
1947	Montreal	11	1	2	3	10	....	....	....
1948	Boston	5	1	2	3	2	....	....	....
1949	Boston	4	0	1	1	0	....	....	....
1950◆	Detroit	8	0	2	2	0	....	....	....
1951	Detroit	6	0	0	0	0	....	....	....
1953	Chicago	7	0	1	1	4	....	....	....
1954◆	Detroit	10	0	0	0	0	....	....	....
Playoff Totals		**60**	**5**	**9**	**14**	**22**	....	....	....
PETERSON, Brent	Center								
1982	Buffalo	4	1	0	1	12	1	0	0
1983	Buffalo	10	1	2	3	28	0	0	1
1984	Buffalo	3	0	1	1	4	0	0	0
1985	Buffalo	5	0	0	0	6	0	0	0
1986	Vancouver	3	2	0	2	9	1	0	0
1988	Hartford	4	0	0	0	2	0	0	0
1989	Hartford	2	0	1	1	4	0	0	0
Playoff Totals		**31**	**4**	**4**	**8**	**65**	**2**	**0**	**1**
PETERSON, Brent *No playoffs*	Left wing								
PETIT, Michel	Defense								
1984	Vancouver	1	0	0	0	0	0	0	0
1989	NY Rangers	4	0	2	2	27	0	0	0
1996	Tampa Bay	6	0	0	0	20	0	0	0
1997	Philadelphia	3	0	0	0	6	0	0	0
1998	Phoenix	5	0	0	0	8	0	0	0
Playoff Totals		**19**	**0**	**2**	**2**	**61**	**0**	**0**	**0**
PETRENKO, Sergei *No playoffs*	Left wing								
PETROV, Oleg	Right wing								
1993◆	Montreal	1	0	0	0	0	0	0	0
1994	Montreal	2	0	0	0	0	0	0	0
1996	Montreal	5	0	1	1	0	0	0	0
Playoff Totals		**8**	**0**	**1**	**1**	**0**	**0**	**0**	**0**
PETROVICKY, Robert	Center								
1997	St. Louis	2	0	0	0	0	0	0	0
Playoff Totals		**2**	**0**	**0**	**0**	**0**	**0**	**0**	**0**
PETTERSSON, Jorgen	Left wing								
1981	St. Louis	11	4	3	7	0	1	0	2
1982	St. Louis	7	1	2	3	0	1	0	0
1983	St. Louis	4	1	1	2	0	1	0	0
1984	St. Louis	11	7	3	10	2	2	0	1
1985	St. Louis	3	1	1	2	0	0	0	0
1986	Washington	8	1	2	3	2	1	0	0
Playoff Totals		**44**	**15**	**12**	**27**	**4**	**6**	**0**	**3**
PETTINGER, Eric	Left wing/center								
1929	Toronto	4	1	0	1	8	....	....	....
Playoff Totals		**4**	**1**	**0**	**1**	**8**	....	....	....
PETTINGER, Gord	Center								
1933◆	NY Rangers	8	0	0	0	0	....	....	....
1934	Detroit	7	1	0	1	2	....	....	....
1936◆	Detroit	7	2	2	4	0	....	....	....
1937◆	Detroit	10	0	2	2	2	....	....	....
1938	Boston	3	0	0	0	0	....	....	....
1939◆	Boston	12	1	1	2	7	....	....	....
Playoff Totals		**47**	**4**	**5**	**9**	**11**	....	....	....
PHAIR, Lyle	Left wing								
1988	Los Angeles	1	0	0	0	0	0	0	0
Playoff Totals		**1**	**0**	**0**	**0**	**0**	**0**	**0**	**0**
PHILLIPOFF, Harold	Left wing								
1978	Atlanta	2	0	1	1	2	0	0	0
1979	Chicago	4	0	1	1	7	0	0	0
Playoff Totals		**6**	**0**	**2**	**2**	**9**	**0**	**0**	**0**
PHILLIPS, Batt	Center								
1930	Mtl. Maroons	4	0	0	0	2	0	0	0
Playoff Totals		**4**	**0**	**0**	**0**	**2**	**0**	**0**	**0**

PHILLIPS, Charlie *No playoffs* Defense

PHILLIPS, Chris Defense

Season	Club	GP	G	A	Pts	PIM	PP	SH	GW
1998	Ottawa	11	0	2	2	2	0	0	0
1999	Ottawa	3	0	0	0	0	0	0	0
Playoff Totals		**14**	**0**	**2**	**2**	**2**	**0**	**0**	**0**

PHILLIPS, Meryn J. Center

Season	Club	GP	G	A	Pts	PIM	PP	SH	GW
1926◆	Mtl. Maroons	8	4	1	5	4	....	....	....
1927	Mtl. Maroons	2	0	0	0	0	....	....	....
1928	Mtl. Maroons	9	2	1	3	9	....	....	....
1930	Mtl. Maroons	4	0	0	0	2	....	....	....
1931	Mtl. Maroons	1	0	0	0	2	....	....	....
1932	Mtl. Maroons	4	0	0	0	2	....	....	....
Playoff Totals		**28**	**6**	**2**	**8**	**19**	....	....	....

PICARD, Michel Left wing

Season	Club	GP	G	A	Pts	PIM	PP	SH	GW
1999	St. Louis	5	0	0	0	2	0	0	0
Playoff Totals		**5**	**0**	**0**	**0**	**2**	**0**	**0**	**0**

PICARD, Noel Defense

Season	Club	GP	G	A	Pts	PIM	PP	SH	GW
1965◆	Montreal	3	0	1	1	0	0	0	0
1968	St. Louis	13	0	3	3	46	0	0	0
1969	St. Louis	12	1	4	5	30	0	0	0
1970	St. Louis	16	0	2	2	65	0	0	0
1971	St. Louis	6	1	1	2	26	1	0	0
Playoff Totals		**50**	**2**	**11**	**13**	**167**	**1**	**0**	**0**

PICARD, Robert Defense

Season	Club	GP	G	A	Pts	PIM	PP	SH	GW
1981	Montreal	1	0	0	0	0	0	0	0
1982	Montreal	5	1	1	2	7	0	0	0
1983	Montreal	3	0	0	0	0	0	0	0
1984	Winnipeg	3	0	0	0	12	0	0	0
1985	Winnipeg	8	2	2	4	8	1	0	0
1986	Quebec	3	0	2	2	2	0	0	0
1987	Quebec	13	2	10	12	10	1	0	0
Playoff Totals		**36**	**5**	**15**	**20**	**39**	**2**	**0**	**0**

PICARD, Roger *No playoffs* Right wing

PICHETTE, Dave Defense

Season	Club	GP	G	A	Pts	PIM	PP	SH	GW
1981	Quebec	1	0	0	0	14	0	0	0
1982	Quebec	16	2	4	6	22	1	0	1
1983	Quebec	2	0	1	1	0	0	0	0
1984	St. Louis	9	1	2	3	18	0	0	0
Playoff Totals		**28**	**3**	**7**	**10**	**54**	**1**	**0**	**1**

PICKETTS, Hal *No playoffs* Right wing

PIDHIRNY, Harry *No playoffs* Center

PIERCE, Randy Right wing

Season	Club	GP	G	A	Pts	PIM	PP	SH	GW
1978	Colorado	2	0	0	0	0	0	0	0
Playoff Totals		**2**	**0**	**0**	**0**	**0**	**0**	**0**	**0**

PIKE, Alf Left wing/center

Season	Club	GP	G	A	Pts	PIM	PP	SH	GW
1940◆	NY Rangers	12	3	1	4	6	....	....	....
1941	NY Rangers	3	0	1	1	2	....	....	....
1942	NY Rangers	6	1	0	1	4	....	....	....
Playoff Totals		**21**	**4**	**2**	**6**	**12**	....	....	....

PILON, Richard Defense

Season	Club	GP	G	A	Pts	PIM	PP	SH	GW
1993	NY Islanders	15	0	0	0	50	0	0	0
Playoff Totals		**15**	**0**	**0**	**0**	**50**	**0**	**0**	**0**

PILOTE, Pierre Defense

Season	Club	GP	G	A	Pts	PIM	PP	SH	GW
1959	Chicago	6	0	2	2	10	0	0	0
1960	Chicago	4	0	1	1	8	0	0	0
1961◆	Chicago	12	3	*12	*15	8	1	0	0
1962	Chicago	12	0	7	7	8	0	0	0
1963	Chicago	6	0	8	8	8	0	0	0
1964	Chicago	7	2	6	8	6	0	0	1
1965	Chicago	12	0	7	7	22	0	0	0
1966	Chicago	6	0	2	2	10	0	0	0
1967	Chicago	6	2	4	6	6	0	0	0
1968	Chicago	11	1	3	4	12	1	0	0
1969	Toronto	4	0	1	1	4	0	0	0
Playoff Totals		**86**	**8**	**53**	**61**	**102**	**2**	**0**	**1**

PINDER, Gerry Left wing

Season	Club	GP	G	A	Pts	PIM	PP	SH	GW
1970	Chicago	8	0	4	4	4	0	0	0
1971	Chicago	9	0	0	0	2	0	0	0
Playoff Totals		**17**	**0**	**4**	**4**	**6**	**0**	**0**	**0**

PIRUS, Alex Right wing

Season	Club	GP	G	A	Pts	PIM	PP	SH	GW
1977	Minnesota	2	0	1	1	2	0	0	0
Playoff Totals		**2**	**0**	**1**	**1**	**2**	**0**	**0**	**0**

PITLICK, Lance Defense

Season	Club	GP	G	A	Pts	PIM	PP	SH	GW
1997	Ottawa	7	0	0	0	4	0	0	0
1998	Ottawa	11	0	1	1	17	0	0	0
1999	Ottawa	2	0	0	0	0	0	0	0
Playoff Totals		**20**	**0**	**1**	**1**	**21**	**0**	**0**	**0**

PITRE, Didier Right wing/defense

Season	Club	GP	G	A	Pts	PIM	PP	SH	GW
1918	Mtl. Canadiens	2	0	0	0	13	....	....	....
1919	Mtl. Canadiens	10	2	6	8	6	....	....	....
1923	Mtl. Canadiens	2	0	0	0	0	....	....	....
Playoff Totals		**14**	**2**	**6**	**8**	**19**	....	....	....

PITTIS, Domenic *No playoffs* Center

PIVONKA, Michal Center

Season	Club	GP	G	A	Pts	PIM	PP	SH	GW
1987	Washington	7	1	1	2	2	0	0	0
1988	Washington	14	4	9	13	4	2	0	0
1989	Washington	6	3	1	4	10	0	1	0
1990	Washington	11	0	2	2	6	0	0	0
1991	Washington	11	2	3	5	8	0	0	0
1992	Washington	7	1	5	6	13	1	0	1
1993	Washington	6	0	2	2	0	0	0	0
1994	Washington	7	4	4	8	4	1	0	0
1995	Washington	7	1	4	5	21	0	0	0
1996	Washington	6	3	2	5	18	1	0	0
1998	Washington	13	0	3	3	0	0	0	0
Playoff Totals		**95**	**19**	**36**	**55**	**86**	**5**	**1**	**1**

PLAGER, Barclay Defense

Season	Club	GP	G	A	Pts	PIM	PP	SH	GW
1968	St. Louis	18	2	5	7	*73	0	1	0
1969	St. Louis	12	0	4	4	31	0	0	0
1970	St. Louis	13	0	2	2	20	0	0	0
1971	St. Louis	6	0	3	3	10	0	0	0
1972	St. Louis	11	1	4	5	21	1	0	1
1973	St. Louis	5	0	1	1	0	0	0	0
1975	St. Louis	2	0	1	1	14	0	0	0
1976	St. Louis	1	0	0	0	13	0	0	0
Playoff Totals		**68**	**3**	**20**	**23**	**182**	**1**	**1**	**1**

PLAGER, Bill Defense

Season	Club	GP	G	A	Pts	PIM	PP	SH	GW
1968	Minnesota	12	0	2	2	8	0	0	0
1969	St. Louis	4	0	0	0	4	0	0	0
1970	St. Louis	3	0	0	0	0	0	0	0
1971	St. Louis	1	0	0	0	2	0	0	0
1972	St. Louis	11	0	0	0	12	0	0	0
Playoff Totals		**31**	**0**	**2**	**2**	**26**	**0**	**0**	**0**

PLAGER, Bob Defense

Season	Club	GP	G	A	Pts	PIM	PP	SH	GW
1968	St. Louis	18	1	2	3	69	0	0	0
1969	St. Louis	9	0	4	4	47	0	0	0
1970	St. Louis	16	0	3	3	46	0	0	0
1971	St. Louis	6	0	2	2	4	0	0	0
1972	St. Louis	11	1	4	5	5	0	0	0
1973	St. Louis	5	0	2	2	2	0	0	0
1975	St. Louis	2	0	0	0	20	0	0	0
1976	St. Louis	3	0	0	0	2	0	0	0
1977	St. Louis	4	0	0	0	0	0	0	0
Playoff Totals		**74**	**2**	**17**	**19**	**195**	**0**	**0**	**0**

PLAMONDON, Gerry Left wing

Season	Club	GP	G	A	Pts	PIM	PP	SH	GW
1946◆	Montreal	1	0	0	0	0	....	....	....
1949	Montreal	7	5	1	6	0	....	....	....
1950	Montreal	3	0	1	1	2	....	....	....
Playoff Totals		**11**	**5**	**2**	**7**	**2**	....	....	....

PLANTE, Cam *No playoffs* Defense

PLANTE, Dan Right wing

Season	Club	GP	G	A	Pts	PIM	PP	SH	GW
1994	NY Islanders	1	1	0	1	2	0	0	0
Playoff Totals		**1**	**1**	**0**	**1**	**2**	**0**	**0**	**0**

PLANTE, Derek Center

Season	Club	GP	G	A	Pts	PIM	PP	SH	GW
1994	Buffalo	7	1	0	1	0	0	0	0
1997	Buffalo	12	4	6	10	4	0	0	0
1998	Buffalo	11	0	3	3	10	0	0	0
1999◆	Dallas	6	1	0	1	4	0	0	0
Playoff Totals		**36**	**6**	**9**	**15**	**18**	**0**	**0**	**0**

PLANTE, Pierre Right wing

Season	Club	GP	G	A	Pts	PIM	PP	SH	GW
1973	St. Louis	5	2	0	2	15	0	0	0
1975	St. Louis	2	0	0	0	8	0	0	0
1976	St. Louis	3	0	0	0	6	0	0	0
1977	St. Louis	4	0	0	0	2	0	0	0
1978	Chicago	1	0	0	0	0	0	0	0
1979	NY Rangers	18	0	6	6	20	0	0	0
Playoff Totals		**33**	**2**	**6**	**8**	**51**	**0**	**0**	**0**

PLANTERY, Mark *No playoffs* Defense

PLAVSIC, Adrien Defense

Season	Club	GP	G	A	Pts	PIM	PP	SH	GW
1992	Vancouver	13	1	7	8	4	0	0	0
Playoff Totals		**13**	**1**	**7**	**8**	**4**	**0**	**0**	**0**

PLAXTON, Hugh *No playoffs* Left wing

PLAYFAIR, Jim *No playoffs* Defense

PLAYFAIR, Larry Defense

Season	Club	GP	G	A	Pts	PIM	PP	SH	GW
1980	Buffalo	14	0	2	2	29	0	0	0
1981	Buffalo	8	0	0	0	26	0	0	0
1982	Buffalo	4	0	0	0	22	0	0	0
1983	Buffalo	5	0	1	1	11	0	0	0
1984	Buffalo	3	0	0	0	0	0	0	0
1985	Buffalo	5	0	3	3	9	0	0	0
1988	Los Angeles	3	0	0	0	14	0	0	0
1989	Buffalo	1	0	0	0	0	0	0	0
Playoff Totals		**43**	**0**	**6**	**6**	**111**	**0**	**0**	**0**

PLEAU, Larry Center

Season	Club	GP	G	A	Pts	PIM	PP	SH	GW
1972	Montreal	4	0	0	0	0	0	0	0
Playoff Totals		**4**	**0**	**0**	**0**	**0**	**0**	**0**	**0**

PLETSCH, Charles *No playoffs* Defense

PLETT, Willi Right wing

Season	Club	GP	G	A	Pts	PIM	PP	SH	GW
1977	Atlanta	3	1	0	1	19	0	0	0
1979	Atlanta	2	1	0	1	29	0	0	0
1980	Atlanta	4	1	0	1	15	1	0	0
1981	Calgary	15	8	4	12	89	5	0	3
1982	Calgary	3	1	2	3	39	1	0	0
1983	Minnesota	9	1	3	4	38	0	0	0
1984	Minnesota	16	6	2	8	51	1	0	0
1985	Minnesota	9	3	6	9	67	1	0	0
1986	Minnesota	5	0	1	1	45	0	0	0
1988	Boston	17	2	4	6	74	0	0	1
Playoff Totals		**83**	**24**	**22**	**46**	**466**	**9**	**0**	**4**

PLUMB, Rob *No playoffs* Left wing

PLUMB, Ron *No playoffs* Defense

POAPST, Steve Defense

Season	Club	GP	G	A	Pts	PIM	PP	SH	GW
1996	Washington	6	0	0	0	0	0	0	0
Playoff Totals		**6**	**0**	**0**	**0**	**0**	**0**	**0**	**0**

POCZA, Harvie *No playoffs* Left wing

PODDUBNY, Walt Left wing

Season	Club	GP	G	A	Pts	PIM	PP	SH	GW
1983	Toronto	4	3	1	4	0	2	0	1
1986	Toronto	9	4	1	5	4	0	0	3
1987	NY Rangers	6	0	0	0	8	0	0	0
Playoff Totals		**19**	**7**	**2**	**9**	**12**	**2**	**0**	**4**

PODEIN, Shjon Left wing

Season	Club	GP	G	A	Pts	PIM	PP	SH	GW
1995	Philadelphia	15	1	3	4	10	0	0	0
1996	Philadelphia	12	1	2	3	50	0	0	1
1997	Philadelphia	19	4	3	7	16	0	0	1
1998	Philadelphia	5	0	0	0	10	0	0	0
1999	Colorado	19	1	1	2	12	0	0	0
Playoff Totals		**70**	**7**	**9**	**16**	**98**	**0**	**0**	**2**

PODLOSKI, Ray *No playoffs* Center

PODOLLAN, Jason *No playoffs* Right wing

PODOLSKY, Nels Left wing

Season	Club	GP	G	A	Pts	PIM	PP	SH	GW
1949	Detroit	7	0	0	0	4	0	0	0
Playoff Totals		**7**	**0**	**0**	**0**	**4**	**0**	**0**	**0**

POESCHEK, Rudy Right wing/Defense

Season	Club	GP	G	A	Pts	PIM	PP	SH	GW
1996	Tampa Bay	3	0	0	0	12	0	0	0
1998	St. Louis	2	0	0	0	6	0	0	0
Playoff Totals		**5**	**0**	**0**	**0**	**18**	**0**	**0**	**0**

POETA, Tony *No playoffs* Right wing

POILE, Bud Right wing

Season	Club	GP	G	A	Pts	PIM	PP	SH	GW
1943	Toronto	6	2	4	6	4	....	....	....
1947◆	Toronto	7	2	0	2	2	....	....	....
1949	Detroit	10	0	1	1	2	....	....	....
Playoff Totals		**23**	**4**	**5**	**9**	**8**	....	....	....

POILE, Don Center

Season	Club	GP	G	A	Pts	PIM	PP	SH	GW
1958	Detroit	4	0	0	0	0	0	0	0
Playoff Totals		**4**	**0**	**0**	**0**	**0**	**0**	**0**	**0**

POIRER, Gordie *No playoffs* Center

POLANIC, Tom Defense

Season	Club	GP	G	A	Pts	PIM	PP	SH	GW
1970	Minnesota	5	1	1	2	4	0	0	0
Playoff Totals		**5**	**1**	**1**	**2**	**4**	**0**	**0**	**0**

POLICH, John *No playoffs* Right wing

POLICH, Mike Center/left wing

Season	Club	GP	G	A	Pts	PIM	PP	SH	GW
1977◆	Montreal	5	0	0	0	0	0	0	0
1980	Minnesota	15	2	1	3	2	0	0	0
1981	Minnesota	3	0	0	0	0	0	0	0
Playoff Totals		**23**	**2**	**1**	**3**	**2**	**0**	**0**	**0**

POLIS, Greg Left wing

Season	Club	GP	G	A	Pts	PIM	PP	SH	GW
1972	Pittsburgh	4	0	2	2	0	0	0	0
1975	NY Rangers	3	0	0	0	6	0	0	0
Playoff Totals		**7**	**0**	**2**	**2**	**6**	**0**	**0**	**0**

POLIZIANI, Daniel Right wing

Season	Club	GP	G	A	Pts	PIM	PP	SH	GW
1959	Boston	3	0	0	0	0	0	0	0
Playoff Totals		**3**	**0**	**0**	**0**	**0**	**0**	**0**	**0**

POLONICH, Dennis Center/right wing

Season	Club	GP	G	A	Pts	PIM	PP	SH	GW
1978	Detroit	7	1	0	1	19	0	0	0
Playoff Totals		**7**	**1**	**0**	**1**	**19**	**0**	**0**	**0**

POOLEY, Paul *No playoffs* Center

POPEIN, Larry Center

Season	Club	GP	G	A	Pts	PIM	PP	SH	GW
1956	NY Rangers	5	0	1	1	2	0	0	0
1957	NY Rangers	5	0	3	3	0	0	0	0
1958	NY Rangers	6	1	0	1	4	0	0	0
Playoff Totals		**16**	**1**	**4**	**5**	**6**	**0**	**0**	**0**

POPIEL, Poul Defense

Season	Club	GP	G	A	Pts	PIM	PP	SH	GW
1968	Los Angeles	3	1	0	1	4	0	0	0
1970	Detroit	1	0	0	0	0	0	0	0
Playoff Totals		**4**	**1**	**0**	**1**	**4**	**0**	**0**	**0**

POPOVIC, Peter Defense

Season	Club	GP	G	A	Pts	PIM	PP	SH	GW
1994	Montreal	6	0	1	1	0	0	0	0
1996	Montreal	6	0	2	2	4	0	0	0
1997	Montreal	3	0	0	0	2	0	0	0
1998	Montreal	10	1	1	2	2	0	0	0
Playoff Totals		**25**	**1**	**4**	**5**	**8**	**0**	**0**	**0**

Season	Club	GP	G	A	Pts	PIM	PP	SH	GW
PORTLAND, Jack									Defense
1934	Mtl. Canadiens	2	0	0	0	0	....	....	....
1937	Boston	3	0	0	0	4	....	....	....
1938	Boston	3	0	0	0	4	....	....	....
1939♦	Boston	12	0	0	0	11	....	....	....
1940	Chicago	2	0	0	0	2	....	....	....
1941	Montreal	3	0	1	1	2	....	....	....
1942	Montreal	3	0	0	0	0	....	....	....
1943	Montreal	5	1	2	3	2	....	....	....
Playoff Totals		**33**	**1**	**3**	**4**	**25**	....	....	....
PORVARI, Jukka *No playoffs*									Right wing
POSA, Victor *No playoffs*									Left wing/defense
POSAVAD, Mike *No playoffs*									Defense
POTI, Tom									Defense
1999	Edmonton	4	0	1	1	2	0	0	0
Playoff Totals		**4**	**0**	**1**	**1**	**2**	**0**	**0**	**0**
POTOMSKI, Barry *No playoffs*									Left wing
POTVIN, Denis									Defense
1975	NY Islanders	17	5	9	14	30	3	1	0
1976	NY Islanders	13	5	*14	19	32	2	0	1
1977	NY Islanders	12	6	4	10	20	2	0	0
1978	NY Islanders	7	2	2	4	6	0	0	0
1979	NY Islanders	10	4	7	11	8	0	0	1
1980♦	NY Islanders	21	6	13	19	24	4	0	1
1981♦	NY Islanders	18	8	17	25	16	6	1	2
1982♦	NY Islanders	19	5	16	21	30	3	0	0
1983♦	NY Islanders	20	8	12	20	22	4	0	1
1984	NY Islanders	20	1	5	6	28	1	0	0
1985	NY Islanders	10	3	2	5	10	1	0	1
1986	NY Islanders	3	0	1	1	0	0	0	0
1987	NY Islanders	10	2	2	4	21	1	0	0
1988	NY Islanders	5	1	4	5	6	1	0	0
Playoff Totals		**185**	**56**	**108**	**164**	**253**	**28**	**2**	**7**
POTVIN, Jean									Defense
1975	NY Islanders	15	2	4	6	9	0	0	0
1976	NY Islanders	13	0	1	1	2	0	0	0
1977	NY Islanders	11	0	4	4	6	0	0	0
Playoff Totals		**39**	**2**	**9**	**11**	**17**	**0**	**0**	**0**
POTVIN, Marc									Right wing
1991	Detroit	6	0	0	0	32	0	0	0
1992	Detroit	1	0	0	0	0	0	0	0
1993	Los Angeles	1	0	0	0	0	0	0	0
1996	Boston	5	0	1	1	18	0	0	0
Playoff Totals		**13**	**0**	**1**	**1**	**50**	**0**	**0**	**0**
POUDRIER, Daniel *No playoffs*									Defense
POULIN, Daniel *No playoffs*									Defense
POULIN, Dave									Center
1983	Philadelphia	3	1	3	4	9	0	0	0
1984	Philadelphia	3	0	0	0	2	0	0	0
1985	Philadelphia	11	3	5	8	6	0	2	0
1986	Philadelphia	5	2	0	2	2	1	0	0
1987	Philadelphia	15	3	3	6	14	1	1	0
1988	Philadelphia	7	2	6	8	4	1	0	1
1989	Philadelphia	19	6	5	11	16	0	2	2
1990	Boston	18	8	5	13	8	2	0	2
1991	Boston	16	0	9	9	20	0	0	0
1992	Boston	15	3	3	6	22	1	0	1
1993	Boston	4	1	1	2	10	0	1	0
1994	Washington	11	2	2	4	19	0	0	0
1995	Washington	2	0	0	0	0	0	0	0
Playoff Totals		**129**	**31**	**42**	**73**	**132**	**6**	**6**	**6**
POULIN, Patrick									Center
1992	Hartford	7	2	1	3	0	1	0	0
1994	Chicago	4	0	0	0	0	0	0	0
1995	Chicago	16	4	1	5	8	1	0	0
1996	Tampa Bay	2	0	0	0	0	0	0	0
1998	Montreal	3	0	0	0	0	0	0	0
Playoff Totals		**32**	**6**	**2**	**8**	**8**	**2**	**0**	**0**
POUZAR, Jaroslav									Left wing
1983	Edmonton	1	2	0	2	0	1	0	1
1984♦	Edmonton	14	1	2	3	12	0	0	1
1985♦	Edmonton	9	2	1	3	2	0	0	0
1987♦	Edmonton	5	1	1	2	2	0	0	0
Playoff Totals		**29**	**6**	**4**	**10**	**16**	**1**	**0**	**2**
POWELL, Ray *No playoffs*									Center
POWIS, Geoff *No playoffs*									Center
POWIS, Lynn									Center
1974	Chicago	1	0	0	0	0	0	0	0
Playoff Totals		**1**	**0**	**0**	**0**	**0**	**0**	**0**	**0**
PRAJSLER, Petr									Defense
1989	Los Angeles	1	0	0	0	0	0	0	0
1990	Los Angeles	3	0	0	0	0	0	0	0
Playoff Totals		**4**	**0**	**0**	**0**	**0**	**0**	**0**	**0**

Season	Club	GP	G	A	Pts	PIM	PP	SH	GW
PRATT, Babe									Defense
1937	NY Rangers	9	3	1	4	11	....	....	....
1938	NY Rangers	2	0	0	0	2	....	....	....
1939	NY Rangers	7	1	2	3	9	....	....	....
1940♦	NY Rangers	12	3	1	4	18	....	....	....
1941	NY Rangers	3	1	1	2	6	....	....	....
1942	NY Rangers	6	1	3	4	24	....	....	....
1943	Toronto	6	1	2	3	8	....	....	....
1944	Toronto	5	0	3	3	4	....	....	....
1945♦	Toronto	13	2	4	6	8	....	....	....
Playoff Totals		**63**	**12**	**17**	**29**	**90**	....	....	....
PRATT, Jack									Center/defense
1931	Boston	4	0	0	0	0	0	0	0
Playoff Totals		**4**	**0**	**0**	**0**	**0**	**0**	**0**	**0**
PRATT, Kelly *No playoffs*									Right wing
PRATT, Nolan									Defense
1999	Carolina	3	0	0	0	2	0	0	0
Playoff Totals		**3**	**0**	**0**	**0**	**2**	**0**	**0**	**0**
PRATT, Tracy									Defense
1970	Pittsburgh	10	0	1	1	51	0	0	0
1973	Buffalo	6	0	0	0	6	0	0	0
1975	Vancouver	3	0	0	0	5	0	0	0
1976	Vancouver	2	0	0	0	0	0	0	0
1977	Toronto	4	0	0	0	0	0	0	0
Playoff Totals		**25**	**0**	**1**	**1**	**62**	**0**	**0**	**0**
PRENTICE, Dean									Left wing
1956	NY Rangers	5	1	0	1	2	0	0	0
1957	NY Rangers	5	0	2	2	4	0	0	0
1958	NY Rangers	6	1	3	4	4	0	0	0
1962	NY Rangers	3	0	2	2	0	0	0	0
1966	Detroit	12	5	5	10	4	2	0	0
1970	Pittsburgh	10	2	5	7	8	1	0	0
1972	Minnesota	7	3	0	3	0	0	0	1
1973	Minnesota	6	1	0	1	16	1	0	0
Playoff Totals		**54**	**13**	**17**	**30**	**38**	**4**	**0**	**1**
PRENTICE, Eric *No playoffs*									Left wing
PRESLEY, Wayne									Right wing
1986	Chicago	3	0	0	0	0	0	0	0
1987	Chicago	4	1	0	1	9	0	0	0
1988	Chicago	5	0	0	0	4	0	0	0
1989	Chicago	14	7	5	12	18	1	3	1
1990	Chicago	19	9	6	15	29	1	1	1
1991	Chicago	6	0	1	1	38	0	0	0
1992	Buffalo	7	3	3	6	14	0	0	0
1993	Buffalo	8	1	0	1	6	0	1	1
1994	Buffalo	7	2	1	3	14	1	0	1
1995	Buffalo	5	3	1	4	8	0	1	1
1996	Toronto	5	0	0	0	2	0	0	0
Playoff Totals		**83**	**26**	**17**	**43**	**142**	**3**	**6**	**5**
PRESTON, Rich									Right wing
1980	Chicago	7	0	3	3	2	0	0	0
1981	Chicago	3	0	1	1	0	0	0	0
1982	Chicago	15	2	4	6	21	0	0	0
1983	Chicago	13	2	7	9	25	0	0	1
1984	Chicago	5	0	1	1	4	0	0	0
1987	Chicago	4	0	2	2	4	0	0	0
Playoff Totals		**47**	**4**	**18**	**22**	**56**	**0**	**0**	**1**
PRESTON, Yves *No playoffs*									Left wing
PRIAKIN, Sergei									Right wing
1989♦	Calgary	1	0	0	0	0	0	0	0
Playoff Totals		**1**	**0**	**0**	**0**	**0**	**0**	**0**	**0**
PRICE, Jack									Defense
1953	Chicago	4	0	0	0	0	0	0	0
Playoff Totals		**4**	**0**	**0**	**0**	**0**	**0**	**0**	**0**
PRICE, Noel									Defense
1959	Toronto	5	0	0	0	2	0	0	0
1966♦	Montreal	3	0	1	1	0	0	0	0
1974	Atlanta	4	0	0	0	6	0	0	0
Playoff Totals		**12**	**0**	**1**	**1**	**8**	**0**	**0**	**0**
PRICE, Pat									Defense
1977	NY Islanders	10	0	1	1	2	0	0	0
1978	NY Islanders	5	0	1	1	2	0	0	0
1979	NY Islanders	7	0	1	1	25	0	0	0
1980	Edmonton	3	0	0	0	11	0	0	0
1981	Pittsburgh	5	1	1	2	21	0	0	0
1982	Pittsburgh	5	0	0	0	28	0	0	0
1983	Quebec	4	0	0	0	14	0	0	0
1984	Quebec	9	1	0	1	10	0	0	0
1985	Quebec	17	0	4	4	51	0	0	0
1986	Quebec	3	0	1	1	4	0	0	0
1987	NY Rangers	6	0	1	1	27	0	0	0
Playoff Totals		**74**	**2**	**10**	**12**	**195**	**0**	**0**	**0**
PRICE, Tom *No playoffs*									Defense
PRIESTLAY, Ken									Center
1988	Buffalo	6	0	0	0	11	0	0	0
1989	Buffalo	3	0	0	0	2	0	0	0
1990	Buffalo	5	0	0	0	8	0	0	0
Playoff Totals		**14**	**0**	**0**	**0**	**21**	**0**	**0**	**0**

Season	Club	GP	G	A	Pts	PIM	PP	SH	GW
PRIMEAU, Joe									Center
1931	Toronto	2	0	0	0	0	....	....	....
1932♦	Toronto	7	0	*6	6	2	....	....	....
1933	Toronto	8	0	1	1	4	....	....	....
1934	Toronto	5	2	4	6	6	....	....	....
1935	Toronto	7	0	3	3	0	....	....	....
1936	Toronto	9	3	4	7	0	....	....	....
Playoff Totals		**38**	**5**	**18**	**23**	**12**	....	....	....
PRIMEAU, Keith									Center
1991	Detroit	5	1	1	2	25	0	0	0
1992	Detroit	11	0	0	0	14	0	0	0
1993	Detroit	7	0	2	2	26	0	0	0
1994	Detroit	7	0	2	2	6	0	0	0
1995	Detroit	17	4	5	9	45	2	0	0
1996	Detroit	17	1	4	5	28	0	0	0
1999	Carolina	6	0	3	3	6	0	0	0
Playoff Totals		**70**	**6**	**17**	**23**	**150**	**2**	**0**	**0**
PRIMEAU, Kevin *No playoffs*									Right wing
PRIMEAU, Wayne									Center
1997	Buffalo	9	0	0	0	6	0	0	0
1998	Buffalo	14	1	3	4	6	0	0	0
1999	Buffalo	19	3	4	7	6	1	0	0
Playoff Totals		**42**	**4**	**7**	**11**	**18**	**1**	**0**	**0**
PRINGLE, Ellie *No playoffs*									Defense
PROBERT, Bob									Left wing
1987	Detroit	16	3	4	7	63	1	0	1
1988	Detroit	16	8	13	21	51	5	0	1
1991	Detroit	6	1	2	3	50	0	0	0
1992	Detroit	11	1	6	7	28	0	0	0
1993	Detroit	7	0	3	3	10	0	0	0
1994	Detroit	7	1	1	2	8	0	0	0
1996	Chicago	10	0	2	2	23	0	0	0
1997	Chicago	6	2	1	3	41	0	0	0
Playoff Totals		**79**	**16**	**32**	**48**	**274**	**6**	**0**	**2**
PROCHAZKA, Martin *No playoffs*									Right wing
PRODGERS, Goldie *No playoffs*									Forward/Defense
PROKHOROV, Vitali									Left wing
1994	St. Louis	4	0	0	0	0	0	0	0
Playoff Totals		**4**	**0**	**0**	**0**	**0**	**0**	**0**	**0**
PROKOPEC, Mike *No playoffs*									Right wing
PRONGER, Chris									Defense
1996	St. Louis	13	1	5	6	16	0	0	0
1997	St. Louis	6	1	1	2	22	0	0	0
1998	St. Louis	10	1	9	10	26	0	0	0
1999	St. Louis	13	1	4	5	28	1	0	0
Playoff Totals		**42**	**4**	**19**	**23**	**92**	**1**	**0**	**0**
PRONGER, Sean									Center
1997	Anaheim	9	0	2	2	4	0	0	0
1998	Pittsburgh	5	0	0	0	4	0	0	0
Playoff Totals		**14**	**0**	**2**	**2**	**8**	**0**	**0**	**0**
PRONOVOST, Andre									Left wing
1957♦	Montreal	8	1	0	1	4	....	....	....
1958♦	Montreal	10	2	0	2	16	....	....	....
1959♦	Montreal	11	2	1	3	6	....	....	....
1960♦	Montreal	8	1	2	3	0	....	....	....
1963	Detroit	11	1	4	5	6	....	....	....
1964	Detroit	14	4	3	7	26	....	....	....
1968	Minnesota	8	0	1	1	0	0	0	0
Playoff Totals		**70**	**11**	**11**	**22**	**58**	....	....	....
PRONOVOST, Jean									Right wing
1970	Pittsburgh	10	3	4	7	2	1	1	0
1972	Pittsburgh	4	1	1	2	0	0	1	0
1975	Pittsburgh	9	3	3	6	6	0	0	0
1976	Pittsburgh	3	0	0	0	2	0	0	0
1977	Pittsburgh	3	2	1	3	2	1	0	0
1979	Atlanta	2	2	0	2	0	1	0	0
1980	Atlanta	4	0	0	0	2	0	0	0
Playoff Totals		**35**	**11**	**9**	**20**	**14**	**3**	**2**	**0**
PRONOVOST, Marcel									Defense
1950♦	Detroit	9	0	1	1	10	....	....	....
1951	Detroit	6	0	0	0	0	....	....	....
1952♦	Detroit	8	0	1	1	10	....	....	....
1953	Detroit	6	0	0	0	6	....	....	....
1954♦	Detroit	12	2	3	5	12	....	....	....
1955♦	Detroit	11	1	2	3	6	....	....	....
1956	Detroit	10	0	2	2	8	....	....	....
1957	Detroit	5	0	0	0	6	....	....	....
1958	Detroit	4	0	1	1	4	....	....	....
1960	Detroit	6	1	1	2	2	....	....	....
1961	Detroit	9	2	3	5	0	....	....	....
1963	Detroit	11	1	4	5	8	....	....	....
1964	Detroit	14	0	2	2	14	....	....	....
1965	Detroit	7	0	3	3	4	....	....	....
1966	Toronto	4	0	0	0	6	....	....	....
1967♦	Toronto	12	1	0	1	8	....	....	....
Playoff Totals		**134**	**8**	**23**	**31**	**104**	....	....	....

Season	Club	GP	G	A	Pts	PIM	PP	SH	GW
PROPP, Brian	Left wing								
1980	Philadelphia	19	5	10	15	29	3	0	0
1981	Philadelphia	12	6	6	12	32	0	0	0
1982	Philadelphia	4	2	2	4	4	0	0	1
1983	Philadelphia	3	1	2	3	8	1	0	0
1984	Philadelphia	3	0	1	1	6	0	0	0
1985	Philadelphia	19	8	10	18	6	4	1	2
1986	Philadelphia	5	0	2	2	4	0	0	0
1987	Philadelphia	26	12	16	28	10	5	1	3
1988	Philadelphia	7	4	2	6	8	0	0	0
1989	Philadelphia	18	14	9	23	14	5	1	1
1990	Boston	20	4	9	13	2	1	0	2
1991	Minnesota	23	8	15	23	28	8	0	3
1992	Minnesota	1	0	0	0	0	0	0	0
Playoff Totals		**160**	**64**	**84**	**148**	**151**	**27**	**3**	**12**
PROSPAL, Vaclav	Center								
1997	Philadelphia	5	1	3	4	4	0	0	0
1998	Ottawa	6	0	0	0	0	0	0	0
1999	Ottawa	4	0	0	0	0	0	0	0
Playoff Totals		**15**	**1**	**3**	**4**	**4**	**0**	**0**	**0**
PROULX, Christian *No playoffs*	Defense								
PROVOST, Claude	Right wing								
1956♦	Montreal	10	3	3	6	12	....	....	....
1957♦	Montreal	10	0	1	1	8	....	....	....
1958♦	Montreal	10	1	3	4	8	....	....	....
1959♦	Montreal	11	6	2	8	2	....	....	....
1960♦	Montreal	8	1	1	2	0	....	....	....
1961	Montreal	6	1	3	4	4	....	....	....
1962	Montreal	6	2	2	4	2	....	....	....
1963	Montreal	5	0	1	1	2	....	....	....
1964	Montreal	7	2	2	4	22	....	....	....
1965♦	Montreal	13	2	6	8	12	....	....	....
1966♦	Montreal	10	2	3	5	2	....	....	....
1967	Montreal	7	1	1	2	0	....	....	....
1968♦	Montreal	13	2	8	10	10	1	0	1
1969♦	Montreal	10	2	2	4	2	0	0	0
Playoff Totals		**126**	**25**	**38**	**63**	**86**	....	....	....
PRPIC, Joel *No playoffs*	Center								
PRYOR, Chris *No playoffs*	Defense								
PRYSTAI, Metro	Center								
1951	Detroit	3	1	0	1	0	....	....	....
1952♦	Detroit	8	2	*5	*7	0	....	....	....
1953	Detroit	6	4	4	8	2	....	....	....
1954♦	Detroit	12	2	3	5	0	....	....	....
1956	Detroit	9	1	2	3	6	....	....	....
1957	Detroit	5	2	0	2	0	....	....	....
Playoff Totals		**43**	**12**	**14**	**26**	**8**	....	....	....
PUDAS, Al *No playoffs*	Right/left wing								
PULFORD, Bob	Left wing								
1959	Toronto	12	4	4	8	8	....	....	....
1960	Toronto	10	4	1	5	10	....	....	....
1961	Toronto	5	0	0	0	8	....	....	....
1962♦	Toronto	12	7	1	8	24	....	....	....
1963♦	Toronto	10	2	5	7	14	....	....	....
1964♦	Toronto	14	5	3	8	20	....	....	....
1965	Toronto	6	1	1	2	16	....	....	....
1966	Toronto	4	1	1	2	12	....	....	....
1967♦	Toronto	12	1	*10	11	12	....	....	....
1969	Toronto	4	0	0	0	2	0	0	0
Playoff Totals		**89**	**25**	**26**	**51**	**126**	....	....	....
PULKKINEN, Dave *No playoffs*	Left wing/defense								
PURPUR, Fido	Right wing								
1944	Chicago	9	1	1	2	0	....	....	....
1945	Detroit	7	0	1	1	4	....	....	....
Playoff Totals		**16**	**1**	**2**	**3**	**4**	....	....	....
PURVES, John *No playoffs*	Right wing								
PUSHOR, Jamie	Defense								
1997♦	Detroit	5	0	1	1	5	0	0	0
1999	Anaheim	4	0	0	0	6	0	0	0
Playoff Totals		**9**	**0**	**1**	**1**	**11**	**0**	**0**	**0**
PUSIE, Jean	Defense								
1931♦	Mtl. Canadiens	3	0	0	0	0	0	0	0
1935	Boston	4	0	0	0	0	0	0	0
Playoff Totals		**7**	**0**	**0**	**0**	**0**	**0**	**0**	**0**
PYATT, Nelson *No playoffs*	Center								
QUACKENBUSH, Bill	Defense								
1944	Detroit	2	1	0	1	0	....	....	....
1945	Detroit	14	0	2	2	2	....	....	....
1946	Detroit	5	0	1	1	0	....	....	....
1947	Detroit	5	0	0	0	2	....	....	....
1948	Detroit	10	0	2	2	0	....	....	....
1949	Detroit	11	1	1	2	0	....	....	....
1951	Boston	6	0	1	1	0	....	....	....
1952	Boston	7	0	3	3	0	....	....	....
1953	Boston	11	0	4	4	4	....	....	....
1954	Boston	4	0	0	0	0	....	....	....
1955	Boston	5	0	5	5	0	....	....	....
Playoff Totals		**80**	**2**	**19**	**21**	**8**	....	....	....
QUACKENBUSH, Max	Defense								
1951	Boston	6	0	0	0	4	0	0	0
Playoff Totals		**6**	**0**	**0**	**0**	**4**	**0**	**0**	**0**

Season	Club	GP	G	A	Pts	PIM	PP	SH	GW
QUENNEVILLE, Joel	Defense								
1979	Toronto	6	0	1	1	4	0	0	0
1986	Hartford	10	0	2	2	12	0	0	0
1987	Hartford	6	0	0	0	0	0	0	0
1988	Hartford	6	0	2	2	2	0	0	0
1989	Hartford	4	0	3	3	4	0	0	0
Playoff Totals		**32**	**0**	**8**	**8**	**22**	**0**	**0**	**0**
QUENNEVILLE, Leo	Left wing/center								
1930	NY Rangers	3	0	0	0	0	0	0	0
Playoff Totals		**3**	**0**	**0**	**0**	**0**	**0**	**0**	**0**
QUILTY, John	Center								
1941	Montreal	3	0	2	2	0	....	....	....
1942	Montreal	3	0	1	1	0	....	....	....
1947	Montreal	7	3	2	5	9	....	....	....
Playoff Totals		**13**	**3**	**5**	**8**	**9**	....	....	....
QUINN, Dan	Center								
1984	Calgary	8	3	5	8	4	1	0	0
1985	Calgary	3	0	0	0	0	0	0	0
1986	Calgary	18	8	7	15	10	5	1	2
1989	Pittsburgh	11	6	3	9	10	4	0	1
1991	St. Louis	13	4	7	11	32	2	0	1
1996	Philadelphia	12	1	4	5	6	1	0	0
Playoff Totals		**65**	**22**	**26**	**48**	**62**	**13**	**1**	**4**
QUINN, Pat	Defense								
1969	Toronto	4	0	0	0	13	0	0	0
1974	Atlanta	4	0	0	0	6	0	0	0
1976	Atlanta	2	0	1	1	2	0	0	0
1977	Atlanta	1	0	0	0	0	0	0	0
Playoff Totals		**11**	**0**	**1**	**1**	**21**	**0**	**0**	**0**
QUINNEY, Ken *No playoffs*	Right wing								
QUINT, Deron	Defense								
1997	Phoenix	7	0	2	2	0	0	0	0
Playoff Totals		**7**	**0**	**2**	**2**	**0**	**0**	**0**	**0**
QUINTAL, Stephane	Defense								
1991	Boston	3	0	1	1	7	0	0	0
1992	St. Louis	4	1	2	3	6	1	0	0
1993	St. Louis	9	0	0	0	8	0	0	0
1996	Montreal	6	0	1	1	6	0	0	0
1997	Montreal	5	0	1	1	6	0	0	0
1998	Montreal	9	0	2	2	4	0	0	0
Playoff Totals		**36**	**1**	**7**	**8**	**37**	**1**	**0**	**0**
QUINTIN, Jean-Francois *No playoffs*	Left wing								
RACHUNEK, Karel *No playoffs*	Defense								
RACINE, Yves	Defense								
1991	Detroit	7	2	0	2	0	2	0	0
1992	Detroit	11	2	1	3	10	1	0	1
1993	Detroit	7	1	3	4	27	0	0	0
Playoff Totals		**25**	**5**	**4**	**9**	**37**	**3**	**0**	**1**
RADLEY, Yip *No playoffs*	Defense								
RAFALSKI, Brian *No playoffs*	Defense								
RAGLAN, Herb	Right wing								
1986	St. Louis	10	1	1	2	24	0	0	0
1987	St. Louis	4	0	0	0	2	0	0	0
1988	St. Louis	10	1	3	4	11	0	0	0
1989	St. Louis	8	1	2	3	13	0	0	0
Playoff Totals		**32**	**3**	**6**	**9**	**50**	**0**	**0**	**0**
RAGLAN, Rags	Defense								
1953	Chicago	3	0	0	0	0	0	0	0
Playoff Totals		**3**	**0**	**0**	**0**	**0**	**0**	**0**	**0**
RAGNARSSON, Marcus	Defense								
1998	San Jose	6	0	0	0	4	0	0	0
1999	San Jose	6	0	1	1	6	0	0	0
Playoff Totals		**12**	**0**	**1**	**1**	**10**	**0**	**0**	**0**
RALEIGH, Don	Center								
1948	NY Rangers	6	2	0	2	2	....	....	....
1950	NY Rangers	12	4	5	9	4	....	....	....
Playoff Totals		**18**	**6**	**5**	**11**	**6**	....	....	....
RAMAGE, Rob	Defense								
1983	St. Louis	4	0	3	3	22	0	0	0
1984	St. Louis	11	1	8	9	32	1	0	1
1985	St. Louis	3	1	3	4	6	0	1	0
1986	St. Louis	19	1	10	11	66	0	0	0
1987	St. Louis	6	2	2	4	21	2	0	0
1988	Calgary	9	1	3	4	21	1	0	0
1989♦	Calgary	20	1	11	12	26	1	0	0
1990	Toronto	5	1	2	3	20	0	0	0
1993♦	Montreal	7	0	0	0	4	0	0	0
Playoff Totals		**84**	**8**	**42**	**50**	**218**	**5**	**1**	**1**
RAMSAY, Beattie *No playoffs*	Defense								

Season	Club	GP	G	A	Pts	PIM	PP	SH	GW
RAMSAY, Craig	Left wing								
1973	Buffalo	6	1	1	2	0	0	0	0
1975	Buffalo	17	5	7	12	2	1	1	1
1976	Buffalo	9	1	2	3	2	0	1	0
1977	Buffalo	6	0	4	4	0	0	0	0
1978	Buffalo	8	3	1	4	9	1	0	1
1979	Buffalo	3	1	0	1	2	0	0	0
1980	Buffalo	10	0	6	6	4	0	0	0
1981	Buffalo	8	2	4	6	4	0	0	1
1982	Buffalo	4	1	1	2	0	0	0	1
1983	Buffalo	10	2	3	5	4	0	0	0
1984	Buffalo	3	0	1	1	0	0	0	0
1985	Buffalo	5	1	1	2	0	0	0	0
Playoff Totals		**89**	**17**	**31**	**48**	**27**	**2**	**2**	**4**
RAMSAY, Les *No playoffs*	Left wing								
RAMSEY, Mike	Defense								
1980	Buffalo	13	1	2	3	12	1	0	1
1981	Buffalo	8	0	3	3	20	0	0	0
1982	Buffalo	4	1	1	2	14	0	0	0
1983	Buffalo	10	4	4	8	15	0	0	1
1984	Buffalo	3	0	1	1	6	0	0	0
1985	Buffalo	5	0	1	1	23	0	0	0
1988	Buffalo	6	0	3	3	29	0	0	0
1989	Buffalo	5	1	0	1	11	1	0	0
1990	Buffalo	6	0	1	1	8	0	0	0
1991	Buffalo	5	1	0	1	12	0	0	1
1992	Buffalo	7	0	2	2	8	0	0	0
1993	Pittsburgh	12	0	6	6	4	0	0	0
1994	Pittsburgh	1	0	0	0	0	0	0	0
1995	Detroit	15	0	1	1	4	0	0	0
1996	Detroit	15	0	4	4	10	0	0	0
Playoff Totals		**115**	**8**	**29**	**37**	**176**	**2**	**0**	**3**
RAMSEY, Wayne *No playoffs*	Defense								
RANDALL, Ken	Right wing/defense								
1918♦	Toronto	7	2	1	3	*33	....	....	....
1921	Toronto	2	0	0	0	11	....	....	....
1922♦	Toronto	6	2	0	2	23	....	....	....
Playoff Totals		**15**	**4**	**1**	**5**	**67**	....	....	....
RANHEIM, Paul	Left wing								
1990	Calgary	6	1	3	4	2	0	0	0
1991	Calgary	7	2	2	4	0	0	0	0
1993	Calgary	6	0	1	1	0	0	0	0
1999	Carolina	6	0	0	0	2	0	0	0
Playoff Totals		**25**	**3**	**6**	**9**	**4**	**0**	**0**	**0**
RANIERI, George *No playoffs*	Left wing								
RASMUSSEN, Erik	Center								
1999	Buffalo	21	2	4	6	18	0	0	1
Playoff Totals		**21**	**2**	**4**	**6**	**18**	**0**	**0**	**1**
RATCHUK, Peter *No playoffs*	Defense								
RATELLE, Jean	Center								
1967	NY Rangers	4	0	0	0	2	0	0	0
1968	NY Rangers	6	0	4	4	2	0	0	0
1969	NY Rangers	4	1	0	1	0	1	0	0
1970	NY Rangers	6	1	3	4	0	0	0	0
1971	NY Rangers	13	2	9	11	8	0	0	0
1972	NY Rangers	6	0	1	1	0	0	0	0
1973	NY Rangers	10	2	7	9	0	1	0	0
1974	NY Rangers	13	2	4	6	0	0	0	1
1975	NY Rangers	3	1	5	6	2	1	0	0
1976	Boston	12	8	8	16	4	5	0	1
1977	Boston	14	5	12	17	4	1	0	1
1978	Boston	15	3	7	10	0	0	0	0
1979	Boston	11	7	6	13	2	2	0	2
1980	Boston	3	0	0	0	0	0	0	0
1981	Boston	3	0	0	0	0	0	0	0
Playoff Totals		**123**	**32**	**66**	**98**	**24**	**11**	**0**	**5**
RATHJE, Mike	Defense								
1994	San Jose	1	0	0	0	0	0	0	0
1995	San Jose	11	5	2	7	4	5	0	0
1998	San Jose	6	1	0	1	6	1	0	0
1999	San Jose	6	0	0	0	4	0	0	0
Playoff Totals		**24**	**6**	**2**	**8**	**14**	**6**	**0**	**0**
RATHWELL, John *No playoffs*	Right wing								
RATUSHNY, Dan *No playoffs*	Defense								
RAUSSE, Errol *No playoffs*	Left wing								
RAUTAKALLIO, Pekka	Defense								
1980	Atlanta	4	0	1	1	2	0	0	0
1981	Calgary	16	2	4	6	6	1	0	0
1982	Calgary	3	0	0	0	0	0	0	0
Playoff Totals		**23**	**2**	**5**	**7**	**8**	**1**	**0**	**0**
RAVLICH, Matt	Defense								
1965	Chicago	14	1	4	5	14	1	0	0
1966	Chicago	6	0	1	1	2	0	0	0
1968	Chicago	4	0	0	0	0	0	0	0
Playoff Totals		**24**	**1**	**5**	**6**	**16**	**1**	**0**	**0**

Season	Club	GP	G	A	Pts	PIM	PP	SH	GW
RAY, Rob	Right wing								
1991	Buffalo	6	1	1	2	56	0	0	1
1992	Buffalo	7	0	0	0	2	0	0	0
1994	Buffalo	7	1	0	1	43	0	0	0
1995	Buffalo	5	0	0	0	14	0	0	0
1997	Buffalo	12	0	1	1	28	0	0	0
1998	Buffalo	10	0	0	0	24	0	0	0
1999	Buffalo	5	1	0	1	0	0	0	1
Playoff Totals		**52**	**3**	**2**	**5**	**167**	**0**	**0**	**2**
RAYMOND, Armand	*No playoffs* Defense								
RAYMOND, Paul	Right wing								
1934	Mtl. Canadiens	2	0	0	0	0	0	0	0
1939	Mtl. Canadiens	3	0	0	0	2	0	0	0
Playoff Totals		**5**	**0**	**0**	**0**	**2**	**0**	**0**	**0**
READ, Mel	*No playoffs* Center								
REARDON, Ken	Defense								
1941	Montreal	3	0	0	0	4	....	....	....
1942	Montreal	3	0	0	0	4	....	....	....
1946♦	Montreal	9	1	1	2	4	....	....	....
1947	Montreal	7	1	2	3	20	....	....	....
1949	Montreal	7	0	0	0	18	....	....	....
1950	Montreal	2	0	2	2	12	....	....	....
Playoff Totals		**31**	**2**	**5**	**7**	**62**	....	....	....
REARDON, Terry	Center/right wing								
1940	Boston	1	0	1	1	0	....	....	....
1941♦	Boston	11	2	4	6	6	....	....	....
1942	Montreal	3	2	2	4	2	....	....	....
1946	Boston	10	4	0	4	2	....	....	....
1947	Boston	5	0	3	3	2	....	....	....
Playoff Totals		**30**	**8**	**10**	**18**	**12**	....	....	....
REASONER, Marty	*No playoffs* Center								
REAUME, Marc	Defense								
1955	Toronto	4	0	0	0	2	0	0	0
1956	Toronto	5	0	2	2	6	0	0	0
1959	Toronto	10	0	0	0	0	0	0	0
1960	Detroit	2	0	0	0	0	0	0	0
Playoff Totals		**21**	**0**	**2**	**2**	**8**	**0**	**0**	**0**
REAY, Billy	Center								
1946♦	Montreal	9	1	2	3	4	....	....	....
1947	Montreal	11	6	1	7	14	....	....	....
1949	Montreal	7	1	5	6	4	....	....	....
1950	Montreal	4	0	1	1	0	....	....	....
1951	Montreal	11	3	3	6	10	....	....	....
1952	Montreal	10	2	2	4	7	....	....	....
1953♦	Montreal	11	0	2	2	4	....	....	....
Playoff Totals		**63**	**13**	**16**	**29**	**43**	....	....	....
RECCHI, Mark	Right wing								
1991♦	Pittsburgh	24	10	24	34	33	5	0	2
1996	Montreal	6	3	3	6	0	3	0	0
1997	Montreal	5	4	2	6	2	0	0	0
1998	Montreal	10	4	8	12	6	0	0	2
1999	Philadelphia	6	0	1	1	2	0	0	0
Playoff Totals		**51**	**21**	**38**	**59**	**43**	**8**	**0**	**4**
REDAHL, Gord	*No playoffs* Right wing								
REDDEN, Wade	Defense								
1997	Ottawa	7	1	3	4	2	0	0	0
1998	Ottawa	9	0	2	2	2	0	0	0
1999	Ottawa	4	1	2	3	2	1	0	0
Playoff Totals		**20**	**2**	**7**	**9**	**6**	**1**	**0**	**0**
REDDING, George	*No playoffs* Left wing/defense								
REDMOND, Craig	Defense								
1985	Los Angeles	3	1	0	1	2	0	0	0
Playoff Totals		**3**	**1**	**0**	**1**	**2**	**0**	**0**	**0**
REDMOND, Dick	Defense								
1973	Chicago	13	4	2	6	2	0	0	2
1974	Chicago	11	1	7	8	8	1	0	0
1975	Chicago	8	2	3	5	0	1	0	0
1976	Chicago	4	0	2	2	4	0	0	0
1977	Chicago	2	0	1	1	0	0	0	0
1978	Atlanta	2	1	0	1	0	0	0	0
1979	Boston	11	1	3	4	2	0	1	0
1980	Boston	10	0	3	3	9	0	0	0
1981	Boston	3	0	1	1	2	0	0	0
1982	Boston	2	0	0	0	0	0	0	0
Playoff Totals		**66**	**9**	**22**	**31**	**27**	**2**	**1**	**2**
REDMOND, Keith	*No playoffs* Left wing								
REDMOND, Mickey	Right wing								
1968♦	Montreal	2	0	0	0	0	0	0	0
1969♦	Montreal	14	2	3	5	2	0	1	1
Playoff Totals		**16**	**2**	**3**	**5**	**2**	**0**	**1**	**1**
REEDS, Mark	Right wing								
1982	St. Louis	10	0	1	1	2	0	0	0
1983	St. Louis	4	1	0	1	2	0	0	0
1984	St. Louis	11	3	3	6	15	0	1	1
1985	St. Louis	3	0	0	0	0	0	0	0
1986	St. Louis	19	4	4	8	2	0	0	1
1987	St. Louis	6	0	1	1	2	0	0	0
Playoff Totals		**53**	**8**	**9**	**17**	**23**	**0**	**1**	**2**
REEKIE, Joe	Defense								
1988	Buffalo	2	0	0	0	4	0	0	0
1994	Washington	11	2	1	3	29	0	1	1
1995	Washington	7	0	0	0	2	0	0	0
1998	Washington	21	1	2	3	20	0	0	0
Playoff Totals		**41**	**3**	**3**	**6**	**55**	**0**	**1**	**1**
REGAN, Bill	Defense								
1930	NY Rangers	4	0	0	0	0	0	0	0
1931	NY Rangers	4	0	0	0	2	0	0	0
Playoff Totals		**8**	**0**	**0**	**0**	**2**	**0**	**0**	**0**
REGAN, Larry	Right wing								
1957	Boston	8	0	2	2	10	....	....	....
1958	Boston	12	3	8	11	6	....	....	....
1959	Toronto	8	1	1	2	2	....	....	....
1960	Toronto	10	3	3	6	0	....	....	....
1961	Toronto	4	0	0	0	0	....	....	....
Playoff Totals		**42**	**7**	**14**	**21**	**18**	....	....	....
REGEHR, Robyn	*No playoffs* Defense								
REGIER, Darcy	*No playoffs* Defense								
REIBEL, Earl	Center								
1954♦	Detroit	9	1	3	4	0	1	0	1
1955♦	Detroit	11	5	7	12	2	1	0	1
1956	Detroit	10	0	2	2	2	0	0	0
1957	Detroit	5	0	2	2	0	0	0	0
1959	Boston	4	0	0	0	0	0	0	0
Playoff Totals		**39**	**6**	**14**	**20**	**4**	**2**	**0**	**2**
REICHEL, Robert	Center								
1991	Calgary	6	1	1	2	0	1	0	0
1993	Calgary	6	2	4	6	2	2	0	0
1994	Calgary	7	0	5	5	0	0	0	0
1995	Calgary	7	2	4	6	4	0	0	1
1999	Phoenix	7	1	3	4	2	0	0	0
Playoff Totals		**33**	**6**	**17**	**23**	**8**	**3**	**0**	**1**
REICHERT, Craig	*No playoffs* Right wing								
REID, Dave	Left wing								
1985	Boston	5	1	0	1	0	0	0	0
1987	Boston	2	0	0	0	0	0	0	0
1990	Toronto	3	0	0	0	0	0	0	0
1992	Boston	15	2	5	7	4	0	0	1
1994	Boston	13	2	1	3	2	0	1	0
1995	Boston	5	0	0	0	0	0	0	0
1996	Boston	5	0	2	2	2	0	0	0
1997	Dallas	7	1	0	1	4	0	0	0
1998	Dallas	5	0	3	3	2	0	0	0
1999♦	Dallas	23	2	8	10	14	0	0	0
Playoff Totals		**83**	**8**	**19**	**27**	**28**	**0**	**1**	**1**
REID, Dave	*No playoffs* Center								
REID, Gerry	Center								
1949	Detroit	2	0	0	0	2	0	0	0
Playoff Totals		**2**	**0**	**0**	**0**	**2**	**0**	**0**	**0**
REID, Gord	*No playoffs* Defense								
REID, Reg	Left wing								
1925	Toronto	2	0	0	0	0	0	0	0
Playoff Totals		**2**	**0**	**0**	**0**	**0**	**0**	**0**	**0**
REID, Tom	Defense								
1968	Chicago	9	0	0	0	2	0	0	0
1970	Minnesota	6	0	1	1	4	0	0	0
1971	Minnesota	12	0	6	6	20	0	0	0
1972	Minnesota	7	1	4	5	17	0	0	0
1973	Minnesota	6	0	2	2	4	0	0	0
1977	Minnesota	2	0	0	0	2	0	0	0
Playoff Totals		**42**	**1**	**13**	**14**	**49**	**0**	**0**	**0**
REIERSON, Dave	*No playoffs* Defense								
REIGLE, Ed	*No playoffs* Defense								
REINHART, Paul	Defense								
1981	Calgary	16	1	14	15	16	1	0	0
1982	Calgary	3	0	1	1	2	0	0	0
1983	Calgary	9	6	3	9	2	4	1	0
1984	Calgary	11	6	11	17	2	0	1	0
1985	Calgary	4	1	1	2	0	0	0	0
1986	Calgary	21	5	13	18	4	4	0	0
1987	Calgary	4	0	1	1	6	0	0	0
1988	Calgary	8	2	7	9	6	1	0	0
1989	Vancouver	7	2	3	5	4	1	0	2
Playoff Totals		**83**	**23**	**54**	**77**	**42**	**11**	**2**	**2**
REINIKKA, Ollie	*No playoffs* Center/right wing								
REIRDEN, Todd	*No playoffs* Defense								
REISE Jr., Leo	Defense								
1947	Detroit	5	0	1	1	4	....	....	....
1948	Detroit	10	2	1	3	12	....	....	....
1949	Detroit	11	1	0	1	4	....	....	....
1950♦	Detroit	14	2	0	2	19	....	....	....
1951	Detroit	6	2	3	5	2	....	....	....
1952♦	Detroit	6	1	0	1	*27	....	....	....
Playoff Totals		**52**	**8**	**5**	**13**	**68**	....	....	....
REISE Sr., Leo	Defense								
1929	NY Americans	2	0	0	0	0	0	0	0
1930	NY Rangers	4	0	0	0	16	0	0	0
Playoff Totals		**6**	**0**	**0**	**0**	**16**	**0**	**0**	**0**
RENAUD, Mark	*No playoffs* Defense								
RENBERG, Mikael	Right wing								
1995	Philadelphia	15	6	7	13	6	2	0	0
1996	Philadelphia	11	3	6	9	14	1	0	0
1997	Philadelphia	18	5	6	11	4	2	0	0
1999	Philadelphia	6	0	1	1	0	0	0	0
Playoff Totals		**50**	**14**	**20**	**34**	**24**	**5**	**0**	**0**
REYNOLDS, Bobby	*No playoffs* Left wing								
RHEAUME, Pascal	Left wing								
1998	St. Louis	10	1	3	4	8	1	0	0
1999	St. Louis	5	1	0	1	4	0	0	0
Playoff Totals		**15**	**2**	**3**	**5**	**12**	**1**	**0**	**0**
RIBBLE, Pat	Defense								
1977	Atlanta	2	0	0	0	6	0	0	0
1978	Atlanta	2	0	1	1	2	0	0	0
1979	Chicago	4	0	0	0	4	0	0	0
Playoff Totals		**8**	**0**	**1**	**1**	**12**	**0**	**0**	**0**
RIBEIRO, Mike	*No playoffs* Center								
RICCI, Mike	Center								
1993	Quebec	6	0	6	6	8	0	0	0
1995	Quebec	6	1	3	4	8	0	0	0
1996♦	Colorado	22	6	11	17	18	3	0	1
1997	Colorado	17	2	4	6	17	0	0	1
1998	San Jose	6	1	3	4	6	0	0	0
1999	San Jose	6	2	3	5	10	1	0	0
Playoff Totals		**63**	**12**	**30**	**42**	**67**	**4**	**0**	**2**
RICE, Steven	Right wing								
1991	NY Rangers	2	2	1	3	6	1	0	0
Playoff Totals		**2**	**2**	**1**	**3**	**6**	**1**	**0**	**0**
RICHARD, Henri	Center								
1956♦	Montreal	10	4	4	8	21	....	....	....
1957♦	Montreal	10	2	6	8	10	....	....	....
1958♦	Montreal	10	1	7	8	11	....	....	....
1959♦	Montreal	11	3	8	11	13	....	....	....
1960♦	Montreal	8	3	9	*12	9	....	....	....
1961	Montreal	6	2	4	6	22	....	....	....
1963	Montreal	5	1	1	2	2	....	....	....
1964	Montreal	7	1	1	2	9	....	....	....
1965♦	Montreal	13	7	4	11	24	....	....	....
1966♦	Montreal	8	1	4	5	2	....	....	....
1967	Montreal	10	4	6	10	2	....	....	....
1968♦	Montreal	13	4	4	8	4	1	0	0
1969♦	Montreal	14	2	4	6	8	0	0	0
1971♦	Montreal	20	5	7	12	20	0	0	1
1972	Montreal	6	0	3	3	4	0	0	0
1973♦	Montreal	17	6	4	10	14	0	0	2
1974	Montreal	6	2	2	4	2	0	0	0
1975	Montreal	6	1	2	3	4	0	0	0
Playoff Totals		**180**	**49**	**80**	**129**	**181**	....	....	....
RICHARD, Jacques	Left wing								
1974	Atlanta	4	0	0	0	2	0	0	0
1976	Buffalo	9	1	1	2	7	0	0	0
1979	Buffalo	3	1	0	1	0	0	0	1
1981	Quebec	5	2	4	6	14	1	0	0
1982	Quebec	10	1	0	1	9	0	0	0
1983	Quebec	4	0	0	0	2	0	0	0
Playoff Totals		**35**	**5**	**5**	**10**	**34**	**1**	**0**	**1**
RICHARD, Jean-Marc	*No playoffs* Defense								
RICHARD, Maurice	Right wing								
1944♦	Montreal	9	*12	5	17	10	....	....	....
1945	Montreal	6	6	2	8	10	....	....	....
1946♦	Montreal	9	*7	4	11	15	....	....	....
1947	Montreal	10	*6	5	*11	*44	....	....	....
1949	Montreal	7	2	1	3	14	....	....	....
1950	Montreal	5	1	1	2	6	....	....	....
1951	Montreal	11	*9	4	*13	13	....	....	....
1952	Montreal	11	4	2	6	6	....	....	....
1953♦	Montreal	12	7	1	8	2	....	....	....
1954	Montreal	11	3	0	3	22	....	....	....
1956♦	Montreal	10	5	9	14	*24	....	....	....
1957♦	Montreal	10	8	3	11	8	....	....	....
1958♦	Montreal	10	*11	4	15	10	....	....	....
1959♦	Montreal	4	0	0	0	2	....	....	....
1960♦	Montreal	8	1	3	4	2	....	....	....
Playoff Totals		**133**	**82**	**44**	**126**	**188**	....	....	....
RICHARD, Mike	*No playoffs* Center								
RICHARDS, Todd	Defense								
1991	Hartford	6	0	0	0	2	0	0	0
1992	Hartford	5	0	3	3	4	0	0	0
Playoff Totals		**11**	**0**	**3**	**3**	**6**	**0**	**0**	**0**
RICHARDS, Travis	*No playoffs* Defense								
RICHARDSON, Dave	*No playoffs* Left wing								
RICHARDSON, Glen	*No playoffs* Left wing								
RICHARDSON, Ken	*No playoffs* Center								

Season	Club	GP	G	A	Pts	PIM	PP	SH	GW
RICHARDSON, Luke	Defense								
1988	Toronto	2	0	0	0	0	0	0	0
1990	Toronto	5	0	0	0	22	0	0	0
1992	Edmonton	16	0	5	5	45	0	0	0
1997	Edmonton	12	0	2	2	14	0	0	0
1998	Philadelphia	5	0	0	0	0	0	0	0
Playoff Totals		**40**	**0**	**7**	**7**	**81**	**0**	**0**	**0**
RICHER, Bob *No playoffs*	Center								
RICHER, Stephane	Defense								
1993	Boston	3	0	0	0	0	0	0	0
Playoff Totals		**3**	**0**	**0**	**0**	**0**	**0**	**0**	**0**
RICHER, Stephane	Right wing								
1986◆	Montreal	16	4	1	5	23	3	0	1
1987	Montreal	5	3	2	5	0	0	0	1
1988	Montreal	8	7	5	12	6	1	0	2
1989	Montreal	21	6	5	11	14	2	0	3
1990	Montreal	9	7	3	10	2	1	0	1
1991	Montreal	13	9	5	14	6	1	0	1
1992	New Jersey	7	1	2	3	0	0	0	0
1993	New Jersey	5	2	2	4	2	1	0	0
1994	New Jersey	20	7	5	12	6	3	0	2
1995◆	New Jersey	19	6	15	21	2	3	1	2
1997	Montreal	5	0	0	0	0	0	0	0
Playoff Totals		**128**	**52**	**45**	**97**	**61**	**15**	**1**	**13**
RICHMOND, Steve	Defense								
1984	NY Rangers	4	0	0	0	12	0	0	0
Playoff Totals		**4**	**0**	**0**	**0**	**12**	**0**	**0**	**0**
RICHTER, Barry *No playoffs*	Defense								
RICHTER, Dave	Defense								
1984	Minnesota	8	0	0	0	20	0	0	0
1985	Minnesota	9	1	0	1	39	0	0	0
1986	Philadelphia	5	0	0	0	21	0	0	0
Playoff Totals		**22**	**1**	**0**	**1**	**80**	**0**	**0**	**0**
RIDLEY, Mike	Center								
1986	NY Rangers	16	6	8	14	26	2	0	1
1987	Washington	7	2	1	3	6	0	0	1
1988	Washington	14	6	5	11	10	1	0	0
1989	Washington	6	0	5	5	2	0	0	0
1990	Washington	14	3	4	7	8	0	1	0
1991	Washington	11	3	4	7	8	1	0	1
1992	Washington	7	0	11	11	0	0	0	0
1993	Washington	6	1	5	6	0	1	0	0
1994	Washington	11	4	6	10	6	0	0	0
1995	Toronto	7	3	1	4	2	1	0	1
1996	Vancouver	5	0	0	0	2	0	0	0
Playoff Totals		**104**	**28**	**50**	**78**	**70**	**6**	**1**	**4**
RILEY, Bill *No playoffs*	Right wing								
RILEY, Jack	Center								
1934	Mtl. Canadiens	2	0	1	1	0	0	0	0
1935	Mtl. Canadiens	2	0	2	2	0	0	0	0
Playoff Totals		**4**	**0**	**3**	**3**	**0**	**0**	**0**	**0**
RILEY, Jim *No playoffs*	Left wing								
RIOPELLIE, Rip	Left wing								
1949	Montreal	7	1	1	2	2	....	....	....
1950	Montreal	1	0	0	0	0	....	....	....
Playoff Totals		**8**	**1**	**1**	**2**	**2**	....	....	....
RIOUX, Gerry *No playoffs*	Right wing								
RIOUX, Pierre *No playoffs*	Right wing								
RIPLEY, Vic	Left wing								
1930	Chicago	2	0	0	0	2	....	....	....
1931	Chicago	9	2	1	3	4	....	....	....
1932	Chicago	2	0	0	0	0	....	....	....
1933	Boston	5	1	0	1	0	....	....	....
1934	NY Rangers	2	1	0	1	4	....	....	....
Playoff Totals		**20**	**4**	**1**	**5**	**10**	....	....	....
RISEBROUGH, Doug	Center								
1975	Montreal	11	3	5	8	37	0	0	0
1976◆	Montreal	13	0	3	3	30	0	0	0
1977◆	Montreal	12	2	3	5	16	0	0	0
1978◆	Montreal	15	2	2	4	17	0	1	1
1979◆	Montreal	15	1	6	7	32	0	0	1
1981	Montreal	3	1	0	1	0	1	0	0
1982	Montreal	5	2	1	3	11	0	0	0
1983	Calgary	9	1	3	4	18	0	0	0
1984	Calgary	11	2	1	3	25	0	0	0
1985	Calgary	4	0	3	3	12	0	0	0
1986	Calgary	22	7	9	16	38	0	1	1
1987	Calgary	4	0	1	1	2	0	0	0
Playoff Totals		**124**	**21**	**37**	**58**	**238**	**1**	**2**	**3**
RISSLING, Gary	Left wing								
1981	Pittsburgh	5	0	1	1	4	0	0	0
Playoff Totals		**5**	**0**	**1**	**1**	**4**	**0**	**0**	**0**
RITCHIE, Bob *No playoffs*	Left wing								
RITCHIE, Byron *No playoffs*	Center								
RITCHIE, Dave	Defense								
1925	Mtl. Canadiens	1	0	0	0	0	0	0	0
Playoff Totals		**1**	**0**	**0**	**0**	**0**	**0**	**0**	**0**
RITSON, Alex *No playoffs*	Center								
RITTINGER, Alan *No playoffs*	Right/left wing								
RIVARD, Bob *No playoffs*	Center/left wing								
RIVERS, Gus	Right wing								
1930◆	Mtl. Canadiens	6	1	0	1	2	....	....	....
1931◆	Mtl. Canadiens	10	1	0	1	0	....	....	....
Playoff Totals		**16**	**2**	**0**	**2**	**2**	....	....	....
RIVERS, Jamie	Defense								
1999	St. Louis	9	1	1	2	2	1	0	1
Playoff Totals		**9**	**1**	**1**	**2**	**2**	**1**	**0**	**1**
RIVERS, Shawn *No playoffs*	Defense								
RIVERS, Wayne *No playoffs*	Right wing								
RIVET, Craig	Defense								
1997	Montreal	5	0	1	1	14	0	0	0
1998	Montreal	5	0	0	0	2	0	0	0
Playoff Totals		**10**	**0**	**1**	**1**	**16**	**0**	**0**	**0**
RIZZUTO, Garth *No playoffs*	Center								
ROACH, Mickey *No playoffs*	Center								
ROBERGE, Mario	Left wing								
1991	Montreal	12	0	0	0	24	0	0	0
1993◆	Montreal	3	0	0	0	0	0	0	0
Playoff Totals		**15**	**0**	**0**	**0**	**24**	**0**	**0**	**0**
ROBERGE, Serge *No playoffs*	Right wing								
ROBERT, Claude *No playoffs*	Left wing								
ROBERT, Rene	Right wing								
1973	Buffalo	6	5	3	8	2	1	0	1
1975	Buffalo	16	5	8	13	16	0	0	3
1976	Buffalo	9	3	2	5	6	0	0	0
1977	Buffalo	6	5	2	7	20	1	0	0
1978	Buffalo	7	2	0	2	23	0	0	0
1979	Buffalo	3	2	2	4	4	0	0	0
1981	Toronto	3	0	2	2	2	0	0	0
Playoff Totals		**50**	**22**	**19**	**41**	**73**	**2**	**0**	**4**
ROBERTO, Phil	Right wing								
1971◆	Montreal	15	0	1	1	36	0	0	0
1972	St. Louis	11	7	6	13	29	3	0	1
1973	St. Louis	5	2	1	3	4	0	0	0
Playoff Totals		**31**	**9**	**8**	**17**	**69**	**3**	**0**	**1**
ROBERTS, David	Left wing								
1994	St. Louis	3	0	0	0	12	0	0	0
1995	St. Louis	6	0	0	0	4	0	0	0
Playoff Totals		**9**	**0**	**0**	**0**	**16**	**0**	**0**	**0**
ROBERTS, Doug	Right wing								
1969	Oakland	7	0	1	1	34	0	0	0
1970	Oakland	4	0	2	2	6	0	0	0
1973	Boston	5	2	0	2	6	0	0	0
Playoff Totals		**16**	**2**	**3**	**5**	**46**	**0**	**0**	**0**
ROBERTS, Gary	Left wing								
1987	Calgary	2	0	0	0	4	0	0	0
1988	Calgary	9	2	3	5	29	0	0	0
1989◆	Calgary	22	5	7	12	57	0	0	0
1990	Calgary	6	2	5	7	41	0	0	0
1991	Calgary	7	1	3	4	18	0	0	0
1993	Calgary	5	1	6	7	43	1	0	0
1994	Calgary	7	2	6	8	24	1	0	1
1999	Carolina	6	1	1	2	8	0	0	0
Playoff Totals		**64**	**14**	**31**	**45**	**224**	**2**	**0**	**1**
ROBERTS, Gordie	Defense								
1980	Hartford	3	1	1	2	2	0	0	0
1981	Minnesota	19	1	5	6	17	0	1	0
1982	Minnesota	4	0	3	3	27	0	0	0
1983	Minnesota	9	1	5	6	14	0	0	0
1984	Minnesota	15	3	7	10	23	1	1	0
1985	Minnesota	9	1	6	7	6	0	0	0
1986	Minnesota	5	0	4	4	8	0	0	0
1988	St. Louis	10	1	2	3	33	0	0	0
1989	St. Louis	10	1	7	8	8	0	0	0
1990	St. Louis	10	0	2	2	26	0	0	0
1991◆	Pittsburgh	24	1	2	3	63	0	0	0
1992◆	Pittsburgh	19	0	2	2	32	0	0	0
1993	Boston	4	0	0	0	6	0	0	0
1994	Boston	12	0	1	1	8	0	0	0
Playoff Totals		**153**	**10**	**47**	**57**	**273**	**1**	**2**	**0**
ROBERTS, Jim	Left wing								
1977	Minnesota	2	0	0	0	0	0	0	0
Playoff Totals		**2**	**0**	**0**	**0**	**0**	**0**	**0**	**0**
ROBERTS, Jimmy	Defense/right wing								
1964	Montreal	7	0	1	1	14	0	0	0
1965◆	Montreal	13	0	0	0	30	0	0	0
1966◆	Montreal	10	1	1	2	10	0	1	0
1967	Montreal	4	1	0	1	0	0	0	0
1968	St. Louis	18	4	1	5	20	0	0	1
1969	St. Louis	12	1	4	5	10	0	0	0
1970	St. Louis	16	2	3	5	29	0	0	0
1971	St. Louis	6	2	1	3	11	0	0	0
1972	Montreal	6	1	0	1	0	0	0	1
1973◆	Montreal	17	0	2	2	22	0	0	0
1974	Montreal	6	0	0	0	4	0	0	0
1975	Montreal	11	2	2	4	2	0	0	0
1976◆	Montreal	13	3	1	4	2	0	1	0
1977◆	Montreal	14	3	0	3	6	0	1	1
Playoff Totals		**153**	**20**	**16**	**36**	**160**	**0**	**3**	**3**
ROBERTSON, Fred	Defense								
1932◆	Toronto	7	0	0	0	0	0	0	0
Playoff Totals		**7**	**0**	**0**	**0**	**0**	**0**	**0**	**0**
ROBERTSON, Geordie *No playoffs*	Right wing								
ROBERTSON, George *No playoffs*	Left wing/center								
ROBERTSON, Torrie	Left wing								
1986	Hartford	10	1	0	1	67	0	0	0
1988	Hartford	6	0	1	1	6	0	0	0
1989	Detroit	6	1	0	1	17	0	0	0
Playoff Totals		**22**	**2**	**1**	**3**	**90**	**0**	**0**	**0**
ROBERTSSON, Bert *No playoffs*	Defense								
ROBIDAS, Stephane *No playoffs*	Defense								
ROBIDOUX, Florent *No playoffs*	Left wing								
ROBINSON, Doug	Left wing								
1964	Chicago	4	0	0	0	0	0	0	0
1968	Los Angeles	7	4	3	7	0	0	0	0
Playoff Totals		**11**	**4**	**3**	**7**	**0**	**0**	**0**	**0**
ROBINSON, Earl	Right wing/center								
1930	Mtl. Maroons	4	0	0	0	0	....	....	....
1933	Mtl. Maroons	2	0	0	0	0	....	....	....
1934	Mtl. Maroons	4	2	0	2	0	....	....	....
1935◆	Mtl. Maroons	7	2	2	4	0	....	....	....
1936	Mtl. Maroons	3	0	0	0	0	....	....	....
1937	Mtl. Maroons	5	1	2	3	0	....	....	....
Playoff Totals		**25**	**5**	**4**	**9**	**0**	....	....	....
ROBINSON, Larry	Defense								
1973◆	Montreal	11	1	4	5	9	0	0	1
1974	Montreal	6	0	1	1	26	0	0	0
1975	Montreal	11	0	4	4	27	0	0	0
1976◆	Montreal	13	3	3	6	10	0	0	1
1977◆	Montreal	14	2	10	12	12	1	0	0
1978◆	Montreal	15	4	*17	*21	6	2	0	0
1979◆	Montreal	16	6	9	15	8	1	0	1
1980	Montreal	10	0	4	4	2	0	0	0
1981	Montreal	3	0	1	1	2	0	0	0
1982	Montreal	5	0	1	1	8	0	0	0
1983	Montreal	3	0	0	0	2	0	0	0
1984	Montreal	15	0	5	5	22	0	0	0
1985	Montreal	12	3	8	11	8	1	0	0
1986◆	Montreal	20	0	13	13	22	0	0	0
1987	Montreal	17	3	17	20	6	2	0	0
1988	Montreal	11	1	4	5	4	0	0	0
1989	Montreal	21	2	8	10	12	0	0	0
1990	Los Angeles	10	2	3	5	10	0	0	0
1991	Los Angeles	12	1	4	5	15	0	0	0
1992	Los Angeles	2	0	0	0	0	0	0	0
Playoff Totals		**227**	**28**	**116**	**144**	**211**	**7**	**0**	**3**
ROBINSON, Moe *No playoffs*	Defense								
ROBINSON, Rob *No playoffs*	Defense								
ROBINSON, Scott *No playoffs*	Right wing								
ROBITAILLE, Luc	Left wing								
1987	Los Angeles	5	1	4	5	2	0	0	0
1988	Los Angeles	5	2	5	7	18	2	0	1
1989	Los Angeles	11	2	6	8	10	0	0	1
1990	Los Angeles	10	5	5	10	10	1	0	1
1991	Los Angeles	12	12	4	16	22	5	0	2
1992	Los Angeles	6	3	4	7	12	1	0	1
1993	Los Angeles	24	9	13	22	28	4	0	2
1995	Pittsburgh	12	7	4	11	26	0	0	2
1996	NY Rangers	11	1	5	6	8	0	0	0
1997	NY Rangers	15	4	7	11	4	0	0	0
1998	Los Angeles	4	1	2	3	6	0	0	0
Playoff Totals		**115**	**47**	**59**	**106**	**146**	**13**	**0**	**10**
ROBITAILLE, Mike	Defense								
1973	Buffalo	6	0	0	0	0	0	0	0
1975	Vancouver	5	0	1	1	2	0	0	0
1976	Vancouver	2	0	0	0	2	0	0	0
Playoff Totals		**13**	**0**	**1**	**1**	**4**	**0**	**0**	**0**
ROBITAILLE, Randy	Center								
1999	Boston	1	0	0	0	0	0	0	0
Playoff Totals		**1**	**0**	**0**	**0**	**0**	**0**	**0**	**0**
ROCHE, Dave	Center								
1996	Pittsburgh	16	2	7	9	26	0	0	0
Playoff Totals		**16**	**2**	**7**	**9**	**26**	**0**	**0**	**0**

Season	Club	GP	G	A	Pts	PIM	PP	SH	GW
ROCHE, Des *No playoffs*	Right wing								
ROCHE, Earl	Left wing								
1931	Mtl. Maroons	2	0	0	0	0	0	0	0
Playoff Totals		**2**	**0**	**0**	**0**	**0**	**0**	**0**	**0**
ROCHE, Ernie *No playoffs*	Defense								
ROCHEFORT, Dave *No playoffs*	Center								
ROCHEFORT, Leon	Right wing								
1966♦	Montreal	4	1	1	2	4	0	0	0
1967	Montreal	10	1	1	2	4	0	0	0
1968	Philadelphia	7	2	0	2	2	0	0	1
1969	Philadelphia	3	0	0	0	0	0	0	0
1971♦	Montreal	10	0	0	0	6	0	0	0
1975	Vancouver	5	0	2	2	0	0	0	0
Playoff Totals		**39**	**4**	**4**	**8**	**16**	**0**	**0**	**1**
ROCHEFORT, Normand	Defense								
1981	Quebec	5	0	0	0	4	0	0	0
1982	Quebec	16	0	2	2	10	0	0	0
1983	Quebec	1	0	0	0	2	0	0	0
1984	Quebec	6	1	0	1	6	0	0	0
1985	Quebec	18	2	1	3	8	0	0	1
1987	Quebec	13	2	1	3	26	0	0	1
1990	NY Rangers	10	2	1	3	26	0	1	0
Playoff Totals		**69**	**7**	**5**	**12**	**82**	**0**	**1**	**2**
ROCKBURN, Harvey *No playoffs*	Defense								
RODDEN, Eddie	Center								
1927	Chicago	2	0	1	1	0	0	0	0
Playoff Totals		**2**	**0**	**1**	**1**	**0**	**0**	**0**	**0**
RODGERS, Marc *No playoffs*	Right wing								
ROENICK, Jeremy	Center								
1989	Chicago	10	1	3	4	7	1	0	1
1990	Chicago	20	11	7	18	8	4	0	1
1991	Chicago	6	3	5	8	4	1	0	1
1992	Chicago	18	12	10	22	12	4	0	3
1993	Chicago	4	1	2	3	2	0	0	0
1994	Chicago	6	1	6	7	2	0	0	1
1995	Chicago	8	1	2	3	16	0	0	0
1996	Chicago	10	5	7	12	2	1	0	1
1997	Phoenix	6	2	4	6	4	0	0	0
1998	Phoenix	6	5	3	8	4	2	2	2
1999	Phoenix	1	0	0	0	0	0	0	0
Playoff Totals		**95**	**42**	**49**	**91**	**61**	**13**	**2**	**10**
ROEST, Stacy *No playoffs*	Center								
ROGERS, John *No playoffs*	Right wing								
ROGERS, Mike	Center								
1980	Hartford	3	0	3	3	0	0	0	0
1982	NY Rangers	9	1	6	7	2	0	0	0
1983	NY Rangers	1	0	0	0	0	0	0	0
1984	NY Rangers	1	0	0	0	0	0	0	0
1985	NY Rangers	3	0	4	4	4	0	0	0
Playoff Totals		**17**	**1**	**13**	**14**	**6**	**0**	**0**	**0**
ROHLICEK, Jeff *No playoffs*	Center								
ROHLIN, Leif	Defense								
1996	Vancouver	5	0	0	0	0	0	0	0
Playoff Totals		**5**	**0**	**0**	**0**	**0**	**0**	**0**	**0**
ROHLOFF, Jon	Defense								
1995	Boston	5	0	0	0	6	0	0	0
1996	Boston	5	1	2	3	2	1	0	0
Playoff Totals		**10**	**1**	**2**	**3**	**8**	**1**	**0**	**0**
ROLFE, Dale	Defense								
1968	Los Angeles	7	0	1	1	14	0	0	0
1969	Los Angeles	10	0	4	4	8	0	0	0
1970	Detroit	4	0	2	2	8	0	0	0
1971	NY Rangers	13	0	1	1	14	0	0	0
1972	NY Rangers	16	4	3	7	16	0	0	1
1973	NY Rangers	8	0	5	5	6	0	0	0
1974	NY Rangers	13	1	8	9	23	0	0	0
Playoff Totals		**71**	**5**	**24**	**29**	**89**	**0**	**0**	**1**
ROLSTON, Brian	Center								
1995♦	New Jersey	6	2	1	3	4	1	0	0
1997	New Jersey	10	4	1	5	6	1	2	0
1998	New Jersey	6	1	0	1	2	0	1	0
1999	New Jersey	7	1	0	1	2	0	1	0
Playoff Totals		**29**	**8**	**2**	**10**	**14**	**2**	**4**	**0**
ROMANCHYCH, Larry	Right wing								
1974	Atlanta	4	2	2	4	4	0	0	0
1976	Atlanta	2	0	0	0	0	0	0	0
1977	Atlanta	1	0	0	0	0	0	0	0
Playoff Totals		**7**	**2**	**2**	**4**	**4**	**0**	**0**	**0**
ROMANIUK, Russell	Left wing								
1993	Winnipeg	1	0	0	0	0	0	0	0
1996	Philadelphia	1	0	0	0	0	0	0	0
Playoff Totals		**2**	**0**	**0**	**0**	**0**	**0**	**0**	**0**
ROMBOUGH, Doug *No playoffs*	Center								
ROMINSKI, Dale *No playoffs*	Right wing								

Season	Club	GP	G	A	Pts	PIM	PP	SH	GW
ROMNES, Doc	Left wing/center								
1931	Chicago	9	1	1	2	2	....	....	....
1932	Chicago	2	0	0	0	0	....	....	....
1934♦	Chicago	8	2	*7	9	0	....	....	....
1935	Chicago	2	0	0	0	0	....	....	....
1936	Chicago	2	1	2	3	0	....	....	....
1938♦	Chicago	12	2	4	6	2	....	....	....
1939	Toronto	10	1	4	5	0	....	....	....
Playoff Totals		**45**	**7**	**18**	**25**	**4**	....	....	....
RONAN, Ed	Right wing								
1993♦	Montreal	14	2	3	5	10	0	0	0
1994	Montreal	7	1	0	1	0	0	0	0
1997	Buffalo	6	1	0	1	6	0	0	0
Playoff Totals		**27**	**4**	**3**	**7**	**16**	**0**	**0**	**0**
RONAN, Skene *No playoffs*	Defense/center								
RONNING, Cliff	Center								
1986	St. Louis	5	1	1	2	2	1	0	0
1987	St. Louis	4	0	1	1	0	0	0	0
1989	St. Louis	7	1	3	4	0	1	0	0
1991	Vancouver	6	6	3	9	12	2	0	2
1992	Vancouver	13	8	5	13	6	1	0	1
1993	Vancouver	12	2	9	11	6	0	0	0
1994	Vancouver	24	5	10	15	16	2	0	2
1995	Vancouver	11	3	5	8	2	1	0	2
1996	Vancouver	6	0	2	2	6	0	0	0
1997	Phoenix	7	0	7	7	12	0	0	0
1998	Phoenix	6	1	3	4	4	0	0	0
Playoff Totals		**101**	**27**	**49**	**76**	**66**	**8**	**0**	**7**
RONSON, Len *No playoffs*	Left wing								
RONTY, Paul	Center								
1948	Boston	5	0	4	4	0	....	....	....
1949	Boston	5	1	2	3	2	....	....	....
1951	Boston	6	0	1	1	2	....	....	....
1955	Montreal	5	0	0	0	2	....	....	....
Playoff Totals		**21**	**1**	**7**	**8**	**6**	....	....	....
ROONEY, Steve	Left wing								
1985	Montreal	11	2	2	4	19	0	0	0
1986♦	Montreal	1	0	0	0	0	0	0	0
1987	Winnipeg	8	0	0	0	34	0	0	0
1988	Winnipeg	5	1	0	1	33	0	0	0
Playoff Totals		**25**	**3**	**2**	**5**	**86**	**0**	**0**	**0**
ROOT, Bill	Defense								
1986	Toronto	7	0	2	2	13	0	0	0
1987	Toronto	13	1	0	1	12	0	0	0
1988	Philadelphia	2	0	0	0	0	0	0	0
Playoff Totals		**22**	**1**	**2**	**3**	**25**	**0**	**0**	**0**
ROSA, Pavel *No playoffs*	Right wing								
ROSS, Art *No playoffs*	Defense								
ROSS, Jim *No playoffs*	Defense								
ROSSIGNOL, Roly	Right wing								
1945	Montreal	1	0	0	0	2	0	0	0
Playoff Totals		**1**	**0**	**0**	**0**	**2**	**0**	**0**	**0**
ROTA, Darcy	Left wing								
1974	Chicago	11	3	0	3	11	0	0	0
1975	Chicago	7	0	1	1	24	0	0	0
1976	Chicago	4	1	0	1	2	1	0	0
1977	Chicago	2	0	0	0	0	0	0	0
1978	Chicago	4	0	0	0	2	0	0	0
1979	Atlanta	2	0	1	1	26	0	0	0
1980	Vancouver	4	2	0	2	8	0	0	0
1981	Vancouver	3	2	1	3	14	1	0	0
1982	Vancouver	17	6	3	9	54	2	0	1
1983	Vancouver	3	0	0	0	6	0	0	0
1984	Vancouver	3	0	1	1	0	0	0	0
Playoff Totals		**60**	**14**	**7**	**21**	**147**	**4**	**0**	**1**
ROTA, Randy	Center/left wing								
1974	Los Angeles	5	0	1	1	0	0	0	0
Playoff Totals		**5**	**0**	**1**	**1**	**0**	**0**	**0**	**0**
ROTHSCHILD, Sam	Left wing								
1926♦	Mtl. Maroons	8	0	0	0	0	0	0	0
1927	Mtl. Maroons	2	0	0	0	0	0	0	0
Playoff Totals		**10**	**0**	**0**	**0**	**0**	**0**	**0**	**0**
ROULSTON, Rolly *No playoffs*	Left wing/defense								
ROULSTON, Tom	Center/right wing								
1982	Edmonton	5	1	0	1	2	0	0	0
1983	Edmonton	16	1	2	3	0	0	0	0
Playoff Totals		**21**	**2**	**2**	**4**	**2**	**0**	**0**	**0**
ROUPE, Magnus *No playoffs*	Left wing								

Season	Club	GP	G	A	Pts	PIM	PP	SH	GW
ROUSE, Bob	Defense								
1986	Minnesota	3	0	0	0	0	0	0	0
1989	Washington	6	2	0	2	4	0	0	0
1990	Washington	15	2	3	5	47	1	0	0
1993	Toronto	21	3	8	11	29	1	0	1
1994	Toronto	18	0	3	3	29	0	0	0
1995	Detroit	18	0	3	3	8	0	0	0
1996	Detroit	7	0	1	1	4	0	0	0
1997♦	Detroit	20	0	0	0	55	0	0	0
1998♦	Detroit	22	0	3	3	16	0	0	0
1999	San Jose	6	0	0	0	6	0	0	0
Playoff Totals		**136**	**7**	**21**	**28**	**198**	**2**	**0**	**1**
ROUSSEAU, Bobby	Right wing								
1962	Montreal	6	0	2	2	0	0	0	0
1963	Montreal	5	0	1	1	2	0	0	0
1964	Montreal	7	1	1	2	2	0	1	1
1965♦	Montreal	13	5	8	13	24	5	0	2
1966♦	Montreal	10	4	4	8	6	2	0	0
1967	Montreal	10	1	7	8	4	1	0	1
1968♦	Montreal	13	2	4	6	8	0	0	1
1969♦	Montreal	14	3	2	5	8	0	2	1
1971	Minnesota	12	2	6	8	0	1	0	1
1972	NY Rangers	16	6	11	17	7	0	0	1
1973	NY Rangers	10	2	3	5	4	0	0	0
1974	NY Rangers	12	1	8	9	4	1	0	0
Playoff Totals		**128**	**27**	**57**	**84**	**69**	**10**	**3**	**8**
ROUSSEAU, Guy *No playoffs*	Left wing								
ROUSSEAU, Roland *No playoffs*	Defense								
ROUTHIER, Jean-Marc *No playoffs*	Right wing								
ROWE, Bobby *No playoffs*	Right wing/defense								
ROWE, Mike *No playoffs*	Defense								
ROWE, Ron *No playoffs*	Center/left wing								
ROWE, Tom	Right wing								
1980	Hartford	3	2	0	2	0	0	0	0
Playoff Totals		**3**	**2**	**0**	**2**	**0**	**0**	**0**	**0**
ROY, Andre *No playoffs*	Left wing								
ROY, Jean-Yves *No playoffs*	Right wing								
ROY, Stephane *No playoffs*	Center								
ROYER, Remi *No playoffs*	Defense								
ROZSIVAL, Michal *No playoffs*	Defense								
ROZZINI, Gino	Center								
1945	Boston	6	1	2	3	6	....	....	....
Playoff Totals		**6**	**1**	**2**	**3**	**6**	....	....	....
RUCCHIN, Steve	Center								
1997	Anaheim	8	1	2	3	10	0	0	0
1999	Anaheim	4	0	3	3	0	0	0	0
Playoff Totals		**12**	**1**	**5**	**6**	**10**	**0**	**0**	**0**
RUCINSKI, Mike *No playoffs*	Defense								
RUCINSKI, Mike	Center								
1988	Chicago	2	0	0	0	0	0	0	0
Playoff Totals		**2**	**0**	**0**	**0**	**0**	**0**	**0**	**0**
RUCINSKY, Martin	Left wing								
1993	Quebec	6	1	1	2	4	1	0	0
1997	Montreal	5	0	0	0	4	0	0	0
1998	Montreal	10	3	0	3	4	1	0	0
Playoff Totals		**21**	**4**	**1**	**5**	**12**	**2**	**0**	**0**
RUELLE, Bernie *No playoffs*	Left wing								
RUFF, Jason *No playoffs*	Left wing								
RUFF, Lindy	Defense/Left wing								
1980	Buffalo	8	1	1	2	19	0	0	0
1981	Buffalo	6	3	1	4	23	1	0	1
1982	Buffalo	4	0	0	0	28	0	0	0
1983	Buffalo	10	4	2	6	47	0	0	0
1984	Buffalo	3	1	0	1	9	0	0	0
1985	Buffalo	5	2	4	6	15	1	0	0
1988	Buffalo	6	0	2	2	23	0	0	0
1989	NY Rangers	2	0	0	0	17	0	0	0
1990	NY Rangers	8	0	3	3	12	0	0	0
Playoff Totals		**52**	**11**	**13**	**24**	**193**	**2**	**0**	**1**
RUHNKE, Kent *No playoffs*	Right wing								
RUMBLE, Darren *No playoffs*	Defense								
RUNDQVIST, Thomas *No playoffs*	Center								
RUNGE, Paul	Center/left wing								
1936	Boston	2	0	0	0	2	0	0	0
1937	Mtl. Maroons	5	0	0	0	4	0	0	0
Playoff Totals		**7**	**0**	**0**	**0**	**6**	**0**	**0**	**0**
RUOTSALAINEN, Reijo	Defense								
1982	NY Rangers	10	4	5	9	2	2	0	1
1983	NY Rangers	9	4	2	6	6	1	0	1
1984	NY Rangers	5	1	1	2	2	1	0	1
1985	NY Rangers	3	2	0	2	6	1	0	0
1986	NY Rangers	16	0	8	8	6	0	0	0
1987♦	Edmonton	21	2	5	7	10	1	0	1
1990♦	Edmonton	22	2	11	13	12	1	0	0
Playoff Totals		**86**	**15**	**32**	**47**	**44**	**7**	**0**	**4**

Season	Club	GP	G	A	Pts	PIM	PP	SH	GW
RUPP, Duane	Defense								
1970	Pittsburgh	6	2	2	4	2	0	0	0
1972	Pittsburgh	4	0	0	0	6	0	0	0
Playoff Totals		**10**	**2**	**2**	**4**	**8**	**0**	**0**	**0**
RUSKOWSKI, Terry	Center								
1980	Chicago	4	0	0	0	22	0	0	0
1981	Chicago	3	0	2	2	11	0	0	0
1982	Chicago	11	1	2	3	53	0	0	0
1985	Los Angeles	3	0	2	2	0	0	0	0
Playoff Totals		**21**	**1**	**6**	**7**	**86**	**0**	**0**	**0**
RUSSELL, Cam	Defense								
1990	Chicago	1	0	0	0	0	0	0	0
1991	Chicago	1	0	0	0	0	0	0	0
1992	Chicago	12	0	2	2	2	0	0	0
1993	Chicago	4	0	0	0	0	0	0	0
1995	Chicago	16	0	3	3	8	0	0	0
1996	Chicago	6	0	0	0	2	0	0	0
1997	Chicago	4	0	0	0	4	0	0	0
Playoff Totals		**44**	**0**	**5**	**5**	**16**	**0**	**0**	**0**
RUSSELL, Church	*No playoffs* Left wing/center								
RUSSELL, Phil	Defense								
1973	Chicago	16	0	3	3	49	0	0	0
1974	Chicago	9	0	1	1	41	0	0	0
1975	Chicago	8	1	3	4	23	0	0	0
1976	Chicago	4	0	1	1	17	0	0	0
1977	Chicago	2	0	1	1	2	0	0	0
1979	Atlanta	2	0	0	0	9	0	0	0
1980	Atlanta	4	0	1	1	6	0	0	0
1981	Calgary	16	2	7	9	29	0	0	0
1982	Calgary	3	0	1	1	2	0	0	0
1983	Calgary	9	1	4	5	24	0	0	0
Playoff Totals		**73**	**4**	**22**	**26**	**202**	**0**	**0**	**0**
RUUTTU, Christian	Center								
1988	Buffalo	6	2	5	7	4	1	0	0
1989	Buffalo	2	0	0	0	2	0	0	0
1990	Buffalo	6	0	0	0	4	0	0	0
1991	Buffalo	6	1	3	4	29	0	1	0
1992	Buffalo	3	0	0	0	6	0	0	0
1993	Chicago	4	0	0	0	2	0	0	0
1994	Chicago	6	0	0	0	2	0	0	0
1995	Vancouver	9	1	1	2	0	0	1	0
Playoff Totals		**42**	**4**	**9**	**13**	**49**	**1**	**2**	**0**
RUUTU, Jarkko	*No playoffs* Left wing								
RUZICKA, Vladimir	Center								
1991	Boston	17	2	11	13	0	1	0	2
1992	Boston	13	2	3	5	2	2	0	0
Playoff Totals		**30**	**4**	**14**	**18**	**2**	**3**	**0**	**2**
RYAN, Terry	*No playoffs* Left wing								
RYCHEL, Warren	Left wing								
1991	Chicago	3	1	3	4	2	1	0	1
1993	Los Angeles	23	6	7	13	39	0	0	2
1995	Toronto	3	0	0	0	0	0	0	0
1996♦	Colorado	12	1	0	1	23	0	0	0
1997	Anaheim	11	0	2	2	19	0	0	0
1998	Colorado	6	0	0	0	24	0	0	0
1999	Colorado	12	0	1	1	14	0	0	0
Playoff Totals		**70**	**8**	**13**	**21**	**121**	**1**	**0**	**3**
RYMSHA, Andy	*No playoffs* Defense								
SAARINEN, Simo	*No playoffs* Defense								
SABOL, Shaun	*No playoffs* Defense								
SABOURIN, Bob	*No playoffs* Left wing								
SABOURIN, Gary	Right wing								
1968	St. Louis	18	4	2	6	30	1	0	1
1969	St. Louis	12	6	5	11	12	1	2	0
1970	St. Louis	16	5	0	5	10	0	1	1
1972	St. Louis	11	3	3	6	6	0	0	0
1973	St. Louis	5	1	1	2	0	0	0	1
Playoff Totals		**62**	**19**	**11**	**30**	**58**	**2**	**3**	**3**
SABOURIN, Ken	Defense								
1989♦	Calgary	1	0	0	0	0	0	0	0
1991	Washington	11	0	0	0	34	0	0	0
Playoff Totals		**12**	**0**	**0**	**0**	**34**	**0**	**0**	**0**
SACCO, David	*No playoffs* Right wing								
SACCO, Joe	Right wing								
1997	Anaheim	11	2	0	2	2	0	0	0
Playoff Totals		**11**	**2**	**0**	**2**	**2**	**0**	**0**	**0**
SACHARUK, Lawrence	Defense								
1975	St. Louis	2	1	1	2	2	0	0	0
Playoff Totals		**2**	**1**	**1**	**2**	**2**	**0**	**0**	**0**
SAGANIUK, Rocky	Right wing/center								
1979	Toronto	3	1	0	1	5	0	0	0
1980	Toronto	3	0	0	0	10	0	0	0
Playoff Totals		**6**	**1**	**0**	**1**	**15**	**0**	**0**	**0**
ST. AMOUR, Martin	*No playoffs* Left wing								

Season	Club	GP	G	A	Pts	PIM	PP	SH	GW
ST. LAURENT, Andre	Center								
1975	NY Islanders	15	2	2	4	6	1	0	0
1976	NY Islanders	13	1	5	6	15	0	0	0
1977	NY Islanders	12	1	2	3	6	0	0	1
1978	Detroit	7	1	1	2	4	0	0	0
1980	Los Angeles	4	1	0	1	0	0	1	1
1981	Los Angeles	3	0	1	1	9	0	0	0
1982	Pittsburgh	5	2	1	3	8	0	0	0
Playoff Totals		**59**	**8**	**12**	**20**	**48**	**1**	**1**	**2**
ST. LAURENT, Dollard	Defense								
1952	Montreal	9	0	3	3	6	....	....	....
1953♦	Montreal	12	0	3	3	4	....	....	....
1954	Montreal	10	1	2	3	8	....	....	....
1955	Montreal	12	0	5	5	12	....	....	....
1956♦	Montreal	4	0	0	0	2	....	....	....
1957♦	Montreal	7	0	1	1	13	....	....	....
1958♦	Montreal	5	0	0	0	10	....	....	....
1959	Chicago	6	0	1	1	2	....	....	....
1960	Chicago	4	0	1	1	0	....	....	....
1961♦	Chicago	11	1	2	3	12	....	....	....
1962	Chicago	12	0	4	4	18	....	....	....
Playoff Totals		**92**	**2**	**22**	**24**	**87**	....	....	....
ST. LOUIS, Martin	*No playoffs* Right wing								
ST. MARSEILLE, Frank	Right wing								
1968	St. Louis	18	5	8	13	0	4	0	0
1969	St. Louis	12	3	3	6	2	0	0	0
1970	St. Louis	15	6	7	13	4	3	1	0
1971	St. Louis	6	2	1	3	4	2	0	1
1972	St. Louis	11	3	5	8	6	1	0	0
1974	Los Angeles	5	0	0	0	0	0	0	0
1975	Los Angeles	3	0	1	1	0	0	0	0
1976	Los Angeles	9	0	0	0	0	0	0	0
1977	Los Angeles	9	1	0	1	2	0	0	0
Playoff Totals		**88**	**20**	**25**	**45**	**18**	**10**	**1**	**1**
ST. SAUVEUR, Claude	Center								
1976	Atlanta	2	0	0	0	0	0	0	0
Playoff Totals		**2**	**0**	**0**	**0**	**0**	**0**	**0**	**0**
SAKIC, Joe	Center								
1993	Quebec	6	3	3	6	2	1	0	0
1995	Quebec	6	4	1	5	0	1	1	1
1996♦	Colorado	22	*18	16	*34	14	6	0	6
1997	Colorado	17	8	*17	25	14	3	0	0
1998	Colorado	6	2	3	5	6	0	1	2
1999	Colorado	19	6	13	19	8	1	1	1
Playoff Totals		**76**	**41**	**53**	**94**	**44**	**12**	**3**	**10**
SALEI, Ruslan	Defense								
1999	Anaheim	3	0	0	0	4	0	0	0
Playoff Totals		**3**	**0**	**0**	**0**	**4**	**0**	**0**	**0**
SALESKI, Don	Right wing								
1973	Philadelphia	11	1	2	3	4	0	0	0
1974♦	Philadelphia	17	2	7	9	24	0	0	0
1975♦	Philadelphia	17	2	3	5	25	0	0	1
1976	Philadelphia	16	6	5	11	47	0	1	1
1977	Philadelphia	10	0	0	0	12	0	0	0
1978	Philadelphia	11	2	0	2	19	0	0	1
Playoff Totals		**82**	**13**	**17**	**30**	**131**	**0**	**1**	**3**
SALMING, Borje	Defense								
1974	Toronto	4	0	1	1	4	0	0	0
1975	Toronto	7	0	4	4	6	0	0	0
1976	Toronto	10	3	4	7	9	1	0	0
1977	Toronto	9	3	6	9	6	2	0	0
1978	Toronto	6	2	2	4	6	0	0	1
1979	Toronto	6	0	1	1	8	0	0	0
1980	Toronto	3	1	1	2	2	1	0	0
1981	Toronto	3	0	2	2	4	0	0	0
1983	Toronto	4	1	4	5	10	1	0	0
1986	Toronto	10	1	6	7	14	0	0	0
1987	Toronto	13	0	3	3	14	0	0	0
1988	Toronto	6	1	3	4	8	0	0	0
Playoff Totals		**81**	**12**	**37**	**49**	**91**	**5**	**0**	**1**
SALO, Sami	Defense								
1999	Ottawa	4	0	0	0	0	0	0	0
Playoff Totals		**4**	**0**	**0**	**0**	**0**	**0**	**0**	**0**
SALOVAARA, John	*No playoffs* Defense								
SALVIAN, Dave	Right wing								
1977	NY Islanders	1	0	1	1	2	0	0	0
Playoff Totals		**1**	**0**	**1**	**1**	**2**	**0**	**0**	**0**
SAMIS, Phil	Defense								
1948♦	Toronto	5	0	1	1	2	0	0	0
Playoff Totals		**5**	**0**	**1**	**1**	**2**	**0**	**0**	**0**
SAMPSON, Gary	Left wing								
1984	Washington	8	1	0	1	0	0	0	0
1985	Washington	4	0	0	0	0	0	0	0
Playoff Totals		**12**	**1**	**0**	**1**	**0**	**0**	**0**	**0**
SAMSONOV, Sergei	Left wing								
1998	Boston	6	2	5	7	0	0	0	1
1999	Boston	11	3	1	4	0	0	0	0
Playoff Totals		**17**	**5**	**6**	**11**	**0**	**0**	**0**	**1**

Season	Club	GP	G	A	Pts	PIM	PP	SH	GW
SAMUELSSON, Kjell	Defense								
1986	NY Rangers	9	0	1	1	8	0	0	0
1987	Philadelphia	26	0	4	4	25	0	0	0
1988	Philadelphia	7	2	5	7	23	0	0	1
1989	Philadelphia	19	1	3	4	24	0	0	0
1992♦	Pittsburgh	15	0	3	3	12	0	0	0
1993	Pittsburgh	12	0	3	3	2	0	0	0
1994	Pittsburgh	6	0	0	0	26	0	0	0
1995	Pittsburgh	11	0	1	1	32	0	0	0
1996	Philadelphia	12	1	0	1	24	0	0	0
1997	Philadelphia	5	0	0	0	2	0	0	0
1998	Philadelphia	1	0	0	0	0	0	0	0
Playoff Totals		**123**	**4**	**20**	**24**	**178**	**0**	**0**	**1**
SAMUELSSON, Ulf	Defense								
1986	Hartford	10	1	2	3	38	0	0	1
1987	Hartford	5	0	1	1	41	-2	0	0
1988	Hartford	5	0	0	0	8	0	0	0
1989	Hartford	4	0	2	2	4	0	0	0
1990	Hartford	7	1	0	1	2	0	0	0
1991♦	Pittsburgh	20	3	2	5	34	1	0	1
1992♦	Pittsburgh	21	0	2	2	39	0	0	0
1993	Pittsburgh	12	1	5	6	24	0	0	0
1994	Pittsburgh	6	0	1	1	18	0	0	0
1995	Pittsburgh	7	0	2	2	8	0	0	0
1996	NY Rangers	11	1	5	6	16	0	0	0
1997	NY Rangers	15	0	2	2	30	0	0	0
1999	Detroit	9	0	3	3	10	0	0	0
Playoff Totals		**132**	**7**	**27**	**34**	**272**	**-1**	**0**	**2**
SANDELIN, Scott	*No playoffs* Defense								
SANDERSON, Derek	Center								
1968	Boston	4	0	2	2	9	0	0	0
1969	Boston	9	*8	2	10	36	0	2	3
1970♦	Boston	14	5	4	9	*72	1	0	2
1971	Boston	7	2	1	3	13	0	0	0
1972♦	Boston	11	1	1	2	44	0	1	0
1973	Boston	5	1	2	3	13	0	0	0
1975	NY Rangers	3	0	0	0	0	0	0	0
1976	St. Louis	3	1	0	1	0	1	0	0
Playoff Totals		**56**	**18**	**12**	**30**	**187**	**2**	**3**	**5**
SANDERSON, Geoff	Left wing								
1991	Hartford	3	0	0	0	0	0	0	0
1992	Hartford	7	1	0	1	2	0	0	0
1998	Buffalo	14	3	1	4	4	1	0	1
1999	Buffalo	19	4	6	10	14	0	0	1
Playoff Totals		**43**	**8**	**7**	**15**	**20**	**1**	**0**	**2**
SANDFORD, Ed	Left wing								
1948	Boston	5	1	0	1	0	....	....	....
1949	Boston	5	1	3	4	2	....	....	....
1951	Boston	6	0	1	1	4	....	....	....
1952	Boston	7	2	2	4	0	....	....	....
1953	Boston	11	*8	3	*11	11	....	....	....
1954	Boston	3	0	1	1	4	....	....	....
1955	Boston	5	1	1	2	6	....	....	....
Playoff Totals		**42**	**13**	**11**	**24**	**27**	....	....	....
SANDLAK, Jim	Right wing								
1986	Vancouver	3	0	1	1	0	0	0	0
1989	Vancouver	6	1	1	2	2	0	0	0
1992	Vancouver	13	4	6	10	22	2	0	0
1993	Vancouver	6	2	2	4	4	0	0	0
1996	Vancouver	5	0	0	0	2	0	0	0
Playoff Totals		**33**	**7**	**10**	**17**	**30**	**2**	**0**	**0**
SANDS, Charlie	Center/right wing								
1933	Toronto	9	2	2	4	2	....	....	....
1934	Toronto	5	1	0	1	0	....	....	....
1935	Boston	4	0	0	0	0	....	....	....
1936	Boston	2	0	0	0	0	....	....	....
1937	Boston	3	1	2	3	0	....	....	....
1938	Boston	3	1	1	2	0	....	....	....
1939♦	Boston	1	0	0	0	0	....	....	....
1941	Montreal	2	1	0	1	0	....	....	....
1942	Montreal	3	0	1	1	2	....	....	....
1943	Montreal	2	0	0	0	0	....	....	....
Playoff Totals		**34**	**6**	**6**	**12**	**4**	....	....	....
SANDSTROM, Tomas	Right wing								
1985	NY Rangers	3	0	2	2	0	0	0	0
1986	NY Rangers	16	4	6	10	20	0	0	1
1987	NY Rangers	6	1	2	3	20	0	0	0
1989	NY Rangers	4	3	2	5	12	2	0	0
1990	Los Angeles	10	5	4	9	19	0	0	0
1991	Los Angeles	10	4	4	8	14	3	0	0
1992	Los Angeles	6	0	3	3	8	0	0	0
1993	Los Angeles	24	8	17	25	12	2	0	2
1994	Pittsburgh	6	0	0	0	4	0	0	0
1995	Pittsburgh	12	3	3	6	16	2	0	0
1996	Pittsburgh	18	4	2	6	30	0	0	1
1997♦	Detroit	20	0	4	4	24	0	0	0
1999	Anaheim	4	0	0	0	4	0	0	0
Playoff Totals		**139**	**32**	**49**	**81**	**183**	**9**	**0**	**4**
SANDWITH, Terran	*No playoffs* Defense								
SANIPASS, Everett	Left wing								
1988	Chicago	2	2	0	2	2	0	0	0
1989	Chicago	3	0	0	0	2	0	0	0
Playoff Totals		**5**	**2**	**0**	**2**	**4**	**0**	**0**	**0**

Season	Club	GP	G	A	Pts	PIM	PP	SH	GW
SAPRYKIN, Oleg *No playoffs* Center									
SARAULT, Yves Left wing									
1997	Colorado	5	0	0	0	2	0	0	0
Playoff Totals		**5**	**0**	**0**	**0**	**2**	**0**	**0**	**0**
SARGENT, Gary Defense									
1977	Los Angeles	9	3	4	7	6	2	0	0
1978	Los Angeles	2	0	0	0	0	0	0	0
1980	Minnesota	4	2	1	3	2	1	0	1
1983	Minnesota	5	0	2	2	0	0	0	0
Playoff Totals		**20**	**5**	**7**	**12**	**8**	**3**	**0**	**1**
SARICH, Cory *No playoffs* Defense									
SARNER, Craig *No playoffs* Right wing									
SARRAZIN, Dick Right wing									
1969	Philadelphia	4	0	0	0	0	0	0	0
Playoff Totals		**4**	**0**	**0**	**0**	**0**	**0**	**0**	**0**
SASKAMOOSE, Fred *No playoffs* Center									
SASSER, Grant *No playoffs* Center									
SATAN, Miroslav Left wing									
1997	Buffalo	7	0	0	0	0	0	0	0
1998	Buffalo	14	5	4	9	4	4	0	1
1999	Buffalo	12	3	5	8	2	1	0	1
Playoff Totals		**33**	**8**	**9**	**17**	**6**	**5**	**0**	**2**
SATHER, Glen Left wing									
1968	Boston	3	0	0	0	0	0	0	0
1969	Boston	10	0	0	0	18	0	0	0
1970	Pittsburgh	10	0	2	2	17	0	0	0
1971	NY Rangers	13	0	1	1	18	0	0	0
1972	NY Rangers	16	0	1	1	22	0	0	0
1973	NY Rangers	9	0	0	0	7	0	0	0
1975	Montreal	11	1	1	2	4	0	0	0
Playoff Totals		**72**	**1**	**5**	**6**	**86**	**0**	**0**	**0**
SAUNDERS, Bernie *No playoffs* Left wing									
SAUNDERS, David *No playoffs* Left wing									
SAUNDERS, Ted *No playoffs* Right wing									
SAUVE, Jean-Francois Center									
1981	Buffalo	5	2	0	2	0	1	0	0
1982	Buffalo	2	0	2	2	0	0	0	0
1984	Quebec	9	2	5	7	2	2	0	1
1985	Quebec	18	5	5	10	8	2	0	0
1986	Quebec	2	0	0	0	0	0	0	0
Playoff Totals		**36**	**9**	**12**	**21**	**10**	**5**	**0**	**1**
SAVAGE, Andre *No playoffs* Center									
SAVAGE, Brian right wing									
1994	Montreal	3	0	2	2	0	0	0	0
1996	Montreal	6	0	2	2	2	0	0	0
1997	Montreal	5	1	1	2	0	0	0	0
1998	Montreal	9	0	2	2	6	0	0	0
Playoff Totals		**23**	**1**	**7**	**8**	**8**	**0**	**0**	**0**
SAVAGE, Joel *No playoffs* Right wing									
SAVAGE, Reggie *No playoffs* Center									
SAVAGE, Tony Defense									
1935	Mtl. Canadiens	2	0	0	0	0	0	0	0
Playoff Totals		**2**	**0**	**0**	**0**	**0**	**0**	**0**	**0**
SAVARD, Andre Center									
1974	Boston	16	3	2	5	24	0	0	0
1975	Boston	3	1	1	2	2	0	0	1
1976	Boston	12	1	4	5	9	0	0	0
1977	Buffalo	6	0	1	1	2	0	0	0
1978	Buffalo	6	0	0	0	4	0	0	0
1979	Buffalo	3	0	2	2	2	0	0	0
1980	Buffalo	8	1	1	2	2	0	0	0
1981	Buffalo	8	4	2	6	17	1	0	0
1982	Buffalo	4	0	1	1	5	0	0	0
1983	Buffalo	10	0	4	4	8	0	0	0
1984	Quebec	9	3	0	3	2	0	2	1
Playoff Totals		**85**	**13**	**18**	**31**	**77**	**1**	**2**	**2**
SAVARD, Denis Center									
1981	Chicago	3	0	0	0	0	0	0	0
1982	Chicago	15	11	7	18	52	5	0	2
1983	Chicago	13	8	9	17	22	3	0	1
1984	Chicago	5	1	3	4	9	0	0	0
1985	Chicago	15	9	20	29	20	3	0	0
1986	Chicago	3	4	1	5	6	2	0	0
1987	Chicago	4	1	0	1	12	0	0	0
1988	Chicago	5	4	3	7	17	0	1	1
1989	Chicago	16	8	11	19	10	2	1	1
1990	Chicago	20	7	15	22	41	4	0	1
1991	Montreal	13	2	11	13	35	1	0	0
1992	Montreal	11	3	9	12	8	1	0	0
1993◆	Montreal	14	0	5	5	4	0	0	0
1995	Chicago	16	7	11	18	10	3	0	0
1996	Chicago	10	1	2	3	8	0	0	0
1997	Chicago	6	0	2	2	2	0	0	0
Playoff Totals		**169**	**66**	**109**	**175**	**256**	**24**	**2**	**6**
SAVARD, Jean *No playoffs* Center									
SAVARD, Marc *No playoffs* Center									
SAVARD, Serge Defense									
1968◆	Montreal	6	2	0	2	0	0	2	1
1969◆	Montreal	14	4	6	10	24	1	1	0
1972	Montreal	6	0	0	0	10	0	0	0
1973◆	Montreal	17	3	8	11	22	0	0	0
1974	Montreal	6	1	1	2	4	0	0	0
1975	Montreal	11	1	7	8	2	0	0	0
1976◆	Montreal	13	3	6	9	6	1	1	2
1977◆	Montreal	14	2	7	9	2	1	0	1
1978◆	Montreal	15	1	7	8	8	0	0	0
1979◆	Montreal	16	2	7	9	6	1	0	1
1980	Montreal	2	0	0	0	0	0	0	0
1981	Montreal	3	0	0	0	0	0	0	0
1982	Winnipeg	4	0	0	0	2	0	0	0
1983	Winnipeg	3	0	0	0	2	0	0	0
Playoff Totals		**130**	**19**	**49**	**68**	**88**	**4**	**4**	**5**
SAVOIA, Ryan *No playoffs* Center									
SAWYER, Kevin *No playoffs* Left wing									
SCAMURRA, Peter *No playoffs* Defense									
SCATCHARD, Dave *No playoffs* Center									
SCEVIOUR, Darin *No playoffs* Right wing									
SCHAEFER, Peter *No playoffs* Left wing									
SCHAEFFER, Butch *No playoffs* Defense									
SCHAMEHORN, Kevin *No playoffs* Right wing									
SCHASTLIVY, Petr *No playoffs* Left wing									
SCHELLA, John *No playoffs* Defense									
SCHERZA, Chuck *No playoffs* Left wing/center									
SCHINKEL, Ken Right wing									
1962	NY Rangers	2	1	0	1	0	0	0	0
1967	NY Rangers	4	0	1	1	0	0	0	0
1970	Pittsburgh	10	4	1	5	4	1	0	0
1972	Pittsburgh	3	2	0	2	0	0	0	0
Playoff Totals		**19**	**7**	**2**	**9**	**4**	**1**	**0**	**0**
SCHLEGEL, Brad Defense									
1992	Washington	7	0	1	1	2	0	0	0
Playoff Totals		**7**	**0**	**1**	**1**	**2**	**0**	**0**	**0**
SCHLIEBENER, Andy Defense									
1982	Vancouver	3	0	0	0	0	0	0	0
1984	Vancouver	3	0	0	0	0	0	0	0
Playoff Totals		**6**	**0**	**0**	**0**	**0**	**0**	**0**	**0**
SCHMAUTZ, Bobby Right wing									
1968	Chicago	11	2	3	5	2	0	0	1
1974	Boston	16	3	6	9	44	0	0	0
1975	Boston	3	1	5	6	6	0	0	0
1976	Boston	11	2	8	10	13	0	0	1
1977	Boston	14	*11	1	12	10	4	0	1
1978	Boston	15	7	8	15	11	2	0	1
1979	Boston	11	2	2	4	6	1	0	0
1981	Vancouver	3	0	0	0	0	0	0	0
Playoff Totals		**84**	**28**	**33**	**61**	**92**	**7**	**0**	**4**
SCHMAUTZ, Cliff *No playoffs* Right wing									
SCHMIDT, Clarence *No playoffs* Right wing									
SCHMIDT, Jackie Left wing									
1943	Boston	5	0	0	0	0	0	0	0
Playoff Totals		**5**	**0**	**0**	**0**	**0**	**0**	**0**	**0**
SCHMIDT, Joseph *No playoffs* Defense									
SCHMIDT, Milt Center/defense									
1937	Boston	3	0	0	0	0	....	....	....
1938	Boston	3	0	0	0	0	....	....	....
1939◆	Boston	12	3	3	6	2	....	....	....
1940	Boston	6	0	0	0	0	....	....	....
1941◆	Boston	11	5	6	*11	9	....	....	....
1946	Boston	10	3	5	8	2	....	....	....
1947	Boston	5	3	1	4	4	....	....	....
1948	Boston	5	2	5	7	2	....	....	....
1949	Boston	4	0	2	2	8	....	....	....
1951	Boston	6	0	1	1	7	....	....	....
1952	Boston	7	2	1	3	0	....	....	....
1953	Boston	10	5	1	6	6	....	....	....
1954	Boston	4	1	0	1	20	....	....	....
Playoff Totals		**86**	**24**	**25**	**49**	**60**	....	....	....
SCHMIDT, Norm *No playoffs* Defense									
SCHNARR, Werner *No playoffs* Center									
SCHNEIDER, Andy *No playoffs* Left wing									
SCHNEIDER, Mathieu Defense									
1990	Montreal	9	1	3	4	31	1	0	0
1991	Montreal	13	2	7	9	18	1	0	0
1992	Montreal	10	1	4	5	6	1	0	0
1993◆	Montreal	11	1	2	3	16	0	0	0
1994	Montreal	1	0	0	0	0	0	0	0
1996	Toronto	6	0	4	4	8	0	0	0
Playoff Totals		**50**	**5**	**20**	**25**	**79**	**3**	**0**	**0**
SCHOCK, Danny Left wing									
1970◆	Boston	1	0	0	0	0	0	0	0
Playoff Totals		**1**	**0**	**0**	**0**	**0**	**0**	**0**	**0**
SCHOCK, Ron Center									
1968	St. Louis	12	1	2	3	0	0	0	1
1969	St. Louis	12	1	2	3	6	0	0	0
1970	Pittsburgh	10	1	6	7	7	0	0	0
1972	Pittsburgh	4	1	0	1	6	0	0	0
1975	Pittsburgh	9	0	4	4	10	0	0	0
1976	Pittsburgh	3	0	1	1	0	0	0	0
1977	Pittsburgh	3	0	1	1	0	0	0	0
1978	Buffalo	2	0	0	0	0	0	0	0
Playoff Totals		**55**	**4**	**16**	**20**	**29**	**0**	**0**	**1**
SCHOENFELD, Jim Defense									
1973	Buffalo	6	2	1	3	4	0	0	0
1975	Buffalo	17	1	4	5	38	1	0	0
1976	Buffalo	8	0	3	3	33	0	0	0
1977	Buffalo	6	0	0	0	12	0	0	0
1978	Buffalo	8	0	1	1	28	0	0	0
1979	Buffalo	3	0	1	1	0	0	0	0
1980	Buffalo	14	0	3	3	18	0	0	0
1981	Buffalo	8	0	0	0	14	0	0	0
1985	Buffalo	5	0	0	0	4	0	0	0
Playoff Totals		**75**	**3**	**13**	**16**	**151**	**1**	**0**	**0**
SCHOFIELD, Dwight Defense									
1984	St. Louis	4	0	0	0	26	0	0	0
1985	St. Louis	2	0	0	0	15	0	0	0
1986	Washington	3	0	0	0	14	0	0	0
Playoff Totals		**9**	**0**	**0**	**0**	**55**	**0**	**0**	**0**
SCHREIBER, Wally *No playoffs* Right wing									
SCHRINER, Sweeney Left wing									
1936	NY Americans	5	3	1	4	2	....	....	....
1938	NY Americans	6	1	0	1	0	....	....	....
1939	NY Americans	2	0	0	0	30	....	....	....
1940	Toronto	9	1	3	4	4	....	....	....
1941	Toronto	7	2	1	3	4	....	....	....
1942◆	Toronto	13	6	3	9	10	....	....	....
1943	Toronto	4	2	2	4	0	....	....	....
1945◆	Toronto	13	3	1	4	4	....	....	....
Playoff Totals		**59**	**18**	**11**	**29**	**54**	....	....	....
SCHULTE, Paxton *No playoffs* Left wing									
SCHULTZ, Dave Left wing									
1973	Philadelphia	11	1	0	1	*51	0	0	0
1974◆	Philadelphia	17	2	4	6	*139	0	0	1
1975◆	Philadelphia	17	2	3	5	*83	0	0	0
1976	Philadelphia	16	2	2	4	*90	0	0	0
1977	Los Angeles	9	1	1	2	45	1	0	0
1979	Buffalo	3	0	2	2	4	0	0	0
Playoff Totals		**73**	**8**	**12**	**20**	**412**	**1**	**0**	**1**
SCHULTZ, Ray *No playoffs* Defense									
SCHURMAN, Maynard *No playoffs* Left wing									
SCHUTT, Rod Left wing									
1979	Pittsburgh	7	2	0	2	4	0	0	0
1980	Pittsburgh	5	2	1	3	6	0	0	0
1981	Pittsburgh	5	3	3	6	16	1	0	1
1982	Pittsburgh	5	1	2	3	0	0	0	0
Playoff Totals		**22**	**8**	**6**	**14**	**26**	**1**	**0**	**1**
SCISSONS, Scott Center									
1993	NY Islanders	1	0	0	0	0	0	0	0
Playoff Totals		**1**	**0**	**0**	**0**	**0**	**0**	**0**	**0**
SCLISIZZI, Enio Left wing									
1947	Detroit	1	0	0	0	0	0	0	0
1948	Detroit	6	0	0	0	4	0	0	0
1949	Detroit	6	0	0	0	2	0	0	0
Playoff Totals		**13**	**0**	**0**	**0**	**6**	**0**	**0**	**0**
SCOTT, Ganton *No playoffs* Right wing									
SCOTT, Laurie *No playoffs* Left wing/center									
SCOVILLE, Darryl *No playoffs* Defense									
SCREMIN, Claudio *No playoffs* Defense									
SCRUTON, Howard *No playoffs* Defense									
SEABROOKE, Glen *No playoffs* Center									
SECORD, Al Left wing									
1979	Boston	4	0	0	0	4	0	0	0
1980	Boston	10	0	3	3	65	0	0	0
1981	Chicago	3	4	0	4	14	0	0	0
1982	Chicago	15	2	5	7	61	2	0	1
1983	Chicago	12	4	7	11	66	1	0	0
1984	Chicago	5	3	4	7	28	0	0	1
1985	Chicago	15	7	9	16	42	1	0	1
1986	Chicago	2	0	2	2	26	0	0	0
1987	Chicago	4	0	0	0	21	0	0	0
1988	Toronto	6	1	0	1	16	0	0	0
1989	Philadelphia	14	0	4	4	31	0	0	0
1990	Chicago	12	0	0	0	8	0	0	0
Playoff Totals		**102**	**21**	**34**	**55**	**382**	**4**	**0**	**3**
SEDLBAUER, Ron Left wing									
1975	Vancouver	5	0	0	0	10	0	0	0
1976	Vancouver	2	0	0	0	0	0	0	0
1979	Vancouver	3	0	1	1	9	0	0	0
1980	Chicago	7	1	1	2	6	1	0	1
1981	Toronto	2	0	1	1	2	0	0	0
Playoff Totals		**19**	**1**	**3**	**4**	**27**	**1**	**0**	**1**

SEFTEL, Steve *No playoffs* Left wing

SEGUIN, Dan *No playoffs* Left wing

SEGUIN, Steve *No playoffs* Left/right wing

SEIBERT, Earl Defense

Season	Club	GP	G	A	Pts	PIM	PP	SH	GW
1932	NY Rangers	7	1	2	3	14	....	....	....
1933♦	NY Rangers	8	1	0	1	14	....	....	....
1934	NY Rangers	2	0	0	0	4	....	....	....
1935	NY Rangers	4	0	0	0	6	....	....	....
1936	Chicago	2	2	0	2	0	....	....	....
1938♦	Chicago	10	5	2	7	12	....	....	....
1940	Chicago	2	0	1	1	8	....	....	....
1941	Chicago	5	0	0	0	12	....	....	....
1942	Chicago	3	0	0	0	0	....	....	....
1944	Chicago	9	0	2	2	2	....	....	....
1945	Detroit	14	2	1	3	4	....	....	....
Playoff Totals		**66**	**11**	**8**	**19**	**76**	....	....	....

SEILING, Ric Right wing/center

Season	Club	GP	G	A	Pts	PIM	PP	SH	GW
1978	Buffalo	8	0	2	2	7	0	0	0
1979	Buffalo	3	0	1	1	2	0	0	0
1980	Buffalo	14	5	4	9	6	0	0	0
1981	Buffalo	8	2	2	4	2	0	0	0
1982	Buffalo	4	1	1	2	2	1	0	0
1983	Buffalo	10	2	3	5	6	0	0	0
1984	Buffalo	3	0	0	0	2	0	0	0
1985	Buffalo	5	4	1	5	4	0	0	0
1987	Detroit	7	0	0	0	5	0	0	0
Playoff Totals		**62**	**14**	**14**	**28**	**36**	**1**	**0**	**0**

SEILING, Rod Defense

Season	Club	GP	G	A	Pts	PIM	PP	SH	GW
1968	NY Rangers	6	1	1	2	4	0	0	0
1969	NY Rangers	4	1	0	1	2	0	0	0
1970	NY Rangers	2	0	0	0	0	0	0	0
1971	NY Rangers	13	1	0	1	12	0	0	0
1972	NY Rangers	16	1	4	5	10	1	0	0
1974	NY Rangers	13	0	2	2	19	0	0	0
1975	Toronto	7	0	0	0	0	0	0	0
1976	Toronto	10	0	1	1	6	0	0	0
1977	St. Louis	4	0	0	0	2	0	0	0
1979	Atlanta	2	0	0	0	0	0	0	0
Playoff Totals		**77**	**4**	**8**	**12**	**55**	**1**	**0**	**0**

SEJBA, Jiri *No playoffs* Left wing

SELANNE, Teemu Right wing

Season	Club	GP	G	A	Pts	PIM	PP	SH	GW
1993	Winnipeg	6	4	2	6	2	2	0	2
1997	Anaheim	11	7	3	10	4	3	0	1
1999	Anaheim	4	2	2	4	2	1	0	0
Playoff Totals		**21**	**13**	**7**	**20**	**8**	**6**	**0**	**3**

SELBY, Brit Left wing

Season	Club	GP	G	A	Pts	PIM	PP	SH	GW
1966	Toronto	4	0	0	0	0	0	0	0
1968	Philadelphia	7	1	1	2	4	0	0	0
1969	Toronto	4	0	0	0	4	0	0	0
1971	St. Louis	1	0	0	0	0	0	0	0
Playoff Totals		**16**	**1**	**1**	**2**	**8**	**0**	**0**	**0**

SELF, Steve *No playoffs* Center

SELIVANOV, Alex Right wing

Season	Club	GP	G	A	Pts	PIM	PP	SH	GW
1996	Tampa Bay	6	2	2	4	6	0	0	1
1999	Edmonton	2	0	1	1	2	0	0	0
Playoff Totals		**8**	**2**	**3**	**5**	**8**	**0**	**0**	**1**

SELWOOD, Brad Defense

Season	Club	GP	G	A	Pts	PIM	PP	SH	GW
1972	Toronto	5	0	0	0	4	0	0	0
1980	Los Angeles	1	0	0	0	0	0	0	0
Playoff Totals		**6**	**0**	**0**	**0**	**4**	**0**	**0**	**0**

SEMAK, Alexander Center

Season	Club	GP	G	A	Pts	PIM	PP	SH	GW
1992	New Jersey	1	0	0	0	0	0	0	0
1993	New Jersey	5	1	1	2	0	0	0	0
1994	New Jersey	2	0	0	0	0	0	0	0
Playoff Totals		**8**	**1**	**1**	**2**	**0**	**0**	**0**	**0**

SEMCHUK, Brandy *No playoffs* Right wing

SEMENKO, Dave Left wing

Season	Club	GP	G	A	Pts	PIM	PP	SH	GW
1980	Edmonton	3	0	0	0	2	0	0	0
1981	Edmonton	8	0	0	0	5	0	0	0
1982	Edmonton	4	0	0	0	2	0	0	0
1983	Edmonton	15	1	1	2	69	0	0	0
1984♦	Edmonton	19	5	5	10	44	0	0	1
1985♦	Edmonton	14	0	0	0	39	0	0	0
1986	Edmonton	6	0	0	0	32	0	0	0
1987	Hartford	4	0	0	0	15	0	0	0
Playoff Totals		**73**	**6**	**6**	**12**	**208**	**0**	**0**	**1**

SEMENOV, Anatoli Center/Left wing

Season	Club	GP	G	A	Pts	PIM	PP	SH	GW
1990♦	Edmonton	2	0	0	0	0	0	0	0
1991	Edmonton	12	5	5	10	6	0	0	0
1992	Edmonton	8	1	1	2	6	0	0	0
1993	Vancouver	12	1	3	4	0	0	0	0
1995	Philadelphia	15	2	4	6	0	0	0	0
Playoff Totals		**49**	**9**	**13**	**22**	**12**	**0**	**0**	**0**

SENICK, George *No playoffs* Left wing

SEPPA, Jyrki *No playoffs* Defense

SERAFINI, Ron *No playoffs* Defense

SEROWIK, Jeff *No playoffs* Defense

SERVINIS, George *No playoffs* Left wing

SEVCIK, Jaroslav *No playoffs* Left wing

SEVERYN, Brent Left wing

Season	Club	GP	G	A	Pts	PIM	PP	SH	GW
1997	Colorado	8	0	0	0	12	0	0	0
Playoff Totals		**8**	**0**	**0**	**0**	**12**	**0**	**0**	**0**

SEVIGNY, Pierre Left wing

Season	Club	GP	G	A	Pts	PIM	PP	SH	GW
1994	Montreal	3	0	1	1	0	0	0	0
Playoff Totals		**3**	**0**	**1**	**1**	**0**	**0**	**0**	**0**

SHACK, Eddie Left wing

Season	Club	GP	G	A	Pts	PIM	PP	SH	GW
1961	Toronto	4	0	0	0	2	0	0	0
1962♦	Toronto	9	0	0	0	18	0	0	0
1963♦	Toronto	10	2	1	3	11	0	0	2
1964♦	Toronto	13	0	1	1	25	0	0	0
1965	Toronto	5	1	0	1	8	0	0	0
1966	Toronto	4	2	1	3	33	1	0	0
1967♦	Toronto	8	0	0	0	8	0	0	0
1968	Boston	4	0	1	1	6	0	0	0
1969	Boston	9	0	2	2	23	0	0	0
1972	Pittsburgh	4	0	1	1	15	0	0	0
1974	Toronto	4	1	0	1	2	0	0	0
Playoff Totals		**74**	**6**	**7**	**13**	**151**	**1**	**0**	**2**

SHACK, Joe *No playoffs* Left wing

SHAFRANOV, Konstantin *No playoffs* Right wing

SHAKES, Paul *No playoffs* Defense

SHALDYBIN, Yevgeny *No playoffs* Defense

SHANAHAN, Brendan Left wing

Season	Club	GP	G	A	Pts	PIM	PP	SH	GW
1988	New Jersey	12	2	1	3	44	1	0	0
1990	New Jersey	6	3	3	6	20	1	0	1
1991	New Jersey	7	3	5	8	12	2	0	0
1992	St. Louis	6	2	3	5	14	1	0	0
1993	St. Louis	11	4	3	7	18	2	0	0
1994	St. Louis	4	2	5	7	4	0	0	0
1995	St. Louis	5	4	5	9	14	1	0	1
1997♦	Detroit	20	9	8	17	43	2	0	2
1998♦	Detroit	20	5	4	9	22	3	0	2
1999	Detroit	10	3	7	10	6	1	0	1
Playoff Totals		**101**	**37**	**44**	**81**	**197**	**14**	**0**	**7**

SHANAHAN, Sean *No playoffs* Center/right wing

SHAND, Dave Defense

Season	Club	GP	G	A	Pts	PIM	PP	SH	GW
1977	Atlanta	3	0	0	0	33	0	0	0
1978	Atlanta	2	0	0	0	4	0	0	0
1979	Atlanta	2	0	0	0	20	0	0	0
1980	Atlanta	4	0	1	1	0	0	0	0
1981	Toronto	3	0	0	0	0	0	0	0
1983	Toronto	4	1	0	1	13	0	0	0
1984	Washington	8	0	1	1	13	0	0	0
Playoff Totals		**26**	**1**	**2**	**3**	**83**	**0**	**0**	**0**

SHANK, Daniel Right wing

Season	Club	GP	G	A	Pts	PIM	PP	SH	GW
1992	Hartford	5	0	0	0	22	0	0	0
Playoff Totals		**5**	**0**	**0**	**0**	**22**	**0**	**0**	**0**

SHANNON, Chuck *No playoffs* Defense

SHANNON, Darrin Left wing

Season	Club	GP	G	A	Pts	PIM	PP	SH	GW
1989	Buffalo	2	0	0	0	0	0	0	0
1990	Buffalo	6	0	1	1	4	0	0	0
1991	Buffalo	6	1	2	3	4	0	0	0
1992	Winnipeg	7	0	1	1	10	0	0	0
1993	Winnipeg	6	2	4	6	6	1	0	0
1996	Winnipeg	6	1	0	1	6	0	0	0
1997	Phoenix	7	3	1	4	4	0	0	1
1998	Phoenix	5	0	1	1	4	0	0	0
Playoff Totals		**45**	**7**	**10**	**17**	**38**	**1**	**0**	**1**

SHANNON, Darryl Defense

Season	Club	GP	G	A	Pts	PIM	PP	SH	GW
1997	Buffalo	12	2	3	5	8	0	0	0
1998	Buffalo	15	2	4	6	8	0	1	0
1999	Buffalo	2	0	0	0	0	0	0	0
Playoff Totals		**29**	**4**	**7**	**11**	**16**	**0**	**1**	**0**

SHANNON, Gerry Left wing

Season	Club	GP	G	A	Pts	PIM	PP	SH	GW
1935	Boston	4	0	0	0	2	0	0	0
1937	Mtl. Maroons	5	0	1	1	0	0	0	0
Playoff Totals		**9**	**0**	**1**	**1**	**2**	**0**	**0**	**0**

SHANTZ, Jeff Center

Season	Club	GP	G	A	Pts	PIM	PP	SH	GW
1994	Chicago	6	0	0	0	6	0	0	0
1995	Chicago	16	3	1	4	2	0	0	0
1996	Chicago	10	2	3	5	6	0	0	0
1997	Chicago	6	0	4	4	6	0	0	0
Playoff Totals		**38**	**5**	**8**	**13**	**20**	**0**	**0**	**0**

SHARIFIJANOV, Vadim Right wing

Season	Club	GP	G	A	Pts	PIM	PP	SH	GW
1999	New Jersey	4	0	0	0	0	0	0	0
Playoff Totals		**4**	**0**	**0**	**0**	**0**	**0**	**0**	**0**

SHARPLES, Jeff Defense

Season	Club	GP	G	A	Pts	PIM	PP	SH	GW
1987	Detroit	2	0	0	0	2	0	0	0
1988	Detroit	4	0	3	3	4	0	0	0
1989	Detroit	1	0	0	0	0	0	0	0
Playoff Totals		**7**	**0**	**3**	**3**	**6**	**0**	**0**	**0**

SHARPLEY, Glen Center

Season	Club	GP	G	A	Pts	PIM	PP	SH	GW
1977	Minnesota	2	0	0	0	4	0	0	0
1980	Minnesota	9	1	6	7	4	0	0	0
1981	Chicago	1	0	2	2	0	0	0	0
1982	Chicago	15	6	3	9	16	0	0	0
Playoff Totals		**27**	**7**	**11**	**18**	**24**	**0**	**0**	**0**

SHAUNESSY, Scott *No playoffs* Defense/left wing

SHAW, Brad Defense

Season	Club	GP	G	A	Pts	PIM	PP	SH	GW
1989	Hartford	3	1	0	1	0	0	0	0
1990	Hartford	7	2	5	7	0	1	0	0
1991	Hartford	6	1	2	3	2	0	0	0
1992	Hartford	3	0	1	1	4	0	0	0
1999	St. Louis	4	0	0	0	0	0	0	0
Playoff Totals		**23**	**4**	**8**	**12**	**6**	**1**	**0**	**0**

SHAW, David Defense

Season	Club	GP	G	A	Pts	PIM	PP	SH	GW
1989	NY Rangers	4	0	2	2	30	0	0	0
1991	NY Rangers	6	0	0	0	11	0	0	0
1992	Minnesota	7	2	2	4	10	1	0	0
1993	Boston	4	0	1	1	6	0	0	0
1994	Boston	13	1	2	3	16	0	0	1
1995	Boston	5	0	1	1	4	0	0	0
1996	Tampa Bay	6	0	1	1	4	0	0	0
Playoff Totals		**45**	**3**	**9**	**12**	**81**	**1**	**0**	**1**

SHAY, Norman *No playoffs* Defense/right wing

SHEA, Pat *No playoffs* Defense

SHEDDEN, Doug *No playoffs* Center

SHEEHAN, Bobby Center

Season	Club	GP	G	A	Pts	PIM	PP	SH	GW
1971♦	Montreal	6	0	0	0	0	0	0	0
1976	Chicago	4	0	0	0	0	0	0	0
1979	NY Rangers	15	4	3	7	8	1	0	0
Playoff Totals		**25**	**4**	**3**	**7**	**8**	**1**	**0**	**0**

SHEEHY, Neil Defense

Season	Club	GP	G	A	Pts	PIM	PP	SH	GW
1984	Calgary	4	0	0	0	4	0	0	0
1986	Calgary	22	0	2	2	79	0	0	0
1987	Calgary	6	0	0	0	21	0	0	0
1988	Hartford	1	0	0	0	7	0	0	0
1989	Washington	6	0	0	0	19	0	0	0
1990	Washington	13	0	1	1	92	0	0	0
1991	Washington	2	0	0	0	19	0	0	0
Playoff Totals		**54**	**0**	**3**	**3**	**241**	**0**	**0**	**0**

SHEEHY, Tim *No playoffs* Right wing

SHELTON, Doug *No playoffs* Right wing

SHEPPARD, Frank *No playoffs* Center/left wing

SHEPPARD, Gregg Center

Season	Club	GP	G	A	Pts	PIM	PP	SH	GW
1973	Boston	5	2	1	3	0	0	1	1
1974	Boston	16	11	8	19	4	0	2	2
1975	Boston	3	3	1	4	5	0	0	0
1976	Boston	12	5	6	11	6	1	0	1
1977	Boston	14	5	7	12	8	1	1	2
1978	Boston	15	2	10	12	6	0	0	0
1979	Pittsburgh	7	1	2	3	0	1	0	0
1980	Pittsburgh	5	1	1	2	0	0	0	0
1981	Pittsburgh	5	2	4	6	2	1	0	0
Playoff Totals		**82**	**32**	**40**	**72**	**31**	**4**	**4**	**6**

SHEPPARD, Johnny Left wing

Season	Club	GP	G	A	Pts	PIM	PP	SH	GW
1929	NY Americans	2	0	0	0	0	0	0	0
1934♦	Chicago	8	0	0	0	0	0	0	0
Playoff Totals		**10**	**0**	**0**	**0**	**0**	**0**	**0**	**0**

SHEPPARD, Ray Right wing

Season	Club	GP	G	A	Pts	PIM	PP	SH	GW
1988	Buffalo	6	1	1	2	2	1	0	0
1989	Buffalo	1	0	1	1	0	0	0	0
1992	Detroit	11	6	2	8	4	3	0	0
1993	Detroit	7	2	3	5	0	2	0	0
1994	Detroit	7	2	1	3	4	0	0	0
1995	Detroit	17	4	3	7	5	2	0	0
1996	Florida	21	8	8	16	4	3	0	0
1997	Florida	5	2	0	2	0	1	0	0
1999	Carolina	6	5	1	6	2	1	0	1
Playoff Totals		**81**	**30**	**20**	**50**	**21**	**13**	**0**	**1**

SHERF, John Left wing

Season	Club	GP	G	A	Pts	PIM	PP	SH	GW
1937♦	Detroit	5	0	1	1	2	0	0	0
1939	Detroit	3	0	0	0	0	0	0	0
Playoff Totals		**8**	**0**	**1**	**1**	**2**	**0**	**0**	**0**

SHERO, Fred Defense

Season	Club	GP	G	A	Pts	PIM	PP	SH	GW
1948	NY Rangers	6	0	1	1	6	0	0	0
1950	NY Rangers	7	0	1	1	2	0	0	0
Playoff Totals		**13**	**0**	**2**	**2**	**8**	**0**	**0**	**0**

SHERRITT, Gordon *No playoffs* Defense

SHERVEN, Gord Center

Season	Club	GP	G	A	Pts	PIM	PP	SH	GW
1985	Minnesota	3	0	0	0	0	0	0	0
Playoff Totals		**3**	**0**	**0**	**0**	**0**	**0**	**0**	**0**

SHEVALIER, Jeff *No playoffs* Left wing

SHEWCHUCK, Jack Defense

Season	Club	GP	G	A	Pts	PIM	PP	SH	GW
1940	Boston	6	0	0	0	0	0	0	0
1942	Boston	5	0	1	1	7	0	0	0
1943	Boston	9	0	0	0	12	0	0	0
Playoff Totals		**20**	**0**	**1**	**1**	**19**	**0**	**0**	**0**

SHIBICKY, Alex Right wing

Season	Club	GP	G	A	Pts	PIM	PP	SH	GW
1937	NY Rangers	9	1	4	5	0	....	....	....
1938	NY Rangers	3	2	0	2	2	....	....	....
1939	NY Rangers	7	3	1	4	2	....	....	....
1940♦	NY Rangers	11	2	5	7	4	....	....	....
1941	NY Rangers	3	1	0	1	2	....	....	....
1942	NY Rangers	6	3	2	5	2	....	....	....
Playoff Totals		**39**	**12**	**12**	**24**	**12**	....	....	....

Season	Club	GP	G	A	Pts	PIM	PP	SH	GW
SHIELDS, Al	Defense								
1928	Ottawa	2	0	0	0	0	0	0	0
1930	Ottawa	2	0	0	0	0	0	0	0
1935◆	Mtl. Maroons	7	0	1	1	6	0	0	0
1936	Mtl. Maroons	3	0	0	0	6	0	0	0
1937	Boston	3	0	0	0	2	0	0	0
Playoff Totals		**17**	**0**	**1**	**1**	**14**	**0**	**0**	**0**
SHILL, Bill	Right wing								
1946	Boston	7	1	2	3	2	....	....	....
Playoff Totals		**7**	**1**	**2**	**3**	**2**	....	....	....
SHILL, Jack	Center								
1934	Toronto	2	0	0	0	0	....	....	....
1935	Boston	2	0	0	0	0	....	....	....
1936	Toronto	9	0	3	3	8	....	....	....
1937	Toronto	2	0	0	0	0	....	....	....
1938◆	Chicago	10	1	3	4	15	....	....	....
Playoff Totals		**25**	**1**	**6**	**7**	**23**	....	....	....
SHINSKE, Rick *No playoffs*	Center								
SHIRES, Jim *No playoffs*	Left wing								
SHMYR, Paul	Defense								
1970	Chicago	8	1	2	3	0	0	0	0
1971	Chicago	9	0	0	0	17	0	0	0
1980	Minnesota	14	2	1	3	23	1	0	1
1981	Minnesota	3	0	0	0	4	0	0	0
Playoff Totals		**34**	**3**	**3**	**6**	**44**	**1**	**0**	**1**
SHOEBOTTOM, Bruce	Defense								
1988	Boston	4	1	0	1	42	0	0	1
1989	Boston	10	0	2	2	35	0	0	0
Playoff Totals		**14**	**1**	**2**	**3**	**77**	**0**	**0**	**1**
SHORE, Eddie	Defense								
1927	Boston	8	1	1	2	*40	....	....	....
1928	Boston	2	0	0	0	8	....	....	....
1929◆	Boston	5	1	1	2	*28	....	....	....
1930	Boston	6	1	0	1	*26	....	....	....
1931	Boston	5	2	1	3	24	....	....	....
1933	Boston	5	0	1	1	14	....	....	....
1935	Boston	4	0	1	1	2	....	....	....
1936	Boston	2	1	1	2	12	....	....	....
1938	Boston	3	0	1	1	6	....	....	....
1939◆	Boston	12	0	4	4	19	....	....	....
1940	NY Americans	3	0	2	2	2	....	....	....
Playoff Totals		**55**	**6**	**13**	**19**	**181**	....	....	....
SHORE, Hamby *No playoffs*	Defense/left wing								
SHORT, Steve *No playoffs*	Left wing								
SHUCHUK, Gary	Right wing								
1991	Detroit	3	0	0	0	0	0	0	0
1993	Los Angeles	17	2	2	4	12	0	0	1
Playoff Totals		**20**	**2**	**2**	**4**	**12**	**0**	**0**	**1**
SHUDRA, Ron *No playoffs*	Defense								
SHUTT, Steve	Left wing								
1973◆	Montreal	1	0	0	0	0	0	0	0
1974	Montreal	6	5	3	8	9	1	0	0
1975	Montreal	9	1	6	7	4	0	0	0
1976◆	Montreal	13	7	8	15	2	3	0	0
1977◆	Montreal	14	8	10	18	2	2	0	3
1978◆	Montreal	15	9	8	17	20	3	0	0
1979◆	Montreal	11	4	7	11	6	1	0	0
1980	Montreal	10	6	3	9	6	2	0	2
1981	Montreal	3	2	1	3	4	0	0	0
1983	Montreal	3	1	0	1	0	0	0	0
1984	Montreal	11	7	2	9	8	2	0	0
1985	Los Angeles	3	0	0	0	4	0	0	0
Playoff Totals		**99**	**50**	**48**	**98**	**65**	**14**	**0**	**5**
SIEBERT, Babe	Left wing/defense								
1926◆	Mtl. Maroons	8	2	2	4	6	....	....	....
1927	Mtl. Maroons	2	1	0	1	2	....	....	....
1928	Mtl. Maroons	9	2	0	2	26	....	....	....
1930	Mtl. Maroons	3	0	0	0	0	....	....	....
1931	Mtl. Maroons	2	0	0	0	6	....	....	....
1932	Mtl. Maroons	4	0	1	1	4	....	....	....
1933◆	NY Rangers	8	1	0	1	12	....	....	....
1935	Boston	4	0	0	0	6	....	....	....
1936	Boston	2	0	1	1	0	....	....	....
1937	Mtl. Canadiens	5	1	2	3	2	....	....	....
1938	Mtl. Canadiens	3	1	1	2	0	....	....	....
1939	Mtl. Canadiens	3	0	0	0	0	....	....	....
Playoff Totals		**53**	**8**	**7**	**15**	**64**	....	....	....
SILK, Dave	Right wing								
1982	NY Rangers	9	2	4	6	4	0	0	1
1984	Boston	3	0	0	0	7	0	0	0
1986	Winnipeg	1	0	0	0	2	0	0	0
Playoff Totals		**13**	**2**	**4**	**6**	**13**	**0**	**0**	**1**
SILLINGER, Mike	Center								
1991	Detroit	3	0	1	1	0	0	0	0
1992	Detroit	8	2	2	4	2	0	0	0
1996	Vancouver	6	0	0	0	2	0	0	0
1998	Philadelphia	3	1	0	1	0	0	0	0
Playoff Totals		**20**	**3**	**3**	**6**	**4**	**0**	**0**	**0**
SILTALA, Mike *No playoffs*	Right wing								

Season	Club	GP	G	A	Pts	PIM	PP	SH	GW
SILTANEN, Risto	Defense								
1980	Edmonton	2	0	0	0	2	0	0	0
1981	Edmonton	9	2	0	2	8	2	0	1
1982	Edmonton	5	3	2	5	10	1	0	0
1986	Quebec	3	0	1	1	2	0	0	0
1987	Quebec	13	1	9	10	8	1	0	0
Playoff Totals		**32**	**6**	**12**	**18**	**30**	**4**	**0**	**1**
SIM, Jonathan	Center								
1999◆	Dallas	4	0	0	0	0	0	0	0
Playoff Totals		**4**	**0**	**0**	**0**	**0**	**0**	**0**	**0**
SIM, Trevor *No playoffs*	Right wing								
SIMARD, Martin *No playoffs*	Right wing								
SIMMER, Charlie	Left wing								
1979	Los Angeles	2	1	0	1	2	1	0	0
1980	Los Angeles	3	2	0	2	0	1	0	0
1982	Los Angeles	10	4	7	11	22	1	0	1
1985	Boston	5	2	2	4	2	0	0	0
1986	Boston	3	0	0	0	4	0	0	0
1987	Boston	1	0	0	0	2	0	0	0
Playoff Totals		**24**	**9**	**9**	**18**	**32**	**3**	**0**	**1**
SIMMONS, Al	Defense								
1974	Boston	1	0	0	0	0	0	0	0
Playoff Totals		**1**	**0**	**0**	**0**	**0**	**0**	**0**	**0**
SIMON, Chris	Left wing								
1993	Quebec	5	0	0	0	26	0	0	0
1995	Quebec	6	1	1	2	19	0	0	1
1996◆	Colorado	12	1	2	3	11	0	0	0
1998	Washington	18	1	0	1	26	0	0	0
Playoff Totals		**41**	**3**	**3**	**6**	**82**	**0**	**0**	**1**
SIMON, Cully	Defense								
1943◆	Detroit	9	0	1	1	4	0	0	0
1944	Detroit	5	0	0	0	2	0	0	0
Playoff Totals		**14**	**0**	**1**	**1**	**6**	**0**	**0**	**0**
SIMON, Jason *No playoffs*	Left wing								
SIMON, Thain *No playoffs*	Defense								
SIMON, Todd	Center								
1994	Buffalo	5	1	0	1	0	1	0	1
Playoff Totals		**5**	**1**	**0**	**1**	**0**	**1**	**0**	**1**
SIMONETTI, Frank	Defense								
1985	Boston	5	0	1	1	2	0	0	0
1986	Boston	3	0	0	0	0	0	0	0
1987	Boston	4	0	0	0	6	0	0	0
Playoff Totals		**12**	**0**	**1**	**1**	**8**	**0**	**0**	**0**
SIMPSON, Bobby	Left wing								
1977	Atlanta	2	0	1	1	0	0	0	0
1978	Atlanta	2	0	0	0	2	0	0	0
1982	Pittsburgh	2	0	0	0	0	0	0	0
Playoff Totals		**6**	**0**	**1**	**1**	**2**	**0**	**0**	**0**
SIMPSON, Cliff	Center								
1947	Detroit	1	0	0	0	0	0	0	0
1948	Detroit	1	0	0	0	2	0	0	0
Playoff Totals		**2**	**0**	**0**	**0**	**2**	**0**	**0**	**0**
SIMPSON, Craig	Left wing								
1988◆	Edmonton	19	13	6	19	26	3	0	3
1989	Edmonton	7	2	0	2	10	1	0	1
1990◆	Edmonton	22	*16	15	*31	8	6	0	3
1991	Edmonton	18	5	11	16	12	1	0	0
1992	Edmonton	1	0	0	0	0	0	0	0
Playoff Totals		**67**	**36**	**32**	**68**	**56**	**11**	**0**	**7**
SIMPSON, Joe	Defense								
1929	NY Americans	2	0	0	0	0	0	0	0
Playoff Totals		**2**	**0**	**0**	**0**	**0**	**0**	**0**	**0**
SIMPSON, Reid	Left wing								
1997	New Jersey	5	0	0	0	29	0	0	0
Playoff Totals		**5**	**0**	**0**	**0**	**29**	**0**	**0**	**0**
SIMPSON, Todd *No playoffs*	Defense								
SIMS, Al	Defense								
1974	Boston	16	0	0	0	12	0	0	0
1976	Boston	1	0	0	0	0	0	0	0
1977	Boston	2	0	0	0	0	0	0	0
1978	Boston	8	0	0	0	0	0	0	0
1979	Boston	11	0	2	2	0	0	0	0
1980	Hartford	3	0	0	0	2	0	0	0
Playoff Totals		**41**	**0**	**2**	**2**	**14**	**0**	**0**	**0**
SINCLAIR, Reg	Right wing/center								
1953	Detroit	3	1	0	1	0	....	....	....
Playoff Totals		**3**	**1**	**0**	**1**	**0**	....	....	....
SINGBUSH, Alex	Defense								
1941	Montreal	3	0	0	0	4	0	0	0
Playoff Totals		**3**	**0**	**0**	**0**	**4**	**0**	**0**	**0**

Season	Club	GP	G	A	Pts	PIM	PP	SH	GW
SINISALO, Ilkka	Right wing								
1982	Philadelphia	4	0	2	2	0	0	0	0
1983	Philadelphia	3	1	1	2	0	0	0	0
1984	Philadelphia	2	2	0	2	0	1	0	0
1985	Philadelphia	19	6	1	7	0	2	0	3
1986	Philadelphia	5	2	2	4	2	0	0	0
1987	Philadelphia	18	5	1	6	4	0	0	1
1988	Philadelphia	7	4	2	6	0	1	0	0
1989	Philadelphia	8	1	1	2	0	0	1	1
1991	Los Angeles	2	0	1	1	0	0	0	0
Playoff Totals		**68**	**21**	**11**	**32**	**6**	**4**	**1**	**5**
SIREN, Ville	Defense								
1989	Minnesota	4	0	0	0	4	0	0	0
1990	Minnesota	3	0	0	0	2	0	0	0
Playoff Totals		**7**	**0**	**0**	**0**	**6**	**0**	**0**	**0**
SIROIS, Bob *No playoffs*	Right wing								
SITTLER, Darryl	Center								
1971	Toronto	6	2	1	3	31	1	0	0
1972	Toronto	3	0	0	0	2	0	0	0
1974	Toronto	4	2	1	3	6	1	0	0
1975	Toronto	7	2	1	3	15	1	0	0
1976	Toronto	10	5	7	12	19	2	0	1
1977	Toronto	9	5	16	21	4	3	0	0
1978	Toronto	13	3	8	11	12	2	0	0
1979	Toronto	6	5	4	9	17	2	0	0
1980	Toronto	3	1	2	3	10	1	0	0
1981	Toronto	3	0	0	0	4	0	0	0
1982	Philadelphia	4	3	1	4	6	1	0	0
1983	Philadelphia	3	1	0	1	4	0	0	0
1984	Philadelphia	3	0	2	2	7	0	0	0
1985	Detroit	2	0	2	2	0	0	0	0
Playoff Totals		**76**	**29**	**45**	**74**	**137**	**14**	**0**	**1**
SJOBERG, Lars-Erik *No playoffs*	Defense								
SJODIN, Tommy *No playoffs*	Defense								
SKAARE, Bjorn *No playoffs*	Center								
SKALDE, Jarrod *No playoffs*	Center								
SKARDA, Randy *No playoffs*	Defense								
SKILTON, Raymie *No playoffs*	Defense								
SKINNER, Alf	Right wing								
1918◆	Toronto	7	8	3	11	27	....	....	....
Playoff Totals		**7**	**8**	**3**	**11**	**27**	....	....	....
SKINNER, Larry	Center								
1978	Colorado	2	0	0	0	0	0	0	0
Playoff Totals		**2**	**0**	**0**	**0**	**0**	**0**	**0**	**0**
SKOPINTSEV, Andrei *No playoffs*	Defense								
SKOULA, Martin *No playoffs*	Defense								
SKOV, Glen	Center/left wing								
1951	Detroit	6	0	0	0	0	....	....	....
1952◆	Detroit	8	1	4	5	16	....	....	....
1953	Detroit	6	1	0	1	2	....	....	....
1954◆	Detroit	12	1	2	3	16	....	....	....
1955◆	Detroit	11	2	0	2	8	....	....	....
1959	Chicago	6	2	1	3	4	....	....	....
1960	Chicago	4	0	0	0	2	....	....	....
Playoff Totals		**53**	**7**	**7**	**14**	**48**	....	....	....
SKRASTINS, Karlis *No playoffs*	Defense								
SKRBEK, Pavel *No playoffs*	Defense								
SKRIKO, Petri	Left wing								
1986	Vancouver	3	0	0	0	0	0	0	0
1989	Vancouver	7	1	5	6	0	0	0	0
1991	Boston	18	4	4	8	4	3	0	0
Playoff Totals		**28**	**5**	**9**	**14**	**4**	**3**	**0**	**0**
SKRUDLAND, Brian	Center								
1986◆	Montreal	20	2	4	6	76	0	0	1
1987	Montreal	14	1	5	6	29	0	0	0
1988	Montreal	11	1	5	6	24	0	0	0
1989	Montreal	21	3	7	10	40	0	0	0
1990	Montreal	11	3	5	8	30	0	0	1
1991	Montreal	13	3	10	13	42	1	0	0
1992	Montreal	11	1	1	2	20	0	0	0
1993	Calgary	6	0	3	3	12	0	0	0
1996	Florida	21	1	3	4	18	0	0	0
1998	Dallas	17	0	1	1	16	0	0	0
1999◆	Dallas	19	0	2	2	16	0	0	0
Playoff Totals		**164**	**15**	**46**	**61**	**323**	**1**	**0**	**2**
SLANEY, John	Defense								
1994	Washington	11	1	1	2	2	1	0	0
Playoff Totals		**11**	**1**	**1**	**2**	**2**	**1**	**0**	**0**
SLEAVER, John *No playoffs*	Center								
SLEGR, Jiri	Defense								
1993	Vancouver	5	0	3	3	4	0	0	0
1998	Pittsburgh	6	0	4	4	2	0	0	0
1999	Pittsburgh	13	1	3	4	12	0	0	1
Playoff Totals		**24**	**1**	**10**	**11**	**18**	**0**	**0**	**1**

Season	Club	GP	G	A	Pts	PIM	PP	SH	GW
SLEIGHER, Louis									Right wing
1983	Quebec	4	0	0	0	4	0	0	0
1984	Quebec	7	1	1	2	42	0	0	0
1985	Boston	5	0	0	0	4	0	0	0
1986	Boston	1	0	0	0	14	0	0	0
Playoff Totals		**17**	**1**	**1**	**2**	**64**	**0**	**0**	**0**
SLOAN, Blake									Right wing
1999◆	Dallas	19	0	2	2	8	0	0	0
Playoff Totals		**19**	**0**	**2**	**2**	**8**	**0**	**0**	**0**
SLOAN, Tod									Center/Right wing
1951◆	Toronto	11	4	5	9	18	....	....	....
1952	Toronto	4	0	0	0	10	....	....	....
1954	Toronto	5	1	1	2	4	....	....	....
1955	Toronto	4	0	0	0	2	....	....	....
1956	Toronto	2	0	0	0	5	....	....	....
1959	Chicago	6	3	5	8	0	....	....	....
1960	Chicago	3	0	0	0	0	....	....	....
1961◆	Chicago	12	1	1	2	8	....	....	....
Playoff Totals		**47**	**9**	**12**	**21**	**47**	....	....	....
SLOBODZIAN, Peter	*No playoffs*								Defense
SLOWINSKI, Eddie									Right wing
1948	NY Rangers	4	0	0	0	0	....	....	....
1950	NY Rangers	12	2	*6	8	6	....	....	....
Playoff Totals		**16**	**2**	**6**	**8**	**6**	....	....	....
SLY, Darryl	*No playoffs*								Defense
SMAIL, Doug									Left wing
1982	Winnipeg	4	0	0	0	0	0	0	0
1983	Winnipeg	3	0	0	0	6	0	0	0
1984	Winnipeg	3	0	1	1	7	0	0	0
1985	Winnipeg	8	2	1	3	4	0	1	0
1986	Winnipeg	3	1	0	1	0	0	0	0
1987	Winnipeg	10	4	0	4	10	0	1	0
1988	Winnipeg	5	1	0	1	22	0	0	0
1990	Winnipeg	5	1	0	1	0	0	0	0
1991	Minnesota	1	0	0	0	0	0	0	0
Playoff Totals		**42**	**9**	**2**	**11**	**49**	**0**	**2**	**0**
SMART, Alex	*No playoffs*								Left wing
SMEDSMO, Dale	*No playoffs*								Left wing
SMEHLIK, Richard									Defense
1993	Buffalo	8	0	4	4	2	0	0	0
1994	Buffalo	7	0	2	2	10	0	0	0
1995	Buffalo	5	0	0	0	2	0	0	0
1997	Buffalo	12	0	2	2	4	0	0	0
1998	Buffalo	15	0	2	2	6	0	0	0
1999	Buffalo	21	0	3	3	10	0	0	0
Playoff Totals		**68**	**0**	**13**	**13**	**34**	**0**	**0**	**0**
SMILLIE, Don	*No playoffs*								Left wing
SMITH, Alex									Defense
1926	Ottawa	2	0	0	0	14	0	0	0
1927◆	Ottawa	6	0	0	0	8	0	0	0
1928	Ottawa	2	0	0	0	4	0	0	0
1930	Ottawa	2	0	0	0	4	0	0	0
1932	Detroit	2	0	0	0	4	0	0	0
1933	Boston	5	0	2	2	6	0	0	0
Playoff Totals		**19**	**0**	**2**	**2**	**40**	**0**	**0**	**0**
SMITH, Art									Defense
1929	Toronto	4	1	1	2	8	....	....	....
Playoff Totals		**4**	**1**	**1**	**2**	**8**	....	....	....
SMITH, Barry	*No playoffs*								Center
SMITH, Bobby									Center
1980	Minnesota	15	1	13	14	9	1	0	0
1981	Minnesota	19	8	17	25	13	2	0	0
1982	Minnesota	4	2	4	6	5	0	0	0
1983	Minnesota	9	6	4	10	17	3	0	2
1984	Montreal	15	2	7	9	8	1	0	1
1985	Montreal	12	5	6	11	30	3	0	1
1986◆	Montreal	20	7	8	15	22	3	0	3
1987	Montreal	17	9	9	18	19	2	0	0
1988	Montreal	11	3	4	7	8	1	0	0
1989	Montreal	21	11	8	19	46	5	0	1
1990	Montreal	11	1	4	5	6	0	0	0
1991	Minnesota	23	8	8	16	56	2	0	5
1992	Minnesota	7	1	4	5	6	1	0	0
Playoff Totals		**184**	**64**	**96**	**160**	**245**	**24**	**0**	**13**
SMITH, Brad									Right wing
1985	Detroit	3	0	1	1	5	0	0	0
1986	Toronto	6	2	1	3	20	1	0	0
1987	Toronto	11	1	1	2	24	0	0	1
Playoff Totals		**20**	**3**	**3**	**6**	**49**	**1**	**0**	**1**
SMITH, Brandon	*No playoffs*								Defense
SMITH, Brian D.									Left wing
1968	Los Angeles	7	0	0	0	0	0	0	0
Playoff Totals		**7**	**0**	**0**	**0**	**0**	**0**	**0**	**0**
SMITH, Brian S.									Left wing
1960	Detroit	5	0	0	0	0	0	0	0
Playoff Totals		**5**	**0**	**0**	**0**	**0**	**0**	**0**	**0**
SMITH, Carl	*No playoffs*								Right wing
SMITH, Clint									Center
1938	NY Rangers	3	2	0	2	0	....	....	....
1939	NY Rangers	7	1	2	3	0	....	....	....
1940◆	NY Rangers	11	1	3	4	2	....	....	....
1941	NY Rangers	3	0	0	0	0	....	....	....
1942	NY Rangers	5	0	0	0	0	....	....	....
1944	Chicago	9	4	8	12	0	....	....	....
1946	Chicago	4	2	1	3	0	....	....	....
Playoff Totals		**42**	**10**	**14**	**24**	**2**	....	....	....
SMITH, D.J.	*No playoffs*								Defense
SMITH, Dallas									Defense
1968	Boston	4	0	2	2	0	0	0	0
1969	Boston	10	0	3	3	16	0	0	0
1970◆	Boston	14	0	3	3	19	0	0	0
1971	Boston	7	0	3	3	26	0	0	0
1972◆	Boston	15	0	4	4	22	0	0	0
1973	Boston	5	0	2	2	2	0	0	0
1974	Boston	16	1	7	8	20	0	0	0
1975	Boston	3	0	2	2	4	0	0	0
1976	Boston	11	2	2	4	19	0	0	1
1978	NY Rangers	1	0	1	1	0	0	0	0
Playoff Totals		**86**	**3**	**29**	**32**	**128**	**0**	**0**	**1**
SMITH, Dan	*No playoffs*								Defense
SMITH, Dennis	*No playoffs*								Defense
SMITH, Derek									Center/left wing
1976	Buffalo	1	0	0	0	0	0	0	0
1978	Buffalo	8	3	3	6	7	0	0	0
1980	Buffalo	13	5	7	12	4	3	0	1
1981	Buffalo	8	1	4	5	2	1	0	0
Playoff Totals		**30**	**9**	**14**	**23**	**13**	**4**	**0**	**1**
SMITH, Derrick									Left wing
1985	Philadelphia	19	2	5	7	16	0	0	0
1986	Philadelphia	4	0	0	0	10	0	0	0
1987	Philadelphia	26	6	4	10	26	0	0	1
1988	Philadelphia	7	0	0	0	6	0	0	0
1989	Philadelphia	19	5	2	7	12	0	2	1
1992	Minnesota	7	1	0	1	9	0	0	1
Playoff Totals		**82**	**14**	**11**	**25**	**79**	**0**	**2**	**3**
SMITH, Des									Defense
1939	Mtl. Canadiens	3	0	0	0	4	....	....	....
1940	Boston	6	0	0	0	0	....	....	....
1941◆	Boston	11	0	2	2	12	....	....	....
1942	Boston	5	1	2	3	2	....	....	....
Playoff Totals		**25**	**1**	**4**	**5**	**18**	....	....	....
SMITH, Don A.									Left wing/center
1950	NY Rangers	1	0	0	0	0	0	0	0
Playoff Totals		**1**	**0**	**0**	**0**	**0**	**0**	**0**	**0**
SMITH, Don	*No playoffs*								Left wing/center
SMITH, Doug									Center
1982	Los Angeles	10	3	2	5	11	1	0	0
1985	Los Angeles	3	1	0	1	4	0	0	0
1988	Buffalo	1	0	0	0	0	0	0	0
1989	Vancouver	4	0	0	0	6	0	0	0
Playoff Totals		**18**	**4**	**2**	**6**	**21**	**1**	**0**	**0**
SMITH, Floyd									Right wing
1963	Detroit	11	2	3	5	4	0	0	0
1964	Detroit	14	4	3	7	4	2	0	0
1965	Detroit	7	1	3	4	4	0	0	0
1966	Detroit	12	5	2	7	4	2	0	1
1969	Toronto	4	0	0	0	0	0	0	0
Playoff Totals		**48**	**12**	**11**	**23**	**16**	**4**	**0**	**1**
SMITH, Geoff									Defense
1990◆	Edmonton	3	0	0	0	0	0	0	0
1991	Edmonton	4	0	0	0	0	0	0	0
1992	Edmonton	5	0	1	1	6	0	0	0
1996	Florida	1	0	0	0	2	0	0	0
Playoff Totals		**13**	**0**	**1**	**1**	**8**	**0**	**0**	**0**
SMITH, Glen	*No playoffs*								Right wing
SMITH, Glenn	*No playoffs*								Defense
SMITH, Gord	*No playoffs*								Defense
SMITH, Greg									Defense
1980	Minnesota	12	0	1	1	9	0	0	0
1981	Minnesota	19	1	5	6	39	0	1	0
1984	Detroit	4	1	0	1	8	0	0	0
1985	Detroit	3	0	0	0	7	0	0	0
1986	Washington	9	2	1	3	9	0	1	0
1987	Washington	7	0	0	0	11	0	0	0
1988	Washington	9	0	0	0	23	0	0	0
Playoff Totals		**63**	**4**	**7**	**11**	**106**	**0**	**2**	**0**
SMITH, Hooley									Center/right wing
1926	Ottawa	2	0	0	0	14	....	....	....
1927◆	Ottawa	6	1	0	1	16	....	....	....
1928	Mtl. Maroons	9	2	1	3	23	....	....	....
1930	Mtl. Maroons	4	1	1	2	14	....	....	....
1932	Mtl. Maroons	4	2	1	3	2	....	....	....
1933	Mtl. Maroons	2	2	0	2	2	....	....	....
1934	Mtl. Maroons	4	0	1	1	6	....	....	....
1935◆	Mtl. Maroons	6	0	0	0	14	....	....	....
1936	Mtl. Maroons	3	0	0	0	2	....	....	....
1937	Boston	3	0	0	0	0	....	....	....
1938	NY Americans	6	0	3	3	0	....	....	....
1939	NY Americans	2	0	0	0	14	....	....	....
1940	NY Americans	3	3	1	4	2	....	....	....
Playoff Totals		**54**	**11**	**8**	**19**	**109**	....	....	....
SMITH, Jason									Defense
1994	New Jersey	6	0	0	0	7	0	0	0
1999	Edmonton	4	0	1	1	4	0	0	0
Playoff Totals		**10**	**0**	**1**	**1**	**11**	**0**	**0**	**0**
SMITH, Kenny									Left wing
1945	Boston	7	3	4	7	0	....	....	....
1946	Boston	8	0	4	4	0	....	....	....
1947	Boston	5	3	0	3	2	....	....	....
1948	Boston	5	2	3	5	0	....	....	....
1949	Boston	5	0	2	2	4	....	....	....
Playoff Totals		**30**	**8**	**13**	**21**	**6**	....	....	....
SMITH, Nakina	*No playoffs*								Center
SMITH, Randy	*No playoffs*								Center
SMITH, Rick									Defense
1969	Boston	9	0	0	0	6	0	0	0
1970◆	Boston	14	1	3	4	17	0	0	0
1971	Boston	6	0	0	0	0	0	0	0
1976	St. Louis	3	0	1	1	4	0	0	0
1977	Boston	14	0	9	9	14	0	0	0
1978	Boston	15	1	5	6	18	0	0	0
1979	Boston	11	0	4	4	12	0	0	0
1980	Boston	6	1	1	2	2	0	0	0
Playoff Totals		**78**	**3**	**23**	**26**	**73**	**0**	**0**	**0**
SMITH, Rodger									Defense
1926	Pittsburgh	2	1	0	1	0	....	....	....
1928	Pittsburgh	2	2	0	2	0	....	....	....
Playoff Totals		**4**	**3**	**0**	**3**	**0**	....	....	....
SMITH, Ron	*No playoffs*								Defense
SMITH, Sid									Left wing
1948◆	Toronto	2	0	0	0	0	....	....	....
1949◆	Toronto	6	5	2	7	0	....	....	....
1950	Toronto	7	0	3	3	2	....	....	....
1951◆	Toronto	11	7	3	10	0	....	....	....
1952	Toronto	4	0	0	0	0	....	....	....
1954	Toronto	5	1	1	2	0	....	....	....
1955	Toronto	4	3	1	4	0	....	....	....
1956	Toronto	5	1	0	1	0	....	....	....
Playoff Totals		**44**	**17**	**10**	**27**	**2**	....	....	....
SMITH, Stan									Center
1940◆	NY Rangers	1	0	0	0	0	0	0	0
Playoff Totals		**1**	**0**	**0**	**0**	**0**	**0**	**0**	**0**
SMITH, Steve	*No playoffs*								Defense
SMITH, Steve									Defense
1986	Edmonton	6	0	1	1	14	0	0	0
1987◆	Edmonton	15	1	3	4	45	0	0	0
1988◆	Edmonton	19	1	11	12	55	1	0	0
1989	Edmonton	7	2	2	4	20	0	0	1
1990◆	Edmonton	22	5	10	15	37	0	1	1
1991	Edmonton	18	1	2	3	45	1	0	0
1992	Chicago	18	1	11	12	16	1	0	0
1993	Chicago	4	0	0	0	10	0	0	0
1995	Chicago	16	0	1	1	26	0	0	0
1996	Chicago	6	0	0	0	16	0	0	0
1997	Chicago	3	0	0	0	4	0	0	0
Playoff Totals		**134**	**11**	**41**	**52**	**288**	**3**	**1**	**2**
SMITH, Stu									Left wing
1941	Montreal	1	0	0	0	0	0	0	0
Playoff Totals		**1**	**0**	**0**	**0**	**0**	**0**	**0**	**0**
SMITH, Stu	*No playoffs*								Defense
SMITH, Tommy	*No playoffs*								Center
SMITH, Vern	*No playoffs*								Defense
SMITH, Wayne									Defense
1967	Chicago	1	0	0	0	0	0	0	0
Playoff Totals		**1**	**0**	**0**	**0**	**0**	**0**	**0**	**0**
SMOLINSKI, Bryan									Center/Right wing
1993	Boston	4	1	0	1	2	0	0	0
1994	Boston	13	5	4	9	4	2	0	0
1995	Boston	5	0	1	1	4	0	0	0
1996	Pittsburgh	18	5	4	9	10	0	0	1
Playoff Totals		**40**	**11**	**9**	**20**	**20**	**2**	**0**	**1**
SMRKE, John	*No playoffs*								Left wing
SMRKE, Stan	*No playoffs*								Left wing

Season	Club	GP	G	A	Pts	PIM	PP	SH	GW
SMYL, Stan	Right wing								
1979	Vancouver	2	1	1	2	0	0	0	0
1980	Vancouver	4	0	2	2	14	0	0	0
1981	Vancouver	3	1	2	3	0	0	0	0
1982	Vancouver	17	9	9	18	25	1	0	1
1983	Vancouver	4	3	2	5	12	1	0	1
1984	Vancouver	4	2	1	3	4	0	0	0
1989	Vancouver	7	0	0	0	9	0	0	0
Playoff Totals		**41**	**16**	**17**	**33**	**64**	**2**	**0**	**2**
SMYLIE, Rod	Right/left wing								
1921	Toronto	2	0	0	0	0	....	....	....
1922◆	Toronto	6	1	*3	4	2	....	....	....
1925	Toronto	1	0	0	0	0	....	....	....
Playoff Totals		**9**	**1**	**3**	**4**	**2**	....	....	....
SMYTH, Brad *No playoffs*	Right wing								
SMYTH, Greg	Defense								
1987	Philadelphia	1	0	0	0	2	0	0	0
1988	Philadelphia	5	0	0	0	38	0	0	0
1994	Chicago	6	0	0	0	0	0	0	0
Playoff Totals		**12**	**0**	**0**	**0**	**40**	**0**	**0**	**0**
SMYTH, Kevin *No playoffs*	Left wing								
SMYTH, Ryan	Left wing								
1997	Edmonton	12	5	5	10	12	1	0	2
1998	Edmonton	12	1	3	4	16	1	0	0
1999	Edmonton	3	3	0	3	0	2	0	0
Playoff Totals		**27**	**9**	**8**	**17**	**28**	**4**	**0**	**2**
SNELL, Chris *No playoffs*	Defense								
SNELL, Ron *No playoffs*	Right wing								
SNELL, Ted *No playoffs*	Right wing								
SNEPSTS, Harold	Defense								
1976	Vancouver	2	0	0	0	4	0	0	0
1979	Vancouver	3	0	0	0	0	0	0	0
1980	Vancouver	4	0	2	2	8	0	0	0
1981	Vancouver	3	0	0	0	8	0	0	0
1982	Vancouver	17	0	4	4	50	0	0	0
1983	Vancouver	4	1	1	2	8	0	0	0
1984	Vancouver	4	0	1	1	15	0	0	0
1985	Minnesota	9	0	0	0	24	0	0	0
1987	Detroit	11	0	2	2	18	0	0	0
1988	Detroit	10	0	0	0	40	0	0	0
1989	Vancouver	7	0	1	1	6	0	0	0
1990	St. Louis	11	0	3	3	38	0	0	0
1991	St. Louis	8	0	0	0	12	0	0	0
Playoff Totals		**93**	**1**	**14**	**15**	**231**	**0**	**0**	**0**
SNOW, Sandy *No playoffs*	Right wing								
SNUGGERUD, Dave	Right wing								
1990	Buffalo	6	0	0	0	2	0	0	0
1991	Buffalo	6	1	3	4	4	0	1	0
Playoff Totals		**12**	**1**	**3**	**4**	**6**	**0**	**1**	**0**
SOBCHUK, Dennis *No playoffs*	Center								
SOBCHUK, Gene *No playoffs*	Left wing/center								
SOLHEIM, Ken	Left wing								
1981	Minnesota	2	1	0	1	0	0	0	0
1982	Minnesota	1	0	1	1	2	0	0	0
Playoff Totals		**3**	**1**	**1**	**2**	**2**	**0**	**0**	**0**
SOLINGER, Bob *No playoffs*	Right/left wing								
SOMERS, Art	Center								
1930	Chicago	2	0	0	0	2	....	....	....
1931	Chicago	9	0	0	0	0	....	....	....
1932	NY Rangers	7	0	1	1	8	....	....	....
1933◆	NY Rangers	8	1	*4	5	8	....	....	....
1934	NY Rangers	2	0	0	0	0	....	....	....
1935	NY Rangers	2	0	0	0	2	....	....	....
Playoff Totals		**30**	**1**	**5**	**6**	**20**	....	....	....
SOMMER, Roy *No playoffs*	Left wing/center								
SONGIN, Tom *No playoffs*	Right wing								
SONMOR, Glen *No playoffs*	Left wing								
SONNENBERG, Martin *No playoffs*	Left wing								
SOPEL, Brent *No playoffs*	Defense								
SOROCHAN, Lee *No playoffs*	Defense								
SORRELL, John	Left wing								
1932	Detroit	2	1	0	1	0	....	....	....
1933	Detroit	4	2	2	4	4	....	....	....
1934	Detroit	8	0	2	2	0	....	....	....
1936◆	Detroit	7	3	4	7	0	....	....	....
1937◆	Detroit	10	2	4	6	2	....	....	....
1938	NY Americans	6	4	0	4	2	....	....	....
1939	NY Americans	2	0	0	0	0	....	....	....
1940	NY Americans	3	0	3	3	2	....	....	....
Playoff Totals		**42**	**12**	**15**	**27**	**10**	....	....	....
SOURAY, Sheldon	Defense								
1998	New Jersey	3	0	1	1	2	0	0	0
1999	New Jersey	2	0	1	1	0	0	0	0
Playoff Totals		**5**	**0**	**2**	**2**	**2**	**0**	**0**	**0**
SPACEK, Jaroslav *No playoffs*	Defense								
SPARROW, Emory *No playoffs*	Right wing/center								
SPECK, Fred *No playoffs*	Center								

Season	Club	GP	G	A	Pts	PIM	PP	SH	GW
SPEER, Bill	Defense								
1970◆	Boston	8	1	0	1	4	0	0	0
Playoff Totals		**8**	**1**	**0**	**1**	**4**	**0**	**0**	**0**
SPEERS, Ted *No playoffs*	Right wing								
SPENCE, Gordon *No playoffs*	Left wing								
SPENCER, Brian	Left wing								
1971	Toronto	6	0	1	1	17	0	0	0
1975	Buffalo	16	0	4	4	8	0	0	0
1976	Buffalo	9	1	0	1	4	0	0	0
1977	Buffalo	6	0	0	0	0	0	0	0
Playoff Totals		**37**	**1**	**5**	**6**	**29**	**0**	**0**	**0**
SPENCER, Irv	Defense								
1962	NY Rangers	1	0	0	0	2	0	0	0
1964	Detroit	11	0	0	0	0	0	0	0
1965	Detroit	1	0	0	0	4	0	0	0
1966	Detroit	3	0	0	0	2	0	0	0
Playoff Totals		**16**	**0**	**0**	**0**	**8**	**0**	**0**	**0**
SPEYER, Chris *No playoffs*	Defense								
SPRING, Corey *No playoffs*	Right wing								
SPRING, Don	Defense								
1982	Winnipeg	4	0	0	0	4	0	0	0
1983	Winnipeg	2	0	0	0	6	0	0	0
Playoff Totals		**6**	**0**	**0**	**0**	**10**	**0**	**0**	**0**
SPRING, Frank *No playoffs*	Right wing								
SPRING, Jesse	Defense								
1926	Pittsburgh	2	0	2	2	2	0	0	0
Playoff Totals		**2**	**0**	**2**	**2**	**2**	**0**	**0**	**0**
SPRUCE, Andy	Left wing								
1978	Colorado	2	0	2	2	0	0	0	0
Playoff Totals		**2**	**0**	**2**	**2**	**0**	**0**	**0**	**0**
SRSEN, Tomas *No playoffs*	Right wing								
STACKHOUSE, Ron	Defense								
1975	Pittsburgh	9	2	6	8	10	1	0	0
1976	Pittsburgh	3	0	0	0	0	0	0	0
1977	Pittsburgh	3	2	1	3	0	0	0	0
1979	Pittsburgh	7	0	0	0	4	0	0	0
1980	Pittsburgh	5	1	0	1	18	1	0	0
1981	Pittsburgh	4	0	1	1	6	0	0	0
1982	Pittsburgh	1	0	0	0	0	0	0	0
Playoff Totals		**32**	**5**	**8**	**13**	**38**	**2**	**0**	**0**
STACKHOUSE, Ted	Defense								
1922◆	Toronto	5	0	0	0	0	0	0	0
Playoff Totals		**5**	**0**	**0**	**0**	**0**	**0**	**0**	**0**
STAHAN, Butch	Defense								
1945	Montreal	3	0	1	1	2	0	0	0
Playoff Totals		**3**	**0**	**1**	**1**	**2**	**0**	**0**	**0**
STAIOS, Steve	Defense/Right wing								
1996	Boston	3	0	0	0	0	0	0	0
Playoff Totals		**3**	**0**	**0**	**0**	**0**	**0**	**0**	**0**
STAJDUHAR, Nick *No playoffs*	Defense								
STALEY, Al *No playoffs*	Center								
STAMLER, Lorne *No playoffs*	Left wing								
STANDING, George *No playoffs*	Right wing								
STANFIELD, Fred	Left wing								
1965	Chicago	14	2	1	3	2	0	0	0
1966	Chicago	5	0	0	0	2	0	0	0
1967	Chicago	1	0	0	0	0	0	0	0
1968	Boston	4	0	1	1	0	0	0	0
1969	Boston	10	2	2	4	0	1	0	0
1970◆	Boston	14	4	12	16	6	2	0	0
1971	Boston	7	3	4	7	0	1	0	0
1972◆	Boston	15	7	9	16	0	1	0	0
1973	Boston	5	1	1	2	0	0	0	0
1975	Buffalo	17	2	4	6	0	0	0	0
1976	Buffalo	9	0	1	1	0	0	0	0
1977	Buffalo	5	0	0	0	0	0	0	0
Playoff Totals		**106**	**21**	**35**	**56**	**10**	**5**	**0**	**0**
STANFIELD, Jack	Left wing								
1966	Chicago	1	0	0	0	0	0	0	0
Playoff Totals		**1**	**0**	**0**	**0**	**0**	**0**	**0**	**0**
STANFIELD, Jim *No playoffs*	Center/right wing								
STANKIEWICZ, Ed *No playoffs*	Center								
STANKIEWICZ, Myron	Left wing								
1969	Philadelphia	1	0	0	0	0	0	0	0
Playoff Totals		**1**	**0**	**0**	**0**	**0**	**0**	**0**	**0**

Season	Club	GP	G	A	Pts	PIM	PP	SH	GW
STANLEY, Allan	Defense								
1950	NY Rangers	12	2	5	7	10	....	....	....
1958	Boston	12	1	3	4	6	....	....	....
1959	Toronto	12	0	3	3	2	....	....	....
1960	Toronto	10	2	3	5	2	....	....	....
1961	Toronto	5	0	3	3	0	....	....	....
1962◆	Toronto	12	0	3	3	6	....	....	....
1963◆	Toronto	10	1	6	7	8	....	....	....
1964◆	Toronto	14	1	6	7	20	....	....	....
1965	Toronto	6	0	1	1	12	....	....	....
1966	Toronto	1	0	0	0	0	....	....	....
1967◆	Toronto	12	0	2	2	10	....	....	....
1969	Philadelphia	3	0	1	1	4	0	0	0
Playoff Totals		**109**	**7**	**36**	**43**	**80**	....	....	....
STANLEY, Barney *No playoffs*	Right wing								
STANLEY, Daryl	Defense/left wing								
1984	Philadelphia	3	0	0	0	19	0	0	0
1986	Philadelphia	1	0	0	0	2	0	0	0
1987	Philadelphia	13	0	0	0	9	0	0	0
Playoff Totals		**17**	**0**	**0**	**0**	**30**	**0**	**0**	**0**
STANOWSKI, Wally	Defense								
1940	Toronto	10	1	0	1	2	....	....	....
1941	Toronto	7	0	3	3	2	....	....	....
1942◆	Toronto	13	2	8	10	2	....	....	....
1945◆	Toronto	13	0	1	1	5	....	....	....
1947◆	Toronto	8	0	0	0	0	....	....	....
1948◆	Toronto	9	0	2	2	2	....	....	....
Playoff Totals		**60**	**3**	**14**	**17**	**13**	....	....	....
STANTON, Paul	Defense								
1991◆	Pittsburgh	22	1	2	3	24	0	0	0
1992◆	Pittsburgh	21	1	7	8	42	0	0	0
1993	Pittsburgh	1	0	1	1	0	0	0	0
Playoff Totals		**44**	**2**	**10**	**12**	**66**	**0**	**0**	**0**
STAPLETON, Brian *No playoffs*	Right wing								
STAPLETON, Mike	Center								
1987	Chicago	4	0	0	0	2	0	0	0
1993	Pittsburgh	4	0	0	0	0	0	0	0
1996	Winnipeg	6	0	0	0	21	0	0	0
1997	Phoenix	7	0	0	0	14	0	0	0
1998	Phoenix	6	0	0	0	2	0	0	0
1999	Phoenix	7	1	0	1	0	0	0	0
Playoff Totals		**34**	**1**	**0**	**1**	**39**	**0**	**0**	**0**
STAPLETON, Pat	Defense								
1966	Chicago	6	2	3	5	4	1	0	0
1967	Chicago	6	1	1	2	12	0	0	0
1968	Chicago	11	0	4	4	4	0	0	0
1971	Chicago	18	3	14	17	4	1	1	0
1972	Chicago	8	2	2	4	4	2	0	0
1973	Chicago	16	2	*15	17	10	1	0	0
Playoff Totals		**65**	**10**	**39**	**49**	**38**	**5**	**1**	**0**
STARIKOV, Sergei *No playoffs*	Defense								
STARR, Harold	Defense								
1930	Ottawa	2	1	0	1	0	....	....	....
1932	Mtl. Maroons	4	0	0	0	0	....	....	....
1933	Mtl. Canadiens	2	0	0	0	2	....	....	....
1934	Mtl. Maroons	3	0	0	0	0	....	....	....
1935	NY Rangers	4	0	0	0	2	....	....	....
Playoff Totals		**15**	**1**	**0**	**1**	**4**	....	....	....
STARR, Wilf	Center								
1934	Detroit	7	0	2	2	2	0	0	0
Playoff Totals		**7**	**0**	**2**	**2**	**2**	**0**	**0**	**0**
STASIUK, Vic	Left wing								
1952◆	Detroit	7	0	2	2	0	....	....	....
1955◆	Detroit	11	5	3	8	6	....	....	....
1957	Boston	10	2	1	3	2	....	....	....
1958	Boston	12	0	5	5	13	....	....	....
1959	Boston	7	4	2	6	11	....	....	....
1961	Detroit	11	2	5	7	4	....	....	....
1963	Detroit	11	3	0	3	4	....	....	....
Playoff Totals		**69**	**16**	**18**	**34**	**40**	....	....	....
STASTNY, Anton	Left wing								
1981	Quebec	5	4	3	7	2	2	0	0
1982	Quebec	16	5	10	15	10	3	0	0
1983	Quebec	4	2	2	4	0	0	0	0
1984	Quebec	9	2	5	7	7	0	0	0
1985	Quebec	16	3	3	6	6	1	0	1
1986	Quebec	3	1	1	2	0	0	0	0
1987	Quebec	13	3	8	11	6	0	0	0
Playoff Totals		**66**	**20**	**32**	**52**	**31**	**6**	**0**	**1**
STASTNY, Marian	Right wing								
1982	Quebec	16	3	14	17	5	1	0	0
1983	Quebec	2	0	0	0	0	0	0	0
1984	Quebec	9	2	3	5	2	0	0	1
1985	Quebec	2	0	0	0	0	0	0	0
1986	Toronto	3	0	0	0	0	0	0	0
Playoff Totals		**32**	**5**	**17**	**22**	**7**	**1**	**0**	**1**

Season	Club	GP	G	A	Pts	PIM	PP	SH	GW
STASTNY, Peter									Center
1981	Quebec	5	2	8	10	7	1	0	0
1982	Quebec	12	7	11	18	10	4	0	1
1983	Quebec	4	3	2	5	10	1	0	0
1984	Quebec	9	2	7	9	31	2	0	0
1985	Quebec	18	4	19	23	24	1	0	2
1986	Quebec	3	0	1	1	2	0	0	0
1987	Quebec	13	6	9	15	12	2	1	1
1990	New Jersey	6	3	2	5	2	1	0	1
1991	New Jersey	7	3	4	7	2	1	0	2
1992	New Jersey	7	3	7	10	19	0	0	0
1993	New Jersey	5	0	2	2	2	0	0	0
1994	St. Louis	4	0	0	0	2	0	0	0
Playoff Totals		**93**	**33**	**72**	**105**	**123**	**13**	**1**	**7**
STASZAK, Ray *No playoffs*									Right wing
STEELE, Frank *No playoffs*									Right wing/defense
STEEN, Anders *No playoffs*									Center
STEEN, Thomas									Center
1982	Winnipeg	4	0	4	4	2	0	0	0
1983	Winnipeg	3	0	2	2	0	0	0	0
1984	Winnipeg	3	0	1	1	9	0	0	0
1985	Winnipeg	8	2	3	5	17	2	0	0
1986	Winnipeg	3	1	1	2	4	0	1	0
1987	Winnipeg	10	3	4	7	8	0	1	1
1988	Winnipeg	5	1	5	6	2	1	0	0
1990	Winnipeg	7	2	5	7	16	1	0	0
1992	Winnipeg	7	2	4	6	2	2	0	0
1993	Winnipeg	6	1	3	4	2	1	0	0
Playoff Totals		**56**	**12**	**32**	**44**	**62**	**7**	**2**	**1**
STEFAN, Patrik *No playoffs*									Center
STEFANIW, Morris *No playoffs*									Center
STEFANSKI, Bud *No playoffs*									Center
STEINBERG, Trevor									Right wing
1986	Quebec	1	0	0	0	0	0	0	0
Playoff Totals		**1**	**0**	**0**	**0**	**0**	**0**	**0**	**0**
STEMKOWSKI, Pete									Center
1965	Toronto	6	0	3	3	7	0	0	0
1966	Toronto	4	0	0	0	26	0	0	0
1967◆	Toronto	12	5	7	12	20	2	0	2
1970	Detroit	4	1	1	2	6	0	0	1
1971	NY Rangers	13	3	2	5	6	0	0	2
1972	NY Rangers	16	4	8	12	18	0	0	1
1973	NY Rangers	10	4	2	6	6	1	0	1
1974	NY Rangers	13	6	6	12	35	1	0	0
1975	NY Rangers	3	1	0	1	10	0	0	0
1978	Los Angeles	2	1	0	1	2	0	0	0
Playoff Totals		**83**	**25**	**29**	**54**	**136**	**4**	**0**	**7**
STENLUND, Vern *No playoffs*									Center
STEPHENS, Phil *No playoffs*									Center/defense
STEPHENSON, Bob *No playoffs*									Right wing
STERN, Ron									Right wing
1989	Vancouver	3	0	1	1	17	0	0	0
1991	Calgary	7	1	3	4	14	0	0	0
1993	Calgary	6	0	0	0	43	0	0	0
1994	Calgary	7	2	0	2	12	0	0	0
1995	Calgary	7	3	1	4	8	1	1	0
1996	Calgary	4	0	2	2	8	0	0	0
1999	San Jose	6	0	0	0	6	0	0	0
Playoff Totals		**40**	**6**	**7**	**13**	**108**	**1**	**1**	**0**
STERNER, Ulf *No playoffs*									Left wing
STEVENS, John *No playoffs*									Defense
STEVENS, Kevin									Left wing
1989	Pittsburgh	11	3	7	10	16	0	0	0
1991◆	Pittsburgh	24	*17	16	33	53	7	0	4
1992◆	Pittsburgh	21	13	15	28	28	4	0	3
1993	Pittsburgh	12	5	11	16	22	4	0	0
1994	Pittsburgh	6	1	1	2	10	0	0	0
1995	Pittsburgh	12	4	7	11	21	3	0	1
Playoff Totals		**86**	**43**	**57**	**100**	**150**	**18**	**0**	**8**
STEVENS, Mike *No playoffs*									Left wing
STEVENS, Scott									Defense
1983	Washington	4	1	0	1	26	0	0	0
1984	Washington	8	1	8	9	21	1	0	0
1985	Washington	5	0	1	1	20	0	0	0
1986	Washington	9	3	8	11	12	2	0	2
1987	Washington	7	0	5	5	19	0	0	0
1988	Washington	13	1	11	12	46	0	0	0
1989	Washington	6	1	4	5	11	0	0	0
1990	Washington	15	2	7	9	25	1	0	0
1991	St. Louis	13	0	3	3	36	0	0	0
1992	New Jersey	7	2	1	3	29	2	0	1
1993	New Jersey	5	2	2	4	10	1	0	0
1994	New Jersey	20	2	9	11	42	2	0	1
1995◆	New Jersey	20	1	7	8	24	0	0	1
1997	New Jersey	10	0	4	4	2	0	0	0
1998	New Jersey	6	1	0	1	8	0	0	0
1999	New Jersey	7	2	1	3	10	2	0	0
Playoff Totals		**155**	**19**	**71**	**90**	**341**	**11**	**0**	**5**
STEVENSON, Jeremy *No playoffs*									Left wing
STEVENSON, Shayne *No playoffs*									Right wing

Season	Club	GP	G	A	Pts	PIM	PP	SH	GW
STEVENSON, Turner									Right wing
1994	Montreal	3	0	2	2	0	0	0	0
1996	Montreal	6	0	1	1	2	0	0	0
1997	Montreal	5	1	1	2	2	0	0	0
1998	Montreal	10	3	4	7	12	0	0	0
Playoff Totals		**24**	**4**	**8**	**12**	**16**	**0**	**0**	**0**
STEWART, Allan *No playoffs*									Left wing
STEWART, Bill									Defense
1978	Buffalo	8	0	2	2	0	0	0	0
1979	Buffalo	1	0	1	1	0	0	0	0
1981	St. Louis	4	1	0	1	11	0	0	0
Playoff Totals		**13**	**1**	**3**	**4**	**11**	**0**	**0**	**0**
STEWART, Blair *No playoffs*									Center
STEWART, Bob									Defense
1980	Pittsburgh	5	1	1	2	2	0	0	0
Playoff Totals		**5**	**1**	**1**	**2**	**2**	**0**	**0**	**0**
STEWART, Cam									Left wing
1994	Boston	8	0	3	3	7	0	0	0
1996	Boston	5	1	0	1	2	0	0	0
Playoff Totals		**13**	**1**	**3**	**4**	**9**	**0**	**0**	**0**
STEWART, Gaye									Left wing
1942◆	Toronto	1	0	0	0	0	....	....	....
1943	Toronto	4	0	2	2	4	....	....	....
1947◆	Toronto	11	2	5	7	8	....	....	....
1951	Detroit	6	0	2	2	4	....	....	....
1954	Montreal	3	0	0	0	0	....	....	....
Playoff Totals		**25**	**2**	**9**	**11**	**16**	....	....	....
STEWART, Jack									Defense
1940	Detroit	5	0	0	0	4	....	....	....
1941	Detroit	9	1	2	3	8	....	....	....
1942	Detroit	12	0	1	1	12	....	....	....
1943◆	Detroit	10	1	2	3	*35	....	....	....
1946	Detroit	5	0	0	0	14	....	....	....
1947	Detroit	5	0	1	1	12	....	....	....
1948	Detroit	9	1	3	4	6	....	....	....
1949	Detroit	11	1	1	2	*32	....	....	....
1950◆	Detroit	14	1	4	5	20	....	....	....
Playoff Totals		**80**	**5**	**14**	**19**	**143**	....	....	....
STEWART, John									Left wing
1974	Atlanta	4	0	0	0	10	0	0	0
Playoff Totals		**4**	**0**	**0**	**0**	**10**	**0**	**0**	**0**
STEWART, John *No playoffs*									Center
STEWART, Ken *No playoffs*									Defense
STEWART, Nels									Center
1926◆	Mtl. Maroons	8	*6	*3	*9	24	....	....	....
1927	Mtl. Maroons	2	0	0	0	4	....	....	....
1928	Mtl. Maroons	9	2	2	4	13	....	....	....
1930	Mtl. Maroons	4	1	1	2	2	....	....	....
1931	Mtl. Maroons	2	1	0	1	6	....	....	....
1932	Mtl. Maroons	4	0	1	1	2	....	....	....
1933	Boston	5	2	0	2	4	....	....	....
1935	Boston	4	0	1	1	0	....	....	....
1936	NY Americans	5	1	2	3	4	....	....	....
1938	NY Americans	6	2	3	5	2	....	....	....
1939	NY Americans	2	0	0	0	0	....	....	....
1940	NY Americans	3	0	0	0	0	....	....	....
Playoff Totals		**54**	**15**	**13**	**28**	**61**	....	....	....
STEWART, Paul *No playoffs*									Left wing/defense
STEWART, Ralph									Center
1975	NY Islanders	13	3	3	6	2	1	0	0
1976	NY Islanders	6	1	1	2	0	1	0	0
Playoff Totals		**19**	**4**	**4**	**8**	**2**	**2**	**0**	**0**
STEWART, Ron									Center
1954	Toronto	5	0	1	1	10	....	....	....
1955	Toronto	4	0	0	0	2	....	....	....
1956	Toronto	5	1	1	2	2	....	....	....
1959	Toronto	12	3	3	6	6	....	....	....
1960	Toronto	10	0	2	2	2	....	....	....
1961	Toronto	5	1	0	1	2	....	....	....
1962◆	Toronto	11	1	6	7	4	....	....	....
1963◆	Toronto	10	4	0	4	2	....	....	....
1964◆	Toronto	14	0	4	4	24	....	....	....
1965	Toronto	6	0	1	1	2	....	....	....
1968	NY Rangers	6	1	1	2	2	0	0	0
1969	NY Rangers	4	0	1	1	0	0	0	0
1970	NY Rangers	6	0	0	0	2	0	0	0
1971	NY Rangers	13	1	0	1	0	0	1	0
1972	NY Rangers	8	2	1	3	0	0	0	0
Playoff Totals		**119**	**14**	**21**	**35**	**60**	....	....	....
STEWART, Ryan *No playoffs*									Center
STILES, Tony *No playoffs*									Defense
STILLMAN, Cory									Center
1996	Calgary	2	1	1	2	0	0	0	0
Playoff Totals		**2**	**1**	**1**	**2**	**0**	**0**	**0**	**0**
STOCK, P.J. *No playoffs*									Left wing
STODDARD, Jack *No playoffs*									Right wing

Season	Club	GP	G	A	Pts	PIM	PP	SH	GW
STOJANOV, Alek									Right wing
1995	Vancouver	5	0	0	0	2	0	0	0
1996	Pittsburgh	9	0	0	0	19	0	0	0
Playoff Totals		**14**	**0**	**0**	**0**	**21**	**0**	**0**	**0**
STOLTZ, Roland *No playoffs*									Right wing
STONE, Steve *No playoffs*									Right wing
STORM, Jim *No playoffs*									Left wing
STOTHERS, Mike									Defense
1986	Philadelphia	3	0	0	0	4	0	0	0
1987	Philadelphia	2	0	0	0	7	0	0	0
Playoff Totals		**5**	**0**	**0**	**0**	**11**	**0**	**0**	**0**
STOUGHTON, Blaine									Right wing
1975	Toronto	7	4	2	6	2	1	0	1
1980	Hartford	1	0	0	0	0	0	0	0
Playoff Totals		**8**	**4**	**2**	**6**	**2**	**1**	**0**	**1**
STOYANOVICH, Steve *No playoffs*									Center
STRAIN, Neil *No playoffs*									Left wing/Center
STRAKA, Martin									Center
1993	Pittsburgh	11	2	1	3	2	0	0	0
1994	Pittsburgh	6	1	0	1	2	0	0	0
1996	Florida	13	2	2	4	2	0	0	0
1997	Florida	4	0	0	0	0	0	0	0
1998	Pittsburgh	6	2	0	2	2	0	1	0
1999	Pittsburgh	13	6	9	15	6	1	0	0
Playoff Totals		**53**	**13**	**12**	**25**	**14**	**1**	**1**	**0**
STRATE, Gord *No playoffs*									Defense
STRATTON, Art									Center/left wing
1968	Philadelphia	5	0	0	0	0	0	0	0
Playoff Totals		**5**	**0**	**0**	**0**	**0**	**0**	**0**	**0**
STROBEL, Art *No playoffs*									Left wing
STRONG, Ken *No playoffs*									Left wing
STRUCH, David *No playoffs*									Center
STRUDWICK, Jason *No playoffs*									Defense
STRUEBY, Todd *No playoffs*									Left wing
STUART, Billy									Defense
1921	Toronto	2	0	0	0	0	....	....	....
1922◆	Toronto	7	1	3	4	6	....	....	....
1927	Boston	8	0	0	0	6	....	....	....
Playoff Totals		**17**	**1**	**3**	**4**	**12**	....	....	....
STUART, Brad *No playoffs*									Defense
STUMPEL, Jozef									Center
1994	Boston	13	1	7	8	4	0	0	0
1995	Boston	5	0	0	0	0	0	0	0
1996	Boston	5	1	2	3	0	0	0	0
1998	Los Angeles	4	1	2	3	2	0	0	0
Playoff Totals		**27**	**3**	**11**	**14**	**6**	**0**	**0**	**0**
STUMPF, Robert *No playoffs*									Right wing/defense
STURGEON, Peter *No playoffs*									Left wing
STURM, Marco									Center
1998	San Jose	2	0	0	0	0	0	0	0
1999	San Jose	6	2	2	4	4	0	0	1
Playoff Totals		**8**	**2**	**2**	**4**	**4**	**0**	**0**	**1**
SUCHY, Radoslav *No playoffs*									Defense
SUIKKANEN, Kai *No playoffs*									Defense
SULLIMAN, Doug									Right wing
1981	NY Rangers	3	1	0	1	0	0	0	0
1988	New Jersey	9	0	3	3	2	0	0	0
1989	Philadelphia	4	0	0	0	0	0	0	0
Playoff Totals		**16**	**1**	**3**	**4**	**2**	**0**	**0**	**0**
SULLIVAN, Barry *No playoffs*									Right wing
SULLIVAN, Bob *No playoffs*									Left wing
SULLIVAN, Brian *No playoffs*									Right wing
SULLIVAN, Frank *No playoffs*									Defense
SULLIVAN, Mike									Center
1994	Calgary	7	1	1	2	8	0	1	0
1995	Calgary	7	3	5	8	2	0	1	1
1996	Calgary	4	0	0	0	0	0	0	0
1998	Boston	6	0	1	1	2	0	0	0
1999	Phoenix	5	0	0	0	2	0	0	0
Playoff Totals		**29**	**4**	**7**	**11**	**14**	**0**	**2**	**1**
SULLIVAN, Peter *No playoffs*									Center
SULLIVAN, Red									Center
1951	Boston	2	0	0	0	2	0	0	0
1952	Boston	7	0	0	0	0	0	0	0
1953	Boston	3	0	0	0	0	0	0	0
1957	NY Rangers	5	1	2	3	4	0	0	0
1958	NY Rangers	1	0	0	0	0	0	0	0
Playoff Totals		**18**	**1**	**2**	**3**	**6**	**0**	**0**	**0**
SULLIVAN, Steve									Center
1999	Toronto	13	3	3	6	14	2	0	0
Playoff Totals		**13**	**3**	**3**	**6**	**14**	**2**	**0**	**0**
SUMMANEN, Raimo									Left wing
1984◆	Edmonton	5	1	4	5	0	0	0	0
1986	Edmonton	5	1	1	2	0	0	0	0
Playoff Totals		**10**	**2**	**5**	**7**	**0**	**0**	**0**	**0**

SUMMERHILL, Bill Right wing

Season	Club	GP	G	A	Pts	PIM	PP	SH	GW
1938	Mtl. Canadiens	1	0	0	0	0	0	0	0
1939	Mtl. Canadiens	2	0	0	0	2	0	0	0
Playoff Totals		**3**	**0**	**0**	**0**	**2**	**0**	**0**	**0**

SUNDBLAD, Niklas *No playoffs* Right wing

SUNDIN, Mats Center/Right wing

Season	Club	GP	G	A	Pts	PIM	PP	SH	GW
1993	Quebec	6	3	1	4	6	1	0	0
1995	Toronto	7	5	4	9	4	2	0	1
1996	Toronto	6	3	1	4	4	2	0	1
1999	Toronto	17	8	8	16	16	3	0	2
Playoff Totals		**36**	**19**	**14**	**33**	**30**	**8**	**0**	**4**

SUNDIN, Ronnie *No playoffs* Defense

SUNDSTROM, Niklas Left wing

Season	Club	GP	G	A	Pts	PIM	PP	SH	GW
1996	NY Rangers	11	4	3	7	4	1	0	0
1997	NY Rangers	9	0	5	5	2	0	0	0
Playoff Totals		**20**	**4**	**8**	**12**	**6**	**1**	**0**	**0**

SUNDSTROM, Patrik Center

Season	Club	GP	G	A	Pts	PIM	PP	SH	GW
1983	Vancouver	4	0	0	0	2	0	0	0
1984	Vancouver	4	0	1	1	7	0	0	0
1986	Vancouver	3	1	0	1	0	1	0	0
1988	New Jersey	18	7	13	20	14	3	0	1
1990	New Jersey	6	1	3	4	2	0	0	0
1991	New Jersey	2	0	0	0	0	0	0	0
Playoff Totals		**37**	**9**	**17**	**26**	**25**	**4**	**0**	**1**

SUNDSTROM, Peter Left wing

Season	Club	GP	G	A	Pts	PIM	PP	SH	GW
1984	NY Rangers	5	1	3	4	0	1	0	0
1985	NY Rangers	3	0	0	0	0	0	0	0
1986	NY Rangers	1	0	0	0	2	0	0	0
1988	Washington	14	2	0	2	6	0	1	1
Playoff Totals		**23**	**3**	**3**	**6**	**8**	**1**	**1**	**1**

SUOMI, Al *No playoffs* Left wing

SUTER, Gary Defense

Season	Club	GP	G	A	Pts	PIM	PP	SH	GW
1986	Calgary	10	2	8	10	8	0	0	1
1987	Calgary	6	0	3	3	10	0	0	0
1988	Calgary	9	1	9	10	6	0	1	0
1989♦	Calgary	5	0	3	3	10	0	0	0
1990	Calgary	6	0	1	1	14	0	0	0
1991	Calgary	7	1	6	7	12	1	0	0
1993	Calgary	6	2	3	5	8	0	1	0
1994	Chicago	6	3	2	5	6	2	0	0
1995	Chicago	12	2	5	7	10	1	0	0
1996	Chicago	10	3	3	6	8	2	0	1
1997	Chicago	6	1	4	5	8	0	0	0
Playoff Totals		**83**	**15**	**47**	**62**	**100**	**6**	**2**	**2**

SUTHERLAND, Bill Center

Season	Club	GP	G	A	Pts	PIM	PP	SH	GW
1963	Montreal	2	0	0	0	0	0	0	0
1968	Philadelphia	7	1	3	4	0	1	0	0
1969	Philadelphia	4	1	1	2	0	1	0	0
1971	St. Louis	1	0	0	0	0	0	0	0
Playoff Totals		**14**	**2**	**4**	**6**	**0**	**2**	**0**	**0**

SUTHERLAND, Max *No playoffs* Left wing

SUTTER, Brent Center

Season	Club	GP	G	A	Pts	PIM	PP	SH	GW
1982♦	NY Islanders	19	2	6	8	36	0	0	0
1983♦	NY Islanders	20	10	11	21	26	3	0	0
1984	NY Islanders	20	4	10	14	18	0	1	3
1985	NY Islanders	10	3	3	6	14	1	0	2
1986	NY Islanders	3	0	1	1	2	0	0	0
1987	NY Islanders	5	1	0	1	4	1	0	0
1988	NY Islanders	6	2	1	3	18	0	1	1
1990	NY Islanders	5	2	3	5	2	2	0	1
1992	Chicago	18	3	5	8	22	1	0	1
1993	Chicago	4	1	1	2	4	0	0	0
1994	Chicago	6	0	0	0	2	0	0	0
1995	Chicago	16	1	2	3	4	0	0	0
1996	Chicago	10	1	1	2	6	0	0	0
1997	Chicago	2	0	0	0	6	0	0	0
Playoff Totals		**144**	**30**	**44**	**74**	**164**	**8**	**2**	**8**

SUTTER, Brian Left wing

Season	Club	GP	G	A	Pts	PIM	PP	SH	GW
1977	St. Louis	4	1	0	1	14	0	0	0
1980	St. Louis	3	0	0	0	4	0	0	0
1981	St. Louis	11	6	3	9	77	3	0	0
1982	St. Louis	10	8	6	14	49	0	0	1
1983	St. Louis	4	2	1	3	10	2	0	0
1984	St. Louis	11	1	5	6	22	1	0	0
1985	St. Louis	3	2	1	3	2	2	0	0
1986	St. Louis	9	1	2	3	22	0	0	0
1988	St. Louis	10	0	3	3	49	0	0	0
Playoff Totals		**65**	**21**	**21**	**42**	**249**	**8**	**0**	**1**

SUTTER, Darryl Left wing

Season	Club	GP	G	A	Pts	PIM	PP	SH	GW
1980	Chicago	7	3	1	4	2	2	0	1
1981	Chicago	3	3	1	4	2	1	0	0
1982	Chicago	3	0	1	1	2	0	0	0
1983	Chicago	13	4	6	10	8	0	0	0
1984	Chicago	5	1	1	2	0	0	0	0
1985	Chicago	15	12	7	19	12	2	0	4
1986	Chicago	3	1	2	3	0	1	0	0
1987	Chicago	2	0	0	0	0	0	0	0
Playoff Totals		**51**	**24**	**19**	**43**	**26**	**6**	**0**	**5**

SUTTER, Duane Right wing

Season	Club	GP	G	A	Pts	PIM	PP	SH	GW
1980♦	NY Islanders	21	3	7	10	74	0	0	0
1981♦	NY Islanders	12	3	1	4	10	0	0	0
1982♦	NY Islanders	19	5	5	10	57	0	0	2
1983♦	NY Islanders	20	9	12	21	43	2	0	1
1984	NY Islanders	21	1	3	4	48	0	0	0
1985	NY Islanders	10	0	2	2	47	0	0	0
1986	NY Islanders	3	0	0	0	16	0	0	0
1987	NY Islanders	14	1	0	1	26	0	0	0
1988	Chicago	5	0	0	0	21	0	0	0
1989	Chicago	16	3	1	4	15	0	0	2
1990	Chicago	20	1	1	2	48	0	0	0
Playoff Totals		**161**	**26**	**32**	**58**	**405**	**2**	**0**	**5**

SUTTER, Rich Right wing

Season	Club	GP	G	A	Pts	PIM	PP	SH	GW
1984	Philadelphia	3	0	0	0	15	0	0	0
1985	Philadelphia	11	3	0	3	10	0	0	0
1986	Philadelphia	5	2	0	2	19	0	0	0
1989	Vancouver	7	2	1	3	12	0	0	0
1990	St. Louis	12	2	1	3	39	0	1	1
1991	St. Louis	13	4	2	6	16	0	0	1
1992	St. Louis	6	0	0	0	8	0	0	0
1993	St. Louis	11	0	1	1	10	0	0	0
1994	Chicago	6	0	0	0	2	0	0	0
1995	Toronto	4	0	0	0	2	0	0	0
Playoff Totals		**78**	**13**	**5**	**18**	**133**	**0**	**1**	**2**

SUTTER, Ron Center

Season	Club	GP	G	A	Pts	PIM	PP	SH	GW
1984	Philadelphia	3	0	0	0	22	0	0	0
1985	Philadelphia	19	4	8	12	28	0	0	1
1986	Philadelphia	5	0	2	2	10	0	0	0
1987	Philadelphia	16	1	7	8	12	0	0	0
1988	Philadelphia	7	0	1	1	26	0	0	0
1989	Philadelphia	19	1	9	10	51	0	0	0
1992	St. Louis	6	1	3	4	8	1	0	0
1996	Boston	5	0	0	0	8	0	0	0
1998	San Jose	6	1	0	1	14	0	0	0
1999	San Jose	6	0	0	0	4	0	0	0
Playoff Totals		**92**	**8**	**30**	**38**	**183**	**1**	**0**	**1**

SUTTON, Andy *No playoffs* Defense

SUTTON, Ken Defense

Season	Club	GP	G	A	Pts	PIM	PP	SH	GW
1991	Buffalo	6	0	1	1	2	0	0	0
1992	Buffalo	7	0	2	2	4	0	0	0
1993	Buffalo	8	3	1	4	8	0	0	0
1994	Buffalo	4	0	0	0	2	0	0	0
1996	St. Louis	1	0	0	0	0	0	0	0
Playoff Totals		**26**	**3**	**4**	**7**	**16**	**0**	**0**	**0**

SUZOR, Mark *No playoffs* Defense

SVARTVADET, Per *No playoffs* Center

SVEHLA, Robert Defense

Season	Club	GP	G	A	Pts	PIM	PP	SH	GW
1996	Florida	22	0	6	6	32	0	0	0
1997	Florida	5	1	4	5	4	1	0	0
Playoff Totals		**27**	**1**	**10**	**11**	**36**	**1**	**0**	**0**

SVEJKOVSKY, Jaroslav Right wing

Season	Club	GP	G	A	Pts	PIM	PP	SH	GW
1998	Washington	1	0	0	0	2	0	0	0
Playoff Totals		**1**	**0**	**0**	**0**	**2**	**0**	**0**	**0**

SVENSSON, Leif *No playoffs* Defense

SVENSSON, Magnus *No playoffs* Defense

SVOBODA, Petr Defense

Season	Club	GP	G	A	Pts	PIM	PP	SH	GW
1985	Montreal	7	1	1	2	12	0	0	0
1986♦	Montreal	8	0	0	0	21	0	0	0
1987	Montreal	14	0	5	5	10	0	0	0
1988	Montreal	10	0	5	5	12	0	0	0
1989	Montreal	21	1	11	12	16	0	0	0
1990	Montreal	10	0	5	5	7	0	0	0
1991	Montreal	2	0	1	1	2	0	0	0
1992	Buffalo	7	1	4	5	6	0	1	0
1994	Buffalo	3	0	0	0	4	0	0	0
1995	Philadelphia	14	0	4	4	8	0	0	0
1996	Philadelphia	12	0	6	6	22	0	0	0
1997	Philadelphia	16	1	2	3	16	0	0	0
1998	Philadelphia	3	0	1	1	4	0	0	0
Playoff Totals		**127**	**4**	**45**	**49**	**140**	**0**	**1**	**0**

SWAIN, Garry *No playoffs* Center

SWARBRICK, George *No playoffs* Right wing

SWEENEY, Bill *No playoffs* Center

SWEENEY, Bob Center/Right wing

Season	Club	GP	G	A	Pts	PIM	PP	SH	GW
1987	Boston	3	0	0	0	0	0	0	0
1988	Boston	23	6	8	14	66	1	1	1
1989	Boston	10	2	4	6	19	0	0	0
1990	Boston	20	0	2	2	30	0	0	0
1991	Boston	17	4	2	6	45	0	0	1
1992	Boston	14	1	0	1	25	0	1	0
1993	Buffalo	8	2	2	4	8	0	0	1
1994	Buffalo	1	0	0	0	0	0	0	0
1995	Buffalo	5	0	0	0	4	0	0	0
1996	Calgary	2	0	0	0	0	0	0	0
Playoff Totals		**103**	**15**	**18**	**33**	**197**	**1**	**2**	**3**

SWEENEY, Don Defense

Season	Club	GP	G	A	Pts	PIM	PP	SH	GW
1990	Boston	21	1	5	6	18	1	0	0
1991	Boston	19	3	0	3	25	0	0	0
1992	Boston	15	0	0	0	10	0	0	0
1993	Boston	4	0	0	0	4	0	0	0
1994	Boston	12	2	1	3	4	0	0	1
1995	Boston	5	0	0	0	4	0	0	0
1996	Boston	5	0	2	2	6	0	0	0
1999	Boston	11	3	0	3	6	1	0	0
Playoff Totals		**92**	**9**	**8**	**17**	**77**	**2**	**0**	**1**

SWEENEY, Tim Left wing

Season	Club	GP	G	A	Pts	PIM	PP	SH	GW
1993	Boston	3	0	0	0	0	0	0	0
1996	Boston	1	0	0	0	2	0	0	0
Playoff Totals		**4**	**0**	**0**	**0**	**2**	**0**	**0**	**0**

SYDOR, Darryl Defense

Season	Club	GP	G	A	Pts	PIM	PP	SH	GW
1993	Los Angeles	24	3	8	11	16	2	0	0
1997	Dallas	7	0	2	2	0	0	0	0
1998	Dallas	17	0	5	5	14	0	0	0
1999♦	Dallas	23	3	9	12	16	1	0	1
Playoff Totals		**71**	**6**	**24**	**30**	**46**	**3**	**0**	**1**

SYKES, Bob *No playoffs* Left wing

SYKES, Phil Left wing

Season	Club	GP	G	A	Pts	PIM	PP	SH	GW
1985	Los Angeles	3	0	1	1	4	0	0	0
1987	Los Angeles	5	0	1	1	8	0	0	0
1988	Los Angeles	4	0	0	0	0	0	0	0
1989	Los Angeles	3	0	0	0	8	0	0	0
1990	Winnipeg	4	0	0	0	0	0	0	0
1992	Winnipeg	7	0	1	1	9	0	0	0
Playoff Totals		**26**	**0**	**3**	**3**	**29**	**0**	**0**	**0**

SYKORA, Michal Defense

Season	Club	GP	G	A	Pts	PIM	PP	SH	GW
1997	Chicago	1	0	0	0	0	0	0	0
Playoff Totals		**1**	**0**	**0**	**0**	**0**	**0**	**0**	**0**

SYKORA, Petr *No playoffs* Center

SYKORA, Petr Center

Season	Club	GP	G	A	Pts	PIM	PP	SH	GW
1997	New Jersey	2	0	0	0	2	0	0	0
1998	New Jersey	2	0	0	0	0	0	0	0
1999	New Jersey	7	3	3	6	4	0	0	1
Playoff Totals		**11**	**3**	**3**	**6**	**6**	**0**	**0**	**1**

SYLVESTER, Dean *No playoffs* Right wing

SZURA, Joe Center

Season	Club	GP	G	A	Pts	PIM	PP	SH	GW
1969	Oakland	7	2	3	5	2	1	0	0
Playoff Totals		**7**	**2**	**3**	**5**	**2**	**1**	**0**	**0**

TAFT, John *No playoffs* Defense

TAGLIANETTI, Peter Defense

Season	Club	GP	G	A	Pts	PIM	PP	SH	GW
1985	Winnipeg	1	0	0	0	0	0	0	0
1986	Winnipeg	3	0	0	0	2	0	0	0
1988	Winnipeg	5	1	1	2	12	0	0	0
1990	Winnipeg	5	0	0	0	6	0	0	0
1991♦	Pittsburgh	19	0	3	3	49	0	0	0
1993	Pittsburgh	11	1	2	3	16	0	0	0
1994	Pittsburgh	5	0	2	2	16	0	0	0
1995	Pittsburgh	4	0	0	0	2	0	0	0
Playoff Totals		**53**	**2**	**8**	**10**	**103**	**0**	**0**	**0**

TALAFOUS, Dean Right wing

Season	Club	GP	G	A	Pts	PIM	PP	SH	GW
1977	Minnesota	2	0	0	0	0	0	0	0
1980	NY Rangers	5	1	2	3	9	1	0	0
1981	NY Rangers	14	3	5	8	2	0	0	0
Playoff Totals		**21**	**4**	**7**	**11**	**11**	**1**	**0**	**0**

TALAKOSKI, Ron *No playoffs* Right wing

TALBOT, Jean-Guy Defense

Season	Club	GP	G	A	Pts	PIM	PP	SH	GW
1956♦	Montreal	9	0	2	2	4	0	0	0
1957♦	Montreal	10	0	2	2	10	0	0	0
1958♦	Montreal	10	0	3	3	12	0	0	0
1959♦	Montreal	11	0	1	1	10	0	0	0
1960♦	Montreal	8	1	1	2	8	0	0	0
1961	Montreal	6	1	1	2	10	1	0	0
1962	Montreal	6	1	1	2	10	0	0	0
1963	Montreal	5	0	0	0	8	0	0	0
1964	Montreal	7	0	2	2	10	0	0	0
1965♦	Montreal	13	0	1	1	22	0	0	0
1966♦	Montreal	10	0	2	2	8	0	0	0
1967	Montreal	10	0	0	0	0	0	0	0
1968	St. Louis	17	0	2	2	8	0	0	0
1969	St. Louis	12	0	2	2	6	0	0	0
1970	St. Louis	16	1	6	7	16	0	0	0
Playoff Totals		**150**	**4**	**26**	**30**	**142**	**1**	**0**	**0**

TALLON, Dale Defense

Season	Club	GP	G	A	Pts	PIM	PP	SH	GW
1974	Chicago	11	1	3	4	29	1	0	0
1975	Chicago	8	1	3	4	4	0	0	0
1976	Chicago	4	0	1	1	8	0	0	0
1977	Chicago	2	0	1	1	0	0	0	0
1978	Chicago	4	0	2	2	0	0	0	0
1980	Pittsburgh	4	0	0	0	4	0	0	0
Playoff Totals		**33**	**2**	**10**	**12**	**45**	**1**	**0**	**0**

TAMBELLINI, Steve Center

Season	Club	GP	G	A	Pts	PIM	PP	SH	GW
1984	Calgary	2	0	1	1	0	0	0	0
Playoff Totals		**2**	**0**	**1**	**1**	**0**	**0**	**0**	**0**

Season	Club	GP	G	A	Pts	PIM	PP	SH	GW
TAMER, Chris									Defense
1994	Pittsburgh	5	0	0	0	2	0	0	0
1995	Pittsburgh	4	0	0	0	18	0	0	0
1996	Pittsburgh	18	0	7	7	24	0	0	0
1997	Pittsburgh	4	0	0	0	4	0	0	0
1998	Pittsburgh	6	0	1	1	4	0	0	0
Playoff Totals		**37**	**0**	**8**	**8**	**52**	**0**	**0**	**0**
TANABE, David	*No playoffs*								Defense
TANCILL, Chris									Center
1995	San Jose	11	1	1	2	8	0	0	0
Playoff Totals		**11**	**1**	**1**	**2**	**8**	**0**	**0**	**0**
TANGUAY, Alex	*No playoffs*								Center
TANGUAY, Chris	*No playoffs*								Right wing
TANNAHILL, Don	*No playoffs*								Left wing
TANTI, Tony									Right wing
1983	Vancouver	4	0	1	1	0	0	0	0
1984	Vancouver	4	1	2	3	0	0	0	0
1986	Vancouver	3	0	1	1	11	0	0	0
1989	Vancouver	7	0	5	5	4	0	0	0
1991	Buffalo	5	2	0	2	8	1	0	0
1992	Buffalo	7	0	3	3	4	0	0	0
Playoff Totals		**30**	**3**	**12**	**15**	**27**	**1**	**0**	**0**
TARDIF, Marc									Left wing
1971♦	Montreal	20	3	1	4	40	0	0	0
1972	Montreal	6	2	3	5	9	0	0	1
1973♦	Montreal	14	6	6	12	6	2	0	2
1981	Quebec	5	1	3	4	2	0	0	0
1982	Quebec	13	1	2	3	16	0	0	0
1983	Quebec	4	0	0	0	2	0	0	0
Playoff Totals		**62**	**13**	**15**	**28**	**75**	**2**	**0**	**3**
TARDIF, Patrice	*No playoffs*								Center
TATARINOV, Mikhail	*No playoffs*								Defense
THATCHELL, Spence	*No playoffs*								Defense
TAYLOR Jr., Billy	*No playoffs*								Center
TAYLOR Sr., Billy									Center
1940	Toronto	2	1	0	1	0	....	....	....
1941	Toronto	7	0	3	3	5	....	....	....
1942♦	Toronto	13	2	*8	10	4	....	....	....
1943	Toronto	6	2	2	4	0	....	....	....
1947	Detroit	5	1	5	6	4	....	....	....
Playoff Totals		**33**	**6**	**18**	**24**	**13**	....	....	....
TAYLOR, Bob	*No playoffs*								Right wing
TAYLOR, Chris	*No playoffs*								Center
TAYLOR, Dave									Right wing
1978	Los Angeles	2	0	0	0	5	0	0	0
1979	Los Angeles	2	0	0	0	2	0	0	0
1980	Los Angeles	4	2	1	3	4	0	0	0
1981	Los Angeles	4	2	2	4	10	1	0	0
1982	Los Angeles	10	4	6	10	20	3	0	0
1985	Los Angeles	3	2	2	4	8	0	0	0
1987	Los Angeles	5	2	3	5	6	1	0	0
1988	Los Angeles	5	3	3	6	6	2	0	0
1989	Los Angeles	11	1	5	6	19	1	0	0
1990	Los Angeles	6	4	4	8	2	2	0	0
1991	Los Angeles	12	2	1	3	12	0	0	1
1992	Los Angeles	6	1	1	2	20	0	0	0
1993	Los Angeles	22	3	5	8	31	0	2	0
Playoff Totals		**92**	**26**	**33**	**59**	**145**	**10**	**2**	**1**
TAYLOR, Harry									Center
1949♦	Toronto	1	0	0	0	0	0	0	0
Playoff Totals		**1**	**0**	**0**	**0**	**0**	**0**	**0**	**0**
TAYLOR, Mark									Center
1983	Philadelphia	3	0	0	0	0	0	0	0
1986	Washington	3	0	0	0	0	0	0	0
Playoff Totals		**6**	**0**	**0**	**0**	**0**	**0**	**0**	**0**
TAYLOR, Ralph									Defense
1930	NY Rangers	4	0	0	0	10	0	0	0
Playoff Totals		**4**	**0**	**0**	**0**	**10**	**0**	**0**	**0**
TAYLOR, Ted	*No playoffs*								Left wing
TAYLOR, Tim									Center
1995	Detroit	6	0	1	1	12	0	0	0
1996	Detroit	18	0	4	4	4	0	0	0
1997♦	Detroit	2	0	0	0	0	0	0	0
1998	Boston	6	0	0	0	10	0	0	0
1999	Boston	12	0	3	3	8	0	0	0
Playoff Totals		**44**	**0**	**8**	**8**	**34**	**0**	**0**	**0**
TEAL, Jeff	*No playoffs*								Right wing
TEAL, Skip	*No playoffs*								Center
TEAL, Vic	*No playoffs*								Right wing
TEBBUTT, Greg	*No playoffs*								Defense
TEPPER, Stephen	*No playoffs*								Right wing
TERBENCHE, Paul									Defense
1968	Chicago	6	0	0	0	0	0	0	0
1973	Buffalo	6	0	0	0	0	0	0	0
Playoff Totals		**12**	**0**	**0**	**0**	**0**	**0**	**0**	**0**
TERRION, Greg									Left wing
1981	Los Angeles	3	1	0	1	4	1	0	0
1983	Toronto	4	1	2	3	2	0	0	0
1986	Toronto	10	0	3	3	17	0	0	0
1987	Toronto	13	0	2	2	14	0	0	0
1988	Toronto	5	0	2	2	4	0	0	0
Playoff Totals		**35**	**2**	**9**	**11**	**41**	**1**	**0**	**0**
TERRY, Bill	*No playoffs*								Center
TERTYSHNY, Dimitri									Defense
1999	Philadelphia	1	0	0	0	0	0	0	0
Playoff Totals		**1**	**0**	**0**	**0**	**0**	**0**	**0**	**0**
TESSIER, Orval	*No playoffs*								Center
TEZIKOV, Alexei	*No playoffs*								Defense
THEBERGE, Greg									Defense
1983	Washington	4	0	1	1	0	0	0	0
Playoff Totals		**4**	**0**	**1**	**1**	**0**	**0**	**0**	**0**
THELIN, Mats									Defense
1985	Boston	5	0	0	0	6	0	0	0
Playoff Totals		**5**	**0**	**0**	**0**	**6**	**0**	**0**	**0**
THELVEN, Michael									Defense
1986	Boston	3	0	0	0	0	0	0	0
1988	Boston	21	3	3	6	26	1	0	0
1989	Boston	10	1	7	8	8	0	0	1
Playoff Totals		**34**	**4**	**10**	**14**	**34**	**1**	**0**	**1**
THERIEN, Chris									Defense
1995	Philadelphia	15	0	0	0	10	0	0	0
1996	Philadelphia	12	0	0	0	18	0	0	0
1997	Philadelphia	19	1	6	7	6	0	0	1
1998	Philadelphia	5	0	1	1	4	0	0	0
1999	Philadelphia	6	0	0	0	6	0	0	0
Playoff Totals		**57**	**1**	**7**	**8**	**44**	**0**	**0**	**1**
THERRIEN, Gaston									Defense
1982	Quebec	9	0	1	1	4	0	0	0
Playoff Totals		**9**	**0**	**1**	**1**	**4**	**0**	**0**	**0**
THIBAUDEAU, Gilles									Center
1988	Montreal	8	3	3	6	2	1	0	0
Playoff Totals		**8**	**3**	**3**	**6**	**2**	**1**	**0**	**0**
THIBEAULT, Lorran	*No playoffs*								Left wing
THIFFAULT, Leo									Left wing
1968	Minnesota	5	0	0	0	0	0	0	0
Playoff Totals		**5**	**0**	**0**	**0**	**0**	**0**	**0**	**0**
THOMAS, Cy	*No playoffs*								Left/right wing
THOMAS, Reg	*No playoffs*								Left wing
THOMAS, Scott	*No playoffs*								Right wing
THOMAS, Steve									Left wing
1986	Toronto	10	6	8	14	9	3	0	0
1987	Toronto	13	2	3	5	13	0	0	0
1988	Chicago	3	1	2	3	6	0	0	0
1989	Chicago	12	3	5	8	10	1	0	2
1990	Chicago	20	7	6	13	33	1	0	3
1991	Chicago	6	1	2	3	15	0	0	0
1993	NY Islanders	18	9	8	17	37	0	0	0
1994	NY Islanders	4	1	0	1	8	1	0	0
1997	New Jersey	10	1	1	2	18	0	0	0
1998	New Jersey	6	0	3	3	2	0	0	0
1999	Toronto	17	6	3	9	12	2	0	1
Playoff Totals		**119**	**37**	**41**	**78**	**163**	**8**	**0**	**6**
THOMLINSON, Dave									Left wing
1991	St. Louis	9	3	1	4	4	1	0	1
Playoff Totals		**9**	**3**	**1**	**4**	**4**	**1**	**0**	**1**
THOMPSON, Brent									Defense
1992	Los Angeles	4	0	0	0	4	0	0	0
Playoff Totals		**4**	**0**	**0**	**0**	**4**	**0**	**0**	**0**
THOMPSON, Cliff	*No playoffs*								Defense
THOMPSON, Errol									Left wing
1974	Toronto	2	0	1	1	0	0	0	0
1975	Toronto	6	0	0	0	9	0	0	0
1976	Toronto	10	3	3	6	0	2	1	0
1977	Toronto	9	2	0	2	0	0	0	1
1978	Detroit	7	2	1	3	2	1	0	1
Playoff Totals		**34**	**7**	**5**	**12**	**11**	**3**	**1**	**2**
THOMPSON, Kenneth	*No playoffs*								Left wing/center
THOMPSON, Paul									Left wing
1927	NY Rangers	2	0	0	0	0	....	....	....
1928♦	NY Rangers	8	0	0	0	30	....	....	....
1929	NY Rangers	6	0	*2	2	6	....	....	....
1930	NY Rangers	4	0	0	0	2	....	....	....
1931	NY Rangers	4	3	0	3	2	....	....	....
1932	Chicago	2	0	0	0	2	....	....	....
1934♦	Chicago	8	4	3	7	6	....	....	....
1935	Chicago	2	0	0	0	0	....	....	....
1936	Chicago	2	0	3	3	0	....	....	....
1938♦	Chicago	10	4	3	7	6	....	....	....
Playoff Totals		**48**	**11**	**11**	**22**	**54**	....	....	....
THOMSON, Rhys	*No playoffs*								Defense
THOMPSON, Rocky	*No playoffs*								Right wing
THOMS, Bill									Center
1933	Toronto	9	1	1	2	4	....	....	....
1934	Toronto	5	0	2	2	0	....	....	....
1935	Toronto	7	2	0	2	0	....	....	....
1936	Toronto	9	3	*5	8	0	....	....	....
1937	Toronto	2	0	0	0	0	....	....	....
1938	Toronto	7	0	1	1	0	....	....	....
1940	Chicago	1	0	0	0	0	....	....	....
1942	Chicago	3	0	1	1	0	....	....	....
1945	Boston	1	0	0	0	2	....	....	....
Playoff Totals		**44**	**6**	**10**	**16**	**6**	....	....	....
THOMSON, Bill									Center/right wing
1944	Detroit	2	0	0	0	0	0	0	0
Playoff Totals		**2**	**0**	**0**	**0**	**0**	**0**	**0**	**0**
THOMSON, Floyd									Left wing
1973	St. Louis	5	0	1	1	2	0	0	0
1975	St. Louis	2	0	1	1	0	0	0	0
1977	St. Louis	3	0	0	0	4	0	0	0
Playoff Totals		**10**	**0**	**2**	**2**	**6**	**0**	**0**	**0**
THOMSON, Jim									Right wing
1993	Los Angeles	1	0	0	0	0	0	0	0
Playoff Totals		**1**	**0**	**0**	**0**	**0**	**0**	**0**	**0**
THOMSON, Jimmy									Defense
1947♦	Toronto	11	0	1	1	22	....	....	....
1948♦	Toronto	9	1	1	2	9	....	....	....
1949♦	Toronto	9	1	5	6	10	....	....	....
1950	Toronto	7	0	2	2	7	....	....	....
1951♦	Toronto	11	0	1	1	*34	....	....	....
1952	Toronto	4	0	0	0	25	....	....	....
1954	Toronto	3	0	0	0	2	....	....	....
1955	Toronto	4	0	0	0	16	....	....	....
1956	Toronto	5	0	3	3	10	....	....	....
Playoff Totals		**63**	**2**	**13**	**15**	**135**	....	....	....
THORNBURY, Tom	*No playoffs*								Defense
THORNTON, Joe									Center
1998	Boston	6	0	0	0	9	0	0	0
1999	Boston	11	3	6	9	4	2	0	2
Playoff Totals		**17**	**3**	**6**	**9**	**13**	**2**	**0**	**2**
THORNTON, Scott									Center
1992	Edmonton	1	0	0	0	0	0	0	0
1997	Montreal	5	1	0	1	2	0	0	0
1998	Montreal	9	0	2	2	10	0	0	0
Playoff Totals		**15**	**1**	**2**	**3**	**12**	**0**	**0**	**0**
THORSTEINSON, Joe	*No playoffs*								Right wing
THURIER, Fred	*No playoffs*								Center
THURLBY, Tom	*No playoffs*								Defense
THYER, Mario									Center
1990	Minnesota	1	0	0	0	2	0	0	0
Playoff Totals		**1**	**0**	**0**	**0**	**2**	**0**	**0**	**0**
TICHY, Milan	*No playoffs*								Defense
TIDEY, Alex									Right wing
1977	Buffalo	2	0	0	0	0	0	0	0
Playoff Totals		**2**	**0**	**0**	**0**	**0**	**0**	**0**	**0**
TIKKANEN, Esa									Left wing
1985♦	Edmonton	3	0	0	0	2	0	0	0
1986	Edmonton	8	3	2	5	7	0	0	0
1987♦	Edmonton	21	7	2	9	22	1	0	1
1988♦	Edmonton	19	10	17	27	72	5	0	1
1989	Edmonton	7	1	3	4	12	0	0	0
1990♦	Edmonton	22	13	11	24	26	2	2	0
1991	Edmonton	18	12	8	20	24	3	0	3
1992	Edmonton	16	5	3	8	8	1	0	1
1994♦	NY Rangers	23	4	4	8	34	0	0	1
1995	St. Louis	7	2	2	4	20	1	0	1
1996	Vancouver	6	3	2	5	2	2	0	0
1997	NY Rangers	15	9	3	12	26	3	1	3
1998	Washington	21	3	3	6	20	1	0	0
Playoff Totals		**186**	**72**	**60**	**132**	**275**	**19**	**3**	**11**
TILEY, Brad									Defense
1999	Phoenix	1	0	0	0	0	0	0	0
Playoff Totals		**1**	**0**	**0**	**0**	**0**	**0**	**0**	**0**
TILLEY, Tom									Defense
1989	St. Louis	10	1	2	3	17	0	0	0
1994	St. Louis	4	0	1	1	2	0	0	0
Playoff Totals		**14**	**1**	**3**	**4**	**19**	**0**	**0**	**0**
TIMANDER, Mattias									Defense
1999	Boston	4	1	1	2	2	0	0	0
Playoff Totals		**4**	**1**	**1**	**2**	**2**	**0**	**0**	**0**
TIMGREN, Ray									Left wing
1949♦	Toronto	9	3	3	6	2	....	....	....
1950	Toronto	6	0	4	4	2	....	....	....
1951♦	Toronto	11	0	1	1	2	....	....	....
1952	Toronto	4	0	1	1	0	....	....	....
Playoff Totals		**30**	**3**	**9**	**12**	**6**	....	....	....
TIMONEN, Kimmo	*No playoffs*								Defense

Season	Club	GP	G	A	Pts	PIM	PP	SH	GW
TINORDI, Mark	Defense								
1989	Minnesota	5	0	0	0	0	0	0	0
1990	Minnesota	7	0	1	1	16	0	0	0
1991	Minnesota	23	5	6	11	78	4	0	0
1992	Minnesota	7	1	2	3	11	0	0	0
1995	Washington	1	0	0	0	2	0	0	0
1996	Washington	6	0	0	0	16	0	0	0
1998	Washington	21	1	2	3	42	0	0	0
Playoff Totals		**70**	**7**	**11**	**18**	**165**	**4**	**0**	**0**
TIPPETT, Dave	Left wing								
1986	Hartford	10	2	2	4	4	0	1	0
1987	Hartford	6	0	2	2	4	0	0	0
1988	Hartford	6	0	0	0	2	0	0	0
1989	Hartford	4	0	1	1	0	0	0	0
1990	Hartford	7	1	3	4	2	0	0	0
1991	Washington	10	2	3	5	8	0	0	0
1992	Washington	7	0	1	1	0	0	0	0
1993	Pittsburgh	12	1	4	5	14	0	0	0
Playoff Totals		**62**	**6**	**16**	**22**	**34**	**0**	**1**	**0**
TITANIC, Morris *No playoffs*	Left wing								
TITOV, German	Center								
1994	Calgary	7	2	1	3	4	1	0	0
1995	Calgary	7	5	3	8	10	0	1	0
1996	Calgary	4	0	2	2	0	0	0	0
1999	Pittsburgh	11	3	5	8	4	0	0	0
Playoff Totals		**29**	**10**	**11**	**21**	**18**	**1**	**1**	**0**
TKACHUK, Keith	Left wing								
1992	Winnipeg	7	3	0	3	30	0	0	0
1993	Winnipeg	6	4	0	4	14	1	0	0
1996	Winnipeg	6	1	2	3	22	0	0	0
1997	Phoenix	7	6	0	6	7	2	0	0
1998	Phoenix	6	3	3	6	10	0	0	0
1999	Phoenix	7	1	3	4	13	1	0	0
Playoff Totals		**39**	**18**	**8**	**26**	**96**	**4**	**0**	**0**
TKACZUK, Walt	Center								
1969	NY Rangers	4	0	1	1	6	0	0	0
1970	NY Rangers	6	2	1	3	17	1	0	0
1971	NY Rangers	13	1	5	6	14	0	0	1
1972	NY Rangers	16	4	6	10	35	0	0	2
1973	NY Rangers	10	7	2	9	8	1	0	1
1974	NY Rangers	13	0	5	5	22	0	0	0
1975	NY Rangers	3	1	2	3	5	0	0	0
1978	NY Rangers	3	0	2	2	0	0	0	0
1979	NY Rangers	18	4	7	11	10	0	1	0
1980	NY Rangers	7	0	1	1	2	0	0	0
Playoff Totals		**93**	**19**	**32**	**51**	**119**	**2**	**1**	**4**
TOAL, Mike *No playoffs*	Center								
TOCCHET, Rick	Right wing								
1985	Philadelphia	19	3	4	7	72	0	0	2
1986	Philadelphia	5	1	2	3	26	0	0	0
1987	Philadelphia	26	11	10	21	72	0	1	2
1988	Philadelphia	5	1	4	5	55	2	1	0
1989	Philadelphia	16	6	6	12	69	2	0	1
1992◆	Pittsburgh	14	6	13	19	24	3	0	1
1993	Pittsburgh	12	7	6	13	24	1	0	0
1994	Pittsburgh	6	2	3	5	20	1	0	1
1996	Boston	5	4	0	4	21	3	0	1
1998	Phoenix	6	6	2	8	25	3	0	0
1999	Phoenix	7	0	3	3	8	0	0	0
Playoff Totals		**121**	**47**	**53**	**100**	**416**	**15**	**2**	**8**
TODD, Kevin	Center								
1991	New Jersey	1	0	0	0	6	0	0	0
1992	New Jersey	7	3	2	5	8	1	0	0
1997	Anaheim	4	0	0	0	2	0	0	0
Playoff Totals		**12**	**3**	**2**	**5**	**16**	**1**	**0**	**0**
TOMALTY, Glenn *No playoffs*	Left wing								
TOMLAK, Mike	Center/Left wing								
1990	Hartford	7	0	1	1	2	0	0	0
1991	Hartford	3	0	0	0	2	0	0	0
Playoff Totals		**10**	**0**	**1**	**1**	**4**	**0**	**0**	**0**
TOMLINSON, Dave *No playoffs*	Center								
TOMLINSON, Kirk *No playoffs*	Center								
TOMS, Jeff	Left wing								
1998	Washington	1	0	0	0	0	0	0	0
Playoff Totals		**1**	**0**	**0**	**0**	**0**	**0**	**0**	**0**
TOMSON, Jack	Defense								
1939	NY Americans	2	0	0	0	0	0	0	0
Playoff Totals		**2**	**0**	**0**	**0**	**0**	**0**	**0**	**0**
TONELLI, John	Left wing								
1979	NY Islanders	10	1	6	7	0	0	0	0
1980◆	NY Islanders	21	7	9	16	18	0	0	0
1981◆	NY Islanders	16	5	8	13	16	0	0	2
1982◆	NY Islanders	19	6	10	16	18	1	0	1
1983◆	NY Islanders	20	7	11	18	20	0	0	2
1984	NY Islanders	17	1	3	4	31	0	0	0
1985	NY Islanders	10	1	8	9	10	0	0	0
1986	Calgary	22	7	9	16	49	1	0	1
1987	Calgary	3	0	0	0	4	0	0	0
1988	Calgary	6	2	5	7	8	2	0	1
1989	Los Angeles	6	0	0	0	8	0	0	0
1990	Los Angeles	10	1	2	3	6	0	0	0
1991	Los Angeles	12	2	4	6	12	1	0	0
Playoff Totals		**172**	**40**	**75**	**115**	**200**	**5**	**0**	**7**
TOOKEY, Tim	Center								
1987	Philadelphia	10	1	3	4	2	0	0	0
Playoff Totals		**10**	**1**	**3**	**4**	**2**	**0**	**0**	**0**
TOOMEY, Sean *No playoffs*	Left wing								
TOPOROWSKI, Shayne *No playoffs*	Right wing								
TOPPAZZINI, Jerry	Right wing								
1953	Boston	11	0	3	3	9	....	....	....
1957	Boston	10	0	1	1	2	....	....	....
1958	Boston	12	9	3	12	2	....	....	....
1959	Boston	7	4	2	6	0	....	....	....
Playoff Totals		**40**	**13**	**9**	**22**	**13**	....	....	....
TOPPAZZINI, Zellio	Right wing								
1949	Boston	2	0	0	0	0	0	0	0
Playoff Totals		**2**	**0**	**0**	**0**	**0**	**0**	**0**	**0**
TORGAYEV, Pavel	Left wing								
1996	Calgary	1	0	0	0	0	0	0	0
Playoff Totals		**1**	**0**	**0**	**0**	**0**	**0**	**0**	**0**
TORKKI, Jari *No playoffs*	Left wing								
TORMANEN, Antti *No playoffs*	Right wing								
TOUHEY, Bill	Left wing								
1930	Ottawa	2	1	0	1	0	....	....	....
Playoff Totals		**2**	**1**	**0**	**1**	**0**	....	....	....
TOUPIN, Jacques	Right wing								
1944	Chicago	4	0	0	0	0	0	0	0
Playoff Totals		**4**	**0**	**0**	**0**	**0**	**0**	**0**	**0**
TOWNSEND, Art *No playoffs*	Defense								
TOWNSHEND, Graeme *No playoffs*	Right wing								
TRADER, Larry	Defense								
1985	Detroit	3	0	0	0	0	0	0	0
Playoff Totals		**3**	**0**	**0**	**0**	**0**	**0**	**0**	**0**
TRAINOR, Wes *No playoffs*	Center/left wing								
TRAPP, Bob	Defense								
1927	Chicago	2	0	0	0	4	0	0	0
Playoff Totals		**2**	**0**	**0**	**0**	**4**	**0**	**0**	**0**
TRAPP, Doug *No playoffs*	Left wing								
TRAUB, Percy	Defense								
1927	Chicago	2	0	0	0	6	0	0	0
1929	Detroit	2	0	0	0	0	0	0	0
Playoff Totals		**4**	**0**	**0**	**0**	**6**	**0**	**0**	**0**
TRAVERSE, Patrick *No playoffs*	Defense								
TREBIL, Daniel	Defense								
1997	Anaheim	9	0	1	1	6	0	0	0
1999	Anaheim	1	0	0	0	2	0	0	0
Playoff Totals		**10**	**0**	**1**	**1**	**8**	**0**	**0**	**0**
TREDWAY, Brock	Right wing								
1982	Los Angeles	1	0	0	0	0	0	0	0
Playoff Totals		**1**	**0**	**0**	**0**	**0**	**0**	**0**	**0**
TREMBLAY, Brent *No playoffs*	Defense								
TREMBLAY, Gilles	Left wing								
1961	Montreal	6	1	3	4	0	0	0	0
1962	Montreal	6	1	0	1	2	0	0	0
1963	Montreal	5	2	0	2	0	2	0	1
1964	Montreal	2	0	0	0	0	0	0	0
1966◆	Montreal	10	4	5	9	0	3	0	1
1967	Montreal	10	0	1	1	0	0	0	0
1968◆	Montreal	9	1	5	6	2	0	0	0
Playoff Totals		**48**	**9**	**14**	**23**	**4**	**5**	**0**	**2**
TREMBLAY, J.C.	Defense								
1961	Montreal	5	0	0	0	2	0	0	0
1962	Montreal	6	0	2	2	2	0	0	0
1963	Montreal	5	0	0	0	0	0	0	0
1964	Montreal	7	2	1	3	9	0	1	0
1965◆	Montreal	13	1	*9	10	18	0	1	0
1966◆	Montreal	10	2	9	11	2	2	0	0
1967	Montreal	10	2	4	6	2	0	0	0
1968◆	Montreal	13	3	6	9	2	0	1	1
1969◆	Montreal	13	1	4	5	6	0	1	0
1971◆	Montreal	20	3	14	17	15	1	0	3
1972	Montreal	6	0	2	2	0	0	0	0
Playoff Totals		**108**	**14**	**51**	**65**	**58**	**3**	**4**	**4**
TREMBLAY, Marcel *No playoffs*	Right wing								
TREMBLAY, Mario	Right wing								
1975	Montreal	11	0	1	1	7	0	0	0
1976◆	Montreal	10	0	1	1	27	0	0	0
1977◆	Montreal	14	3	0	3	9	0	0	0
1978◆	Montreal	5	2	1	3	16	0	0	1
1979◆	Montreal	13	3	4	7	13	0	0	1
1980	Montreal	10	0	11	11	14	0	0	0
1981	Montreal	3	0	0	0	9	0	0	0
1982	Montreal	5	4	1	5	24	0	0	1
1983	Montreal	3	0	1	1	7	0	0	0
1984	Montreal	15	6	3	9	31	0	0	1
1985	Montreal	12	2	6	8	30	1	0	0
Playoff Totals		**101**	**20**	**29**	**49**	**187**	**1**	**0**	**4**
TREMBLAY, Nils	Center								
1945	Montreal	2	0	0	0	0	0	0	0
Playoff Totals		**2**	**0**	**0**	**0**	**0**	**0**	**0**	**0**
TREMBLAY, Yannick *No playoffs*	Defense								
TREPANIER, Pascal *No playoffs*	Defense								
TRIMPER, Tim	Left wing								
1980	Chicago	1	0	0	0	2	0	0	0
1982	Winnipeg	1	0	0	0	0	0	0	0
Playoff Totals		**2**	**0**	**0**	**0**	**2**	**0**	**0**	**0**
TRNKA, Pavel	Defense								
1999	Anaheim	4	0	1	1	2	0	0	0
Playoff Totals		**4**	**0**	**1**	**1**	**2**	**0**	**0**	**0**
TROTTIER, Bryan	Center								
1976	NY Islanders	13	1	7	8	8	0	0	0
1977	NY Islanders	12	2	8	10	2	0	0	0
1978	NY Islanders	7	0	3	3	4	0	0	0
1979	NY Islanders	10	2	4	6	13	0	0	1
1980◆	NY Islanders	21	*12	17	*29	16	4	2	2
1981◆	NY Islanders	*18	11	*18	29	34	4	2	1
1982◆	NY Islanders	19	6	*23	*29	40	2	0	2
1983◆	NY Islanders	17	8	12	20	18	3	0	1
1984	NY Islanders	21	8	6	14	49	1	0	0
1985	NY Islanders	10	4	2	6	8	1	0	1
1986	NY Islanders	3	1	1	2	2	0	0	0
1987	NY Islanders	14	8	5	13	12	3	0	2
1988	NY Islanders	6	0	0	0	10	0	0	0
1990	NY Islanders	4	1	0	1	4	0	0	0
1991◆	Pittsburgh	23	3	4	7	49	0	0	2
1992◆	Pittsburgh	21	4	3	7	8	0	0	0
1994	Pittsburgh	2	0	0	0	0	0	0	0
Playoff Totals		**221**	**71**	**113**	**184**	**277**	**18**	**4**	**12**
TROTTIER, Dave	Left wing								
1930	Mtl. Maroons	4	0	2	2	8	....	....	....
1931	Mtl. Maroons	2	0	0	0	6	....	....	....
1932	Mtl. Maroons	4	1	0	1	0	....	....	....
1933	Mtl. Maroons	2	0	0	0	6	....	....	....
1934	Mtl. Maroons	4	0	0	0	6	....	....	....
1935◆	Mtl. Maroons	7	2	1	3	4	....	....	....
1936	Mtl. Maroons	3	0	0	0	4	....	....	....
1937	Mtl. Maroons	5	1	0	1	5	....	....	....
Playoff Totals		**31**	**4**	**3**	**7**	**39**	....	....	....
TROTTIER, Guy	Right wing								
1971	Toronto	5	0	0	0	0	0	0	0
1972	Toronto	4	1	0	1	16	0	0	0
Playoff Totals		**9**	**1**	**0**	**1**	**16**	**0**	**0**	**0**
TROTTIER, Rocky *No playoffs*	Right wing								
TRUDEL, Lou	Left wing								
1934◆	Chicago	7	0	0	0	0	....	....	....
1935	Chicago	2	0	0	0	0	....	....	....
1936	Chicago	2	0	0	0	2	....	....	....
1938◆	Chicago	10	0	3	3	2	....	....	....
1939	Mtl. Canadiens	3	1	0	1	0	....	....	....
Playoff Totals		**24**	**1**	**3**	**4**	**4**	....	....	....
TRUDELL, Rene	Right wing								
1948	NY Rangers	5	0	0	0	2	0	0	0
Playoff Totals		**5**	**0**	**0**	**0**	**2**	**0**	**0**	**0**
TSULYGIN, Nikolai *No playoffs*	Defense								
TSYGUROV, Denis *No playoffs*	Defense								
TSYPLAKOV, Vladimir	Left wing								
1998	Los Angeles	4	0	1	1	8	0	0	0
Playoff Totals		**4**	**0**	**1**	**1**	**8**	**0**	**0**	**0**
TUCKER, Darcy	Center								
1997	Montreal	4	0	0	0	0	0	0	0
Playoff Totals		**4**	**0**	**0**	**0**	**0**	**0**	**0**	**0**
TUCKER, John	Center								
1984	Buffalo	3	1	0	1	0	0	0	0
1985	Buffalo	5	1	5	6	0	0	0	0
1988	Buffalo	6	7	3	10	18	4	0	2
1989	Buffalo	3	0	3	3	0	0	0	0
1990	Washington	12	1	7	8	4	0	0	0
1996	Tampa Bay	2	0	0	0	2	0	0	0
Playoff Totals		**31**	**10**	**18**	**28**	**24**	**4**	**0**	**2**
TUDIN, Connie *No playoffs*	Center								

Season	Club	GP	G	A	Pts	PIM	PP	SH	GW
TUDOR, Rob									Right wing/center
1979	Vancouver	2	0	0	0	0	0	0	0
1980	Vancouver	1	0	0	0	0	0	0	0
Playoff Totals		**3**	**0**	**0**	**0**	**0**	**0**	**0**	**0**
TUER, Allan	*No playoffs*								Defense
TUOMAINEN, Marko	*No playoffs*								Right wing
TURCOTTE, Alfie									Center
1985	Montreal	5	0	0	0	0	0	0	0
Playoff Totals		**5**	**0**	**0**	**0**	**0**	**0**	**0**	**0**
TURCOTTE, Darren									Center
1989	NY Rangers	1	0	0	0	0	0	0	0
1990	NY Rangers	10	1	6	7	4	0	0	1
1991	NY Rangers	6	1	2	3	0	1	0	0
1992	NY Rangers	8	4	0	4	6	2	1	0
1998	St. Louis	10	0	0	0	2	0	0	0
Playoff Totals		**35**	**6**	**8**	**14**	**12**	**3**	**1**	**1**
TURGEON, Pierre									Center
1988	Buffalo	6	4	3	7	4	3	0	0
1989	Buffalo	5	3	5	8	2	1	0	0
1990	Buffalo	6	2	4	6	2	0	0	1
1991	Buffalo	6	3	1	4	6	1	0	0
1993	NY Islanders	11	6	7	13	0	0	0	0
1994	NY Islanders	4	0	1	1	0	0	0	0
1996	Montreal	6	2	4	6	2	0	0	0
1997	St. Louis	5	1	1	2	2	1	0	0
1998	St. Louis	10	4	4	8	2	2	0	0
1999	St. Louis	13	4	9	13	6	0	0	2
Playoff Totals		**72**	**29**	**39**	**68**	**26**	**8**	**0**	**3**
TURGEON, Sylvain									Left wing
1986	Hartford	9	2	3	5	4	0	0	0
1987	Hartford	6	1	2	3	4	0	0	0
1988	Hartford	6	0	0	0	4	0	0	0
1989	Hartford	4	0	2	2	4	0	0	0
1990	New Jersey	1	0	0	0	0	0	0	0
1991	Montreal	5	0	0	0	2	0	0	0
1992	Montreal	5	1	0	1	4	0	0	0
Playoff Totals		**36**	**4**	**7**	**11**	**22**	**0**	**0**	**0**
TURLICK, Gord	*No playoffs*								Left wing/center
TURNBULL, Ian									Defense
1974	Toronto	4	0	0	0	8	0	0	0
1975	Toronto	7	0	2	2	4	0	0	0
1976	Toronto	10	2	9	11	29	1	0	0
1977	Toronto	9	4	4	8	10	4	0	0
1978	Toronto	13	6	10	16	10	1	0	0
1979	Toronto	6	0	4	4	27	0	0	0
1980	Toronto	3	0	3	3	2	0	0	0
1981	Toronto	3	1	0	1	4	0	0	0
Playoff Totals		**55**	**13**	**32**	**45**	**94**	**6**	**0**	**0**
TURNBULL, Perry									Center
1980	St. Louis	3	1	1	2	2	1	0	0
1982	St. Louis	5	3	2	5	11	1	0	0
1983	St. Louis	4	1	0	1	14	0	0	0
1984	Montreal	9	1	2	3	10	0	0	0
1985	Winnipeg	8	0	1	1	26	0	0	0
1986	Winnipeg	3	0	1	1	11	0	0	0
1987	Winnipeg	1	0	0	0	10	0	0	0
1988	St. Louis	1	0	0	0	2	0	0	0
Playoff Totals		**34**	**6**	**7**	**13**	**86**	**2**	**0**	**0**
TURNBULL, Randy	*No playoffs*								Defense
TURNER, Bob									Defense
1956◆	Montreal	10	0	1	1	10	0	0	0
1957◆	Montreal	6	0	1	1	0	0	0	0
1958◆	Montreal	10	0	0	0	2	0	0	0
1959◆	Montreal	11	0	2	2	20	0	0	0
1960◆	Montreal	8	0	0	0	0	0	0	0
1961	Montreal	5	0	0	0	0	0	0	0
1962	Chicago	12	1	0	1	6	0	1	0
1963	Chicago	6	0	0	0	6	0	0	0
Playoff Totals		**68**	**1**	**4**	**5**	**44**	**0**	**1**	**0**
TURNER, Brad	*No playoffs*								Defense
TURNER, Dean	*No playoffs*								Defense
TUSTIN, Norm	*No playoffs*								Left wing
TUTEN, Aut	*No playoffs*								Defense
TUTT, Brian	*No playoffs*								Defense
TUTTLE, Steve									Right wing
1989	St. Louis	6	1	2	3	0	0	0	0
1990	St. Louis	5	0	1	1	2	0	0	0
1991	St. Louis	6	0	3	3	0	0	0	0
Playoff Totals		**17**	**1**	**6**	**7**	**2**	**0**	**0**	**0**
TUZZOLINO, Tony	*No playoffs*								Right wing
TVERDOVSKY, Oleg									Defense
1996	Winnipeg	6	0	1	1	0	0	0	0
1997	Phoenix	7	0	1	1	0	0	0	0
1998	Phoenix	6	0	7	7	0	0	0	0
1999	Phoenix	6	0	2	2	6	0	0	0
Playoff Totals		**25**	**0**	**11**	**11**	**6**	**0**	**0**	**0**

Season	Club	GP	G	A	Pts	PIM	PP	SH	GW
TWIST, Tony									Left wing
1995	St. Louis	1	0	0	0	6	0	0	0
1996	St. Louis	10	1	1	2	16	0	0	0
1997	St. Louis	6	0	0	0	0	0	0	0
1999	St. Louis	1	0	0	0	0	0	0	0
Playoff Totals		**18**	**1**	**1**	**2**	**22**	**0**	**0**	**0**
UBRIACO, Gene									Left wing/center
1969	Oakland	7	2	0	2	2	0	0	0
1970	Chicago	4	0	0	0	2	0	0	0
Playoff Totals		**11**	**2**	**0**	**2**	**4**	**0**	**0**	**0**
ULANOV, Igor									Defense
1992	Winnipeg	7	0	0	0	39	0	0	0
1993	Winnipeg	4	0	0	0	4	0	0	0
1995	Washington	2	0	0	0	4	0	0	0
1996	Tampa Bay	5	0	0	0	15	0	0	0
1998	Montreal	10	1	4	5	12	0	0	0
Playoff Totals		**28**	**1**	**4**	**5**	**74**	**0**	**0**	**0**
ULLMAN, Norm									Center
1956	Detroit	10	1	3	4	13	....	....	....
1957	Detroit	5	1	1	2	6	....	....	....
1958	Detroit	4	0	2	2	4	....	....	....
1960	Detroit	6	2	2	4	0	....	....	....
1961	Detroit	11	0	4	4	4	....	....	....
1963	Detroit	11	4	*12	*16	14	....	....	....
1964	Detroit	14	7	10	17	6	....	....	....
1965	Detroit	7	6	4	10	2	....	....	....
1966	Detroit	12	*6	9	*15	12	....	....	....
1969	Toronto	4	1	0	1	0	0	0	0
1971	Toronto	6	0	2	2	2	0	0	0
1972	Toronto	5	1	3	4	2	0	0	0
1974	Toronto	4	1	1	2	0	0	0	0
1975	Toronto	7	0	0	0	2	0	0	0
Playoff Totals		**106**	**30**	**53**	**83**	**67**	....	....	....
UNGER, Garry									Center
1970	Detroit	4	0	1	1	6	0	0	0
1971	St. Louis	6	3	2	5	20	0	1	0
1972	St. Louis	11	4	5	9	35	2	0	1
1973	St. Louis	5	1	2	3	2	0	0	0
1975	St. Louis	2	1	3	4	6	0	0	0
1976	St. Louis	3	2	1	3	7	0	0	0
1977	St. Louis	4	0	1	1	2	0	0	0
1980	Atlanta	4	0	3	3	2	0	0	0
1981	Edmonton	8	0	0	0	2	0	0	0
1982	Edmonton	4	1	0	1	23	0	0	0
1983	Edmonton	1	0	0	0	0	0	0	0
Playoff Totals		**52**	**12**	**18**	**30**	**105**	**2**	**1**	**1**
USTORF, Stefan									Center
1996	Washington	5	0	0	0	0	0	0	0
Playoff Totals		**5**	**0**	**0**	**0**	**0**	**0**	**0**	**0**
VACHON, Nick	*No playoffs*								Center
VADNAIS, Carol									Left wing/Defense
1967	Montreal	1	0	0	0	2	0	0	0
1968◆	Montreal	1	0	0	0	0	0	0	0
1969	Oakland	7	1	4	5	10	1	0	0
1970	Oakland	4	2	1	3	15	2	0	0
1972◆	Boston	15	0	2	2	43	0	0	0
1973	Boston	5	0	0	0	8	0	0	0
1974	Boston	16	1	12	13	42	1	0	0
1975	Boston	3	1	5	6	0	0	0	0
1978	NY Rangers	3	0	2	2	16	0	0	0
1979	NY Rangers	18	2	9	11	13	0	0	0
1980	NY Rangers	9	1	2	3	6	0	0	0
1981	NY Rangers	14	1	3	4	26	0	0	0
1982	NY Rangers	10	1	0	1	4	0	0	0
Playoff Totals		**106**	**10**	**40**	**50**	**185**	**4**	**0**	**0**
VAIC, Lubomir	*No playoffs*								Center
VAIL, Eric									Left wing
1974	Atlanta	1	0	0	0	2	0	0	0
1976	Atlanta	2	0	0	0	0	0	0	0
1977	Atlanta	3	1	3	4	0	0	0	1
1978	Atlanta	2	1	1	2	0	0	0	0
1979	Atlanta	2	0	1	1	2	0	0	0
1980	Atlanta	4	3	1	4	2	1	0	1
1981	Calgary	6	0	0	0	0	0	0	0
Playoff Totals		**20**	**5**	**6**	**11**	**6**	**1**	**0**	**2**
VAIL, Sparky									Defense/left wing
1929	NY Rangers	6	0	0	0	2	0	0	0
1930	NY Rangers	4	0	0	0	0	0	0	0
Playoff Totals		**10**	**0**	**0**	**0**	**2**	**0**	**0**	**0**
VAIVE, Rick									Right wing
1980	Toronto	3	1	0	1	11	0	0	0
1981	Toronto	3	1	0	1	4	0	0	0
1983	Toronto	4	2	5	7	6	0	0	0
1986	Toronto	9	6	2	8	9	3	0	0
1987	Toronto	13	4	2	6	23	1	0	0
1988	Chicago	5	6	2	8	38	5	0	0
1989	Buffalo	5	2	1	3	8	2	0	0
1990	Buffalo	6	4	2	6	6	4	0	1
1991	Buffalo	6	1	2	3	6	1	0	0
Playoff Totals		**54**	**27**	**16**	**43**	**111**	**16**	**0**	**1**

Season	Club	GP	G	A	Pts	PIM	PP	SH	GW
VALENTINE, Chris									Center
1983	Washington	2	0	0	0	4	0	0	0
Playoff Totals		**2**	**0**	**0**	**0**	**4**	**0**	**0**	**0**
VALICEVIC, Robert	*No playoffs*								Right wing
VALIQUETTE, Jack									Center
1976	Toronto	10	2	3	5	2	0	0	0
1978	Toronto	13	1	3	4	2	1	0	0
Playoff Totals		**23**	**3**	**6**	**9**	**4**	**1**	**0**	**0**
VALK, Garry									Left wing
1991	Vancouver	5	0	0	0	20	0	0	0
1992	Vancouver	4	0	0	0	5	0	0	0
1993	Vancouver	7	0	1	1	12	0	0	0
1999	Toronto	17	3	4	7	22	0	0	1
Playoff Totals		**33**	**3**	**5**	**8**	**59**	**0**	**0**	**1**
VALLIS, Lindsay	*No playoffs*								Defense
VAN ALLEN, Shaun									Center
1997	Ottawa	7	0	1	1	4	0	0	0
1998	Ottawa	11	0	1	1	10	0	0	0
1999	Ottawa	4	0	0	0	0	0	0	0
Playoff Totals		**22**	**0**	**2**	**2**	**14**	**0**	**0**	**0**
VAN BOXMEER, John									Defense
1974	Montreal	1	0	0	0	0	0	0	0
1978	Colorado	2	0	1	1	2	0	0	0
1980	Buffalo	14	3	5	8	12	2	0	2
1981	Buffalo	8	1	8	9	7	0	0	0
1982	Buffalo	4	0	1	1	6	0	0	0
1983	Buffalo	9	1	0	1	10	1	0	0
Playoff Totals		**38**	**5**	**15**	**20**	**37**	**3**	**0**	**2**
VANDENBUSSCHE, Ryan	*No playoffs*								Right wing
VAN DORP, Wayne									Left wing
1987◆	Edmonton	3	0	0	0	2	0	0	0
1989	Chicago	16	0	1	1	17	0	0	0
1990	Chicago	8	0	0	0	23	0	0	0
Playoff Totals		**27**	**0**	**1**	**1**	**42**	**0**	**0**	**0**
VAN DRUNEN, David	*No playoffs*								Defense
VAN IMPE, Darren									Defense
1997	Anaheim	9	0	2	2	16	0	0	0
1998	Boston	6	2	1	3	0	1	0	1
1999	Boston	11	1	2	3	4	1	0	0
Playoff Totals		**26**	**3**	**5**	**8**	**20**	**2**	**0**	**1**
VAN IMPE, Ed									Defense
1967	Chicago	6	0	0	0	8	0	0	0
1968	Philadelphia	7	0	4	4	11	0	0	0
1969	Philadelphia	1	0	0	0	17	0	0	0
1971	Philadelphia	4	0	1	1	8	0	0	0
1973	Philadelphia	11	0	0	0	16	0	0	0
1974◆	Philadelphia	17	1	2	3	41	0	0	0
1975◆	Philadelphia	17	0	4	4	28	0	0	0
1976	Pittsburgh	3	0	1	1	2	0	0	0
Playoff Totals		**66**	**1**	**12**	**13**	**131**	**0**	**0**	**0**
VARADA, Vaclav									Right wing
1998	Buffalo	15	3	4	7	18	0	0	0
1999	Buffalo	21	5	4	9	14	1	0	0
Playoff Totals		**36**	**8**	**8**	**16**	**32**	**1**	**0**	**0**
VARIS, Petri	*No playoffs*								Left wing
VARLAMOV, Sergei	*No playoffs*								Left wing
VARVIO, Jarkko	*No playoffs*								Right wing
VASILEVSKY, Alexander	*No playoffs*								Right wing
VASILJEVS, Herbert	*No playoffs*								Center
VASILYEV, Andrei	*No playoffs*								Left wing
VASKE, Dennis									Defense
1993	NY Islanders	18	0	6	6	14	0	0	0
1994	NY Islanders	4	0	1	1	2	0	0	0
Playoff Totals		**22**	**0**	**7**	**7**	**16**	**0**	**0**	**0**
VASKO, Elmer									Defense
1959	Chicago	6	0	1	1	4	0	0	0
1960	Chicago	4	0	0	0	0	0	0	0
1961◆	Chicago	12	1	1	2	23	1	0	1
1962	Chicago	12	0	0	0	4	0	0	0
1963	Chicago	6	0	1	1	8	0	0	0
1964	Chicago	7	0	0	0	4	0	0	0
1965	Chicago	14	1	2	3	20	0	0	0
1966	Chicago	3	0	0	0	4	0	0	0
1968	Minnesota	14	0	2	2	6	0	0	0
Playoff Totals		**78**	**2**	**7**	**9**	**73**	**1**	**0**	**1**
VASKO, Rick	*No playoffs*								Defense
VAUTOUR, Yvon	*No playoffs*								Right wing
VAYDIK, Greg	*No playoffs*								Center
VEITCH, Darren									Defense
1984	Washington	5	0	1	1	15	0	0	0
1985	Washington	5	0	1	1	4	0	0	0
1987	Detroit	12	3	4	7	8	2	0	1
1988	Detroit	11	1	5	6	6	1	0	0
Playoff Totals		**33**	**4**	**11**	**15**	**33**	**3**	**0**	**1**

Season	Club	GP	G	A	Pts	PIM	PP	SH	GW
VELISCHEK, Randy	Defense								
1983	Minnesota	9	0	0	0	0	0	0	0
1984	Minnesota	1	0	0	0	0	0	0	0
1985	Minnesota	9	2	3	5	8	0	0	0
1988	New Jersey	19	0	2	2	20	0	0	0
1990	New Jersey	6	0	0	0	4	0	0	0
Playoff Totals		**44**	**2**	**5**	**7**	**32**	**0**	**0**	**0**
VELLUCCI, Mike *No playoffs*	Defense								
VENASKY, Vic	Center								
1976	Los Angeles	9	0	1	1	6	0	0	0
1977	Los Angeles	9	1	4	5	6	1	0	0
1978	Los Angeles	1	0	0	0	0	0	0	0
1979	Los Angeles	2	0	0	0	0	0	0	0
Playoff Totals		**21**	**1**	**5**	**6**	**12**	**1**	**0**	**0**
VENERUZZO, Gary	Right/left wing								
1968	St. Louis	9	0	2	2	2	0	0	0
Playoff Totals		**9**	**0**	**2**	**2**	**2**	**0**	**0**	**0**
VERBEEK, Pat	Right/Left wing								
1988	New Jersey	20	4	8	12	51	2	0	1
1990	Hartford	7	2	2	4	26	1	0	1
1991	Hartford	6	3	2	5	40	2	0	0
1992	Hartford	7	0	2	2	12	0	0	0
1995	NY Rangers	10	4	6	10	20	3	0	0
1996	NY Rangers	11	3	6	9	12	1	0	0
1997	Dallas	7	1	3	4	16	1	0	0
1998	Dallas	17	3	2	5	26	2	0	1
1999♦	Dallas	18	3	4	7	14	0	0	1
Playoff Totals		**103**	**23**	**35**	**58**	**217**	**12**	**0**	**4**
VERMETTE, Mark *No playoffs*	Right wing								
VERRET, Claude *No playoffs*	Center								
VERSTRAETE, Leigh *No playoffs*	Right wing								
VERVERGAERT, Dennis	Right wing								
1975	Vancouver	1	0	0	0	0	0	0	0
1976	Vancouver	2	1	0	1	4	1	0	0
1979	Philadelphia	3	0	2	2	2	0	0	0
1980	Philadelphia	2	0	0	0	0	0	0	0
Playoff Totals		**8**	**1**	**2**	**3**	**6**	**1**	**0**	**0**
VESEY, Jim *No playoffs*	Center/Right wing								
VEYSEY, Sid *No playoffs*	Center								
VIAL, Dennis *No playoffs*	Left wing								
VICKERS, Steve	Left wing								
1973	NY Rangers	10	5	4	9	4	0	0	0
1974	NY Rangers	13	4	4	8	17	2	0	0
1975	NY Rangers	3	2	4	6	6	0	0	0
1978	NY Rangers	3	2	1	3	0	0	0	0
1979	NY Rangers	18	5	3	8	13	1	0	1
1980	NY Rangers	9	2	2	4	4	0	0	1
1981	NY Rangers	12	4	7	11	14	1	0	0
Playoff Totals		**68**	**24**	**25**	**49**	**58**	**4**	**0**	**2**
VIGNEAULT, Alain	Defense								
1983	St. Louis	4	0	1	1	26	0	0	0
Playoff Totals		**4**	**0**	**1**	**1**	**26**	**0**	**0**	**0**
VIITAKOSKI, Vesa *No playoffs*	Left wing								
VILGRAIN, Claude	Right wing								
1990	New Jersey	4	0	0	0	0	0	0	0
1992	New Jersey	7	1	1	2	17	0	0	0
Playoff Totals		**11**	**1**	**1**	**2**	**17**	**0**	**0**	**0**
VINCELETTE, Daniel	Left wing								
1987	Chicago	3	0	0	0	0	0	0	0
1988	Chicago	4	0	0	0	0	0	0	0
1989	Chicago	5	0	0	0	4	0	0	0
Playoff Totals		**12**	**0**	**0**	**0**	**4**	**0**	**0**	**0**
VIPOND, Pete *No playoffs*	Left wing								
VIRTA, Hannu	Defense								
1982	Buffalo	4	0	1	1	0	0	0	0
1983	Buffalo	10	1	2	3	4	0	0	0
1984	Buffalo	3	0	0	0	2	0	0	0
Playoff Totals		**17**	**1**	**3**	**4**	**6**	**0**	**0**	**0**
VIRTUE, Terry *No playoffs*	Defense								
VISHEAU, Mark *No playoffs*	Defense								
VISHNEVSKI, Vitaly *No playoffs*	Defense								
VITOLINSH, Harijs *No playoffs*	Center								
VIVEIROS, Emanuel *No playoffs*	Defense								
VOKES, Ed *No playoffs*	Left wing								
VOLCAN, Mickey *No playoffs*	Defense								
VOLCHKOV, Alexander *No playoffs*	Center								
VOLEK, David	Left/Right wing								
1990	NY Islanders	5	1	4	5	0	0	0	0
1993	NY Islanders	10	4	1	5	2	0	0	0
Playoff Totals		**15**	**5**	**5**	**10**	**2**	**0**	**0**	**0**
VOLMAR, Doug	Right wing								
1970	Detroit	2	1	0	1	0	0	0	0
Playoff Totals		**2**	**1**	**0**	**1**	**0**	**0**	**0**	**0**
VON STEFENELLI, Phil *No playoffs*	Defense								
VOPAT, Jan	Defense								
1998	Los Angeles	2	0	1	1	2	0	0	0
Playoff Totals		**2**	**0**	**1**	**1**	**2**	**0**	**0**	**0**
VOPAT, Roman *No playoffs*	Center								
VOROBIEV, Vladimir	Left wing								
1999	Edmonton	1	0	0	0	0	0	0	0
Playoff Totals		**1**	**0**	**0**	**0**	**0**	**0**	**0**	**0**
VOSS, Carl	Center								
1933	Detroit	4	1	1	2	0	....	....	....
1936	NY Americans	5	0	0	0	0	....	....	....
1937	Mtl. Maroons	5	1	0	1	0	....	....	....
1938♦	Chicago	10	3	2	5	0	....	....	....
Playoff Totals		**24**	**5**	**3**	**8**	**0**	....	....	....
VUJTEK, Vladimir *No playoffs*	Left wing								
VUKOTA, Mick	Right wing								
1988	NY Islanders	2	0	0	0	23	0	0	0
1990	NY Islanders	1	0	0	0	17	0	0	0
1993	NY Islanders	15	0	0	0	16	0	0	0
1994	NY Islanders	4	0	0	0	17	0	0	0
1998	Montreal	1	0	0	0	0	0	0	0
Playoff Totals		**23**	**0**	**0**	**0**	**73**	**0**	**0**	**0**
VYAZMIKIN, Igor *No playoffs*	Right/left wing								
WADDELL, Don *No playoffs*	Defense								
WAITE, Frank *No playoffs*	Center								
WALKER, Gord *No playoffs*	Right wing								
WALKER, Howard *No playoffs*	Defense								
WALKER, Jack *No playoffs*	Forward								
WALKER, Kurt	Defense								
1976	Toronto	6	0	0	0	24	0	0	0
1978	Toronto	10	0	0	0	10	0	0	0
Playoff Totals		**16**	**0**	**0**	**0**	**34**	**0**	**0**	**0**
WALKER, Russ *No playoffs*	Right wing								
WALKER, Scott *No playoffs*	Center								
WALL, Bob	Defense								
1965	Detroit	1	0	0	0	0	0	0	0
1966	Detroit	6	0	0	0	2	0	0	0
1968	Los Angeles	7	0	1	1	0	0	0	0
1969	Los Angeles	8	0	2	2	0	0	0	0
Playoff Totals		**22**	**0**	**3**	**3**	**2**	**0**	**0**	**0**
WALLIN, Peter	Right wing								
1981	NY Rangers	14	2	6	8	6	0	0	0
Playoff Totals		**14**	**2**	**6**	**8**	**6**	**0**	**0**	**0**
WALSH, Jim *No playoffs*	Defense								
WALSH, Mike *No playoffs*	Left wing								
WALTER, Ryan	Center/Left wing								
1983	Montreal	3	0	0	0	11	0	0	0
1984	Montreal	15	2	1	3	4	1	0	1
1985	Montreal	12	2	7	9	13	1	0	0
1986♦	Montreal	5	0	1	1	2	0	0	0
1987	Montreal	17	7	12	19	10	2	1	1
1988	Montreal	11	2	4	6	6	2	0	1
1989	Montreal	21	3	5	8	6	0	1	2
1990	Montreal	11	0	2	2	0	0	0	0
1991	Montreal	5	0	0	0	2	0	0	0
1992	Vancouver	13	0	3	3	8	0	0	0
Playoff Totals		**113**	**16**	**35**	**51**	**62**	**5**	**2**	**5**
WALTON, Bobby *No playoffs*	Center/right wing								
WALTON, Mike	Center								
1967♦	Toronto	12	4	3	7	2	3	0	1
1969	Toronto	4	0	0	0	4	0	0	0
1971	Boston	5	2	0	2	19	1	0	0
1972♦	Boston	15	6	6	12	13	1	0	2
1973	Boston	5	1	1	2	2	0	0	0
1976	Vancouver	2	0	0	0	5	0	0	0
1979	Chicago	4	1	0	1	0	0	0	0
Playoff Totals		**47**	**14**	**10**	**24**	**45**	**5**	**0**	**3**
WALZ, Wes	Center								
1991	Boston	2	0	0	0	0	0	0	0
1994	Calgary	6	3	0	3	2	0	0	0
1995	Calgary	1	0	0	0	0	0	0	0
Playoff Totals		**9**	**3**	**0**	**3**	**2**	**0**	**0**	**0**
WAPPEL, Gord	Defense								
1980	Atlanta	2	0	0	0	4	0	0	0
Playoff Totals		**2**	**0**	**0**	**0**	**4**	**0**	**0**	**0**
WARD, Aaron	Defense								
1997♦	Detroit	19	0	0	0	17	0	0	0
1999	Detroit	8	0	1	1	8	0	0	0
Playoff Totals		**27**	**0**	**1**	**1**	**25**	**0**	**0**	**0**
WARD, Dixon	Right wing								
1993	Vancouver	9	2	3	5	0	2	0	0
1997	Buffalo	12	2	3	5	6	0	0	0
1998	Buffalo	15	3	8	11	6	0	0	0
1999	Buffalo	21	7	5	12	32	0	2	3
Playoff Totals		**57**	**14**	**19**	**33**	**44**	**2**	**2**	**3**
WARD, Don *No playoffs*	Defense								
WARD, Ed *No playoffs*	Right wing								
WARD, Jason *No playoffs*	Right wing								
WARD, Jimmy	Right wing								
1928	Mtl. Maroons	9	1	1	2	6	....	....	....
1930	Mtl. Maroons	4	0	1	1	12	....	....	....
1931	Mtl. Maroons	2	0	0	0	2	....	....	....
1932	Mtl. Maroons	4	2	1	3	0	....	....	....
1933	Mtl. Maroons	2	0	0	0	0	....	....	....
1934	Mtl. Maroons	4	0	0	0	0	....	....	....
1935♦	Mtl. Maroons	7	1	1	2	0	....	....	....
1936	Mtl. Maroons	3	0	0	0	6	....	....	....
1939	Mtl. Canadiens	1	0	0	0	0	....	....	....
Playoff Totals		**36**	**4**	**4**	**8**	**26**	....	....	....
WARD, Joe *No playoffs*	Center								
WARD, Ron *No playoffs*	Center								
WARE, Jeff *No playoffs*	Defense								
WARE, Michael *No playoffs*	Right wing								
WARES, Eddie	Defense/right wing								
1939	Detroit	6	1	0	1	8	....	....	....
1940	Detroit	5	0	0	0	0	....	....	....
1941	Detroit	9	0	0	0	0	....	....	....
1942	Detroit	12	1	3	4	22	....	....	....
1943♦	Detroit	10	3	3	6	4	....	....	....
1946	Chicago	3	0	1	1	0	....	....	....
Playoff Totals		**45**	**5**	**7**	**12**	**34**	....	....	....
WARNER, Bob	Defense								
1976	Toronto	2	0	0	0	0	0	0	0
1977	Toronto	2	0	0	0	0	0	0	0
Playoff Totals		**4**	**0**	**0**	**0**	**0**	**0**	**0**	**0**
WARNER, Jim *No playoffs*	Right wing								
WARRENER, Rhett	Defense								
1996	Florida	21	0	1	1	0	0	0	0
1997	Florida	5	0	0	0	0	0	0	0
1999	Buffalo	20	1	3	4	32	0	0	0
Playoff Totals		**46**	**1**	**4**	**5**	**32**	**0**	**0**	**0**
WARRINER, Todd	Left wing								
1996	Toronto	6	1	1	2	2	0	0	0
1999	Toronto	9	0	0	0	2	0	0	0
Playoff Totals		**15**	**1**	**1**	**2**	**4**	**0**	**0**	**0**
WARWICK, Bill *No playoffs*	Left wing								
WARWICK, Grant	Right wing								
1942	NY Rangers	6	0	1	1	2	....	....	....
1948	Boston	5	0	3	3	4	....	....	....
1949	Boston	5	2	0	2	0	....	....	....
Playoff Totals		**16**	**2**	**4**	**6**	**6**	....	....	....
WASHBURN, Steve	Center								
1996	Florida	1	0	1	1	0	0	0	0
Playoff Totals		**1**	**0**	**1**	**1**	**0**	**0**	**0**	**0**
WASNIE, Nick	Right wing								
1930♦	Mtl. Canadiens	6	2	2	4	12	....	....	....
1931♦	Mtl. Canadiens	4	4	1	5	8	....	....	....
1932	Mtl. Canadiens	4	0	0	0	0	....	....	....
Playoff Totals		**14**	**6**	**3**	**9**	**20**	....	....	....
WATSON, Bill	Right wing								
1986	Chicago	2	0	1	1	0	0	0	0
1987	Chicago	4	0	1	1	0	0	0	0
Playoff Totals		**6**	**0**	**2**	**2**	**0**	**0**	**0**	**0**
WATSON, Bryan	Defense								
1964	Montreal	6	0	0	0	2	0	0	0
1966	Detroit	12	2	0	2	30	0	0	0
1970	Pittsburgh	10	0	0	0	17	0	0	0
1972	Pittsburgh	4	0	0	0	21	0	0	0
Playoff Totals		**32**	**2**	**0**	**2**	**70**	**0**	**0**	**0**
WATSON, Dave *No playoffs*	Left wing								
WATSON, Harry	Left wing								
1943♦	Detroit	7	0	0	0	0	....	....	....
1946	Detroit	5	2	0	2	0	....	....	....
1947♦	Toronto	11	3	2	5	6	....	....	....
1948♦	Toronto	9	5	2	7	9	....	....	....
1949♦	Toronto	9	4	2	6	2	....	....	....
1950	Toronto	7	0	0	0	2	....	....	....
1951♦	Toronto	5	1	2	3	4	....	....	....
1952	Toronto	4	1	0	1	2	....	....	....
1954	Toronto	5	0	1	1	2	....	....	....
Playoff Totals		**62**	**16**	**9**	**25**	**27**	....	....	....
WATSON, Jim *No playoffs*	Defense								
WATSON, Jimmy	Defense								
1973	Philadelphia	2	0	0	0	0	0	0	0
1974♦	Philadelphia	17	1	2	3	41	1	0	0
1975♦	Philadelphia	17	1	8	9	10	0	0	0
1976	Philadelphia	16	1	8	9	6	0	0	0
1977	Philadelphia	10	1	2	3	2	0	0	1
1978	Philadelphia	12	1	7	8	6	0	0	0
1979	Philadelphia	8	0	2	2	2	0	0	0
1980	Philadelphia	15	0	4	4	20	0	0	0
1982	Philadelphia	4	0	1	1	2	0	0	0
Playoff Totals		**101**	**5**	**34**	**39**	**89**	**1**	**0**	**1**

Season	Club	GP	G	A	Pts	PIM	PP	SH	GW
WATSON, Joe									Defense
1968	Philadelphia	7	1	1	2	28	0	0	0
1969	Philadelphia	4	0	0	0	0	0	0	0
1971	Philadelphia	1	0	0	0	0	0	0	0
1973	Philadelphia	11	0	2	2	12	0	0	0
1974♦	Philadelphia	17	1	4	5	24	0	0	0
1975♦	Philadelphia	17	0	4	4	6	0	0	0
1976	Philadelphia	16	1	1	2	10	0	0	0
1977	Philadelphia	10	0	0	0	2	0	0	0
1978	Philadelphia	1	0	0	0	0	0	0	0
Playoff Totals		**84**	**3**	**12**	**15**	**82**	**0**	**0**	**0**
WATSON, Phil									Right wing/center
1937	NY Rangers	9	0	2	2	9	....	....	....
1938	NY Rangers	3	0	2	2	0	....	....	....
1939	NY Rangers	7	1	1	2	7	....	....	....
1940♦	NY Rangers	12	3	6	*9	16	....	....	....
1941	NY Rangers	3	0	2	2	9	....	....	....
1942	NY Rangers	6	1	4	5	8	....	....	....
1944♦	Montreal	9	3	5	8	16	....	....	....
1948	NY Rangers	5	2	3	5	2	....	....	....
Playoff Totals		**54**	**10**	**25**	**35**	**67**	....	....	....
WATT, Mike *No playoffs*									Left wing
WATTERS, Tim									Defense
1982	Winnipeg	4	0	1	1	8	0	0	0
1983	Winnipeg	3	0	0	0	2	0	0	0
1984	Winnipeg	3	1	0	1	2	0	0	0
1985	Winnipeg	8	0	1	1	16	0	0	0
1987	Winnipeg	10	0	0	0	21	0	0	0
1988	Winnipeg	4	0	0	0	4	0	0	0
1989	Los Angeles	11	0	1	1	6	0	0	0
1990	Los Angeles	4	0	0	0	6	0	0	0
1991	Los Angeles	7	0	0	0	12	0	0	0
1992	Los Angeles	6	0	0	0	8	0	0	0
1993	Los Angeles	22	0	2	2	30	0	0	0
Playoff Totals		**82**	**1**	**5**	**6**	**115**	**0**	**0**	**0**
WATTS, Brian *No playoffs*									Left wing
WEBB, Steve *No playoffs*									Right wing
WEBSTER, Aubrey *No playoffs*									Right wing
WEBSTER, Don									Left wing
1944	Toronto	5	0	0	0	12	0	0	0
Playoff Totals		**5**	**0**	**0**	**0**	**12**	**0**	**0**	**0**
WEBSTER, John *No playoffs*									Center
WEBSTER, Tom									Right wing
1969	Boston	1	0	0	0	0	0	0	0
Playoff Totals		**1**	**0**	**0**	**0**	**0**	**0**	**0**	**0**
WEIGHT, Doug									Center
1991	NY Rangers	1	0	0	0	0	0	0	0
1992	NY Rangers	7	2	2	4	0	1	0	0
1997	Edmonton	12	3	8	11	8	0	0	0
1998	Edmonton	12	2	7	9	14	2	0	1
1999	Edmonton	4	1	1	2	15	0	0	0
Playoff Totals		**36**	**8**	**18**	**26**	**37**	**3**	**0**	**1**
WEILAND, Cooney									Center
1929♦	Boston	5	2	0	2	2	....	....	....
1930	Boston	6	1	*5	*6	2	....	....	....
1931	Boston	5	*6	3	*9	2	....	....	....
1934	Detroit	9	2	2	4	4	....	....	....
1936	Boston	2	1	0	1	2	....	....	....
1937	Boston	3	0	0	0	0	....	....	....
1938	Boston	3	0	0	0	0	....	....	....
1939♦	Boston	12	0	0	0	0	....	....	....
Playoff Totals		**45**	**12**	**10**	**22**	**12**	....	....	....
WEINRICH, Eric									Defense
1990	New Jersey	6	1	3	4	17	0	0	0
1991	New Jersey	7	1	2	3	6	1	0	0
1992	New Jersey	7	0	2	2	4	0	0	0
1994	Chicago	6	0	2	2	6	0	0	0
1995	Chicago	16	1	5	6	4	0	0	0
1996	Chicago	10	1	4	5	10	1	0	0
1997	Chicago	6	0	1	1	4	0	0	0
Playoff Totals		**58**	**4**	**19**	**23**	**51**	**2**	**0**	**0**
WEIR, Stan									Center
1976	Toronto	9	1	3	4	0	1	0	1
1977	Toronto	7	2	1	3	0	1	0	1
1978	Toronto	13	3	1	4	0	1	0	1
1980	Edmonton	3	0	0	0	2	0	0	0
1981	Edmonton	5	0	0	0	2	0	0	0
Playoff Totals		**37**	**6**	**5**	**11**	**4**	**3**	**0**	**3**
WEIR, Wally									Defense
1981	Quebec	3	0	0	0	15	0	0	0
1982	Quebec	15	0	0	0	45	0	0	0
1983	Quebec	4	0	1	1	19	0	0	0
1984	Quebec	1	0	0	0	17	0	0	0
Playoff Totals		**23**	**0**	**1**	**1**	**96**	**0**	**0**	**0**
WELLINGTON, Alex *No playoffs*									Right wing
WELLS, Chris									Center
1997	Florida	3	0	0	0	0	0	0	0
Playoff Totals		**3**	**0**	**0**	**0**	**0**	**0**	**0**	**0**

Season	Club	GP	G	A	Pts	PIM	PP	SH	GW
WELLS, Jay									Defense
1980	Los Angeles	4	0	0	0	11	0	0	0
1981	Los Angeles	4	0	0	0	27	0	0	0
1982	Los Angeles	10	1	3	4	41	0	0	0
1985	Los Angeles	3	0	1	1	0	0	0	0
1987	Los Angeles	5	1	2	3	10	1	0	0
1988	Los Angeles	5	1	2	3	21	0	0	0
1989	Philadelphia	18	0	2	2	51	0	0	0
1990	Buffalo	6	0	0	0	12	0	0	0
1991	Buffalo	1	0	1	1	0	0	0	0
1992	NY Rangers	13	0	2	2	10	0	0	0
1994♦	NY Rangers	23	0	0	0	20	0	0	0
1995	NY Rangers	10	0	0	0	8	0	0	0
1996	St. Louis	12	0	1	1	2	0	0	0
Playoff Totals		**114**	**3**	**14**	**17**	**213**	**1**	**0**	**0**
WENSINK, John									Left wing
1977	Boston	13	0	3	3	8	0	0	0
1978	Boston	15	2	2	4	54	0	0	0
1979	Boston	8	0	1	1	19	0	0	0
1980	Boston	4	0	0	0	5	0	0	0
1981	Quebec	3	0	0	0	0	0	0	0
Playoff Totals		**43**	**2**	**6**	**8**	**86**	**0**	**0**	**0**
WENTWORTH, Cy									Defense
1931	Chicago	9	1	1	2	14	....	....	....
1932	Chicago	2	0	0	0	0	....	....	....
1933	Mtl. Maroons	2	0	1	1	0	....	....	....
1934	Mtl. Maroons	4	0	2	2	2	....	....	....
1935♦	Mtl. Maroons	7	3	2	*5	0	....	....	....
1936	Mtl. Maroons	3	0	0	0	0	....	....	....
1937	Mtl. Maroons	5	1	0	1	0	....	....	....
1939	Mtl. Canadiens	3	0	0	0	4	....	....	....
Playoff Totals		**35**	**5**	**6**	**11**	**20**	....	....	....
WERENKA, Brad									Defense
1998	Pittsburgh	6	1	0	1	8	0	1	0
1999	Pittsburgh	13	1	1	2	6	0	0	0
Playoff Totals		**19**	**2**	**1**	**3**	**14**	**0**	**1**	**0**
WESENBERG, Brian *No playoffs*									Right wing
WESLEY, Blake									Defense
1983	Quebec	4	0	0	0	2	0	0	0
1984	Quebec	9	1	2	3	20	0	0	1
1985	Quebec	6	1	0	1	8	0	0	0
Playoff Totals		**19**	**2**	**2**	**4**	**30**	**0**	**0**	**1**
WESLEY, Glen									Defense
1988	Boston	23	6	8	14	22	4	1	0
1989	Boston	10	0	2	2	4	0	0	0
1990	Boston	21	2	6	8	36	0	0	1
1991	Boston	19	2	9	11	19	2	0	0
1992	Boston	15	2	4	6	16	0	0	0
1993	Boston	4	0	0	0	0	0	0	0
1994	Boston	13	3	3	6	12	1	0	0
1999	Carolina	6	0	0	0	2	0	0	0
Playoff Totals		**111**	**15**	**32**	**47**	**111**	**7**	**1**	**1**
WESTFALL, Ed									Defense/Right wing
1968	Boston	4	2	0	2	2	0	0	0
1969	Boston	10	3	7	10	11	0	0	2
1970♦	Boston	14	3	5	8	4	0	1	1
1971	Boston	7	1	2	3	2	0	1	0
1972♦	Boston	15	4	3	7	10	0	2	1
1975	NY Islanders	17	5	10	15	12	2	1	2
1976	NY Islanders	8	2	3	5	0	1	0	0
1977	NY Islanders	12	1	5	6	0	0	1	0
1978	NY Islanders	2	0	0	0	0	0	0	0
1979	NY Islanders	6	1	2	3	0	0	0	0
Playoff Totals		**95**	**22**	**37**	**59**	**41**	**3**	**6**	**6**
WESTLUND, Tommy *No playoffs*									Right wing
WHARRAM, Kenny									Right wing/center
1959	Chicago	6	0	2	2	2	....	....	....
1960	Chicago	4	1	1	2	0	....	....	....
1961♦	Chicago	12	3	5	8	12	....	....	....
1962	Chicago	12	3	4	7	8	....	....	....
1963	Chicago	6	1	5	6	0	....	....	....
1964	Chicago	7	2	2	4	6	....	....	....
1965	Chicago	12	2	3	5	4	....	....	....
1966	Chicago	6	1	0	1	4	....	....	....
1967	Chicago	6	2	2	4	2	....	....	....
1968	Chicago	9	1	3	4	0	0	0	0
Playoff Totals		**80**	**16**	**27**	**43**	**38**	....	....	....
WHARTON, Len *No playoffs*									Defense
WHEELDON, Simon *No playoffs*									Center
WHELDON, Donald *No playoffs*									Defense
WHELTON, Bill *No playoffs*									Defense
WHISTLE, Rob									Defense
1986	NY Rangers	3	0	0	0	2	0	0	0
1988	St. Louis	1	0	0	0	0	0	0	0
Playoff Totals		**4**	**0**	**0**	**0**	**2**	**0**	**0**	**0**

Season	Club	GP	G	A	Pts	PIM	PP	SH	GW
WHITE, Bill									Defense
1968	Los Angeles	7	2	2	4	4	0	0	1
1969	Los Angeles	11	1	4	5	8	0	0	0
1970	Chicago	8	1	2	3	8	0	0	0
1971	Chicago	18	1	4	5	20	0	0	1
1972	Chicago	8	0	3	3	6	0	0	0
1973	Chicago	16	1	6	7	10	0	1	0
1974	Chicago	11	1	7	8	14	1	0	0
1975	Chicago	8	0	3	3	4	0	0	0
1976	Chicago	4	0	1	1	2	0	0	0
Playoff Totals		**91**	**7**	**32**	**39**	**76**	**1**	**1**	**2**
WHITE, Brian *No playoffs*									Defense
WHITE, Colin *No playoffs*									Defense
WHITE, Moe *No playoffs*									Left wing/center
WHITE, Peter *No playoffs*									Center
WHITE, Sherman *No playoffs*									Center
WHITE, Tex									Right wing
1928	Pittsburgh	2	0	0	0	2	0	0	0
1929	NY Americans	2	0	0	0	2	0	0	0
Playoff Totals		**4**	**0**	**0**	**0**	**4**	**0**	**0**	**0**
WHITE, Todd *No playoffs*									Center
WHITE, Tony *No playoffs*									Left wing
WHITELAW, Bob									Defense
1941	Detroit	8	0	0	0	0	0	0	0
Playoff Totals		**8**	**0**	**0**	**0**	**0**	**0**	**0**	**0**
WHITLOCK, Bob *No playoffs*									Center
WHITNEY, Ray									Left wing
1994	San Jose	14	0	4	4	8	0	0	0
1995	San Jose	11	4	4	8	2	0	0	1
Playoff Totals		**25**	**4**	**8**	**12**	**10**	**0**	**0**	**1**
WHYTE, Sean *No playoffs*									Right wing
WICKENHEISER, Doug									Center
1984	St. Louis	11	2	2	4	2	0	1	1
1986	St. Louis	19	2	5	7	12	1	0	1
1987	St. Louis	6	0	0	0	2	0	0	0
1989	Washington	5	0	0	0	2	0	0	0
Playoff Totals		**41**	**4**	**7**	**11**	**18**	**1**	**1**	**2**
WIDING, Juha									Center
1974	Los Angeles	5	1	0	1	2	0	0	1
1975	Los Angeles	3	0	2	2	0	0	0	0
Playoff Totals		**8**	**1**	**2**	**3**	**2**	**0**	**0**	**1**
WIDMER, Jason *No playoffs*									Defense
WIEBE, Art									Defense
1935	Chicago	2	0	0	0	2	....	....	....
1936	Chicago	2	0	0	0	0	....	....	....
1938♦	Chicago	10	0	1	1	2	....	....	....
1940	Chicago	2	1	0	1	2	....	....	....
1941	Chicago	4	0	0	0	0	....	....	....
1942	Chicago	3	0	0	0	0	....	....	....
1944	Chicago	8	0	2	2	4	....	....	....
Playoff Totals		**31**	**1**	**3**	**4**	**10**	....	....	....
WIEMER, Jason									Center
1996	Tampa Bay	6	1	0	1	28	1	0	0
Playoff Totals		**6**	**1**	**0**	**1**	**28**	**1**	**0**	**0**
WIEMER, Jim									Defense
1983	Buffalo	1	0	0	0	0	0	0	0
1985	NY Rangers	1	0	0	0	0	0	0	0
1986	NY Rangers	8	1	0	1	6	1	0	1
1988♦	Edmonton	2	0	0	0	2	0	0	0
1989	Los Angeles	10	2	1	3	19	0	0	1
1990	Boston	8	0	1	1	4	0	0	0
1991	Boston	16	1	3	4	14	1	0	0
1992	Boston	15	1	3	4	14	0	0	1
1993	Boston	1	0	0	0	4	0	0	0
Playoff Totals		**62**	**5**	**8**	**13**	**63**	**2**	**0**	**3**
WILCOX, Archie									Right wing/defense
1930	Mtl. Maroons	4	1	0	1	2	....	....	....
1931	Mtl. Maroons	2	0	0	0	2	....	....	....
1932	Mtl. Maroons	4	0	0	0	4	....	....	....
1933	Mtl. Maroons	2	0	0	0	0	....	....	....
Playoff Totals		**12**	**1**	**0**	**1**	**8**	....	....	....
WILCOX, Barry *No playoffs*									Right wing
WILDER, Arch *No playoffs*									Left wing
WILEY, Jim *No playoffs*									Center
WILKIE, Bob *No playoffs*									Defense
WILKIE, David									Defense
1996	Montreal	6	1	2	3	12	0	0	0
1997	Montreal	2	0	0	0	2	0	0	0
Playoff Totals		**8**	**1**	**2**	**3**	**14**	**0**	**0**	**0**
WILKINS, Barry									Defense
1975	Pittsburgh	3	0	0	0	0	0	0	0
1976	Pittsburgh	3	0	1	1	4	0	0	0
Playoff Totals		**6**	**0**	**1**	**1**	**4**	**0**	**0**	**0**
WILKINSON, John *No playoffs*									Defense

Season	Club	GP	G	A	Pts	PIM	PP	SH	GW
WILKINSON, Neil — Defense									
1990	Minnesota	7	0	2	2	11	0	0	0
1991	Minnesota	22	3	3	6	12	1	0	0
1994	Chicago	4	0	0	0	0	0	0	0
1996	Pittsburgh	15	0	1	1	14	0	0	0
1997	Pittsburgh	5	0	0	0	4	0	0	0
Playoff Totals		**53**	**3**	**6**	**9**	**41**	**1**	**0**	**0**
WILKS, Brian *No playoffs* — Center									
WILLARD, Rod *No playoffs* — Left wing									
WILLIAMS, Burr — Defense									
1934	Detroit	7	0	0	0	8	0	0	0
Playoff Totals		**7**	**0**	**0**	**0**	**8**	**0**	**0**	**0**
WILLIAMS, Darryl *No playoffs* — Left wing									
WILLIAMS, David *No playoffs* — Defense									
WILLIAMS, Fred *No playoffs* — Center									
WILLIAMS, Gord *No playoffs* — Right wing									
WILLIAMS, Sean *No playoffs* — Center									
WILLIAMS, Tiger — Left wing									
1975	Toronto	7	1	3	4	25	1	0	0
1976	Toronto	10	0	0	0	75	0	0	0
1977	Toronto	9	3	6	9	29	0	0	1
1978	Toronto	12	1	2	3	*63	0	0	0
1979	Toronto	6	0	0	0	*48	0	0	0
1980	Vancouver	3	0	0	0	20	0	0	0
1981	Vancouver	3	0	0	0	20	0	0	0
1982	Vancouver	17	3	7	10	*116	0	0	2
1983	Vancouver	4	0	3	3	12	0	0	0
1984	Vancouver	4	1	0	1	13	0	0	0
1985	Los Angeles	3	0	0	0	4	0	0	0
1987	Los Angeles	5	3	2	5	30	0	0	1
Playoff Totals		**83**	**12**	**23**	**35**	**455**	**1**	**0**	**4**
WILLIAMS, Tom — Left wing									
1974	Los Angeles	5	3	1	4	0	1	0	0
1975	Los Angeles	3	0	0	0	0	0	0	0
1976	Los Angeles	9	2	2	4	2	0	0	0
1977	Los Angeles	9	3	4	7	2	1	0	0
1978	Los Angeles	2	0	0	0	0	0	0	0
1979	Los Angeles	1	0	0	0	0	0	0	0
Playoff Totals		**29**	**8**	**7**	**15**	**4**	**2**	**0**	**0**
WILLIAMS, Tommy — Right wing									
1968	Boston	4	1	0	1	2	0	0	0
1970	Minnesota	6	1	5	6	0	0	0	0
Playoff Totals		**10**	**2**	**5**	**7**	**2**	**0**	**0**	**0**
WILLIAMS, Warren *No playoffs* — Right wing									
WILLIS, Shane *No playoffs* — Right wing									
WILLSIE, Brian *No playoffs* — Right wing									
WILLSON, Don — Center									
1938	Mtl. Canadiens	3	0	0	0	0	0	0	0
Playoff Totals		**3**	**0**	**0**	**0**	**0**	**0**	**0**	**0**
WILM, Clarke *No playoffs* — Center									
WILSON, Behn — Defense									
1979	Philadelphia	5	1	0	1	8	0	0	0
1980	Philadelphia	19	4	9	13	66	0	0	2
1981	Philadelphia	12	2	10	12	36	1	0	0
1982	Philadelphia	4	1	4	5	10	1	0	0
1983	Philadelphia	3	0	1	1	2	0	0	0
1984	Chicago	4	0	0	0	0	0	0	0
1985	Chicago	15	4	5	9	60	1	0	1
1986	Chicago	2	0	0	0	2	0	0	0
1988	Chicago	3	0	0	0	6	0	0	0
Playoff Totals		**67**	**12**	**29**	**41**	**190**	**3**	**0**	**3**
WILSON, Bert — Left wing									
1976	Los Angeles	8	0	0	0	24	0	0	0
1977	Los Angeles	8	0	2	2	12	0	0	0
1978	Los Angeles	2	0	0	0	2	0	0	0
1980	Los Angeles	2	0	0	0	4	0	0	0
1981	Calgary	1	0	0	0	0	0	0	0
Playoff Totals		**21**	**0**	**2**	**2**	**42**	**0**	**0**	**0**
WILSON, Bob *No playoffs* — Defense									
WILSON, Carey — Center									
1984	Calgary	6	3	1	4	2	0	0	1
1985	Calgary	4	0	0	0	0	0	0	0
1986	Calgary	9	0	2	2	2	0	0	0
1987	Calgary	6	1	1	2	6	0	0	0
1988	Hartford	6	2	4	6	2	1	0	1
1989	NY Rangers	4	1	2	3	2	0	0	0
1990	NY Rangers	10	2	1	3	0	1	0	0
1991	Calgary	7	2	2	4	0	1	0	0
Playoff Totals		**52**	**11**	**13**	**24**	**14**	**3**	**0**	**2**
WILSON, Cully — Right wing									
1927	Chicago	2	1	0	1	6	....	....	....
Playoff Totals		**2**	**1**	**0**	**1**	**6**	....	....	....

Season	Club	GP	G	A	Pts	PIM	PP	SH	GW
WILSON, Doug — Defense									
1978	Chicago	4	0	0	0	0	0	0	0
1980	Chicago	7	2	8	10	6	0	0	0
1981	Chicago	3	0	3	3	2	0	0	0
1982	Chicago	15	3	10	13	32	0	1	1
1983	Chicago	13	4	11	15	12	0	1	0
1984	Chicago	5	0	3	3	2	0	0	0
1985	Chicago	12	3	10	13	12	2	0	0
1986	Chicago	3	1	1	2	2	0	0	0
1987	Chicago	4	0	0	0	0	0	0	0
1989	Chicago	4	1	2	3	0	1	0	0
1990	Chicago	20	3	12	15	18	1	0	1
1991	Chicago	5	2	1	3	2	2	0	0
Playoff Totals		**95**	**19**	**61**	**80**	**88**	**6**	**2**	**2**
WILSON, Gord — Left wing									
1955	Boston	2	0	0	0	0	0	0	0
Playoff Totals		**2**	**0**	**0**	**0**	**0**	**0**	**0**	**0**
WILSON, Hub *No playoffs* — Left wing									
WILSON, Jerry *No playoffs* — Center									
WILSON, Johnny — Left wing									
1950◆	Detroit	8	0	1	1	0	....	....	....
1951	Detroit	1	0	0	0	0	....	....	....
1952◆	Detroit	8	4	1	5	5	....	....	....
1953	Detroit	6	2	5	7	0	....	....	....
1954◆	Detroit	12	3	0	3	0	....	....	....
1955◆	Detroit	11	0	1	1	0	....	....	....
1958	Detroit	4	2	1	3	0	....	....	....
1960	Toronto	10	1	2	3	2	....	....	....
1962	NY Rangers	6	2	2	4	4	....	....	....
Playoff Totals		**66**	**14**	**13**	**27**	**11**	....	....	....
WILSON, Landon — Right wing									
1998	Boston	1	0	0	0	0	0	0	0
1999	Boston	8	1	1	2	8	1	0	1
Playoff Totals		**9**	**1**	**1**	**2**	**8**	**1**	**0**	**1**
WILSON, Larry — Center									
1950◆	Detroit	4	0	0	0	0	0	0	0
Playoff Totals		**4**	**0**	**0**	**0**	**0**	**0**	**0**	**0**
WILSON, Mike — Defense									
1997	Buffalo	10	0	1	1	2	0	0	0
1998	Buffalo	15	0	1	1	13	0	0	0
Playoff Totals		**25**	**0**	**2**	**2**	**15**	**0**	**0**	**0**
WILSON, Mitch *No playoffs* — Center									
WILSON, Murray — Left wing									
1973◆	Montreal	16	2	4	6	6	0	0	1
1974	Montreal	5	1	0	1	2	0	0	0
1975	Montreal	5	0	3	3	4	0	0	0
1976◆	Montreal	12	1	1	2	6	0	0	0
1977◆	Montreal	14	1	6	7	14	0	0	0
1979	Los Angeles	1	0	0	0	0	0	0	0
Playoff Totals		**53**	**5**	**14**	**19**	**32**	**0**	**0**	**1**
WILSON, Rick — Defense									
1975	St. Louis	2	0	0	0	0	0	0	0
1976	St. Louis	1	0	0	0	0	0	0	0
Playoff Totals		**3**	**0**	**0**	**0**	**0**	**0**	**0**	**0**
WILSON, Rik — Defense									
1982	St. Louis	9	0	3	3	14	0	0	0
1984	St. Louis	11	0	0	0	9	0	0	0
1985	St. Louis	2	0	1	1	0	0	0	0
Playoff Totals		**22**	**0**	**4**	**4**	**23**	**0**	**0**	**0**
WILSON, Roger *No playoffs* — Defense									
WILSON, Ron — Defense									
1979	Toronto	3	0	1	1	0	0	0	0
1980	Toronto	3	1	2	3	2	1	0	0
1985	Minnesota	9	1	6	7	2	1	0	0
1986	Minnesota	5	2	4	6	4	1	0	0
Playoff Totals		**20**	**4**	**13**	**17**	**8**	**3**	**0**	**0**
WILSON, Ron — Center									
1983	Winnipeg	3	2	2	4	2	0	0	0
1985	Winnipeg	8	4	2	6	2	0	0	1
1986	Winnipeg	1	0	0	0	0	0	0	0
1987	Winnipeg	10	1	2	3	0	0	0	0
1988	Winnipeg	1	0	0	0	2	0	0	0
1990	St. Louis	12	3	5	8	18	2	0	0
1991	St. Louis	7	0	0	0	28	0	0	0
1992	St. Louis	6	0	1	1	0	0	0	0
1993	St. Louis	11	0	0	0	12	0	0	0
1994	Montreal	4	0	0	0	0	0	0	0
Playoff Totals		**63**	**10**	**12**	**22**	**64**	**2**	**0**	**1**
WILSON, Wally — Center									
1948	Boston	1	0	0	0	0	0	0	0
Playoff Totals		**1**	**0**	**0**	**0**	**0**	**0**	**0**	**0**
WING, Murray *No playoffs* — Defense									
WINNES, Chris — Right wing									
1991	Boston	1	0	0	0	0	0	0	0
Playoff Totals		**1**	**0**	**0**	**0**	**0**	**0**	**0**	**0**
WISEMAN, Brian *No playoffs* — Center									

Season	Club	GP	G	A	Pts	PIM	PP	SH	GW
WISEMAN, Eddie — Right wing									
1933	Detroit	2	0	0	0	0	....	....	....
1934	Detroit	7	0	1	1	4	....	....	....
1936	NY Americans	4	2	1	3	0	....	....	....
1938	NY Americans	6	0	4	4	10	....	....	....
1939	NY Americans	2	0	0	0	0	....	....	....
1940	Boston	6	2	1	3	2	....	....	....
1941◆	Boston	11	6	2	8	0	....	....	....
1942	Boston	5	0	1	1	0	....	....	....
Playoff Totals		**43**	**10**	**10**	**20**	**16**	....	....	....
WISTE, Jim *No playoffs* — Center									
WITEHALL, Johan *No playoffs* — Left wing									
WITHERSPOON, Jim *No playoffs* — Defense									
WITIUK, Steve *No playoffs* — Right wing									
WITT, Brendan — Defense									
1998	Washington	16	1	0	1	14	0	0	0
Playoff Totals		**16**	**1**	**0**	**1**	**14**	**0**	**0**	**0**
WOIT, Benny — Right wing/defense									
1951	Detroit	4	0	0	0	2	....	....	....
1952◆	Detroit	8	1	1	2	2	....	....	....
1953	Detroit	6	1	3	4	0	....	....	....
1954◆	Detroit	12	0	1	1	8	....	....	....
1955◆	Detroit	11	0	1	1	6	....	....	....
Playoff Totals		**41**	**2**	**6**	**8**	**18**	....	....	....
WOJCIECHOWSKI, Steven — Right wing									
1945	Detroit	6	0	1	1	0	0	0	0
Playoff Totals		**6**	**0**	**1**	**1**	**0**	**0**	**0**	**0**
WOLANIN, Craig — Defense									
1988	New Jersey	18	2	5	7	51	1	0	0
1993	Quebec	4	0	0	0	4	0	0	0
1995	Quebec	6	1	1	2	4	0	0	0
1996◆	Colorado	7	1	0	1	8	0	0	1
Playoff Totals		**35**	**4**	**6**	**10**	**67**	**1**	**0**	**1**
WOLF, Bennett *No playoffs* — Defense									
WONG, Mike *No playoffs* — Center									
WOOD, Dody *No playoffs* — Center									
WOOD, Randy — Left wing/Center									
1987	NY Islanders	13	1	3	4	14	0	0	1
1988	NY Islanders	5	1	0	1	6	0	0	0
1990	NY Islanders	5	1	1	2	4	0	0	0
1992	Buffalo	7	2	1	3	6	0	0	0
1993	Buffalo	8	1	4	5	4	1	0	0
1994	Buffalo	6	0	0	0	0	0	0	0
1995	Toronto	7	2	0	2	6	1	0	1
Playoff Totals		**51**	**8**	**9**	**17**	**40**	**2**	**0**	**2**
WOOD, Robert *No playoffs* — Defense									
WOODLEY, Dan *No playoffs* — Right wing									
WOODS, Paul — Left wing									
1978	Detroit	7	0	5	5	4	0	0	0
Playoff Totals		**7**	**0**	**5**	**5**	**4**	**0**	**0**	**0**
WOOLLEY, Jason — Defense									
1994	Washington	4	1	0	1	4	0	0	1
1996	Florida	13	2	6	8	14	1	0	1
1997	Pittsburgh	5	0	3	3	0	0	0	0
1998	Buffalo	15	2	9	11	12	1	0	1
1999	Buffalo	21	4	11	15	10	2	0	1
Playoff Totals		**58**	**9**	**29**	**38**	**40**	**4**	**0**	**4**
WORRELL, Peter *No playoffs* — Left wing									
WORTMAN, Kevin *No playoffs* — Defense									
WOTTON, Mark — Defense									
1995	Vancouver	5	0	0	0	4	0	0	0
Playoff Totals		**5**	**0**	**0**	**0**	**4**	**0**	**0**	**0**
WOYTOWICH, Bob — Defense									
1968	Minnesota	14	0	1	1	18	0	0	0
1970	Pittsburgh	10	1	2	3	2	0	0	0
Playoff Totals		**24**	**1**	**3**	**4**	**20**	**0**	**0**	**0**
WREN, Bob *No playoffs* — Center									
WRIGHT, Jamie — Left wing									
1998	Dallas	5	0	0	0	0	0	0	0
Playoff Totals		**5**	**0**	**0**	**0**	**0**	**0**	**0**	**0**
WRIGHT, John *No playoffs* — Center									
WRIGHT, Keith *No playoffs* — Left wing									
WRIGHT, Larry *No playoffs* — Center									
WRIGHT, Tyler — Center									
1998	Pittsburgh	6	0	1	1	4	0	0	0
1999	Pittsburgh	13	0	0	0	19	0	0	0
Playoff Totals		**19**	**0**	**1**	**1**	**23**	**0**	**0**	**0**
WYCHERLEY, Ralph *No playoffs* — Left wing									
WYLIE, Duane *No playoffs* — Center									
WYLIE, William *No playoffs* — Center									
WYROZUB, Randy *No playoffs* — Center									
YACHMENEV, Vitali *No playoffs* — Right wing									
YACKEL, Ken — Right wing									
1959	Boston	2	0	0	0	2	0	0	0
Playoff Totals		**2**	**0**	**0**	**0**	**2**	**0**	**0**	**0**

Season	Club	GP	G	A	Pts	PIM	PP	SH	GW
YAKE, Terry									Center
1991	Hartford	6	1	1	2	16	0	1	0
1998	St. Louis	10	2	1	3	6	2	0	1
1999	St. Louis	13	1	2	3	14	1	0	0
Playoff Totals		**29**	**4**	**4**	**8**	**36**	**3**	**1**	**1**
YAKUSHIN, Dmitri	*No playoffs*								Defense
YAREMCHUK, Gary	*No playoffs*								Center
YAREMCHUK, Ken									Center
1984	Chicago	1	0	0	0	0	0	0	0
1985	Chicago	15	5	5	10	37	0	0	1
1986	Chicago	3	1	1	2	2	0	0	0
1987	Toronto	6	0	0	0	0	0	0	0
1988	Toronto	6	0	2	2	10	0	0	0
Playoff Totals		**31**	**6**	**8**	**14**	**49**	**0**	**0**	**1**
YASHIN, Alexei									Center
1997	Ottawa	7	1	5	6	2	1	0	0
1998	Ottawa	11	5	3	8	8	3	0	2
1999	Ottawa	4	0	0	0	10	0	0	0
Playoff Totals		**22**	**6**	**8**	**14**	**20**	**4**	**0**	**2**
YATES, Ross	*No playoffs*								Center
YAWNEY, Trent									Defense
1988	Chicago	5	0	4	4	8	0	0	0
1989	Chicago	15	3	6	9	20	0	1	0
1990	Chicago	20	3	5	8	27	3	0	1
1991	Chicago	1	0	0	0	0	0	0	0
1993	Calgary	6	3	2	5	6	1	0	0
1994	Calgary	7	0	0	0	16	0	0	0
1995	Calgary	2	0	0	0	2	0	0	0
1996	Calgary	4	0	0	0	2	0	0	0
Playoff Totals		**60**	**9**	**17**	**26**	**81**	**4**	**1**	**1**
YEGOROV, Alexei	*No playoffs*								Right wing
YELLE, Stephane									Center
1996♦	Colorado	22	1	4	5	8	0	1	0
1997	Colorado	12	1	6	7	2	0	0	0
1998	Colorado	7	1	0	1	12	0	0	0
1999	Colorado	10	0	1	1	6	0	0	0
Playoff Totals		**51**	**3**	**11**	**14**	**28**	**0**	**1**	**0**
YLONEN, Juha									Center
1999	Phoenix	2	0	2	2	2	0	0	0
Playoff Totals		**2**	**0**	**2**	**2**	**2**	**0**	**0**	**0**
YORK, Harry									Center
1997	St. Louis	5	0	0	0	2	0	0	0
Playoff Totals		**5**	**0**	**0**	**0**	**2**	**0**	**0**	**0**
YORK, Jason									Defense
1997	Ottawa	7	0	0	0	4	0	0	0
1998	Ottawa	7	1	1	2	7	1	0	0
1999	Ottawa	4	1	1	2	4	0	0	0
Playoff Totals		**18**	**2**	**2**	**4**	**15**	**1**	**0**	**0**
YORK, Michael	*No playoffs*								Center
YOUNG, B.J.	*No playoffs*								Right wing
YOUNG, Brian	*No playoffs*								Defense
YOUNG, C.J.	*No playoffs*								Right wing
YOUNG, Doug									Defense
1932	Detroit	2	0	0	0	2	....	....	....
1933	Detroit	4	1	1	2	0	....	....	....
1934	Detroit	9	0	0	0	10	....	....	....
1936♦	Detroit	7	0	2	2	0	....	....	....
1939	Detroit	6	0	2	2	4	....	....	....
Playoff Totals		**28**	**1**	**5**	**6**	**16**	....	....	....
YOUNG, Howie									Right wing
1961	Detroit	11	2	2	4	*30	0	0	0
1963	Detroit	8	0	2	2	16	0	0	0
Playoff Totals		**19**	**2**	**4**	**6**	**46**	**0**	**0**	**0**
YOUNG, Scott									Right wing
1988	Hartford	4	1	0	1	0	0	0	0
1989	Hartford	4	2	0	2	4	0	0	0
1990	Hartford	7	2	0	2	2	0	0	0
1991♦	Pittsburgh	17	1	6	7	2	1	0	0
1993	Quebec	6	4	1	5	0	0	0	2
1995	Quebec	6	3	3	6	2	0	1	0
1996♦	Colorado	22	3	12	15	10	0	0	0
1997	Colorado	17	4	2	6	14	2	0	0
1999	St. Louis	13	4	7	11	10	1	0	1
Playoff Totals		**96**	**24**	**31**	**55**	**44**	**4**	**1**	**3**
YOUNG, Tim									Center
1977	Minnesota	2	1	1	2	2	0	0	0
1980	Minnesota	15	2	5	7	4	1	1	0
1981	Minnesota	12	3	14	17	9	0	0	1
1982	Minnesota	4	1	1	2	10	0	0	0
1983	Minnesota	2	0	2	2	2	0	0	0
1984	Winnipeg	1	0	1	1	0	0	0	0
Playoff Totals		**36**	**7**	**24**	**31**	**27**	**1**	**1**	**1**

Season	Club	GP	G	A	Pts	PIM	PP	SH	GW
YOUNG, Warren	*No playoffs*								Center
YOUNGHANS, Tom									Right wing
1977	Minnesota	2	0	0	0	0	0	0	0
1980	Minnesota	15	2	1	3	17	0	2	0
1981	Minnesota	5	0	0	0	4	0	0	0
1982	NY Rangers	2	0	0	0	0	0	0	0
Playoff Totals		**24**	**2**	**1**	**3**	**21**	**0**	**2**	**0**
YSEBAERT, Paul									Center
1991	Detroit	2	0	2	2	0	0	0	0
1992	Detroit	10	1	0	1	10	0	0	0
1993	Detroit	7	3	1	4	2	0	1	1
1994	Chicago	6	0	0	0	8	0	0	0
1996	Tampa Bay	5	0	0	0	0	0	0	0
Playoff Totals		**30**	**4**	**3**	**7**	**20**	**0**	**1**	**1**
YUSHKEVICH, Dimitri									Defense
1995	Philadelphia	15	1	5	6	12	0	0	0
1996	Toronto	4	0	0	0	0	0	0	0
1999	Toronto	17	1	5	6	22	1	0	0
Playoff Totals		**36**	**2**	**10**	**12**	**34**	**1**	**0**	**0**
YZERMAN, Steve									Center
1984	Detroit	4	3	3	6	0	1	0	1
1985	Detroit	3	2	1	3	2	0	0	0
1987	Detroit	16	5	13	18	8	1	0	0
1988	Detroit	3	1	3	4	6	0	0	0
1989	Detroit	6	5	5	10	2	2	0	0
1991	Detroit	7	3	3	6	4	1	0	0
1992	Detroit	11	3	5	8	12	0	1	1
1993	Detroit	7	4	3	7	4	1	1	1
1994	Detroit	3	1	3	4	0	0	0	0
1995	Detroit	15	4	8	12	0	2	0	1
1996	Detroit	18	8	12	20	4	4	0	1
1997♦	Detroit	20	7	6	13	4	3	0	2
1998♦	Detroit	22	6	*18	*24	22	3	1	0
1999	Detroit	10	9	4	13	0	4	0	2
Playoff Totals		**145**	**61**	**87**	**148**	**68**	**22**	**3**	**9**
ZABRANSKY, Libor	*No playoffs*								Defense
ZAHARKO, Miles									Defense
1978	Atlanta	1	0	0	0	0	0	0	0
1981	Chicago	2	0	0	0	0	0	0	0
Playoff Totals		**3**	**0**	**0**	**0**	**0**	**0**	**0**	**0**
ZAINE, Rod	*No playoffs*								Center
ZALAPSKI, Zarley									Defense
1989	Pittsburgh	11	1	8	9	13	1	0	0
1991	Hartford	6	1	3	4	8	0	0	1
1992	Hartford	7	2	3	5	6	0	0	0
1994	Calgary	7	0	3	3	2	0	0	0
1995	Calgary	7	0	4	4	4	0	0	0
1996	Calgary	4	0	1	1	10	0	0	0
1998	Montreal	6	0	1	1	4	0	0	0
Playoff Totals		**48**	**4**	**23**	**27**	**47**	**1**	**0**	**1**
ZAMUNER, Rob									Left wing
1996	Tampa Bay	6	2	3	5	10	0	1	0
Playoff Totals		**6**	**2**	**3**	**5**	**10**	**0**	**1**	**0**
ZANUSSI, Joe									Defense
1976	Boston	4	0	1	1	2	0	0	0
Playoff Totals		**4**	**0**	**1**	**1**	**2**	**0**	**0**	**0**
ZANUSSI, Ron									Right wing
1980	Minnesota	14	0	4	4	17	0	0	0
1981	Toronto	3	0	0	0	0	0	0	0
Playoff Totals		**17**	**0**	**4**	**4**	**17**	**0**	**0**	**0**
ZAVISHA, Brad	*No playoffs*								Left wing
ZEDNIK, Richard									Left wing
1998	Washington	17	7	3	10	16	2	0	0
Playoff Totals		**17**	**7**	**3**	**10**	**16**	**2**	**0**	**0**
ZEHR, Jeff	*No playoffs*								Left wing
ZEIDEL, Larry									Defense
1952♦	Detroit	5	0	0	0	0	0	0	0
1968	Philadelphia	7	0	1	1	12	0	0	0
Playoff Totals		**12**	**0**	**1**	**1**	**12**	**0**	**0**	**0**
ZELEPUKIN, Valeri									Left wing
1992	New Jersey	4	1	1	2	2	0	0	0
1993	New Jersey	5	0	2	2	0	0	0	0
1994	New Jersey	20	5	2	7	14	1	0	0
1995♦	New Jersey	18	1	2	3	12	0	0	1
1997	New Jersey	8	3	2	5	2	1	0	1
1998	Edmonton	8	1	2	3	2	0	0	0
1999	Philadelphia	4	1	0	1	4	0	0	1
Playoff Totals		**67**	**12**	**11**	**23**	**36**	**2**	**0**	**3**
ZEMLAK, Richard									Right wing
1989	Pittsburgh	1	0	0	0	10	0	0	0
Playoff Totals		**1**	**0**	**0**	**0**	**10**	**0**	**0**	**0**
ZENIUK, Ed	*No playoffs*								Defense

Season	Club	GP	G	A	Pts	PIM	PP	SH	GW
ZENT, Jason	*No playoffs*								Left wing
ZETTERSTROM, Lars	*No playoffs*								Defense
ZETTLER, Rob									Defense
1995	Philadelphia	1	0	0	0	2	0	0	0
1996	Toronto	2	0	0	0	0	0	0	0
Playoff Totals		**3**	**0**	**0**	**0**	**2**	**0**	**0**	**0**
ZEZEL, Peter									Center
1985	Philadelphia	19	1	8	9	28	1	0	0
1986	Philadelphia	5	3	1	4	4	1	0	1
1987	Philadelphia	25	3	10	13	10	1	1	1
1988	Philadelphia	7	3	2	5	7	0	0	0
1989	St. Louis	10	6	6	12	4	1	1	1
1990	St. Louis	12	1	7	8	4	1	0	0
1993	Toronto	20	2	1	3	6	0	0	0
1994	Toronto	18	2	4	6	8	0	0	1
1995	Dallas	3	1	0	1	0	0	0	0
1996	St. Louis	10	3	0	3	2	0	1	0
1997	New Jersey	2	0	0	0	10	0	0	0
Playoff Totals		**131**	**25**	**39**	**64**	**83**	**5**	**3**	**4**
ZHAMNOV, Alexei									Center
1993	Winnipeg	6	0	2	2	2	0	0	0
1996	Winnipeg	6	2	1	3	8	0	0	0
Playoff Totals		**12**	**2**	**3**	**5**	**10**	**0**	**0**	**0**
ZHITNIK, Alexei									Defense
1993	Los Angeles	24	3	9	12	26	2	0	1
1995	Buffalo	5	0	1	1	14	0	0	0
1997	Buffalo	12	1	0	1	16	0	0	0
1998	Buffalo	15	0	3	3	36	0	0	0
1999	Buffalo	21	4	11	15	*52	4	0	2
Playoff Totals		**77**	**8**	**24**	**32**	**144**	**6**	**0**	**3**
ZHOLTOK, Sergei									Center
1997	Ottawa	7	1	1	2	0	1	0	0
1998	Ottawa	11	0	2	2	0	0	0	0
Playoff Totals		**18**	**1**	**3**	**4**	**0**	**1**	**0**	**0**
ZMOLEK, Doug									Defense
1994	Dallas	7	0	1	1	4	0	0	0
1995	Dallas	5	0	0	0	10	0	0	0
1998	Los Angeles	2	0	0	0	2	0	0	0
Playoff Totals		**14**	**0**	**1**	**1**	**16**	**0**	**0**	**0**
ZABROSKI, Marty	*No playoffs*								Defense
ZOMBO, Rick									Defense
1987	Detroit	7	0	1	1	9	0	0	0
1988	Detroit	16	0	6	6	55	0	0	0
1989	Detroit	6	0	1	1	16	0	0	0
1991	Detroit	7	1	0	1	10	0	0	0
1992	St. Louis	6	0	2	2	12	0	0	0
1993	St. Louis	11	0	1	1	12	0	0	0
1994	St. Louis	4	0	0	0	11	0	0	0
1995	St. Louis	3	0	0	0	2	0	0	0
Playoff Totals		**60**	**1**	**11**	**12**	**127**	**0**	**0**	**0**
ZUBOV, Sergei									Defense
1994♦	NY Rangers	22	5	14	19	0	2	0	0
1995	NY Rangers	10	3	8	11	2	1	0	0
1996	Pittsburgh	18	1	14	15	26	1	0	0
1997	Dallas	7	0	3	3	2	0	0	0
1998	Dallas	17	4	5	9	2	3	0	1
1999♦	Dallas	23	1	12	13	4	0	0	0
Playoff Totals		**97**	**14**	**56**	**70**	**36**	**7**	**0**	**1**
ZUBRUS, Dainius									Right wing
1997	Philadelphia	19	5	4	9	12	1	0	1
1998	Philadelphia	5	0	1	1	2	0	0	0
Playoff Totals		**24**	**5**	**5**	**10**	**14**	**1**	**0**	**1**
ZUKE, Mike									Center
1980	St. Louis	3	0	0	0	2	0	0	0
1981	St. Louis	11	4	5	9	4	3	0	0
1982	St. Louis	8	1	1	2	2	0	0	0
1983	St. Louis	4	1	0	1	4	0	0	1
Playoff Totals		**26**	**6**	**6**	**12**	**12**	**3**	**0**	**1**
ZUNICH, Rudy	*No playoffs*								Defense
ZYUZIN, Andrei									Defense
1998	San Jose	6	1	0	1	14	0	0	1
Playoff Totals		**6**	**1**	**0**	**1**	**14**	**0**	**0**	**1**

CHAPTER 24

Goaltender Register

Career NHL Playoff Records, 1918–1999

Abbreviations: Avg – average; **GA** – goals against; **GP** – games played; **L** – losses; **Mins** – minutes played; **S%** – save percentage; **SA** – shots against; **SAPG** – shots against per 60 minutes; **SO** – shutouts; **T** – ties; **W** – wins; * – league-leading total; ♦ – member of Stanley Cup winning team.
Player Register begins on page 131.

Season	Club	GP	W	L	T	Mins	GA	SO	Avg	SA	S%	SAPG
ABBOTT, George *No playoffs*												
ADAMS, John *No playoffs*												
AIKEN, John *No playoffs*												
AITKENHEAD, Andy												
1933♦	NY Rangers	8	*6	1	1	488	13	*2	1.60	....	....	....
1934	NY Rangers	2	0	1	1	120	2	1	1.00	....	....	....
Playoff Totals		**10**	**6**	**2**	**2**	**608**	**15**	**3**	**1.48**	....	....	....
ALMAS, Red												
1947	Detroit	5	1	3	....	263	13	0	2.97	....	....	....
Playoff Totals		**5**	**1**	**3**	....	**263**	**13**	**0**	**2.97**	....	....	....
ANDERSON, Lorne *No playoffs*												
ASKEY, Tom												
1999	Anaheim	1	0	1	....	30	2	0	4.00	11	.818	22.0
Playoff Totals		**1**	**0**	**1**	....	**30**	**2**	**0**	**4.00**	**11**	**.818**	**22.0**
ASTROM, Hardy *No playoffs*												
AUBIN, Jean-Sebastien *No playoffs*												
BACH, Ryan *No playoffs*												
BAILEY, Scott *No playoffs*												
BAKER, Steve												
1981	NY Rangers	14	7	7	....	826	55	0	4.00	....	....	....
Playoff Totals		**14**	**7**	**7**	....	**826**	**55**	**0**	**4.00**	....	....	....
BALES, Mike *No playoffs*												
BANNERMAN, Murray												
1982	Chicago	10	5	4	....	555	35	0	3.78	....	....	....
1983	Chicago	8	4	4	....	480	32	0	4.00	....	....	....
1984	Chicago	5	2	3	....	300	17	0	3.40	171	.901	34.2
1985	Chicago	15	9	6	....	906	72	0	4.77	547	.868	36.2
1986	Chicago	2	0	1	....	81	9	0	6.67	40	.775	29.6
Playoff Totals		**40**	**20**	**18**	....	**2322**	**165**	**0**	**4.26**	....	....	....
BARON, Marco												
1981	Boston	1	0	1	....	20	3	0	9.00	....	....	....
Playoff Totals		**1**	**0**	**1**	....	**20**	**3**	**0**	**9.00**	....	....	....
BARRASSO, Tom												
1984	Buffalo	3	0	2	....	139	8	0	3.45	59	.864	25.5
1985	Buffalo	5	2	3	....	300	22	0	4.40	151	.854	30.2
1988	Buffalo	4	1	3	....	224	16	0	4.29	120	.867	32.1
1989	Pittsburgh	11	7	4	....	631	40	0	3.80	389	.897	37.0
1991♦	Pittsburgh	20	12	7	....	1175	51	*1	*2.60	629	.919	32.1
1992♦	Pittsburgh	*21	*16	5	....	*1233	58	1	2.82	622	.907	30.3
1993	Pittsburgh	12	7	5	....	722	35	*2	2.91	370	.905	30.7
1994	Pittsburgh	6	2	4	....	356	17	0	2.87	162	.895	27.3
1995	Pittsburgh	2	0	1	....	80	8	0	6.00	41	.805	30.8
1996	Pittsburgh	10	4	5	....	558	26	1	2.80	337	.923	36.2
1998	Pittsburgh	6	2	4	....	376	17	0	2.71	171	.901	27.3
1999	Pittsburgh	13	6	7	....	787	35	1	2.67	350	.900	26.7
Playoff Totals		**113**	**59**	**50**	....	**6581**	**333**	**6**	**3.04**	**3401**	**.902**	**31.0**
BASSEN, Hank												
1961	Detroit	4	1	2	....	220	9	0	2.45	....	....	....
1966	Detroit	1	0	1	....	54	2	0	2.22	....	....	....
Playoff Totals		**5**	**1**	**3**	....	**274**	**11**	**0**	**2.41**	....	....	....
BASTIEN, Baz *No playoffs*												
BAUMAN, Gary *No playoffs*												
BEAUPRE, Don												
1981	Minnesota	6	4	2	....	360	26	0	4.33	....	....	....
1982	Minnesota	2	0	1	....	60	4	0	4.00	....	....	....
1983	Minnesota	4	2	2	....	245	20	0	4.90	....	....	....
1984	Minnesota	13	6	7	....	782	40	1	3.07	380	.895	29.2
1985	Minnesota	4	1	1	....	184	12	0	3.91	80	.850	26.1
1986	Minnesota	5	2	3	....	300	17	0	3.40	158	.892	31.6
1990	Washington	8	4	3	....	401	18	0	2.69	187	.904	28.0
1991	Washington	11	5	5	....	624	29	*1	2.79	294	.901	28.3
1992	Washington	7	3	4	....	419	22	0	3.15	212	.896	30.4
1993	Washington	2	1	1	....	119	9	0	4.54	65	.862	32.8
1994	Washington	8	5	2	....	429	21	1	2.94	191	.890	26.7
1996	Toronto	2	0	0	....	20	2	0	6.00	13	.846	39.0
Playoff Totals		**72**	**33**	**31**	....	**3943**	**220**	**3**	**3.35**	....	....	....
BEAUREGARD, Stephane												
1990	Winnipeg	4	1	3	....	238	12	0	3.03	105	.886	26.5
Playoff Totals		**4**	**1**	**3**	....	**238**	**12**	**0**	**3.03**	**105**	**.886**	**26.5**
BEDARD, Jim *No playoffs*												

Season	Club	GP	W	L	T	Mins	GA	SO	Avg	SA	S%	SAPG
BEHREND, Marc												
1984	Winnipeg	2	0	2	0	121	9	0	4.46	91	.901	45.1
1985	Winnipeg	4	1	1	0	179	10	0	3.35	98	.898	32.8
1986	Winnipeg	1	0	0	0	12	0	0	0.00	7	.000	35.0
Playoff Totals		**7**	**1**	**3**	**0**	**312**	**19**	**0**	**3.65**	**196**	**.903**	**37.7**
BELANGER, Yves *No playoffs*												
BELFOUR, Ed												
1990	Chicago	9	4	2	....	409	17	0	2.49	200	.915	29.3
1991	Chicago	6	2	4	....	295	20	0	4.07	183	.891	37.2
1992	Chicago	18	12	4	....	949	39	1	*2.47	398	.902	25.2
1993	Chicago	4	0	4	....	249	13	0	3.13	97	.866	23.4
1994	Chicago	6	2	4	....	360	15	0	2.50	191	.921	31.8
1995	Chicago	16	9	7	....	1014	37	1	2.19	479	.923	28.3
1996	Chicago	9	6	3	....	666	23	1	2.07	323	.929	29.1
1998	Dallas	17	10	7	....	1039	31	1	*1.79	399	.922	23.0
1999♦	Dallas	*23	*16	7	....	*1544	43	*3	*1.67	617	.930	24.0
Playoff Totals		**108**	**61**	**42**	....	**6525**	**238**	**7**	**2.19**	**2887**	**.918**	**26.5**
BELHUMEUR, Michel												
1973	Philadelphia	1	0	0	....	10	1	0	6.00	....	....	....
Playoff Totals		**1**	**0**	**0**	....	**10**	**1**	**0**	**6.00**	....	....	....
BELL, Gordie												
1956	NY Rangers	2	1	1	....	120	9	0	4.50	....	....	....
Playoff Totals		**2**	**1**	**1**	....	**120**	**9**	**0**	**4.50**	....	....	....
BENEDICT, Clint												
1919	Ottawa	5	1	4	0	300	26	0	5.20	....	....	....
1920♦	Ottawa	*5	*3	2	0	*300	11	*1	*2.20	....	....	....
1921♦	Ottawa	*7	*5	2	0	*420	12	*2	*1.71	....	....	....
1922	Ottawa	2	0	1	1	120	5	1	2.50	....	....	....
1923♦	Ottawa	*8	*6	2	0	*480	10	*3	*1.25	....	....	....
1924	Ottawa	2	0	2	0	120	5	0	2.50	....	....	....
1926♦	Mtl. Maroons	*8	*5	1	2	480	8	*4	*1.00	....	....	....
1927	Mtl. Maroons	2	0	1	1	132	2	0	0.91	....	....	....
1928	Mtl. Maroons	*9	*5	3	1	*555	8	*4	*0.86	....	....	....
Playoff Totals		**48**	**25**	**18**	**5**	**2907**	**87**	***15**	**1.80**	....	....	....
BENNETT, Harvey *No playoffs*												
BERGERON, Jean-Claude *No playoffs*												
BERNHARDT, Tim *No playoffs*												
BERTHIAUME, Daniel												
1986	Winnipeg	1	0	1	....	68	4	0	3.53	43	.907	37.9
1987	Winnipeg	8	4	4	....	439	21	0	2.87	210	.900	28.7
1988	Winnipeg	5	1	4	....	300	25	0	5.00	154	.838	30.8
Playoff Totals		**14**	**5**	**9**	....	**807**	**50**	**0**	**3.72**	**407**	**.877**	**30.3**
BESTER, Allan												
1987	Toronto	1	0	0	....	39	1	0	1.54	17	.941	26.2
1988	Toronto	5	2	3	....	253	21	0	4.98	135	.844	32.0
1990	Toronto	4	0	3	....	196	14	0	4.29	120	.883	36.7
1991	Detroit	1	0	0	....	20	1	0	3.00	12	.917	36.0
Playoff Totals		**11**	**2**	**6**	....	**508**	**37**	**0**	**4.37**	**284**	**.870**	**33.5**
BEVERIDGE, Bill												
1937	Mtl. Maroons	5	2	3	....	300	11	0	2.20	....	....	....
Playoff Totals		**5**	**2**	**3**	....	**300**	**11**	**0**	**2.20**	....	....	....
BIBEAULT, Paul												
1942	Montreal	3	1	2	....	180	8	*1	2.67	....	....	....
1943	Montreal	5	1	4	....	320	18	1	3.38	....	....	....
1944	Toronto	5	1	4	....	300	23	0	4.60	....	....	....
1945	Boston	7	3	4	....	437	22	0	3.02	....	....	....
Playoff Totals		**20**	**6**	**14**	....	**1237**	**71**	**2**	**3.44**	....	....	....
BIERK, Zac *No playoffs*												
BILLINGTON, Craig												
1993	New Jersey	2	0	1	....	78	5	0	3.85	39	.872	30.0
1995	Boston	1	0	0	....	25	1	0	2.40	10	.900	24.0
1996	Boston	1	0	1	....	60	6	0	6.00	28	.786	28.0
1997	Colorado	1	0	0	....	20	1	0	3.00	13	.923	39.0
1998	Colorado	1	0	0	....	1	0	0	0.00	0	.000	0.0
1999	Colorado	1	0	0	....	9	1	0	6.67	6	.833	40.0
Playoff Totals		**7**	**0**	**2**	....	**193**	**14**	**0**	**4.35**	**96**	**.854**	**29.8**
BINETTE, Andre *No playoffs*												
BINKLEY, Les												
1970	Pittsburgh	7	5	2	....	428	15	0	2.10	....	....	....
Playoff Totals		**7**	**5**	**2**	....	**428**	**15**	**0**	**2.10**	....	....	....
BIRON, Martin *No playoffs*												

Season	Club	GP	W	L	T	Mins	GA	SO	Avg	SA	S%	SAPG
BITTNER, Richard *No playoffs*												
BLAKE, Mike *No playoffs*												
BLUE, John												
1993	Boston	2	0	1	....	96	5	0	3.13	49	.898	30.6
Playoff Totals		**2**	**0**	**1**	....	**96**	**5**	**0**	**3.13**	**49**	**.898**	**30.6**
BOISVERT, Gilles *No playoffs*												
BOUCHARD, Dan												
1974	Atlanta	1	0	1	....	60	4	0	4.00	....	....	....
1976	Atlanta	2	0	2	....	120	3	0	1.50	....	....	....
1977	Atlanta	1	0	1	....	60	5	0	5.00	....	....	....
1978	Atlanta	2	0	2	....	120	7	0	3.50	....	....	....
1979	Atlanta	2	0	2	....	100	9	0	5.40	....	....	....
1980	Atlanta	4	1	3	....	241	14	0	3.49	....	....	....
1981	Quebec	5	2	3	....	286	19	*1	3.99	....	....	....
1982	Quebec	11	4	7	....	677	38	0	3.37	....	....	....
1983	Quebec	4	1	3	....	242	11	0	2.73	....	....	....
1984	Quebec	9	5	4	....	543	25	0	2.76	224	.888	24.8
1985	Quebec	1	0	1	....	60	7	0	7.00	24	.708	24.0
1986	Winnipeg	1	0	1	....	40	5	0	7.50	22	.773	33.0
Playoff Totals		**43**	**13**	**30**	....	**2549**	**147**	**1**	**3.46**	....	....	....
BOUCHER, Brian *No playoffs*												
BOURQUE, Claude												
1939	Montreal	3	1	2	....	188	8	1	2.55	....	....	....
Playoff Totals		**3**	**1**	**2**	....	**188**	**8**	**1**	**2.55**	....	....	....
BOUTIN, Rollie *No playoffs*												
BOUVRETTE, Lionel *No playoffs*												
BOWER, Johnny												
1959	Toronto	*12	5	7	....	*746	39	0	3.14	....	....	....
1960	Toronto	*10	4	6	....	*645	31	0	2.88	....	....	....
1961	Toronto	3	0	3	....	180	9	0	3.00	....	....	....
1962◆	Toronto	10	*6	3	....	579	22	0	*2.28	....	....	....
1963◆	Toronto	10	*8	2	....	600	16	*2	*1.60	....	....	....
1964◆	Toronto	*14	*8	6	....	*850	30	*2	*2.12	....	....	....
1965	Toronto	5	2	3	....	321	13	0	2.43	....	....	....
1966	Toronto	2	0	2	....	120	8	0	4.00	....	....	....
1967◆	Toronto	4	2	0	....	183	5	*1	1.64	....	....	....
1969	Toronto	4	0	2	....	154	11	0	4.29	....	....	....
Playoff Totals		**74**	**35**	**34**	....	**4378**	**184**	**5**	**2.52**	....	....	....
BRANIGAN, Andy *No playoffs*												Defense
BRATHWAITE, Fred *No playoffs*												
BRIMSEK, Frank												
1939◆	Boston	*12	*8	4	....	*863	18	1	*1.25	....	....	....
1940	Boston	6	2	4	....	360	15	0	2.50	....	....	....
1941◆	Boston	*11	*8	3	....	*678	23	*1	*2.04	....	....	....
1942	Boston	5	2	3	....	307	16	0	3.13	....	....	....
1943	Boston	9	4	5	....	560	33	0	3.54	....	....	....
1946	Boston	*10	5	5	....	*650	29	0	2.68	....	....	....
1947	Boston	5	1	4	....	343	16	0	2.80	....	....	....
1948	Boston	5	1	4	....	317	20	0	3.79	....	....	....
1949	Boston	5	1	4	....	316	16	0	3.04	....	....	....
Playoff Totals		**68**	**32**	**36**	....	**4394**	**186**	**2**	**2.54**	....	....	....
BROCHU, Martin *No playoffs*												
BRODA, Turk												
1937	Toronto	2	0	2	....	133	5	0	2.26	....	....	....
1938	Toronto	7	4	3	....	452	13	1	1.73	....	....	....
1939	Toronto	10	5	5	....	617	20	*2	1.94	....	....	....
1940	Toronto	10	6	4	....	657	19	1	1.74	....	....	....
1941	Toronto	7	3	4	....	438	15	0	2.05	....	....	....
1942◆	Toronto	*13	*8	5	....	*780	31	*1	2.38	....	....	....
1943	Toronto	6	2	4	....	439	20	0	2.73	....	....	....
1947◆	Toronto	*11	*8	3	....	680	27	*1	2.38	....	....	....
1948◆	Toronto	9	*8	1	....	557	20	*1	*2.15	....	....	....
1949◆	Toronto	9	*8	1	....	574	15	*1	*1.57	....	....	....
1950	Toronto	7	3	4	....	450	10	*3	*1.33	....	....	....
1951◆	Toronto	8	*5	1	....	492	9	*2	1.10	....	....	....
1952	Toronto	2	0	2	....	120	7	0	3.50	....	....	....
Playoff Totals		**101**	**60**	**39**	....	**6389**	**211**	**13**	**1.98**	....	....	....
BRODERICK, Ken *No playoffs*												
BRODERICK, Len *No playoffs*												
BRODEUR, Martin												
1992	New Jersey	1	0	1	....	32	3	0	5.63	15	.800	28.1
1994	New Jersey	17	8	9	....	1171	38	1	1.95	531	.928	27.2
1995◆	New Jersey	*20	*16	4	....	*1222	34	*3	*1.67	463	.927	22.7
1997	New Jersey	10	5	5	....	659	19	2	*1.73	268	.929	24.4
1998	New Jersey	6	2	4	....	366	12	0	1.97	164	.927	26.9
1999	New Jersey	7	3	4	....	425	20	0	2.82	139	.856	19.6
Playoff Totals		**61**	**34**	**27**	....	**3875**	**126**	**6**	**1.95**	**1580**	**.920**	**24.5**
BRODEUR, Richard												
1981	Vancouver	3	0	3	....	185	13	0	4.22	....	....	....
1982	Vancouver	17	11	6	....	1089	49	0	2.70	....	....	....
1983	Vancouver	3	0	3	....	193	13	0	4.04	....	....	....
1984	Vancouver	4	1	3	....	222	12	1	3.24	115	.896	31.1
1986	Vancouver	2	0	2	....	120	12	0	6.00	79	.848	39.5
1988	Hartford	4	1	3	....	200	12	0	3.60	87	.862	26.1
Playoff Totals		**33**	**13**	**20**	....	**2009**	**111**	**1**	**3.32**	....	....	....
BROMLEY, Gary												
1979	Vancouver	3	1	2	....	180	14	0	4.67	....	....	....
1980	Vancouver	4	1	3	....	180	11	0	3.67	....	....	....
Playoff Totals		**7**	**2**	**5**	....	**360**	**25**	**0**	**4.17**	....	....	....
BROOKS, Arthur *No playoffs*												

Season	Club	GP	W	L	T	Mins	GA	SO	Avg	SA	S%	SAPG
BROOKS, Ross												
1973	Boston	1	0	0	....	20	3	0	9.00	....	....	....
Playoff Totals		**1**	**0**	**0**	....	**20**	**3**	**0**	**9.00**	....	....	....
BROPHY, Frank *No playoffs*												
BROWN, Andy *No playoffs*												
BROWN, Ken *No playoffs*												
BRUNETTA, Mario *No playoffs*												
BULLOCK, Bruce *No playoffs*												
BURKE, Sean												
1988	New Jersey	17	9	8	....	1001	57	*1	3.42	515	.889	30.9
1990	New Jersey	2	0	2	....	125	8	0	3.84	57	.860	27.4
1998	Philadelphia	5	1	4	....	283	17	0	3.60	121	.860	25.7
Playoff Totals		**24**	**10**	**14**	....	**1409**	**82**	**1**	**3.49**	**693**	**.882**	**29.5**
BUZINSKI, Steve *No playoffs*												
CALEY, Don *No playoffs*												
CAPRICE, Frank *No playoffs*												
CAREY, Jim												
1995	Washington	7	2	4	....	358	25	0	4.19	151	.834	25.3
1996	Washington	3	0	1	....	97	10	0	6.19	39	.744	24.1
Playoff Totals		**10**	**2**	**5**	....	**455**	**35**	**0**	**4.62**	**190**	**.816**	**25.1**
CARON, Jacques												
1972	St. Louis	9	4	5	....	499	26	0	3.13	....	....	....
1973	St. Louis	3	0	2	....	140	8	0	3.43	....	....	....
Playoff Totals		**12**	**4**	**7**	....	**639**	**34**	**0**	**3.19**	....	....	....
CARTER, Lyle *No playoffs*												
CASEY, Jon												
1989	Minnesota	4	1	3	....	211	16	0	4.55	121	.868	34.4
1990	Minnesota	7	3	4	....	415	21	1	3.04	219	.904	31.7
1991	Minnesota	*23	*14	7	....	*1205	61	*1	3.04	571	.893	28.4
1992	Minnesota	7	3	4	....	437	22	0	3.02	225	.902	30.9
1994	Boston	11	5	6	....	698	34	0	2.92	308	.890	26.5
1995	St. Louis	2	0	1	....	30	2	0	4.00	10	.800	20.0
1996	St. Louis	12	6	6	....	747	36	1	2.89	378	.905	30.4
Playoff Totals		**66**	**32**	**31**	....	**3743**	**192**	**3**	**3.08**	**1832**	**.895**	**29.4**
CHABOT, Frederic *No playoffs*												
CHABOT, Lorne												
1927	NY Rangers	2	0	1	1	120	3	1	1.50	....	....	....
1928◆	NY Rangers	6	2	2	1	321	8	1	1.50	....	....	....
1929	Toronto	4	2	2	0	242	5	0	1.24	....	....	....
1931	Toronto	2	0	1	1	139	4	0	1.73	....	....	....
1932◆	Toronto	*7	*5	1	1	438	15	0	2.05	....	....	....
1933	Toronto	*9	4	5	0	*686	18	*2	1.57	....	....	....
1934	Mtl. Canadiens	2	0	1	1	131	4	0	1.83	....	....	....
1935	Chicago	2	0	1	1	124	1	1	0.48	....	....	....
1936	Mtl. Maroons	3	0	3	0	297	6	0	*1.21	....	....	....
Playoff Totals		**37**	**13**	**17**	**6**	**2498**	**64**	**5**	**1.54**	....	....	....
CHADWICK, Ed *No playoffs*												
CHAMPOUX, Bob												
1964	Detroit	1	1	0	....	55	4	0	4.36	....	....	....
Playoff Totals		**1**	**1**	**0**	....	**55**	**4**	**0**	**4.36**	....	....	....
CHEEVERS, Gerry												
1968	Boston	4	0	4	....	240	15	0	3.75	....	....	....
1969	Boston	9	6	3	....	572	16	*3	1.68	....	....	....
1970◆	Boston	*13	*12	1	....	*781	29	0	2.23	....	....	....
1971	Boston	6	3	3	....	360	21	0	3.50	....	....	....
1972◆	Boston	8	*6	2	....	483	21	*2	2.61	....	....	....
1976	Boston	6	2	4	....	392	14	1	2.14	....	....	....
1977	Boston	*14	8	5	....	*858	44	1	3.08	....	....	....
1978	Boston	12	8	4	....	731	35	1	2.87	....	....	....
1979	Boston	6	4	2	....	360	15	0	2.50	....	....	....
1980	Boston	10	4	6	....	619	32	0	3.10	....	....	....
Playoff Totals		**88**	**53**	**34**	....	**5396**	**242**	**8**	**2.69**	....	....	....
CHEVELDAE, Tim												
1991	Detroit	7	3	4	....	398	22	0	3.32	208	.894	31.4
1992	Detroit	11	3	7	....	597	25	*2	2.51	277	.910	27.8
1993	Detroit	7	3	4	....	423	24	0	3.40	200	.880	28.4
Playoff Totals		**25**	**9**	**15**	....	**1418**	**71**	**2**	**3.00**	**685**	**.896**	**29.0**
CHEVRIER, Alain												
1989	Chicago	16	9	7	....	1013	44	0	2.61	484	.909	28.7
Playoff Totals		**16**	**9**	**7**	....	**1013**	**44**	**0**	**2.61**	**484**	**.909**	**28.7**
CLANCY, King												Defense
1923◆	Ottawa	1	0	0	0	2	0	0	0.00	....	....	....
Playoff Totals		**1**	**0**	**0**	**0**	**2**	**0**	**0**	**0.00**	....	....	....
CLEGHORN, Odie *No playoffs*												Right wing/Center
CLEGHORN, Sprague *No playoffs*												Defense
CLIFFORD, Chris *No playoffs*												
CLOUTIER, Dan *No playoffs*												
CLOUTIER, Jacques												
1989	Buffalo	4	1	3	....	238	10	1	2.52	108	.907	27.2
1990	Chicago	4	0	2	....	175	8	0	2.74	75	.893	25.7
Playoff Totals		**8**	**1**	**5**	....	**413**	**18**	**1**	**2.62**	**183**	**.902**	**26.6**
COLVIN, Les *No playoffs*												
CONACHER, Charlie *No playoffs*												Right wing

Season	Club	GP	W	L	T	Mins	GA	SO	Avg	SA	S%	SAPG
CONNELL, Alex												
1926	Ottawa	2	0	1	1	120	2	0	*1.00	....	....	....
1927♦	Ottawa	6	*3	0	3	400	4	*2	*0.60	....	....	....
1928	Ottawa	2	0	2	0	120	3	0	1.50	....	....	....
1930	Ottawa	2	0	1	1	120	6	0	3.00	....	....	....
1932	Detroit	2	0	1	1	120	3	0	1.50	....	....	....
1935♦	Mtl. Maroons	*7	*5	0	2	429	8	*2	*1.12	....	....	....
Playoff Totals		**21**	**8**	**5**	**8**	**1309**	**26**	**4**	***1.19**	....	....	....
CORSI, Jim *No playoffs*												
COURTEAU, Maurice *No playoffs*												
COUSINEAU, Marcel *No playoffs*												
COWLEY, Wayne *No playoffs*												
COX, Abbie *No playoffs*												
CRAIG, Jim *No playoffs*												
CRHA, Jiri												
1980	Toronto	2	0	2	....	121	10	0	4.96	....	....	....
1981	Toronto	3	0	2	....	65	11	0	10.15	....	....	....
Playoff Totals		**5**	**0**	**4**	....	**186**	**21**	**0**	**6.77**	....	....	....
CROZIER, Roger												
1964	Detroit	3	0	2	....	126	5	0	2.38	....	....	....
1965	Detroit	7	3	4	....	420	23	0	3.29	....	....	....
1966	Detroit	*12	6	5	....	*668	26	*1	2.34	....	....	....
1970	Detroit	1	0	1	....	34	3	0	5.29	....	....	....
1973	Buffalo	4	2	2	....	249	11	0	2.65	....	....	....
1975	Buffalo	5	3	2	....	292	14	0	2.88	....	....	....
Playoff Totals		**32**	**14**	**16**	....	**1789**	**82**	**1**	**2.75**	....	....	....
CUDE, Wilf												
1934	Detroit	*9	4	5	0	*593	21	1	2.12	....	....	....
1935	Mtl. Canadiens	2	0	1	1	120	6	0	3.00	....	....	....
1937	Mtl. Canadiens	5	2	3	....	352	13	0	2.22	....	....	....
1938	Mtl. Canadiens	3	1	2	....	192	11	0	3.44	....	....	....
Playoff Totals		**19**	**7**	**11**	**1**	**1257**	**51**	**1**	**2.43**	....	....	....
CUTTS, Don *No playoffs*												
CYR, Claude *No playoffs*												
DADSWELL, Doug *No playoffs*												
DAFOE, Byron												
1994	Washington	2	0	2	....	118	5	0	2.54	39	.872	19.8
1995	Washington	1	0	0	....	20	1	0	3.00	3	.667	9.0
1998	Boston	6	2	4	....	422	14	1	1.99	159	.912	22.6
1999	Boston	12	6	6	....	768	26	2	2.03	330	.921	25.8
Playoff Totals		**21**	**8**	**12**	....	**1328**	**46**	**3**	**2.08**	**531**	**.913**	**24.0**
D'ALESSIO, Corrie *No playoffs*												
DALEY, Joe *No playoffs*												
DAMORE, Nick *No playoffs*												
D'AMOUR, Marc *No playoffs*												
DARRAGH, Jack *No playoffs*												
DASKALAKIS, Cleon *No playoffs*												
DAVIDSON, John												
1975	St. Louis	1	0	1	....	60	4	0	4.00	....	....	....
1978	NY Rangers	2	1	1	....	122	7	0	3.44	....	....	....
1979	NY Rangers	*18	11	7	....	*1106	42	*1	2.28	....	....	....
1980	NY Rangers	9	4	5	....	541	21	0	2.33	....	....	....
1982	NY Rangers	1	0	0	....	33	3	0	5.45	....	....	....
Playoff Totals		**31**	**16**	**14**	....	**1862**	**77**	**1**	**2.48**	....	....	....
DECOURCY, Robert *No playoffs*												
DEFELICE, Norm *No playoffs*												
DEJORDY, Denis												
1964	Chicago	1	0	0	....	20	2	0	6.00	....	....	....
1965	Chicago	2	0	1	....	80	9	0	6.75	....	....	....
1967	Chicago	4	1	2	....	184	10	0	3.26	....	....	....
1968	Chicago	11	5	6	....	662	34	0	3.08	....	....	....
Playoff Totals		**18**	**6**	**9**	....	**946**	**55**	**0**	**3.49**	....	....	....
DELGUIDICE, Matt *No playoffs*												
DENIS, Marc *No playoffs*												
DeROUVILLE, Philippe *No playoffs*												
DESJARDINS, Gerry												
1969	Los Angeles	9	3	4	....	431	28	0	3.90	....	....	....
1972	Chicago	1	1	0	....	60	5	0	5.00	....	....	....
1975	Buffalo	*15	7	5	....	760	43	0	3.39	....	....	....
1976	Buffalo	9	4	5	....	563	28	0	2.98	....	....	....
1977	Buffalo	1	0	1	....	60	4	0	4.00	....	....	....
Playoff Totals		**35**	**15**	**15**	....	**1874**	**108**	**0**	**3.46**	....	....	....
DICKIE, Bill *No playoffs*												
DION, Connie												
1944	Detroit	5	1	4	....	300	17	0	3.40	....	....	....
Playoff Totals		**5**	**1**	**4**	....	**300**	**17**	**0**	**3.40**	....	....	....
DION, Michel												
1982	Pittsburgh	5	2	3	....	304	22	0	4.34	....	....	....
Playoff Totals		**5**	**2**	**3**	....	**304**	**22**	**0**	**4.34**	....	....	....
DOLSON, Dolly												
1929	Detroit	2	0	2	0	120	7	0	3.50	....	....	....
Playoff Totals		**2**	**0**	**2**	**0**	**120**	**7**	**0**	**3.50**	....	....	....
DOPSON, Robert *No playoffs*												
DOWIE, Bruce *No playoffs*												

Season	Club	GP	W	L	T	Mins	GA	SO	Avg	SA	S%	SAPG
DRAPER, Tom												
1992	Buffalo	7	3	4	....	433	19	1	2.63	201	.905	27.9
Playoff Totals		**7**	**3**	**4**	....	**433**	**19**	**1**	**2.63**	**201**	**.905**	**27.9**
DRYDEN, Dave												
1966	Chicago	1	0	0	....	13	0	0	0.00	....	....	....
1973	Buffalo	2	0	2	....	120	9	0	4.50	....	....	....
Playoff Totals		**3**	**0**	**2**	....	**133**	**9**	**0**	**4.06**	....	....	....
DRYDEN, Ken												
1971♦	Montreal	*20	*12	8	....	*1221	61	0	3.00	....	....	....
1972	Montreal	6	2	4	....	360	17	0	2.83	....	....	....
1973♦	Montreal	*17	*12	5	....	*1039	50	1	2.89	....	....	....
1975	Montreal	11	6	5	....	688	29	2	2.53	....	....	....
1976♦	Montreal	*13	*12	1	....	*780	25	1	*1.92	....	....	....
1977♦	Montreal	*14	*12	2	....	849	22	*4	*1.55	....	....	....
1978♦	Montreal	*15	*12	3	....	*919	29	*2	*1.89	....	....	....
1979♦	Montreal	16	*12	4	....	990	41	0	2.48	....	....	....
Playoff Totals		**112**	**80**	**32**	....	**6846**	**274**	**10**	**2.40**	....	....	....
DUFFUS, Parris *No playoffs*												
DUMAS, Michel												
1975	Chicago	1	0	0	....	19	1	0	3.16	....	....	....
Playoff Totals		**1**	**0**	**0**	....	**19**	**1**	**0**	**3.16**	....	....	....
DUNHAM, Mike *No playoffs*												
***DUPUIS, Bob** *No playoffs*												
DURNAN, Bill												
1944♦	Montreal	*9	*8	1	....	*549	14	*1	*1.53	....	....	....
1945	Montreal	6	2	4	....	373	15	0	2.41	....	....	....
1946♦	Montreal	9	*8	1	....	581	20	0	*2.07	....	....	....
1947	Montreal	*11	6	5	....	*720	23	*1	*1.92	....	....	....
1949	Montreal	7	3	4	....	468	17	0	2.18	....	....	....
1950	Montreal	3	0	3	....	180	10	0	3.33	....	....	....
Playoff Totals		**45**	**27**	**18**	....	**2871**	**99**	**2**	**2.07**	....	....	....
DYCK, Ed *No playoffs*												
EDWARDS, Don												
1977	Buffalo	5	2	3	....	300	15	0	3.00	....	....	....
1978	Buffalo	8	3	5	....	482	22	0	2.74	....	....	....
1980	Buffalo	6	3	3	....	360	17	1	2.83	....	....	....
1981	Buffalo	8	4	4	....	503	28	0	3.34	....	....	....
1982	Buffalo	4	1	3	....	214	16	0	4.49	....	....	....
1983	Calgary	5	1	2	....	226	22	0	5.84	....	....	....
1984	Calgary	6	2	1	....	217	12	0	3.32	133	.910	36.8
Playoff Totals		**42**	**16**	**21**	....	**2302**	**132**	**1**	**3.44**	....	....	....
EDWARDS, Gary												
1974	Los Angeles	1	1	0	....	60	1	0	1.00	....	....	....
1976	Los Angeles	2	1	1	....	120	9	0	4.50	....	....	....
1980	Minnesota	7	3	3	....	337	22	0	3.92	....	....	....
1981	Edmonton	1	0	0	....	20	2	0	6.00	....	....	....
Playoff Totals		**11**	**5**	**4**	....	**537**	**34**	**0**	**3.80**	....	....	....
EDWARDS, Marv *No playoffs*												
EDWARDS, Roy												
1970	Detroit	4	0	3	....	206	11	0	3.20	....	....	....
Playoff Totals		**4**	**0**	**3**	....	**206**	**11**	**0**	**3.20**	....	....	....
ELIOT, Darren												
1987	Los Angeles	1	0	0	....	40	7	0	10.50	29	.759	43.5
Playoff Totals		**1**	**0**	**0**	....	**40**	**7**	**0**	**10.50**	**29**	**.759**	**43.5**
ELLACOTT, Ken *No playoffs*												
ERICKSON, Chad *No playoffs*												
ESCHE, Robert *No playoffs*												
ESPOSITO, Tony												
1969♦	Montreal	....	....	....	....	....	....	....	....	....	....	....
1970	Chicago	8	4	4	....	480	27	0	3.38	....	....	....
1971	Chicago	18	11	7	....	1151	42	*2	*2.19	....	....	....
1972	Chicago	5	2	3	....	300	16	0	3.20	....	....	....
1973	Chicago	15	10	5	....	895	46	1	3.08	....	....	....
1974	Chicago	10	6	4	....	584	28	*2	2.88	....	....	....
1975	Chicago	8	3	5	....	472	34	0	4.32	....	....	....
1976	Chicago	4	0	4	....	240	13	0	3.25	....	....	....
1977	Chicago	2	0	2	....	120	6	0	3.00	....	....	....
1978	Chicago	4	0	4	....	252	19	0	4.52	....	....	....
1979	Chicago	4	0	4	....	243	14	0	3.46	....	....	....
1980	Chicago	6	3	3	....	373	14	0	2.25	....	....	....
1981	Chicago	3	0	3	....	215	15	0	4.19	....	....	....
1982	Chicago	7	3	3	....	381	16	*1	2.52	....	....	....
1983	Chicago	5	3	2	....	311	18	0	3.47	....	....	....
Playoff Totals		**99**	**45**	**53**	....	**6017**	**308**	**6**	**3.07**	....	....	....
ESSENSA, Bob												
1990	Winnipeg	4	2	1	....	206	12	0	3.50	100	.880	29.1
1992	Winnipeg	1	0	0	....	33	3	0	5.45	17	.824	30.9
1993	Winnipeg	6	2	4	....	367	20	0	3.27	183	.891	29.9
1994	Detroit	2	0	2	....	109	9	0	4.95	43	.791	23.7
1998	Edmonton	1	0	0	....	27	1	0	2.22	11	.909	24.4
Playoff Totals		**14**	**4**	**7**	....	**742**	**45**	**0**	**3.64**	**354**	**.873**	**28.6**
EVANS, Claude *No playoffs*												
EXELBY, Randy *No playoffs*												
FANKHOUSER, Scott *No playoffs*												
FARR, Rocky *No playoffs*												

Season	Club	GP	W	L	T	Mins	GA	SO	Avg	SA	S%	SAPG
FAVELL, Doug												
1968	Philadelphia	2	0	2	....	120	8	0	4.00	....	....	....
1969	Philadelphia	1	0	1	....	60	5	0	5.00	....	....	....
1971	Philadelphia	2	0	2	....	120	8	0	4.00	....	....	....
1973	Philadelphia	11	5	6	....	669	29	1	2.60	....	....	....
1974	Toronto	3	0	3	....	181	10	0	3.31	....	....	....
1978	Colorado	2	0	2	....	120	6	0	3.00	....	....	....
Playoff Totals		**21**	**5**	**16**	....	**1270**	**66**	**1**	**3.12**	....	....	....
FERNANDEZ, Manny												
1998	Dallas	1	0	0	....	2	0	0	0.00	0	.000	0.0
Playoff Totals		**1**	**0**	**0**	....	**2**	**0**	**0**	**0.00**	**0**	**.000**	**0.0**
FICHAUD, Eric *No playoffs*												
FISET, Stephane												
1993	Quebec	1	0	0	....	21	1	0	2.86	12	.917	34.3
1995	Quebec	4	1	2	....	209	16	0	4.59	115	.861	33.0
1996♦	Colorado	1	0	0	....	1	0	0	0.00	0	.000	0.0
1998	Los Angeles	2	0	2	....	93	7	0	4.52	61	.885	39.4
Playoff Totals		**8**	**1**	**4**	....	**324**	**24**	**0**	**4.44**	**188**	**.872**	**34.8**
FITZPATRICK, Mark												
1990	NY Islanders	4	0	2	....	152	13	0	5.13	71	.817	28.0
1993	NY Islanders	3	0	1	....	77	4	0	3.12	23	.826	17.9
1996	Florida	2	0	0	....	60	6	0	6.00	30	.800	30.0
Playoff Totals		**9**	**0**	**3**	....	**289**	**23**	**0**	**4.78**	**124**	**.815**	**25.7**
FLAHERTY, Wade												
1995	San Jose	7	2	3	....	377	31	0	4.93	221	.860	35.2
Playoff Totals		**7**	**2**	**3**	....	**377**	**31**	**0**	**4.93**	**221**	**.860**	**35.2**
FORBES, Jake												
1921	Toronto	2	0	2	0	120	7	0	3.50	....	....	....
Playoff Totals		**2**	**0**	**2**	**0**	**120**	**7**	**0**	**3.50**	....	....	....
FORD, Brian *No playoffs*												
FOSTER, Norm *No playoffs*												
FOUNTAIN, Mike *No playoffs*												
FOWLER, Hec *No playoffs*												
FRANCIS, Emile *No playoffs*												
FRANKS, Jim												
1937♦	Detroit	1	0	1	....	30	2	0	4.00	....	....	....
Playoff Totals		**1**	**0**	**1**	....	**30**	**2**	**0**	**4.00**	....	....	....
FREDERICK, Ray *No playoffs*												
FRIESEN, Karl *No playoffs*												
FROESE, Bob												
1984	Philadelphia	3	0	2	....	154	11	0	4.29	77	.857	30.0
1985	Philadelphia	4	0	1	....	146	11	0	4.52	71	.845	29.2
1986	Philadelphia	5	2	3	....	293	15	0	3.07	125	.880	25.6
1987	NY Rangers	4	1	1	....	165	10	0	3.64	96	.896	34.9
1989	NY Rangers	2	0	2	....	72	8	0	6.67	51	.843	42.5
Playoff Totals		**18**	**3**	**9**	....	**830**	**55**	**0**	**3.98**	**420**	**.869**	**30.4**
FUHR, Grant												
1982	Edmonton	5	2	3	....	309	26	0	5.05	....	....	....
1983	Edmonton	1	0	0	....	11	0	0	0.00	....	....	....
1984♦	Edmonton	16	11	4	....	883	44	1	2.99	491	.910	33.4
1985♦	Edmonton	*18	*15	3	....	1064	55	0	3.10	522	.895	29.4
1986	Edmonton	9	5	4	....	541	28	0	3.11	273	.897	30.3
1987♦	Edmonton	19	14	5	....	1148	47	0	2.46	511	.908	26.7
1988♦	Edmonton	*19	*16	2	....	*1136	55	0	2.90	471	.883	24.9
1989	Edmonton	7	3	4	....	417	24	1	3.45	227	.894	32.7
1990♦	Edmonton	....	....	....	....	....	....	....	....	....	....	....
1991	Edmonton	17	8	7	....	1019	51	0	3.00	488	.895	28.7
1993	Buffalo	8	3	4	....	474	27	1	3.42	216	.875	27.3
1996	St. Louis	2	1	0	....	69	1	0	0.87	45	.978	39.1
1997	St. Louis	6	2	4	....	357	13	2	2.18	183	.929	30.8
1998	St. Louis	10	6	4	....	616	28	0	2.73	297	.906	28.9
1999	St. Louis	13	6	6	....	790	31	1	2.35	305	.898	23.2
Playoff Totals		**150**	**92**	**50**	....	**8834**	**430**	**6**	**2.92**	....	....	....
GAGE, Joaquin *No playoffs*												
GAGNON, David *No playoffs*												
GAMBLE, Bruce												
1967♦	Toronto	....	....	....	....	....	....	....	....	....	....	....
1969	Toronto	3	0	2	....	86	13	0	9.07	....	....	....
1971	Philadelphia	2	0	2	....	120	12	0	6.00	....	....	....
Playoff Totals		**5**	**0**	**4**	....	**206**	**25**	**0**	**7.28**	....	....	....
GAMBLE, Troy												
1991	Vancouver	4	1	3	....	249	16	0	3.86	133	.880	32.0
Playoff Totals		**4**	**1**	**3**	....	**249**	**16**	**0**	**3.86**	**133**	**.880**	**32.0**
GARDINER, Bert												
1939	NY Rangers	6	3	3	....	433	12	0	1.66	....	....	....
1941	Montreal	3	1	2	....	214	8	0	2.24	....	....	....
Playoff Totals		**9**	**4**	**5**	....	**647**	**20**	**0**	**1.85**	....	....	....
GARDINER, Chuck												
1930	Chicago	2	0	1	1	172	3	0	1.05	....	....	....
1931	Chicago	9	5	3	1	638	14	*2	1.32	....	....	....
1932	Chicago	2	1	1	0	120	6	*1	3.00	....	....	....
1934♦	Chicago	8	*6	1	1	542	12	*2	*1.33	....	....	....
Playoff Totals		**21**	**12**	**6**	**3**	**1472**	**35**	**5**	**1.43**	....	....	....
GARDNER, George *No playoffs*												
GARNER, Tyrone *No playoffs*												

Season	Club	GP	W	L	T	Mins	GA	SO	Avg	SA	S%	SAPG
GARRETT, John												
1980	Hartford	1	0	1	....	60	8	0	8.00	....	....	....
1982	Quebec	5	3	2	....	323	21	0	3.90	....	....	....
1983	Vancouver	1	1	0	....	60	4	0	4.00	....	....	....
1984	Vancouver	2	0	0	....	18	0	0	0.00	5	.000	16.7
Playoff Totals		**9**	**4**	**3**	....	**461**	**33**	**0**	**4.30**	....	....	....
GATHERUM, Dave *No playoffs*												
GAUTHIER, Paul *No playoffs*												
GAUTHIER, Sean *No playoffs*												
GELINEAU, Jack												
1951	Boston	4	1	2	....	260	7	1	1.62	....	....	....
Playoff Totals		**4**	**1**	**2**	....	**260**	**7**	**1**	**1.62**	....	....	....
GIACOMIN, Ed												
1967	NY Rangers	4	0	4	....	246	14	0	3.41	....	....	....
1968	NY Rangers	6	2	4	....	360	18	0	3.00	....	....	....
1969	NY Rangers	3	0	3	....	180	10	0	3.33	....	....	....
1970	NY Rangers	5	2	3	....	276	19	0	4.13	....	....	....
1971	NY Rangers	12	7	5	....	759	28	0	2.21	....	....	....
1972	NY Rangers	*10	*6	4	....	*600	27	0	2.70	....	....	....
1973	NY Rangers	10	5	4	....	539	23	1	2.56	....	....	....
1974	NY Rangers	13	7	6	....	788	37	0	2.82	....	....	....
1975	NY Rangers	2	0	2	....	86	4	0	2.79	....	....	....
Playoff Totals		**65**	**29**	**35**	....	**3834**	**180**	**1**	**2.82**	....	....	....
GIGUERE, Jean-Sebastien *No playoffs*												
GILBERT, Gilles												
1973	Minnesota	1	0	1	....	60	4	0	4.00	....	....	....
1974	Boston	16	10	6	....	977	43	1	2.64	....	....	....
1975	Boston	3	1	2	....	188	12	0	3.83	....	....	....
1976	Boston	6	3	3	....	360	19	*2	3.17	....	....	....
1977	Boston	1	0	1	....	20	3	0	9.00	....	....	....
1979	Boston	5	3	2	....	314	16	0	3.06	....	....	....
Playoff Totals		**32**	**17**	**15**	....	**1919**	**97**	**3**	**3.03**	....	....	....
GILL, Andre *No playoffs*												
GOODMAN, Paul												
1938♦	Chicago	1	0	1	....	60	5	0	5.00	....	....	....
1940	Chicago	2	0	2	....	127	5	0	2.36	....	....	....
Playoff Totals		**3**	**0**	**3**	....	**187**	**10**	**0**	**3.21**	....	....	....
GORDON, Scott *No playoffs*												
GOSSELIN, Mario												
1985	Quebec	17	9	8	....	1059	54	0	3.06	473	.886	26.8
1986	Quebec	1	0	1	....	40	5	0	7.50	22	.773	33.0
1987	Quebec	11	7	4	....	654	37	0	3.39	326	.887	29.9
1990	Los Angeles	3	0	2	....	63	3	0	2.90	23	.870	21.9
Playoff Totals		**32**	**16**	**15**	....	**1816**	**99**	**0**	**3.27**	**844**	**.883**	**27.9**
GOVERDE, David *No playoffs*												
GRAHAME, John *No playoffs*												
GRAHAME, Ron												
1978	Boston	4	2	1	....	202	7	0	2.08	....	....	....
Playoff Totals		**4**	**2**	**1**	....	**202**	**7**	**0**	**2.08**	....	....	....
GRANT, Ben *No playoffs*												
GRANT, Doug *No playoffs*												
GRATTON, Gilles *No playoffs*												
GRAY, Gerry *No playoffs*												
GRAY, Harrison *No playoffs*												
GREENLAY, Mike *No playoffs*												
GUENETTE, Steve *No playoffs*												
HACKETT, Jeff												
1995	Chicago	2	0	0	....	26	1	0	2.31	11	.909	25.4
1996	Chicago	1	0	1	....	60	5	0	5.00	32	.844	32.0
1997	Chicago	6	2	4	....	345	25	0	4.35	190	.868	33.0
Playoff Totals		**9**	**2**	**5**	....	**431**	**31**	**0**	**4.32**	**233**	**.867**	**32.4**
HAINSWORTH, George												
1927	Mtl. Canadiens	4	1	1	2	252	6	1	1.43	....	....	....
1928	Mtl. Canadiens	2	0	1	1	128	3	0	1.41	....	....	....
1929	Mtl. Canadiens	3	0	3	0	180	5	0	1.67	....	....	....
1930♦	Mtl. Canadiens	*6	*5	0	1	*481	6	*3	*0.75	....	....	....
1931♦	Mtl. Canadiens	*10	*6	4	0	*722	21	*2	1.75	....	....	....
1932	Mtl. Canadiens	4	1	3	0	300	13	0	2.60	....	....	....
1933	Mtl. Canadiens	2	0	1	1	120	8	0	4.00	....	....	....
1934	Toronto	5	2	3	0	302	11	0	2.19	....	....	....
1935	Toronto	*7	3	4	0	*460	12	*2	1.57	....	....	....
1936	Toronto	*9	4	5	0	*541	27	0	2.99	....	....	....
Playoff Totals		**52**	**22**	**25**	**5**	**3486**	**112**	**8**	**1.93**	....	....	....

Season	Club	GP	W	L	T	Mins	GA	SO	Avg	SA	S%	SAPG
HALL, Glenn												
1956	Detroit	*10	5	5	....	*604	28	0	2.78	....	....	....
1957	Detroit	5	1	4	....	300	15	0	3.00	....	....	....
1959	Chicago	6	2	4	....	360	21	0	3.50	....	....	....
1960	Chicago	4	0	4	....	249	14	0	3.37	....	....	....
1961♦	Chicago	*12	*8	4	....	*772	27	*2	*2.10	....	....	....
1962	Chicago	*12	*6	6	....	*720	31	*2	2.58	....	....	....
1963	Chicago	6	2	4	....	360	25	0	4.17	....	....	....
1964	Chicago	7	3	4	....	408	22	0	3.24	....	....	....
1965	Chicago	*13	*7	6	....	*760	28	1	2.21	....	....	....
1966	Chicago	6	2	4	....	347	22	0	3.80	....	....	....
1967	Chicago	3	1	2	....	176	8	0	2.73	....	....	....
1968	St. Louis	*18	8	10	....	*1111	45	*1	2.43	....	....	....
1969	St. Louis	3	0	2	....	131	5	0	2.29	....	....	....
1970	St. Louis	7	4	3	....	421	21	0	2.99	....	....	....
1971	St. Louis	3	0	3	....	180	9	0	3.00	....	....	....
Playoff Totals		**115**	**49**	**65**	....	**6899**	**321**	**6**	**2.79**	....	....	....
HAMEL, Pierre	*No playoffs*											
HANLON, Glen												
1980	Vancouver	2	0	0	....	60	3	0	3.00	....	....	....
1982	St. Louis	3	0	2	....	109	9	0	4.95	....	....	....
1983	NY Rangers	1	0	1	....	60	5	0	5.00	....	....	....
1984	NY Rangers	5	2	3	....	308	13	1	2.53	166	.922	32.3
1985	NY Rangers	3	0	3	....	168	14	0	5.00	99	.859	35.4
1986	NY Rangers	3	0	0	....	75	6	0	4.80	32	.813	25.6
1987	Detroit	8	5	2	....	467	13	*2	*1.67	227	.943	29.2
1988	Detroit	8	4	3	....	431	22	*1	3.06	171	.871	23.8
1989	Detroit	2	0	1	....	78	7	0	5.38	47	.851	36.2
Playoff Totals		**35**	**11**	**15**	....	**1756**	**92**	**4**	**3.14**	....	....	....
HARRISON, Paul												
1979	Toronto	2	0	1	....	91	7	0	4.62	....	....	....
1981	Toronto	1	0	0	....	40	1	0	1.50	....	....	....
1982	Buffalo	1	0	0	....	26	1	0	2.31	....	....	....
Playoff Totals		**4**	**0**	**1**	....	**157**	**9**	**0**	**3.44**	....	....	....
HASEK, Dominik												
1991	Chicago	3	0	0	....	69	3	0	2.61	39	.923	33.9
1992	Chicago	3	0	2	....	158	8	0	3.04	70	.886	26.6
1993	Buffalo	1	1	0	....	45	1	0	1.33	24	.958	32.0
1994	Buffalo	7	3	4	....	484	13	2	*1.61	261	.950	32.4
1995	Buffalo	5	1	4	....	309	18	0	3.50	131	.863	25.4
1997	Buffalo	3	1	1	....	153	5	0	1.96	68	.926	26.7
1998	Buffalo	15	10	5	....	948	32	1	2.03	514	.938	32.5
1999	Buffalo	19	13	6	....	1217	36	2	1.77	587	.939	28.9
Playoff Totals		**56**	**29**	**22**	....	**3383**	**116**	**5**	**2.06**	**1694**	**.932**	**30.0**
HAYWARD, Brian												
1983	Winnipeg	3	0	3	....	160	14	0	5.25	....	....	....
1985	Winnipeg	6	2	4	....	309	23	0	4.47	156	.853	30.3
1986	Winnipeg	2	0	1	....	68	6	0	5.29	31	.806	27.4
1987	Montreal	13	6	5	....	708	32	0	2.71	308	.896	26.1
1988	Montreal	4	2	2	....	230	9	0	2.35	85	.894	22.2
1989	Montreal	2	1	1	....	124	7	0	3.39	54	.870	26.1
1990	Montreal	1	0	0	....	33	2	0	3.64	18	.889	32.7
1991	Minnesota	6	0	2	....	171	11	0	3.86	75	.853	26.3
Playoff Totals		**37**	**11**	**18**	....	**1803**	**104**	**0**	**3.46**	....	....	....
HEAD, Don	*No playoffs*											
HEALY, Glenn												
1988	Los Angeles	4	1	3	....	240	20	0	5.00	128	.844	32.0
1989	Los Angeles	3	0	1	....	97	6	0	3.71	59	.898	36.5
1990	NY Islanders	4	1	2	....	166	9	0	3.25	79	.886	28.6
1993	NY Islanders	18	9	8	....	1109	59	0	3.19	524	.887	28.4
1994♦	NY Rangers	2	0	0	....	68	1	0	0.88	17	.941	15.0
1995	NY Rangers	5	2	1	....	230	13	0	3.39	93	.860	24.3
1999	Toronto	1	0	0	....	20	0	0	0.00	5	.000	15.0
Playoff Totals		**37**	**13**	**15**	....	**1930**	**108**	**0**	**3.36**	**905**	**.881**	**28.1**
HEBERT, Guy												
1993	St. Louis	1	0	0	....	2	0	0	0.00	1	.000	30.0
1997	Anaheim	9	4	4	....	534	18	1	2.02	255	.929	28.7
1999	Anaheim	4	0	3	....	208	15	0	4.33	124	.879	35.8
Playoff Totals		**14**	**4**	**7**	....	**744**	**33**	**1**	**2.66**	**380**	**.913**	**30.6**
HEBERT, Sammy												
1918♦	Toronto	....	....	....	....	....	....	....	....	....	....	....
Playoff Totals		....	....	....	....	....	....	....	....	....	....	....
HEINZ, Rick												
1984	St. Louis	1	0	0	....	8	1	0	7.50	....	....	....
Playoff Totals		**1**	**0**	**0**	....	**8**	**1**	**0**	**7.50**	....	....	....
HENDERSON, John												
1955	Boston	2	0	2	....	120	8	0	4.00	....	....	....
Playoff Totals		**2**	**0**	**2**	....	**120**	**8**	**0**	**4.00**	....	....	....
HENRY, Gord												
1951	Boston	2	0	2	....	120	10	0	5.00	....	....	....
1953	Boston	3	0	2	....	163	11	0	4.05	....	....	....
Playoff Totals		**5**	**0**	**4**	....	**283**	**21**	**0**	**4.45**	....	....	....
HENRY, Jim												
1942	NY Rangers	6	2	4	....	360	13	*1	*2.17	....	....	....
1952	Boston	7	3	4	....	448	18	1	2.41	....	....	....
1953	Boston	*9	5	4	....	*510	26	0	3.06	....	....	....
1954	Boston	4	0	4	....	240	16	0	4.00	....	....	....
1955	Boston	3	1	2	....	183	8	0	2.62	....	....	....
Playoff Totals		**29**	**11**	**18**	....	**1741**	**81**	**2**	**2.79**	....	....	....

Season	Club	GP	W	L	T	Mins	GA	SO	Avg	SA	S%	SAPG
HERRON, Denis												
1977	Pittsburgh	3	1	2	....	180	11	0	3.67	....	....	....
1979	Pittsburgh	7	2	5	....	421	24	0	3.42	....	....	....
1980	Montreal	5	2	3	....	300	15	0	3.00	....	....	....
Playoff Totals		**15**	**5**	**10**	....	**901**	**50**	**0**	**3.33**	....	....	....
HEXTALL, Ron												
1987	Philadelphia	*26	15	11	....	*1540	71	*2	2.77	769	.908	30.0
1988	Philadelphia	7	2	4	....	379	30	0	4.75	196	.847	31.0
1989	Philadelphia	15	8	7	....	886	49	0	3.32	445	.890	30.1
1993	Quebec	6	2	4	....	372	18	0	2.90	211	.915	34.0
1994	NY Islanders	3	0	3	....	158	16	0	6.08	80	.800	30.4
1995	Philadelphia	15	10	5	....	897	42	0	2.81	437	.904	29.2
1996	Philadelphia	12	6	6	....	760	27	0	2.13	319	.915	25.2
1997	Philadelphia	8	4	3	....	444	22	0	2.97	203	.892	27.4
1998	Philadelphia	1	0	0	....	20	1	0	3.00	8	.875	24.0
Playoff Totals		**93**	**47**	**43**	....	**5456**	**276**	**2**	**3.04**	**2668**	**.897**	**29.3**
HIGHTON, Hec	*No playoffs*											
HIMES, Normie	*No playoffs*											Center
HIRSCH, Corey												
1996	Vancouver	6	2	3	....	338	21	0	3.73	166	.873	29.5
Playoff Totals		**6**	**2**	**3**	....	**338**	**21**	**0**	**3.73**	**166**	**.873**	**29.5**
HNILICKA, Milan	*No playoffs*											
HODGE, Charlie												
1955	Montreal	4	1	1	....	83	6	0	4.34	....	....	....
1959♦	Montreal	....	....	....	....	....	....	....	....	....	....	....
1960♦	Montreal	....	....	....	....	....	....	....	....	....	....	....
1964	Montreal	7	3	4	....	420	16	1	2.29	....	....	....
1965♦	Montreal	5	3	2	....	300	10	1	2.00	....	....	....
1966♦	Montreal	....	....	....	....	....	....	....	....	....	....	....
Playoff Totals		**16**	**7**	**7**	....	**803**	**32**	**2**	**2.39**	....	....	....
HODSON, Kevin												
1998♦	Detroit	1	0	0	....	1	0	0	0.00	0	.000	0.0
Playoff Totals		**1**	**0**	**0**	....	**1**	**0**	**0**	**0.00**	**0**	**.000**	**0.0**
HOFFORT, Bruce	*No playoffs*											
HOGANSON, Paul	*No playoffs*											
HOGOSTA, Goran	*No playoffs*											
HOLDEN, Mark	*No playoffs*											
HOLLAND, Ken	*No playoffs*											
HOLLAND, Robbie	*No playoffs*											
HOLMES, Harry												
1918♦	Toronto	*7	*4	3	0	*420	28	0	*4.00	....	....	....
Playoff Totals		**7**	**4**	**3**	**0**	**420**	**28**	**0**	**4.00**	....	....	....
HORNER, Red	*No playoffs*											Defense
HRIVNAK, Jim	*No playoffs*											
HRUDEY, Kelly												
1985	NY Islanders	5	1	3	....	281	8	0	1.71	149	.946	31.8
1986	NY Islanders	2	0	2	....	120	6	0	3.00	59	.898	29.5
1987	NY Islanders	14	7	7	....	842	38	0	2.71	464	.918	33.1
1988	NY Islanders	6	2	4	....	381	23	0	3.62	154	.851	24.3
1989	Los Angeles	10	4	6	....	566	35	0	3.71	293	.881	31.1
1990	Los Angeles	9	4	4	....	539	39	0	4.34	265	.853	29.5
1991	Los Angeles	12	6	6	....	798	37	0	2.78	382	.903	28.7
1992	Los Angeles	6	2	4	....	355	22	0	3.72	179	.877	30.3
1993	Los Angeles	20	10	10	....	1261	74	0	3.52	656	.887	31.2
1998	San Jose	1	0	0	....	20	1	0	3.00	6	.833	18.0
Playoff Totals		**85**	**36**	**46**	....	**5163**	**283**	**0**	**3.29**	**2607**	**.891**	**30.3**
ING, Peter	*No playoffs*											
INNESS, Gary												
1975	Pittsburgh	9	5	4	....	540	24	0	2.67	....	....	....
Playoff Totals		**9**	**5**	**4**	....	**540**	**24**	**0**	**2.67**	....	....	....
IRBE, Arturs												
1994	San Jose	14	7	7	....	806	50	0	3.72	399	.875	29.7
1995	San Jose	6	2	4	....	316	27	0	5.13	184	.853	34.9
1997	Dallas	1	0	0	....	13	0	0	0.00	4	.000	18.5
1999	Carolina	6	2	4	....	408	15	0	2.21	181	.917	26.6
Playoff Totals		**27**	**11**	**15**	....	**1543**	**92**	**0**	**3.58**	**768**	**.880**	**29.9**
IRELAND, Randy	*No playoffs*											
IRONS, Robbie	*No playoffs*											
IRONSTONE, Joe	*No playoffs*											
JABLONSKI, Pat												
1991	St. Louis	3	0	0	....	90	5	0	3.33	35	.857	23.3
1996	Montreal	1	0	0	....	49	1	0	1.22	17	.941	20.8
Playoff Totals		**4**	**0**	**0**	....	**139**	**6**	**0**	**2.59**	**52**	**.885**	**22.4**
JACKSON, Doug	*No playoffs*											
JACKSON, Percy	*No playoffs*											
JAKS, Pauli	*No playoffs*											
JANASZAK, Steve	*No playoffs*											
JANECYK, Bob												
1985	Los Angeles	3	0	3	....	184	10	0	3.26	100	.900	32.6
Playoff Totals		**3**	**0**	**3**	....	**184**	**10**	**0**	**3.26**	**100**	**.900**	**32.6**
JENKINS, Roger	*No playoffs*											Right wing/defense
JENSEN, Al												
1983	Washington	3	1	2	....	139	10	0	4.32	....	....	....
1984	Washington	6	3	1	....	258	14	0	3.26	120	.883	27.9
1985	Washington	3	1	2	....	201	8	0	2.39	86	.907	25.7
Playoff Totals		**12**	**5**	**5**	....	**598**	**32**	**0**	**3.21**	....	....	....

Season	Club	GP	W	L	T	Mins	GA	SO	Avg	SA	S%	SAPG
JENSEN, Darren *No playoffs*												
JOHNSON, Bob *No playoffs*												
JOHNSON, Brent *No playoffs*												
JOHNSTON, Eddie												
1969	Boston	1	0	1	....	65	4	0	3.69	....	....	....
1970◆	Boston	1	0	1	....	60	4	0	4.00	....	....	....
1971	Boston	1	0	1	....	60	7	0	7.00	....	....	....
1972◆	Boston	7	*6	1	....	420	13	1	*1.86	....	....	....
1973	Boston	3	1	2	....	160	9	0	3.38	....	....	....
1974	Toronto	1	0	1	....	60	6	0	6.00	....	....	....
1975	St. Louis	1	0	1	....	60	5	0	5.00	....	....	....
1977	St. Louis	3	0	2	....	138	9	0	3.91	....	....	....
Playoff Totals		**18**	**7**	**10**	....	**1023**	**57**	**1**	**3.34**	....	....	....
JOSEPH, Curtis												
1990	St. Louis	6	4	1	....	327	18	0	3.30	167	.892	30.6
1992	St. Louis	6	2	4	....	379	23	0	3.64	217	.894	34.4
1993	St. Louis	11	7	4	....	715	27	*2	2.27	438	.938	36.8
1994	St. Louis	4	0	4	....	246	15	0	3.66	158	.905	38.5
1995	St. Louis	7	3	3	....	392	24	0	3.67	178	.865	27.2
1997	Edmonton	12	5	7	....	767	36	2	2.82	405	.911	31.7
1998	Edmonton	12	5	7	....	716	23	3	1.93	319	.928	26.7
1999	Toronto	17	9	8	....	1011	41	1	2.43	440	.907	26.1
Playoff Totals		**75**	**35**	**38**	....	**4553**	**207**	**8**	**2.73**	**2322**	**.911**	**30.6**
JUNKIN, Joe *No playoffs*												
KAARELA, Jari *No playoffs*												
KAMPURRI, Hannu *No playoffs*												
KARAKAS, Mike												
1936	Chicago	2	1	1	0	120	7	0	3.50	....	....	....
1938◆	Chicago	*8	*6	2	....	*525	15	*2	1.71	....	....	....
1944	Chicago	*9	4	5	....	*549	24	*1	2.62	....	....	....
1946	Chicago	4	0	4	....	240	26	0	6.50	....	....	....
Playoff Totals		**23**	**11**	**12**	**0**	**1434**	**72**	**3**	**3.01**	....	....	....
KEANS, Doug												
1980	Los Angeles	1	0	1	....	40	7	0	10.50	....	....	....
1982	Los Angeles	2	0	1	....	32	1	0	1.88	....	....	....
1985	Boston	4	2	2	....	240	15	0	3.75	110	.864	27.5
1987	Boston	2	0	2	....	120	11	0	5.50	58	.810	29.0
Playoff Totals		**9**	**2**	**6**	....	**432**	**34**	**0**	**4.72**	....	....	....
KEENAN, Don *No playoffs*												
KERR, Dave												
1931	Mtl. Maroons	2	0	2	0	120	8	0	4.00	....	....	....
1933	Mtl. Maroons	2	0	2	0	120	5	0	2.50	....	....	....
1934	Mtl. Maroons	4	1	2	1	240	7	1	1.75	....	....	....
1935	NY Rangers	4	1	1	2	240	10	0	2.50	....	....	....
1937	NY Rangers	*9	*6	3	....	*553	10	*4	*1.08	....	....	....
1938	NY Rangers	3	1	2	....	262	8	0	1.83	....	....	....
1939	NY Rangers	1	0	1	....	119	2	0	1.01	....	....	....
1940◆	NY Rangers	*12	*8	4	....	*770	20	*3	*1.56	....	....	....
1941	NY Rangers	3	1	2	....	192	6	0	1.88	....	....	....
Playoff Totals		**40**	**18**	**19**	**3**	**2616**	**76**	**8**	**1.74**	....	....	....
KHABIBULIN, Nikolai												
1996	Winnipeg	6	2	4	....	359	19	0	3.18	214	.911	35.8
1997	Phoenix	7	3	4	....	426	15	1	2.11	222	.932	31.3
1998	Phoenix	4	2	1	....	185	13	0	4.22	106	.877	34.4
1999	Phoenix	7	3	4	....	449	18	0	2.41	236	.924	31.5
Playoff Totals		**24**	**10**	**13**	....	**1419**	**65**	**1**	**2.75**	**778**	**.916**	**32.9**
KIDD, Trevor												
1995	Calgary	7	3	4	....	434	26	1	3.59	181	.856	25.0
1996	Calgary	2	0	1	....	83	9	0	6.51	40	.775	28.9
Playoff Totals		**9**	**3**	**5**	....	**517**	**35**	**1**	**4.06**	**221**	**.842**	**25.6**
KING, Scott *No playoffs*												
KLEISINGER, Terry *No playoffs*												
KLYMKIW, Julian *No playoffs*												
KNICKLE, Rick *No playoffs*												
KOLZIG, Olaf												
1995	Washington	2	1	0	....	44	1	0	1.36	21	.952	28.6
1996	Washington	5	2	3	....	341	11	0	*1.94	167	.934	29.4
1998	Washington	21	12	9	....	1351	44	*4	1.95	740	.941	32.9
Playoff Totals		**28**	**15**	**12**	....	**1736**	**56**	**4**	**1.94**	**928**	**.940**	**32.1**
KUNTAR, Les *No playoffs*												
KURT, Gary *No playoffs*												
LABRECQUE, Patrick *No playoffs*												
LACHER, Blaine												
1995	Boston	5	1	4	....	283	12	0	2.54	125	.904	26.5
Playoff Totals		**5**	**1**	**4**	....	**283**	**12**	**0**	**2.54**	**125**	**.904**	**26.5**
LACROIX, Albert *No playoffs*												
LAFERRIERE, Rick *No playoffs*												
LaFOREST, Mark												
1988	Philadelphia	2	1	0	....	48	1	0	1.25	12	.917	15.0
Playoff Totals		**2**	**1**	**0**	....	**48**	**1**	**0**	**1.25**	**12**	**.917**	**15.0**
LALIME, Patrick *No playoffs*												
LAMOTHE, Marc *No playoffs*												
LANGKOW, Scott *No playoffs*												

Season	Club	GP	W	L	T	Mins	GA	SO	Avg	SA	S%	SAPG
LAROCQUE, Michel												
1974	Montreal	6	2	4	....	364	18	0	2.97	....	....	....
1976◆	Montreal	....	....	....	....	....	....	....	....	....	....	....
1977◆	Montreal	....	....	....	....	....	....	....	....	....	....	....
1978◆	Montreal	....	....	....	....	....	....	....	....	....	....	....
1979◆	Montreal	1	0	0	....	20	0	0	0.00	....	....	....
1980	Montreal	5	4	1	....	300	11	1	2.20	....	....	....
1981	Toronto	2	0	1	....	75	8	0	6.40	....	....	....
Playoff Totals		**14**	**6**	**6**	....	**759**	**37**	**1**	**2.92**	....	....	....
LASKOWSKI, Gary *No playoffs*												
LAXTON, Gord *No playoffs*												
LeBLANC, Ray *No playoffs*												
LEDUC, Albert *No playoffs*												Defense
LEGACE, Manny *No playoffs*												
LEGRIS, Claude *No playoffs*												
LEHMAN, Hugh												
1927	Chicago	2	0	1	1	120	10	0	5.00	....	....	....
Playoff Totals		**2**	**0**	**1**	**1**	**120**	**10**	**0**	**5.00**	....	....	....
LEMELIN, Reggie												
1979	Atlanta	1	0	0	....	20	0	0	0.00	....	....	....
1981	Calgary	6	3	3	....	366	22	0	3.61	....	....	....
1983	Calgary	7	3	3	....	327	27	0	4.95	....	....	....
1984	Calgary	8	4	4	....	448	32	0	4.29	290	.890	38.8
1985	Calgary	4	1	3	....	248	15	1	3.63	128	.883	31.0
1986	Calgary	3	0	1	....	109	7	0	3.85	48	.854	26.4
1987	Calgary	2	0	1	....	101	6	0	3.56	47	.872	27.9
1988	Boston	17	11	6	....	1027	45	*1	*2.63	430	.895	25.1
1989	Boston	4	1	3	....	252	16	0	3.81	112	.857	26.7
1990	Boston	3	0	1	....	135	13	0	5.78	57	.772	25.3
1991	Boston	2	0	0	....	32	0	0	0.00	18	.000	33.8
1992	Boston	2	0	0	....	54	3	0	3.33	23	.870	25.6
Playoff Totals		**59**	**23**	**25**	....	**3119**	**186**	**2**	**3.58**	....	....	....
LENARDUZZI, Mike *No playoffs*												
LESSARD, Mario												
1979	Los Angeles	2	0	2	....	126	8	0	3.81	....	....	....
1980	Los Angeles	4	1	2	....	207	14	0	4.06	....	....	....
1981	Los Angeles	4	1	3	....	220	20	0	5.45	....	....	....
1982	Los Angeles	10	4	5	....	583	41	0	4.22	....	....	....
Playoff Totals		**20**	**6**	**12**	....	**1136**	**83**	**0**	**4.38**	....	....	....
LEVASSEUR, Jean-Louis *No playoffs*												
LEVINSKY, Alex *No playoffs*												Defense
LINDBERGH, Pelle												
1983	Philadelphia	3	0	3	....	180	18	0	6.00	....	....	....
1984	Philadelphia	2	0	1	....	26	3	0	6.92	13	.769	30.0
1985	Philadelphia	*18	12	6	....	1008	42	*3	2.50	490	.914	29.2
Playoff Totals		**23**	**12**	**10**	....	**1214**	**63**	**3**	**3.11**	....	....	....
LINDSAY, Bert *No playoffs*												
LITTMAN, David *No playoffs*												
LIUT, Mike												
1980	St. Louis	3	0	3	....	193	12	0	3.73	....	....	....
1981	St. Louis	11	5	6	....	685	50	0	4.38	....	....	....
1982	St. Louis	10	5	3	....	494	27	0	3.28	....	....	....
1983	St. Louis	4	1	3	....	240	15	0	3.75	....	....	....
1984	St. Louis	11	6	5	....	714	29	1	2.44	362	.920	30.4
1986	Hartford	8	5	2	....	441	14	*1	*1.90	226	.938	30.7
1987	Hartford	6	2	4	....	332	25	0	4.52	159	.843	28.7
1988	Hartford	3	1	1	....	160	11	0	4.13	82	.866	30.8
1990	Washington	9	4	4	....	507	28	0	3.31	223	.874	26.4
1991	Washington	2	0	1	....	48	4	0	5.00	30	.867	37.5
Playoff Totals		**67**	**29**	**32**	....	**3814**	**215**	**2**	**3.38**	....	....	....
LOCKETT, Ken												
1975	Vancouver	1	0	1	....	60	6	0	6.00	....	....	....
Playoff Totals		**1**	**0**	**1**	....	**60**	**6**	**0**	**6.00**	....	....	....
LOCKHART, Howard *No playoffs*												
LOPRESTI, Pete												
1977	Minnesota	2	0	2	....	77	6	0	4.68	....	....	....
Playoff Totals		**2**	**0**	**2**	....	**77**	**6**	**0**	**4.68**	....	....	....
LOPRESTI, Sam												
1941	Chicago	5	2	3	....	343	12	0	2.10	....	....	....
1942	Chicago	3	1	2	....	187	5	*1	1.60	....	....	....
Playoff Totals		**8**	**3**	**5**	....	**530**	**17**	**1**	**1.92**	....	....	....
LORENZ, Danny *No playoffs*												
LOUSTEL, Ron *No playoffs*												
LOW, Ron												
1978	Detroit	4	1	3	....	240	17	0	4.25	....	....	....
1980	Edmonton	3	0	3	....	212	12	0	3.40	....	....	....
Playoff Totals		**7**	**1**	**6**	....	**452**	**29**	**0**	**3.85**	....	....	....
LOZINSKI, Larry *No playoffs*												

Season	Club	GP	W	L	T	Mins	GA	SO	Avg	SA	S%	SAPG
LUMLEY, Harry												
1945	Detroit	*14	7	7	....	*871	31	2	*2.14	....	....	....
1946	Detroit	5	1	4	....	309	16	*1	3.11	....	....	....
1948	Detroit	*10	4	6	....	*600	30	0	3.00	....	....	....
1949	Detroit	*11	4	7	....	*726	26	0	2.15	....	....	....
1950♦	Detroit	*14	*8	6	....	910	28	*3	1.85	....	....	....
1954	Toronto	5	1	4	....	321	15	0	2.80	....	....	....
1955	Toronto	4	0	4	....	240	14	0	3.50	....	....	....
1956	Toronto	5	1	4	....	304	14	1	2.76	....	....	....
1958	Boston	1	0	1	....	60	5	0	5.00	....	....	....
1959	Boston	7	3	4	....	436	20	0	2.75	....	....	....
Playoff Totals		**76**	**29**	**47**	....	**4777**	**199**	**7**	**2.50**	....	....	....
LUONGO, Roberto *No playoffs*												
MacKENZIE, Shawn *No playoffs*												
MADELEY, Darrin *No playoffs*												
MALARCHUK, Clint												
1986	Quebec	3	0	2	....	143	11	0	4.62	81	.864	34.0
1987	Quebec	3	0	2	....	140	8	0	3.43	56	.857	24.0
1988	Washington	4	0	2	....	193	15	0	4.66	95	.842	29.5
1989	Buffalo	1	0	1	0	59	5	0	5.08	32	.844	32.5
1991	Buffalo	4	2	2	....	246	17	0	4.15	116	.853	28.3
Playoff Totals		**15**	**2**	**9**	**0**	**781**	**56**	**0**	**4.30**	**380**	**.853**	**29.2**
MANELUK, George *No playoffs*												
MANIAGO, Cesare												
1961	Toronto	2	1	1	....	145	6	0	2.48	....	....	....
1968	Minnesota	14	7	7	....	893	39	0	2.62	....	....	....
1970	Minnesota	3	1	2	....	180	6	*1	2.00	....	....	....
1971	Minnesota	8	3	5	....	480	28	0	3.50	....	....	....
1972	Minnesota	4	1	3	....	238	12	0	3.03	....	....	....
1973	Minnesota	5	2	3	....	309	9	*2	*1.75	....	....	....
Playoff Totals		**36**	**15**	**21**	....	**2245**	**100**	**3**	**2.67**	....	....	....
MARACLE, Norm												
1999	Detroit	2	0	0	....	58	3	0	3.10	22	.864	22.8
Playoff Totals		**2**	**0**	**0**	....	**58**	**3**	**0**	**3.10**	**22**	**.864**	**22.8**
MAROIS, Jean *No playoffs*												
MARTIN, Seth												
1968	St. Louis	2	0	0	....	73	5	0	4.11	....	....	....
Playoff Totals		**2**	**0**	**0**	....	**73**	**5**	**0**	**4.11**	....	....	....
MASON, Bob												
1987	Washington	4	2	2	....	309	9	1	1.75	143	.937	27.8
1988	Chicago	1	0	1	....	60	3	0	3.00	31	.903	31.0
Playoff Totals		**5**	**2**	**3**	....	**369**	**12**	**1**	**1.95**	**174**	**.931**	**28.3**
MASON, Chris *No playoffs*												
MATTSON, Markus *No playoffs*												
MAY, Darrell *No playoffs*												
MAYER, Gilles *No playoffs*												
McAULEY, Ken *No playoffs*												
McCARTAN, Jack *No playoffs*												
McCOOL, Frank												
1945♦	Toronto	13	*8	5	....	807	30	*4	2.23	....	....	....
Playoff Totals		**13**	**8**	**5**	....	**807**	**30**	**4**	**2.23**	....	....	....
McDUFFE, Peter												
1972	St. Louis	1	0	1	....	60	7	0	7.00	....	....	....
Playoff Totals		**1**	**0**	**1**	....	**60**	**7**	**0**	**7.00**	....	....	....
McGRATTAN, Tom *No playoffs*												
McKAY, Ross *No playoffs*												
McKENZIE, Bill *No playoffs*												
McKICHAN, Steve *No playoffs*												
McLACHLAN, Murray *No playoffs*												
McLEAN, Kirk												
1989	Vancouver	5	2	3	....	302	18	0	3.58	167	.892	33.2
1991	Vancouver	2	1	1	....	123	7	0	3.41	66	.894	32.2
1992	Vancouver	13	6	7	....	785	33	*2	2.52	364	.909	27.8
1993	Vancouver	12	6	6	....	754	42	0	3.34	369	.886	29.4
1994	Vancouver	*24	15	9	....	*1544	59	*4	2.29	820	.928	31.9
1995	Vancouver	11	4	7	....	660	36	0	3.27	336	.893	30.5
1996	Vancouver	1	0	1	....	21	3	0	8.57	12	.750	34.3
Playoff Totals		**68**	**34**	**34**	....	**4189**	**198**	**6**	**2.84**	**2134**	**.907**	**30.6**
McLELLAND, Dave *No playoffs*												
McLENNAN, Jamie												
1994	NY Islanders	2	0	1	....	82	6	0	4.39	47	.872	34.4
1998	St. Louis	1	0	0	....	14	1	0	4.29	4	.750	17.1
1999	St. Louis	1	0	1	....	37	0	0	0.00	7	.000	11.4
Playoff Totals		**4**	**0**	**2**	....	**133**	**7**	**0**	**3.16**	**58**	**.879**	**26.2**
McLEOD, Don *No playoffs*												
McLEOD, Jim *No playoffs*												
McNAMARA, Gerry *No playoffs*												
McNEIL, Gerry												
1950	Montreal	2	1	1	....	135	5	0	2.22	....	....	....
1951	Montreal	*11	*5	6	....	*785	25	1	1.91	....	....	....
1952	Montreal	*11	4	7	....	*688	23	1	2.01	....	....	....
1953♦	Montreal	8	*5	3	....	486	16	*2	1.98	....	....	....
1954	Montreal	3	2	1	....	190	3	1	0.95	....	....	....
1957♦	Montreal	....	....	....	....	....	....	....	....	....	....	....
1958♦	Montreal	....	....	....	....	....	....	....	....	....	....	....
Playoff Totals		**35**	**17**	**18**	....	**2284**	**72**	**5**	**1.89**	....	....	....

Season	Club	GP	W	L	T	Mins	GA	SO	Avg	SA	S%	SAPG
McRAE, Gord												
1975	Toronto	7	2	5	....	441	21	0	2.86	....	....	....
1976	Toronto	1	0	0	....	13	1	0	4.62	....	....	....
Playoff Totals		**8**	**2**	**5**	....	**454**	**22**	**0**	**2.91**	....	....	....
MELANSON, Rollie												
1981♦	NY Islanders	3	1	0	....	92	6	0	3.91	....	....	....
1982♦	NY Islanders	3	0	1	....	64	5	0	4.69	....	....	....
1983♦	NY Islanders	5	2	2	....	238	10	0	2.52	....	....	....
1984	NY Islanders	6	0	1	....	87	5	0	3.45	32	.844	22.1
1987	Los Angeles	5	1	4	....	260	24	0	5.54	154	.844	35.5
1988	Los Angeles	1	0	1	....	60	9	0	9.00	50	.820	50.0
Playoff Totals		**23**	**4**	**9**	....	**801**	**59**	**0**	**4.42**	....	....	....
MELOCHE, Gilles												
1980	Minnesota	11	5	4	....	564	34	1	3.62	....	....	....
1981	Minnesota	13	8	5	....	802	47	0	3.52	....	....	....
1982	Minnesota	4	1	2	....	184	8	0	2.61	....	....	....
1983	Minnesota	5	2	3	....	319	18	0	3.39	....	....	....
1984	Minnesota	4	1	2	....	200	11	0	3.30	88	.875	26.4
1985	Minnesota	8	4	3	....	395	25	1	3.80	256	.902	38.9
Playoff Totals		**45**	**21**	**19**	....	**2464**	**143**	**2**	**3.48**	....	....	....
MICALEF, Corrado												
1984	Detroit	1	0	0	....	7	2	0	17.14	5	.600	42.9
1985	Detroit	2	0	0	....	42	6	0	8.57	18	.667	25.7
Playoff Totals		**3**	**0**	**0**	....	**49**	**8**	**0**	**9.80**	**23**	**.652**	**28.2**
MICHAUD, Alfie *No playoffs*												
MIDDLEBROOK, Lindsay *No playoffs*												
MILLAR, Al *No playoffs*												
MILLEN, Greg												
1980	Pittsburgh	5	2	3	....	300	21	0	4.20	....	....	....
1981	Pittsburgh	5	2	3	....	325	19	0	3.51	....	....	....
1985	St. Louis	1	0	1	....	60	2	0	2.00	35	.943	35.0
1986	St. Louis	10	6	3	....	586	29	0	2.97	330	.912	33.8
1987	St. Louis	4	1	3	....	250	10	0	2.40	122	.918	29.3
1988	St. Louis	10	5	5	....	600	38	0	3.80	252	.849	25.2
1989	St. Louis	10	5	5	....	649	34	0	3.14	308	.890	28.5
1990	Chicago	14	6	6	....	613	40	0	3.92	300	.867	29.4
Playoff Totals		**59**	**27**	**29**	....	**3383**	**193**	**0**	**3.42**	....	....	....
MILLER, Joe												
1928♦	NY Rangers	3	2	1	0	180	3	1	1.00	....	....	....
Playoff Totals		**3**	**2**	**1**	**0**	**180**	**3**	**1**	**1.00**	....	....	....
MIO, Eddie												
1982	NY Rangers	8	4	3	....	443	28	0	3.79	....	....	....
1983	NY Rangers	8	5	3	....	480	32	0	4.00	....	....	....
1984	Detroit	1	0	1	....	63	3	0	2.86	24	.875	22.9
Playoff Totals		**17**	**9**	**7**	....	**986**	**63**	**0**	**3.83**	....	....	....
MITCHELL, Ivan *No playoffs*												
MOFFATT, Mike												
1982	Boston	11	6	5	....	663	38	0	3.44	....	....	....
Playoff Totals		**11**	**6**	**5**	....	**663**	**38**	**0**	**3.44**	....	....	....
MOOG, Andy												
1981	Edmonton	9	5	4	....	526	32	0	3.65	....	....	....
1983	Edmonton	16	11	5	....	949	48	0	3.03	....	....	....
1984♦	Edmonton	7	4	0	....	263	12	0	2.74	110	.891	25.1
1985♦	Edmonton	2	0	0	....	20	0	0	0.00	3	.000	9.0
1986	Edmonton	1	1	0	....	60	1	0	1.00	27	.963	27.0
1987♦	Edmonton	2	2	0	....	120	8	0	4.00	37	.784	18.5
1988	Boston	7	1	4	....	354	25	0	4.24	166	.849	28.1
1989	Boston	6	4	2	....	359	14	0	2.34	136	.897	22.7
1990	Boston	20	13	7	....	1195	44	*2	*2.21	486	.909	24.4
1991	Boston	19	10	9	....	1133	60	0	3.18	569	.895	30.1
1992	Boston	15	8	7	....	866	46	1	3.19	385	.881	26.7
1993	Boston	3	0	3	....	161	14	0	5.22	67	.791	25.0
1994	Dallas	4	1	3	....	246	12	0	2.93	121	.901	29.5
1995	Dallas	5	1	4	....	277	16	0	3.47	169	.905	36.6
1997	Dallas	7	3	4	....	449	21	0	2.81	214	.902	28.6
1998	Montreal	9	4	5	....	474	24	1	3.04	204	.882	25.8
Playoff Totals		**132**	**68**	**57**	....	**7452**	**377**	**4**	**3.04**	....	....	....
MOORE, Alfie												
1938♦	Chicago	1	1	0	....	60	1	0	1.00	....	....	....
1939	NY Americans	2	0	2	....	120	6	0	3.00	....	....	....
Playoff Totals		**3**	**1**	**2**	....	**180**	**7**	**0**	**2.33**	....	....	....
MOORE, Robbie												
1979	Philadelphia	5	3	2	....	268	18	0	4.03	....	....	....
Playoff Totals		**5**	**3**	**2**	....	**268**	**18**	**0**	**4.03**	....	....	....
MORISETTE, Jean-Guy *No playoffs*												
MOSS, Tyler *No playoffs*												
MOWERS, Johnny												
1941	Detroit	9	4	5	....	561	20	0	2.14	....	....	....
1942	Detroit	12	7	5	....	720	38	0	3.17	....	....	....
1943♦	Detroit	*10	*8	2	....	*679	22	*2	*1.94	....	....	....
1947	Detroit	1	0	1	....	40	5	0	7.50	....	....	....
Playoff Totals		**32**	**19**	**13**	....	**2000**	**85**	**2**	**2.55**	....	....	....
MRAZEK, Jerome *No playoffs*												
MUMMERY, Harry *No playoffs*												Defense
MUNRO, Dunc *No playoffs*												Defense
MURPHY, Hal *No playoffs*												
MURRAY, Mickey *No playoffs*												
MUZZATTI, Jason *No playoffs*												

Season	Club	GP	W	L	T	Mins	GA	SO	Avg	SA	S%	SAPG
MYLLYS, Jarmo *No playoffs*												
MYLNIKOV, Sergei *No playoffs*												
MYRE, Phil												
1971◆	Montreal	....	....	....	....	....	....	....	....	....	....	....
1974	Atlanta	3	0	3	....	186	13	0	4.19	....	....	....
1977	Atlanta	2	1	1	....	120	5	0	2.50	....	....	....
1980	Philadelphia	6	5	1	....	384	16	1	2.50	....	....	....
1983	Buffalo	1	0	0	....	57	7	0	7.37	....	....	....
Playoff Totals		**12**	**6**	**5**	....	**747**	**41**	**1**	**3.29**	....	....	....
NABOKOV, John *No playoffs*												
NEWTON, Cam *No playoffs*												
NORRIS, Jack *No playoffs*												
OLESCHUK, Bill *No playoffs*												
OLESEVICH, Dan *No playoffs*												
O'NEILL, Mike *No playoffs*												
OSGOOD, Chris												
1994	Detroit	6	3	2	....	307	12	1	2.35	110	.891	21.5
1995	Detroit	2	0	0	....	68	2	0	1.76	25	.920	22.1
1996	Detroit	15	8	7	....	936	33	2	2.12	322	.898	20.6
1997◆	Detroit	2	0	0	....	47	2	0	2.55	21	.905	26.8
1998◆	Detroit	*22	*16	6	....	*1361	48	2	2.12	588	.918	25.9
1999	Detroit	6	4	2	....	358	14	1	2.35	172	.919	28.8
Playoff Totals		**53**	**31**	**17**	....	**3077**	**111**	**6**	**2.16**	**1238**	**.910**	**24.1**
OUIMET, Ted *No playoffs*												
PAGEAU, Paul *No playoffs*												
PAILLE, Marcel *No playoffs*												
PALMATEER, Mike												
1977	Toronto	6	3	3	....	360	16	0	2.67	....	....	....
1978	Toronto	13	6	7	....	795	32	*2	2.42	....	....	....
1979	Toronto	5	2	3	....	298	17	0	3.42	....	....	....
1980	Toronto	1	0	1	....	60	7	0	7.00	....	....	....
1983	Toronto	4	1	3	....	252	17	0	4.05	....	....	....
Playoff Totals		**29**	**12**	**17**	....	**1765**	**89**	**2**	**3.03**	....	....	....
PANG, Darren												
1988	Chicago	4	1	3	....	240	18	0	4.50	130	.862	32.5
1989	Chicago	2	0	0	....	10	0	0	0.00	4	.000	24.0
Playoff Totals		**6**	**1**	**3**	....	**250**	**18**	**0**	**4.32**	**134**	**.866**	**32.2**
PARENT, Bernie												
1968	Philadelphia	5	2	3	....	355	8	0	*1.35	....	....	....
1969	Philadelphia	3	0	3	....	180	12	0	4.00	....	....	....
1971	Toronto	4	2	2	....	235	9	0	2.30	....	....	....
1972	Toronto	4	1	3	....	243	13	0	3.21	....	....	....
1974◆	Philadelphia	*17	*12	5	....	*1042	35	*2	2.02	....	....	....
1975◆	Philadelphia	*15	*10	5	....	*922	29	*4	*1.89	....	....	....
1976	Philadelphia	8	4	4	....	480	27	0	3.38	....	....	....
1977	Philadelphia	3	0	3	....	123	8	0	3.90	....	....	....
1978	Philadelphia	12	7	5	....	722	33	0	2.74	....	....	....
Playoff Totals		**71**	**38**	**33**	....	**4302**	**174**	**6**	**2.43**	....	....	....
PARENT, Bob *No playoffs*												
PARENT, Rich *No playoffs*												
PARRO, Dave *No playoffs*												
PASSMORE, Steve *No playoffs*												
PATRICK, Lester Manager/Coach												
1928◆	NY Rangers	1	1	0	0	46	1	0	1.30	....	....	....
Playoff Totals		**1**	**1**	**0**	**0**	**46**	**1**	**0**	**1.30**	....	....	....
PEETERS, Pete												
1980	Philadelphia	13	8	5	....	799	37	1	2.78	....	....	....
1981	Philadelphia	3	2	1	....	180	12	0	4.00	....	....	....
1982	Philadelphia	4	1	2	....	220	17	0	4.64	....	....	....
1983	Boston	*17	9	8	....	*1024	61	1	3.57	....	....	....
1984	Boston	3	0	3	....	180	10	0	3.33	68	.853	22.7
1985	Boston	1	0	1	....	60	4	0	4.00	26	.846	26.0
1986	Washington	9	5	4	....	544	24	0	2.65	253	.905	27.9
1987	Washington	3	1	2	....	180	9	0	3.00	76	.882	25.3
1988	Washington	12	7	5	....	654	34	0	3.12	326	.896	29.9
1989	Washington	6	2	4	....	359	24	0	4.01	164	.854	27.4
Playoff Totals		**71**	**35**	**35**	....	**4200**	**232**	**2**	**3.31**	....	....	....
PELLETIER, Jean-Marc *No playoffs*												
PELLETIER, Marcel *No playoffs*												
PENNEY, Steve												
1984	Montreal	15	9	6	....	871	32	*3	*2.20	354	.910	24.4
1985	Montreal	12	6	6	....	733	40	1	3.27	300	.867	24.6
Playoff Totals		**27**	**15**	**12**	....	**1604**	**72**	**4**	**2.69**	**654**	**.890**	**24.5**
PERREAULT, Bob *No playoffs*												
PETTIE, Jim *No playoffs*												
PIETRANGELO, Frank												
1991◆	Pittsburgh	5	4	1	....	288	15	*1	3.13	148	.899	30.8
1992	Hartford	7	3	4	....	425	19	0	2.68	244	.922	34.4
Playoff Totals		**12**	**7**	**5**	....	**713**	**34**	**1**	**2.86**	**392**	**.913**	**33.0**

Season	Club	GP	W	L	T	Mins	GA	SO	Avg	SA	S%	SAPG
PLANTE, Jacques												
1953◆	Montreal	4	3	1	....	240	7	1	*1.75	....	....	....
1954	Montreal	8	5	3	....	480	15	*2	1.88	....	....	....
1955	Montreal	*12	6	4	....	640	30	0	2.81	....	....	....
1956◆	Montreal	*10	*8	2	....	600	18	*2	*1.80	....	....	....
1957◆	Montreal	*10	*8	2	....	*616	18	1	*1.75	....	....	....
1958◆	Montreal	10	*8	2	....	618	20	*1	*1.94	....	....	....
1959◆	Montreal	11	*8	3	....	670	28	0	*2.51	....	....	....
1960◆	Montreal	8	*8	0	....	489	11	*3	*1.35	....	....	....
1961	Montreal	6	2	4	....	412	16	0	2.33	....	....	....
1962	Montreal	6	2	4	....	360	19	0	3.17	....	....	....
1963	Montreal	5	1	4	....	300	14	0	2.80	....	....	....
1969	St. Louis	*10	*8	2	....	*589	14	*3	1.43	....	....	....
1970	St. Louis	6	4	1	....	324	8	*1	*1.48	....	....	....
1971	Toronto	3	0	2	....	134	7	0	3.13	....	....	....
1972	Toronto	1	0	1	....	60	5	0	5.00	....	....	....
1973	Boston	2	0	2	....	120	10	0	5.00	....	....	....
Playoff Totals		**112**	**71**	**37**	....	**6652**	**240**	**14**	**2.16**	....	....	....
PLASSE, Michel												
1973◆	Montreal	....	....	....	....	....	....	....	....	....	....	....
1976	Pittsburgh	3	1	2	....	180	8	1	2.67	....	....	....
1981	Quebec	1	0	0	....	15	1	0	4.00	....	....	....
Playoff Totals		**4**	**1**	**2**	....	**195**	**9**	**1**	**2.77**	....	....	....
PLAXTON, Hugh *No playoffs* Left wing												
POTVIN, Felix												
1993	Toronto	*21	11	10	....	*1308	62	1	2.84	636	.903	29.2
1994	Toronto	18	9	9	....	1124	46	3	2.46	520	.912	27.8
1995	Toronto	7	3	4	....	424	20	1	2.83	253	.921	35.8
1996	Toronto	6	2	4	....	350	19	0	3.26	198	.904	33.9
Playoff Totals		**52**	**25**	**27**	....	**3206**	**147**	**5**	**2.75**	**1607**	**.909**	**30.1**
PRONOVOST, Claude *No playoffs*												
PUPPA, Daren												
1988	Buffalo	3	1	1	....	142	11	0	4.65	67	.836	28.3
1990	Buffalo	6	2	4	....	370	15	0	2.43	192	.922	31.1
1991	Buffalo	2	0	1	....	81	10	0	7.41	46	.783	34.1
1993	Toronto	1	0	0	....	20	1	0	3.00	7	.857	21.0
1996	Tampa Bay	4	1	3	....	173	14	0	4.86	86	.837	29.8
Playoff Totals		**16**	**4**	**9**	....	**786**	**51**	**0**	**3.89**	**398**	**.872**	**30.4**
PUSEY, Chris *No playoffs*												
RACICOT, Andre												
1991	Montreal	2	0	1	....	12	2	0	10.00	14	.857	70.0
1992	Montreal	1	0	0	....	1	0	0	0.00	1	.000	60.0
1993◆	Montreal	1	0	0	....	18	2	0	6.67	9	.778	30.0
Playoff Totals		**4**	**0**	**1**	....	**31**	**4**	**0**	**7.74**	**24**	**.833**	**46.5**
RACINE, Bruce												
1996	St. Louis	1	0	0	....	1	0	0	0.00	0	.000	0.0
Playoff Totals		**1**	**0**	**0**	....	**1**	**0**	**0**	**0.00**	**0**	**.000**	**0.0**
RAM, Jamie *No playoffs*												
RANFORD, Bill												
1986	Boston	2	0	2	....	120	7	0	3.50	44	.841	22.0
1987	Boston	2	0	2	....	123	8	0	3.90	55	.855	26.8
1988◆	Edmonton	....	....	....	....	....	....	....	....	....	....	....
1990◆	Edmonton	*22	*16	6	....	*1401	59	1	2.53	672	.912	28.8
1991	Edmonton	3	1	2	....	135	8	0	3.56	78	.897	34.7
1992	Edmonton	16	8	8	....	909	51	*2	3.37	484	.895	31.9
1996	Boston	4	1	3	....	239	16	0	4.02	112	.857	28.1
1999	Detroit	4	2	2	....	183	10	1	3.28	105	.905	34.4
Playoff Totals		**53**	**28**	**25**	....	**3110**	**159**	**4**	**3.07**	....	....	....
RAYMOND, Alain *No playoffs*												
RAYNER, Chuck												
1948	NY Rangers	6	2	4	....	360	17	0	2.83	....	....	....
1950	NY Rangers	12	7	5	....	775	29	1	2.25	....	....	....
Playoff Totals		**18**	**9**	**9**	....	**1135**	**46**	**1**	**2.43**	....	....	....
REAUGH, Daryl *No playoffs*												
REDDICK, Pokey												
1987	Winnipeg	3	0	2	....	166	10	0	3.61	74	.865	26.7
1990◆	Edmonton	1	0	0	....	2	0	0	0.00	1	.000	30.0
Playoff Totals		**4**	**0**	**2**	....	**168**	**10**	**0**	**3.57**	**75**	**.867**	**26.8**
REDDING, George *No playoffs*												
REDQUEST, Greg *No playoffs*												
REECE, Dave *No playoffs*												
REESE, Jeff												
1990	Toronto	2	1	1	....	108	6	0	3.33	50	.880	27.8
1993	Calgary	4	1	3	....	209	17	0	4.88	91	.813	26.1
1996	Tampa Bay	5	1	1	....	198	12	0	3.64	100	.880	30.3
Playoff Totals		**11**	**3**	**5**	....	**515**	**35**	**0**	**4.08**	**241**	**.855**	**28.1**
RESCH, Glenn												
1975	NY Islanders	12	8	4	....	692	25	1	2.17	....	....	....
1976	NY Islanders	7	3	3	....	357	18	0	3.03	....	....	....
1977	NY Islanders	3	1	1	....	144	5	0	2.08	....	....	....
1978	NY Islanders	7	3	4	....	388	15	0	2.32	....	....	....
1979	NY Islanders	5	2	3	....	300	11	*1	2.20	....	....	....
1980◆	NY Islanders	4	0	2	....	120	9	0	4.50	....	....	....
1986	Philadelphia	1	0	0	....	7	1	0	8.57	1	.000	8.6
1987	Philadelphia	2	0	0	....	36	1	0	1.67	12	.917	20.0
Playoff Totals		**41**	**17**	**17**	....	**2044**	**85**	**2**	**2.50**	....	....	....
RHEAUME, Herb *No playoffs*												

Season	Club	GP	W	L	T	Mins	GA	SO	Avg	SA	S%	SAPG
RHODES, Damian												
1994	Toronto	1	0	0	....	1	0	0	0.00	0	.000	0.0
1998	Ottawa	10	5	5	....	590	21	0	2.14	236	.911	24.0
1999	Ottawa	2	0	2	....	150	6	0	2.40	65	.908	26.0
Playoff Totals		**13**	**5**	**7**	....	**741**	**27**	**0**	**2.19**	**301**	**.910**	**24.4**
RICCI, Nick *No playoffs*												
RICHARDSON, Terry *No playoffs*												
RICHTER, Mike												
1989	NY Rangers	1	0	1	....	58	4	0	4.14	30	.867	31.0
1990	NY Rangers	6	3	2	....	330	19	0	3.45	182	.896	33.1
1991	NY Rangers	6	2	4	....	313	14	*1	2.68	182	.923	34.9
1992	NY Rangers	7	4	2	....	412	24	1	3.50	226	.894	32.9
1994♦	NY Rangers	23	*16	7	....	1417	49	*4	2.07	623	.921	26.4
1995	NY Rangers	7	2	5	....	384	23	0	3.59	189	.878	29.5
1996	NY Rangers	11	5	6	....	661	36	0	3.27	308	.883	28.0
1997	NY Rangers	15	9	6	....	939	33	*3	2.11	488	.932	31.2
Playoff Totals		**76**	**41**	**33**	....	**4514**	**202**	**9**	**2.68**	**2228**	**.909**	**29.6**
RIDLEY, Curt												
1976	Vancouver	2	0	2	....	120	8	0	4.00	....	....	....
Playoff Totals		**2**	**0**	**2**	....	**120**	**8**	**0**	**4.00**	....	....	....
RIENDEAU, Vincent												
1990	St. Louis	8	3	4	....	397	24	0	3.63	223	.892	33.7
1991	St. Louis	13	6	7	....	687	35	*1	3.06	294	.881	25.7
1992	Detroit	2	1	0	....	73	4	0	3.29	30	.867	24.7
1994	Boston	2	1	1	....	120	8	0	4.00	42	.810	21.0
Playoff Totals		**25**	**11**	**12**	....	**1277**	**71**	**1**	**3.34**	**589**	**.879**	**27.7**
RIGGIN, Dennis *No playoffs*												
RIGGIN, Pat												
1981	Calgary	11	6	4	....	629	37	0	3.53	....	....	....
1982	Calgary	3	0	3	....	194	10	0	3.09	....	....	....
1983	Washington	3	0	1	....	101	8	0	4.75	....	....	....
1984	Washington	5	1	3	....	230	9	0	2.35	81	.889	21.1
1985	Washington	2	1	1	....	122	5	0	2.46	39	.872	19.2
1986	Boston	1	0	1	....	60	3	0	3.00	23	.870	23.0
Playoff Totals		**25**	**8**	**13**	....	**1336**	**72**	**0**	**3.23**	....	....	....
RING, Bob *No playoffs*												
RIVARD, Fern *No playoffs*												
ROACH, John Ross												
1922♦	Toronto	*7	*4	2	1	*425	13	*2	*1.84	....	....	....
1925	Toronto	2	0	2	0	120	5	0	*2.50	....	....	....
1929	NY Rangers	*6	3	2	1	*392	5	*3	0.77	....	....	....
1930	NY Rangers	4	1	2	1	309	7	0	1.36	....	....	....
1931	NY Rangers	4	2	2	0	240	4	1	*1.00	....	....	....
1932	NY Rangers	*7	3	4	0	*480	27	*1	3.38	....	....	....
1933	Detroit	4	2	2	0	240	8	1	2.00	....	....	....
Playoff Totals		**34**	**15**	**16**	**3**	**2206**	**69**	**8**	**1.88**	....	....	....
ROBERTS, Moe *No playoffs*												
ROBERTSON, Earl												
1937♦	Detroit	6	3	2	....	340	8	2	1.41	....	....	....
1938	NY Americans	6	3	3	....	475	12	0	*1.52	....	....	....
1940	NY Americans	3	1	2	....	180	9	0	3.00	....	....	....
Playoff Totals		**15**	**7**	**7**	....	**995**	**29**	**2**	**1.75**	....	....	....
ROLLINS, Al												
1951♦	Toronto	4	3	1	....	210	6	0	1.71	....	....	....
1952	Toronto	2	0	2	....	120	6	0	3.00	....	....	....
1953	Chicago	7	3	4	....	425	18	0	2.54	....	....	....
Playoff Totals		**13**	**6**	**7**	....	**755**	**30**	**0**	**2.38**	....	....	....
ROLOSON, Dwayne												
1999	Buffalo	4	1	1	....	139	10	0	4.32	67	.851	28.9
Playoff Totals		**4**	**1**	**1**	....	**139**	**10**	**0**	**4.32**	**67**	**.851**	**28.9**
ROMANO, Roberto *No playoffs*												
ROSATI, Mike *No playoffs*												
ROUSSEL, Dominic												
1995	Philadelphia	1	0	0	....	23	0	0	0.00	8	.000	20.9
Playoff Totals		**1**	**0**	**0**	....	**23**	**0**	**0**	**0.00**	**8**	**.000**	**20.9**
ROY, Patrick												
1986♦	Montreal	20	*15	5	....	1218	39	*1	1.92	506	.923	24.9
1987	Montreal	6	4	2	....	330	22	0	4.00	173	.873	31.5
1988	Montreal	8	3	4	....	430	24	0	3.35	218	.890	30.4
1989	Montreal	19	13	6	....	1206	42	2	*2.09	528	.920	26.3
1990	Montreal	11	5	6	....	641	26	1	2.43	292	.911	27.3
1991	Montreal	13	7	5	....	785	40	0	3.06	394	.898	30.1
1992	Montreal	11	4	7	....	686	30	1	2.62	312	.904	27.3
1993♦	Montreal	20	*16	4	....	1293	46	0	*2.13	647	.929	30.0
1994	Montreal	6	3	3	....	375	16	0	2.56	228	.930	36.5
1996♦	Colorado	*22	*16	6	....	*1454	51	*3	2.10	649	.921	26.8
1997	Colorado	17	10	7	....	1034	38	*3	2.21	559	.932	32.4
1998	Colorado	7	3	4	....	430	18	0	2.51	191	.906	26.7
1999	Colorado	19	11	8	....	1173	52	1	2.66	650	.920	33.2
Playoff Totals		***179**	***110**	**67**	....	***11055**	**444**	**12**	**2.41**	**5347**	**.917**	**29.0**
RUPP, Pat *No playoffs*												
RUTHERFORD, Jim												
1972	Pittsburgh	4	0	4	....	240	14	0	3.50	....	....	....
1978	Detroit	3	2	1	....	180	12	0	4.00	....	....	....
1981	Los Angeles	1	0	0	....	20	2	0	6.00	....	....	....
Playoff Totals		**8**	**2**	**5**	....	**440**	**28**	**0**	**3.82**	....	....	....

Season	Club	GP	W	L	T	Mins	GA	SO	Avg	SA	S%	SAPG
RUTLEDGE, Wayne												
1968	Los Angeles	3	1	1	....	149	8	0	3.22	....	....	....
1969	Los Angeles	5	1	3	....	229	12	0	3.14	....	....	....
Playoff Totals		**8**	**2**	**4**	....	**378**	**20**	**0**	**3.17**	....	....	....
ST. CROIX, Rick												
1981	Philadelphia	9	4	5	....	541	27	*1	2.99	....	....	....
1982	Philadelphia	1	0	1	....	20	1	0	3.00	....	....	....
1983	Toronto	1	0	0	....	1	1	0	60.00	....	....	....
Playoff Totals		**11**	**4**	**6**	....	**562**	**29**	**1**	**3.10**	....	....	....
ST. LAURENT, Sam												
1988	Detroit	1	0	0	....	10	1	0	6.00	7	.857	42.0
Playoff Totals		**1**	**0**	**0**	....	**10**	**1**	**0**	**6.00**	**7**	**.857**	**42.0**
SALO, Tommy												
1999	Edmonton	4	0	4	....	296	11	0	2.23	149	.926	30.2
Playoff Totals		**4**	**0**	**4**	....	**296**	**11**	**0**	**2.23**	**149**	**.926**	**30.2**
SANDS, Charlie *No playoffs* Center/right wing												
SANDS, Mike *No playoffs*												
SARJEANT, Geoff *No playoffs*												
SAUVE, Bob												
1979	Buffalo	3	1	2	....	181	9	0	2.98	....	....	....
1980	Buffalo	8	6	2	....	501	17	*2	*2.04	....	....	....
1983	Buffalo	10	6	4	....	545	28	*2	3.08	....	....	....
1984	Buffalo	2	0	1	....	41	5	0	7.32	14	.643	20.5
1986	Chicago	2	0	2	....	99	8	0	4.85	61	.869	37.0
1987	Chicago	4	0	4	....	245	15	0	3.67	136	.890	33.3
1988	New Jersey	5	2	1	....	238	13	0	3.28	118	.890	29.7
Playoff Totals		**34**	**15**	**16**	....	**1850**	**95**	**4**	**3.08**	....	....	....
SAWCHUK, Terry												
1951	Detroit	6	2	4	....	463	13	1	1.68	....	....	....
1952♦	Detroit	*8	*8	0	....	480	5	*4	*0.63	....	....	....
1953	Detroit	6	2	4	....	372	21	1	3.39	....	....	....
1954♦	Detroit	*12	*8	4	....	*751	20	*2	*1.60	....	....	....
1955♦	Detroit	11	*8	3	....	*660	26	*1	*2.36	....	....	....
1958	Detroit	4	0	4	....	252	19	0	4.52	....	....	....
1960	Detroit	6	2	4	....	405	20	0	2.96	....	....	....
1961	Detroit	8	5	3	....	465	18	1	2.32	....	....	....
1963	Detroit	*11	5	6	....	*660	36	0	3.27	....	....	....
1964	Detroit	13	6	5	....	677	31	1	2.75	....	....	....
1965	Toronto	1	0	1	....	60	3	0	3.00	....	....	....
1966	Toronto	2	0	2	....	120	6	0	3.00	....	....	....
1967♦	Toronto	*10	*6	4	....	*565	25	0	2.65	....	....	....
1968	Los Angeles	5	2	3	....	280	18	*1	3.86	....	....	....
1970	NY Rangers	3	0	1	....	80	6	0	4.50	....	....	....
Playoff Totals		**106**	**54**	**48**	....	**6290**	**267**	**12**	**2.55**	....	....	....
SCHAEFER, Joe *No playoffs*												
SCHAFER, Paxton *No playoffs*												
SCHWAB, Corey *No playoffs*												
SCOTT, Ron												
1990	Los Angeles	1	0	0	....	32	4	0	7.50	10	.600	18.8
Playoff Totals		**1**	**0**	**0**	....	**32**	**4**	**0**	**7.50**	**10**	**.600**	**18.8**
SEVIGNY, Richard												
1981	Montreal	3	0	3	....	180	13	0	4.33	....	....	....
1983	Montreal	1	0	0	....	28	0	0	0.00	....	....	....
Playoff Totals		**4**	**0**	**3**	....	**208**	**13**	**0**	**3.75**	....	....	....
SHARPLES, Scott *No playoffs*												
SHIELDS, Al *No playoffs* Defense												
SHIELDS, Steve												
1997	Buffalo	10	4	6	....	570	26	1	2.74	334	.922	35.2
1999	San Jose	1	0	1	....	60	6	0	6.00	36	.833	36.0
Playoff Totals		**11**	**4**	**7**	....	**630**	**32**	**1**	**3.05**	**370**	**.914**	**35.2**
SHTALENKOV, Mikhail												
1997	Anaheim	4	0	3	....	211	10	0	2.84	162	.938	46.1
Playoff Totals		**4**	**0**	**3**	....	**211**	**10**	**0**	**2.84**	**162**	**.938**	**46.1**
SHULMISTRA, Richard *No playoffs*												
SIDORKIEWICZ, Peter												
1989	Hartford	2	0	2	....	124	8	0	3.87	45	.822	21.8
1990	Hartford	7	3	4	....	429	23	0	3.22	193	.881	27.0
1991	Hartford	6	2	4	....	359	24	0	4.01	174	.862	29.1
Playoff Totals		**15**	**5**	**10**	....	**912**	**55**	**0**	**3.62**	**412**	**.867**	**27.1**
SIMMONS, Don												
1957	Boston	*10	5	5	....	600	29	*2	2.90	....	....	....
1958	Boston	*11	6	5	....	*671	27	*1	2.41	....	....	....
1962♦	Toronto	3	2	1	....	165	8	0	2.91	....	....	....
1963♦	Toronto	....	....	....	....	....	....	....	....	....	....	....
1964♦	Toronto	....	....	....	....	....	....	....	....	....	....	....
Playoff Totals		**24**	**13**	**11**	....	**1436**	**64**	**3**	**2.67**	....	....	....
SIMMONS, Gary												
1977	Los Angeles	1	0	0	....	20	1	0	3.00	....	....	....
Playoff Totals		**1**	**0**	**0**	....	**20**	**1**	**0**	**3.00**	....	....	....
SKIDMORE, Paul *No playoffs*												
SKORODENSKI, Warren												
1985	Chicago	2	0	0	....	33	6	0	10.91	28	.786	50.9
Playoff Totals		**2**	**0**	**0**	....	**33**	**6**	**0**	**10.91**	**28**	**.786**	**50.9**
SKUDRA, Peter *No playoffs*												

Season	Club	GP	W	L	T	Mins	GA	SO	Avg	SA	S%	SAPG
SMITH, Al												
1970	Pittsburgh	3	1	2	....	180	10	0	3.33	....	....	....
1976	Buffalo	1	0	0	....	17	1	0	3.53	....	....	....
1980	Hartford	2	0	2	....	120	10	0	5.00	....	....	....
Playoff Totals		**6**	**1**	**4**	....	**317**	**21**	**0**	**3.97**	....	....	....
SMITH, Billy												
1975	NY Islanders	6	1	4	....	333	23	0	4.14	....	....	....
1976	NY Islanders	8	4	3	....	437	21	0	2.88	....	....	....
1977	NY Islanders	10	7	3	....	580	27	0	2.79	....	....	....
1978	NY Islanders	1	0	0	....	47	1	0	1.28	....	....	....
1979	NY Islanders	5	4	1	....	315	10	*1	*1.90	....	....	....
1980◆	NY Islanders	*20	*15	4	....	*1198	56	1	2.80	....	....	....
1981◆	NY Islanders	*17	*14	3	....	*994	42	0	*2.54	....	....	....
1982◆	NY Islanders	*18	*15	3	....	*1120	47	*1	2.52	....	....	....
1983◆	NY Islanders	*17	*13	3	....	962	43	*2	*2.68	....	....	....
1984	NY Islanders	*21	*12	8	....	*1190	54	0	2.72	567	.905	28.6
1985	NY Islanders	6	3	3	....	342	19	0	3.33	182	.896	31.9
1986	NY Islanders	1	0	1	....	60	4	0	4.00	34	.882	34.0
1987	NY Islanders	2	0	0	....	67	1	0	0.90	22	.955	19.7
Playoff Totals		**132**	**88**	**36**	....	**7645**	**348**	**5**	**2.73**	....	....	....
SMITH, Gary												
1969	Oakland	7	3	4	....	420	23	0	3.29	....	....	....
1970	Oakland	4	0	4	....	248	13	0	3.15	....	....	....
1972	Chicago	2	1	1	....	120	3	1	1.50	....	....	....
1973	Chicago	2	0	1	....	65	5	0	4.62	....	....	....
1975	Vancouver	4	1	3	....	257	14	0	3.27	....	....	....
1977	Minnesota	1	0	0	....	43	4	0	5.58	....	....	....
Playoff Totals		**20**	**5**	**13**	....	**1153**	**62**	**1**	**3.23**	....	....	....
SMITH, Norman												
1936◆	Detroit	7	*6	1	0	538	12	*2	1.34	....	....	....
1937◆	Detroit	5	3	1	....	282	6	1	1.28	....	....	....
Playoff Totals		**12**	**9**	**2**	**0**	**820**	**18**	**3**	**1.32**	....	....	....
SNEDDON, Bob *No playoffs*												
SNOW, Garth												
1995	Quebec	1	0	0	....	9	1	0	6.67	3	.667	20.0
1996	Philadelphia	1	0	0	....	1	0	0	0.00	0	.000	0.0
1997	Philadelphia	12	8	4	....	699	33	0	2.83	305	.892	26.2
Playoff Totals		**14**	**8**	**4**	....	**709**	**34**	**0**	**2.88**	**308**	**.890**	**26.1**
SODERSTROM, Tommy *No playoffs*												
SOETAERT, Doug												
1982	Winnipeg	2	1	1	....	120	8	0	4.00	....	....	....
1983	Winnipeg	1	0	0	....	20	0	0	0.00	....	....	....
1984	Winnipeg	1	0	1	....	20	5	0	15.00	19	.737	57.0
1985	Montreal	1	0	0	....	20	1	0	3.00	9	.889	27.0
1986◆	Montreal	....	....	....	....	....	....	....	....	....	....	....
Playoff Totals		**5**	**1**	**2**	....	**180**	**14**	**0**	**4.67**	....	....	....
SOUCY, Christian *No playoffs*												
SPOONER, Red *No playoffs*												
SPRING, Jesse *No playoffs*												Defense
STANIOWSKI, Ed												
1976	St. Louis	3	1	2	....	206	7	0	2.04	....	....	....
1977	St. Louis	3	0	2	....	102	9	0	5.29	....	....	....
1982	Winnipeg	2	0	2	....	120	12	0	6.00	....	....	....
Playoff Totals		**8**	**1**	**6**	....	**428**	**28**	**0**	**3.93**	....	....	....
STARR, Harold *No playoffs*												Defense
STAUBER, Robb												
1993	Los Angeles	4	3	1	....	240	16	0	4.00	157	.898	39.3
Playoff Totals		**4**	**3**	**1**	....	**240**	**16**	**0**	**4.00**	**157**	**.898**	**39.3**
STEFAN, Greg												
1984	Detroit	3	1	2	....	210	8	0	2.29	86	.907	24.6
1985	Detroit	3	0	3	....	138	17	0	7.39	69	.754	30.0
1987	Detroit	9	4	5	....	508	24	0	2.83	252	.905	29.8
1988	Detroit	10	5	4	....	531	32	*1	3.62	236	.864	26.7
1989	Detroit	5	2	3	....	294	18	0	3.67	151	.881	30.8
Playoff Totals		**30**	**12**	**17**	....	**1681**	**99**	**1**	**3.53**	**794**	**.875**	**28.3**
STEIN, Phil *No playoffs*												
STEPHENSON, Wayne												
1973	St. Louis	3	1	2	....	160	14	0	5.25	....	....	....
1975◆	Philadelphia	2	2	0	....	123	4	1	1.95	....	....	....
1976	Philadelphia	8	4	4	....	494	22	0	2.67	....	....	....
1977	Philadelphia	9	4	3	....	532	23	1	2.59	....	....	....
1979	Philadelphia	4	0	3	....	213	16	0	4.51	....	....	....
Playoff Totals		**26**	**11**	**12**	....	**1522**	**79**	**2**	**3.11**	....	....	....
STEVENSON, Doug *No playoffs*												
STEWART, Charles *No playoffs*												
STEWART, Jim *No playoffs*												
STORR, Jamie												
1998	Los Angeles	3	0	2	....	145	9	0	3.72	77	.883	31.9
Playoff Totals		**3**	**0**	**2**	....	**145**	**9**	**0**	**3.72**	**77**	**.883**	**31.9**
STUART, Herb *No playoffs*												
SYLVESTRI, Don *No playoffs*												
TABARACCI, Rick												
1992	Winnipeg	7	3	4	....	387	26	0	4.03	212	.877	32.9
1993	Washington	4	1	3	....	304	14	0	2.76	160	.913	31.6
1994	Washington	2	0	2	....	111	6	0	3.24	50	.880	27.0
1995	Calgary	1	0	0	....	19	0	0	0.00	9	.000	28.4
1996	Calgary	3	0	3	....	204	7	0	2.06	84	.917	24.7
Playoff Totals		**17**	**4**	**12**	....	**1025**	**53**	**0**	**3.10**	**515**	**.897**	**30.1**
TAKKO, Kari												
1989	Minnesota	3	0	1	....	105	7	0	4.00	55	.873	31.4
1990	Minnesota	1	0	0	....	4	0	0	0.00	0	.000	0.0
Playoff Totals		**4**	**0**	**1**	....	**109**	**7**	**0**	**3.85**	**55**	**.873**	**30.3**
TALLAS, Robbie *No playoffs*												
TANNER, John *No playoffs*												
TATARYN, Dave *No playoffs*												
TAYLOR, Bobby												
1974◆	Philadelphia	....	....	....	....	....	....	....	....	....	....	....
Playoff Totals		....	....	....	....	....	....	....	....	....	....	....
TENO, Harvey *No playoffs*												
TERRERI, Chris												
1990	New Jersey	4	2	2	....	238	13	0	3.28	103	.874	26.0
1991	New Jersey	7	3	4	....	428	21	0	2.94	216	.903	30.3
1992	New Jersey	7	3	3	....	386	23	0	3.58	203	.887	31.6
1993	New Jersey	4	1	3	....	219	17	0	4.66	118	.856	32.3
1994	New Jersey	4	3	0	....	200	9	0	2.70	111	.919	33.3
1995◆	New Jersey	1	0	0	....	8	0	0	0.00	2	.000	15.0
1997	Chicago	2	0	0	....	44	3	0	4.09	28	.893	38.2
Playoff Totals		**29**	**12**	**12**	....	**1523**	**86**	**0**	**3.39**	**781**	**.890**	**30.8**
THEODORE, Jose												
1997	Montreal	2	1	1	....	168	7	0	2.50	108	.935	38.6
1998	Montreal	3	0	1	....	120	1	0	0.50	35	.971	17.5
Playoff Totals		**5**	**1**	**2**	....	**288**	**8**	**0**	**1.67**	**143**	**.944**	**29.8**
THIBAULT, Jocelyn												
1995	Quebec	3	1	2	....	148	8	0	3.24	76	.895	30.8
1996	Montreal	6	2	4	....	311	18	0	3.47	188	.904	36.3
1997	Montreal	3	0	3	....	179	13	0	4.36	101	.871	33.9
1998	Montreal	2	0	0	....	43	4	0	5.58	16	.750	22.3
Playoff Totals		**14**	**3**	**9**	....	**681**	**43**	**0**	**3.79**	**381**	**.887**	**33.6**
THOMAS, Wayne												
1976	Toronto	10	5	5	....	587	34	1	3.48	....	....	....
1977	Toronto	4	1	2	....	202	12	0	3.56	....	....	....
1978	NY Rangers	1	0	1	....	60	4	0	4.00	....	....	....
Playoff Totals		**15**	**6**	**8**	....	**849**	**50**	**1**	**3.53**	....	....	....
THOMPSON, Tiny												
1929◆	Boston	5	*5	0	0	300	3	*3	*0.60	....	....	....
1930	Boston	*6	3	3	0	432	12	0	1.67	....	....	....
1931	Boston	5	2	3	0	343	13	0	2.27	....	....	....
1933	Boston	5	2	3	0	438	9	0	*1.23	....	....	....
1935	Boston	4	1	3	0	273	7	1	1.54	....	....	....
1936	Boston	2	1	1	0	120	8	1	4.00	....	....	....
1937	Boston	3	1	2	....	180	8	1	2.67	....	....	....
1938	Boston	3	0	3	....	212	6	0	1.70	....	....	....
1939	Detroit	6	3	3	....	374	15	1	2.41	....	....	....
1940	Detroit	5	2	3	....	300	12	0	2.40	....	....	....
Playoff Totals		**44**	**20**	**24**	**0**	**2972**	**93**	**7**	**1.88**	....	....	....
TOPPAZZINI, Jerry *No playoffs*												Right wing
TORCHIA, Mike *No playoffs*												
TREFILOV, Andrei												
1997	Buffalo	1	0	0	....	5	0	0	0.00	4	.000	48.0
Playoff Totals		**1**	**0**	**0**	....	**5**	**0**	**0**	**0.00**	**4**	**.000**	**48.0**
TREMBLAY, Vincent *No playoffs*												
TUCKER, Ted *No playoffs*												
TUGNUTT, Ron												
1992	Edmonton	2	0	0	....	60	3	0	3.00	34	.912	34.0
1994	Montreal	1	0	1	....	59	5	0	5.08	25	.800	25.4
1997	Ottawa	7	3	4	....	425	14	1	1.98	169	.917	23.9
1998	Ottawa	2	0	1	....	74	6	0	4.86	25	.760	20.3
1999	Ottawa	2	0	2	....	118	6	0	3.05	41	.854	20.8
Playoff Totals		**14**	**3**	**8**	....	**736**	**34**	**1**	**2.77**	**294**	**.884**	**24.0**
TUREK, Roman												
1999◆	Dallas	....	....	....	....	....	....	....	....	....	....	....
Playoff Totals		....	....	....	....	....	....	....	....	....	....	....
TURNER, Joe *No playoffs*												
VACHON, Rogie												
1967	Montreal	9	*6	3	....	555	22	0	*2.38	....	....	....
1968◆	Montreal	2	1	1	....	113	4	0	2.12	....	....	....
1969◆	Montreal	8	7	1	....	507	12	1	1.42	....	....	....
1971◆	Montreal	....	....	....	....	....	....	....	....	....	....	....
1974	Los Angeles	4	0	4	....	240	7	0	1.75	....	....	....
1975	Los Angeles	3	1	2	....	199	7	0	2.11	....	....	....
1976	Los Angeles	7	4	3	....	438	17	1	2.33	....	....	....
1977	Los Angeles	9	4	5	....	520	36	0	4.15	....	....	....
1978	Los Angeles	2	0	2	....	120	11	0	5.50	....	....	....
1981	Boston	3	0	2	....	164	16	0	5.85	....	....	....
1982	Boston	1	0	0	....	20	1	0	3.00	....	....	....
Playoff Totals		**48**	**23**	**23**	....	**2876**	**133**	**2**	**2.77**	....	....	....

Season	Club	GP	W	L	T	Mins	GA	SO	Avg	SA	S%	SAPG
VANBIESBROUCK, John												
1984	NY Rangers	1	0	0	....	1	0	0	0.00	0	.000	0.0
1985	NY Rangers	1	0	0	....	20	0	0	0.00	12	.000	36.0
1986	NY Rangers	16	8	8	....	899	49	*1	3.27	477	.897	31.8
1987	NY Rangers	4	1	3	....	195	11	1	3.38	110	.900	33.8
1989	NY Rangers	2	0	1	....	107	6	0	3.36	55	.891	30.8
1990	NY Rangers	6	2	3	....	298	15	0	3.02	153	.902	30.8
1991	NY Rangers	1	0	0	....	52	1	0	1.15	22	.955	25.4
1992	NY Rangers	7	2	5	....	368	23	0	3.75	179	.872	29.2
1996	Florida	*22	12	10	....	1332	50	1	2.25	735	.932	33.1
1997	Florida	5	1	4	....	328	13	1	2.38	184	.929	33.7
1999	Philadelphia	6	2	4	....	369	9	1	1.46	146	.938	23.7
Playoff Totals		**71**	**28**	**38**	....	**3969**	**177**	**5**	**2.68**	**2073**	**.915**	**31.3**
VEISOR, Mike												
1974	Chicago	2	0	1	....	80	5	0	3.75	....	....	....
1980	Chicago	1	0	1	....	60	6	0	6.00	....	....	....
1984	Winnipeg	1	0	0	....	40	4	0	6.00	29	.862	43.5
Playoff Totals		**4**	**0**	**2**	....	**180**	**15**	**0**	**5.00**	....	....	....
VERNON, Mike												
1986	Calgary	*21	12	*9	....	*1229	60	0	2.93	583	.897	28.5
1987	Calgary	5	2	3	....	263	16	0	3.65	136	.882	31.0
1988	Calgary	9	4	4	....	515	34	0	3.96	210	.838	24.5
1989♦	Calgary	*22	*16	5	....	*1381	52	*3	2.26	550	.905	23.9
1990	Calgary	6	2	3	....	342	19	0	3.33	150	.873	26.3
1991	Calgary	7	3	4	....	427	21	0	2.95	204	.897	28.7
1993	Calgary	4	1	1	....	150	15	0	6.00	81	.815	32.4
1994	Calgary	7	3	4	....	466	23	0	2.96	220	.895	28.3
1995	Detroit	18	12	6	....	1063	41	1	2.31	370	.889	20.9
1996	Detroit	4	2	2	....	243	11	0	2.72	81	.864	20.0
1997♦	Detroit	*20	*16	4	....	*1229	36	1	1.76	494	.927	24.1
1998	San Jose	6	2	4	....	348	14	1	2.41	138	.899	23.8
1999	San Jose	5	2	3	....	321	13	0	2.43	172	.924	32.1
Playoff Totals		**134**	**77**	**52**	....	**7977**	**355**	**6**	**2.67**	**3389**	**.895**	**25.5**
VEZINA, Georges												
1918	Mtl. Canadiens	2	1	1	0	120	10	0	5.00	....	....	....
1919	Mtl. Canadiens	*10	*6	3	1	*636	37	*1	*3.49	....	....	....
1923	Mtl. Canadiens	2	1	1	0	120	3	0	1.50	....	....	....
1924♦	Mtl. Canadiens	*6	*6	0	0	*360	6	*2	*1.00	....	....	....
1925	Mtl. Canadiens	*6	*3	3	0	*360	18	*1	3.00	....	....	....
Playoff Totals		**26**	**17**	**8**	**1**	**1596**	**74**	**4**	**2.78**	....	....	....
VILLEMURE, Gilles												
1969	NY Rangers	1	0	1	....	60	4	0	4.00	....	....	....
1971	NY Rangers	2	0	1	....	80	6	0	4.50	....	....	....
1972	NY Rangers	6	4	2	....	360	14	0	2.33	....	....	....
1973	NY Rangers	2	0	1	....	61	2	0	1.97	....	....	....
1974	NY Rangers	1	0	0	....	1	0	0	0.00	....	....	....
1975	NY Rangers	2	1	0	....	94	6	0	3.83	....	....	....
Playoff Totals		**14**	**5**	**5**	....	**656**	**32**	**0**	**2.93**	....	....	....
VOKOUN, Tomas *No playoffs*												
WAITE, Jimmy												
1994	San Jose	2	0	0	....	40	3	0	4.50	17	.824	25.5
1998	Phoenix	4	0	3	....	171	11	0	3.86	97	.887	34.0
Playoff Totals		**6**	**0**	**3**	....	**211**	**14**	**0**	**3.98**	**114**	**.877**	**32.4**
WAKALUK, Darcy												
1991	Buffalo	2	0	1	....	37	2	0	3.24	22	.909	35.7
1994	Dallas	5	4	1	....	307	15	0	2.93	168	.911	32.8
1995	Dallas	1	0	0	....	20	1	0	3.00	9	.889	27.0
Playoff Totals		**8**	**4**	**2**	....	**364**	**18**	**0**	**2.97**	**199**	**.910**	**32.8**
WAKELY, Ernie												
1970	St. Louis	4	0	4	....	216	17	0	4.72	....	....	....
1971	St. Louis	3	2	1	....	180	7	1	2.33	....	....	....
1972	St. Louis	3	0	1	....	113	13	0	6.90	....	....	....
Playoff Totals		**10**	**2**	**6**	....	**509**	**37**	**1**	**4.36**	....	....	....
WALSH, James												
1930	Mtl. Maroons	4	1	3	0	312	11	1	2.12	....	....	....
1932	Mtl. Maroons	4	1	1	2	258	5	*1	*1.16	....	....	....
Playoff Totals		**8**	**2**	**4**	**2**	**570**	**16**	**2**	**1.68**	....	....	....

Season	Club	GP	W	L	T	Mins	GA	SO	Avg	SA	S%	SAPG
WAMSLEY, Rick												
1982	Montreal	5	2	3	....	300	11	0	*2.20	....	....	....
1983	Montreal	3	0	3	....	152	7	0	2.76	....	....	....
1984	Montreal	1	0	0	....	32	0	0	0.00	12	.000	22.5
1985	St. Louis	2	0	2	....	120	7	0	3.50	56	.875	28.0
1986	St. Louis	10	4	6	....	569	37	0	3.90	307	.879	32.4
1987	St. Louis	2	1	1	....	120	5	0	2.50	54	.907	27.0
1988	Calgary	1	0	1	....	33	2	0	3.64	8	.750	14.5
1989♦	Calgary	1	0	1	....	20	2	0	6.00	10	.800	30.0
1990	Calgary	1	0	1	....	49	9	0	11.02	23	.609	28.2
1991	Calgary	1	0	0	....	2	1	0	30.00	2	.500	60.0
Playoff Totals		**27**	**7**	**18**	....	**1397**	**81**	**0**	**3.48**	....	....	....
WATT, Jim *No playoffs*												
WEEKES, Kevin *No playoffs*												
WEEKS, Steve												
1981	NY Rangers	1	0	0	....	14	1	0	4.29	....	....	....
1982	NY Rangers	4	1	2	....	127	9	0	4.25	....	....	....
1986	Hartford	3	1	2	....	169	8	0	2.84	64	.875	22.7
1987	Hartford	1	0	0	....	36	1	0	1.67	22	.955	36.7
1989	Vancouver	3	1	1	....	140	8	0	3.43	79	.899	33.9
Playoff Totals		**12**	**3**	**5**	....	**486**	**27**	**0**	**3.33**	....	....	....
WETZEL, Carl *No playoffs*												
WHITMORE, Kay												
1989	Hartford	2	0	2	....	135	10	0	4.44	73	.863	32.4
1992	Hartford	1	0	0	....	19	1	0	3.16	5	.800	15.8
1995	Vancouver	1	0	0	....	20	2	0	6.00	18	.889	54.0
Playoff Totals		**4**	**0**	**2**	....	**174**	**13**	**0**	**4.48**	**96**	**.865**	**33.1**
WILKINSON, Derek *No playoffs*												
WILLIS, Jordan *No playoffs*												
WILSON, Dunc *No playoffs*												
WILSON, Lefty *No playoffs*												
WINKLER, Hal												
1927	Boston	*8	2	2	4	*520	13	*2	1.50	....	....	....
1928	Boston	2	0	1	1	120	5	0	2.50	....	....	....
Playoff Totals		**10**	**2**	**3**	**5**	**640**	**18**	**2**	**1.69**	....	....	....
WOLFE, Bernie *No playoffs*												
WOOD, Alex *No playoffs*												
WORSLEY, Gump												
1956	NY Rangers	3	0	3	....	180	15	0	5.00	....	....	....
1957	NY Rangers	5	1	4	....	316	22	0	4.18	....	....	....
1958	NY Rangers	6	2	4	....	365	28	0	4.60	....	....	....
1962	NY Rangers	6	2	4	....	384	22	0	3.44	....	....	....
1965♦	Montreal	8	5	3	....	501	14	*2	*1.68	....	....	....
1966♦	Montreal	10	*8	2	....	602	20	*1	*1.99	....	....	....
1967	Montreal	2	0	1	....	80	2	0	1.50	....	....	....
1968♦	Montreal	12	*11	0	....	669	21	*1	1.88	....	....	....
1969♦	Montreal	7	5	1	....	370	14	0	2.27	....	....	....
1970	Minnesota	3	1	2	....	180	14	0	4.67	....	....	....
1971	Minnesota	4	3	1	....	240	13	0	3.25	....	....	....
1972	Minnesota	4	2	1	....	194	7	1	2.16	....	....	....
Playoff Totals		**70**	**40**	**26**	....	**4081**	**192**	**5**	**2.82**	....	....	....
WORTERS, Roy												
1926	Pittsburgh	2	0	1	1	120	6	0	3.00	....	....	....
1928	Pittsburgh	2	1	1	0	120	6	0	3.00	....	....	....
1929	NY Americans	2	0	1	1	150	1	1	0.40	....	....	....
1936	NY Americans	5	2	3	0	300	11	*2	2.20	....	....	....
Playoff Totals		**11**	**3**	**6**	**2**	**690**	**24**	**3**	**2.09**	....	....	....
WORTHY, Chris *No playoffs*												
WREGGET, Ken												
1986	Toronto	10	6	4	....	607	32	*1	3.16	323	.901	31.9
1987	Toronto	13	7	6	....	761	29	1	2.29	368	.921	29.0
1988	Toronto	2	0	1	....	108	11	0	6.11	62	.823	34.4
1989	Philadelphia	5	2	2	....	268	10	0	2.24	139	.928	31.1
1992♦	Pittsburgh	1	0	0	....	40	4	0	6.00	16	.750	24.0
1995	Pittsburgh	11	5	6	....	661	33	1	3.00	349	.905	31.7
1996	Pittsburgh	9	7	2	....	599	23	0	2.30	328	.930	32.9
1997	Pittsburgh	5	1	4	....	297	18	0	3.64	211	.915	42.6
Playoff Totals		**56**	**28**	**25**	....	**3341**	**160**	**3**	**2.87**	**1796**	**.911**	**32.3**
YOUNG, Doug *No playoffs*												Defense
YOUNG, Wendell												
1986	Vancouver	1	0	1	....	60	5	0	5.00	32	.844	32.0
1989	Pittsburgh	1	0	0	....	39	1	0	1.54	11	.909	16.9
1991♦	Pittsburgh	....	....	....	....	....	....	....	....	....	....	....
1992♦	Pittsburgh	....	....	....	....	....	....	....	....	....	....	....
Playoff Totals		**2**	**0**	**1**	....	**99**	**6**	**0**	**3.64**	....	....	....
ZANIER, Mike *No playoffs*												